Supersite

LEARNING IS
JUST A CLICK AWAY

The **Sag mal Supersite**—everything you need to motivate students and support language learning.

- Engages and focuses students
- Improves student performance
- Saves you time with auto-grading, quick setup, and reporting tools
- Provides flexibility to personalize your course
- Offers cost-saving digital options
- Includes vText—the online, interactive Student Edition

 Go to vhlcentral.com to get started

THIRD EDITION

SAG MAL

AN INTRODUCTION TO GERMAN LANGUAGE AND CULTURE

Christine Anton

Tobias Barske

VISTA®
HIGHER LEARNING

Boston, Massachusetts

Creative Director: José A. Blanco
Publisher: Sharla Zwirek
Editorial Development: Judith Bach, Carlos Calvo, Sarah Wu
Project Management: Erik Restrepo, Faith Ryan
Rights Management: Jorgensen Fernandez, Annie Pickert Fuller
Technology Production: David Duque, Egle Gutiérrez
Design: Paula Díaz, Sara Gutiérrez, Radoslav Mateev, Gabriel Noreña, Andrés Vanegas
Production: Oscar Díez, Sebastián Díez, Andrés Escobar, Daniel Lopera

Student Text ISBN: 978-1-54331-028-3
Teacher's Edition ISBN: 978-1-54331-030-6
Library of Congress Control Number: 2019932364

1 2 3 4 5 6 7 8 9 TC 24 23 22 21 20 19
Printed in Canada.

Contents

INSTRUCTOR'S ANNOTATED EDITION

The Vista Higher Learning Story

Your Specialized Foreign Language Publisher

Independent, specialized, and privately owned, Vista Higher Learning was founded in 2000 with one mission: to raise the teaching and learning of world languages to a higher level. This mission is based on the following beliefs:

- It is essential to prepare students for a world in which learning another language is a necessity, not a luxury.
- Language learning should be fun and rewarding, and all students should have the tools they need to achieve success.
- Students who experience success learning a language will be more likely to continue their language studies both inside and outside the classroom.

With this in mind, we decided to take a fresh look at all aspects of language instructional materials. Because we are specialized, we dedicate 100 percent of our resources to this goal and base every decision on how well it supports language learning.

That is where you come in. Since our founding, we have relied on the invaluable feedback of language instructors and students nationwide. This partnership has proved to be the cornerstone of our success, allowing us to constantly improve our programs to meet your instructional needs.

The result? Programs that make language learning exciting, relevant, and effective through:

- unprecedented access to resources
- a wide variety of contemporary, authentic materials
- the integration of text, technology, and media
- a bold and engaging textbook design

By focusing on our singular passion, we let you focus on yours.

The Vista Higher Learning Team

VISTA®
HIGHER LEARNING

500 Boylston Street, Suite 620, Boston, MA 02116-3736 TOLL-FREE: 800-618-7375
TELEPHONE: 617-426-4910 FAX: 617-426-5209 www.vistahigherlearning.com

Getting to Know SAG MAL Third Edition

Vibrant and original, **SAG MAL**, Third Edition, takes a fresh, student-friendly approach to introductory German, aimed at making students' learning and instructors' teaching easier, more enjoyable, and more successful. **SAG MAL** develops students' speaking, listening, reading, and writing skills so that they will be able to express their own ideas and interact with others meaningfully and in real-life contexts.

NEW to the Third Edition

- Additional Instructor Resources, including expanded Testing Program with new A-B versions of lesson tests, chapter tests, and exams, Integrated Performance Assessment, and Video Virtual Chats audioscripts

- Interactive Grammar Tutorials and grammar practice tests with Diagnostics

- Twenty three new **Kontext** audio activities

- Five new authentic **Zapping** TV-clips

- New **Kurzfilm**, *Fünf Minuten Freundschaft,* in Chapter 12

- Twelve realia-based activities

- Video virtual chats

- Three new **Lesen** readings with audio-sync recording in Chapters 8, 10, and 11

- New music feature **Musik, Musik**

- Twelve web-only activities for new music feature

- Revised textbook content—with increased scaffolding, and practice of the three modes of communication

Plus, the original hallmark features of SAG MAL

- A unique, easy-to-navigate design with color-coded lesson sections and visually engaging textbook pages featuring content designed for instructional impact and visual appeal

- Distinctive and cohesive integration of video—from a specially shot **Fotoroman** dramatic series to authentic TV clips and short films in the **Zapping** or **Kurzfilm** feature in every chapter

- A unique vocabulary practice sequence that alternates between recognition and production practice at every level of discourse: words, phrases or sentences, and dialogues, including listening comprehension activities in each lesson

- A unique four-part practice sequence for every grammar point, moving from form focused **Jetzt sind Sie dran!** activities to directed **Anwendung** activities, to communicative, interactive **Kommunikation** activities, and finallly, to open-ended activities in **Wiederholung** that recycle previously learned material

- **Tipp** and **Achtung** boxes with linguistic and cultural notes, **More activities** boxes with correlations to student supplements and **Querverweis** boxes with grammar cross-references

- Systematic development of reading and writing skills, incorporating learning strategies and a process approach

- A rich, contemporary cultural presentation of the everyday lives of German speakers

- Groundbreaking technology designed to expand learning and teaching options, including online textbook and web-only activities, with Partner Chats and Video Virtual Chats for pair activities

- vText—the interactive, online text—perfect for hybrid courses

*Students must use a computer for audio recording and select presentations and tools that require Flash or Shockwave.

KONTEXT

FOTOROMAN

KULTUR

STRUKTUREN

WEITER GEHT'S

KONTEXT   FOTOROMAN

KULTUR	STRUKTUREN	WEITER GEHT'S

KONTEXT

FOTOROMAN

KONTEXT

FOTOROMAN

KULTUR	STRUKTUREN	WEITER GEHT'S

There's more to SAG MAL than meets the page

The **SAG MAL** Supersite provides a learning environment designed especially for world language instruction. Password-protected and program-specific, this website provides seamless textbook-technology integration that helps build students' love for language learning.

For students:

- engaging media
- motivating user experience
- superior performance
- helpful resources
- plenty of practice

For educators:

- proven instructional design
- powerful course management
- time-saving tools
- enhanced support

Integrated content means a more powerful student experience

- Streaming videos—episodic dramatic series, authentic TV clips, and authentic short films
- All program audio in downloadable MP3 format
- Textbook activities and additional online-only practice—most with automatic feedback
- Interactive Grammar Tutorials with quick checks
- Grammar practice tests with diagnostics
- Video Virtual Chat and Partner Chat activities for conversational skills practice
- Vocabulary Tools for personalized language study
- Audio-sync readings for all **Lesen** selections
- Cultural readings and literary selections
- Online Student Activities Manual fully integrated with the Supersite gradebook

Specialized resources ensure a successful implementation

- Online assessments and Testing Program files in an editable format
- Audioscripts and videoscripts with English translations
- Grammar presentation slides
- Editable block and standard lesson plans
- IPAs with grading rubrics
- Digital Image Bank
- Answer keys

Educator tools facilitate instruction and save time

Video Virtual Chat

In-line editing

Easy course management

A powerful setup wizard lets you customize your class settings, copy previous courses to save time, and create your all-in-one gradebook. Grades for teacher-created assignments (e.g., pop quizzes, class participation) can be incorporated for a true, up-to-date cumulative grade.

Customized content

Tailor the Supersite to fit your needs. Create your own open-ended or video Partner Chat activities, add video or outside resources, and modify existing content with your own personalized notes.

Grading tools

Grade efficiently via spot-checking, student-by-student, and question-by-question options. Use in-line editing tools to give targeted feedback and voice comments—it's the perfect tool for busy language educators!

Assessment solutions

Administer online tests and exams. Use any pre-built assessment "as is" or customize them to meet your specific needs, including: adding or removing questions from a section, reordering sections or questions, and changing point values for questions.

Plus!

- A communication center for announcements, notifications, and student help requests

- Forums for oral assignments, group discussions, homework, and more

- Reporting tools for summarizing student data

- Single sign-on for easy integration with your school's Learning Management System*

- Live Chat for video chat, audio chat, and instant messaging with students

* available for select LMSs

upersite

Each section of your textbook comes with activities on the **SAG MAL** Supersite, many of which are auto-graded with immediate feedback. Visit vhlcentral.com to explore the wealth of exciting resources.

KONTEXT	• Image-based vocabulary activities with audio • Additional activities for extra practice • **Aussprache und Rechtschreibung** presentation followed by record-compare activities	• Textbook activities • Chat activities for conversational skill-building and oral practice
FOTOROMAN	• Streaming video for all episodes of the **Fotoroman** with teacher-controlled options for subtitles • Textbook activities	• **Zusammenfassung** section with key vocabulary and grammar from the episode • Additional activities for extra practice
KULTUR	• Culture reading • Internet search activity	• Textbook activities • Additional activities for extra practice
STRUKTUREN	• Grammar presentations • Interactive Grammar Tutorials with quick checks • Additional activities for extra practice	• Chat activities for conversational skill-building and oral practice • Textbook activities
WIEDERHOLUNG	• Grammar practice tests with diagnostics	
ZAPPING/KURZFILM	• Streaming video of TV clip and short film	
WEITER GEHT'S	**Panorama** • Interactive map with statistics and cultural notes • Additional activity for extra practice **Im Internet** • Internet search activity **Musik Musik** • Music feature with online activity	**Lesen** • Audio-sync reading • Additional activities for extra practice • Textbook activities **Hören** • Textbook activities • Additional activities for extra practice **Schreiben** • Submit your writing assignment online
WORTSCHATZ	• Audio recordings of all vocabulary items	• Vocabulary Tools to create lists and flashcards

Plus! Also found on the Supersite:

- All textbook and lab audio MP3 files
- Communication center for teacher notifications and feedback
- A single gradebook for all Supersite activities

- WebSAM online Workbook/Video Manual and Lab Manual
- **vText** online, interactive student edition with access to Supersite activities, audio, and video

*Students must use a computer for audio-recording.

Program Components for the Student

COMPONENT TITLE	WHAT IS IT?	▯	Ⓢ
Student Edition	Core instruction for students	•	•
Audio-synced Readings	Audio to accompany all Lesen sections		•
Dictionary	Easy digital access to a dictionary		•
End-of-lesson Vocabulary Lists	Core vocabulary for each lesson, with linked audio online		•
Flashcards	Provide an easy way to study vocabulary (available as part of Vocabulary Tools)		•
Fotoroman Video	Engaging storyline video		•
Interactive Grammar Tutorials	Animated grammar presentations with quick checks		•
Lab Manual Activities Audio	Audio to accompany the Lab Manual portion of the Student Activities Manual		•
Vocabulary Tools	A variety of tools to practice vocabulary		•
Partner Chats	Work with a partner online to record a conversation via video or audio and submit for grading		•
Student Activities Manual	Combined Workbook/Lab Manual/Video Manual aligned to each lesson	•	•
Textbook Audio	Audio to accompany all textbook listening activities		•
Textbook Mouse Activities	Textbook activities that can also be completed digitally; many provide immediate feedback		•
Video Virtual Chats	Record and submit a simulated video conversation with a native speaker for online grading		•
Vocabulary Hot Spots	Vocabulary presentations with embedded audio		•
Forums	Collaborative spaces for oral assignments, group discussions, homework, and projects		•
vText	Virtual interactive textbook for browser-based exploration • Links to all mouse-icon activities, audio, and video • Note-taking capabilities		•
WebSAM	Online version of the Student Activities Manual, embedded in the online gradebook, with many auto-graded options		•
Web-only Activities	Additional online practice for students		•
Zapping/Kurzfilm Video	Authentic TV clips and short films from across the German-speaking world		•

Print   Ⓢ Supersite

Interactive Grammar Tutorials

Research shows that a little humor is engaging, stimulates the brain, and helps with memory retention. Interactive grammar tutorials, **NEW!** for **SAG MAL, Third Edition**, feature the Professor, an amusing character who grabs your attention with his humorous gags and lighthearted approach to grammar. The tutorials entertain and inform by pairing grammar rules with fun explanations and examples. The Professor always uses the new grammar in a humorous way at the end of each tutorial.

There are five learning scenarios: the classroom, the library, the theater, the café, and the Professor's living room. These settings offer opportunities for humor and for cultural references.

The Professor explains the grammar in an informal, conversational way. The Narrator pronounces words in charts and reads example sentences. Animation features such as color and pulsing emphasize the grammar being taught. The examples often appear with pictures that illustrate their meaning.

Longer tutorials with more complex explanations have one or two Quick Checks, which are pauses in the instruction to give you a chance to react to what has just been presented. It's a way to make sure you understand one concept before tackling the next one. Each tutorial ends with a **Versuchen Sie es!** activity that can be submitted for a grade.

The *Fotoroman* Episodes

Fully integrated with your textbook, the **SAG MAL Fotoroman** contains 24 dramatic episodes—one for each lesson of the text. The episodes relate the adventures of four students who are studying in Berlin.

The **Fotoroman** dialogues in the printed textbook lesson are an abbreviated version of the dramatic episode featured in the video. Therefore, each Fotoroman section can be used as preparation before you view the corresponding video episode, as post-viewing reinforcement, or as a stand-alone section.

As you watch the video, you will see the characters interact using the vocabulary and grammar you are studying. Their conversations incorporate new vocabulary and grammar with previously taught language. At the conclusion of each episode, the **Zusammenfassung** segment summarizes the key language functions and grammar points used in the episode.

THE CAST

Learn more about each of the characters you'll meet
in **SAG MAL Fotoroman:**

George
is from Milwaukee, Wisconsin.
He is studying Architecture.

Meline
is from Vienna.
She is studying Business.

Hans
is from Straubing, in Bavaria.
He studies Political Science and History.

Sabite
is from Berlin.
She studies Art.

Zapping

About *Zapping* TV Clips

A TV clip from the German-speaking world appears in the first **Lektion** of each **Kapitel** up to Chapter 9. The purpose of this feature is to expose students to the language and culture contained in authentic media pieces. The following list of the television commercials is organized by **Kapitel.**

Kapitel 1

Deutsche Bahn
(29 seconds)

Kapitel 2

Kein Wohnraum: Studenten Schlafen in Hotels Bahn
(2 minutes, 34 seconds)

Kapitel 3

Naturkost für Hund und Katze
(58 seconds)

Kapitel 4

Yello Strom
(39 seconds)

Kapitel 5

Penny
(36 seconds)

Kapitel 6

Neustart: Möbel bauen statt Kinder erziehen
(4 minutes)

Kapitel 7

Wetterbericht
(1 minute, 15 seconds)

Kapitel 8

Deutschen Automarken
(35 seconds)

Kapitel 9

Gesundheit bewegt uns
(25 seconds)

About *Kurzfilm* Short Films

A short film from the German-speaking world appears in the first **Lektion** of **Kapitels 10-12.** The purpose of this feature is to expose students to the language and culture contained in authentic films. The following list of short films is organized by **Kapitel.**

Kapitel 10

Bienenstich ist aus
(15 minutes)

Kapitel 11

Die Berliner Mauer
(15 minutes)

Kapitel 12

Fünf Minuten Freundschaft
(9 minutes, 30 seconds)

Icons

Familiarize yourself with these icons that appear throughout **SAG MAL.**

1 Richtig oder f
or falsch.
1. Sabite hat eine
2. Meline hat zwe
3. Melines Nichte

5 Beschreibur
Compare your an

8 Familienpo
Use possessive
everyone has s
the rest of the

6 Die Trauml
Partner / einer
Sie so viele De
Partner / Ihre

 Online Activities

The mouse icon indicates when an activity is also available on the Supersite.

Pair Activities

Two heads indicate a pair activity.

Group Activities

Three heads indicate a group activity.

Recycle

The recycling icon indicates that you will need to use vocabulary and grammar learned in previous lessons.

6 Partnersu
discuss with a
a better matcl
to the class.

4 Hören Sie
each statemen

3 Arbeitsbla
worksheet with
a different nan
your findings w

5 Diskutiere
will give you a
Ask questions
the two picture

Partner and Video Virtual Chat Activities

Two heads with a speech bubble indicate that the activity may be assigned as a Partner Chat or a Video Virtual Chat activity on the Supersite.

Listening

The listening icon indicates that audio is available on the Supersite.

Worksheets

The activities marked with these icons require worksheets that your teacher will provide for you to complete the activity in a group.

Info Gap Activities

Two heads with a puzzle piece indicate an activity which will be done with a partner using a handout your teacher will provide.

More activities

More activities boxes tell you exactly what print and digital resources you can use to reinforce and expand on every section of the textbook lesson with page numbers where applicable.

WB	**Workbook**	Additional vocabulary and grammar
LM	**Lab Manual**	practice; audio activities; and pre-,
VM	**Video Manual**	while-, and post-viewing activities for the video programs

Supersite
Additional practice on the Supersite, not included in the textbook

Beginning with
the student in mind

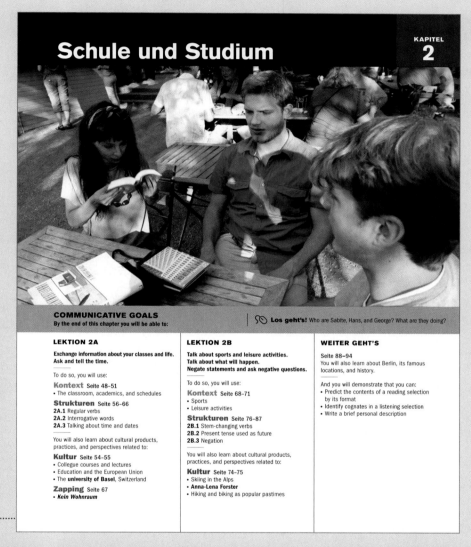

Schule und Studium

KAPITEL
2

COMMUNICATIVE GOALS
By the end of this chapter you will be able to:

🔊 **Los geht's!** Who are Sabite, Hans, and George? What are they doing?

LEKTION 2A

Exchange information about your classes and life.
Ask and tell the time.

To do so, you will use:

Kontext Seite 48–51
• The classroom, academics, and schedules

Strukturen Seite 56–66
2A.1 Regular verbs
2A.2 Interrogative words
2A.3 Talking about time and dates

You will also learn about cultural products, practices, and perspectives related to:

Kultur Seite 54–55
• Collegue courses and lectures
• Education and the European Union
• The **university of Basel**, Switzerland

Zapping Seite 67
• *Kein Wohnraum*

LEKTION 2B

Talk about sports and leisure activities.
Talk about what will happen.
Negate statements and ask negative questions.

To do so, you will use:

Kontext Seite 68–71
• Sports
• Leisure activities

Strukturen Seite 76–87
2B.1 Stem-changing verbs
2B.2 Present tense used as future
2B.3 Negation

You will also learn about cultural products, practices, and perspectives related to:

Kultur Seite 74–75
• Skiing in the Alps
• **Anna-Lena Forster**
• Hiking and biking as popular pastimes

WEITER GEHT'S

Seite 88–94
You will also learn about Berlin, its famous locations, and history.

And you will demonstrate that you can:
• Predict the contents of a reading selection by its format
• Identify cognates in a listening selection
• Write a brief personal description

Chapter opener photos highlight scenes that illustrate the chapter theme. They are snapshots of the characters that students will come to know throughout the program.

Communicative goals highlight the real-life tasks students will be able to carry out in German by the end of each chapter. Communicative goals break down each chapter into its two lessons and one **Weiter Geht's** section, giving an at-a-glance summary of the vocabulary, grammar, cultural topics, and language skills covered.

Ⓢupersite

Supersite resources are available for every section of each chapter at **vhlcentral.com**. Icons show you which textbook activities are also available online, and where additional practice activities are available. The description next to the Ⓢ icon indicates what additional resources are available for each section: videos, audio recordings, readings, presentations, and more!

Setting the stage
for communication

Illustrations introduce high-frequency vocabulary through expansive, full-color images.

Wortschatz sidebars call out important theme-related vocabulary in easy-to-reference German-English lists.

More practice boxes indicate what print and technology ancillaries reinforce and expand on every section of every lesson.

Achtung boxes provide additional information about how and when to use certain vocabulary words or grammar structures.

Kontext always contains two audio activities that accompany the **Anwendung** practice activities. **Anwendung** follows a pedagogical sequence that starts with simpler, shorter, discrete recognition activities and builds toward longer, more complex production activities.

Ⓢupersite

- Audio recordings of all vocabulary items
- Audio for **Kontext** listening activities
- Image-based vocabulary activity with audio
- Textbook activities
- Additional online-only practice activities

Engaging students in
active communication

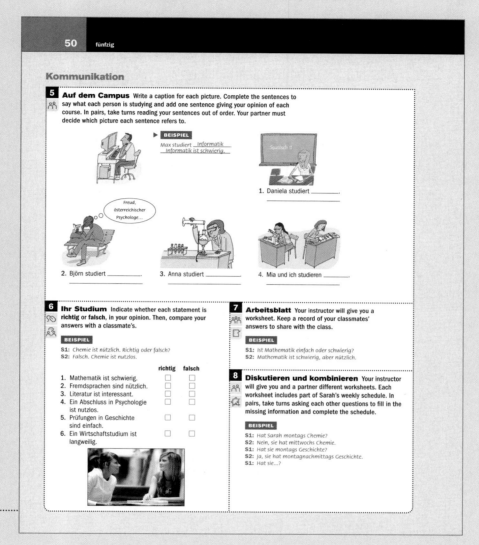

Kommunikation activities make use of discourse-level prompts, encouraging the creative use of vocabulary in interactions with a partner, a small group, or the entire class.

Pair and group icons indicate communicative activities—such as role play, games, personal questions, interviews, and surveys—for interpersonal and presentational practice.

ⓢupersite

- Chat activities for conversational skill-building and oral practice

Authenticity
in pronunciation and spelling

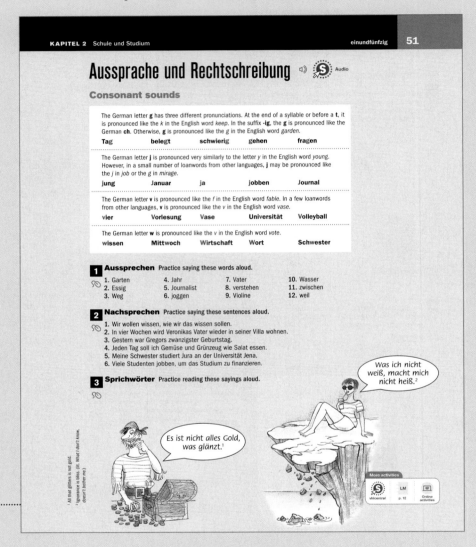

Explanations of German pronunciation and spelling are presented clearly, with abundant model words and phrases. The red highlighting feature focuses students' attention on the target structure.

Practice pronunciation and spelling at the word- and sentence-levels. The final activity features illustrated sayings and proverbs that present the target structures in an entertaining cultural context.

The audio icon at the top of the page indicates that the explanation and activities are recorded for convenient use in or outside of class.

Supersite

- Audio recording of the **Aussprache und Rechtschreibung** presentation
- Record-and-compare activities

Fotoroman
bridges language and culture

Fotoroman is a versatile episodic video that can be assigned as homework, presented in class, or used as review.

Conversations reinforce vocabulary from **Kontext**. They also preview structures from the upcoming **Strukturen** section in context.

Personen features the cast of recurring **Fotoroman** characters, including four students living in Berlin: George, Sabite, Meline, and Hans.

Nützliche Ausdrücke calls out the most important words and expressions from the **Fotoroman** episode that have not been formally presented. This vocabulary is not tested. The blue numbers refer to the grammar structures presented in the lesson.

Übungen activities include comprehension questions, a communicative task, and a research-based task.

Supersite

- Streaming video for all episodes of the **Fotoroman**
- End-of-video **Zusammenfassung** section where key vocabulary and grammar from the episode are called out
- Textbook activities

Culture
presented in context

Im Fokus presents an in-depth reading about the lesson's cultural theme. Full-color photos bring to life important aspects of the topic, while charts support the main text with statistics and additional information.

Porträt spotlights notable people, places, events, and products from the German-speaking world. This article is thematically linked to the lesson.

Deutsch im Alltag presents additional vocabulary related to the lesson theme, showcasing words and phrases used in everyday spoken German. This vocabulary is not tested.

Die deutschsprachige Welt focuses on the people, places, dialects, and traditions in regions where German is spoken. This short article is thematically linked to the lesson.

Im Internet boxes, with provocative questions and photos, feature additional cultural explorations online.

Übungen activities include comprehension questions, each followed by a discussion question.

Supersite

- **Kultur** reading
- **Im Internet** research activity expands on the chapter theme
- Textbook activities

Grammar
as a tool not a topic

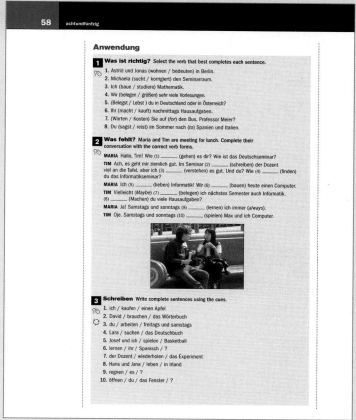

Startblock eases into each grammar explanation, with definitions of grammatical terms and reminders about grammar concepts which are already familiar.

Querverweis boxes call out information covered in earlier lessons or provide cross-references to related topics that will be covered in future lessons.

Achtung boxes clarify potential sources of confusion and provide supplementary information.

Jetzt sind Sie dran! is the first opportunity to practice the new grammar point.

Anwendung offers a wide range of guided activities that combine lesson vocabulary and previously learned material with the new grammar point.

Kommunikation activities provide opportunities for self-expression using the lesson grammar and vocabulary. These activities feature interaction with a partner, in small groups, or with the whole class.

Ⓢupersite

- Grammar presentations
- Interactive grammar tutorials (see page IAE-18)
- Textbook activities

- Additional online-only practice activities
- Chat activities for conversational skill-building and oral practice

Carefully scaffolded
lesson review

Wiederholung activities integrate the lesson's grammar points and vocabulary with previously learned vocabulary and structures, providing consistent, built-in review. It includes a realia-based activity.

Pair and group icons indicate communicative activities—such as role play, games, personal questions, interviews, and surveys for interpersonal and presentational practice.

Information gap activities, identified by interlocking puzzle pieces, engage partners in problem-solving situations.

Recycling icons call out activities that practice the lesson's grammar and vocabulary along with previously learned material.

Mein Wörterbuch in the B lesson of each chapter offers the opportunity to increase vocabulary comprehension and the contextualization of new words.

Supersite

- Chat activities for conversational skill-building and oral practice
- Grammar practice tests with diagnostics

Authentic cultural media
for interpretive communication

Zapping presents TV commercials from the German-speaking world. Post-viewing activities check comprehension.

Kurzfilm in Chapters 10, 11, and 12 features short films from contemporary German-speaking filmmakers.

Summary provides context for each video clip.

Photos and captions provide key information to facilitate comprehension.

Analyse post-viewing activities encourage exploration of the broader idea presented in each video clip.

Supersite

- Streaming video of the TV clip or short film with teacher-controlled subtitle options
- Textbook activities

Perspective
through geography

Panorama offers interesting facts about the featured city, region, or country.

Maps point out major geographical features and situate the featured region in the context of its immediate surroundings.

Readings explore different aspects of the featured region's culture, such as history, landmarks, fine art, literature, and insight into everyday life.

Unglaublich, aber wahr! highlights an intriguing fact about the featured region.

Musik, Musik introduces contemporary musicians and singers from different musical genres of the German-speaking world.

Comprehension questions and **discussion activities** check your understanding of key ideas.

Supersite

- Map with statistics and cultural notes
- Textbook activities
- **Im Internet** research activity

Reading skills
developed in context

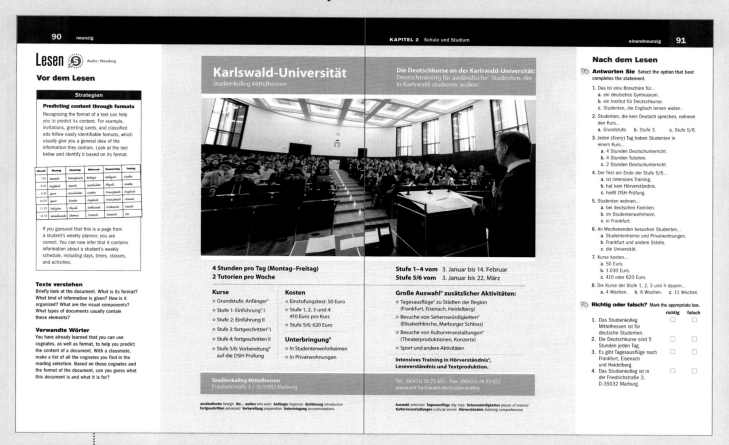

Vor dem Lesen presents useful strategies and activities that help develop stronger reading abilities.

Readings are tied to the chapter theme. The selections recycle vocabulary and grammar learned.

Nach dem Lesen consists of post-reading activities that check comprehension.

ⓢupersite

- Audio-sync reading that highlights text as it is being read
- Textbook activities

Listening and writing skills
developed in context

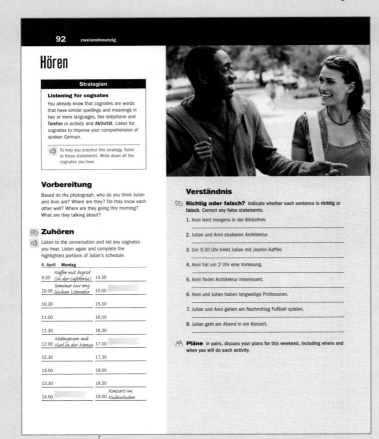

92 zweiundneunzig

Hören

Strategien

Listening for cognates

You already know that cognates are words that have similar spellings and meanings in two or more languages, like *telephone* and **Telefon** or *activity* and **Aktivität**. Listen for cognates to improve your comprehension of spoken German.

To help you practice this strategy, listen to these statements. Write down all the cognates you hear.

Vorbereitung

Based on the photograph, who do you think Julian and Anni are? Where are they? Do they know each other well? Where are they going this morning? What are they talking about?

Zuhören

Listen to the conversation and list any cognates you hear. Listen again and complete the highlighted portions of Julian's schedule.

4. April Montag		
9.30	*Kaffee mit Ingrid (in der Cafeteria)*	14.30
10.00	*Seminar zur englischen Literatur*	15.00
10.30		15.30
11.00		16.00
11.30		16.30
12.00	*Mittagessen mit Karl in der Mensa*	17.00
12.30		17.30
13.00		18.00
13.30		18.30
14.00		19.00 *Konzert im Kulturladen*

Verständnis

Richtig oder falsch? Indicate whether each sentence is **richtig** or **falsch**. Correct any false statements.

1. Anni lernt morgens in der Bibliothek.

2. Julian und Anni studieren Architektur.

3. Um 9.30 Uhr trinkt Julian mit Jasmin Kaffee.

4. Anni hat um 2 Uhr eine Vorlesung.

5. Anni findet Architektur interessant.

6. Anni und Julian haben langweilige Professoren.

7. Julian und Anni gehen am Nachmittag Fußball spielen.

8. Julian geht am Abend in ein Konzert.

Pläne In pairs, discuss your plans for this weekend, including where and when you will do each activity.

KAPITEL 2 Schule und Studium   dreiundneunzig **93**

Schreiben

Strategien

Brainstorming

Brainstorming can help you generate ideas on a specific topic. Before you begin writing, you should spend 10-15 minutes brainstorming, jotting down any ideas about the topic that occur to you. Whenever possible, try to write down your ideas in German. Express your ideas in single words or phrases, and jot them down in any order. While brainstorming, do not worry about whether your ideas are good or bad. Selecting and organizing ideas should be the second stage of your writing. The more ideas you write down while you are brainstorming, the more options you will have to choose from later on, when you start to organize your ideas.

Hobbys:
laufen
campen gehen
Tennis spielen
kochen
tanzen
schreiben
schwimmen
Fahrrad fahren

Thema

Eine persönliche Beschreibung

Write a description of yourself to post on a Web site in order to find a German-speaking e-pal. Your description should include:

• your name and where you are from.

• your birthday.

• the name of your school and where it is located.

• the courses you are currently taking and your opinion of each one.

• your hobbies and pastimes.

• any other information you would like to include.

Hallo!

Ich heiße Erik Schneider und ich komme aus Köln. Ich studiere Physik an der Technischen Universität in Berlin. Ich fahre Ski, spiele Tennis und fahre Fahrrad...

Hören uses a recorded conversation or narration to develop listening skills in German, while **Strategien** and **Vorbereitung** are preparation for an audio listening activity.

Zuhören serves as a guide to the recorded segment, and **Verständnis** checks comprehension.

In the **Schreiben** section, **Strategien** provides useful preparation for the writing task presented in **Thema**.

Thema presents a writing topic and includes suggestions for approaching it. It also provides words and phrases that may be useful in writing about the topic.

Supersite

• Audio for **Hören** activities

• Textbook activities

• Additional online-only practice activity

• Composition writing activity for **Schreiben**

Vocabulary

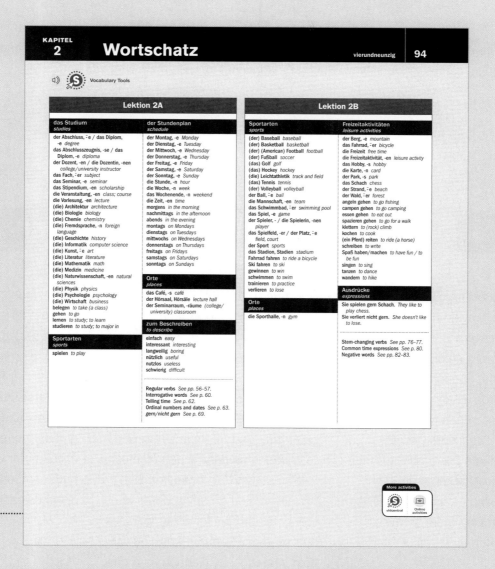

Wortschatz presents the chapter's active vocabulary in logical groupings, including notation of plural forms. Words are separated by corresponding A and B lessons.

Supersite

- Audio recordings of all vocabulary items
- Vocabulary Tools

Six-step instructional design

Take advantage of the unique, powerful six-step instructional design in **SAG MAL.** With a focus on personalization, authenticity, cultural immersion, and the seamless integration of text and technology, language learning comes to life in ways that are meaningful to each and every student.

STEP 1

Context

Begin each lesson by asking students to provide from their own experience words, concepts, categories, and opinions related to the theme. Spend quality time evoking words, images, ideas, phrases, and sentences; group and classify concepts. You are giving students the "hook" for their learning, focusing them on their most interesting topic— themselves— and encouraging them to invest personally in their learning.

STEP 2

Vocabulary

Now turn to the vocabulary section, inviting students to experience it as a new linguistic code to express what they already know and experience in the context of the lesson theme. Vocabulary concepts are presented in context, carefully organized, and frequently reviewed to reinforce student understanding. Involve students in brainstorming, classifying and grouping words and thoughts, and personalizing phrases and sentences. In this way, you will help students see German as a new tool for self-expression.

STEP 3

Media

Once students see that German is a tool for expressing their own ideas, bridge their experiences to those of German speakers through the **Fotoroman** section. The **Fotoroman** storyline video presents and reviews vocabulary and structure in accurate cultural contexts for effective training in both comprehension and personal communication.

STEP 4

Culture

Now bring students into the experience of culture as seen from the perspective of those living in it. Here we share German-speaking cultures' unique geography, history, products, perspectives, and practices. Through **Zapping** and **Kurzfilm** students experience and reflect on cultural experiences beyond their own.

STEP 5

Structure

Through context, media and culture, students have incorporated both previously learned and new grammatical structures into their personalized communication. Now a formal presentation of relevant grammar demonstrates that grammar is a tool for clearer and more effective communication. Clear presentations and invitations to compare German to English build confidence, fluency, and accuracy.

STEP 6

Skill synthesis

Pulling all their learning together, students now integrate context, personal experience, communication tools, and cultural products, perspectives, and practices. Through extended reading, writing, listening, speaking, and cultural exploration in scaffolded progression, students apply all their skills for a rich, personalized experience of German.

World-Readiness Standards
for Learning Languages

SAG MAL blends the underlying principles of ACTFL's World-Readiness Standards with features and strategies tailored specifically to build students' language and cultural competencies.

THE FIVE C'S OF FOREIGN LANGUAGE LEARNING	
COMMUNICATION	**Students:** 1. Interact and negotiate meaning in spoken, signed, or written conversations to share information, reactions, feelings, and opinions. (Interpersonal mode) 2. Understand, interpret, and analyze what is heard, read, or viewed on a variety of topics. (Interpretive mode) 3. Present information, concepts, and ideas to inform, explain, persuade, and narrate on a variety of topics using appropriate media and adapting to various audiences of listeners, readers, or viewers. (Presentational mode)
CULTURES	**Students use German to investigate, explain, and reflect on:** 1. The relationship of the practices and perspectives of the culture studied. 2. The relationship of the products and perspectives of the culture studied.
CONNECTIONS	**Students:** 1. Build, reinforce, and expand their knowledge of other disciplines while using German to develop critical thinking and to solve problems creatively. 2. Access and evaluate information and diverse perspectives that are available through German and its cultures.
COMPARISONS	**Students use German to investigate, explain, and reflect on:** 1. The nature of language through comparisons of the German language and their own. 2. The concept of culture through comparisons of the cultures studied and their own.
COMMUNITIES	**Students:** 1. Use German both within and beyond the school to interact and collaborate in their community and the globalized world. 2. Set goals and reflect on their progress in using languages for enjoyment, enrichment, and advancement.

Adapted from ACTFL's Standards for Foreign Language Learning in the 21st Century

Learning to Use Your
Instructor's Annotated Edition

SAG MAL offers you a comprehensive, thoroughly developed Instructor's Annotated Edition (IAE). It features student text pages overprinted with answers to all activities with discrete responses. Each page also contains annotations for a few selected activities that were written to complement and support varied teaching styles, to extend the already rich contents of the student textbook, and to save you time in class preparation and course management.

Because the **SAG MAL** IAE is different from instructor's editions available with other German programs, this section is designed as a quick orientation to the principal types of instructor annotations it contains. As you familiarize yourself with them, it is important to know that the annotations are suggestions only. Any German question, sentence, model, or simulated instructor-student exchange is not meant to be prescriptive or limiting. You are encouraged to view these suggested "scripts" as flexible points of departure that will help you achieve your instructional goals.

For the Chapter Opening Page

- **Suggestion** A discussion topic idea, based on the Chapter Opener photo

For the Lessons

- **Suggestion** Teaching suggestions for working with on-page materials, carrying out specific activities, and presenting new vocabulary or grammar

- **Expansion** Expansions and variations on activities

- **Vorbereitung** Suggestions for talking about the **Fotoroman** pages before students have watched the video or studied the pages

- **Nützliche Ausdrücke** A list of expressions taken from the **Fotoroman** that students may need to study before watching the episode

- **Partner and Video Virtual Chats** Assignments that develop students' communication skills with the convenience of the Supersite

- **Communication Icons** are tagged to activities that engage students in one of the three different modes of communication:

     Interpretive communication Exercises that target students' reading or listening skills and assess their comprehension

     Presentational communication Ideas and contexts that require students to produce a written or verbal presentation in the target language

     Interpersonal communication Activities that provide students with opportunities to carry out language functions in simulated real-life contexts or engage in personalized communication with others

 Please check the **SAG MAL** Supersite at **vhlcentral.com** for additional teaching support.

Course Planning

The entire **SAG MAL,** Third Edition, program was developed with an eye to flexibility and ease of use in a wide variety of course configurations. **SAG MAL,** Third Edition, can be used in courses taught on semester or quarter systems, and in courses that complete the book in two or three semesters. Here are some sample course plans that illustrate how **SAG MAL,** Third Edition, can be used in different academic situations. You should, of course, feel free to organize your courses in the way that best suits your students' needs and your instructional objectives.

Two-Semester System

The following chart illustrates how **SAG MAL,** Third Edition, can be completed in a two-semester course.

Semester 1	Semester 2
Chapters 1–6	Chapters 7–12

Three-Semester or Quarter System

This chart shows how **SAG MAL,** Third Edition, can be used in a three-semester or quarter course. The chapters are divided over each semester/quarter, allowing students to absorb the material at a steady pace.

Semester/Quarter 1	Semester/Quarter 2	Semester/Quarter 3
Chapters 1–4	Chapters 5–8	Chapters 9–12

Four-Semester System

This chart shows how **SAG MAL,** Third Edition, can be used in a four-semester course.

Semester 1	Semester 2	Semester 3	Semester 1
Chapters 1–3	Chapters 4–6	Chapters 7–9	Chapters 10–12

SAMPLE LESSON PLAN AND SYLLABUS

The sample two-semester syllabus and **Kapitel 2** lesson plan for **SAG MAL,** Third Edition, are available on the instructor's section of the **SAG MAL,** Third Edition, Supersite at **vhlcentral.com**. You will find general suggestions, as well as plans for the two lessons in each chapter and end-of-chapter **Weiter geht's** section. The sample syllabus and lesson plan are not intended to be prescriptive. You should feel free to present lesson materials as you see fit, tailoring them to your own teaching preferences and to your students' learning styles. It is our hope that you will find the **SAG MAL,** Third Edition, program very flexible: simply pick and choose from its array of instructional resources, and sequence the material in the way that makes the most sense for your course.

General Teaching Considerations

Orienting Students to the Student Textbook

Because **SAG MAL,** Third Edition, treats interior and graphic design as an integral part of students' language-learning experience, you may want to take a few minutes to orient students to the student textbook. Have them flip through one chapter, and point out that the chapters are all organized exactly the same way, with two short lessons and a concluding **Weiter geht's** section. Also point out that the major sections of each lesson are color-coded for easy navigation: green for **Kontext;** orange for **Fotoroman;** red for **Kultur**; blue for **Strukturen, Zapping, Kurzfilm,** and **Wiederholung**; and purple for **Weiter geht's** and **Wortschatz.** Because of these design elements, students can be confident that they will always know "where they are" in their textbook.

Emphasize that sections are self-contained, occupying either a full page or a spread of two facing pages, thereby eliminating "bad breaks." Finally, call students' attention to the use of color to highlight key information in elements such as charts, diagrams, word lists, activity models, titles, and help boxes such as **Achtung!, Tipp,** and **Querverweis.**

Flexible Lesson Organization

SAG MAL, Third Edition, uses a flexible lesson organization designed to meet the needs of diverse teaching styles, instructional goals, and institutional requirements. For example, you can begin with the chapter opening page and progress sequentially through a chapter. If you do not want to devote class time to grammar, you can assign the **Strukturen** explanations for outside study, freeing up class time for other purposes, such as developing oral communication skills; building listening, reading, and writing skills; learning more about the German-speaking world; or working with the video program. You might decide to work with the Weiter geht's section in order to focus on students' reading skills and their knowledge of German-speaking regions. On the other hand, you might prefer to skip these sections entirely, or to draw from them selectively, depending on your classroom needs and the interests of your students. If you plan on using the **SAG MAL,** Third Edition, Testing Program, however, be aware that its tests and exams check students' command of language presented in **Kontext** and vocabulary called out in text and charts on the **Strukturen** pages. The language presented in the **Nützliche Ausdrücke** boxes of the **Fotoroman** and the Deutsch im **Alltag** boxes on **Kultur** pages is not tested.

Identifying Active Vocabulary

All words and expressions taught in the **Kontext** illustrations and lists are considered active, testable vocabulary. Likewise, new vocabulary called out in **Strukturen**, including tables, charts, and boxes, is considered active and testable. At the end of each chapter, **Wortschatz** provides a convenient one-page summary of the items that students should know and that may appear on tests or exams. The phrases and expressions in **Fotoroman** are not part of the active vocabulary load. You will want to point this out to students.

Taking into Account
the Affective Dimension

While many factors contribute to the quality and success rate of learning experiences, two factors are particularly germane to language learning. One is students' beliefs about how language is learned; the other is language-learning anxiety.

As studies show and experienced instructors know, students often come to modern language courses either with a lack of knowledge about how to approach language learning or with mistaken notions about how to do so. For example, many students believe that making mistakes when speaking the target language must be avoided because doing so will lead to permanent errors. Others are convinced that learning another language is like learning any other academic subject. In other words, they believe that success is guaranteed, provided they attend class regularly, learn the assigned vocabulary words and grammar rules, and study for exams. In fact, in a study of college-level beginning language learners in the United States, over one third of the participants thought that they could become fluent if they studied the language for only one hour a day for two years or less. Mistaken and unrealistic beliefs such as these can cause frustration and ultimately demotivation, thereby significantly undermining students' ability to achieve a successful language-learning experience.

Another factor that can negatively impact students' language-learning experiences is language-learning anxiety. As Professor Elaine K. Horwitz of The University of Texas at Austin and Senior Consulting Editor of **VISTAS,** First Edition, wrote, "Surveys indicate that up to one-third of American foreign language students feel moderately to highly anxious about studying another language. Physical symptoms of foreign language anxiety can include heart-pounding or palpitations, sweating, trembling, fast breathing, and general feelings of unease." The late Dr. Philip Redwine Donley, **VISTAS** co-author and author of articles on language-learning anxiety, spoke with many students who reported feeling nervous or apprehensive in their classes. They mentioned freezing when called on by their instructors or going inexplicably blank when taking tests. Some so dreaded their classes that they skipped them or dropped the course.

Based on what Vista Higher Learning learned from instructors and students using our highly successful introductory Spanish and French programs, **SAG MAL,** Third Edition, contains several features aimed at reducing students' language anxiety and supporting their successful language learning. First of all, the highly structured, visually dramatic interior design of the **SAG MAL,** Third Edition, student text was conceived as a learning tool to make students feel comfortable with the content and confident about navigating the lessons. In addition, the student text provides marginal boxes that assist students by making relevant connections with new information or reminding them of previously learned concepts.

General Suggestions for Using the
SAG MAL *Fotoroman* Video Episodes

The **Fotoroman** section in each lesson and the **Fotoroman** video were created as interlocking pieces. All photos in **Fotoroman** are actual video stills from the corresponding video episode, while the printed conversations are abbreviated versions of the dramatic segment. Both the **Fotoroman** conversations and their expanded video versions represent comprehensible input at the discourse level; they were purposely written to use language from the corresponding lesson's **Kontext** and **Strukturen** sections. Thus, as of **Episode 2** in **Lektion 1B,** they recycle known language, preview grammar points students will study later in the lesson, and, in keeping with **Krashen's** concept of "i + 1," contain some amount of unknown language.

Because the **Fotoroman** textbook sections and the dramatic episodes of the **Fotoroman** video are so closely connected, you may use them in many different ways. For instance, you can use **Fotoroman** as a preview, presenting it before showing the video episode. You can also show the video episode first and follow up with **Fotoroman.** You can even use **Fotoroman** as a stand-alone, video-independent section.

Depending on your teaching preferences and campus facilities, you might decide to show all video episodes in class or to assign them solely for viewing outside the classroom. You could begin by showing the first one or two episodes in class to familiarize yourself and students with the characters, storyline, style, and **Zusammenfassung** sections. After that, you could work in class only with **Fotoroman** and have students view the remaining video episodes outside of class. No matter which approach you choose, students have ample materials to support viewing the video independently and processing it in a meaningful way. For each video episode, there are activities in the **Fotoroman** section of the corresponding textbook lesson, as well as additional activities in the **SAG MAL,** Third Edition, Video Manual section of the Student Activities Manual.

You might also want to use the **Fotoroman** video in class when working with the **Strukturen** sections. You could play the parts of the dramatic episode that correspond to the video stills in the grammar explanations or show selected scenes and ask students to identify certain grammar points.

You could also focus on the **Zusammenfassung** sections that appear at the end of each episode to summarize the key language functions and grammar points used. In class, you could play the parts of the **Zusammenfassung** section that exemplify individual grammar points as you progress through each **Strukturen** section. You could also wait until you complete a **Strukturen** section and review it and the lesson's **Kontext** section by showing the corresponding **Zusammenfassung** section in its entirety.

On the **SAG MAL,** Third Edition, Supersite, instructors can control what, if any, subtitles students can see. They are available in German or in English, and in transcript format.

When showing the **Fotoroman** video segments in your classes, you might want to implement a process approach. You could start with an activity that prepares students for the video segment, implementing the vocabulary they learned in the **Kontext** section. This could be followed by an activity that students do while you play parts of, or the entire, video segment. The final activity, done in the same class period or in the next one as warm-up, could recap what students saw and heard and move beyond the video segment's topic. The following suggestions for using the **Fotoroman** video segments in class are in addition to those on the individual pages of the Instructor's Annotated Edition, and they can be carried out as described or expanded upon in any number of ways.

Before viewing

- Ask students to guess what the segment might be about based on what they've learned in Kontext or by asking them to look at the video stills.

- Have pairs make a list of the lesson vocabulary they expect to hear in the video.

- Read a list of true-false or multiple-choice questions about the video to the class, and have students use what they know about the characters to guess the answers. Have them confirm their guesses after watching the segment.

While viewing

- Show the video segment with the audio turned off and ask students to use lesson vocabulary and previously learned structures to describe what they see. Have them confirm their guesses by showing the segment again with the audio on.

- Have students refer to the list of words they brainstormed before viewing the video and put a check in front of any words they actually hear or see in the segment.

- First, have students simply watch the video. Then, show it again and ask students to take notes on what they see and hear. Finally, have them compare their notes in pairs or groups for confirmation.

- Print the episoce's videoscript from the Supersite and white out words and expressions related to the lesson theme. Distribute the scripts for pairs or groups to complete as cloze paragraphs.

- Show the video segment before moving on to Kontext to jump-start the lesson's vocabulary, grammar, and cultural focus. Have students tell you what vocabulary and grammar they recognize from previous lessons.

After viewing

- Have students say what aspects of the information presented in the corresponding textbook lesson are included in the video segment.

- Ask groups to write a brief summary of the content of the video segment. Have them exchange papers with another group for peer review.

- Have students pick one new aspect of the corresponding textbook lesson's cultural theme that they learned about from watching the video segment. Then ask them to research more about that topic and write a list or paragraph to expand on it.

About strategies
in *Lesen, Hören*, and *Schreiben*

SAG MAL, Third Edition, takes a process approach to the development of reading, listening, and writing skills. These are lists of the different strategies taught in each chapter so that you may refer to them in one convenient place.

Lesen

Kapitel 1 Recognizing cognates	**Kapitel 7** Predicting content from the title
Kapitel 2 Predicting content through formats	**Kapitel 8** Identifying borrowed words: anglicisms
Kapitel 3 Predicting content from visuals	**Kapitel 9** Reading for the main idea
Kapitel 4 Scanning	**Kapitel 10** Analyzing repetition
Kapitel 5 Skimming	**Kapitel 11** Analyzing characters
Kapitel 6 Recognizing word families	**Kapitel 12** Analyzing imagery

Hören

Kapitel 1 Listening for words you know	**Kapitel 7** Using visual cues
Kapitel 2 Listening for cognates	**Kapitel 8** Recognizing the genre of spoken discourse
Kapitel 3 Asking for repetition	**Kapitel 9** Using background information
Kapitel 4 Listening for the gist	**Kapitel 10** Guessing the meaning of words from context
Kapitel 5 Listening for key words	**Kapitel 11** Listening for linguistic clues
Kapitel 6 Using background knowledge	**Kapitel 12** Taking notes

Schreiben

Kapitel 1 Writing in German	**Kapitel 7** Making an outline
Kapitel 2 Brainstorming	**Kapitel 8** Expressing and supporting opinions
Kapitel 3 Using idea maps	**Kapitel 9** Using linking words
Kapitel 4 Adding details	**Kapitel 10** Using note cards
Kapitel 5 Using a dictionary	**Kapitel 11** Writing strong introductions and conclusions
Kapitel 6 Reporting on an interview	**Kapitel 12** Considering audience and purpose

Acknowledgments

Acknowledgments

On behalf of its authors and editors, Vista Higher Learning expresses its sincere appreciation to the instructors nationwide who reviewed materials from **SAG MAL.** Their input and suggestions were vitally helpful in forming and shaping the Third Edition in its final, published form.

We also extend a special thank you to the contributing writers of **SAG MAL,** Third Edition, whose hard work was central to the publication.

Reviewers

Tim Altanero
Eastern Florida State College, TX

Jennifer Aykens
Northern VA Community College, VA

Professor K. Bowen
Spring Arbor University, MI

Annette Budzinski-Luftig
Towson University, MD

Nicole L. Butler
Morehouse College, GA

Lisa Coffield, M.S.
Idaho State University, ID

Dr. David Dowdey, Professor of German
Pepperdine University, CA

Janet Dickey Lein
Central Michigan University, MI

Gregory Divers, PhD
Saint Louis University, MO

Devon Donohue-Bergeler
The University of Texas at Austin, TX

Cordula Drossel-Brown, Ph.D.
Bellevue College, WA

Lara Ducate
University of South Carolina, SC

Karen Ewing
UT Austin, TX

Jennifer M. Gully
William & Mary, VA

Michelle Kendrick
Pacific Union College, CA

Sara Lee
Arizona State University, AZ

Erich Lichtscheidl
Montgomery County Community College, PA

Hannes Mandel
University of Texas at Austin

Dr. Janya Martin
Baylor University, TX

Bette M. Miller
Northeast Texas Community College, TX

Rita Morandi
American University, Washington D.C.

Timothy K. Nixon, Ph.D.
Shepherd University, WV

Eva Norling
Bellevue College, WA

Dr. Stephanie G. Ortega
Concordia University Texas, TX

Hanne Pardos
Arkansas State University, AR

Lukas Pawelek
University of South Carolina Beaufort, SC

James L Raskob
UWM – SCE, WI

Dr. Christine Rinne
University of South Alabama, AL

Eckhard Rölz
South Dakota State University, SD

Christopher Ruwe
University of Cincinnati Clermont College, OH

Prisilla Sanchez
University of Oregon, OR

Patricia Schempp
Penn State University, PA

Mariagrazia Spina
UCF, FL

Leslie Taylor
Pima Community College, AZ

Matthias W. Vogel
University of Oregon, OR

Anja Wright, MA
George Mason University, VA

THIRD EDITION

SAG MAL

AN INTRODUCTION TO GERMAN LANGUAGE AND CULTURE

COMMUNICATIVE GOALS
By the end of this chapter you will be able to:

Los geht's! What are these people doing?
How do you greet your friends?

LEKTION 1A

Greet people and say good-bye.
Make introductions and use polite expressions.

To do so, you will use:

Kontext Seite 2–5
• Greetings and polite expressions
• Introductions

Strukturen Seite 10–20
1A.1 Gender, articles, and nouns
1A.2 Plurals
1A.3 Subject pronouns, **sein**, and the nominative case

You will also learn about cultural products, practices, and perspectives related to:

Kultur Seite 8–9
• Regional differences for common polite phrases
• The **Brandenburger Tor**

Zapping Seite 21
• *Deutsche Bahn*

LEKTION 1B

Talk about classes and schedules.

To do so, you will use:

Kontext Seite 22–25
• Classroom vocabulary
• Places
• People

Strukturen Seite 30–39
1B.1 Haben and the accusative case
1B.2 Word order
1B.3 Numbers

You will also learn about cultural products, practices, and perspectives related to:

Kultur Seite 28–29
• The German school system
• The first day of school
• The school day in Germany

WEITER GEHT'S

Seite 40–46
You will also learn about countries that have German as an official language, the Alps, the Berlin Wall, Swiss chocolate, and the Hanseatic League.

And you will demonstrate that you can:
• Recognize cognates in a reading selection
• Listen for words you know in a listening selection
• Write a list of important phone numbers and addresses

Suggestion Tell students that the people in the photo are characters from the Fotoroman. Introduce them as George, Sabite, and Meline and ask students what they might be saying to one another. Ask if students know any German greetings.

Wie geht's?

 Vocabulary Tools

Active vocabulary Point out that all expressions used in the illustration are glossed in the **Wortschatz** on p.46. Tell students that they are responsible for learning all terms listed in the **Wortschatz**, as well as vocabulary introduced on the **Strukturen** pages. This is the content they will be expected to know for tests and quizzes.

Wortschatz

Begrüßung und Abschied	*hellos and good-byes*
Guten Morgen.	*Good morning.*
Guten Abend.	*Good evening.*
Gute Nacht.	*Good night.*
Bis dann.	*See you later.*
Bis gleich.	*See you soon.*
Bis morgen.	*See you tomorrow.*
Auf Wiedersehen.	*Good-bye.*
Schönen Tag noch!	*Have a nice day!*
Prima.	*Great.*
Es geht.	*So-so.*
(Nicht) schlecht.	*(Not) bad.*
Mir geht's nicht (so) gut.	*I'm not (so) well.*

Suggestion Point out that **Morgen** with a capital *M* means *morning*, as in **Guten Morgen**, while **morgen** with a lowercase *m* means *tomorrow*, as in **bis morgen**.

Höflichkeiten	*polite expressions*
Gern geschehen.	*My pleasure.*
Entschuldigung.	*Excuse me.*
Entschuldigen Sie.	*Excuse me. (form.)*
Es tut mir leid.	*I'm sorry.*
ja	*yes*
nein	*no*

Suggestion Point out that the informal question **Wie heißt du?** is used in the dialogue between Markus and Anna on p.3.

sich vorstellen	*introducing oneself*
Wie heißen Sie?	*What is your name? (form.)*
Schön dich/Sie kennen zu lernen.	*Nice to meet you. (inf./form.)*

Personen	*people*
die Frau	*woman*
der Freund / die Freundin	*friend (m./f.)*
der Junge	*boy*
das Mädchen	*girl*
der Mann	*man*

Suggestion Point out that **Frau** is used to address a woman regardless of her marital status.

Herr	*Mr.*
Frau	*Mrs.; Ms.*
wo?	*where?*
hier	*here*
da/dort	*there*

Suggestion Explain that German speakers often end a phone conversation with **Auf Wiederhören** (*Until we hear each other again*) instead of **Auf Wiedersehen** (*Until we see each other again*).

MICHAEL Guten Tag, Herr Brenner, wie geht es Ihnen?
HERR BRENNER Hallo, Michael! Es geht mir ziemlich gut. Und dir?
MICHAEL Mir auch, danke.

Suggestion Point out that **Gut(en)** means *good* and **Tag** means *day*. Tell students that this greeting can be used from morning to afternoon.

PAUL Vielen Dank!
JOHANNES Bitte!

MARIA Bis später, Lukas!
LUKAS Tschüss, Maria. Bis bald!

Suggestion Explain to students the differences between **bis bald**, **bis gleich**, **bis dann**, and **bis später**.

CHRISTOPH Guten Tag, Herr Arnold. Das ist Christina Schöller.
HERR ARNOLD Guten Tag, Frau Schöller!
CHRISTINA Freut mich.

ACHTUNG

ACHTUNG

There are formal and informal ways of saying *you* in German. Use **du** and its plural, **ihr**, in informal situations; use **Sie** in formal situations.

MARKUS Guten Tag, ich heiße Markus. Und du? Wie heißt du?
ANNA Ich heiße Anna.
MARKUS Angenehm, Anna.

Suggestion Have students take turns greeting each other and introducing themselves using vocabulary from this section.

SOFIA Guten Tag, Katrin!
KATRIN Hallo, Sofia!
SOFIA Wie geht's?
KATRIN Mir geht's gut, danke! Und wie geht es dir? Alles klar?
SOFIA Sehr gut, danke!

Anwendung

1 **Was passt?** Put these expressions into the correct categories.

1 Suggestion Ask students to suggest additional items from this section that could be listed in each category.

Bitte!	die Frau	der Mann
Danke.	der Freund	Tschüss!
Entschuldigung.	Guten Tag!	Wie geht's?

Polite expressions	**People**	**Hellos and good-byes**
Danke.	die Frau	Wie geht's?
Entschuldigung.	der Mann	Guten Tag!
Bitte!	der Freund	Tschüss!

2 **Was fehlt?** Complete each conversation with the appropriate word.

1. —_____Vielen_____ Dank!
   —_____Gern_____ geschehen!
2. —Guten Morgen. Ich _____heiße_____ Daniel.
   —Guten _____Morgen_____, Daniel.
3. —Hallo, Lina! _____Wie_____ geht's?
   —_____Sehr_____ gut.
4. —Auf _____Wiedersehen_____, Frau Stein. Schönen Tag noch!
   —_____Danke/Vielen Dank_____.
5. —Hallo, David! Das _____ist_____ Lara.
   —Hallo, Lara! Schön, dich _____kennen_____ zu lernen!
6. —Guten Abend, Herr Klein. Wie geht es _____Ihnen_____?
   —Hallo, Tom. Es geht _____mir_____ gut, danke. Und dir?

2 Expansion Have students write two more lines of dialogue for each conversation. Remind them to pay careful attention to the use of **du** and **Sie**.

3 **Kurze Gespräche** Listen to the conversations and decide whether each conversation is **formell** (*formal*) or **informell** (*informal*).

	formell	**informell**
1.	☐	☑
2.	☑	☐
3.	☐	☑
4.	☐	☑
5.	☑	☐
6.	☐	☑

3 Suggestion Before playing the audio recording, ask students to brainstorm ways of indicating formal and informal speech, such as the use of titles and last names versus first names.

4 **Antworten Sie** Provide an appropriate response to each question or statement you hear.

1. Ich heiße [name]. _____
2. Gut, danke. _____
3. Freut mich. _____
4. Gern geschehen. _____
5. Tschüss. _____
6. Danke. _____

4 Suggestion Have students listen to the recording and respond out loud to each prompt. Then, have them listen again and write down their answers.

Kommunikation

NATIONAL communication STANDARDS

5 Minidialoge
Select the response that best completes each conversation, then role-play the mini-dialogues with a partner.

5 Suggestion Before playing the audio recording, ask students to brainstorm ways of indicating formal and informal speech, such as the use of titles and last names versus first names.

1. —Guten Tag, Frau Meier!
   a. —Hallo, Frau Schneider! **b.** —Nicht schlecht.
2. —Danke, Sabine.
   a. —Bitte. **b.** —Bis bald!
3. —Auf Wiedersehen!
   a. —Prima. **b.** —Tschüss!
4. —Wie heißen Sie?
   a. —Ich heiße Paul. b. —Vielen Dank.
5. —Wie geht es Ihnen, Herr Huber?
   a. —Bis dann. **b.** —Danke, gut.
6. —Ich heiße Anka.
   a. —Freut mich. b. —Entschuldigung.
7. —Gute Nacht, Lara. Bis morgen.
   a. —Ja, bis dann. b. —Freut mich.
8. —Guten Tag, Herr Melchior. Das ist mein Freund.
   a. —Gern geschehen. **b.** —Angenehm.

6 Begrüßungen
In small groups, look at the illustrations, then act out a short dialogue in which the people greet each other, ask each other's names, and ask each other how they are. Pay attention to the use of **du** and **Sie**. Act out the dialogues in front of the class. Answers will vary.

BEISPIEL

S1: Das ist Frau Sperber.
S2: Guten Tag, Frau Sperber.
S3: ...

1. Professor Fink

2. Frau Sperber

3. Anja

4. Franz

7 Diskutieren und kombinieren
Your instructor will give you and a partner worksheets with descriptions of five people. Use the information from your worksheet to introduce yourself and talk about how you are. Role-play each of the five people on your worksheet. Answers will vary.

BEISPIEL

S1: Hallo, ich heiße Martin. Und du?
S2: Hallo, ich heiße Sandra. Wie geht's?
S1: Ziemlich gut. Und dir?

8 Kennen lernen
In groups of three, introduce yourself and ask your partners how they are. Then introduce your partners to the members of another group. Answers will vary.

BEISPIEL

S1: Hallo, ich heiße Sina. Und wie heißt du?
S2: Hallo, Sina. Ich heiße Katja.
S1: Und wie geht's dir?
S2: Prima, danke. Und wie geht's dir?
S1: Ziemlich gut. Katja, das hier ist Thomas.
S3: Hallo, Katja. Schön dich kennen zu lernen.

Aussprache und Rechtschreibung Audio

The German alphabet

The German alphabet is made up of the same 26 letters as the English alphabet. Although the alphabet is the same, many of the letters (**Buchstaben**) are pronounced differently.

Buchstabe	Beispiel	Buchstabe	Beispiel	Buchstabe	Beispiel
a (ah)	**Abend**	i (ih)	**Idee**	r (err)	**Regen**
b (beh)	**Butter**	j (yot)	**ja**	s (ess)	**singen**
c (tseh)	**Celsius,**	k (kah)	**Katze**	t (teh)	**tanzen**
	Café	l (ell)	**lesen**	u (ooh)	**Universität**
d (deh)	**danke**	m (emm)	**Mutter**	v (fau)	**Vogel, Vase**
e (eh)	**Elefant**	n (enn)	**Nase**	w (veh)	**Wasser**
f (eff)	**finden**	o (oh)	**Oper**	x (iks)	**Xylophon**
g (geh)	**gut**	p (peh)	**Papier**	y (üpsilon)	**Yacht, Typ**
h (hah)	**hallo**	q (koo)	**Quatsch**	z (tset)	**Zelt**

The symbol **ß** (**Eszett** or **scharfes s**) is used instead of a double **s** in certain words. **Eszett** is never used at the beginning of a word. It is capitalized as **SS**.

ß (Eszett, scharfes S)   **Straße** (*street*)

An **Umlaut** (¨) can be added to the vowels **a**, **o**, and **u**, changing their pronunciation.

a	**Apfel**	ä	(a-Umlaut)	**Äpfel**
o	**Ofen**	ö	(o-Umlaut)	**Öfen**
u	**Mutter**	ü	(u-Umlaut)	**Mütter**

In German, all nouns are capitalized, no matter where they appear in a sentence. When spelling aloud, say **großes a** for *capital a*, or **kleines a** for *lowercase a*. To ask how a word is spelled, say: **Wie schreibt man das?** (lit. *How does one write this?*)

Suggestion Pronounce the words **Buchstabe** and **Beispiel** for students and ask them what they think these words mean.

Suggestion Tell students that, except in words or names of foreign origin, the letter *c* is only used in the letter combinations *ch* and *sch*. Also point out that the letter *c* before the vowels *e* and *i* is pronounced **tseh** but before *a*, *o*, and *u* is pronounced **kah**.

Suggestion Tell students that the letter *v* is pronounced like an English *v* in words of foreign origin. Ex.: **Vanille, Viktor, Vatikan, Venedig.**

Suggestion Tell students that ß is not used at all in Switzerland. In Swiss German, **Straße** is written as **Strasse**.

Suggestion Explain that the words with umlauts in these examples are the plural forms of the words to their left. Also point out that when used as a vowel, the letter **y** is pronounced like **ü**. Ex.: **Typ, typisch.**

1 **Aussprechen** Practice saying the German alphabet and sample words aloud.

2 **Buchstabieren** Spell these words aloud in German.

1. hallo
2. Morgen
3. studieren
4. Explosion
5. typisch
6. Universität
7. Bäcker
8. Straße
9. Juwelen
10. Frühling
11. tanzen
12. Querflöte

2 **Expansion** Ask students to identify cognates. Tell students the meanings of any unfamiliar words.

3 **Sprichwörter** Practice reading these sayings aloud.

Wer A sagt, muss auch B sagen.[1]

Übung macht den Meister.[2]

[1] You have to finish what you've started. (lit. *Whoever says A must also say B.*)
[2] Practice makes perfect.

More activities

vhlcentral   LM p. 2   Online activities

Willkommen in Berlin! Video

Meline und George kommen nach Berlin. Hier treffen sie Sabite und Hans.
Ist es eine freundliche Begrüßung (*friendly welcome*)?

Vorbereitung Before showing the video, have students preview the images and text on the page and guess the content of the episode. Encourage them to focus on overall comprehension of the video, and not to worry if they don't understand every word.

1

MELINE (*am Telefon*) Lukas... ah, Kreuzberg, okay. Lukas...

2

SABITE Hallo?
GEORGE Hallo. Ich bin George. Wie heißt du?
SABITE Ich heiße Sabite. Nett dich kennen zu lernen.
GEORGE Nett dich kennen zu lernen, Sabite.

3

SABITE Alles in Ordnung?
GEORGE Hier sind die Schlüssel. Danke, vielen Dank.
SABITE Gern geschehen. Keine Ursache. Bis später.

4

GEORGE *Talk to you later.*
Auf Wiederhören.

5

HANS Entschuldigung. Was für ein Chaos! Hier ist die Bürste... und der Lippenstift. Und hier ist das Handy.
MELINE (*am Telefon*) Tschüss, Lukas.

HANS Ich heiße Hans. Schönen Tag!

6

1 **Richtig oder falsch?** Choose whether each statement is **richtig** (*true*) or **falsch** (*false*).

1. Sabite hilft (*helps*) Hans. Falsch.
2. Meline ist am Flughafen (*airport*). Falsch.
3. George hat (*has*) die Schlüssel. Richtig.
4. Meline telefoniert mit (*calls*) Lukas. Richtig.
5. George trifft (*meets*) Sabite. Richtig.

6. Hans geht es ganz okay. Falsch.
7. Meline geht nach (*is going to*) Kreuzberg. Richtig.
8. Meline hat eine Bürste, einen Lippenstift und ein Handy. Richtig.
9. Sabite geht es gut. Richtig.
10. Hans sagt: „Willkommen in München." Falsch.

PERSONEN George Hans Meline Sabite

MELINE Ich bin's, Meline.
SABITE Meline, hallo. Nett dich kennen zu lernen.
MELINE Freut mich. Wie geht es dir?
SABITE Mir geht es gut.

SABITE Oh, das ist George. Hallo, George. Das ist Meline. Meline, George.
GEORGE Hallo.
MELINE Nett dich kennen zu lernen.
GEORGE Freut mich.

HANS George?
GEORGE Ja!
HANS Hallo! Ich bin Hans. Willkommen in Deutschland. Nett dich kennen zu lernen. Wie geht's?
GEORGE Ganz okay.

GEORGE Das ist Sabite.
SABITE Hallo.
HANS Hi.

Nützliche Ausdrücke

- **Wie heißt du?**
  What's your name?
- **Nett dich kennen zu lernen.**
  Nice to meet you.
- **Ist jemand da?**
  Anyone there?
- **Keine Ursache.**
  Don't mention it.
- **Auf Wiederhören.**
  Talk to you later.
- **Was für ein Chaos!**
  What a mess!
- **der Lippenstift**
  lipstick
- **das Handy**
  cell phone
- **Freut mich.**
  It's a pleasure.
- **Willkommen in Deutschland.**
  Welcome to Germany.

1A.1
- **Hier ist die Bürste.**
  Here's the brush.

1A.2
- **Hier sind die Schlüssel.**
  Here are the keys.

1A.3
- **Ich bin George.**
  I'm George.

Suggestion Tell students that they will learn more about the grammar structures previewed in each episode in the lesson's **Strukturen** section.

---

2 **Zum Besprechen** Imagine that you and your partner are exchange students meeting for the first time. Greet each other, give your names, and be sure to include an appropriate goodbye. Be prepared to present your conversation to the class. Answers will vary.

2 **Partner Chat** You can also assign activity 2 on the Supersite. Students work in pairs to record the activity online. The pair's recorded conversation will appear in your gradebook.

2 **Suggestion** This activity can also be done with groups of three or more.

3 **Vertiefung** Germans often shake hands when they meet. Do you and your friends often shake hands? Why or why not? Answers will vary.

More activities

vhlcentral | VM p. 1 | Online activities

IM FOKUS

Hallo, Deutschland!

 Reading

SAYING "HELLO" CAN BE A COMPLEX social interaction. Should you shake hands? Kiss cheeks? Keep your distance? The answers depend on where you are, who you are, and who you're talking to.

In general, Germans shake hands more than Americans do, and eye contact is an important feature of this gesture. If you've just been introduced to someone, shake hands, look him or her in the eye, and say **Freut mich**. In a business setting, a handshake is more or less obligatory, but friends may or may not shake hands when greeting. As in North America, friends in Germany, Austria, and Switzerland can often be seen greeting each other with a hug or a kiss on the cheek.

Greetings vary depending on time of day, level of formality, and region. In formal situations, you can say **Guten Morgen** in the morning, **Guten Tag** from morning to late afternoon, and **Guten Abend** in the evening. In Bavaria or Austria, you are likely to hear **Grüß Gott°** at any time of day. **Hallo**, **Tag**, and **Grüß dich°** are all common informal greetings. In Bavaria and Austria, use **Servus°** to say hello or good-bye to friends.

Deciding between informal and polite forms of address requires some judgment. In general, use the familiar forms **du** and **ihr** with children, teenagers, family members, and fellow

students. Use the polite form **Sie** with anyone else until they invite you to call them **du**. Always use **Sie** with people with whom you are not on a first-name basis. Address men as **Herr** and women as **Frau**, regardless of their marital status.

Grüß Gott *Hello. (lit. Greet God)* **Grüß dich** *Hello. (lit. Greet you (inf.))* **Servus** *Hello; Goodbye (inf.)*

1 **Im Fokus** Indicate whether each statement is **richtig** (*true*) or **falsch** (*false*). Correct the false statements. Then discuss the last question with a partner.

1. Germans shake hands more readily than Americans.
   Richtig.
2. **Grüß Gott** is a general greeting in Bavaria and Austria.
3. The **Sie**-form should be used with German adults until one gets to know them better and is prompted to use the **du**-form.
   Richtig.

Diskussion How do you and your friends greet other people? How do your practices differ from those in German-speaking countries?

2 **Die deutschsprachige Welt** Indicate whether each statement is **richtig** or **falsch**. Correct the false statements. Then discuss the last question with a partner.

1. Modern spoken German is very standardized.
   Falsch. Spoken German has many dialects.
2. **Uf Widerluege** is Austrian German for *Good-bye*.
   Falsch. It is a Swiss German way of saying "Goodbye."
3. **Auf Wiedersehen** will be understood in all German-speaking countries.
   Richtig.

Diskussion Have you heard any of these regional greetings? What regional differences exist in your native language?

Deutsch im Alltag Have students take turns practicing the greetings
from the list. Remind them that these items are not active vocabulary.

DEUTSCH IM ALLTAG

Wie geht's?

Geht's dir gut?	*Are you all right? (inf.)*
Und dir?	*And you? (inf.)*
Geht es Ihnen gut?	*Are you all right? (form.)*
Und Ihnen?	*And you? (form.)*
So weit, so gut.	*So far, so good.*
Spitze!	*Great!*
Schön dich zu sehen.	*Nice to see you. (inf.)*
Schön Sie zu sehen.	*Nice to see you. (form.)*
Herzlich willkommen.	*Welcome.*
Was geht?	*What's up?*

DIE DEUTSCHSPRACHIGE WELT

Auf Wiedersehen, Goodbye

One characteristic feature of the German
language is its wealth of regional differences.
Many dialects have their own greetings, from
Moin Moin along the North Sea Coast to
Switzerland's **Grüezi mitenand**. But how do
German speakers say goodbye?

- **Auf Wiedersehen** and **tschüss** are the
  most standard goodbyes.
- The formal Swiss counterpart is
  Uf Widerluege.
- The informal **Mach's gut** is similar in
  meaning to *Take care.*
- In Baden-Württemberg and the Saarland,
  Ade is common.
- In Austria, **Pfiati** is often used
  among friends.

Die deutschsprachige Welt Have students locate the
countries and regions mentioned here in the map on p. 40 of their textbooks.

PORTRÄT

Das Brandenburger Tor°

On December 22, 1989, thousands cheered as West German Chancellor Helmut Kohl
walked through the Brandenburg Gate to shake hands with East German Prime Minister
Hans Modrow. It was the first time since the construction of the **Berliner Mauer°** in 1961
that East and West Germans had been permitted to pass through the gate.

Built in 1791, the **Brandenburger Tor** was one of fourteen toll gates that encircled the city.
Over the next two centuries, the **Tor** withstood an invasion by Napoleon's soldiers, falling
bombs in World War II, and the Cold War partition of East and West Germany. Today, the
Tor is one of Berlin's most popular attractions, a symbol of German unity, and a monument
to Berlin's tumultuous past. Suggestion Tell students the origin and meaning of some regional greetings: **Moin
Moin** derives from a Dutch word meaning *good* or *beautiful*. **Grüezi mitenand** means

Tor *Gate* **Berliner Mauer** *Berlin Wall* *Hello everyone* and is used to greet multiple people. **Pfiati** is derived from **Pfüat di**,
meaning (May God) protect you. **Tschüss** is derived from *ciao*, and **Ade** from *adieu*.

🔗 IM INTERNET

Fashionably late isn't always fashionable. How
do German and American manners differ when it
comes to punctuality, greetings, and formality?

Find out more at **vhlcentral.com**.

3 Expansion Show students pictures of various people (an elderly person,
a child, a teacher, etc.) and ask how they would greet each person.

---

3 **Porträt** Indicate whether each statement is **richtig** or **falsch**. Correct
the false statements. Then discuss the last question with a partner.

🔗 1. The **Brandenburger Tor** dates from the late 18ᵗʰ century.
Richtig.

2. The Brandenburg Gate is now a symbol of German militarism. Falsch. The
Brandenburg Gate now symbolizes German unity, yet it also stands as a reminder of Berlin's tumultuous political past.

3. The **Berliner Mauer** lasted almost 30 years.
Richtig.

Diskussion Why do we build walls and gates? Where do you find them
in your community, and why do they exist? How do they affect you?

Suggestion To avoid political debate in class, remind students that walls and gates exist in
everyday life, e.g., room and house doors, picket fences.

4 **Hallo!** Write a brief conversation for these people. How would they greet
each other and say goodbye? What else would they say? Choose the
appropriate level of formality.

1. Die Studentin Becky trifft (*meets*) Professor Kent.

2. Professor Kent trifft Professor Meyer.

3. Becky trifft ihre Freundin Anna.

Strukturen

1A.1

Gender, articles, and nouns

 Grammar Tutorial

Teaching Tip You may want to assign the grammar tutorial **1A.1 Gender, articles, and nouns** on the Supersite for students to watch before they come to class.

Startblock Like English nouns, German nouns can be either singular or plural and may be preceded by a definite or indefinite article. Unlike English nouns, all German nouns have a gender. German nouns are always capitalized, regardless of where they appear in a sentence.

Was für **ein Chaos!**

Hier ist **die Bürste**. Hier ist **das Handy**.

Suggestion Point out that nouns taught in this text are listed with their corresponding singular definite articles. Encourage students to memorize the article along with each noun, in order to remember its gender.

Gender

- All German nouns have a gender: masculine, feminine, or neuter. While most nouns referring to males are masculine and most nouns referring to females are feminine, the genders of nouns representing objects and ideas need to be memorized.

MASCULINE	FEMININE	NEUTER
der **Mann**	die **Frau**	das **Buch**
the man	*the woman*	*the book*
der **Junge**	die **Blume**	das **Mädchen**
the boy	*the flower*	*the girl*

Suggestion Give students examples of nouns with the feminine endings -**heit** and -**ung**. Ex: **die Freiheit**, **die Wohnung**.

- Nouns ending with -**in** that refer to people are always feminine.

die Freund**in**	die Student**in**	die Professor**in**
*the (**female**) friend*	*the (**female**) student*	*the (**female**) professor*

ACHTUNG

Nouns ending with -**chen** are always neuter.

- Other feminine noun endings include -**ei**, -**heit**, -**schaft**, -**ung**, and -**tät**.

die **Bäckerei**	die **Freundschaft**	die **Universität**
*the **bakery***	*the **friendship***	*the **university***

Definite and indefinite articles

- The definite article, equivalent to *the* in English, precedes a noun and indicates its gender. The masculine article is **der**, the feminine article is **die**, and the neuter article is **das**.

MASCULINE	FEMININE	NEUTER
der **Tisch**	die **Tür**	das **Fenster**
the table	*the door*	*the window*

- The definite article **die** is used with all plural nouns, regardless of gender.

QUERVERWEIS

You will learn more about forming plurals in **1A.2**.

	SINGULAR		PLURAL	
MASCULINE	der Tisch		die Tische	*the tables*
FEMININE	die Tür		die Türen	*the doors*
NEUTER	das Fenster		die Fenster	*the windows*

- The indefinite article **ein(e)** corresponds to *a* or *an* in English. It precedes the noun and matches its gender. Note that both masculine and neuter nouns take the form **ein**, while feminine nouns take **eine**.

MASCULINE	FEMININE	NEUTER
ein Tisch	**eine** Tür	**ein** Fenster
a table	*a door*	*a window*
ein Mann	**eine** Frau	**ein** Mädchen
a man	*a woman*	*a girl*

- There is no plural form of the indefinite article.

Er ist **ein Mann**.   ▶   Sie sind **Männer**.
*He is **a man**.*   *They are **men**.*

Compound nouns

- Compound words are very common in German. As in English, two or more simple nouns can be combined to form a compound noun.

die Nacht   +   das Hemd   =   **das Nachthemd**
night   *shirt*   *nightshirt*

Hier ist **der Lippenstift**.

- The gender and number of a compound noun is determined by the last noun in the compound.

das Haus   +   **die** Aufgabe   =   **die Hausaufgabe**
house   *assignment*   *homework*

die Nacht   +   **der** Tisch   =   **der Nachttisch**
night   *table*   *night table*

Jetzt sind Sie dran! Tell students that all the nouns listed are singular.

Expansion Give students additional examples of nouns that can combine to form compounds. Have them figure out the appropriate articles for the compound forms. Ex.: **das Land** (*the country*) **+ die Karte** (*the map*) **= die Landkarte** (*the (country) map*); **der Arm** (*the arm*) **+ das Band** (*the strap*) **+ die Uhr** (*the clock*) **= die Armbanduhr** (*the watch*).

More activities

vhlcentral

WB
pp. 3–4

LM
p. 3

Online activities

Jetzt sind Sie dran!   Indicate the gender of each noun: **Maskulinum, Femininum,** or **Neutrum.**

	Maskulinum	Femininum	Neutrum		Maskulinum	Femininum	Neutrum
1. der Mann	☑	☐	☐	7. eine Frau	☐	☑	☐
2. die Freundin	☐	☑	☐	8. ein Mädchen	☐	☐	☑
3. der Junge	☑	☐	☐	9. ein Tisch	☑	☐	☐
4. das Hemd	☐	☐	☑	10. eine Nacht	☐	☑	☐
5. die Aufgabe	☐	☑	☐	11. die Universität	☐	☑	☐
6. ein Freund	☑	☐	☐	12. ein Buch	☐	☐	☑

Anwendung

1 **Was fehlt?** Write the appropriate article.

der, die, das	ein, eine
1. _das_ Fenster	5. _eine_ Frau
2. _der_ Tisch	6. _eine_ Tür
3. _der_ Student	7. _ein_ Mann
4. _die_ Freundschaft	8. _ein_ Mädchen

2 **Ergänzen Sie** Write each noun in the appropriate column. Include the definite and indefinite article.

Bäckerei	Haus
Buch	Hemd
Freund	Junge
Freundin	Studentin

Maskulinum	Femininum	Neutrum
der Mann; ein Mann	die Bäckerei; eine Bäckerei	das Buch; ein Buch
der Freund; ein Freund	die Freundin; eine Freundin	das Haus; ein Haus
der Junge; ein Junge	die Studentin; eine Studentin	das Hemd; ein Hemd

3 **Sätze** Complete each sentence with the appropriate definite or indefinite article.

1. _Der_ Junge heißt Paul.
2. Wie heißt _die_ Professorin?
3. Jasmin ist _ein_ Mädchen.
4. _Das_ Buch ist prima!
5. _Die_ Türen sind hier.
6. Lara ist _eine_ gute Studentin.

4 **Bilden Sie Wörter** Write the compound word with the appropriate definite article.

▶ **BEISPIEL**
das Haus + die Aufgabe =
die Hausaufgabe

1. die Kinder + der Garten
= _der Kindergarten_

2. der Schlaf (*sleep*) +
das Zimmer (*room*) =
das Schlafzimmer

3. das Telefon +
die Nummer =
die Telefonnummer

4. der Computer +
das Spiel (*game*) =
das Computerspiel

Kommunikation

5 **Was ist das?** In pairs, take turns identifying each person or object. Provide both the definite and indefinite articles.

▶ **BEISPIEL**
S1: *der Junge*
S2: *ein Junge*

1.
das Buch, ein Buch

2.
die Frau, eine Frau

3.
der Mann, ein Mann

4.
die Tür, eine Tür

5.
das Fenster, ein Fenster

6.
das Mädchen, ein Mädchen

6 **Was passt zusammen?** In pairs, take turns creating compound nouns using the words below. Include the appropriate article. Sample answers are provided.

der Schlüssel   der Ring

▶ **BEISPIEL**
S1: *der Schlüssel / der Ring*
S2: *der Schlüsselring*
der Handschuh, die Hauskatze, der Nachtbus, der Eisbär

die Hand   der Schuh   die Nacht   der Bus

das Haus   die Katze   das Eis   der Bär

7 **Was zeichne ich?** Take turns drawing pictures of nouns you've learned so far, for your partners to guess. The person who guesses correctly is the next to draw. Answers will vary.

▶ **BEISPIEL**
S1: *Das ist ein Buch.*
S2: *Nein.*
S1: *Ein Fenster?*
S2: *Ja!*

8 **Gedächtnisspiel** Play a memory game. The first player says a noun with the appropriate definite or indefinite article, and the next player repeats the previous noun and says his or her own. Go around the class until someone forgets an item or uses the wrong article. That player starts the next round. Answers will vary.

6 Suggestion Tell students the compounds they come up with don't have to be real words in German. Have them read out loud the compound words they created. Then, share with them the actual compounds (provided as sample answers) that can be made from combining the words listed, and have students guess their meanings.

1A.2 **Plurals** Grammar Tutorial

Startblock Plurals in German follow several patterns. These patterns can help you remember the plural form of each noun you learn.

- In German dictionaries and vocabulary lists, singular nouns are listed along with a notation that indicates how to form the plural. There are five main patterns for forming plural nouns.

notation	singular	plural
- ¨	das Fenster ⟶ die Mutter (*mother*) ⟶	die Fenster die Mütter
-e ¨e	der Freund ⟶ der Stuhl (*chair*) ⟶	die Freunde die Stühle
-er ¨er	das Kind (*child*) ⟶ der Mann ⟶	die Kinder die Männer
-n -en -nen	der Junge ⟶ die Frau ⟶ die Freundin ⟶	die Jungen die Frauen die Freundinnen
-s	der Park ⟶	die Parks

- Most masculine and neuter nouns form the plural by adding -e or -er. Plurals with the -er ending always add an **Umlaut** when the vowel in the singular form is **a**, **o**, or **u**.

    der Tag (*day*) ⟶ die Tage   das Buch ⟶ die Bücher

- If the singular form of a noun ends in -el, -en, or -er, there is no additional plural ending, but an **Umlaut** is added to the stem vowel **a**, **o**, or **u**.

    der Apfel (*apple*) ⟶ die Äpfel   das Zimmer (*room*) ⟶ die Zimmer

- For feminine nouns ending with -in, add -nen to form the plural.

    die Freundin ⟶ die Freundinnen   die Studentin ⟶ die Studentinnen

- For most other feminine nouns, add -n if the singular form ends in -e, -el, or -er. Add -en if it does not. Note that feminine plurals with these endings never add an **Umlaut**.

    die Blume (*flower*) ⟶ die Blumen   die Frau ⟶ die Frauen

- The -s ending is added to most words borrowed from other languages and to most nouns ending with vowels other than **e**.

    das Sofa ⟶ die Sofas   das Auto ⟶ die Autos

Jetzt sind Sie dran! Write the plural form of each singular noun and vice versa.

Singular
1. das Café ___die Cafés___
2. die Studentin ___die Studentinnen___
3. der Stuhl ___die Stühle___
4. die Tochter ___die Töchter___

Plural
5. die Zimmer ___das Zimmer___
6. die Universitäten ___die Universität___
7. die Äpfel ___der Apfel___
8. die Studenten ___der Student___

Anwendung und Kommunikation

1 **Schreiben** Write the plural form.

1. das Buch _____die Bücher_____
2. der Mann _____die Männer_____
3. der Tag _____die Tage_____
4. die Blume _____die Blumen_____
5. die Mutter _____die Mütter_____

6. das Auto _____die Autos_____
7. der Junge _____die Jungen_____
8. die Tür _____die Türen_____
9. das Kind _____die Kinder_____
10. der Park _____die Parks_____

2 **Plural** Complete each sentence with the plural form of the appropriate word.

BEISPIEL Holiday Inn und Marriott sind _____Hotels_____.

Apfel	Buch	Freundin
Auto	Computer	Hotel
Blume	Freund	Tag

1. BMW und Volkswagen sind _____Autos_____.
2. Rosen und Tulpen (*tulips*) sind _____Blumen_____.
3. Dell, HP und Acer sind _____Computer_____.
4. Granny Smith und Macintosh sind _____Äpfel_____.
5. Eine Woche (*week*) hat sieben (*seven*) _____Tage_____.
6. Anna, Monika und Emma sind _____Freundinnen_____.
7. *Harry Potter* und *Sag mal* sind _____Bücher_____.
8. Lukas und Felix sind _____Freunde_____.

3 **Was ist das?** In pairs, take turns identifying each object, place, or person. Give both singular and plural forms. Share your answers with the class. Sample answers are provided.

BEISPIEL
S1: *die Blume*
S2: *die Blumen*

1. das Mädchen, die Mädchen/ das Kind, die Kinder
2. der Park, die Parks
3. der Junge, die Jungen / das Kind, die Kinder
4. das Auto, die Autos
5. das Fenster, die Fenster
6. die Tür, die Türen
7. der Stuhl, die Stühle

2 **Suggestion** Remind students that they learned in **1A.1** that there is no plural form of the indefinite article.

3 **Expansion** Write nouns from this lesson's vocabulary on the back of note cards and distribute them to students. Have each student make a drawing of their noun on the opposite side of the card. Then have them take turns identifying each other's drawings and giving the plural form of each noun.

1A.3

Subject pronouns, *sein*, and the nominative case

 Grammar Tutorial

Lukas, **du bist**...

Ich bin George.

Subject pronouns

QUERVERWEIS

German speakers often use the third-person singular pronoun **man** where English speakers would say *one* or *you*.

You will learn more about the use of **man** in **7B.3**.

- In German, as in English, any noun can be replaced with an equivalent pronoun. A subject pronoun replaces a noun that functions as the subject of a sentence.

Maria ist nett.   **Sie** ist nett.   **Der Junge** ist groß.   **Er** ist groß.
Maria is nice.   *She is nice.*   *The boy is tall.*   *He is tall.*

subject pronouns		singular		plural
1ˢᵗ person		ich *I*		wir *we*
2ⁿᵈ person		du *you* (inf.) Sie *you* (form.)		ihr *you* (inf.) Sie *you* (form.)
3ʳᵈ person		er *he/it* sie *she/it* es *it*		sie *they*

Suggestion Tell students that **ich** is capitalized only when it begins a sentence, unlike the pronoun *I* in English. Remind them that the formal **Sie** is always capitalized.

- The gender of a noun determines the gender of the pronoun that replaces it. German uses **er** for all masculine nouns, **sie** for all feminine nouns, and **es** for all neuter nouns.

Der Tisch ist klein. ▶ **Er** ist klein.   **Das Buch** ist neu. ▶ **Es** ist neu.
The table is small.   *It's small.*   *The book is new.*   *It's new.*

Suggestion Give students additional examples using **sie** and **Sie** and ask them to figure out the intended meaning based on the context.

- The pronoun **Sie/sie** can mean *you, she, it,* or *they,* depending on context. Write **Sie** with a capital **S** to mean *you* in a formal context, and **sie** with a lowercase **s** to mean *she, it,* or *they.*

Das ist Frau Hansen.
   Sie ist Professorin.
That's Mrs. Hansen. **She** *is a professor.*

Das sind Lara und Jonas.
   Sie sind Studenten.
That's Lara and Jonas. **They're** *students.*

Woher kommen **Sie**?
Where are **you** *from?*

The verb *sein*

- **Sein** (*to be*) is an irregular verb: its conjugation does not follow a predictable pattern.

Suggestion
Explain to students that the conjugation of a verb is the set of verb forms corresponding to the different possible subjects.

sein (*to be*)			
singular		**plural**	
ich **bin**	*I am*	wir **sind**	*we are*
du **bist**	*you are* (inf.)	ihr **seid**	*you are* (inf.)
Sie **sind**	*you are* (form.)	Sie **sind**	*you are* (form.)
er/sie/es **ist**	*he/she/it is*	sie **sind**	*they are*

Ich bin Amerikaner.
I'm American.

Sie ist Deutsche.
She's German.

Wir sind Freunde.
We are friends.

The nominative case

- German has four *cases* that indicate the function of each noun in a sentence. The case of a noun determines the form of the definite or indefinite article that precedes the noun, the form of any adjectives that modify the noun, and the form of the pronoun that can replace the noun.

German cases		
Nominativ	Der Mann ist alt.	*The man is old.*
Akkusativ	Ich verstehe **den** Mann.	*I understand the man.*
Dativ	Der Assistent zeigt **dem** Mann den neuen Computer.	*The assistant is showing the man the new computer.*
Genitiv	Das ist der Assistent **des** Manns.	*This is the man's assistant.*

- The grammatical subject of a sentence is always in the nominative case (**der Nominativ**). Subject pronouns are, by definition, nominative pronouns. The nominative case is also used for nouns that follow a form of **sein**, **werden** (*to become*), or **bleiben** (*to stay, to remain*).

Das ist **eine gute Idee**.
*That's **a good idea**.*

Wir bleiben **Freunde**.
*We're still **friends**.*

- The definite and indefinite articles you learned in **1A.1** are the forms used with nouns in the nominative case.

nominative articles				
	masculine	**feminine**	**neuter**	**plural**
definite	der Junge	die Frau	das Mädchen	die Jungen
indefinite	ein Junge	eine Frau	ein Mädchen	– Jungen

Suggestion Point out that the conjugated form of **sein** is the same for **wir**, **Sie**, and **sie** (*pl.*). Tell students that all verbs have the same conjugated form for these three subjects.

Suggestion Point out that **Amerikaner** and **Deutsche** are nouns, even though they are translated as adjectives in this context. Tell students that the feminine form of **Amerikaner** is **Amerikanerin**, and the masculine form of **Deutsche** is **Deutscher**.

QUERVERWEIS

You will learn more about cases in **1B.1**, **3B.2**, **4B.1**, **4B.2**, and **8B.1**.

Suggestions

- Tell students that dictionaries and vocabulary lists always give nouns in their nominative form.
- Tell students that the set of forms that change depending on the number, case, and gender of a word are called declensions (**die Deklination, -en**).

Students will learn more about cases in **Vol. 2, 4B.1**.

More activities

vhlcentral

WB
pp. 7–8

LM
p. 5

Online activities

Jetzt sind Sie dran! For each noun, write the correct subject pronoun. For each pronoun, write the appropriate form of sein.

1. der Apfel ___er___
2. das Haus ___es___
3. die Jungen ___sie___
4. die Hausaufgabe ___sie___
5. Brigitte und ich ___wir___
6. die Studentin und du ___ihr___
7. wir ___sind___
8. ihr ___seid___
9. du ___bist___
10. Sie ___sind___
11. ich ___bin___
12. er ___ist___

Anwendung

1 **Was ist richtig?** Select the appropriate subject pronoun.

1. (**Ihr** / Wir) seid in Deutschland.
2. (**Er** / Ich) ist Katjas Freund.
3. (Du / **Sie**) sind nett!
4. (**Ihr** / Ich) seid Amerikaner.

5. (**Wir** / Ich) sind Deutsche.
6. (**Ich** / Du) bin Studentin.
7. (Es / **Du**) bist prima!
8. (Ihr / **Sie**) ist intelligent.

2 **Expansion** Have students transform the subjects of items 1, 4, 6, and 8 into subject pronouns.

2 **Was fehlt?** Write the correct form of **sein**.

1. Herr und Frau Schlüter ____sind____ dort.
2. Lena und ich ____sind____ hier.
3. Ich ____bin____ Anna.
4. Du ____bist____ Student.
5. Herr Doktor, Sie ____sind____ Experte.
6. Das Buch ____ist____ sehr interessant.
7. Ihr ____seid____ Kinder.
8. Das Fenster und die Tür ____sind____ offen (*open*).

3 **Sätze ergänzen** Write the pronoun and the appropriate form of **sein**.

▶ **BEISPIEL**

____Sie sind____ im (*at the*)
Restaurant.

1. ____Sie sind____
Freundinnen.

2. ____Er ist____
Deutschprofessor.

3. Mia, Tim und ich,
____sind____ Studenten.

4. Sara, ____du bist____
allein (*alone*).

5. ____Sie ist____
müde (*tired*).

6. Jan und du,
____ihr seid____ Freunde.

4 **Bilden Sie Sätze** Write complete sentences using **sein**. Then, replace the subjects with subject pronouns, where possible.

BEISPIEL Samuel / intelligent
Samuel ist intelligent. Er ist intelligent.

1. Lukas und ich / Studenten
Lukas und ich sind Studenten. Wir sind Studenten.
2. du / nett
Du bist nett.
3. es / ein gutes (*good*) Buch
Es ist ein gutes Buch.
4. Michael und du / in Deutschland
Michael und du seid in Deutschland. Ihr seid in Deutschland.

5. Danielle und Johanna / Deutsche
Danielle und Donna sind Deutsche. Sie sind Deutsche.
6. ich / Amerikaner
Ich bin Amerikaner.
7. Sie / unfair, Frau Henke
Sie sind unfair, Frau Henke.
8. das Haus / gigantisch
Das Haus ist gigantisch. Es ist gigantisch.

Kommunikation

5 **Was sehen Sie?** These pictures have been mislabeled. Correct the labels. Then compare your answers with a partner. Answers will vary.

▶ **BEISPIEL** Kinder

S1: Das sind Kinder.
S2: Nein, das sind Studentinnen.

1. Stühle

2. ein Tisch

3. ein Professor

4. Autos

5. Männer

6. ein Fenster

6 **Beschreibungen** Tell your partner that you are like each of the people listed. Answers will vary.

BEISPIEL   Paul / in Amerika (du)
                      Jan und Sara / tolerant (ihr)

S1: Paul ist in Amerika, und du?
S2: Ich bin auch in Amerika. Jan und Sara sind tolerant, und ihr?
S1: Wir sind auch tolerant.

1. die Professorin / intelligent (du)   3. Felix / romantisch (du)
2. Klara und Tim / Freunde (ihr)   4. Max und Lisa / Studenten (ihr)

7 **Freut mich!** In groups of three, role-play these situations. Each person should say something about him-/herself using a form of **sein**.

BEISPIEL

S1: Hallo, ich bin Max.
S2: Hallo, Max! Schön dich kennen zu lernen.
        Ich bin Sara und das ist Julia. Wir sind Studentinnen.

1. You are meeting your classmates for the first time. Introduce yourself and ask how each person is doing.

2. You and your friend are invited to a birthday party. Exchange greetings and introduce yourselves to other guests.

5 **Video Virtual Chat** You can also assign activity 5 on the Supersite. Students record individual responses that appear in your gradebook.

6 **Suggestion** Model pronunciation of the cognates used in this activity.

7 **Expansion** Have group members introduce themselves to the rest of the class.

Wiederholung

4 Expansions
- Repeat this activity using the cards students created for **Memory-Spiel**.
- Divide the class into teams and play Pictionary using the lesson vocabulary.

1

Memory-Spiel With a partner, create a set of cards to play Memory, featuring ten nouns you learned in this lesson. For each noun you draw, create a matching card showing the word with the definite article. Shuffle the cards and place them face down. Take turns matching pictures and words. Answers will vary.

der Apfel

Freut mich! In pairs, practice introducing yourselves in formal and informal situations. Answers will vary.

BEISPIEL

S1: Ich heiße Frau Schmidt.
S2: Angenehm. Ich heiße Luisa.
S1: Freut mich.

2 Partner Chat You can also assign activity 2 on the Supersite.

3

Schatzsuche With a partner, find one word or phrase from this lesson that corresponds to each description. Compete against other pairs to see which team can complete their list first. Remember: all words must be spelled correctly, nouns must be preceded by the appropriate definite article, and no word or phrase can be used more than once. Answers will vary.

BEISPIEL

S1: a feminine plural noun
die Blumen

1. a formal greeting
2. an informal way to say goodbye
3. a neuter noun that refers to a person
4. a response to the question "**Wie geht's**?"
5. a plural noun ending in -**s**
6. a sentence using a subject pronoun with **sein**
7. a noun that has identical singular and plural forms

4

Was ist das? In pairs, take turns identifying the objects and people.

▶ **BEISPIEL**

S1: Was ist das?
S2: Das ist ein Auto.

1. Das ist ein Buch.　　2. Das ist eine Blume./Das sind Blumen.

3. Das ist ein Fenster.　　4. Das ist ein Sofa.

5. Das ist ein Park.　　6. Das sind Kinder.

---

5 **Diskutieren und kombinieren** Your instructor will give you and a partner two worksheets with different images and labels. Work together to form the compound words.

---

6 **Arbeitsblatt** Your instructor will give you a worksheet (**das Arbeitsblatt**). Ask your classmates to say their names and spell them for you. Don't forget to greet them, ask how they are, and say thank you! Answers will vary.

BEISPIEL

S1: Guten Morgen!
S2: Hallo!
S1: Wie geht's?
S2: Es geht mir gut.
S1: Wie heißt du?
S2: Ich heiße Nadia.
S1: Wie schreibt man das?
S2: N-A-D-I-A.
S1: Wie ist dein Nachname (last name)?
S2: Mueller. M-U-E-L-L-E-R.
S1: Danke!

Video

Deutsche Bahn

Suggestion After showing students the video, ask questions to facilitate comprehension. Ex: In the first scene, why do some of the people in the child's drawing have blank faces? In the second scene, why are the children happier?

Vorbereitung Take a look at the picture and answer the questions.

1. Who is in the photo?
2. Where are these people?

Deutsche Bahn (DB) is the German railway company, based in Berlin. The **Deutsche Bahn** offers a **Sparpreis** (*discount price*) for families. Children under age 15 ride free when accompanied by an adult and pay half-price fares when traveling alone. This presents the **Deutsche Bahn** as a convenient and comfortable transportation option for families, allowing parents and children to interact and enjoy themselves on the way to their destination.

Familien fahren besser mit der Bahn.

Nützliche Ausdrücke	
die Familie	*family*
die Eltern	*parents*
der Euro	*euro*
das Gratiseis	*free popsicle*
das Kind, -er	*child*
Zug (m.) fahren	*to ride a train*

Verständnis Choose the correct answers.

1. How much does the DB family package cost?

   (a.) 49 Euro   b. 60 Euro   c. 39 Euro   d. 55 Euro

2. What do children riding the train receive?

   a. Bücher   b. Äpfel   (c.) Eis   d. Blumen

3 Diskussion Discuss the following questions with a partner.

1. What is train service like in your country? How do you think it compares with the services offered by the **Deutsche Bahn**?
2. Does this commercial make you want to travel by train in Germany? Why or why not?

4 Schreiben Write a short conversation between two people who meet on a train in a German-speaking country. Be sure to use the correct form of address.

BEISPIEL

Frau Schulze (45) trifft (meets) Tina (16).
Tina: Guten Tag. Wie geht es Ihnen?
Fr. Schulze: Danke. Gut. Und dir?

Suggestion Review the different levels of formality with students before they begin writing.

In der Schule

Vocabulary Tools

Wortschatz

im Unterricht	*in class*
der Computer, -	*computer*
das Ergebnis, -se	*result; score*
das Foto, -s	*photo*
die Frage, -n	*question*
die Hausaufgabe, -n	*homework*
der Kalender, -	*calendar*
die Klasse, -n	*class*
der Kuli, -s	*ball-point pen*
das Lehrbuch, ⁻er	*(university) textbook*
die Note, -n	*grade (on an assignment)*
die Notiz, -en	*note*
das Problem, -e	*problem*
die Prüfung, -en	*test; exam*
der Radiergummi, -s	*eraser*
die Sache, -n	*thing*
das Schulbuch, ⁻er	*(K–12) textbook*
die Stunde, -n	*lesson*
der Taschenrechner, -	*calculator*
der Tisch, -e	*table; desk*
die Tür, -en	*door*
das Zeugnis, -se	*report card; grade report*
Da ist/sind...	*There is/are...*
Ist/Sind hier...?	*Is/Are there... here?*
Hier ist/sind...	*Here is/are...*
Was ist das?	*What is that?*
Orte	***places***
die Bibliothek, -en	*library*
das Klassenzimmer, -	*classroom*
die Mensa, Mensen	*(university) cafeteria*
die Schule, -n	*school*
die Universität, -en	*university, college*
Personen	***people***
Wer ist das?	*Who is it?*
der Klassenkamerad, -en / die Klassenkameradin, -nen	*(K-12) classmate*
der Kommilitone, -n / die Kommilitonin, -nen	*(university) classmate*
der Professor, -en / die Professorin, -nen	*professor*
der Student, -en / die Studentin, -nen	*(university) student*

Suggestion Point out that many of these vocabulary items are compound nouns. Ask students to identify the compound nouns, then help them to figure out the meaning of the component words.

Suggestion Tell students that **Schüler(in)** refers to a student in elementary school through high school, while **Student(in)** refers to a college university student

ACHTUNG

Don't confuse **Da ist...** (*There is...*) with **Das ist...** (*This is...*).

die Uhr, -en

der Bleistift, -e

das Fenster, -

der Schüler, -

das Buch, ⁻er

die Schülerin, -nen

das Heft, -e

der Rucksack, ⁻e

der Stift, -e

das Wörterbuch, ⁻er
dictionary

der Papierkorb, ⁻e

das Blatt Papier,
(*pl.* Blätter Papier)
sheet of paper

die Tafel, -n

DEUTSCHLAND

LIECHTENSTEIN

DIE SCHWEIZ   ÖSTERREICH

die Karte, -n

der Lehrer, -
(die Lehrerin, -nen f.)

er Schreibtisch, -e

der Stuhl, ⁓e

Anwendung

1 Expansion Ask students what other words from the lesson vocabulary could be included in each group.

1 Was passt nicht? Select the word that doesn't belong.

1. der Professor / (das Problem) / die Universität / die Studentin
2. (das Fenster) / das Schulbuch / die Notizen / das Heft
3. der Stift / der Bleistift / (der Papierkorb) / der Kuli
4. die Tafel / der Schreibtisch / der Stuhl / (die Prüfung)
5. die Tür / (das Ergebnis) / der Tisch / die Uhr
6. das Problem / (der Radiergummi) / die Frage / das Ergebnis

2 Was ist das? Label each item.

3 Suggestion Have students identify items in your own classroom. Ask students: **Ist hier eine Uhr? Wo ist die Tür?**, etc.

▶ **BEISPIEL**   *der Bleistift*

1. ___der Stift/der Kuli___
2. ___das Buch/das Schulbuch/ das Lehrbuch/das Wörterbuch___
3. ___der Stuhl___
4. ___der Rucksack___
5. ___die Uhr___
6. ___die Tür___

3 Zuordnungen Write each word you hear in the correct category.

Orte	Personen
1. ___die Schule___	5. ___die Freundin___
2. ___die Mensa___	6. ___der Lehrer___
3. ___das Klassenzimmer___	7. ___die Professorin___
4. ___die Universität___	8. ___der Schüler___

3 Expansion Have students give the plural form of each word.

4 Logisch? Listen to the sentences and decide if they make sense.

	Logisch	Unlogisch		Logisch	Unlogisch
1.	☑	☐	4.	☑	☐
2.	☐	☑	5.	☐	☐
3.	☑	☐	6.	☑	☐

5 Ergänzen Sie Select the words that best complete each sentence.

Bücher	die Lehrerin	die Prüfung	die Schülerin	Tische

1. Anika ist... die Schülerin
2. Der Test ist... eine Prüfung
3. Im Rucksack sind... Bücher
4. Frau Meier ist... die Lehrerin
5. Im Klasseszimmer sind... Tische/Bücher

Kommunikation

 6 **Was ist das?** In pairs, take turns pointing at items and people in your classroom and asking each other to identify them. Answers will vary.

BEISPIEL

S1: Was ist das?
S2: Das ist ein Bleistift. Wer ist das?
S1: Das ist der Professor.

6 **Expansion** Repeat the activity as a class, having students ask and answer questions about items in the classroom.

---

7 **Im Rucksack** List six items that are in your backpack. Then, work with a partner and compare lists. Answers will vary.

1. In meinem Rucksack ist ein Buch.
2. _____
3. _____
4. _____
5. _____
6. _____

1. In Annas Rucksack sind Bücher.
2. _____
3. _____
4. _____
5. _____
6. _____

WERKZEUG

To say that something belongs to someone, add an **-s** to the person's name (**Marias Heft**; **Julians Buch**). Add an apostrophe if the name already ends in **-s** (**Niklas' Heft**; **Tobias' Buch**).

7 **Expansion** Bring in a bag filled with items such as pens, a calendar, a calculator, and so on. Pull them out one by one and ask students: **Ist das ein Bleistift oder ein Kuli? Ist das eine Uhr oder ein Taschenrechner? Ein Schulbuch oder ein Wörterbuch?** etc.

---

8 **Ist da...?** In pairs, take turns asking each other questions about what you see in the illustration. Answers will vary.

BEISPIEL

S1: Ist da ein Papierkorb?
S2: Nein. Da ist ein Bleistift. Ist da...?

8 **Partner Chat** You can also assign activity 7 on the Supersite. Students work in pairs to record the activity online. The pair's recorded conversation will appear in your gradebook.

9 **Ratespiel** Play Pictionary as a class. Answers will vary.

- Take turns going to the board and drawing images representing words from the lesson vocabulary.
- The person drawing may not write any letters or numbers.
- The person who correctly identifies the drawing in German gets to go next.

Aussprache und Rechtschreibung Audio

The vowels *a*, *e*, *i*, *o*, and *u*

Each German vowel may be pronounced with either a long or a short sound. A vowel followed by **h** is always long. A double **oo**, **aa**, or **ee** also indicates a long vowel sound. In some words, long **i** is spelled **ie**.

Fahne	wen	ihn	doof	Mut	diese

A vowel followed by two or more consonant sounds is usually short.

Pfanne	wenn	in	Sonne	Mutter	singst

When the German letter **e** appears in the unstressed syllable at the end of a word, it is pronounced like the e in the English word *the*.

danke	Schule	Frage	Klasse	Dinge	Vase

In certain words, an **Umlaut** (¨) is added to the vowel **a**, **o**, or **u**, changing the pronunciation of the vowel.

Bank	Bänke	schon	schön	Bruder	Brüder

Suggestion To produce the **ü** sound, tell students to round their lips as if to pronounce the letter **u**, but then make the long **i** sound.

1 **Aussprechen** Practice saying these words aloud.

1. Kahn / kann
2. beten / Betten
3. Robe / Robbe
4. Buch / Butter
5. den / denn
6. Saat / satt
7. Rogen / Roggen
8. Sack / Säcke
9. Wort / Wörter
10. Stuhl / Stühle
11. Hefte
12. Tage

1 **Expansion** Tell students the meanings of any unfamiliar words.

2 **Nachsprechen** Practice saying these sentences aloud.

1. Der Mann kam ohne Kamm.
2. Wir essen Bienenstich und trinken Kaffee.
3. Am Sonntag und am Montag scheint die Sonne.
4. Das U-Boot ist unter Wasser.
5. Ich habe viele Freunde in der Schule.
6. Der Mantel mit den fünf Knöpfen ist schöner als die Mäntel mit einem Knopf.

3 **Sprichwörter** Practice reading these sayings aloud.

Sag mir, mit wem du gehst, und ich sage dir, wer du bist.[1]

Der frühe Vogel fängt den Wurm.[2]

[1] Tell me who your friends are, and I will tell you who you are.
[2] The early bird catches the worm.

More activities

S vhlcentral LM p. 7 Online activities

Fotoroman

Oh, George! Video

George und Hans treffen *(meet)* Meline und Sabite im Biergarten.
Melines Handy klingelt...

Vorbereitung Have students review the **Nützliche Ausdrücke** before watching the video, in order to preview the episode content.

SABITE Wer ist es?
MELINE Lukas.
SABITE Oh, dein Freund?
MELINE Ja. Nein. Ja.

MELINE Wir haben Probleme.

MELINE Hast du einen Freund?
SABITE Ja. Torsten. Er ist Student.
MELINE Hast du ein Bild?

GEORGE Sabite? Sabite, hallo.
SABITE Hallo.
HANS Hallo.
SABITE Was ist da drin?
GEORGE Lehrbücher! Wörterbuch... Hefte...
  Stifte... Kalender.
HANS Hast du auch einen Computer?

KELLNERIN Bitte schön?
HANS Ein Wasser, bitte.
GEORGE Einen Kaffee und ein
  Stück Strudel.

MELINE Ich habe keinen Freund mehr.
SABITE Wie geht's dir?
MELINE Mir geht es sehr gut.

---

1 **Richtig oder falsch?** Indicate whether each statement is richtig or falsch.

1. George hat ein Wörterbuch. Richtig.
2. Sabite hat ein Bild von *(of)* Torsten. Richtig.
3. George will *(wants)* das Brandenburger Tor sehen *(to see)*. Richtig.
4. Im Bauhaus-Museum gibt es viele Bücher. Falsch.
5. Meline telefoniert mit Lukas. Richtig.

6. Die Kellnerin hat einen Freund. Richtig.
7. Torsten ist Student. Richtig.
8. Hans hat einen Stadtplan. Richtig.
9. Die Kellnerin heißt Laura. Falsch.
10. George bestellt *(orders)* Kaffee und Steak. Falsch.

PERSONEN

 George

 Hans

 Meline

 Sabite

 Kellnerin

7

> **GEORGE** Ich habe eine Idee. Hast du einen Stadtplan?
> **HANS** Ja!
> **GEORGE** Was muss ich in Berlin sehen? Das Brandenburger Tor!
> **HANS** Checkpoint Charlie!

8

> **SABITE** Potsdamer Platz!
> **GEORGE** Marlene-Dietrich-Platz!
> **KELLNERIN** Das Bode-Museum. Und das Jüdische Museum!

9

> **HANS** Wie viele Kurse hast du belegt?
> **SABITE** Ah, vier.
> **MELINE** Bauhaus-Museum.
> **HANS** Ja!
> **MELINE** Im Bauhaus-Museum gibt es viele...
> **SABITE** Stühle! Viele Stühle. Und Tische.

10

> **GEORGE** Wie heißt sie?
> **SABITE** Ähm, Leyna? Oh, George.
> **HANS** Sie hat einen Freund?
> **GEORGE** Ja.

Nützliche Ausdrücke

- **Prost!**
  Cheers!
- **Wer ist es?**
  Who is it?
- **Hast du ein Bild?**
  Do you have a picture?
- **Was ist da drin?**
  What's in there?
- **Hast du auch einen Computer?**
  Do you have a computer, too?
- **die Kellnerin**
  waitress
- **Bitte schön?**
  May I take your order?; May I help you?
- **das Wasser**   **der Kaffee**
  water   *coffee*
- **das Stück Strudel**
  a piece of strudel
- **Ich habe keinen Freund mehr.**
  I don't have a boyfriend anymore.
- **die Idee**   **der Stadtplan**
  idea   *city map*
- **Was muss ich in Berlin sehen?**
  What do I have to see in Berlin?
- **Ist alles in Ordnung?**
  Is everything alright?
- **Wie heißt sie?**
  What's her name?

1B.1
- **Wir haben Probleme.**
  We have problems.

1B.2
- **Hast du einen Stadtplan?**
  Do you have a city map?

1B.3
- **—Wie viele Kurse hast du?**
  —How many classes are you taking?
- **—Vier.**
  —Four.

---

2 Zum Besprechen With a partner, role-play a scene where one of you plays the waiter (**Kellner**) or waitress at a **Biergarten** and the other plays a customer ordering food. Here are some common items to order.
Answers will vary.

eine Cola	ein Stück Strudel
einen Kaffee	einen Tee
einen Saft (*juice*)	ein Wasser

2 Suggestion This activity can also be done with groups of three or more. Have students take turns playing the roles of server and customers.

2 Partner Chat You can also assign activity 2 on the Supersite.

3 Vertiefung The characters mention several important sites and museums in Berlin. Research these and other monuments and plan a day of sightseeing in Berlin to present to the class. Mention at least three sites that interest you, their names in German, and why you want to visit them.
Answers will vary.

3 Suggestion Preview the expression **es gibt** and encourage students to list some of the things they can see at each site.

More activities

S vhlcentral | VM p. 2 | Online activities

IM FOKUS

Die Schulzeit Reading

Suggestion Explain that the **Abitur** is awarded based on a points system. For each course and each exam they take, students can earn a maximum of 15 points. At the completion of all courses and exams, the points are tallied, and students are awarded a final grade from 1 to 6. The minimum qualifying score for the **Abitur** is 280 points (out of 840).

THE WORD AND THE CONCEPT OF **KIN-dergarten** were invented by **Friedrich Fröbel**, a teacher in 19th-century Germany. However, **Vorschule** is the term used in Germany today, while **Kindergärten** are the equivalent of preschool.

Public school for German children starts at age six, with **Grundschule°**. For the first four years, all **Grundschüler** attend school together. But after age ten, students are streamed into three different kinds of schools, usually as recommended by their teacher.

The most academically rigorous option is **Gymnasium**. **Gymnasium** lasts eight years, and graduates need to pass difficult exit exams to earn their **Abitur°**. The "Abi" gives students access to competitive internships and a university education.

A more vocationally-oriented option is **Hauptschule**. Students typically finish **Hauptschule** at age 15 or 16. They may then attend **Berufsfachschule°**, where they can train for a variety of professions, from mechanics to physical therapy.

The third option is **Realschule**, which has stricter academic requirements than **Hauptschule**. After graduation, students may seek further schooling that will lead them into careers such as banking, IT, or social work.

This three-track system has been in use for decades, but it has come under serious criticism. The **Abitur** is associated with higher social status, and more and more families push to have their children admitted into **Gymnasium**. **Realschule** still generally leads to solid employment opportunities, but there is a stigma attached to **Hauptschule**, which makes the job search more difficult for its graduates.

In some states, there is a fourth option for secondary school students: the **Gesamtschule°**. These comprehensive schools have no entrance requirements. They offer college preparatory classes for students who perform well, general education classes for students with average performance, and remedial courses for those who need additional support. **Gesamtschulen** were introduced in 1969 with the hope of eliminating inequalities associated with the three-track system, but they have been slow to take root.

Grundschule *elementary school* **Abitur** *high school diploma* **Berufsfachschule** *vocational school* **Gesamtschule** *comprehensive school*

1 **Im Fokus** Indicate whether each statement is **richtig** or **falsch**. Correct the false statements.

1. Students who complete the **Hauptschule** may then go on to a vocational school.
   Richtig.
2. Students who complete the **Realschule** go on to **Hauptschule**.
   Falsch. After **Realschule** students typically find white-collar jobs.
3. Enrolling at a German university requires the **Abitur**.
   Richtig.

Diskussion How does the German education system compare with your experience? What are the pros and cons of each system?

2 **Die deutschsprachige Welt** Indicate whether each statement is **richtig** or **falsch**. Correct the false statements.

1. Students beginning the **Grundschule** are called **Erstklässler**.
   Richtig.
2. The **Schultüte** contains books and the school uniform.
   Falsch. It contains candies, chocolates, and school supplies.
3. Scoring a **2** in Germany means you are a better-than-average student.
   Richtig.

Diskussion Do you remember your first day of grade school? Compare your experience with the German tradition of **Schultüte**.

DEUTSCH IM ALLTAG

Die Schule

die Abschlussfeier, -n	graduation party
die Pause, -n	recess
der Schulleiter, -	(male) principal
die Schulleiterin, -nen	(female) principal
bestehen	to pass a test
durchfallen	to flunk; to fail
schwänzen	to cut class
langweilig	boring

DIE DEUTSCHSPRACHIGE WELT

Ein süßer° Beginn

In German-speaking countries, the first day of school is a festive occasion. Excited **Erstklässler°** are presented with **Schultüten** by their parents on the morning of their first day of school. The **Schultüte** is a decorated paper cone, filled with candies, chocolates, school supplies, and other treats. With their unopened **Tüten** in hand, the **Erstklässler** set off for **Grundschule. Alles Gute für den ersten Schultag!°**

süßer sweet **Erstklässler** first-graders **Alles Gute für den ersten Schultag!** Best wishes on your first day of school!

Noten in Deutschland

Deutsche Noten:	1	2	3	4	5/6
US-Äquivalente:	A/A+	A-/B+	B/B-	C/D	D-/F

Suggestion Tell students that the grading systems are different in other German-speaking countries. In Switzerland 5 is the best grade.

PORTRÄT

Der Schultag

The school day in Germany typically lasts from 7:30 or 8:00 in the morning until 1:00 in the afternoon, with a 15-20 minute mid-morning break, called the **Große Pause**. Many schools do not have cafeterias, since students go home at lunch time. They then have the afternoon to do homework and participate in extracurricular activities. Students have only 6 weeks of summer vacation, but they get longer breaks during the school year, with 2 weeks off in the fall, 2 weeks for Christmas, and 2 weeks in the spring.

Die Deutschsprachige Welt Tell students that children often craft their own **Schultüten** in **Kindergarten.** Their parents then fill the **Tüten** before the first day of **Grundschule.**

TIPP

The German word for *one* is **eins**. A straight-A student is called **ein(e) Einserschüler(in)**.

🔗 IM INTERNET

Subjects: What subjects do students study at **Gymnasium**? What are **Pflichtfächer**? What are **Wahlfächer**?

Find out more at **vhlcentral.com**.

---

3 **Porträt** Indicate whether each statement is **richtig** or **falsch**. Correct the false statements.

1. The German school day lasts from 8:30 until 2:00 in the afternoon, with continuous classes. Falsch. It lasts from 7:30 or 8:00 until 1:00 in the afternoon, with a mid-morning break called **die Große Pause.**
2. The German spring break is typically longer than that of U.S. public schools. Richtig.
3. German schools are closed for two weeks in winter. Richtig.

Diskussion Discuss and compare your school day or vacations with those of German students. What are the differences? Which do you prefer?

4 **Meine deutsche Schule** Research a German **Realschule** or **Gymnasium** and present it to the class. Compare what you have learned about the German school system and the school you researched. What other differences did you find? You may make your presentation in English.

1B.1

Haben and the accusative case Grammar Tutorial

Suggestion Point out that in everyday speech, the final **e** is frequently dropped from the **ich** form. Ex.: **Ich hab' ein Buch.**

Startblock To describe what someone or something has, use the irregular verb **haben** with the accusative case.

Haben

haben (*to have*)			
ich **habe**	*I have*	wir **haben**	*we have*
du **hast**	*you have* (inf.)	ihr **habt**	*you have* (inf.)
Sie **haben**	*you have* (form.)	Sie **haben**	*you have* (form.)
er/sie/es **hat**	*he/she/it has*	sie **haben**	*they have*

Ich **habe** ein Buch.
*I **have** a book.*

Greta **hat** eine Karte.
*Greta **has** a map.*

Wir **haben** eine Frage.
*We **have** a question.*

ACHTUNG

A direct object receives the action of a verb directly and answers the question *what?* or *whom?*

The accusative case

- In **1A.3**, you learned that the function of a noun in a sentence determines its case, as well as the case of any article or adjective that modifies it. A noun that functions as a direct object is in the accusative case (**der Akkusativ**).

QUERVERWEIS

The accusative case is also used following certain prepositions. You will learn more about this usage in **3B.2**.

definite articles				
	masculine	**feminine**	**neuter**	**plural**
nominative	der Stuhl	die Tür	das Fenster	die Notizen
accusative	den Stuhl	die Tür	das Fenster	die Notizen

indefinite articles				
	masculine	**feminine**	**neuter**	**plural**
nominative	ein Stuhl	eine Tür	ein Fenster	– Notizen
accusative	einen Stuhl	eine Tür	ein Fenster	– Notizen

Der Lehrer hat **den Stift**.
*The teacher has **the pen**.*

Ich kaufe **ein Bleistift**.
*I'm buying **a pencil**.*

Sie öffnet **die Tür**.
*She's opening **the door**.*

Wir haben hier **ein Problem**.
*We have **a problem** here.*

Suggestion Give students additional examples to illustrate the use of the accusative with direct objects and the nominative with predicate nouns. Ex.: **Markus ist ein guter Freund. Sabine hat einen guten Freund.**

Jetzt sind Sie dran! In the first column, complete the sentences using **haben**. In the second column, indicate whether each underlined phrase is in the **Nominativ (N)** or **Akkusativ (A)** case.

1. Wir ___haben___ die Bücher.
2. Ich ___habe___ Fotos.
3. Herr Müller ___hat___ ein Haus.
4. Ihr ___habt___ morgen Schule.
5. Max und Julia ___haben___ viele Hausaufgaben.
6. Lena ___hat___ eine Theorie.

___N___ 7. Sie ist eine gute Schülerin.
___A___ 8. David hat eine Frage.
___A___ 9. Ich habe ein Problem.
___A___ 10. Du hast einen Stuhl.
___N___ 11. Ihr seid Studenten.
___A___ 12. Herr Meier trinkt ein Glas Wasser.

Anwendung und Kommunikation

1 **Bilden Sie Sätze** Write complete sentences.

BEISPIEL ich / haben / ein Radiergummi

Ich habe einen Radiergummi.

1. du / haben / ein Computer Du hast einen Computer.
2. ihr / haben / ein Taschenrechner Ihr habt einen Taschenrechner.
3. der Lehrer / haben / ein Buch Der Lehrer hat ein Buch.
4. wir / haben / ein Problem Wir haben ein Problem.
5. ich / haben / eine Frage Ich habe eine Frage.
6. das Mädchen / haben / ein Freund Das Mädchen hat einen Freund.

2 **Was haben wir?** Rewrite each sentence using **haben** with the subject provided.

BEISPIEL Das ist ein Computer. (Inge)

Inge hat einen Computer.

1. Das ist ein Rucksack. (Peter) Peter hat einen Rucksack.
2. Das ist ein Kuli. (ich) Ich habe einen Kuli.
3. Das ist ein Schulbuch. (ihr) Ihr habt ein Schulbuch.
4. Das sind Fotos. (du) Du hast Fotos.
5. Das ist ein Wörterbuch. (Erik und Nina) Erik und Nina haben ein Wörterbuch.
6. Das ist eine Karte. (wir) Wir haben eine Karte.

3 **Was haben sie?** With a partner, take turns saying what each person has.

BEISPIEL

Patrick hat Fotos.

Patrick

1. du

Du hast Bücher.

2. die Kommilitonen

Die Kommilitonen/Sie haben Hefte.

3 Video Virtual Chat
You can also assign activity 3 on the Supersite. Students record individual responses that appear in your gradebook.

3. Bettina

Bettina/Sie hat eine Uhr.

4. ich

Ich habe einen Taschenrechner.

5. du und Abdel

Du und Abdel/Ihr habt einen Rucksack.

6. wir

Wir haben einen Computer.

4 **Im Klassenzimmer** In groups, take turns discussing what items are in your classroom and what each of you has brought to class. Answers will vary.

BEISPIEL

S1: *Was haben wir hier?*
S2: *Wir haben Stühle und Bänke.*

S1: *Was hast du?*
S2: *Ich habe ein Heft.*

4 Expansion Call on individual students and have them describe what they and their group members have brought to class. Ex.: **Er hat ein Heft und einen Bleistift. Ich habe auch ein Heft und sie hat einen Kuli.**

1B.2

QUERVERWEIS

You will learn more about word order and conjunctions in **6A.3** and **10A.1**.

You will learn how to form negative statements in **2B.3**.

More activities

vhlcentral

WB
pp. 13–14

LM
p. 9

Online activities

Word order Grammar Tutorial

Startblock By changing the order of words in a sentence, you can shift emphasis or turn a statement into a yes-or-no question.

Statements

- In German, the verb is always the second element in a statement. The first element is often the subject, but it can also be a time expression or a prepositional phrase.

1ST	2ND	3RD
Ich	**habe**	heute Abend viele Hausaufgaben.

*I **have** a lot of homework tonight.*

Heute Abend	**habe**	ich viele Hausaufgaben.

*Tonight I **have** a lot of homework.*

- A direct or indirect object may be placed in first position, but this is a less common phrasing, used to place emphasis on the object. When the subject is not the first element in the sentence, it immediately follows the verb.

1ST	2ND	3RD
Viele Hausaufgaben	**habe**	ich heute Abend.

*I **have** a lot of homework tonight.*

- You can use the conjunctions **und** (*and*), **aber** (*but*), and **oder** (*or*) to combine two statements into one sentence, without affecting the word order of either statement.

Heute Abend haben wir viele
Hausaufgaben **und** morgen haben wir Unterricht.
*Tonight we have a lot of homework **and** tomorrow we have class.*

Yes-or-no questions

- To turn a statement into a yes-or-no question, move the verb to the first position. Move the subject to the second position, since it must immediately follow the verb. Use **ja** or **nein** to respond to this type of question.

STATEMENT	QUESTION
Die Professorin ist nett. *The professor is nice.*	▶ **Ist die Professorin** nett? *Is the professor nice?*
Jetzt habt ihr einen Computer. *Now you have a computer.*	▶ **Habt ihr jetzt** einen Computer? *Do you have a computer now?*

Jetzt sind Sie dran! — Turn each statement into a yes-or-no question.

1. Ich habe ein Buch.
   Habe ich ein Buch?/Hast du ein Buch? /Haben Sie ein Buch?

2. Ich bin Studentin.
   Bin ich Studentin?/Bist du Studentin?/Sind Sie Studentin?

3. Das sind Kommilitonen.
   Sind das Kommilitonen?

4. Der Apfel ist gut.
   Ist der Apfel gut?

5. Wir haben viele Fotos.
   Haben wir viele Fotos?/Habt ihr viele Fotos?/Haben Sie viele Fotos?

6. Tobias und Jasmin haben Rucksäcke.
   Haben Tobias und Jasmin Rucksäcke?

7. Lukas hat einen Taschenrechner.
   Hat Lukas einen Taschenrechner?

8. Ich habe ein Problem.
   Habe ich ein Problem?/Hast du ein Problem? /Haben Sie ein Problem?

Anwendung und Kommunikation

1 **Sätze** Combine each pair of sentences using **oder**, **aber**, or **und**, as indicated.

 BEISPIEL Ben hat gute Noten. David hat schlechte Noten. (aber)

Ben hat gute Noten, aber David hat schlechte Noten.

1. Du hast ein Blatt Papier. Ich habe einen Bleistift. (und) Du hast ein Blatt Papier und ich habe einen Bleistift.
2. Ist das Buch gut? Ist es schlecht? (oder) Ist das Buch gut oder ist es schlecht?
3. Es geht mir ziemlich gut. Ich habe ein Problem. (aber) Es geht mir ziemlich gut, aber ich habe ein Problem.
4. Ist Ela da? Ist sie im Unterricht? (oder) Ist Ela da oder ist sie im Unterricht?
5. Wir haben heute viele Hausaufgaben. Morgen haben wir eine Prüfung. (und)
Wir haben heute viele Hausaufgaben und morgen haben wir eine Prüfung
6. Ich heiße Sophia. Das ist Mia. (und) Ich heiße Sophia und das ist Mia.

2 **Noch einmal** Rewrite each sentence twice, changing the order of the underlined elements.

 BEISPIEL <u>Ich</u> habe <u>heute</u> (*today*) <u>eine Prüfung</u>.

Heute habe ich eine Prüfung.
Eine Prüfung habe ich heute.

1. <u>Tim</u> hat <u>heute Abend</u> <u>Deutschhausaufgaben</u>. Heute Abend hat Tim Deutschhausaufgaben. Deutschhausaufgaben
hat Tim heute Abend.
2. <u>Max und Lisa</u> haben <u>ein Haus</u> <u>in Berlin</u>. Ein Haus haben Max und Lisa in Berlin. In Berlin haben
Max und Lisa ein Haus. Max und Lisa haben in Berlin ein Haus.
3. <u>Wir</u> sind <u>jetzt</u> <u>im Unterricht.</u> Jetzt sind wir im Unterricht. Im Unterricht sind wir jetzt.
4. <u>Ich</u> bin <u>jetzt</u> <u>in Berlin</u>. Jetzt bin ich in Berlin. In Berlin bin ich jetzt.

3 **Wer hat was?** In pairs, take turns asking and answering questions.

 BEISPIEL Junge / Problem (nein / Frage)

S1: *Hat der Professor ein Problem?*
S2: *Nein, er hat eine Frage.*

 1. Frau / Blatt Papier (nein / Foto) Hat die Frau ein Blatt Papier? Nein, sie hat ein Foto.
2. Emil und ich / Bleistifte (ja) Haben Emil und ich Bleistifte? Ja, ihr habt Bleistifte.
3. Lehrerin / Kalender (ja) Hat die Lehrerin (einen) Kalender? Ja, sie hat (einen) Kalender.
4. Schüler / Buch (nein / Heft) Hat der Schüler/Haben die Schüler ein Buch? Nein, er hat/sie haben ein Heft.

4 **Was ist los?** In groups, take turns asking and answering yes-or-no questions about the image. Answers will vary.

 BEISPIEL

S1: *Haben die Schüler Bücher?*
S2: *Ja, sie haben Bücher.*

3 **Partner Chat** You can also assign activity 3 on the Supersite. Students work in pairs to record the activity online. The pair's recorded conversation will appear in your gradebook.

1B.3 | Numbers Grammar Tutorial

Startblock As in English, numbers in German follow patterns. Memorizing the numbers from **1** to **20** will help you learn numbers **21** and above.

Sabite hat **vier** Kurse.

George ist **21** Jahre alt.

- Every number up to one million is written as a single word. Numbers from **13** to **19** follow a pattern similar to English, adding the ending **-zehn** to each single-digit number. Numbers from **21** to **99** repeat this pattern, adding **und** plus the number in the tens place to each single-digit number: [ones] + **und** + [tens].

25 = **fünf** + **und** + zwanzig ▶ **fünf**und**zwanzig**

0	null	**10**	zehn	**20**	zwanzig	**30**	dreißig
1	eins	**11**	elf	**21**	einundzwanzig	**31**	einunddreißig
2	zwei	**12**	zwölf	**22**	zweiundzwanzig	**40**	vierzig
3	drei	**13**	dreizehn	**23**	dreiundzwanzig	**45**	fünfundvierzig
4	vier	**14**	vierzehn	**24**	vierundzwanzig	**50**	fünfzig
5	fünf	**15**	fünfzehn	**25**	fünfundzwanzig	**60**	sechzig
6	sechs	**16**	sechzehn	**26**	sechsundzwanzig	**70**	siebzig
7	sieben	**17**	siebzehn	**27**	siebenundzwanzig	**80**	achtzig
8	acht	**18**	achtzehn	**28**	achtundzwanzig	**90**	neunzig
9	neun	**19**	neunzehn	**29**	neunundzwanzig	**99**	neunundneunzig

numbers 0–99

- Note that the **s** in **eins** is dropped at the beginning of a compound word.

41 = ein**s** + vierzig ▶ **ein**und**vierzig**   **81** = ein**s** + achtzig ▶ **ein**und**achtzig**

- Likewise, **sechs** and **sieben** are shortened when they precede the letter **z**.

16 = **sech**zehn   **66** = sechsund**sech**zig
17 = **sieb**zehn   **77** = siebenund**sieb**zig

- In German, decimals are indicated by a comma (**Komma**), not a period (**Punkt**). When giving a unit of measurement (length, currency, etc.), say the unit instead of **Komma**. Note that units of currency are usually written after the number.

25,4 = fünfundzwanzig **Komma** vier   **0,5** = null **Komma** fünf
4,99 € = vier **Euro** neunundneunzig   **10,18 m** = zehn **Meter** achtzehn

QUERVERWEIS

You will learn more about interrogative words in **2A.2**.

- Use **Wie viel?** to ask *How much?* and **Wie viele?** to ask *How many?*

Wie viel kostet das Buch?   **Wie viele** Blätter Papier habt ihr?
How much does the book cost?   *How many pieces of paper do you have?*

numbers 100 and higher			
100	(ein)hundert	1.000	(ein)tausend
101	hunderteins	1.300	tausenddreihundert
128	hundertachtundzwanzig	5.000	fünftausend
200	zweihundert	10.000	zehntausend
300	dreihundert	50.000	fünfzigtausend
400	vierhundert	100.000	hunderttausend
500	fünfhundert	460.000	vierhundertsechzigtausend
600	sechshundert	1.000.000	eine Million
700	siebenhundert	1.050.000	eine Million fünfzigtausend
800	achthundert	7.000.000	sieben Millionen
900	neunhundert	1.000.000.000	eine Milliarde

Suggestion Have students practice reading these numbers aloud.

- Note that German uses a period where English typically uses a comma to separate thousands, millions, etc.

2.320.000	1.999,99 €	5.225,00 $
2,320,000	*€1,999.99*	*$5,225.00*

- Numbers in the millions and higher are written as separate words.

2.016.000   **1.000.050.000**
zwei Millionen sechzehntausend   **eine Milliarde fünfzigtausend**

Mathematical expressions

- Use these expressions to talk about math.

mathematical expressions					
+	plus	×	mal	=	ist (gleich)
–	minus	÷	geteilt durch	%	Prozent

ACHTUNG

Note that German speakers typically use the symbol · to indicate multiplication and the symbol : to indicate division.

6 + 7 = 13 ▶ **Sechs plus sieben ist dreizehn.**
Six plus seven is thirteen.

8 – 2 = 6 ▶ **Acht minus zwei ist gleich sechs.**
Eight minus two equals six.

3 · 3 = 9 ▶ **Drei mal drei (ist) gleich neun.**
Three times three equals nine.

20 : 5 = 4 ▶ **Zwanzig geteilt durch fünf ist vier.**
Twenty divided by five is four.

More activities

vhlcentral

WB
pp. 15–16

LM
p. 10

Online activities

Jetzt sind Sie dran!   Write each number or equation in words.

1. 37
   siebenunddreißig

2. 212
   zweihundertzwölf

3. 49
   neunundvierzig

4. 368
   dreihundertachtundsechzig

5. 24
   vierundzwanzig

6. 75
   fünfundsiebzig

7. 1991
   eintausendneunhunderteinundneunzig

8. 587
   fünfhundertsiebenundachtzig

9. 16 + 15 = 31
   Sechzehn plus fünfzehn ist (gleich) einunddreißig.

10. 97 – 17 = 80
    Siebenundneunzig minus siebzehn ist achtzig.

11. 18 : 9 = 2
    Achtzehn geteilt durch neun ist zwei.

12. 12 · 3 = 36
    Zwölf mal drei ist sechsunddreißig.

Anwendung

1 **Eins, zwei, drei...** Fill in the missing number, then write the number in words.

BEISPIEL 0, 5, 10, __15__ , 20; ___fünfzehn___

1. 2, 4, __6__, 8, 10; ___sechs___
2. 0, 10, 20, __30__, 40; ___dreißig___
3. 670, 671, 672, 673, __674__; ___sechshundertvierundsiebzig___
4. 3.456, 3.457, 3.458, __3.459__, 3.460; ___dreitausendvierhundertneunundfünfzig___
5. 35, 40, 45, 50, __55__; ___fünfundfünfzig___
6. 1.899.996, 1.899.997, 1.899.998, 1.899.999, __1.900.000__; ___eine Million neunhunderttausend___

2 **Wie alt bist du?** With a partner, take turns asking and saying how old each person is.

BEISPIEL Anna: 16
S1: *Wie alt ist Anna?*
S2: *Sie ist sechzehn. / Sie ist sechzehn Jahre alt.*

1. Tim: 19 Er ist neunzehn (Jahre alt).
2. Sara: 11 Sie ist elf (Jahre alt).
3. Herr Wolf: 73 Er ist dreiundsiebzig (Jahre alt).
4. Frau Öztürk: 101 Sie ist hundertundein (Jahre alt).

5. Niklas: 5 Er ist fünf (Jahre alt).
6. Herr Braun: 42 Er ist zweiundvierzig (Jahre alt).
7. Jasmin: 21 Sie ist einundzwanzig (Jahre alt).
8. Frau Schröder: 67 Sie ist siebenundsechzig (Jahre alt).

3 **Was sehen Sie?** Write how many there are of each item.

▶ **BEISPIEL**
(860) Student
Da sind achthundertsechzig Studenten.

(5.937) Buch
1. Da sind fünftausendneunhundertsiebenunddreißig Bücher.

(16) Mädchen
2. Da sind sechzehn Mädchen.

(217) Tisch
3. Da sind zweihundertsiebzehn Tische.

(54) Auto
4. Da sind vierundfünfzig Autos.

(12) Stuhl
5. Da sind zwölf Stühle.

(4) Studentin
6. Da sind vier Studentinnen.

4 **Matheprofi** In pairs, take turns reading the equations out loud.

1. $67 + 4 = 71$
2. $16 + 28 = 44$
3. $91 - 6 = 85$
4. $45 - 7 = 38$
5. $24 : 4 = 6$
6. $989 : 43 = 23$
7. $58 \cdot 2 = 116$
8. $213 \cdot 3 = 639$

1. Siebenundsechzig plus vier ist (gleich) einundsiebzig.
2. Sechzehn plus achtundzwanzig ist (gleich) vierundvierzig.
3. Einundneunzig minus sechs ist (gleich) fünfundachtzig.
4. Fünfundvierzig minus sieben ist (gleich) achtunddreißig.
5. Vierundzwanzig geteilt durch vier ist (gleich) sechs.
6. Neunhundertneunundachtzig geteilt durch dreiundvierzig ist (gleich) dreiundzwanzig.
7. Achtundfünfzig mal zwei ist (gleich) (ein) hundertsechzehn.
8. Zweihundertdreizehn mal drei ist (gleich) sechshundertneununddreißig.

1 Expansion Distribute blank Bingo cards and have students fill them in with numbers from 0–30 in random order. Pick numbers from a hat and call them out in German. The first student to get five numbers in a row wins.

4 Expansion Ask students to write out their own equations. Have them take turns reading their equations and figuring out the answers.

Kommunikation

5 **Wie viele Einwohner hat...?** In pairs, discuss the population of each city.

BEISPIEL München: 1.456.039

S1: Wie viele Einwohner (*inhabitants*) hat München?
S2: München hat eine Million vierhundertsechsundfünfzigtausendneununddreißig Einwohner.

1. Berlin: 3.613.495 Berlin hat drei Millionen sechshundertdreizehntausendvierhundertfünfundneunzig Einwohner.
2. Gelsenkirchen: 260.368 Gelsenkirchen hat zweihundertsechzigtausenddreihundertachtundsechzig Einwohner.
3. Hamburg: 1.830.584 Hamburg hat eine Million achthundertdreißigtausendfünfhundertvierundachtzig Einwohner.
4. Dresden: 543.825 Dresden hat fünfhundertdreiundvierzigtausendachthundertfünfundzwanzig Einwohner.
5. Stuttgart: 628.032 Stuttgart hat sechshundertachtundzwanzigtausendzweiunddreißig Einwohner.

6 **Wie viel kostet...?** In pairs, take turns asking about and saying the cost of each item. Answers will vary.

BEISPIEL

S1: Wie viel kostet ein Computer?
S2: Er kostet eintausenddreihundertvierundzwanzig Euro siebzehn.

Auto	Apfel
Haus	Blume
Tisch	Heft
Computer	Stuhl

7 **Wie viel sind...?** In pairs, discuss these exchange rates.

BEISPIEL $120 = 104,22 €

S1: Wie viel sind hundertzwanzig Dollar in Euro?
S2: Das sind (ein)hundertvier Euro zweiundzwanzig.

1. $450 = 390,65 €
2. $573 = 562,22 CHF (Schweizer Franken)
3. 781,45 € = 86.074,17 ¥ (Yen)
4. $1.628,50 = £1.275,32 (Pfund Sterling)
5. 3.816 € = £3.321,67
6. 6.487,15 CHF = $6.608,22
7. $14.005,90 = 12.163,88 €
8. £251.029 = $320.545,76

8 **Ich habe mehr!** In small groups, take turns exaggerating the number of items you have at home.

BEISPIEL

S1: Ich habe sieben Kulis.
S2: Ich habe dreihundertfünfundneunzig Taschenrechner!
S3: Und ich habe neuntausendvierundzwanzig Stifte!

1.253.687

6 Suggestion Bring in price listings from German-language web sites and have students read the prices aloud.

7 Answers
1. vierhundertfünfzig Dollar/dreihundertneunzig Euro fünfundsechzig.
2. fünfhundertdreiundsiebzig Dollar/fünfhundertzweiundsechzig (Schweizer) Franken zweiundzwanzig.
3. siebenhunderteinundachtzig Euro fünfundvierzig/sechsundachtzigtausendvierundsiebzig Yen siebzehn.
4. eintausendsechshundertachtundzwanzig Dollar fünfzig/eintausendzweihundertfünfundsiebzig Pfund (Sterling) zweiunddreißig.
5. dreitausendachthundertsechzehn Euro/dreitausenddreihunderteinundzwanzig Pfund Sterling siebenundsechzig.
6. sechstausendvierhundertsiebenundachtzig Schweizer Franken fünfzehn/sechstausendsechshundertacht Franken zweiundzwanzig.
7. vierzehntausendfünf Dollar neunzig/zwölftausendeinhundertdreiundsechzig Euro achtundachtzig.
8. zweihunderteinundfünfzigtausendneunundzwanzig Pfund Sterling/dreihundertzwanzigtausendfünfhundertfünfundvierzig Dollar sechsundsiebzig.

7 Video Virtual Chat You can also assign activity 7 on the Supersite.

8 Expansion Ask each student to make a list of items and quantities before beginning this activity. (Ex: **7 Kulis, 86 Rucksäcke, 98 Taschenrechner**....) As they do the activity, have students write down the numbers they hear and then compare with what their partner actually said.

Wiederholung

1 Fragespiel

Fragespiel In pairs, play a question game (**Fragespiel**) using the lesson vocabulary. Choose a person or object in the classroom. Your partner will ask yes-or-no questions to figure out the word you've chosen. Answers will vary.

BEISPIEL

S1: *Bist du eine Sache?*
S2: *Nein.*
S1: *Bist du eine Person?*
S2: *Ja.*
S1: *Hast du einen Schreibtisch?*
S2: *Ja.*
S1: *Bist du ein Lehrer?*
S2: *Genau (Exactly)!*

1 Suggestion Help students to select vocabulary that they can ask questions about. Circulate around the room to ensure that everyone is forming appropriate questions.

1 Partner Chat You can also assign activity 1 on the Supersite. Students work in pairs to record the activity online. The pair's recorded conversation will appear in your gradebook.

2 Mathe

Mathe Write two numbers between 1 and 100 on separate index cards. Then, in small groups, make a pile of everyone's cards, shuffle, and take turns drawing two cards from the pile. The person who draws must create a math problem using the numbers. The first person to answer the math problem correctly draws next. Answers will vary.

BEISPIEL

S1: *(draws 55 and 5)* *Fünfundfünfzig geteilt durch fünf.*
S2: *Fünfundfünfzig geteilt durch fünf ist elf.*

2 Expansion Have the whole class play this game, as a group or in teams.

$$55 : 5 =$$

3 Ratespiel

Ratespiel In small groups, collect the items listed. One student leaves the group while the others distribute the items among themselves. The student then returns and tries to guess who has each item. Answers will vary.

BEISPIEL

S1: *Hast du den Radiergummi?*
S2: *Nein.*
S1: *Hat Megan den Radiergummi?*
S2: *Nein, Simon hat den Radiergummi.*

3 Suggestion Remind students to pay attention to articles when using nouns in the accusative case.

der Bleistift	der Radiergummi
das Buch	der Rucksack
das Heft	der Taschenrechner
der Kuli	die Uhr

4 Im Schreibwarenladen

Im Schreibwarenladen In groups of three, make a shopping list of school supplies. Then, role-play a trip to the store to buy the items you need. Present your scene to the class. Answers will vary.

BEISPIEL

S1: *Guten Tag.*
S2: *Guten Tag. Haben Sie hier Hefte und Bleistifte?*
S1: *Ja, wir haben hier Hefte und Bleistifte.*
S3: *Wie viel kosten die Hefte?*
S1: *Sie kosten fünf Euro neunzig.*

5 Diskutieren und kombinieren

Diskutieren und kombinieren Your instructor will give you and your partner worksheets with different pictures of a classroom. Do not look at each other's pictures. Ask and answer questions to identify seven differences (**Unterschiede**) between the two pictures. Answers will vary.

BEISPIEL

S1: *Ich habe zwei Türen. Hast du auch zwei Türen?*
S2: *Nein. Ich habe eine Tür. Hast du einen Lehrer?*
S1: *Ja, ich habe auch einen Lehrer. Hast du...?*

6 Arbeitsblatt

Arbeitsblatt Your instructor will give you a game board. Play the game with your partners. Count the spaces aloud in German as you play.

7 **Schreibutensilien** Pelikan Group is a worldwide leading brand-name company of quality paper, office and stationery supplies. The strength of the Pelikan brand is its over 180 years of experience and expertise. Generations of customers have grown up with the brand. Take a look at the brand logo and talk about the supplies you recognize and other supplies you have.

BEISPIEL

S1: *Das ist ein Radiergummi. Hast du einen Radiergummi?*
S2: *Ja. Ich habe einen Radiergummi./Nein, aber ich habe einen Computer.*

Suggestion Write on the board the German words that students won't know for supplies in the graphic, and ask students to add them to **Vocabulary Tools** on the **Sag mal** Supersite.

Expansion Encourage students to research the **Pelikan** company and report back to the class.

8 **Galgenmännchen** In small groups, play Hangman using the vocabulary you learned in **Lektion 1A** and **Lektion 1B**. For nouns, include the definite article. Give your partners a hint about each word. Answers will vary.

BEISPIEL

S1: *Es ist eine Person / eine Sache / ein Ort / ein Ausdruck (expression).*
S2: *Hat das Wort ein S?*
S1: *Nein. / Ja, das Wort hat zwei S.*

8 Suggestion Tell students that letters of the alphabet are neuter.

⟨S⟩ Mein Wörterbuch

Personalize your vocabulary. Add five words related to the themes **an der Universität** and **Sport und Freizeit** to the online Vocabulary Tools.

Lektion 2B

German	English	Definition
+ add word		
✎ Sehr erfreut.	Pleased to meet you.	Freut mich./ Angenehm./Schön dich/Sie kennen zu lernen.

ä   ö   ü   ß   ALL CAPS

Encourage students to keep a personalized dictionary either in a notebook or in the Vocabulary Tools on the Supersite, where they can create flashcards. They will be able to create entries that are relevant to them.

Panorama Interactive Map

Die deutschsprachige Welt°

Länder° mit Deutsch als Amtssprache°

▶ Belgien
▶ Deutschland
▶ Italien (Region: Südtirol)
▶ Liechtenstein
▶ Luxemburg
▶ Österreich
▶ die Schweiz

Bevölkerung°

▶ **Belgien:** *11,4 Millionen Einwohner° (77.000 deutsche Muttersprachler°)*
▶ **Deutschland:** *82,8 Millionen Einwohner*
▶ **Italien:** *60,5 Millionen Einwohner (336.000 deutsche Muttersprachler)*
▶ **Liechtenstein:** *38.111 Einwohner*
▶ **Luxemburg:** *602.005 Einwohner (474.000 deutsche Muttersprachler)*
▶ **Österreich:** *8,6 Millionen Einwohner*
▶ **die Schweiz:** *8,5 Millionen Einwohner (5,4 Millionen deutsche Muttersprachler)*

QUELLE: das Haus der deutschen Sprache

Hauptstädte°

▶ **Belgien:** *Brüssel*
▶ **Deutschland:** *Berlin*
▶ **Liechtenstein:** *Vaduz*
▶ **Luxemburg:** *Luxemburg*
▶ **Österreich:** *Wien*
▶ **die Schweiz:** *Bern*

More activities

vhlcentral

Online activities

Wien, Österreichs Hauptstadt

Bern, Hauptstadt der Schweiz

Landesgrenzen
• Stadt
◉ Landeshauptstadt
✹ Hauptstadt

0   50 Meilen
0   50 Kilometer

Unglaublich, aber wahr!

Belgien hat drei offizielle Sprachen°: Französisch, Niederländisch und Deutsch. Die deutschsprachige Region ist im Osten Belgiens. Circa° 77.000 Menschen leben° hier. Viele Belgier sprechen mindestens° zwei Sprachen.

deutschsprachige Welt *German-speaking world* **Länder** *countries*
Amtssprache *official language* **Bevölkerung** *population*
Einwohner *inhabitants* **Muttersprachler** *native speakers*
Hauptstädte *capitals* **Sprachen** *languages* **Circa** *Approximately*
leben *live* **mindestens** *at least*

Österreich

Die Alpen

Die Alpen sind das höchste Gebirge° in Europa. Es ist circa 1.200 Kilometer lang, und 29% sind in Österreich. Deshalb heißt Österreich auch die „Alpenrepublik". In Österreich leben circa 4 Millionen Menschen° in den Alpen. Das sind fast 50% aller Österreicher. Der höchste Berg° in Österreich ist der Großglockner. Er ist 3.798 Meter hoch.

Deutschland

Die Berliner Mauer°

Die Berliner Mauer
Tell students that *3,40 Meter* is read out loud as **drei Meter vierzig**.

Vom 13. August 1961 bis 9. November 1989 ist die Berliner Mauer eine Grenze° zwischen° Ost- und Westberlin. Die Mauer umgibt° ganz Westberlin und kreiert eine Insel°. Sie ist das Symbol des Kalten Krieges°. Die Mauer ist 156,4 Kilometer lang. Sie ist zwischen 3,40 Meter und 4,20 Meter hoch. Rund um Westberlin stehen 302 Beobachtungstürme°.

Die Schweiz

Schokolade

Die Schweiz ist bekannt für Banken, Uhren, Messer° und natürlich° Schokolade. Die bekanntesten Schokoladenfirmen sind Lindt, Tobler, Sprüngli und Suchard. Pro Jahr isst° jeder Schweizer 10,5 Kilogramm Schokolade. Niemand° auf der Welt isst mehr Schokolade als° die Schweizer. In Deutschland isst man fast genauso viel°, nämlich 10 Kilogramm Schokolade pro Person, in Österreich 6,3 und in den USA nur 5 Kilogramm.

Geschichte

Die Hanse

Die Hanse Point out that the Hanse was the precursor to the European Union and one of the first international trade unions.

Die Deutsche Hanse ist eine Union von Kaufleuten°. Sie existiert zwischen Mitte des 12. Jahrhunderts° und Mitte des 17. Jahrhunderts. Bis zu 200 Städte im nördlichen Europa sind in der Union, wie zum Beispiel Zuidersee (heutiges° Holland), Hamburg, Bremen und Lübeck (heutiges Deutschland), Stockholm (heutiges Schweden), Danzig (heutiges Polen) und Riga (heutiges Lettland°). Diese Städte liegen° vor allem an der Nordsee und der Ostsee°.

Musik Musik

2raumwohnung

Inga Humpe und **Tommi Eckert** sind seit° 2001 das Berliner Popduo **2raumwohnung**. Der englische Punkrock, New Wave und die deutsche Technomusik beeinflussen° den Musikstil von **2raumwohnung**.

Go to **vhlcentral.com** to find out more about **2raumwohnung** and their music.

---

höchste Gebirge *highest mountain range* **Menschen** *people* **Berg** *mountain* **Mauer** *Wall* **Grenze** *border* **zwischen** *between* **umgibt** *surrounds* **kreiert eine Insel** *creates an island* **des Kalten Krieges** *of the Cold War* **Beobachtungstürme** *watchtowers* **Messer** *knives* **natürlich** *of course* **isst** *eats* **Niemand** *Nobody* **mehr... als** *more... than* **fast genauso viel, nämlich...** *almost as much, in fact...* **von Kaufleuten** *of merchants* **des 12. Jahrhunderts** *of the 12th century* **heutiges** *present-day* **Lettland** *Latvia* **liegen** *are located* **Ostsee** *Baltic Sea* **seit** *since* **beeinflussen** *influence*
Die Berliner Mauer Tell students that the dates **13. August** and **9. November** are read out loud as **der dreizehnte August** and **der neunte November**. Explain that students will learn more about reading and writing dates in 2A.3.

---

1 **Was haben Sie gelernt?** Indicate whether each statement is richtig or falsch.

 1. In Belgien gibt es zwei offizielle Sprachen.
   Falsch. In Belgien gibt es drei offizielle Sprachen: Französisch, Niederländisch und Deutsch.

2. Ein anderer (*other*) Name für Österreich ist die Alpenrepublik.
   Richtig

3. Der Großglockner ist der höchste Berg in der Schweiz.
   Falsch. Das ist der höchste Berg in Österreich.

4. Amerikaner essen mehr Schokolade als die Schweizer.
   Falsch. Die Schweizer essen mehr Schokolade

5. Berlin und München sind Hansestädte.
   Falsch. Hamburg, Bremen und Lübeck sind Hansestädte.

2 **Was meinen Sie?** Reflect on these questions. Discuss your thoughts with a partner.

 • Many countries have more than one official language. Why do you think this is so? What do you think are the pros and cons?

• What are the advantages of studying another language? Why do you study German?

Lesen

Audio: Reading

Vor dem Lesen

Strategien

Recognizing cognates

Cognates are words in two or more languages that are similar in meaning and in spelling. Look for cognates to increase your comprehension when you read in German. However, watch out for false cognates. For example, you've already learned that in German, **Note** means *grade*, not *note*. Likewise, **bald** means *soon*, not *bald*, and **fast** means *almost*, not *fast*. Can you guess the meaning of these German words?

das Café	das Programm
der Doktor	das Restaurant
das Hotel	der Sommer
der Juli	das Telefon
das Museum	das Theater

Untersuchen Sie den Text

Look at this text. What kind of information does it present? Where do you usually find such information? Can you guess what this is?

Suchen Sie verwandte Wörter

Read the list of cognates in **Strategien** again. How many of them can you find in the reading? Do you see any additional cognates? Can you guess their English equivalents?

Raten Sie die Bedeutung

Besides using cognates and words you already know, you can also use context to guess the meaning of unfamiliar words. Find the following words in the reading and try to figure out what they mean. Compare your answers with a classmate's.

ägyptisch	Platz
Abakus	Straße

Suggestion Point out that in German, the digits in phone numbers are listed in pairs. Have students practice reading the phone numbers for these listings out loud.

Adressbuch

Ägyptisches Museum

✉ **Residenzstraße 1**
80333 München
☎ (089) 29 85 46

Christian Hunner

✉ **Pfarrstraße 16**
80667 München
☎ (089) 2 10 28 84

Sparda-Bank

✉ **Arnulfstraße 15**
80335 München
☎ (089) 5 51 42 – 4 00

Heideck Apotheke°

✉ **Heideckstraße 31**
80637 München
☎ (089) 1 57 52 52

Il Galeone Ristorante Pizzeria

✉ **Hornsteinstraße 18**
81679 München
☎ (089) 94 46 47 03

Andreas Spitzauer

✉ **Appenzeller Straße 95**
81475 München
☎ (089) 75 67 19

Suggestion Point out to students that in German addresses, the house number follows the street name. Also, the state, or **Land**, is not included, and the postal code precedes the city.

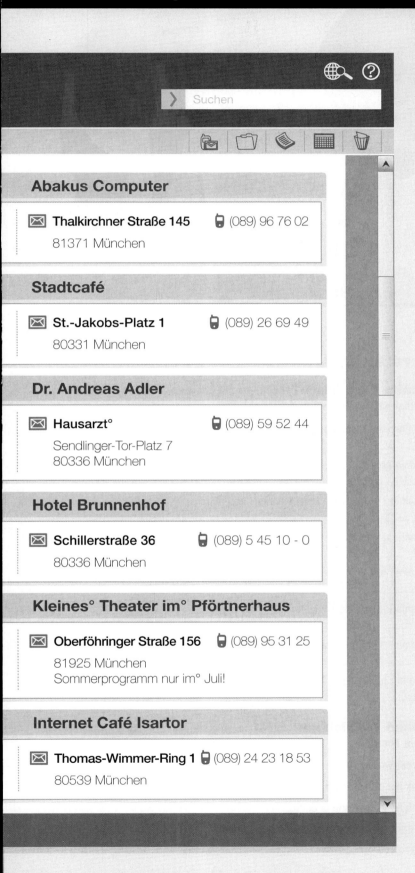

Abakus Computer

✉ **Thalkirchner Straße 145**   📱 (089) 96 76 02
81371 München

Stadtcafé

✉ **St.-Jakobs-Platz 1**   📱 (089) 26 69 49
80331 München

Dr. Andreas Adler

✉ **Hausarzt°**   📱 (089) 59 52 44
Sendlinger-Tor-Platz 7
80336 München

Hotel Brunnenhof

✉ **Schillerstraße 36**   📱 (089) 5 45 10 - 0
80336 München

Kleines° Theater im° Pförtnerhaus

✉ **Oberföhringer Straße 156**   📱 (089) 95 31 25
81925 München
Sommerprogramm nur im° Juli!

Internet Café Isartor

✉ **Thomas-Wimmer-Ring 1** 📱 (089) 24 23 18 53
80539 München

Nach dem Lesen

Wohin gehen sie? Say where each of these people should go, based on the clues.

> **BEISPIEL** Lena loves to eat pasta but hates to cook.
> Il Galeone Ristorante Pizzeria

1. Frau Scholz needs to reserve some hotel rooms.
   Hotel Brunnenhof

2. Christiane's computer is broken.
   Abakus Computer

3. Herr Meier thinks he has the flu.
   Dr. Adler/Heideck Apotheke/Hausarzt

4. Nina would like to see some ancient Egyptian art.
   Ägyptisches Museum

5. Herr and Frau Hansel want to go somewhere for coffee or tea.
   Stadtcafé/Internet Café Isartor

6. Andrea is meeting some friends for Italian food.
   Il Galeone Ristorante Pizzeria

7. Frau Müller needs to buy some aspirin for her daughter.
   Heideck Apotheke

8. Thomas wants to take his girlfriend to a play.
   Kleines Theater im Pförtnerhaus

9. Herr Trüb needs to deposit his paycheck.
   Sparda-Bank

10. Sebastian's computer is broken, but he needs to send an e-mail.
    Internet Café Isartor/Abakus Computer

 Unsere Einträge Select three listings from the reading and use them as models to create similar listings in German that advertise places or services in your area.

> **BEISPIEL**
>
> *Stonydale Bank*
> *Hunter Straße 206*
> *50555 Stonydale*
> *Tel. (555) 337-0665*

Suggestion You may want to have students complete this activity in pairs.

Apotheke *pharmacy* **Hausarzt** *family physician* **Kleines** *Small* **im** *in (the)* **nur im** *only in (the)*

Hören

Strategien

Listening for words you know

You can get the gist of a conversation by listening for words and phrases you already know.

 To help you practice this strategy, listen to these statements and make a list of the words you have already learned.

_____   _____

_____   _____

Vorbereitung

Where are the people in the photograph? What are they doing? Do you think they know each other? Why or why not? What do you think they are talking about?

 ## Zuhören

 As you listen, check the words you associate with Tanja and those you associate with Rainer.

Tanja	Rainer
✓ der Taschenrechner	___ der Radiergummi
___ der Computer	✓ die Hausaufgaben
✓ das Blatt Papier	___ das Heft
✓ zwei Bleistifte	✓ das Problem
___ die Prüfung	___ die Karte

Verständnis

 Richtig oder falsch? Based on the conversation you heard, indicate whether each statement is **richtig** or **falsch**.

1. Rainer ist Deutschprofessor.
   Falsch. _____

2. Tanja geht es gut.
   Richtig. _____

3. Rainer braucht (*needs*) einen Taschenrechner.
   Richtig. _____

4. Tanja hat ein Problem mit den Hausaufgaben.
   Falsch. _____

5. Rainer hat einen Bleistift für Tanja.
   Falsch. _____

6. Tanja hat ein Blatt Papier für Rainer.
   Richtig. _____

7. Tanja hat zwei Bleistifte.
   Richtig. _____

8. Rainer hilft (*helps*) Tanja bei den Hausaufgaben.
   Falsch. _____

Stellen Sie sich vor! Introduce yourself in German to a classmate you do not know well.

- Greet your partner.
- Ask his or her name.
- Ask how he or she is doing.
- Introduce your partner to another student.
- Say good-bye.

Suggestion Students often gravitate towards other students they already know. Make sure to direct students to new partners.

Schreiben

Strategien Emphasize the importance of outlining ideas in German, instead of translating from English. Encourage students to use the vocabulary and grammar they already know to complete this **Thema**.

Thema

 Schreiben Sie eine Liste

 A group of German-speaking students will be spending a year at your school. Put together a list of people and places that might be useful or interesting to them. Your list should include:

- Your name, address, phone number(s), and e-mail address
- The names of two or three other students in your German class, their addresses, phone numbers, and e-mail addresses
- Your German instructor's name, office phone number, and e-mail address
- The names, addresses, and phone numbers of three places near your school where students like to go (a bookstore, a café or restaurant, a movie theater, etc.)

NAME: *Prof. Reinhard (Deutschprofessor)*
ADRESSE: *Stonydale School*
TELEFONNUMMER: *(555) 654-3458 (Büro)*
HANDY: *(555) 919-0040*
E-MAIL-ADRESSE: *prof.reinhard@stonydale.edu*
NOTIZEN: *Ist aus Hamburg*

NAME: *Zest Coffee House*
ADRESSE: *8970 McNeil Road*
TELEFONNUMMER: *(555) 654-0349*
HANDY: *–*
E-MAIL-ADRESSE: *info@zest.com*
NOTIZEN: *Hat sehr guten Kaffee und gute Musik*

Vocabulary Tools

Lektion 1A

Begrüßung und Abschied
hellos and good-byes

Hallo./Guten Tag. *Hello.*
Guten Morgen. *Good morning.*
Guten Abend. *Good evening.*
Gute Nacht. *Good night.*
Bis bald./Bis gleich. *See you soon.*
Bis dann./Bis später. *See you later.*
Bis morgen. *See you tomorrow.*
Auf Wiedersehen. *Good-bye.*
Schönen Tag noch! *Have a nice day!*
Tschüss. *Bye.*
Alles klar? *Is everything OK?*
Wie geht's (dir)? *How are you? (inf.)*
Wie geht es Ihnen? *How are you? (form.)*
Prima. *Great.*
Sehr gut. *Very well.*
Ziemlich gut. *Fine.*
Und dir/Ihnen? *And you?*
Mir auch. *Me, too.*
Es geht. *So-so.*
(Nicht) schlecht. *(Not) bad.*
Mir geht's (sehr) gut. *I'm (very) well.*
Mir geht's nicht (so) gut. *I'm not (so) well.*

sich vorstellen
introducing oneself

Wie heißt du? *What is your name? (inf.)*
Wie heißen Sie? *What is your name? (form.)*
Und du/Sie? *And you? (inf./form.)*
Das ist.../Das sind... *This is.../These are...*
Ich heiße... *My name is...*
Freut mich./Angenehm. *Pleased to meet you.*
Schön dich/Sie kennen zu lernen. *Nice to meet you. (inf./form.)*

Personen
people

die Frau, -en *woman*
der Freund, -e / die Freundin, -nen *friend*
der Junge, -n *boy*
das Mädchen, - *girl*
der Mann, ⸚er *man*
Herr *Mr.*
Frau *Mrs.; Ms.*

Höflichkeiten
polite expressions

Danke. *Thank you.*
Vielen Dank. *Thank you very much.*
Bitte. *Please./You're welcome.*
Gern geschehen. *My pleasure.*
Entschuldigung. *Excuse me.*
Entschuldigen Sie. *Excuse me. (form.)*
Es tut mir leid. *I'm sorry.*
ja *yes*
nein *no*

Orte
places

wo? *where?*
hier *here*
da / dort *there*

Nouns and articles *See pp. 10–11.*
Compound nouns *See p. 11.*
Plurals *See p. 14.*
Subject pronouns *See p. 16.*
sein *See p. 17.*
Nominative articles *See p. 17.*

Lektion 1B

im Unterricht
in class

das Blatt Papier, (*pl.* Blätter Papier) *sheet of paper*
der Bleistift, -e *pencil*
das Buch, ⸚er *book*
der Computer, - *computer*
das Ergebnis, -se *result; score*
das Fenster, - *window*
das Foto, -s *photo*
die Frage, -n *question*
die Hausaufgabe, -n *homework*
das Heft, -e *notebook*
der Kalender, - *calendar*
die Karte, -n *map*
die Klasse, -n *class*
das Klassenzimmer, - *classroom*
der Kuli, -s *ball-point pen*
das Lehrbuch, ⸚er *(university) textbook*
die Note, -n *grade (on an assignment)*
die Notiz, -en *note*
der Papierkorb, ⸚e *wastebasket*
das Problem, -e *problem*
die Prüfung, -en *test; exam*
der Radiergummi, -s *eraser*
der Rucksack, ⸚e *backpack*
der Schreibtisch, -e *desk*
die Sache, -n *thing*
das Schulbuch, ⸚er *(K–12) textbook*
der Stift, -e *pen*
der Stuhl, ⸚e *chair*
die Stunde, -n *lesson*
die Tafel, -n *(black/white) board*
der Taschenrechner, - *calculator*
der Tisch, -e *table; desk*
die Tür, -en *door*
die Uhr, -en *clock*
das Wörterbuch, ⸚er *dictionary*
das Zeugnis, -se *report card; grade report*
Da ist/sind... *There is/are...*
Ist/Sind...hier? *Is/Are there... here?*
Hier ist/sind... *Here is/are...*
Was ist das? *What is that?*

Orte

die Bibliothek, -en *library*
die Mensa, Mensen *(university) cafeteria*
die Schule, -n *school*
die Universität, -en *university, college*

Personen

der Klassenkamerad, -en /die Klassenkameradin, -nen *(K–12) classmate*
der Kommilitone, -n / die Kommilitonin, -nen *(university) classmate*
der Lehrer, - / die Lehrerin, -nen *teacher*
der Professor, -en / die Professorin, -nen *professor*
der Schüler, - / die Schülerin, -nen *(K–12) student*
der Student, -en / die Studentin, -nen *(university) student*
Wer ist das? *Who is it?*

haben *See p. 30.*
Accusative articles *See p. 30.*
Yes-or-no questions *See p. 32.*
Numbers and math expressions *See pp. 34–35.*

COMMUNICATIVE GOALS
By the end of this chapter you will be able to:

Los geht's! Who are Sabite, Hans, and George? What are they doing?

LEKTION 2A

Exchange information about your classes and life.
Ask and tell the time.

To do so, you will use:

Kontext Seite 48–51
• The classroom, academics, and schedules

Strukturen Seite 56–66
2A.1 Regular verbs
2A.2 Interrogative words
2A.3 Talking about time and dates

You will also learn about cultural products, practices, and perspectives related to:

Kultur Seite 54–55
• Collegue courses and lectures
• Education and the European Union
• The **university of Basel**, Switzerland

Zapping Seite 67
• *Kein Wohnraum*

LEKTION 2B

Talk about sports and leisure activities.
Talk about what will happen.
Negate statements and ask negative questions.

To do so, you will use:

Kontext Seite 68–71
• Sports
• Leisure activities

Strukturen Seite 76–87
2B.1 Stem-changing verbs
2B.2 Present tense used as future
2B.3 Negation

You will also learn about cultural products, practices, and perspectives related to:

Kultur Seite 74–75
• Skiing in the Alps
• **Anna-Lena Forster**
• Hiking and biking as popular pastimes

WEITER GEHT'S

Seite 88–94
You will also learn about Berlin, its famous locations, and history.

And you will demonstrate that you can:
• Predict the contents of a reading selection by its format
• Identify cognates in a listening selection
• Write a brief personal description

Suggestion Ask students who the people in the photo are, where they are, and what they are doing.

An der Universität

 Vocabulary Tools

Wortschatz

das Studium	studies
der Abschluss, ¨e/	degree
das Diplom, -e	
das Abschlusszeugnis, -se/	diploma
das Diplom, -e	
der Dozent, -en /	college/university
die Dozentin, -nen	instructor
das Fach, ¨er	subject
die Literatur	literature
das Seminar, -e	seminar
das Stipendium, -en	scholarship
die Veranstaltung, -en	class; course
die Vorlesung, -en	lecture
belegen	to take (a class)
gehen	to go
lernen	to study; to learn
studieren	to study; to major in
Orte	**places**
das Café, -s	café
der Hörsaal, Hörsäle	lecture hall
der Seminarraum, -räume	college classroom
die Sporthalle, -n	gym
zum Beschreiben	**to describe**
einfach	easy
interessant	interesting
langweilig	boring
nützlich / nutzlos	useful / useless
schwierig	difficult
der Stundenplan	**schedule**
der Montag, -e	Monday
der Dienstag, -e	Tuesday
der Mittwoch, -e	Wednesday
der Donnerstag, -e	Thursday
der Freitag, -e	Friday
der Samstag, -e	Saturday
der Sonntag, -e	Sunday
die Stunde, -n	hour
die Woche, -n	week
das Wochenende, -n	weekend
die Zeit, -en	time
montags/dienstags/	on Mondays/Tuesdays/
mittwochs	Wednesdays
morgens	in the morning
nachmittags	in the afternoon
abends	in the evening

More activities

 vhlcentral | WB pp. 17–18 | LM p. 11 | Online activities

Tell students that **an der Universität** means *at the university*. Point out that **der** is a feminine article in the dative case, and that the dative is used in certain phrases describing locations, including the expressions **in der Schule** (*at school*) and **im Unterricht** (*in class*) from **1B Kontext**. They will learn more about the dative case in **Lektion 4B**.

Suggestion Explain to students that the **Abschlusszeugnis** is a document similar to a transcript, itemizing the course credits required to obtain a degree, including grades and GPA.

Suggestion Explain that a **Diplom** is one of the degrees awarded by universities, in addition to others such as the **Bachelor**, the **Magister**, and the **Staatsexamen**.

(die) Biologie

(die) Architektur

Ich studiere Physik (f.) und Chemie (f.).

Was studierst du?

(die) Künste *art*

(die) Mathematik

(die) Informatik *computer science*

ACHTUNG

Don't use an article when talking about a school subject or sport, or identifying someone's profession.

Julian studiert Psychologie.
Julian is studying psychology.

Anna spielt Basketball.
Anna plays basketball.

Herr Fischer ist Pilot.
Mr. Fischer is a pilot.

(die) Psychologie

(die) Fremdsprachen (f., pl.)
foreign languages

(die) Wirtschaft
business

(die) Geschichte
history

(die) Naturwissenschaften (f., pl.)
natural sciences

Suggestion Emphasize that **studieren** means *to study* in the sense of examining something or pursuing an academic subject, while **lernen** is used in the context of learning information or studying for a test.

Anwendung

Suggestion Explain that the term **Veranstaltungen** can refer to **Vorlesungen**, **Seminare**, or other scheduled events.

1 Richtig oder falsch? Indicate **richtig** if the word you hear is an academic subject or **falsch** if it's not.

	Richtig	Falsch
1.	☑	☐
2.	☑	☐
3.	☐	☑
4.	☑	☐
5.	☐	☑
6.	☑	☐

1 Expansion Ask students about their courses and schedule, and which courses they find interesting or boring, easy or difficult.

2 Was passt zusammen? Match related words in the two columns.

_f_ 1. der Computer
_c_ 2. die Vorlesung
_d_ 3. die Biologie
_e_ 4. das Diplom
_g_ 5. Montag, Dienstag, Mittwoch...
_a_ 6. Deutsch
_b_ 7. der Basketball

a. die Fremdsprache
b. die Sporthalle
c. der Hörsaal
d. die Naturwissenschaft
e. der Abschluss
f. die Informatik
g. die Woche

3 Das Unileben Listen to the conversation between Hannah and Mehmet and indicate which classes each of them is taking this semester.

Veranstaltungen	Mehmet	Hannah
Mathematik	X	
Physik	X	
Geschichte	X	X
Literatur	X	X
Kunst	X	
Psychologie		X
Medizin		X

4 Was fehlt? Complete the sentences. Use each word once.

Dozentin	Seminarraum
Fremdsprachen	Stipendium
Hörsaal	Wirtschaft

1. Die Vorlesung von Professor Huber ist im _____Hörsaal_____ C.
2. Frau Klein ist _____Dozentin_____ an der Uni.
3. Für ein Studium in __Wirtschaft/Naturwissenschaften__ ist Mathematik nützlich.
4. Spanisch, Italienisch und Chinesisch sind _____Fremdsprachen_____.
5. Wir haben eine Veranstaltung in diesem (*this*) _____Seminarraum_____.
6. Eva hat ein _____Stipendium_____ und studiert in England.

Kommunikation

5 **Auf dem Campus** Write a caption for each picture. Complete the sentences to say what each person is studying and add one sentence giving your opinion of each course. In pairs, take turns reading your sentences out of order. Your partner must decide which picture each sentence refers to. Sample answers are provided.

5 **Suggestion** Before students do this activity, you may want to have them preview the conjugation of **studieren**, taught in **2A.1**. Call on individual students and ask: **Was studierst du?**

▶ **BEISPIEL**

Max studiert <u>Informatik</u>.
<u>Informatik ist schwierig.</u>

Spanisch II

1. Daniela studiert <u>Spanisch</u>.
   <u>Spanisch ist nützlich.</u>

Freud, österreichischer Psychologe…

2. Björn studiert <u>Psychologie</u>.
   <u>Psychologie ist einfach.</u>

3. Anna studiert <u>Chemie</u>.
   <u>Chemie ist nutzlos.</u>

4. Mia und ich studieren <u>Architektur</u>.
   <u>Architektur ist interessant.</u>

6 **Ihr Studium** Indicate whether each statement is **richtig** or **falsch**, in your opinion. Then, compare your answers with a classmate's. Answers will vary.

6 **Video Virtual Chat** You can also assign activity 6 on the Supersite.

BEISPIEL

S1: Chemie ist nützlich. Richtig oder falsch?
S2: Falsch. Chemie ist nutzlos.

	richtig	falsch
1. Mathematik ist schwierig.	☐	☐
2. Fremdsprachen sind nützlich.	☐	☐
3. Literatur ist interessant.	☐	☐
4. Ein Abschluss in Psychologie ist nutzlos.	☐	☐
5. Prüfungen in Geschichte sind einfach.	☐	☐
6. Ein Wirtschaftstudium ist langweilig.	☐	☐

7 **Arbeitsblatt** Your instructor will give you a worksheet. Keep a record of your classmates' answers to share with the class.

BEISPIEL

S1: Ist Mathematik einfach oder schwierig?
S2: Mathematik ist schwierig, aber nützlich.

8 **Diskutieren und kombinieren** Your instructor will give you and a partner different worksheets. Each worksheet includes part of Sarah's weekly schedule. In pairs, take turns asking each other questions to fill in the missing information and complete the schedule.

BEISPIEL

S1: Hat Sarah montags Chemie?
S2: Nein, sie hat mittwochs Chemie.
S1: Hat sie montags Geschichte?
S2: Ja, sie hat montagnachmittags Geschichte.
S1: Hat sie…?

7 **Expansion** Read the statements out loud and have students vote on whether each is **richtig** or **falsch**. Then have a class discussion about the results of the poll.

Aussprache und Rechtschreibung Audio

Consonant sounds

The German letter **g** has three different pronunciations. At the end of a syllable or before a **t**, it is pronounced like the *k* in the English word *keep*. In the suffix **-ig**, the **g** is pronounced like the German **ch**. Otherwise, **g** is pronounced like the *g* in the English word *garden*.

| Tag | belegt | schwierig | gehen | fragen |

The German letter **j** is pronounced very similarly to the letter *y* in the English word *young*. However, in a small number of loanwords from other languages, **j** may be pronounced like the *j* in *job* or the *g* in *mirage*.

| jung | Januar | ja | jobben | Journal |

The German letter **v** is pronounced like the *f* in the English word *fable*. In a few loanwords from other languages, **v** is pronounced like the *v* in the English word *vase*.

| vier | Vorlesung | Vase | Universität | Volleyball |

The German letter **w** is pronounced like the *v* in the English word *vote*.

| wissen | Mittwoch | Wirtschaft | Wort | Schwester |

Although most German consonants sound very similar to their English counterparts, there are five letters that represent different sounds than they do in English: **g, j, v, w,** and initial **c,** which will be discussed in **6B**.

Suggestion Tell students that the pronunciation of the final **-ig** sound has several regional variations.

Suggestion Have students look at the sample words and sentences on this page to identify cognates and words they already know. Tell students the meanings of any unfamiliar words or phrases.

1 **Aussprechen** Practice saying these words aloud.

1. Garten
2. Essig
3. Weg
4. Jahr
5. Journalist
6. joggen
7. Vater
8. verstehen
9. Violine
10. Wasser
11. zwischen
12. weil

2 **Nachsprechen** Practice saying these sentences aloud.

1. Wir wollen wissen, wie wir das wissen sollen.
2. In vier Wochen wird Veronikas Vater wieder in seiner Villa wohnen.
3. Gestern war Gregors zwanzigster Geburtstag.
4. Jeden Tag soll ich Gemüse und Grünzeug wie Salat essen.
5. Meine Schwester studiert Jura an der Universität Jena.
6. Viele Studenten jobben, um das Studium zu finanzieren.

3 **Sprichwörter** Practice reading these sayings aloud.

Es ist nicht alles Gold, was glänzt.[1]

Was ich nicht weiß, macht mich nicht heiß.[2]

[1] All that glitters is not gold.
[2] Ignorance is bliss. (lit. *What I don't know, doesn't bother me.*)

More activities

vhlcentral   LM p. 12   Online activities

Checkpoint Charlie Video

George und Hans reden über (*talk about*) das Studium und über Meline und Sabite. Ist Hans in Sabite verliebt (*in love*)?

Vorbereitung Have students look at scene 7 and try to guess what Hans is reacting to. After they have watched the video, have them review their predictions.

1

GEORGE Woher kommst du?
HANS Ich komme aus Straubing. Das ist in Bayern.
GEORGE Wie viele Menschen leben dort?
HANS Hmm... etwa 100.000.

2

HANS Woher kommst du?
GEORGE Milwaukee, Wisconsin.
HANS Wie viel Uhr ist es dort?
GEORGE Wie viel Uhr ist es hier?
HANS Es ist Viertel vor zwei.
GEORGE Der Zeitunterschied ist sieben Stunden. Also Viertel vor sieben morgens.

3

HANS Alles in Ordnung?
GEORGE Ich studiere Architektur, belege Kurse in Städtebau, Physik, Mathematik und Philosophie!

4

HANS Und du belegst einen Deutschkurs, nicht wahr? Studieren ist nicht leicht. George, du bist ein Mitbewohner und Freund. Ich helfe dir.
GEORGE Wann?
HANS Morgens. Um 5.00 Uhr!

5

GEORGE Hey! Wir sind da!
HANS Check...
GEORGE ...point Charlie.

GEORGE Sabite kommt aus Prenzlauer Berg. Und Meline?
HANS Was ist mit Meline?
GEORGE Woher kommt sie?
HANS Wien.

6

ÜBUNGEN

1 **Wer ist das?** Which character does each statement describe: George, Meline, Sabite, or Hans?

1. _George_ hält ein Referat über Architektur und Kunst.
2. _Meline_ kommt aus Wien.
3. _George_ belegt einen Deutschkurs.
4. _Hans_ kommt aus Straubing.
5. _George_ studiert Architektur.

6. _George_ ist Hans' Mitbewohner und Freund.
7. _Sabite_ liest Bücher über Kunst und Mode.
8. _Sabite_ kommt aus Prenzlauer Berg.
9. _George_ kommt aus Milwaukee.
10. _Hans_ hilft (*helps*) George morgens um 5.00 Uhr.

PERSONEN

George　　　Hans

7

HANS Sabite ist ganz anders. Sie liest Bücher über Kunst und Mode.
GEORGE Mode ist nutzlos. Ich halte am 20. Oktober ein Referat über Architektur und Kunst in Berlin. Sabite hilft mir.
HANS Was?
GEORGE Sabite studiert Kunst. Ich halte bald das Referat. Sie hilft mir.

8

GEORGE Alles in Ordnung, Hans?
HANS Ja, alles klar. Lernst du Philosophie mit Meline?
GEORGE Wo liegt das Problem?
HANS Was?
GEORGE Hans, findest du Sabite...

9

HANS Sabite ist nur eine Freundin.
GEORGE Okay.
HANS Also, ähm... hat Sabite einen Freund? Nein?
GEORGE Ich glaube nicht, dass sie einen hat.

10

HANS Du und Sabite, ihr seid nicht...?
GEORGE Nein!
HANS Okay.
GEORGE Okay.

Nützliche Ausdrücke

- **etwa**
  about
- **Wie viel Uhr ist es dort?**
  What time is it there?
- **der Zeitunterschied**
  time difference
- **Und du belegst einen Deutschkurs, nicht wahr?**
  And you're taking a German class, aren't you?
- **Ich helfe dir.**
  I'll help you.
- **Was ist mit Meline?**
  What's with Meline?
- **ein Referat halten**
  to give a presentation
- **Alles klar!**
  All right!
- **Wo liegt das Problem?**
  Where's the problem?
- **Sabite ist nur eine Freundin.**
  Sabite's just a friend.
- **Ich glaube nicht, dass sie einen hat.**
  I don't think she has one.

2A.1
- **Sabite studiert Kunst.**
  Sabite is studying art.

2A.2
- **Woher kommst du?**
  Where are you from?

2A.3
- **Es ist Viertel vor zwei.**
  It's a quarter to two.

---

2 **Zum Besprechen** In this episode, the characters talk about their classes. With a partner, discuss your classes and schedule. Mention what you are studying, how many courses you are taking, and which courses you have in the morning, afternoon, or evenings.
Answers will vary.

BEISPIEL

 S1: *Welche Fächer hast du?*
S2: *Ich habe Fremdsprachen und Geschichte. Und du?*

2 **Partner Chat** You can also assign activity 2 on the Supersite.

3 **Vertiefung** George and Hans visit Checkpoint Charlie on their walk in Berlin. Find out more about this well-known landmark. What is its significance? What streets are nearby? What does "Charlie" refer to? Would you want to visit Checkpoint Charlie? Why or why not?
Sample answers: It was the main crossing point of the Berlin Wall; it is located at the junction of Friedrichstraße, Zimmerstraße, and Mauerstraße; "Charlie" comes from the letter C in the NATO phonetic alphabet.

More activities

vhlcentral　　　VM p. 3　　　Online activities

IM FOKUS

Uni-Zeit, Büffel-Zeit° Reading

Historically, university education in Germany has been government-funded and free for all students. In the past few decades, some states introduced modest tuition fees—usually 500 Euros per semester. However, the fees proved so unpopular that they have since been abolished. As of October 2014, all public universities are again tuition-free, even for foreign students.

Apart from cost, there are other significant differences between German and American university life. German universities typically offer only a limited amount of dormitory housing. Most students live off campus, either commuting from home or renting an apartment shared with other students. Unlike in most American universities, students must decide on a major before they begin their studies, and there is little flexibility in the choice of courses.

In the past few decades, there has been an initiative to standardize degree requirements between countries. Part of this restructuring has included a push to transition from 4- to 6-year **Diplom** and **Magister°** degrees to 3-year **Bachelor** degrees. This change has been met with resistance from students, including complaints that it simply compresses the original curriculum into a shorter time frame. Many students also object to the shift toward a heavier workload with more frequent testing.

The percentage of students studying at private universities remains very small, but it is gradually increasing. Whereas public universities have had problems with over-crowding, private institutions can offer smaller class sizes, giving students more contact with professors.

Statistische Informationen zum Thema Studium	
Neue Studenten pro Jahr°	ca. 508.800
Studenten, die nach dem° Bachelor weiter studieren°	78%
Bachelor-Studenten, die zum Studieren ins Ausland gehen°	ca. 7,4%
Bachelor-Absolventen°, die 1,5 Jahre nach dem Abschluss Arbeit° haben	ca. 25%

QUELLE: Der Tagesspiegel

Büffel-Zeit cramming time **Diplom, Magister** degrees available before the education reform **pro Jahr** per year **die nach dem** who after the **weiter studieren** continue their studies **ins Ausland gehen** go abroad **Absolventen** graduates **Arbeit** work

---

ÜBUNGEN

1 **Im Fokus** Indicate whether each statement is **richtig** or **falsch**. Correct the false statements. Then discuss the last question with a partner.

1. Most universities in Germany are public.
   Richtig.
2. German students have embraced the changes to make the curriculum more similar to the curriculum in other countries. Falsch. German students are not happy about these changes and the greater workload resulting from the shorter time frame.
3. There are more options for German students to choose their courses than at American universities.
   Falsch. There is little flexibility in the choice of courses at German universities.

Diskussion Do you think college students should choose a major before they begin their studies? What are the advantages and disadvantages?

2 **Die deutschsprachige Welt** Indicate whether each statement is **richtig** or **falsch**. Correct the false statements. Then discuss the last question with a partner.

1. Viele Länder müssen ihre Hochschulbildung standardisieren.
   Richtig.
2. Die neuen Abschluss-Standards begannen schon 1999.
   Falsch. Nur der Prozess began 1999. Die Standardisierung ist erst seit 2010 Realität.
3. Studenten sollen in ihren Heimatländern studieren.
   Falsch. Die Mobilität der Studenten in der Europäischen Union ist besonders wichtig.

Diskussion How does the **Bologna-Prozess** make studying in Europe simpler? Why is mobility important for European students?

Die Uni

der Besserwisser, -	*know-it-all*
der Mitbewohner, - / die Mitbewohnerin, -nen	*roommate*
das Referat, -e	*presentation*
das Schwarze Brett	*bulletin board*
das Studentenwohnheim, -e	*dormitory*
die Studiengebühr, -en	*tuition fee*
büffeln	*to cram (for a test)*

Der Bologna-Prozess

Die Bildungsminister° der Europäischen Union treffen sich erstmals° 1999 in Bologna in Italien. Das Ziel°: international einheitliche° Universitäts-Abschlüsse in ganz Europa und hohe° Mobilität für Studenten. In Europa müssen° Universitäten die Hochschulbildung° standardisieren. Im März 2010 wird der gemeinsame° europäische Hochschulraum in Budapest und Wien offiziell eröffnet°. 47 Mitgliedsländer° nehmen daran teil°.

Bildungsminister *secretaries of education* **treffen... erstmals** *meet for the first time* **Ziel** *goal* **einheitliche** *standardized* **hohe** *high* **müssen** *must* **Hochschulbildung** *higher education* **gemeinsame** *common* **Hochschulraum** *Higher Education Area* **eröffnet** *opened* **Mitgliedsländer** *member countries* **nehmen... teil** *participate*

Uni Basel

Die Uni Basel ist die älteste° Universität der Schweiz. Sie bietet° schon seit ihrer Gründung° im Jahr 1460 die Studienfächer° Theologie, Jura und Medizin an. Zudem gibt es die Artistenfakultät°, die Grundwissen° vermittelt und dadurch auf das Studium der anderen Fächer vorbereitet°. Diese wird später zur Philosophischen Fakultät. Mittlerweile° kann man hier auch Geschichte, Naturwissenschaften und Psychologie studieren. Der Bologna-Prozess führt auch hier zu einigen wesentlichen° Veränderungen°. Heute ist die Uni Basel unter anderem bekannt für ihre Forschungen°, vor allem im Bereich° der Life Sciences, in dem sie auch von ihrer guten internationalen Vernetzung° profitiert.

älteste *oldest* **bietet** *offers* **Gründung** *founding* **Studienfächer** *courses of study* **Artistenfakultät** *school of arts* **Grundwissen** *basic knowledge* **vorbereitet** *prepares* **Mittlerweile** *now* **wesentlichen** *essential* **Veränderungen** *changes* **Forschungen** *research* **im Bereich** *in the area* **Vernetzung** *networking*

IM INTERNET

Österreichische Universitäten. Wie ist das Studium in Österreich? Ist es mit dem (*with the*) deutschen System vergleichbar (*comparable*)?

Find out more at **vhlcentral.com**.

Expansion Have students search online for more information about the people mentioned in this article, as well as other famous intellectuals from Basel. Have them share their findings with the class.

---

3 **Porträt** Indicate whether each statement is **richtig** or **falsch**. Correct the false statements. Then discuss the last question with a partner.

 1. Die Uni Basel existiert schon seit 1600.
    Falsch. Sie existiert schon seit 1460.

 2. Die Schweizer Universitäten machen beim Bologna-Prozess nicht mit (don't participate).
    Falsch. Der Bologna-Prozess gilt auch für Universitäten in der Schweiz.

3. An der Uni Basel studiert man nur Naturwissenschaften.
    Falsch. An der Uni Basel studiert man auch Jura, Geschichte, Psychologie und andere Fächer.

Diskussion Which subjects can you study at the **Uni Basel**? Compare them with the subjects at your university. Would you like to study in Basel? Why or why not?

4 **Mein Auslandsjahr (*Year abroad*)** Briefly talk about your (likely) major and how a year in a German-speaking country might fit your plans. What would be your main reason for studying abroad? Where would you consider studying?.

2A.1

QUERVERWEIS

In **Kapitel 1**, you learned the irregular verbs **sein** and **haben**. You will learn more about irregular verbs in **2B.1**.

ACHTUNG

Depending on the context, **sie lernt** can be translated as *she studies, she is studying,* or *she does study.*

QUERVERWEIS

As in English, the simple present can sometimes be used to talk about a future action. You will learn more about this usage in **2B.2**.

Regular verbs Grammar Tutorial

Startblock Most German verbs follow predictable conjugation patterns in which a set of endings is added to the verb stem.

Ich **studiere** Architektur.

Lernst du Philosophie mit Meline?

- To form the present tense of a regular verb, drop the **-en** or **-n** ending from the infinitive and add **-e**, **-st**, **-t**, or **-en/-n** to the stem.

	lernen *(to study)*		wandern *(to hike)*	
ich	lerne	*I study*	wandere	*I hike*
du	lernst	*you study*	wanderst	*you hike*
Sie	lernen	*you study*	wandern	*you hike*
er/sie/es	lernt	*he/she studies*	wandert	*he/she hikes*
wir	lernen	*we study*	wandern	*we hike*
ihr	lernt	*you study*	wandert	*you hike*
Sie	lernen	*you study*	wandern	*you hike*
sie	lernen	*they study*	wandern	*they hike*

Lernst du Physik?
Are you studying physics?

Sie wandern im Sommer.
They go hiking in the summer.

- Regular verbs whose stems end in **-d** or **-t** add an **e** before the endings **-st** or **-t** for ease of pronunciation.

arbeiten *(to work)*			
ich arbeite	*I work*	wir arbeiten	*we work*
du arbeitest	*you work*	ihr arbeitet	*you work*
Sie arbeiten	*you work*	Sie arbeiten	*you work*
er/sie/es arbeitet	*he/she/it works*	sie arbeiten	*they work*

Lena **arbeitet** in München.
Lena works in Munich.

Findest du Mathematik interessant?
Do you find math interesting?

Wartet ihr auf eure Freunde?
Are you waiting for your friends?

Die Hefte **kosten** zu viel.
The notebooks cost too much.

- Verbs whose stems end in **-gn** or **-fn** also add an **-e** before the endings **-st** and **-t**.

Es regnet morgen.
It's going to rain tomorrow.

Öffnest du das Fenster?
Are you opening the window?

- If a verb stem ends in **-s**, **-ß**, **-x**, or **-z**, the **-s** is dropped from the second person singular ending.

heißen (*to be named*)			
ich heiße	*I am named*	wir heißen	*we are named*
du heißt	*you are named*	ihr heißt	*you are named*
Sie heißen	*you are named*	Sie heißen	*you are named*
er/sie/es heißt	*he/she/it is named*	sie heißen	*they are named*

Du heißt Jonas, nicht wahr?
Your name is Jonas, right?

Mein Hund heißt Fritz.
My dog's name is Fritz.

Martin **reist** oft in die Schweiz.
Martin often travels to Switzerland.

Ihr **grüßt** den Professor nicht?
You're not going to greet the professor?

common regular verbs (present tense)			
antworten	*to answer*	leben	*to live*
bauen	*to build*	lernen	*to learn; to study*
bedeuten	*to mean*	lieben	*to love*
begrüßen	*to greet*	machen	*to do; to make*
belegen	*to take (a class)*	öffnen	*to open*
brauchen	*to need*	regnen	*to rain*
bringen	*to bring*	reisen	*to travel*
finden	*to find*	sagen	*to say*
fragen	*to ask*	schreiben	*to write*
gehen	*to go*	spielen	*to play*
hören	*to hear; to listen to*	suchen	*to look for*
kaufen	*to buy*	verstehen	*to understand*
kommen	*to come*	warten	*to wait*
korrigieren	*to correct*	wiederholen	*to repeat*
kosten	*to cost*	wohnen	*to live (somewhere)*

More activities

vhlcentral

WB
pp. 19–20

LM
p. 13

Online activities

Kaufst du Kaffee im Supermarkt?
Do you buy coffee at the supermarket?

Was **bedeutet** das auf Englisch?
What does that mean in English?

Ich **lerne** Deutsch.
I'm learning German.

Wir **belegen** Biologie.
We're taking Biology.

Jetzt sind Sie dran! **Write the appropriate form of the verb.**

1. Wir ___lernen___ (lernen) Deutsch.
2. Der Student ___wiederholt___ (wiederholen) den Satz (*sentence*).
3. Ich ___warte___ (warten) auf den Bus.
4. Die Lehrerin ___korrigiert___ (korrigieren) die Prüfungen.
5. Du ___belegst___ (belegen) fünf Veranstaltungen.
6. Das Universitätsstudium ___kostet___ (kosten) sehr viel.

7. Ihr ___versteht___ (verstehen) Mathematik.
8. Wir ___brauchen___ (brauchen) viel Papier und viele Bleistifte für den Unterricht.
9. Anja und Thomas ___begrüßen___ (begrüßen) den Dozenten.
10. Ich ___kaufe___ (kaufen) eine Tasse Kaffee in der Mensa.
11. Wir ___machen___ (machen) nachmittags Hausaufgaben.
12. Du ___öffnest___ (öffnen) die Tür.

Anwendung

1 Was ist richtig? Select the verb that best completes each sentence.

1. Astrid und Jonas (wohnen)/ bedeuten) in Berlin.
2. Michaela (sucht)/ korrigiert) den Seminarraum.
3. Ich (baue / (studiere) Mathematik.
4. Wir (belegen)/ grüßen) sehr viele Vorlesungen.
5. (Belegst / (Lebst)) du in Deutschland oder in Österreich?
6. Ihr (macht)/ kauft) nachmittags Hausaufgaben.
7. (Warten)/ Kosten) Sie auf (*for*) den Bus, Professor Meier?
8. Du (sagst / (reist)) im Sommer nach (*to*) Spanien und Italien.

2 Expansion Have students write their own dialogues about the courses they are taking.

2 Was fehlt? Maria and Tim are meeting for lunch. Complete their conversation with the correct verb forms.

MARIA Hallo, Tim! Wie (1) __geht__ (gehen) es dir? Wie ist das Deutschseminar?

TIM Ach, es geht mir ziemlich gut. Im Seminar (2) __schreibt__ (schreiben) der Dozent viel an die Tafel, aber ich (3) __verstehe__ (verstehen) es gut. Und du? Wie (4) __findest__ (finden) du das Informatikseminar?

MARIA Ich (5) __liebe__ (lieben) Informatik! Wir (6) __bauen__ (bauen) heute einen Computer.

TIM Vielleicht (*Maybe*) (7) __belege__ (belegen) ich nächstes Semester auch Informatik. (8) __Machst__ (Machen) du viele Hausaufgaben?

MARIA Ja! Samstags und sonntags (9) __lerne__ (lernen) ich immer (*always*).

TIM Oje. Samstags und sonntags (10) __spielen__ (spielen) Max und ich Computer.

3 Schreiben Write complete sentences using the cues.

1. ich / kaufen / einen Apfel Ich kaufe einen Apfel.
2. David / brauchen / das Wörterbuch David braucht das Wörterbuch.
3. du / arbeiten / freitags und samstags Du arbeitest freitags und samstags.
4. Lara / suchen / das Deutschbuch Lara sucht das Deutschbuch.
5. Josef und ich / spielen / Basketball Josef und ich spielen Basketball.
6. lernen / ihr / Spanisch / ? Lernt ihr Spanisch?
7. der Dozent / wiederholen / das Experiment Der Dozent wiederholt das Experiment.
8. Hans und Jana / leben / in Irland Hans und Jana leben in Irland.
9. regnen / es / ? Regnet es?
10. öffnen / du / das Fenster / ? Öffnest du das Fenster?

Kommunikation

4 **Was fehlt?** Complete the sentences, and then, with a partner, take turns asking and explaining what each person is doing.

▶ **BEISPIEL**

Du ___hörst___ Musik.
S1: *Was mache ich?*
S2: *Du hörst Musik.*

1. Herr Becker __arbeitet__.

2. Wir __spielen__ Tennis.

3. Ihr__lernt__ viel.

4. Ich __kaufe__ ein neues Fahrrad.

5. Heinrich __begrüßt__ den Mann.

6. Hans __liebt__ Emma.

5 **Bilden Sie Sätze** In pairs, use items from each column to create six sentences. You may use some items more than once. Answers will vary.

BEISPIEL *Ich höre Musik.*

A	B	C
ich	hören	Deutsch
du	lernen	Hausaufgaben
Alena	lieben	Kunst
Anna und ich	machen	Musik
ihr	spielen	Naturwissenschaft
die Studenten	verstehen	Tennis

6 **Persönliche Fragen** In pairs, take turns asking and answering the questions.
Answers will vary.

BEISPIEL **S1:** *Studierst du Chemie?*
S2: *Nein, ich studiere Physik.*

1. Wie viele Kurse belegst du?

2. Lernst du Fremdsprachen?

3. Gehst du oft in die Sporthalle?

4. Was machst du morgens?

5. Was machst du nachmittags?

6. Was machst du abends?

7 **Gespräch** In pairs, fill in Student 2's half of the dialogue, then continue the conversation with your partner using at least four more regular verbs. Then present your conversation to the class. Answers will vary.

> **S1:** Hallo! Studierst du hier an der Uni?
> **S2:** …
> **S1:** Ich auch! Was studierst du?
> **S2:** …
> **S1:** Ist Wirtschaft schwierig?
> **S2:** …
> **S1:** Montags und mittwochs habe ich Geschichte. Und du?
> **S2:** …

6 **Expansion** Have students write a paragraph about themselves, including their name, age, major, and class schedule.

6 **Video Virtual Chat** You can also assign activity 6 on the Supersite. Students record individual responses that appear in your gradebook.

2A.2 Interrogative words Grammar Tutorial

Startblock Use interrogative words to ask for information.

ACHTUNG

In **1B.3**, you learned to use **wie viel** with a singular noun and **wie viele** with a plural noun.

Wie viel Zeit haben wir?
Wie viele Bücher kauft er?

The word **viel(e)** by itself means a *lot (of)/many*.
Ich studiere viele Fächer.
Du arbeitest viel.

QUERVERWEIS

Answers to questions that ask **Wie...?** or **Wo...?** may require the dative case. You will learn about the dative in **4B.1** and **4B.2**.

You will learn more about **wohin**, **woher**, and related words in **6A.2**.

Welcher is a **der**-word. You will learn about **der**-words in **8B.2**.

Wie viele Menschen leben dort?

Was ist mit Meline?

Suggestion Ask students additional questions using interrogatives from the list, and have students answer. Ex.: **Was ist das? Wer ist sie?**, etc.

interrogatives			
wann?	*when?*	**wie?**	*how?*
warum?	*why?*	**wie viel(e)?**	*how much/many?*
was?	*what?*	**wo?**	*where?*
welcher/welche/welches?	*which?*	**woher?**	*where (from)?*
wer/wen?	*who/whom?*	**wohin?**	*where (to)?*

- To ask an information question (one that cannot be answered with **ja** or **nein**), begin the question with an interrogative word.

  Wann beginnen wir?　　**Warum** machst du das?　　**Wo** ist Frau Schultz?
  When do we start?　　*Why are you doing that?*　　*Where is Mrs. Schultz?*

- Use **wer** when the person you're asking about is the grammatical subject of the verb and **wen** when the person is the direct object of the verb.

  Wer begrüßt den Professor?　　　　**Wen** begrüßt der Professor?
  Who is greeting the professor?　　　*Who(m) is the professor greeting?*

- The form of **welcher** depends on the gender and number of the noun it modifies. Its three forms (**welcher/welche/welches**) have the same endings as the masculine, feminine/plural, and neuter forms of the definite article (**der/die/das**).

  Welche Professorin lehrt Mathematik?　　**Welcher Student** belegt Mathematik?
  Which professor teaches mathematics?　　*Which student is taking math?*

- Use **woher** to ask people where they are from and **wohin** to ask where they are going.

  —**Woher** kommen Sie?　　　　—**Wohin** geht ihr?
  —Ich komme **aus Wien**.　　　—Wir gehen **in die Bibliothek**.
  —*Where are you from?*　　　　—*Where are you going?*
  —*I'm from Vienna.*　　　　　　—*We're going to the library.*

More activities

vhlcentral

WB pp. 21–22

LM p. 14

Online activities

Jetzt sind Sie dran! Select the appropriate interrogative for each question. **Expansion** Have students take turns asking each other the questions and giving logical answers, where possible.

1. (Woher / Wer) kommst du?
2. (Wohin / Wann) haben wir Deutsch?
3. (Was / Wohin) reisen wir?
4. (Wer / Wo) braucht ein Blatt Papier?
5. (Welche / Woher) Seminare sind einfach?
6. (Wer / Wen) liebst du?

Anwendung und Kommunikation

1 **Was fehlt?** Complete each sentence with an appropriate interrogative word.

1. ___Wann/Wo___ spielen wir Tennis?
2. ___Wann/Woher___ kommt die Dozentin?
3. ___Was___ kaufst du für das Studium?
4. ___Warum/Wann___ brauchst du einen Computer?
5. ___Wo/Wann/Wie viel/Was___ lernst du?
6. ___Wie___ alt bist du?
7. ___Welche/Wie viele___ Kurse belegst du?
8. ___Wie viel___ Zeit haben wir abends?

2 **Schreiben** Write questions using the cues. Pay attention to word order.

BEISPIEL Marie und Alex / woher / kommen
Woher kommen Marie und Alex?

1. der Hörsaal / wo / ist Wo ist der Hörsaal?
2. wie / die Deutschvorlesung / ist Wie ist die Deutschvorlesung?
3. gehen / wann / wir / in die Bibliothek Wann gehen wir in die Bibliothek?
4. einen Kuli / wer / braucht Wer braucht einen Kuli?
5. machst / was / du / samstags Was machst du samstags?
6. wohin / gehen / nachmittags / die Studenten Wohin gehen die Studenten nachmittags?
7. welches / belegt / Seminar / ihr Welches Seminar belegt ihr?
8. lernt / warum / Paul / so viel Warum lernt Paul so viel?

3 **Fragen** In pairs, write a question for each response. Sample answers are provided.

BEISPIEL Ich komme **aus Wien**.
Woher kommst du?

1. Karl hat <u>montags, mittwochs und freitags</u> Vorlesungen. Wann hat Karl Vorlesungen?
2. Die Bibliothek hat <u>3.726</u> Bücher. Wie viele Bücher hat die Bibliothek?
3. <u>Das Seminar</u> ist langweilig. Was ist langweilig?
4. Das Heft kostet <u>3,50 €</u>. Wie viel kostet das Heft?
5. Ich brauche das Buch <u>*Siddhartha*</u> für die Literaturvorlesung. Welches Buch brauchst du für die Literaturvorlesung?
6. Ich wohne <u>in Berlin</u>. Wo wohnst du?
7. <u>Der Dozent</u> wiederholt die Frage. Wer wiederholt die Frage?
8. Anna liebt <u>Paul</u>. Wen liebt Anna?

4 **Interview** Prepare six questions about school life using interrogative words. Then, survey your classmates. Summarize your findings for the class. Answers will vary.

4 **Expansion** Have each group of students make a set of flashcards with interrogative pronouns. One student chooses a card and asks a question with the selected word to someone in the group. That person must answer the question and select the next card.

4 **Partner Chat** You can also assign activity 4 on the Supersite.

2A.3 **Talking about time and dates** Grammar Tutorial

Startblock Like English, German uses cardinal numbers (*one, two, three*) to tell time and ordinal numbers (*first, second, third*) to give dates.

Telling time

- To ask *What time is it?*, say **Wie spät ist es?** or **Wie viel Uhr ist es?**. To answer, say **Es ist** + [*hour*] + **Uhr** + [*minutes*].

Es ist ein Uhr./
Es ist eins.

Es ist zwei Uhr./
Es ist zwei.

Es ist zwölf Uhr./
Es ist Mittag/Mitternacht.

- Use **vor** and **nach** to indicate minutes before and after the hour. Use **Viertel vor** for *quarter to* and **Viertel nach** for *quarter past*. In these constructions, omit the word **Uhr**.

Es ist **Viertel vor** elf./
Es ist zehn Uhr fünfundvierzig.

Es ist **zwanzig nach** vier./
Es ist vier Uhr zwanzig.

- Use **halb** to mean *half an hour before*. Note that it is not equivalent to the English phrase *half past*.

Es ist **halb zehn**.
Es ist neun Uhr dreißig.

Es ist **halb sieben**.
Es ist sechs Uhr dreißig.

- Use the 24-hour clock when talking about train schedules, movie listings, and official timetables. Do not use the expressions **Viertel vor, Viertel nach,** or **halb** with the 24-hour clock.

  20.30 Uhr = zwanzig Uhr dreißig
  8:30 p.m.

  18.45 Uhr = achtzehn Uhr fünfundvierzig
  6:45 p.m.

- To specify the time at which an event or activity will take place, use **um** + [*time*].

  —**Um wie viel Uhr** beginnt der Film?
  —***What time*** does the movie start?

  —**Um** sechzehn Uhr zehn.
  —*At four-ten p.m.*

Ordinal numbers

- The ordinal numbers (**die Ordinalzahlen**) from 1st to 19th are formed, with a few exceptions, by adding **-te** to the corresponding cardinal numbers. To form all other ordinals, add **-ste** to the cardinal forms. Use a period to indicate the abbreviated form of an ordinal number.

ordinal numbers								
1.	erste	*first*	7.	siebte	*seventh*	19.	neunzehnte	*nineteenth*
2.	zweite	*second*	8.	achte	*eighth*	20.	zwanzigste	*twentieth*
3.	dritte	*third*	9.	neunte	*ninth*	31.	einunddreißigste	*thirty-first*
4.	vierte	*fourth*	10.	zehnte	*tenth*	55.	fünfundfünfzigste	*fifty-fifth*
5.	fünfte	*fifth*	11.	elfte	*eleventh*	100.	hundertste	*hundredth*
6.	sechste	*sixth*	12.	zwölfte	*twelfth*	1000.	tausendste	*thousandth*

der **erste** Dozent
*the **first** instructor*

die **zweite** Vorlesung
*the **second** lecture*

das **dritte** Fach
*the **third** subject*

Dates

die Monate (*months*)			
Januar	April	Juli	Oktober
Februar	Mai	August	November
März	Juni	September	Dezember

Januar ist der erste Monat.
January is the first month.

Dezember ist der zwölfte Monat.
December is the twelfth month.

- Answer the question **Der Wievielte ist heute?** (*What is the date today?*) with **Heute ist der** + [*ordinal number* (+ *month*)].

  Heute ist **der erste Mai**.
  *Today is **May first**.*

  Heute ist **der einunddreißigste**.
  *Today is **the thirty-first**.*

  23. März 2010 ⟶ **23.3.2010**
  March 23rd, 2010 ⟶ *3/23/2010*

  7. Oktober 2014 ⟶ **7.10.2014**
  October 7th, 2014 ⟶ *10/7/2014*

- To specify the day on which an event or activity takes place, use **am** before the date, and add **-n** to the ordinal number. Use the question **Wann hast du Geburtstag?** to ask someone when their birthday is.

  Ich habe **am 7. (siebten) Juli** Geburtstag.
  *My birthday is **on July 7th**.*

  Am 1. (ersten) Januar beginnt das neue Jahr.
  *The new year begins **on January 1st**.*

- The pattern **am** + [*time expression*] is also used with days of the week.

  am Montag
  on Monday

  am Dienstag
  on Tuesday

  am Wochenende
  on the weekend

- Like English, German uses cardinal numbers to refer to a particular year.

  1895 = achtzehnhundertfünfundneunzig

  2016 = zweitausendsechzehn

QUERVERWEIS

To form the accusative of ordinal numbers, add **-n** before masculine nouns. The feminine and neuter forms do not change.

Du trinkst deinen zweiten Kaffee.
You're having your second coffee.

Ich antworte auf die dritte Frage.
I'm answering the third question.

You will learn more about nominative and accusative adjective endings in **3A.2**.

ACHTUNG

In writing, the day also comes before the month. Remember that an ordinal number is indicated by putting a period after the number.

More activities

vhlcentral

WB
pp. 23–24

LM
p. 15

Online activities

Jetzt sind Sie dran!

Expansion Write some additional times and dates on the board and have students read them aloud.

Suggestion Show students this alternative question/answer pattern for recognition purposes only: **Den Wievielten haben wir heute? Heute haben wir den zweiundzwanzigsten Juni.** Point out the use of the accusative article and the **-n** added to the ordinal number.

A. Select the correct time.

1. **7:15 a.m.** Es ist (Viertel nach / Viertel vor) sieben.
2. **2:00 p.m.** Es ist zwei Uhr (morgens / nachmittags).
3. **10:30 a.m.** Es ist (halb zehn / halb elf) vormittags.
4. **12:00 p.m.** Es ist (Mittag/Mitternacht).
5. **7:55 a.m.** Es ist (acht/sieben) Uhr fünfundfünfzig.
6. **8:37 p.m.** Es ist (zwanzig Uhr/ achtzehn Uhr) siebenunddreißig.

B. Write the correct date.

7. **14. Februar** Heute ist der ___vierzehnte___ Februar.
8. **28. Dezember** Heute ist der ___achtundzwanzigste___ Dezember.
9. **3. Juli** Heute ist der ___dritte___ Juli.
10. **30. Mai** Heute ist der ___dreißigste___ Mai.
11. **11. Oktober** Heute ist der ___elfte___ Oktober.
12. **7. August** Heute ist der ___siebte___ August.

Anwendung

1 Was ist richtig? Select the sentence that refers to the time shown.

1. Es ist zwei Uhr. / Es ist drei Uhr.

2. Es ist Viertel vor eins. / Es ist zwölf Uhr vierzig.

3. Es ist fünf Uhr zwanzig. / Es ist zehn vor drei.

4. Es ist zwei Uhr fünfundvierzig. / Es ist Viertel vor zwei.

2 Wie spät ist es? Write a sentence indicating the time shown on each clock or watch.

> **BEISPIEL**
> *Es ist Viertel nach vier.*

p.m.

1. Es ist halb eins. / Es ist zwölf Uhr dreißig.

2. Es ist ein Uhr. / Es ist eins.

p.m.   p.m.   a.m.   a.m.

3. Es ist Viertel nach fünf. / Es ist siebzehn Uhr fünfzehn.

4. Es ist zehn nach acht. / Es ist zwanzig Uhr zehn.

5. Es ist halb sechs. / Es ist fünf Uhr dreißig.

6. Es ist Viertel vor elf. / Es ist zehn Uhr fünfundvierzig.

a.m.   a.m.

7. Es ist zwölf nach zwei. / Es ist vierzehn Uhr zwölf.

8. Es ist fünf nach sieben. / Es ist sieben Uhr fünf.

9. Es ist fünf vor vier. / Es ist drei Uhr fünfundfünfzig.

10. Es ist elf Uhr fünfunddreißig.

3 Wer hat Geburtstag? Write out the date indicated to say when each person's birthday is.

BEISPIEL Angela Merkel hat am (17.) *siebzehnten* Juli Geburtstag.

1. Arnold Schwarzenegger hat am (30.) _____dreißigsten_____ Juli Geburtstag.

2. Heidi Klum hat am (1.) _____ersten_____ Juni Geburtstag.

3. Karl Lagerfeld hat am (10.) _____zehnten_____ September Geburtstag.

4. Michael Fassbender hat am (2.) _____zweiten_____ April Geburtstag.

5. Die Tennisspielerin Steffi Graf hat am (14.) _____vierzehnten_____ Juni Geburtstag.

6. Der Fußballspieler Mesut Özil hat am (15.) _____fünfzehnten_____ Oktober Geburtstag.

7. Die Musikerin Nena hat am (24.) _____vierundzwanzigsten_____ März Geburtstag.

8. Der Musiker Herbert Grönemeyer hat am (12.) _____zwölften_____ April Geburtstag.

9. Der Schauspieler (*actor*) Christoph Waltz hat am (4.) _____vierten_____ Oktober Geburtstag.

10. Die Schauspielerin Sibel Kekilli hat am (16.) _____sechzehnten_____ Juni Geburtstag.

Kommunikation

4 **Um wie viel Uhr...?** Look at the class schedule. In pairs, take turns asking and answering questions about the start times of classes. *Answers will vary.*

BEISPIEL

S1: Wann und um wie viel Uhr ist Literatur?
S2: Literatur ist dienstags und donnerstags um halb neun.

	Montag	Dienstag	Mittwoch	Donnerstag	Freitag
8.30		Literatur		Literatur	Chemie
9.25	Biologie	Biologie	Biologie		Chemie
10.20		Kunst		Kunst	
11.15	Informatik		Informatik		Informatik
12.10	Mathematik	Deutsch	Deutsch	Deutsch	Mathematik

5 **Der Wievielte ist heute?** In pairs, take turns pointing at different dates on the calendar and having your partner tell you the date. *Answers will vary.*

BEISPIEL

S1: Der Wievielte ist heute?
S2: Heute ist der dritte Oktober.

Oktober						
Montag	Dienstag	Mittwoch	Donnerstag	Freitag	Samstag	Sonntag
		1	2	3	4	5
6	7	8	9	10	11	12
13	14	15	16	17	18	19
20	21	22	23	24	25	26
27	28	29	30	31		

6 **Geburtstage** Ask your classmates when their birthdays are. Find out whose birthday is closest to yours. Share what you learn about your classmates. *Answers will vary.*

BEISPIEL

S1: Wann hast du Geburtstag?
S2: Ich habe am siebten Dezember Geburtstag. Und wann hast du Geburtstag?
S1: Ich habe am neunten Oktober Geburtstag.

7 **Interview** In pairs, role-play an interview for the class. Use the following questions and add your own. *Answers will vary.*

BEISPIEL

S1: Wann hast du Geschichte?
S2: Montags, mittwochs und freitags um Viertel nach elf. Und du?

1. Welcher Tag ist heute?
2. Wann hast du Geburtstag?
3. Wann gehst du in die Sporthalle?
4. Wie spät ist es?
5. Um wie viel Uhr gehst du in die Mensa?
6. Wann hast du Unterricht?

4 **Expansion** Ask students to describe their own schedules. In pairs, have them take turns asking and answering questions about their own classes and activities.

5 **Expansion** Bring an example of movie listings, TV schedules, or course schedules from a German school. In pairs, have students ask and answer questions about the schedules.

5 **Suggestion** Point out that on German calendars and schedules, **Montag** is listed as the first day of the week and **Sonntag** as the last.

7 **Video Virtual Chat** You can also assign activity 7 on the Supersite. Students record individual responses that appear in your gradebook.

Wiederholung

4 Expansion Show a time zone map and ask what time it is in a given place. Ex.: **Wie viel Uhr ist es in Bangkok?**

1 Graffiti
In small groups, take turns drawing items from the lesson vocabulary and guessing what they are. Answers will vary.

BEISPIEL

S1: *Ist das ein Diplom?*
S2: *Nein!*
S3: *Ist das ein Stipendium?*
S2: *Ja, richtig!*

2 Verabredungen
Take turns asking and answering questions using the cues and the images. Answers will vary.

▶ **BEISPIEL**

S1: *Wohin reist du im Sommer?*
S2: *Ich reise nach Spanien.*

reisen

1. gehen   2. lernen   3. kosten

4. kaufen   5. hören   6. begrüßen

3 Feste
Ask your classmates on what date these holidays fall. Add three additional holidays. Answers will vary.

BEISPIEL Weihnachten (*Christmas*)

S1: *Wann ist Weihnachten?*
S2: *Weihnachten ist am 25. Dezember.*

3 Suggestion Provide students with a calendar to consult for this activity.

- Silvester (*New Year's Eve*)
- Neujahrstag (*New Year's Day*)
- Columbus-Tag
- Halloween
- Veteranentag
- Heiligabend (*Christmas Eve*)

3 Suggestion Tell students about the German celebrations of **Aprilscherz, der Tag der Arbeit, and Erntedankfest** and explain how they differ from their American equivalents.

4 Zeitzonen
In pairs, take turns telling your partner what time it is in each North American city and asking what time it is in a German-speaking country. Answers will vary.

4 Partner Chat You can also assign activity 4 on the Supersite.

BEISPIEL

S1: *In Pittsburgh ist es fünfzehn Uhr zwölf. Wie spät ist es in Österreich?*
S2: *In Österreich ist es einundzwanzig Uhr zwölf. In Calgary ist es halb vier. Wie spät ist es in Deutschland?*

Uhrzeit in...	Uhrzeit in Deutschland / in Österreich / in der Schweiz
Pittsburgh, PA: 15.12	+ 6 Stunden
Calgary, AB: 3.30	+ 8 Stunden
Fairbanks, AK: 22.54	+ 11 Stunden
Ft. Stockton, TX: 11.45	+ 7 Stunden
Hope, BC: 15.28	+ 9 Stunden
London, ON: 3.09	+ 6 Stunden
Needles, CA: 12.30	+ 9 Stunden
Tifton, FL: 21.36	+ 6 Stunden
Winnipeg, MB: 20.15	+ 7 Stunden

5 Arbeitsblatt
Your instructor will give you a worksheet. Talk with your classmates to figure out the starting lineup of a race.

5 Suggestion Make sure students understand that **der Wievielte** is the masculine form and **die Wievielte** is the feminine form.

BEISPIEL

S1: *Der Wievielte bist du?*
S2: *Ich bin der vierzehnte. Die Wievielte bist du?*
S1: *Ich bin die achte.*
S1 schreibt: *Ben ist der vierzehnte.*
S2 schreibt: *Sarah ist die achte.*

6 Diskutieren und kombinieren
You and your partner each have two schedules. One shows your activities. The other shows a partial list of your partner's activities, with one activity missing each day. Ask and answer questions to complete both schedules.

BEISPIEL

S1: *Was machst du am Sonntag um neun Uhr morgens?*
S2: *Ich mache Hausaufgaben. Und was machst du am Freitag um vier Uhr nachmittags?*
S1: *Ich mache Yoga.*

Video

Kein Wohnraum: Studenten schlafen in Hotels

1

Vorbereitung Discuss the questions with a partner.
Answers will vary.
1. Where and with whom do you live?
2. What are three things on which you spend most of your money?

Students enrolling at a German university are not assigned a dorm room. **Studentenwerk**, the student affairs association, oversees about 1,000 dorms in Germany and provides temporary accommodations to first-year students who have not found a place to live. Intense competition has led to soaring rent prices, so most students rent private rooms or share an apartment (**Wohngemeinschaft**). While larger cities have seen student housing prices rise, smaller cities are more affordable.

Viele Studienanfänger suchen eine Bleibe (*housing*).

Nützliche Ausdrücke

die Hilfe	help
die Lösung, -en	solution
die Miete, -en	rent
das Schwarze Brett	bulletin board
die Wohnung, -en	apartment
das Wohnheim, -e	dormitory

2

Richtig oder falsch Indicate whether each statement is **richtig** or **falsch**. Correct the false statements.

	Richtig	Falsch	
1. The students in the video say it's easy to find housing.	☐	☑	Falsch. They say it's difficult: **Es ist schwer, eine Wohnung zu finden./Ich finde einfach keine richtige Wohnung.**
2. Some students stay in hotels.	☑	☐	
3. Anna Backhaus studies German.	☐	☑	Falsch. Anna studies French and philosophy.
4. Anna will live in a hotel for two weeks.	☑	☐	

3

Diskussion Discuss the following questions with a partner.
1. A student needs €850 per month. What do you think this money is spent on?
2. Would you rather get a dorm room on campus or a car for your commute? Why?

4

Vergleich (*Comparison*) Compare your living situation with that of the students in the video. Where do you live? How did you find your room? Answers will vary.

Sport und Freizeit Vocabulary Tools

Remind students to omit the article when talking about a sport: **Stefan spielt Basketball.** Point out that **der Basketball** refers to the actual ball: **Julia kauft einen Basketball.**

Wortschatz

Sportarten	*sports*
(der) (American) Football	*football*
(das) Golf	*golf*
(das) Hockey	*hockey*
(der) Volleyball	*volleyball*
das Schwimmbad, ⁻er	*swimming pool*
das Spiel, -e	*game*
der Sport	*sports*
das Stadion, Stadien	*stadium*
Fahrrad fahren (fährt)	*to ride a bicycle*
Ski fahren	*to ski*
schwimmen	*to swim*
trainieren	*to practice*
Freizeitaktivitäten	*leisure activities*
der Berg, -e	*mountain*
das Fahrrad, ⁻er	*bicycle*
die Freizeit	*free time*
das Hobby, -s	*hobby*
der Park, -s	*park*
der Strand, ⁻e	*beach*
der Wald, ⁻er	*forest*
angeln gehen	*to go fishing*
campen gehen	*to go camping*
essen gehen	*to eat out*
spazieren gehen	*to go for a walk*
klettern	*to (rock) climb*
kochen	*to cook*
(ein Pferd) reiten	*to ride (a horse)*
schreiben	*to write*
Spaß haben/machen	*to have fun / to be fun*
singen	*to sing*
tanzen	*to dance*
wandern	*to hike*

Suggestion Have students preview the conjugation of **fahren**, which will be covered in **2B.1**. Explain that **fahren** is listed with its third-person singular form because it has a stem change in the present tense.

More activities

vhlcentral | WB pp. 25–26 | LM p. 16 | Online activities

die Spielerinnen (*sing.* **die Spielerin**) *players (f)*

Sie spielen Tennis (*n.*)**.** *They are playing tennis.*

der Ball, ⁻e

das Spielfeld, -er/ der Platz, ⁻e

die Mannschaft, -en *team*

der Spieler, - *player (m)*

Er spielt Fußball. (**spielen**) *He is playing soccer.*

Sie verliert nicht gern. (**verlieren**) *She doesn't like to lose.*

Er gewinnt. (**gewinnen**) *He is winning.*

die Karten (*sing.* **die Karte**) *cards*

ACHTUNG

Infinitives can be used as nouns in German. **Freitags habe ich Schwimmen. Samstags habe ich Reiten.** Infinitives used as nouns are neuter.

ACHTUNG

Use **gern** or **nicht gern** after a verb to say that you *like* or *don't like* doing something.

Lisa singt gern.
Lisa likes to sing.

Ich spiele nicht gern Tennis.
I don't like playing tennis.

You will learn more about the uses of **gern** in **Lektion 4A.**

Basketball (*m.*)

der Basketball

Sie spielen gern Schach (*n.*).
They like playing chess.

Baseball (*m.*)

Leichtathletik (*f.*)
track and field

Anwendung

3 **Expansion** Have students correct the false statements. Ask students what else people do at these locations: **in einem Stadion; in den Bergen; am Strand; im Schwimmbad.** Then ask what people do at locations not mentioned in the audio: **im Park; im Wald.**

1 Was passt nicht? Indicate the word that doesn't belong.

1. a. Basketball
   b. Schach
   c. Golf
   d. Tennis
2. a. der Strand
   b. der Spieler
   c. das Stadion
   d. der Platz
3. a. reiten
   b. schwimmen
   c. singen
   d. klettern
4. a. der Rucksack
   b. das Camping
   c. der Berg
   d. das Spielfeld
5. a. spazieren gehen
   b. kochen
   c. wandern
   d. reiten
6. a. die Freizeit
   b. die Schule
   c. die Aktivität
   d. das Hobby

2 Was fehlt? Complete the sentences with words from the list.

1. Serena und Venus Williams sind ___Tennisspielerinnen___.
2. Ski fahren macht im Winter viel ___Spaß___.
3. Wir schwimmen im ___Schwimmbad___.
4. Auf dem Spielfeld spielen wir ___Fußball___.
5. Im Park gehen wir ___spazieren___.

Fußball
Schwimmbad
Spaß
spazieren
Tennisspielerinnen

3 Richtig oder falsch? Listen to the statements and decide if they are **richtig** or **falsch**.

	Richtig	Falsch		Richtig	Falsch
1.	☐	☑	4.	☑	☐
2.	☑	☐	5.	☐	☑
3.	☑	☐	6.	☐	☑

4 Zuordnen Write the activity that describes each picture.

Sample answers are provided.

▶ **BEISPIEL**

Leichtathletik trainieren

4 **Expansion** Ask students what they do in their free time. Ex.: **Spielen Sie Baseball oder Basketball? Fahren Sie Ski? Gehen Sie im Park spazieren?**

1. Ski fahren
2. campen gehen
3. Fahrrad fahren
4. Basketball spielen

5 Das Wochenende Listen to the conversation between Lukas, Max, and Michaela, and indicate who will be doing each activity.

1. Tennis spielen ___Max___
2. kochen ___Michaela___
3. lernen ___Max, Michaela___
4. tanzen ___Max, Michaela___
5. klettern ___Lukas___
6. Videospiele spielen ___Lukas___

Kommunikation

6 Berühmte Sportler
Match the athletes with the descriptions. Then check your answers with a partner.

BEISPIEL

S1: Er spielt Fußball und kommt aus England.
S2: Es ist David Beckham.

_c_ 1. Er kommt aus der Schweiz und spielt Tennis.
_f_ 2. Er spielt Basketball.
_b_ 3. Sie ist eine Tennisspielerin aus Deutschland.
_d_ 4. Er schwimmt und hat viele olympische Medaillen (*medals*).
_a_ 5. Sie ist eine Skifahrerin aus Amerika.
_e_ 6. Er kommt aus Kalifornien und spielt Golf.

a. Lindsay Vonn
b. Steffi Graf
c. Roger Federer
d. Michael Phelps
e. Tiger Woods
f. LeBron James

6 Expansion Have students come up with their own prompts, real or fictitious. Ex.: **Sie ist groß und blond und sie spielt Gitarre und singt.** (Taylor Swift) **Er ist Hogwarts-Schüler.** (Harry Potter) **Sein Alter Ego heißt „Slim Shady".** (Eminem)

7 Machst du das gern?
In pairs, take turns telling each other whether you like or dislike each activity. Sample answers are provided.

7 Video Virtual Chat You can also assign activity 7 on the Supersite. Students record individual responses that appear in your gradebook.

BEISPIEL

S1: Ich schwimme gern. Und du?
S2: Ich schwimme auch gern. /
Ich schwimme nicht gern.

1.
Ich spiele (nicht) gern Schach.

2.
Ich tanze (nicht) gern.

3.
Ich spiele (nicht) gern Fußball.

4.
Ich reite (nicht) gern.

8 Pantomime
Play charades in groups of four. Take turns acting out activities from the lesson vocabulary. The person who guesses the activity goes next. Answers will vary.

8 Suggestion Tell students to find at least one person for each activity.

BEISPIEL

S1: Ist es Baseball?
S2: Nein.
S3: Ist es Tennis?
S2: Ja, es ist Tennis!

9 Arbeitsblatt
Your instructor will give you a worksheet with information about activities. Ask your classmates what they like to do in their free time. Share your results with the class.

BEISPIEL Volleyball spielen

S1: Spielst du gern Volleyball?
S2: Ja. Ich spiele gern Volleyball./Nein. Ich spiele nicht gern Volleyball.

angeln gehen	reiten	Fußball spielen
campen gehen	schwimmen	Schach spielen
kochen	singen	tanzen
spazieren gehen	Baseball spielen	Tennis trainieren
klettern	Basketball spielen	wandern

Aussprache und Rechtschreibung 🔊 Audio

Diphthongs: *au, ei/ai, eu/äu*

When one vowel sound glides into another vowel sound in the same syllable, the complex sound produced is called a diphthong. In German, this complex sound is said quickly and is not drawn out as it is in English. There are three diphthongs in German: **au**, **ei/ai**, and **eu/äu**.

faul	aus	Leine	Mais	neun	täuschen

The German diphthong written **au** begins with the vowel sound of the *o* in the English word *pod* and ends with a sound similar to the *oo* in the English word *loose*.

auf	Frau	Bauch	Haus	auch

The German diphthong written as **ei** or **ai** is pronounced very similarly to the *i* in the English word *time*. Remember that the German **ie** is not a diphthong, but simply a way of writing the long **i** sound, as in the word **sieben**.

Freitag	Zeit	Mai	Eis	schreiben

The German diphthong written as **eu** or **äu** is pronounced very similarly to the *oi* in the English word *coin*.

Zeugnis	Freund	Häuser	Europa	Deutsch

1 **Aussprechen** Practice saying these words aloud.

1. laufen
2. Kaufhaus
3. Rauch
4. Maus
5. mein
6. Wein
7. Mainz
8. reiten
9. treu
10. freuen
11. Leute
12. läuft

Suggestion Have students look at the sample words and sentences on this page to identify cognates and words they already know. Tell students the meanings of any unfamiliar words or phrases.

2 **Nachsprechen** Practice saying these sentences aloud.

1. Die Mäuse laufen einfach im Zimmer herum.
2. Tausende Leute gehen an uns vorbei.
3. Am Freitag habe ich leider keine Zeit.
4. Paul macht eine Europareise mit Freunden.
5. Meine Frau kauft ein neues Haus außerhalb von Mainz.
6. Für den Sauerbraten brauchen wir Rotweinessig.

3 **Sprichwörter** Practice reading these sayings aloud.

Schuster, bleib bei deinen Leisten.[1]

Einem geschenkten Gaul schaut man nicht ins Maul.[2]

[1] Stick with what you know. (lit. Cobbler, stick with your shoe stretchers.)

[2] Don't look a gift horse in the mouth.

More activities

🅢 vhlcentral | LM p. 17 | 📶 Online activities

Ein Picknick im Park Video

George und Meline treffen Sabite und Torsten im Park. Sie sprechen über Sport und ihre Hobbys. Kommt Meline Torsten zu nahe (*too close*)?

Vorbereitung Have students preview the images and write down three questions they want to have answered when they watch the video.

TORSTEN Das Fußballspiel beginnt um halb acht.
SABITE Es ist Viertel nach sechs. Niemand ist hier. George kommt von der Uni.

TORSTEN Spielt er Fußball?
SABITE Er spielt Baseball in der Freizeit. Er ist in einer Uni-Mannschaft.
TORSTEN Hat Meline Hobbys?
SABITE Sie fährt Ski und spielt Tennis. Sie gewinnt alles.

GEORGE Oh, vielen Dank! Wo sind Hans und Meline?
SABITE Meline kommt aus der Bibliothek. Hans hat eine Vorlesung.
GEORGE Studierst du auch, Torsten?
TORSTEN Ja. Ich studiere Chemie und Biologie.

MELINE Ich bringe Dessert!
GEORGE Sabite, ich glaube, Hans...
MELINE Hans. Hallo, Torsten, nett dich kennen zu lernen.
TORSTEN Gleichfalls, Meline.

MELINE Du studierst Medizin?
TORSTEN Biologie.
MELINE Fährst du Ski?
TORSTEN Nee, meine Familie fährt nicht Ski. Aber ich wandere und klettere.

MELINE Ich komme aus Wien. Alle fahren Ski in den österreichischen Alpen. Wir haben viele Sportarten: Skifahren, Klettern, Fahrradfahren, Golf und Tennis. Spielst du auch Tennis?
SABITE Äh, Meline?
MELINE Hmmm?
SABITE Gehen wir spazieren.

ÜBUNGEN

1 **Was ist richtig?** Choose the words that best complete the sentences.

1. Torsten und Sabite sind (im Park / im Café).
2. George kommt (aus dem Stadion / von der Uni).
3. Meline fährt Ski und spielt (Golf / Tennis).
4. Torsten studiert Chemie und (Biologie / Physik).
5. Meline bringt (Kaffee / Dessert).

6. Alle fahren (Ski / Bob) in den österreichischen Alpen.
7. Sabite ist eifersüchtig auf (*jealous of*) (Meline / Torsten).
8. Meline trennt keine (Klassenkameraden / Paare).
9. (Frau Yilmaz / Herr Yilmaz) macht morgen Sauerbraten.
10. Hans weiß nicht, dass Sabite einen (Mitbewohner / Freund) hat.

Expansion Have students write simple sentences with the words that were not chosen.

PERSONEN   Torsten   Sabite   George   Meline

7

SABITE Meline. Wir sind Mitbewohnerinnen.
Freundinnen.
MELINE Und?
SABITE „Spielst du auch Tennis?"

8

MELINE Sabite. Keine Sorge. Ich trenne
keine Paare.
SABITE Es ist okay, ich verstehe.

9

SABITE George, Meline, meine Mutter
macht morgen Sauerbraten. Kommt ihr
zum Abendessen?
MELINE Oh, danke, Sabite. Wir kommen.
TORSTEN Frau Yilmaz ist eine gute Köchin.
GEORGE Wow, vielen Dank. Und Hans?
SABITE Ich frage ihn.

10

MELINE Hans weiß nicht, dass Sabite einen
Freund hat, oder?
GEORGE Er hat keine Ahnung.

Nützliche Ausdrücke

- **Niemand ist hier.**
  Nobody's here.
- **die Uni-Mannschaft**
  varsity team
- **Sie gewinnt alles.**
  She wins at everything.
- **glauben**
  to believe
- **aber**
  but
- **Alle fahren Ski in den
  österreichischen Alpen.**
  Everyone in the Austrian Alps skis.
- **Gehen wir spazieren.**
  Let's go for a walk.
- **Keine Sorge.**
  Don't worry.
- **das Abendessen**
  dinner
- **der Koch / die Köchin**
  cook
- **Hans weiß nicht, dass Sabite einen
  Freund hat, oder?**
  *Hans doesn't know Sabite has a boyfriend,
  does he?*
- **Er hat keine Ahnung.**
  He doesn't have a clue.

2B.1
- **Meine Familie fährt nicht Ski.**
  My family doesn't ski.

2B.2
- **Meine Mutter macht
  morgen Sauerbraten.**
  My mother is making sauerbraten tomorrow.

2B.3
- **Ich trenne keine Paare.**
  I wouldn't break up a couple.

2 **Zum Besprechen** In this episode, the characters talk about their
favorite sports and pastimes. Interview your classmates to find out
who shares your interests. Who likes the same sports? Who has the
same hobbies? Answers will vary.

2 Suggestion Refer students to the
script for scenes 3, 5, and 6 for model
questions they can use to interview
their classmates.

3 **Vertiefung** Fußball is one of the most popular sports in Germany.
What is the name of the German national soccer league? Find the names
of four prominent German soccer teams. Which team won last year's
championship? Do you like **Fußball**? Why or why not?

(Fußball-)Bundesliga; Sample answers: FC Bayern München, VfL Wolfsburg, Bayer
Leverkusen, Borussia Mönchengladbach; Answers will vary.

3 Expansion Have students
research popular soccer players from
Germany, Austria, and Switzerland
and share their names with the class.

More activities

S vhlcentral   VM p. 4   Online activities

Skifahren im Blut°

 Reading

IN ALPINE VILLAGES, LEARNING TO SKI is like learning to walk. Almost everyone does it, starting at a very young age. The beginner slopes are full of pre-school-aged children taking their first lessons. Skiing courses were required in Austrian schools until 1995, and many schools in Bavaria and Austria still offer **Skiwoche°**, a chaperoned week-long ski trip, as part of their curriculum.

Many of the world's best skiers come from German-speaking countries. Carina Vogt is a German **Skisprung-Weltmeisterin°** and **Olympiasiegerin°**.

Vogt won the first gold medal ever awarded for women's ski jumping at the 2014 Sochi Winter Olympic Games, and in 2015 she won two World Cup gold medals for ski jumping, coming in third overall in women's events. In honor of her achievements, there is now a street named after her in her home town of Degenfeld in Baden-Württemberg.

Austrian Marcel Hirscher specializes in slalom and giant slalom. The son of two ski instructors, Hirscher has been skiing since age 2. In 2015, at the age of 26, he became the first **Weltmeister** ever to win the overall World Cup title for men's ski events four times in a row. In 2018, he won the gold medal for giant slalom in Pyeongchang.

While the Alpine skiing tradition remains strong, environmental and economic sustainability have become major concerns. Ski tourism has had a serious impact on the ecology of the Alpine regions. With rising temperatures due to climate change, lack of snow is also becoming an issue. Snowmaking is expensive and uses vast amounts of water. And, while large ski resorts continue to draw visitors from all over the world, skiing is becoming less affordable for locals, with some smaller ski areas struggling to remain in business.

Österreich: Ski-Paradies	
Jährliche Anzahl an° Skitouristen	16,2 Millionen
Jährliche Einnahmen° durch Skifahren	13,3 Milliarden Euro
Skigebiete in Österreich	439
Alpine Skiweltmeisterschaft 2017: Medaillen für Österreich	9 (3 Gold, 4 Silber, 2 Bronze)

QUELLE: Statista

Blut *blood* **Skiwoche** *ski week* **Skisprung-Weltmeisterin** *ski jump world champion* **Olympiasiegerin** *Olympic gold medalist* **Jährliche Anzahl an** *Annual number of* **mehr als** *more than* **Einnahmen** *revenue* **Arbeitsplätze** *jobs*

1 **Im Fokus** Indicate whether each statement is **richtig** or **falsch**. Correct the false statements. Then discuss the last question with a partner.

 1. In Bavaria and Austria, schoolchildren can opt for a week-long hiking trip.
Falsch. They can opt for a week-long ski trip.

 2. There are more than 500 ski resorts in Austria.
Falsch. There are 439 ski resorts in Austria.

3. More than 16 million tourists head for Austria's ski slopes every year.
Richtig.

Diskussion How do sports programs where you grew up compare with those that promote winter sports in Austria and Bavaria?

2 **Die deutschsprachige Welt** Indicate whether each statement is **richtig** or **falsch**. Correct the false statements. Then discuss the last question with a partner.

1. Germans have 5 hours of leisure time per day on average.
Falsch. They have 6 hours and 34 minutes of leisure time per day on average.

2. Bicycling is an important recreational activity in Germany.
Richtig.

3. Germany has many country roads but few bike paths.
Falsch. It has a lot of bike paths.

Diskussion Which sport or other recreational activity do you like to do most in your spare time?

DEUTSCH IM ALLTAG

Mehr Freizeit

der Fan, -s	*fan*
die Meisterschaft, -en	*championship*
der Spielstand, ⁻e	*score*
das Tor, -e	*goal (in soccer, etc.)*
faulenzen	*to relax; to be lazy*
joggen	*to jog*
fit	*in good shape*
sportlich	*athletic*
Los!	*Start!; Go!*

DIE DEUTSCHSPRACHIGE WELT

Die Deutschen und das Fahrrad

In Deutschland hat man im Schnitt° 6 Stunden und 34 Minuten Freizeit am Tag. Populäre Hobbys der Deutschen sind Videospiele, Lesen und natürlich° Sport. Die Deutschen sind leidenschaftliche° Fahrradfahrer. Kilometerlange Radwege° durchkreuzen° das Land, wie etwa° die Romantische Straße° in Bayern: sie führt an Schlössern° und vielseitigen Landschaften° vorbei°.

im Schnitt *on average* **natürlich** *of course*
leidenschaftliche *passionate* **Radwege** *bike trails*
durchkreuzen *cross* **wie etwa** *such as* **Straße** *road*
Schlössern *castles* **vielseitigen Landschaften** *varied*
landscapes **führt an... vorbei** *leads past*
Suggestion Tell students that **die Romantische Straße** is
a road with an adjacent bike path that runs 350 km from Würzburg to Füssen.

PORTRÄT

Anna-Lena Forster

Die 24 Jahre alte Monobobskifahrerin° Anna-Lena Forster ist Mitglied° des deutschen Paralympics-Teams. Sie kommt aus Radolfzell am Bodensee° und hat schon seit ihrem sechsten Lebensjahr Skierfahrung°. Sie spezialisiert sich auf Abfahrt° und Slalom und hat bei den Paralympischen Spielen 2014 and 2018 und bei verschiedenen Weltcups Medaillen gewonnen°. Möglich ist so eine enorme Leistung°, da Forster hochmotiviert° ist und intensiv trainiert. Allerdings ist das Training einer paralympischen Athletin auch mit hohen Kosten verbunden°, wobei ihre Familie sie sehr unterstützt°. Forsters Konkurrentin°, die etwas ältere Paralympierin Anna Schaffelhuber, ist auch ihr großes Vorbild im Skisport.

Monobobskifahrerin *monoskier* **Mitglied** *member*
Bodensee *Lake Constance* **Skierfahrung** *skiing*
experience **Abfahrt** *downhill* **gewonnen** *won*
Leistung *achievement* **hochmotiviert** *highly motivated*
verbunden *associated with* **unterstützt** *supports*
Konkurrentin *competition* **Vorbild** *role model*

 IM INTERNET

Wandern: Was sind beliebte Wanderwege° in der Schweiz?

beliebte Wanderwege *popular hiking trails*

Find out more at **vhlcentral.com**.

---

3 **Porträt** Indicate whether each statement is **richtig** or **falsch**. Correct the false statements. Then discuss the last question with a partner.

 1. Anna-Lena Forster hat seit ihrem sechsten Lebensjahr eine Behinderung.
   Falsch. Sie ist von Geburt an behindert.

 2. Anna-Lena Forsters Familie hilft finanziell.
   Richtig.

3. Forster spezialisiert sich im Sport auf Slalom und Abfahrt.
   Richtig.

 Diskussion Which winter sport would you like to learn if you could spend a winter in the Alps? What other sports do you like?

4 **Spitzensportler** Research a German, Austrian, or Swiss athlete on the Internet and write a brief biography in German. What is his or her sport? Where is he or she from? How old is he or she? Is this athlete a role model outside of sports as well? Present your mini-bio to the class.

 Suggestion Encourage students to choose non-superstar as well as superstar athletes.

2B.1 Stem-changing verbs Grammar Tutorial

QUERVERWEIS

See **2A.1** to review the present-tense conjugations of regular verbs.

ACHTUNG

The formal **Sie** forms are the same as the plural **sie** forms for all verbs. Starting in this lesson, **Sie** and **sie** (*pl.*) forms will be listed together in verb tables.

Startblock Certain irregular verbs follow predictable patterns of spelling changes in their present-tense conjugations. These verbs use the regular endings, but have changes to their stem vowels in the **du** and **er/sie/es** forms. Most stem-changing verbs follow one of four patterns in the present tense.

- a ⟶ ä

schlafen (*to sleep*)			
ich schlafe	*I sleep*	wir schlafen	*we sleep*
du schläfst	*you sleep*	ihr schlaft	*you sleep*
er/sie/es schläft	*he/she/it sleeps*	Sie/sie schlafen	*you/they sleep*

Schläfst du jede Nacht acht Stunden?
*Do you **sleep** eight hours every night?*

Sie **schlafen** im Studentenwohnheim.
*They **sleep** in the dormitory.*

- au ⟶ äu

laufen (*to run*)			
ich laufe	*I run*	wir laufen	*we run*
du läufst	*you run*	ihr lauft	*you run*
er/sie/es läuft	*he/she/it runs*	Sie/sie laufen	*you/they run*

Mehmet **läuft** am Strand.
*Mehmet **runs** on the beach.*

Sie **laufen** über das Spielfeld.
*They're **running** across the field.*

- e ⟶ i

	essen (*to eat*)			sprechen (*to speak*)	
ich	esse	*I eat*		spreche	*I speak*
du	isst	*you eat*		sprichst	*you speak*
er/sie/es	isst	*he/she/it eats*		spricht	*he/she/it speaks*
wir	essen	*we eat*		sprechen	*we speak*
ihr	esst	*you eat*		sprecht	*you speak*
Sie/sie	essen	*you/they eat*		sprechen	*you/they speak*

Wir **essen** in der Mensa.
*We're **eating** in the cafeteria.*

Sprichst du Englisch?
*Do you **speak** English?*

- Besides an e ⟶ i vowel change, **nehmen** (*to take*) and **werden** (*to become*) have additional changes in the **du** and **er/sie/es** forms.

ACHTUNG

Remember: when the verb stem ends in **-s**, drop the **-s** from the second-person singular ending.

	nehmen (*to take*)			werden (*to become*)	
ich	nehme	*I take*		werde	*I become*
du	nimmst	*you take*		wirst	*you become*
er/sie/es	nimmt	*he/she/it takes*		wird	*he/she/it becomes*
wir	nehmen	*we take*		werden	*we become*
ihr	nehmt	*you take*		werdet	*you become*
Sie/sie	nehmen	*you/they take*		werden	*you/they become*

Du **nimmst** jeden Tag den Bus.
*You **take** the bus every day.*

Ein Anfänger **wird** mit der Zeit Experte.
*A beginner **becomes** an expert over time.*

- e ⟶ ie

	lesen (*to read*)		sehen (*to see*)	
ich	lese	*I read*	sehe	*I see*
du	liest	*you read*	siehst	*you see*
er/sie/es	liest	*he/she/it reads*	sieht	*he/she/it sees*
wir	lesen	*we read*	sehen	*we see*
ihr	lest	*you read*	seht	*you see*
Sie/sie	lesen	*you/they read*	sehen	*you/they see*

Du **liest** viele Bücher.
*You **read** a lot of books.*

Seht ihr die Spieler?
*Do you **see** the players?*

- This table summarizes some common verbs with stem changes in the present tense. When a verb with a present-tense stem change is presented in this text, it will be listed with its third-person singular form: **lesen (liest)**.

common stem-changing verbs (present tense)			
a ⟶ ä		**e ⟶ i**	
braten	*to fry*	brechen	*to break*
fahren	*to go*	essen	*to eat*
fallen	*to fall*	geben	*to give*
fangen	*to catch*	helfen	*to help*
lassen	*to let, to allow*	nehmen	*to take*
schlafen	*to sleep*	sprechen	*to speak*
tragen	*to carry; to wear*	treffen	*to hit; to meet*
waschen	*to wash*	vergessen	*to forget*
		werden	*to become*
		werfen	*to throw*
au ⟶ äu		**e ⟶ ie**	
laufen	*to run*	empfehlen	*to recommend*
		lesen	*to read*
		sehen	*to see*
		stehlen	*to steal*

Fährst du nach Berlin?
*Are you **going** to Berlin?*

Es **gibt** dort ein sehr gutes Café.
*There **is** a very good café there.*

Suggestion Remind students that new verbs are also vocabulary items. Tell students that they should be able to recognize these verbs in all of their present-tense forms, but they will learn more about how to use them in later chapters.

ACHTUNG

The verb **geben** is used in certain idiomatic expressions, such as **Es gibt** (*There is/There are*). Idiomatic expressions do not translate literally to English.

More activities

S
vhlcentral

WB
pp. 27–28

LM
p. 18

Online activities

Jetzt sind Sie dran! **Write the appropriate form of the verb.**

1. Ich ___esse___ (essen) viele Äpfel.
2. Du ___hilfst___ (helfen) Sophie.
3. Ich ___gebe___ (geben) Tobias ein Buch.
4. Peter ___nimmt___ (nehmen) ein Taxi.
5. Ihr ___fahrt___ (fahren) gern Fahrrad.
6. Wir ___tragen___ (tragen) Rucksäcke.

7. Anna ___wird___ (werden) Informatikprofessorin.
8. Du ___liest___ (lesen) viele Bücher.
9. Er ___schläft___ (schlafen) bis 8 Uhr morgens.
10. Ihr ___sprecht___ (sprechen) Deutsch.
11. Die Schüler ___sehen___ (sehen) einen Film.
12. Du ___vergisst___ (vergessen) die Hausaufgaben.

Anwendung

1 **Was ist richtig?** Select the verb that best completes each sentence.

1. Hannah (schläft / isst) viele Äpfel.
2. Ich (lese / brate) ein Schnitzel.
3. Du (fährst / triffst) einen Porsche.
4. Wir (helfen / waschen) den Hund.
5. Alena und Daniel (treffen / sprechen) Deutsch, Englisch und Polnisch.
6. Ihr (lauft / fangt) 8 Kilometer.
7. Du (liest / wird) viele Bücher.
8. Du (gibst / triffst) Jasmin im Café.

2 **Schreiben** Write complete sentences using the cues.

1. Herr Schmidt / empfehlen / das Schnitzel
   Herr Schmidt empfiehlt das Schnitzel.
2. ich / wissen / die Antwort
   Ich weiß die Antwort.
3. du / fahren / das Auto
   Du fährst das Auto.
4. wir / treffen / Katrina und Paul
   Wir treffen Katrina und Paul.
5. Angela / lesen / gern
   Angela liest gern.
6. du / sprechen / Deutsch
   Du sprichst Deutsch.
7. ich / werden / Architekt
   Ich werde Architekt.
8. Peter / stehlen / einen Apfel
   Peter stiehlt einen Apfel.

3 **Was sehen Sie?** Complete the sentences. Sample answers are provided.

▶ **BEISPIEL**

Peter ___läuft___ gern im Park.

1. Sie ___schlafen___ in der Hängematte.

2. Tobi ___wäscht___ das Auto.

3. Der Footballspieler ___fängt___ den Ball.

4. Hans ___liest___ das Buch.

5. Er ___isst___ eine Bratwurst.

6. Ingrid ___trifft___ Rolf im Museum.

Kommunikation

4 **Wie bitte?** Adele is talking to her mother on the phone. You see only Adele's side of the conversation. Reconstruct her mother's questions. Then check your answers with a partner. Sample answers are provided.

BEISPIEL Ich fahre am Wochenende nach Hause (*home*).

Wann fährst du nach Hause?

1. Ja, ich schlafe gut.
   Schläfst du gut?
2. Ich esse um 7 Uhr abends.
   Wann isst du?
3. Ja, ich lese viel.
   Liest du viel?
4. Ich sehe Matthias im Unterricht.
   Wo siehst du Matthias? / Wen siehst du im Unterricht?

5. Ja, wir sprechen im Unterricht Deutsch.
   Sprecht ihr im Unterricht Deutsch?
6. Ja, Matthias und ich nehmen zusammen (*together*) den Bus.
   Nehmt ihr zusammen den Bus?
7. Ich treffe Matthias nachmittags im Café.
   Wo/Wann triffst du Matthias?
8. Ja, ich fahre oft Fahrrad.
   Fährst du oft Fahrrad?

5 **Bilden Sie Sätze** In pairs, create six logical sentences with items from each column. Some items may be used more than once. Answers will vary.

BEISPIEL *Du empfiehlst die Torte.*

A	B	C
ich	empfehlen	Fußball im Stadion
du	lesen	Goethes *Faust*
Nina	sehen	die Torte
Elsa und ich	spielen	23 Jahre alt
Bianca und du	sprechen	viele Fremdsprachen
Olivia und Markus	werden	einen Film

6 **Im Park** In pairs, write a paragraph that describes the activities of the people shown. Use each of the verbs from the list at least once. Answers will vary.

BEISPIEL

S1: *Die Frauen gehen im Park spazieren.*
S2: *Die Kinder reiten im Park.*

fahren	sehen
laufen	gehen
reiten	spielen
schlafen	treffen

7 **Wer macht was?** Use the cues to ask your classmates whether they participate in these activities. Answers will vary.

BEISPIEL

S1: *Spielst du Fußball im Stadion?*
S2: *Nein, aber ich laufe im Park. Läufst du auch im Park?*

Fahrrad fahren	im Park laufen	im Stadion Fußball spielen
Ski fahren	im Schwimmbad schwimmen	Bälle werfen und fangen
viele Bücher lesen	den Bus nehmen	Freunde im Café treffen

7 **Expansion** Have students take notes on their classmates' answers and report their findings to the class. Ex.: **Michael spielt Baseball im Stadion. Anna fährt Fahrrad im Park.**

2B.2

Present tense used as future

 Grammar Tutorial

Startblock In German, as in English, you can use the present tense with certain time expressions to talk about the future.

Heute Abend spielen wir Fußball.

Morgen macht meine Mutter Sauerbraten.

ACHTUNG

To talk about *this morning*, you can say either **heute Morgen** or **heute früh**. Use **früh** (*early; in the morning*) instead of **Morgen** with the adverbs **morgen** and **übermorgen**.

Heute Morgen habe ich Biologie.
This morning I have biology.

Morgen früh habe ich Chemie.
Tomorrow morning I have chemistry.

QUERVERWEIS

Note that all of the words for seasons are masculine nouns. You will learn more vocabulary related to the seasons in **Lektion 7A**.

You will learn more about adjectives and adverbs in **3A.2** and **4A.1**.

More activities

vhlcentral

WB
pp. 29–30

LM
p. 19

Online activities

- The adverbs **heute** (*today*), **morgen** (*tomorrow*), and **übermorgen** (*the day after tomorrow*) are commonly used with the present tense to express future ideas. Use them with these time expressions to specify the time of day at which a future action will occur.

common time expressions			
Morgen	*morning*	**Nachmittag**	*afternoon*
Vormittag	*midmorning*	**Abend**	*evening*
Mittag	*noon*	**Nacht**	*night*

Morgen gehen wir einkaufen.
Tomorrow we're going shopping.

Heute Nachmittag gehe ich schwimmen.
This afternoon I'm going swimming.

- In **2A.3**, you learned to use **am** before dates and days of the week. Also use **am** with **Morgen, Vormittag, Mittag, Nachmittag, Abend**, or **Wochenende** to specify when something will occur. When both the day of the week and the time of day are specified, they form a compound noun: **Dienstagmittag, Mittwochabend**.

Am Wochenende gehen wir angeln.
*We're going fishing **this weekend**.*

Am Freitagnachmittag gehe ich zum Arzt.
*I'm going to the doctor's **Friday afternoon**.*

- Use **im** with months and seasons (**Frühling, Sommer, Herbst, Winter**).

Im Februar fahre ich Ski.
*I'm going skiing **in February**.*

Im Frühling gehe ich wandern.
*I'm going hiking **this spring**.*

- The adjective **nächste** (*next*) can be used with time-related nouns such as days of the week, seasons, and months. In this usage, it takes accusative endings.

nächsten Sommer
next summer

nächste Woche
next week

nächstes Jahr
next year

Jetzt sind Sie dran! Select the appropriate word or phrase.

1. Wir fahren (nächstes /(nächste)) Woche nach Polen.
2. (Am)/ Im) Montagvormittag gehe ich spazieren.
3. (Heute Abend)/ Abend) spielt ihr Karten.
4. Ursula fährt (am /(im)) Februar Ski.
5. Wir wandern ((nächsten)/ nächstes) Freitag im Wald.
6. ((Morgen Nachmittag)/ Nachmittag) fahre ich Fahrrad.
7. Wir gehen (Nacht /(übermorgen)) klettern.
8. (Nächsten /(Nächstes)) Wochenende spielst du Tennis.

Anwendung und Kommunikation

1 **Was passt?** Select the appropriate time expression.

1. Die nächste Prüfung ist (Nachmittag / übermorgen).
2. Ich fahre (im / am) März in Urlaub.
3. Spielst du (am / im) Abend Hockey?
4. Peter und Bettina fahren (nächstes / nächste) Wochenende in die Berge.
5. Gehst du (Nachmittag / heute Nachmittag) klettern?
6. (Nächstes / Nächsten) Sommer fahren wir an den Strand.

2 **Bilden Sie Sätze** Write sentences using the cues. Answers will vary.

1. ich / gehen / heute Nachmittag / angeln   Ich gehe heute Nachmittag angeln.
2. übermorgen / spielen / Roland / Baseball   Übermorgen spielt Roland Baseball.
3. nächstes Jahr / fahren / Anja / an den Strand   Nächstes Jahr fährt Anja an den Strand.
4. Patrick / treffen / Bianca / am Abend   Patrick trifft Bianca am Abend.
5. am Sonntagabend / kochen / wir   Am Sonntagabend kochen wir.
6. du / fahren / im Winter / Ski   Du fährst im Winter Ski.

3 **Fernsehen** In pairs, decide which TV programs you want to watch, and take turns asking each other when they will be on. Share your answers with the class. Answers will vary.

BEISPIEL

S1: *Wann kommt TV total?*
S2: *TV total kommt morgen Abend / Mittwochabend.*

	Dienstag (heute)	**Mittwoch**	**Donnerstag**
10.00 Uhr	Reisen für Genießer	Lindenstraße	Türkisch für Anfänger
15.00 Uhr	Sport Aktuell	Das Supertalent	Die Sendung mit der Maus
19.00 Uhr	Formel 1	Hallo Deutschland	Deutschland sucht den Superstar
23.00 Uhr	Bauer sucht Frau	TV total	Familien im Brennpunkt

4 **Sätze** In pairs, use items from each column to make up sentences describing what each person is going to do. Answers will vary.

BEISPIEL

Wir sehen heute Abend einen Film.

A	B	C	D
ich	Fahrrad fahren	am Freitag	für einen Marathonlauf
du	gehen	heute Nacht	im Park
Angelika	spazieren gehen	im Dezember	nach Österreich
wir	reisen	im Frühling	Freunde im Restaurant
ihr	trainieren	morgen Nachmittag	in die Disko
Otto und Gabi	treffen	nächstes Jahr	in den Bergen

3 **Partner Chat** You can also assign activity 3 on the Supersite. Students work in pairs to record the activity online. The pair's recorded conversation will appear in your gradebook.

3 **Expansion** Tell students that **Lindenstraße** is a long-running TV drama. The show started in 1985 and has over 1,700 episodes.

4 **Expansion** Have students ask each other about their own plans for each of the times listed in column C. Ex.: **Was macht du am Freitag?**

2B.3 | **Negation** Grammar Tutorial

Startblock In 1B.2, you learned to make affirmative statements and ask yes-or-no questions. To negate a statement or ask a negative question, use **nicht** or **kein**.

Nein, meine Familie fährt **nicht** Ski.

Ich trenne **keine** Paare.

Nicht

QUERVERWEIS

You have already learned to use **nicht** in the expressions **nicht schlecht** and **nicht (so) gut** (in **1A Kontext**) and **nicht gern** (in **2B Kontext**).

• In negative statements or questions, place **nicht** after the subject, conjugated verb, direct object, and definite time expressions, but before other sentence elements.

Ich gehe heute in die Sporthalle. ▶ Ich gehe heute **nicht** in die Sporthalle.
I'm going to the gym today. *I'm **not** going to the gym today.*

Brauchst du den Fußball? ▶ Brauchst du den Fußball **nicht**?
Do you need the soccer ball? *Don't you need the soccer ball?*

Die Spieler sind hier. ▶ Die Spieler sind **nicht** hier.
The players are here. *The players are **not** here.*

Mathematik ist einfach ▶ Mathematik ist **nicht** einfach.
Math is easy. *Math is **not** easy.*

• In some cases, the placement of **nicht** depends on which element of a statement the speaker wants to emphasize.

Ich spiele **nicht** Golf mit Tobias.   Ich spiele **nicht** mit Tobias Golf.
  Ich spiele mit Tobias Tennis.   Ich spiele mit Moritz Golf.
*I'm **not** playing golf with Tobias.*   *I'm **not** playing golf with Tobias.*
  I'm playing tennis with Tobias.   *I'm playing golf with Moritz.*

Wir sehen den Film heute **nicht**.   Wir sehen den Film morgen, **nicht** heute.
*We're **not** seeing the film today.*   *We're seeing the film tomorrow, **not** today.*

Die Studenten essen **nicht** in der Mensa.   Die Studenten essen in der Mensa **nicht** gern.
The students aren't eating in the   *The students don't like to eat in the*
  dining hall.   *dining hall.*

Hans weiß es **nicht**?

Er hat **keine** Ahnung.

Kein

- **Kein** is the negative form of the indefinite article **ein**. Use **kein** to negate a noun preceded by an indefinite article or by no article.

—Haben Sie Zeit?
—*Do you have time?*

—Nein, wir haben **keine** Zeit.
—*No, we don't have time.*

—Hat er ein Hobby?
—*Does he have a hobby?*

—Nein, er hat **keine** Hobbys.
—*No, he has **no** hobbies.*

- **Kein** follows the same patterns of gender and case endings as **ein**. Note that, unlike **ein**, **kein** has a plural form.

QUERVERWEIS

Words that have the same endings as **ein** are often called **ein**-words. You will learn about other **ein**-words in **3A.1**.

kein				
	masculine	**feminine**	**neuter**	**plural**
nominative	kein Ball	keine Freizeit	kein Spiel	keine Karten
accusative	kein**en** Ball	keine Freizeit	kein Spiel	keine Karten

—Hast du **einen** Fußball?
—*Do you have **a** soccer ball?*

—Nein, ich habe **keinen** Fußball.
—*No, I don't have **a** soccer ball.*

—Ist das **ein** Stadion?
—*Is that **a** stadium?*

—Nein, das ist **kein** Stadion.
—*No, that's **not a** stadium.*

—Sind das Basketballspieler?
—*Are those guys basketball players?*

—Nein, das sind **keine** Basketballspieler.
—*No, those aren't basketball players.*

Suggestion Point out that the responses **Ja**, **Nein**, and **Doch** at the beginning of a sentence do not affect subject-verb word order.

Doch

- The word **doch** has no exact equivalent in English. Use it to contradict a negative question or statement.

—Ich habe **keine** Freunde.
—*I don't have **any** friends.*

—**Doch**, du hast viele Freunde!
—**No**, *you have lots of friends!*

—Gehst du **nicht** zum Strand?
—*Aren't you going to the beach?*

—**Doch**, ich gehe zum Strand.
—**Yes**, *I'm going to the beach.*

More activities

vhlcentral

WB
pp. 31–32

LM
p. 20

Online activities

Jetzt sind Sie dran! **Complete the sentences with the appropriate form of nicht or kein.**

1. Der Volleyballspieler ist __*nicht*__ so fit.
2. Stefan hat __keinen__ Fußball.
3. Wir machen die Hausaufgaben __nicht__.
4. Übermorgen habe ich __keine__ Vorlesung.
5. Uwe trainiert __nicht__ und verliert das Spiel.
6. Ich habe __kein__ Foto.

7. Bernhard spielt viel Fußball, aber er gewinnt __keine__ Spiele.
8. Du schwimmst __nicht__ im Schwimmbad.
9. Wir sehen den Film __nicht__.
10. Ihr habt __keine__ Freizeit.
11. Am Donnerstag fahren wir __nicht__ in die Berge.
12. Es gibt hier __kein__ Stadion.

Anwendung

1 **Verneinen Sie** Negate the sentences using **nicht**.

1. Wir haben die Karten.
   Wir haben die Karten nicht.
2. Ich vergesse die Hausaufgaben.
   Ich vergesse die Hausaufgaben nicht.
3. Wir reiten am Wochenende.
   Wir reiten am Wochenende nicht.
4. Simon und Katrina sind hier.
   Simon und Katrina sind nicht hier.
5. Du gehst in die Bibliothek.
   Du gehst nicht in die Bibliothek.

6. Ihr verliert das Volleyballspiel.
   Ihr verliert das Volleyballspiel nicht.
7. Thomas und Brigitte schwimmen am Nachmittag.
   Thomas und Brigitte schwimmen am Nachmittag nicht.
8. Am Sonntag gehen wir angeln.
   Am Sonntag gehen wir nicht angeln.

2 **Antworten Sie** Answer the questions using **kein**.

BEISPIEL

S1: *Hast du Hobbys?*
S2: *Nein, ich habe keine Hobbys.*

1. Hat Peter ein Fahrrad?
   Nein, Peter hat kein Fahrrad.
2. Habt ihr Freizeit?
   Nein, wir haben keine Freizeit.
3. Sind das Spielerinnen?
   Nein, das sind keine Spielerinnen.
4. Ist Berlin ein Land (*country*)?
   Nein, Berlin ist kein Land.
5. Ist Alexandra eine Hockeyspielerin?
   Nein, Alexandra ist keine Hockeyspielerin.

6. Hast du einen Basketball?
   Nein, ich habe keinen Basketball.
7. Gibt es dort ein Stadion?
   Nein, es gibt dort kein Stadion.
8. Spielst du Volleyball?
   Nein, ich spiele keinen Volleyball.
9. Ist Salzburg ein Berg?
   Nein, Salzburg ist kein Berg.
10. Haben Sie Karten?
    Nein, ich habe keine Karten.

3 **Was fehlt?** Complete the conversation with **nicht**, **kein**, or **doch**.

KARIN Hallo, Alina! Geht's dir gut? Kommst du heute Abend (1) ___nicht___ zum Training?

ALINA Heute Abend? (2) ___Doch___! Aber morgen komme ich (3) ___nicht___.

KARIN Warum (4) ___nicht___?

ALINA Ich habe (5) ___keine___ Zeit! Wir haben sehr viele Biologiehausaufgaben und übermorgen habe ich auch eine Chemieprüfung!

KARIN Belegst du nicht vier Veranstaltungen?

ALINA (6) ___Doch___, ich habe Biologie, Chemie, Physik und auch Mathematik.

Kommunikation

4 **Das stimmt nicht!** Make false statements about the photos. In pairs, correct your partner's false statements by negating them; then supply the correct answer. Answers will vary.

BEISPIEL
S1: Die Frau fährt Auto.
S2: Nein, sie fährt nicht Auto. Sie fährt Fahrrad.

1.

2.

3.

4.

5.

6.

5 **Partnerinterview** In pairs, take turns asking each other questions. Contradict your partner's questions using **nicht**, **kein**, or **doch**. Sample answers are provided.

BEISPIEL
S1: Hast du einen Basketball?
S2: Nein, ich habe keinen Basketball.
S1: Tanzt du nicht am Wochenende?
S2: Doch, ich tanze am Wochenende.

1. Spielst du Hockey?
   Nein, ich spiele kein/nicht Hockey.
2. Wanderst du im Wald?
   Nein, ich wandere nicht im Wald.
3. Fährst du im Dezember Fahrrad?
   Nein, im Dezember fahre ich nicht Fahrrad.
4. Hast du keine Hobbys?
   Doch, ich habe viele Hobbys.
5. Trainierst du für den Marathon?
   Nein, ich trainiere nicht für den Marathon.
6. Hast du nicht viele Hausaufgaben?
   Doch, ich habe viele Hausaufgaben.
7. Schwimmst du im Schwimmbad?
   Nein, ich schwimme nicht im Schwimmbad.
8. Bist du Tennisspieler(in)?
   Nein, ich bin kein Tennisspieler / keine Tennisspielerin.

6 **Ich habe es schlecht** In pairs, take turns coming up with exaggerations using **nicht** and **kein**. Contradict your partner's exaggerations using **doch**. Answers will vary.

BEISPIEL
S1: Wir haben keine Freizeit!
S2: Doch, wir haben viel Freizeit!

7 **Trauriger Jörn** In small groups, explain why Jörn is sad, using negative statements. Share your group's answers with the class. Answers will vary.

BEISPIEL
S1: Jörn hat keine Freunde.
S2: Er lernt nicht und hat keine guten Noten.

5 Expansion Have students create their own questions to ask their partners.

5 Video Virtual Chat You can also assign activity 5 on the Supersite. Students record individual responses that appear in your gradebook.

6 Partner Chat You can also assign activity 6 on the Supersite. Students work in pairs to record the activity online. The pair's recorded conversation will appear in your gradebook.

Wiederholung

1 Expansion Have students add their partner's name to the list and ask questions in order to fill out their partner's row in the chart.

Gute Freunde In pairs, look at the information provided about each person. Decide which of them are friends, based on their interests. Answers will vary.

BEISPIEL
Heidi fährt Ski und Florian fährt auch Ski.
Heidi und Florian sind Freunde.

	Tennis spielen	Musik hören	Bücher lesen	Ski fahren	Fahrrad fahren	Fremdsprachen sprechen
Heidi	✓		✓	✓		✓
Daniela	✓	✓	✓	✓		✓
Magda	✓		✓	✓	✓	✓
Klaus		✓		✓	✓	
Florian	✓	✓	✓		✓	✓
Oliver		✓			✓	✓

Begriffe raten In small groups, take turns drawing pictures based on words or phrases you learned in **Lektionen 2A** and **2B**. The first person to guess the word or phrase draws next. Answers will vary.

BEISPIEL
S1: Spielt er Schach?
S2: Nein. Er spielt nicht Schach.
S3: Spielt er Karten?
S2: Ja, richtig!

3 **Viele Fragen** Start a conversation with a classmate using the questions as prompts. Ask follow-up questions using time expressions. Answers will vary.

BEISPIEL
S1: Machst du viele Hausaufgaben?
S2: Ja, ich mache viele Hausaufgaben.
S1: Hast du heute Hausaufgaben in Geschichte?
S2: Nein, ich habe heute keine Hausaufgaben in Geschichte.

1. Liest du viele Bücher?
2. Reist du im Winter nach Kanada?
3. Sprichst du Deutsch?
4. Verstehst du Mathematik?
5. Machst du viel Sport?
6. Spielst du Schach?
7. Isst du viel Pizza?
8. Fährst du viel Fahrrad?

3 Video Virtual Chat
You can also assign activity 3 on the Supersite. Students record individual responses that appear in your gradebook.

4 **Diskutieren und kombinieren** Your instructor will give you and your partner different worksheets showing two schedules. Take turns asking and answering questions to find out the missing information from your partner's schedule.

BEISPIEL
S1: Wann gehst du ins Stadion?
S2: Nächsten Montag um halb fünf.

5 **Vermischtes** Use the cues to form questions. Then, in pairs, take turns asking and answering the questions. Answers will vary.

BEISPIEL
S1: Hast du heute Abend Zeit?
S2: Nein, ich habe heute Abend keine Zeit.

1. angeln gehen / du / am Sonntag
2. Tennis spielen / du / samstags
3. gehen / du / oft / in die Sporthalle
4. Tennisschuhe / haben / keine / du
5. du / reiten / am Wochenende
6. du / schlafen / viel / sonntags
7. für die Prüfung / lernen / nicht / du
8. du / nicht / aus Berlin / kommen

6 **Arbeitsblatt** Your instructor will give you and your partner each a worksheet. Take turns asking questions to find each other's battleships.

BEISPIEL
S1: Liest Otto ein Buch?
S2: Treffer (*Hit*)! Er liest ein Buch./ Nein, kein Treffer. Er liest nicht.

	lesen	arbeiten
Otto		
Lukas und Maria		🚢

7 **Stundenplan** In Germany, you can pick up schedules like this one for free in many stores. Map out your classes and compare your **Stundenplan** with that of a partner.

BEISPIEL

S1: Dienstags habe ich … Wann hast du …?
S2: Ich habe … Um wie viel Uhr hast du …?

Expansion Encourage students to research class schedules at a few German universities. What time are the classes at each university? Um wie viel Uhr sind/beginnen die Vorlesungen an jeder Universität? **Wann/Um wie viel Uhr ist/beginnt die erste Vorlesung am Morgen? Wann/Um wie viel Uhr ist/ beginnt die letzte Vorlesung am Abend? An welchen Tagen können Sie zu Vorlesungen gehen?**

Zeit	Montag	Dienstag	Mittwoch	Donnerstag	Freitag
1					
2					
3					
4					
5					
6					
7					

8 **Minigeschichte** In small groups, make up a story about the people in the picture. Be as detailed as possible. You may want to give the people names.
Answers will vary.

BEISPIEL

S1: Es ist Samstag und viele Studenten trainieren im Stadion.
S2: Niklas und David sind Basketballspieler, aber sie trainieren nicht...

fangen	laufen	trainieren	verlieren
gewinnen	spielen	treffen	werfen

Mein Wörterbuch

Personalize your vocabulary list. Add five words related to the themes **an der Universität** and **Sport und Freizeit** to the online Vocabulary Tools.

Lektion 2B

German	English	Definition
+ add word		
die Klausur, -en	exam	die Prüfung, das Examen

ä   ö   ü   ß   ALL CAPS

Panorama Interactive Map

Berlin

Die Stadt in Zahlen

- ▶ **Fläche:** *892 km² (Quadratkilometer)*
- ▶ **Einwohner° der Stadt Berlin:** *3.624.930*
- ▶ **Ausländer° in Berlin:** *652.997*
- ▶ **Touristen (2018):** *über 10 Millionen*
- ▶ **Fastfood:** *Döner Kebap, erfunden° 1972 von Kadir Nurman in Berlin; über 1.000 Verkaufsstellen° in Berlin Currywurst, erfunden 1949 von Herta Heuwer in Berlin.*
- ▶ **Touristenattraktionen:** *das Brandenburger Tor, der Reichstag, die Gedächtniskirche, der Gendarmenmarkt, der Alexanderplatz, das Holocaust-Mahnmal, die Museumsinsel, der Potsdamer Platz, das Nikolaiviertel.*

QUELLE: Amt für Statistik Berlin Brandenburg

Berühmte Berliner

- ▶ **Friedrich II. (Friedrich der Große),** *König von Preußen° (1712–1786)*
- ▶ **Alexander von Humboldt,** *Naturforscher° (1769–1859)*
- ▶ **Gustav Langenscheidt,** *Deutschlehrer und Verlagsbuchhändler° (1832–1895)*
- ▶ **Berthold Brecht,** *Dramatiker° (1898–1956)*
- ▶ **Marlene Dietrich,** *Schauspielerin° und Sängerin° (1901–1992)*
- ▶ **Thomas „Icke" Häßler,** *Fußballspieler (1966–)*
- ▶ **Franziska van Almsick,** *Schwimmerin (1978–)*

More activities

vhlcentral

Online activities

Suggestion You may want to play Herbert Grönemeyer's song *Currywurst* for the class.

Expansion Ask students questions to review numbers. Ex.: **Wie viele Touristen besuchen Berlin 2018? Wie alt ist Franziska von Almsick?**

Expansion Ask students to plan a trip to Berlin for next year. Ask them what sites they will visit and what they will do on their trip.

Einwohner *inhabitants* Ausländer *foreigners* **erfunden** *invented*
Verkaufsstellen *points of sale* König von Preußen *King of Prussia*
Naturforscher *naturalist* Verlagsbuchhändler *publisher*
Dramatiker *playwright* Schauspielerin *actress* Sängerin *singer*
Weltkrieg *World War* in Trümmern *in ruins* Gebäude zerstört *buildings destroyed* Wohnungen *apartments* Krankenhäuser *hospitals*
beschädigt *damaged*

das Brandenburger Tor

der Alexanderplatz

die Museumsinsel

die Gedächtniskirche

Unglaublich aber wahr!

Am 2. Mai 1945 endet der 2. Weltkrieg° in Berlin. 28.5 km² der Stadt liegen in Trümmern°. Im Zentrum sind etwa 50% der Gebäude zerstört°. Etwa 600.000 Wohnungen° sind komplett zerstört. Die Infrastruktur der Stadt, Straßen, Schulen und Krankenhäuser° sind schwer beschädigt°. In Berlin leben noch 2,8 Millionen Menschen, vor dem Krieg sind es 4,3 Millionen.

Geschichte

Das DDR Museum

Seit 1989 sind Berlin und ganz Deutschland nicht mehr geteilt°. Das DDR Museum beleuchtet° das Leben in der ehemaligen° DDR: die Mauer, die Stasi° und den Alltag°. Die Ausstellung ist interaktiv. Man kann sich in einen echten° Trabant° oder ein authentisches DDR-Wohnzimmer° setzen. Geschichte zum Anfassen°!

Architektur

Der Reichstag°

Zwischen 1884 und 1894 errichtet der Architekt Paul Wallot den Reichstag. Er ist das wichtigste° Gebäude der deutschen Politik: Bis 1918 trifft sich hier der Reichstag des Deutschen Kaiserreichs°, danach das Parlament der Weimarer Republik, und seit 1999 der Deutsche Bundestag. 1933 ist der legendäre Reichstagsbrand°. Heute besuchen Touristen oft die Glaskuppel. Sie ist 23,5 Meter hoch°, 40 Meter breit° und 800 Tonnen schwer°. Im Sommer 1995 verhüllen° die Künstler Christo und Jeanne-Claude den Reichstag komplett. Jedes Jahr kommen 3 Millionen Besucher° nach Berlin, um den Reichstag zu sehen.

Kultur

Karneval der Kulturen

Berlin ist eine internationale Stadt mit mehr als 700.000 Menschen aus 130 Ländern. Seit 1996 gibt es jedes Jahr ein Fest, um die Internationalität und Kulturenvielfalt° Berlins zu feiern: den Karneval der Kulturen. Es gibt einen großen Umzug° mit etwa 4.000 Teilnehmern und ein viertägiges Straßenfest mit mehr als 800 Künstlern – Musik, Tanz, Performance. 2018 besuchen fast 1 Million Menschen das Event in Berlin-Kreuzberg. Mehr als 500.000 sehen den Umzug. An den vier Tagen kann man viele kulinarische und handwerkliche° Sachen genießen°.

Sport

Olympische Spiele 1936

Die Olympischen Sommerspiele 1936 finden vom 1. bis 16. August 1936 in Berlin statt°. 3.961 Athleten aus 49 Nationen nehmen an den Spielen teil° – ein neuer Rekord. Der bekannteste° Sportler dieser Spiele ist der amerikanische Leichtathlet Jesse Owens. Er gewinnt vier Goldmedaillen. Der erfolgreichste° deutsche Athlet ist der Kunstturner° Konrad Frey mit drei Goldmedaillen, einer Silbermedaille und zwei Bronzemedaillen. Die Nationalsozialisten missbrauchen° die Spiele als Propaganda.

Musik Musik

Nena

Nenas Hit "99 Luftballons" ist ein Höhepunkt der musikalischen Ära der Neuen Deutschen Welle in den achtziger Jahren.

Go to **vhlcentral.com** to find out more about **Nena** and her band.

geteilt *divided* **beleuchtet** *illuminates* **ehemaligen** *former* **Stasi** *secret police* **Alltag** *everyday* **echten** *real* **Trabant** *car produced in East Germany* **Wohnzimmer** *living room* **zum Anfassen** *to touch* **finden... statt** *take place* **nehmen... teil** *participate* **bekannteste** *most well-known* **erfolgreichste** *most successful* **Kunstturner** *gymnast* **missbrauchen** *misuse* **Reichstag** *parliament building* **wichtigste** *most important* **des Deutschen Kaiserreichs** *of the German empire* **Reichstagsbrand** *Reichstag fire* **hoch** *high* **breit** *wide* **schwer** *heavy* **verhüllen** *cover with fabric* **Besucher** *visitors* **Kulturenvielfalt** *cultural diversity* **Umzug** *parade* **handwerkliche** *crafts* **genießen** *enjoy*

---

1 **Richtig oder falsch?** Indicate whether each statement is **richtig** or **falsch**. Correct the false statements.

1. Vor dem 2. Weltkrieg wohnen fast 4,3 Millionen Leute in Berlin.
   Richtig.
2. In Berlin gibt es ein DDR Museum.
   Richtig.
3. Der Reichstag ist das wichtigste Gebäude der deutschen Kultur.
   Falsch. Der Reichstag ist das wichtigste Gebäude der deutschen Politik.
4. Die Olympischen Sommerspiele finden 1938 in Berlin statt.
   Falsch. Die Olympischen Sommerspiele finden 1936 in Berlin statt.
5. 2018 besuchen fast 1 Million Menschen den Berliner Karneval der Kulturen.
   Richtig.

2 **Denken Sie nach.** In a small group, discuss an annual cultural celebration in your city. How is it like the **Karneval der Kulturen?** What cultures are usually represented? How do people showcase their cultures?

Lesen   Audio: Reading

Vor dem Lesen

Strategien

Predicting content through formats

Recognizing the format of a text can help you to predict its content. For example, invitations, greeting cards, and classified ads follow easily identifiable formats, which usually give you a general idea of the information they contain. Look at the text below and identify it based on its format.

Uhrzeit	Montag	Dienstag	Mittwoch	Donnerstag	Freitag
7.55	Deutsch	Französisch	Biologie	Religion	Mathe
8.40	Englisch	Musik	Geschichte	Physik	Mathe
9.40	Sport	Geschichte	Mathe	Französisch	Englisch
10.25	Sport	Mathe	Englisch	Französisch	Chemie
11.25	Religion	Physik	Erdkunde	Erdkunde	Musik
12.10	Sozialkunde	Chemie	Deutsch	Deutsch	Bio

If you guessed that this is a page from a student's weekly planner, you are correct. You can now infer that it contains information about a student's weekly schedule, including days, times, classes, and activities.

Texte verstehen

Briefly look at the document. What is its format? What kind of information is given? How is it organized? What are the visual components? What types of documents usually contain these elements?

Verwandte Wörter

You have already learned that you can use cognates, as well as format, to help you predict the content of a document. With a classmate, make a list of all the cognates you find in the reading selection. Based on these cognates and the format of the document, can you guess what this document is and what it is for?

Karlswald-Universität
Studienkolleg Mittelhessen

4 Stunden pro Tag (Montag–Freitag)
2 Tutorien pro Woche

Kurse
- Grundstufe: Anfänger°
- Stufe 1: Einführung° I
- Stufe 2: Einführung II
- Stufe 3: fortgeschritten° I
- Stufe 4: fortgeschritten II
- Stufe 5/6: Vorbereitung° auf die DSH-Prüfung

Kosten
- Einstufungstest: 50 Euro
- Stufe 1, 2, 3 und 4: 410 Euro pro Kurs
- Stufe 5/6: 620 Euro

Unterbringung°
- In Studentenwohnheimen
- In Privatwohnungen

Studienkolleg Mittelhessen
Friedrichstraße 3 | D-35032 Marburg

ausländische *foreign* **die... wollen** *who want* **Anfänger** *beginner* **Einführung** *introduction*
fortgeschritten *advanced* **Vorbereitung** *preparation* **Unterbringung** *accommodations*

Die Deutschkurse an der Karlswald-Universität:
Deutschtraining für ausländische° Studenten, die in Karlswald studieren wollen°.

Stufe 1–4 vom 3. Januar bis 14. Februar
Stufe 5/6 vom 3. Januar bis 22. März

Große Auswahl° zusätzlicher Aktivitäten:

- Tagesausflüge° zu Städten der Region (Frankfurt, Eisenach, Heidelberg)
- Besuche von Sehenswürdigkeiten° (Elisabethkirche, Marburger Schloss)
- Besuche von Kulturveranstaltungen° (Theaterproduktionen, Konzerte)
- Sport und andere Aktivitäten

Suggestion Encourage students to record unfamiliar words and phrases that they learn from this reading in their personalized dictionaries.

Intensives Training in Hörverständnis°, Leseverständnis und Textproduktion.

Tel.: (06421) 28 23 651 · Fax.: (06421) 28 23 652
www.uni-karlswald.de/studienkolleg

Auswahl *selection* **Tagesausflüge** *day trips* **Sehenswürdigkeiten** *places of interest*
Kulturveranstaltungen *cultural events* **Hörverständnis** *listening comprehension*

Nach dem Lesen

Antworten Sie Select the option that best completes the statement.

1. Das ist eine Broschüre für...
   a. ein deutsches Gymnasium.
   b. ein Institut für Deutschkurse.
   c. Studenten, die Englisch lernen wollen.

2. Studenten, die kein Deutsch sprechen, nehmen den Kurs...
   a. Grundstufe.   b. Stufe 3.   c. Stufe 5/6.

3. Jeden (*Every*) Tag haben Studenten in einem Kurs...
   a. 4 Stunden Deutschunterricht.
   b. 4 Stunden Tutorien.
   c. 2 Stunden Deutschunterricht.

4. Der Test am Ende der Stufe 5/6...
   a. ist intensives Training.
   b. hat kein Hörverständnis.
   c. heißt DSH-Prüfung.

5. Studenten wohnen...
   a. bei deutschen Familien.
   b. im Studentenwohnheim.
   c. in Frankfurt.

6. An Wochenenden besuchen Studenten...
   a. Studentenheime und Privatwohnungen.
   b. Frankfurt und andere Städte.
   c. die Universität.

7. Kurse kosten...
   a. 50 Euro.
   b. 1.030 Euro.
   c. 410 oder 620 Euro.

Suggestion Go over the answers with the whole class or have students check their answers in pairs.

8. Die Kurse der Stufe 1, 2, 3 und 4 dauern...
   a. 4 Wochen.   **b.** 6 Wochen.   c. 11 Wochen.

Richtig oder falsch? Mark the appropriate box.

	richtig	falsch
1. Das Studienkolleg Mittelhessen ist für deutsche Studenten.	☐	☑
2. Die Deutschkurse sind 5 Stunden jeden Tag.	☐	☑
3. Es gibt Tagesausflüge nach Frankfurt, Eisenach und Heidelberg.	☑	☐
4. Das Studienkolleg ist in der Friedrichstraße 3, D-35032 Marburg.	☑	☐

Hören

Strategien

Listening for cognates

You already know that cognates are words that have similar spellings and meanings in two or more languages, like *telephone* and **Telefon** or *activity* and **Aktivität**. Listen for cognates to improve your comprehension of spoken German.

 To help you practice this strategy, listen to these statements. Write down all the cognates you hear.

Vorbereitung

Based on the photograph, who do you think Julian and Anni are? Where are they? Do they know each other well? Where are they going this morning? What are they talking about?

Zuhören

 Listen to the conversation and list any cognates you hear. Listen again and complete the highlighted portions of Julian's schedule.

4. April   Montag

9.30	*Kaffee mit Ingrid (in der Cafeteria)*	14.30	
10.00	*Seminar zur englischen Literatur*	15.00	lernen mit David
10.30		15.30	
11.00		16.00	
11.30		16.30	
12.00	*Mittagessen mit Karl in der Mensa*	17.00	Fußball spielen
12.30		17.30	
13.00		18.00	
13.30		18.30	
14.00	Englischvorlesung	19.00	*Konzert im Kulturladen*

Verständnis

 Richtig oder falsch? Indicate whether each sentence is **richtig** or **falsch**. Correct any false statements.

1. Anni lernt morgens in der Bibliothek.
   Richtig.

2. Julian und Anni studieren Architektur.
   Falsch. Julian studiert englische Literatur und Anni studiert Architektur.

3. Um 9.30 Uhr trinkt Julian mit Jasmin Kaffee.
   Falsch. Um 9.30 Uhr trinkt Julian mit Ingrid Kaffee.

4. Anni hat um 2 Uhr eine Vorlesung.
   Falsch. Julian hat um 2 Uhr eine Vorlesung.

5. Anni findet Architektur interessant.
   Richtig.

6. Anni und Julian haben langweilige Professoren.
   Richtig.

7. Julian und Anni gehen am Nachmittag Fußball spielen.
   Falsch. Julian geht am Nachmittag Fußball spielen.

8. Julian geht am Abend in ein Konzert.
   Richtig.

Pläne In pairs, discuss your plans for this weekend, including where and when you will do each activity.

Suggestion To check answers for **Zuhören**, have students work in pairs and ask each other questions about Julian's schedule.

Schreiben

Brainstorming

Brainstorming can help you generate ideas on a specific topic. Before you begin writing, you should spend 10–15 minutes brainstorming, jotting down any ideas about the topic that occur to you. Whenever possible, try to write down your ideas in German. Express your ideas in single words or phrases, and jot them down in any order. While brainstorming, do not worry about whether your ideas are good or bad. Selecting and organizing ideas should be the second stage of your writing. The more ideas you write down while you are brainstorming, the more options you will have to choose from later on, when you start to organize your ideas.

Hobbys...
laufen
campen gehen
Tennis spielen
kochen
tanzen
schreiben
schwimmen
Fahrrad fahren

Thema

 Eine persönliche Beschreibung

Write a description of yourself to post on a Web site in order to find a German-speaking e-pal. Your description should include:

- your name and where you are from.
- your birthday.
- the name of your school and where it is located.
- the courses you are currently taking and your opinion of each one.
- your hobbies and pastimes.
- any other information you would like to include.

Hallo!

Ich heiße Erik Schneider und ich komme aus Köln. Ich studiere Physik an der Technischen Universität in Berlin. Ich fahre Ski, spiele Tennis und fahre Fahrrad...

Vocabulary Tools

Lektion 2A

das Studium
studies

der Abschluss, ⁻e / das Diplom, -e *degree*
das Abschlusszeugnis, -se / das Diplom, -e *diploma*
der Dozent, -en / die Dozentin, -nen *college/university instructor*
das Fach, ⁻er *subject*
das Seminar, -e *seminar*
das Stipendium, -en *scholarship*
die Veranstaltung, -en *class; course*
die Vorlesung, -en *lecture*
(die) Architektur *architecture*
(die) Biologie *biology*
(die) Chemie *chemistry*
(die) Fremdsprache, -n *foreign language*
(die) Geschichte *history*
(die) Informatik *computer science*
(die) Kunst, ⁻e *art*
(die) Literatur *literature*
(die) Mathematik *math*
(die) Medizin *medicine*
(die) Naturwissenschaft, -en *natural sciences*
(die) Physik *physics*
(die) Psychologie *psychology*
(die) Wirtschaft *business*
belegen *to take (a class)*
gehen *to go*
lernen *to study; to learn*
studieren *to study; to major in*

Sportarten
sports

spielen *to play*

der Stundenplan
schedule

der Montag, -e *Monday*
der Dienstag, -e *Tuesday*
der Mittwoch, -e *Wednesday*
der Donnerstag, -e *Thursday*
der Freitag, -e *Friday*
der Samstag, -e *Saturday*
der Sonntag, -e *Sunday*
die Stunde, -n *hour*
die Woche, -n *week*
das Wochenende, -n *weekend*
die Zeit, -en *time*
morgens *in the morning*
nachmittags *in the afternoon*
abends *in the evening*
montags *on Mondays*
dienstags *on Tuesdays*
mittwochs *on Wednesdays*
donnerstags *on Thursdays*
freitags *on Fridays*
samstags *on Saturdays*
sonntags *on Sundays*

Orte
places

das Café, -s *café*
der Hörsaal, Hörsäle *lecture hall*
der Seminarraum, -räume *(college/university) classroom*

zum Beschreiben
to describe

einfach *easy*
interessant *interesting*
langweilig *boring*
nützlich *useful*
nutzlos *useless*
schwierig *difficult*

Regular verbs *See pp. 56–57.*
Interrogative words *See p. 60.*
Telling time *See p. 62.*
Ordinal numbers and dates *See p. 63.*
gern/nicht gern *See p. 69.*

Lektion 2B

Sportarten
sports

(der) Baseball *baseball*
(der) Basketball *basketball*
(der) (American) Football *football*
(der) Fußball *soccer*
(das) Golf *golf*
(das) Hockey *hockey*
(die) Leichtathletik *track and field*
(das) Tennis *tennis*
(der) Volleyball *volleyball*
der Ball, ⁻e *ball*
die Mannschaft, -en *team*
das Schwimmbad, ⁻er *swimming pool*
das Spiel, -e *game*
der Spieler, - / die Spielerin, -nen *player*
das Spielfeld, -er / der Platz, ⁻e *field, court*
der Sport *sports*
das Stadion, Stadien *stadium*
Fahrrad fahren *to ride a bicycle*
Ski fahren *to ski*
gewinnen *to win*
schwimmen *to swim*
trainieren *to practice*
verlieren *to lose*

Orte
places

die Sporthalle, -n *gym*

Freizeitaktivitäten
leisure activities

der Berg, -e *mountain*
das Fahrrad, ⁻er *bicycle*
die Freizeit *free time*
die Freizeitaktivität, -en *leisure activity*
das Hobby, -s *hobby*
die Karte, -n *card*
der Park, -s *park*
das Schach *chess*
der Strand, ⁻e *beach*
der Wald, ⁻er *forest*
angeln gehen *to go fishing*
campen gehen *to go camping*
essen gehen *to eat out*
spazieren gehen *to go for a walk*
klettern *to (rock) climb*
kochen *to cook*
(ein Pferd) reiten *to ride (a horse)*
schreiben *to write*
Spaß haben/machen *to have fun / to be fun*
singen *to sing*
tanzen *to dance*
wandern *to hike*

Ausdrücke
expressions

Sie spielen gern Schach. *They like to play chess.*
Sie verliert nicht gern. *She doesn't like to lose.*

Stem-changing verbs *See pp. 76–77.*
Common time expressions *See p. 80.*
Negative words *See pp. 82–83.*

COMMUNICATIVE GOALS
By the end of this chapter you will be able to:

🔊 **Los geht's!** Wo sind George, Meline und Hans? Was machen sie?

LEKTION 3A

Discuss family relationships and describe people. Express ownership.

To do so, you will use:

Kontext Seite 96-99
• Family relationships, marital status, and pets

Strukturen Seite 104-113
3A.1 Possessive adjectives
3A.2 Descriptive adjectives and adjective agreement

You will also learn about cultural products, practices, and perspectives related to:

Kultur Seite 102–103
• German families
• Regional expressions about love
• The **Albrecht** brothers and **Aldi**

Zapping Seite 113
• *Naturkost für Hund und Katze*

LEKTION 3B

Talk about professions.
Express an attitude about an action.
Give instructions.

To do so, you will use:

Kontext Seite 114-117
• Personal descriptions
• Professions

Strukturen Seite 122-133
3B.1 Modals
3B.2 Prepositions with the accusative
3B.3 The imperative

You will also learn about cultural products, practices, and perspectives related to:

Kultur Seite 120–121
• Friendship in Germany
• Regional differences in marriage traditions
• **Herbert Grönemeyer**

WEITER GEHT'S

Seite 134-140
You will learn about the influence of people from German-speaking countries on the United States and Canada.

And you will demonstrate that you can:
• Predict content from visuals
• Ask for repetition
• Use idea maps

Suggestion Ask students to identify the people they already know and guess who the man at the head of the table is. Solicit other statements about what they see. Supply vocabulary as needed. Answers: **George, Meline und Hans essen. Der Mann ist Sabites Vater.**

Kontext

Johanna Schmidts Familie Vocabulary Tools

Walter Gärtner

mein Großvater/Opa (m.)

Wortschatz

die Familie	*family*
das Baby, -s	*baby*
die Eltern	*parents*
die Geschwister	*siblings*
die Großeltern	*grandparents*
der Halbbruder, ⁒	*half brother*
die Halbschwester, -n	*half sister*
das Kind, -er	*child*
der Nachname, -n	*last name*
das Paar, -e	*couple*
der Schwager, ⁒	*brother-in-law*
die Schwägerin, -nen	*sister-in-law*
die Schwiegermutter, ⁒	*mother-in-law*
der Schwiegervater, ⁒	*father-in-law*
der Stiefbruder, ⁒	*stepbrother*
die Stiefmutter, ⁒	*stepmother*
die Stiefschwester, -n	*stepsister*
der Stiefsohn, ⁒e	*stepson*
die Stieftochter, ⁒	*stepdaughter*
der Stiefvater, ⁒	*stepfather*
der / die Verwandte, -n	*relative*
der Zwilling, -e	*twin*
die Haustiere	*pets*
der Fisch, -e	*fish*
der Hund, -e	*dog*
die Katze, -n	*cat*
der Vogel, ⁒	*bird*
der Familienstand	*marital status*
die Witwe, -n	*widow*
der Witwer, -	*widower*
geschieden	*divorced*
getrennt	*separated*
ledig	*single*
verheiratet	*married*
verlobt	*engaged*
zusammen	*together*
heiraten	*to marry*
zum Beschreiben	*to describe*
blaue/grüne/braune Augen	*blue/green/brown eyes*
blonde/braune/ schwarze Haare	*blond/brown/ black hair*
dunkel / hell	*dark / light*

Suggestion Point out to students that both **Eltern** and **Geschwister** are plural nouns and have no singular form. Model this usage by asking individual students whether they have any siblings. Ex.: **Hast du noch Geschwister? Ja, ich habe eine Schwester und zwei Brüder.**

Point out that whereas *hair* in English is a collective singular noun, **die Haare** is a plural noun. Explain that **das Haar** refers to a single hair, or to hair in general.

Peter Schmidt   **Marianne Schmidt**

mein Vater (m.), Mariannes Mann (m.)   **meine Mutter (f.), Walter und Hannas Tochter (f.)**

Michaela Schmidt   **Daniel Schmidt**   **Johanna Schmidt**

meine Schwägerin   **mein Bruder (m.)**   **ich, Peter und Mariannes Tochter**

Jonas Schmidt   **Greta Schmidt**

mein Neffe (m.)   **meine Nichte (f.)**
Peter und Mariannes Enkelkinder

ACHTUNG

To say *my big/little brother/sister*, use **mein großer/kleiner Bruder** or **meine große/kleine Schwester**.

Hanna Gärtner

meine Großmutter/Oma (f.)

2 Expansion Ask students if they have a favorite uncle/aunt (**Lieblingsonkel, Lieblingstante**), cousin, etc.

Dieter Gärtner

mein Onkel (m.), Walter und Hannas Sohn (m.)

Renate Gärtner

meine Tante (f.), Dieters Frau (f.)

Simon Gärtner

mein Cousin (m.), Walter und Hannas Enkelsohn (m.)

Sophia Gärtner

meine Cousine (f.), Simon und Klaras Schwester (f.)

Klara Gärtner

meine Cousine, Simon und Sophias Schwester, Walter und Hannas Enkeltochter (f.)

Zeus

Simon, Sophia und Klaras Hund

Anwendung

1 Expansion Get students started by asking them questions about their own families. Ex.: **Haben Sie Geschwister?**

1 Kombinieren Match the people with the descriptions.

- _d_ 1. Daniels Frau
- _a_ 2. Marianne und Peter
- _c_ 3. Dieter und Renates Sohn
- _f_ 4. Mariannes Vater
- _e_ 5. Daniels Tochter
- _b_ 6. Dieters Frau

- a. Johannas Eltern
- b. Johannas Tante
- c. Johannas Cousin
- d. Johannas Schwägerin
- e. Johannas Nichte
- f. Johannas Opa

2 Ja oder nein? Write **Ja** if the word you hear indicates a family member and **Nein** if it does not.

1. _Ja_
2. _Nein_
3. _Ja_
4. _Ja_
5. _Nein_
6. _Nein_
7. _Ja_
8. _Nein_
9. _Ja_

3 Identifizieren Write each person's family relationship to Dieter Gärtner.

BEISPIEL Hanna: _die Mutter_

1. Sophia: _die Tochter_
2. Marianne: _die Schwester_
3. Daniel: _der Neffe_
4. Peter: _der Schwager_
5. Simon: _der Sohn_
6. Johanna: _die Nichte_
7. Walter und Hanna: _die Eltern_
8. Renate: _die Frau_

4 Kategorien List at least four roles each person could have in a family.

Sample answers are provided.

BEISPIEL eine Frau, 40 Jahre alt

eine Mutter   _eine Tante_   _eine Cousine_   _eine Tochter_

1. ein Mann, 62 Jahre alt:

ein Schwager   ein Großvater   ein Schwiegervater   ein Vater

2. ein Kind, 3 Jahre alt:

ein Sohn   ein Neffe   ein Enkelsohn   ein Bruder

3. ein Mädchen, 15 Jahre alt:

eine Cousine   eine Schwester   eine Tochter   eine Enkeltochter

4. eine Frau, 50 Jahre alt:

eine Oma   eine Tante   eine Schwägerin   eine Mutter

5 Hören Sie zu Listen to Johanna's descriptions and indicate whether each statement is **richtig** or **falsch**, based on her family tree.

	richtig	falsch		richtig	falsch
1.	✓		5.		✓
2.		✓	6.		✓
3.	✓		7.	✓	
4.	✓		8.		✓

Kommunikation

6 **Beschreibungen** Use words from the list to describe the images. Compare your answers with a classmate's, and correct each other's work. Sample answers are provided.

> Enkelkinder | Großeltern | Neffe | Sohn | heiraten | verlobt | Zwillinge

▶ **BEISPIEL**

Das Paar ist verlobt.

5 Suggestion Give students cues to help them complete this activity. Ask them questions about the pictures. Ex.: **Wer sind die Leute? Wie alt ist das Kind?**

1. Das Kind ist der Neffe.

2. Die Babys sind Zwillinge.

3. Der Mann und die Frau heiraten.

4. Die Mutter hat einen Sohn.

5. Die Großmutter hat drei Enkelkinder.

6. Die Großeltern begrüßen die Familie.

7 **Brieffreunde** Read Eva's letter to her penpal. Then, in pairs, take turns answering the questions. Sample answers are provided.

> *Liebe Andrea,*
>
> *hast du eine große Familie? Meine Familie ist nicht sehr groß. Ich habe eine große Schwester Nicole und einen kleinen Halbbruder Peter. Und wir haben einen Hund, Cäsar, und Miezi, unsere kleine Katze.*
>
> *Nicole studiert Sportmedizin in Heidelberg. Peter ist fünf und geht in den Kindergarten.*
>
> *Meine Familie ist sehr sportlich. Mein Stiefvater spielt Golf, meine Mutter und Nicole spielen Tennis, Peter spielt Fußball und ich mache Ballett.*
>
> *Und wie ist deine Familie?*
>
> *Liebe Grüße,*
> *deine Eva*

1. Wie viele Personen wohnen mit Eva zusammen? Drei Personen wohnen mit Eva zusammen: der Stiefvater, die Mutter, der Halbbruder.
2. Hat sie auch Haustiere? Ja, sie hat zwei Haustiere: einen Hund und eine Katze.
3. Wie alt ist Peter? Er ist fünf (Jahre alt).
4. Was macht Evas Familie in der Freizeit? Der Stiefvater spielt Golf, die Mutter und die Schwester spielen Tennis, der Halbbruder spielt Fußball und Eva macht Ballett.
5. Wie groß ist Ihre (*your*) Familie? Answers will vary.

8 **Arbeitsblatt** Your instructor will give you a worksheet with statements about family relationships. Use the cues to ask your classmates about their families. Then present one classmate to the class.

BEISPIEL Ich habe zwei Schwestern.

S1: Hast du zwei Schwestern?
S2: Ja, ich habe zwei Schwestern. (*You write his/her name.*)
OR
S2: Nein, ich habe keine Schwestern. (*You ask another classmate.*)

8 Suggestion Ask volunteers to share their results with the class.

9 **Was machen sie gern?** Use the vocabulary you learned in **Kapitel 2** to talk with a classmate about what your family members enjoy doing. **9 Partner Chat** You can also assign activity 9 on the Supersite.

BEISPIEL

S1: Mein Bruder spielt gern Tennis. Was macht dein Bruder?
S2: Mein Bruder liest gern Bücher.

7 Expansion Have students write their own responses to Eva's letter. You might provide them with real postcards which they have to "mail" back to you. Encourage volunteers to read their letters aloud to the class.

Aussprache und Rechtschreibung Audio

Final consonants

The German consonants **b**, **d**, and **g** generally sound quite similar to their English counterparts.

Ball	Bruder	Dezember	bringen	Golf

However, when **b** appears at the end of a word or syllable, or before a **t**, it is pronounced like a **p**.

ab	habt	gelb	Staub	liebt

When **d** appears at the end of a word or syllable, it is pronounced like a **t**. The **-dt** letter combination is also pronounced **t**.

Geld	Hund	Stadt	sind	Fahrrad

As you learned in **2A**, when **g** appears at the end of a word or before a **t**, it is pronounced like a **k**. In standard German, **-ig** at the end of a word is pronounced like the German **ch**.

klug	bringt	Tag	sagt	zwanzig

Suggestion Remind students that the pronunciation of the final **-ig** sound has several regional variations.
For more about the **ch** sound, see **Lektion 6A**.

1 **Aussprechen** Practice saying these words aloud.

1. Bank
2. sieben
3. Laub
4. lobt
5. danken
6. Boden
7. Abend
8. gehen
9. Junge
10. Berg
11. fragt
12. schwierig

2 **Nachsprechen** Practice saying these sentences aloud.

1. Der Dieb klaut ein Fahrrad.
2. Der Besucher fragt Manfred ruhig um Rat.
3. Bernds Geschwister sind freundlich und großzügig.
4. Viele Diebe klauen viele Fahrräder.
5. Ingrids böser Bruder ist gierig und gemein.
6. Jörg sitzt im Zug und singt ein Lied.

Suggestion Have students look at the sample words and sentences on this page to identify cognates and words they already know. Tell students the meanings of any unfamiliar words or phrases.

3 **Sprichwörter** Practice reading these sayings aloud.

Kindermund tut Wahrheit kund.[1]

Geld regiert die Welt.[2]

[1] Out of the mouths of babes. (lit. The mouths of children make known the truth.)
[2] Money rules the world.

More activities

vhlcentral | LM p. 22 | Online activities

Fotoroman

Ein Abend mit der Familie Video

Die Freunde essen bei Familie Yilmaz. Alle wissen (*know*), Torsten ist
Sabites Freund. Alle, nur einer nicht.

Vorbereitung Have students scan the images on the pages before they watch the video and try to guess what this episode will be about.

ANKE Hallo! Willkommen, ich bin Sabites Mutter.
GEORGE Freut mich sehr, Sie kennen zu lernen, Frau Yilmaz. Ich bin George Bachman.

SABITE George, das ist meine jüngere Schwester, Zeynep.
GEORGE Hallo, Zeynep, nett dich kennen zu lernen.
SABITE Und das ist unser Vater.
GEORGE Herr Yilmaz, freut mich.

ANKE Das sind die Patatesli Sigara Böregi von Faiks Großmutter.
MELINE Herr Yilmaz, Ihre Familie kommt aus der Türkei?
FAIK Ja. Ich komme aus Ankara. Ich habe dort Cousins und einen Onkel. Haben Sie Geschwister?
MELINE Ich habe drei ältere Schwestern. Eine ist verheiratet, eine ist getrennt, eine ist verlobt. Ich habe auch eine Nichte, sie heißt Ava und ist 12.

GEORGE Meine Eltern sind geschieden. Meine Urgroßeltern kommen aus Heidelberg.
TORSTEN Mein Onkel lebt in Heidelberg. Er ist Professor. Es ist eine schöne Stadt.

SABITE Hallo, Hans.
HANS Tut mir leid, dass ich zu spät komme.

HANS Hallo!
SABITE Hans, das sind meine Eltern, Anke und Faik.
HANS Guten Abend, Herr Yilmaz. Guten Abend, Frau Yilmaz. Für Sie.
ANKE Danke.
HANS Sehr erfreut.

ÜBUNGEN

1 **Richtig oder falsch?** Indicate whether each statement is **richtig** or **falsch**.

1. Sabite hat einen jüngeren Bruder. Falsch.
2. Meline hat zwei ältere Schwestern. Falsch.
3. Melines Nichte heißt Ava. Richtig.
4. Faik kommt aus Ankara. Richtig.
5. Es gibt Sauerbraten bei Familie Yilmaz. Richtig.
6. Georges Eltern sind verheiratet. Falsch.
7. Torstens Onkel lebt in München. Falsch.
8. Georges Urgroßeltern kommen aus Berlin. Falsch.
9. Hans' Familie kommt aus Bayern. Richtig.
10. Max ist 18 und spielt Basketball. Falsch.

PERSONEN Anke   Faik   George   Hans   Meline   Sabite   Torsten Zeynep

HANS Bist du ihr Bruder?
TORSTEN Nein, Sabite ist meine Freundin. Ich bin Torsten. Nett dich kennen zu lernen.
HANS Freut mich.
MELINE Börek?
HANS Nein danke.

MELINE Frau Yilmaz, Ihr Sauerbraten ist köstlich.
ANKE Danke, Meline. Hans? Alles in Ordnung? Du isst nichts.
HANS Hmm? Ja, danke.

FAIK Hans, Ihre Familie kommt aus Bayern?
HANS Ja.
TORSTEN Ich habe eine Tante in München. Hast du Geschwister, Hans?
HANS Mein Bruder, Max, ist 18. Er ist sportlich und spielt gern Fußball.
MELINE Hat er eine Freundin?

SABITE Hans, alles in Ordnung?
MELINE Sabite!
SABITE Was?
MELINE Hans.
SABITE Was ist mit Hans? Oh. Ooooh.
ANKE Wir haben Strudel!

Nützliche Ausdrücke

- **Freut mich sehr, Sie kennen zu lernen.**
  Pleased to meet you.
- **Das ist meine jüngere Schwester.**
  This is my younger sister.
- **die Türkei**
  Turkey
- **Haben Sie Geschwister?**
  Do you have any siblings?
- **die Urgroßeltern**
  great-grandparents
- **Tut mir leid, dass ich zu spät komme.**
  Sorry for being late.
- **der Sauerbraten**
  marinated beef
- **Ihr Sauerbraten ist köstlich.**
  Your sauerbraten is delicious.
- **Er ist sportlich und spielt gern Fußball.**
  He's athletic and likes to play soccer.
- **Alles in Ordnung?**
  Everything OK?
- **einladen**
  to invite
- **das Abendessen**
  dinner

  3A.1
- **Das ist unser Vater.**
  This is our father.

  3A.2
- **Es ist eine schöne Stadt.**
  It's a beautiful city.

2 **Zum Besprechen** Draw your family tree. Include your parents, siblings, aunts, uncles, and grandparents. Then "introduce" your family to a classmate. Answers will vary.

BEISPIEL

S1: *Das ist meine Tante. Sie heißt Paula. Sie wohnt in New Jersey.*
S2: *Das ist mein Onkel. Er heißt...*

2 **Expansion** Have students present their partners' families to another pair.

3 **Erweiterung** Börek are a popular Turkish snack with many varieties. In pairs, research another popular Turkish dish, and share your findings with the class. Do you like trying new foods from different cultures? Why or why not? Answers will vary.

More activities

vhlcentral VM p. 5 Online activities

IM FOKUS

Eine deutsche Familie Reading

TANJA UND JENS KRONE SIND EIN deutsches Ehepaar mit zwei Kindern. Sie haben zwei Söhne, Finn und Lukas. Finn ist 11 Jahre alt und in der 5. Klasse. Lukas ist zwei Jahre älter als Finn und geht schon° in die 7. Klasse. Die Familie hat eine große Wohnung° und einen schönen Garten vor dem Haus. Jens arbeitet den ganzen Tag in einem Büro°. Tanja arbeitet als Krankenschwester°, aber sie ist nachmittags immer zu Hause, wenn Finn und Lukas um eins von der Schule nach Hause kommen. Abends spielen sie zusammen Fußball im Park oder fahren Fahrrad am Rhein.

In der Familie macht auch Jens Hausarbeit°, aber Tanja kocht und putzt° trotzdem mehr. Die Familie fährt einmal im Jahr zusammen in den Urlaub°.

Sind Jens und Tanja also eine „typisch" deutsche Familie? Das Leben in Deutschland ist vielfältiger geworden°. In der Wohnung links neben Jens und Tanja lebt eine Einwandererfamilie°, rechts von ihnen lebt ein allein erziehender° Vater mit seiner Tochter. Was ist also „typisch" für die deutsche Familie von heute? Vielleicht einfach Zusammenhalt° und Liebe.

schon *already* **Wohnung** *apartment* **Büro** *office* **Krankenschwester** *nurse* **Hausarbeit** *housework* **putzt** *cleans* **Urlaub** *vacation* **ist vielfältiger geworden** *has become more diverse* **Einwandererfamilie** *family of immigrants* **allein erziehender** *single parent* **Zusammenhalt** *sticking together* **Mit wem** *With whom* **sonstige** *miscellaneous*

Mit wem° die Deutschen leben (%)				
	Eltern	**allein**	**Partner**	**allein mit Kind**	**sonstige°**
18–24	63,5	15,9	15,8	1,4	3,4
25–29	19,8	25,2	48,6	3,1	3,3
30–34	6,8	20,1	66,9	4,5	1,7
35–44	3,3	14,9	74,1	6,3	1,4
45–54	1,3	13,6	78,8	5,0	1,4
55–64	0,3	16,9	79,4	2,2	1,3
65–74	0,1	25,0	70,8	2,1	2,1
75–79	0	41,8	52,0	2,2	3,9
80+	0	58,7	30,1	2,5	3,4

QUELLE: Bundesministerium

Expansion Have students read the data in the chart aloud to practice saying numbers.

1 **Im Fokus** Indicate whether each statement is **richtig** or **falsch**. Correct the false statements. Then discuss the last question with a partner.

1. Familie Krone wohnt in einer kleinen Wohnung.
   Falsch. Sie wohnt in einer großen Wohnung mit Garten.
2. Beide Eltern arbeiten.
   Richtig.
3. Lukas und Finn sehen ihre Mutter nachmittags nach der Schule.
   Richtig.

Diskussion What is a "typical" family? How much of the description of a typical German family applies to you? Compare your families.

1 Im Fokus Encourage students to answer in German. Write these phrases on the board: Eine typische Familie hat...; Meine Familie ist...; Ich habe... Schwestern/Brüder; Wie viele...?

2 **Die deutschsprachige Welt** Indicate whether each statement is **richtig** or **falsch**. Correct the false statements. Then discuss the last question with a partner.

1. Auf Kölsch sagt man „Bussi" für einen Kuss.
   Falsch. Man sagt „Bütz."
2. In der Schweiz, in Österreich und in Deutschland sagt man „Kuss".
   Richtig.

Diskussion What regional or generational differences have you observed in the English language? What words, phrases or expressions have you used or heard that differ from standard English?

DEUTSCH IM ALLTAG

Die Familie

die Ehe	marriage
das Einzelkind	only child
die Hochzeit	wedding
die Lebenspartner (pl.)	life partners
die Mama	mom
der erste/zweite Mann	first/second husband
der Papa	dad
die Urgroßeltern	great-grandparents
der / die Verlobte	fiancé(e)
adoptieren	to adopt

DIE DEUTSCHSPRACHIGE WELT

Die Liebe

Ein Kuss° ist nicht nur° ein Kuss. In den meisten Teilen° Deutschlands sagt man „Kuss". Aber es gibt andere Möglichkeiten°, „Kuss" in der deutschsprachigen Welt zu sagen. **In der Schweiz** und **in Liechtenstein** sagt man „Müntschi". **In Österreich** und **in Bayern** ist ein Kuss ein „Bussi" oder ein „Busserl". **Auf Kölsch** (der Dialekt von Köln) ist das ein „Bütz".

Und wie sagt man „Ich liebe dich"? Ein paar° Varianten: **In Bayern** und **in Österreich** sagt man „I mog di". **In der Schweiz** geht das so: „I liäbä di". Und **die Berliner** sagen „Ick liebe Dir".

Kuss kiss **nur** only **meisten Teilen** most parts
Möglichkeiten possibilities **Ein paar** A couple of

PORTRÄT

Aldi

Der deutsche Lebensmittel°-Discounter **Aldi** hat seine Anfänge° in der Stadt Essen. 1946, unmittelbar° nach dem Zweiten Weltkrieg, übernehmen° die Brüder Theo und Karl die Geschäftsführung° des Familienunternehmens° **Albrecht Discount** und expandieren.

Die Brüder zerstreiten sich und teilen das Unternehmen 1961 in **Aldi –Nord** und **Aldi-Süd** auf°. Theos Aldi-Nord und Karls Aldi-Süd haben weiterhin° großen Erfolg. Allein in Deutschland gibt es heute um die 4.000 Aldi-Filialen. Auch international expandieren die Brüder. 1979 kauft° Theo die kalifornische Kette **Trader Joe´s**, die bis heute zu Aldi-Nord gehört°. Auch Aldi-Süd ist in den U.S.A. präsent°, und seit 2017 gibt es die Geschäfte sogar in China. Die Familie Albrecht zählt zu den reichsten° Familien in Deutschland.

Lebensmittel grocery **Anfänge** origins **unmittelbar** immediately **übernehmen** take over
Geschäftsführung management **des Familienunternehmens** of the family business
teilen... auf split **weiterhin** still **kauft** buys **gehört** belongs to **präsent** present **reichsten** richest

🔗 IM INTERNET

Scheidung (*Divorce*): Eine Epidemie in den deutschsprachigen Ländern?

Find out more at **vhlcentral.com**.

---

3 **Porträt** Indicate whether each statement is **richtig** or **falsch**. Correct the false statements. Then discuss the last question with a partner.

🔗 1. Aldi gibt es nur in Deutschland.
Falsch. Aldi gibt es in aller Welt.

👥 2. Seit den sechziger Jahren gibt es Aldi-Nord und Aldi-Süd.
Richtig.

3. Die Brüder haben großen Erfolg mit ihren Geschäften.
Richtig.

👥 **Diskussion** Where do you buy your groceries? Do you shop at discount supermarkets, or do you favor smaller, family-run stores? Try to answer in German. Use these phrases: **Ich kaufe... bei (*at*)...; Es gibt dort...**

4 **Ihre Familie** In small groups, ask and answer each other's questions about your families.

🔗 • Wer sind Ihre Eltern?

👥 • Wo arbeiten Ihre Eltern?

• Haben Sie Geschwister?

NATIONAL STANDARDS
comparisons

3A.1

Teaching Tip You may want to assign the grammar tutorial **3A.1 Possessive adjectives** on the Supersite for students to watch before they come to class.

QUERVERWEIS

In **Kontext 3A**, you learned some possessive adjectives used with family vocabulary: **mein Großvater**, **meine Mutter**, **meine Eltern**.

Possessive adjectives Grammar Tutorial

Startblock In both English and German, possessive adjectives indicate ownership or belonging.

Sabite ist **meine** Freundin.

Herr Yilmaz, **Ihre** Familie kommt aus der Türkei?

- In **1A.1**, you learned about indefinite articles. Possessive adjectives are also referred to as **ein**-words since they take the same endings as the indefinite article **ein**. Each personal pronoun has a corresponding possessive adjective.

personal pronouns	possessive adjectives	
ich	mein	*my*
du	dein	*your* (sing., inf.)
er	sein	*his*
sie	ihr	*her*
es	sein	*its*
wir	unser	*our*
ihr	euer	*your* (pl., inf.)
Sie	Ihr	*your* (sing./pl., form.)
sie	ihr	*their*

Meine Schwester ist 16 Jahre alt.	Wo ist **dein** Vater?
My sister is 16 years old.	*Where is **your** father?*

- Possessive adjectives always precede the nouns they modify.

meine Mutter	**deine** Mutter	**unsere** Mutter	**seine** Mutter
my mother	*your mother*	*our mother*	*his mother*

Meine Schwester ist sehr sportlich.
My sister is very athletic.

- Like other **ein**-words, their endings change according to the gender, case, and number of the object possessed.

deine Mutter	**dein** Vater	**dein** Baby	**deine** Eltern
your mother	*your father*	*your baby*	*your parents*

Mein Großvater liebt **seine** Enkelkinder.
*My grandfather loves **his** grandchildren.*

- Like other **ein**-words, possessive adjectives have no added endings before singular masculine or neuter nouns in the nominative, or before singular neuter nouns in the accusative.

nominative and accusative of *ein*-words				
	masculine	**feminine**	**neuter**	**plural**
nominative	**ein** Vater **unser** Vater	**eine** Mutter **unsere** Mutter	**ein** Kind **unser** Kind	**keine** Brüder **unsere** Brüder
accusative	**einen** Vater **unseren** Vater	**eine** Mutter **unsere** Mutter	**ein** Kind **unser** Kind	**keine** Brüder **unsere** Brüder

Ihr Kind ist 3 Jahre alt.
Her child is 3 years old.

Tobias liebt **seinen** Bruder.
*Tobias loves **his** brother.*

- The formal possessive adjective **Ihr** corresponds to the formal personal pronoun **Sie**. The possessive adjective **ihr** can mean either *her* or *their*, depending on context.

Wo sind **Ihre** Eltern?
*Where are **your** parents?*

Rolf und Heike kochen für **ihre** Kinder.
*Rolf and Heike cook for **their** children.*

Christa kocht für **ihre** Enkelkinder.
*Christa cooks for **her** grandchildren.*

- The possessive adjective **euer** drops the second e when an ending is added. The possessive adjective **unser** may drop the e in the stem when an ending is added, but this form is rare.

euer Enkelsohn
your grandson

eure Familie
your family

unser Sohn
our son

uns(e)re Tochter
our daughter

More activities

vhlcentral

WB
pp. 35-36

LM
p. 23

Online activities

⊘ **Jetzt sind Sie dran!**   Write the correct forms of the possessive adjectives.

Nominativ	**Akkusativ**	**Nominativ**	**Akkusativ**
mein	**mein**	**unser**	**unser**
1. _meine_ Idee	5. _meinen_ Bruder	9. _unser_ Fahrrad	13. _uns(e)re_ Verwandten
dein	**dein**	**euer**	**euer**
2. _deine_ Eltern	6. _deine_ Frage	10. _eure_ Mannschaft	14. _euren_ Sohn
sein	**sein**	**ihr**	**Ihr**
3. _sein_ Wörterbuch	7. _seine_ Familie	11. _Ihr_ Nachname	15. _Ihre_ Hunde
ihr	**ihr**	**ihr**	**ihr**
4. _ihr_ Familienstand	8. _ihr_ Kind	12. _ihre_ Hausaufgaben	16. _ihr_ Problem

Anwendung

1 **Was ist richtig?** Select the appropriate form of the possessive adjective.

1. (Mein / Meine) Eltern essen gern Spaghetti.
2. (Unser / Unsere) Sohn spielt gut Fußball.
3. Markus und Sabine lieben (ihren / ihre) Eltern.
4. Andrea liebt (euren / euer) Hund.
5. Hat (dein / deinen) Bruder einen Sohn?
6. Sind (Ihr / Ihre) Großeltern hier?
7. Ich lese (mein / meine) Bücher nicht.
8. Mein Vater und (sein / seinen) Freund spielen Schach.

2 **Was fehlt?** Complete each sentence with the appropriate possessive adjective.

BEISPIEL Treffen Sie ___Ihren___ Mann im Restaurant?

1. Das Baby braucht ___seine___ Mutter.
2. Ali und Lara suchen ___ihren___ Hund.
3. Ich heiße Jan, und ___mein___ Nachname ist Bauer.
4. Sarah und ___ihre___ Schwester kochen gern zusammen.
5. Herr Schulz und ___seine___ Frau sind getrennt.
6. Siehst du ___deine___ Großeltern oft?
7. Wir lieben ___unsere___ Verwandten.
8. Kinder, wo sind ___eure___ Eltern?

3 Expansion Model using possessive adjectives with students' belongings. Ex.: **Ist das sein Kuli? Nein, das ist ihr Kuli.**

3 **Schreiben** Write a sentence about each item saying whose it is.

BEISPIEL

Das sind meine Hefte.

ich

1. du Das ist dein Computer.

2. er Das ist sein Fahrrad.

3. wir Das sind unsere Bleistifte.

4. sie Das ist ihr Rucksack.

5. Sie Das ist Ihr Buch.

6. ihr Das ist eure Tafel.

4 **Antworten Sie** Answer the questions with complete sentences. Answers will vary.

BEISPIEL Wo wohnen Ihre Eltern? Meine Eltern wohnen in Dallas.

1. Wo wohnen Ihre Großeltern
2. Wie heißt Ihre Mutter?
3. Wie ist ihr Nachname?
4. Wie alt ist Ihr Vater?
5. Welche Sportarten spielt Ihre Familie gern?
6. Spielen Ihre Großeltern Schach?
7. Wie heißt Ihr bester Freund / Ihre beste Freundin?
8. Welche Bücher lesen Ihre Freunde gern?

Kommunikation

5 **Meine Familie** Use the cues to form questions. Then interview your classmates about their family members. Sample answers are provided.

> **BEISPIEL**
>
> **S1:** Spricht deine Mutter Deutsch?
> **S2:** Ja, meine Mutter spricht Deutsch.
> **S3:** Nein, meine Mutter spricht kein Deutsch.

1. Bruder / spielen / Fußball Spielt dein Bruder Fußball?
2. Vater / haben / ein Hund Hat dein Vater einen Hund?
3. Eltern / lesen / Bücher Lesen deine Eltern Bücher?
4. Großmutter / spielen / Tennis Spielt deine Großmutter Tennis?
5. Schwester / haben / grüne Augen Hat deine Schwester grüne Augen?
6. Onkel und Tante / fahren / Ski Fahren dein Onkel und deine Tante Ski?
7. Verwandte / schreiben / E-Mails Schreiben deine Verwandten E-Mails?
8. Familie / sein / groß Ist deine Familie groß?

6 **Familie und Freunde** With your partner, take turns asking and answering these questions. Answers will vary.

> **BEISPIEL**
>
> **S1:** Hat deine Mutter Haustiere?
> **S2:** Ja, meine Mutter hat zwei Haustiere. Ihre Katze
>   heißt Muffin und ihr Hund heißt Sam. Wie ist dein Vater?
> **S1:** Mein Vater ist Lehrer. Er ist vierzig Jahre alt
>   und hat zwei Brüder.

1. Hat deine Mutter Haustiere?
2. Wie ist dein Vater?
3. Wieviele Kinder haben deine Eltern?
4. Wo wohnt deine Familie?
5. Was machen deine Freunde am Samstag?
6. Was studiert dein bester Freund oder deine beste Freundin?

7 **Ich sehe etwas** Tell the class about something of yours that you can see in the classroom. Then, repeat what the people before you said they saw. Answers will vary.

> **BEISPIEL**
>
> **S1:** Ich sehe meinen Fußball.
> **S2:** Ich sehe mein Buch und Stefan sieht seinen Fußball.
> **S3:** Ich sehe meine Fotos, Maria sieht ihr Buch und
>   Stefan sieht seinen Fußball.

8 **Familienporträt** In small groups, take turns describing your families. Use possessive pronouns in the nominative and accusative case. After everyone has spoken, take turns describing your group's families to the rest of the class. Answers will vary.

> **BEISPIEL**
>
> **S1:** Das ist Inga. Ihre Mutter ist
>   Krankenschwester.
> **S2:** Das ist Michael. Seine Mutter ist Lehrerin.

5 **Expansion** If students answer a question negatively, encourage them to mention a different family member for whom the statement is true. Ex.: **Spricht deine Mutter Deutsch? Nein, meine Mutter spricht kein Deutsch. Aber mein Vater spricht Deutsch.**

6 **Expansion** After pairs have shared their answers, ask them to repeat what has been said, using the appropriate possessive adjective. Ex.: **S1: Meine Mutter hat braune Augen. S2: Seine/Ihre Mutter hat braune Augen.**

6 **Partner Chat** You can also assign activity 6 on the Supersite. Students work in pairs to record the activity online. The pair's recorded conversation will appear in your gradebook.

3A.2

Descriptive adjectives and adjective agreement

Grammar Tutorial

Startblock Adjectives can describe people, places, or things. Here are some adjectives commonly used to describe people and their physical attributes.

physical description			
alt	*old*	hübsch	*pretty*
blond	*blond*	jung	*young*
braunhaarig	*brown-haired*	klein	*small; short (stature)*
dick	*fat; thick*	kurz	*short (hair)*
dunkelhaarig	*dark-haired*	lang	*long (hair)*
dünn	*thin*	lockig	*curly*
glatt	*straight (hair)*	rothaarig	*red-headed*
groß	*big; tall*	schlank	*slim*
großartig	*terrific*	schön	*pretty; beautiful*
gut aussehend	*handsome*	schwarzhaarig	*black-haired*
hässlich	*ugly*	sportlich	*athletic*

QUERVERWEIS

In **2A Kontext**, you learned a few adjectives to describe school subjects. In **3A Kontext**, you learned some additional adjectives to describe eye color, hair color, and marital status.

- Use an adjective with no added endings after the verbs **sein** and **werden**.

  Mein Bruder ist **klein**.
  *My brother is **short**.*

  Deine Schwester wird **groß**.
  *Your sister is getting **tall**.*

- When you use an adjective before a noun, you need to include an adjective ending.

  Meine **großen** Schwestern spielen Fußball.
  *My **big** sisters play soccer.*

  Das ist eine **schöne** Katze.
  *That's a **pretty** cat.*

Suggestion Tell students that **der**-words include the definite articles, **dieser** (*this*), **mancher** (*some*), **jeder** (*each*), and **solcher** (*such*), while **ein**-words include the indefinite articles, **kein**, and possessive adjectives.

- Adjective endings depend on the case, number, and gender of the noun they modify, and whether they are preceded by a **der**-word, an **ein**-word, or neither.

  Sie lieben ihren **jungen** Sohn.
  *They love their **young** son.*

  Das **kleine** Baby hat **blaue** Augen.
  *The **little** baby has **blue** eyes.*

QUERVERWEIS

For more about **der**-words, see **8B.2**.

- Adjectives after a **der**-word have these endings.

after *der*-words			
	masculine	**feminine**	**neuter**	**plural**
nominative	der **große** Bruder	die **blonde** Schwester	das **junge** Kind	die **alten** Großeltern
accusative	den **großen** Bruder	die **blonde** Schwester	das **junge** Kind	die **alten** Großeltern

Der **alte** Mann dort ist mein Opa.
*The **old** man over there is my grandpa.*

Ich liebe die **schönen** Häuser
  in dieser Straße.
*I love the **pretty** houses on this street.*

Die **große** Frau ist meine Tante.
*The **tall** woman is my aunt.*

Irene sucht den **kleinen** Hund.
*Irene is looking for the **little** dog.*

- Adjectives preceded by an **ein**-word have these endings.

after *ein*-words				
	masculine	**feminine**	**neuter**	**plural**
nominative	ein **groß**er Bruder	eine **blonde** Schwester	ein **junges** Kind	meine **alten** Großeltern
accusative	einen **großen** Bruder	eine **blonde** Schwester	ein **junges** Kind	meine **alten** Großeltern

Mein **großer** Bruder ist ein **guter** Golfspieler.
*My **big** brother is a **good** golf player.*

Herr Wirth hat eine **sportliche** Tochter.
*Mr. Wirth has an **athletic** daughter.*

Ist deine **kleine** Schwester hier?
*Is your **little** sister here?*

Seine Großmutter hat einen **schönen** Vogel.
*His grandmother has a **beautiful** bird.*

- Unpreceded adjectives have these endings.

unpreceded				
	masculine	**feminine**	**neuter**	**plural**
nominative	**rot**er Wein	**dicke** Milch	**altes** Brot	**große** Fische
accusative	**roten** Wein	**dicke** Milch	**altes** Brot	**große** Fische

Kleine Kinder brauchen **gute** Eltern.
*Small children need **good** parents.*

Mein Vater hat **braune** Augen.
*My father has **brown** eyes.*

Altes Brot schmeckt nicht so gut.
Old bread doesn't taste so good.

Unsere Geschwister haben **lockige** Haare.
*Our siblings have **curly** hair.*

- If multiple adjectives precede the same noun, they all take the same ending.

Ist das **kleine, rothaarige** Mädchen deine Schwester?
*Is the **little, red-headed** girl your sister?*

Sie hat einen **großen, gut aussehenden** Bruder.
*She has a **tall, good-looking** brother.*

- Use **sehr** before an adjective to mean *very*. The adverb **sehr** does not take any additional endings.

Ihre Haare sind **sehr** lang.
*Her hair is **very** long.*

Ich lese ein **sehr** gutes Buch.
*I'm reading a **very** good book.*

Jetzt sind Sie dran! Write the nominative or accusative form of the adjectives.

Nominativ

1. der ___schlanke___ (schlank) Vater
2. ein ___verheirateter___ (verheiratet) Mann
3. die ___große___ (groß) Familie
4. eine ___alte___ (alt) Schwägerin
5. das ___verlobte___ (verlobt) Paar
6. die ___sportlichen___ (sportlich) Enkelkinder

Akkusativ

7. einen ___jungen___ (jung) Vater
8. die ___ledigen___ (ledig) Verwandten
9. einen ___dünnen___ (dünn) Hund
10. ein ___hübsches___ (hübsch) Mädchen
11. den ___kleinen___ (klein) Sohn
12. das ___blonde___ (blond) Kind

Anwendung

1 Kombinieren Match each adjective with its opposite.

_d_ 1. hässlich   a. jung
_f_ 2. kurz   b. dick
_e_ 3. blond   c. klein
_a_ 4. alt   d. schön
_c_ 5. groß   e. schwarzhaarig
_b_ 6. dünn   f. lang
_g_ 7. lockig   g. glatt

2 Was fehlt? Complete the sentences.

1. Ich habe einen ____großen____ (groß) Bruder.
2. Mein ____großer____ (groß) Bruder spielt Fußball.
3. Er hat einen ____kleinen____ (klein) Hund.
4. Der ____kleine____ (klein) Hund hat sehr ____kurze____ Haare.
5. Seine ____kurzen____ (kurz) Haare sind auch sehr ____dünn____ (dünn).
6. Hast du auch so einen ____kleinen____ (klein), ____schönen____ (schön) Hund?

3 Was ist richtig? Select the adjective that best completes each sentence.

BEISPIEL Martin ist sehr nett und freundlich.
Er ist ein ____großartiger____ (hässlicher, sportlicher, großartiger) Junge.

1. Sein Vater fährt viel Fahrrad und Ski. Er ist ein sehr ____sportlicher____ (sportlicher, alter, blonder) Mann.
2. Deine Schwester hat schöne Haare. Sie ist ein ____hübsches____ (großes, hässliches, hübsches) Mädchen.
3. Meine Mutter hat keine lockigen Haare. Sie hat ____glatte____ (kleine, lange, glatte) Haare.
4. Meine Eltern sind nicht mehr zusammen. Ich habe ____geschiedene____ (verheiratete, kurze, geschiedene) Eltern.
5. Ihre Enkeltochter ist 2 Jahre alt. Sie ist ein ____junges____ (junges, hässliches, dickes) Kind.
6. Die Großeltern sind 80 Jahre alt. Die ____alten____ (hübschen, alten, kleinen) Großeltern spielen Schach am Wochenende.

4 Schreiben Replace the underlined words with the words in parentheses and make any necessary changes.

BEISPIEL <u>Das</u> kleine Mädchen ist sehr sportlich. (die)
Die kleinen Mädchen sind sehr sportlich.

1. <u>Der</u> rothaarige Sohn spielt Fußball. (mein)   Mein rothaariger Sohn spielt Fußball.
2. Ihr Großvater liest <u>das</u> lange Buch. (ein)   Ihr Großvater liest ein langes Buch.
3. Ich belege <u>einen</u> schwierigen Kurs. (den)   Ich belege den schwierigen Kurs.
4. <u>Der</u> kurze, dünne Junge ist nicht sehr sportlich. (die)   Die kurzen, dünnen Jungen sind nicht sehr sportlich.
5. Siehst du <u>die</u> kleinen Kinder? (das)   Siehst du das kleine Kind?

Kommunikation

5 **Die Familie Müller** Describe the members of the Müller family.
Then compare your descriptions with a partner. Answers will vary.

BEISPIEL

Moritz ist alt und klein.

Michael *Petra* *Inez*

Rex

Moritz

Alexander

6 **Ein guter Freund** Interview a classmate to learn about one of his/her
friends. Use the questions below and add three more of your own. Answers will vary.

BEISPIEL

S1: *Hat deine beste Freundin lange Haare?*
S2: *Nein, sie hat kurze Haare.*

- Wie heißt er/sie?
- Wie alt ist er/sie?
- Ist er/sie groß oder klein?
- Hat er/sie blaue Augen?
- Ist er/sie dunkelhaarig?
- Ist er/sie sportlich?
- Ist er ein guter Student? / Ist sie eine gute Studentin?

7 **Raten Sie** Choose a famous person. In small groups, take turns asking
yes-or-no questions to determine the identity of each person. Answers will vary.

▶ **BEISPIEL**

S1: *Ist sie eine Frau?*
S2: *Ja.*
S3: *Hat sie blaue Augen?*
S2: *Nein.*

8 **Beschreiben** Pick one of your family members and describe him or her
to your partner. Take notes on your partner's description, and be prepared
to describe his or her family member to the class. Answers will vary.

BEISPIEL

Mein Onkel ist ein großer Mann. Er hat kurze schwarze Haare...

- Wie alt ist er/sie?
- Wie ist sein/ihr Familienstand?
- Hat er/sie Kinder?
- Macht er/sie Sport?
- Hat er/sie Haustiere?
- Woher kommt er/sie?

5 **Partner Chat** You can
also assign activity 5 on
the Supersite.

6 **Expansions**
• Have students bring in photos
 of their family or friends.
 Ask students to describe
 the people in the photos
 to classmates.
 Ex.: **Das ist mein sportlicher
 Vater und hier ist meine
 hübsche Mutter.**
• Have students describe their
 partners' friends to the class.

6 **Partner Chat** You can
also assign activity 6 on
the Supersite.

8 **Suggestion** Tell students
they can describe an actual
family member or invent a
fictional person.

Wiederholung

1 Wer ist wer?
In pairs, take turns choosing a person from the list and giving clues to help your partner guess which person you've chosen. Answers will vary.

BEISPIEL

S1: *Mein Vater ist ihr Mann. Meine Schwester ist ihre Tochter. Wer ist sie?*
S2: *Sie ist deine Mutter.*

1 Partner Chat You can also assign activity 1 on the Supersite.

Bruder	Schwester
Cousin	Schwiegermutter
Enkeltochter	Sohn
Großvater	Tante
Schwager	Vater

2 Saras Familie
In pairs, say what each person in Sara's family is like and what he or she likes to do. Use vocabulary from **Kontext 2B**. Answers will vary.

BEISPIEL

S1: *Wie ist Saras Bruder?*
S2: *Ihr Bruder ist groß. Er spielt gern Tennis.*

Bruder

1. Cousin   2. Neffe   3. Tante

4. Onkel   5. Großvater   6. Schwägerin

3 Arbeitsblatt
Your instructor will give you a worksheet with instructions to play Family Bingo. Get a different name for each square of the grid, then share your findings with the class. Answers will vary.

BEISPIEL

S1: *Paula, hast du einen großen Bruder?*
S2: *Ja, mein Bruder Stefan ist sehr groß.*
S1: *Paula hat einen großen Bruder.*

4 Verschiedene Menschen
In small groups, take turns picking someone in the illustration and describing him/her. The next person repeats the description and adds to it. Keep going around the group, trying to add as many details as possible. Answers will vary.

BEISPIEL

S1: *Die Frau heißt Fatima. Sie ist hübsch.*
S2: *Die Frau heißt Fatima. Sie ist hübsch und liest gern.*
S3: *Die Frau heißt Fatima. Sie ist hübsch und liest gern. Morgen geht sie spazieren.*

Daniel   Fatima   Annika
Mert und Lara   Yusuf und Tobias
Emil und Eva   Jana und Alexander

5 Diskutieren und kombinieren
Your instructor will give you and your partner each a picture of a family. Ask questions to find the six differences between the two pictures. Answers will vary.

BEISPIEL

S1: *Ist Renate blond?*
S2: *Nein. Renate ist nicht blond. Sie ist dunkelhaarig.*

6 Stammbaum
Create an illustrated family tree and share it with a classmate. Tell your partner about each of your family members, including their names, how they are related to you, what they are like, and what they like or don't like to do. Answers will vary.

BEISPIEL

S1: *Das ist meine Schwester. Sie heißt Steffi. Sie ist sehr sportlich.*
S2: *Fährt Steffi gern Fahrrad?*

Video

 Zapping

Naturkost für Hund und Katze

Vorbereitung Answer the following questions. Answers will vary.

1. Do you prefer dogs or cats? Why?
2. Which organic pet foods are you familiar with?
   Do you eat organic food yourself?

Minkas und Charlys Naturkost offers healthy cat and dog food, distributed exclusively by the online pet supply store ZooRoyal. These tasty and nutritious meals are made in the German countryside near the Northern coast using only carefully selected local products. Combining the desire to support local businesses with the love for man's furry friends, **Minkas und Charlys Naturkost's** home grown products do not add any artificial preservatives or flavoring.

Naturkost für Hund und Katze ganz aus frischen und natürlichen Zutaten

Nützliche Ausdrücke

an der Küste	on the coast
der Anteil, -e	amount, proportion, percentage
auf dem Land	in the country
ausgewogen	balanced
frisch	fresh
gesund	healthy
heimisch	local, native
die Naturkost	health food
natürlich	natural
die Zutat, -en	ingredient

Richtig oder falsch Watch the video about the pet food and decide whether the following statements are **richtig** or **falsch**. Correct the false statements.

	Richtig	Falsch
1. David does not live in the countryside.	☑	☐
2. **Minkas und Charlys Naturkost** is produced in the city. Minkas und Charlys Naturkost is produced in the countryside.	☐	☑
3. **Minkas und Charlys Naturkost** contains a low percentage of animal proteins.	☐	☑
4. **Minkas und Charlys Naturkost** for dogs and cats is made entirely from natural ingredients.	☑	☐

Minkas und Charlys Naturkost contains a high percentage of protein.

Expansion Distribute a list of additional questions about the video. Have the students watch it again and jot down the answers to the questions. You may want to assign only one or two questions to each student. Discuss the answers as a class. **Wie heißt die Katze? Wie heißt der Hund? Welche Zutaten sind in Minkas und Charlys Naturkost? Woher kommen diese Zutaten? Was hat in dieser Naturkost nichts zu suchen? Warum nicht?**

Diskussion Discuss these questions with a partner. Answers will vary.

1. What are the advantages and disadvantages of natural foods for pets?
2. Do you think it is a good idea to support local products? Why or why not?

Präsentation Write a script for a TV or online commercial that features a new product using only natural ingredients. Use these questions to guide your writing. Answers will vary.

Wie heißt Ihr Produkt?   Für wen ist es?   Beschreiben Sie das Produkt.

Wie sind sie? Vocabulary Tools

Wortschatz

persönliche Beschreibungen	*personal descriptions*
(un)angenehm	*(un)pleasant*
arm	*poor; unfortunate*
bescheiden	*modest*
egoistisch	*selfish*
ernst	*serious*
freundlich	*friendly*
gemein	*mean*
gierig	*greedy*
großzügig	*generous*
intellektuell	*intellectual*
intelligent	*intelligent*
langsam	*slow*
mutig	*brave*
naiv	*naïve*
nervös	*nervous*
nett	*nice*
neugierig	*curious*
reich	*rich*
schlecht	*bad*
schüchtern	*shy*
schwach	*weak*
stolz	*proud*
toll	*great*
lächeln	*to smile*
lachen	*to laugh*
weinen	*to cry*
Berufe	*professions*
der Architekt, -en / die Architektin, -nen	*architect*
der Geschäftsmann (*pl.* Geschäftsleute) / die Geschäftsfrau, -en	*businessman / businesswoman*
der Ingenieur, -e / die Ingenieurin, -nen	*engineer*
der Journalist, -en / die Journalistin, -nen	*journalist*
der Rechtsanwalt, ⸚e / die Rechtsanwältin, -nen	*lawyer*

Er ist stark. *He is strong.*

der Kellner, - **(die Kellnerin, -nen)**

Er ist schnell. *He is fast.*

Sie sind faul. *They are lazy.*

Er ist fleißig. *He is hardworking.*

der Besitzer, - **(die Besitzerin, -nen)** *owner*

diskret

müde *tired*

eifersüchtig *jealous*

Sie ist besorgt. *She is worried.*

Er ist traurig. *He is sad.*

More activities

 vhlcentral | WB pp. 39-40 | LM p. 25 | Online activities

ACHTUNG

Note that the plural of **der Geschäftsmann** is **die Geschäftsleute; die Leute** means *people*.

die Friseurin, -nen
(der Friseur, -e)
hairdresser

Er ist lustig.
He is funny.

Sie sind glücklich/froh.
They are happy.

Sie ist süß.
She is sweet.

der Musiker, -
(die Musikerin, -nen)

Anwendung

1 **Expansion** Bring in pictures of famous people with different professions and ask students: **Wie heißt diese Person? Was ist ihr/sein Beruf?**

1 Kombinieren Match these famous people with their professions.

1 **Expansion** Play the audio again and have students correct the false statements.

d 1. Sheryl Sandberg	a. Architekt
f 2. Ferdinand Porsche	b. Rechtsanwältin
a 3. Walter Gropius	c. Musiker
e 4. Diane Sawyer	d. Geschäftsfrau
c 5. Ludwig van Beethoven	e. Journalistin
b 6. Sonia Sotomayor	f. Ingenieur

2 Ja oder nein? Write Ja if the word you hear indicates a profession and Nein if it does not.

1. __Ja__
2. __Nein__
3. __Nein__
4. __Ja__

5. __Ja__
6. __Nein__
7. __Ja__
8. __Ja__

3 Gegenteile Complete each sentence with the opposite adjective.

1. Der Geschäftsmann ist nicht <u>arm</u>, er ist __reich__.
2. Die Besitzerin ist nicht <u>gierig</u>, sie ist __großzügig__.
3. Die Tennisspieler sind nicht <u>schwach</u>, sie sind __stark__.
4. Der Rechtsanwalt ist nicht <u>fleißig</u>, er ist __faul__.
5. Die Architektin ist nicht <u>stolz</u>, sie ist __bescheiden__.
6. Unser Hund ist nicht <u>gemein</u>, er ist __freundlich/nett__.

3 **Expansion** Introduce adjectives with visuals: **Ist diese Person schnell oder langsam? Sportlich oder unsportlich? Freundlich oder gemein?** etc.

4 Was fehlt? Select the word that best describes each person.

faul	glücklich	neugierig
fleißig	müde	traurig

1. Klara arbeitet viel und schnell. Sie ist __fleißig__.
2. Emma lacht und lächelt viel. Sie ist __glücklich__.
3. Maria macht keine Hausaufgaben. Sie ist __faul__.
4. Tom schläft nicht viel. Er ist __müde__.
5. Erik weint. Er ist __traurig__.
6. Greta hat viele Fragen. Sie ist __neugierig__.

5 Identifizieren Listen to the audio and write down the occupation that best fits each description.

Ingenieure	Rechtsanwalt
Geschäftsleute	Journalisten
Architekten	Musiker

1. __Musiker__
2. __Architekten__
3. __Geschäftsleute__

4. __Ingenieure__
5. __Journalisten__
6. __Rechtsanwalt__

Kommunikation

7 Suggestion Have students brainstorm a list of adjectives to describe themselves and their ideal partner before they start composing their ads.

---

6 Berufe In pairs, take turns replying to the questions based on the images.

▶ **BEISPIEL**

S1: Ist Karl Musiker?
S2: Nein, er ist Kellner.

1. Ist Helga Ingenieurin?
Nein, sie ist Geschäftsfrau/Rechtsanwältin.

2. Ist Ulrich Architekt?
Nein, er ist Friseur.

3. Sind Markus, Jan und Tobias Rechtsanwälte?
Nein, sie sind Musiker.

4. Ist Birgit Kellnerin?
Nein, sie ist Journalistin.

5. Ist Stefan Friseur?
Nein, er ist Geschäftsmann.

6. Ist Claudia Musikerin?
Nein, sie ist Ingenieurin/Architektin.

---

7 Partnersuche

Read Georg's personal ad and discuss with a partner whether Maria or Jessica would be a better match for him. Be ready to defend your opinion to the class. Answers will vary. **7 Partner Chat** You can also assign activity 7 on the Supersite.

Georg, 32 Jahre

Hallo! Ich heiße Georg, ich bin 32 Jahre alt, 182 cm groß, schlank, dunkelhaarig und habe braune Augen. Ich bin ein netter Mann, optimistisch und intelligent. Ich habe viele Hobbys, spiele Fußball, Tennis und Handball, sehe gern Filme und koche auch gern und gut. Ich bin geschieden und habe eine kleine Tochter. Meine ideale Partnerin ist zwischen 26 und 32 Jahre alt, nicht zu klein (ca. 168 cm), blond, schlank, aktiv und sportlich. Sie muss gern essen und sie muss Kinder gern haben! Wenn du das bist, dann schicke mir eine E-Mail an nettergeorg@gvz.de.

Maria
23 Jahre
groß (182 cm)
lustig
schüchtern
aktiv

Jessica
28 Jahre
klein (165 cm)
sportlich
intellektuell
schlank

7 Expansion Ask students to explain their choice of the ideal partner for Georg. Encourage them to use opposite adjectives. Ex.: **Jessica ist nicht groß, sie ist klein**.

9 Suggestion As a class, brainstorm some of the questions partners will need to ask for this activity. Ex.: **Wo wohnst du? Was ist dein Beruf? Bist du verheiratet? Wie viele Kinder hast du?** Have pairs act out their conversations for the class.

---

8 Wunschpartner

Use Georg's ad as a model and describe yourself and your ideal partner. Include details such as profession, age, physical characteristics, etc. Then take turns reading the ads and guessing who wrote them.

---

9 Klassentreffen

Imagine you are at the 10th reunion for your high-school class. With a partner, role-play a conversation between two old friends who haven't seen each other since graduation.

BEISPIEL

S1: Wo wohnst du, Sabine? Was ist dein Beruf?
S2: Ich wohne jetzt in Hamburg. Ich arbeite als Journalistin. Und du?

- Find out where your friend now lives and what his or her profession is.
- Ask about your friend's marital status, whether he or she has children, and, if so, what they are like.
- Ask your friend to describe his or her significant other.

---

10 Klatsch und Tratsch

Heike is catching up with her cousin Lisa, who is a real **Klatschbase** (*gossip*). With a partner, write a conversation in which Lisa gives her opinion of the guests at a recent family wedding. Answers will vary.

BEISPIEL

S1: Wie ist Peters Frau?
S2: Sie ist hübsch und sehr schlank, aber eine unangenehme Person und ein bisschen gemein.

10 Expansion Hand out pictures of famous people to pairs or groups of students and ask them to write some gossip about each person.

Aussprache und Rechtschreibung Audio

Consonant clusters

Some German consonant combinations are not common in English. In the clusters **gn**, **kn**, **pf**, and **ps**, both consonants are pronounced. Do not add a vowel sound between these consonants when you pronounce them.

Gnom	Knödel	Pferd	Napf	psychisch

The German **ng** is always pronounced like the English *ng* in *singer*, never like the consonant combination in *finger*, regardless of where it appears in a word.

Ring	fangen	jung	Prüfungen	entlang

Some German letters represent the sound of a consonant cluster. The letter **x** is pronounced like the consonant combination **ks**. The letter **z** and the consonant combinations **tz** and **ts** are pronounced like the *ts* in the English word *hats*. The letter combination **qu** is pronounced *kv*.

extra	Zahn	Qualität	sitzt	Äquator

1 **Aussprechen** Practice saying these words aloud.

1. Gnade
2. knicken
3. Pfeil
4. Topf
5. Pseudonym
6. lang
7. bringen
8. Examen
9. Zoo
10. Mozart
11. Quatsch
12. Aquarell

Suggestion Have students look at the sample words and sentences on this page to identify cognates and words they already know. Tell students the meanings of any unfamiliar words or phrases.

2 **Nachsprechen** Practice saying these sentences aloud.

1. Die Katze streckt sich und legt den Kopf in den Nacken.
2. Felix fängt eine Qualle aus dem Ozean.
3. Der Zoowärter zähmt ein quergestreiftes Zebra.
4. Herr Quast brät Knödel in der Pfanne.
5. Der Gefangene bittet Xerxes um Gnade.
6. Das Taxi fährt kreuz und quer durch die Schweiz.

3 **Sprichwörter** Practice reading these sayings aloud.

Pferde lassen sich zum Wasser bringen, aber nicht zum Trinken zwingen.[1]

Nachts sind alle Katzen grau.[2]

[1] You can lead a horse to water, but you can't make it drink.
[2] At night, all cats are grey.

More activities

vhlcentral   LM p. 26   Online activities

Unsere Mitbewohner Video

George trifft Meline im Museum und Hans trifft Sabite am Brandenburger Tor.
Sie reden über ihre Mitbewohner. Oder reden sie über mehr?

Vorbereitung Before showing the video, ask students to brainstorm what adjectives they would use to describe each of the characters. Write these words on the board.

GEORGE Hallo, Meline. Wer ist das?
MELINE Fritz Sommer. Langweilig. George, du sollst nicht immer alles so ernst nehmen.
GEORGE Du bist lustig.
MELINE Und du bist süß, mein kleiner amerikanischer Freund.

HANS Hallo, Sabite!
SABITE Hallo, Hans! Wie geht's? Oh, sei nicht traurig. Du bist nett und großzügig. Können wir Freunde sein?

MELINE Oh, armer Hans!
GEORGE Sei nicht gemein, Meline.
MELINE Bin ich nicht. Sabite ist künstlerisch, lebhaft und verrückt.

GEORGE Ist Sabite eine gute Mitbewohnerin?
MELINE Sabite ist eine liebenswürdige und bescheidene Person. Ihre Kunst ist hässlich und schlecht!

SABITE Ich bin so stolz auf dich, Hans. Du bist ein echter Freund. Danke, dass du mir hilfst.
HANS Keine Ursache.
SABITE Meline ist gemein.
HANS Meline ist unangenehm.

MELINE Hans ist intellektuell, aber naiv.
GEORGE Ihn als Mitbewohner zu haben, ist langweilig. Er liest und sieht fern bis um zwei Uhr früh. Ich habe morgens Uni.
MELINE Kann er nicht ohne Fernsehen lernen?
GEORGE Nein, das kann er nicht.

ÜBUNGEN

1 **Wer ist das?** Which character does each statement describe: George, Meline, Sabite, or Hans?

1. _____George_____ ist besorgt um seine Noten.
2. _____Meline_____ hat schöne Augen.
3. _____Sabite_____ macht hässliche und schlechte Kunst.
4. Jungen finden _____Meline_____ geheimnisvoll und faszinierend.
5. _____Hans_____ ist nett und großzügig.
6. _____Hans_____ ist ein echter Freund.
7. _____George_____ ist ein netter Typ.
8. _____Sabite_____ ist künstlerisch, lebhaft und verrückt.
9. _____George_____ ist süß.
10. _____Hans_____ ist intellektuell, aber naiv.

PERSONEN George Hans Meline Sabite

7

SABITE Ich möchte, dass sie einen neuen Freund hat.
HANS Bist du eifersüchtig?
SABITE Was?
HANS Sie ist lebhaft und hübsch. Sie hat sehr schöne Augen. Jungen finden sie geheimnisvoll und faszinierend.

8

SABITE Ist George ein guter Mitbewohner?
HANS Er ist ein netter Typ. Er ist besorgt um seine Noten. Ich sehe nachts fern und lese und er lernt bis zwei Uhr morgens.

9

SABITE Findest du sie hübsch?
HANS Wen?
SABITE Meline.
HANS Ich weiß nicht.

10

GEORGE Meline, Sabite meint es ernst mit Torsten. Du darfst nicht...
MELINE Ich finde nicht, dass sie gut zusammenpassen. Aber mach dir keine Sorgen. Ich kann sie nicht auseinanderbringen. Sie machen bald Schluss, auch ohne meine Hilfe.

Nützliche Ausdrücke

- **etwas ernst nehmen**
  to take something seriously
- **Du bist lustig.**
  You should talk. (lit. You're funny.)
- **Ihn als Mitbewohner zu haben, ist langweilig.**
  Having him as a roommate is boring.
- **Sei nicht traurig.**
  Don't be sad.
- **Danke, dass du mir hilfst.**
  Thanks for helping me.
- **Keine Ursache.**
  You're welcome.
- **Ich möchte, dass sie einen neuen Freund hat.**
  I want her to get a new boyfriend.
- **Jungen finden sie geheimnisvoll und faszinierend.**
  Boys find her mysterious and fascinating.
- **besorgt sein um**
  to be worried about
- **Du darfst nicht...**
  You mustn't...
- **Ich finde nicht, dass sie gut zusammenpassen.**
  I don't think they're a good match.
- **Schluss machen**
  to break up

3B.1
- **Ich kann sie nicht auseinanderbringen.**
  I can't break them up.

3B.2
- **Er ist besorgt um seine Noten.**
  He's worried about his grades.

3B.3
- **Mach dir keine Sorgen.**
  Don't worry.

---

2 **Schreiben** Write a brief description of a well-known person in your school or community, using as many descriptive adjectives as you can. Do not mention his/her name. Be prepared to read your description to the class, who will guess this person's identity. Answers will vary.

freundlich	intellektuell	schüchtern
glücklich	lustig	traurig
großzügig	mutig	...

3 **Vertiefung** Research a famous German person and present him/her to the class. Use adjectives to describe his/her physical appearance and personality. Explain why you chose this person. Be prepared to share your description with your classmates. Answers will vary.

3 Suggestion You may wish to assign individuals for students to research, such as Diane Kruger, Hermann Hesse, Wilhelm Röntgen, Hugo Boss, etc.

You might also want students to use a visual aid for their presentation.

More activities

vhlcentral   VM p. 6   Online activities

Suggestion Point out to students that, as they have seen in the **Fotoroman**, German speakers also use **Freund/Freundin** to refer to a boyfriend or girlfriend. Encourage students to think about misunderstandings that might arise from the different ways that Americans and Germans use the word "friend."

IM FOKUS

Auf unsere Freunde! Reading

TIPP

In German, many adjectives can be transformed into nouns.

bekannt → **der / die Bekannte**
known — *acquaintance*

besonders → **(etwas) Besonderes**
special — *something special*

gleich → **das Gleiche**
same — *the same one/the same thing*

IN DIESER° FACEBOOK-ZEIT HABEN wir alle viele „Freunde". Was ist also ein Kumpel°, mit dem Sie hin und wieder auf Partys gehen, und was ist ein echter° Freund? Deutsche sagen nicht so schnell „Freund" wie Amerikaner. In Deutschland ist es etwas Besonderes° ein „Freund" zu sein.

Wirklich gute Freunde hat man in Deutschland wahrscheinlich höchstens° vier oder fünf. Ein echter Freund zu sein bedeutet, dass° man sich sehr gut und vielleicht auch schon sehr lange kennt°. Die meisten Leute in Deutschland sagen, dass sie ihre Freunde schon aus der Schule oder aus der Kinderzeit kennen. Nur

weil° man einmal zusammen Kaffee getrunken hat°, ist man noch lange kein Freund.

In der Gruppe kennen sich alle mehr oder weniger gut. Trotzdem° nennen sich die Leute in einer Gruppe „Kumpel", nicht „Freunde". Die anderen Leute, die man kennt, nennt man meistens „Bekannte".

Es gibt also drei Gruppen von Menschen um eine Person: Die meisten Menschen sind Bekannte. Die größere Gruppe sind die Kumpel. Und nur eine sehr kleine Gruppe sind richtige Freunde. Aber mit diesen Freunden kann man alles teilen°. Also: Auf Freunde!

Auf unsere Freunde! *Here's to our friends!* **dieser** *this* **Kumpel** *buddy* **echter** *real* **etwas Besonderes** *something special* **wahrscheinlich höchstens** *probably at most* **bedeutet, dass** *means that* **sich... kennt** *know each other* **Nur weil** *Just because* **getrunken hat** *has drunk* **Trotzdem** *Nevertheless* **teilen** *share*

---

1 **Im Fokus** Indicate whether each statement is **richtig** or **falsch**. Correct the false statements. Then discuss the last question with a partner.

1. Mit einem Kumpel geht man hin und wieder ins Kino oder auf Partys.
   Richtig.
2. Mit Bekannten kann man alles teilen.
   Falsch. Mit echten Freunden kann man alles teilen.

 Diskussion How many friends do you have? How many acquaintances? How do you like to spend your time together?

2 **Die deutschsprachige Welt** Indicate whether each statement is **richtig** or **falsch**. Correct the false statements. Then discuss the last question with a partner.

1. Nur in Bayern gibt es das Brautstehlen.
   Falsch. Das Brautstehlen gibt es auch in Österreich und in der Schweiz.
2. Der Bräutigam findet seine Braut in einer Gaststätte.
   Richtig.

 Diskussion What typically happens at a wedding reception in your country? How are the traditions different in Germany?

DEUTSCH IM ALLTAG

Wie wir Menschen sind

aufrichtig	sincere
besserwisserisch	know-it-all (adj.)
eingebildet	arrogant
geduldig	patient
geizig	stingy
liebevoll	loving
locker	easy-going
oberflächlich	superficial
ruhig	calm
weise	wise
zuverlässig	reliable

DIE DEUTSCHSPRACHIGE WELT

Es wird geheiratet!°

Wie wünscht° man dem neuen Paar ein frohes Eheleben°? In **Bayern**, **Österreich** und **in der Schweiz** ist das **Brautstehlen°** eine lustige Tradition. Freunde stehlen die Braut und bringen sie von Gaststätte° zu Gaststätte. Der Bräutigam° muss sie finden... und alle Getränke bezahlen°! Die **Deutschen** und die **Österreicher** tragen den Ring meistens an der rechten° Hand. Aber **in der Schweiz** trägt man ihn an der linken° Hand. Die ist dem Herzen näher°.

Es wird geheiratet! *Someone's getting married!* **wünscht** *wishes* **Eheleben** *married life* **Brautstehlen** *stealing of the bride* **Gaststätte** *restaurant* **Bräutigam** *groom* **Getränke bezahlen** *pay for the drinks* **rechten** *right* **linken** *left* **dem Herzen näher** *closer to the heart*

Herbert Grönemeyer

Seit den siebziger Jahren° ist Herbert Grönemeyer ein Begriff° für Deutsche, und etwas später wird er auch im Ausland durch seine Rolle in dem Kriegsfilm° *Das Boot* (1981) bekannt°. Der jetzige° Sänger°, Schauspieler°, Komponist° und Produzent° lebt als Kind in der Industriestadt° Bochum und bekommt schon früh Musikunterricht°. Er studiert einige Jahre an der Universität in Bochum, macht aber keinen Abschluss, sondern geht ans° Theater und singt nebenbei°. Am Anfang° war er nicht erfolgreich° als Musiker, aber nun schreibt er seine eigenen° Songs und wird dann durch sein Album *4630 Bochum* bekannt. Seitdem hat er parallele Karrieren° als Schauspieler und Musiker und komponiert° sogar den Soundtrack zu dem Hollywood-Film *The American* (mit George Clooney). Sein Album *Mensch* (2002) macht ihn zum kommerziell° erfolgreichsten° zeitgenössischen° Musiker in Deutschland.

erfolgreich *successful* **Seit den siebziger Jahren** *Since the 1970s* **Begriff** *concept* **Kriegsfilm** *WWII movie* **bekannt** *well-known* **jetzige** *current* **Sänger** *singer* **Schauspieler** *actor* **Komponist** *composer* **Produzent** *producer* **Industriestadt** *industrial city* **Musikunterricht** *music lessons* **geht ans** *pursued* **nebenbei** *on the side* **Am Anfang** *initially* **erfolgreich** *successful* **eigenen** *own* **Karrieren** *careers* **komponiert** *composes* **komerziell** *comercially* **erfolgreichsten** *most successful* **zeitgenössischen** *contemporary*

IM INTERNET

Sind die Hochzeitsbräuche (*wedding traditions*) anders (*different*) in Deutschland als in den USA?

Find out more at **vhlcentral.com**.

3 **Suggestion** You may want to teach students the expression **ich glaube**.

3 **Porträt** Indicate whether each statement is **richtig** or **falsch**. Correct the false statements. Then discuss the last question with a partner.

1. Herbert Grönemeyer interessiert sich nur für Musik.
   Falsch. Er interessiert sich für Musik, Film und Theater.
2. Grönemeyer hat nie an einer Universität studiert.
   Falsch. Er hat einige Semester an der Universität in Bochum studiert.

Diskussion How important is music in your life? Do you play an instrument or sing? What kind of music do you like to listen to? Discuss in German.

spielen *to play...* **singen** *to sing* **tanzen** *to dance*

4 **Deutschsprachige Musiker** Write a brief synopsis of the life of a famous contemporary German, Austrian, or Swiss musician.

Die deutschsprachige Welt Tell students that weddings in Germany typically have two parts: the legal ceremony (which is required) at the **Standesamt**, and the church wedding. Before the wedding day, friends and family may gather in front of the bride's home to break pottery, because "**Scherben bringen Glück**" (*shards bring luck*).

3B.1

Modals ⓢ Grammar Tutorial

Teaching Tip You may want to assign the grammar tutorial **3B.1 Modals** on the Supersite for students to watch before they come to class.

Startblock In both English and German, modal verbs modify the meaning of another verb.

Können wir Freunde sein?

Oh, George, du **darfst** nicht so ernst sein.

- Modals express an attitude towards an action, such as permission, obligation, ability, desire, or necessity. *May*, *can*, and *must* are examples of English modals.

Suggestion Explain to students that there are six modals in total. The modal **mögen** will be presented in **4A.2**.

modals	
dürfen	*to be allowed to, may*
können	*to be able to, can*
müssen	*to have to, must*
sollen	*to be supposed to*
wollen	*to want to*

- Except for **sollen**, all of the German modals are irregular in their present tense singular forms.

modals in the present tense					
	dürfen	**können**	**müssen**	**sollen**	**wollen**
ich	darf	kann	muss	soll	will
du	darfst	kannst	musst	sollst	willst
er/sie/es	darf	kann	muss	soll	will
wir	dürfen	können	müssen	sollen	wollen
ihr	dürft	könnt	müsst	sollt	wollt
Sie/sie	dürfen	können	müssen	sollen	wollen

Expansion Give students example sentences in English, with and without modals, to illustrate their use. Ex.: *He does his homework. He should do his homework. He must do his homework. He can do his homework. He wants to do his homework. He is allowed to do his homework.* Point out how each modal changes the meaning of the sentence.

- When you use a modal to modify the meaning of another verb, put the conjugated form of the modal in second position. Put the infinitive of the other verb at the end of the sentence.

Ich **muss** Französisch **lernen**.
*I **have to study** French.*

Ich **will** Französisch **lernen**.
*I **want to learn** French.*

- To form a yes-or-no question, move the modal verb to the beginning of the sentence, while the verb it modifies remains at the end.

  Willst du Wasser **trinken**?
  *Do you **want to drink** water?*

  Könnt ihr eurer Mutter **helfen**?
  *Can you **help** your mother?*

- **Dürfen** expresses permission.

  Mama, **darf** ich heute Nachmittag schwimmen gehen?
  *Mom, **may** I go swimming this afternoon?*

  Nein, Lina, du **darfst** heute nicht schwimmen gehen.
  *No, Lina, you **may** not go swimming today.*

- **Können** expresses ability.

  Peter **kann** Ski fahren.
  *Peter **can** ski.*

  Kannst du Fahrrad fahren?
  Can you ride a bicycle?

- **Müssen** expresses obligation.

  Jasmin und Moritz **müssen** viel lernen.
  *Jasmin and Moritz **have to** study a lot.*

  Muss Maria Spanisch lernen?
  *Does Maria **have to** learn Spanish?*

- **Sollen** conveys the expectation that a task be completed (*to be supposed to*). Note that, unlike the English *should* or *ought*, **sollen** implies an expectation that comes from someone other than the subject.

  Du **sollst** das Buch lesen.
  *You **are supposed to** read the book.*

  Soll ich nach Hause gehen?
  ***Should** I go home?*

- **Wollen** expresses desire.

  Sie **wollen** Musikerinnen werden.
  *They **want to** become musicians.*

  Willst du eine Katze haben?
  *Do you **want to** get a cat?*

More activities

vhlcentral

WB
pp. 41-42

LM
p. 27

Online activities

Jetzt sind Sie dran! Complete the sentences.

1. Die Lehrerin ___soll___ (sollen) langsam sprechen.
2. Ihr ___sollt___ (sollen) eure Hausaufgaben nicht vergessen.
3. Was ___sollen___ (sollen) wir heute machen?
4. Der Musiker ___kann___ (können) Gitarre spielen.
5. Ich ___kann___ (können) meinen Rucksack nicht finden.
6. ___Kannst___ (Können) du nach Deutschland reisen?
7. Du ___musst___ (müssen) ein Wörterbuch kaufen.
8. Ein Geschäftsmann ___muss___ (müssen) sehr fleißig sein.
9. Wir ___müssen___ (müssen) das Matheproblem an die Tafel schreiben.
10. Das Paar ___darf___ (dürfen) heiraten.
11. Die Kinder ___dürfen___ (dürfen) hier Fußball spielen.
12. Du ___darfst___ (dürfen) nicht in das Klassenzimmer gehen.
13. Ich ___will___ (wollen) Architektin werden.
14. Die Kinder ___wollen___ (wollen) Fremdsprachen studieren.
15. ___Wollt___ (Wollen) ihr die Fotos sehen?

Anwendung

1 **Entscheiden Sie** Select the correct form of the modal.

1. Ich (sollen / (soll)) Gitarre spielen.
2. Wir ((dürfen) / darf) keine Schokolade essen.
3. ((Willst) / Wollt) du in die Bibliothek gehen?
4. Ihr (musst / (müsst)) eure Großeltern begrüßen.
5. Annika ((kann) / können) ihre Cousine nicht finden.
6. Max und Nils (kann / (können)) samstags lange schlafen.

2 **Was fehlt?** Complete the sentences.

1. Die Kellner _____sollen_____ (sollen) das Essen bringen.
2. Du _____kannst_____ (können) Deutsch lernen.
3. Wir _____müssen_____ (müssen) einen Beruf finden.
4. Ihr _____dürft_____ (dürfen) einen Film sehen.
5. Ich _____will_____ (wollen) Journalist werden.

3 **Schreiben** Rewrite the sentences using the cues.

BEISPIEL Antonia ist Musikerin. (wollen)
Antonia will Musikerin sein.

1. Die Ingenieure bauen eine neue Maschine. (müssen) Die Ingenieure müssen eine neue Maschine bauen.
2. Der Journalist reist nach Deutschland. (dürfen) Der Journalist darf nach Deutschland reisen.
3. Die Geschäftsfrau und der Geschäftsmann sind nicht gierig. (sollen)
Die Geschäftsfrau und der Geschäftsmann sollen nicht gierig sein.
4. Meine Tante und ich tanzen Tango. (können) Meine Tante und ich können Tango tanzen.
5. Ich werde Friseurin. (wollen) Ich will Friseurin werden.

4 **Expansion** Have students use these questions as the basis for a partner interview. Instead of using the subjects given, have them pose the questions to one another.
Ex.: **Darfst du schwimmen gehen? Ja, ich darf schwimmen gehen.**

4 **Fragen** Use the cues to form questions about the images.

BEISPIEL
ich / schwimmen
gehen / dürfen

Darf ich schwimmen gehen?

1. du / Ski fahren / können
Kannst du Ski fahren?

2. ich / jetzt lernen / sollen
Soll ich jetzt lernen?

3. Erika / Fußball spielen / wollen
Will Erika Fußball spielen?

4. wir / Musik hören / dürfen
Dürfen wir Musik hören?

5. Thomas / Musiker werden / wollen
Will Thomas Musiker werden?

6. ihr / viele Bücher lesen / müssen
Müsst ihr viele Bücher lesen?

Kommunikation

5 **Viele Wünsche** In pairs, take turns saying what each person wants to do. Then, imagine what they must or should do to achieve that goal.

Sample answers are provided.

BEISPIEL mein Bruder / nach Deutschland fahren

S1: *Mein Bruder will nach Deutschland fahren.*
S2: *Er soll Deutsch lernen.*

1. meine Freundin / Architektin werden Meine Freundin will Architektin werden.
2. ich / das Fußballspiel gewinnen Ich will das Fußballspiel gewinnen.
3. wir / einen Hund haben Wir wollen einen Hund haben.
4. mein Vater / ein neues Auto kaufen Mein Vater will ein neues Auto kaufen.
5. meine Schwester / gute Noten haben Meine Schwester will gute Noten haben.
6. mein Onkel / kurze Haare haben Mein Onkel will kurze Haare haben.

6 **Berufe** With a partner, offer advice to help these people get the jobs they want. Answers will vary.

BEISPIEL Mira und Maria / Ingenieurinnen

S1: *Mira und Maria wollen Ingenieurinnen werden.*
S2: *Sie sollen viel lernen.*

1. Emil und Hasan / Rechtsanwälte
2. David und Hanna / Musiker
3. Julia / Journalistin
4. Greta und Dilara / Geschäftsfrauen

7 **Einladungen** In small groups, take turns inviting each other to take part in these activities. If you turn down an invitation, explain what you want to do, should do, or must do instead, and suggest a different activity. Answers will vary.

▶ **BEISPIEL**

S1: *Willst du Tennis spielen?*
S2: *Ich kann nicht. Ich muss Hausaufgaben machen.*
Aber wir können morgen spazieren gehen.

1.

2.

3.

4.

5.

6.

5 **Expansion** Have students say what they want to do and let other students give them advice. Ex.: **Ich will gute Noten bekommen. Du musst viel lernen.**

5 **Partner Chat** You can also assign activity 5 on the Supersite.

3B.2 | **Prepositions with the accusative** Grammar Tutorial

Startblock In **1B.1**, you learned the accusative endings for definite and indefinite articles. You also learned that the direct object in German always takes the accusative case. In addition, the objects of certain prepositions are always in the accusative case.

Das Trinkgeld ist **für den Kellner**.
*The tip is **for the waiter**.*

Der Hund läuft **durch die Wälder**.
*The dog is running **through the woods**.*

- Prepositions and prepositional phrases describe time, manner, and place, and answer the questions *when*, *how*, and *where*.

um 8 Uhr
at 8 o'clock

ohne meinen Bruder
without my brother

gegen die Wand
against the wall

- Here are some common accusative prepositions.

prepositions with the accusative							
bis	*until, to*	entlang	*along*	gegen	*against*	pro	*per*
durch	*through*	für	*for*	ohne	*without*	um	*around; at (time)*

Der Besitzer kommt **durch die Tür**.
*The owner is coming **through the door**.*

Was hast du **gegen meinen Freund**?
*What do you have **against my boyfriend**?*

- The prepositions **durch**, **für**, and **um**, when followed by the neuter definite article **das**, may be contracted to **durchs**, **fürs**, and **ums**. These contractions are frequently used in speech and are acceptable in writing.

Das Spielzeug ist **fürs** Baby.
*The toy is **for the baby**.*

Die Kinder laufen **ums** Haus.
*The kids are running **around** the house.*

- The accusative preposition **bis** is frequently used with time expressions. When **bis** comes before a proper noun, such as **Samstag** or **März**, no article is necessary.

Ich bin **bis April** in Deutschland.
*I'm in Germany **until April**.*

Wir **bleiben bis nächsten Monat** in Köln.
*We are **staying** in Cologne **until next month**.*

- **Pro** is also an accusative preposition. The object it precedes takes no article.

Der Kellner verdient 300 Euro **pro Woche**.
*The waiter earns 300 euros **per week**.*

Das Auto fährt 230 Kilometer **pro Stunde**.
*The car goes 230 kilometers **per hour**.*

- The accusative is also used with objects that precede **entlang**.

Wir gehen **den Fluss entlang**.
*We are going **down the river**.*

Ich fahre **die Straße entlang**.
*I'm driving **along the road**.*

Suggestion Help students remember the most common accusative prepositions with the mnemonic **DOGFU: durch, ohne, gegen, für, um** or by having them sing "**durch, für, gegen, ohne, um**" to the tune of "Raindrops keep falling on my head."

More activities

S
vhlcentral

WB
pp. 43–44

LM
p. 28

Online activities

Jetzt sind Sie dran! **Select the preposition that best completes each sentence.**

1. Die Frau geht (ohne / pro) ihren Mann einkaufen.
2. Der Hund läuft (durch / gegen) den Park.
3. Die Mutter braucht ein Spielzeug (um / für) ihre Tochter.
4. Was haben die Besitzer (gegen / bis) die Musik?
5. Die Kellnerin geht (durch / um) den Tisch.

6. Die Taxifahrt kostet 2 € (für / pro) Kilometer.
7. Ich gehe den Fluss (entlang / bis).
8. Die Journalisten arbeiten (gegen / bis) Mitternacht.

Anwendung und Kommunikation

1 Was ist richtig? Select the preposition that best completes each sentence.

| bis | entlang | für | gegen | ohne | um |

1. ___Um___ 8 Uhr muss ich arbeiten.
2. Der kleine Junge wirft den Ball ___gegen___ die Wand.
3. ___Ohne___ meine Schwester gehe ich nicht campen.
4. Das Auto fährt die Straße ___entlang___.
5. Sara kauft einen Kaffee ___für___ ihre Mutter.
6. Mein Onkel spielt ___bis___ 6 Uhr Fußball.

2 Bilden Sie Sätze Write eight sentences using items from each column. Pay attention to word order and accusative endings. Use each preposition once.

BEISPIEL Herr und Frau Becker / heute Abend eine Party geben / um / 8 Uhr
Heute Abend um 8 Uhr geben Herr und Frau Becker eine Party.

der Besitzer	angeln gehen	bis	Haustiere
du	beginnen	durch	Woche
ich	in Berlin bleiben	entlang	der Park
die Journalistin	50 Stunden arbeiten	für	19 Uhr
das Konzert	fahren	gegen	Samstag
Herr Bauer	laufen	ohne	die Straße
meine Schwester	lernen	pro	mein Bruder
wir	sein	um	die Prüfung

3 Umfrage In pairs, take turns asking and answering the questions. Answers will vary.

BEISPIEL

S1: *Um wie viel Uhr fährst du zur Uni?*
S2: *Ich fahre um 8 Uhr zur Uni.*

1. Um wie viel Uhr beginnt dein Unterricht?
2. Wie viele Stunden schläfst du pro Nacht?
3. Für wen kaufst du gern Blumen?
4. Ohne was kannst du nicht leben?
5. Gegen welche Mannschaften spielst du gern?

4 Die Geburtstagsfeier In small groups, write four sentences describing the illustration. Use at least four prepositions with the accusative.

BEISPIEL

Die Familie geht ohne den Hund spazieren.

Possible answers: Der Hund läuft durch das Spielfeld. Die Äpfel sind für die Kinder. Die Jungen spielen ohne ihre Schwester. Die Eltern wollen um 12 Uhr essen.

3 Video Virtual Chat You can also assign activity 3 on the Supersite.

3B.3 | **The imperative** Grammar Tutorial

Startblock Imperatives are used to express commands, requests, suggestions, directions, and instructions.

Sei nicht traurig.

Mach dir keine Sorgen!

- The imperative forms are based on the present-tense conjugation patterns of **du**, **wir**, **ihr**, and **Sie**.

the *Imperativ* conjugation	
Indikativ	**Imperativ**
du kaufst	kauf(e)
ihr kauft	kauft
Sie kaufen	kaufen Sie
wir kaufen	kaufen wir

Mach deine Hausaufgaben!   **Backen wir** einen Kuchen!
Do your homework!   *Let's bake a cake!*

ACHTUNG

Verbs that contain a double **s** in the infinitive do not drop an **s** in the informal singular imperative.

Iss das Gemüse, Tanja!
Eat your vegetables, Tanja!

- To form an informal singular command, drop the **-st** from the present-tense **du** form of the verb. As in English, omit the subject pronoun with the second-person imperative.

Antworte auf die Frage!   **Schreib** deinen Eltern eine E-Mail.
Answer the question!   *Write your parents an email.*

- Verbs with an **a** to **ä** vowel change do not retain this change in the imperative. However, **e** to **ie** and **e** to **i** changes are retained in the imperative for **du**.

Fahr langsam!   **Lies** das Buch.   **Nimm** den Bleistift.
Drive slowly!   *Read the book.*   *Take the pencil.*

- The informal plural **ihr** command is identical to the present-tense form, without the pronoun.

Esst die Äpfel, Kinder!   **Lernt** für die Prüfung.
Eat the apples, kids!   *Study for the exam.*

- For formal commands, keep the subject **Sie** and invert the subject/verb word order of the present tense. Remember that the singular and plural forms are identical.

Probieren Sie den Kuchen!   **Warten Sie** bitte hier.
Try the cake!   *Please wait here.*

- The first person plural command is equivalent to the English *Let's....* As with **Sie**, invert the subject/verb order of the present tense for **wir**.

Essen wir den Kuchen.   **Gehen wir** spazieren.
Let's eat the cake.   *Let's go for a walk.*

- In a negative command, **nicht** or **kein** follows the imperative form.

QUERVERWEIS

See **2B.3** to review the use of **nicht** and **kein**.

Fahren Sie nicht so schnell! *Don't drive so fast!*	**Arbeite nicht** so langsam! *Don't work so slowly!*
Hör keine laute Musik! *Don't listen to loud music!*	**Macht kein** Theater! *Don't make a fuss!*

- Use **bitte** to soften a command and make it polite. **Bitte** can be placed almost anywhere in a sentence, as long as it doesn't separate the verb from the subject pronoun **wir** or **Sie**.

Öffnen Sie **bitte** Ihren Rucksack. *Open your backpack, **please**.*	Geh nach Hause, **bitte**. *Go home, **please**.*
Schlaft **bitte** nicht im Unterricht! ***Please** don't sleep in class!*	**Bitte** nehmen Sie Platz. ***Please** take a seat.*

- The modals **können** and **wollen** are often used instead of the imperative for polite requests.

Können Sie mir helfen? ***Can** you help me?*	**Wollen** wir gehen? ***Shall** we go?*

- The verbs **sein, haben**, and **werden** have irregular imperative forms.

Sei lieb! ***Be** good! (sing., inf.)*	**Hab** keine Angst! ***Don't be** afraid!*	**Werd(e)** nicht faul! ***Don't get** lazy!*
Seid diskret! ***Be** discreet! (pl., inf.)*	**Habt** Geduld! ***Be** patient!*	**Werdet** fleißiger! ***Get** busier!*
Seien Sie mutig! ***Be** brave! (form.)*	**Haben Sie** Mut! ***Be** courageous!*	**Werden Sie** besser! ***Get** better!*
Seien wir realistisch! ***Let's be** realistic!*	**Haben wir** Spaß! ***Let's have** fun!*	**Werden wir** nicht traurig! ***Let's not get** sad!*

- On signs or labels, and in recipes or printed instructions, infinitives are often used instead of imperatives. Here are some common commands and instructions found in everyday situations. Notice that in some cases, a command is conveyed by using an infinitive or the word **verboten** (*forbidden*), rather than the imperative.

common commands			
Drücken.	*Push.*	Türen schließen.	*Keep doors closed.*
Ziehen.	*Pull.*	Rauchen verboten.	*No smoking.*
Bring mir....	*Bring me...*	Betreten des Rasens verboten.	*Keep off the grass.*
Langsam fahren.	*Slow down.*	Keine Zufahrt.	*Do not enter.*
Warte.	*Wait.*	Parkverbot.	*No parking.*
Sprechen Sie bitte langsamer.	*Please speak more slowly.*		

More activities

vhlcentral

WB
pp. 45-46

LM
p. 29

Online activities

 Jetzt sind Sie dran! Select the correct imperative form to complete each sentence.

1. Herr Braun, (sprecht / (sprechen Sie)) bitte langsamer.
2. Schüler, (öffnen Sie / (öffnet)) eure Bücher auf Seite 34.
3. Philip, ((vergiss) / vergessen wir) deine Hausaufgaben nicht!
4. Kinder, ((seid) / sei) freundlich und nett!
5. Wir haben morgen eine Prüfung. ((Lernen wir) / Lernt) zusammen!
6. Nina, (fahrt / (fahr)) nicht so schnell!
7. Herr und Frau Schmidt, (warte / (warten Sie)) bitte einen Moment.
8. Wir haben Hunger. ((Essen wir) / Iss) den Strudel!

Anwendung

1 Was fehlt? Complete the sentences using the imperative.

BEISPIEL Sebastian, _____Komm_____ (kommen)!

1. Herr Schneider, _____wiederholen Sie_____ (wiederholen) bitte.
2. Marie und Lukas, _____esst_____ (essen) langsamer!
3. Felix, _____sei_____ (sein) nicht gemein!
4. Frau Fischer und Herr Wagner, _____nehmen Sie_____ (nehmen) bitte eine Karte!
5. Paul und Else, _____macht_____ (machen) bitte kein Theater!
6. _____Sprechen_____ (sprechen) wir Deutsch!

2 Bilden Sie Sätze Write imperative commands for each person using the cues.

BEISPIEL Herr Braun: nicht so schnell fahren
Herr Braun, fahren Sie nicht so schnell!

1. Klara: Tennis mit Jan spielen   Klara, spiel Tennis mit Jan!
2. Wir: durch den Park gehen   Gehen wir durch den Park!
3. Max und Lara: den Text auf Seite 27 lesen   Max und Lara, lest/lesen Sie den Text auf Seite 27!
4. Herr Gärtner: heute bis 8 Uhr bleiben   Herr Gärtner, beiben Sie heute bis 8 Uhr!
5. Frau Weber: nicht nervös sein   Frau Weber, seien Sie nicht nervös!
6. Niklas: um 6 Uhr nach Hause kommen   Niklas, komm um 6 Uhr nach Hause!

3 Schreiben Tell these people not to do what they are doing. Sample answers are provided.

BEISPIEL Lara ist eifersüchtig.
Sei nicht eifersüchtig, Lara!

3 Expansion Have students give additional affirmative commands for this activity. Ex.: **1. Seien Sie nicht gierig, Herr Becker! Seien Sie großzügig und nett!**

1. Herr Becker ist gierig.
Seien Sie nicht gierig, Herr Becker!
2. Tom und Jonas weinen.
Weint nicht, Tom und Jonas!
3. Lukas spielt schlechte Musik.
Spiel keine schlechte Musik, Lukas!
4. Frau Weber kauft hässliche Sachen.
Kaufen Sie keine hässlichen Sachen, Frau Weber!

5. Max und Lukas schreiben an die Wand.
Schreibt nicht an die Wand, Max und Lukas!
6. Wir bleiben hier.
Bleiben wir nicht hier!
7. Hanna telefoniert 4 Stunden pro Tag.
Hanna, telefonier nicht 4 Stunden pro Tag!
8. Otto und Emma essen den Kuchen.
Esst den Kuchen nicht, Otto und Emma!

4 Konjugieren Write a command for each image using the cues. Sample answers are provided.

1. wir   Tanzen wir.

2. Nils   Nils, wirf den Ball!

3. Kinder / eure Bücher
Kinder, öffnet eure Bücher.

4. Frau Schulze / ein Glas Wasser
Frau Schulze, trinken Sie ein Glas Wasser.

5. wir   Gehen wir spazieren.

6. Greta / ein Bonbon
Greta, nimm ein Bonbon.

Kommunikation

5 **Befehle** In small groups, write eight sentences using **sollen**. Then, trade lists with another group and convert their sentences into commands. Answers will vary.

BEISPIEL

S1: Du sollst deine Hausaufgaben machen.
S2: Mach deine Hausaufgaben.

6 **Guter Rat** In pairs, use the imperative to give advice to each person or group. Answers will vary.

BEISPIEL deine Lehrerin

Sprechen Sie bitte langsamer.

1. deine Mitschüler

2. deine beste Freundin oder dein bester Freund

3. deine Eltern oder deine Großeltern

4. dein Bruder oder deine Schwester

5. dein Schuldirektor oder deine Schuldirektorin

6. deine Katze oder dein Hund

7 **Ein paar Ratschläge** In pairs, list ten pieces of advice that you would give to a new German exchange student at your school. Use the affirmative and negative forms of the imperative. Answers will vary.

BEISPIEL

S1: Sei fleißig, aber nicht zu ernst!
S2: Vergiss nicht deine Hausaufgaben!

8 **Simon sagt** In groups of five, play Simon Says. One student gives commands using the **du**, **Sie**, **ihr**, and **wir** forms. The group members must perform or mime the activity, but only if the speaker says "**Simon sagt**". The first person to make a mistake becomes the new leader. Answers will vary.

BEISPIEL

S1: Simon sagt: „Tanzen wir!"
OR
S1: Laura und Michael, lauft um den Tisch!

essen	laufen	schreiben
fahren	nehmen	sprechen
hören	öffnen	tanzen
fangen	sagen	weinen
lachen	schlafen	wiederholen

6 **Partner Chat** You can also assign activity 6 on the Supersite.

8 **Suggestion** If nobody makes a mistake, tell students to change leaders after three commands.

8 **Expansion** You may want to introduce students to the traditional German game **Kommando Pimperle**, similar to Simon Says.

Wiederholung

1 Etwas unternehmen In pairs, make plans for what you will do today in each location. Use prepositions with the accusative. Answers will vary.

> **BEISPIEL**
>
> **S1:** Um 10 Uhr gehen wir in die Bibliothek.
> **S2:** Ja, dort können wir gute Bücher für das Referat finden.

1 Partner Chat You can also assign activity 1 on the Supersite.

bis	gegen
durch	ohne
entlang	um
für	

1.

2.

3.

4.

2 Wollen und sollen In small groups, take turns saying one thing that you want to do today, one thing you must do, one thing you can do, one thing you may do, and one thing you are supposed to do. Answers will vary.

> **BEISPIEL**
>
> **S1:** Ich will heute Abend in die Sporthalle gehen, aber ich muss Hausaufgaben machen.
> **S2:** Ich soll für meinen Deutschkurs lernen, aber ich kann auch Tennis spielen.
> **S3:** Ich kann nicht Tennis spielen. Ich muss...

3 Diskutieren und kombinieren Your instructor will give you and a partner different worksheets with a list of occupations and profiles of several students. Take turns describing the students and matching their qualities to appropriate occupations. Answers will vary.

> **BEISPIEL**
>
> **S1:** Jana ist kreativ und gut in Mathe.
> **S2:** Ah, dann ist Jana eine gute Architektin.

3 Expansion After partners have matched each student to the profession indicated, have them brainstorm alternative professions that would be compatible with the qualities listed.

4 Meine ideale Familie Survey your classmates about their ideal family situation, and write down their answers. Then, in pairs, compare your results. Answers will vary.

> **BEISPIEL**
>
> **S1:** Wie ist deine ideale Familie?
> **S2:** Meine ideale Familie ist sehr groß...

5 Arbeitsblatt Your instructor will give you a worksheet with several activities listed. Survey your classmates to find someone who would like to do each of the activities with you. When someone says "yes", agree on a time and date. If someone says "no", they must give an excuse, explaining what they have to or are supposed to do instead. Answers will vary.

> **BEISPIEL**
>
> **S1:** Gehen wir morgen Abend ins Theater!
> **S2:** Ich kann nicht. Ich muss für die Prüfung lernen.
> **S3:** Ich komme gern. Gehen wir morgen um 7 Uhr!

6 Geschwister In pairs, role-play a conversation between two siblings. The younger sibling asks to do things, and the older sibling tells him/her what to do and what not to do. Answers will vary.

> **BEISPIEL**
>
> **S1:** Darf ich Fußball spielen?
> **S2:** Nein, das darfst du nicht! Iss dein Abendessen!

6 Partner Chat You can also assign activity 6 on the Supersite.

7 Zooplus

Zooplus Imagine you own a cat and you're shopping for your pet online. Discuss with a partner what you can buy at zooplus.de. Answers will vary.

BEISPIEL

S1: Hast du einen Katze?
S2: IJa, und sie heißt Luna.
S1: Wo kaufst du das Katzenfutter für Luna?
S2: Ich kaufe es bei zooplus. Es kostet...

7 Suggestion Write on the board the German words that students won't know for pets, and ask students to add them to the **Vocabulary Tools** on the **Sag mal** Supersite.

© 2019 by zooplus AG

8 Am Wochenende

Am Wochenende In small groups, prepare a skit in which a group of friends makes plans for the weekend. Use vocabulary from **Kapitel 2**. Answers will vary.

BEISPIEL

S1: Ich spiele gern Basketball! Können wir morgen Basketball spielen?
S2: Nein, bleiben wir hier! Wir müssen unsere Hausaufgaben machen!
S3: Ihr könnt hier bleiben, aber ich will...

8 Suggestion Before dividing students into groups, have the class brainstorm a list of possible activities that could take place in the locations pictured.

Mein Wörterbuch

Add five words related to **die Familie** and **persönliche Beschreibungen** to your personalized dictionary.

Lektion 3B		
German	English	Definition
+ add word		
klug	smart	intelligent

Panorama Interactive Map

Die Vereinigten Staaten und Kanada

connections
cultures
NATIONAL STANDARDS

Anteil der Amerikaner mit deutschen Wurzeln: 15% (50 Millionen)

- **Kalifornien:** *5.517.470*
- **Pennsylvania:** *3.491.269*
- **Ohio:** *3.231.788*
- **Illinois:** *2.668.955*
- **Texas:** *2.542.996*
- **Wisconsin:** *2.455.980*
- **Michigan:** *2.271.091*
- **Florida:** *2.270.456*
- **New York:** *2.250.309*
- **Minnesota:** *1.949.346*
- **Indiana:** *1.629.766*
- **Missouri:** *1.576.813*

QUELLE: U.S. Census 2010

Anteil der Kanadier mit deutschen Wurzeln: 10% (3 Millionen)

- **Toronto:** *220.135*
- **Vancouver:** *187.410*
- **Winnipeg:**: *109.355*
- **Kitchener:** *93.325*
- **Montreal:** *83.850*

QUELLE: Canadian Census 2011

Die ersten deutschen Siedler in Kanada kommen zwischen 1750 und 1753 nach Nova Scotia. Die meisten von ihnen° sind Bauern und Kaufleute°. Zwischen 1919 und 1939 kommen fast 100.000 Deutsche nach Kanada. Auch von ihnen sind die meisten Bauern. Sie alle bringen ihre Familien mit und starten ein neues Leben in Nordamerika.

Berühmte Deutschamerikaner und Deutschkanadier

- **Levi Strauss,** *Unternehmer° (1829–1902)*
- **Frederick Louis Maytag I,** *Unternehmer (1857–1937)*
- **Dwight D. Eisenhower,** *Fünf-Sterne General und US-Präsident (1890–1969)*
- **Lou Gehrig,** *Baseballspieler (1903–1941)*
- **Henry Kissinger,** *Politiker (1923–)*
- **Almuth Lütkenhaus,** *Künstlerin° (1930–1996)*
- **Dany Heatley,** *Eishockeyspieler (1981–)*
- **Justin Bieber,** *Sänger° (1994–)*

Die meisten von ihnen *most of them* **Kaufleute** *tradespeople*
Unternehmer *entrepreneur* **Künstlerin** *artist* **Sänger** *singer*
verlässt *leaves* **Flöten** *flutes* **Immobilien** *real estate*
Fellhandel *fur trade* **reichste** *richest* **Vermögen** *fortune*

Eine Straße in Minocqua, Wisconsin

Eine Bratwurst mit Salat und Senf

Nova Scotia
Minnesota
Wisconsin
New York
Vancouver
Winnipeg
Michigan
Montreal
Toronto
Kitchener
Illinois
Ohio
Indiana
Missouri
Pennsylvania
Kalifornien
Texas
Florida

0 — 1.000 Meilen
0 — 1.000 Kilometer

0 — 200 Meilen
0 — 200 Kilometer

Tänzer auf dem Oktoberfest in Hollywood Beach, Florida

Suggestion Ask students from German American families where they live, whether they have any German traditions in their family, and whether they prepare any German dishes. This is a good opportunity to explore the richness of German American culture in the United States, and also to point out how some German customs have evolved.

Unglaublich, aber wahr!

1784 verlässt° **John Jacob Astor** (1763–1848) das Dorf Walldorf in Deutschland mit $25 und 7 Flöten° in Richtung USA. Durch Immobilien°– und Fellhandel° wird er reich und ist zur Zeit seines Todes der reichste° Mann Amerikas. Sein Vermögen° beträgt ungefähr $90 Millionen.

Menschen

Sandra Bullock

Sandra Bullock wurde 1964 in Arlington, Virginia geboren°. Ihre Mutter ist Helga D. Meyer, eine deutsche Opernsängerin. Deshalb verbringt° Bullock, die neben Englisch fließend° Deutsch spricht, auch die ersten 12 Jahre ihres Lebens in der deutschen Stadt Fürth, bevor sie mit ihrer Familie in die USA zieht. Ihre erfolgreiche Karriere beinhaltet Filme wie *Gravity, Speed, Blind Side – Die große Chance* und *Ocean's 8*.

Geschichte

Deutsche in Texas

1848 gibt es in Deutschland und vielen anderen europäischen Ländern (Frankreich, Dänemark, Österreich) Revolutionen und Aufstände° auf Grund von sozialen und wirtschaftlichen° Problemen. Nach der Mairevolution verlassen° viele Revolutionäre Deutschland und gehen in die USA. Sie leben in Städten wie zum Beispiel New Braunfels und Fredericksburg in Texas. Diesen deutschen Einfluss° kann man heute hier immer noch sehen. Unter anderem gibt es in Texas eine Form des Deutschen, die man Texas-Deutsch nennt.

Essen

Hamburger

Der Hamburger – ein Sandwich aus einer Frikadelle° in einer Semmel° mit einem Salatblatt und einer Scheibe Tomate – hat etwas mit der Stadt Hamburg zu tun. Als deutsche Immigranten und Matrosen° Ende des 18. Jahrhunderts nach New York kommen, bekommen Sie hier „Steak im Hamburger Stil". Diese Steaks damals hatten mit heutigen Hamburgern außer dem Namen noch nicht viel zu tun. Erst mit der Erfindung des Fleischwolfs° im 19. Jahrhunderts werden aus Steaks im Hamburger Stil die heutigen Hamburger.

Feiern

German Fest

Das German Fest in Milwaukee ist das größte „deutsche" Event Nordamerikas. Seit 1981 feiern die Menschen hier am letzten Juliwochenende Kultur deutschsprachiger° Länder und Regionen wie Österreich, Deutschland, Liechtenstein, Südtirol und der Schweiz. Besucher° tragen teilweise Dirndl und Lederhosen, hören traditionelle Blaskapellen° oder moderne Popmusik und bekommen Informationen über ihre deutsche Abstammung°. Die Besucher des German Festes essen unter anderem 20.000 Bratwürste, 9.000 Knödel°, 200 Spanferkel° und 15.000 Stück Strudel.

Musik Musik

Hans Zimmer

Hans Zimmer ist ein deutscher Filmkomponist und Musikproduzent, der in Los Angeles wohnt und arbeitet. 2010 bekam er einen Stern auf dem *Hollywood Walk of Fame*. Er ist einer der einflussreichsten° Filmkomponisten in der Geschichte Hollywoods.

Go to **vhlcentral.com** to find out more about **Hans Zimmer** and his music.

---

wurde… geboren *was born* **verbringt** *spends (time)* **fließend** *fluent* **Aufstände** *uprisings* **wirtschaftlichen** *economic* **verlassen** *leave* **Einfluss** *influence* **Frikadelle** *meatball* **Semmel** *bun* **Matrosen** *sailors* **Erfindung des Fleischwolfs** *invention of the meat grinder* **deutschsprachiger** *German-speaking* **Besucher** *Visitors* **Blaskapellen** *brass bands* **Abstammung** *descent* **Knödel** *dumplings* **Spanferkel** *suckling pigs* **einflussreichsten** *most influential*

---

1 **Was haben Sie gelernt?** Indicate whether each statement is richtig or falsch.

1. Zu seiner Zeit ist John Jacob Astor der reichste Mann Kanadas.
   Falsch. Er wird der reichste Mann Amerikas.
2. Sandra Bullock kann ein bisschen (*a little*) Deutsch sprechen.
   Falsch. Sie kann fließend Deutsch sprechen.
3. New Braunfels, Texas, ist eine Stadt mit starkem (*strong*) deutschen Einfluss.
   Richtig.
4. Der Hamburger kommt nicht direkt aus Hamburg.
   Richtig.
5. Die Kultur, die Musik und das Essen deutschsprachiger Länder werden auf dem *German Fest* in Milwaukee gefeiert.   Richtig.

2 **Was meinen Sie?** Discuss your thoughts with a partner.

Where do you encounter cultural products, practices, or perspectives from German-speaking countries in your life? Think about the media, entertainment, food, and other areas of daily life.

Lesen Audio: Reading

Vor dem Lesen

Strategien

Predicting content from visuals

When you read in German, look for visual cues that can help you figure out the content and purpose of what you are reading. Photos and illustrations, for example, can give you a good idea of the main points of the reading. You may also encounter helpful visuals that summarize large amounts of data in a way that is easy to comprehend; these visuals include bar graphs, pie charts, flow charts, lists of percentages, and other diagrams.

Die beliebtesten° Haustiere

In Deutschland gibt es Haustiere in mehr als° 12 Millionen Haushalten.

Katzen	**16,5%** der Haushalte
Hunde	**13,8%** der Haushalte
Kleintiere	**5,9%** der Haushalte
Vögel	**5,7%** der Haushalte
Aquarien°	**5,7%** der Haushalte

Auch in Österreich und der Schweiz sind Katzen und Hunde die beliebtesten Haustiere.

beliebtesten *most popular* **mehr als** *more than*
Aquarien *fish tanks*

 Texte verstehen Take a quick look at the visual elements of the article in order to generate a list of ideas about its content. Then compare your list with a classmate's. What elements did you both notice? What aspects did your partner notice that didn't catch your eye? Discuss and consolidate your ideas to produce a final list to share with the class.

Hunde und Katzen

Für viele Deutsche, Österreicher und Schweizer sind Haustiere sehr wichtig. Allerdings gibt es in diesen Ländern weit weniger vierbeinige° Freunde als in anderen europäischen Ländern. Zum Beispiel hat in Deutschland nur etwa jeder Vierte ein Haustier.

Welche Tiere findet man bei Deutschen, Österreichern und Schweizern am häufigsten°? Oft hört man, der Hund ist des Deutschen bester Freund. Statistiken zeigen° allerdings, dass nicht Hunde, sondern Katzen das Haustier Nummer 1 im deutschsprachigen Raum sind. Hunde stehen nur an Nummer 2.

vierbeinige *four-legged* **am häufigsten** *most frequently* **zeigen** *show*

Außerdem geht der allgemeine° Trend hin zu mehr° Katzen und weniger° Hunden. Andere beliebte Tiere sind Kleintiere wie Kaninchen° und Hamster. Vögel singen immer weniger in deutschsprachigen Haushalten°.

Haustiere sind oft ein wichtiger Teil° der Familie. Kinder lernen durch sie, soziale Kontakte zu pflegen°. Großstadtkinder, die mit einem Hund leben, haben später° oft weniger Probleme mit Kriminalität. Vor allem bei Singles sind Katzen beliebt, da sie alleine sein können, aber auch eine Art Partnerersatz sind.

Wer hat welches Haustier?

Status	Katzen	Hunde	Fische	Vögel
Ledig	23%	18%	7%	5%
Verheiratet	18%	18%	6%	5%
Frauen	17%	18%	7%	5%
Männer	17%	18%	6%	5%

allgemeine *general* **mehr** *more* **weniger** *fewer* **Kaninchen** *bunnies* **Haushalten** *households*
ein wichtiger Teil *an important part* **pflegen** *to cultivate* **später** *later*

Nach dem Lesen

 Richtig oder falsch? Indicate whether each statement is **richtig** or **falsch**.
Expansion Have students correct the false statements.

	richtig	falsch
1. Fast jede Familie in Deutschland hat ein Haustier. Jeder Vierte in Deutschland hat ein Haustier.	☐	☑
2. Katzen sind das Haustier Nummer 1.	☑	☐
3. Der Trend in den nächsten Jahren geht zu mehr Hunden. Der Trend in den nächsten Jahren geht zu mehr Katzen.	☐	☑
4. Immer weniger Menschen haben Vögel.	☑	☐
5. Großstadtkinder mit Hunden haben mehr Probleme. Großstadtkinder mit Hunden haben weniger Probleme.	☐	☑
6. Viele Ledige haben Katzen als Haustiere.	☑	☐

 Was ist richtig? Select the correct response according to the article.

1. Wie viel Prozent der Deutschen besitzen ein Haustier?
   a. 10%–20%   (b.) 20%–30%   c. 30%–40%

2. Welche Haustiere werden immer beliebter?
   (a.) Katzen   b. Vögel   c. Hunde

3. Welches Tier passt in die Kategorie Kleintiere?
   a. Katzen   b. Hunde   (c.) Hamster

4. Welches Haustier besitzen die meisten Deutschen?
   a. Hunde   b. Fische   (c.) Katzen

5. Welche Bevölkerungsgruppe hat die meisten Haustiere?
   a. Frauen   (b.) Ledige   c. Verheiratete

 Meine Haustiere With a partner, talk about the pets you or your family and friends have. Use the verb **haben** and possessive adjectives.

BEISPIEL

S1: *Hast du eine Katze?*
S2: *Nein, ich habe einen Fisch, aber mein Onkel hat zwei Katzen…*

Hören

Vorbereitung

Based on the photograph, where do you think Lena and Jasmin are? What do you think they are talking about?

Zuhören

Now you are going to hear Lena and Jasmin's conversation. Write **M** next to adjectives that describe Jasmin's friend Maria. Write **T** next to adjectives that describe Lena's ex-boyfriend, Tobias. Some adjectives will not be used.

_M_	fleißig	___	langweilig
___	hübsch	_M_	intelligent
_T_	eifersüchtig	_T_	egoistisch
___	sportlich	___	langsam
_M_	großartig	_T_	verlobt
___	ernst	___	faul

Vor dem Hören Ask students questions about the two women in the picture to help them guess what they might be talking about. Brainstorm possible topics for the women's conversation and write them on the board. Ex.: **Über was sprechen Lena und Jasmin? Über die Arbeit? Über Familie? Über die Liebe?**

Verständnis

Wer ist das? Write the name of the person described by each statement.

1. _Maria_ ist Jasmins neue Freundin.
2. _Tobias_ ist egoistisch und eifersüchtig.
3. _Jasmin_ lernt mit Maria für die Literaturprüfungen.
4. _Lena_ ist allein glücklich.
5. _Tobias_ ist mit Antonia verlobt.
6. _Jasmin_ will mit Lena schwimmen gehen.

Richtig oder falsch Indicate whether each statement is **richtig** or **falsch**. Correct the false statements.

1. Lena studiert Literatur. Falsch. Jasmin studiert Literatur.
2. Tobias hilft Jasmin. Falsch. Maria hilft Jasmin.
3. Maria ist großartig. Richtig.
4. Lena ist ledig. Richtig.
5. Geschichte ist Jasmins Hobby. Richtig.
6. Tobias ist intelligent und fleißig. Falsch. Tobias ist egoistisch und eifersüchtig.

Schreiben

Strategien

Using idea maps

How do you organize ideas for a first draft? Often, the organization of ideas represents the most challenging part of the writing process. Idea maps are useful for organizing information. Here is an example of an idea map you could use when writing.

IDEA MAP

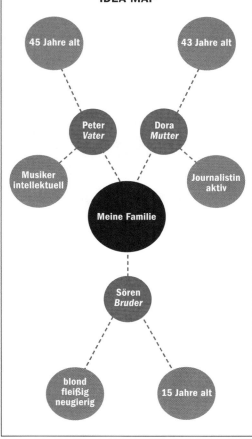

Successful Language Learning Remind students to write their notes in German. Emphasize that they should not translate directly from English. Encourage them to use words and phrases they are familiar with and not rely too heavily on the dictionary.

Thema

Briefe schreiben

 A German friend you met online wants to know about your family. Using the verbs and grammar structures you learned in this chapter, write a brief description of your family or an imaginary family, including:

- Names and relationships
- Physical characteristics
- Hobbies and interests

Suggestion Tell students that it may be helpful to write their idea maps on note cards, so that they can easily rearrange the ideas if necessary.

Here are some useful expressions for writing a letter or e-mail in German:

Salutations

Lieber Erik,	Dear Erik,
Liebe Anna,	Dear Anna,

Asking for a response

Ich hoffe, bald von dir zu hören.	I hope to hear from you soon.
Erzähl, was es Neues bei dir gibt!	Let me know what's new with you!

Closings

Bis bald!/Tschüss!	So long!
Mach's gut!	All the best!
Mit freundlichen Grüßen	Yours sincerely
Hochachtungsvoll	Respectfully

Suggestion Tell students that when the salutation ends with a comma, it is considered part of the first sentence of the letter, and the word that follows is not capitalized (unless it's a noun). Point out that an exclamation mark can be used instead of a comma, in which case the text that follows does start with a capitalized word.

Suggestion Point out the differences in formality in the closing expressions. For example, **Tschüss!** and **Mach's gut!** should only be used with friends and family, whereas **Mit freundlichen Grüßen** or **Hochachtungsvoll** are more formal.

Vocabulary Tools

Lektion 3A

die Familie
family

das Baby, -s *baby*
der Bruder, ⸗ *brother*
der Cousin, -s *cousin (m.)*
die Cousine, -n *cousin (f.)*
die Eltern *parents*
das Enkelkind, -er *grandchild*
der Enkelsohn, ⸗e *grandson*
die Enkeltochter, ⸗ *granddaughter*
die Frau, -en *wife*
das Geschwister, - *sibling*
die Großeltern *grandparents*
die Großmutter, ⸗ *grandmother*
der Großvater, ⸗ *grandfather*
der Halbbruder, ⸗ *half brother*
die Halbschwester, -n *half sister*
das Kind, -er *child*
der Lebenspartner, - *life partner*
die Lebenspartnerin, -nen *life partner*
der Mann, ⸗er *husband*
die Mutter, ⸗ *mother*
der Nachname, -n *last name*
der Neffe, -n *nephew*
die Nichte, -n *niece*
die Oma, -s *grandma*
der Onkel, - *uncle*
der Opa, -s *grandpa*
das Paar, -e *couple*
der Schwager, ⸗ *brother-in-law*
die Schwägerin, -nen *sister-in-law*
die Schwester, -n *sister*
die Schwiegermutter, ⸗ *mother-in-law*
der Schwiegervater, ⸗ *father-in-law*
der Sohn, ⸗e *son*
der Stiefbruder, ⸗ *stepbrother*
die Stiefmutter, ⸗ *stepmother*
die Stiefschwester, -n *stepsister*
der Stiefsohn, ⸗e *stepson*
die Stieftochter, ⸗ *stepdaughter*
der Stiefvater, ⸗ *stepfather*
die Tante, -n *aunt*
die Tochter, ⸗ *daughter*
der Vater, ⸗ *father*
der / die Verwandte, -n *relative*
der Zwilling, -e *twin*

der Familienstand
marital status

die Witwe, -n *widow*
der Witwer, - *widower*
geschieden *divorced*
getrennt *separated*
ledig *single*
verheiratet *married*
verlobt *engaged*
zusammen *together*
heiraten *to marry*

die Haustiere
pets

der Fisch, -e *fish*
der Hund, -e *dog*
die Katze, -n *cat*
der Vogel, ⸗ *bird*

zum Beschreiben
to describe

blaue / grüne / braune Augen
  blue / green / brown eyes
blonde / braune / schwarze Haare
  blond / brown / black hair
dunkel *dark*
hell *light*

....

Possessive adjectives *See p. 104.*
Descriptive adjectives *See p. 108.*

Lektion 3B

zum Beschreiben
to describe

(un)angenehm *(un)pleasant*
arm *poor; unfortunate*
bescheiden *modest*
besorgt *worried*
diskret *discreet*
egoistisch *selfish*
eifersüchtig *jealous*
ernst *serious*
faul *lazy*
fleißig *hard-working*
freundlich *friendly*
froh *happy*
gemein *mean*
gierig *greedy*
glücklich *happy*
großzügig *generous*
intellektuell *intellectual*
intelligent *intelligent*
langsam *slow*
lustig *funny*
müde *tired*
mutig *brave*
naiv *naïve*
nervös *nervous*
nett *nice*
neugierig *curious*
reich *rich*
schlecht *bad*
schnell *fast*
schüchtern *shy*
schwach *weak*
stark *strong*
stolz *proud*
süß *sweet; cute*
toll *great*
traurig *sad*
lächeln *to smile*
lachen *to laugh*
weinen *to cry*

Berufe
professions

der Architekt, -en / die Architektin, -nen
  architect
der Besitzer, - / die Besitzerin, -nen
  owner
der Friseur, -e / die Friseurin, -nen
  hairdresser
der Geschäftsmann (*pl.* Geschäftsleute)
  / die Geschäftsfrau, -en
  businessman / businesswoman
der Ingenieur, -e / die Ingenieurin, -nen
  engineer
der Journalist, -en / die Journalistin, -nen
  journalist
der Kellner, - / die Kellnerin, -nen
  waiter / waitress
der Musiker, - / die Musikerin, -nen
  musician
der Rechtsanwalt, ⸗e / die
  Rechtsanwältin, -nen *lawyer*

Modalverben
modal verbs

dürfen *to be allowed to, may*
können *to be able to, can*
müssen *to have to, must*
sollen *to be supposed to*
wollen *to want to*

....

Prepositions with the accusative
  See p. 126.
Common commands *See p. 129.*

More activities
vhlcentral | Online activities

COMMUNICATIVE GOALS
By the end of this chapter you will be able to:

🔊 **Los geht's!** Wo sind George und Hans? Was machen sie?

LEKTION 4A

Talk about food and grocery shopping.

To do so, you will use:

Kontext Seite 142-145
- Food
- Stores

Strukturen Seite 150-161
4A.1 Adverbs
4A.2 The modal **mögen**
4A.3 Separable and inseparable prefix verbs

You will also learn about cultural products, practices, and perspectives related to:

Kultur Seite 148-149
- **der Wiener Naschmarkt**
- Regional differences for food words
- **Wolfgang Puck**

Zapping Seite 161
- *Yello Strom*

LEKTION 4B

Talk about food and meals.
Describe flavors.

To do so, you will use:

Kontext Seite 162-165
- Descriptions of food
- Meals and drinks
- Restaurant words and phrases

Strukturen Seite 170-177
4B.1 The dative
4B.2 Prepositions with the dative

You will also learn about cultural products, practices, and perspectives related to:

Kultur Seite 168-169
- **Wiener Kaffeehäuser**
- **Ausländische Spezialitäten**
- **Restaurant Tian**

WEITER GEHT'S

You will learn about Austria, famous Austrians, and Austrian culture.

Panorama Seite 178-184
- Österreich

And you will demonstrate that you can:
Lesen: Scan a written text for information
Hören: Listen for the main theme
Schreiben: Add details to your writing

Suggestion Have students look at the photo and items they see. Ask them what they think this chapter will be about.

Lebensmittel

 Vocabulary Tools

Wortschatz

Geschäfte	stores
die Bäckerei, -en	bakery
die Eisdiele, -n	ice cream shop
das Feinkostgeschäft, -e	delicatessen
das Fischgeschäft, -e	fish store
die Konditorei, -en	pastry shop
das Lebensmittelgeschäft, -e	grocery store
der Markt, ̈e	market
die Metzgerei, -en	butcher shop
der Supermarkt, ̈e	supermarket
einkaufen gehen	to go shopping
verkaufen	to sell
Essen	food
das Brot, -e	bread
das Brötchen, -	roll
die Butter	butter
der Joghurt, -s	yogurt
der Käse, -	cheese
das Öl, -e	oil
das Olivenöl, -e	olive oil
die Pasta	pasta
der Reis	rice
das Rezept, -e	recipe
die Zutat, -en	ingredient
Fleisch und Fisch	meat and fish
die Garnele, -n	shrimp
das Hähnchen, -	chicken
die Meeresfrüchte (pl.)	seafood
das Rindfleisch	beef
der Schinken, -	ham
das Schweinefleisch	pork
der Thunfisch	tuna
das Würstchen, -	sausage
Obst und Gemüse	fruits and vegetables
die Ananas, -	pineapple
die Artischocke, -n	artichoke
die Himbeere, -n	raspberry
die Melone, -n	melon
die Traube, -n	grape

Suggestion Tell students that many German speakers treat **Paprika** as a masculine noun and that some also treat **Joghurt** as a feminine or neuter noun, especially in Austria and Switzerland.

Suggestion Tell students that Germans typically buy fresh bread from a bakery, rather than the supermarket.

die Orange, -n

die Birne, -n
pear

die Erdbeere, -n
strawberries

der Pfirsich, -e
peach

Obst

die Banane, -n

der Apfel, ̈
apple

die Kartoffel, -n
potato

Gemüse

die Zwiebel, -n
onion

die rote Paprika
(*pl.* die roten Paprika)
red pepper

die Karotte, -n

die Aubergine, -n
eggplant

die grüne Bohne
(*pl.* die grünen Bohnen)
green beans

der Knoblauch
garlic

der Pilz, -e

die Tomate, -n

Suggestion Tell students that some words have more than one accepted plural form. Ex.: **die Ananas/die Ananasse; die Paprika/die Paprikas**.

More activities

 vhlcentral | WB pp. 47–48 | LM p. 30 | Online activities

Anwendung

ACHTUNG

Note that **der Salat** can refer to either *salad* or *lettuce*. A head of *lettuce* is **ein Salatkopf** (*m.*).

die Marmelade, -n

der Kuchen, -

die grüne Paprika
(*pl.* die grünen Paprika)
green pepper

der Salat, -e

das Ei, -er

---

1   **Was passt zusammen?** Welche Wörter in Liste 1 passen zu (*match*) den Wörtern in Liste 2?

	Liste 1		Liste 2
_d_	**1.** die Paprika	**a.**	der Fisch
_b_	**2.** der Schinken	**b.**	das Fleisch
_c_	**3.** die Banane	**c.**	das Obst
_a_	**4.** der Thunfisch	**d.**	das Gemüse
_c_	**5.** die Traube		
_b_	**6.** das Würstchen		

1 **Expansion** Go over the answers to this activity as a class. Ex.: **Die Paprika: Ist das Obst, Gemüse, Fleisch, Fisch? Und das Rindfleisch? Ist das eine Sorte Gemüse? Nein? Was ist das?**

---

2   **Hören Sie zu** Kann ein Veganer diese Lebensmittel essen?

	Ja	Nein		Ja	Nein
1.	☑	☐	**4.**	☑	☐
2.	☐	☑	**5.**	☐	☑
3.	☑	☐	**6.**	☐	☑

---

3   **Lebensmittel** Schreiben Sie die Namen der Lebensmittel unter die Fotos.

▶ **BEISPIEL**   *die Tomaten*

1. _die Orangen_

2. _die Garnelen_   **3.** _das Brot_   **4.** _der Käse_   **5.** _die Würstchen_

---

4   **Was essen Sie gern?** Schreiben Sie die Namen der Lebensmittel, die (*that*) Sie gern, nicht so gern und nicht gern essen. Answers will vary.

	gern	nicht so gern	nicht gern
1.	_____	_____	_____
2.	_____	_____	_____
3.	_____	_____	_____

---

5   **Samstag ist Markttag** Hören Sie die Dialoge an und entscheiden Sie (*decide*), ob die Sätze (*sentences*) **richtig** oder **falsch** sind.

		richtig	falsch
1.	Annika geht im Supermarkt einkaufen.	☐	☑
2.	Sie kauft Garnelen und Thunfisch.	☐	☑
3.	Thunfisch ist heute im Angebot (*on sale*).	☑	☐
4.	Ein Kilo Garnelen kostet 8,30 €.	☑	☐
5.	Am Obststand kauft Annika nur Äpfel und Bananen.	☐	☑
6.	Annika macht einen Salat.	☑	☐

4 **Expansion** Survey the class to find out which foods are most popular. Ex.: **Wer isst gern Pizza? Heben Sie die Hand. Wer isst gern Brokkoli?**

Kommunikation

6 Was kann man hier kaufen? Welche drei Lebensmittel können

Sie in den Geschäften kaufen? Vergleichen Sie (*Compare*) die Antworten mit einem Partner / einer Partnerin. Answers will vary.

▶ **BEISPIEL**

in der Eisdiele
das Eis
der Kaffee
die Cola

6 Expansion Check students' answers by asking:
**Was kauft man beim Bäcker? Was kauft man in
der Metzgerei? Was kauft man auf dem Markt?**

1. beim Bäcker
_____
_____
_____

TIPP

Auf Deutsch sagt man:

Ich kaufe Brot **beim** Bäcker.

Ich kaufe Fleisch **in
der** Metzgerei.

Ich kaufe Fisch
im Fischgeschäft/
im Supermarkt.

Ich kaufe Obst und
Gemüse **auf dem** Markt.

2. in der Metzgerei
_____
_____
_____

3. auf dem Markt
_____
_____
_____

4. im Supermarkt
_____
_____
_____

5. im Fischgeschäft
_____
_____
_____

7 Kochen mit Freunden Sie und Ihre Freunde
wollen am Abend zusammen kochen. Diskutieren Sie,
was Sie alles brauchen und wer was kaufen soll
(*who should buy what*). Answers will vary.

BEISPIEL

S1: Wer bringt Obst und Gemüse?
S2: Ich bringe Salat. Thomas, bringst du das Obst?
S3: Ja, ich kann Trauben und Birnen bringen.

8 Arbeitsblatt Sie sind Geschäftsbesitzer und Ihre
Mitstudenten müssen erraten (*guess*), was man bei
Ihnen kaufen kann und welches Geschäft Sie haben.

BEISPIEL

S1: Verkaufen Sie Bananen?
S2: Nein.
S3: Verkaufen Sie Wurst?
S2: Ja.
S1: Haben Sie eine Metzgerei?

9 Essen und trinken Fragen Sie Ihre Mitstudenten,
was sie gern oder nicht gern essen und trinken. Finden
Sie mindestens (*at least*) eine Person, die denselben
Geschmack (*the same taste*) hat wie Sie. Answers will vary.

BEISPIEL

S1: Ich esse gern Brot und Nutella am Morgen. Isst du
auch Nutella?
S2: Nein, ich esse nicht gern Nutella.
S3: Ich esse gern Brot und Nutella. Und ich trinke morgens
Kaffee. Du auch?

Aussprache und Rechtschreibung Audio

The German *s*, *z*, and *c*

The *s* sound in German is represented by **s**, **ss**, or **ß**. At the end of a word, **s**, **ss**, and **ß** are pronounced like the *s* in the English word *yes*. Before a vowel, **s** is pronounced like the *s* in the English word *please*.

| **Reis** | **Professor** | **weiß** | **Supermarkt** | **Käse** |

The German **z** is pronounced like the *ts* in the English word *bats*, whether it appears at the beginning, middle, or end of a word. The combination **tz** is also pronounced *ts*. The ending -**tion** is always pronounced -*tsion*.

| **Pilze** | **Zwiebel** | **Platz** | **Besitzer** | **Kaution** |

Only in loan words does the letter **c** appear directly before a vowel. Before **e** or **i**, the letter **c** is usually pronounced *ts*. Before other vowels, it is usually pronounced like the *c* in *cat*. The letter combination **ck** is pronounced like the *ck* in the English word *packer*.

| **Cent** | **Celsius** | **Computer** | **backen** | **Bäckerei** |

Suggestion Tell students that people in Southern Germany, Austria, and Switzerland typically pronounce **s** like the *s* in *yes*, even before vowels.

1 **Aussprechen** Wiederholen Sie die Wörter, die Sie hören.

1. lassen
2. lasen
3. weißer
4. weiser
5. sinnlos
6. seitens
7. selbst
8. Zeile
9. Katzen
10. letztes
11. Campingplatz
12. Fleck

2 **Nachsprechen** Wiederholen Sie die Sätze, die Sie hören.

1. Der Musiker geht am Samstag zum Friseur.
2. Es geht uns sehr gut.
3. Die Zwillinge essen eine Pizza mit Pilzen, Zwiebeln und Tomaten.
4. Jetzt ist es Zeit in den Zoo zu gehen.
5. Der Clown sitzt im Café und spielt Computerspiele.
6. Ich esse nur eine Portion Eis.

2 Suggestion Tell students that tuna, eggs, shrimp, and corn are all common pizza toppings in Germany.

3 **Sprichwörter** Wiederholen Sie die Sprichwörter, die Sie hören.

Aus den Augen, aus dem Sinn.[1]

Gegensätze ziehen sich an.[2]

[1] Out of sight, out of mind.
[2] Opposites attract.

More activities

vhlcentral | LM p. 31 | Online activities

Fotoroman

Börek für alle Video

George und Hans treffen Meline und Sabite im Supermarkt. George hat eine
Idee: Er macht Börek für seine Freunde. Aber kann George kochen?

Vorbereitung Have students scan the images and
try to guess what the characters will buy. Have them
create a grocery shopping list for the boys and another
one for the girls.

NATIONAL communication cultures STANDARDS

1

GEORGE Was möchtest du heute essen?
HANS Hmmm. Ich esse gerne Fleisch.
Rindfleisch, Schweinefleisch und Wurst...
GEORGE Los! Auf zur Fleischtheke!
HANS Ja!

2

SABITE Ich esse gern Tofu mit Pilzen
und Erdbeeren.
HANS Erdbeeren und was?
SABITE Pilze. Mit Tofu.

3

GEORGE Sabite, welche Zutaten kommen
in die Börek von deiner Mutter? Wir können
sie kochen.
SABITE Hmm. Lass mich überlegen. Kartoffeln,
Blätterteig, Zwiebeln. Kartoffeln kochen,
Zwiebeln braten, Teig aufrollen. Backen.

4

GEORGE Ich mache heute Abend Börek!
SABITE Wir bringen Käse und Brot mit. Wann
sollen wir kommen?
GEORGE Kommt um halb sieben vorbei.
SABITE Perfekt.
MELINE Was ist perfekt?

5

MELINE Müssen wir mit Hans und
George essen?
SABITE Ach, Meline, sei nett.

HANS Muss Meline mit uns essen? Sie ist
extrem unangenehm. Ich finde, das ist
eine ausgesprochen schlechte Idee.
GEORGE Meline ist lustig. Du magst
sie bestimmt.
HANS Das glaube ich kaum.
GEORGE Sie mag dich bestimmt.

6

1 **Was fehlt?** Ergänzen Sie die Sätze mit den richtigen Informationen.

1. Hans isst gern Schweinefleisch und (Rindfleisch / Tofu).
2. Sabite isst gern Tofu mit Pilzen und (Wurst / Erdbeeren).
3. In die Börek von Frau Yilmaz kommen (Pilze / Zwiebeln).
4. Man muss die Zwiebeln (waschen / braten).
5. Meline und Sabite sollen um (zehn nach sieben / halb sieben)
bei Hans und George sein.

6. Sie bringen (Käse und Brot / Käse und Wurst) mit.
7. Hans findet die Idee ausgesprochen (schlecht / gut).
8. In Georges Börek ist kein (Blätterteig / Schafskäse).
9. Sabite ruft morgen (ihre Mutter / ihre Oma) an.
10. Hans und George haben noch (Milch und Äpfel / Joghurt
und Bananen).

PERSONEN George Hans Meline Sabite

> **GEORGE** Tada! Prost!
> **HANS** Prost!

> **SABITE** George! Was...
> **GEORGE** Ich weiß es nicht!

> **SABITE** Wo ist der Schafskäse? Er gibt ihnen erst noch den Geschmack.
> **GEORGE** Schafskäse? Wieso...
> **SABITE** Oh, nein. Oh, George, es tut mir leid! Ich rufe morgen meine Mutter an und schreibe es dann auf.

> **GEORGE** Es ist schon okay. Der Butterkäse und das Brot liegen dort.
> **MELINE** Ich brate Eier und Kartoffeln.
> **HANS** Gute Idee. Wir haben hier oben noch Joghurt und Bananen.
> **SABITE** Hier stehen noch Butter und Marmelade für das Brot!

Nützliche Ausdrücke

- **die Wurst**
  cold cuts
- **Los! Auf zur Fleischtheke!**
  Let's go! To the butcher's counter!
- **der Blätterteig**
  phyllo dough
- **aufrollen**
  roll up
- **Kommt um halb sieben vorbei!**
  Come over at half past six!
- **Brauchen wir noch etwas?**
  Do we need anything else?
- **Ich finde, das ist eine ausgesprochen schlechte Idee.**
  I think it's an extremely bad idea.
- **Das glaube ich kaum.**
  I hardly think so.
- **Ich weiß es nicht!**
  I don't know!
- **der Schafskäse**
  Feta cheese

4A.1
- **Ich mache heute Abend Börek!**
  I'm making boreks tonight!

4A.2
- **Du magst sie bestimmt.**
  You really will like her.

4A.3
- **Ich rufe morgen meine Mutter an und schreibe es dann auf.**
  I'll call my mother tomorrow, and I'll write it down.

Suggestion Explain to students that **Wurst** can refer to either sausage or cold cuts.

---

2 **Zum Besprechen** Sie und ein Freund möchten heute Abend eine Party geben. Spielen Sie mit einem Partner einen Dialog. Welches Essen wollen Sie servieren? Welche Zutaten brauchen Sie? Müssen Sie einkaufen gehen? Wie kochen Sie das Essen? Answers will vary.

2 **Partner Chat** You can also assign activity 2 on the Supersite.

2 **Expansion** Have students work in groups to talk about German food. Have they ever tried German food? What dishes have they heard of? Are there any German stores or restaurants in your area? Invite students from German-American families to share family recipes with the class.

3 **Vertiefung** Suchen Sie bekannte Lebensmittelhersteller (*food brands*) in Deutschland, wie Knorr, Maggi oder Haribo. Finden Sie drei bekannte Produkte und sagen Sie, welche Produkte Sie gern probieren (*try*) und warum. Präsentieren Sie Ihre Resultate im Kurs. Answers will vary.

More activities

vhlcentral   VM p. 7   Online activities

Suggestion Before reading, ask students about their own shopping habits: **Wo kaufen Sie Ihr Essen? Hat Ihre Stadt einen „Farmer's Market"? Was kann man da kaufen?**

Der Wiener Naschmarkt Reading

IN DEUTSCHLAND, ÖSTERREICH und der Schweiz hat fast jede Stadt° einen Marktplatz°. Er ist normalerweise im Zentrum der Stadt.

Stände am Naschmarkt	
Lebensmittel	40
Gastronomie°	27
Obst und Gemüse	11
Backwaren°	5
Fisch	5
Fleischwaren	3
Milchprodukte	1
Wein	1
Bier	1
Sonstiges°	1

QUELLE: http://www.wienernaschmarkt.eu

Große Städte haben oft mehr als einen Marktplatz. Berühmte° Marktplätze sind der Viktualienmarkt in München, der Alexanderplatz in Berlin, der Helvetiaplatz in Zürich und der Naschmarkt in Wien.

Der Naschmarkt ist einer der 26 Märkte in Wien. Er existiert seit über° 80 Jahren und liegt° sehr zentral. Viele Stände° auf dem Naschmarkt sind von Montag bis Samstag zwischen° 9 und 21 Uhr offen. Vor allem° samstagmorgens bei gutem Wetter° findet man alte und junge Menschen an den Ständen. Die Atmosphäre ist lebendig°: Menschen unterhalten sich° und Kunden handeln mit den Verkäufern°.

Märkte wie der Wiener Naschmarkt haben auch viele verschiedene° Waren: Es gibt Käse, Fleisch, Wurst, Obst und Gemüse. Natürlich gibt es auch Milchprodukte wie Käse und Joghurt. Außerdem° kann man Blumen oder Seife° kaufen. Der Markt ist auch sehr international mit italienischen, griechischen, türkischen und asiatischen Ständen.

fast jede Stadt almost every city **Marktplatz** market square **Berühmte** Famous **existiert seit über** has existed for more than **liegt** is located **Stände** stands **zwischen** between **Vor allem** Especially **bei gutem Wetter** when the weather is nice **lebendig** lively **unterhalten sich** chat **Kunden handeln mit den Verkäufern** buyers negotiate with the vendors **verschiedene** different **Außerdem** In addition **Seife** soap **Gastronomie** prepared foods **Backwaren** baked goods **Sonstiges** Other

1 **Im Fokus** Richtig oder falsch? Korrigieren Sie die falschen Aussagen. Diskutieren Sie dann die letzte Frage mit einem Partner/einer Partnerin.

1. Jede Stadt in Deutschland, Österreich und der Schweiz hat einen Helvetiaplatz.
   Falsch. Jede Stadt hat einen Marktplatz.
2. An fünf Ständen am Naschmarkt kann man Fisch kaufen.
   Richtig.
3. Am Naschmarkt gibt es keine Waren für Vegetarier.
   Falsch. Es gibt Obst, Gemüse, Käse und Milchprodukte.

Diskussion Was sind die Unterschiede (*differences*) und Ähnlichkeiten (*similarities*) zwischen einem traditionellen Marktplatz in Deutschland und einem amerikanischen „Farmer's Market" in Ihrer Stadt?

2 **Die deutschsprachige Welt** Richtig oder falsch? Korrigieren Sie die falschen Aussagen. Diskutieren Sie dann die letzte Frage mit einem Partner/einer Partnerin.

1. In Österreich heißen Tomaten „Paradeiser."
   Richtig.
2. In Deutschland sagt man „Obers."
   Falsch. Man sagt „Sahne."
3. In Österreich und in Deutschland sagt man „Aprikose."
   Falsch. Man sagt „Aprikose" nur in Deutschland.

Diskussion Welche regionalen Wörter und Ausdrücke benutzen Sie? Vergleichen Sie Ihre Wörtern mit Wörtern aus anderen Regionen.

DEUTSCH IM ALLTAG

Auf dem Markt

Ich hätte gern...	I would like...
ein Dutzend Eier	a dozen eggs
ein Pfund Kartoffeln	a pound of potatoes
100 Gramm Käse	100 grams of cheese
Das macht 3,80 €.	That's € 3.80.
Sonst noch etwas?	Anything else?
Was wünschen Sie?	What would you like?
Wie viel kostet das?	How much is that?

DIE DEUTSCHSPRACHIGE WELT

Das ist eine Tomate, oder?

Deutsche und Österreicher sprechen Deutsch, aber es gibt verschiedene Vokabeln. Deutsche sagen „Tomate". Was sagen Österreicher? Hier ist eine kurze Liste mit Essensvokabeln:

In Deutschland	In Österreich
die Aprikose°	die Marille
grüne Bohnen	Fisolen
das Brötchen	die Semmel
das Hackfleisch°	das Faschierte
die Kartoffel	der Erdapfel
der Meerrettich°	der Kren
der Quark°	der Topfen
die Sahne°	der Obers
die Tomate	der Paradeiser

Aprikose apricot **Hackfleisch** ground meat **Meerrettich** horseradish **Quark** curd cheese **Sahne** cream

PORTRÄT

Wolfgang Puck

Wolfgang Puck ist ein österreichischer Koch°. Er lebt und arbeitet in den USA, hat aber auch Restaurants in Toronto, Dubai, London, Singapur und Tokio. Er ist sehr erfolgreich°: Der Umsatz° seiner Firmen ist mehr als 600 Millionen Dollar pro Jahr. In den USA hat er mehr als 70 Restaurants: Bistros, Cafés und Gourmetrestaurants. Ein sehr berühmtes und sehr teures° Restaurant ist das Spago in Beverly Hills. Das Essen in seinen Restaurants ist nicht nur amerikanisch. In fast jedem Restaurant kann man neben amerikanischen Burgern auch Wiener Schnitzel° und Kärntner Kasnudeln° bestellen.

Koch chef **erfolgreich** successful **Umsatz** total revenue **teures** expensive
Wiener Schnitzel Viennese schnitzel **Kärntner Kasnudeln** South Austrian cheese noodles

∞ IM INTERNET

Wie viele Christkindlmärkte gibt es in Österreich? Wo sind sie? Welche Christkindlmärkte sind sehr berühmt?

Find out more at **vhlcentral.com**.

---

3 **Porträt** Richtig oder falsch? Korrigieren Sie die falschen Aussagen. Diskutieren Sie dann die letzte Frage mit einem Partner/ einer Partnerin.

1. Wolfgang Puck ist ein österreichischer Koch.
   Richtig.
2. Wolfgang Puck lebt in Österreich.
   Falsch. Er lebt und arbeitet in den USA.
3. Pucks Firmen sind in Nordamerika, Europa und Asien präsent.
   Richtig.

Diskussion Welche Star-Köche kennen Sie aus dem Fernsehen (TV)? Haben sie ein bekanntes Restaurant? Was kochen sie?

4 **Auf dem Naschmarkt** Schreiben Sie einen Dialog zwischen einem Kunden (customer) und einem Verkäufer auf dem Naschmarkt. Integrieren Sie die folgenden Informationen: Begrüßung, eine Obstsorte oder ein Milchprodukt, eine Gemüsesorte oder ein Fleischprodukt, Preise, Bezahlung und Abschied. Lesen Sie den Dialog der Klasse vor. Answers will vary.

BEISPIEL

S1: *Guten Tag.*
S2: *Grüß Gott. Kann ich Ihnen helfen?*
S1: *Ja. Ich hätte gerne...*

Suggestion Students should partner up to write their dialogues and either read their dialogue standing before the class or remain within grupos of four to avoid repetition.

More activities

vhlcentral | Online activities

4A.1

Adverbs Grammar Tutorial

Startblock In German, as in English, adverbs are words or phrases that modify a verb, an adjective, or another adverb. Adverbs describe *when*, *how*, or *where* an action takes place.

Ich gehe **wirklich gern** einkaufen.

Ich mache **heute Abend** Börek!

Teaching Tip You may want to assign the grammar tutorial **4A.1 Adverbs** on the Supersite for students to watch before they come to class.

Suggestion Teach students the mnemonic device "TMP" to help them remember that adverbs of <u>T</u>ime come before adverbs of <u>M</u>anner, which come before adverbs of <u>P</u>lace.

QUERVERWEIS

In **2B**, you learned to use the adverb **gern(e)** (*lit.* gladly) with a verb to say that you enjoy an activity.

See **1B.2** to review basic word order in German.

See **2A.3** to review other adverbs related to time and date.

- An adverb usually comes immediately before the adjective or adverb it modifies. Adverbs that frequently modify adjectives or other adverbs include **fast** (*almost*), **noch** (*yet; still; in addition*), **nur** (*only*), **schon** (*already*), **sehr, so** (*so*), **wirklich** (*really*), **ziemlich** (*quite*), and **zu** (*too*).

Der Kuchen ist **fast** fertig.	Du isst **viel zu** schnell.
*The cake is **almost** ready.*	*You eat **much too** quickly.*

- When an adverb modifies a verb, it generally comes immediately after the verb it modifies. Adverbs of time or place can also come directly before the verb.

Ich esse **täglich** Gemüse.	**Morgens** trinken wir **immer** Kaffee.
*I eat vegetables **every day.***	*We **always** drink coffee **in the morning.***

- Here are some common adverbs of time, manner, and place.

Suggestion On the board, write the sentence: **Ein Student fährt heute Nachmittag zu schnell zum Supermarkt.** Have students underline the adverbial phrases and identify which one describes time, which describes manner, and which describes place.

adverbs					
Wann?		**Wie?**		**Wo?**	
immer	*always*	allein	*alone*	da/dort	*there*
jetzt	*now*	bestimmt	*definitely*	drüben	*over there*
nie	*never*	leider	*unfortunately*	hier	*here*
oft	*often*	vielleicht	*maybe*	überall	*everywhere*
selten	*rarely*	zusammen	*together*	woanders	*somewhere else*
täglich	*daily*				

- Adverbs of time indicate *when* or *how frequently* an event occurs and answer the questions **wann?** and **wie oft?** (*how often?*).

Wir gehen **morgen** einkaufen.	Ich esse **selten** Kuchen.
*We're going shopping **tomorrow.***	*I **rarely** eat cake.*

- If there is more than one time expression in a sentence, general time references are placed before adverbs of specific time.

Die Bäckerei öffnet **am Sonntag um 9 Uhr**.	**Samstag morgens um 11 Uhr** frühstücke ich mit meinem Vater.
*The bakery opens at **9 o'clock on Sunday.***	*I have breakfast with my father **every Saturday morning at 11 o'clock.***

ACHTUNG

In English, you can turn an adjective into an adverb by adding the ending -*ly*.

In German, you can turn an adjective into an adverb by placing it after the verb you want to modify:

Peter ist ein gesunder Junge.
Peter is a healthy boy.

Peter isst sehr gesund.
Peter eats very healthily.

- Adverbs of manner indicate *how* an action is done. They answer the question **wie?**

<table>
<tr><td>Ich mache das allein.
I'm doing this by myself.</td><td>Du spielst wirklich gut Tennis.
You play tennis really well.</td></tr>
</table>

- Adverbs of place describe locations or directions and answer the questions **wo?**, **wohin?**, and **woher?**

<table>
<tr><td>Woher kommst du?
Where are you from?</td><td>Ich komme aus Deutschland.
I'm from Germany.</td></tr>
<tr><td>Wohin geht ihr?
Where are you going?</td><td>Wir gehen in die Eisdiele.
We're going to the ice cream shop.</td></tr>
</table>

- When there is more than one adverbial expression in a sentence, adverbs of time come first, followed by adverbs of manner, then adverbs of place.

<table>
<tr><td>Papa kauft heute in der Konditorei eine Geburtstagstorte.
Dad is getting a birthday cake today at the pastry shop.</td><td>Wir fahren zusammen zum Supermarkt.
We're going to the supermarket together.</td></tr>
<tr><td>Heute Abend esse ich vielleicht im Restaurant.
Maybe I'll eat at a restaurant tonight.</td><td>Sie essen morgen Abend bestimmt woanders.
They are definitely eating somewhere else tomorrow night.</td></tr>
</table>

- In **2B.3** you learned how to negate sentences with **nicht**. In sentences with adverbial expressions, **nicht** usually *precedes* general expressions of time, manner, and place, but *follows* adverbs of specific time.

<table>
<tr><td>Wir kaufen nicht oft Fleisch im Supermarkt.
We don't often buy meat at the supermarket.</td><td>Ich will am Montag nicht in die Schule gehen.
I don't want to go to school on Monday.</td></tr>
<tr><td>Die Gäste sind noch nicht hier.
The guests aren't here yet.</td><td>Wir können nicht mehr hier warten.
We can't wait here anymore.</td></tr>
</table>

More activities

vhlcentral

WB
pp. 49–50

LM
p. 32

Online activities

Jetzt sind Sie dran!   **Geben Sie an (Indicate), ob die Adverbien die Zeit, die Art und Weise (manner) oder den Ort beschreiben.**

1. Wir kochen heute Abend <u>zusammen</u>. _Art und Weise_
2. Marina ist <u>immer</u> besorgt. _Zeit_
3. Die Eltern trinken <u>gern</u> Rotwein. _Art und Weise_
4. Das Lebensmittelgeschäft ist <u>dort drüben</u>. _Ort_
5. Meine Schwester isst <u>nie</u> Obst und Gemüse. _Zeit_
6. Ihr trinkt <u>selten</u> Kaffee. _Zeit_

7. Du machst deine Hausaufgaben <u>allein</u>. _Art und Weise_
8. Ich fahre <u>schnell</u> zur Universität. _Art und Weise_
9. Petra hat <u>jetzt</u> keine Zeit. _Zeit_
10. Ich esse <u>oft</u> Käse und Brot. _Zeit_
11. Kann man Auberginen <u>überall</u> kaufen? _Ort_
12. Wir bleiben <u>hier</u> in Berlin. _Ort_

Suggestion Point out to students that adverbs can make their speech and writing more informative and expressive. Give them a sample sentence, such as **Anna geht spazieren**. Ask them to make it more vivid by adding adverbs that describe where, how, and when the action takes place.

Anwendung

1 **Was ist richtig?** Wählen Sie (*Choose*) das adverbiale Element, das am besten passt.

> **BEISPIEL** Ich gehe (die ganze Nacht / im Restaurant / morgens) in den Unterricht.

1. Yusuf macht (in der Bibliothek)/ im Fitnessstudio / in der Bäckerei) Hausaufgaben.
2. Wir möchten später (selten / beim Bäcker / im Park) ein Picknick machen.
3. Efe geht (im Hörsaal / im Supermarkt)/ im Café) einkaufen.
4. Das Restaurant ist (oft)/ überall / zusammen) voll (*crowded*).
5. Das Rezept ist (jetzt/ fast / wirklich) einfach.
6. Thomas isst (dort / selten) / allein) Fleisch.
7. Der Kuchen ist (abends / am Wochenende / sehr) gut.
8. Zum Mittagessen gehen wir (leider / in die Mensa)/ überall).

2 **Auf dem Campus** Setzen Sie das Adverb an die richtige Stelle.

> **BEISPIEL** Wir essen um 6 Uhr. (immer)
> *Wir essen immer um 6 Uhr.*

1. David vergisst immer seine Hausaufgaben. (fast)
   David vergisst fast immer seine Hausaufgaben.

2. Ich gehe im Supermarkt einkaufen. (oft)
   Ich gehe oft im Supermarkt einkaufen.

3. Paula geht nachmittags spazieren. (auf dem Campus)
   Paula geht nachmittags auf dem Campus spazieren.

4. Die Studenten essen in der Mensa. (nicht gern)
   Die Studenten essen nicht gern in der Mensa.

5. Ihr lernt in der Bibliothek. (abends)
   Ihr lernt abends in der Bibliothek.

6. Du gehst freitags tanzen. (im Club)
   Du gehst freitags im Club tanzen.

7. Die Professorin korrigiert die Prüfungen. (am Sonntag)
   Die Professorin korrigiert am Sonntag die Prüfungen./Die Professorin korrigiert die Prüfungen am Sonntag.

8. Julius fährt nach Berlin. (am Wochenende)
   Julius fährt am Wochenende nach Berlin.

3 Suggestion Remind students that they do not need to use words from each column in every sentence. Create one sentence together as a class, before having students work in groups.

3 **Was machen diese Leute?** Bilden Sie Sätze mit zwei Adverbien. Setzen Sie die Wörter in die richtige Reihenfolge (*order*). Answers will vary.

Subjekt	Objekt	Verb	Adverbien	
ich	das Auto	backen	gern	selten
du	die Hausaufgaben	fahren	jetzt	im Sommer
mein Vater	den Hund	kaufen	nächstes Jahr	überall
wir	einen Kuchen	machen	nie	um 9 Uhr
du und Dieter	einen Obstsalat	wandern	oft	am Wochenende
meine Freunde	einen Snack	waschen	schnell	zusammen

Kommunikation

4 **Wie und warum?** Was machen die Personen, wie machen Sie das und warum? Erfinden Sie (*Make up*) ein kurzes Szenario. Benutzen Sie (*Use*) jedes der folgenden Adverbien nur einmal (*once*): allein, langsam, oft, selten, vielleicht, zusammen. Sample answers are provided.

1. Sie lernen zusammen.

► **BEISPIEL**

S1: Wie geht er?
S2: Er geht schnell. Wohin geht er?
S3: Er geht vielleicht in den Park.

2. Er liest allein.

3. Er kocht vielleicht Reis.

4. Sie fährt langsam.

5. Sie fährt oft Fahrrad.

5 **Partnergespräch** Stellen Sie Ihrem Partner / Ihrer Partnerin Fragen. Answers will vary.

BEISPIEL

S1: Wie oft kochst du?
S2: Ich koche sehr oft. / Ich koche selten.

1. Wann lernst du?
2. Wann sind deine Kurse?
3. Wie oft gehst du in die Mensa?
4. Wann machst du deine Mittagspause?
5. Wie oft gehst du tanzen?
6. Wie oft fährst du zu den Großeltern?

6 **Meine Mitstudenten** Finden Sie für jede Aktivität eine Person aus Ihrem Kurs.

BEISPIEL

S1: Isst du oft Fisch?
S2: Nein, ich esse nicht oft Fisch.
S3: Und du?

oft / Fisch essen
gut / Gitarre spielen
täglich / in der Sporthalle trainieren
selten / Gemüse essen
gern / am Wochenende tanzen gehen
oft / Schokomilch trinken
nie / samstags im Haus bleiben
immer / Eier zum Frühstück essen
gut / kochen können

5 **Video Virtual Chat** You can also assign activity 5 on the Supersite.

6 **Suggestion** Before students begin the activity, make sure they know how to form the questions properly. Emphasize that they must answer using complete sentences. During the activity, circulate around the room and interact with students, asking them questions and keeping them on task.

NATIONAL comparisons STANDARDS

4A.2   # The modal *mögen* Grammar Tutorial

Startblock In **2B Kontext**, you learned to express likes and dislikes using **gern** and **nicht gern**. Another way of expressing liking is with the modal **mögen**.

Hey! Ich **mag** das! Danke.

Meline ist lustig. Du **magst** sie bestimmt.

ACHTUNG

While **gern** is always used with a verb, **mögen** is typically used with a noun:
Wir mögen Erdbeeren.
But: **Wir essen gern Erdbeeren.**

Ich mag keinen Tee.
But: **Ich trinke nicht gern Tee.**

Since **gern** is an adverb, it can also be used in combination with **mögen**, for emphasis:

Was magst du gern?
Das mag ich nicht so gern.

QUERVERWEIS

See **3B.1** to review the other modal verbs: **dürfen, können, müssen, sollen,** and **wollen**.

See **2B.3** to review negation.

You will learn more about subjunctive forms in **9B.1**.

• Like all the modal verbs, **mögen** is irregular in the singular.

Suggestion Point out that, as with other modals, the **er/sie/es** form of **mögen** is identical to its **ich** form.

mögen (*to like*)			
ich mag	*I like*	wir mögen	*we like*
du magst	*you like*	ihr mögt	*you like*
er/sie/es mag	*he/she/it likes*	Sie/sie mögen	*you/they like*

• While most modals modify another verb, **mögen** almost always modifies a noun.

Mögt ihr diesen Joghurt?
*Do you **like** this yogurt?*

Nein, diesen Joghurt **mögen** wir **nicht**.
*No, we **don't like** that yogurt.*

• Depending on context, you can use either **nicht** or **kein** to negate a statement with **mögen**.

Ich **mag keine** grünen Paprika.
*I **don't like** green peppers.*

Magst du rote Paprika?
*Do you **like** red peppers?*

Nein, rote Paprika **mag** ich auch **nicht**.
*No, I **don't like** red peppers either.*

• **Möchten** is the subjunctive form of **mögen**. Use **möchten** for polite requests and to say what you *would like* to have or do. **Möchten** may be followed by either a verb or a noun.

More activities

S vhlcentral

WB pp. 51–52

LM p. 33

Online activities

möchten			
ich möchte	*I would like*	wir möchten	*we would like*
du möchtest	*you would like*	ihr möchtet	*you would like*
er/sie/es möchte	*he/she/it would like*	Sie/sie möchten	*you/they would like*

Wir **möchten** Fußball spielen.
*We **would like** to play soccer.*

Möchten Sie Kaffee oder Tee?
***Would** you **like** coffee or tea?*

Suggestion Explain to students that "**Ich mag keine grünen Paprika.**", "**Grüne Paprika mag ich nicht.**", and "**Ich mag grüne Paprika nicht gern.**" all convey the same idea, but with slightly different emphasis.

Jetzt sind Sie dran!   **Ergänzen Sie die Lücken mit den richtigen Formen der Modalverben mögen oder möchten.**

1. Die Kinder __mögen__ (mögen) Schokolade.
2. Ich __mag__ (mögen) keinen Fußball.
3. Julia __möchte__ (möchten) in die Konditorei gehen.
4. __Möchtest__ (Möchten) du Pasta oder Reis?
5. Anne __mag__ (mögen) russische Literatur.
6. __Möchten__ (Möchten) Sie einen Tisch am Fenster?
7. Ihr __möchtet__ (möchten) zur Bäckerei gehen.
8. __Magst__ (Mögen) du Meeresfrüchte nicht?
9. Ich __möchte__ (möchten) kein Fleisch essen.
10. Unsere Katzen __mögen__ (mögen) unseren Hund nicht.
11. __Mögt__ (Mögen) ihr Garnelen?
12. Wir __möchten__ (möchten) Pasta.

Anwendung und Kommunikation

1 **Wer mag was?** Schreiben Sie die Sätze um. Benutzen Sie **mögen** anstatt **essen** oder **trinken gern.** Some answers may vary.

> **BEISPIEL** Ich esse nicht gern Garnelen.
>
> *Ich mag keine Garnelen. / Ich mag Garnelen nicht.*

1. Meine Schwester isst gern Schokolade. Meine Schwester mag Schokolade.
2. Meine Eltern essen gern Bananen zum Frühstück. Meine Eltern mögen Bananen zum Frühstück.
3. Ich esse nicht gern Auberginen. Ich mag Auberginen nicht./Ich mag keine Auberginen.
4. Mein Mann und ich essen gern Pizza. Mein Mann und ich mögen Pizza.
5. Esst ihr gern Würstchen? Mögt ihr Würstchen?
6. Trinkst du nicht gern Kaffee? Magst du keine Kaffee?/Magst du Kaffee nicht?

2 **Pläne** Ergänzen Sie die Sätze mit der richtigen Form von **möchten** und mit Wörtern aus der Liste.

am Wochenende Fußball spielen	schlafen
im Biergarten essen	tanzen
heiraten	Tennis spielen

> ▶ **BEISPIEL**
>
> Ben und Simon
>
> *möchten am Wochenende Fußball spielen.*

1. Elias und Emma möchten heiraten.

2. Paula, du möchtest schlafen.

3. Professor Klein möchte Tennis spielen.

4. Alex und du, ihr möchtet tanzen.

5. Marie und ich, wir möchten im Biergarten essen.

3 **Was magst du?** Fragen Sie Ihren Partner / Ihre Partnerin, was er/sie (nicht) mag. Fragen Sie auch nach den anderen Personen in seiner/ihrer Familie. Answers will vary.

> **BEISPIEL**
>
> **S1:** *Magst du Thunfisch?*
> **S2:** *Nein, aber ich mag Käse.*
> **S1:** *Und dein Bruder? Mag er Thunfisch?*
> **S2:** *Nein, aber er mag Würstchen.*

3 Suggestion You may want to teach students the words **igitt** and **lecker** for use in this activity.

2 Expansion Have students write 5 sentences about what *they* would like to do this weekend, using **möchten**.

3 Partner Chat You can also assign activity 3 on the Supersite. Students work in pairs to record the activity online. The pair's recorded conversation will appear in your gradebook.

4A.3

Separable and inseparable prefix verbs

 Grammar Tutorial

Startblock In German, many verbs have a prefix in their infinitive form.

> Ich gehe wirklich gern **einkaufen**.

> Lass mich **überlegen**.

- A verb with a prefix has the same conjugations as its base form, but the added prefix changes the meaning.

  Sucht ihr eure Eltern?
  *Are you **looking for** your parents?*

  Besucht ihr eure Verwandten?
  *Do you **visit** your relatives?*

- Some prefixes are always attached to the verb and others can be separated from it.

  Jakob **verkauft** sein Fahrrad.
  *Jakob **is selling** his bike.*

  Ich **kaufe** im Supermarkt **ein**.
  *I **shop** at the supermarket.*

- Here are some of the most common separable and inseparable prefix verbs.

verbs with separable prefixes	
anfangen	*to begin*
ankommen	*to arrive*
anrufen	*to call*
aufstehen	*to get up*
ausgehen	*to go out*
einkaufen	*to shop*
einschlafen	*to fall asleep*
mitbringen	*to bring along*
mitkommen	*to come along*
vorbereiten	*to prepare*
vorstellen	*to introduce*
zuschauen	*to watch*
zurückkommen	*to come back*

verbs with inseparable prefixes	
beantworten	*to answer*
besprechen	*to discuss*
bestellen	*to order*
besuchen	*to visit*
bezahlen	*to pay (for)*
erklären	*to explain*
verkaufen	*to sell*
verbringen	*to spend (time)*
überlegen	*to think over*
wiederholen	*to repeat*

- Separable prefixes are generally prepositions (**an**, **aus**, **mit**) or other parts of speech that carry meaning and can stand alone. In contrast, most inseparable prefixes (**be-**, **er-**, **ver-**) have no independent meaning and never stand alone.

  Heute Abend **gehen** wir zusammen **aus**.
  *Tonight we're **going out** together.*

  Ich **bestelle** die Pasta mit Garnelen.
  *I'm **ordering** the pasta with shrimp.*

  Stefan **steht** jeden Morgen um 6 Uhr **auf**.
  *Stefan **gets up** at 6 o'clock every morning.*

  Ihr **verkauft** euer Auto?
  *You're **selling** your car?*

QUERVERWEIS

See **2B.1** to review the present tense of irregular verbs like **fangen** and **schlafen**.

The verb **vorstellen** is often used reflexively. You will learn more about reflexive verbs in **9A.1** and **9A.2**.

Suggestion Give students the name of a celebrity and ask them to write sentences about what this celebrity does on a typical Saturday, using 5-6 separable or inseparable prefix verbs. Create the first sentence as a class.

ACHTUNG

When speaking, place the stress on the prefix of a separable prefix verb: **anrufen**, **einschlafen**. The prefix of an inseparable prefix verb is never stressed: **verkaufen**, **wiederholen**.

- When using a separable prefix verb in the present tense or the imperative, move the prefix to the end of the sentence or clause.

Wir **kaufen** auf dem Markt **ein**.
We're shopping at the market.

Bitte **stellen** Sie die Frau **vor**.
Please introduce the woman.

Kommst du **zurück**?
Are you coming back?

Ruf deine Eltern **an**!
Call your parents!

Wir **bringen** Käse und Brot **mit**.

Wir **laden** Meline und Sabite zu uns zu Börek **ein**?

ACHTUNG

In this book, separable prefix verbs will be presented with their third person present-tense form in parentheses: **einkaufen (kauft... ein)**

- To make the sentence negative, add **nicht** immediately before the separable prefix.

Ich komme **nicht** zurück.
I'm not coming back.

Ruf deine Eltern **nicht** an!
Don't call your parents!

- When using a modal with a separable prefix verb, move the infinitive of the separable prefix verb to the end of the sentence.

Die Mädchen **möchten** morgen Abend **ausgehen**.
The girls want to go out tomorrow night.

Ich **muss** mit meinen Hausaufgaben **anfangen**.
I need to start my homework.

Expansion Before they begin the **Jetzt sind Sie dran!** activity, have students identify which verbs have separable prefixes and which do not.

- The prefix of an inseparable prefix verb always remains attached to the beginning of the verb.

Ich **bezahle** die Lebensmittel.
I'll pay for the groceries.

Wiederholen Sie den Satz.
Repeat the sentence.

More activities

vhlcentral

WB
pp. 53–54

LM
p. 34

Online activities

Jetzt sind Sie dran! Schreiben Sie die richtige Form des Verbs in Klammern.

1. Ich __wiederhole__ den Satz. (wiederholen)
2. Wir __rufen__ unsere Freunde __an__. (anrufen)
3. Erwin und Marta __verkaufen__ ihr Haus. (verkaufen)
4. Du musst heute Abend noch __einkaufen__. (einkaufen)
5. Der Student __stellt__ seine Eltern __vor__. (vorstellen)

6. __Gehen__ wir am Wochenende __aus__? (ausgehen)
7. Papa __bestellt__ gern Meeresfrüchte. (bestellen)
8. Ich __verbringe__ eine Woche in Zürich. (verbringen)
9. Kannst du Brot __mitbringen__? (mitbringen)
10. Wir __besuchen__ unsere Verwandten in Salzburg. (besuchen)

Anwendung

1 **Befehle** Geben Sie Befehle (*commands*) in der **Sie**-Form.

 BEISPIEL

aufstehen
Stehen Sie auf.

1. anrufen   Rufen Sie an.
2. einkaufen   Kaufen Sie ein.
3. bezahlen   Bezahlen Sie.
4. zuschauen   Schauen Sie zu.
5. nicht mitkommen   Kommen Sie nicht mit.

6. überlegen   Überlegen Sie.
7. anfangen   Fangen Sie an.
8. nicht einschlafen   Schlafen Sie nicht ein.
9. zurückkommen   Kommen Sie zurück.
10. nicht ausgehen   Gehen Sie nicht aus.

2 **Fragen** Formulieren Sie die Fragen um und benutzen Sie (*use*) dabei die angegebenen (*indicated*) Modalverben.

 BEISPIEL

Kommst du mit? (können)
Kannst du mitkommen?

1. Gehst du aus? (wollen)   Willst du ausgehen?
2. Kaufen wir ein? (sollen)   Sollen wir einkaufen?
3. Kommt Lisa mit? (müssen)   Muss Lisa mitkommen?

4. Fangt ihr an? (möchten)   Möchtet ihr anfangen?
5. Schläfst du ein? (dürfen)   Darfst du einschlafen?
6. Schaut Nils zu? (können)   Kann Nils zuschauen?

3 **Was machen sie?** Schreiben Sie zu jedem (*each*) Foto einen Satz und benutzen Sie Präfixverben.

> Freunde anrufen
> heute Abend ausgehen
> die Bücher bezahlen
> einkaufen
> einschlafen
> die Grammatik erklären
> euren Hund mitbringen

▶ **BEISPIEL**
Herr Schröder
Herr Schröder erklärt die Grammatik.

ich
1. Ich schlafe ein.

Jana und Lina
2. Jana und Lina rufen Freunde an.

Emma und ihre Freunde
3. Emma und ihre Freunde gehen heute Abend aus.

Stefanie
4. Stefanie bezahlt die Bücher.

Frau Neumann und ihre Tochter
5. Frau Neumann und ihre Tochter kaufen ein.

ihr
6. Ihr bringt euren Hund mit.

Kommunikation

4 **Mein Tag** Füllen Sie einen Terminkalender mit Ihren Informationen aus und diskutieren Sie dann mit Ihrem Partner / Ihrer Partnerin, was Sie täglich so machen. Answers will vary.

BEISPIEL

S1: Ich stehe um 8 Uhr auf. Und du?
S2: Ich stehe um 8.30 Uhr auf. Meine erste Vorlesung fängt um 10 Uhr an. Und deine?

8.00	*Ich stehe auf.*
9.00	
10.00	
11.00	
12.00	
13.00	
14.00	
15.00	

5 **Wer ist das?** Wählen Sie eine Person und schreiben Sie zwei Dinge auf, die diese (*this*) Person macht. Ihre Mitstudenten müssen raten (*guess*), wer es ist. Answers will vary.

BEISPIEL

S1: Sie kommt um 8 Uhr zur Uni.
Sie erklärt die Hausaufgaben und beantwortet unsere Fragen.
S2: Ist es die Professorin?

anfangen	ausgehen	besuchen	erklären	verbringen
ankommen	beantworten	bezahlen	mitbringen	vorbereiten
anrufen	besprechen	einkaufen	mitkommen	zurückkommen

6 **Ein Picknick machen** Sie und Ihre Freunde planen ein Picknick. Diskutieren Sie, wer was kauft, wer was mitbringt und was Sie alles machen müssen. Answers will vary.

BEISPIEL

S1: Sollen wir viele Freunde anrufen?
S2: Ja, und wir müssen auch viel Essen mitbringen.
S3: Ich bringe Wurst und Käse mit!

4 **Partner Chat** You can also assign activity 4 on the Supersite. Students work in pairs to record the activity online. The pair's recorded conversation will appear in your gradebook.

Wiederholung

1 **Expansion** Ask students to brainstorm other good food combinations and then have the class vote on the best one.

1 **Was magst du?** Fragen Sie einen Partner / eine Partnerin, was er/sie mag oder nicht mag. Answers will vary.

1 **Partner Chat** You can also assign activity 1 on the Supersite.

BEISPIEL

S1: *Magst du Hähnchen mit Reis?*
S2: *Ja, ich mag Hähnchen mit Reis. Und du?*
S1: *Nein, ich mag Hähnchen mit Reis nicht. Magst du...?*

Würstchen mit Brot	Schweinefleisch mit Kartoffeln
Thunfisch mit Zwiebeln	Auberginen mit Tomaten
Pasta mit Pilzen	Schinken mit Brot
Hähnchen mit Reis	Pasta mit Käse
Garnelen mit Tomaten	Rindfleisch mit Salat

2 **Das Wochenende** Sagen Sie, was die Personen am Wochenende machen möchten. Wechseln Sie sich (*Take turns*) mit einem Partner / einer Partnerin ab. Answers will vary.

▶ **BEISPIEL**

S1: *Was möchte Klara am Wochenende machen?*
S2: *Klara möchte am Wochenende gern lesen.*

Klara

1. Petra und Klaus

2. Paul, Manfred, Andrea und Monika

3. Inge

4. Robert

3 **Arbeitsblatt** Fragen Sie Ihre Mitstudenten, wie oft, wie und wo sie diese Lebensmittel essen. Answers will vary.

BEISPIEL

S1: *Wie oft isst du Eier in der Mensa?*
S2: *Ich esse selten Eier in der Mensa.*

4 **Was machen sie?** Ein Student / Eine Studentin spielt eine Situation. Die anderen Studenten raten (*guess*) die Situation. Benutzen Sie vollständige (*complete*) Sätze. Answers will vary.

BEISPIEL

S1: *Fährst du Fahrrad?*
S2: *Nein.*
S1: *Reitest du ein Pferd?*
S2: *Ja.*

4 **Suggestion** Remind students of the stem-vowel change in the verbs **fahren** and **schlafen**. Model correct pronunciation in both the **ich** and **du** forms.

aufstehen	im Restaurant	einschlafen
ausgehen	bestellen	Fahrrad fahren
einen Kuchen	einen Freund	ein Pferd reiten
backen	besuchen	Volleyball spielen

5 **Diskutieren und kombinieren** Sie bekommen eine Tabelle von Ihrem Professor / Ihrer Professorin. Fragen Sie einen Partner / eine Partnerin, wann die Personen die Aktivitäten machen.

BEISPIEL

S1: *Wann geht Alex Lebensmittel einkaufen?*
S2: *Alex geht am Samstag Lebensmittel einkaufen.*

6 **Der Wochenplan** Entscheiden Sie (*Decide*), was Sie diese Woche machen wollen. Suchen Sie andere Studenten in der Gruppe, die das Gleiche planen und finden Sie eine gemeinsame Zeit, wann sie das machen können. Answers will vary.

BEISPIEL

S1: *Willst du diese Woche einkaufen gehen?*
S2: *Ja, ich will diese Woche einkaufen gehen.*
S1: *Können wir zusammen einkaufen gehen?*
S2: *Ja, gern.*
S1: *Hast du am Mittwoch Zeit?*
S2: *Nein, am Mittwoch habe ich keine Zeit. Hast du am Donnerstag Zeit?*
S1: *Ja, am Donnerstag habe ich Zeit. Um wie viel Uhr...*

6 **Suggestion** Have students brainstorm activities before they begin the exercise.

6 **Expansion** Instead of working in small groups, have students stand up and circulate throughout the entire class.

Video

Yello Strom

1 **Vorbereitung** Besprechen Sie zu zweit die Fragen. Answers will vary.

1. Wo kaufen Sie oder Ihre Familie Obst und Gemüse?
2. Was kaufen Sie online?
3. Wer kocht bei Ihnen? Kochen Sie mit Gas oder mit Strom?

Wechseln Sie zum Yello Strom!

Yello Strom ist eine kreative deutsche Stromfirma mit neuen Ideen. Kundenservice ist sehr wichtig für Yello Strom. In ihrem Werbeclip zeigt die Firma, dass Kunden bei Yello Strom nur mit echten Menschen reden.

Nützliche Ausdrücke	
gelb	*yellow*
der Kunde, -n	*customer*
die Stromfirma, Stromfirmen	*electric power company*
zeigen	*to show*

2 **Richtig oder falsch?** Sehen Sie sich das Video an und entscheiden Sie, ob die Aussagen richtig oder falsch sind. Korrigieren Sie die falschen Aussagen.

	richtig	falsch	
1. Der Verkäufer begrüßt die Frau mit „Guten Tag".	☐	☑	Der Mann sagt: „Hallo! Und willkommen!".
2. Die Frau möchte drei Äpfel kaufen.	☑	☐	
3. Yello Strom ist gut und günstig.	☑	☐	
4. Yello Strom war schon dreimal Testsieger.	☐	☑	Yello Strom war zweimal Testsieger.

3 **Diskussion** Diskutieren Sie zu zweit die Fragen. Answers will vary.

1. Wie finden Sie die Werbung (*commercial*)?
2. Wie finden Sie Telefonmenüs? Funktionieren sie gut? Sind sie praktisch oder frustrierend?

4 **Präsentation** Spielen Sie zu zweit ein Telefonangespäch beim Kundenservice. Sie sind der Verkäufer / die Verkäuferin und Ihr Partner / Ihre Partnerin ist Kunde / Kundin. Schreiben Sie einige Stichworte (*key words*) auf bevor Sie das Gespräch beginnen. Answers will vary.

- **Begrüßung:** Guten Tag. / Mein Name ist ...
- **Problem:** Mein Rucksack ist kaput (*broken*).
- **Lösung (*solution*):** Ich bekomme mein Geld zurück.

More activities

vhlcentral

Online activities

Im Restaurant

 Vocabulary Tools

Wortschatz

im Restaurant	*at the restaurant*
die Beilage, -n	side dish
das Besteck	silverware
die Flasche, -n	bottle
der erste/zweite Gang	first/second course
das Gericht, -e	dish
die Hauptspeise, -n	main course
der Nachtisch, -e	dessert
die Rechnung, -en	check
die Tasse, -n	cup
das Trinkgeld	tip
die Vorspeise, -n	appetizer
Mahlzeiten	*meals*
das Abendessen	dinner
das Frühstück	breakfast
das Mittagessen	lunch
der Snack, -s	snack
Getränke	*drinks*
das Bier	beer
der Kaffee	coffee
die Milch	milk
das Mineralwasser	sparkling water
der Saft, ⁻e	juice
der Tee	tea
das stille Wasser	still water
der Wein	wine
Essen beschreiben	*talking about food*
der Geschmack, ⁻e	flavor; taste
fade	bland
lecker	delicious
leicht	light
salzig	salty
scharf	spicy
schwer	rich, heavy
süß	sweet
Ausdrücke	*expressions*
Ich hätte gern(e)...	I would like...
auf Diät sein	to be on a diet
hausgemacht	homemade

Explain that **ein Gericht** refers to a particular food item whereas **ein Teller** is the plate on which it is served.

Suggestion Point out the compound words **Hauptspeise**, **Vorspeise**, and **Speisekarte**. Ask students for a synonym for **Speise**.

Suggestion Point out that the word **Snack** has come into German from English. Tell students that Germans also use the word **die Zwischenmahlzeit**, while Austrians often say **die Jause**.

Suggestion Point out that the noun **Geschmack** comes from the verb **schmecken**.

der Koch, ⁻e
(die Köchin, -nen *f.*)

Die Suppe schmeckt gut.
(schmecken)
The soup tastes good.

der Kellner, -
(die Kellnerin, -nen *f.*)

die Gabel, -n

die Speisekarte, -n

die Serviette, -n

der Teller, -

das Messer, -

die Tischdecke, -n
tablecloth

Anwendung

1 Was passt nicht? Welches Wort passt nicht zu den anderen?

1. die Gabel / das Messer / (die Serviette) / der Löffel
2. die Milch / der Saft / der Kaffee / (das Salz)
3. (die Speisekarte) / die Flasche / die Tasse / das Glas
4. salzig / (stolz) / scharf / süß
5. die Kellnerin / die Köchin / (der Saft) / der Koch
6. das Mittagessen / (die Beilage) / das Abendessen / das Frühstück

2 Stimmt das oder nicht? Hören Sie zu und entscheiden Sie, ob die Sätze stimmen (make sense).

	Stimmt	Stimmt nicht		Stimmt	Stimmt nicht
1.	✓		4.		✓
2.	✓		5.	✓	
3.		✓	6.		✓

3 Wie schmeckt's? Beschreiben Sie (Describe) den Geschmack der Lebensmittel. Sample answers are provided.

▶ **BEISPIEL** Die Bratwurst ist _scharf_.

1. Der Saft ist _süß_.
2. Die Suppe ist _schwer_.
3. Der Salat ist _leicht_.

4. Der Käse ist _salzig_.
5. Das Brot ist _fade_.
6. Der Kuchen ist _lecker_.

4 Was bestellen wir? Hören Sie den Dialog an und markieren Sie, was Tom, Klara und Murat bestellen.

Essen	Tom	Klara	Murat
1. Steak	✓		
2. Cola			✓
3. Meeresfrüchtesalat		✓	
4. stilles Wasser	✓		
5. gemischter Salat	✓		
6. Brot		✓	

Sie bestellen. (bestellen) They are ordering.

das Salz   das Glas, ̈-er
der Pfeffer
der Esslöffel, -
der Teelöffel, -

Suggestion Tell students that a soup spoon may also be referred to as **der Suppenlöffel.**

Kommunikation

5 **Verschiedene Mahlzeiten** Fragen Sie Ihren Partner / Ihre Partnerin, welche Mahlzeiten auf den Fotos zu sehen sind. Wechseln Sie sich ab (*Take turns*). Sample answers are provided.

5 **Video Virtual Chat** You can also assign activity 5 on the Supersite.

▶ **BEISPIEL**

das Frühstück
S1: Ist das das Frühstück?
S2: Nein, das ist das Abendessen.

1. **die Vorspeise**
Ist das die Vorspeise?
Nein, das ist der Nachtisch.

2. **die Hauptspeise**
Ist das die Hauptspeise?
Nein, das ist ein Getränk.

3. **der Nachtisch**
Ist das der Nachtisch?
Nein, das ist das Mittagessen.

4. **das Abendessen**
Ist das das Abendessen?
Nein, das ist das Frühstück.

5. **ein Snack**
Ist das ein Snack?
Nein, das ist das Abendessen.

6. **das Mittagessen**
Ist das das Mittagessen?
Nein, das ist ein Snack.

Wo möchten wir heute Abend essen? Sie möchten heute Abend ins Restaurant essen gehen. Lesen Sie die Speisekarte und überlegen Sie, was Sie zu jedem (*for each*) Gang bestellen wollen. Answers will vary.

Suggestion Explain to students that **Nachspeise** and **Dessert** are synonyms for **Nachtisch** commonly used on restaurant menus.

BEISPIEL

S1: Ich möchte gern den Tomatensalat mit Mozzarella als ersten Gang.
S2: Ich auch! Und als zweiten Gang bestelle ich das Hähnchen mit Reis.
S3: Wollt ihr auch Getränke bestellen?

8 **Expansion** Have students work in groups to create a commercial for their "ideal restaurant" and present it to the class. You may want to provide prompts. Ex.: **Unser Restaurant ist/hat... Das Essen ist... Wir servieren... In unserem Restaurant kann man... Die Atmosphäre ist... Die Kellner sind...**

Speisekarte

Vorspeisen
Tagessuppe
Chef-Salat mit Schinken, Käse und Ei
Bauern-Salat mit Schafskäse, Zwiebeln und Oliven
Tomatensalat mit Mozzarella

Beilagen
Kartoffelsalat
Karottensalat
Grüner Salat
Kartoffelpuffer
Sauerkraut

Nachspeisen
Apfelkuchen
Bananen mit Schokolade
hausgemachter Joghurt mit Himbeermarmalade
Obstsalat

Hauptspeisen
Würstchen mit Brötchen
Thunfisch mit Salat
Hähnchen mit Reis
Rindfleisch mit Pommes frites
Schweinefleisch mit Kartoffeln
Pasta mit Garnelen
Pasta mit Käse

Getränke
stilles Wasser
Mineralwasser
Orangensaft
Milch
Kaffee
Tee

---

7 **Stress im Restaurant!** Sie sind im Restaurant und der Kellner bringt Ihr Essen. Aber auf dem Tisch gibt es kein Besteck, kein Brot, keine Getränke, kein Salz und so weiter. Sagen Sie dem Kellner, was er noch alles bringen soll. Answers will vary.

BEISPIEL

S1: Kann ich bitte auch Messer und Gabel haben?
S2: Und bitte zwei Glas Wasser!
S3: Natürlich. Möchten sie noch etwas (*anything else*)?

8 **Diskutieren und kombinieren** Wie sind die Restaurants „Zum Grünen Baum" und „Zur Stadtmauer"? Fragen Sie Ihren Partner / Ihre Partnerin, und ergänzen Sie die fehlenden (*missing*) Informationen.

BEISPIEL

S1: Was für ein Restaurant ist „Zur Stadtmauer"?
S2: Es ist ein vegetarisches Bistro. Und was für ein Restaurant ist „Zum Grünen Baum"?
S1: Dort gibt es traditionelle deutsche Gerichte. Welche Vorspeisen gibt es im Bistro?

Aussprache und Rechtschreibung Audio

The German *s* in combination with other letters

The letter combination **sch** is pronounced like the *sh* in the English word *fish*.

| Fisch | Schinken | Geschäft | Fleisch | Schule |

When an **s** appears at the beginning of a word in front of the letter **p** or **t**, it is also pronounced like the *sh* in *fish*. A prefix added to the word will not change the pronunciation of the **s**. However, if the **sp** or **st** letter combination occurs in the middle or at the end of a word, the **s** is pronounced like the *s* in the English word *restore*.

| Speise | stoppen | versprechen | Aspirin | Fenster |

In a few words borrowed from other languages, **sh** and **ch** are also pronounced like the *sh* in *fish*.

| Chauffeur | Cashewnuss | Shampoo | Champignon | charmant |

At the beginning of a word, the letter combination **tsch** is pronounced like the *ch* in *chat*. In the middle or at the end of a word, **tsch** is pronounced like the *tch* in *catch*.

| tschüss | Tschad | Tschechien | Rutsch | Klatschbase |

---

1 **Aussprechen** Wiederholen Sie die Wörter, die Sie hören.

1. Schaft
2. waschen
3. Sport
4. Strudel
5. aufstehen
6. Kasten
7. Aspekt
8. Putsch
9. platschen
10. Kutscher

2 **Nachsprechen** Wiederholen Sie die Sätze, die Sie hören.

1. Im Lebensmittelgeschäft kaufst du Schinken und Fisch.
2. In der Schule schwimmen alle Schüler im Schwimmbad.
3. Studenten spielen gern Videospiele.
4. Auf der Speisekarte steht Käsespätzle.
5. Der Tscheche sagt nicht mal tschüss.
6. Ich wünsche dir einen guten Rutsch ins neue Jahr!

3 **Sprichwörter** Wiederholen Sie die Sprichwörter, die Sie hören.

Besser spät als nie.[1]

Reden ist Silber; Schweigen ist Gold.[2]

> **2 Suggestion** Point out that **Einen guten Rutsch ins neue Jahr!** is a common New Year's greeting in German.
>
> **2 Expansion** Item 2 is a tongue twister. Have students take turns trying to say it as quickly as possible. You may also want to teach students the tongue twister **Fischers Fritz fischt frische Fische.**

[1] Better late than never.
[2] Talk is silver; silence is golden.

More activities

vhlcentral | LM p. 36 | Online activities

Fotoroman

Die Rechnung, bitte! Video

Torsten und Sabite sind bei einem romantischen Abendessen in einem
schönen Restaurant. Aber es bleibt nicht so romantisch...

Vorbereitung Have students scan the script to find
words and expressions related to food.

NATIONAL communication cultures STANDARDS

KELLNER Wir bieten eine leckere hausgemachte
Pilzsuppe an. Nicht zu schwer.
SABITE Davon nehme ich einen Teller,
bitte. Und als zweiten Gang nehme ich
die Rindsrouladen.
KELLNER Sehr gerne. Und für Sie, mein Herr?
TORSTEN Als Vorspeise nehme ich den Salat
und als Hauptspeise das Wiener Schnitzel,
mit Salzkartoffeln, bitte.
KELLNER Ausgezeichnet.

SABITE Sie haben sehr gutes Essen in
diesem Restaurant.
TORSTEN Ja. Meine ältere Schwester empfiehlt
es guten Freunden wärmstens.

KELLNER Möchten Sie gerne noch
einen Nachtisch?
MELINE Ach, ich muss auf meine Figur achten!
KELLNER Oh, nein, Sie sind doch extrem...
LORENZO Wir nehmen ein Stück Schwarzwälder
Kirschtorte. Zwei Gabeln.
MELINE Und zwei Kaffee bitte.

SABITE Hallo!
MELINE Sabite! Hallo! Sabite, das ist Lorenzo.
Lorenzo, das ist meine Mitbewohnerin, Sabite.
LORENZO Ciao.

LORENZO Ich komme aus Milano.
MELINE Lorenzo ist geschäftlich in
Berlin. Er arbeitet im Bereich
internationale Finanzen.
LORENZO Bist du auch Studentin?
SABITE Ja, ich studiere Kunst.

SABITE Ich liebe die Kunst von Kandinsky
und Klee. Aber Italien hat die Meister...
Michelangelo... Da Vinci...
LORENZO Ja. Du musst sie mal aus der
Nähe sehen.
SABITE Ich hoffe, sie eines Tages sehen
zu können. Mein Vater kommt aus
der Türkei. Ich möchte dort gern ein
Semester lang studieren.

ÜBUNGEN

1 **Richtig oder falsch?** Entscheiden Sie, ob die folgenden Sätze
richtig oder **falsch** sind.

1. Sabite nimmt die Pilzsuppe und die Roulade. Richtig.
2. Torsten bestellt ein Schnitzel mit Salzkartoffeln. Richtig.
3. Torstens Schwester empfiehlt ihren Freunden das Restaurant. Richtig.
4. Meline und Lorenzo bestellen zwei Stück Schwarzwälder Kirschtorte. Falsch.
5. Lorenzo kommt aus Italien. Richtig.

6. Er studiert Kunst. Falsch.
7. Sabite mag die Kunst von Klee und Picasso. Falsch.
8. Sie möchte ein Jahr in der Türkei studieren. Falsch.
9. Sie möchte Istanbul kennen lernen. Richtig.
10. Sabite findet Torsten egoistisch. Richtig.

1 **Expansion** Have students correct the false sentences.

PERSONEN

 Torsten   **Sabite**   **Meline**   **Lorenzo**   **Kellner**

7

SABITE Torsten, ist alles in Ordnung?
TORSTEN Türkei? Du möchtest in der Türkei studieren?
SABITE Ich möchte Istanbul kennen lernen.

8

SABITE Hör auf. Noch studiert niemand in der Türkei. Entschuldige bitte.
TORSTEN Sabite!

9

SABITE Torsten ist... ist... ist so egoistisch!

10

TORSTEN Frauen. Und du bist also nicht Lukas?
LORENZO Die Rechnung, bitte!

Nützliche Ausdrücke

- **anbieten**
  to offer

- **Davon nehme ich einen Teller, bitte.**
  I would like a bowl of that, please.

- **die Rindsroulade**
  beef roulade

- **die Salzkartoffeln**
  boiled potatoes

- **Ich muss auf meine Figur achten.**
  I have to watch my weight.

- **die Schwarzwälder Kirschtorte**
  Black Forest cake

- **Er ist geschäftlich in Berlin.**
  He's in Berlin on business.

- **Er arbeitet im Bereich internationale Finanzen.**
  He works in international finance.

- **Ich hoffe, sie eines Tages sehen zu können.**
  I hope to see them someday.

- **ein Semester lang**
  for one semester

- **Hör auf!**
  Cut it out!

- **Noch studiert niemand in der Türkei.**
  No one's studying in Turkey just yet.

4B.1
- **Meine ältere Schwester empfiehlt es guten Freunden wärmstens.**
  My older sister highly recommends it to her close friends.

4B.2
- **Du musst sie mal aus der Nähe sehen.**
  You should see them up close.

---

2 **Zum Besprechen** Wählen Sie zu dritt ein Gericht aus Deutschland, Österreich oder der Schweiz und machen Sie eine Liste mit Zutaten. Präsentieren Sie dann die Liste im Kurs. Ihre Kommilitonen müssen das Gericht erraten (*guess*).   Answers will vary.

2 **Expansion** Name some well-known German, Austrian or Swiss dishes (**Kaiserschmarrn, Sauerbraten, Knödel,** etc.), and ask students to find the main ingredients. Write any new words on the board.

3 **Vertiefung** Das Wiener Schnitzel ist ein bekanntes (*well known*) Gericht aus einem deutschsprachigen Land. Wissen Sie, woher es kommt? Kennen Sie andere Gerichte, die den Namen einer deutschen oder amerikanischen Stadt haben?

Sample answers: Wiener Schnitzel: Wien (*Vienna*); Frankfurter (Würstchen), Hamburger, Nürnberger (Bratwürstchen), Berliner (*jelly doughnut*), Kassler (*smoked pork chop*). Philadelphia cheesesteak sandwich, New York cheesecake, Boston cream pie, Texas toast.

More activities

vhlcentral | VM p. 8 | Online activities

IM FOKUS

Wiener Kaffeehäuser Reading

KAFFEEHÄUSER IN ÖSTERREICH HABEN eine lange Tradition. Kaffeehäuser gibt es seit dem 18. Jahrhundert. In Wien findet man heute ungefähr 1.000 Kaffeehäuser. Typischerweise serviert ein Kellner einen Kaffee auf einem silbernen Tablett° mit einem Löffel, einem Glas Wasser und einem Keks. In den Kaffeehäusern trinkt man aber auch andere Getränke wie Kakao, Wasser und Wein. Zum Kaffee isst man oft Apfelstrudel, Gugelhupf° oder Sachertorte°. Oft besuchen Gäste° ein Kaffeehaus, bestellen einen Kaffee und bleiben viele Stunden. Hier diskutieren Gäste auch über Politik, Sport und andere Themen.

Wiener Kaffeehäuser haben spezielle Vokabeln: Sahne° heißt Obers. Ein kleiner oder großer Brauner ist ein Kaffee serviert mit Obers in einer kleinen Schale°. Eine Melange ist halb° Kaffee und halb geschäumte° Milch. Ein Kapuziner ist ein kleiner Mokka (ein Schwarzer oder Espresso pur) mit wenig Milch.

Es gibt auch andere Cafés in Wien. In einer Espresso-Bar trinkt man vor allem° Espresso und Cappuccino wie in Italien. In Stehcafés trinken Gäste Kaffee sehr schnell oder nehmen den Kaffee mit. Café-Konditoreien sind nicht nur Cafés. In der Konditorei kaufen Kunden hausgemachte Kuchen und Süßigkeiten°. Die neueste Version eines Cafés ist der amerikanische Import Starbucks. Hier findet man vor allem jüngere Österreicher.

Typische Cafépreise	
Kleiner Mokka	3,30 €
Kleiner Brauner	3,30 €
Melange	4,10 €
Großer Mokka	4,80 €
Großer Brauner	4,80 €
Einspänner	5,50 €
Kapuziner	5,50 €
Pharisäer	7,20 €

QUELLE: Café Korb in Wien

ungefähr *around* **Tablett** *tray* **Gugelhupf** *Bundt cake* **Sachertorte** *chocolate torte* **Gäste** *guests* **Sahne** *cream* **Schale** *dish* **halb** *half* **geschäumte** *foamed* **vor allem** *above all* **Süßigkeiten** *sweets*

ÜBUNGEN

1 Im Fokus Richtig oder falsch? Korrigieren Sie die falschen Aussagen. Diskutieren Sie dann die letzte Frage mit einem Partner/ einer Partnerin.

1. Wiener Kaffeehäuser gibt es seit dem 17. Jahrhundert.
   Falsch. Es gibt sie seit dem 18. Jahrhundert.
2. In Stehcafés kauft man Kaffee zum mitnehmen.
   Richtig.
3. In einer Café-Konditorei gibt es hausgemachte Kuchen und Torten.
   Richtig.

Diskussion Was sind die Unterschiede (*differences*) und Ähnlichkeiten (*similarities*) zwischen einem traditionellen Kaffeehaus in Wien und einem amerikanischen Café in Ihrer Stadt?

2 Die deutschsprachige Welt Richtig oder falsch? Korrigieren Sie die falschen Aussagen. Diskutieren Sie dann die letzte Frage mit einem Partner/ einer Partnerin.

1. Die beliebtesten (*most popular*) internationalen Restaurants in Deutschland sind italienisch.
   Richtig.
2. In der Schweiz besteht die Bevölkerung zu 8% aus Ausländern.
   Falsch. Die Bevölkerung dort besteht zu 25% aus Ausländern

Diskussion Wo essen Sie gern? Was bestellen Sie dort zu essen und trinken? Wie viel Prozent Trinkgeld (*tip*) geben Sie?

DEUTSCH IM ALLTAG

Am Tisch

Die Rechnung, bitte!	*Check, please!*
Die Speisekarte, bitte!	*The menu, please!*
Guten Appetit!	*Enjoy your meal!*
Noch einen Wunsch?	*Anything else?*
Herr Ober!	*Waiter!*
Prost!	*Cheers!*
Zum Wohl!	*Cheers!*

DIE DEUTSCHSPRACHIGE WELT

Ausländische Spezialitäten

In Deutschland besteht die Bevölkerung° ungefähr zu 13% aus° Ausländern°, in der Schweiz sind es fast 25%. Die Ausländer kommen aus vielen Ländern wie Italien, Griechenland°, der Türkei, Nordafrika und dem ehemaligen° Jugoslawien. Deshalb° ist die Restaurantszene in Deutschland, Österreich und der Schweiz auch sehr international. In jeder° Stadt gibt es Restaurants mit italienischen, griechischen und verschiedenen° asiatischen Speisen. Vor allem in Großstädten ist die Auswahl° sehr groß. Die populärsten Restaurants sind definitiv italienisch, aber man findet auch sehr viele asiatische Restaurants.

Bevölkerung *population* **besteht... aus** *consists of* **Ausländern** *foreigners* **Griechenland** *Greece* **ehemaligen** *former* **Deshalb** *Therefore* **jeder** *every* **verschiedenen** *various* **Auswahl** *selection*

PORTRÄT

Restaurant Tian

Wer in Wien gut, aber ohne Fleisch essen will und biologisch angebaute° Zutaten wichtig findet, sollte einmal beim° vegetarischen Restaurant Tian reservieren°. Dort kocht Paul Ivic ohne genmanipulierte° Lebensmittel und plädiert° auch generell für den Bio-Anbau° in Österreich. Wie er meint°, schmeckt so das Essen im Alltag° einfach besser° und ist auch gesünder°. Zuhause° isst der Küchenchef gern Fleisch, aber im Tian kocht Ivic gern mit Tomaten und Artischocken°. Aber „natürlich" zu essen ist auch teurer°, und so zahlt° der Gast etwa 140 bis 200 € für ein Abendmenü° mit acht Gängen und Wein. Tian ist das einzige° vegetarische Restaurant in Österreich, das von Michelin mit einem Stern° ausgezeichnet° ist.

biologisch angebaute *organically grown* **beim** *at the* **reservieren** *book a table* **genmanipulierte** *genetically modified* **plädiert...für** *make the case for* **Bio-Anbau** *organic cultivation* **meint** *argues* **im Alltag** *every day* **besser** *better* **gesünder** *healthier* **Zuhause** *at home* **Artischocken** *artichokes* **teurer** *more expensive* **zahlt** *pays* **Abendmenü** *dinner* **einzige** *only* **Stern** *star* **ausgezeichnet** *awarded*

IM INTERNET

Suchen Sie Informationen über die Mensa an der Universität Wien. Was können Studenten essen? Was können Studenten trinken? Wie viel kostet das Essen?

Find out more at **vhlcentral.com**.

4 **Expansion** After each group creates a menu, have them act out a short restaurant role-play using phrases from the **Deutsch im Alltag** box. Have students request the menu, order their food, and finally pay for it.

3 **Porträt** Richtig oder falsch? Korrigieren Sie die falschen Aussagen. Diskutieren Sie dann die letzte Frage mit einem Partner / einer Partnerin.

1. Im Restaurant Tian kostet ein Abendessen 140 bis 200 Euro.
   Richtig.
2. Österreicher essen nur biologisch angebaute Lebensmittel.
   Falsch. Sie essen auch genmanipulierte Lebensmittel.
3. In Österreich gibt es viele vegetarische Restaurants mit einem Michelin-Stern.
   Falsch. In Österreich gibt es nur ein vegetarisches Restaurant mit einem Michelin-Stern.

Diskussion Essen Sie Fleisch oder sind Sie Vegetarier/Vegetarierin? Wie wichtig sind biologisch angebaute Lebensmittel für Sie? Welche vegetarischen Gerichte essen Sie sehr gern?

4 **Mein Kaffeehaus** Schreiben Sie eine Speisekarte mit Preisen für Ihr Wiener Kaffeehaus. Ihr Kaffeehaus darf auch italienische und amerikanische Spezialitäten haben. Stellen Sie dann im Kurs Ihr Kaffeehaus vor.

BEISPIEL

S1: *In meinem Kaffeehaus gibt es 15 Kaffeespezialitäten. Ein Mokka kostet...*

More activities

vhlcentral

Online activities

4B.1

QUERVERWEIS

See **1A.3** and **1B.1** to review the use of the nominative and accusative case.

You will learn more about verbs that take dative objects in **5A.3**.

The dative

Startblock In **1B.1**, you learned that the direct object of a verb is always in the accusative case. When a verb has an indirect object, it is always in the dative case.

- An object in the dative case indicates *to whom* or *for whom* an action is performed.

  Ich bringe **dem Lehrer** einen Apfel.
  *I'm bringing **the teacher** an apple.*

  Zeig **der Professorin** deine Arbeit.
  *Show your work **to the professor.***

- Verbs that are frequently used with a dative object include **zeigen** (*to show*), **geben**, **bringen**, **empfehlen**, and **gehören** (*to belong to*). Note that the verbs **helfen** and **danken** also take a dative object, even though their English equivalents normally take a direct object.

  Wir helfen **den Kindern**.
  *We're helping (giving help to) **the kids**.*

  Sie dankt **dem Kellner**.
  *She's thanking (giving thanks to) **the waiter**.*

- The forms of the definite and indefinite articles that accompany dative nouns differ from the forms in the nominative or accusative case.

definite articles				
	masculine	**feminine**	**neuter**	**plural**
nominative	der Kellner	die Kellnerin	das Kind	die Kinder
accusative	den Kellner	die Kellnerin	das Kind	die Kinder
dative	dem Kellner	der Kellnerin	dem Kind	den Kindern

indefinite articles				
	masculine	**feminine**	**neuter**	**plural**
nominative	ein Kellner	eine Kellnerin	ein Kind	keine Kinder
accusative	einen Kellner	eine Kellnerin	ein Kind	keine Kinder
dative	einem Kellner	einer Kellnerin	einem Kind	keinen Kindern

Der Kellner bringt **der Frau** einen Salat.
*The waiter is bringing **the woman** a salad.*

Ich empfehle **einem Freund** das Restaurant.
*I'm recommending the restaurant **to a friend**.*

- The endings for possessive adjectives are the same as the endings for the indefinite articles.

QUERVERWEIS

See **3A.1** to review the use of possessive adjectives.

possessive adjectives				
	masculine	**feminine**	**neuter**	**plural**
nominative	mein Koch	meine Köchin	mein Kind	meine Kinder
accusative	meinen Koch	meine Köchin	mein Kind	meine Kinder
dative	meinem Koch	meiner Köchin	meinem Kind	meinen Kindern

Der Kellner bringt **meiner Frau** einen Salat.
*The waiter is bringing **my wife** a salad.*

Wir empfehlen unseren **Freunden** das Restaurant.
*We recommend the restaurant **to our friends**.*

- When using plural nouns in the dative case, add **-n** to any noun whose plural form does not already end in **-n** or **-s**.

nominative plural	dative plural
die Teller	den Tellern
die Esslöffel	den Esslöffeln
die Kaffees	den Kaffees
die Rechnungen	den Rechnungen

- A small number of singular masculine nouns also add the ending **-n** or **-en** in the accusative and dative cases. The n-nouns you have learned so far are: **der Architekt, der Journalist, der Junge, der Neffe**, and **der Student**.

Nils backt **seinem Neffen** einen Apfelkuchen.
*Nils is baking an apple pie **for his nephew**.*

Ich schreibe **dem Journalisten** eine E-Mail.
*I'm writing an e-mail **to the journalist**.*

- In the dative case, an adjective preceded by an **ein**-word or a **der**-word always ends in **-en**.

Anna kauft **dem kleinen** Jungen ein Eis.
*Anna is buying an ice cream for **the little** boy.*

Ich gebe **meiner kleinen** Schwester eine Banane.
*I'm giving **my little** sister a banana.*

- Adjectives in the dative that are not preceded by an article have endings similar to the definite article endings.

unpreceded adjective endings				
	masculine	**feminine**	**neuter**	**plural**
nominative	süßer Kuchen	süße Melone	süßes Getränk	süße Äpfel
accusative	süßen Kuchen	süße Melone	süßes Getränk	süße Äpfel
dative	süßem Kuchen	süßer Melone	süßem Getränk	süßen Äpfeln

Ich biete **guten** Freunden immer gutes Essen an.
*I always serve good food to **good** friends.*

Die Lehrerin hilft **neuen** Studenten gern.
*The teacher likes to help **new** students.*

- Use the dative question word **wem** to ask *to whom?*

nominative	accusative	dative
wer?	**wen?**	**wem?**

Wem gibst du das Geschenk?
***To whom** are you giving the present?*

Ich gebe **meiner Mutter** das Geschenk.
*I'm giving the present **to my mother**.*

Wem gehört diese Tasse?
***Who** does this cup belong **to**?*

Sie gehört **meinem Opa**.
*It belongs to **my grandpa**.*

Suggestion Students often forget to add **-n** in the dative plural. Write sentences on the board in which the **n** is missing, and ask students to find the mistakes. Ex.: **Der Koch kocht den** <u>Kinder</u> **eine leckere Suppe. Die Kinder bringen ihren** <u>Freunde</u> **viele Geschenke.**

QUERVERWEIS

You will learn more about **n**-nouns in **8B.1**.

See **3A.2** to review adjective agreement in the nominative and accusative case.

See **2A.2** to review question words.

ACHTUNG

In sentences with both direct and indirect objects, the dative object comes before the accusative object.

Suggestion Point out to students that these endings are similar to the endings of the definite articles, and also follow the "rese, nese, mrmn" pattern.

More activities

S vhlcentral

WB pp. 57–58

LM p. 37

Online activities

Jetzt sind Sie dran! **Wählen Sie den richtigen Artikel.**

1. Mama dankt (der /(dem)) Kellner.
2. Ich gebe (dem /(der)) Professorin die Hausaufgaben.
3. Moritz gibt ((seiner)/ seinem) Mutter ein Parfüm.

4. Die Professorin hilft ((ihren)/ ihrem) Studenten mit der Grammatik.
5. Die Großmutter backt ((ihrem)/ ihrer) Enkelkind einen Kuchen.
6. Ich schreibe ((dem)/ der) Besitzer eine E-Mail.

Anwendung

1 **Was fehlt?** Ergänzen Sie die Sätze mit den richtigen Substantivformen im Dativ.

BEISPIEL deine Freundin: Kaufst du _deiner Freundin_ einen MP3-Player?

1. meine Partnerin: Ich zeige _meiner Partnerin_ die Hausaufgaben.
2. ihr Mann: Sie gibt _ihrem Mann_ einen Kuss.
3. die Freunde: Er macht _den Freunden_ ein leckeres Essen.
4. unser Opa: Ich schreibe _unserem Opa_ eine lange E-Mail.
5. die alte Frau: Er bringt _der alten Frau_ ein Mineralwasser.
6. die Kellnerin: Der Koch gibt _der Kellnerin_ eine Tasse Tee.

2 **Pluralformen** Geben Sie die richtigen Pluralformen im Dativ an.

1. dem alten Hund: _den alten Hunden_
2. seiner lieben Tante: _seinen lieben Tanten_
3. der netten Katze: _den netten Katzen_
4. einem neugierigen Journalisten: _neugierigen Journalisten_
5. dem kleinen Mädchen: _den kleinen Mädchen_
6. keiner stolzen Frau: _keinen stolzen Frauen_
7. dem mutigen Kind: _den mutigen Kindern_
8. ihrem großen Neffen: _ihren großen Neffen_
9. meinem faulen Bruder: _meinen faulen Brüdern_

3 **Dativobjekte** Ergänzen Sie die Sätze mit der richtigen Form im Dativ.

1. Die Kellnerin empfiehlt _meinen Brüdern_ (meine Brüder) die Vorspeise.
2. _Wem_ (Wer) bringst du die Flasche Apfelsaft?
3. Ich gebe _der Kellnerin_ (die Kellnerin) ein Trinkgeld.
4. Der gute Student hilft _schlechten Studenten_ (schlechte Studenten) oft.
5. Du gibst _einem schönen Mädchen_ (ein schönes Mädchen) rote Rosen.
6. _Wem_ (Wer) soll ich das Besteck geben?
7. Kannst du _meiner Mutter_ (meine Mutter) einen Nachtisch empfehlen?
8. Ich zeige _meinem Freund_ (mein Freund) die Rechnung.
9. Die Kinder helfen _ihren Eltern_ (ihre Eltern) gern.
10. Der Junge gibt _den alten Hunden_ (die alten Hunde) Würstchen.

4 **Nettigkeiten** Bilden Sie Sätze. Sample answers are provided.

BEISPIEL sie / der Kellner / ein Trinkgeld / geben
Sie geben dem Kellner ein Trinkgeld.

1. die Frau / ihre Mutter / ein Kuchen / backen   Die Frau backt ihrer Mutter einen Kuchen.
2. ich / der Hund / sein Essen / geben   Ich gebe dem Hund sein Essen.
3. der Schüler / die Lehrerin / eine Postkarte / schreiben   Der Schüler schreibt der Lehrerin eine Postkarte.
4. er / seine Tochter / eine Vorspeise / bestellen   Er bestellt seiner Tochter eine Vorspeise.
5. die Köchin / das Kind / ein Brötchen / geben   Die Köchin gibt dem Kind ein Brötchen.
6. meine Frau / die Oma / eine Beilage / mitbringen   Meine Frau bringt der Oma eine Beilage mit.

Kommunikation

5 **Geschenke** Sehen Sie sich die Speisekarte auf Seite 164 an und erzählen Sie Ihrem Partner / Ihrer Partnerin, welche Gerichte Sie Ihrer Familie und Ihren Freunden empfehlen. Answers will vary.

 BEISPIEL meine Tante

S1: *Ich empfehle meiner Tante den Chef-Salat.*
Was empfiehlst du deiner Oma?
S2: *Ich empfehle meiner Oma einen kleinen*
Tomatensalat mit Mozzarella!

1. Mutter/Vater
2. Großeltern
3. Lehrer/Lehrerin
4. Cousin/Cousine

5. Onkel/Tante
6. bester Freund/beste Freundin
7. Bruder/Schwester
8. Kommilitonen

6 **Was für ein Chaos!** Ihr Haus ist ein totales Chaos. Fragen Sie Ihren Partner / Ihre Partnerin, wem die Sachen gehören, die im Haus herumliegen. Answers will vary.

▶ **BEISPIEL**

S1: *Wem gehört der Pullover?*
S2: *Er gehört meiner Schwester.*

| meine Eltern | der Kellner | meine Schwester |
| eine Freundin | die Köchin | ein Student |

1.   2.   3.

4.   5.   6.

7 **Wem tust du einen Gefallen?** Beantworten Sie die Fragen von Ihrem Partner / Ihrer Partnerin. Answers will vary.

BEISPIEL

S1: *Wem zeigst du dein Zeugnis?*
S2: *Ich zeige meinen Eltern mein Zeugnis. Und du?*

1. Wem schreibst du Postkarten im Sommer?
2. Wem kochst du ein Essen?
3. Wem kaufst du ein Buch?

4. Wem hilfst du bei den Hausaufgaben?
5. Wem stellst du deine Eltern vor?
6. Wem backst du einen Kuchen?

5 Suggestions
• Even if students have been working well with the accusative and dative in isolation, they often have difficulty when they must use both cases in the same sentence. It may be helpful to have charts on the board, and to emphasize that the person who receives the recommendation will be in the dative, while the recommended dish will be in the accusative.
• Give students a few minutes to look at the menu on p. 164 and decide on their recommendations before they begin working with partners. Emphasize that they will be working with *both* the accusative and the dative. Ask a student volunteer to put an example on the board.

6 **Video Virtual Chat** You can also assign activity 6 on the Supersite.

4B.2

Prepositions with the dative

 Grammar Tutorial

Startblock Certain prepositions are always followed by an object in the dative case.

Mein Vater kommt **aus der Türkei**.

Ich glaube, es ist alles okay **mit den beiden**.

Suggestion Teach students the mnemonic device of singing the dative prepositions in alphabetical order to the tune of Strauss's *Donauwalzer* ("Blue Danube").

QUERVERWEIS

See **3B.2** to review prepositions that take an object in the accusative case.

ACHTUNG

The prepositions **nach** and **zu** are also used in the set expressions **nach Hause** (*home*) and **zu Hause** (*at home*). **Ich gehe jetzt nach Hause. Er bleibt immer zu Hause.**

Suggestion Emphasize that the phrases **zu Hause** and **nach Hause** are idiomatic and should be memorized as "sound bites".

More activities

vhlcentral

WB
pp. 59–60

LM
p. 38

Online activities

- Most dative prepositional phrases provide information about time and location.

prepositions with the dative			
aus	*from*	nach	*after; to*
außer	*except for*	seit	*since; for*
bei	*at; near; with*	von	*from*
mit	*with*	zu	*to; for; at*

Willst du **bei meinen Eltern** essen?
*Do you want to eat **at my parents' house**?*

Zum Geburtstag bekomme ich Geschenke.
*I get presents **on my birthday**.*

- Use **nach** before the names of countries or cities. Use **zu** with people, businesses, or other locations.

Wir fliegen morgen **nach Berlin**.
*We're flying **to Berlin** tomorrow.*

Gehst du **zur Bäckerei**?
*Are you going **to the bakery**?*

- The preposition **seit** is used with time expressions to indicate *since when* or *for how long* something has been taking place.

Seit wann wohnst du in Berlin?
Since when have you been living in Berlin?

Ich wohne **seit einem Jahr** in Berlin.
*I've been living in Berlin **for one year**.*

- The prepositions **bei**, **von**, and **zu** can combine with the definite article **dem** to form contractions. The preposition **zu** also forms a contraction with the definite article **der**.

bei + dem = **beim**   zu + dem = **zum**
von + dem = **vom**   zu + der = **zur**

Wir kaufen oft **beim** Supermarkt ein.
*We often shop **at the** supermarket.*

Ich esse immer Eier **zum** Frühstück.
*I always have eggs **for** breakfast.*

Jetzt sind Sie dran! **Wählen Sie die passenden Präpositionen.**

1. Der beste Tisch ist (aus dem / beim) Fenster.
2. Wann fährst du (zum / mit dem) Supermarkt?
3. (Vom / Außer dem) Supermarkt gibt es hier keine Geschäfte.
4. Deine Familie kommt (mit / aus) den USA.
5. (Seit / Außer) zwei Jahren lerne ich Spanisch.
6. Ninas Freund fährt (nach der / zur) Universität.
7. Ich wohne (zu / bei) meinen Eltern.
8. Wir essen Pizza (mit / bei) Besteck.

Anwendung und Kommunikation

1 Was ist richtig? Wählen Sie die passenden Präpositionen.

BEISPIEL Wir wohnen (**seit**/ um) fünf Jahren hier.

1. Daniel kommt (mit /**aus**) Hamburg.
2. Er studiert (bei /**seit**) sechs Semestern an der Uni Heidelberg.
3. Er wohnt (**mit**/ von) drei Freunden zusammen.
4. Alle drei Monate fährt er (**nach**/ zu) Hause zu seinen Eltern.
5. Seine Mutter ist immer extrem glücklich, wenn ihr Sohn (nach /**zu**) Hause ist.
6. Am Wochenende spielt er (aus /**mit**) seinem Vater Tennis.
7. (**Außer**/ Aus) seinen Eltern besucht er auch seine Großeltern.
8. Daniel hat nächste Woche Geburtstag und er bekommt (nach /**von**) seinem Opa ein neues Auto.

2 Wer ist das? Setzen Sie die fehlenden Dativpräpositionen ein.

Christoph Waltz kommt (1) ____aus____ Österreich. Seine Großmutter arbeitet als junge Frau als Schauspielerin (*actress*) (2) ____bei____ einem Theater. (3) ____Von____ dieser Großmutter hat er sein Talent. Waltz ist (4) ____seit____ vielen Jahren als ein großartiger Schauspieler berühmt. Für seine Rollen in den Filmen *Inglourious Basterds* und *Django Unchained* gewinnt er zwei Oscars. Beide Filme sind (5) ____von____ Quentin Tarantino. Waltz wohnt (6) ____mit____ seiner Frau in Hollywood, London und Berlin.

3 Seit wann? Seit wann macht Ihr Partner / Ihre Partnerin die folgenden Aktivitäten? Answers will vary.

BEISPIEL heute Vorlesungen haben

S1: *Seit wann hast du heute Vorlesungen?*
S2: *Ich habe seit 10 Uhr Vorlesungen. Und du?*

1. hier studieren
2. Deutsch lernen
3. Kaffee trinken
4. einen Computer haben
5. ein Handy haben
6. Auto fahren

4 Fotoalbum Sehen Sie sich die Fotos an und beantworten Sie die Fragen von Ihrem Partner / Ihrer Partnerin. Answers will vary.

▶ **BEISPIEL**

S1: *Woher kommt Eriks Opa?*
S2: *Er kommt aus der Schweiz.*

1. Mit wem spricht Anna?
2. Wohin reisen Lena und Jasmin?
3. Wohin geht Annika?
4. Seit wann arbeitet Felix im Restaurant?

3 Suggestion Native speakers of English often try to use the present perfect with **seit**. Remind students to use the present tense in this exercise.

3 Partner Chat You can also assign activity 3 on the Supersite. Students work in pairs to record the activity online. The pair's recorded conversation will appear in your gradebook.

4 Suggestion Have students take turns asking and answering the questions. Make sure they understand that they should base their answers on the pictures, but that there is no single correct answer for each question, and they are welcome to respond imaginatively.

Wiederholung

1 Ankes Familie
Ankes Familie ist in einem Restaurant. Was bringt der Kellner den Familienmitgliedern (*family members*) zu trinken? Answers will vary.

BEISPIEL die Schwester

S1: *Was bringt der Kellner Ankes Schwester?*
S2: *Er bringt ihrer Schwester ein Glas Milch.*

der Kaffee	das Mineralwasser	das stille Wasser
die Milch	der Orangensaft	der Tee

1. der Onkel 3. der Bruder 5. die Tante
2. die Eltern 4. die Oma 6. der Opa

2 Der Koch
Fragen Sie den Koch, was er den Personen zum Essen macht. Wechseln Sie sich ab. Sample answers are provided.

2 Partner Chat You can also assign activity 2 on the Supersite.

BEISPIEL

S1: *Herr Müller, was machen Sie dem Musiker zum Frühstück?*
S2: *Ich mache dem Musiker ein Schinkenbrot.*

der Musiker / das Frühstück

1. die Journalistin / das Abendessen
Herr Müller, was machen Sie der Journalistin zum Abendessen? Ich mache der Journalistin eine Suppe.

2. die Architektin / das Mittagessen
Herr Müller, was machen Sie der Architektin zum Mittagessen? Ich mache der Architektin Rindfleisch.

3. die Friseurin / das Mittagessen
Herr Müller, was machen Sie der Friseurin zum Mittagessen? Ich mache der Friseurin einen kleinen Salat.

4. der Geschäftsmann / das Abendessen
Herr Müller, was machen Sie dem Geschäftsmann zum Abendessen? Ich mache dem Geschäftsmann Fisch mit Garnelen.

5. die Dozentin / das Abendessen
Herr Müller, was machen Sie der Dozentin zum Abendessen? Ich mache der Dozentin Hähnchen mit Kartoffeln.

6. der Ingenieur / das Mittagessen
Herr Müller, was machen Sie dem Ingenieur zum Mittagessen? Ich mache dem Ingenieur Pasta.

3 Wie schmeckt's?
Sagen Sie einem Partner / einer Partnerin, was die Personen essen und wie sie es finden. Answers will vary.

▶ **BEISPIEL**

S1: *Wie findet die Frau die Erdbeeren?*
S2: *Sie sind der Frau zu süß.*

fade	lecker	leicht	salzig	scharf	süß

1. der Mann 2. die Frau 3. das Mädchen

4. die Studenten 5. der Junge 6. die Kinder

4 Diskutieren und kombinieren
Sie sind Kellner / Kellnerin im Restaurant. Was sollen Sie den Gästen bringen? Fragen Sie Ihren Partner / Ihre Partnerin. Answers will vary.

BEISPIEL

S1: *Was braucht der junge Mann?*
S2: *Bring dem jungen Mann eine Serviette.*
S1: *Was braucht die alte Frau?*
S2: *Bring der alten Frau eine Gabel.*

4 Suggestion Briefly review vocabulary, to make sure students recall the names and genders of all the items pictured before beginning this activity.

5 Arbeitsblatt
Sie bekommen von Ihrem Professor / Ihrer Professorin eine Liste mit diversen Aktivitäten. Suchen Sie Kommilitonen, die diese Aktivitäten machen. Answers will vary.

BEISPIEL

S1: *Isst du täglich Eier zum Frühstück?*
S2: *Ja, ich esse täglich Eier zum Frühstück.*
OR
S1: *Wohnst du bei deinen Eltern?*
S2: *Nein, ich wohne nicht bei meinen Eltern.*

6 **Essen in Österreich** Die Österreicher lieben Fleisch. Etwa zwei Drittel der Bevölkerung isst täglich Fleisch, und nur ca. 3% sind Vegetarier oder Veganer. Aber fettarmes und gemüsereiches Essen werden immer beliebter. Diskutieren Sie zu zweit und mit Hilfe der Grafik die österreichischen Essgewohnheiten (*eating habits*) und vergleichen Sie sie mit Ihren eigenen (*your own*).

BEISPIEL

S1: Das Lieblingsobst der Österreicher sind Tomaten. Was ist dein Lieblingsobst?
S2: Ich esse gern... Und du?
S1: Ich mag..

Expansion Ask students how often they eat meat or fruit and vegetables, and what they think of a vegetarian or vegan diet. Also ask them to research Austrian cuisine and its influences, and what regional specialties are typically found on an Austrian menu.

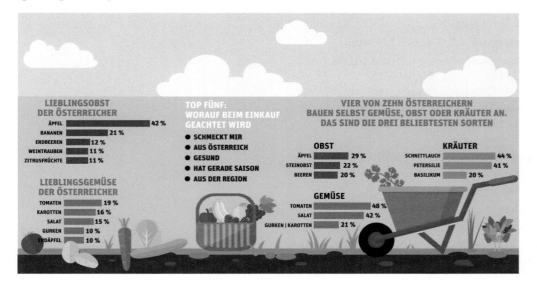

LIEBLINGSOBST DER ÖSTERREICHER

ÄPFEL	42 %
BANANEN	21 %
ERDBEEREN	12 %
WEINTRAUBEN	11 %
ZITRUSFRÜCHTE	11 %

LIEBLINGSGEMÜSE DER ÖSTERREICHER

TOMATEN	19 %
KAROTTEN	16 %
SALAT	15 %
GURKEN	10 %
ERDÄPFEL	10 %

TOP FÜNF: WORAUF BEIM EINKAUF GEACHTET WIRD

● SCHMECKT MIR
● AUS ÖSTERREICH
● GESUND
● HAT GERADE SAISON
● AUS DER REGION

VIER VON ZEHN ÖSTERREICHERN BAUEN SELBST GEMÜSE, OBST ODER KRÄUTER AN. DAS SIND DIE DREI BELIEBTESTEN SORTEN

OBST

ÄPFEL	29 %
STEINOBST	22 %
BEEREN	20 %

KRÄUTER

SCHNITTLAUCH	44 %
PETERSILIE	41 %
BASILIKUM	20 %

GEMÜSE

TOMATEN	48 %
SALAT	42 %
GURKEN | KAROTTEN	21 %

7 **Interview** Stellen Sie sich gegenseitig (*each other*) diese Fragen und beantworten Sie sie. Answers will vary.

BEISPIEL

S1: Bei wem wohnst du im Sommer?
S2: Ich wohne bei meinem Bruder.

1. Woher kommst du?
2. Seit wann studierst du an der Uni?
3. Gehst du gern im Supermarkt einkaufen?
4. Mit wem telefonierst du gern?
5. Bei wem wohnst du im Sommer?
6. Wohin möchtest du reisen?

8 **Poetische Präpositionen** Schreiben Sie zu zweit ein Gedicht aus fünf Sätzen. Beginnen Sie die ersten vier Zeilen (*lines*) mit einer Dativ- oder Akkusativpräposition.

BEISPIEL

Mit dem Ball spiele ich.
Bei dem Metzger kaufen wir ein.
Durch die Stadt läuft die Mutter.
Außer Anton isst die Familie.
Der Hund schläft ein.

⑤ Mein Wörterbuch

Personalize your vocabulary. Add five words related to the themes **an der Universität** and **Sport und Freizeit** to the online Vocabulary Tools.

Lektion 2B

German	English	Definition
+ add word		

✎ der Mais, -	corn	Aus Mais kann man Popcorn machen.

↓ 🗑

[ä] [ö] [ü] [ß] ☐ ALL CAPS

Panorama Interactive Map

Österreich

NATIONAL connections cultures STANDARDS

Österreich in Zahlen

Suggestion Point out that Austria is slightly smaller than the state of Maine.

▶ **Fläche°:** *83.879 km² (Quadratkilometer) (60% der Fläche sind gebirgig°)*

▶ **Bevölkerung:** *8,7 Millionen Menschen*

▶ **9 Bundesländer°:** *Burgenland, Kärnten, Niederösterreich, Oberösterreich, Salzburg, Steiermark, Tirol, Vorarlberg, Wien*

▶ **Städte:** *Wien (1,8 Mio. Einwohner), Graz (270.000), Linz (194.000), Salzburg (147.000) und Innsbruck (125.000)*

▶ **Berge:** *der Großglockner (3.797 m), die Wildspitze (3.774 m)*

▶ **Flüsse°:** *die Donau, der Inn*

▶ **Währung°:** *der Euro (€) (seit 2002)*

▶ **Wichtige Industriezweige°:** *Banken, Tourismus*

▶ **Touristenattraktionen:** *Bergsport, Salzburger Festspiele°, Spanische Hofreitschule°, Wintertourismus*

Touristen können in Städten wie Wien und Salzburg viel Kultur genießen° oder in den Alpen Berg- und Wintersport betreiben. Für Firmen ist Österreich interessant, weil die Unternehmenssteuer° sehr niedrig° ist.

QUELLE: Österreichische Botschaft, Washington

Berühmte Österreicher

▶ **Maria Theresia,** *Kaiserin° (1717–1780)*

▶ **Wolfgang Amadeus Mozart,** *Komponist (1756–1791)*

▶ **Sigmund Freud,** *Neurologe (1856–1939)*

▶ **Gustav Klimt,** *Künstler° (1862–1918)*

▶ **Lise Meitner,** *Physikerin (1878–1968)*

▶ **Friedensreich Hundertwasser,** *Architekt (1928–2000)*

▶ **Elfriede Jelinek,** *Autorin (1946–)*

▶ **Falco,** *Musiker (1957–1998)*

Suggestion With books closed, tell students: **Wir sprechen sehr oft von Deutschland. Wie heißen die anderen Länder, in denen man Deutsch spricht?** After they answer, ask students what they already know about Austria: rivers, capital, size, money, famous Austrians, dialect, etc. Then have them open their books to the **Panorama** section and review the statistics. Ask comprehension questions: **Wie groß ist Österreich? Wie viele Menschen leben in Österreich?**

More activities
vhlcentral
Online activities

Fläche *surface area* **gebirgig** *mountainous* **Bundesländer** *states* **Flüsse** *rivers* **Währung** *currency* **Wichtige Industriezweige** *Important industries* **Festspiele** *festivals* **Hofreitschule** *Riding School* **genießen** *enjoy* **Unternehmenssteuer** *business tax* **niedrig** *low* **Kaiserin** *empress* **Künstler** *artist* **Pfefferminzbonbons** *peppermint candies* **Geschmacksrichtung** *flavor* **jedem** *every* **Lakritz** *licorice* **Köpfe** *heads* **Spendern** *dispensers*

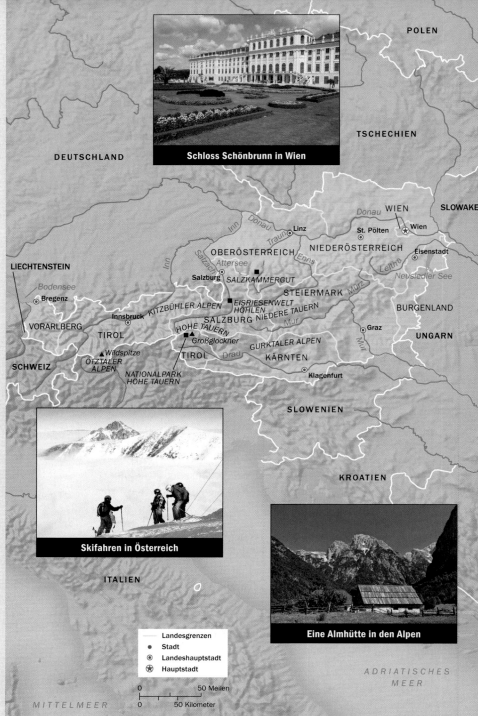

POLEN

DEUTSCHLAND

TSCHECHIEN

Schloss Schönbrunn in Wien

Donau **WIEN** SLOWAKE

Inn Donau Linz St. Pölten Wien

LIECHTENSTEIN Traun **OBERÖSTERREICH** Enns **NIEDERÖSTERREICH** Eisenstadt

Bodensee Attersee Salzach

Bregenz Salzburg SALZKAMMERGUT Leitha Neusiedler See

STEIERMARK BURGENLAND

Innsbruck KITZBÜHLER ALPEN EISRIESENWELT HÖHLEN Mürz

VORARLBERG SALZBURG NIEDERE TAUERN UNGARN

TIROL HOHE TAUERN Mur Graz

Großglockner GURKTALER ALPEN

Wildspitze TIROL Drau **KÄRNTEN**

ÖTZTALER ALPEN

SCHWEIZ NATIONALPARK HOHE TAUERN Klagenfurt

SLOWENIEN

Skifahren in Österreich

KROATIEN

Eine Almhütte in den Alpen

ITALIEN

— Landesgrenzen
• Stadt
◎ Landeshauptstadt
✳ Hauptstadt

ADRIATISCHES MEER

0 50 Meilen
0 50 Kilometer

MITTELMEER

Unglaublich, aber wahr!

Der Österreicher Eduard Haas III. fängt 1927 an, Pfefferminzbonbons° mit dem Namen PEZ zu verkaufen. Der Name PEZ kommt von der ersten Geschmacksrichtung°, PfeffErminZ. PEZ gibt es heute mit jedem° Geschmack, sogar Chlorophyll und Lakritz°! Seit 1957 gibt es lustige Köpfe° auf den Spendern° wie Mickey Mouse und Donald Duck.

Politik

Internationale Institutionen in Wien

Politisch ist Österreich ein neutrales Land. Es ist Mitglied° in der Europäischen Union, aber nicht in der NATO. Seit 1980 ist Wien einer von vier Hauptsitzen° der Vereinten Nationen°. Die anderen Hauptsitze sind New York, Genf und Nairobi. Andere internationale Organisationen in Wien sind die IAEA (Internationale Organisation für Atomenergie) und die OPEC.

Sport

Olympische Spiele

Olympische Spiele und Österreich bedeuten vor allem° Olympische Winterspiele und alpiner Skisport. 1964 und 1976 treffen sich° Sportler aus aller Welt zu den Olympischen Winterspielen in Innsbruck. Erfolgreiche° österreichische Olympioniken° sind Felix Gottwald (nordischer Kombinierer°) mit drei Gold-, einer Silber- und drei Bronzemedaillen. Der Skispringer° Thomas Morgenstern und der Skifahrer Toni Sailer gewinnen jeweils° drei Goldmedaillen. In alpinen Skidisziplinen gewinnen Österreicher mehr Medaillen als jedes andere Land der Welt (34 Gold-, 39 Silber- und 41 Bronzemedaillen).

Architektur

Friedensreich Hundertwasser

Hundertwasser ist ein kontroverser österreichischer Architekt und Künstler. Er beginnt in den 50er Jahren in Österreich als Künstler mit revolutionären Ideen. Die Beziehung° zwischen Mensch und Natur ist ein zentrales Thema in seiner Kunst. Heute kann man seine Häuser in der ganzen Welt finden. Das Hundertwasserhaus in Wien und die Fassade der Müllverbrennungsanlage° Spittelau ist sehr berühmt.

Familie

Familie von Trapp in Amerika

Viele kennen° die Familie von Trapp aus dem Film *The Sound of Music*. Aber was passiert° mit der Familie nach der Emigration? 1939 emigriert die Familie mit nur vier Dollar in der Tasche° nach Amerika. Die von Trapps machen als „Trapp Family Singers" Karriere und kaufen 1942 eine Farm in Stowe, Vermont. Auch heute kann man die Farm als Gasthaus° besuchen — und man kann mit den von Trapps Weihnachten° feiern.

Musik Musik

Andreas Gabalier

Andreas Gabalier ist Österreichs „Alpen Elvis". Er singt seine Lieder auf Deutsch, aber nicht Hochdeutsch, sondern in österreichischem Dialekt. Er trägt (*wears*) bei seinen Konzerten am liebsten Lederhosen und karierte Holzfällerhemden (*plaid lumberjack shirts*).

Go to **vhlcentral.com** to find out more about **Andreas Gabalier** and his music.

Mitglied *member* **Hauptsitzen** *head offices* **Vereinten Nationen** *United Nations* **vor allem** *especially* **treffen sich** *meet* **Erfolgreiche** *Successful* **Olympioniken** *Olympic champions* **nordischer Kombinierer** *Nordic combined skier* **Skispringer** *ski jumper* **jeweils** *each* **kennen** *know* **passiert** *happens* **Tasche** *pocket* **Gasthaus** *inn* **Weihnachten** *Christmas* **Beziehung** *relationship* **Müllverbrennungsanlage** *waste incineration plant*

1 **Was haben Sie gelernt?** Entscheiden Sie, ob die Sätze richtig oder falsch sind. Korrigieren Sie die falschen Sätze.

1. Alle PEZ Bonbons schmecken nach Pfefferminz.
   Falsch. Es gibt viele verschiedene Geschmacksrichtungen.
2. Die Vereinten Nationen haben einen Sitz in Wien.
   Richtig.
3. In Österreich gibt es keine guten Skifahrer.
   Falsch. Österreich hat viele erfolgreiche Skifahrer.
4. Die Familie von Trapp besitzt (*owns*) ein Gasthaus in Kalifornien.
   Falsch. Sie besitzt ein Gasthaus in Vermont.
5. Hundertwasser ist bekannt für seine revolutionären Ideen in Architektur.
   Richtig.

2 **Was meinen Sie?** Denken Sie über diese Frage nach. Besprechen Sie die Antwort mit einem Partner/einer Partnerin.

Österreich und Deutschland sind sich ähnlich (*similar*), aber sie sind auch ziemlich verschieden (*different*). Wie sind sie ähnlich? Wie sind sie verschieden? Würden (*would*) Sie Österreich gern besuchen? Warum (nicht)?

Lesen Audio: Reading

Vor dem Lesen

Strategien

Scanning

Scanning involves glancing over a document in search of specific information. For example, you can scan a document to identify its format, to find cognates, to locate visual clues about the document's content, or to find specific facts. Scanning allows you to learn a great deal about a text without having to read it word for word.

 Textart Was für ein Text ist das? Erklären Sie Ihre Antwort einem Partner / einer Partnerin.

eine E-Mail	**(ein Blog)**
eine Broschüre	ein Memo
eine Einkaufsliste	ein Artikel

 Auf einen Blick Sehen Sie sich mit einem Partner / einer Partnerin den Text an.

A. Schreiben Sie drei Aktivitäten auf, die Sie im Text finden. *Sample answers are provided.*

schlafen
Inlineskates fahren
klettern

B. Welche Lehnwörter (*loan words*) und Kognate können Sie im Text finden? Diskutieren Sie Ihre Antworten. *Sample answers are provided.*

Sofas	Musik
Konzerthalle	Brunch
Jamsession	Inlineskates

Die ersten Monate in Graz

über mich	Hauptseite	Fotos	Kontakt

Besuch! 12. Oktober

Das Kunsthaus

Am Freitag besuchen mich meine Freunde Lukas, Jan und Paul für ein Wochenende in Graz. Super! Vier Jahre lang haben wir zusammen in Wien studiert. Jetzt sehen wir uns nur selten. Jan wohnt in Linz, Lukas arbeitet in Wien und Paul studiert immer noch. Alle können bei mir übernachten. Ich habe ein Gästezimmer° und zwei Sofas im Wohnzimmer°. Das funktioniert prima! Schlafen werden wir an diesem Wochenende ohnehin° nicht! Am Freitag geht's erstmal in die Hopfenlaube, eine tolle Konzerthalle, für eine Jamsession. Da ist die Musik immer toll und wir können über die guten alten Zeiten reden. Am Samstag geht's dann ins Café Schwalbennest frühstücken. Nach der langen Nacht ist ein guter Brunch extrem wichtig°. Das Café ist ganz in der Nähe° meiner Wohnung°. Anschließend° gehen wir bei schönem Wetter° eine Runde im Volksgarten Inlineskates fahren.

Gästezimmer *guest bedroom* **Wohnzimmer** *living room* **ohnehin** *anyhow* **wichtig** *important* **in der Nähe** *near to* **Wohnung** *apartment* **Anschließend** *Afterwards* **bei schönem Wetter** *in nice weather*

☆ ▼ · (Suche 🔍)

Der Volksgarten ist total schön und sehr zentral gelegen°. Später können wir auch noch die Treppen° zum Grazer Schlossberg hochklettern°. Vom Uhrturm kann man die ganze Stadt super sehen inklusive der wunderschönen Innenstadt. Und was machen wir bei Regen°? Dann können wir das Kunsthaus Graz besuchen. Dort gibt es immer moderne Ausstellungen°. Ich freue mich schon auf° das Wochenende und auf meine alten Freunde.

Archiv

▶ Prüfungsstress ☹
▶ Glücklich!
▶ Die Uni
▶ Es ist schon wieder° Montag...
▶ September
▶ August
▶ Juli
▶ Juni
▶ Mai
▶ April
▶ März

Der Uhrturm

zentral gelegen *centrally located* **Treppen** *stairs* **hochklettern** *to climb up*
Regen *rain* **Ausstellungen** *exhibits* **freue mich...auf** *look forward to*
schon wieder *once again*

Nach dem Lesen

 Das richtige Wort Ergänzen Sie
 die Aussagen mit den richtigen Informationen.

1. Am Freitag besuchen drei Freunde die Stadt
   ___Graz___ für ein Wochenende.

2. Am ___Freitag___ gehen die Freunde in
   die Hopfenlaube.

3. Am Samstag essen die Freunde ___Frühstück/Brunch___
   im Café Schwalbennest.

4. Anschließend gehen sie Inlineskates fahren im
   ___Volksgarten___.

5. Später können sie die ___Treppen___ zum Grazer
   Schlossberg hochklettern.

6. Bei Regen besuchen sie ___das Kunsthaus Graz___.

 Informationen Schreiben Sie die richtigen
Antworten. Schreiben Sie ganze Sätze.
Sample answers are provided.

BEISPIEL Wo wohnt Lukas?

Lukas wohnt in Wien.

1. Wer besucht Graz am Wochenende?
   Lukas, Jan und Paul besuchen Graz.

2. Warum wollen die Freunde in die
   Hopfenlaube gehen?
   Die Musik da ist toll.

3. Wann frühstücken die Freunde im
   Café Schwalbennest?
   Sie frühstücken dort am Samstag.

4. Was machen die Freunde im Volksgarten?
   Die Freunde fahren im Volksgarten Inlineskates.

5. Was kann man vom Uhrturm sehen?
   Man kann die ganze Stadt super sehen.

6. Was kann man im Kunsthaus Graz sehen?
   Im Kunsthaus Graz kann man moderne Ausstellungen sehen.

 Ihre Heimatstadt Stellen Sie einem
Partner / einer Partnerin Fragen: Was kann oder
soll man in Ihrer Heimatstadt (*hometown*) machen?

BEISPIEL

S1: *Was muss man in deiner Heimatstadt sehen?*
S2: *In meiner Heimatstadt muss man das
Kunstmuseum sehen.*
S1: *Wo kann man gut essen?*

Suggestion Give students a minute to prepare their lists of
sights, and provide them with vocabulary as needed.

Partner Chat You can also assign this activity on the
Supersite. Students work in pairs to record the activity
online. The pair's recorded conversation will appear in
your gradebook.

Hören

Strategien

Listening for the gist

When you listen to a conversation in German, try to figure out the main ideas that are being expressed, rather than trying to catch every word. Listening for the gist can help you follow what someone is saying, even if you can't hear or understand some of the words.

 To help you practice this strategy, you will listen to three sentences. Jot down a brief summary of what you hear.

Vorbereitung

Schauen Sie sich das Foto an. Wer ist auf dem Foto? Wo sind sie? Was machen sie?

Zuhören

Hören Sie sich den Podcast mit Andrea und der Reporterin an. Lesen Sie dann die Liste. Hören Sie sich den Podcast ein zweites Mal an und markieren Sie die Zutaten, die Sie hören.

(Pilze)	(Nudeln)
Kartoffel	(Zwiebeln)
(Butter)	(Salz)
(Milch)	Pfirsiche
Tomaten	Paprika
(Schinken)	(Pfeffer)
Knoblauch	Eier

Verständnis

Eine Zusammenfassung
Ergänzen Sie die Zusammenfassung (*summary*) von dem Podcast mit Wörtern von der Liste.

den Schinken	die Nudeln	eine Reporterin
findet	frische Pilze	salzig
lecker	einen Podcast	schmeckt
Pfeffer	probieren	Zwiebeln

1. Wir hören ___einen Podcast___ mit der Köchin Andrea.
2. In der Küche sind Andrea und ___eine Reporterin___.
3. Im Moment kann man auf dem Markt ___frische Pilze___ kaufen.
4. Heute kocht Andrea Nudeln mit Pfifferlingen (*chanterelles*). Sie sind sehr ___lecker___.
5. Die Pfifferlinge passen gut zum Schinken — er ist ziemlich ___salzig___.
6. Man braucht auch Vollmilch, Butter und ___Zwiebeln___.
7. Erst kocht Andrea ___die Nudeln___.
8. Dann brät sie ___den Schinken___ mit Butter.
9. Am Ende kommen noch Salz und ___Pfeffer___ dazu.
10. Die Reporterin ___findet___ das Gericht lecker!

Und Sie?
Bereiten Sie mit einem Partner / einer Partnerin ein Rezept für eine Pizza vor. Welche Zutaten sollen auf die Pizza?

BEISPIEL

S1: *Was soll alles auf die Pizza?*
S2: *Pilze, Zwiebeln, Tomaten…*

Schreiben

Strategien

Adding details

How can you make your writing more informative or more interesting? You can add details by answering the "W" questions: Who? What? When? Where? Why? The answers to these questions will provide useful information that can be incorporated into your writing. Here are some useful question words that you have already learned.

Wer?	Wo?
Was?	Warum?
Wann?	Wie?

Compare these two statements.

„Ich muss einkaufen gehen.“

„Nach der Schule muss ich Eier kaufen. Mit den Eiern kann ich eine leckere Omelette kochen.“

While both statements give the same basic information (the writer needs to go shopping), the details provided in the second statement are much more informative.

Suggestion Remind students that adverbs, like the ones they learned in **4A.2**, can make their speech and writing more informative and expressive.

Thema

Grüße nach Salzburg

Sie entschließen sich (*decide*), ein Jahr in Österreich zu verbringen und bei einer Familie zu leben. Schreiben Sie eine Karte an Ihre Gastfamilie (*host family*). Sagen Sie der Familie, was Sie gern sehen wollen und was Sie machen wollen. Schreiben Sie fünf Sätze. Nennen Sie (*Give*) Details. Beantworten Sie dabei Fragen mit **wer?**, **was?**, **wo?**, **wie?** und **wann?**

Liebe Gastfamilie, bald komme ich nach Salzburg. Dann können wir zusammen den Uhrturm besuchen...

Expansion Before students start writing, have them come up with an ending to the sample sentence that answers each of the questions **was?**, **wo?**, **wer?**, **wie?**, and **wann?** Write the sentence on the board, underline the answers to each question, and label them with the appropriate interrogative term.

Vocabulary Tools

Lektion 4A

Obst und Gemüse
fruit and vegetables

die Ananas, - *pineapple*
der Apfel, ⸚ *apple*
die Artischocke, -n *artichoke*
die Aubergine, -n *eggplant*
die Banane, -n *banana*
die Birne, -n *pear*
die grüne Bohne (*pl.* die grünen
 Bohnen) *green bean*
die Erdbeere, -n *strawberry*
die Himbeere, -n *raspberry*
die Karotte, -n *carrot*
die Kartoffel, -n *potato*
der Knoblauch *garlic*
die Melone, -n *melon*
die Orange, -n *orange*
die grüne Paprika (*pl.* die grünen
 Paprika) *green pepper*
die rote Paprika (*pl.* die roten
 Paprika) *red pepper*
der Pfirsich, -e *peach*
der Pilz, -e *mushroom*
der Salat, -e *lettuce; salad*
die Tomate, -n *tomato*
die Traube, -n *grape*
die Zwiebel, -n *onion*

Geschäfte
stores

die Bäckerei, -en *bakery*
die Eisdiele, -n *ice cream shop*
das Feinkostgeschäft, -e *delicatessen*
das Fischgeschäft, -e *fish store*
die Konditorei, -en *pastry shop*
das Lebensmittelgeschäft, -e
 grocery store
der Markt, ⸚e *market*
die Metzgerei, -en *butcher shop*
der Supermarkt, ⸚e *supermarket*
einkaufen gehen *to go shopping*
verkaufen *to sell*

Essen
food

das Brot, -e *bread*
das Brötchen, - *roll*
die Butter *butter*
das Ei, -er *egg*
der Joghurt, -s *yogurt*
der Käse, - *cheese*
der Kuchen, - *cake; pie*
die Marmelade, -n *jam*
das Öl, -e *oil*
das Olivenöl, -e *olive oil*
die Pasta *pasta*
der Reis *rice*
das Rezept, -e *recipe*
die Zutat, -en *ingredient*

Fleisch und Fisch
meat and fish

die Garnele, -n *shrimp*
das Hähnchen, - *chicken*
die Meeresfrüchte (*pl.*) *seafood*
das Rindfleisch *beef*
der Schinken, - *ham*
das Schweinefleisch *pork*
der Thunfisch *tuna*
das Würstchen, - *sausage*

Ausdrücke
expressions

mögen *to like*

im Restaurant
in the restaurant

der Pfeffer *pepper*
bestellen *to order*

Adverbs *See p. 150.*
Separable and inseparable prefix
 verbs *See p. 156.*

Lektion 4B

im Restaurant

die Beilage, -n *side dish*
das Besteck *silverware*
der Esslöffel, - *soup spoon*
die Flasche, -n *bottle*
die Gabel, -n *fork*
der erste/zweite Gang, ⸚ *first/second
 course*
das Glas, ⸚er *glass*
das Gericht, -e *dish*
die Hauptspeise, -n *main course*
der Kellner, - / die Kellnerin,
 -nen *waiter / waitress*
der Koch, ⸚e / die Köchin, -nen *cook*
das Messer, - *knife*
der Nachtisch, -e *dessert*
die Rechnung, -en *check*
das Salz *salt*
die Serviette, -n *napkin*
die Speisekarte, -n *menu*
die Suppe, -n *soup*
die Tasse, -n *cup*
der Teelöffel, - *teaspoon*
der Teller, - *plate*
die Tischdecke, -n *tablecloth*
das Trinkgeld *tip*
die Vorspeise, -n *appetizer*
schmecken *to taste*

Mahlzeiten
meals

das Abendessen *dinner*
das Frühstück *breakfast*
das Mittagessen *lunch*
der Snack, -s *snack*

Getränke
drinks

das Bier *beer*
der Kaffee *coffee*
die Milch *milk*
das Mineralwasser *sparkling water*
der Saft, ⸚e *juice*
der Tee *tea*
das stille Wasser *still water*
der Wein *wine*

Essen beschreiben
talking about food

der Geschmack, ⸚e *flavor; taste*
fade *bland*
lecker *delicious*
leicht *light*
salzig *salty*
scharf *spicy*
schwer *rich, heavy*
süß *sweet*

Ausdrücke

Ich hätte gern(e)... / Ich möchte
 I would like...
auf Diät sein *to be on a diet*
hausgemacht *homemade*

Dative articles and possessive
 adjectives *See pp. 170–171.*
Dative prepositions *See p. 174.*

COMMUNICATIVE GOALS
By the end of this chapter you will be able to:

Los geht's! Was machen Meline, Hans und Sabite?

LEKTION 5A

Talk about celebrations of life events.
Talk about holidays.

To do so, you will use:

Kontext Seite 186–189
• Celebrations
• Special Occasions

Strukturen Seite 194–203
5A.1 The **Perfekt** (Part 1)
5A.2 Accusative pronouns
5A.3 Dative pronouns

You will also learn about cultural products, practices, and perspectives related to:

Kultur Seite 192–193
• **Das Oktoberfest**
• German Christmas traditions
• Die Sternsinger

Zapping *Penny*

LEKTION 5B

Describe clothing.
Talk about clothes shopping.

To do so, you will use:

Kontext Seite 204–207
• Articles of clothing
• Descriptions of clothing
• Shopping words and phrases

Strukturen Seite 212–223
5B.1 The **Perfekt** (Part 2)
5B.2 **Wissen** and **kennen**
5B.3 Two-way prepositions

You will also learn about cultural products, practices, and perspectives related to:

Kultur Seite 210–211
• **Die deutsche Modewelt**
• Traditional Costumes
• **Guido Maria Kretschmer**

WEITER GEHT'S

You will learn about the region of Bavaria, famous Bavarians, and Bavarian culture and industry.

Panorama Seite 224–230
• **Bayern**

And you will demonstrate that you can:
Lesen: Scan a written text for information
Hören: Listen for key words
Schreiben: Use a dictionary

Suggestion Have students guess the meaning of the chapter title **Feiern** based on the image shown. Ask: **Was feiern Meline, Hans und Sabite?**

Feste feiern

 Vocabulary Tools

Wortschatz

Feste	*celebrations*
der Feiertag, -e	*holiday*
die Karte, -n	*card*
die Party, -s	*party*
das Zimmer, -	*room*
anstoßen (stößt... an)	*to toast*
bekommen	*to receive*
einladen (lädt... ein)	*to invite*
feiern	*to celebrate*
eine Party geben	*to throw a party*
(keinen) Spaß haben	*(not) to have fun*
schenken	*to give (a gift)*
überraschen	*to surprise*
Herzlichen Glückwunsch!	*Congratulations!*
besondere Anlässe	*special occasions*
die Ehe, -n	*marriage*
der/die Frischvermählte, -n	*newlywed*
die Geburt, -en	*birth*
der Geburtstag, -e	*birthday*
die Hochzeit, -en	*wedding*
der Hochzeitstag, -e	*wedding anniversary*
der Jahrestag, -e	*anniversary*
(das/der) Silvester	*New Year's Eve*
(das) Weihnachten	*Christmas*
in Rente gehen	*to retire*
einen Abschluss machen	*to graduate*
Ausdrücke	*expressions*
die Freundschaft, -en	*friendship*
das Glück	*happiness*
der Kuss, ¨e	*kiss*
die Liebe	*love*

Suggestion Point out to students that **Anlässe** is the plural form of **der Anlass**.

Suggestion Tell students that many German speakers also treat **Silvester** as a masculine noun.

Suggestion Tell students that the phrase **Ich lade dich ein** can also mean *It's my treat.*

Suggestion Teach students the verb form **küssen**.

Expansion Ask students to cut out pictures from magazines that depict words on the vocabulary list and bring them to class. Have students work in groups, taking turns asking about and identifying the pictures.

Suggestion Tell students that because of the influence of English, one often sees the plural form **Parties** on blogs and in advertising. Remind them that the correct plural form is still **Partys**.

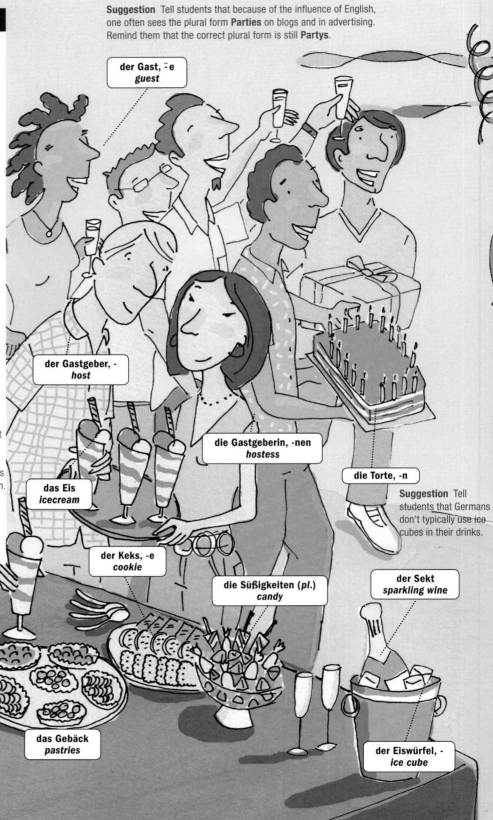

der Gast, ¨e *guest*

der Gastgeber, - *host*

die Gastgeberin, -nen *hostess*

die Torte, -n

Suggestion Tell students that Germans don't typically use ice cubes in their drinks.

das Eis *icecream*

der Keks, -e *cookie*

die Süßigkeiten (pl.) *candy*

der Sekt *sparkling wine*

das Gebäck *pastries*

der Eiswürfel, - *ice cube*

Herzlichen Glückwunsch zum Geburtstag, Hans!

der Ballon, -s

die Überraschung, -en
surprise

Suggestion Tell students that the plural form **die Ballone** is also used, especially in Southern Germany, Austria, and Switzerland.

das Geschenk, -e
present/gift

ACHTUNG

Use the preposition **zu** to say *on Christmas* or *on New Year's Eve:*
Zu Silvester feiern wir bei meinem Bruder.

Expansion Bring in a box with one or more objects inside and tell students it is an **Überraschung.** Have them ask yes-or-no questions to figure out what the object is.

Anwendung

1 Suggestion Go over the first few items together, as a class.

1 Was passt zusammen? Welche Wörter in der linken Spalte (*column*) passen am besten zu den Wörtern in der rechten Spalte?

- a/b 1. der Geburtstag
- d 2. der Gast
- e 3. die Ehe
- a 4. die Torte
- c 5. das Weihnachten

- a. der Kuchen
- b. die Karte
- c. das Silvester
- d. die Gastgeberin
- e. die Frischvermählten

2 Ja oder nein? Kann man die Dinge, die Sie hören, essen?

	Ja	Nein		Ja	Nein
1.	☐	☑	4.	☐	☑
2.	☑	☐	5.	☐	☑
3.	☑	☐	6.	☑	☐

Expansion Ask students how they celebrate their birthday, Christmas, with whom they celebrate New Year's, and what presents they give and receive.

3 Feste und Feiertage Ergänzen Sie die Sätze.

1. An nationalen __Feiertagen__ muss man nicht arbeiten.
2. An Halloween kommen Kinder an die Haustür und man gibt ihnen __Süßigkeiten__.
3. Zum Geburtstag bekommt man __Geschenke/Karten__.
4. An Silvester stößt man um Mitternacht mit __Sekt__ an.
5. Nach 50 Ehejahren feiert man die goldene __Hochzeit__.

4 Eine Party für Max Hören Sie sich den Dialog an und markieren Sie dann die richtigen Aussagen.

4 Expansion Have students write a second dialogue that takes place at Max's surprise party, then act it out for the class.

	richtig	falsch
1. Max hat nächsten Monat Geburtstag.	☐	☑
2. Max braucht ein bisschen Spaß.	☑	☐
3. Max plant seine Geburtstagsparty selbst.	☐	☑
4. Max spielt in der Basketballmannschaft.	☑	☐
5. Zum Geburtstag kommen zehn Personen.	☐	☑
6. Die Party ist bei Emil.	☑	☐
7. Die Freunde kaufen das Geschenk zusammen.	☑	☐
8. Zum Geburtstag bekommt Max einen Baseball.	☐	☑

5 Satzsalat Bilden Sie Sätze mit den diversen Elementen.

Answers will vary. Sample answers are provided.

BEISPIEL *Die Eltern bereiten eine Geburtstagsparty vor.*

5 Suggestion Have students identify the separable prefix verbs before they complete this activity.

die Eltern	anstoßen	die Kinder
die Gäste	bekommen	eine Geburtstagsparty
der Gastgeber	einladen	eine Geburtstagstorte
das Geburtstagskind	mitbringen	ein Geschenk
die Verwandten	vorbereiten	mit einem Getränk

5 Answers 1. Die Verwandten bringen ein Geschenk mit. 2. Das Geburtstagskind bekommt eine Geburtstagstorte. 3. Die Gäste bereiten das Essen vor. 4. Die Gastgeber laden die Kinder ein. 5. Die Gäste stoßen mit einem Getränk an. 6. Die Eltern laden die Kinder ein.

8 Suggestion Write the following useful phrases on the board: **Auf meinem Bild sind ...**, **Mein Bild hat ...**, and **Hast du das auch auf deinem Bild?** Make sure students understand that they should not show each other their pictures. Model this by protectively holding your sheet of paper and saying: **Mein Partner darf mein Bild nicht sehen.**

Kommunikation

Besondere Anlässe Was feiern die Personen auf den Bildern? Bilden Sie mit Ihrem Partner / Ihrer Partnerin zusammen einen Satz zu jedem Bild. Answers will vary. Sample answers are provided.

▶ **BEISPIEL**

Matthias hat heute Geburtstag.

6 Suggestion Encourage students to be inventive and detailed in their descriptions.

Matthias

1. Lena
Lena macht ihren Abschluss.

2. Kerstin und Simon
Kerstin und Simon feiern ihre Hochzeit.

3. die Familie Hartmann
Die Familie Hartmann feiert Weihnachten.

4. Andreas und seine Freunde Andreas gibt eine Silvesterparty für seine Freunde.

5. Herr Aydin
Herr Aydin ist jetzt in Rente.

6. Martin
Martin gibt seiner Freundin einen Kuss.

7

Eine Einladung Lesen Sie Kiaras Einladung an ihre Verwandten und beantworten Sie mit Ihrem Partner / Ihrer Partnerin die Fragen zum Text.
Answers will vary. Sample answers are provided.

Von:	Kiara Gökda
An:	Familie Özer; Familie Celik; Murat Gökda; Familie Gökda; Ela Cengiz; Kenan Cengiz; Alik Aymaz; Familie Yilmaz
Betreff:	Feier für meine Eltern

Hallo an alle,

im Mai feiern unsere Eltern ihre silberne Hochzeit. 25 Jahre – unglaublich! Mein Bruder Murat und ich planen eine Feier für sie am Samstag, dem 5. Mai, im Restaurant „Zum Alten Markt" hier in München. Unsere Idee ist, dass wir alle, wir beide und ihr, ihnen eine Reise nach Marokko schenken. Die Reise ist für eine Woche und kostet 520 Euro pro Person.

Wir hoffen, ihr könnt kommen und macht bei dem Geschenk mit.

Kiara

1. **Warum schreibt Kiara die E-Mail?** Sie plant eine Feier für ihre Eltern.
2. **Wie lange sind die Eltern verheiratet?** Sie sind 25 Jahre verheiratet.
3. **Was wollen sie den Eltern schenken?** Sie wollen den Eltern eine Reise nach Marokko schenken.
4. **Von wem ist das Geschenk?** Das Geschenk ist von Kiara und Murat und den Verwandten.
5. **Wie viel Geld braucht Kiara für das Geschenk?** Sie braucht 1.040 Euro für das Geschenk.
6. **Wann und wo ist die Feier?**
Sie ist am 5. Mai im Restaurant „Zum Alten Markt" in München.

8

Diskutieren und kombinieren Finden Sie die sieben kleinen Unterschiede auf den Bildern, die Sie von Ihrem Professor / Ihrer Professorin bekommen. Answers will vary.

BEISPIEL

S1: *Auf meinem Bild sind fünf Personen. Wie viele Personen sind auf deinem Bild?*
S2: *Auf meinem Bild sind sechs Personen.*

9

Feiern wir! Sie planen eine Party. Diskutieren Sie, wo Sie die Party machen wollen, wen Sie einladen, was Sie alles brauchen, wer Essen macht, wer die Getränke kauft, welche Musik Sie hören möchten und so weiter. Lesen Sie die Pläne für Ihre Party im Kurs vor. Answers will vary.

BEISPIEL

S1: *Bei wem wollen wir die Party machen?*
S2: *Bei Hanna? Sie wohnt bei ihren Eltern, und ihr Haus ist ziemlich groß. Und wen wollen wir einladen?*
S3: *Wir können unsere Freunde vom Basketball einladen.*

9 Expansion Have students plan an actual party as the culmination of this chapter. Make sure students use German to discuss the plans.

Aussprache und Rechtschreibung   Audio

The consonantal *r*

To pronounce the German consonant **r**, start by placing the tip of your tongue against your lower front teeth. Then, raise the back of your tongue toward the roof of your mouth. Let air flow from the back of your throat over your tongue creating a soft vibrating sound from the roof of your mouth.

Rock	**rot**	**Brille**	**Freund**	**Jahrestag**

Note that the consonant **r** sound always precedes a vowel.

Orange	**frisch**	**fahren**	**Rucksack**	**Paprika**

When the German **r** comes at the end of a word or a syllable, it sounds more like a vowel than a consonant.

Suggestion Tell students that in some parts of Bavaria and Austria, the **r** sound is produced with the tongue at the front of the mouth, and sounds similar to the Spanish r.

1 **Aussprechen** Wiederholen Sie die Wörter, die Sie hören.

1. Rente
2. rosa
3. reden
4. Schrank
5. schreiben
6. sprechen
7. Sprudel
8. Straße
9. gestreift
10. frisch
11. Bruder
12. tragen
13. grau
14. Haare
15. Amerika
16. studieren

2 **Nachsprechen** Wiederholen Sie die Sätze, die Sie hören.

1. Veronika trägt einen roten Rock.
2. Mein Bruder schreibt einen Brief.
3. Rolf reist mit Rucksack nach Rosenheim.
4. Regensburg und Bayreuth liegen in Bayern.
5. Warum fahren Sie nicht am Freitag?
6. Marie und Robert sprechen Russisch.
7. Drei Krokodile fressen frische Frösche.
8. Im Restaurant bestellt die Frau Roggenbrot mit Radieschen.

3 **Sprichwörter** Wiederholen Sie die Sprichwörter, die Sie hören.

1 You learn how to do something by doing it. (lit. Speak, if you want to learn how to speak.)

2 If you overdo it, you'll wear yourself out. (lit. The pitcher goes to the well until it breaks.)

More activities
vhlcentral   LM p. 40   Online activities

Frohes neues Jahr! Video

Vorbereitung Have students preview the scenes and write down one adjective to describe each scene.

Meline und Sabite wollen Silvester feiern, aber Torsten und Lorenzo haben andere Pläne. Da klingelt es plötzlich an der Tür...

1

SABITE Torsten! Es ist Silvester! Aber es sind Weihnachtsferien! Die Uni fängt erst wieder in zwei Wochen an. Warte mal.

2

MELINE Niemand lernt an Silvester. Man geht auf Partys und hat Spaß. Du hast eine wunderschöne Freundin, Torsten. Verlange nicht von ihr, das neue Jahr ohne dich zu beginnen. Bist du ihr immer noch böse?

3

SABITE Torsten? Dir auch ein frohes neues Jahr!

4

MELINE Lorenzo ist in der Stadt. Wir gehen später am Abend essen und danach gehen wir zu einer Party am Brandenburger Tor.
SABITE Schön, dass du Silvester mit ihm feierst.
MELINE Wir haben Spaß zusammen. Wieso kommst du nicht mit uns mit? Es sind bestimmt eine Million Leute da.
SABITE Ich mag keine Menschenmassen. Danke für die Einladung.

5

MELINE Sind Hans und George schon aus Bayern zurück? Wo ist Lorenzo?
SABITE Er ist nicht da! Es wird langsam spät.
MELINE Voicemail.
SABITE Nur die Ruhe, Meline.
MELINE Lorenzo!

GEORGE UND HANS Frohes neues Jahr!!!!
GEORGE Wir haben die Party einfach zu euch gebracht!
HANS George hat das Licht in eurer Wohnung gesehen.
GEORGE Hans hat Meline schreien gehört.
MELINE Ich habe nicht geschrien.
HANS Wo ist Lorenzo?
MELINE Ha, ha, ha, Hans. Wo ist denn deine neue Freundin?

6

ÜBUNGEN

1 Richtig oder falsch? Entscheiden Sie, ob die folgenden Sätze richtig oder falsch sind.

1. Torsten will an Silvester lernen. Richtig.
2. Lorenzo ist in der Stadt. Richtig.
3. Meline und Lorenzo wollen ins Kino gehen. Falsch.
4. Es sind eine Million Leute am Fernsehturm. Falsch.
5. George und Hans haben Licht in der Wohnung gesehen. Richtig.

6. Hans hat Meline singen gehört. Falsch.
7. George und Hans sind auf einer Party in Kreuzberg gewesen. Richtig.
8. Meline möchte, dass Hans und George zurück zur Party gehen. Falsch.
9. Hans hat Kekse gebacken. Falsch.
10. George möchte mit seinen Freunden anstoßen. Richtig.

PERSONEN George Hans Meline Sabite

HANS Gut, dann gehen wir eben zurück zur Party in Kreuzberg.
SABITE Ah, ah! Geht nicht. Ich bin so froh, dass ihr hier seid. Frohes neues Jahr, Hans, George.
MELINE Bitte geht nicht. Ich habe Sekt.

HANS Ich habe einen Stollen für uns gebacken.
SABITE Oh, sieht lecker aus. Bitte schön.
HANS Danke. Hier, reich mal rüber.
MELINE Oh, Hans, er schmeckt genau wie der von meiner Mutter!

MELINE Es ist Mitternacht! Frohes neues Jahr!

GEORGE Ich möchte gern mit euch anstoßen, meine neuen Freunde. *Happy New Year!*
SABITE *Mutlu yillar.*

Nützliche Ausdrücke

- **Silvester**
  New Year's Eve
- **die Weihnachtsferien**
  winter break
- **Die Uni fängt erst wieder in zwei Wochen an.**
  Classes don't begin for two weeks.
- **wunderschön**
  gorgeous
- **Bist du ihr immer noch böse?**
  Are you still mad at her?
- **Frohes neues Jahr!**
  Happy New Year!
- **die Menschenmassen**
  crowds
- **Nur die Ruhe!**
  Relax!
- **Hans hat Meline schreien gehört.**
  Hans heard Meline yelling.
- **Reich mal rüber!**
  Hand it over!

5A.1
- **Ich habe einen Stollen für uns gebacken.**
  I baked a stollen for us.

5A.2
- **Verlange nicht von ihr, das neue Jahr ohne dich zu beginnen.**
  Don't make her start the new year without you.

5A.3
- **Schön, dass du Silvester mit ihm feierst.**
  It's great that you're celebrating New Year's with him.

---

 2 **Zum Besprechen** Planen Sie zu dritt eine Silvesterparty. Machen Sie eine Einkaufsliste und eine Gästeliste. Soll die Party ein Motto (*theme*) haben? Was müssen die Gäste mitbringen? Answers will vary.

Suggestion Explain to students that Hans speaks in Bavarian at the end of this episode: **Is' scho' recht. A guat's Nei's! (Ist schon recht. Ein gutes Neues!)**

3 **Vertiefung** Finden Sie heraus (*Find out*), warum der letzte Tag im Jahr in der deutschsprachigen Welt Silvester heißt. Woher kommt der Name? Seit wann heißt der Tag so? Vergleichen Sie dann die deutschen Silvestertraditionen mit Ihren eigenen (*your own*).
 Wo feiern Sie Silvester? Gehen Sie auf Partys oder bleiben Sie mit Freunden zu Hause?

More activities

 vhlcentral   VM p. 9   Online activities

Kultur

IM FOKUS

Das Oktoberfest

 Reading

AM 12. OKTOBER 1810 HEIRATET Kronprinz Ludwig (der spätere König Ludwig I. von Bayern) Prinzessin Therese. Vor den Toren Münchens° feiern Menschen aus ganz Bayern die königliche Hochzeit auf einem Feld. Dieses Feld heißt heute noch Theresienwiese. Viele Menschen nennen es einfach die Wiesn, ein Wort aus der bayerischen Umgangssprache°. 1810 kann man Pferderennen° auf der Theresienwiese sehen und in den nächsten Jahren wiederholt man diese Pferderennen. Das ist der Anfang des Oktoberfests.

Im Jahr 1818 gibt es das erste Karussell° beim Oktoberfest. Heute findet man neben Karussells und Festzelten° auch Willenborgs Riesenrad° und einen Flohzirkus° für Kinder. Aus Wettergründen° beginnt das Oktoberfest bereits im September. Traditionell ist der erste Tag immer der erste Samstag nach dem 15. September. Der Oberbürgermeister° Münchens zapft° das erste Bierfass° an und sagt dann: „O'zapft is!" Das ist Bayerisch und bedeutet „Es ist angezapft!" Der letzte Tag ist der erste Sonntag im Oktober. In über 200 Jahren findet das Oktoberfest 24-mal wegen° Cholera oder Kriegen° nicht statt°.

Das Oktoberfest	
Erstes Oktoberfest:	1810
Ort:	Theresienwiese
Fläche:	0,42 km² (Quadratkilometer)
Besucher:	mehr als 6,3 Millionen Gäste
Festzelte:	16 große und 22 kleine
Schweinswürste:	140,225 Paar
Schweinshaxen°:	75.456
Abfall°:	mehr als 1.000 Tonnen
Verlorene Gegenstände°:	300 Brillen° und 480 Handys

QUELLE: offizielles Stadtportal für München

den Toren Münchens *the gates of Munich* bayerischen Umgangssprache *Bavarian vernacular* Pferderennen *horse races* Karussell *merry-go-round* Festzelten *pavilions* Riesenrad *Ferris wheel* Flohzirkus *flea circus* aus Wettergründen *due to weather concerns* Oberbürgermeister *mayor* zapft... an *taps* Bierfass *beer barrel* wegen *due to* Kriegen *wars* findet... statt *takes place* Schweinshaxen *pork knuckles* Abfall *garbage* Verlorene Gegenstände *Lost items* Brillen *eyeglasses*

ÜBUNGEN

1 **Im Fokus** Richtig oder falsch? Korrigieren Sie die falschen Aussagen. Diskutieren Sie dann die letzte Frage mit einem Partner / einer Partnerin.

1. Die Menschen feiern die Hochzeit von Kronprinz Ludwig und Prinzessin Therese auf einem Feld vor der Stadt München. **Richtig.**

2. Heute beginnt das Oktoberfest am 1. Oktober. **Falsch.** Heute beginnt das Oktoberfest schon am ersten Samstag nach dem 15. September.

3. Der Präsident des Fußball-Clubs „Bayern München" zapft das erste Bierfass an. **Falsch.** Der Münchner Oberbürgermeister zapft das erste Bierfass an.

Diskussion Vergleichen Sie (*compare*) Feste in Ihrem Land mit dem Oktoberfest.

2 **Die deutschsprachige Welt** Richtig oder falsch? Korrigieren Sie die falschen Aussagen. Diskutieren Sie dann die letzte Frage mit einem Partner / einer Partnerin.

1. Am 6. Dezember besucht Sankt Nikolaus die Kinder. **Richtig.**

2. Die Kinder bekommen ihre Geschenke am 25. Dezember. **Falsch.** Sie bekommen ihre Geschenke schon am 24. Dezember.

3. Brave Kinder bekommen am 6. Dezember oft Süßigkeiten. **Richtig.**

Diskussion Welche Feste feiern Sie im Winter? Welche Familientraditionen gibt es bei diesen Festen?

DEUTSCH IM ALLTAG

Herzlichen Glückwunsch

Alles Gute zum Geburtstag!	*Happy birthday!*
Ein gutes neues Jahr!	*Happy New Year!*
Frohe Ostern!	*Happy Easter!*
Frohe Weihnachten!	*Merry Christmas!*
Gute Besserung!	*Get well!*
Hals- und Beinbruch!	*Break a leg!*
Viel Glück!	*Good luck!*

DIE DEUTSCHSPRACHIGE WELT

Weihnachten

Am 6. Dezember besucht Sankt Nikolaus Kinder in vielen Gegenden° Deutschlands, Österreichs und der Schweiz. Brave° Kinder bekommen Schokolade, Nüsse° und andere Süßigkeiten. Sankt Nikolaus kommt oft mit einer zweiten Gestalt°. Diese Gestalt heißt Krampus im Süden und Knecht Ruprecht im Norden und soll böse° Kinder erschrecken°.

Die Weihnachtsfeiertage sind der 25. und 26. Dezember. Geschenke bekommen Kinder aber schon am 24. Dezember, dem Heiligen Abend. Das Christkind bringt Geschenke, und Familien öffnen sie am gleichen Abend.

in vielen Gegenden *in many areas* **Brave** *Well-behaved* **Nüsse** *nuts* **Gestalt** *figure* **böse** *naughty* **erschrecken** *scare*

PORTRÄT

Die Sternsinger

Suggestion Ask students what differences they've noticed between Christmas as it is celebrated in their country and Christmas in German-speaking countries.

Vor allem in Bayern und Österreich sind die Sternsinger ein sehr bekanntes Brauchtum°. Drei Kinder oder junge Leute verkleiden sich° als die Heiligen Drei Könige° Caspar, Melchior und Balthasar. Sie gehen zwischen dem 27. Dezember und dem 6. Januar, dem Tag des Dreikönigsfestes, von Haus zu Haus. Sie singen Lieder in den Häusern, sprechen ein Gebet° und sagen ein Gedicht° auf. Dann schreiben sie mit Kreide° einen Segen° über° die Haustür. In Deutschland sammeln° die Sternsinger seit dem 16. Jahrhundert Geld für wohltätige Zwecke°, vor allem für Kinder in Not°. Die Aktion Dreikönigssingen ist weltweit° die größte organisierte Hilfsaktion von Kindern für Kinder. Alleine im Jahr 2017 sammeln die Sternsinger über 75 Millionen Euro.

Brauchtum *tradition* **verkleiden sich** *dress up* **Könige** *kings* **Gebet** *prayer* **Gedicht** *poem* **Kreide** *chalk* **Segen** *blessing* **über** *over* **sammeln** *collect* **wohltätige Zwecke** *charitable causes* **in Not** *in need* **weltweit** *worldwide*

ꙅ IM INTERNET

Welche anderen Feste und Festivals werden in Deutschland, Österreich und der Schweiz gefeiert?

Find out more at **vhlcentral.com**.

---

3 **Porträt** Richtig oder falsch? Korrigieren Sie die falschen Aussagen. Diskutieren Sie dann die letzte Frage mit einem Partner / einer Partnerin.

1. Die Sternsinger sind vor allem eine süddeutsche und österreichische Tradition. Richtig.
2. Die Sternsinger verkleiden sich als Kinder in Not. **Falsch.** Die Sternsinger verkleiden sich als die Drei Könige.
3. Die Sternsinger kommen kurz nach Weihnachten in die Häuser. Richtig.

Diskussion Sind Traditionen wichtig? Welche Bräuche (*customs*) gibt es in Ihrer Familie oder Ihrem Freundeskreis? Vergleichen Sie Ihre Traditionen mit denen Ihres Partners / Ihrer Partnerin.

4 **Deutsche Feste** Machen Sie eine Liste von deutschen und amerikanischen Feiertagen. Beschreiben Sie die Feiertage und diskutieren Sie die Unterschiede (*differences*) und Ähnlichkeiten (*similarities*) in kleinen Gruppen. Lesen Sie dann Ihre Beschreibungen im Kurs vor. Können Ihre Mitstudenten die Feiertage erraten?

BEISPIEL

S1: *Das Christkind kommt und es gibt Geschenke.*

S2: *Das ist Weihnachten.*

Suggestion Assign a set of months to each group so each group is researching holidays for a different part of the year.

More activities

vhlcentral · Online activities

5A.1

Teaching Tip You may want to assign the grammar tutorial **5A.1 The *Perfekt* (Part 1)** on the Supersite for students to watch before they come to class.

QUERVERWEIS

In **6A.1** and **6B.1**, you will learn about the **Präteritum**, a past tense used mainly in writing.

QUERVERWEIS

Most verbs form the **Perfekt** with **haben**. You will learn about forming the **Perfekt** with **sein** in **5B.1**.

ACHTUNG

The **-et** ending is added to verb stems ending in **-d**, **-t**, or a consonant cluster, to make pronunciation easier: **Es hat geregnet**.

Suggestion Write on the board: **ge-** + stem + **-t** and have students copy it down in their notes. Give students the infinitives of other weak verbs, and have them figure out the past participles, based on the pattern. Ex.: **kochen, machen**.

The *Perfekt* (Part 1) Grammar Tutorial

Startblock In English, there are several ways of talking about events in the past: *I ate, I have eaten, I was eating.* In German, all of these meanings can be expressed with the **Perfekt** tense.

Wir **haben** die Party einfach zu euch **gebracht**.

Ich **habe** einen Stollen für uns **gebacken**.

The *Perfekt* tense

- To form the **Perfekt**, use a present tense form of **haben** or **sein** with the *past participle* of the verb that expresses the action.

   Ich **habe** zu viel Kuchen **gegessen**.
   *I **ate** too much cake.*

   Wir **haben** den Kindern Geschenke **gekauft**.
   *We **bought** the kids presents.*

Forming past participles

- German verbs can be grouped into three main categories, based on the way their past participles are formed.

   Ich **habe** eine Torte **gemacht**.
   *I **made** a cake.*

   Wir **haben** Kekse **gegessen**.
   *We **ate** cookies.*

   Er **hat** eine CD **gebrannt**.
   *He **burned** a CD.*

- Most German verbs are *weak*. Form the past participle of a weak verb by adding **ge-** before the verb stem and **-t** or **-et** after the stem.

common weak verbs			
infinitive	past participle	infinitive	past participle
arbeiten	gearbeitet	lernen	gelernt
feiern	gefeiert	öffnen	geöffnet
hören	gehört	sagen	gesagt
kaufen	gekauft	spielen	gespielt
lachen	gelacht	tanzen	getanzt

   Haben Sie eine Flasche Wasser **gekauft**?
   *** Did** you **buy** a bottle of water?*

   Ich **habe** mit den Gästen **geredet**.
   *I **chatted** with the guests.*

- Verbs ending in **-ieren** are almost always weak. Their past participles end in **-t**, but omit the **ge-** prefix.

   Der Lehrer **hat** die Hausaufgaben **korrigiert**.
   *The teacher **corrected** the homework.*

   Wie lange **habt** ihr in Deutschland **studiert**?
   *How long **did** you **study** in Germany?*

   Suggestion Point out that the past participle of **verlieren** is an exception: **Ich habe verloren**.

- To form the past participle of a *strong* verb, add **ge-** before the verb stem and **-en** after. Strong verbs may be regular or irregular in the present, but verbs that have a stem change in the present tense are almost always strong verbs in the **Perfekt**.

Wir **haben** unsere Freunde **gesehen**.
*We **saw** our friends.*

Ich **habe** meinen Eltern **geholfen**.
*I **helped** my parents.*

- Note that many strong verbs have a stem change in the past participle.

common strong verbs			
infinitive	past participle	infinitive	past participle
essen	gegessen	schlafen	geschlafen
finden	gefunden	schreiben	geschrieben
geben	gegeben	sprechen	gesprochen
heißen	geheißen	tragen	getragen
helfen	geholfen	treffen	getroffen
lesen	gelesen	trinken	getrunken
nehmen	genommen	waschen	gewaschen

Habt Ihr den Bus nach Hause **genommen**?
*Did you **take** the bus home?*

Sie **hat** viele Bücher **geschrieben**.
*She's **written** a lot of books.*

Hast du gut **geschlafen**?
*Did you **sleep** well?*

Was **habt** ihr auf der Party **getragen**?
*What **did** you **wear** to the party?*

- There is a small group of verbs called *mixed* verbs. The past participles of mixed verbs have a **ge-** prefix and end in **-t** like weak verbs, but they have irregular stems like many strong verbs.

common mixed verbs	
infinitive	past participle
brennen (*to burn*)	gebrannt
bringen	gebracht
denken (*to think*)	gedacht
nennen (*to name*)	genannt
rennen (*to run*)	gerannt

Habt ihr an die Hochzeit **gedacht**?
*Were you **thinking** about the wedding?*

Sie **haben** ihr Kind Johanna **genannt**.
*They **named** their child Johanna.*

Suggestion Show students the verb list in **Appendix A**. Give them the infinitive of a strong or mixed verb, and have them check the appendix to find the past participle.

Suggestion Tell students that there are 10 vowel change patterns for the past forms of strong verbs, which will become more apparent when they learn the **Präteritum** in **Kapitel 2**: **ei-e-ie, ei-i-i, i-a-u, i-a-o, ie-o-o, e-a-o, e-a-e, e-o-o, a-u-a, a-ie-a**. Emphasize that while it is useful to be aware of these patterns, they still need to memorize which verbs are strong or mixed and what if any stem changes they have.

ACHTUNG

You cannot tell which category a verb belongs to by looking at the infinitive. You must learn the past participle of a verb along with its present tense forms.

QUERVERWEIS

See **Appendix A** for a complete list of past participles for all strong and mixed verbs taught in this book.

More activities

vhlcentral

WB
pp. 63–64

LM
p. 41

Online activities

Jetzt sind Sie dran! Ergänzen Sie die Sätze mit den richtigen Formen der Hilfsverben und der Partizipien.

1. Wir ___haben___ Monikas Geburtstag ___gefeiert___. (feiern)
2. Die Katzen ___haben___ viel Milch ___getrunken___. (trinken)
3. Unsere Freunde ___haben___ viel Spaß ___gehabt___. (haben)
4. Jens ___hat___ mit seinen Geschenken ___gespielt___. (spielen)
5. Ich ___habe___ am Montag ___gearbeitet___. (arbeiten)
6. Peter ___hat___ vier Jahre an der Uni ___studiert___. (studieren)

7. Die Gäste ___haben___ dem Geburtstagskind viele Geschenke ___gegeben___. (geben)
8. ___Habt___ ihr die Bücher ___gelesen___? (lesen)
9. ___Hast___ du an die Pläne ___gedacht___? (denken)
10. Wir ___haben___ sehr viel ___gelacht___. (lachen)
11. ___Habt___ ihr Süßigkeiten ___gegessen___? (essen)
12. Meine Freundin ___hat___ einen Hund ___adoptiert___. (adoptieren)

Anwendung

1 **Was passt zusammen?** Welche Verben in Spalte 1 entsprechen (*match*) den Partizipien in Spalte 2?

_c_ 1. essen	a. gebracht
_f_ 2. finden	b. geholfen
_b_ 3. helfen	c. gegessen
_e_ 4. schreiben	d. genommen
_a_ 5. bringen	e. geschrieben
_d_ 6. nehmen	f. gefunden

2 **Das Perfekt** Setzen Sie die Verben ins Perfekt.

BEISPIEL tanzen (ich)
ich habe getanzt

1. kaufen (du) du hast gekauft
2. lernen (wir) wir haben gelernt
3. feiern (er) er hat gefeiert
4. arbeiten (Sie) Sie haben gearbeitet
5. hören (ihr) ihr habt gehört
6. regnen (es) es hat geregnet
7. kochen (sie, *sing.*) sie hat gekocht
8. denken (ich) ich habe gedacht

3 **Was haben sie gemacht?** Ergänzen Sie die Sätze mit der richtigen Form von **haben** und dem passenden Partizip.

1. Ich ___habe___ einen neuen Rucksack ___gekauft___. (kaufen)
2. Julius ___hat___ seine Freunde ___getroffen___. (treffen)
3. ___Habt___ ihr das Fußballspiel mit Paul ___diskutiert___? (diskutieren)
4. Der Koch ___hat___ die Kartoffeln ___gewaschen___. (waschen)
5. ___Hast___ du mit deinem Bruder ___gesprochen___? (sprechen)
6. Anna ___hat___ ihre Tochter zum Friseur ___gebracht___. (bringen)
7. Kiara ___hat___ eine Party ___gegeben___. (geben)
8. Professor Schulz, ___haben___ Sie meine Arbeit ___korrigiert___? (korrigieren)

4 **Am Wochenende** Was haben diese Personen am Wochenende gemacht? Schreiben Sie zu jedem Foto einen Satz im Perfekt. Answers will vary. Sample answers are provided.

▶ **BEISPIEL**
meine Eltern und ich
Meine Eltern und ich haben Karten gespielt.

1. Herr Peters
Herr Peters hat gelesen.

2. Erik und Emil
Erik und Emil haben Tee getrunken.

3. Jessica
Jessica hat geschlafen.

4. Nina
Nina hat getanzt.

5. Hasan
Hasan hat sein Auto gewaschen.

6. Sara und Max
Sara und Max haben im Restaurant gegessen.

Kommunikation

5 **Letzten Sommer** Fragen Sie Ihren Partner / Ihre Partnerin, was er/sie letzten Sommer gemacht hat. Answers will vary.

 BEISPIEL

S1: *Hast du eine Reise gemacht?*
S2: *Ja, ich habe eine Reise in die Schweiz gemacht.*

1. Hast du viel geschlafen?
2. Hast du viel gegessen?
3. Hast du gearbeitet? Wo?
4. Hast du Deutsch gelernt?
5. Hast du Sport gemacht?
6. Hast du oft Freunde getroffen?
7. Hast du etwas gekauft? Was?
8. Hast du viele Filme gesehen? Welche?

6 **Auf Dieters Geburtstagsparty** Sehen Sie mit einem Partner / einer Partnerin das Bild (*picture*) an. Was haben die Personen auf Dieters Geburtstagsparty gemacht?

 BEISPIEL

S1: *Jutta hat Karaoke gesungen.*
S2: *Ja, und ihre Freunde haben viel gelacht.*

7 **Im Deutschkurs** Fragen Sie Ihre Mitstudenten, was man heute im Deutschkurs gemacht hat. Vergleichen Sie die Antworten in Ihrer Gruppe.

BEISPIEL

S1: *Habt ihr gelesen?*
S2: *Ja, wir haben gelesen.*
S3: *Wer hat gelacht?*
S1: *Ben hat gelacht!*

antworten	schlafen
diskutieren	schreiben
essen	singen
lachen	spielen
lernen	sprechen
lesen	trinken

8 **Meine Großeltern** Erzählen Sie den Mitstudenten in Ihrer Gruppe, was Ihre Großeltern gemacht haben, als sie jünger waren (*when they were younger*).

 BEISPIEL

S1: *Mein Großvater hat immer viele Geschenke für seine Kinder gekauft.*
S2: *Meine Großmutter hat jeden Tag Kuchen oder Kekse gebacken.*
S3: *Meine Großeltern haben oft Karten gespielt.*

5 **Video Virtual Chat** You can also assign activity 5 on the Supersite. Students record individual responses that appear in your gradebook.

7 **Suggestion** Divide students into small groups and ask each group to come up with their own sample question, using verbs from the word bank. Write their suggestions on the board.

8 **Suggestion** Smaller groups are recommended for this activity. Tell students that if they don't know much about their grandparents, they can be creative and make something up.

5A.2 Accusative pronouns

Startblock Just as nouns in the nominative case can be replaced by nominative pronouns, nouns in the accusative case can be replaced by accusative pronouns.

QUERVERWEIS

See **Lektion 1A.3** to review the nominative pronouns.

Suggestion Give students a moment to read through the list of accusative pronouns. Then, with their books closed, have them provide the accusative form of each nominative pronoun you give them.

Suggestion Remind students that a noun following the verb **sein** is *not* a direct object and is in the nominative case.

Suggestion The song **"Ich will"** by Rammstein is full of pronouns and features ample repetition. Give students a fill-in-the-blanks worksheet containing the song lyrics, with the pronouns omitted. Have students listen to the song and fill in the missing pronouns.

personal pronouns					
	nominative			**accusative**	
singular	ich	*I*		mich	*me*
	du	*you* (inf.)		dich	*you* (inf.)
	Sie	*you* (form.)		Sie	*you* (form.)
	er/sie/es	*he/she/it*		ihn/sie/es	*him/her/it*
plural	wir	*we*		uns	*us*
	ihr	*you* (inf.)		euch	*you* (inf.)
	Sie	*you* (form.)		Sie	*you* (form.)
	sie	*they*		sie	*them*

Wer hat **die Torte** gebacken?   Ich habe **sie** gebacken.
*Who baked **the cake**?*   *I baked **it**.*

- Direct objects are always in the accusative case. An accusative pronoun replaces a noun that functions as a direct object.

  Er hat **mich** überrascht.   Hast du **ihn** geküsst?
  *He surprised **me**.*   *Did you kiss **him**?*

- Certain prepositions are always followed by the accusative. A pronoun that follows an accusative preposition must be in the accusative case.

  Wir haben eine Überraschung **für dich**.   Ihr fahrt **ohne mich** zur Hochzeit.
  *We have a surprise **for you**.*   *You're going to the wedding **without me**.*

More activities

vhlcentral

WB pp. 65–66

LM p. 42

Online activities

- In simple sentences, accusative pronouns go directly after the conjugated verb. If the sentence has a modal verb, the accusative pronoun goes after the conjugated modal verb.

  Ich sehe **euch** jeden Tag.   Ich muss **es** heute machen.
  *I see **you** every day.*   *I have to do **it** today.*

- In the **Perfekt**, place the accusative pronoun directly after the conjugated helping verb.

  Sie haben **uns** zur Party eingeladen.   Wir haben **sie** mit einer Torte überrascht.
  *They invited **us** to the party.*   *We surprised **them** with a cake.*

- In sentences with inverted word order, such as yes-or-no questions, place the accusative pronoun after the subject.

  Siehst du **sie** oft?   Morgen rufe ich **dich** an.
  *Do you see **her** often?*   *I'll call **you** tomorrow.*

Jetzt sind Sie dran!   Wählen Sie die richtigen Pronomen.

1. Das Buch? Du sollst (es)/ ihn) lesen.
2. Da sind die Ballons. Siehst du (sie)/ uns) nicht?
3. Ihr müsst ohne (uns)/ euch) ins Kino gehen.
4. Ich finde Paul süß und habe (uns / ihn)) geküsst.
5. Jana und dich? Wir finden (euch)/ sie) nett.
6. Sophia, warte! Ich habe eine Karte für (dich)/ ihn).
7. Die große Liebe? Gibt es (uns / sie)?
8. Nina, liebst du (mich)/ dich)?

Anwendung und Kommunikation

1 **Bei meinen Eltern** Ersetzen Sie (*Substitute*) die unterstrichenen Wörter mit Akkusativpronomen.

> **BEISPIEL** Ich sehe <u>Peter</u>.
> *Ich sehe ihn.*

1. Ich rufe <u>meinen Freund</u> an.
   Ich rufe ihn an.
2. Mein Freund besucht <u>mich und meine Familie</u>.
   Mein Freund besucht uns.
3. Mein Bruder kocht <u>das Essen</u> für uns.
   Mein Bruder kocht es für uns.
4. Mein Vater isst <u>die Suppe</u> gern.
   Mein Vater isst sie gern.
5. Meine Schwester kauft <u>die Erdbeeren</u> auf dem Markt.
   Meine Schwester kauft sie auf dem Markt.
6. Mein Freund sagt: „Ich besuche <u>dich und deine Eltern</u> gern.“
   Mein Freund sagt: „Ich besuche euch gern.“

2 **Sätze bilden** Bilden Sie logische Sätze mit den angegebenen Wörtern. Ersetzen Sie die Wörter in Klammern (*parentheses*) mit Akkusativpronomen.
Answers may vary. Sample answers are provided.

> ▶ **BEISPIEL** (die Erdbeeren) essen wollen
> *Ich will sie essen.*

1. (das Buch) lesen müssen
   Ich muss es lesen.

2. (Lisa) einladen wollen
   Ich will sie einladen.
3. (der Film) sehen möchten
   Ich möchte ihn sehen.
4. (das Auto) kaufen sollen
   Ich soll es kaufen.
5. (Hausaufgaben) machen müssen
   Ich muss sie machen.

3 **Die Überraschungsparty** Ihr Partner / Ihre Partnerin fragt Sie über die Party am Samstag bei Max. Beantworten Sie die Fragen und benutzen Sie Akkusativpronomen. Answers may vary. Sample answers are provided.

> **BEISPIEL** **S1:** *Ruft ihr Emil und Maria an?*
> **S2:** *Ja, wir rufen sie an.*

1. Ist es eine Party für Max?
   Ja, es ist eine Party für ihn.
2. Lädst du Erik ein?
   Ja, ich lade ihn ein.
3. Kommt Erik ohne seine Freundin?
   Ja, er kommt ohne sie.
4. Hast du das Geschenk schon gekauft?
   Ja, ich habe es schon gekauft.
5. Bringst du deine Cousins mit?
   Nein, ich bringe sie nicht mit.
6. Soll ich den Kuchen mitbringen?
   Ja, du sollst ihn mitbringen.
7. Können wir dort laute Musik hören?
   Ja, ihr könnt sie dort hören.
8. Überraschen wir Max?
   Ja, wir überraschen ihn.

4 **Der Computer** Erstellen Sie ein Gespräch mit den angegebenen Wörtern. Benutzen Sie Akkusativpronomen. Answers will vary.

> **BEISPIEL** der Computer
> **S1:** *Meine Eltern haben ihn für mich gekauft.*
> **S2:** *Ohne ihn kann ich nicht lernen.*
> **S3:** *Ich finde ihn schlecht.*

das Eis	das Geschenk
der Gastgeber	die Karten
der Geburtstag	die Kekse

3 **Suggestion** Students are sometimes confused when answering **wir** questions with **ihr**. You may wish to do item 7 together as a class.

3 **Video Virtual Chat** You can also assign activity 3 on the Supersite. Students record individual responses that appear in your gradebook.

5A.3   Dative pronouns   Grammar Tutorial

Startblock Use dative pronouns in place of dative nouns to indicate *to whom* or *for whom* an action is done.

ACHTUNG

Be careful when deciding whether the pronoun you need is a direct or an indirect object.

Ich sehe ihn.
[direct object]

Ich gebe ihm das Buch.
[indirect object]

QUERVERWEIS

In **2B** and **4A.2**, you learned to use **gern** and **mögen** to express liking. Use **gefallen** to say that you like the way something looks or sounds.

Die Musik gefällt mir.
Der Film hat mir gefallen.

ACHTUNG

Certain prepositions are always followed by the dative case. If a dative preposition is followed by a pronoun, use a dative pronoun: **mit mir, von ihnen, bei uns**

- Indirect objects are always in the dative case. When the indirect object is a pronoun rather than a noun, use a dative pronoun.

Suggestion Give students two or three simple sentences that feature pronouns, and have them identify the subjects, the direct objects, the indirect objects, and any objects of prepositions. Use humorous or dramatic sentences to keep students engaged.

personal pronouns			
	nominative	accusative	dative
singular	ich du Sie er/sie/es	mich dich Sie ihn/sie/es	mir dir Ihnen ihm/ihr/ihm
plural	wir ihr Sie sie	uns euch Sie sie	uns euch Ihnen ihnen

Musst du **ihr** eine E-Mail schreiben?
*Do you have to write **her** an e-mail?*

Wir wollen **euch** die Stadt zeigen.
*We want to show **you** the city.*

- The verbs **helfen, danken,** and **gehören** always take an object in the dative case. Here are some other verbs that always take a dative object.

antworten	*to answer*	glauben	*to believe*
folgen	*to follow*	gratulieren	*to congratulate*
gefallen (gefällt)	*to please*	passen	*to fit*

Das gefällt **mir** sehr gut.
I like that a lot.

Ich glaube **dir** nicht.
*I don't believe **you**.*

Gehört das **euch**?
*Does this belong to **you**?*

Antworte **mir**!
*Answer **me**!*

- When one object is a noun and the other is a pronoun, place the pronoun first.

Gib **mir** einen Kuss!
*Give **me** a kiss!*

Zeig **es** dem Lehrer!
*Show **it** to the teacher!*

- When a sentence has both a direct and an indirect object and both are pronouns, place the dative pronoun after the accusative pronoun.

Ich habe **dem Gastgeber das Geschenk** gegeben.
*I gave **the present** to the host.*

Ich habe **es ihm** gegeben.
*I gave **it** to **him**.*

More activities

vhlcentral

WB
pp. 67–68

LM
p. 43

Online activities

Suggestion Point out to students that in item 4, **Backen** is used as a noun. Explain that in this context, **beim Backen** means *with the baking*.

Jetzt sind Sie dran!   Wählen Sie den richtigen Fall (*case*) für die unterstrichenen Wörter: Nominativ (N), Akkusativ (A), oder Dativ (D).

  D   1. Er hat <u>ihr</u> eine Blume gegeben.

  N   2. <u>Wir</u> bringen Wein und Käse zur Party mit.

  A   3. Hast du <u>sie</u> zu Weihnachten besucht?

  D   4. Kannst du <u>mir</u> beim Backen helfen?

  D   5. Ich danke <u>euch</u> für die Fotos von der Hochzeit.

  N   6. Vielleicht glaubt <u>seine Mutter</u> ihm nicht.

  A   7. Gabi besucht <u>dich</u> am Wochenende, nicht?

  D   8. Das Geschenk ist von <u>ihr</u>.

Anwendung und Kommunikation

1 **Meine Tante** Ersetzen Sie die Dativobjekte mit Dativpronomen.

BEISPIEL Meine Tante hat mit meiner Mutter telefoniert.
Meine Tante hat mit ihr telefoniert.

1. Ich habe viel von meiner Tante Marie gelernt. <small>Ich habe viel von ihr gelernt.</small>
2. Ich habe oft bei Tante Marie und Onkel Hans geschlafen. <small>Ich habe oft bei ihnen geschlafen.</small>
3. Sie haben immer mit mir und meinem Bruder gespielt. <small>Sie haben immer mit uns gespielt.</small>
4. Mein Onkel hat meinem Bruder oft geholfen. <small>Mein Onkel hat ihm oft geholfen.</small>
5. „Tante Marie, kann ich bei dir und Onkel Hans wohnen?" <small>„Tante Marie, kann ich bei euch wohnen?"</small>

2 **Was ist richtig?** Wählen Sie in jedem Satz das richtige Pronomen.

1. Wir haben (ihr / sie) das Geschenk gegeben.
2. Gehören (euch / ihn) die Karten?
3. Hast du (ihn / ihm) zum Geburtstag gratuliert?
4. Haben die Gäste mit (sie / ihnen) angestoßen?
5. Wer hat außer (dir / dich) Kuchen gegessen?
6. Und das Baby? Habt ihr (ihm / es) auch gesehen?
7. Wann feiert ihr die Hochzeit? Feiert ihr (sie / ihr) im Sommer?
8. Lädst du (mich / mir) auch ein?

3 **Alles Gute zum Geburtstag!** Erzählen Sie Ihrem Partner / Ihrer Partnerin, was Sie diesen Personen zum Geburtstag schenken. <small>Answers will vary.</small>

BEISPIEL

Ihre Mutter
S1: *Was schenkst du deiner Mutter zum Geburtstag?*
S2: *Ich schenke ihr einen kleinen Hund! Und deiner Mutter?*
S1: *Meine Mutter mag Hunde nicht. Ich schenke ihr einen Computer.*

1. Ihr Bruder
2. Ihre Großeltern
3. Ihre Schwester

4. Ihre Katze
5. Ihr Vater
6. Ihr Professor / Ihre Professorin

4 **Danke schön!** Erfinden Sie mit Ihren Kommilitonen eine Geschichte (*story*) über die Personen auf dem Bild. Lesen Sie dann der Klasse die Geschichte vor. <small>Answers will vary.</small>

BEISPIEL

S1: *Die junge Frau ruft ihre Schwester an.*
S2: *Sie dankt ihr für das Geburtstagsgeschenk.*
S3: *Nein! Sie gratuliert ihr zu ihrem Abschluss...*

anrufen	einladen	gratulieren (zu)
antworten (auf)	gefallen	helfen
danken (für)	gehören	kaufen
einkaufen	glauben	schreiben

3 **Partner Chat** You can also assign activity 3 on the Supersite. Students work in pairs to record the activity online. The pair's recorded conversation will appear in your gradebook.

4 **Suggestion** Circulate among groups and provide vocabulary as needed. Allow students to focus on content and comprehensibility rather than on accuracy.

4 **Expansion** Have students write their stories down, this time paying closer attention to grammatical correctness. Have them read their stories out loud to the class.

Wiederholung

1 Auf der Party
Wer hat dieses Essen gemacht und diese Geschenke gekauft? Answers will vary.

BEISPIEL

S1: *Wer hat den Apfelsaft gekauft?*
S2: *Anja hat ihn gekauft.*

backen	kaufen
bringen	machen
gehören	schenken

1 Partner Chat You can also assign activity 1 on the Supersite.

2 Suggestion Before beginning this activity, have students review the gender of each food item listed, to make sure they apply the appropriate pronouns in the accusative.

Anja Emma Mehmet Nina
Ali Niklas Jan
Tobias Yusuf Daniel

2 Was isst du gern?
Was isst Ihr Partner / Ihre Partnerin gern? Benutzen Sie Wörter aus der Liste in den Fragen und Akkusativpronomen in den Antworten. Answers will vary.

BEISPIEL

S1: *Isst du gern Garnelen?*
S2: *Nein, ich esse sie nicht gern.*

2 Expansion Have students jot down which foods their partner likes and report back to the class.

Auberginen	Pilze
Eis	Schinken
Gebäck	Schweinefleisch
Kekse	Süßigkeiten
Knoblauch	Torten
Meeresfrüchte	Trauben
Pfirsiche	Würstchen

3 Arbeitsblatt
Wer hat in Ihrem Kurs diese Aktivitäten gemacht? Schreiben Sie die Namen der Mitstudenten auf. Fragen Sie dann weiter nach mehr Informationen. Answers will vary.

3 Suggestion You may wish to set a time limit for this activity, or encourage students to go as quickly as possible, to help them stay on task.

BEISPIEL

S1: *Hast du zu viel gegessen? Wann?*
S2: *Ich habe an Thanksgiving zu viel gegessen.*

4 Geschenke
Was haben Sie und Ihr Partner / Ihre Partnerin Freunden und Familie zum Geburtstag oder zu Weihnachten geschenkt? Answers will vary.

BEISPIEL

S1: *Was hast du deiner Mutter zum Geburtstag geschenkt?*
S2: *Ich habe ihr einen schönen Terminkalender geschenkt.*

5 Diskutieren und kombinieren
Sie und Ihr Partner / Ihre Partnerin bekommen unterschiedliche Blätter mit Bildern von einer Party. Beschreiben Sie mit Ihrem Partner / Ihrer Partnerin Laras Aktivitäten. Answers will vary.

BEISPIEL

S1: *Um halb acht hat Lara mit einem Freund gesprochen. Was hat sie um acht Uhr gemacht?*
S2: *Um acht Uhr hat sie gesungen.*

6 Und Sie?
Was haben Sie auf der letzten Party gemacht? Was haben die anderen in der Gruppe gemacht? Answers will vary.

BEISPIEL

S1: *Auf der Party am Freitagabend habe ich getanzt. Und du? Hast du auf der letzten Party getanzt?*
S2: *Nein, ich habe nicht getanzt. Aber ich habe auf der Party am Samstagabend Musik gehört. Das mache ich gern.*

Geschenke kaufen
essen
(keinen) Spaß haben
Musik hören
kochen
lachen
mit Freunden reden
tanzen

4 Suggestion Emphasize correct use of case. Students may need a moment to formulate their questions in writing before they speak with their partners.

Video

Penny

Expansion Have students identify the English words in the ad. Ask students about helpful apps or shopping online: **Benutzen Sie Apps beim Einkaufen? Was ist Ihr Lieblingsapp?** Ask students to compare discount grocery stores such as **Penny** with full-service **Supermärkte** such as **Tengelmann, Rewe, Edeka** and **Wochenmärkte**. Ask: **Wo hat man mehr Auswahl? Wo ist alles immer frisch?**

1

Vorbereitung Besprechen Sie mit Ihrem Partner / Ihrer Partnerin die folgenden Fragen. Answers will vary.

1. Wo kaufen Sie Lebensmittel, Kleidung und Schuhe?

2. Wie benutzen Sie Ihr Handy beim Einkaufen?

3. Finden Sie es einfach oder schwierig, Geld zu sparen? Warum?

Einkaufen bei Penny

Penny ist ein deutscher Lebensmittel-Discounter mit über 2.200 Filialen°. Discounter bieten immer sehr günstige Preise und tolle Schnäppchen° an, und mit Couponing wird alles noch billiger°.

Filialen *chain stores* **Schnäppchen** *bargains* **billiger** *cheaper*

Nützliche Ausdrücke

der Anfänger, -	*rookie*
die Auswahl	*choice, variety, selection*
das Geld, -er	*money*
das Handy, -s	*cell phone*
sparen	*to save*

2

Verständnis Beantworten Sie die Fragen mit den Informationen aus dem Video.

1. Der Werbeclip spielt in _____.

    a. einem Feinkostgeschäft   ⓑ einem Lebensmittelgeschäft   c. einer Mensa

2. Warum ist der junge Mann irritiert? Er hat _____.

    a. kein Handy   b. kein Geld   ⓒ nicht viel Zeit

3. Warum ist der junge Mann überrascht? Die Frau _____.

    a. will nicht bezahlen   ⓑ bezahlt mit ihrem Handy   c. ist seine Lehrerin

4. Was benutzt die Frau?

    a. eine Penny Kreditkarte   b. Euros   ⓒ die Penny App

3

Diskussion Besprechen Sie zu zweit die Fragen. Answers will vary.

1. Wie können Sie mit Apps beim Einkaufen Geld sparen? Welche Apps sind das?

2. Bei Discountern findet man billige Produkte und günstige Preise. Andere Supermärkte oder Geschäfte müssen daher oft ihre eigenen Preise senken (*lower*), wenn sie keine Kunden verlieren möchten. Finden Sie das gut oder fair? Warum (nicht)?

4

Präsentation Schreiben Sie Ihrer Großmutter eine Email. Erklären Sie ihr, wie Mobile-Couponing funktioniert. Answers will vary.

More activities

vhlcentral

Online activities

Kleidung Vocabulary Tools

Wortschatz

Kleidung	clothing
die Bluse, -n	blouse
die Brille, -n	glasses
der Handschuh, -e	glove
die Jeans, -	jeans
der Mantel, ⸚	coat
der Pullover, -	sweater
die Socke, -n	sock
der Stiefel, -	boot
das Sweatshirt, -s	sweatshirt
das Trägerhemd, -en	tank top
das T-Shirt, -s	T-shirt
die Unterwäsche	underwear

Suggestion Tell students that **Jeans** may be used in the singular (**Ich trage eine Jeans**) or plural (**Meine Jeans sind alt**).

Einkaufen	shopping
die Baumwolle	cotton
die Farbe, -n	color
die Kleidergröße, -n	size
das Leder	leather
der Kunde, -n / die Kundin, -nen	customer
die Seide	silk
der Verkäufer, - / die Verkäuferin, -nen	salesperson
die Wolle	wool
im Angebot	on sale
einfarbig	solid colored
eng	tight
gestreift	striped
kurzärmlig	short-sleeved
langärmlig	long-sleeved
weit	loose; big
anziehen (zieht... an)	to put on

Suggestion Tell students that **Kleider** can also mean clothing, in general. Ex: **Hast du neue Kleider gekauft?**

Suggestion Give students sample sentences using the verb anziehen. Ex.: **Ich ziehe eine Jacke an.**

ACHTUNG

You can add the prefix **hell** (*light; bright*) or **dunkel** (*dark*) to any color word, to form a compound adjective: **dunkelbraun**, **hellblau**.

der Hut, ⸚e

der Badeanzug, ⸚e
bathing suit

Er ist teuer.
It is expensive.

die Krawatte, -n

das Kleid, -er

der Gürtel, -

das Hemd, -en
shirt

die kurze Hose
(*pl.* die kurzen Hosen)
shorts

Er trägt einen Anzug
(*pl.* ⸚e). (tragen)
He is wearing a suit.

die Handtasche, -n

die Turnschuhe
(*sing.* der Turnschuh)
sneakers

gelb · grün · lila · rosa · grau

orange · schwarz

blau · braun · weiß

rot

Suggestion Use items in the classroom to practice color, or bring a bag of assorted colorful objects and ask students to name the colors they see. Ask: **Welche Farbe hat der Tisch? Welche Farbe hat die Tafel? Welche Farbe hat Jakes Sweatshirt?**

Anwendung

1 **Was passt nicht?** Welches Wort passt nicht zu den anderen?

1. (die Unterwäsche), der Mantel, die Jacke
2. teuer, günstig, (langärmlig)
3. das Leder, die Seide, (die Farbe)
4. die Schuhe, (die Halsketten), die Stiefel
5. (die Verkäuferin), die Mütze, der Schal
6. das Kleid, der Rock, (die Krawatte)

2 **Was fehlt?** Hören Sie sich die Sätze an und ergänzen Sie die fehlenden Wörter.

1. Der Mann trägt einen braunen ___Anzug___.
2. Der ___grüne___ Rock passt nicht.
3. Ich mag die lila ___Bluse___.
4. Die blaue ___Krawatte___ ist schön.
5. Das rosa Kleid ist ___eng___.
6. Der ___Gürtel___ ist schwarz.

3 **Farben bezeichnen** Nennen Sie die Farben von den Dingen, die Sie auf den Fotos sehen.

1. ___gelb___   2. ___weiß___   3. ___rot___

4. ___rosa___   5. ___braun___   6. ___schwarz/dunkelgrau___

**Illustration labels:**

die Sonnenbrille, -n
sunglasses

die Mütze, -n
cap

die Halskette, -n
necklace

der Schal, -s
scarf

Es ist günstig.
It is inexpensive.

die Jacke, -n
jacket

der Rock, ¨e
skirt

die Hose, -n
pants

der Schuh, -e

4 **Passende Kleidungsstücke** Welche Kleidungsstücke trägt man in diesen Situationen? Answers will vary. Sample answers are provided.

1. Hasan trägt am Strand seine ___Sonnenbrille___.
2. Zum Wandern in den Alpen soll man ___gute Schuhe___ tragen.
3. Im Winter trägt Alexandra ihren ___Mantel___ und ihren Pullover.
4. Zum Schwimmen trägt Lena ihren ___Badeanzug___.
5. Für ihren Abschlussball kauft Emma ein schönes ___Kleid___.

5 **Manfreds Urlaub** Hören Sie sich an, was Manfred sagt und markieren Sie die Kleidungsstücke, die er kaufen will.

___ 1. einen Pullover   _X_ 3. eine Jeans   _X_ 5. eine Skihose
_X_ 2. Skistiefel   ___ 4. eine Lederjacke   ___ 6. eine Skijacke

Kommunikation

6 Was tragen die Leute?
Beschreiben Sie mit Ihrem Partner / Ihrer Partnerin die Kleidungsstücke von den Personen auf den Fotos. Answers will vary. Sample answers are provided.

die Tennisspielerin

▶ **BEISPIEL**

Die Tennisspielerin trägt ein weißes Trägerhemd und einen weißen Tennisrock.

6 Suggestion Give students sample adjective phrases that model correct endings for all genders in the accusative. Ex.: *masculine:* **einen roten Rock;** *feminine:* **eine gelbe Bluse;** *neuter:* **ein weißes Hemd;** *plural:* **grüne Socken.**

1. Thomas Thomas trägt einen grauen Mantel, Jeans und einen schwarzen Pullover.

2. der Geschäftsmann Der Geschäftsmann trägt ein blaues Hemd und eine schwarze Hose.

3. die Studentin Die Studentin trägt einen roten Pullover, eine dunkle Hose und einen braunen Rucksack.

4. die Kinder Die Kinder tragen weiße T-Shirts, grüne kurze Hosen, weiße Socken und Turnschuhe.

5. Frau Walter Frau Walter trägt einen hellbraunen Mantel, einen hellbraunen Schal und eine schwarze Handtasche.

6. Herr Huber Herr Huber trägt einen hellen Anzug und einen dunklen Hut.

7 Diskutieren und kombinieren
Finden Sie die sieben kleinen Unterschiede auf den Bildern, die Sie von Ihrem Professor / Ihrer Professorin bekommen. Answers will vary.

BEISPIEL

S1: *Trägt die Person auf deinem Bild (picture) eine Jeans?*
S2: *Nein, sie trägt einen Rock.*

8 Wir gehen auf eine Party!
Annika lädt Ihren Deutschkurs zu einer Party ein. Besprechen Sie mit Ihren Mitstudenten, was für eine Party es wird und was Sie für die Fete anziehen wollen. Answers will vary.

BEISPIEL

S1: *Annikas Fete ist morgen Abend. Was soll ich anziehen? Vielleicht meine enge, schwarze Jeans und ein schwarzes T-Shirt.*
S2: *Hmm, ganz in schwarz? Ich bringe auch einen Badeanzug mit. Sie hat ein Schwimmbad im Garten.*
S3: *Soll ich dann auch einen Hut und eine Sonnenbrille mitnehmen?*

8 Suggestion Have each group report back to the class about who will be wearing what to the party.

9 Im Kaufhaus
Schreiben Sie in kleinen Gruppen einen Dialog im Kaufhaus. Sprechen Sie mit dem Verkäufer / der Verkäuferin über die Kleider, die Sie brauchen, aus welchem Material sie sein sollen, für welchen Anlass Sie einkaufen und so weiter. Spielen Sie das Gespräch im Kurs vor (*present*). Answers will vary.

BEISPIEL

S1: *Guten Tag. Kann ich Ihnen helfen?*
S2: *Ja, ich brauche für eine Hochzeitsfeier ein passendes Kleid.*
S3: *Und ich brauche einen Anzug. Schwarz oder dunkelgrau.*

ein baumwollenes Nachthemd
ein dunkelblaues Abendkleid
gute Wanderschuhe
einen rot gestreiften Badeanzug
eine flexible Skibrille
traditionelle Lederhosen
warme Stiefel
weiße Tenniskleidung

7 Expansion Draw a **Strichmännchen** wearing assorted items of clothing, but do not show students the picture. Ask them to draw a stick figure and clothe him or her according to your oral description. Then, reveal your drawing so students can compare it to their own.

Aussprache und Rechtschreibung Audio

The letter combination *ch* (Part 1)

The letter combination **ch** has two distinct pronunciations, which depend on its placement within a word. To pronounce **ch** after the vowels **a**, **o**, **u**, and **au**, start by pressing the tip of your tongue against your lower front teeth and raising the back of the tongue to the roof of the mouth. Then blow out air through the small space between the back of the tongue and the roof of the mouth.

| Nachname | Tochter | Buch | brauchen | acht |

Expansion Have students come up with a class motto including as many **ch**-sounds following a back vowel as possible.

In loanwords, **ch** may appear at the beginning of a word. In these words, the **ch** is sometimes pronounced like the *k* in the English word *king*. It may also be pronounced like the *sh* in the English word *ship*.

| Chaos | Chor | Christ | Chance | Chef |

1 **Aussprechen** Wiederholen Sie die Wörter, die Sie hören.

1. lachen
2. nach
3. auch
4. gesprochen
5. geflochten
6. brauchen
7. fluchen
8. Tuch
9. flache

2 **Nachsprechen** Wiederholen Sie die Sätze, die Sie hören.

1. Wir haben schon wieder Krach mit den Nachbarn.
2. Christians Tochter macht die Nachspeise.
3. Die Kinder waren nass bis auf die Knochen.
4. Hast du Bauchweh?
5. Der Schüler sucht ein Buch über Fremdsprachen.
6. Jochen kocht eine Suppe mit Lauch.

Vorgetan und nachgedacht hat manchem großes Leid gebracht.[2]

3 **Sprichwörter** Wiederholen Sie die Sprichwörter, die Sie hören.

Wo Rauch ist, da ist auch Feuer.[1]

[1] Where there's smoke, there's fire.
[2] Look before you leap. (*lit.* Doing before thinking has brought great suffering to many.)

More activities

vhlcentral   LM p. 45   Online activities

Sehr attraktiv, George! Video

Meline findet Georges Stil nicht sehr attraktiv. Kann sie ihm helfen, attraktive Kleidung zu finden?

Vorbereitung Ask students to describe what George and Meline are wearing in each scene.

communication cultures NATIONAL STANDARDS

GEORGE Hallo, Meline.
MELINE Hallo, George.
GEORGE Wer ist das gewesen?
MELINE Esteban Aurelio Gómez de la Garza. Kommt aus Madrid. Langweilig.
GEORGE Hast du seit Silvester mit Lorenzo gesprochen?
MELINE Lorenzo ist unhöflich gewesen. Ich habe ihn gelöscht.

GEORGE Ich gehe zur Kaiser-Wilhelm-Gedächtnis-Kirche. Möchtest du gern mitkommen?
MELINE Ja.

GEORGE Franz Schwechten hat das Originalbauwerk entworfen.
MELINE Im neuromanischen Baustil.
GEORGE Du weißt viel über Architektur.
MELINE Ich kann lesen. Das steht hier alles. Dort ist eine Tafel!

MELINE George, lass es bleiben. Komm. Ich weiß, wie ich dir helfen kann.
GEORGE Mir mit was helfen?
MELINE George, du bist nicht in den USA. Männer in Europa tragen keine Jeans und Turnschuhe. Schau.

GEORGE Woher hast du gewusst, dass das passiert?
MELINE Du kennst deine Architektur. Und ich kenne die Menschen. Gehen wir.

MELINE Wie sieht's aus da drin, George? George?
GEORGE Okay?
MELINE Komm, lass mich mal sehen!

1 **Was fehlt?** Ergänzen Sie die Sätze mit den richtigen Informationen.

1. Esteban Aurelio Gómez de la Garza kommt aus (Madrid / Barcelona).
2. George möchte zur (Berliner Mauer / Kaiser-Wilhelm-Gedächtnis-Kirche) gehen.
3. (Franz Beckenbauer / Franz Schwechten) hat das Originalbauwerk entworfen.
4. George weiß viel über (Kleidung / Architektur).
5. Meline kann George mit seiner (Kleidung / Hausaufgabe) helfen.

6. Männer in Europa tragen keine (Jeans und Turnschuhe / Seidenkrawatten).
7. Meline findet die Kleidung im Geschäft zu (teuer / hässlich).
8. George empfiehlt Meline einen Freund aus einem anderen (Land / Beruf).
9. Mit dem Hut und der (Sonnenbrille / Jacke) sieht George sehr europäisch aus.
10. Meline hat eine schöne (Halskette / Handtasche) gesehen.

PERSONEN

George   Meline

MELINE Dieser Pullover ist zu eng. Die Hosen sind zu lang. Du musst ein gestreiftes Hemd unter dem Pullover anziehen, kein einfarbiges. Was meinst du?
GEORGE Mir gefallen die Stiefel?
MELINE Das ist alles falsch. Zu teuer, zu teuer. Diese sind ein Schnäppchen. Wo ist der Verkäufer?
GEORGE Warum bin ich in diesen Laden gekommen? Ich sehe lächerlich aus.

MELINE Blau? Nein. Schwarz? Nein. Grün? Nein. Okay. Zieh dieses Hemd... und diese Hose an... mit... dieser Seidenkrawatte. Komm schon! Wir haben nicht den ganzen Tag Zeit.

GEORGE Wie wäre es du denn mal mit einer Person aus einem anderen Beruf?
MELINE Wie Architektur?
GEORGE Ähmm... nein. Literatur oder Philosophie. Informatik oder Geschichte? Wie Hans.

MELINE Sehr attraktiv, George. Setz diese Sonnenbrille auf. Hut. So sieht ein europäischer Mann aus.
GEORGE Hast du gehört, was ich gesagt habe?
MELINE Zieh schnell deine Jeans wieder an. Ich habe eine Handtasche gesehen. Die muss ich unbedingt kaufen. Hans. Also wirklich.

Nützliche Ausdrücke

- **die Kirche**
  church
- **Franz Schwechten hat das Originalbauwerk entworfen.**
  Franz Schwechten designed the original structure.
- **Im neuromanischen Baustil.**
  In the neo-Romanesque style.
- **die Tafel**
  plaque
- **George, lass es bleiben.**
  George, don't even try.
- **Mir mit was helfen?**
  Help me with what?
- **Woher hast du gewusst, dass das passiert?**
  How did you know that was going to happen?
- **Wie sieht's aus da drin, George?**
  How's it going in there, George?
- **lächerlich**
  ridiculous
- **Wir haben nicht den ganzen Tag Zeit.**
  We don't have all day.
- **unbedingt**
  at all costs

5B.1
- **Wer ist das gewesen?**
  Who was that?

5B.2
- **Du weißt viel über Architektur.**
  You know a lot about architecture.
- **Und ich kenne die Menschen.**
  And I know people.

5B.3
- **George, du bist nicht in den USA.**
  George, you're not in the U.S.
- **Warum bin ich in diesen Laden gekommen?**
  Why did I come into this store?

---

 2 **Zum Besprechen** Bilden Sie Gruppen zu dritt und diskutieren Sie: Was denken Sie über Mode? Ist sie Ihnen wichtig? Was ist Ihre Lieblingskleidung? Answers will vary.

3 **Vertiefung** Suchen Sie einen bekannten Designer oder eine bekannte Designerin aus Deutschland, Österreich, der Schweiz oder Liechtenstein und finden Sie Informationen zu ihm/ihr im Internet. Warum gefällt Ihnen dieser Designer / diese Designerin? Stellen Sie seine / Ihre Mode im Kurs vor.

3 **Suggestion** Encourage students to bring photos of their chosen designer and his/her fashions to share with the class.

More activities

vhlcentral   VM p. 10   Online activities

Suggestion Ask students if they have a favorite designer. Also ask them which countries they associate with fashion. Are they familiar with any German clothing brands, department stores or designers?

IM FOKUS

Deutsche Modewelt°

 Reading

TIPP

The symbol **m²** stands for **Quadratmeter** (*square meters*).

FRANKREICH UND ITALIEN SIND klassische Modeländer. Aber in Deutschland entwirft° und produziert man auch viel Mode und Kleidung. Ähnlich wie° in Frankreich und Italien gibt es berühmte Modedesigner:

Karl Lagerfeld, Wolfgang Joop und Jil Sander sind internationale Stars. Deutsche Marken° wie Hugo Boss, Bogner und Escada sind weltweit° bekannt.

Mode spielt in Deutschland eine große Rolle für die Wirtschaft. Deutschland gehört heute zu den führenden° Mode-Exporteuren. Jedes Jahr importieren deutsche Firmen aber auch Kleidung im Wert von 44,9 Milliarden Euro nach Deutschland: Deutschland ist einer der größten internationalen Kleiderimporteure. Im Bereich° der Sportmode sind deutsche Firmen wie Adidas und Puma überall bekannt. Diese beiden Firmen haben ihren Hauptsitz° in Herzogenaurach, einer kleinen Stadt in Bayern. In Berlin

findet man das größte Warenhaus° auf dem europäischen Kontinent: das Kaufhaus des Westens (KaDeWe), mit rund 60.000 m² Verkaufsfläche°. Die wichtigsten Modestädte in Deutschland sind Berlin und Düsseldorf. Auch München wird für Mode immer wichtiger.

Deutschland ist ein Magnet für Modeexperten aus der ganzen Welt. In Düsseldorf findet zweimal pro Jahr die CPD (Collections Premieren Düsseldorf) statt°. Das ist die größte Modemesse° weltweit. In München kommen Fachbesucher° aus über 120 Ländern zweimal pro Jahr zur ISPO (Internationale Fachmesse für Sportartikel und Sportmode), wo rund 2.900 Aussteller° neue Sportkleidung und Accessoires präsentieren. Die PREMIUM Internationale Fachmesse für Mode findet in Berlin auch zweimal pro Jahr statt. Hier findet man viele junge Modeschöpfer°.

Kleidergrößen

Frauenkleider		Männerhosen	
Deutschland	USA	Deutschland	USA (Bundweite/Länge in Zoll°)
30	2	44	30/32
32	4	46	32/32
34	6	48	33/32
36	8	50	34/32
38	10	52	36/34
40	12	54	38/34
42	14	56	40/34
44	16		

Modewelt *world of fashion* **entwirft** *designs* **Ähnlich wie** *Similar to* **Marken** *brands* **weltweit** *worldwide* **führenden** *leading* **Bereich** *area* **Hauptsitz** *headquarters* **Warenhaus** *department store* **Verkaufsfläche** *sales floor* **findet... statt** *takes place* **Modemesse** *fashion trade fair* **Fachbesucher** *trade visitors* **Aussteller** *exhibitors* **Modeschöpfer** *fashion designers* **Zoll** *inches*

---

1 **Im Fokus** Richtig oder falsch? Korrigieren Sie die falschen Aussagen.

1. Deutschland und Dänemark sind die klassischen Modeländer.
Falsch. Frankreich und Italien sind die klassischen Modeländer.
2. Jetzt sind viele deutsche Modemarken weltweit bekannt. **Richtig.**
3. Deutschland ist einer der größten internationalen Kleiderexporteure.
Falsch. Deutschland ist einer der größten internationalen Modeimporteure.

Diskussion Welche Mode finden Sie toll? Welche Mode gefällt Ihnen nicht?

2 **Die deutschsprachige Welt** Richtig oder falsch? Korrigieren Sie die falschen Aussagen.

1. Eine Tracht ist traditionelle und historische Kleidung. **Richtig.**
2. Historisch waren Dirndl und Lederhosen Kleidung für feierliche Anlässe.
Falsch. Dirndl und Lederhosen waren Arbeitskleidung.
3. Lederhosen kommen aus Berlin. **Falsch.** Lederhosen kommen aus Bayern und Österreich.

Diskussion Wo finden Sie traditionelle oder moderne Trachten in Ihrem Land?

Suggestion Remind students that when dealing with long sentences, identifying the subject and verb can help them to figure out the gist.

DEUTSCH IM ALLTAG

Modevokabeln

der letzte Schrei	the latest thing
der Stil	style
angesagt	trendy
ausgefallen	offbeat
elegant	elegant
gut gekleidet	well-dressed
modisch	fashionable
schlecht gekleidet	badly dressed

DIE DEUTSCHSPRACHIGE WELT

Die Tracht

Das Wort „Tracht" bezeichnet° oft traditionelle oder historische Kleidung. In der Alpenregion, genauer gesagt° in Bayern und in Österreich, bezieht sich° das Wort heute auf Lederhosen für Männer und Dirndl für Frauen. Männer tragen neben° Lederhosen Hosenträger°, Haferlschuhe° und Bundhosenstrümpfe°. Frauen in Dirndl tragen eine weiße Bluse mit Puffärmeln° und ein Kropfband°. Ursprünglich° waren Lederhosen und Dirndl Arbeitskleidung, aber heute sieht man sie bei Umzügen° wie dem Oktoberfest.

bezeichnet denotes **genauer gesagt** more precisely **bezieht sich** refers to **neben** in addition to **Hosenträger** suspenders **Haferlschuhe** brogue shoes **Bundhosenstrümpfe** long socks **Puffärmeln** puffed sleeves **Kropfband** choker **Ursprünglich** originally **Umzügen** parades

PORTRÄT

Guido Maria Kretschmer

Wer sich für Filmstars und andere Prominente° interessiert, sieht einige von ihnen sicher in den Designs von Guido Maria Kretschmer. Kretschmers Modeimperium hat klein angefangen°: auf einem Hippiemarkt auf der spanischen Mittelmeerinsel Ibiza, wo er selbstgenähte Kleidungsstücke verkauft hat. Und er hat Glück gehabt, als der deutsche Rockmusiker Udo Lindenberg für seine Tournee eine Anzahl von Jacken bei ihm bestellt hat°. Bald haben er und seine Mitarbeiter Uniformen für Unternehmen wie die Fluggesellschaft Hapag Lloyd und die Deutsche Telekom genäht°. Auch für die Aufführungen° von Opern hat Kretschmer Kostüme entworfen°, und er ist sogar mit diversen Gastrollen° in der Filmwelt zu sehen. In der Stadt München kann man sich seit 2009 in Kretschmers eigener Boutique etwas Glamouröses kaufen.

Prominente well-known people **hat... angefangen** began **bestellt hat** ordered **haben... genäht** sewed **Aufführungen** performances **entworfen** designed **Gastrollen** guest roles

🔗 IM INTERNET

Suchen Sie Namen bekannter Designer in Deutschland, Österreich und der Schweiz.

Find out more at **vhlcentral.com**.

---

3 **Porträt** Richtig oder falsch? Korrigieren Sie die falschen Aussagen.

1. Guido Maria Kretschmer hat seine Karriere als Modeschöpfer begonnen. Richtig.
2. Kretschmer hat Unterstützung von einem Rocker bekommen. **Richtig.**
3. Kretschmer ist ein talentierter Opernsänger. **Falsch.** Er hat Kostüme für Opern entworfen.

Diskussion Beschreiben Sie ein erfolgreiches (*successful*) Start-up-Unternehmen (*business*).

4 **Modische Kleidung** Besprechen Sie die Fragen mit Ihrem Partner/Ihrer Partnerin. Schreiben Sie dann einen kurzen Text und lesen Sie ihn im Kurs vor.

- Was tragen Sie normalerweise, wenn Sie mit Freunden ausgehen?
- Zu welchen Anlässen tragen Sie etwas Besonderes *something special*?

BEISPIEL Modische Kleidung ist mir (nicht) wichtig *important*. Ich trage...

5B.1

QUERVERWEIS

See **1B.1** to review the function of direct objects.

The *Perfekt* (Part 2) Grammar Tutorial

Startblock Most verbs form the **Perfekt** with **haben**. However, certain types of verbs form the **Perfekt** with **sein**.

Wer **ist** das **gewesen**?

Sie **ist** vor sechs Monaten von Köln nach Berlin **gezogen**.

The *Perfekt* with *sein*

- Only a few verbs form the **Perfekt** with **sein**. They are all verbs that indicate a change of condition or location. These verbs never take a direct object.

Die Pflanzen **sind** schnell **gewachsen**.
*The plants **grew** quickly.*

Peter **ist** krank **gewesen**.
*Peter **got** sick.*

Wir **sind** zusammen nach Innsbruck **gefahren**.
*We **drove** to Innsbruck together.*

Ich **bin** vom Fahrrad **gefallen**.
*I **fell** off my bike.*

ACHTUNG

Use the adverb **gestern** to say that something happened *yesterday*.

Gestern sind wir zum Park gelaufen.
Paul ist gestern Abend auf eine Party gegangen.

- To form the **Perfekt** tense of a verb with **sein**, use a conjugated form of **sein** plus the past participle of the verb that expresses the action.

Amira **ist** schon nach Hause **gegangen**.
*Amira already **went** home.*

Mein Opa **ist** gestern nach München **gefahren**.
*My grandpa **went** to Munich yesterday.*

Sie **sind** gestern Abend **gekommen**.
*They **came** last night.*

Letzten Sommer **sind** wir nach Italien **gereist**.
*Last summer we **traveled** to Italy.*

Suggestion Remind students that this rule is helpful as a general guideline, but that ultimately, they will need to memorize the correct participles and auxiliaries on a verb-by-verb basis.

- Both **sein** and **bleiben** are conjugated with **sein** in the **Perfekt**. Note that the past participle of **sein** is **gewesen**.

Ich **bin** in der Bibliothek **geblieben**.
*I **stayed** in the library.*

Vor zwei Jahren **bin** ich in Istanbul **gewesen**.
*Two years ago I **was** in Istanbul.*

Suggestion Point out to students that **bleiben** and **sein** are an exception to the "change of condition or location" rule.

- Here is a list of common verbs that take **sein** in the **Perfekt**. Note that most are strong verbs.

verbs that form the *Perfekt* with *sein*			
infinitive	past participle	infinitive	past participle
bleiben	geblieben	reisen	gereist
fahren	gefahren	sein	gewesen
fallen	gefallen	steigen (*to climb*)	gestiegen
gehen	gegangen	sterben (*to die*)	gestorben
kommen	gekommen	wachsen (*to grow*)	gewachsen
laufen	gelaufen	wandern	gewandert
passieren (*to happen*)	passiert	werden	geworden

Was **ist passiert**?
*What **happened**?*

Ich **bin** gerade zwanzig **geworden**.
*I just **turned** twenty.*

Word order in the *Perfekt*

- The conjugated verb is always in second position in a statement and in first position in a yes-or-no question. In the **Perfekt**, the conjugated form of **haben** or **sein** is always in second position for statements and first in yes-or-no questions.

Hast du seit Silvester mit Lorenzo **gesprochen**?

Lorenzo **ist** unhöflich **gewesen**.

More activities

vhlcentral

WB
pp. 71–72

LM
p. 46

Online activities

Die roten Schuhe **haben** nicht viel **gekostet**.
*The red shoes **didn't cost** very much.*

Seid ihr im Sommer viel **gereist**?
*Did you **travel** a lot over the summer?*

- In statements and questions, always place the past participle at the end of the sentence or clause.

Ich **habe** gestern ein neues Kleid **gekauft**.
*I **bought** a new dress yesterday.*

Wo **hast** du die tollen Stiefel **gekauft**?
*Where **did** you **buy** those awesome boots?*

Jetzt sind Sie dran! **Wählen Sie das passende Hilfsverb.**

1. Wir (sind / haben) den ganzen Abend bei unseren Eltern gewesen.
2. Ich (bin / habe) nicht lange auf der Party geblieben.
3. (Ist / Hat) Philip eine teure Sonnenbrille gekauft?
4. Leider (ist / hat) Jasmins Katze letzte Woche gestorben.
5. Wann (seid / habt) ihr nach Italien gereist?
6. Ich (bin / habe) einen schicken Rock aus Seide getragen.

7. (Bist / Hast) du die Kleider gewaschen?
8. Michael (ist / hat) zum Kaufhof gefahren.
9. Meine Eltern (sind / haben) mir Handschuhe geschenkt.
10. Leider (ist / hat) mein Bleistift ins Wasser gefallen.
11. Ihr (seid / habt) nicht viel gelaufen.
12. (Bist / Hast) du ohne Brille ins Theater gegangen?

Anwendung

1 Perfektformen Ergänzen Sie die Sätze mit den richtigen Formen von sein und den Partizipien.

1. Ich ____bin____ am Samstag zu Michaela ____gegangen____. (gehen)
2. Meine Mutter ____ist____ fünf Kilometer ____gelaufen____. (laufen)
3. Die Wintermonate ____sind____ sehr warm ____gewesen____. (sein)
4. Wann ____ist____ Sigmund Freud ____gestorben____? (sterben)
5. Jan und Klara, ihr ____seid____ zu spät ____gekommen____. (kommen)
6. Zu Silvester ____sind____ wir zu Hause ____geblieben____. (bleiben)
7. ____Bist____ du letzten Sommer durch Europa ____gereist____? (reisen)
8. Professor Schmidt, wann ____sind____ Sie nach Hause ____gefahren____? (fahren)

2 Letzten Juli Beschreiben Sie, was diese Personen letzten Juli gemacht haben. Answers may vary. Sample answers are provided.

> | nach Nürnberg fahren | am Strand laufen |
> | von einem Stuhl fallen | nach Europa reisen |
> | nach Hause kommen | schwimmen gehen |

BEISPIEL Mein Bruder Max
ist am Strand gelaufen.

1. Anja
ist nach Hause gekommen

2. Mein Neffe Emil
ist von einem Stuhl gefallen

3. Professor Aydin
ist nach Europa gereist

4. Frau Weber
ist nach Nürnberg gefahren

5. Meine Cousins
sind schwimmen gegangen

3 In letzter Zeit Bilden Sie Sätze im Perfekt. Benutzen Sie sein als Hilfsverb. Answers may vary. Sample answers are provided.

BEISPIEL meine Oma / kommen / zu meiner Abschlussfeier
Meine Oma ist zu meiner Abschlussfeier gekommen.

1. fahren / du / nach Hause
Bist du nach Hause gefahren?
2. meine Eltern und ich / reisen / im Januar / nach Österreich
Meine Eltern und ich sind im Januar nach Österreich gereist.
3. mein Freund / bleiben / bei seinen Eltern / in Berlin
Mein Freund ist bei seinen Eltern in Berlin geblieben.
4. ich / werden / nach der Party / sehr müde
Ich bin nach der Party sehr müde geworden.
5. dein Baby / wachsen / so schnell
Dein Baby ist so schnell gewachsen!
6. gehen / ihr / auf die Hochzeit / von Nils und Julia
Seid ihr auf die Hochzeit von Nils und Julia gegangen?

Kommunikation

4 **Bilden Sie Sätze** Was hat Ihrer Partner / Ihre Partnerin zu Silvester gemacht? Stellen Sie ihm/ihr sechs logische Fragen darüber. Benutzen Sie das Perfekt und verwenden Sie Wörter aus jeder Spalte. Answers will vary.

BEISPIEL

S1: Bist du mit deinen Freunden auf eine Party gegangen?
S2: Ja, wir sind zusammen auf eine Party gegangen!

A	B	C
ich	bleiben	mit dem Auto
du	fahren	nicht
das Wetter	gehen	neue Kleider
der/die Gastgeber(in)	kommen	bei deinen Eltern
ihr	passieren	mit deinen Freunden
deine Freunde	sein	warm
was?	tragen	zu spät

5 **Historische Personen** Beschreiben Sie mit Ihrer Gruppe, was jede von diesen historischen Personen in ihrem Leben gemacht hat. Answers will vary. Sample answers are provided.

BEISPIEL George Washington
    Er ist Präsident von Amerika gewesen.

fallen	laufen	sein
gehen	reisen	spielen
helfen	schreiben	werden

1. Julia Child / Kochbücher
   Sie hat Kochbücher geschrieben.
2. Babe Ruth / Baseball
   Er hat Baseball gespielt.
3. Mesut Özil / Fußballer
   Er ist Fußballer geworden.

4. Humpty Dumpty / die Mauer
   Er ist von der Mauer gefallen.
5. Mutter Teresa / arme Leute
   Sie hat armen Leuten geholfen.
6. Marco Polo / nach China
   Er ist nach China gereist.

6 **Semesterferien** Fragen Sie Ihren Partner / Ihre Partnerin, was er/sie in den Semesterferien (*semester break*) gemacht hat. Answers will vary.

BEISPIEL

S1: Bist du in den Semesterferien gereist?
S2: Nein, ich bin hier geblieben. Ich habe in einer Pizzeria gearbeitet. Und du?
S1: Meine Familie und ich sind nach Deutschland gefahren.

arbeiten	spazieren gehen
bleiben	kommen
fahren	reisen
einkaufen gehen	sein
schwimmen gehen	wandern

7 **Als Kind** Machen Sie ein Interview über Ihre Kindheit (*childhood*) in der Grundschule (*elementary school*). Wenn Sie fertig sind, tauschen Sie die Rollen. Spielen Sie ihre Interviews im Kurs vor.

BEISPIEL gern zur Schule gehen

S1: Bist du gern zur Schule gegangen?
S2: Ja, ich bin gern zur Schule gegangen. Aber meine Hausaufgaben habe ich nicht immer gern gemacht!

1. ein guter Schüler / eine gute Schülerin sein

2. nach der Schule mit Freunden spielen

3. oft zu spät zur Schule kommen

4. Fahrrad fahren

5. im Sommer mit den Eltern reisen

6. gern ins Schwimmbad gehen

7. am Wochenende zu Hause bleiben

8. einen Hund oder eine Katze haben

5 **Expansion** For homework, have students research biographical information about a famous person of their choice and write ten simple sentences about that person in the **Perfekt**. In class, students must present their sentences and have classmates guess who the person is.

6 **Partner Chat** You can also assign activity 6 on the Supersite. Students work in pairs to record the activity online. The pair's recorded conversation will appear in your gradebook.

7 **Suggestion** If you hear many mistakes in the formation of participles or use of the correct auxiliary, interrupt this activity to form some sample questions together with the class.

5B.2

Wissen and kennen Grammar Tutorial

Startblock In German, the verbs **wissen** and **kennen** are used to express different types of knowledge.

Du **weißt** viel über Architektur.

Ich **kenne** die Menschen.

QUERVERWEIS

The verb **wissen** is often used with dependent clauses. You will learn about dependent clauses in **10A.3**.

ACHTUNG

The verb **wissen** is used in many common idiomatic expressions:

Weißt du was?
You know what?

Weißt du das bestimmt?
Are you sure about that?

Woher soll ich das wissen?
How should I know?

QUERVERWEIS

To review the formation of mixed verbs, see **5A.1**.

More activities

vhlcentral

WB
pp. 73–74

LM
p. 47

Online activities

- Use **wissen** to express the idea of *knowing a fact* or piece of information. **Wissen** is irregular in its present-tense singular forms.

wissen (*to know information*)			
ich weiß	*I know*	wir wissen	*we know*
du weißt	*you know*	ihr wisst	*you know*
er/sie/es weiß	*he/she/it knows*	Sie/sie wissen	*you/they know*

Michael **weiß** die Antwort nicht.
*Michael doesn't **know** the answer.*

Weißt du Saras Telefonnummer?
*Do you **know** Sara's phone number?*

- Use **kennen** to express the idea of *being familiar with* someone or something. **Kennen** always takes a direct object, usually a person or place. It is regular in the present tense.

kennen (*to know, to be familiar with*)			
ich kenne	*I know*	wir kennen	*we know*
du kennst	*you know*	ihr kennt	*you know*
er/sie/es kennt	*he/she/it knows*	Sie/sie kennen	*you/they know*

Ich **kenne** viele Leute.
*I **know** a lot of people.*

Du **kennst** Jana schon seit zwei Jahren.
*You've **known** Jana for two years.*

- In the **Perfekt**, both **kennen** and **wissen** are mixed verbs; their past participles end in **-t**, but their stems are irregular.

Jan **hat** den Professor sehr gut **gekannt**.
*Jan **knew** the professor very well.*

Mein Opa **hat** viel über Kunst **gewusst**.
*My grandpa **knew** a lot about art.*

Das **habe** ich nicht **gewusst**.
*I **didn't know** that.*

Hast du deine Urgroßeltern **gekannt**?
*Did you **know** your great grandparents?*

Jetzt sind Sie dran! Wählen Sie das richtige Verb.

1. (Wisst / Kennt) ihr was?
2. Wir (wissen / kennen) die Musik von Mozart.
3. (Wisst / Kennt) ihr die neue Studentin?
4. (Weiß / Kennt) er das bestimmt?

5. Woher sollen wir das (wissen / kennen)?
6. Du (weißt / kennst) die Antwort nicht.
7. Ich habe ihn nicht gut (gewusst / gekannt).
8. Ich habe das nicht (gewusst / gekannt).

Anwendung und Kommunikation

1 **Wissen und kennen** Ergänzen Sie die richtigen Formen von **kennen** und **wissen**.

Präsens

1. sie (*sing.*) ___kennt___ (kennen)
2. ihr ___wisst___ (wissen)
3. wir ___kennen___ (kennen)
4. du ___weißt___ (wissen)
5. er ___weiß___ (wissen)
6. ich ___kenne___ (kennen)

Perfekt

7. Sie ___haben gewusst___ (wissen)
8. du ___hast gekannt___ (kennen)
9. ihr ___habt gekannt___ (kennen)
10. er ___hat gewusst___ (wissen)
11. ich ___habe gekannt___ (kennen)
12. wir ___haben gewusst___ (wissen)

2 **Wissen oder kennen?** Wählen Sie das passende Verb und ergänzen Sie die Sätze mit den richtigen Formen von **wissen** oder **kennen**.

1. ___Weißt___ du die Telefonnummer von Marie?
2. Wir ___kennen___ ihren Freund, aber wir ___wissen___ nicht viel über ihn.
3. ___Wisst___ ihr das bestimmt?
4. Meine Freundin ___kennt___ Berlin sehr gut.
5. ___Habt___ ihr euch schon letztes Semester ___gekannt___? (Perfekt)
6. Einstein ___hat___ sehr viel über Physik ___gewusst___! (Perfekt)

3 **Die Stadt und der Campus** Fragen Sie Ihren Partner / Ihre Partnerin nach Ihrer Stadt und Ihrem Campus. Wen oder was kennen Sie dort? Was wissen Sie darüber? Answers will vary.

BEISPIEL

S1: *Kennst du ein schönes Café?*
S2: *Ja, ich kenne ein sehr schönes Café!*
S1: *Weißt du auch die Adresse?*
S2: *Natürlich weiß ich die: Schillerstraße 5.*

> unsere Stadt
> die Telefonnummer von Professor... / Professorin...
> ein gutes und nicht so teures Restaurant
> die E-mail-Adressen von deinen Kommilitonen
> einen guten Friseur

3 **Suggestion** Formulate the first few questions and answers together as a class.

3 **Partner Chat** You can also assign activity 3 on the Supersite. Students work in pairs to record the activity online. The pair's recorded conversation will appear in your gradebook.

4 **Ihre Kommilitonen** Finden Sie ein paar Informationen über die Personen in Ihrer Gruppe.

BEISPIEL

S1: *Wo wohnst du?*
S2: *Ich wohne in Brooklyn.*
S1: *Kennst du Herrn Schmidt?*
S2: *Nein, ich kenne ihn nicht.*

Name: Caroline

Ich weiß:
1. ihren Namen. (Caroline)
2. ihre Adresse. (24 Kennedy Avenue)
3. ihre Telefonnummer.

Ich kenne:
4. ihre Freundin Katia.
5. ihren Freund Jeffrey. (Sie spielen Tennis zusammen.)
6. ihr Lieblingsrestaurant. (Blue Moon)

NATIONAL comparisons STANDARDS

5B.3

Two-way prepositions Grammar Tutorial

Startblock Certain prepositions are always followed by the accusative case, while others are always followed by the dative case. A small number of prepositions can be followed by either the dative or the accusative, depending on the situation.

Was machst du **in diesem Teil** der Stadt?

Warum bin ich **in diesen Laden** gekommen?

- Prepositions that can be followed by either the dative or the accusative are called *two-way prepositions*.

two-way prepositions			
an	*at, on*	über	*above, over*
auf	*on, on top of*	unter	*under*
hinter	*behind*	vor	*in front of*
in	*in, into*	zwischen	*between*
neben	*next to*		

Ich trage ein T-Shirt **unter dem Pullover**.
*I'm wearing a T-shirt **under my sweater**.*

Stell deine Schuhe nicht **auf den Tisch!**
*Don't put your shoes **on the table!***

- Whether you choose a dative or an accusative object to follow a two-way preposition depends on the meaning of the sentence. If the verb indicates *movement toward* a destination, use an object in the accusative.

Ich **fahre** das Auto **in die Garage**.
*I'm driving the car **into the garage**.*

Der Hund **geht in die Küche**.
*The dog **is going into the kitchen**.*

- If the verb does *not* indicate movement toward a destination, use an object in the dative case.

Warum **bist** du heute **auf dem** Kurfürstendamm?

Er **arbeitet im Bereich** internationale Finanzen.

Das Auto **ist in der Garage**.
*The car **is in the garage**.*

Der Hund **isst in der Küche**.
*The dog **eats in the kitchen**.*

- When you use a two-way preposition with a pronoun, make sure to select a pronoun in the appropriate case.

Ich sitze **neben dem alten Mann**.
*I'm sitting **next to the old man**.*

Ich sitze **neben ihm**.
*I'm sitting **next to him**.*

Er hat den Teller **vor seinen Sohn** gestellt.
*He put the plate **in front of his son**.*

Er hat den Teller **vor ihn** gestellt.
*He put the plate **in front of him**.*

- Here are some common contractions of two-way prepositions and definite articles.

an	+	das	⟶	**ans**
auf	+	das	⟶	**aufs**
in	+	das	⟶	**ins**
an	+	dem	⟶	**am**
in	+	dem	⟶	**im**

- The question **wohin?** (*where to?*) asks about movement. When you answer this question with a two-way preposition, always use an object in the accusative case.

Wohin fahren wir morgen?
***Where** are we going tomorrow?*

Wir fahren morgen **in die Stadt**.
*We're going **to the city** tomorrow.*

Wohin gehen die Leute?
***Where** are the people going?*

Sie gehen **ins Konzert**.
*They're going **to the concert**.*

- The question **wo?** (*where?*) asks about location. When you answer this question with a two-way preposition, always use an object in the dative case.

Wo ist mein Schal?
***Where** is my scarf?*

Dein Schal liegt **auf dem Tisch**.
*Your scarf is lying **on the table**.*

- Use the dative after a two-way preposition with a verb that indicates where something is located. Use the accusative with a verb that indicates where something is being placed.

wo?	
hängen	*to hang, to be hanging*
liegen	*to lie*
sitzen	*to sit*
stehen	*to stand*

wohin?	
hängen	*to hang (something)*
legen	*to lay (down)*
setzen	*to set (down)*
stellen	*to put (down)*

Das Bild **hängt an der** Wand.
*The picture **is hanging on the** wall.*

Ich **hänge** das Bild **an die** Wand.
*I'm **hanging** the picture **on the** wall.*

QUERVERWEIS

To review the forms of dative and accusative pronouns, see **5A.2** and **5A.3**.

See **3B.2** to review contractions with accusative prepositions. See **4B.2** to review contractions with dative prepositions.

Suggestion Make sure students understand that the "**wo**" verbs all describe location (place) and the "**wohin**" verbs all describe the process of placing something somewhere (placement).

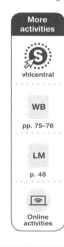

More activities

vhlcentral

WB
pp. 75–76

LM
p. 48

Online activities

Jetzt sind Sie dran! **Wählen Sie den richtigen Artikel.** **Suggestion** Remind students that they need to look at the verb in order to make a decision about case. Students may have difficulty with item 7 because of the motion verb **fahren**. Point out that the car is your *location*, not your *destination*. You are *in the car*, not moving *towards the car*.

1. Wir wohnen über (einer/ eine) Bäckerei.
2. Ich lege den gestreiften Hut auf (den / dem) Tisch.
3. Aha! Unter (den / dem) Tisch liegt meine Mütze.
4. Die Verkäuferin hängt das kurzärmlige Kleid zwischen (die / den) langärmligen Kleider und die Blusen.
5. Matthias trägt selten ein Sweatshirt über (sein / seinem) T-Shirt.
6. Dein Schal hängt neben (die / der) Tür.
7. Ich bin in (meinem/ mein) Auto gefahren.
8. Frau Vögele braucht Unterwäsche und geht in (ein/ einem) Geschäft.
9. Die Katze sitzt gern auf (meine / meiner) Jacke.
10. Seid ihr am Montag wieder in (ein/ einem) Konzert gegangen?

Anwendung

1 Präpositionen Ergänzen Sie die Sätze mit den richtigen bestimmten (*definite*) Artikeln.

> **BEISPIEL** Die neue Bäckerei ist zwischen __der__ Metzgerei und __dem__ Supermarkt.

1. Die warme Jacke hängt an ___der___ Tür.
2. Hast du dein Fahrrad hinter ___das___ Haus gestellt?
3. Der Kellner geht um ___den___ Tisch.
4. Trägst du ein Trägerhemd unter ___dem___ T-Shirt?
5. Ich gehe in ___die___ Bibliothek.
6. Sophia und Hans laufen morgens durch ___den___ Park.
7. Die Katze liegt gern neben ___dem___ Fenster.
8. Der Hund ist hinter ___das___ Auto gelaufen.

2 Wo macht man das? Schreiben Sie zu jedem Foto, wo man diese Aktivitäten machen kann.

> die Berge | ein altes Haus | das Restaurant
> die Bibliothek | der Park | das Stadion

> ▶ **BEISPIEL** lesen
> *in der Bibliothek*

1. Fußball spielen
   im Stadion

2. essen
   im Restaurant

3. Ski fahren
   in den Bergen

4. spazieren gehen
   im Park

5. wohnen
   in einem alten Haus

3 Überraschung beim Abendessen Bilden Sie Sätze. Sample answers are provided.

> **BEISPIEL** das Trinkgeld / liegen / auf / der Tisch
> *Das Trinkgeld liegt auf dem Tisch.*

1. der Pizzaservice / bringen / die Pizza / an / die Haustür
   Der Pizzaservice bringt die Pizza an die Haustür.
2. die Großmutter / stellen / Teller und Gläser / auf / der Tisch
   Die Großmutter stellt Teller und Gläser auf den Tisch.
3. die Kinder / sitzen / zwischen / die Eltern
   Die Kinder sitzen zwischen den Eltern.
4. die kleine Lisa / setzen / ihre neue Barbie / neben / ihr großer Bruder
   Die kleine Lisa setzt ihre neue Barbie neben ihren großen Bruder.
5. die leckere Pizza / sein / schon / auf / der Tisch
   Die leckere Pizza ist schon auf dem Tisch.
6. eine kleine Maus / laufen / über / die Teller
   Eine kleine Maus ist über die Teller gelaufen.
7. der Vater / bringen / schnell / die Katze / in / das Zimmer
   Der Vater hat schnell die Katze ins Zimmer gebracht.
8. was / finden / die Familie / später / unter / der Tisch
   Was hat die Familie später unter dem Tisch gefunden?

Kommunikation

4 **Auf dem Campus** Beantworten Sie die Fragen von Ihrem Partner / Ihrer Partnerin. Answers will vary.

BEISPIEL

S1: *Wohin hast du deinen Rucksack gelegt?*
S2: *Ich habe ihn unter den Tisch gelegt.*

1. Wohin können wir zum Kaffee trinken gehen?
2. Wo lernen die Studenten Fremdsprachen?
3. Wohin gehen die Studenten zum Mittagessen?
4. Wo kann ich ein leckeres Eis kaufen?
5. Wohin sollen die Studenten ihre Fahrräder stellen?
6. Wo wanderst du gern?

5 **Wohin gehst du?** Sie wollen diese Aktivitäten machen. Fragen Sie die Studenten in Ihrer Gruppe, wohin Sie gehen müssen. Answers will vary.

BEISPIEL frühstücken

S1: *Ich will frühstücken. Wohin muss ich gehen?*
S2: *Du musst in die Cafeteria gehen.*
S3: *Ja, in der Cafeteria kannst du Mittag essen.*

1. Deutsch lernen
2. Basketball spielen
3. ein Fußballspiel sehen
4. schwimmen

5. Lebensmittel kaufen
6. Bücher lesen
7. Gebäck kaufen
8. mit Freunden zum Essen ausgehen

6 **Hier auf dem Campus** Sarah ist neu an Ihrer Uni. Erfinden Sie mit Ihrem Partner / Ihrer Partnerin zusammen sechs Ratschläge (*pieces of advice*) für Sarah. Sie können auch andere Verben benutzen. Answers will vary.

BEISPIEL Die Mensa is nicht sehr gut. (essen)
Iss nicht in der Mensa. Geh ins Café!

1. Das Café ist leider teuer. (bestellen)
2. Dein Zimmer ist sehr warm. (öffnen)
3. Der Deutschkurs ist nicht einfach. (lernen)
4. Parken ist ein Problem. (stellen)
5. Der Park ist abends sehr dunkel. (laufen)

7 **Was passiert alles im Restaurant?** Erfinden Sie eine Geschichte (*story*) mit den Studenten / Studentinnen in Ihrer Gruppe über die Personen auf dem Bild. Benutzen Sie Präpositionen. Answers will vary.

BEISPIEL

S1: *Die junge Frau ist mit ihrem Mann ins Restaurant gekommen.*
S2: *Sie sitzt neben ihrem Mann am Tisch.*
S3: *Ein Kellner stellt einen Teller auf den Tisch...*

4 **Suggestion** Make sure partners take turns asking and answering questions.

4 **Video Virtual Chat** You can also assign activity 4 on the Supersite. Students record individual responses that appear in your gradebook.

6 **Suggestion** Briefly review formation of the **du**-imperative for each verb.

7 **Suggestion** Make sure students understand that they need to use a preposition in each sentence. You may wish to set a time limit and have groups compete to create the most correct sentences.

Wiederholung

1 Kleidung zu jedem Anlass

Beschreiben Sie mit einem Partner / einer Partnerin, was Tobias und Anna zu jedem (*each*) Anlass tragen. Answers will vary.

BEISPIEL

S1: Was trägt Tobias zur Geburtstagsfeier im Restaurant?
S2: Zur Geburtstagsfeier im Restaurant trägt er eine grüne Hose und ein oranges T-shirt. Und was trägt Anna?

> im Regen (*rain*)
> im Rockkonzert
> in den Bergen, zum Ski fahren
> ins Schwimmbad
> zur Geburtstagsfeier im Restaurant
> zur Sporthalle

2 Arbeitsblatt

Ihr Professor / Ihre Professorin gibt Ihnen ein Blatt mit einigen Fragen und Fakten. Finden Sie eine Person, die die Antwort weiß.

BEISPIEL

S1: Wie heißt der längste (*longest*) Fluss in Österreich?
S2: Ich weiß es nicht. / Ich weiß es. Das ist die Donau.

3 Diskutieren und kombinieren

Sie und ein Partner / eine Partnerin bekommen zwei verschiedene Blätter. Sehen Sie die Bilder an und antworten Sie auf die Fragen von Ihrem Partner / Ihrer Partnerin.

BEISPIEL

S1: Wohin ist Jasmin gegangen?
S2: Sie ist ins Stadion gegangen.
S1: Was macht sie in dem Stadion?
S2: Sie sieht ein Fußballspiel an.

4 Lenas Großeltern

Erzählen Sie mit einem Partner / einer Partnerin von Lenas Großeltern. Benutzen Sie die angegebenen Daten und erfinden Sie (*invent*) weitere (*additional*) Informationen.

BEISPIEL

S1: Lenas Großeltern sind 1967 auf die Uni gegangen.
S2: Im Deutschseminar hat die Oma den Opa gesehen.
S1: Sie hat gedacht: „Er ist der Mann für mich!"

1967	1973	1975	1976	2020
Die Oma sieht den Opa im Deutschseminar.	Oma und Opa machen den Abschluss.	Oma und Opa heiraten.	Die Frischvermählten reisen nach Indien.	Beide gehen in Rente.

5 Unsere Woche

Schreiben Sie auf, was Sie in der letzten Woche gemacht haben. Fragen Sie Ihren Partner / Ihre Partnerin, was er/sie gemacht hat.

BEISPIEL

S1: Am Montag bin ich in die Bibliothek gegangen. Und du, Monika, was hast du gemacht?
S2: Ich bin auf meinem Zimmer geblieben.

	meine Woche	
	ich	*mein Partner / meine Partnerin*
Montag	Ich bin in die Bibliothek gegangen.	Monika ist auf ihrem Zimmer geblieben.
Dienstag		
Mittwoch		
Donnerstag		
Freitag		
Samstag		
Sonntag		

6 Kennst du diese Person?

Beschreiben Sie eine bekannte Person. Die Gruppe soll erraten, wer es ist.

BEISPIEL

S1: Er hat 2015 einen Oscar gewonnen. Kennt ihr ihn?
S2: Ja, ich kenne ihn. Das ist Eddie Redmayne.

7 **Tracht tragen ist in** In Süddeutschland, Österreich und der Schweiz sieht man an Festtagen oft Frauen im Dirndl und Männer in traditionellen Lederhosen. Mode im Trachtenstil ist vor allem bei jungen Menschen wieder im Trend. Fragen Sie Ihren Partner / Ihre Partnerin, wie er / sie diese Mode findet.

BEISPIEL

S1: Wie findest du das Dirndl (die Lederhose)?
S2: Ich finde das Dirndl (die Hose) ... Und du?
S1: Ich mag (nicht) ...

Expansion: Ask students what they typically wear during the week and what for special events. Ask them to research **Trachten** in Bavaria, Austria, and Switzerland and describe the various styles.

Suggestion Have students review clothing vocabulary before beginning this activity.

8 **Das Klassenzimmer** Beschreiben Sie, wo die Gegenstände (*objects*) und Personen in Ihrem Klassenzimmer sind.

BEISPIEL

S1: Vor der Tafel steht der Professor.
S2: Unter dem Tisch...

 Mein Wörterbuch

Schreiben Sie noch fünf weitere Wörter in Ihr persönliches Wörterbuch zu den Themen **Feste feiern** und **Kleidung**.

Lektion 5B		
German	English	Definition
+ add word		
das Bekleidungsgeschäft, -e	Übersetzung clothing store	Synonyme der Klamottenladen

ä ö ü ß ☐ ALL CAPS

Panorama Interactive Map

Bayern

Bayern in Zahlen

▶ **Fläche:** *70.549 km² (größtes deutsches Bundesland)*

▶ **Bevölkerung:** *12,9 Millionen Menschen (zweite Stelle° hinter Nordrhein-Westfalen)*

▶ **Religion:** *römisch-katholisch 67,2 %, evangelisch-lutherisch 24,1%*

▶ **Städte:** *München (1,5 Mio. Einwohner), Nürnberg (509.975), Augsburg (286.370), Würzburg (124.873) und Regensburg (145.500)*

▶ **Berge:** *die Zugspitze (2.962 m) (höchster Berg Deutschlands), Hochfrottspitze (2.649 m), Großer Arber (1.456 m)*

▶ **Niedrigster Punkt:** *Kahl am Main (107 m)*

▶ **Flüsse:** *die Donau, der Inn*

▶ **Wichtige Industriezweige:** *Automobil, IT, Medien und Verlage°, Finanzindustrie, Tourismus*

▶ **Touristenattraktionen:** *Befreiungshalle (Kelheim), Fuggerei (Augsburg), Marienplatz (München), Schloss Neuschwanstein (Füssen), Steinerne Brücke (Regensburg), Walhalla (Donaustauf)*
Touristen können in Städten wie München, Augsburg und Regensburg viel Kultur genießen. In den Alpen oder dem Bayerischen Wald können sie Berg- und Wintersport treiben. Wirtschaftlich entwickelt sich° Bayern in den letzten Jahrzehnten von einem Agrar- zu einem Technologieland.

QUELLE: Bayerisches Landesportal

Berühmte Bayern

▶ **Adam Ries,** *Mathematiker (1492/93–1559)*

▶ **Levi Strauss,** *Erfinder° der Jeans (1829–1902)*

▶ **Elizabeth „Sisi",** *Kaiserin° von Österreich und Ungarn (1837–1898)*

▶ **Ludwig II.,** *König von Bayern (1845–1886)*

▶ **Lena Christ,** *Autorin (1881–1920)*

▶ **Franz Josef Strauß,** *Politiker (1915–1988)*

▶ **Dirk Nowitzki,** *Basketballspieler (1978–)*

▶ **Magdalena Neuner,** *Biathletin (1987–)*

Stelle *position* **Verlage** *publishing companies* **entwickelt sich** *evolves* **Erfinder** *inventor* **Kaiserin** *empress* **Weltkulturerbe** *World Heritage Site* **herrscht** *exists* **Dialektpfleger** *dialect conservator* **Ortseingängen** *city limit* **Verbotsschilder** *ban signs*

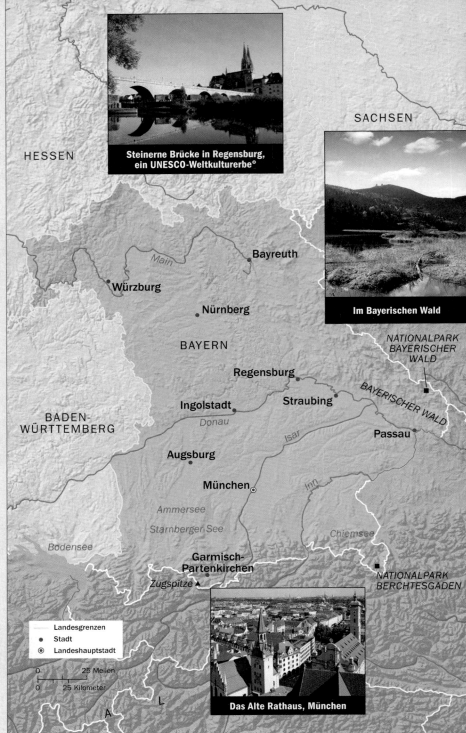

Steinerne Brücke in Regensburg, ein UNESCO-Weltkulturerbe°

Im Bayerischen Wald

Das Alte Rathaus, München

Unglaublich, aber wahr!

„Auf Wiedersehen" heißt im bayerischen Dialekt „Servus". In Norddeutschland kann man „Tschüss" (oder „Tschüß") sagen. In dem bayerischen Dorf Gotzing herrscht° ein Tschüss-Verbot oder eine „Tschüss-freie Zone". Hans Triebel, ein Dialektpfleger°, installiert deshalb an den Ortseingängen° „Tschüss"-Verbotsschilder°.

"Tschüß" freie Zone

Kunst

Bayreuther Festspiele

Die Bayreuther Festspiele heißen auch Richard-Wagner-Festspiele. Sie finden jedes Jahr in der Stadt Bayreuth im Festspielhaus auf dem Grünen Hügel statt. Die Werke von Richard Wagner, einem berühmten deutschen Komponisten°, kann man während dieses weltberühmten Events seit 1876 sehen. Bei den ersten Festspielen inszeniert Richard Wagner seine Oper° „Der Ring des Nibelungen". Jedes Jahr besuchen 58.000 Zuschauer eine von zweiunddreißig Aufführungen° in Bayreuth. Allerdings versuchen° jedes Jahr 500.000 Menschen Karten zu kaufen. Deshalb dauert es bis zu zehn Jahre, bis man eine Karte bekommt.

Städte

Die sieben Hügel° von Bamberg

Bamberg ist eine Stadt in Franken, einer Region in Bayern. Seit 1993 ist sie ein UNESCO-Weltkulturerbe wegen des größten unversehrt erhaltenen° historischen Stadtzentrums in Deutschland. Genauso wie° Rom ist Bamberg auf sieben Hügeln gebaut. Deshalb trägt es auch den Namen „das Fränkische Rom". Die sieben Hügel Bambergs sind der Altenburger Berg, der Domberg, der Michaelsberg, der Abtsberg, der Jakobsberg, der Kaulberg und der Stephansberg. Auf dem Domberg kann man den mächtigen°, viertürmigen Dom° aus dem 13. Jahrhundert° finden.

Suggestion Ask students which other German car brands they are familiar with.

Industrie

Audi

Die Autofirma Audi hat ihren Hauptsitz° in Ingolstadt, Oberbayern. Neben VW, Porsche, BMW und Opel ist Audi einer der wichtigsten Autoproduzenten Deutschlands. Audi baut besonders sportliche Autos. Zwischen 2000 und 2014 haben Audis das Autosport Rennen Le Mans dreizehn Mal° gewonnen. 2018 fängt Audi an, sich auf Formel E, die Rennserie mit elektrischen Rennwagen, zu konzentrieren. Im Jahr 2017 arbeiten 90.000 Mitarbeiter bei Audi.

Architektur

Die Schlösser° von Ludwig II.

Ludwig II. ist der bekannteste König Bayerns. Er ist in erster Linie für seine Schlösser weltberühmt. Neben dem bekanntesten Schloss, Schloss Neuschwanstein, ist er auch für das Königshaus am Schachen und Schloss Linderhof verantwortlich°. Die Schlösser sind heute die bedeutendsten touristischen Attraktionen Bayerns.

Musik Musik

Tim Bendzko

Tim Bendzko ist ein deutscher Sänger und Songwriter. Er wurde überregional bekannt als er 2011 den Bundesvision Song Contest gewann. Im selben Jahr spielte er auch im Vorprogramm bei Elton Johns Deutschlandtournee.

Go to **vhlcentral.com** to find out more about **Tim Bendzko.**

Komponisten *composer* **Oper** *opera* **Aufführungen** *performances* **versuchen** *try* **Hügel** *hills* **unversehrt erhaltenen** *preserved undamaged* **Genauso wie** *Just like* **mächtigen** *mighty* **viertürmigen Dom** *cathedral with four towers* **Jahrhundert** *century* **Hauptsitz** *headquarters* **Mal** *times* **Schlösser** *castles* **verantwortlich** *responsible* **wichtig** *important* **Stahlbau** *steel construction* **Licht** *light*

---

1 **Was haben Sie gelernt?** Entscheiden Sie, ob die Sätze richtig oder falsch sind. Korrigieren Sie die falschen Sätze.

1. „Auf Wiedersehen" heißt auf Bayerisch „Tschüß"
   Falsch. „Auf Wiedersehen" heißt auf Bayerisch „Servus"
2. Bei den ersten Bayreuther Festspielen inszeniert Gustav Mahler seine Oper „Der Ring des Nibelungen." Falsch. Richard Wagner inszeniert den „Ring des Nibelungen."
3. Genauso wie Rom ist Bamberg auf sieben Hügeln gebaut. Richtig.
4. Das bekannteste Schloss von König Ludwig II. ist Schloss Linderhof.
   Falsch. Sein bekanntestes Schloss ist Schloss Neuschwanstein.
5. Der Hauptsitz der Firma Audi ist in Ingolstadt. Richtig.

2 **Denken Sie nach** Welche Touristenattraktionen gibt es in Ihrem Staat (*state*)? Vergleichen Sie sie mit den Touristenattraktionen in Bayern.

Lesen Audio: Reading

Vor dem Lesen

Strategien

Skimming

Skimming involves quickly reading through a document to absorb its general meaning. This allows you to understand the main ideas without having to read word for word. When you skim a text, look at its title and subtitles and read the first sentence of each paragraph.

Untersuchen Sie den Text Lesen Sie den Text schnell. Was ist der Titel des Texts? Wie viele Teile hat der Text? Wie heißen die Teile? Sehen Sie sich jetzt die Fotos an. Was ist das Thema des Texts?

Lehnwörter Sehen Sie sich mit einem Partner / einer Partnerin den Text an und machen Sie eine Liste mit englischen Lehnwörtern (*loanwords*) und Kognaten. Sample answers are provided.
Trend, Internet, Web, traditionell, Millionen, Accessoires, hier, Alternative, Probleme, Internetpräsenz, coole

Suchen Sehen Sie sich mit einem Partner / einer Partnerin den Text an. Stehen die Informationen im Text oder nicht? Markieren Sie **ja** oder **nein**.

	ja	nein
1. wo Deutsche Kleider kaufen	☑	☐
2. das Internet	☑	☐
3. Modenschauen	☐	☑
4. Designer	☐	☑
5. Warenhäuser	☑	☐
6. Boutiquen	☐	☑
7. Modeketten	☑	☐
8. Flohmärkte	☑	☐

Deutschland heute

Hauptseite   **Politik**   **Wirtschaft**

WO KAUFEN DEUTSCHE HEUTE IHRE KLEIDUNG?

In den letzten Jahren gibt es einen neuen Trend: Deutsche kaufen ihre Kleider immer öfter im Internet. Neben dem Web besuchen Deutsche aber auch weiterhin° traditionelle Geschäfte wie Warenhäuser° und Kleidergeschäfte. Nur noch wenige° Deutsche finden ihre Kleidung auf Flohmärkten°.

INTERNET, DAS GROSSE GESCHÄFT

Im Jahr 2017 sind 70 Millionen Deutsche online shoppen gegangen. Mehr als 65 Prozent dieser Internetkäufer haben Bekleidung und Accessoires im Web gekauft. Vor allem Frauen kaufen hier gerne ein; im Jahr 2018 haben mehr als siebzig Prozent aller Frauen Kleidung oder Sportartikel im Internet gekauft. Bei den Männern sind es fast sechzig Prozent.

WARENHÄUSER WERDEN IMMER WENIGER

Warenhäuser wie Karstadt und Galeria Kaufhof sind immer noch eine Alternative für den Kleiderkauf. In den letzten Jahren haben Warenhäuser aber immer größere wirtschaftliche Probleme und viele Warenhäuser schließen°. Seit 2018 gehören Karstadt und Kaufhof zur selben Firma.

DH

Kultur   Sport   Gesundheit

MODEKETTEN° HABEN ERFOLG°

Kleidergeschäfte wie H&M, Zara, Esprit und Orsay kann man heute in allen großen deutschen Städten finden. Diese Ketten sind bei jungen Menschen besonders beliebt. C & A ist der Marktführer° in Deutschland. H&M ist an zweiter Stelle.° Alle Modeketten haben immer mehr Internetpräsenz.

AUF DEM FLOHMARKT

Es gibt immer noch eine kleine Gruppe Deutscher, die am Samstagmorgen früh aufsteht°, um Flohmärkte zu besuchen. Hier kann man unter anderem gebrauchte° Kleidung günstig kaufen. Es gibt sie in jeder Stadt besonders im Sommer. Vor allem coole Klamotten° aus den 60er und 70er Jahren findet man hier für wenig Geld.

weiterhin *still* **Warenhäuser** *department stores* **wenige** *few*
Flohmärkten *flea markets* **schließen** *close* **Modeketten** *Fashion chains* **Erfolg** *success* **Marktführer** *market leader* **an zweiter Stelle** *in second place* **gemeinsam** *in common* **aufsteht** *gets up* **gebrauchte** *used* **Klamotten** *clothes (colloquial)*

Nach dem Lesen

Was fehlt? Ergänzen Sie die Sätze.

1. Deutsche kaufen Kleider vor allem ___im Internet___, in Warenhäusern und in Kleidergeschäften.

2. ___70 Millionen___ Deutsche sind 2017 im Internet einkaufen gegangen.

3. Mehr ___Frauen___ als Männer kaufen Kleider im Internet.

4. Kaufhof und ___Karstadt___ sind eine Firma.

5. Der Marktführer der Modeketten in Deutschland ist ___C&A___.

6. Flohmärkte gibt es besonders im ___Sommer___.

Richtig oder falsch? Sind die Aussagen richtig oder falsch? Korrigieren Sie die falschen Sätze. Sample answers are provided.

	richtig	falsch
1. Deutsche kaufen Mode immer öfter im Internet.	☑	☐
2. Fast 60 Prozent aller Frauen haben Kleidung oder Sportartikel im Internet gekauft.	☐	☑

Fast 60 Prozent aller Männer haben Kleidung oder Sportartikel im Internet gekauft.

	richtig	falsch
3. Karstadt und Galeria Kaufhof sind deutsche Warenhäuser.	☑	☐
4. Junge Menschen kaufen nicht gern bei H&M ein.	☐	☑

Diese Kette ist bei jungen Menschen beliebt.

	richtig	falsch
5. Alle Modeketten verkaufen Kleidung auch im Internet.	☑	☐
6. Auf dem Flohmarkt ist Kleidung teuer.	☐	☑

Auf dem Flohmarkt ist Kleidung günstig.

Was tragen Sie? Besprechen Sie in einer Gruppe: Was tragen Sie gern zu verschiedenen Anlässen (in der Uni, bei einer Party, zu Hause)? Wo kaufen Sie Ihre Kleider?

BEISPIEL

S1: *Zu Hause trage ich gerne Jeans und T-Shirts.*
S2: *Wo kaufst du deine Jeans?*
S1: *Meine Jeans kaufe ich im Internet.*
S3: *Ich trage im Sommer gern Kleider.*

Hören

NATIONAL communication cultures STANDARDS

Strategien

Listening for key words

By listening for key words (**Schlüsselwörter**) or phrases, you can identify the subject and main ideas of a conversation or speech, as well as some of the details.

🔊 To practice this strategy, you will listen to a short radio spot. Jot down the key words that help you identify the subject of the radio spot and its main ideas.

Vorbereitung

Schauen Sie sich das Foto an. Wer ist in dem Foto? Wo sind sie? Was machen sie?

🔊 Zuhören

Hören Sie sich an, wie Marion Scholz ihre neue Mode beschreibt. Lesen Sie dann die Liste. Hören Sie sich die Beschreibung ein zweites Mal an. Welche Kleidungsartikel tragen die Models?

1. ___ Mütze
2. ✓ Anzug
3. ✓ Hemd
4. ✓ Kleid
5. ___ Stiefel
6. ___ Jacke

7. ___ Rock
8. ✓ Gürtel
9. ___ Bluse
10. ✓ Hut
11. ___ Badeanzug
12. ✓ Socken

Verständnis

🔊 **Was fehlt?** Ergänzen Sie die Sätze mit den richtigen Informationen.

braun Handtasche	hellblau kurz	lange orange	Sandalen schwarz	Seide weiten

1. Robert trägt einen ___weiten___ Anzug.
2. Die Farbe des Anzugs ist ___hellblau___.
3. Die Sandalen sind ___schwarz___.
4. Elizabeth trägt ein Kleid aus ___Seide___.
5. Am Arm trägt sie eine ___Handtasche___.
6. Ihre ___Sandalen___ sind braun.
7. Carolas Hose und T-Shirt sind ___kurz___.
8. Ihre Hose und ihr T-Shirt sind ___orange___ und gelb.
9. Thomas trägt ___lange___ Socken zu seiner kurzen Hose.
10. Die Kleidung von Thomas ist ___braun___.

👥 **Ein Star, ein Fest** Wählen Sie einen Star und einen besonderen Anlass. Was trägt der Star zu diesem Anlass? Beschreiben Sie den Star einem Partner / einer Partnerin.

Expansion Show students pictures of celebrities at a **Preisverleihung** such as the Grammy Awards. Have students describe what the celebrities are wearing and then have them vote on the best and worst outfits.

Schreiben

Strategien

Using a dictionary

The dictionary is a useful tool that can provide valuable information about vocabulary. However, in order to use the dictionary correctly, you must understand the elements of each entry.

If you glance at an English-German dictionary, you will notice that its format is similar to that of an English dictionary. Most words are listed with several different definitions, organized by part of speech. The most frequently used meanings are usually listed first.

To find the best word for your needs, refer to the abbreviations and explanatory notes that appear next to each entry. For example, imagine that you are writing about fashion. You want to write *The man is wearing a suit*, but you don't know the German word for *suit*. In the dictionary, you might find an entry like this one:

> **suit** *n.* 1. der Anzug, Anzüge; (*woman's*) das Kostüm, -e 2. der Prozess, -e (*Jur*); 3. die Farbe, -n (*Cards*)

The abbreviation key at the front of the dictionary says that *n.* corresponds to **Substantiv** (*noun*). The second translation is **der Prozess** followed by the abbreviation *Jur*, indicating that it's a law term, and thus that **der Prozess** is a *law suit*. The third word is **die Farbe**, followed by the word *Cards*, indicating that **die Farbe** is a *suit* in a card game. Since **der Anzug** is listed first, you can assume that this is the main translation of the word. The first definition also specifies the difference between a suit for a man, **der Anzug**, and a suit for a woman, **das Kostüm**. Since the other two meanings do not apply to clothing, these details tell you that **der Anzug** is the best choice for your needs.

Thema

Beschreiben Sie

Sehen Sie sich das Bild an. Beschreiben Sie dann in einem Absatz (*paragraph*) den Mann oder die Frau für einen Artikel in einem Modejournal.

Beschreiben Sie das Aussehen (*look*) im Detail. Aus welchem Material sind die Kleider? Wie sind die Kleider geschnitten (*cut*)? Welche Muster (*patterns*) und Farben haben die Kleider? Wo kann man diese Kleider tragen? Sagen Sie auch etwas über den Designer und darüber, wo man die Kleider kaufen kann. Am Ende schreiben Sie Ihre Meinung über die Kleidung. Geben Sie dem Artikel einen Titel.

Bevor Sie den Artikel schreiben, machen Sie sich Notizen. Suchen Sie Vokabeln, die Sie brauchen, in einem Wörterbuch.

- Material
- Schnitt
- Muster
- Farben
- Wo kann man es tragen?
- Wo kann man es kaufen?

Neueste Mode

Lederjacken sind wieder in. Dieser Mann trägt eine schwarze Lederjacke mit einem weißen Trägerhemd. Der Schnitt ist…

Vocabulary Tools

Lektion 5A

Feste
celebrations

der Ballon, -s *balloon*
der Feiertag, -e *holiday*
der Gast, ¨e *guest*
der Gastgeber, - / die Gastgeberin, -nen *host / hostess*
das Geschenk, -e *gift*
die Karte, -n *card*
die Party, -s *party*
die Überraschung, -en *surprise*
das Zimmer, - *room*
anstoßen (stößt... an) *to toast*
bekommen *to receive*
einladen (lädt... ein) *to invite*
feiern *to celebrate*
eine Party geben *to throw a party*
(keinen) Spaß haben *(not) to have fun*
schenken *to give (a gift)*
überraschen *to surprise*
Herzlichen Glückwunsch! *Congratulations!*

besondere Anlässe
special occasions

die Ehe, -n *marriage*
der / die Frischvermählte, -n *newlywed*
die Geburt, -en *birth*
der Geburtstag, -e *birthday*
die Hochzeit, -en *wedding*
der Hochzeitstag, -e *wedding anniversary*
der Jahrestag, -e *anniversary*
(das) Silvester *New Year's Eve*
(das) Weihnachten *Christmas*
in Rente gehen *to retire*
einen Abschluss machen *to graduate*

Essen und Trinken
food and drink

das Eis *ice cream*
der Eiswürfel, - *ice cube*
das Gebäck *pastries; baked goods*
der Keks, -e *cookie*
der Sekt *champagne*
die Süßigkeiten (*pl.*) *candy*
die Torte, -n *cake*

Ausdrücke
expressions

die Freundschaft, -en *friendship*
das Glück *happiness*
der Kuss, ¨e *kiss*
die Liebe *love*

Past participles with **haben** See pp. 194–195.
Accusative pronouns See p. 198
Dative pronouns See p. 200.

Lektion 5B

Kleidung
clothing

der Anzug, ¨e *suit*
der Badeanzug, ¨e *bathing suit*
die Bluse, -n *blouse*
die Brille, -n *glasses*
der Gürtel, - *belt*
die Halskette, -n *necklace*
der Handschuh, -e *glove*
die Handtasche, -n *purse*
das Hemd, -en *shirt*
die Hose, -n *pants*
die kurze Hose (*pl.* die kurzen Hosen) *shorts*
der Hut, ¨e *hat*
die Jacke, -n *jacket*
die Jeans, - *jeans*
das Kleid, -er *dress*
die Krawatte, -n *tie*
der Mantel, ¨ *coat*
die Mütze, -n *cap*
der Pullover, - *sweater*
der Rock, ¨e *skirt*
der Schal, -s *scarf*
der Schuh, -e *shoe*
die Socke, -n *sock*
die Sonnenbrille, -n *sunglasses*
der Stiefel, - *boot*
das Sweatshirt, -s *sweatshirt*
das Trägerhemd, -en *tank top*
das T-Shirt, -s *T-shirt*
der Turnschuh, -e *sneakers*
die Unterwäsche *underwear*

Farben
colors

blau *blue*
braun *brown*
gelb *yellow*
grau *gray*
grün *green*
lila *purple*
orange *orange*
rosa *pink*
rot *red*
schwarz *black*
weiß *white*

Einkaufen
shopping

die Baumwolle *cotton*
die Farbe, -n *color*
die Kleidergröße, -n *size*
der Kunde, -n / die Kundin, -nen *customer*
das Leder *leather*
die Seide *silk*
der Verkäufer, - / die Verkäuferin, -nen *salesperson*
die Wolle *wool*
im Angebot *on sale*
günstig *inexpensive*
einfarbig *solid colored*
eng *tight*
gestreift *striped*
kurzärmlig *short-sleeved*
langärmlig *long-sleeved*
teuer *expensive*
weit *loose; big*
anziehen (zieht... an) *to put on*
tragen (trägt) *to wear*

Past participles with **sein** See p. 213.
Wissen and **kennen** See p. 216.
Two-way prepositions See p. 218.

Trautes Heim

COMMUNICATIVE GOALS
By the end of this chapter you will be able to:

Los geht's! Wo ist George?

LEKTION 6A

Describe your home.
Talk about living arrangements.

To do so, you will use:

Kontext Seite 232–235
• Rooms and furniture
• Places to live

Strukturen Seite 240–250
6A.1 The **Präteritum**
6A.2 Da-, wo-, hin-, and **her-** compounds
6A.3 Coordinating conjunctions

You will also learn about cultural products, practices, and perspectives related to:

Kultur Seite 238–239
• Fribourg
• Chalets
• César Ritz

Zapping Seite 251
• *Möbel bauen statt Kinder erziehen*

LEKTION 6B

Talk about household chores.
Talk about appliances.

To do so, you will use:

Kontext Seite 252–255
• Housework
• Household items
• Words and phrases related to cleaning

Strukturen Seite 260–269
6B.1 Perfekt versus **Präteritum**
6B.2 Separable and inseparable prefix verbs in the **Perfekt**

You will also learn about cultural products, practices, and perspectives related to:

Kultur Seite 258–259
• **Haushaltsgeräte**
• **Fachleute Hauswirtschaft**
• **Martin Suter**

WEITER GEHT'S

Seite 270–276
You will learn about Switzerland, its languages, and Swiss culture and industry. You will also learn about the principality of Liechtenstein.

Panorama Seite 270–271
• **Die Schweiz und Liechtenstein**

And you will demonstrate that you can:
Lesen: Recognize word families
Hören: Use background knowledge when listening
Schreiben: Format a written interview

Suggestion Ask students to guess what **Trautes Heim** means. Teach them the saying **Trautes Heim, Glück allein**. What is the equivalent saying in English? Note the difference between **Haus** and **Heim**.

Suggestion Ask students to name the objects they see in the photo and to guess what food or meal they think George might be preparing.

Zu Hause Vocabulary Tools

Wortschatz

Zimmer	rooms
das Arbeitszimmer, -	home office
der Dachboden, ⸚	attic
das Erdgeschoss, -e	first floor/ground floor
das Esszimmer, -	dining room
der Flur, -e	hall
die Küche, -n	kitchen
der erste/zweite Stock	second/third floor

Möbel	furniture
das Bild, -er	picture
das Möbelstück, -e	piece of furniture
der Nachttisch, -e	night table
der Schrank, ⸚e	cabinet; closet
die Schublade, -n	drawer
die Treppe, -n	stairway

Orte	places
das Haus, ⸚er	house
das Wohnheim, -e	dorm
die Wohnung, -en	apartment

nach rechts/links	to the right/left

Ausdrücke	expressions
mieten	to rent
umziehen (zieht... um)	to move
wohnen	to live

ACHTUNG

Note that **mieten** means to rent *from* someone, while **vermieten** means to rent *to* someone. **Ich miete eine kleine Wohnung in der Stadt. Die Familie vermietet ein Zimmer in ihrem Haus.**

Expansion Have students play a memory game to internalize the new vocabulary. The first student starts with **In meiner Wohnung gibt es...** and names an item of furniture. The next student repeats the previous item(s) and adds one. If a student can't repeat the entire sequence, he or she is eliminated. Remind students to use the accusative with **Es gibt.**

der Vorhang, ⸚e

Suggestion Point out that **das Möbel,-** is a countable noun in German, but that *furniture* is a non-countable noun in English. Explain that German speakers typically use **Möbel** to refer to furniture in general and **Möbelstück** to refer to a piece of furniture.

Suggestion Point out that many Germans in big cities live in apartments, not single-family homes.

der Balkon, -e

die Toilette, -n

das Badezimmer, - *bathroom*

der Spiegel, -

das Poster, -

die Badewanne, -n

das Sofa, -s

der Teppich, -e

der Sessel, -

die Blume, -n

die Vase, -n

der Keller, - *basement*

das Wohnzimmer, - *living room*

die Pflanze, -n *plant*

Suggestion Point out that what Americans call the "first floor" is the **Erdgeschoss** in Germany, and when Germans say **erster Stock**, they mean the floor above. Ask students to tell you, in German, which floor your classroom is on.

Suggestion Make sure that students understand the difference between **der Stock** and **der Boden**. Point out that **der Dachboden** is a compound of **das Dach** (*roof*) and **der Boden**.

Anwendung

1 Expansion Give students a description of a mixed-up apartment and ask them to tell you where things ought to be. Ex.: **Mein Sofa ist in der Garage. Wo sollte es sein? Mein Bett ist in der Küche. Wo sollte es sein? Meine Bücher sind unter dem Bett. Wo sollten sie sein?**

das Bücherregal, -e
bookshelf

die Wand, ̈e
wall

die Lampe, -n

das Bett, -en
bed

die Kommode, -n
dresser

der Boden, ̈
floor

das Schlafzimmer, -
bedroom

die Garage, -n

Suggestion Ask students where they do various activities. Ex.: **Wo schläfst du? Wo isst du? Wo kochst du?**

Expansion Have students create their own **wo**-question using items from the lesson vocabulary. Remind students to use the dative with two-way prepositions since they will be describing location.

1 Paare finden Welche Objekte assoziieren Sie mit welchen Zimmern?

_b_ 1. die Küche   a. das Sofa
_a_ 2. das Wohnzimmer   b. die Lebensmittel
_d_ 3. das Esszimmer   c. die Kommode
_e_ 4. das Badezimmer   d. der Esstisch
_c_ 5. das Schlafzimmer   e. die Toilette

2 Emmas neue Wohnung Hören Sie sich die Beschreibung von Emmas neuer Wohnung an und ergänzen Sie die Sätze.

1. Emma mietet ein Zimmer in ___Hamburg___.
2. Das Zimmer hat ___16/sechzehn___ Quadratmeter.
3. Im Zimmer gibt es ein Bett, eine ___Kommode___, und einen Stuhl.
4. Die Wohnung hat Bad, Toilette und ___Küche___.
5. Das Haus hat ___4/vier___ Stockwerke.
6. Die Miete ist inklusive Wasser und ___Elektrizität___.

3 Bilder beschriften Wie heißen die verschiedenen Bereiche (*parts*)?

3 Expansion Have students compile a list of what they have and would like to have in their rooms and share with the class or a partner. Provide a model to demonstrate use of the accusative and of **kein**.

1. ___der Dachboden___   4. ___die Küche___
2. ___der Balkon___   5. ___das Wohnzimmer___
3. ___das Schlafzimmer___   6. ___das Badezimmer___

4 Was ist richtig? Hören Sie die Definitionen und wählen Sie das Wort, das am besten passt.

1. Flur / (Küche)   4. (Garage) / Dachboden   7. (Haus) / Esszimmer
2. Wand / (Vorhang)   5. Rucksack / (Vase)   8. Bücherregal /
3. (Badezimmer) /   6. (Bild) / Kommode   (Lampe)
   Wohnzimmer

4 Expansion Play a guessing game using vocabulary items not mentioned in the recording. Ex.: **Ich denke an ein Möbelstück. Da schlafe ich. Was ist das?**

Kommunikation

Wo ich wohne Arbeiten Sie mit einem Partner / einer Partnerin. Benutzen Sie die Wörter aus den drei Spalten und beschreiben Sie Ihr Zimmer, Ihre Wohnung oder Ihr Haus. Answers will vary.

BEISPIEL

S1: *Meine Wohnung ist ziemlich groß und hat einen kleinen Balkon.*
S2: *Mein Zimmer ist klein. Aber alle meine Möbel sind neu.*

5 **Partner Chat** You can also assign activity 4 on the Supersite. Students work in pairs to record the activity online. The pair's recorded conversation will appear in your gradebook.

5 **Expansion** After students have put the dialogue in the correct order, have two volunteers read it aloud.

A	B	C
mein Haus mein Zimmer meine Wohnung	ist (nicht) hat (kein)	Badezimmer Balkon Fenster Garage Küche Schlafzimmer Schreibtisch groß/klein alt/neu modern/unmodern

Janas Haus Klara besucht Jana in ihrem neuen Haus. Bringen Sie den Dialog in eine logische Reihenfolge (*order*). Wenn Sie fertig sind, vergleichen Sie Ihr Haus oder Ihre Wohnung mit Janas Haus.

   4   **JANA** Sechs Zimmer. Das hier ist das Wohnzimmer und dann hier links die Küche und das Esszimmer.

   1   **KLARA** Jana, dein neues Haus ist wirklich schön.

   6   **JANA** Ja, die Küche gefällt meinem Mann sehr gut. Er kocht so gern! So, und hier rechts siehst du den Flur zu den drei Schlafzimmern und den zwei Badezimmern. Es gibt nur den einen Stock.

   3   **KLARA** Das stimmt. Wie viele Zimmer hat es?

   7   **KLARA** Ihr braucht ja auch nicht noch mehr Zimmer. Also, ich muss sagen, du hast ein ganz tolles Haus gefunden.

   2   **JANA** Danke schön! Es ist ziemlich groß. Die alte Wohnung in der Stadt war einfach zu klein.

   5   **KLARA** Die Küche ist auch super. Da kann dein Mann leckeres Essen kochen.

8 **Expansion** Review the differences between **stellen**, **legen**, and **hängen**. Place a classroom eraser horizontally on the desk and say: **Ich lege den Schwamm auf den Tisch.** Then stand the eraser on one end and say: **Ich stelle den Schwamm auf den Tisch.** Finally, tape the **Schwamm** to the wall and say: **Ich hänge den Schwamm an die Wand.**

7 **Mein Zimmer** Beschreiben Sie zwei Mitstudenten Ihr Zimmer. Answers will vary.

BEISPIEL

S1: *In meinem Zimmer habe ich ein Bett und einen Schreibtisch.*
S2: *Ich habe auch ein Bett, aber ich habe keinen Schreibtisch.*
S3: *Ich habe in meinem Zimmer einen grünen Teppich...*

8 **Diskutieren und kombinieren** Arbeiten Sie mit einem Partner / einer Partnerin. Ihr Professor / Ihre Professorin gibt Ihnen zwei verschiedene Blätter mit dem Grundriss (*floor plan*) von Ihrer neuen Wohnung. Sagen Sie Ihrem Partner / Ihrer Partnerin, was Sie alles mitgebracht haben. Er/Sie wird Ihnen sagen, in welche Zimmer Sie die Sachen stellen sollen. Answers will vary.

BEISPIEL

S1: *Ich habe Balkonpflanzen mitgebracht.*
S2: *Stell sie auf den Balkon. Er ist rechts von der Küche. Ich habe...*

8 **Suggestion** Remind students to use the accusative with two-way prepositions when they tell each other where to place an item.

Aussprache und Rechtschreibung Audio

The letter combination *ch* (Part 2)

To pronounce the soft **ch** after the vowel sounds **i/ie**, **e**, **ä**, **ö**, **ü**, or **ei**, start by placing the tip of your tongue behind your lower teeth. Then pronounce the *h* sound while breathing out forcefully.

Chemie	rechts	Teppich	Küche	leicht

Use the same soft **ch** sound when pronouncing the **g** in the suffix **-ig** at the end of a word. However, when there is an adjective ending after the **-ig**, the **g** is pronounced like the hard *g* in the word *garden*. In the combination **-iglich**, the **g** is pronounced like the *k* in the word *kind*. The soft **ch** is also used in the suffix **-lich**, whether or not there is an ending after it.

dreckig	schmutzig	billige	königlich	freundlichen

When **ch** appears before an **s**, the letter combination is pronounced like the *x* in the word *fox*. Do not confuse **chs** with the combination **sch**, which is pronounced like the *sh* in the word *shade*.

sechs	wachsen	schlafen	waschen	Dachs

When **ch** appears at the beginning of loanwords, its pronunciation varies.

Charakter	Chip	Chef	Charterflug	Chronik

---

1   **Aussprechen** Wiederholen Sie die Wörter, die Sie hören.

1. Bücher
2. freundlich
3. China
4. zwanzig
5. braunhaarige
6. lediglich
7. höchste
8. Achsel
9. Ochse
10. Chaos
11. checken
12. Charme

2   **Nachsprechen** Wiederholen Sie die Sätze, die Sie hören.

1. Die königliche Köchin schläft wieder in der Küche.
2. Mein neugieriger Nachbar will täglich mit mir sprechen.
3. Den Rechtsanwalt finden wir freundlich und zuverlässig.
4. Der Chef schickt mich nächstes Jahr nach China.
5. Der Dachs hat einen schlechten Charakter.

2 Suggestion Have students take turns reading the sentences aloud. Explain the meaning of any unfamiliar words.

3   **Sprichwörter** Wiederholen Sie die Sprichwörter, die Sie hören.

Liebe deinen Nächsten wie dich selbst.[1]

Jedem Tierchen sein Pläsierchen.[2]

[1] Love thy neighbor as thyself.
[2] To each his/her own. (lit. For every creature its own pleasure.)

More activities

vhlcentral   LM p. 50   Online activities

Besuch von Max Video

Hans' kleiner Bruder Max kommt ihn in Berlin besuchen. Meline ist froh, Max kennen zu lernen. Zu froh, in den Augen von Hans.

communication cultures
NATIONAL STANDARDS

Vorbereitung Have students read the title of the episode and discuss in pairs what they expect to happen in the episode.

GEORGE Max!
MAX Hallo, George!
GEORGE Schön, dich wiederzusehen! Wie viele Nächte schläfst du auf unserem Sofa?
MAX Zwei. Ich bin übers Wochenende in Berlin. Doch bis Sonntagabend muss ich wieder in Straubing sein.

HANS Warum lernst du eigentlich nicht an deinem Schreibtisch in deinem Zimmer?
GEORGE Es ist bequemer im Wohnzimmer, denn die Küche ist gleich nebenan. Und es ist schön hell hier.
HANS Da ist was dran.
MAX Wir gehen in den Biergarten. Komm doch mit.

Suggestion Explain to students that **Servus!** means both *Hello!* and *Goodbye!* in Bavaria and Austria.

MAX Wir bleiben bestimmt lange dort.
GEORGE Nach dieser Lektion komme ich herunter.
HANS Alles klar! Okay! Servus!

MAX Das tut mir leid.
MELINE Es ist schon okay. Kein Problem.
HANS Meline, das ist mein kleiner Bruder Max.
MELINE Hallo.
MAX Wir gehen in den Biergarten. Komm doch mit uns.
MELINE Ich muss nur noch schnell die Lebensmittel in die Küche bringen.

MELINE Max, ich kann das Regalbrett nicht erreichen. Kannst du mir das dort oben hinstellen?
MAX Deine Wohnung gefällt mir.
MELINE Ja. Die Lampen und Vorhänge gehören Sabite. Und die ganzen Gemälde.

MAX Du bist aus Wien?
MELINE Ja. Hast du das an meinem Akzent erkannt?
MAX Ja. Als Hans zu Weihnachten nach Hause kam, sprach er übrigens von dir.
MELINE Wirklich? Was hat er gesagt?

1 **Wer ist das?** Welche Person(en) beschreiben die folgenden Sätze: George, Hans, Max, Meline oder Sabite?

1. Er/Sie ist übers Wochenende in Berlin. Max
2. Er/Sie lernt im Wohnzimmer, denn die Küche ist gleich nebenan. George
3. Sie wollen in den Biergarten gehen. Hans und Max
4. Nach einer Lektion kommt er/sie herunter. George

5. Er/Sie muss Lebensmittel in die Küche bringen. Meline
6. Die Wohnung gefällt ihm/ihr. Max
7. Ihm/Ihr gehören die Vorhänge, die Lampen und die Gemälde. Sabite
8. Weihnachten sprach er/sie von Meline. Hans
9. Er/Sie war satt und konnte nicht schlafen. George
10. Er/Sie überlegt, ob (*whether*) Hans und Max wirklich Brüder sind. Meline

PERSONEN

 George   Hans   Meline   Max

GEORGE Wir hatten Heiligabend ein riesiges Essen.
HANS Es war drei Uhr früh, am Weihnachtsmorgen.
GEORGE Ich war ja noch total satt und konnte nicht einschlafen.
HANS Es war ja noch total dunkel im Haus.

GEORGE Ich ging den Gang hinunter und hörte ein Geräusch.
HANS Max, meine Familie und ich, wir schliefen in unseren Zimmern.
GEORGE Ich ging in die Küche, und am Herd stand ihr Großvater.
HANS Opa Otto bereitete die Weihnachtsgans zu. George überraschte ihn und... „Ja! Wo kommst du denn her?"

GEORGE Sie war köstlich! Wo ist Sabite heute Abend?
MELINE Mit Torsten weg.
GEORGE Sind sie immer noch zusammen?
MELINE Ja, aber es ist schwierig seit den Feiertagen.

MELINE Ich mag Torsten, aber man sagt an Silvester keine Verabredung ab.
HANS So wie Lorenzo?
MELINE Wer?
HANS Na, Lorenzo. Der Italiener.
MELINE Seid ihr wirklich Brüder?

Nützliche Ausdrücke

- **Doch bis Sonntagabend muss ich wieder in Straubing sein.**
  But by Sunday evening I have to be back in Straubing.

- **Da ist was dran.**
  You have a point there.

- **Servus!**
  So long!

- **Ich kann das Regalbrett nicht erreichen.**
  I can't reach the shelf.

- **Kannst du mir das dort oben hinstellen?**
  Can you put this up there for me?

- **das Gemälde**
  painting

- **Hast du das an meinem Akzent erkannt?**
  Could you tell from my accent?

- **riesig**   • **satt**
  huge   *full (of food)*

- **das Geräusch**   • **der Herd**
  noise   *stove*

- **Opa Otto bereitete die Weihnachtsgans zu.**
  Grandpa Otto was preparing the Christmas goose.

6A.1
- **Als Hans zu Weihnachten nach Hause kam, sprach er übrigens von dir.**
  When Hans was home for Christmas, he talked about you, by the way.

6A.2
- **Nach dieser Lektion komme ich herunter.**
  After this lesson, I'll come down.

6A.3
- **Es ist bequemer im Wohnzimmer, denn die Küche ist gleich nebenan.**
  The living room is more convenient, because it's right next to the kitchen.

---

2 **Zum Besprechen** George trifft Opa Otto an Heiligabend in der Küche. Bereiten Sie mit einem Partner / einer Partnerin einen kurzen Dialog zwischen George und Opa Otto vor. Präsentieren Sie Ihren Dialog im Kurs. Answers will vary.

Suggestion After each pair has presented their role play, have the class vote on the most interesting, realistic, and convincing performances.

3 **Vertiefung** Suchen Sie im Internet Informationen über die Weihnachtsgans. Woher kommt diese Tradition? In welchen Ländern isst man Weihnachtsgans? Was isst man als Beilage? Vergleichen Sie dieses traditionelle deutsche Weihnachtsessen mit einem Festessen in Ihrer Kultur. Welche Gemeinsamkeiten (*similarities*) und welche Unterschiede (*differences*) gibt es? Schreiben Sie einen Aufsatz oder berichten Sie (*report*) im Kurs. Answers will vary.

More activities

 vhlcentral   VM p. 11   Online activities

IM FOKUS

Fribourg Reading

TIPP

The abbreviation **St.** stands for **Sankt**, meaning *Saint*.

Die Architektur Fribourgs bietet° Beispiele vieler historischer Epochen. Die Altstadt im Zentrum ist eines der größten geschlossenen Ortsbilder° des mittelalterlichen° Europa. Die St.-Niklaus-Kathedrale, gebaut zwischen 1283 und 1490, ist das Symbol Fribourgs. Es ist ein Beispiel gotischer Architektur. Die Stadt hat über 200 gotische Gebäude. Den Renaissancestil kann man im Ratzéhof sehen, gebaut zwischen 1581 und 1585. Heute ist dieses Gebäude die Heimat° des Museums für Kunst und Geschichte. Neben den vielen alten Teilen der Stadt kann man auch neue Gebäude finden wie zum Beispiel die Universität (1889) oder die Villenviertel° im Gembachquartier. Viele Villen sind Jugendstil-Bauten°. Bekannt sind in Fribourg auch die alten Brücken° und seine zwölf historischen Brunnen°.

FRIBOURG LIEGT GENAU AN DER Grenze° zwischen deutschsprachiger und französischsprachiger Schweiz. Die Saane fließt° durch die Stadt und trennt sie in zwei Teile°. Im westlichen Teil spricht man Französisch und im östlichen Teil Deutsch. Etwa 66% der Bevölkerung spricht Französisch und 33% spricht Deutsch. Studenten können hier in beiden Sprachen studieren und machen einen großen Teil der 39.000 Einwohner aus. Die Stadt ist sehr alt und existiert bereits seit 1157. Damals war Fribourg noch deutschsprachig.

Wohnen in der Schweiz

Wohnungen: 4,5 Millionen (2017)	
durchschnittliche° Größe: 99 m²	
durchschnittlicher Kaufpreis für Wohnungen	
• **Bern:** SFr (Schweizer Franken) 1,09 Millionen	
• **Zürich:** SFr 1,64 Millionen	
• **durchschnittlicher Mietpreis:** SFr 1.329	
• **Mieteranteil°:** 59%	

QUELLE: Schweizerisches Bundesamt für Statistik

Grenze *border* **fließt** *flows* **Teile** *parts* **bietet** *offers* **geschlossenen Ortsbilder** *complete townscapes* **mittelalterlichen** *medieval* **Heimat** *home* **Villenviertel** *mansion district* **Jugendstil-Bauten** *Art Nouveau buildings* **Brücken** *bridges* **Brunnen** *wells* **durchschnittliche** *average* **Mieteranteil** *percentage of renters*

ÜBUNGEN

1 Im Fokus Richtig oder falsch? Korrigieren Sie die falschen Aussagen. Diskutieren Sie dann die letzte Frage mit einem Partner/ einer Partnerin.

1. Fribourg liegt an der Grenze zwischen der deutschsprachigen und französischsprachigen Schweiz. Richtig.
2. In Fribourg wohnen etwa 39.000 Studenten.
   Falsch. In Fribourg wohnen 39.000 Menschen.
3. Die ganze Stadt ist im mittelalterlichen Stil gebaut.
   Falsch. Man sieht in der Stadt gotische, Renaissance und Jugendstil-Architektur.

Diskussion Welchen architektonischen Stil mögen Sie? Finden Sie Beispiele von zwei Stilen im Internet und vergleichen Sie die Stile.

2 Die deutschsprachige Welt Richtig oder falsch? Korrigieren Sie die falschen Aussagen. Diskutieren Sie dann die letzte Frage mit einem Partner/ einer Partnerin.

1. Die Chalets der Schweiz sind traditionell aus Holz gebaut. Richtig.
2. Zermatt ist bekannt für seine moderne Architektur.
   Falsch. In Zermatt baut man nur im Chalet-Stil.
3. Chalets waren schon immer Ferienhäuser wie heute.
   Falsch. Früher lebten Hirten in Chalets.

Diskussion Vergleichen Sie ein Schweizer Chalet mit einer Blockhütte (*log cabin*), einer Jurte (*yurt*) oder einem Wohnmobil (*RV*). Was ist gemütlicher? Was bevorzugen (*prefer*) Sie?

DEUTSCH IM ALLTAG

Studentenzimmer

der	
Gemeinschaftsraum	common room
die Kaution	security deposit
die Miete	rent
die Nebenkosten	additional charges
die Wohngemeinschaft (WG)	apartment share
(un)möbliert	(un)furnished
Zimmer frei	vacancy

DIE DEUTSCHSPRACHIGE WELT

Chalets

„Chalet" ist ein französisches Wort und bedeutet Sennhütte°. Man kann diese Häuser im Alpenbereich allgemein, insbesondere° aber in der Schweiz finden. Früher haben Hirten° in Chalets gewohnt. Traditionell sind sie aus Holz° gebaut. In den Schweizer Gemeinden° Lenk, Grindelwald, Saanen und Zermatt darf man nur Chalets bauen. Moderne Architektur will man so in den Alpen verhindern°. Heute nennt man oft auch Ferienhäuser° aus Holz Chalets. Sie müssen nicht in einer Bergregion stehen, und man findet sie überall auf der Welt.

Sennhütte herdsman's hut **insbesondere** especially **Hirten** shepherds **Holz** wood **Gemeinden** townships **verhindern** prevent **Ferienhäuser** vacation homes

PORTRÄT

César Ritz

3 Expansion For homework, have students draw their dream apartments and prepare a written description to present in class.

César Ritz war ein berühmter Schweizer Hotelier. Er wurde am 23. Februar 1850 als dreizehntes Kind einer armen Familie in Niederwald im Goms geboren. Die Schule beendete er nicht. Anfangs arbeitete er als Schuhputzer°, Träger° und Kellner in verschiedenen Hotels. Im Rigi-Kulm-Hotel in der Schweiz wurde er schließlich° Hoteldirektor. 1888 heiratete er die Hotelierstochter Marie-Louise Beck. Er hatte großen Erfolg als Direktor und eröffnete° 1898 das Grandhotel Le Ritz in Paris, 1906 das Hotel Ritz in London und 1910 das Hotel Ritz in Madrid. Alle Hotels gelten° als absolute Luxushotels. Wegen seines großen Erfolgs nannte König Edward VII. César Ritz den „König der Hoteliers und Hotelier der Könige".

Schuhputzer shoeshine boy **Träger** porter **schließlich** eventually **eröffnete** opened **gelten** count

WOHNUNG ZU VERMIETEN

🔗 IM INTERNET

Finden Sie ein Zimmer zum Mieten in einer deutschsprachigen Stadt. Wie groß ist es? Wie viel kostet es? Was ist im Preis inbegriffen (*included*)?

Find out more at **vhlcentral.com**.

3 Suggestion Provide a simple model for this activity describing your own dream apartment. Then ask students about their own preferences. Ex.: **Möchten Sie lieber eine Wohnung mit einem Schwimmbad oder mit einem Atelier? Möchten Sie lieber ein Chalet in den Alpen oder eine Villa am Strand? Möchten Sie lieber ein Schloss in der Schweiz oder eine große Wohnung in Manhattan?**

3 Porträt Richtig oder falsch? Korrigieren Sie die falschen Aussagen. Diskutieren Sie dann die letzte Frage mit einem Partner/ einer Partnerin.

1. César Ritz kam aus einer kleinen Familie.
   Falsch. Er kam aus einer großen Familie mit 13 Kindern.
2. Als junger Mann arbeitete Ritz als Kellner. **Richtig.**
3. Er heiratete Maria-Luise Beck, die Tochter eines Schuhputzers.
   Falsch. Er heiratete Maria-Luise Beck, die Tochter eines Hoteliers.

Diskussion Wo haben Sie in Ihrem letzten Urlaub übernachtet (*stayed overnight*)? Wie war Ihr Zimmer? War es groß, sauber, hell, modern, altmodisch, teuer, usw.? War das in einer Stadt, am Meer oder in den Bergen?

4 Wo wohnen Sie? Schreiben Sie über wo und wie Sie wohnen. Lesen Sie Ihre Beschreibung im Kurs vor.

BEISPIEL *Ich wohne mit zwei Studentinnen in einer Wohnung. Die Wohnung hat ...*

More activities

vhlcentral | Online activities

6A.1

QUERVERWEIS

The **Präteritum** appears most often in writing. You will learn more about the uses of the **Präteritum** in **6B.1**.

ACHTUNG

The **ich** form and the **er/sie/es** form are always identical in the **Präteritum**.

Teaching Tip You may want to assign the grammar tutorial **6A.1 The *Präteritum*** on the Supersite for students to watch before they come to class.

Suggestion Tell students that the **Präteritum** is also frequently called the "simple past". Point out that whereas the perfect tense has two parts --the auxiliary and the participle--, the **Präteritum** only has one.

Suggestion Give students a series of weak verbs and have them guess the simple past forms, based on the pattern shown. Ex: **tanzen, machen, leben, kaufen, mieten, vermieten.**

QUERVERWEIS

See **4A.1** to review the uses of **mögen**.

See **4A.1** to review mixed verbs in the **Perfekt**.

Suggestion Emphasize to students that the past tense forms of mixed and strong verbs must be memorized on a verb-by-verb basis.

The *Präteritum* Grammar Tutorial

Startblock In **5A.1**, you learned to use the **Perfekt** to talk about past events. Another tense, the **Präteritum**, is also used to refer to past events.

- To form the **Präteritum** of weak verbs, add **-te**, **-test**, **-ten**, or **-tet** to the infinitive stem. Add an **-e** before these endings if the stem ends in **-d**, **-t**, or a consonant cluster.

Präteritum of weak verbs			
	sagen	**wohnen**	**arbeiten**
ich	sagte	wohnte	arbeitete
du	sagtest	wohntest	arbeitetest
er/sie/es	sagte	wohnte	arbeitete
wir	sagten	wohnten	arbeiteten
ihr	sagtet	wohntet	arbeitetet
Sie/sie	sagten	wohnten	arbeiteten

Die Kinder **spielten** in ihren Zimmern.
*The children **played** in their rooms.*

Ich **mietete** eine kleine Wohnung.
*I **rented** a small apartment.*

- Modal verbs have the same endings as weak verbs in the **Präteritum**. If the modal stem has an **Umlaut**, the **Umlaut** is dropped.

sollen		dürfen	
ich sollte	wir sollten	ich durfte	wir durften
du solltest	ihr solltet	du durftest	ihr durftet
er/sie/es sollte	Sie/sie sollten	er/sie/es durfte	Sie/sie durften

Warum **wolltet** ihr einen neuen Teppich kaufen?
*Why **did** you **want** to buy a new rug?*

Bianca **musste** ihre Großeltern besuchen.
*Bianca **had** to visit her grandparents.*

- The modal **mögen** has an additional stem change in the **Präteritum**. Be careful not to confuse the **Präteritum** form **mochte** with the polite form **möchte**.

Anna **möchte** eine neue Lampe für ihr Schlafzimmer.
*Anna **would like** a new lamp for her bedroom.*

Als Junge **mochte** Peter das Zimmer auf dem Dachboden.
*As a boy, Peter **liked** the room in the attic.*

- The **Präteritum** stem of a mixed verb is the same as the stem of its past participle.

Perfekt and *Präteritum* of mixed verbs		
Infinitiv	**Perfekt**	**Präteritum**
bringen	er hat gebracht	er brachte
denken	er hat gedacht	er dachte
kennen	er hat gekannt	er kannte
wissen	er hat gewusst	er wusste

Wir **brachten** die Tischlampe ins Arbeitszimmer.
*We **brought** the desk lamp into the office.*

Wusste Daniel Emmas Adresse?
***Did** Daniel **know** Emma's address?*

- Strong verbs in the **Präteritum** have irregular stems and add different endings from those of weak verbs.

beginnen	gefallen	liegen
ich begann	ich gefiel	ich lag
du begannst	du gefielst	du lagst
er/sie/es begann	er/sie/es gefiel	er/sie/es lag
wir begannen	wir gefielen	wir lagen
ihr begannt	ihr gefielt	ihr lagt
Sie/sie begannen	Sie/sie gefielen	Sie/sie lagen

irregular verb stems in the *Präteritum*					
bleiben	blieb	helfen	half	sehen	sah
essen	aß	kommen	kam	sprechen	sprach
fahren	fuhr	lesen	las	sterben	starb
finden	fand	nehmen	nahm	tragen	trug
geben	gab	schlafen	schlief	trinken	trank
gehen	ging	schreiben	schrieb	verstehen	verstand

Wir **blieben** gestern zu Hause.
*We **stayed** home yesterday.*

Ich **aß** ein kleines Stück Kuchen.
*I **ate** a little piece of cake.*

Er **sah** mir in die Augen.
*He **looked** me in the eyes.*

Sie **fuhren** nach Frankfurt.
*They **drove** to Frankfurt.*

- The verbs **sein**, **haben**, and **werden** do not follow the pattern of other irregular verbs.

sein	haben	werden
ich war	ich hatte	ich wurde
du warst	du hattest	du wurdest
er/sie/es war	er/sie/es hatte	er/sie/es wurde
wir waren	wir hatten	wir wurden
ihr wart	ihr hattet	ihr wurdet
Sie/sie waren	Sie/sie hatten	Sie/sie wurden

Es **wurde** schnell dunkel.
*It **got** dark quickly.*

Als Kinder **hatten** wir viele Haustiere.
*We **had** a lot of pets when we were kids.*

Suggestion Have students review the meanings of these verbs before having them practice the simple past forms. Emphasize the vowel change from **bleiben** to **blieb** and **schreiben** to **schrieb**. It may be helpful to remind them that "E-I" says "I" and "I-E" says "E."

ACHTUNG

Note that the **Präteritum** endings for strong verbs follow the same pattern as those of weak and mixed verbs, but without the addition of **-te-** as a past-tense marker.
Also note that the **ich** and **er/sie/es** forms of strong verbs have no added endings in the **Präteritum**.

QUERVERWEIS

See **Appendix A** for a complete list of strong verbs and their **Präteritum** forms.

Suggestion Some students may incorrectly add the **-te** ending to the preterite form of strong verbs, creating nonsense forms such as **begannte** or **gefielte**. Explain that adding -te to a strong verb in its simple past form is like adding the -ed ending to an irregular verb like *sang* or *swam* in English.

More activities

vhlcentral

WB pp. 79–80

LM p. 51

Online activities

Jetzt sind Sie dran!   Ergänzen Sie die Sätze mit den richtigen Formen der Verben im **Präteritum**.

1. Wir ___machten___ (machen) zusammen unsere Hausaufgaben.
2. Die alten Möbel ___waren___ (sein) hässlich.
3. Mein Bruder ___wollte___ (wollen) ein Motorrad zu Weihnachten.
4. Das Mathebuch ___lag___ (liegen) auf dem Schreibtisch.
5. ___Hattet___ (Haben) ihr als Kinder einen Hund?
6. Wolfgang ___trank___ (trinken) Tee zum Frühstück.
7. In der 8. Klasse ___schrieben___ (schreiben) wir jede Woche eine Prüfung.
8. Jan ___kaufte___ (kaufen) die Bluse für seine Freundin.
9. ___Musstest___ (Müssen) du am Donnerstag lange arbeiten?
10. Unsere Eltern ___fuhren___ (fahren) ohne uns in die Türkei.
11. Gestern ___gab___ (geben) es Knödel in der Mensa.
12. Ich ___fand___ (finden) diese Präsentation interessant.

Anwendung

1 **Zeitformen** Wählen Sie für jeden Satz die richtige Zeitform (*tense*).

	Präsens	Perfekt	Präteritum
1. Er ist nach Berlin gereist.	☐	☑	☐
2. Sie arbeitete mit seiner Freundin.	☐	☐	☑
3. Mietet ihr ein Haus am Strand?	☑	☐	☐
4. Hast du schon zu Abend gegessen?	☐	☑	☐
5. Sie hatten viel Spaß auf der Party.	☐	☐	☑
6. Wir kaufen die Möbel bei Ikea.	☑	☐	☐
7. Wie fandest du den Film?	☐	☐	☑
8. Ich konnte gestern nicht kommen.	☐	☐	☑

2 **Sätze umformen** Formen Sie die Sätze vom **Präsens** ins **Präteritum** um.

BEISPIEL Der Fußballspieler spielt in Europa.
Der Fußballspieler spielte in Europa.

1. Die Studentin wohnt bei ihren Eltern.
Die Studentin wohnte bei ihren Eltern.
2. Seid ihr verheiratet?
Wart ihr verheiratet?
3. Ich bringe ihnen eine Zimmerpflanze.
Ich brachte ihnen eine Zimmerpflanze.
4. Die Schüler bauen Legohäuser.
Die Schüler bauten Legohäuser.

5. Du gibst ihr ein Hochzeitsgeschenk.
Du gabst ihr ein Hochzeitsgeschenk.
6. Das Haus hat keinen Keller.
Das Haus hatte keinen Keller.
7. Wir ziehen nach Hamburg um.
Wir zogen nach Hamburg um.
8. Sie bleiben eine Woche in Paris.
Sie blieben eine Woche in Paris.

3 **Der gestrige Tag** Erzählen Sie, was gestern alles passierte. Benutzen Sie das Präteritum.

BEISPIEL ich / wollen / ins Feinkostgeschäft gehen
Ich wollte ins Feinkostgeschäft gehen.

1. die Kinder / dürfen / auf die Geburtstagsfeier gehen Die Kinder durften auf die Geburtstagsfeier gehen.

2. wir / müssen / neue Möbel für das Wohnzimmer kaufen Wir mussten neue Möbel für das Wohnzimmer kaufen.

3. Papa / sollen / seine Hemden in die Schublade legen Papa sollte seine Hemden in die Schublade legen.

4. du / wollen / Blumen für den Balkon kaufen Du wolltest Blumen für den Balkon kaufen.

5. ihr / können / leider nicht lange bei uns bleiben Ihr konntet leider nicht lange bei uns bleiben.

6. Sophia / mögen / die Gemüsesuppe nicht Sophia mochte die Gemüsesuppe nicht.

4 **Ein Märchen** Ergänzen Sie die Sätze mit den richtigen Präteritumsformen.

4 Suggestion Ask students if they can guess which famous fairy tale this is. You may want to share the original version of the **Aschenputtel** (*Cinderella*) story with students, and point out how it differs from modern retellings.

4 Expansion For homework, have students write an ending for the story, based on their knowledge of the fairy tale, or from their imaginations.

Es (1) ___war___ (sein) einmal ein kleines Mädchen. Ihr Name war Aschenputtel. Ihre Mutter (2) ___starb___ (sterben), als sie jung war. Ihr Vater (3) ___fand___ (finden) bald eine neue Frau. Seine neue Frau (4) ___hatte___ (haben) zwei hässliche Töchter. Die Stiefschwestern und die Stiefmutter (5) ___mochten___ (mögen) Aschenputtel nicht. Aschenputtel (6) ___musste___ (müssen) den Boden wischen, die Wäsche waschen und alle Betten machen. Die bösen Stiefschwestern (7) ___trugen___ (tragen) selber schöne Kleider, aber sie (8) ___gaben___ (geben) Aschenputtel nur ein altes, dreckiges Kleid. Eines Tages (*One day*) (9) ___besuchte___ (besuchen) Aschenputtel das Grab (*grave*) ihrer Mutter. Sie (10) ___sprach___ (sprechen) über ihr Unglück (*misfortune*)...

Kommunikation

5 **Das Leben vor hundert Jahren** Wie war das Leben vor hundert Jahren? Arbeiten Sie mit einem Partner / einer Partnerin und bilden Sie logische Sätze mit Wörtern aus jeder Spalte. Answers will vary.

 BEISPIEL

S1: *Jungen konnten allein in den Wald gehen.*
S2: *Frauen konnten nicht an einer Universität studieren.*

Frauen	dürfen	im Garten schlafen
Hunde	können	nicht so viele Prüfungen korrigieren
Jungen	müssen	an einer Universität studieren
Kinder	sollen	allein in den Wald gehen
Mädchen	wollen	viel arbeiten
Männer		in einem großen Kaufhaus einkaufen
Professoren		Brot backen
Studenten		mit dem Auto fahren

6 **Meine Familie** Erzählen Sie Ihrem Partner / Ihrer Partnerin von Ihrem Familienleben als junges Kind. Benutzen Sie das Präteritum. Answers will vary.

▶ **BEISPIEL**

S1: *Meine Familie wohnte in New York. Mein Vater war Musiker. Er arbeitete auch in einer Bibliothek. Wir gingen oft am Wochenende zu meinen Großeltern...*
S2: *Ich wohnte zusammen mit meinen Eltern, meinem kleinen Bruder und meiner Oma...*

7 **Ein schöner Tag** Erzählen Sie Ihrem Partner / Ihrer Partnerin von einem sehr schönen Tag in Ihrem Leben. Benutzen Sie das Präteritum. Answers will vary.

BEISPIEL

S1: *Es war ein Samstag. Das Wetter war schön und ich hatte keine Hausaufgaben. Ich ging in die Stadt...*
S2: *Ein sehr schöner Tag war mein 16. Geburtstag. Meine Eltern hatten ein großes Geschenk für mich und es stand vor der Haustür...*

8 **Ein trauriger Tag** Gestern war ein sehr trauriger Tag für Erik. Schreiben Sie mit zwei Mitstudenten zusammen eine Geschichte über Eriks Tag. Benutzen Sie das Präteritum. Lesen Sie im Kurs Ihre Geschichte vor. Answers will vary.

▶ **BEISPIEL**

Erik ging in die Küche. Er fand ein Blatt Papier. Es war von seiner Freundin...

8 **Expansion** Collect the stories, read them out loud, and have the class guess which group wrote which story. You may want to have students vote for their favorite.

7 **Suggestion** Before having students work with a partner, give them time to take notes and prepare. You might want to give them a list of verbs in the simple past. Ex.: **aß, gab, bekam, ging, fand, trank, machte, sagte, arbeitete, besuchte, spielte, schlief, lag, hatte, war, wohnte, kaufte, verlor.**

7 **Partner Chat** You can also assign activity 7 on the Supersite. Students work in pairs to record the activity online. The pair's recorded conversation will appear in your gradebook.

6A.2

Da-, wo-, hin-, and *her*- compounds

 Grammar Tutorial

Startblock In German, personal pronouns following a preposition can only refer to people. Special forms are used when the object of the preposition refers to a thing or an idea.

Als Hans zu Weihnachten nach Hause kam, sprach er übrigens **von dir**.

Davon nehme ich einen Teller, bitte.

Suggestion Write some common **da**-compounds on the board, along with their English equivalents. Ex.: **darüber** (*about that*), **darunter** (*under that*). Give concrete examples for each, such as: **Hier ist mein Rucksack. Darunter ist der Stuhl und darunter ist der Boden.** Have students guess the meanings of other **da**-compounds. Ex.: **dazwischen, danach, daneben, davor, darauf, dahinter**.

QUERVERWEIS

See **3B.2** to review accusative prepositions, **4B.2** to review dative prepositions, and **5B.3** to review two-way prepositions.

Many German verbs are used idiomatically with certain prepositions. You will learn more about these verbs in **3A.2**.

See **4B.1** to review the use of **wen** and **wem**.

Expansion Give students clues using **da**-compounds and have them guess which item in the classroom you're referring to. Ex.: **Damit schreibt man. Darauf sitzen die Studenten. Darunter sind wir alle. Damit lernen wir Deutsch. Max sitzt daneben.** Have students write their own **da**-compound riddles to share with the class.

ACHTUNG

Note that **warten auf** (*to wait for*), **denken an** (*to think about*), and **sprechen über** (*to talk about*) always take accusative objects.

- Use personal pronouns to refer to the object of a preposition. When the object is a thing or an idea, use a **da**-compound instead.

  Kennst du Alex? Wir sind am Samstag **mit ihm** essen gegangen.
  Do you know Alex? We went out to eat **with him** *on Saturday.*

  Wo ist der Teddybär? Das Baby will **damit** spielen.
  Where's the teddy bear? The baby wants to play **with it**.

- Form a **da**-compound by adding **da**- to a preposition. If the preposition begins with a vowel, insert an -**r**- after **da**-.

common **da**-compounds	
dafür davon davor	daran darauf darin

  Wo ist der Bus? Wir warten seit einer halben Stunde **darauf**.
  Where's the bus? We've been waiting **for it** *for half an hour.*

  —Hat Max dir ein Geschenk gegeben?
  —Ja, und ich habe ihm **dafür** gedankt.
  Did Max give you a present?
  —Yes, and I thanked him **for it**.

- German speakers often drop the -**a**- in **da**-compounds that begin with **dar**-.

  Wer ist da **drin**?
  Who's **in** *there?*

  Denk mal **drüber** nach.
  Think it **over**.

- Use **wen** or **wem** to ask about the object of a preposition when it refers to a person. When you ask about a thing or idea, use a **wo**-compound.

  Mit wem seid ihr ins Restaurant gegangen?
  Who *did you go to the restaurant* **with**?

  Womit spielt die Katze?
  What *is the cat playing* **with**?

- Form a **wo**-compound by combining **wo(r)**- with a preposition.

common **wo**-compounds	
wofür wovon wovor	woran worauf worin

  Wofür braucht sie den Spiegel?
  What *does she need the mirror* **for**?

  Woran denkst du jetzt?
  What *are you thinking* **about** *now?*

  Worüber sprecht ihr?
  What *are you talking* **about**?

- Use **wohin** to ask *where to?* and **woher** to ask *from where?* In conversation, **hin** and **her** can be separated from **wo**, moving to the end of the sentence.

QUERVERWEIS

See **5B.3** to review the difference between **wo** and **wohin**.

Wohin soll ich den Spiegel hängen?
Where should I hang the mirror?

Woher hast du diese Möbel bekommen?
Where did you get this furniture?

Wo gehst du jetzt **hin**?
*Where are you going **to** now?*

Wo kommst du **her**?
*Where are you **from**?*

- Use the adverb **dahin** or **daher** to replace a prepositional phrase expressing motion.

ACHTUNG

The phrase **hin und her** means *back and forth:*
Warum laufen die Kinder hin und her?

Reist ihr **in die Schweiz**?
*Are you going **to Switzerland**?*

Ja, wir reisen **dahin**.
*Yes, we're going **there**.*

- **Hin** or **her** can also be combined with the prefix of a separable prefix verb, to indicate motion. Note that **hin** generally indicates motion *away* from the speaker, while **her** indicates motion *toward* the speaker.

Birgit **geht** die Treppe **hinauf**.
*Birgit **is going up** the stairs.*

Paul **kommt** die Treppe **herunter**.
*Paul **is coming down** the stairs.*

Komm **herein** oder geh **hinaus**!
*Either come **in** or go **out**!*

Rapunzel, lass dein Haar **herunter**!
*Rapunzel, let **down** your hair!*

Suggestion The **Jetzt sind Sie dran!** activity helps to underscore the fact that **da-** and **wo**-compounds are not used when the pronoun refers to a person. Go over the answers as a class, and emphasize that since items 2, 4, and 7 refer to people, they must use the preposition with a personal pronoun.

More activities

vhlcentral

WB
pp. 81–82

LM
p. 52

Online activities

- Compound prefixes like **herauf-**, **herein-**, **herunter-**, or **heraus-** are often shortened in spoken German to **rauf-**, **rein-**, **runter-**, **raus-**, and so on.

Lässt du mich bitte ins Badezimmer **rein**?
*Will you please **let** me **into** the bathroom?*

Papa soll die alte Kommode in den Keller **runterbringen**.
*Dad is supposed to **bring** the old dresser **down** to the basement.*

 Jetzt sind Sie dran!   **Wählen Sie die richtigen Formen.**

1. (Woher / Wohin) kommt das Sprichwort „Zeit ist Geld"?
2. (Womit / Mit wem) hast du auf der Party getanzt?
3. (Womit / Mit wem) sollen wir anfangen?
4. Hast du Herrn Schulz gesehen? Ich denke oft (an ihn / daran).
5. (Wohin / Woher) soll ich die Lampe stellen?
6. (Wofür / Für wen) brauchst du so viele Bleistifte?

7. Marie ist wirklich unangenehm. Ich will nicht (damit / mit ihr) sprechen.
8. So eine schöne Vase! Wir danken euch sehr (für sie / dafür).
9. Die neue Wohnung ist wunderschön! Paul und Fabian haben viel (über sie / darüber) geredet.
10. (Woher / Wohin) bekomme ich das Geld für die Miete?

Anwendung

1 **Ersetzungen** Ersetzen Sie die Satzteile mit den entsprechenden **wo-** oder **da-**Komposita.

1. **wo-**: vor dem Kaufhaus ___wovor___
2. **wo-**: unter dem Teppich ___worunter___
3. **da-**: über das Buch ___darüber___
4. **da-**: gegen die Wand ___dagegen___
5. **wo-**: aus Baumwolle ___woraus___
6. **da-**: für das Geschenk ___dafür___
7. **wo-**: mit dem Fahrrad ___womit___
8. **da-**: hinter der Schule ___dahinter___

2 Suggestion Before they complete the activity, have students identify which noun is being replaced in each sentence.

2 **Was ist richtig?** Wählen Sie die passenden Präposition + Pronomen-Verbindungen oder die passenden **da-**Komposita.

1. Mias Cousinen wohnen in Wels. Letzten Sommer hat sie (bei ihnen / dabei) gewohnt.
2. Laura gab mir ein Geburtstagsgeschenk und ich dankte ihr (für es / dafür).
3. Frank ist gegen diese Idee und seine Freunde sind auch alle (gegen ihn / dagegen).
4. Meine große Schwester hat mir immer bei den Hausaufgaben geholfen. Ich habe sie täglich (mit ihr / damit) zusammen gemacht.
5. Simon spricht selten über Politik. Seine Freundin diskutiert aber gern (über sie / darüber).

3 **Was fehlt?** Ergänzen Sie die Sätze mit den passenden Wörtern. Bilden Sie Kombinationen mit **hin** oder **her.**

▶ **BEISPIEL**

Jasmin ___geht___ die Treppe ___hinauf___ (hinaufgehen).

1. Der Junge ___klettert___ den Baum ___hinauf___ (hinaufklettern).

2. Der Kellner ___kommt___ mit der Speisekarte ___heraus___ (herauskommen).

3. Herr Scholz ___geht___ in die Metzgerei ___hinein___ (hineingehen).

4. Die Blätter (*leaves*) ___fallen___ von den Bäumen ___herunter___ (herunterfallen).

4 **Fragen bilden** Was sind die Fragen zu den Antworten?

BEISPIEL Zur Schule fahre ich mit dem Bus.
Womit fährst du zur Schule?

1. Lukas geht mit seiner Schwester ins Theater.   Mit wem geht Lukas ins Theater?
2. Sarah ist gegen die Gartentür gefahren.   Wogegen ist Sarah gefahren?
3. Das neue Sofa ist aus Leder gemacht.   Woraus ist das neue Sofa gemacht?
4. Die Vorlesung war über Neurobiologie.   Worüber war die Vorlesung?

Kommunikation

5 **Hin oder her?** Entscheiden Sie mit Ihrem Partner / Ihrer Partnerin, welches Verb zu jedem Bild passt, und beantworten Sie die Fragen. Sample answers are provided.

> herauskommen | hinausgehen | hineingehen | hinfallen | hinstellen

> **BEISPIEL** **Was macht der Kellner?**
> *Er stellt das Essen hin.*

1. Was ist der Frau passiert? Sie ist hingefallen.
2. Papa kommt gerade von der Arbeit. Was macht er? Er geht hinein.
3. Was will das Kind machen? Es will hinausgehen.
4. Herr und Frau Koch waren im Konzert. Was machen sie jetzt? Sie kommen heraus.

6 **So bin ich** Stellen Sie Ihrem Partner / Ihrer Partnerin die Fragen. Answers will vary.

> **BEISPIEL** **Worüber lachst du oft?**
> *Ich lache oft über meine Katze. Sie ist immer so lustig.*

1. Woher kommt deine Familie?
2. Worüber sprichst du gern?
3. Wohin gehst du gern?
4. An wen denkst du oft?

7 **Mein bester Freund** Wie ist der beste Freund / die beste Freundin von Ihrem Partner / Ihrer Partnerin? Stellen Sie Fragen und benutzen Sie **wo-Komposita** oder **Präposition + wen/wem**. Answers will vary.

> **BEISPIEL** **sehr viel wissen / über**
> **S1:** *Worüber weiß dein bester Freund sehr viel?*
> **S2:** *Er weiß sehr viel über Rockmusik.*

1. oft denken / an
2. selten Probleme haben / mit
3. gern ausgehen / mit
4. mit dir sprechen / über

8 **Mein Zimmer** Beschreiben Sie Ihr Zimmer. Benutzen Sie **da-Komposita**. Ihr Partner / Ihre Partnerin versucht dann, ein Bild von Ihrem Zimmer zu zeichnen. Dann tauschen Sie die Rollen. Answers will vary.

> **BEISPIEL** *Da ist mein Bett. Darauf liegt eine Bettdecke von meiner Oma, und darüber hängt ein Poster. Mein Nachttisch steht neben dem Bett. Darauf liegt…*

hängen	links davon	an	über	hinter
liegen	rechts davon	auf	unter	vor
stehen	zwischen	in	neben	

6A.3

QUERVERWEIS

You learned the conjunctions **und**, **oder**, and **aber** in **1B.2**.

Suggestion Remind students what conjunctions are, and have them give you examples in English. Tell them that German has three kinds — adverbial, coordinating, and subordinating. Explain that coordinating conjunctions have no impact on word order, and are simply inserted between two clauses like a plus sign.

Suggestion Tell students that whenever *but* can be replaced with *rather* in English, the equivalent German conjunction will be **sondern**.

Coordinating conjunctions Grammar Tutorial

Startblock Use coordinating conjunctions to combine two related sentences, words, or phrases into a single sentence.

> Ich ging in die Küche, **und** am Herd stand ihr Großvater.

> Es ist bequemer hier, **denn** die Küche ist gleich nebenan.

- The most common coordinating conjunctions are **aber**, **denn** (*for, because*), **oder**, **sondern** (*but rather/instead*), and **und**.

> Ich habe eine Wohnung mit großer Küche gemietet, **denn** ich koche gern.
> *I rented an apartment with a big kitchen,* ***because*** *I like to cook.*

> Lina braucht einen Schrank **oder** eine Kommode für ihre Kleider.
> *Lina needs a closet* ***or*** *a dresser for her clothes.*

- Both **aber** and **sondern** correspond to the English word *but*. **Sondern** is used after a negated clause and indicates that the two ideas being coordinated are mutually exclusive.

> Erik hat ein großes Sofa, **aber** er sitzt gern auf dem Boden.
> *Erik has a big sofa,* ***but*** *he likes to sit on the floor.*

> Meine Wohnung ist nicht im Erdgeschoss, **sondern** im ersten Stock.
> *My apartment is not on the ground floor,* ***but rather*** *on the second floor.*

- When two clauses are connected by a coordinating conjunction, both follow normal subject-verb word order. Always use a comma before **aber**, **denn**, and **sondern**.

> Die Katze sitzt auf dem Balkon **und der Hund liegt** auf dem Teppich.
> *The cat is sitting on the balcony* ***and the dog is lying*** *on the carpet.*

> Ihr esst immer im Esszimmer, **aber wir essen** gern in der Küche.
> *You always eat in the dining room,* ***but we like to eat*** *in the kitchen.*

Jetzt sind Sie dran! **Wählen Sie die passende Konjunktion.**

1. Seine Schwester hat einen braunen Sessel (und / sondern) ein blaues Sofa im Wohnzimmer.
2. Im Keller ist es nicht warm, (sondern / aber) kalt.
3. Wir haben ein Haus mit einer großen Garage gekauft, (und / denn) wir haben zwei Autos.
4. Ich liebe Schokolade, (denn / aber) ich bin leider auf Diät.
5. Annika kauft gern Pflanzen für ihr Arbeitszimmer, (aber / denn) sie liebt die Natur.
6. Die Kinder wollen spielen, (sondern / aber) sie müssen ihre Hausaufgaben machen.
7. Wohnst du in einem Haus (oder / sondern) mietest du eine Wohnung?
8. Auf meinem Schreibtisch habe ich eine Lampe (und / denn) ein hübsches Bild von meiner Freundin.
9. Ich parke mein Auto nicht auf der Straße, (sondern / aber) in der Garage.
10. Zieht ihr im Januar (denn / oder) im Februar um?

Anwendung und Kommunikation

1 **Aber oder sondern?** Ergänzen Sie die Sätze mit **aber** oder **sondern**.

1. Nils ist intelligent, ____aber____ ein bisschen schüchtern.

2. Er und seine Frau wohnen in Deutschland, ____aber____ sie kommen aus den USA.

3. Anna studiert nicht mehr an der Universität, ____sondern____ arbeitet jetzt als Architektin.

4. Sie wollten letztes Jahr in ein neues Haus umziehen, ____aber____ es war zu teuer.

5. Ihre Kinder sind nicht in der Schule, ____sondern____ im Kindergarten.

6. Ich gehe heute nicht zu Fuß zur Uni, ____sondern____ ich fahre mit dem Fahrrad.

1 **Suggestion** Remind students that **sondern** follows negative statements, so if the first clause contains the word **nicht**, the correct "but" will be probably be **sondern**.

2 **Was und warum** Bilden Sie logische Sätze aus Spalte A und B und verbinden Sie sie mit **aber, oder, denn, und** oder **sondern**. Lesen Sie Ihre Sätze im Kurs vor. Sample answers are provided.

BEISPIEL	A	B
Ich arbeitete gerne mit Antonia, denn sie war sehr fleißig.	Ich arbeitete immer gerne mit Antonia.	Sie fanden dort einen günstigen Kleiderschrank.
	Sie waren beim Möbelhaus Fischer.	Sie war fleißig.
	Hannes wollte das gestreifte Hemd kaufen.	Er wollte nicht im Erdgeschoss wohnen.
	Sie kauften kein zweites Auto.	Sie kauften ein Fahrrad.
	Er wollte ein Zimmer bei einer Familie mieten.	Es war zu eng.
	Ich bin heute Abend zu Hause geblieben.	Ich war sehr müde.

2 Sample answers: **Sie waren beim Möbelhaus Fischer und sie fanden dort einen günstigen Kleiderschrank. / Hannes wollte das gestreifte Hemd kaufen, aber es war zu eng. / Sie kauften kein zweites Auto, sondern ein Fahrrad. / Er wollte ein Zimmer bei einer Familie mieten, aber er wollte nicht im Erdgeschoss wohnen. / Ich bin heute Abend zu Hause geblieben, denn ich war sehr müde.**

3 **Lara und ihre Familie** Erfinden Sie einen passenden Satz zu jedem Bild, und benutzen Sie dabei die angegebenen Konjunktionen. Vergleichen Sie Ihre Sätze mit einem Partner / einer Partnerin. Answers will vary.

3 **Expansion** Invite students to draw their own simple pictures. Then have them share their pictures in small groups and generate captions together using coordinating conjunctions.

▶ **BEISPIEL** sondern

Lara hat keinen Hund, sondern eine Katze.

1. oder

2. und

3. und

4. oder

Wiederholung

1 Umzug Lena reist viel. Sprechen Sie mit einem Partner / einer Partnerin darüber, wo Lena war und was sie machte. Sample answers are provided.

BEISPIEL München / Oktoberfest besuchen

S1: In München besuchte Lena das Oktoberfest.
S2: In Berlin...

1. Berlin / das Brandenburger Tor sehen In Berlin sah sie das Brandenburger Tor.
2. Hamburg / ein Konzert hören In Hamburg hörte sie ein Konzert.
3. Düsseldorf / in der Königsallee wohnen In Düsseldorf wohnte sie in der Königsallee.
4. Köln / ein Fahrrad kaufen In Köln kaufte sie ein Fahrrad.
5. Heidelberg / Chemie studieren In Heidelberg studierte sie Chemie.

2 Eine laute Party Sie sind auf einer Party, aber die Musik ist sehr laut, und Sie können nicht gut hören. Fragen Sie Ihren Partner / Ihre Partnerin, was er/sie gesagt hat. Answers may vary. Sample answers are provided.

BEISPIEL Am Montag / ins Musikgeschäft gehen möchten

S1: Am Montag möchte ich ins Musikgeschäft gehen.
S2: Wie bitte? Wohin möchtest du gehen?

1. am Dienstag / in der Mensa essen wollen Wo willst du essen?
2. im Sommer / nach Österreich reisen möchten Wohin möchtest du reisen?
3. am Freitag / im Schwimmbad schwimmen können Wo kannst du schwimmen?
4. am Wochenende / für die Physikprüfung lernen sollen Wofür sollst du lernen?
5. nächste Woche / einen Essay über München schreiben müssen Worüber musst du schreiben?
6. morgen Abend / mit den Eltern im Restaurant essen können Mit wem kannst du essen?/Wo kannst du essen?
7. morgen Nachmittag / lange in der Bibliothek bleiben müssen Wo musst du lange bleiben?
8. im Winter / in den Alpen Ski fahren wollen Wo willst du Ski fahren?

3 Expansion Before beginning the info-gap activity, show students a picture of a room and ask true or false questions about the picture using **da**-compounds. Ex.: **Richtig oder falsch? Das Zimmer hat keine Lampe. Es gibt ein Bett. Daneben ist ein Nachttisch. Darauf liegt ein Buch. Darüber hängt ein Poster.**

3 Diskutieren und kombinieren Sie und Ihr Partner / Ihre Partnerin bekommen zwei Blätter mit verschiedenen Bildern. Vergleichen Sie die Bilder, und machen Sie eine Liste mit den sieben Unterschieden auf den Bildern. Answers will vary.

BEISPIEL

S1: Es gibt nur ein Bett und eine Lampe rechts daneben, vor dem Fenster.
S2: Ich habe auch ein Bett, aber ich habe keine Lampe, ...

4 Im Stadtzentrum Erzählen Sie Ihrem Partner / Ihrer Partnerin, was Sie am Dienstag im Stadtzentrum machten. Wählen Sie ein Wort aus jeder Spalte und bilden Sie logische Sätze. Answers will vary.

BEISPIEL

S1: Am Dienstag lasen wir Bücher in der Bibliothek.
S2: An der Uni sprach ich mit...

A	B	C
Bücher	mit Freunden	essen
Meeresfrüchte	Kaffee	fahren
an der Uni	Kleider	finden
im Café	Steak	kaufen
im Modegeschäft	auf dem Markt	kommen
im Restaurant „Tivoli"	durch die Stadt	lesen
mit dem Fahrrad	in der Bibliothek	spazieren
langsam	in die Stadt	sprechen
spät	nach Hause	trinken

5 Arbeitsblatt Fragen Sie Ihre Mitstudenten, ob Sie die Aktivitäten in der Liste gern machen. Finden Sie eine Person für jede Aktivität. Answers will vary.

BEISPIEL

S1: Fährst du gern mit dem Fahrrad?
S2: Ja, ich fahre gern damit.

6 Das Wochenende Erzählen Sie sich gegenseitig, was sie am Wochenende gemacht haben. Nennen Sie mindestens sechs Dinge und auch einen Grund für jede Aktivität. Answers will vary.

BEISPIEL

S1: Am Samstagmorgen war ich drei Stunden in der Bibliothek, denn ich musste einen Essay für mein Literaturseminar schreiben.
S2: Am Samstagmorgen war ich nicht in der Bibliothek, sondern ich sollte mit meiner Mannschaft Fußball spielen...

Video

 Zapping

 NATIONAL communication cultures STANDARDS

 NATIONAL connections communities STANDARDS

 NATIONAL comparisons STANDARDS

Neustart: Möbel bauen statt Kinder erziehen

1 **Vorbereitung** Beschreiben Sie Ihrem Partner / Ihrer Partnerin Ihre Wohnsituation. Answers will vary.

1. Welche Möbelstücke stehen in Ihrem Zimmer/Ihrer Wohnung?
2. Aus welchen Materialien sind die Möbel in Ihrem Zimmer/ Ihrer Wohnung?

Mit den Händen arbeiten

Der Immobilienmarkt° in Deutschland ist eng und es ist nicht leicht eine gute, relativ große und günstige Immobilie zu finden. Ob man eine Immobilie kaufen oder mieten soll, hängt von° verschiedenen Punkten ab. Wie viel Kapital hat man? Wie viele Quadratmeter° braucht man? Muss die Immobilie eine konkrete Funktion erfüllen° und gibt es die nötige° Infrastruktur.

Immobilienmarkt real estate market   **hängt ... von... ab** depends on
Quadratmeter square meter   **erfüllen** fulfill   **nötige** necessary

Nützliche Ausdrücke

der Erzieher, -	educator
der Fußabdruck, -¨	footprint
der Grundriss, -e	floor plan
hinterlassen	to leave (behind)
das Holz, ¨-er	wood
die Leidenschaft, -en	passion
nachhaltig	sustainable
nach Maß	to save
der Kundenauftrag, -¨er	customer order
pleite sein	to be broke
der Tischlermeister, -	master carpenter
über die Runden kommen	to make ends meet
das Umfeld, -er	environment

2 **Richtig oder falsch** Sehen Sie sich das Video über Jonas Winkler an. Sind die folgenden Aussagen richtig oder falsch? Korrigieren Sie die falschen Aussagen.

	Richtig	Falsch	
1. Jonas trägt eine Brille.	☑	☐	
2. Jonas ist Produktdesigner für Software.	☐	☑	Er ist Produktdesigner für Möbel.
3. Einige Fenster in Jonas' Werkstatt sind kaputt.	☑	☐	
4. Jonas fährt mit dem Fahrrad nach Hause.	☐	☑	Er geht zu Fuß nach Hause.
5. Jonas sitzt auf seinem Sofa und arbeitet zu Hause.		☑	Er arbeitet am Esstisch zu Hause.

3 **Diskussion** Diskutieren Sie die folgenden Fragen mit einem Partner / einer Partnerin. Answers will vary.

1. Welche Möbelstücke benutzt man im täglichen Leben?
2. Was kann man machen, um im Leben „einen positiven Fußabdruck" zu hinterlassen?

4 **Präsentation** Machen Sie zu zweit ein Rollenspiel und spielen Sie ihn im Kurs vor. Sie sind Jonas Winkler und Ihr Partner / Ihre Partnerin ist Kunde / Kundin. Answers will vary.

BEISPIEL

S1: *Guten Tag. / Mein Name ist... . Können Sie einen Esstisch machen?*
S2: *Ja! Brauchen Sie auch Stühle?*

Expansion Distribute a list of additional questions about the video. Have the students watch again and jot down the answers to the questions. You may want to assign only one or two questions to each student. Discuss the answers as a class. **Welche Möbel baut Jonas? Hat er schon Aufträge? Kann er von seiner Arbeit leben? Warum macht er seine Designs zu Hause am Computer? Was macht er mit dem Holz in der Badewanne?**

More activities

vhlcentral

Online activities

Hausarbeit Vocabulary Tools

Wortschatz

die Hausarbeit	*housework*
den Tisch decken	*to set the table*
staubsaugen	*to vacuum*
Wäsche waschen	*to do laundry*
Haushaltsartikel	***household items***
die Decke, -n	*blanket*
der Herd, -e	*stove*
die Kaffeemaschine, -n	*coffeemaker*
die Pfanne, -n	*pan*
die Spülmaschine, -n	*dishwasher*
der Staubsauger, -	*vacuum cleaner*
der Toaster, -	*toaster*
der Wäschetrockner, -	*dryer*
die Waschmaschine, -n	*washing machine*
zum Beschreiben	***to describe***
dreckig	*filthy*
ordentlich	*tidy*
sauber	*clean*
schmutzig	*dirty*
Es ist ein Saustall!	*It's a pigsty!*
Verben	***verbs***
aufräumen (räumt... auf)	*to clean up*
putzen	*to clean*
waschen	*to wash*
wischen	*to wipe; to mop*

ACHTUNG

German speakers often shorten a compound when the context is clear:
Anja wirft die Wäsche in den Trockner.
But: **Der Wäschetrockner ist kaputt.**

Suggestion Ask students to describe their house, apartment, or dorm room using three adjectives, including at least one from the **zum Beschreiben** list.

Expansion Play "vocabulary bingo" with your students. Give students a list of 16 words from **6A** and **6B** and have them fill in a 4 X 4 grid with the words in mixed-up order. Then given an oral definition for each word. Ex: **Das ist grün. Es lebt. Es ist in einem Topf in meinem Wohnzimmer. (Die Pflanze.) Das ist wie ein Besen mit einem Motor. Damit mache ich meine Teppiche sauber. (Der Staubsauger)** As you define a word, students call out the answer and everyone gets to put an 'X' in the corresponding box. The first student to complete a row or column calls out **Ich gewinne.**

die Mikrowelle, -n

Sie macht das Bett. (machen) *She is making the bed.*

das Kissen, - *pillow*

die Spüle *kitchen sink*

Er spült Geschirr (n.). (spülen) *He is doing the dishes.*

die Laken (*sing.* das Laken) *sheets*

der Topf, ̈e

der Gefrierschrank, ̈e *freezer*

die Bettdecke, -n

der Ofen, ̈

Sie fegt. (fegen) *She is sweeping.*

der Kühlschrank, ̈e

der Besen, -

die Wäsche *laundry*

Expansion Have students write **wo**-compound questions related to the lesson vocabulary and share them with the class. **Womit mache ich mir einen Toast? Womit fegt man den Boden?**

Er bringt den Müll raus. (rausbringen)
He is taking out the trash.

das Bügeleisen, -
iron

Er bügelt.
(bügeln)
He is ironing.

das Bügelbrett, -er
ironing board

Anwendung

4 Expansion Divide the class into small groups. Assign each group one of the sentences from this activity, and have them turn the sentence into a short dialogue. Have each group perform their dialogue for the class.

1 Was passt nicht? Welches Wort passt nicht zu den anderen?

1. Spülmaschine, Geschirr, Besen, Spüle
2. schmutzig, sauber, unordentlich, dreckig
3. Herd, Kissen, Decke, Laken
4. spülen, waschen, bügeln, mieten
5. fegen, wohnen, wischen, staubsaugen
6. putzen, umziehen, wischen, aufräumen
7. Mikrowelle, Toaster, Staubsauger, Ofen
8. Saustall, Bügeleisen, Wäsche, Bügelbrett

2 Vergleiche Ergänzen Sie die Analogien mit einem Wort aus der Liste.

| faul | Gefrierschrank | staubsaugen | Spülmaschine |
| fegen | Laken | schmutzig | Teppich |

1. Hose → Waschmaschine // Messer → _Spülmaschine_
2. Bügeleisen → bügeln // Besen → _fegen_
3. Wäsche → waschen // Teppich → _staubsaugen_
4. Mantel → Kleid // Decke → _Laken_
5. Ofen → Herd // Kühlschrank → _Gefrierschrank_

3 Nach der Feier Hören Sie sich die Aussagen an und entscheiden Sie, ob diese **logisch** oder **unlogisch** sind. **Expansion** Ask students to correct the false/illogical statements.

	Logisch	Unlogisch		Logisch	Unlogisch
1.	☐	✓	4.	✓	☐
2.	✓	☐	5.	✓	☐
3.	☐	✓	6.	✓	☐

4 Was fehlt? Ergänzen Sie die Sätze mit dem richtigen Wort.

1. In der Küche ist das pure Chaos! Wir müssen sie wirklich heute noch (dreckig / sauber) machen.
2. Ich spüle das Geschirr und du (fegst / bügelst) die Hemden.
3. Wir können die Kleider nicht waschen. Die (Spülmaschine / Waschmaschine) ist kaputt.
4. Die Lasagne bäckt schon seit zwei Stunden im (Ofen / Topf).
5. Die Sonne brennt heute richtig! Gib bitte den (Pflanzen / Decken) auf dem Balkon mehr Wasser.

5 Der Besuch Im Haus von Familie Fuchs ist es noch ein bisschen unordentlich. Hören Sie zu und markieren Sie, welche Hausarbeiten Frau Fuchs den Familienmitgliedern gibt.

5 Suggestion Ask students guiding questions to keep in mind as they listen to the recording. Ex.: **Diese Familie muss das Haus aufräumen. Warum? Wer kommt zu Besuch? Was müssen sie alles machen?**

_b_ 1. Claudia
_e_ 2. Erik
_f_ 3. Frau Fuchs
_b/d_ 4. Lukas
_c_ 5. Nina
_a_ 6. Peter

a. Bad putzen
b. Betten machen
c. Geschirr spülen
d. Hund waschen
e. Müll rausbringen
f. staubsaugen

Kommunikation

5 **Räumen wir auf!** Die Wohnung ist mal wieder ein Saustall! Diskutieren Sie mit zwei Mitstudenten, welche Hausarbeiten jeder von Ihnen heute noch macht. Machen Sie dann auch einen Wochenplan, worin steht, wer in der Woche was machen muss, damit (*so that*) die Wohnung sauber bleibt. <small>Answers will vary.</small>

> **BEISPIEL**
>
> **S1:** *Wer spült das Geschirr?*
> **S2:** *Ich spüle das Geschirr. Und wer…?*

6 **Expansion** After students have completed their partner conversations, ask them whether they think the housework is divided up fairly in their own families.

6 **Hausarbeiten** Besprechen Sie mit Ihrem Partner / Ihrer Partnerin, wer in Ihrer Familie die angegebenen (*indicated*) Hausarbeiten macht. <small>Answers will vary.</small>

> **BEISPIEL**
>
> **Betten machen**
> **S1:** *Bei uns in der Familie macht meine Mutter die Betten.*
> **S2:** *Ich mache mein Bett jeden Morgen.*

1. Geschirr spülen
2. Kleider bügeln
3. Müll rausbringen
4. Staub wischen
5. Toilette putzen
6. Wäsche waschen

7 **Expansion** Have students write about their own experiences from the day before, using modals in the simple past: What did they have to do yesterday? (**Ich musste…**) What did they want to do? (**Ich wollte…**) What could they or could they not do? (**Ich konnte…**) What did they enjoy doing? (**Ich mochte…**)

7 **Diskutieren und kombinieren** Gestern Abend haben Tim und Lara eine große Party gegeben, aber heute müssen sie alles aufräumen. Ihr Professor / Ihre Professorin gibt Ihnen und Ihrem Partner / Ihrer Partnerin zwei verschiedene Blätter mit Informationen über Tim und Laras Tag. Erzählen Sie einander, was Tim und Lara heute machen. Schreiben Sie dann einen kurzen Absatz über ihren Tag.

> **BEISPIEL**
>
> **S1:** *Um Viertel nach zehn räumt Lara den Tisch auf. Was macht Tim um Viertel nach zehn?*
> **S2:** *Um Viertel nach zehn macht Tim das Bett.*

8 **Mein Traumhaus** Beschreiben Sie Ihrem Partner / Ihrer Partnerin Ihr Traumhaus: wo ist es, wie groß ist es, wie viele Stockwerke und Zimmer hat es, welche Möbel und Haushaltsartikel haben Sie, und wer macht die diversen Hausarbeiten? **8** **Video Virtual Chat** You can also assign activity 8 on the Supersite.

> **BEISPIEL**
>
> **S1:** *Mein Traumhaus ist am Strand und es hat fünf Schlafzimmer, vier Badezimmer, ein Studierzimmer und auch eine große Garage für drei Autos. Im Garten ist ein Schwimmbad und ein zweites, kleines Haus für meine acht Hunde.*
> **S2:** *Mein Traumhaus ist in der Stadt. Es hat…*

8 **Suggestion** Give students a few minutes to make notes about their dream house before they work with a partner. Encourage them to be creative and to include lots of detail.

Aussprache und Rechtschreibung Audio

The German *k* sound

The German **k** is pronounced like the *k* in the English word *kind*. At the end of a syllable, this sound may be written as **ck**.

Kaffee	Laken	Decke	Frack	Kreide

In a few loanwords, the **c** at the beginning of a word is pronounced like a **k**. In other loanwords, the initial **c** may be pronounced similarly to the *ts* in *cats* or the *c* in *cello*.

Computer	Caravan	Couch	Celsius	Cello

When the consonant combination **kn** appears at the beginning of a word, both letters are pronounced. In the combination **nk**, the sound is very similar to the *nk* in the English word *thank*.

Knie	knusprig	Knödel	danken	Schrank

Remember that the **ch** sound and the **k/ck** sound are pronounced differently.

dich	dick	Bach	Back

Suggestion Tell students that a distinctive feature of Swiss German is the pronunciation of the initial k sound, as in the word **Kirche**. It is pronounced as a k immediately followed by the back ch sound (IPA [*kx*]).

1 **Aussprechen** Wiederholen Sie die Wörter, die Sie hören.

1. Keller
2. Keramik
3. Stock
4. Container
5. Cola
6. Celsius
7. knackig
8. Knallfrosch
9. Bank
10. Hockey
11. lach
12. Lack

2 **Nachsprechen** Wiederholen Sie die Sätze, die Sie hören.

1. In der Küche backt man Kekse.
2. Deine Kleider hängen im Kleiderschrank.
3. In Frankfurt essen glückliche Kinder knackige Bockwürste.
4. Mein Lieblingsmöbelstück ist diese knallrote Couch.
5. Wir kaufen das Cabriolet in Köln.
6. Kann Klaus Knödel kochen?

3 **Sprichwörter** Wiederholen Sie die Sprichwörter, die Sie hören.

Klappern gehört zum Handwerk.[1]

Kommt Zeit, kommt Rat.[2]

[1] Talking it up is part of the trade. (lit. *Rattling is part of the trade.*)
[2] We'll figure it out with time. (lit. *With time comes counsel.*)

More activities

vhlcentral | LM p. 55 | Online activities

Fotoroman

Ich putze gern! Video

Meline und Sabite wollen die Wohnung aufräumen, doch plötzlich hat Meline eine wichtige Verabredung. Muss Sabite jetzt alleine putzen?

Vorbereitung In preparation for this episode, have students list in German all the chores they typically do around the house.

communication cultures
NATIONAL STANDARDS

MELINE Super. Ich treffe dich dann dort in einer halben Stunde.
SABITE Wohin gehst du?
MELINE Meine Freundin Beatrice besucht ihre Großmutter in Wilmersdorf und sie haben mich zum Tee zu sich eingeladen.
SABITE Wir haben darüber gesprochen, die Wohnung zu putzen. Sie ist ein Saustall.

MELINE Das können wir doch später machen.
SABITE Meline, seit wir hier eingezogen sind, hast du nicht ein Mal bei der Hausarbeit geholfen. Du hast kein Geschirr gewaschen, den Boden nicht gefegt und auch die Möbel nicht abgestaubt.

MELINE Beatrice und ich sind schon sehr lange Freundinnen und ihre Großmutter ist sehr alt. Man kann doch Staubsaugen nicht mit der Zeit vergleichen, die man mit der Familie verbringt.
SABITE Warte. Nimm den Abfall mit raus.

GEORGE Danke. Geht's dir gut?
SABITE Oh, mir geht es gut! Meline und ich hatten vor, heute die Wohnung aufzuräumen, aber sie hat sich aus dem Staub gemacht.
GEORGE Ich helfe dir.

GEORGE Ich wusste nicht, dass Mädchen so...
SABITE Unordentlich sein können?
GEORGE Letzte Woche sah es hier tadellos aus. Was ist passiert?
SABITE Es ist so stressig an der Uni. Wir haben keine Zeit zum Putzen. Und Meline macht keine Hausarbeiten.

SABITE Das kann ich von dir nicht verlangen. Es ist schmutzig hier drin.
GEORGE Ich hatte als Kind ein Zimmer mit meinem Bruder zusammen. Er war superfaul. Ich habe die Betten gemacht und die Wäsche gewaschen.

Suggestion Have students do this activity with their books closed. Divide the class into groups and see how many questions each group can answer correctly.

1 **Richtig oder falsch?** Entscheiden Sie, ob die folgenden Sätze richtig oder falsch sind.

1. Meline besucht eine Freundin in Wilmersdorf. Richtig.
2. Sabite und Meline wollten die Wohnung putzen. Richtig.
3. Meline hilft oft bei der Hausarbeit. Falsch.
4. Meline muss den Abfall mit rausnehmen. Richtig.
5. Sabite ist glücklich darüber, dass Meline nicht hilft. Falsch.
6. George hatte als Kind ein Zimmer allein. Falsch.
7. Er hat die Betten gemacht und die Wäsche gewaschen. Richtig.
8. Sabite und Meline haben keine Zeit zum Putzen. Richtig.
9. George und Sabite haben Melines Wäsche gefaltet. Falsch.
10. Meline muss ihre Bluse bügeln. Falsch.

PERSONEN

George   Meline   Sabite

Suggestion Explain to students that although there is no official progressive verb form in German, the so-called **am-Progressiv** (or **Rheinische Verlaufsform**) is increasingly common in standard German: **Da du gerade am Bügeln bist...** (*Since you're ironing...*).

> **SABITE** Vielen Dank für deine Hilfe, George.
> **GEORGE** Ich putze gern. Aber sag das bitte nicht Hans.
> **MELINE** Oh, George. Ich dachte, dass du Torsten bist. Beatrices Großmutter hat einen Mandelkuchen gebacken. Das wird euch aufheitern.

Suggestion Tell students that the expression **sich aus dem Staub machen** originally referred to soldiers who, wanting to escape from their compulsory military service, would take advantage of the large amounts of dust kicked up during battles to sneak away without being detected.

> **SABITE** Wir haben die Böden gefegt, das Geschirr gewaschen, den Herd geputzt, Staub gesaugt und abgestaubt.
> **GEORGE** Wir haben die Töpfe und Pfannen weggeräumt und eklige Dinge aus dem Kühlschrank und dem Spülbecken entfernt.

> **SABITE** Deine Wäsche haben wir *nicht* gefaltet.

> **MELINE** Ach, dieses Kleid möchte ich heute Abend anziehen. Jetzt muss ich bügeln.
> **SABITE** Oh, Meline, da du gerade am Bügeln bist... Danke!

Nützliche Ausdrücke

- **Sie haben mich zum Tee zu sich eingeladen.**
  They invited me over for tea.
- **einziehen**
  to move in
- **nicht ein Mal**
  not even once
- **Man kann doch Staubsaugen nicht mit der Zeit vergleichen, die man mit der Familie verbringt.**
  You can't compare vacuuming to spending time with family.
- **Sie hat sich aus dem Staub gemacht.**
  She ran away.
- **tadellos**   • **der Mandelkuchen**
  spotless   *almond cake*
- **aufheitern**   • **eklig**
  to cheer up   *disgusting*
- **Da du gerade am Bügeln bist...**
  Since you're ironing...

6B.1

- **Ich habe die Betten gemacht und die Wäsche gewaschen.**
  I made the beds and did the laundry.
- **Ich hatte als Kind ein Zimmer mit meinem Bruder zusammen.**
  I shared a bedroom with my brother when I was a kid.

6B.2

- **Wir haben die Töpfe und Pfannen weggeräumt und eklige Dinge aus dem Kühlschrank und dem Spülbecken entfernt.**
  We put away all the pots and pans, and got rid of disgusting things from the refrigerator and the kitchen sink.

---

2 **Zum Besprechen** Stellen Sie sich vor (*Imagine*), Ihre Wohnung ist so ein „Saustall" wie die von Sabite und Meline. Machen Sie zu dritt einen Plan, um die Wohnung aufzuräumen. Wer macht was? Arbeiten Sie zusammen oder alleine? Was machen Sie zuerst? Answers will vary.

3 **Vertiefung** Ordnung muss sein (*Order is a must*) ist eine deutsche Redensart (*expression*). Wie wichtig ist es Ihnen, eine ordentliche und saubere Wohnung zu haben? Warum?

More activities

vhlcentral   VM p. 12   Online activities

IM FOKUS

Haushaltsgeräte°

 Reading

IM SPÄTEN 19. JAHRHUNDERT KAM ES IN Deutschland zu wichtigen Erfindungen° in der Industrie und der Agrarwirtschaft°. Auch für den Verbraucher° gab es neue elektrische Geräte und Maschinen zu kaufen, die die tägliche Arbeit und den Transport leichter machten. 1899 gründeten° Carl Miele und Reinhard Zinkann einen kleinen Betrieb°, in dem sie zunächst° Maschinen für die Verarbeitung° von Milchprodukten bauten. Ein Jahr später brachten sie die erste elektrische Waschmaschine auf den Markt.

Die Firma Miele zeigte sich früh als innovativer Hersteller° von Haushaltsgeräten und wurde schnell zu einer Qualitätsmarke° in Deutschland und im Ausland. Bald konnte man Küchengeräte wie zum Beispiel Geschirrspülmaschinen und Staubsauger kaufen. Von 1911 bis 1913 produzierte Miele sogar Autos. Nach dem Zweiten Weltkrieg profitierte die vielseitige° Firma vom deutschen „Wirtschaftswunder." Neben Haushaltsgeräten baute sie auch ganze Einbauküchen°, Fahrräder und leichte Motorräder. Mit ihrem Erfolg konnte Miele nun expandieren und andere Betriebe aufkaufen, darunter den italienischen Medizintechnik-Hersteller Steelco sowie eine schweizerische Firma, die Bauausrüstungen° produzierte.

Im Gegensatz° zu vielen anderen Firmen ist Miele inmitten der Globalisierung und der Megafusionen° ein deutscher Familienbetrieb geblieben. Die Familie Miele besitzt° Firmenanteile° von 51,1% und die Familie Zinkann Anteile von 48,9%. Miele hat in Deutschland acht und im Ausland vier Standorte° und ist einer der größten Hersteller von Elektro-Haushaltsgeräten in Europa. Wer sich für die Geschichte der Firma interessiert, kann in der westfälischen Stadt Gütersloh das Miele-Museum besuchen.

Haushaltsgerätehersteller in Deutschland

Bauknecht: Küchengeräte	400 Mitarbeiter in Deutschland und Österreich
Bosch/Siemens: Haushaltsgeräte	137.700 Mitarbeiter in Deutschland
Liebherr: Kühlschränke und Gefriertruhen°	43.700 Mitarbeiter weltweit
Miele: Elektro-Haushaltsgeräte	11.100 Mitarbeiter in Deutschland
Rowenta: Küchen- und Haushaltsgeräte	33.600 Mitarbeiter weltweit

QUELLE: Statistisches Bundesamt Deutschland

Haushaltsgeräte household appliances
Erfindungen inventions **Agrarwirtschaft** agribusiness
Verbraucher consumer **gründeten** founded
Betrieb business operation **zunächst** initially
Verarbeitung processing **Hersteller** manufacturer
Qualitätsmarke quality brand **vielseitige** versatile
Einbauküchen fitted kitchens **Bauausrüstungen** construction equipment **Im Gegensatz zu...** Unlike
Megafusionen mega-mergers **besitzt** owns
Firmenanteile company shares **Standorte** locations

1 Im Fokus Richtig oder falsch? Korrigieren Sie die falschen Aussagen. Diskutieren Sie dann die letzte Frage mit einem Partner/ einer Partnerin.

1. Die Firma Miele baute zuerst Autos und erst später Waschmaschinen.
   Falsch. Sie baute zuerst Waschmaschinen und später Autos.
2. Nach dem Zweiten Weltkrieg expandierte die Firma Miele auch ins Ausland.
   Richtig.
3. Miele ist jetzt eine amerikanische Firma und gehört zu Amazon.
   Falsch. Miele ist eine deutsche Familienfirma.

Diskussion Warum ist Miele eine interessante Firma? Gibt es eine amerikanische Firma mit einer ähnlichen (similar) Geschichte und diversen Produkten? Ist diese Firma auch ein Familienunternehmen?

2 Die deutschsprachige Welt Richtig oder falsch? Korrigieren Sie die falschen Aussagen.

1. Hauswirtschaft ist in der Schweiz ein offizieller Beruf. Richtig.
2. Fachleute Hauswirtschaft arbeiten fast immer in Wohnhäusern.
   Falsch. Sie arbeiten auch oft in Heimen, Krankenhäusern, Hotels und Restaurants.
3. Ein Berufsziel ist, dass man gründlicher und umweltschonender arbeitet. Richtig.

Diskussion Was denken Sie über das Berufsziel „Menschen fühlen sich in ihrer Wohnung wohl"?

Materialien

die Fliesen (*pl.*)	tiles
der Granit	granite
das Holz	wood
die Keramik	ceramic
der Kunststoff	plastic
das Leder	leather
der Marmor	marble
der Stahl	steel

Fachleute Hauswirtschaft°

Ein offizieller Beruf in der Schweiz ist
Fachmann/Fachfrau Hauswirtschaft. Personen
mit diesem Beruf sind Experten für Hausarbeit.
Das Berufsziel°: Menschen fühlen sich in ihrer
Wohnung wohl°. Deshalb putzen sie Zimmer
schnell, gründlich° und umweltschonend°.
Bei Schäden° in Zimmern reparieren sie diese
Schäden. Fachleute Hauswirtschaft arbeiten
in Heimen°, Krankenhäusern°, Hotels und
Restaurants. Die Ausbildung° dauert drei Jahre.
Man muss in einem Betrieb° arbeiten, jede
Woche einen Tag in die Schule gehen und am
Ende Prüfungen machen.

Fachleute Hauswirtschaft *home economics specialists*
Berufsziel *professional aim* **fühlen sich... wohl** *feel
comfortable* **gründlich** *thoroughly* **umweltschonend**
environmentally friendly **Schäden** *damages*
Heimen *(nursing) homes* **Krankenhäusern** *hospitals*
Ausbildung *training* **Betrieb** *firm*

Martin Suter

Martin Suter, geboren 1948 in
Zürich, ist ein vielseitiger Schweizer
Schriftsteller°. Suter schreibt
vorwiegend° Geschichten und
Romane. Seine berufliche Karriere
begann er in einer Werbeagentur° in
Basel, doch in den neunziger Jahren
schlug° er eine literarische Richtung
ein. In den folgenden Jahren schrieb
er Kolumnen für die Zeitungen
Weltwoche und *Tages-Anzeiger* sowie
Reportagen für die Zeitschrift *GEO*.
Sein Erstlingsroman° *Small World*
(1997) brachte ihm Anerkennung°,
und das Buch wurde später in
Frankreich verfilmt°. Auch andere
Bücher, wie zum Beispiel *Ein
perfekter Freund*, und mehrere
Theater-Komödien hatten Erfolg°.
Heute genießt° Suter internationalen
Ruhm° als einer der erfolgreichsten
deutschsprachigen Autoren.

Schriftsteller *author* **vorwiegend** *mostly*
Werbeagentur *advertising agency* **schlug...
ein** *took* **Erstlingsroman** *debut novel*
Anerkennung *recognition* **wurde... verfilmt**
was made into a film **Erfolg** *success*
genießt *enjoyed* **Ruhm** *fame*

🔗 IM INTERNET

Suchen Sie Stellenangebote als Fachmann/frau
Hauswirtschaft in der Schweiz. Was muss man
machen? Schreiben Sie Beispiele auf.

Find out more at **vhlcentral.com**.

Suggestion Before they read the article on Martin Suter, have students
scan the text and underline all the **Präteritum** forms they can find.

---

3 **Porträt** Richtig oder falsch? Korrigieren Sie die falschen Aussagen.
Diskutieren Sie dann die letzte Frage mit einem Partner/ einer Partnerin.

1. Martin Suter begann seine Karriere am Theater.
   Falsch. Er begann seine Karriere in einer Werbeagentur, schrieb aber später fürs Theater.
2. Suter ist literarisch vielseitig. **Richtig.**
3. Suters erster Roman heißt *Weltwoche*. **Falsch.** Sein Erstlingsroman heißt *Small World*.

4 **Hergestellt in Deutschland** Die deutschsprachigen Länder
exportieren nicht nur Autos, sondern auch Filme, Bücher, Musik,
Haushaltsgeräte, Lebensmittel, Getränke, Optik und Computerspiele.
Machen Sie eine Liste mit deutschen Produkten - sie können natürlich
auch aus Österreich, der Schweiz oder Liechtenstein kommen. Wählen
Sie eines der Produkte aus und beschreiben
Sie es. Was finden Sie interessant an dem
Produkt? Wie sind Preis und Qualität? Stellen
Sie ihr Produkt im Kurs vor.

More activities

 vhlcentral   Online activities

6B.1

Perfekt versus *Präteritum* Grammar Tutorial

Startblock You have learned to use both the **Perfekt** and the **Präteritum** to talk about past events. However, these two tenses are not used interchangeably.

Ich **habe** es nicht **verstanden**, aber es **hat** mir **gefallen**.

„Da **warf** ich in ein Eckchen mich, die Eingeweide **brannten**."

- The **Perfekt** tense is most often used in conversation and in informal writing, such as e-mails, blog entries, personal letters, or diaries.

  Habt ihr den Tisch **gedeckt**?
  Did you set the table?

  Nein, aber wir **haben** den Boden **gewischt**.
  No, but we mopped the floor.

- The **Präteritum** is generally used in formal or literary writing, such as novels or newspaper articles, or in other formal contexts, such as news reports or speeches. It is sometimes called the *narrative past*, since it is often used to narrate a series of related past events.

  Es **war** einmal eine junge Frau mit dem Namen Aschenputtel.
  Once upon a time, there was a young woman named Cinderella.

  Jeden Tag **fegte** sie den Boden, **machte** sie die Betten und **spülte** sie das Geschirr.
  Every day, she swept the floors, made the beds, and washed the dishes.

- A few specific verbs are commonly used in the **Präteritum**, even in informal contexts. In conversation, German speakers typically use the **Präteritum** of **sein**, **haben**, and modal verbs, rather than the **Perfekt**.

  Hattet ihr am Mittwoch keine Hausaufgaben?
  Didn't you have any homework on Wednesday?

  Meine alte Wohnung **war** ein Saustall.
  My old apartment was a pigsty.

  Die Kinder **wollten** das Gemüse nicht essen.
  The kids didn't want to eat their vegetables.

  Solltet ihr gestern nicht staubsaugen?
  Weren't you supposed to vacuum yesterday?

- The **Präteritum** is also preferred by most speakers after the subordinating conjunction **als**.

  Als wir Kinder **waren**, haben wir viel Hausarbeit gemacht.
  When we were kids, we did a lot of housework.

  Als ich die Garage **aufräumte**, habe ich viele alte Bücher gefunden.
  When I cleaned up the garage, I found lots of old books.

- German verbs are usually listed in dictionaries and vocabulary lists by their *principal parts* (**Stammformen**): the infinitive, the third-person singular form of the **Präteritum**, and the past participle. For verbs with stem changes in the **Präsens**, the third-person singular form is given in parentheses. For completely regular verbs, only the infinitive is listed.

  geben (gibt)
  to give (gives)

  gab
  gave

  gegeben
  given

- Knowing the principal parts of a verb allows you to produce all of its conjugations in any tense. Here are the principal parts of some of the verbs you've learned so far.

infinitive	*Präteritum*	past participle
bringen	brachte	gebracht
denken	dachte	gedacht
essen (isst)	aß	gegessen
helfen (hilft)	half	geholfen
laufen (läuft)	lief	ist gelaufen
nehmen (nimmt)	nahm	genommen
schlafen (schläft)	schlief	geschlafen
sehen (sieht)	sah	gesehen
sitzen	saß	gesessen
waschen (wäscht)	wusch	gewaschen
wissen (weiß)	wusste	gewusst

Sie **nahm** einen Besen und **gab** ihrem Bruder den Staubsauger.
*She **took** a broom and **gave** her brother the vacuum cleaner.*

Ich **habe** nur einen Keks **genommen** und habe Peter die anderen **gegeben**.
*I only **took** one cookie and **gave** the rest to Peter.*

Suggestion Go over the verbs in this list and make sure students remember their meanings. Then have them close their books and quiz them on the past tense forms. Give them infinitives from the list and have them call out the preterite and perfect forms.

Expansion Give students the first sentence of a story using the preterite. One at a time, have students add a sentence to the story, on a piece of paper folded so that only the previous sentence is visible. When everyone has contributed, unfold the paper and share the story with the class.

QUERVERWEIS

See **Appendix A** for a complete list of strong verbs with their principal parts.

More activities

vhlcentral

WB
pp. 87–88

LM
p. 56

Online activities

Jetzt sind Sie dran! Wählen Sie die richtige Zeitform (*tense*) für die folgenden Sätze.

1. Es war einmal ein Mädchen mit dem Namen Rapunzel. (Perfekt / Präteritum)

2. Der Junge saß allein in seinem Zimmer und weinte. (Perfekt / Präteritum)

3. Donnerstags wusch ich die Wäsche. (Perfekt / Präteritum)

4. Was hast du an der Universität studiert? (Perfekt / Präteritum)

5. Meine Eltern haben ein Haus in München gemietet. (Perfekt / Präteritum)

6. Sie wollten schon immer in Bayern wohnen. (Perfekt / Präteritum)

7. Hast du schon den Balkon gefegt? (Perfekt / Präteritum)

8. Heute Morgen war die Mikrowelle noch sauber. (Perfekt / Präteritum)

9. In meiner alten Wohnung hatte ich eine Spülmaschine. (Perfekt / Präteritum)

10. Die ganze Familie hat Alex bei seinem Umzug geholfen. (Perfekt / Präteritum)

11. In seiner neuen Wohnung konnte er sehr gut schlafen. (Perfekt / Präteritum)

12. Er hat wirklich Glück gehabt. (Perfekt / Präteritum)

Anwendung

1 **Perfekt oder Präteritum?** Welche Zeitform benutzt man gewöhnlich (*generally*) in diesen Situationen?

▶ **BEISPIEL** *Perfekt*

1. _____ Präteritum _____

2. _____ Perfekt _____

3. _____ Perfekt _____

4. _____ Präteritum _____

2 **Was fehlt?** Ergänzen Sie die Tabelle mit den fehlenden Informationen.

	Infinitiv	Präteritum	Perfekt
1.	dürfen	*durfte*	hat gedurft
2.	gehen	ging	*ist gegangen*
3.	*fahren*	fuhr	ist gefahren
4.	nehmen	*nahm*	hat genommen
5.	kommen	kam	*ist gekommen*
6.	*sehen*	sah	hat gesehen
7.	bringen	brachte	*hat gebracht*
8.	*mögen*	mochte	hat gemocht

3 **Ein kurzes Gespräch** Ergänzen Sie die Sätze mit den fehlenden Verbformen im Perfekt oder im Präteritum.

BEISPIEL **SARA** Was ___hast___ du gestern Abend _gemacht_? (*machen*)

ANNA Ich (1) ___sollte___ in die Bibliothek gehen, aber Michael (2) ___wollte___ mit mir spazieren gehen. Es (3) ___war___ langweilig. (sollen, wollen, sein)

SARA Ach ja? (4) ___Musste___ er nicht mit Mira einkaufen gehen? (müssen)

ANNA Mira (5) ___konnte___ nicht, denn ihre Eltern (6) ___sind___ zum Abendessen (7) ___gekommen___. (können, kommen)

SARA Haha! Das (8) ___hat___ sie bestimmt toll (9) ___gefunden___. (finden)

ANNA Das weiß ich nicht. Ich (10) ___habe___ heute nicht mit ihr (11) ___gesprochen___. (sprechen)

Kommunikation

4 **Ein bisschen Geschichte** Erraten Sie zusammen mit Ihrem Partner / Ihrer Partnerin, welches Ereignis (*event*) zu welchem historischen Datum passt.

BEISPIEL

S1: *Was ist im Jahr 2005 passiert?*
S2: *2005 ist Angela Merkel als erste Frau Bundeskanzlerin von Deutschland geworden.*

Historisches Datum	Ereignis
_b_ **1.** 1295	a. Die Berliner Mauer fiel.
_d_ **2.** 1492	b. Marco Polo brachte chinesische Nudeln nach Italien.
_c_ **3.** 1824	c. Ludwig van Beethoven komponierte seine 9. Sinfonie.
_e_ **4.** 1918	d. Christoph Kolumbus reiste nach Amerika.
_a_ **5.** 1989	e. Deutschland verlor den Ersten Weltkrieg (*World War*).
_f_ **6.** 2005	f. Angela Merkel wurde als erste Frau Bundeskanzlerin von Deutschland.

5 **Julians Kalender** Erzählen Sie zusammen mit Ihrem Partner / Ihrer Partnerin, was Julian im April alles gemacht hat. Benutzen Sie das Perfekt und/oder Präteritum. Sample answers are provided.

BEISPIEL

S1: *Am 6. April hat er einen Film gesehen.*
S2: *Und am 7. April war er beim Friseur.*

Am 2. April hat er ein Basketballspiel gehabt. / Am 4. April musste er ein Geschenk kaufen. / Am 6. April ist er ins Kino gegangen. / Am 11. April hatte seine Mutter Geburtstag. / Am 15. April ist er auf die Party bei Tom gegangen. / Am 19. April war er auf dem Coldplay-Konzert. / Am 23. April ist er mit Lara im Restaurant gewesen. / Am 27. April hatte er einen Deutschtest.

APRIL

MO	DI	MI	DO	FR	SA	SO
					1	Basketballspiel 2
3	Geschenk kaufen 4	5	Film „Sophie Scholl" 6	Friseur 7	8	9
10	Mama Geburtstag 11	12	13	14	Party bei Tom 15	16
17	18	Coldplay-Konzert 19	20	21	22	Essen mit Lara 23
24	25	26	Deutsch-test 27	28	29	30

6 **Ein Märchen** Schreiben Sie mit Ihrem Partner / Ihrer Partnerin das Märchen zu Ende. Sie dürfen auch Ihr eigenes Märchen erfinden (*make up*). Schreiben Sie sechs bis acht Sätze im Präteritum. Lesen Sie das Märchen im Kurs vor. Answers will vary.

1. Es war einmal ein junges Mädchen. Sie hatte einen gemeinen Stiefbruder. Eines Tages...

2. Es waren einmal ein Hund, eine Katze, ein Hamster und ein Vogel. Sie wohnten alle bei einer alten Frau. Eines Tages...

3. Es war einmal ein kleiner Hund. Er wohnte allein im Wald und wollte so gern eine Familie haben. Eines Tages...

5 **Suggestion** Verify that students remember how to read dates out loud. Ex.: **am zweiten April, am fünften April, am siebten April.**

5 **Expansion** Have students create their own calendar (real or fictional) for the last month and have them share their activities with the class, using complete sentences in the present perfect.

5 **Video Virtual Chat** You can also assign activity 5 on the Supersite. Students record individual responses that appear in your gradebook.

Suggestion Tell students that **Es war einmal...** is a standard fairy tale beginning in German. Provide them with a standard ending that they can use for their fairy tales, such as: **Und wenn sie nicht gestorben sind, dann leben sie noch heute.**

6B.2

Separable and inseparable prefix verbs in the *Perfekt*

Grammar Tutorial

Startblock You previously learned about separable and inseparable prefix verbs in the present tense. In the **Perfekt**, the past participles of verbs with prefixes are formed slightly differently than those of other verbs.

Du **hast** den Boden nicht gefegt und auch die Möbel nicht **abgestaubt**.

Wir **haben** die Töpfe **weggeräumt** und eklige Dinge aus dem Kühlschrank **entfernt**.

- Verbs with prefixes can be either strong, weak, or mixed.

Ihr **habt** das Zimmer **aufgeräumt**.	Wir **haben** Kuchen **mitgebracht**.	Sie **sind** nach Berlin **umgezogen**.
*You **cleaned up** the room.*	*We **brought** cake.*	*They **moved** to Berlin.*

- To form the past participle of a separable prefix verb, add the separable prefix to the past participle of the root verb, before the **-ge-** prefix.

infinitive	participle	infinitive	participle
anrufen	**an**gerufen	rausbringen	**raus**gebracht
aufräumen	**auf**geräumt	umtauschen	**um**getauscht
ausgehen	(ist) **aus**gegangen	umziehen	(ist) **um**gezogen
einkaufen	**ein**gekauft	vorstellen	**vor**gestellt
mitbringen	**mit**gebracht	wegräumen	**weg**geräumt

Sie **haben** mich zum Tee zu sich **eingeladen**.

Wir **haben** das Geschirr **weggeräumt**.
*We **put away** the dishes.*

Wir **haben** Staub gesaugt und **abgestaubt**.

Ich **habe** den kaputten Staubsauger **umgetauscht**.
*I **exchanged** the broken vacuum cleaner.*

- The past participles of inseparable prefix verbs are formed like those of separable prefix verbs, but without the **-ge-** prefix.

infinitive	participle	infinitive	participle
bedeuten	bedeutet	erklären	erklärt
beginnen	begonnen	gehören	gehört
besuchen	besucht	verkaufen	verkauft
bezahlen	bezahlt	verschmutzen	verschmutzt
entdecken	entdeckt	verstehen	verstanden

Herr Koch **hat** uns einen neuen
  Gefrierschrank **verkauft**.
*Mr. Koch **sold** us a new freezer.*

Der Vermieter **hat** das Loch in der Wand
  entdeckt.
*The landlord **discovered** the hole in the wall.*

Sarahs Bruder **hat** uns einmal **besucht**.
*Sarah's brother **came to visit** us once.*

Ich **habe** die Frage nicht **verstanden**.
*I didn't **understand** the question.*

- Remember that the prefixes of inseparable prefix verbs are never stressed, while the prefixes of separable prefix verbs are always stressed.

Wie viel hast du für den
  Toaster be**zahlt**?
How much did you pay for the toaster?

Wir haben viele
  Gäste **ein**geladen.
We invited a lot of guests.

- Most separable and inseparable prefix verbs are conjugated with **haben**. However, prefixed verbs that indicate a change in condition or location and do not take a direct object are conjugated with **sein**.

Der Hund **hat** den sauberen
  Boden **verschmutzt**.
*The dog **got** the clean floor **dirty**.*

Wir **sind** mit unseren Großeltern in die
  Schweiz **mitgefahren**.
*We **went** to Switzerland with our grandparents.*

Du **hast** den dreckigen Teppich **rausgebracht**.
*You **took out** the dirty rug.*

Tobias **ist** gestern Abend **ausgegangen**.
*Tobias **went out** last night.*

- Since prefixes change the meaning of a verb, in some cases a prefixed verb is conjugated with **sein**, while its base form is conjugated with **haben**.

Sie **sind** vor einem Jahr **umgezogen**.
*They **moved** a year ago.*

Die Hunde **haben** den Schlitten **gezogen**.
*The dogs **pulled** the sled.*

Expansion Have students write a fictional journal entry using the following verbs in the present perfect tense: **aufräumen, verkaufen, einkaufen, anrufen, bekommen, bestellen, verlieren, vergessen.**

Suggestion Point out that, although the verb *vorbereiten* has a separable prefix (*vor-*), the root verb *bereiten* has an inseparable prefix (*be-*). Therefore, the past participle— *vorbereitet*—is formed without adding the *ge-* prefix.

QUERVERWEIS

See **5B.1** to review the formation of the **Perfekt** with **sein**.

More activities

vhlcentral

WB
pp. 89–90

LM
p. 57

Online activities

Jetzt sind Sie dran!   **Ergänzen Sie die Sätze mit den richtigen Formen der Verben im Perfekt.**

Suggestion Before they begin this **Jetzt sind Sie dran!** activity, have students identify the verbs with inseparable prefixes.

1. Paul ___*hat*___ den Müll nicht *rausgebracht*. (rausbringen)
2. Liebe Kinder, ___habt___ ihr eure Zimmer schon ___aufgeräumt___? (aufräumen)
3. Frau Schulz ___hat___ den Wäschetrockner ___verkauft___. (verkaufen)
4. David ___hat___ seine Freundin ___angerufen___. (anrufen)
5. Anna, ___habe___ ich dir meinen neuen Freund ___vorgestellt___? (vorstellen)
6. Mama ___hat___ eine schöne Vase zu Weihnachten ___bekommen___. (bekommen)
7. Du ___hast___ den Ring in der Waschmaschine ___entdeckt___. (entdecken)
8. Ich ___bin___ mit meinem Freund ___ausgegangen___. (ausgehen)
9. Wir ___haben___ eine Kaffeemaschine im Internet ___bestellt___. (bestellen)
10. Wie viel ___habt___ ihr für den Wäschetrockner ___bezahlt___? (bezahlen)
11. Maria, ___hast___ du das Geschirr ___weggeräumt___? (wegräumen)
12. Ich ___habe___ die Hausaufgaben zu Hause ___vergessen___! (vergessen)

Anwendung

1 **Perfektformen** Formen Sie die Sätze vom Präsens ins Perfekt um.

BEISPIEL Er ruft seine Schwester an.
Er hat seine Schwester angerufen.

1. Mein Bruder kommt mit.
Mein Bruder ist mitgekommen.
2. Ich stelle meine Eltern vor.
Ich habe meine Eltern vorgestellt.
3. Georg kommt in Zürich an.
Georg ist in Zürich angekommen.
4. Du besuchst das Museum.
Du hast das Museum besucht.

5. Wir bringen ein Geschenk mit.
Wir haben ein Geschenk mitgebracht.
6. Sara vergisst ihre Handtasche.
Sara hat ihre Handtasche vergessen.
7. Der Professor wiederholt die Grammatik.
Der Professor hat die Grammatik wiederholt.
8. Ihr schaut bei dem Fußballmatch zu.
Ihr habt bei dem Fußballmatch zugeschaut.

2 **Letzten Freitag** Was haben diese Leute letzten Freitag gemacht? Bilden Sie Sätze im Perfekt.

BEISPIEL Paula / ihre Schwester anrufen
Paula hat ihre Schwester angerufen.

1. Klara / nicht früh
aufstehen
Klara ist nicht früh aufgestanden.

2. Moritz /
sein Fahrrad
verkaufen
Moritz hat sein Fahrrad verkauft.

3. Herr Huber /
neue Schuhe
anziehen
Herr Huber hat neue Schuhe angezogen.

4. Ali / sein Zimmer
aufräumen
Ali hat sein Zimmer aufgeräumt.

5. Marie und
ihre Freundin /
ausgehen
Marie und ihre Freundin
sind ausgegangen.

3 **Das war früher anders** Sarah ist heutzutage (*nowadays*) sehr fleißig und nett, aber das war nicht immer so. Erzählen Sie, was Sarah alles gemacht hat, als sie jünger war. Answers will vary. Sample answers are provided.

BEISPIEL Heutzutage ruft sie ihre Mutter oft an.
Früher (Before) hat sie ihre Mutter selten angerufen.

1. Heutzutage steht sie immer früh auf.
Früher ist sie immer spät aufgestanden.
2. Heutzutage geht sie oft einkaufen.
Früher ist sie selten einkaufen gegangen.
3. Heutzutage bereitet sie täglich
Essen vor.
Früher hat sie selten Essen vorbereitet.

4. Heutzutage bringt sie immer
den Müll raus.
Früher hat sie selten den Müll rausgebracht.
5. Heutzutage geht sie nur selten aus.
Früher ist sie oft ausgegangen.
6. Heutzutage schläft sie immer früh ein.
Früher ist sie selten früh eingeschlafen.

4 **Was ist passiert?** Was hat Georg letztes Wochenende in Zürich gemacht? Schreiben Sie acht Sätze im Perfekt. Answers will vary.

BEISPIEL *Georg ist am frühen Morgen in Zürich angekommen.*

ankommen	ausgehen	bezahlen	mitkommen
anrufen	bekommen	einkaufen	vergessen
aufstehen	besuchen	mitbringen	zurückkommen

Kommunikation

5 **Kindheitserinnerungen** Stellen Sie Ihrem Partner / Ihrer Partnerin acht logische Fragen über seine/ihre Kindheit. Benutzen Sie das Perfekt und verwenden Sie Wörter aus jeder Spalte. Sie dürfen auch andere Elemente hinzufügen (*add*). Answers will vary.

BEISPIEL

S1: Wie oft hast du dein Zimmer aufgeräumt?
S2: Ich habe es einmal in der Woche aufgeräumt.

A	B	C
Mit wem?	einmal in der Woche	aufhängen
Wen?	immer sehr spät	aufräumen
Wann?	in ein neues Haus	aufstehen
Was?	Poster von Rockstars	ausgehen
Wie oft?	deine Verwandten	bekommen
Wer?	mit Freunden	besuchen
deine Eltern	immer dein Zimmer	einschlafen
deine Geschwister	im Unterricht	umziehen
du	zum Geburtstag	vorbereiten

6 **Nicht nur Hausarbeiten** Was haben diese Personen am Wochenende gemacht? Schreiben Sie mit Ihrem Partner / Ihrer Partnerin zu jedem Bild einen Satz im Perfekt. Sample answers are provided.

BEISPIEL Greta und Jan
Greta und Jan sind ausgegangen.

1. Martin
Martin hat seine Schwester angerufen.

2. Jonas
Jonas ist spät aufgestanden.

3. Nils und Max
Nils und Max haben den Müll rausgebracht.

4. Frau Lange
Frau Lange hat das Wohnzimmer aufgeräumt.

5. Yusuf
Yusuf hat seine Freundin besucht.

7 **Die neugierige Oma** Ihre Oma will wissen, was Sie dieses Schuljahr schon alles gemacht haben. Spielen Sie mit Ihrem Partner / Ihrer Partnerin einen Dialog und benutzen Sie die Perfektformen. Answers will vary.

BEISPIEL

Kaffee trinken
S1: Hast du viel Kaffee getrunken?
S2: Ja, Oma, ich habe viel Kaffee getrunken.

oft die Eltern anrufen	immer das Bett machen
früh aufstehen	die Badewanne putzen
oft ausgehen	den Müll rausbringen
oft Freunde einladen	die Hausaufgaben vorbereiten
fleißig lernen	die Kleider waschen

8 **Die Haushaltsführung** Schreiben Sie zu zweit einen Dialog. Ein Hotelbesitzer / Eine Hotelbesitzerin spricht mit einem Fachmann / einer Fachfrau Hauswirtschaft über die Haushaltsführung (*housekeeping*). Answers will vary.

BEISPIEL **S1:** Haben Sie den Dachboden aufgeräumt?
S2: Ja, ich habe ihn aufgeräumt und habe auch die Wäsche gewaschen.

Wiederholung

1 **Expansion** Take survey of the class, based on this activity. Ex.: **Haben wir saubere Zimmer? Wie viele von uns haben diese Woche Staub gewischt? Wer hat gestaubsaugt?**, etc.

1 **Suggestion** Before they begin the activity, have students review the past participles of the verbs listed.

1 Hausarbeit Fragen Sie Ihren Partner / Ihre Partnerin, was für Hausarbeit er/sie diese Woche gemacht hat.

1 **Partner Chat** You can also assign activity 1 on the Supersite.

BEISPIEL

S1: Hast du diese Woche den Boden gewischt?
S2: Ja, ich habe den Boden gewischt. Du auch?

Kleider bügeln	den Müll rausbringen
den Tisch decken	Geschirr spülen
die Küche fegen	staubsaugen
das Bett machen	Wäsche waschen
Hausarbeit machen	den Boden wischen

2 Arbeitsblatt Sie bekommen von Ihrem Professor / Ihrer Professorin eine Liste mit Aktivitäten. Fragen Sie Ihre Mitstudenten, ob sie die Aktivitäten letzten Monat gemacht haben. Finden Sie eine Person für jede Aktivität.

BEISPIEL

S1: Hast du letzten Monat deine Eltern angerufen?
S2: Ja, ich habe sie angerufen.

3 Die neue Küche Machen Sie zu dritt ein Rollenspiel. Eine Person spielt einen Hausbesitzer / eine Hausbesitzerin. Die anderen zwei spielen Lieferanten (delivery people) von Haushaltgeräten. Die Lieferanten fragen, wohin sie die Geräte stellen sollen.

BEISPIEL

S1: Wohin sollen wir die Waschmaschine stellen?
S2: Stellen Sie sie links neben die Tür.
S3: Und die Kaffeemaschine?

der Gefrierschrank	die Mikrowelle
der Herd	der Ofen
die Kaffeemaschine	die Spülmaschine
der Kühlschrank	der Wäschetrockner

4 Diskutieren und kombinieren Sie und Ihr Partner / Ihre Partnerin bekommen zwei verschiedene Blätter mit Alexandras Aktivitäten. Ergänzen Sie Alexandras Tageslauf. Schreiben Sie dann eine Erzählung darüber.

BEISPIEL

S1: Um halb fünf ist Alexandra im Park gelaufen.
S2: Danach, um fünf Uhr...

5 Ein Luxushotel Erstellen Sie (Create) mit einem Partner / einer Partnerin einen Text für die Website von einem Luxushotel in der Schweiz. Beschreiben Sie das Hotel, die Zimmer und Aktivitäten im Hotel und in der Gegend (area).

BEISPIEL

DAS HOTEL
Schweiz HOME | ROOMS & SUITES | RESTAURANT

Kommen Sie zu Besuch!

In unseren wunderschönen Zimmern finden Sie Kühlschrank, Mikrowelle und Kaffeemaschine.

6 Die Mitbewohner Schreiben Sie mit Ihrem Partner / Ihrer Partnerin eine Geschichte (story) über zwei Mitbewohner. Ein Mitbewohner ist sehr fleißig, aber der andere ist ganz anders (completely different). Benutzen Sie das Präteritum.

BEISPIEL

Es waren einmal zwei Mitbewohner, Daniel und Fabian. Daniel war sehr fleißig. Er lernte viel, machte jeden Abend seine Hausaufgaben, und machte jedes Wochenende die Hausarbeit. Aber Fabian...

2 **Suggestion** Have students compete to see who can be the first to get a positive answer for all eight questions. Circulate around the classroom, monitoring production and keeping students on task.

7 **Barrierefreies Leben** Seit 2002 gibt es in Deutschland das "Behindertengleichstellungsgesetz" (*Equal Opportunities for Disabled People Act*). Es garantiert, dass Menschen mit Behinderung nicht diskriminiert werden. Vor allem räumliche Barrieren machen es diesen Menschen schwer, sich ohne Hilfe bewegen zu können. Diskutieren Sie zu zweit, für welche Räume in einer Wohnung Barrierefreiheit besonders wichtig ist.

Suggestion Write on the board the German words that students won't know for disabilities, and ask students to add them to **Vocabulary Tools** on the **Sag mal** Supersite.

BEISPIEL

S1: *Ich denke das Badezimmer muss barrierefrei sein. Und du?*
S2: *Ja. Im Bad darf der Spiegel nicht so hoch hängen.*
S1: *Und die Tür muss breit (wide) sein.*

Expansion Ask students if they believe that there are sufficient barrier-free facilities on their campus, if they are well distributed, and what their recommendations would be to improve existing buildings and structures to make them barrier-free.

Kosten Umbau barrierefreier Wohnraum und behindertengerechtes Fahrzeug

insgesamt: 146.000 €

Bad 18.000 €
Schlafzimmer 10.000 €
Treppenlift 29.000 €
Wohnzimmer 20.000 €
Rollstuhl 2.000 €
Küche 12.000 €
Rampe 10.000 €
Auto 45.000 €

8 **Was ist passiert?** Fragen Sie Ihren Partner / Ihre Partnerin, was er/sie letzte Woche gemacht hat. Schreiben Sie dann einen Bericht (*report*) über seine/ihre Aktivitäten. Benutzen Sie das Präteritum. Answers will vary.

BEISPIEL

S1: *Hast du letzte Woche den Boden gefegt?*
S2: *Nein, aber ich habe mein Bett gemacht.*
S1: *(Schreibt) Sie fegte den Boden nicht, aber sie machte ihr Bett.*

9 **Eine Lebensgeschichte** Wählen Sie eine berühmte Person, und schreiben Sie mit einem Partner / einer Partnerin eine kurze Biographie über diese Person. Sie dürfen auch eine Person erfinden (*invent*).

BEISPIEL

Brad Pitt (1963–)

Mit zwei musste er mit seiner Familie nach Springfield Missouri umziehen, denn sein Vater hatte da einen Job. Im Gymnasium hat er...

 Mein Wörterbuch

Schreiben Sie noch fünf weitere Wörter in Ihr persönliches Wörterbuch zu den Themen **zu Hause** und **Hausarbeit**.

Lektion 6B

German	English	Definition
+ add word		
der Staub	dust	Ich putze mein Zimmer, denn es liegt zu viel Staub unterm Bett.

ä ö ü ß ☐ ALL CAPS

Panorama Interactive Map

Die Schweiz und Liechtenstein

connections · cultures · NATIONAL STANDARDS

Die Schweiz in Zahlen

▶ **Fläche:** *41.277 km²*

▶ **Offizielle Sprachen:** *Deutsch (63%), Französisch (22,7%), Italienisch (8,1%), Rätoromanisch° (0,5%)*

▶ **Bevölkerung:** *8,4 Millionen*

▶ **Religion:** *römisch-katholisch 38,2%, evangelisch 26,9%*

▶ **Hauptstadt:** *Bern*

▶ **Städte:** *Zürich (402.760 Einwohner), Genf (199.000), Basel (171.000) und Bern (133.100)*

▶ **Berge:** *Hohe Dufourspitze (4.634 m), Dom (4.545 m), Matterhorn (4.478 m)*

▶ **Flüsse:** *der Rhein, die Aare, die Rhone*

▶ **Wichtige Industriezweige:** *Uhrenindustrie°, Maschinenbau, Banken und Versicherungen°*

▶ **Touristenattraktionen:** *St.-Gotthard-Pass, Burgen von Bellinzona, Schweizerischer Nationalpark, Jungfraujoch bei Grindelwald.*

QUELLE: die Schweiz entdecken

Liechtenstein in Zahlen

▶ **Offizieller Name:** *Fürstentum° Liechtenstein*

▶ **Fläche:** *160 km²*

▶ **Bevölkerung:** *38.114*

▶ **Religion:** *römisch-katholisch 79%, evangelisch 8%*

▶ **Hauptstadt:** *Vaduz (5.500 Einwohner)*

▶ **Berge:** *Vorderer Grauspitz (2.599 m), Naafkopf (2.570 m)*

▶ **Niedrigster Punkt:** *Ruggeller Riet (430 m)*

▶ **Flüsse:** *der Rhein, die Samina*

▶ **Wichtige Industriezweige:** *Maschinenbau, Nahrungsmittel°*

▶ **Touristenattraktionen:** *Schloss Vaduz, Kathedrale St. Florin, Kunstmuseum Liechtenstein.*

QUELLE: Portal des Fürstentums Liechtenstein

Expansion For homework, have students find online pictures of the people and places mentioned on this page. Depending on the size of your class, each student could be responsible for one or two pictures.

Rätoromanisch *Romansch* Uhrenindustrie *clock and watch industry*
Versicherungen *insurance companies* Fürstentum *principality*
Nahrungsmittel *food products* Kriminalitätsrate *crime rate* niedrig *low*
Gefängnissen *prisons* Häftlinge *inmates* Haftstrafen *sentences*

Schloss Vaduz in Liechtenstein

Zürich

Landesgrenzen
● Stadt
◎ Landeshauptstadt
✪ Hauptstadt

Alphörner

Unglaublich, aber wahr!

In Liechtenstein ist die Kriminalitätsrate° extrem niedrig°. In den Gefängnissen° sitzen nur wenige Häftlinge°. Die Kollaboration zwischen Liechtenstein, Österreich und der Schweiz ist sehr eng. Zum Beispiel kommen alle Liechtensteiner Häftlinge mit Haftstrafen° über zwei Jahren in österreichische Gefängnisse.

Suggestion Tell students that **Schweizerdeutsch** can be difficult for Germans to understand, so much so that when Swiss speakers are interviewed for German news, subtitles are often added.

Politik
Fürstentum Liechtenstein

Liechtenstein ist ein Binnenland° in Mitteleuropa. Es liegt in den Alpen zwischen Österreich und der Schweiz. Unabhängig° ist das Land seit 1806. Liechtenstein ist ein Fürstentum. Fürst Hans-Adam II. von und zu Liechtenstein ist das Staatsoberhaupt°, aber Ueli Maurer ist seit 2019 der demokratisch gewählte Regierungschef°. Das Land hat keine Armee. Liechtenstein ist das kleinste deutschsprachige Land. Allerdings ist Deutsch nur in Liechtenstein die alleinige Amts- und Landessprache°.

Menschen
Roger Federer

Roger Federer ist ein Schweizer Tennisspieler. Viele Experten halten° ihn für den besten Tennisspieler aller Zeiten. Er hält mit 20 Grand-Slam-Siegen den Weltrekord im Herren Einzel° und ist einer von sieben Spielern, die in ihrer Karriere alle Grand-Slam-Turniere gewannen. 2008 gewann er zusammen mit Stanislas Wawrinka in Beijing eine olympische Goldmedaille im Doppel. In den Jahren 2005–2008 war er Weltsportler des Jahres. 2019 gewann er seinen 100. Karriere-Titel.

Kultur
Vier Amtssprachen

In der Schweiz gibt es vier offizielle Sprachen: Deutsch, Französisch, Italienisch und Rätoromanisch. Kantone haben aber meistens nur eine Amtssprache. Im Westen, an der Grenze zu Frankreich, dominiert Französisch und im Südosten, an der Grenze zu Italien, Italienisch. Im Norden, Zentrum und Osten dominiert Deutsch. Nur im Kanton Graubünden gibt es drei Amtssprachen: Deutsch, Rätoromanisch und Italienisch. Die meisten Schweizer sprechen nur eine Sprache als Muttersprache. Dafür lernen viele Schweizer mindestens eine weitere° Sprache. Einige sind auch dreisprachig.

Industrie
Präzisionszeitmessgeräte°

In der Schweiz gibt es eine lange Tradition für die Produktion von Präzisionszeitmessgeräten. Ein Beispiel ist das Marinechronometer. Auf einem Schiff° kann man mit diesem Gerät Längengrade bestimmen° und es für astronomische Ortsbestimmungen benutzen. Der Schweizer Uhrmacher° Louis Berthoud (1753–1813) stellte ein Präzisions-Taschenchronometer her°, das Alexander von Humboldt 1799 auf seinen Schiffsreisen testete. Heute müssen Chronometer extrem exakt sein.

Musik Musik

Lo und Leduc

Lo und Leduc ist ein Rapper-Duo aus der Schweiz. Die beiden Musiker Lo (Lorenz Häberli) und Leduc (Luc Oggier) machen seit 2009 zusammen Musik. Anfangs studierten sie nebenher noch Germanistik und Geschichte. Ihr Durchbruch kam 2018, als ihre Single „079" den ersten Platz der Schweizer Hitparade erreichte.

Go to **vhlcentral.com** to find out more about **Lo und Leduc**.

Binnenland *land-locked country* **Unabhängig** *Independent* **Staatsoberhaupt** *head of state* **Regierungschef** *head of government* **Amts- und Landessprache** *official and national language* **Herren Einzel** *men's singles* **weitere** *more* **Präzisionszeitmessgeräte** *precision time measuring instruments* **Schiff** *ship* **Längengrade bestimmen** *determine longitude* **Uhrmacher** *watchmaker* **stellte... her** *produced* **prüfen** *test*

Expansion Teach students a few Swiss German phrases, such as **Uf Widerleuge** (**Auf Wiedersehen**) or **Merci villmool (vielen Dank)**.

1 **Was haben Sie gelernt?** Entscheiden Sie, ob die Sätze **richtig** oder **falsch** sind. Korrigieren Sie die falschen Sätze.

1. Lichtenstein liegt zwischen Österreich und Italien. **Falsch.** Lichtenstein liegt zwischen Österreich und der Schweiz.
2. Liechtenstein hat ein Staatsoberhaupt sowie einen Regierungschef. **Richtig.**
3. Federer gewann 20 Grand-Slam-Siege. **Richtig.**
4. Die vier Amtssprachen der Schweiz sind Deutsch, Französisch, Italienisch und Rätoromanisch. **Richtig.**
5. Alexander von Humboldt testete 1799 ein Schweizer Taschenmesser. **Falsch.** Alexander von Humboldt testete ein Schweizer Präzisions-Taschenchronometer.

2 **Was meinen Sie?** Diskutieren Sie die Frage mit einem Partner/ einer Partnerin.

• Was sind die Ähnlichkeiten und Unterschiede zwischen Liechtenstein und der Schweiz? Welches Land würden Sie gern besuchen? Warum (nicht)?

Lesen Audio: Reading

Vor dem Lesen

Text untersuchen

Suchen Sie im Text ein anderes Wort aus der gleichen Wortfamilie. Answers will vary. Sample answers are provided.

BEISPIEL

Zimmer _Zweizimmerwohnung_

1. Möbel _____Möblierung_____
2. Küche _____Einbauküche_____
3. Monat _____monatlich_____
4. Garage _____Tiefgarage_____
5. Miete _____Kaltmiete_____
6. Wohnung _____Luxuswohnung_____
7. Internet _____Internetanschluss_____
8. Bett _____Bettwäsche_____

Präfixe

Suchen Sie mit einem Partner / einer Partnerin im Text ein neues Verb für jede Wortfamilie.

1. mieten _____vermieten_____ untermieten
2. kaufen verkaufen _____einkaufen_____
3. fangen _____anfangen_____ verfangen
4. _____stehen_____ aufstehen verstehen
5. lassen _____verlassen_____ entlassen
6. _____bieten_____ anbieten verbieten

Suggestion Learning to break down long compound words and identify their roots is an important reading strategy. For homework, have students find long German words online or in a dictionary. Have students write their words on the board, then break them down together into their component words.

Wohnung im historischen Fribourg

SIE SUCHEN eine kuschelige° Wohnung für zwei? Sie möchten das Leben in der historischen Innenstadt Fribourgs nicht verlassen°? Dann ist diese Zweizimmerwohnung ideal!

Die Schlafzimmer sind mit Einbauschränken ausgestattet°. Die Wohnung hat eine moderne Einbauküche mit Gasherd und Backofen. Sie bietet° ein modernes Bad, ein großes Wohn- und Esszimmer mit direktem Zugang° zur Küche. Einkaufen können Sie natürlich bequem° in einem Umkreis von fünf Minuten. Sie haben ein Auto? Kein Problem! Sie können Ihr Auto für monatlich SFr 75 auf einen Parkplatz in der Tiefgarage stellen. Zu vermieten ab Juli für SFr 1.100 Kaltmiete.

SIE SUCHEN FÜR IHRE FAMILIE ein neues Zuhause im Kanton Tessin? Ihnen gefällt die Kombination von Kultur und Natur? Sie lieben traditionelle Architektur, viel Holz und warmes Wetter? Dann ist dieses Einfamilienhaus perfekt!

Das Chalet liegt direkt am Lago Maggiore in der Nähe° von Locarno. Es ist als typisches Chalet mit Holzfassaden gebaut. Für eine Familie bieten Esszimmer, Wohnzimmer, zwei Badezimmer plus drei Schlafzimmer viel Platz. Die Küche mit Einbauküche und Frühstücksecke° ist familienfreundlich. Im Keller stehen Waschmaschine und Trockner. Im Garten können Kinder spielen, Hunde herumlaufen und Eltern Grillpartys feiern. Das Haus liegt fünf Minuten entfernt von Locarnos Innenstadt und in 20 Minuten ist man in den Bergen. Zu vermieten ab August. Die Miete beträgt monatlich SFr 2.000 ohne Nebenkosten°.

Expansion Give students a fictional profile of someone looking for an apartment and have them decide which of the three dwellings would be best for that person. Ex: **Bettina: ledig, ist eine 29-jährige Rechtsberaterin, die von Fribourg nach Zürich umziehen möchte. Sie ist ambitiös und perfektionistisch. Am liebsten mag sie alles schlicht und modern. Sie arbeitet viel und hat keine Zeit zu putzen. Welche Wohnung ist am besten für sie?**

BILIEN +41 56 5559990 SCHWEIZER IMMOBILIEN **+41 56 5559990** S

Hochmoderne Luxuswohnung in Zürich

SIE LEBEN ALLEIN? Nur das Beste ist gut genug? Sie arbeiten in Zürich bei einer Bank oder einer Versicherung? Dann ist diese Luxuswohnung genau das Richtige! Top gestylte, neu renovierte Zweizimmerwohnung in der Nähe des Züricher Bankenviertels ab sofort zu vermieten. Moderne Möblierung. Nur das Beste! Küche mit Espressomaschine und Mikrowelle vorhanden. Im Wohnzimmer stehen ein Fernseher° und eine Bar. Internetanschluss in allen Zimmern. Die wöchentliche Apartmentreinigung und das Wechseln° der Bettwäsche sind im Mietpreis inklusive. Mietverträge° können sofort anfangen. Die Miete beträgt SFr 2.100 pro Monat.

Chalet im Tessin

Nach dem Lesen

Was fehlt? Ergänzen Sie die Sätze.

1. Die Wohnung in Fribourg hat eine Einbauküche mit <u>Gasherd und Backofen</u>.
2. Im <u>Schlafzimmer</u> gibt es Einbauschränke.
3. Die Miete für die Wohnung in Fribourg kostet <u>SFr 1.100</u> inklusive Parkplatz.
4. <u>Das Chalet</u> liegt im Tessin.
5. Im Chalet stehen im Keller <u>Waschmaschine und Trockner</u>.
6. Beim Chalet können Kinder <u>im Garten</u> spielen.
7. In der Wohnung in Zürich stehen <u>ein Fernseher und eine Bar</u> im Wohnzimmer.
8. Die Miete der Züricher Wohnung beträgt <u>SFr 2.100</u> pro Monat.

Richtig oder falsch? Sind die Sätze richtig oder falsch? Korrigieren Sie die falschen Sätze.

Sample answers are provided.

	richtig	falsch
1. Die Wohnung in Fribourg ist ideal für eine Familie. Falsch. Die Wohnung ist ideal für zwei Personen.	☐	☑
2. Einkaufen ist in der Nähe der Fribourger Wohnung sehr schwierig. Falsch. Man kann hier bequem einkaufen.	☐	☑
3. Das Chalet ist ein sehr modernes Haus. Falsch. Das Chalet hat traditionelle Architektur.	☐	☑
4. Die Tessiner Wohnung hat viel Platz.	☑	☐
5. Natur und Stadtleben sind dem Chalet sehr nah.	☑	☐
6. Die Züricher Zweizimmerwohnung ist nicht sehr modern. Falsch. Sie ist top gestylt und neu renoviert.	☐	☑
7. In allen Zimmern der Züricher Wohnung ist ein Internetanschluss.	☑	☐
8. Die Wohnung in Zürich reinigt (cleans) man jede Woche.	☑	☐

Die beste Wohnung Diskutieren Sie in einer kleinen Gruppe: Welche ist die beste Wohnung? Answers will vary.

BEISPIEL

S1: Die Zweizimmerwohnung in Zürich ist klein, aber sie liegt in der Innenstadt. Man braucht kein Auto.
S2: Leider ist sie auch sehr teuer! Ich mag das Haus im Tessin.
S3: Ja, es ist ideal für eine Familie!

kuschelig cozy verlassen leave mit Einbauschränken ausgestattet equipped with built-in cabinets
bietet offers Zugang access bequem conveniently in der Nähe in the vicinity Frühstücksecke breakfast
nook Nebenkosten additional charges Fernseher television Wechseln changing Mietverträge rental agreements

Hören

Strategien

Using background knowledge

If you know the topic being discussed, using knowledge you already have about the subject can help you to predict the kind of information you might hear.

 To help you practice this strategy, you will listen to a commercial for a cleaning product. Before you listen, jot down some key words related to the topic of cleaning that you might expect to hear in the commercial.

Vorbereitung

Sehen Sie sich das Foto an. Wer sind die Menschen auf dem Foto? Was machen sie? Könnte das eine Werbung (*advertisement*) sein?

Zuhören

 Hören Sie der Sprecherin der Firma *Zauber* (*Magic*) bis *sauber* zu. Hören Sie die Werbung ein zweites Mal und wählen Sie die Dienstleistungen (*services*), die die Firma anbietet (*offers*).

1. (staubsaugen)
2. Wäsche waschen
3. bügeln
4. Geschirr spülen
5. (Kühlschränke putzen)
6. den Müll rausbringen
7. (Böden putzen)
8. (Fenster sauber machen)

Suggestion Before students listen to the recording, teach them the words **reinigen** and **Zauber**. Have students practice pronouncing **sauber** and **Zauber**, and make sure they can hear the difference.

Verständnis

 Was fehlt? Welche Wörter oder Ausdrücke fehlen?

arbeiten	Experten	neu
Bad	Fenster	putzen
Böden	kostenloses	sauber
bügeln	Kühlschränke	schnell

1. Die Reinigungsfirma (*cleaning company*) heißt Zauber bis ___sauber___.
2. Die Kunden der Reinigungsfirma ___arbeiten___ oft viel und haben keine Zeit zum Putzen.
3. Andere Kunden ___putzen___ einfach nicht gern.
4. Die Reinigungsfirma ist Experte für Küche, ___Bad___ und Wohnzimmer.
5. Sie staubsaugen und reinigen die ___Böden___.
6. Sie putzen auch ___Kühlschränke___ und Herde.
7. Die Leute der Reinigungsfirma sind ___Experten___ beim Saubermachen.
8. Diese Leute sind ___schnell___ und gründlich (*thorough*).
9. Die Zimmer sehen am Ende immer wie ___neu___ aus.
10. Die Reinigungsfirma gibt Kunden ein ___kostenloses___ Angebot (*offer*).

 Die Reinigungsfirma Entwickeln Sie (*Develop*) zu dritt eine Werbung für ein neues Produkt oder eine Dienstleistung.

BEISPIEL

S1: Mit *Sauberküche* können Sie Ihre Küche einfach reinigen!
S2: Sie brauchen keine anderen Produkte! Mit *Sauberküche* können Sie putzen, waschen, wischen...

Schreiben

Strategien

Reporting on an interview

When you transcribe a conversation in German, you should pay careful attention to format and punctuation. You can indicate a dialogue format by including the names of the speakers, or by using a dash (**der Gedankenstrich**) to indicate a new speaker. Compare these two formats.

> **MARIA** Nina, was hast du gestern Abend gemacht?
> **NINA** Ich war zu Hause.
> **MARIA** Oh, schade! Wolltest du nicht zu Davids Party?
> **NINA** Ja, aber ich musste noch putzen.

> —Hallo, Jonas!
> —Hallo, Sarah!
> —Wie geht's?
> —Gut. Und dir?

Whichever format you choose, your interview should begin with a brief introduction of the person you're interviewing, answering the six W-questions (**Wer?**, **Was?**, **Wann?**, **Wo?**, **Warum?**, and **Wie?**) about the topic of the interview.

Thema

 Schreiben Sie ein Interview

Anton Krüger ist Architekt. Er hat ein neues Buch über energiesparendes (*energy-efficient*) Wohnen geschrieben. Diese Woche gibt er an der Universität eine Präsentation darüber. Sie arbeiten für die Studentenzeitung (*student newspaper*) und interviewen Herrn Krüger.

- Schreiben Sie zuerst 2–3 Sätze über den Autor.

- Schreiben Sie ein erfundenes Gespräch (etwa 10–12 Zeilen) zwischen Ihnen und Anton Krüger. Geben Sie mit einem Gedankenstrich oder mit dem Namen der Person an, wer spricht.

BEISPIEL

> *Anton Krügers Buch kann man in Buchläden und im Internet kaufen. Er hielt diese Woche einen Vortrag...*
>
> **Journalistin** Guten Tag, Herr Krüger! Herzlichen Glückwunsch! Ihr neues Buch ist sehr interessant. Ich habe es wirklich toll gefunden.
>
> **Krüger** Vielen Dank!
>
> **Journalistin** Unsere Leser interessiert: Warum haben Sie dieses Buch geschrieben?

Vocabulary Tools

Lektion 6A

Zimmer
rooms

das Arbeitszimmer, - *home office*
das Badezimmer, - *bathroom*
der Balkon, -e *balcony*
der Dachboden, ∺ *attic*
das Erdgeschoss, -e *ground floor*
das Esszimmer, - *dining room*
der Flur, -e *hall*
die Garage, -n *garage*
der Keller, - *cellar*
die Küche, -n *kitchen*
das Schlafzimmer, - *bedroom*
der erste/zweite Stock *second/third floor*
die Toilette, -n *toilet*
das Wohnzimmer, - *living room*

Orte

das Haus, ∺er *house*
das Wohnheim, -e *dorm*
die Wohnung, -en *apartment*
nach rechts/links *to the right/left*

Verben

mieten *to rent*
umziehen (zieht... um) *to move*
wohnen *to live*

Möbel
furniture

die Badewanne, -n *bathtub*
das Bett, -en *bed*
das Bild, -er *picture*
die Blume, -n *flower*
der Boden, ∺ *floor*
das Bücherregal, -e *bookshelf*
die Kommode, -n *dresser*
die Lampe, -n *lamp*
das Möbelstück, -e *piece of furniture*
der Nachttisch, -e *night table*
die Pflanze, -n *plant*
das Poster, - *poster*
der Schrank, ∺e *cabinet; closet*
die Schublade, -n *drawer*
der Sessel, - *armchair*
das Sofa, -s *sofa*
der Spiegel, - *mirror*
der Teppich, -e *rug*
die Treppe, -n *stairway*
die Vase, -n *vase*
der Vorhang, ∺e *curtain*
die Wand, ∺e *wall*

The **Präteritum** *See pp. 240–241.*
Da-, wo-, hin-, and **her-**
compounds *See pp. 244–245.*
Coordinating conjunctions of verbs
See p. 248.

Lektion 6B

die Hausarbeit
housework

den Tisch decken *to set the table*
das Bett machen *to make the bed*
den Müll rausbringen *to take out the trash*
Geschirr (*n.*) spülen *to do the dishes*
staubsaugen *to vacuum*
Wäsche waschen *to do laundry*

Haushaltsartikel
household items

der Besen, - *broom*
die Bettdecke, - n *duvet*
das Bügelbrett, -er *ironing board*
das Bügeleisen, - *iron*
die Decke, -n *blanket*
der Gefrierschrank, ∺e *freezer*
der Herd, -e *stove*
die Kaffeemaschine, -n *coffeemaker*
das Kissen, - *pillow*
der Kühlschrank, ∺e *refrigerator*
das Laken, - *sheet*
die Mikrowelle, -n *microwave*
der Ofen, ∺ *oven*
die Pfanne, -n *pan*
die Spüle, -n *kitchen sink*
die Spülmaschine, -n *dishwasher*
der Staubsauger, - *vacuum cleaner*
der Toaster, - *toaster*
der Topf, ∺e *pot*
die Wäsche *laundry*
der Wäschetrockner, - *dryer*
die Waschmaschine, -n
   washing machine

zum Beschreiben

dreckig *filthy*
ordentlich *tidy*
sauber *clean*
schmutzig *dirty*
Es ist ein Saustall! *It's a pigsty!*

Verben

aufräumen (räumt... auf) *to clean up*
bügeln *to iron*
fegen *to sweep*
putzen *to clean*
waschen *to wash*
wischen *to wipe; to mop*

Principal parts of verbs *See p. 261.*
Perfekt of verbs with prefixes
   See pp. 264–265.

Urlaub und Ferien

COMMUNICATIVE GOALS
By the end of this chapter you will be able to:

LEKTION 7A

Discuss the weather, seasons, and months.

To do so, you will use:

Kontext Seite 278–281
- Das Datum
- Das Wetter, die Jahreszeiten

Strukturen Seite 286–295
7A.1 Separable and inseparable prefix verbs (**Präteritum**)
7A.2 Prepositions of location; Prepositions in set phrases

You will also learn about cultural products, practices, and perspectives related to:

Kultur Seite 284–285
- Die Windenergie
- Planten un Blomen in Hamburg
- Das Klima in Deutschland

Zapping Seite 295
- *Wetterbericht*

LEKTION 7B

Talk about travel.
Talk about vacations and tourism.

To do so, you will use:

Kontext Seite 296–299
- Am Flughafen
- Die Ferien
- Unterkünfte

Strukturen Seite 304–313
7B.1 Infinitive expressions and clauses
7B.2 Time expressions
7B.3 Indefinite pronouns

You will also learn about cultural products, practices, and perspectives related to:

Kultur Seite 302–303
- Der Flughafen Frankfurt
- Die Insel Sylt
- Der Intercity-Express

WEITER GEHT'S

Seite 314–320
You will learn about Schleswig-Holstein, Hamburg, and Bremen and their traditions, attractions, and famous inhabitants.

Panorama Seite 314–315
- **Schleswig-Holstein, Hamburg und Bremen**

And you will demonstrate that you can:
Lesen: Predict content from titles
Hören: Use visual clues
Schreiben: Create an outline

Suggestion Ask students to look at the photo and describe how George, Meline, Sabite, and Hans are feeling. How does the photo relate to the topic of the chapter?

Jahreszeiten Vocabulary Tools

Wortschatz

das Datum	*date*
das Jahr, -e	*year*
die Jahreszeit, -en	*season*
der Monat, -e	*month*
der Tag, -e	*day*
die Woche, -n	*week*

Suggestion Remind students that they first learned to talk about dates and birthdays in **2A.3**. Point out that they can say either **Ich habe am 23. Mai Geburtstag** or **Mein Geburtstag ist am 23. Mai**.

Wann hast du Geburtstag?	*When is your birthday?*
Am 23. Mai.	*May 23rd.*

das Wetter	***weather***
Wie ist das Wetter?	*What's the weather like?*
Es ist schön draußen.	*It's nice out.*
Das Wetter ist gut/ schlecht.	*The weather is nice/bad.*
Das Wetter ist furchtbar.	*The weather is awful.*
Wie warm/kalt ist es?	*How warm/cold is it?*
Es sind 18 Grad draußen.	*It's 18 degrees out.*

der Blitz, -e	*lightning*
der Donner, -	*thunder*
das Gewitter, -	*thunderstorm*
der Hagel	*hail*
der Nebel, -	*fog; mist*
der Regen	*rain*
der Schnee	*snow*
der Sturm, ⸚e	*storm*
der Wetterbericht, -e	*weather report*
die Wolke, -n	*cloud*

Suggestion Ask students to describe today's weather, using vocabulary from this section.

ACHTUNG

You have already learned to ask **Der Wievielte ist heute?** to find out the date. You can also use the question **Was ist heute?** to ask about the date or the day of the week.

Suggestion Have students review the use of ordinal numbers, taught in **2A.3**.

Suggestion Teach students the song **Immse wimmse Spinne** (the German version of "Eensy Weensy Spider"), which includes references to rain and sun. Lyrics can be found online.

Suggestion Point out that all months and seasons are masculine. Remind students to use **im** to talk about what happens during specific months and seasons. Ex., **im Winter**, **im März**, etc.

Expansion Mime various weather conditions, (ex., fanning yourself to indicate **Es ist heiß.**), and ask students: **Wie ist das Wetter?**

Es schneit. (schneien)
It is snowing.

Es ist kalt.
It is cold.

der Winter: Dezember, Januar, Februar

Es ist sonnig.
It is sunny.

Sommerfest

Es ist heiß.
It is hot.

– Welcher Tag ist heute?
– Der 15. August.
What is today?
August 15th.

der Sommer: Juni, Juli, August

Expansion Have students create a "word chain." The first student names a word from the vocabulary list, such as **Sommer**. The next student names a related word, such as **sonnig** or **heiß**, etc. When a student can't think of a word, the chain is "broken," and he or she must start a new "chain."

Es regnet. (regnen)
It is raining.

der Regenschirm, -e
umbrella

der Regenmantel, ¨
raincoat

der Frühling: März, April, Mai

Es ist wolkig.
It is cloudy.

Es ist kühl.
It is cool.

Es ist windig.
It is windy.

der Herbst: September, Oktober, November

Anwendung

1 Suggestion Students may not be familiar with the Celsius scale. Explain that **8° C** is 46.4° F; **17° C** is 62.6° F; and **25° C** is 77° F. Tell students that the conversion formula is: F = (C x 9/5) + 32; C = (F - 32) x 5/9.

1 Was fehlt? Ergänzen Sie die Sätze.

| regnet | schneit | Sturm | warm | windig | wolkig |

BEISPIEL Nürnberg: **25° C** In Nürnberg ist es sehr warm und _sonnig_

1. **Wien: 8° C** In Wien ist es kühl und _wolkig_.
2. **Genf: 17° C** In Genf ist es _windig_.
3. **Konstanz: 32° C** In Konstanz kommt am Abend ein _Sturm/Gewitter_.
4. **Innsbruck -5° C** In Innsbruck ist es kalt und es _schneit_.
5. **Basel: 12° C** In Basel ist es wolkig und es _regnet_.
6. **Hamburg: 21° C** In Hamburg ist es windig, aber _warm_.

2 Winterwetter Hören Sie zu und wählen Sie **ja**, wenn der Satz einen typischen Wintertag beschreibt.

	Ja	Nein		Ja	Nein
1.	☑	☐	4.	☐	☑
2.	☐	☑	5.	☐	☑
3.	☑	☐	6.	☑	☐

Expansion Ask students additional questions about the weather: **Wie ist das Wetter heute? Was möchten Sie gern bei diesem Wetter machen?**

3 Was ist richtig? Entscheiden Sie, welche Aussage zu welchem Bild passt.

a. Es ist heute wieder furchtbar heiß!
b. Wenn es regnet, braucht man einen Regenschirm.
c. Es kommt ein starker Sturm!
d. Auf dicke Wolken folgt schlechtes Wetter.

1. _c_

2. _a_   3. _b_   4. _d_

4 Der Wetterbericht Hören Sie den Wetterbericht an. Sind die Aussagen richtig oder falsch? **4 Suggestion** Have students correct the false statements.

	richtig	falsch
1. Der Wetterbericht ist für die ganze Woche.	☐	☑
2. Am Freitag beginnt der Winter.	☑	☐
3. Im Norden ist es sonnig.	☐	☑
4. Die Wetterfront im Norden kommt aus Skandinavien.	☑	☐
5. In Stuttgart regnet es am Freitag.	☐	☑

4 Expansion Have students work in small groups to predict the weather for the coming days, using simple sentences. Ex.: **Unsere Wettervorhersage: Am Montag schneit es. Am Dienstag gibt es Regen. Am Mittwoch ist es 18 Grad.**

Kommunikation

5 Suggestion To get students started, find the first statement for each dialogue together as a class.

5 Vom Wetter und den Jahreszeiten

Arbeiten Sie mit einem Partner / einer Partnerin und bringen Sie die Sätze in jedem Dialog in eine logische Reihenfolge (*order*).

5 Expansion After the dialogues have been put in order, have volunteers read them out loud to the class.

Dialog 1

__2__ Schön. Die Sonne scheint und es ist ziemlich warm für die Jahreszeit.

__4__ Es regnet oft und die Sonne kommt selten durch die Wolkendecke hervor.

__1__ Paul, wie ist das Wetter heute in Köln?

__3__ Ja? Wie ist das typische Herbstwetter?

Dialog 2

__3__ April? Da ist es noch kühl und Schnee gibt es auch oft.

__2__ Der Monat, in dem ich Geburtstag habe. Der April.

__1__ Was ist dein Lieblingsmonat?

__4__ Ja, aber die Natur ist grün, die Vögel singen, alles beginnt neu.

6 Gute Ratschläge

Schreiben Sie mit einem Partner / einer Partnerin eine E-Mail an eine Studentin in Deutschland. Sie will im Herbst an Ihrer Universität studieren und möchte etwas über das Wetter und die passende (*appropriate*) Kleidung wissen. Answers will vary.

6 Suggestion Have students peer-edit each other's e-mails.

BEISPIEL

Wetter und Kleidung

Von: Anna Webber [anna.webber@students.uni.edu]
An: Jasmin Peters [peterchen@gigglepost.de]
Datum: 26. Juni
Betreff: Wetter und Kleidung

Hallo Jasmin,
wie geht es dir? Wie läuft es mit deinen Prüfungen?
In deiner letzten E-Mail hast du mich nach dem Wetter hier in Atlanta gefragt. Also, du kommst im August an und da ist es hier einfach nur heiß und sonnig! Ab Mitte September…

8 Expansion Encourage students to choose a German-speaking city and use the Internet to find an actual weather report (in German) for that city.

7 Arbeitsblatt

Fragen Sie acht Personen in der Gruppe, wann sie Geburtstag haben, und schreiben Sie das Datum auf.

BEISPIEL

S1: *Sarah, in welcher Jahreszeit hast du Geburtstag?*
S2: *Ich habe im Frühling Geburtstag. Mein Geburtstag ist am achten April.*

7 Suggestion Before they start the activity, give students a moment to write down their birthdays and to practice pronouncing the date. Provide a model by writing your own birthday on the board.

Alles Gute zum Geburtstag!!!

8 Ein Wetterbericht

Schreiben Sie mit einem Partner / einer Partnerin einen Wetterbericht. Stellen Sie dann im Kurs Ihren Wetterbericht vor.

- Sagen Sie, welches Datum und welche Jahreszeit es ist.
- Berichten Sie über das Wetter für die nächsten sieben Tage.
- Illustrieren Sie Ihren Wetterbericht mit Hilfe von einem Poster.
- Sagen Sie, was man an den einzelnen (*individual*) Tagen machen kann oder soll.

Der Wetterbericht für Juli: Hamburg

Mittwoch, der 14. Juli	Donnerstag, der 15. Juli	Freitag, der 16. Juli
25° C	32° C	30° C
sonnig	sehr wolkig	stürmisch

Heute ist Mittwoch, der 14. Juli. Der Sommer zeigt seine schöne Seite. Die Sonne scheint den ganzen Tag und es ist das perfekte Wetter für das Schwimmbad…

7 Expansion Teach your class a short and simple birthday song, such as **Hoch soll er/sie leben** or **Zum Geburtstag viel Glück**. Lyrics can be found online.

8 Expansion Have students create short videos of their own **Wetterbericht**.

Aussprache und Rechtschreibung Audio

Long and short vowels

German vowels can be either long or short. Long vowels are longer in duration and typically occur before a single consonant, before the letter **h**, or when the vowel is doubled. Short vowels are shorter in duration and usually occur before two consonants.

| **Meter** | **mehr** | **Meer** | **Messer** | **melden** |

The long **a** is pronounced like the *a* in the English word *calm*, but with the mouth wide open. The short **a** sounds almost like the long **a**, but it is held for a shorter period of time and pronounced with the mouth more closed.

| **mahnen** | **Mann** | **lasen** | **lassen** |

The long **e** sounds like the *a* in the English word *late*. The short **e** sounds like the *e* in *pet*. The long **i** may be written as **i** or **ie**. It is pronounced like the *e* in *be*. The short **i** is pronounced like the *i* in *mitt*.

| **wen** | **wenn** | **Visum** | **fliegen** | **Zimmer** |

The long **o** is pronounced like the *o* in *hope*, but with the lips firmly rounded. The short **o** is pronounced like the *o* in *moth*, but with the lips rounded. The long **u** is pronounced like the *u* in *tuna*, but with the lips firmly rounded. The short **u** is pronounced like the *u* in *put*, but with the lips rounded.

| **Zoo** | **Zoll** | **Flug** | **Hund** |

Suggestion Model the mouth position needed to produce the **o** and **u** sounds, with lips rounded and pushed forward.

---

1 **Aussprechen** Wiederholen Sie die Wörter, die Sie hören.

1. Haken / hacken
2. den / denn
3. Bienen / binnen
4. Sohn / Sonne
5. buchen / Bucht

6. Nase / nass
7. fehl / Fell
8. Miete / Mitte
9. wohne / Wonne
10. Humor / Hummer

11. Wagen / Wangen
12. Zehner / Zentner
13. Linie / Linde
14. Lot / Lotto
15. Mus / muss

1 **Expansion** Conduct a dictation based on these word pairs. For each pair, read only one of the words out loud and tell students to circle the word they hear.

---

2 **Nachsprechen** Wiederholen Sie die Sätze, die Sie hören.

1. Viele machen im Sommer Urlaub am Strand.
2. Wolf und Monika wollen den ganzen Tag in der Sonne liegen.
3. Sabine und Michael schwimmen lieber im Meer.
4. Alle sieben Studenten übernachten in einer Jugendherberge.
5. Hast du den Flug schon gebucht?
6. Wenn das Wetter schlecht ist, gehen wir ins Museum.

Ende gut, alles gut.[2]

---

3 **Sprichwörter** Wiederholen Sie die Sprichwörter, die Sie hören.

Liebe geht durch den Magen.[1]

Montag *Dienstag*

More activities

| S vhlcentral | LM p. 59 | Online activities |

[1] The way to the heart is through the stomach. (lit. *Love goes through the stomach.*)

[2] All's well that ends well.

Berlin von oben Video

Sabites Kunst gefällt Meline nicht, aber sie sind trotzdem Freundinnen. George und Hans sprechen über ihre Nachbarinnen und wollen hoch hinaus.

Vorbereitung Have students look closely at scenes 1, 2, 9, and 10 and describe the weather in each one.

SABITE Meline! Hallo.
MELINE Hallo.
SABITE Wie findest du es? Gut, es gefällt dir nicht.
MELINE Wie bitte?
SABITE Ich weiß, dass dir meine Kunst nicht gefällt. Ich mag VWL auch nicht, aber wir sind dennoch Freundinnen.

GEORGE Es ist schön draußen. Ich liebe diese Jahreszeit. Es ist kalt, aber nicht zu windig.
HANS Wie ist das Wetter gerade in Wisconsin?
GEORGE Milwaukee liegt am Lake Michigan. Er beeinflusst das Klima. Ich habe gestern mit meiner Mutter gesprochen. Dort liegen etwa zwei Fuß Schnee, etwa 60 cm.

HANS Wie ist das Wetter im Sommer?
GEORGE Im August ist es heiß und feucht. Es regnet, donnert und hagelt. Ich mag alle vier Jahreszeiten, aber der Frühling ist meine Lieblingsjahreszeit.
HANS Warum?
GEORGE Mein Geburtstag ist am 26. April. Und deiner?
HANS Am 17. Juli.

GEORGE Hey, was meinst du zu dieser Krawatte?
HANS Sie ist ganz okay. Warum?
GEORGE Ich habe mit Meline eingekauft. Sie hat sie ausgewählt. Ich war „zu amerikanisch" angezogen, also probiere ich neue Kleidung aus.

HANS Meline. Magst du sie?
GEORGE Ja. Nein, also nicht auf diese Weise. Zu Hause bin ich nicht mit Frauen befreundet. Wir haben Spaß zusammen. Ich habe gesehen, wie du mit ihr gelacht hast, also magst du sie doch.

SABITE Istanbul ist nicht weit von Berlin. Etwa 2.200 Kilometer. George ist 8.000 Kilometer von zu Hause entfernt.
MELINE George hat auch keine Freundin. Wann hast du zum ersten Mal über die Idee gesprochen?

ÜBUNGEN

1 Richtig oder falsch? Entscheiden Sie, ob die folgenden Sätze richtig oder falsch sind.

1. Meline und Sabite mögen dieselbe (*the same*) Kunst. Falsch.
2. In Milwaukee gibt es keinen Schnee. Falsch.
3. Im August ist es dort heiß und feucht. Richtig.
4. Der Frühling ist Georges Lieblingsjahreszeit. Richtig.
5. Der Geburtstag von Hans ist im Herbst. Falsch.
6. Hans findet Georges Krawatte hässlich. Falsch.
7. Istanbul ist etwa 8.000 Kilometer von Berlin entfernt. Falsch.
8. Sabite hat mit Lorenzo über Istanbul gesprochen. Richtig.
9. Der Berliner Fernsehturm ist das höchste Gebäude in Deutschland. Richtig.
10. Von dort kann man den Reichstag und das Brandenburger Tor sehen. Richtig.

PERSONEN

George   Hans   Meline   Sabite

7

SABITE An dem Abend, als wir dich und Lorenzo im Restaurant gesehen haben. Ich stand auf, ging Richtung Toilette und kam an deinem Tisch vorbei.
MELINE Torsten war also überrascht?
SABITE Ja.
MELINE Das ist das Problem! Du hast es ihm nicht zuerst gesagt.

8

SABITE Das ist doch dumm.
MELINE Sabite. Männer können manchmal dumm sein. Liebst du ihn? Sabite?
SABITE Ich weiß nicht.

GEORGE Der Fernsehturm ist 365 Meter hoch! Von dort kann man den Reichstag und das Brandenburger Tor sehen! Hans, ist alles in Ordnung?
HANS Ja. Mir geht's gut.
GEORGE Dies ist das höchste Gebäude in ganz Deutschland.
HANS Ich weiß.

10

HANS Mir geht's gut. Genieß den Ausblick. Ich bleibe solange hier stehen. Weit weg vom Rand.
GEORGE Hey, ist das Sabite?
HANS Wo?
GEORGE Fühlst du dich besser, Kumpel? Lass uns auf den Turm gehen und von dort oben Berlin sehen.
HANS Wow.

Nützliche Ausdrücke

- **Wie bitte?**
  Excuse me?

- **dennoch**
  nevertheless

- **beeinflussen**
  to influence

- **feucht**
  moist

- **auswählen**
  to choose

- **ausprobieren**
  to try

- **Nein, also nicht auf diese Weise.**
  No, not like that.

- **weit**
  far

- **Du hast es ihm nicht zuerst gesagt.**
  You didn't tell him first.

- **Dies ist das höchste Gebäude in ganz Deutschland.**
  This is the tallest building in all of Germany.

- **genießen**
  to enjoy

- **Fühlst du dich besser, Kumpel?**
  Are you feeling better, buddy?

7A.1
- **Ich stand auf, ging Richtung Toilette und kam an deinem Tisch vorbei.**
  I got up, went towards the restroom, and stopped by your table.

7A.2
- **Milwaukee liegt am Lake Michigan.**
  Milwaukee is on Lake Michigan.

- **Wann hast du zum ersten Mal über die Idee gesprochen?**
  When was the first time you mentioned the idea?

---

2 **Zum Besprechen** Sprechen Sie mit den anderen Studenten in Ihrem Kurs und finden Sie heraus, wer im gleichen Monat Geburtstag hat. Wie ist das Wetter in diesem Monat? Besprechen Sie es mit einem Partner/einer Partnerin. Answers may vary.

Suggestion Tell students that in 1961, West Germany and Turkey signed a labor recruitment agreement which allowed Turkish citizens to move to Germany as guest workers (**Gastarbeiter**). Today, there are at least 3 million people of Turkish descent living in Germany.

3 **Vertiefung** Sabite möchte ein Semester lang in Istanbul studieren. Es ist das Heimatland (*country of origin*) von Faik, Sabites Vater. Finden Sie Informationen über Türken in Deutschland. Wie viele Türken leben in Deutschland? Wann sind sie nach Deutschland gekommen? Answers may vary.

Expansion Tell students that Berlin is home to the largest Turkish community outside of Turkey. There are some 300,000 people with Turkish roots living in Berlin.

More activities

vhlcentral   VM p. 13   Online activities

IM FOKUS

Windenergie Reading

> **TIPP**
>
> The **Deutsche Mark** (**DM** or **D-Mark**) was Germany's currency prior to the adoption of the **Euro** in 2002.

SCHLESWIG-HOLSTEIN LIEGT ZWISCHEN zwei Meeren, der Nordsee und der Ostsee. Dieses Bundesland ist relativ flach° und wegen der Nähe° zum Meer gibt es viel Wind. Schon seit 1982 investiert man hier immer mehr Geld in diese erneuerbare Energiequelle°.

Am Anfang waren es noch fünfzehn Windturbinen in einem Windpark in Braderup. Dreiunddreißig Privatbürger° finanzierten das Projekt mit einem Darlehen° von 12 Millionen DM (etwa 6 Millionen Euro).

Heute gibt es in Schleswig-Holstein über 3.600 Windturbinen. Beinahe die Hälfte des Strombedarfs° produziert man durch Windenergie in dem Bundesland. Aber Windturbinen stehen nicht nur auf dem Land. Seit 2009 kann man die Turbinen auch im Meer° finden. Hier, wo der Wind sehr stark bläst°, installiert man Turbinen in 30 Meter tiefem Wasser. Zwölf Turbinen produzieren bereits den Strom für etwa 50.000 Haushalte.

In Deutschland will man bis zum Jahr 2025 mit Windenergie 25% des Strombedarfs produzieren. 2017 gab es bereits 29.844 Windkraftanlagen in ganz Deutschland. Die Produktion von Strom mit Wind – aber auch mit Sonne, Wasser, Geothermie und Bioenergie – produziert weniger Stickstoff° im Vergleich° mit Atom-, Kohle- und Gaskraftwerken. Man braucht weniger Öl aus anderen Ländern. Und es gibt neue Arbeitsplätze° in Regionen wie Schleswig-Holstein.

Windenergie

	Deutschland	Österreich	Schweiz
Windkraftanlagen°:	29.844	1.313	37
Stromproduktion:	5.300 MW (Megawatt)	3.045 MW	75 MW
Anteil am Strombedarf:	18,8%	11%	0,2%

QUELLE: Bundesverband WindEnergie, IG Windkraft, Suisse Eole

flach *flat* **wegen der Nähe** *due to its closeness* **erneuerbare Energiequelle** *renewable energy source* **Privatbürger** *private citizens* **Darlehen** *loan* **Beinahe die Hälfte des Strombedarfs** *almost half of electricity requirements* **im Meer** *at sea* **bläst** *blows* **Stickstoff** *nitrogen* **Vergleich** *comparison* **Arbeitsplätze** *jobs* **Windkraftanlagen** *wind power plants*

ÜBUNGEN

1 **Im Fokus** Richtig oder falsch? Korrigieren Sie die falschen Aussagen. Diskutieren Sie dann die letzte Frage mit einem Partner/ einer Partnerin.

1. Schleswig-Holstein ist ideal für Windturbinen, weil es hohe Berge hat.
   Falsch. Dieses Bundesland ist ideal für Windenergie, weil es flach ist.
2. In Deutschland will man im Jahr 2025 ein Viertel des Strombedarfs durch Windenergie produzieren können. Richtig.
3. Wind- und Solarenergie sind umweltfreundlicher als Kohle- und Gaskraftwerke. Richtig.

Diskussion Was sind wichtige erneuerbare Energiequellen (energy sources) in Ihrem Land und wo findet man sie?

2 **Die deutschsprachige Welt** Richtig oder falsch? Korrigieren Sie die falschen Aussagen.

1. Im Planten un Blomen gibt es den größten japanischen Garten in Europa. Richtig.
2. Im Apothekergarten findet man wahrscheinlich viele Pflanzen, die für Menschen gesund sind. Richtig.
3. Der Planten un Blomen ist für kleine Kinder nicht so interessant wie für Erwachsene. Falsch. Für Kinder gibt es dort Aktivitäten.

Diskussion Wo kann man in Ihrer Stadt oder Region einen Botanischen Garten besuchen? Beschreiben Sie ihn.

Deutsch im Alltag Ask students: **Welcher Ausdruck passt am besten zu dem heutigen Wetter?**

DEUTSCH IM ALLTAG

Wetterausdrücke

Hundewetter	terrible weather
Kaiserwetter	beautiful, sunny weather
Schmuddelwetter	dreary, wet weather
Es schüttet wie aus Eimern!	It's pouring buckets!
Petrus meint es gut!	The weather's great!

DIE DEUTSCHSPRACHIGE WELT

Planten un Blomen

Im Sommer kann man im Zentrum Hamburgs den berühmten Park Planten un Blomen besuchen. Hier gibt es einen alten Botanischen Garten. Außerdem finden Besucher den größten Japanischen Garten Europas in dem Park. Die einzelnen Gärten haben verschiedene Themen: der Rosengarten, der Apothekergarten° und die Tropengewächshäuser°. Im Musikpavillon finden im Sommer Konzerte statt° und man kann Wasserlichtkonzerte bewundern°. Kinder können auf Spielplätzen oder der Trampolinanlage spielen und auf Ponys reiten.

Suggestion Point out that the name of the park, **Planten un Blomen**, is **Plattdeutsch**. Have students translate the phrase into **Hochdeutsch**.

Apothekergarten apothecary's garden
Tropengewächshäuser tropical greenhouses
finden... statt take place **bewundern** admire

PORTRÄT

Klima in Deutschland

Das Wetter in Deutschland ist gemäßigt°: Im Winter ist es nicht sehr kalt und im Sommer nicht sehr warm. Im Durchschnitt° ist die Jahrestemperatur 8,1° C. Im Januar liegt die Durchschnittstemperatur bei -0,4° C und im Juli bei 16,9° C. Im Jahr fallen etwa 790 Millimeter Regen, besonders viel fällt im Juni. Die absolute Höchsttemperatur gab es 2003 in Karlsruhe und in Freiburg: 40,2° C. Freiburg liegt im Schwarzwald und gilt als° wärmste und sonnigste Stadt Deutschlands. Man kann hier jedes Jahr 1650 Sonnenstunden genießen. Die absolute Tiefsttemperatur gab es 2001 am Funtensee in den Bayrischen Alpen: -45,9° C.

Suggestion Point out that the German annual average of **8,1° C** is equivalent to 46.58˚ F, while the extreme temperatures of **-45,9° C** and **40,2° C** correspond to -50.62˚ F and 104.36˚ F, respectively.

gemäßigt moderate **Durchschnitt** average **gilt als** is regarded as

∞ IM INTERNET

Finden Sie einen Plan von Planten un Blomen in Hamburg. Welche Gärten möchten Sie besuchen? Machen Sie eine Liste und planen Sie eine Tour.

Find out more at **vhlcentral.com**.

---

3 **Porträt** Richtig oder falsch? Korrigieren Sie die falschen Aussagen. Diskutieren Sie dann die letzte Frage mit einem Partner/ einer Partnerin.

1. Deutschlands Klima produziert oft extrem arktische Winter.
Falsch. Der Winter in Deutschland ist nicht sehr kalt.

2. In Deutschland regnet es oft im Juni. **Richtig.**

3. Die Stadt mit den meisten sonnigen Tagen ist Karlsruhe.
Falsch. Freiburg hat die meisten sonnigen Tage.

Diskussion Welche Jahreszeit haben Sie am liebsten? Warum lieben Sie diese Jahreszeit? Welche Kleidung tragen Sie dann? Was machen Sie in dieser Jahreszeit?

4 **Energie** Schreiben Sie einen kurzen Text über alternative Energiequellen. Gibt es an Ihrem Wohnort genug Sonne und Wind? Ist für Sie ein Atomkraftwerk eine gute Alternative oder zu riskant? Lesen Sie Ihren Text der Gruppe vor.

Suggestion Write a few prompts on the board. Ex.: **Wir sollen mehr Windturbinen bauen und Thermalenergie benutzen. In Ohio haben wir nicht so viele sonnige Tage, also ist Sonnenenergie nicht praktisch.**

More activities

vhlcentral   Online activities

7A.1

Teaching Tip You might want to assign the grammar tutorial **6A.1** Separable and inseparable prefix verbs (*Präteritum*) on the Supersite for students to watch before they come to class.

QUERVERWEIS

See **4A.3** to review **Präsens** of separable and inseparable prefix verbs.

See **6B.2** to review the **Perfekt** of verbs with prefixes. To review the difference between **Perfekt** and **Präteritum**, see **6B.1**.

Suggestion Have students brainstorm a list of separable and inseparable prefix verbs they've already learned. Have them write sentences to demonstrate how each type of verb functions in the present and perfect tenses.

QUERVERWEIS

To review the formation of the **Präteritum**, see **6A.1**. See **Appendix A** for a complete list of strong verbs with their principal parts.

Suggestion Review the meaning of these verbs, making sure students recall which prefixes are separable and which are not.

Separable and inseparable prefix verbs (*Präteritum*)

Grammar Tutorial

Startblock Both separable and inseparable prefix verbs can be used in the **Präteritum** to describe past events.

Ich **stand auf**, ging Richtung Toilette und **kam** an deinem Tisch **vorbei**.

Opa Otto **bereitete** die Weihnachtsgans **zu**. George **überraschte** ihn und...

- In the **Präteritum**, just like the **Präsens**, some prefixes are always attached to the verb, and others can be separated from it. When using a separable prefix verb in the **Präteritum**, move the prefix to the end of the sentence or clause.

Jan **verbrachte** den Sommer in der Schweiz.
*Jan **spent** the summer in Switzerland.*

Einmal **brachten** wir unseren Hund zur Schule **mit**.
*Once we **brought** our dog to school.*

Der Lehrer **erklärte** die Aufgabe.
*The teacher **explained** the assignment.*

Jans Schwester **rief** ihn zu seinem Geburtstag **an**.
*Jan's sister **called** him on his birthday.*

- You learned in **6B.2** that verbs with prefixes can be either strong, weak, or mixed. The **Präteritum** of a verb with a prefix is the same as the **Präteritum** of its base verb, but with the prefix added to the front of the conjugated verb, if it is inseparable, or to the end of the clause, if it is separable.

Präteritum of separable and inseparable prefix verbs			
weak verbs			
kaufen →	kaufte	verkaufen →	verkaufte
schauen (*to look*) →	schaute	anschauen (*to watch, look at*) →	schaute an
strong verbs			
finden →	fand	erfinden (*to invent*) →	erfand
sprechen →	sprach	besprechen (*to discuss*) →	besprach
sehen →	sah	fernsehen (*to watch TV*) →	sah fern
mixed verbs			
bringen →	brachte	mitbringen →	brachte mit
		verbringen (*to spend (time)*) →	verbrachte
kennen →	kannte	erkennen (*to recognize*) →	erkannte

Die Lehrerin **schaute** die Schüler **an**.
*The teacher **looked at** the students.*

Ich **erkannte** meine Tante nicht auf
dem alten Foto.
*I didn't **recognize** my aunt in
the old photo.*

Wir **sahen** als Kinder immer am
Samstagmorgen **fern**.
*When we were kids, we always **watched TV**
on Saturday mornings.*

Wer **erfand** das Internet?
*Who **invented** the Internet?*

- Remember that the prefix of a separable prefix verb is always stressed, while the prefix of an inseparable prefix verb is never stressed.

Als wir am Freitag **ausgingen**, regnete es
noch nicht.
*When we **went out** on Friday, it wasn't
raining yet.*

Wir **bestellten** zwei Pizzas zum
Abendessen.
*We **ordered** two pizzas
for dinner.*

- In a negative sentence, put **nicht** before the separable prefix.

Erik **rief** mich gestern **nicht an**.
*Erik **didn't** call me yesterday.*

Meine Mitbewohnerin **räumte** ihre Sachen **nicht auf**.
*My roommate **didn't** pick up her things.*

- When you talk about past events using a modal and a verb with a prefix, put the modal verb in the **Präteritum**. The prefixed verb goes at the end of the sentence in the infinitive form.

Frau Müller **musste** den kaputten
Regenschirm **umtauschen**.
*Mrs. Müller **had to exchange** the
broken umbrella.*

Niklas **wollte** sein altes
Fahrrad **verkaufen**.
*Niklas **wanted to sell** his
old bicycle.*

Suggestion Before they begin the **Jetzt sind Sie dran!** activity, verify that students know the meanings of each of the verbs, and have them identify which verbs have separable prefixes and which do not. Do the first few items as a class.

More
activities

vhlcentral

WB
pp. 93–94

LM
p. 60

Online
activities

 Jetzt sind Sie dran! **Ergänzen Sie die Tabelle mit den Verben im Präteritum.**

Infinitiv	Präteritum		Infinitiv	Präteritum
1. bedeuten	*bedeutete*	7.	wegräumen	räumte weg
2. einschlafen	schlief ein	8.	wiederholen	wiederholte
3. beschreiben	beschrieb	9.	besuchen	besuchte
4. zurückkommen	kam zurück	10.	entdecken	entdeckte
5. umziehen	zog um	11.	mitbringen	brachte mit
6. erkennen	erkannte	12.	verstehen	verstand

Anwendung

1 **Was fehlt?** Ergänzen Sie die Sätze mit den richtigen Formen der Verben im Präteritum.

> **BEISPIEL** Frau Behrens __*rief*__ ihre Tochter jeden Tag __*an*__. (anrufen)

1. Im Sand __entdeckten__ wir eine alte Halskette. (entdecken)
2. Wann __fing__ der Regen __an__? (anfangen)
3. Ich __verkaufte__ mein Auto vor einem Monat. (verkaufen)

4. Meine Großeltern __sahen__ immer nach dem Essen __fern__. (fernsehen)
5. Wir __besuchten__ unsere Cousinen oft im Sommer. (besuchen)
6. Markus __verstand__ als Schüler nichts von Mathematik. (verstehen)

2 **Was für ein Tag** Ergänzen Sie die Sätze mit den richtigen Verben aus der Liste im Präteritum.

> | aufräumen | besuchen | erklären |
> | aufwachen | einkaufen | verkaufen |

> **BEISPIEL** Tobias __*wachte*__ um acht Uhr __*auf*__.

1. Michael __kaufte__ fürs Abendessen __ein__.

2. Am Samstag __besuchte__ Julian seine Schwester in Heidelberg.

3. Frau Hölzel __erklärte__ den Schülern die Aufgabe.

4. Ich __räumte__ mein Zimmer __auf__.

5. Wir __verkauften__ gestern viel Currywurst.

3 **Noch einmal** Schreiben Sie die Sätze im Präteritum. Benutzen Sie dabei das Modalverb in Klammern.

> **BEISPIEL** Wir tauschten unser Geld auf der Bank um. (wollen)
> *Wir wollten unser Geld auf der Bank umtauschen.*

1. Thomas sah den ganzen Morgen fern. (wollen)
   Thomas wollte den ganzen Morgen fernsehen.
2. Wir bereiteten ein schönes Essen vor. (wollen) Wir wollten ein schönes Essen vorbereiten.
3. Erik rief seine Freundin nicht an. (dürfen)
   Erik durfte seine Freundin nicht anrufen.

4. Herr Roth verkaufte sein Auto nicht. (können) Herr Roth konnte sein Auto nicht verkaufen.
5. Die Lehrerin wiederholte den Satz. (müssen)
   Die Lehrerin musste den Satz wiederholen.
6. Ich brachte meinen Computer in den Urlaub mit. (dürfen)
   Ich durfte meinen Computer in den Urlaub mitbringen.

Kommunikation

4 Eine Überraschungsfeier Lukas und Lena planten letzten Herbst eine Überraschungsfeier für ihre Eltern. Bilden Sie mit einem Partner / einer Partnerin zu jedem Bild einen Satz im Präteritum. Answers may vary.

BEISPIEL Lukas und Lena
bereiteten eine
Überraschungsfeier
für ihre Eltern vor.

1. Lukas und Lena
kauften Sachen für die
Feier ein.

2. Lena
lud viele Verwandte und
Freunde ein.

3. Die Gäste
kamen am Nachmittag an.

4. Frau Braun
brachte eine
Schokoladentorte mit.

5. Die Großeltern
überraschten Svens und
Lenas Eltern mit einer
Reise nach Amerika.

5 Historische Personen Bilden Sie mit einem Partner / einer Partnerin logische Fragen im Präteritum. Wechseln Sie sich bei den Fragen und Antworten ab.

BEISPIEL

S1: *Wer entdeckte die Stadt Troja?*
S2: *Heinrich Schliemann.*

Wer...

entdecken / die Allgemeine (*General*) Relativitätstheorie

erklären / die genetischen Regeln (*rules*)

erfinden / den Buchdruck (*printing press*)

bekommen / einen Nobelpreis für Literatur

> Gregor Johann Mendel
> Günter Grass
> Heinrich Schliemann
> Albert Einstein
> Johannes Gutenberg

6 Eine spannende Geschichte Schreiben Sie mit einem Partner / einer Partnerin eine Geschichte. Benutzen Sie das Präteritum und mindestens (*at least*) drei Elemente aus der Liste. Lesen Sie Ihre Geschichte im Kurs vor. Answers will vary.

BEISPIEL Es war eine dunkle und stürmische Nacht.
Ich schlief schlecht und stand um drei Uhr nachts wieder auf.
Ich sah aus dem Fenster hinaus...

den Regenmantel anziehen	hinausgehen
aufräumen	weggehen
aufstehen	das Handy vergessen
Angst bekommen	die Orientierung verlieren
wieder einschlafen	(nicht) verstehen

5 Partner Chat You can also assign activity 5 on the Supersite. Students work in pairs to record the activity online. The pair's recorded conversation will appear in your gradebook.

Sample answers:
Wer entdeckte die Allgemeine Relativitätstheorie?
Albert Einstein
Wer erklärte die genetischen Regeln? Gregor Johann Mendel
Wer erfand den Buchdruck? Johannes Gutenberg
Wer bekam einen Nobelpreis für Literatur? Günter Grass

7A.2

Prepositions of location
Prepositions in set phrases

 Grammar Tutorial

Startblock When describing locations, and in certain fixed expressions, many German prepositions are used in ways that differ from their English counterparts.

Milwaukee liegt **am Lake Michigan**.

Hat Sabite **über mich** gesprochen?

Suggestion English speakers may find phrases like **auf der Post**, **auf der Bank**, and **auf dem Markt** counter-intuitive. Encourage students to simply memorize these phrases as "sound bites."

QUERVERWEIS

See **5B.3** to review two-way prepositions.

Suggestion Remind students that the expression **zu Hause**, which they learned in, **4B.2** is an exception to the general rule of using **in** with enclosed spaces.

Suggestion Point out that most masculine and neuter country names are directly preceded by **in** with no article, but there are a few that always take a definite article, and are thus preceded by **im** in the dative, ex. **Er lebt im Libanon.**

ACHTUNG

Note that the idea of an enclosed space includes the radio, television, or Internet: **Das habe ich im Radio gehört; Das können wir im Internet finden.**

Suggestion Remind students that they have already seen the phrase **Im Internet** in the activity boxes at the end of each **Kultur** section.

QUERVERWEIS

You will learn more about using prepositions with geographical locations in **10B.1**.

Prepositions of location

- In **5B.3** you learned to use two-way prepositions with the dative to indicate location and with the accusative to show movement toward a destination.

  Neben dem Schreibtisch steht ein großes Bücherregal.
  *There's a big bookcase **next to the desk**.*

  Stell den Stuhl bitte **neben den Tisch**.
  *Please put the chair **next to the table**.*

- Use **auf** with the dative to indicate that something is located on a horizontal surface or to describe a location in a public building or open space.

  Deine Bücher liegen **auf dem Tisch**.
  *Your books are **on the table**.*

  Ich war gestern **auf der Bank**.
  *I was **at the bank** yesterday.*

  Greta hat schöne Blumen **auf dem Markt** gekauft.
  *Greta bought beautiful flowers **at the market**.*

- Use **an** with the dative to indicate a location *on* or *at* a border, wall, or body of water.

  An der Wand hängt ein schöner Kalender.
  *There's a nice calendar hanging **on the wall**.*

  Am Strand war es heute kühl und windig.
  *It was cool and windy **at the beach** today.*

- Use **in** with the dative to indicate a location *on* or *in* an enclosed space.

  Die Sonnenbrille ist **in meiner Handtasche**.
  *The sunglasses are **in my purse**.*

  Die Kinder spielen gern **im Park**.
  *The kids like to play **in the park**.*

  Ich wohne **in der Joachimstraße**.
  *I live **on Joachim Street**.*

- To indicate location in a country whose name is feminine or plural, use **in** with the dative form of the definite article, plus the country name.

  Wagner wohnte **in der Schweiz**.
  *Wagner lived **in Switzerland**.*

  Meine Mutter ist jetzt **in den USA**.
  *My mother is **in the U.S.** right now.*

- In **4B.3** you learned that **bei** is always used with the dative case. Use **bei** with a noun referring to a person or business to indicate a location at that person's home or at that place of business.

  Ich kaufe gern **bei Aldi** ein.
  *I like shopping **at Aldi's**.*

  Anna war gestern **beim Friseur**.
  *Anna was **at the hairdresser's** yesterday.*

Als Student wohnte Nils im Sommer **bei seinen Eltern**.
*When he was a student, Nils lived **with his parents** during the summer.*

Heute Abend spielen wir **bei mir** Karten.
*We're playing cards **at my place** tonight.*

- You can also use **bei** to mean *near* a location or *in the presence of* a condition.

Das Restaurant liegt **bei Wilhelmshaven**.
*The restaurant is **near Wilhelmshaven**.*

Bei schönem Wetter gehen wir gern spazieren.
*We like to go for walks **when the weather is nice**.*

Prepositions in set phrases

- Certain combinations of verbs and prepositions have specific, idiomatic meanings. The prepositions in these fixed expressions are always followed by the same case, regardless of whether the verb they are associated with indicates location or movement.

Jasmin **erzählte** uns **von ihren Problemen**.
*Jasmin **told** us **about her problems**.*

Max muss einen Brief **an seine Tante schreiben**.
*Max has to **write** a letter **to his aunt**.*

- Use the *dative* after the following set phrases.

Verb phrases with the dative	
Angst haben vor	to be afraid of
arbeiten an	to work on
erzählen von	to talk about; to tell a story about
fragen nach	to ask about
handeln von	to be about; to have to do with
helfen bei	to help with
träumen von	to dream of

Meine Nichte **hat Angst vor** Hunden.
*My niece **is afraid of** dogs.*

Herr Weiss **arbeitet an** einem neuen Buch.
*Mister Weiss **is working on** a new book.*

- Use the *accusative* after the following expressions.

Verb phrases with the accusative	
antworten auf	to answer
denken an	to think about
schreiben an	to write to
sprechen/reden über	to talk about
warten auf	to wait for

Wir haben lange **auf** den Bus **gewartet**.
*We **waited** a long time **for** the bus.*

Antworte bitte **auf** die Frage.
*Please **answer** the question.*

Jetzt sind Sie dran!   **Wählen Sie die passenden Präpositionen.**

1. Wir haben (mit / (auf) / über) dem Markt Obst gekauft.
2. Mein Hund hat Angst (über / von / (vor)) Donner und Blitz.
3. Nach dem Sturm lag viel Hagel ((auf) / an / in) der Straße.
4. Sara verbringt ihren Sommer (mit / aus / (in)) der Türkei.
5. Wir helfen unserer Mutter ((bei) / vor / in) der Hausarbeit.
6. ((An) / Mit / Unter) der Berliner Mauer gibt es viel Graffiti.
7. Du hast nicht (über / bei / (auf)) meine Frage geantwortet.
8. Wohnt dein Bruder immer noch (an / (bei) / auf) dir?
9. Hast du schon (bei / (an) / nach) Oma geschrieben?
10. Sophia hat mir (mit / nach / (von)) ihrem Wochenende erzählt.

Anwendung

1 **Präpositionen** Ergänzen Sie die passenden Präpositionen.

BEISPIEL ___Bei___ schlechtem Wetter werde ich oft müde.

1. Wir campen jeden Sommer ___auf___ dem Campingplatz.
2. Maria reitet oft ihr Pferd ___im___ Park.
3. Gehst du oft ___bei___ Aldi einkaufen?
4. Cuxhaven liegt ___an___ der Nordsee.
5. Unsere Katze sitzt gern ___auf___ dem Balkon und schaut den Vögeln zu.

2 **Was fehlt?** Ergänzen Sie die Lücken mit den richtigen Präpositionen.

BEISPIEL Meine Schlüssel sind nicht ___in___ meiner Tasche.

1. Meine Hunde haben immer Angst ___vor___ einem Sturm.

2. Der Film handelt ___von___ einer Naturkatastrophe.

3. Im Sommer mieten wir ein kleines Haus ___an___ einem Strand.

4. Die Frau fragt den Verkäufer ___nach___ dem Preis.

5. Elias arbeitet ___an___ seiner Hausaufgabe.

3 **Kombinieren** Ergänzen Sie die passenden Präpositionen und wählen Sie dann die beste Antwort auf jede Frage.

___a___ 1. Hast du das ___im___ Internet gefunden?

___d___ 2. Warum hat deine Mutter Angst ___vor___ Hunden?

___b___ 3. Oma, erzähl mir bitte ___von___ deiner Kindheit.

___e___ 4. Bleibt Daniel die ganzen Semesterferien ___bei___ seinen Eltern?

___c___ 5. Arbeitet Greta schon ___an___ ihrem Referat?

a. Nein, ich habe es im Radio gehört.

b. Ach Kindchen, das war vor so langer Zeit.

c. Ja, sie hat schon damit angefangen.

d. Ich weiß nicht, aber sie mag Katzen.

e. Nein, er macht einen Sprachkurs in Spanien für vier Wochen.

4 **Video Virtual Chat** You can also assign activity 4 on the Supersite. Students record individual responses that appear in your gradebook.

4 **Fragen** Stellen Sie einem Partner / einer Partnerin diese Fragen. Answers will vary.

1. An wen schreibst du oft E-Mails?
2. Worüber redest du mit deinen Freunden?
3. Wo verbringst du deine Semesterferien?
4. Wo kaufst du deine Lebensmittel ein?
5. Wovon träumst du?
6. Wovor hast du Angst?

Kommunikation

5 **Kettenreaktion** Sagen Sie abwechselnd, wo diese Dinge in Ihrem Klassenzimmer sind. Answers will vary.

> **BEISPIEL**
> **S1:** *die Uhr*
> **S2:** *Die Uhr hängt an der Wand.*
> **S3:** *der Stuhl*
> **S4:** *Oliver sitzt auf dem Stuhl.*

der Boden	die Lampen	die Tafel
das Buch	das Poster	die Uhr
der Computer	der Stuhl	die Wand

6 **Was und wo ist das?** Wählen Sie ein Objekt aus dem Bild und beschreiben Sie seine Lage (*location*). Ihr Partner / Ihre Partnerin muss erraten, welchen Ort oder Objekt Sie beschreiben. Answers will vary.

> **BEISPIEL**
> **S1:** *Ein blaues Auto steht davor.*
> **S2:** *Ist es der Supermarkt?*
> **S1:** *Ja.*

das Café · das Hotel · die Bibliothek · das Restaurant · die Bank · das Kino · das Museum · der Supermarkt

7 **Was kann man wo machen?** Entscheiden Sie (*Decide*) mit einem Partner / einer Partnerin, wo Sie die folgenden Aktivitäten machen können. Answers will vary.

> **BEISPIEL**
> **S1:** *Wo kann ich ein Buch kaufen?*
> **S2:** *Das kannst du im Buchgeschäft machen.*

Wo kann ich... ?	Das kannst du... machen.
eine Tasse Kaffee bestellen	beim Bäcker
Obst und Gemüse kaufen	auf der Bank
leckere Brötchen kaufen	in der Bibliothek
in der Sonne liegen	im Café
ein Bild von Picasso sehen	im Internetcafé
ein Wörterbuch finden	im Museum
Geld bekommen	am Strand
im Internet surfen	im Supermarkt

8 **Persönliche Fragen** Machen Sie ein Interview mit einem Partner / einer Partnerin und finden Sie ein paar persönliche Informationen heraus. Präsentieren Sie Ihre Interviews im Kurs. Answers will vary.

1. Hast du Angst vor: ___ Gewitter ___ Hunden? ___ schlechten Noten?

2. Redest du gern über: ___ Politik? ___ Musik? ___ Sport?

3. Arbeitest du heute an: ___ einem Referat? ___ deinen Hausaufgaben? ___ nichts?

4. Denkst du oft an: ___ deine Freunde? ___ deine Kurse? ___ deine Familie?

5. Handeln deine Träume von: ___ deiner Kindheit? ___ deinem Leben jetzt? ___ anderen Situationen?

Wiederholung

1 In der Stadt
Wechseln Sie sich mit einem Partner / einer Partnerin ab: Beschreiben Sie, wo Yusuf gestern in der Stadt war. Sample answers are provided.

▶ **BEISPIEL** *Zuerst war Yusuf auf der Post. Dann war er...*

2 Suggestion Remind students that in sentences beginning with a time expression, the conjugated verb will appear in 2nd position, *before* the subject. Provide model answers that say what you like to do.

1 Suggestion Do the first few sentences together as a class. Remind students that since they will be talking about Yusuf's *location*, they will use the dative with any two-way prepositions.

1. Dann war er auf der Bank.

2. Dann hat er im Restaurant gegessen.

3. Im Park hat er in der Sonne gelegen.

4. In der Metzgerei hat er Wurst gekauft.

5. In der Bäckerei hat er frisches Brot gekauft.

2 Bei so einem Wetter
Fragen Sie Ihren Partner / Ihre Partnerin, was er/sie bei verschiedenem Wetter macht. Answers may vary.

BEISPIEL

S1: *Was machst du bei windigem Wetter?*
S2: *Bei windigem Wetter gehe ich spazieren.*

1. windig
2. sonnig
3. schlecht
4. kalt
5. heiß
6. schön

3 Hausarbeit
Beschreiben Sie mit einem Partner / einer Partnerin, wie Sie und Ihre Geschwister (*siblings*) am Wochenende die Wohnung putzten. Benutzen Sie Vokabeln aus der Liste. Answers will vary.

BEISPIEL

S1: *Am Wochenende mussten wir viel Hausarbeit machen.*
S2: *Im Bad putzte Eric die Toilette und die Badewanne.*

abstauben	Müll rausbringen
aufräumen	Geschirr spülen
fegen	staubsaugen
Bett machen	Wäsche waschen
putzen	wischen

3 Partner Chat You can also assign activity 3 on the Supersite. Students work in pairs to record the activity online. The pair's recorded conversation will appear in your gradebook.

4 Arbeitsblatt
Sie bekommen von Ihrem Professor / Ihrer Professorin ein Arbeitsblatt mit verschiedenen Aktivitäten. Wer in der Gruppe hat diese Aktivitäten gemacht? Answers will vary.

BEISPIEL

S1: *Hast du deinen Freunden von einem guten Buch erzählt?*
S2: *Ja, ich habe meinen Freunden von einem guten Buch erzählt.*

5 Diskutieren und kombinieren
Tauschen Sie mit Ihrem Partner / Ihrer Partnerin Informationen aus: Was machten Paul und Sara gestern? Füllen Sie die Tabelle für Ihren Partner / Ihre Partnerin und sich selber (*yourself*) aus. Answers will vary.

BEISPIEL

S1: *Was hat Sara am Donnerstag gemacht?*
S2: *Sie hat bei A&P eingekauft.*

6 Als ich zehn war
Erzählen Sie Ihrem Partner / Ihrer Partnerin, was Sie machten, als Sie zehn Jahre alt waren. Was machten Sie im Frühling, im Sommer, im Herbst und im Winter?

BEISPIEL

S1: *Was hast du mit zehn im Herbst gemacht?*
S2: *Im Herbst bin ich Fahrrad gefahren. Im Winter...*

Video

Wetterbericht

1 **Vorbereitung** Answers will vary.

1. Wie ist das Wetter heute?

2. Mögen Sie lieber warmes oder kaltes Wetter? Warum?

ZDF heute Christa Stipp
Meteorologin

Der Wetterbericht im Fernsehen

Das Klima in Deutschland ist gemäßigt°. Der Westen Deutschlands ist von atlantischen Einflüssen° geprägt°, und es gibt regenreiche Winter und mäßig warme Sommer. Im Osten Deutschlands gibt es große Temperaturunterschiede° mit heißen Sommern und kalten Wintern. Im Norden Deutschlands zeigt sich der Einfluß der Nordsee. Die Winter sind mild, aber mit starken Stürmen und die Sommer sind regenreich. An der Ostsee jedoch° sind die Sommer trocken und sehr heiß.

gemäßigt *moderate* **Einflüssen** *influences* **geprägt** *shaped* **Temperaturunterschiede** *temperature differences* **jedoch** *however*

Nützliche Ausdrücke

die Böe,-n	*gust of wind*
das Hoch	*high pressure*
die Luft	*air*
das Tief	*low pressure*
die Wetteraussicht, -en	*weather forecast*

Richtig oder falsch Sehen Sie sich das Video über den Wetterbericht an und entscheiden Sie dann, ob die folgenden Aussagen richtig oder falsch sind. Korrigieren Sie danach die falschen Aussagen.

	Richtig	Falsch	
1. Tief Igor bringt mildere Luft.	✓	☐	
2. An der Ostsee steigt die Hochwassergefahr.	☐	✓	Die Hochwassergefahr steigt im Schwarzwald und im Allgäu.
3. Zwischen Schwarzwald und Allgäu regnet es morgen den ganzen Tag.	☐	✓	Es ist richtig sonnig.
4. Am Montag wird es in Bayern und Baden Württemberg viel kühler.	✓	☐	

Expansion Distribute a list of additional questions about the video. Have the students watch again and jot down the answers to the questions. You may want to assign only one or two questions to each student. Discuss the answers as a class. **Wann steigt die Hochwassergefahr und warum? Wo regnet es morgen und wo nicht? Wo wird es am Sonntag richtig warm? Wieviel Grad hat es dort?**

3 **Diskussion** Diskutieren Sie die folgenden Fragen mit einem Partner / einer Partnerin. Answers will vary.

1. Was trägt die Meteorologin im Video? Passt das zum Wetter? Was tragen Sie bei Sonnenschein, Regen oder Schnee?

2. Was machen Sie gern bei Regenwetter? Und bei Sonnenschein? Und im Schnee?

Präsentation Vergleichen Sie das Klima Ihres Landes mit dem Klima in Deutschland. Welche Region in Deutschland ist der Stadt, in der Sie leben oder aus der Sie kommen am ähnlichsten (*most similar to*)? Schreiben Sie einen kurzen Absatz und lesen Sie ihn im Kurs vor. Answers will vary.

More activities

vhlcentral

Online activities

Reisen

 Vocabulary Tools

Wortschatz

am Flughafen	**at the airport**
der Abflug	departure
die Ankunft	arrival
die Businessklasse	business class
der Flug, ⸚e	flight
das Flugticket, -s	ticket
das Gepäck	luggage
der Koffer, -	suitcase
der Passagier, -e	passenger
die Passkontrolle, -n	passport control
der Personalausweis, -e	ID card
die Reise, -n	trip
das Reisebüro, -s	travel agency
die Touristenklasse	economy class
die Verspätung, -en	delay
das Visum (*pl.* die Visa)	visa
der Zoll	customs
fliegen	**to fly**
das Ausland	abroad
pünktlich	on time
die Ferien	**vacation**
die Kreuzfahrt, -en	cruise
der Skiurlaub, -e	ski vacation
packen	**to pack**
übernachten	to spend the night
Unterkünfte	**accommodations**
der Fahrstuhl, ⸚e	elevator
der Gast, ⸚e	(hotel) guest
das (Fünf-Sterne-)Hotel	(five-star) hotel
die Jugendherberge, -n	youth hostel
der Schlüssel, -	key
der Zimmerservice	room service
abbrechen (bricht... ab)	to cancel
buchen	to make a (hotel) reservation
voll besetzt	**fully occupied**

Suggestion Model correct pronunciation of **Passagier**. Point out that the **g** is soft.

Expansion Ask students: **Fliegen Sie gerne? Warum? Warum nicht?** Have them brainstorm a list of things they associate with flying.

der Ausgang, ⸚e
exit

Er liest eine Karte.
He is reading a map.

der Strand, ⸚e
beach

Sonne und Meer

das Meer, -e
ocean

die Reisenden (*pl.*)
(*sing.* der Reisende)
traveler

die Bordkarte, -n

die Zeitung, -en

Sport

das Handgepäck

Es landet. (landen)
It is landing.

Es fliegt ab. (abfliegen)
It is taking off (departing).

das Flugzeug, -e

Sie machen Urlaub.
They are going on a vacation.

Sie stehen Schlange.
They are standing in line.

Die Welt

ACHTUNG

To say *highway map* in German, use **die Landkarte**; for *city map* use **der Stadtplan**. A GPS system is called **das Navi**.

Anwendung

Expansion Have students write and act out short dialogues that take place at an airport, using at least six vocabulary words from this lesson.

1 **Vergleiche** Ergänzen Sie die Vergleiche mit dem richtigen Wort.

1. das Hotel : der Gast :: das Flugzeug : (der Passagier) / der Familienstand)
2. heimkommen : ausgehen :: ankommen : (abfliegen) / aufstehen)
3. früh : spät :: frei : (besorgt / besetzt))
4. buchen : die Reise :: packen : (der Koffer)/ der Keller)
5. das Zimmer : der Schlüssel :: das Ausland : (das Seminar / das Visum))
6. der Skiurlaub : die Alpen :: die Kreuzfahrt : (das Meer)/ der Park)

2 **Kategorien** Schreiben Sie die Wörter aus der Liste in die passenden Kategorien. Answers may vary slightly. **2** **Expansion** Have students add at least one additional word to each category.

die Bordkarte	die Kreuzfahrt	das Reisebüro
das Hotel	die Passkontrolle	der Tourist
die Jugendherberge	der Personalausweis	der Zimmerservice

Unterkunft	**Flughafen**	**Urlaub**
die Jugendherberge	die Bordkarte	das Hotel
das Hotel	der Personalausweis	die Kreuzfahrt
der Zimmerservice	der Tourist	der Tourist
der Personalausweis	die Passkontrolle	das Reisebüro

3 **Hören Sie zu** Welche Dinge hat ein Fluggast logischerweise bei sich?

	Logisch	Unlogisch		Logisch	Unlogisch
1.	✓	☐	4.	☐	✓
2.	☐	✓	5.	☐	✓
3.	✓	☐	6.	✓	☐

3 **Expansion** Ask students additional questions about traveling by plane: **Mit wie vielen Koffern reisen Sie? Warum muss man beim Einchecken den Ausweis zeigen? Warum haben Flugzeuge Verspätung?**

4 **Kombinationen** Kombinieren Sie die Wörter mit ihren Definitionen.

c 1. der Reisende
d 2. der Zoll
f 3. die Verspätung
e 4. die Businessklasse
b 5. die Jugendherberge
a 6. der Pass

a. den braucht man für eine Reise ins Ausland
b. hier kann man billig übernachten
c. eine Person macht eine Reise
d. hier kontrolliert man Importe aus dem Ausland
e. hier sitzt man im Flugzeug mit allem Komfort
f. nicht pünktlich ankommen

5 **Ansagen** Hören Sie die Ansagen (*announcements*) an und entscheiden Sie, welche Ansage am besten zu welchem Satz passt.

Ansage 4 1. Die Passagiere fliegen nach Russland.
Ansage 5 2. Das Flugzeug ist gerade gelandet.
Ansage 1 3. Der Check-in für Air France ist im Terminal 1.
Ansage 3 4. Der Flug nach Hamburg fliegt bald ab.
Ansage 2 5. Die Passagiere kommen mit Verspätung in Rom an.

5 **Suggestion** Students may need to hear the recording several times in order to complete the exercise.

Kommunikation

Reisen Beantworten Sie die Fragen mit ganzen Sätzen. Vergleichen Sie dann Ihre Antworten mit den Antworten Ihres Partners / Ihrer Partnerin. Answers will vary.

1. In welcher Jahreszeit machen Sie gern Urlaub? Warum?
2. Mit wem reisen Sie nicht gern? Warum?
3. Was bringen Sie auf eine Kreuzfahrt nach Europa mit?
4. Was packen Sie normalerweise in Ihr Handgepäck?
5. Wo haben Sie schon Urlaub gemacht?
6. Wohin möchten Sie gern reisen? Warum?

6 Suggestion Have students share their answers to items 5 and 6 with the class.

6 Video Virtual Chat You can also assign activity 5 on the Supersite. Students record individual responses that appear in your gradebook.

7 Diskutieren und kombinieren Ihr Professor / Ihre Professorin gibt Ihnen verschiedene Blätter mit Durchsagen. Fragen Sie Ihren Partner / Ihre Partnerin nach den fehlenden Informationen und wechseln Sie sich dabei ab. Answers will vary.

7 Suggestion Before beginning the activity, clarify the meaning of any unfamiliar vocabulary and practice pronunciation of the longer words.

BEISPIEL

S1: *Wer kann zum Ausgang gehen?*
S2: *Nur Passagiere mit Bordkarten.*

Beschreibungen Schreiben Sie mit einem Partner / einer Partnerin eine Beschreibung (*description*) von jedem (*each*) Bild. Lesen Sie danach einem anderen Paar Ihre Beschreibung vor. Das andere Paar soll erraten, welches Bild zu welcher Beschreibung passt. Answers will vary.

BEISPIEL

S1: *Es ist Abend. Ein Mädchen sitzt auf einem Koffer.*
S1: *Sie liest Zeitung.*
S3: *Das ist Bild 1.*

8 Suggestion Point out that in the expression **Zeitung lesen** the article is not used.

1.

2.

3.

4.

5.

6.

Aussprache und Rechtschreibung Audio

Pure vowels versus diphthongs

German has three diphthongs: **au**, **ai/ei**, and **eu/äu**. In these vowel combinations, two vowel sounds are pronounced together in the same syllable.

Haus	**Mai**	**meine**	**scheu**	**läuft**

All other German vowel sounds are pure vowels. Whether long or short, they never glide into another vowel sound.

kalt	**Schnee**	**Spiel**	**Monat**	**Schule**

Be sure to pronounce the vowels in German words as pure vowel sounds, even when they resemble English words with similar pronunciations.

kann	**Stereo**	**Apfel**	**Boot**	**Schuh**

Suggestion Have students pronounce each German word alongside its English counterpart, to help them hear the difference in the vowel sounds: "**kann**, *can*", "**Stereo**, *stereo*", etc.

---

1 **Aussprechen** Wiederholen Sie die Wörter, die Sie hören.

1. Hagel
2. wann
3. Regen
4. Wetter
5. minus
6. Winter
7. Oktober
8. Sommer
9. Januar
10. Geburtstag
11. August
12. Mai
13. Zeit
14. heute
15. Häuser
16. Gasthaus

2 **Nachsprechen** Wiederholen Sie die Sätze, die Sie hören.

1. Es hat fast den ganzen Tag geregnet.
2. Im Juli ist es am Nachmittag zu heiß.
3. Im Winter gehe ich gern langlaufen.
4. Trink eine Tasse Tee, damit du wieder wach wirst!
5. Im Mai wird es schön warm und sonnig.
6. Im Sommer schwimmen die Kinder im See.
7. Im Herbst muss Max sein Segelboot reparieren lassen.
8. Meine Freundin besucht mich heute.

3 **Sprichwörter** Wiederholen Sie die Sprichwörter, die Sie hören.

Morgen, morgen, nur nicht heute, sagen alle faulen Leute.[1]

Nach Regen kommt Sonnenschein.[2]

[1] Tomorrow, tomorrow, just not today, that is what all lazy people say.
[2] Things will look brighter tomorrow. (lit. *After the rain comes sunshine.*)

More activities

vhlcentral | LM p. 63 | Online activities

Ein Sommer in der Türkei? Video

Anke hat Pläne für den Sommer: Die ganze Familie soll den Sommer in der Türkei verbringen.

NATIONAL
communication cultures
STANDARDS

Vorbereitung Have students look at scene 10, and discuss with a partner why they think Sabite is sad. After they have watched the episode, have students get together with their partners again and check their predictions.

1

ANKE Ich habe eine Überraschung für euch.
ZEYNEP Ich weiß schon, was es ist!
ANKE Zeynep, psst!
SABITE Was ist es denn?
ANKE Wir verbringen den Sommer in der Türkei.
SABITE Warum?
ZEYNEP Ja, warum wohl!

2

ANKE Es ist das Heimatland von deinem Vater. Und du und deine Schwester wart nicht mehr im Ausland seit... unseren Ferien in Frankreich vor drei Jahren. Wir wollen dort etwas über die Kunststudiengänge für dich erfahren, deshalb machen wir die Reise gemeinsam.

3

SABITE Ich kann es kaum erwarten, George, Hans und Meline davon zu erzählen.
ZEYNEP Und Torsten?

4

SABITE Mama, ich brauche deine Hilfe. Kann ich dich was fragen?
ANKE Du bittest mich doch sonst nie um Hilfe. Das muss ein großes Problem sein.

5

SABITE Torsten und ich haben uns gestritten. Ich habe ihm gesagt, dass ich überlege, in der Türkei Kunst zu studieren. Naja, ich habe es zuerst Meline gesagt. Ich habe mich mit Melines Freund über Kunst unterhalten und er stand daneben.

ANKE Du hast es ihm nicht zuerst gesagt. Und jetzt ist er unglücklich?
SABITE Ja. Und jetzt werden wir den Sommer nicht zusammen sein.
ANKE Wir müssen nicht in die Türkei fahren.
ZEYNEP Ähm, doch!
SABITE Oh, doch, das müssen wir. Aber ich will es ihm noch nicht sagen.

6

1 **Was fehlt?** Ergänzen Sie die Sätze mit den richtigen Informationen.

1. Anke möchte den (Sommer / Herbst) in der Türkei verbringen.
2. Die Türkei ist das Heimatland von (Anke / Faik).
3. Sabite und Zeynep waren schon in (Italien / Frankreich) im Urlaub.
4. Familie Yilmaz möchte etwas über (Jugendherbergen / Kunststudiengänge) in der Türkei erfahren.
5. Sabite bittet ihre Mutter um (Hilfe / Geld).

6. Sie hat Meline zuerst davon erzählt, in der Türkei (Kunst zu studieren / Urlaub zu machen).
7. Deshalb (*Therefore*) ist Torsten jetzt (unglücklich / unangenehm).
8. Anke glaubt, dass Beziehungen (einfach / kompliziert) sind.
9. Vor einem (Monat / Jahr) hat Sabite einige Arbeiten bei einer Galerie eingereicht.
10. Meline mag (Zeynep / Torsten) nicht.

PERSONEN

Anke   Sabite   Zeynep

ANKE Was noch? Bei Problemen zwischen zwei Partnern geht es nie nur um eine Sache. Beziehungen sind kompliziert.
SABITE Er versteht meine Kunst nicht.
ZEYNEP Niemand versteht deine Kunst, ohne dass er verrückt ist.
ANKE Hör auf, deine Schwester zu ärgern.

SABITE Er möchte meine Kunst nicht verstehen. Vor einem Monat habe ich einige Arbeiten bei einer Galerie in der Torstraße eingereicht. Torsten sagte... sie werden das niemals ausstellen.

ZEYNEP Das ist gemein.
ANKE Er darf so etwas nicht zu dir sagen.
SABITE Meline mag ihn nicht.
ZEYNEP Meline ist komisch.

SABITE Aber sie versteht, dass ich Künstlerin bin, ohne meine Kunst zu verstehen. Mama, was soll ich tun?
ANKE Liebst du ihn, Sabite?

Nützliche Ausdrücke

- **Heimatland**
  homeland, country of origin
- **der Kunststudiengang**
  art course
- **gemeinsam**
  together
- **erwarten**
  to expect
- **Du bittest mich doch sonst nie um Hilfe.**
  You never ask for my help.
- **Torsten und ich haben uns gestritten.**
  Torsten and I have been fighting.
- **zuerst**
  first
- **daneben**
  aside, on the side
- **zwischen**
  between
- **ausstellen**
  to exhibit
- **komisch**
  weird

7B.1
- **Aber sie versteht, dass ich Künstlerin bin, ohne meine Kunst zu verstehen.**
  But she understands that I'm an artist, without understanding my art.

7B.2
- **Vor einem Monat habe ich einige Arbeiten bei einer Galerie in der Torstraße eingereicht.**
  A month ago, I submitted some work to a gallery on Torstraße.

7B.3
- **Niemand versteht deine Kunst, ohne dass er verrückt ist.**
  Nobody can understand your art, unless they're crazy.

---

2 **Zum Besprechen** Familie Yilmaz möchte zusammen Urlaub in der Türkei machen. Planen Sie mit einem Partner/einer Partnerin die Reise. Besprechen Sie das Ziel (*destination*), die Dauer der Reise, die Transportmittel, die Unterkünfte und weitere Details. Answers will vary.

 2 Expansion Instead of having them write a paragraph, ask students to act out a conversation about vacation planning.

3 **Vertiefung** Anke, Sabite und Zeynep sind im Bauhaus-Museum. Suchen Sie weitere Museen in Berlin und finden Sie heraus (*find out*), welche Ausstellungen zur Zeit dort zu sehen sind. Welche Ausstellung gefällt Ihnen? Was gefällt Ihnen daran? Beschreiben Sie diese Ausstellung im Kurs. Answers will vary.

More activities

vhlcentral   VM p. 14   Online activities

Suggestion Have students figure out the literal English translation of **Kofferwort**.

IM FOKUS

Flughafen Frankfurt

 Reading

TIPP

The Squaire comes from a combination of the English words *square* and *air*. This type of word combination is called a **Kofferwort** in German.

DER FRANKFURT AIRPORT (auch Rhein-Main-Flughafen) ist der größte Flughafen in Deutschland. Fast 70 Millionen Passagiere kamen hier 2018 an oder flogen von hier ab. In München waren es im gleichen Jahr 44,6 Millionen und in Düsseldorf 24,6 Millionen. In Europa fliegen Passagiere nur London-Heathrow und Paris-Charles de Gaulle öfter an.

Weltweit ist der Frankfurter Flughafen die Nummer 14. Der Flughafen ist sehr praktisch für Passagiere, weil es direkt im Flughafen einen Bahnhof° gibt. Man kann Flug und Zugreise bequem miteinander kombinieren. Über dem Bahnhof findet man auch „The Squaire", ein großes Gebäude mit Büros, zwei Hotels und Geschäften.

Neben dem Passagierverkehr° ist der Frankfurt Airport auch für den Cargoverkehr wichtig. Innerhalb Europas werden nur in Paris-Charles de Gaulle mehr Güter° transportiert. Wegen der vielen Passagiere und der Güter nennt man den Frankfurt Airport auch ein wichtiges Luftfahrtdrehkreuz°. Der Flughafen ist aber nicht nur für Passagiere und Cargotransport wichtig. Hier arbeiten 70.000 Menschen. Innerhalb Deutschlands gilt der Flughafen als größte lokale Arbeitsstätte°. Er ist so groß, dass er seine eigene Postleitzahl° hat!

Flughafen	Passagiere (2018)	Flüge (2018)	Fluggesellschaften°
Frankfurt Airport	fast 70 Millionen	463.000	96
London-Heathrow (größter in Europa)	80 Millionen	474.000	81
Atlanta International Airport (größter weltweit)	mehr als 100 Millionen	899.000	61

QUELLEN Frankfurt Airport, Heathrow Airport, Atlanta International Airport

Bahnhof *train station* **Passagierverkehr** *passenger traffic* **Güter** *freight* **Luftfahrtdrehkreuz** *aviation hub* **Arbeitsstätte** *place of employment* **Postleitzahl** *zip code* **Fluggesellschaften** *airline companies*

Suggestion Before they begin the reading, have students describe the picture to you, using as many vocabulary words as possible.

ÜBUNGEN

1 **Im Fokus** Richtig oder falsch? Korrigieren Sie die falschen Aussagen.

1. Der Flughafen Frankfurt hatte 2018 mehr Passagiere als alle anderen Flughäfen in der Welt. **Falsch.** Er hatte weniger Passagiere als der Londoner Flughafen Heathrow und der Atlanta International Airport

2. Der Flughafen Frankfurt hat seinen eigenen Bahnhof. **Richtig.**

3. Der Flughafen Paris-Charles de Gaulle in Frankreich hat mehr Cargoverkehr als der Flughafen Frankfurt. **Richtig.**

Diskussion Vergleichen Sie einen großen Flughafen in Ihrem Land mit dem Flughafen Frankfurt.

2 **Die deutschsprachige Welt** Richtig oder falsch? Korrigieren Sie die falschen Aussagen.

1. Sylt ist die größte deutsche Insel. **Richtig.**

2. Die Insel hat kleine Strände. **Falsch.** Es gibt lange Strände.

3. Sylts Dünen sind bis zu 1.000 Meter hoch. **Falsch.** Sylts Dünen sind nur etwa 35 Meter hoch.

Diskussion Beschreiben Sie einen typischen Studentenurlaub. Wie verbringen Sie Ihre Winter- und Sommerferien? Was machen Sie?

Deutsch im Alltag You may want to teach the verb **zelten**. Ask the class: **Wer zeltet gern?**

DEUTSCH IM ALLTAG

Urlaub für Studenten

die Pension, -en	guesthouse
das Zelt, -e	tent
der Zeltplatz, ⸚e	camping area
der Zug, ⸚e	train
Sofa-surfen	to couch surf
Zimmer frei	vacancy

DIE DEUTSCHSPRACHIGE WELT

Sylt

Sylt ist die größte deutsche Insel in der Nordsee. Sie heißt auch „die Hamburger Badewanne". Jedes Jahr machen hier 850.000 Menschen Urlaub. Berühmt ist Sylt für seine langen Strände (mehr als 40 Kilometer) und die Wanderdünen° in List. Sie sind bis zu 1.000 Meter lang und 35 Meter hoch. Sie „wandern" jedes Jahr bis zu 4 Meter. Interessant ist auch das Wattenmeer, wo viele Fische und Vögel leben. Auf Sylt findet man auch seltene° Pflanzen, Tiere und Schmetterlinge°. Die Heide° ist auch eine bekannte Landschaft° der Insel.

Wanderdünen hiking dunes **seltene** rare
Schmetterlinge butterflies **Heide** heath
Landschaft landscape

PORTRÄT

Der ICE

Der ICE, oder Intercity-Express, ist die schnellste Zugart° in Deutschland. Dieser Zug fährt in Deutschland und 6 Nachbarländern (Belgien, Dänemark, Frankreich, Niederlande, Österreich und der Schweiz) 180 ICE-Bahnhöfe an. Für Passagiere ist der ICE interessant, weil die Züge nicht nur extrem schnell fahren, sondern auch sehr bequem sind. Passagiere haben viel Platz. Alle Wagen haben Klimaanlagen°. Es gibt auch ein Bordrestaurant im Zug und oft ein Abteil° für Kinder. Mit Kopfhörern° kann man Musik- und Sprachprogramme hören und für Computer gibt es Steckdosen°.

Zugart type of train **Klimaanlagen** air conditioning **Abteil** section
Kopfhörern headphones **Steckdosen** electrical outlets

🔗 IM INTERNET

Suchen Sie Informationen über die Vogelfluglinie: Was ist die Vogelfluglinie? Wo liegt sie? Ist sie nur für Vögel?

Find out more at **vhlcentral.com**.

---

3 **Porträt** Richtig oder falsch? Korrigieren Sie die falschen Aussagen. Diskutieren Sie dann die letzte Frage mit einem Partner/ einer Partnerin.

1. Der ICE fährt 180 Bahnhöfe in 25 Nachbarländern an.
   Falsch. Der ICE fährt 180 Bahnhöfe in 6 Nachbarländern an.
2. Der ICE hat nur Automaten mit Getränken und Sandwiches.
   Falsch. Der ICE hat ein Bordrestaurant.
3. Alle Wagen des ICEs sind klimatisiert. **Richtig.**

Diskussion Wo möchten Sie einmal von Deutschland aus in Europa Urlaub machen? Wie kommen Sie an Ihr Reiseziel? Warum wählen Sie diese Form von Transport?

4 **Der ICE** Welche Vorteile (*advantages*) und Nachteile (*disadvantages*) haben das Reisen mit dem Flugzeug und der Bahn? Schreiben Sie einen kurzen Absatz und lesen Sie ihn im Kurs vor.

More activities

vhlcentral / Online activities

7B.1

Infinitive expressions and clauses Grammar Tutorial

Startblock When you use a non-modal verb with an infinitive clause, add the preposition **zu** before the infinitive.

Ich habe Sabite letzte Woche geholfen, ihre Wohnung **zu putzen**.

Ich habe ihm gesagt, dass ich überlege, ein Semester in der Türkei Kunst **zu studieren**.

- When a conjugated modal verb modifies the meaning of another verb, the infinitive moves to the end of the sentence. The preposition **zu** is not needed in this case.

  Ich möchte Checkpoint Charlie **besuchen**.
  *I want **to visit** Checkpoint Charlie.*

  Es regnet. Wir müssen unsere Regenmäntel **anziehen**.
  *It's raining. We need **to put on** our raincoats.*

ACHTUNG

The comma before an infinitive clause is optional. Use it for clarity, especially in longer sentences. Any adverbs that modify the infinitive expression come after the comma: **Es ist schön, im Sommer Eis zu essen.**

- After most other verbs, however, you need to put **zu** before the infinitive clause. Place **zu** plus the infinitive at the end of the sentence.

  Es macht viel Spaß **zu reisen**!
  ***Travelling** is so much fun!*

  Ich hatte keine Zeit, Postkarten **zu schreiben**.
  *I didn't have time **to write** postcards.*

- When using a double verb expression like **spazieren gehen**, put the preposition **zu** between the two verbs.

  Philip hat Angst, **schwimmen zu gehen**.
  *Philip is afraid **to go swimming**.*

  Es ist uns zu teuer, jeden Abend **essen zu gehen**.
  ***Going out to eat** every night is too expensive for us.*

- If the verb in the infinitive clause is a separable prefix verb, place **zu** between the prefix and the main part of the verb.

  Es macht keinen Spaß, die Küche **aufzuräumen**.
  ***Cleaning** the kitchen is no fun.*

  Vergiss bitte nicht, den Müll **rauszubringen**.
  *Please don't forget **to take out** the trash.*

- Infinitive constructions with **zu** often occur after the verbs **anfangen**, **beginnen**, **helfen**, **vergessen**, and **versuchen** (*to try*), the expressions **Lust haben** (*to be in the mood*), **Angst haben**, and **Spaß machen**, and the adjectives **einfach**, **wichtig** (*important*), and **schön**.

  Ich **habe vergessen**, meine Eltern **anzurufen**.
  *I **forgot to call** my parents.*

  Kannst du mir bitte **helfen**, meine Bordkarte **zu finden**?
  *Can you please **help** me **find** my boarding pass?*

  Wir **haben** keine **Lust**, heute Abend **auszugehen**.
  *We don't **feel like going out** this evening.*

  Ich finde es **wichtig**, pünktlich **zu sein**.
  *I think it's **important to be** on time.*

- Impersonal expressions beginning with **Es ist/war...** are also frequently followed by an infinitive clause.

Es war so schön, in einem Fünf-Sterne-Hotel **zu übernachten**.
*It was so nice **to spend the night** at a five-star hotel.*

Es ist nicht gut, bei Nebel **zu fliegen**.
*It's not good **to fly** when it's foggy.*

Expansion Ask students to explain why they are learning German and answer using the expression **um... zu**. Emphasize that **um** sets off the clause, while **zu** and the infinitive appear at the very end.

- The expressions **um... zu** (*in order to*), **ohne... zu** (*without*), and **anstatt... zu** (*instead of*) are frequently used in infinitive clauses. **Anstatt** is often shortened to **statt**, especially in informal conversation.

Ich esse viel Gemüse und gehe jeden Tag schwimmen, **um** fit **zu bleiben**.
*I eat lots of vegetables and swim every day **to stay** fit.*

Man kann einen schönen Urlaub machen, **ohne** ins Ausland **zu fahren**.
*You can have a nice vacation **without going** abroad.*

Sie sind in die Schweiz gefahren, **anstatt** nach Rom **zu fliegen**.
Instead of flying to Rome, they drove to Switzerland.

Fahrt ihr nach Hamburg, **um** eure Freunde **zu besuchen**?
*Are you driving to Hamburg **to visit** your friends?*

- In sentences with **um... zu**, **ohne... zu**, or **(an)statt... zu**, the infinitive clause may be the first element in a sentence. When the infinitive clause is the first element, the conjugated verb becomes the second element, and the subject comes after the conjugated verb.

Statt zu schlafen, **hat Peter** die ganze Nacht gelesen.
Instead of sleeping, Peter spent all night reading.

Um ein Zimmer in diesem Hotel **zu bekommen**, **muss man** sehr früh buchen.
To get a room at that hotel, you have to book early.

Ohne vorher **zu fragen**, **haben sie** die Kekse gegessen.
*They ate the cookies **without asking** first.*

Anstatt meine Hausaufgaben **zu machen**, **bin ich** gestern Abend ausgegangen.
Instead of doing my homework, I went out last night

More activities

vhlcentral

WB
pp. 99–100

LM
p. 64

Online activities

Jetzt sind Sie dran! **Wählen Sie das passende Wort.**

1. Ich bin rausgegangen, (um / (ohne) / anstatt) den Schlüssel mitzunehmen!

2. (Um / Ohne / (Anstatt)) einen Skiurlaub zu machen, fahren wir ans Meer.

3. Der Student hat eine gute Note in seiner Prüfung bekommen, (um / (ohne) / anstatt) dafür zu lernen.

4. (Um / Ohne / (Anstatt)) mit dem Auto zu fahren, fliegt Jana nach Italien.

5. Willst du Deutsch lernen, ((um) / ohne / anstatt) in Deutschland zu studieren?

6. Michael hat das Hotel gefunden, (um / (ohne) / anstatt) auf den Stadtplan zu schauen.

7. (Um / Ohne / (Anstatt)) Zeitung zu lesen, schlafe ich gern im Flugzeug.

8. Der Geschäftsmann bestellte Zimmerservice, (um / (ohne) / anstatt) nach dem Preis zu fragen.

9. Wir fahren zwei Stunden vor unserem Flug zum Flughafen, ((um) / ohne / anstatt) pünktlich zu sein.

10. Nina ist faul und fährt mit dem Fahrstuhl, (um / ohne / (anstatt)) die Treppe zu nehmen.

11. Ich trage einen Mantel bei schlechtem Wetter, ((um) / ohne / anstatt) warm zu bleiben.

12. Das Gute an Jugendherbergen ist, man kann dort übernachten, (um / (ohne) / anstatt) ein Bett zu reservieren.

Anwendung

1 **Was fehlt?** Ergänzen Sie die Sätze mit der richtigen Form des Verbs im Infinitiv.

1. Wir helfen unseren Eltern, die Koffer ___zu packen___. (packen)
2. Mama fängt an, die Zimmer im Hotel ___zu reservieren___. (reservieren)
3. Es macht Spaß, in Europa ___zu reisen___. (reisen)
4. Papa hat vergessen, unsere Personalausweise ___mitzubringen___. (mitbringen)
5. Der Taxifahrer hatte keine Zeit ___zurückzufahren___. (zurückfahren)
6. Er musste sehr schnell fahren, um am Flughafen pünktlich ___anzukommen___. (ankommen)

2 **Ausdrücke** Ergänzen Sie die Sätze mit dem passenden Ausdruck um... zu, ohne... zu oder (an)statt... zu.

BEISPIEL Im Flugzeug lese ich viel, _(an)statt_ zu schlafen.

1. Wir gehen mit unseren Freunden am Abend vor unserer Reise aus, ___(an)statt___ unsere Koffer zu packen.
2. Die Studenten reisen viel, ___um___ verschiedene Länder kennen zu lernen.
3. Maria hat eine gute Note in Deutsch geschrieben, ___ohne___ viel dafür zu lernen.
4. Warum habt ihr stundenlang in der Sonne gestanden, ___ohne___ einen Hut zu tragen?
5. Am Freitag gehen wir ins Theater, ___um___ das neue Theaterstück anzusehen.
6. ___Anstatt / Statt___ ein Hotelzimmer zu buchen, werden wir in der Jugendherberge übernachten.
7. Er hat das Stück Kuchen gegessen ___anstatt/statt___ es seiner Schwester zu geben.

3 **Suggestion** Do the first few items as a class to make sure that students understand the activity.

3 **Wozu braucht man das?** Sagen Sie, wozu man die abgebildeten Dinge braucht. Sample answers are provided.

> fit bleiben
> im Regen trocken bleiben
> | tanzen gehen
> Deutsch lernen
> | E-Mails schreiben
> in den Bergen wandern

▶ **BEISPIEL**
Man braucht einen Badeanzug, um schwimmen zu gehen.

1.
Man soll viel Gemüse essen, um fit zu bleiben.

2.
Man braucht einen Regenschirm, um im Regen trocken zu bleiben.

3.
Man braucht ein Wörterbuch, um Deutsch zu lernen.

4.
Man braucht einen Rucksack, um in den Bergen zu wandern.

5.
Man braucht einen Computer, um E-Mails zu schreiben.

6.
Man braucht ein schönes Kleid, um tanzen zu gehen.

Kommunikation

4 **Viel gereist** Sie waren im Sommer in Deutschland. Besprechen Sie mit einem Partner / einer Partnerin, wo Sie waren und warum Sie dort waren. Answers will vary.

BEISPIEL in München

S1: *Wo warst du im Sommer?*
S2: *Ich war in München, um meine Familie zu besuchen. Meine Schwester wohnt dort.*

in den Alpen	in Hamburg
in Berlin	in Heidelberg
an der Donau	in München
in Füssen	an der Ostseeküste

4 **Expansion** Review various cultural attractions unique to the cities and landmarks on the list. Encourage students to research points of interest on their own or in groups, and share what they have discovered with the class.

5 **Ein schwerer Koffer** Sie haben viel in den Urlaub mitgebracht. Erzählen Sie einem Partner / einer Partnerin, wieso Sie so viel im Gepäck haben. Answers will vary.

BEISPIEL

S1: *Warum hast du eine Gitarre mitgebracht?*
S2: *Um Musik zu machen. Und du? Warum hast du einen Badeanzug gepackt?*
S1: *Um schwimmen zu gehen.*

einen gestreiften Anzug	eine kurze Hose	einen Rucksack
einen Badeanzug	ein Kleid	viele Bücher
die Brille	eine Krawatte	eine Sonnenbrille
eine Gitarre	eine Mütze	ein langärmliges T-Shirt
eine schöne Halskette	einen Regenschirm	Turnschuhe

6 **Wohin wollen wir reisen?** Denken Sie an drei mögliche Urlaubsziele. Fragen Sie Ihren Partner / Ihre Partnerin, wohin er/sie reisen möchte, und besprechen Sie dabei die Sehenswürdigkeiten in jeder Stadt. Answers will vary.

BEISPIEL

S1: *Wo machen wir im Sommer Urlaub?*
S2: *Ich will nach Disneyland fahren, anstatt Museen zu besuchen.*
S1: *Warum?*
S2: *Um Mickey Mouse zu treffen. Ich finde ihn toll!*

6 **Partner Chat** You can also assign activity 6 on the Supersite.

7 **Meiner Meinung nach** Ergänzen Sie die folgenden Aussagen mit Ihrer Meinung. Vergleichen Sie die Antworten mit anderen Studenten.

1. Ich finde es schwer...
2. Es macht mir Spaß...
3. Ich habe keine Lust...
4. Ich versuche immer...
5. Ich finde es wichtig...
6. Es ist schön...

7 **Suggestion** Make sure students know to use a **zu** + infinitive clause in each answer.

7B.2

QUERVERWEIS

See **2A.3** and **3B.2** to review times and dates in German.

___

To review word order with time expressions, see **4A.2**.

Expansion Write on the board: **0X, 1X, 2X, 3X, ...20X**, etc. and have students verbalize what these shorthand forms indicate: **niemals, einmal, zweimal, dreimal, ...zwanzigmal**, etc. You may also wish to introduce the colloquialism **zigmal**, "a zillion times".

Suggestion To practice the use of **seit** and **schon**, ask students how long they've been doing a particular activity and write their responses on the board. Ex.: **Carrie spielt seit einem Jahr Gitarre. Tom lernt seit Januar Deutsch.** Underline the verbs and emphasize that they are in the present tense.

More activities

S vhlcentral

WB pp. 101–102

LM p. 65

Online activities

Expansion Have students work in small groups to write a short travel cartoon using **zuerst, dann, danach,** and **zuletzt**. Remind them of correct verb position.

Time expressions Grammar Tutorial

Suggestion Ask travel-related questions that can be answered with these expressions, such as: **Wie oft waren Sie in Europa? Wie oft waren Sie am Strand? Wie viele Male sind Sie geflogen?**

Startblock German has two main concepts related to expressions of time. **Zeit** describes a span of time, while **Mal** refers to specific occurrences and repetitions.

Ich habe noch **50 Minuten Zeit** vor meinem Flug.
*I still have **50 minutes** before my flight.*

Ich war nur **einmal** in Hamburg.
*I've only been to Hamburg **once**.*

- Many German time expressions use **Mal** or a compound word containing **-mal**:

diesmal	*this time*	**manchmal**	*sometimes*
das erste Mal	*the first time*	**niemals**	*never*
einmal	*once*	**zum ersten/letzten Mal**	*for the first/last time*

- Use the accusative case to talk about a particular span of time or point in time. To describe how long something lasted, use **dauern** with the accusative.

Die Kreuzfahrt dauerte **einen Monat**.
*The cruise lasted **a month**.*

Nächsten Sommer fahren wir an den Strand.
Next summer we're going to the beach.

Letzten Montag haben meine Ferien angefangen.
*My break started **last Monday**.*

Die Leute tanzten **die ganze Nacht**.
*The people danced **all night long**.*

- Use the present tense with **seit** plus a dative time expression or **schon** plus an accusative time expression to indicate how long something has been going on.

Seit einem Monat wohnt Patrick in Berlin.
*Patrick has been living in Berlin **for a month**.*

Er ist **schon zwei Jahre** in Deutschland.
*He's been in Germany **for two years**.*

- The two-way prepositions **an, in,** and **vor** can all be used to answer the question **wann?** Use the dative case with these time expressions.

Vor einem Jahr studierte ich im Ausland.
A year ago I was studying abroad.

Mein Geburtstag ist **am 18. Februar**.
*My birthday is **on February 18**.*

- Use the time expressions **zuerst** (*first*), **dann** (*then*), **danach** (*after that*), and **zuletzt** (*last*) or **schließlich** (*finally*) to narrate a series of events.

Zuerst musst du die wichtigen Papiere in das Handgepäck packen.
***First** you have to pack your important papers in the carry-on bag.*

Dann kannst du die anderen Sachen in den großen Koffer packen.
***Then** you can pack the other things in the big suitcase.*

Jetzt sind Sie dran! **Wählen Sie die passenden Wörter.**

1. (Im / In den) Frühling regnet es viel.
2. In (der / die) Nacht habe ich schlecht geträumt.
3. Laura reist für (ein / einen) Monat nach Österreich.
4. Vor (einer / eine) Woche haben wir unsere Flugtickets bekommen.
5. (Nächster / Nächsten) Sommer musst du in den Urlaub mitkommen.
6. (Am / An das) Wochenende fahre ich nach Zürich.
7. Herr Boas wartet schon (einer / eine) Stunde auf ein Taxi.
8. Wir waren (letzter / letzten) Dienstag nicht zu Hause.
9. Hugo arbeitet seit (ein / einem) Jahr an seinem neuen Buch.
10. In (einer / eine) Woche macht er eine Kreuzfahrt.

Anwendung und Kommunikation

1 **Was fehlt?** Ergänzen Sie die Sätze mit den passenden Zeitergänzungen aus der Liste.

| einmal | das erste Mal | einen Monat |
| letztes Jahr | 35 Minuten | nächste Woche |

1. Saras Geburtstag ist ___nächste Woche___ und dann wird sie zweiundzwanzig.
2. Mit 18 Jahren durfte ich ___das erste Mal___ allein in Urlaub fahren.
3. Silvester ist ___letztes Jahr___ auf einen Sonntag gefallen.
4. Der Flug von München nach Nürnberg dauert nur ___35 Minuten___.
5. Wir haben noch ___einen Monat___ bis zum Ende von unserem Semester.
6. Meine Großeltern planen eine Familienfeier, denn Goldene Hochzeit hat man nur ___einmal___ im Leben.

2 **Ein kleines Interview** Beantworten Sie die Fragen von Ihrem Partner / Ihrer Partnerin. Answers will vary.

BEISPIEL seit wann / Deutsch lernen

S1: *Seit wann lernst du Deutsch?*
S2: *Seit letztem Semester.*

1. wann / Geburtstag haben   Wann hast du Geburtstag?
2. seit wann / hier studieren   Seit wann studierst du hier?
3. was / zuerst machen nach dem Semesterende / Und danach?
   Was machst du zuerst nach dem Semesterende? Und danach?
4. wann und wo / zuletzt am Strand sein
   Wann und wo bist du zuletzt am Strand gewesen?
5. vor wie vielen Jahren / zum ersten Mal im Flugzeug fliegen
   Vor wie vielen Jahren bist du zum ersten Mal im Flugzeug geflogen?
6. wen / einmal kennen lernen möchten   Wen möchtest du einmal kennen lernen?

3 **Reiselust** Erfinden Sie mit Ihren Mitstudenten eine kurze Geschichte über eine Reise. Benutzen Sie Wörter aus der Liste oder Ihre eigenen.

BEISPIEL

Thomas und seine Familie wollten zum ersten Mal eine Kreuzfahrt von Marseille nach Palermo machen. Zuerst...

Zeitausdrücke	Hauptwörter	Verben
danach	die Crew	einkaufen
dann	das Gepäck	einpacken
niemals	das Meer	essen
seit	der Pass	regnen
vor	der Sandstrand	schwimmen
zuerst	das Souvenir	tanzen
zuletzt	das Wetter	vergessen

7B.3

QUERVERWEIS

To review the use of subject, accusative, and dative pronouns, see **1A.3**, **5A.2**, and **5A.3**.

Indefinite pronouns Grammar Tutorial

Startblock Pronouns that refer to an unknown or nonspecific person or thing are called indefinite pronouns.

Alles in Ordnung?

Niemand bestellt Zimmerservice.

Suggestion Provide sample sentences that demonstrate the different case endings. Ex.: **Niemand war im Zimmer. Wir sahen niemanden im Zimmer. Wir gaben niemandem die Blumen.**

Expansion Provide your class with a list of travel destinations and have students find out who has been to those places. Then have them summarize their results. Ex.: **Niemand ist nach Wyoming gereist. Maria war schon in Kuba, aber niemand aus dem Kurs ist in Ecuador gewesen.**

ACHTUNG

In conversation, **etwas** may be shortened to **was**. Ex.: **Kann ich dich was fragen?**

Remember that **man** is singular. When **man** is the subject, always use a verb in the third-person singular.

Suggestion Emphasize that the declension of **alles** parallels the declension of **das**: the nominative form is **alles**, the accusative form is **alles**, and the dative form is **allem**.

- Two indefinite pronouns that refer to people are **jemand** (*someone*) and **niemand** (*no one*). Use the ending **-en** for the accusative case and **-em** for the dative.

  Jemand hat seinen Personalausweis an der Passkontrolle vergessen.
  Someone left his I.D. card at passport control.

  Herr Klein will mit **niemandem** sprechen.
  Mr. Klein doesn't want to speak with anyone.

- To talk about indefinite things, use **alles** (*everything*), **etwas** (*something*), or **nichts** (*nothing*). **Etwas** and **nichts** do not change in different cases; **alles** is declined like the neuter definite article **das**.

  Wir haben noch **nichts** gegessen.
  We haven't eaten anything yet.

  Ich habe **alles** ins Handgepäck gepackt.
  I packed everything in the carry-on.

  Möchten Sie **etwas** zu trinken bestellen?
  Would you like to order something to drink?

  Meine Schwester kann dir mit **allem** helfen.
  My sister can help you with everything.

- Use the pronoun **man** to talk about people in general.

  Man darf im Flugzeug nicht rauchen.
  You're not allowed to smoke on an airplane.

  In Liechtenstein spricht **man** Deutsch.
  In Liechtenstein they speak German.

  In Hamburg ist **man** froh, wenn es im Winter nicht zu viel schneit.
  In Hamburg we're happy if it doesn't snow too much in winter.

  Man soll zwei Stunden vor dem Abflug am Flughafen sein.
  One should be at the airport two hours before departure.

More activities

vhlcentral

WB
pp. 103–104

LM
p. 66

Online activities

Jetzt sind Sie dran! **Wählen Sie das passende Wort.**

1. Anna vergisst oft ihre Hausaufgaben, aber Emil vergisst (nichts / etwas).

2. (Etwas / Niemand) will arbeiten, wenn das Wetter draußen so schön ist.

3. Wenn (man / alles) nicht ins Ausland will, gibt es auch in Deutschland viele schöne Ferienorte (*vacation spots*).

4. (Nichts / Jemand) hat vergessen, das Fenster zu schließen.

5. Hast du (niemand / etwas) gesagt?

6. Ich möchte (alles / man) in dieser Stadt sehen!

7. Ich will im Urlaub (jemand / nichts) machen – nur schlafen und essen!

8. Sollen wir (man / jemanden) fragen, oder findest du die Antwort im Internet?

9. Jasmin ist sehr schüchtern – sie will mit (niemandem / etwas) reden.

10. (Nichts / Man) kann in diesem Geschäft viele schöne Sachen finden.

Suggestion Tell students that **man** cannot be replaced by **er**, and that in the accusative or dative it is replaced by **einen/einem**. Have students write down sample sentences; ex.: **Wenn man traurig ist, dann soll man spazieren gehen. Dann geht es einem besser.**

Anwendung und Kommunikation

1 **Fragen zur Grammatik** Ergänzen Sie die Sätze mit den passenden Wörtern aus der Liste.

alles	nichts
etwas	niemand
jemand	niemandem

1. Hat ___jemand___ noch Fragen zur Grammatik?
2. Herr Krause, können Sie uns ___alles___ noch einmal erklären?
3. ___Niemand___ hat die Grammatik verstanden.
4. Sie haben wirklich ___nichts___ verstanden?
5. Also kann ich leider ___niemandem___ helfen.
6. Sie können ___etwas___ lernen, liebe Studenten, aber nur wenn Sie Ihre Hausaufgaben machen!

2 **Was macht man hier?** Schreiben Sie zu jedem Foto einen Satz mit **man**. Benutzen Sie die angegebenen Wörter.

▶ **BEISPIEL**

hier / können / Medikamente kaufen
Hier kann man Medikamente kaufen.

1. bei Rot / müssen / stoppen
Bei Rot muss man stoppen.

2. hier / kommen / zum Marienplatz
Hier kommt man zum Marienplatz.

3. hier / sprechen / Deutsch
Hier spricht man Deutsch.

4. hier / dürfen / parken
Hier darf man parken.

5. hier / können / einkaufen
Hier kann man einkaufen.

3 **Armer Niklas** Es geht Ihrem Freund Niklas wirklich schlecht. Besprechen Sie mit Ihrem Partner / Ihrer Partnerin, was Niklas machen muss oder was man machen soll, um Niklas zu helfen. Answers will vary. Suggested answers.

▶ **BEISPIEL**

S1: *Niklas hat heute nichts gegessen.*
S2: *Er muss etwas essen!*

1. Niklas muss morgen ein Referat halten und hat noch nichts dazu vorbereitet.
Er muss etwas dazu vorbereiten!
2. Die Lehrerin hat ihm nichts erklärt.
Sie muss ihm alles erklären!
3. Im Unterricht hat er nichts zu sagen.
Er soll im Unterricht etwas sagen.
4. Niemand hilft ihm.
Jemand soll ihm helfen.
5. Er hat Angst vor allem.
Er muss vor nichts Angst haben!
6. Er hat mit niemandem über seine Probleme gesprochen.
Er muss mit jemandem über seine Probleme sprechen.

3 **Suggestion** Make sure students take turns describing Niklas' problems and proposing solutions.

3 **Video Virtual Chat** You can also assign activity 3 on the Supersite. Students record individual responses that appear in your gradebook.

Wiederholung

1 Die vergesslichen Schröders
Sehen Sie sich die Bilder an. Sagen Sie, was die Familie Schröder vergessen hat.

Sample answers are provided.

▶ **BEISPIEL** *Jan hat vergessen, das Geschirr zu spülen.*

1 Expansion Ask students: **Und Sie? Was haben Sie diese Woche vergessen?**

Jan

1. Opa
Opa hat vergessen, den Müll rauszutragen.

2. Tobias Tobias hat vergessen, das Schlafzimmer aufzuräumen.

3. Tante Ingrid Tante Ingrid hat vergessen, das Fenster zu schließen.

4. Onkel Paul Onkel Paul hat vergessen, im Wohnzimmer zu staubsaugen.

5. Greta Greta hat vergessen, ihre Hausaufgaben zu machen.

2 Wie viel verstehst du?
Wie viel verstehen Sie und Ihr Partner / Ihre Partnerin von den Themen auf der Liste? Etwas? Nichts? Alles? Wechseln Sie sich ab.

Answers will vary.

BEISPIEL

S1: *Wie viel verstehst du von Politik?*
S2: *Ich verstehe etwas von Politik. Und du?*

Chemie	Geographie	Popmusik
Fotographie	Geschichte	Skateboard fahren
Fußball spielen	Politik	Tanzen

3 Diskutieren und kombinieren
Sie und Ihr Partner / Ihre Partnerin bekommen zwei verschiedene Arbeitsblätter von Ihrem Lehrer / Ihrer Lehrerin. Finden Sie heraus, warum die einzelnen Personen etwas tun.

Sample answers are provided.

BEISPIEL

S1: *Warum geht Kiara in die Bibliothek?*
S2: *Sie geht dahin, um ein Buch für ein Referat zu suchen.*

4 Arbeitsblatt
Fragen Sie die anderen Studenten, wann sie die Dinge auf der Liste das letzte Mal gemacht haben. Finden Sie zu jedem Wochentag eine Person.

Answers will vary.

BEISPIEL in die Bibliothek gehen

S1: *Wann bist du das letzte Mal in die Bibliothek gegangen?*
S2: *Am Mittwoch bin ich dahin gegangen.*

5 Wie lange?
Fragen Sie Ihren Partner / Ihre Partnerin, wie lange er/sie die Dinge auf der Liste schon macht. Answers will vary.

BEISPIEL Deutsch lernen

S1: *Wie lange lernst du schon Deutsch?*
S2: *Seit 6 Monaten.*

Konzerte besuchen	schwimmen
Auto fahren	ein Musikinstrument spielen
Rad fahren	Videospiele spielen
Bücher lesen	an der Uni studieren

6 Wie oft?
Arbeiten Sie mit einem Partner / einer Partnerin. Fragen Sie nach seinen/ihren Urlaubserfahrungen. Wie oft ist er/sie ins Ausland gereist oder in einem Hotel geblieben? Wie oft hat er/sie einen Nationalpark besucht? Wie oft hat er/sie Familie in einer anderen Stadt besucht? Answers will vary.

BEISPIEL

S1: *Wie oft bist du ins Ausland gereist?*
S2: *Ich bin zweimal ins Ausland gereist, einmal nach Mexiko und einmal nach Frankreich.*

3 Suggestion In this activity, students will be practicing the **um... zu** + infinitive construction. To prepare them, ask a few **warum** questions and write student responses on the board, using **um... zu**.

7 Klimawandel Wissenschaftler prognostizieren (*predict*), dass das Klima trockener (*drier*) und wärmer wird. Sehen Sie sich die Wetterkarte für den 21. März an. Finden Sie die Temperaturen normal? Besprechen Sie zu zweit, welche Temperaturen Sie angenehm finden, und welche Jahreszeiten Sie (nicht) mögen.

BEISPIEL

S1: *Was für eine Temperatur findest du angenehm?*
S2: *Ich finde 22-25 Grad Celsius angenehm. Und du?*

Expansion Encourage your students to talk about climate change and what impact they believe it will have on their future.

Suggestion Write on the board the German words that students won't know for climate change, and ask students to add them to **Vocabulary Tools** on the **Sag mal** Supersite.

Sonnenstunden Deutschland

Eindeutiger Vorteil für Süden

Heute ist es vom südlichen Emsland bis zur Lausitz sowie nördlich davon meist stark bewölkt und örtlich kann es etwas tröpfeln. Nach Süden hin wird es dagegen immer schöner und sonniger. Die Höchstwerte liegen zwischen 9 und 19 Grad.

Wetterbericht für Deutschland (21.03.)

8 Rollenspiel Spielen Sie mit einem Partner / einer Partnerin die Rollen von zwei älteren Menschen, die über ihr Leben nachdenken. Jede Person sagt etwas über einen anderen Abschnitt (*phase*) des Lebens. Answers will vary.

BEISPIEL

8 Partner Chat You can also assign activity 8 on the Supersite.

S1: *Mit 5 zog meine Familie in die USA.*
S2: *Mit 6 ging ich zum ersten Mal in die Schule.*

9 Eine Geschichte Schauen Sie sich das Bild an und schreiben Sie eine Geschichte dazu. Jede Person schreibt zwei Sätze der Geschichte und gibt sein Stück Papier an die nächste Person weiter. Der erste Satz beginnt mit „zuerst", der dritte mit „dann", der fünfte mit „danach" und so weiter. Answers will vary.

BEISPIEL *Zuerst spazierten zwei Freunde auf der Straße...*

⑤ Mein Wörterbuch

Schreiben Sie noch fünf weitere Wörter in Ihr persönliches Wörterbuch zu den Themen **Jahreszeiten** und **Reisen**.

Lektion 7B		
German	English	Definition
+ add word		
der Altweibersommer	Indian summer	der Spätsommer

ä ö ü ß ☐ ALL CAPS

Weiter geht's

Panorama Interactive Map

Schleswig-Holstein, Hamburg und Bremen

(connections cultures — NATIONAL STANDARDS)

Schleswig-Holstein in Zahlen

▶ **Fläche:** *15.800 km²*

▶ **Einwohner:** *2,9 Millionen*

▶ **Sprachen:** *Deutsch (2,7 Millionen), Plattdeutsch (1,3 Millionen), Dänisch (65.000), Friesisch (10.000)*

▶ **Städte:** *Kiel (246.000), Lübeck (217.000)*

▶ **Industrie:** *Landwirtschaft°, Seehandel°, Windenergie*

▶ **Touristenattraktionen:** *Danewerk und Haithabu (Wikingerstätten°), Karl-May-Festspiele° in Bad Segeberg*

Berühmte Schleswig-Holsteiner

▶ **Max Planck,** *Physiker (1858–1947)*

▶ **Thomas Mann,** *Literaturnobelpreisträger (1875–1955)*

Quelle: Landesportal Schleswig-Holstein

Hamburg in Zahlen

▶ **Fläche:** *755.000 km²*

▶ **Einwohner der Hansestadt Hamburg:** *1,8 Millionen*

▶ **Industrie:** *Flugzeugbau, Hafen, Schiffbau, Tourismus*

▶ **Touristenattraktionen:** *Altonaer Fischmarkt, Hamburger Michel, Museumsschiff Rickmer Rickmers*

Berühmte Hamburger

▶ **Johannes Brahms,** *Komponist (1833–1897)*

▶ **Jil Sander,** *Modedesignerin (1943–)*

Quelle: Landesportal Hamburg

Bremen in Zahlen

▶ **Fläche:** *325 km² (kleinstes deutsches Bundesland)*

▶ **Einwohner der Hansestadt Bremen:** *679.000*

▶ **Industrie:** *Außenhandel°, Automobilindustrie*

▶ **Touristenattraktionen:** *Böttcherstraße, Rathaus, Bremer Stadtmusikanten, Marktplatz, Schnoor*

Berühmte Bremer

▶ **Ernst Rowohlt,** *Verleger° (1887–1960)*

▶ **James Last,** *Komponist und Bandleader (1929–)*

Quelle: Landesportal Bremen

Landwirtschaft *agriculture* **Seehandel** *maritime trade* **Wikingerstätten** *Viking sites* **Festspiele** *festivals* **Außenhandel** *foreign trade* **Verleger** *publisher* **Brücken** *bridges* **überqueren** *cross* **Venedig** *Venice*

Suggestion Tell students that Hamburg is home to several German newspapers and magazines, including *Der Spiegel*, *Die Zeit*, and *Stern*.

Suggestion Ask students if they are familiar with any of Brahms' music. You may want to play them part of his **Wiegenlied**.

Sankt Michaelis: „Der Hamburger Michel", die bekannteste Kirche Hamburgs und ein Wahrzeichen der Stadt

Wahrzeichen der alten Hansestadt Lübeck: das Holstentor

Der Schnoor, der älteste Stadtteil Bremens

Expansion For homework, give each student the name of a person or place mentioned in the text. Have them briefly present a picture to the class with a sentence describing the content. Ex.: **Das ist ein Kleid von der Designerin Jil Sander.**

Landesgrenzen	
●	Stadt
◎	Landeshauptstadt

0 — 25 Meilen
0 — 25 Kilometer

Unglaublich, aber wahr!

In Hamburg gibt es mehr als 2.400 Brücken°. Die Brücken überqueren° die Alster, Süderelbe, Norderelbe und Kanäle der Stadt. Es gibt mehr Brücken in Hamburg als in Venedig°, Amsterdam und London zusammen.

Suggestion Tell students that the Beatles spent a few years in Hamburg in the early sixties. They also recorded German versions of "**Komm gib mir deine Hand**" and "**Sie liebt dich**"; videos for both can be found online.

Expansion A series of puppet shows called **Märchen der Welt** is available online, including a production of **Bremer Stadtmusikanten**. Show students the final five minutes, in which the thieves are driven away by the animals.

Märchen
Bremer Stadtmusikanten

Auf dem Marktplatz der Stadt Bremen gibt es eine Statue: Man kann einen Hahn° auf einer Katze auf einem Hund auf einem Esel° stehen sehen. Diese Tiere spielen die Hauptrollen eines Märchens der Gebrüder Grimm mit dem Namen „Die Bremer Stadtmusikanten". Es ist interessant, dass die Tiere in dem Märchen nie in Bremen ankamen. Zwar wollten sie am Anfang der Geschichte nach Bremen, hielten dann aber in einem Haus außerhalb der Stadt an. Trotzdem sind die Stadtmusikanten ein wichtiges Symbol der Stadt.

Natur
Nationalpark Schleswig-Holsteinsches Wattenmeer

Das Wattenmeer liegt in der Nordsee. Große Teile des Wattenmeers stehen unter Naturschutz°. Der Nationalpark Schleswig-Holsteinisches Wattenmeer hat eine Fläche von 4.410 Quadratkilometern und erstreckt sich von der deutsch-dänischen Seegrenze bis zur Elbmündung°. Er ist der größte deutsche Nationalpark. 70% des Nationalparks stehen permanent unter Wasser. Tiere und Pflanzen, die in diesem Nationalpark leben, sind Schweinswale°, Brandgänse° und diverse Seegräser. Seit 2009 ist das Wattenmeer ein UNESCO-Welterbe°.

Piraten
Störtebeker

Klaus Störtebeker ist der berühmteste deutsche Pirat (wahrscheinlich 1360–1401). Viele Legenden existieren über ihn. Der Name Störtebeker (Stürz den Becher) kommt aus dem Niederdeutschen: angeblich konnte Störtebeker einen 4-Liter-Becher° in einem Schluck° austrinken. 1401 exekutierte man Störtebeker mit 30 Gefährten° in Hamburg. Laut einer Sage° durften alle Gefährten weiterleben°, an denen Störtebeker nach seiner Exekution ohne Kopf vorbeilief°. Er schaffte 11 Kameraden! Heute ist das Interesse an diesem Mann immer noch sehr groß. Einige Schiffe tragen seinen Namen und es gibt auch Filme und Festspiele über ihn.

Tradition
Hafengeburtstag Hamburg

Ungefähr 13.000 Seeschiffe aus aller Welt laufen jährlich den zweitgrößten Seehafen° Europas an. Kaiser Friedrich Barbarossa hatte den Hamburgern am 7. Mai 1189 Zollfreiheit° für ihre Schiffe auf der Elbe von der Stadt bis an die Nordsee gewährt. Das Tor zur Welt war damit geöffnet, der Hamburger Hafen geboren. Seit 1977 feiert man Anfang Mai den Hafengeburtstag Hamburg.

Musik Musik

Namika

Namika ist eine deutsche Hip-Hop-Sängerin, deren Eltern beide aus Marokko stammen. Sie singt über Themen wie Identität, Heimat, und Selbstfindung. Die Inspiration für ihre Musik ist ihr Idol Missy Elliot.

Go to **vhlcentral.com** to find out more about **Namika** and her music.

Hahn *rooster* **Esel** *donkey* **Naturschutz** *conservation* **Elbmündung** *Elbe delta* **Schweinswale** *porpoises* **Brandgänse** *shelducks* **Welterbe** *world heritage site* **zweitgrößten Seehafen** *second largest seaport* **Zollfreiheit** *guaranteed duty exemption* **ausgedehnten** *extensive* **Bühnenprogramm** *stage program* **Becher** *mug* **Schluck** *gulp* **Gefährten** *companions* **Sage** *tale* **weiterleben** *be spared* **ohne Kopf vorbeilief** *ran by without his head*

---

1 **Was haben Sie gelernt?** Entscheiden Sie, ob die Sätze richtig oder falsch sind. Korrigieren Sie die falschen Sätze.

1. Im Hamburg gibt es mehr Brücken als in Venedig, Amsterdam, und London zusammen. **Richtig.**

2. Auf dem Bremer Marktplatz gibt es eine Statue mit vier Brüdern. **Falsch.** Auf dem Bremer Marktplatz gibt es eine Statue mit vier Tieren.

3. Der Hamburger Hafen wurde im Jahr 1189 gegründet. **Richtig.**

4. Der berühmteste deutsche Pilot heißt Klaus Störtebeker. **Falsch.** Der berühmteste deutsche Pirat heißt Klaus Störtebeker.

5. Der Nationalpark Wattenmeer ist der größte deutsche Nationalpark. **Richtig.**

2 **Was meinen Sie?** Diskutieren Sie die Frage mit einem Partner/einer Partnerin.

• Was sind die Ähnlichkeiten und Unterschiede zwischen Schleswig-Holstein, Hamburg, und Bremen? Welchen Bundesstaat würden Sie gern besuchen? Warum?

Lesen Audio: Reading

Vor dem Lesen

Strategien

Predicting content from the title

You can often use titles and subheadings to predict the content of a text before you read it. For example, you can usually predict the content of a newspaper article from its headline. Predicting content from titles will help you increase your reading comprehension in German.

Untersuchen Sie den Text

Lesen Sie die Überschriften (*titles*) des Textes. Was für eine Textart ist das? Schreiben Sie mit einem Partner / einer Partnerin eine Liste: welche Informationen können Sie in jedem Teil des Textes finden? Answers will vary.

Überschriften

Lesen Sie die Überschriften: Was ist das Thema des Textes, der dieser Überschrift folgt (*follows*)? Wo kann man diese Überschriften finden (in einer Tageszeitung, einem Magazin, einer Broschüre, einem Reiseführer, etc.)? Sample answers are provided.

Regensburg entdecken
eine Broschüre, ein Reiseführer

Diese Woche in Berlin
eine Tageszeitung

Die Pyramiden Ägyptens in 8 Tagen!
eine Broschüre, ein Reiseführer

DFB-Team verliert Fußball-Länderspiel gegen Frankreich
eine Tageszeitung

Am Frankfurter Flughafen wird gestreikt
eine Tageszeitung

Die 15 besten Rezepte zum Grillen
ein Magazin

Gute Restaurants für Studenten in Kiel
eine Broschüre, ein Reiseführer

Die Nordseeküste° Schleswig-Holsteins in 6 Tagen

6 Tage Naturerlebnis° für 450 Euro!

1. Tag: Hamburg-Büsum Mit dem Bus von Hamburg nach Brunsbüttel. Hier besichtigen° wir die Schleusen° des Nord-Ostsee-Kanals. Weiter geht es mit dem Bus nach Friedrichskoog. Wir besuchen die Seehundstation° Friedrichskoog, die einzige Seehundstation in Schleswig-Holstein. Per Bus geht es weiter nach Büsum, unserer Endstation heute. Am Nachmittag besuchen wir das „Museum am Meer" mit Informationen über das Fischen an der Nordseeküste. Danach gibt es einen Besuch der 'Sturmflutenwelt° Blanker Hans' mit Demonstration der Flutkatastrophe von 1962.

2. Tag: Büsum-Tönning-St. Peter Ording-Husum Nach einer Busfahrt von Büsum nach Tönning besuchen wir das Multimar Wattforum. Hier kann man in Aquarien Wale und andere Tiere des Wattenmeers sehen. Mit dem Bus geht es weiter nach St. Peter Ording. Wir werden einen Spaziergang am Strand machen und dann den Westküstenpark mit Robbinarium° besuchen (bei schlechtem Wetter gehen wir in der Dünentherme im Freizeit- und Erlebnisbad schwimmen). Nach einer weiteren Busfahrt besuchen wir das Schloss° vor Husum und den Schlosspark mit seinen wunderschönen Blumen.

Nordseeküste *North Sea coast* **Naturerlebnis** *nature experience* **besichtigen** *tour* **Schleusen** *locks* **Seehundstation** *harbor seal ward* **Sturmflutwelt** *world of the storm tide* **Robbinarium** *seal zoo* **Schloss** *castle*

3. Tag: Husum-Insel Föhr

In Husum machen wir eine Stadtführung° mit dem Fahrrad: Wo hat der berühmte Autor Theodor Storm gelebt und gearbeitet? Mit dem Bus geht es dann nach Dagebüll und mit einer Fähre° auf die Insel° Föhr. Hier besuchen wir ein typisches friesisches Dorf°: Nieblum.

4. Tag: Insel Föhr-Insel Amrum

Mit der Fähre fahren wir von Föhr zu der Insel Amrum. Wir sehen uns die Stadt Wittdün an, besuchen den Amrumer Leuchtturm° (gebaut 1875) und gehen auf der Kniepsand-Sandbank spazieren.

5. Tag: Insel Amrum-Sylt

Mit der Fähre fahren wir von Amrum nach Sylt. Wir wandern zum Roten Kliff Kampen. Nachmittags besuchen wir eine Einkaufsarkade in Westerland und das Sylt Aquarium mit 2.000 verschiedenen Kreaturen aus dem Meer.

6. Tag: Sylt-Seebüll-Friedrichstadt-Hamburg

Mit der Fähre geht es zurück zur Küste nach Niebüll und dann weiter nach Seebüll. Hier besuchen wir das Emil-Nolde-Museum. Mit dem Bus weiter nach Friedrichstadt. Diese Stadt heißt auch die „Holländerstadt". Die Stadtführung ist inklusive einer Schiffsfahrt° auf den Grachten° und Kanälen der Stadt. Das Ende unserer Tour ist in Hamburg.

Stadtführung *tour of the town* **Fähre** *ferry* **Insel** *island* **friesisches Dorf** *Frisian village*
Leuchtturm *lighthouse* **Schiffsfahrt** *boat tour* **Grachten** *town canals*

Nach dem Lesen

Richtig oder falsch? Korrigieren Sie die falschen Sätze.

	richtig	falsch
1. Den Nord-Ostsee-Kanal kann man in Brunsbüttel besuchen.	☑	☐
2. In Schleswig-Holstein gibt es viele Seehundstationen.	☐	☑
In Schleswig-Holstein gibt es nur in Friedrichskoog eine Seehundstation.		
3. In der Nordsee gibt es keine Wale.	☐	☑
In der Nordsee gibt es Wale.		
4. Im Schlosspark in Husum kann man wunderschöne Blumen sehen.	☑	☐
5. Dagebüll ist ein typisches friesisches Dorf.	☐	☑
Nieblum ist ein typisches friesisches Dorf.		
6. Die Insel Amrum ist für ihre lange Sandbank aus Kniepsand bekannt.	☑	☐
7. Die Insel Amrum ist berühmt für das Rote Kliff.	☐	☑
Die Insel Sylt ist berühmt für das Rote Kliff in Kampen.		
8. In Seebüll, der „Holländerstadt", gibt es viele Grachten und Kanäle.	☐	☑
In Friedrichstadt gibt es viele Grachten und Kanäle.		

Kombinieren Sie Verbinden Sie jede Aktivität mit dem passenden Ort.

_b_ 1. das Emil-Nolde-Museum besuchen

_d_ 2. auf der Kniepsand-Sandbank spazieren gehen

_a_ 3. eine Seehundstation besuchen

_c_ 4. eine Stadtführung mit dem Fahrrad machen

_e_ 5. das „Museum am Meer" besuchen

a. Friedrichskoog
b. Seebüll
c. Husum
d. Insel Amrum
e. Büsum

Suggestion Explain that **Kniepsand** is the name of a wandering sand dune that currently juts up against the western dunes of the island **Amrum**.

Urlaub in Schleswig-Holstein
Führen Sie zu dritt eine Diskussion.

Sie werden Schleswig-Holstein drei Wochen lang besuchen. Sie wollen eine organisierte Tour machen, die in Hamburg beginnt. Sie besuchen das Reisebüro für weitere Informationen. Stellen Sie Fragen über Städte, Aktivitäten, Ausflüge, Hotels, den Transport, etc.

Suggestion Make sure students understand that the group activity is a role-play and that two people in the group will play tourists, while a third will play the travel agent.

Hören

Strategien

Using visual cues

Visual cues can provide useful context to help you make sense of information you hear.

 To practice this strategy, you will listen to an advertisement.
As you listen, jot down information you hear that relates to the image below.

Vorbereitung

Schauen Sie sich das Foto rechts an. Worüber diskutieren Lisa und Martina?

Zuhören

 Hören Sie sich das Gespräch an. Welchen Ort möchte Lisa besuchen und welchen Martina? Wo werden sie Urlaub machen?

Suggestion Before students listen to the conversation, pre-teach the words **gebongt** ("agreed") and **KaDeWe** (**Kaufhaus des Westens**, a large mall in Berlin).

www.wilkommenimurlaub.de

| Hauptseite | Angebote | Preise | Anfrage und Buchung |

Teichhof Fehmarn. Direkt an der Nordsee. 2-Zimmer Wohnung mit Küche, Bad und Seeblick. 100 Euro pro Nacht.

Ferienwohnung Zugspitze. Gelegen in den Bayerischen Alpen. Wohnung für 2 Personen in traditionellem Haus mit Küche, Bad und Balkon. 50 Euro pro Nacht.

Ferienwohnung Schliemannstraße. Sehr zentral am Prenzlauer Berg in Berlin. Moderne Wohnung mit Küche und Bad. 36 Euro pro Person pro Nacht.

Verständnis

  Details Hören Sie sich den Dialog noch einmal an. Wer mag welche Aktivitäten? Wo wollen sie diese Aktivitäten machen?

	wandern	Touristen-attraktionen besuchen	Fahrrad fahren	schwimmen	Theater besuchen	einkaufen
Fehmarn	Lisa		Lisa	Lisa		
Bayerische Alpen	Martina	Martina				
Berlin		Lisa	Martina		Lisa	Martina

 Urlaubsziele Besprechen Sie mit einem Partner / einer Partnerin, wo Sie gerne Urlaub machen und was Sie dort gerne machen. Fahren Sie gerne im Winter, Frühling, Sommer oder Herbst in Urlaub? Wohin fährt Ihr Partner / Ihre Partnerin gerne? Was macht er/sie gerne im Urlaub? Welchen Urlaub wollen Sie gerne zusammen machen?

BEISPIEL

S1: Ich besuche jeden Sommer einen Nationalpark in den USA. Und du?
S2: Ich mag keine Nationalparks. Ich besuche Chicago mit meiner Familie.

Expansion After they complete the chart, ask students why Lisa doesn't want to go to the Alps. Play the audio again, if necessary. (She says: **Ich habe Angst vor hohen Bergen! Und Schlösser finde ich langweilig.**)

Schreiben

Strategien

Making an outline

Making an outline (**eine Gliederung**) before you write helps you to identify topics and subtopics, and provides a framework for presenting the information. Consider the following outline for a travel brochure.

I. Das Urlaubsziel

  A. Das Hotel

    1. Die Lage (*location*)

    2. Die Ausstattung (*facilities*)

    3. Die Bewertung (*rating*)

  B. Die Landschaft

  C. Die Sehenswürdigkeiten

II. Die Reisezeit

  A. Das Klima

  B. Der Preis

Eine Mindmap

Idea maps provide a useful way to help you visualize information before you create an outline. The larger circles in an idea map correspond to the Roman numerals in an outline. The smaller circles correspond to the outline's capital letters, numbers, and so on. Consider the idea map that led to the outline above.

Thema

Schreiben Sie eine Broschüre

Schreiben Sie eine Tour-Broschüre für ein Reiseziel (*destination*) in einem deutschsprachigen Land.

Bevor Sie die Broschüre schreiben, schreiben Sie sich Ideen für die Broschüre auf. Hier ist eine Liste mit wichtigen Fragen:

- Welches Reiseziele wollen Sie beschreiben?
- Wie lange soll die Tour dauern?
- Wie ist das Wetter am Reiseziel?
- Welche Kleidung brauchen die Teilnehmer (*participant*s)?
- Wo übernachten sie?
- Wo kann man essen gehen?
- Was soll man besuchen?
- Welche Aktivitäten gibt es (Sport, Einkaufen etc.)?
- Wie viel kostet der Urlaub pro Person?

Suggestion Tell students that they may use information from the articles in this chapter, and/or do additional research online.

Organisieren Sie Ihre Ideen mit einer Mindmap. Schreiben Sie mit der fertigen Mindmap eine Gliederung. Jetzt können Sie eine Broschüre schreiben. Benutzen Sie Überschriften (*titles*), damit die Leser die Organisation der Broschüre verstehen können. In guten Broschüren sind oft Anschauungsmaterialien (*visual aids*) (Fotos, Tabellen etc.) integriert. Verwenden Sie Vokabeln und Grammatik, die Sie in diesem Kapitel gelernt haben.

Expansion Have students prepare a poster or short PowerPoint presentation in which they talk about a trip to Germany as though they have really taken it, using the past tense. Encourage them to be creative and to use real destinations featured in the chapter.

Vocabulary Tools

Lektion 7A

Jahreszeiten
seasons

der Winter, - *winter*
der Frühling, -e *spring*
der Sommer, - *summer*
der Herbst, -e *fall*

Monate
months

der Januar *January*
der Februar *February*
der März *March*
der April *April*
der Mai *May*
der Juni *June*
der Juli *July*
der August *August*
der September *September*
der Oktober *October*
der November *November*
der Dezember *December*

das Datum
date

Welcher Tag ist heute? *What day is it today?*
Der 15. August. *The 15th of August.*
Wann hast du Geburtstag? *When is your birthday?*
Am 23. Mai. *May 23rd.*
das Jahr, -e *year*
die Jahreszeit, -en *season*
der Monat, -e *month*
der Tag, -e *day*
die Woche, -n *week*

das Wetter
weather

Wie ist das Wetter? *What's the weather like?*
Es ist schön draußen. *It's nice out.*
Das Wetter ist gut/schlecht. *The weather is nice/bad.*
Wie warm/kalt ist es? *How warm/cold is it?*
Es sind 18 Grad draußen. *It's 18 degrees out.*
Es ist heiß. *It's hot.*
Es ist kalt. *It's cold.*
Es ist kühl. *It's cool.*
Es ist sonnig. *It's sunny.*
Es ist windig. *It's windy.*
Es ist wolkig. *It's cloudy.*
Es regnet. *It's raining.*
Es schneit. *It's snowing.*
der Blitz, -e *lightning*
der Donner, - *thunder*
das Gewitter, - *thunderstorm*
der Hagel *hail*
der Nebel, - *fog; mist*
der Regen *rain*
der Regenmantel, ⁻ *raincoat*
der Regenschirm, -e *umbrella*
der Schnee *snow*
der Sturm, ⁻e *storm*
der Wetterbericht, -e *weather report*
die Wolke, -n *cloud*

***Präteritum* of verbs with prefixes** *See p. 286.*
Prepositions of location *See p. 290.*

Lektion 7B

am Flughafen
at the airport

der Abflug *departure*
die Ankunft *arrival*
der Ausgang, ⁻e *exit*
das Ausland *abroad*
die Bordkarte, -n *boarding pass*
die Businessklasse *business class*
der Flug, ⁻e *flight*
das Flugticket, -s *ticket*
das Flugzeug, -e *airplane*
das Gepäck *luggage*
das Handgepäck *carry-on luggage*
der Koffer, - *suitcase*
der Passagier, -e *passenger*
die Passkontrolle, -n *passport control*
der Personalausweis, -e *ID card*
die Reise, -n *trip*
das Reisebüro, -s *travel agency*
der Reisende, -n *traveler*
die Touristenklasse *economy class*
die Verspätung, -en *delay*
das Visum (*pl.* die Visa) *visa*
die Zeitung, -en *newspaper*
der Zoll *customs*

die Ferien
vacation

die Kreuzfahrt, -en *cruise*
das Meer, -e *sea; ocean*
der Skiurlaub, -e *ski vacation*
der Strand, ⁻e *beach*
eine Karte lesen *to read a map*
Urlaub machen *to go on vacation*

Unterkünfte
accommodations

der Fahrstuhl, ⁻e *elevator*
der Gast, ⁻e *(hotel) guest*
das (Fünf-Sterne-) Hotel *(five-star) hotel*
die Jugendherberge, -n *youth hostel*
der Schlüssel, - *key*
der Zimmerservice *room service*

zum Beschreiben

voll besetzt *fully occupied*
pünktlich *on time*

Verben

abbrechen (bricht... ab) *to cancel*
abfliegen (fliegt... ab) *to take off*
buchen *to make a (hotel) reservation*
fliegen *to fly*
landen *to land*
packen *to pack*
Schlange stehen *to stand in line*
übernachten *to spend the night*

Infinitive expressions *See p. 304.*
Time expressions *See p. 308.*
Indefinite pronouns *See p. 310.*

More activities

vhlcentral

Online activities

Verkehrsmittel und Technologie

COMMUNICATIVE GOALS
By the end of this chapter you will be able to:

Los geht's! Wo sind Hans und George? Was machen sie?

LEKTION 8A

Discuss cars, driving, and public transportation.

To do so, you will use:

Kontext Seite 322–325
• Driving
• Means of transportation
• Words related to public transportation

Strukturen Seite 330–339
8A.1 Das Plusquamperfekt
8A.2 Comparatives and superlatives

You will also learn about cultural products, practices, and perspectives related to:

Kultur Seite 328–329
• **Die deutsche Autobahn**
• **Fahrrad fahren**
• **Fräulein Stinnes' Weltreise**

Zapping Seite 339
• *Deutsche Automarken*

LEKTION 8B

Talk about electronic communication and computer technology.

To do so, you will use:

Kontext Seite 340–343
• Words and phrases related to technology
• Words and phrases related to using technology

Strukturen Seite 348–357
8B.1 The genitive case
8B.2 Demonstratives

You will also learn about cultural products, practices, and perspectives related to:

Kultur Seite 346–347
• **Die Max-Planck Gesellschaft**
• **Deutsche Mediengiganten**

WEITER GEHT'S

Seite 358–364
You will learn about Hessen and Thüringen, their culture, industries, and famous inhabitants.

Panorama Seite 358–359
• **Hessen und Thüringen**

And you will demonstrate that you can:
Lesen: Identifying Borrowed Words: Anglicisms
Hören: Recognize the genres of spoken discourse
Schreiben: Express and support your opinions

Suggestion Ask students to identify the type of public transportation shown in the photo.

Auto und Rad fahren Vocabulary Tools

Wortschatz

Auto fahren	*driving*
die Autobahn, -en	*highway*
der Fahrer, - / die Fahrerin, -nen	*driver*
die Straße, -n	*street*
geradeaus fahren	*to go straight ahead*
einen Unfall haben	*to have an accident*
parken	*to park*
rechts/links abbiegen (biegt... ab)	*to turn right/left*
das Verkehrsmittel	*means of transportation*
das Boot, -e	*boat*
der Bus, -se	*bus*
der LKW, -s	*truck*
das Schiff, -e	*ship*
das Taxi, -s	*taxi*
die U-Bahn, -en	*subway*
der Zug, ¨e	*train*
Auto	*cars*
das Benzin	*gas*
die Bremse, -n	*brakes*
das Nummernschild, -er	*license plate*
reparieren	*to repair*
die öffentlichen Verkehrsmittel	*public transportation*
der Bahnsteig, -e	*track; platform*
die Bushaltestelle, -n	*bus stop*
das Bußgeld, -er	*fine*
die erste/zweite Klasse, -n	*first/second class*
der Fahrkartenschalter, -	*ticket office*
der Fahrplan, ¨e	*schedule*
der Schaffner, -	*ticket collector*
(die Fahrkarte) entwerten	*to validate (a ticket)*

Suggestion Tell students that **Rad** means *wheel*. Ask them to guess the meaning of words like **Einrad**, **Dreirad**, and **Motorrad**.

Suggestion Students may be unfamiliar with the process of buying a ticket in advance from an **Automat** and stamping it when entering a bus or tram. Make sure they understand the phrase **die Fahrkarte entwerten**.

Suggestion Remind students that the **-in** suffix is often added to refer to female practitioners of a profession or activity. Say: **Ein Mann, der Autos repariert, ist *Mechaniker*. Wie heißt eine Frau, die Autos repariert?**

die Tankstelle, -n
gas station

das Fahrrad, ¨er

Er tankt. (tanken)
He is filling up.

das Auto, -s

der Kofferraum, ¨e
trunk

das Lenkrad, ¨er
steering wheel

die Motorhaube, -n
hood

der Sicherheitsgurt, -e

der Motor, -en

der Mechaniker, -
(die Mechanikerin, -nen *f.*)

Sie haben einen Platten.
They have a flat tire.

das Öl, -e

Benzin bleifrei | Diesel

More activities

vhlcentral | WB pp. 105–106 | LM p. 67 | Online activities

ACHTUNG

In German-speaking countries, distances are measured in kilometers (**Kilometer**). One kilometer is equal to 0.62 miles (**Meilen**).

der Verkehr
traffic

der Polizist, -en
(die Polizistin, -nen *f.***)**

der Scheibenwischer, -
windshield wipe

die Windschutzscheibe, -n
windshield

der Scheinwerfer, -

Anwendung

Suggestion Have students look at a map of Germany. Give them the distance between two cities in kilometers. Have them convert the distance to miles. Ex.: **Ich fahre von Frankfurt nach Coburg. Das sind ungefähr 164 km. Wie viele Meilen sind das?**

1 **Paare finden** Verbinden Sie das Verb mit dem richtigen Ausdruck (*expression*).

1 *Suggestion* Check comprehension by asking follow-up questions. Ex.: **Ich habe einen Platten. Was mache ich? Ich bin an der Tankstelle. Was mache ich da?**

__d__ 1. entwerten
__c__ 2. packen
__f__ 3. reparieren
__b__ 4. Schlange stehen
__a__ 5. tanken
__e__ 6. parken

a. die Tankstelle
b. die Bushaltestelle
c. der Kofferraum
d. die Fahrkarte
e. die Garage
f. der Mechaniker

2 **Bilder beschriften** Wie heißen die verschiedenen Verkehrsmittel auf den Fotos?

1. ____der Zug____
2. ____das Schiff____
3. ____der Bus____
4. ____das Fahrrad____
5. ____die U-Bahn____
6. ____der LKW____

3 **Hören Sie zu** Was macht man an der Tankstelle?

3 *Expansion* Ask students if they own a car or motorbike, how much they spend on gas each week, and what one can buy at a gas station.

	Ja	Nein		Ja	Nein
1.	☑	☐	4.	☑	☐
2.	☐	☑	5.	☐	☑
3.	☐	☑	6.	☑	☐

4 **Wer, wen, was und wo** Hören Sie die sechs Aussagen an und wählen Sie das Wort, das am besten zu jeder Situation passt. Beantworten Sie danach die Fragen in ganzen Sätzen.
Audio: Es regnet. Was brauchen Sie? (die Scheibenwischer)/ das Lenkrad.
Schreiben Sie: Ich brauche die Scheibenwischer. Answers will vary.

1. (die Polizei)/ den Schaffner
2. der Metzger / (der Mechaniker)
3. im Fahrstuhl / (am Fahrkartenschalter)
4. (ein Bußgeld)/ eine Geldtasche
5. (an der Tankstelle)/ am Bahnsteig
6. auf den Stadtplan / (auf den Fahrplan)

Kommunikation

5 **Aus dem Polizeibericht** Schauen Sie sich das Bild an und lesen Sie den kurzen Zeitungsartikel dazu. Beantworten Sie danach die Fragen. Arbeiten Sie mit einem Partner / einer Partnerin zusammen. Sample answers provided.

5 Suggestion Before they read the article, ask students if there is a **Handyverbot** in their city or state: **Darf man hier sein Handy benützen, während man fährt?**

5 Video Virtual Chat You can also assign activity 5 on the Supersite.

Unfall in Frankfurter Innenstadt

Ein 23-jähriger Peugeotfahrer hat nicht aufgepasst und fuhr am Donnerstagabend bei Rot über die Kreuzung (*intersection*) Kaiserstraße und Friedensstraße. Ein LKW kam von links und die zwei Fahrzeuge sind zusammengestoßen (*collided*). Beim Unfall ist der Peugeotfahrer auch gegen ein geparktes Motorrad gestoßen. Beide Fahrer trugen Sicherheitsgurte und blieben unverletzt (*unhurt*). Der junge Mann sagte aus, er wollte nur schnell auf sein Handydisplay schauen und sah dann den LKW nicht. Der 23-Jährige bekam ein Bußgeld von 400 Euro. Seit 2001 gibt es ein Handyverbot am Steuer. Man darf nicht mit dem Auto fahren und dabei sein Handy benutzen.

1. Was ist am Donnerstagabend passiert? Ein Unfall zwischen einem Peugeot und einem LKW ist passiert.
2. Welche Fahrzeuge waren in den Unfall verwickelt (*involved*)? Ein Peugeot, ein LKW und ein Motorrad waren in den Unfall verwickelt.
3. Warum hat der Peugeotfahrer nicht bei Rot gehalten? Der Peugeotfahrer hat auf sein Handydisplay geschaut.
4. War jemand beim Unfall verletzt? Nein, niemand war verletzt.
5. Musste der Peugeotfahrer ein Bußgeld bezahlen? Ja, er musste 400 Euro Bußgeld bezahlen.
6. Was ist ein Handyverbot? Man darf nicht mit dem Auto fahren und dabei sein Handy benutzen.

7 Suggestion Before beginning the activity, ask students if public transportation is available in their hometowns. Explain that in Germany, the well-developed network of buses, trains, subways, and trams makes it easy to get around without a car.

6 **Diskutieren und kombinieren** Ihr Professor / Ihre Professorin gibt Ihnen zwei verschiedene Blätter. Finden Sie sieben Unterschiede zwischen Ihrem Bild und dem Bild Ihres Partner / Ihrer Partnerin. Answers will vary.

BEISPIEL

S1: *Ich sehe vier Fahrräder.*
S2: *Mein Bild hat zwei Fahrräder. Und es gibt eine Bushaltestelle.*
S1: *Ich sehe keine Bushaltestelle...*

7 **Verkehrsmittel** Diskutieren Sie in kleinen Gruppen, welche Verkehrsmittel Sie nehmen, um an die verschiedenen Orte zu kommen. Machen Sie danach eine Liste mit allen Verkehrsmitteln, die Sie normalerweise (*usually*) benutzen. Vergleichen Sie schließlich Ihre Liste mit der Liste einer anderen Gruppe. Answers will vary.

BEISPIEL

S1: *Um in die Innenstadt zu kommen, nehme ich die U-Bahn.*
S2: *Wirklich? Ich fahre mit meinem Fahrrad.*
S3: *Ich gehe zu Fuß, aber...*

Verkehrsmittel	Orte
das Auto	das Ausland
der Bus	das Haus von meinen Eltern
das Fahrrad	das Fußballstadion
das Flugzeug	der Supermarkt
zu Fuß	die Diskothek
das Taxi	die Innenstadt
die U-Bahn	die Unibibliothek
der Zug	?

Aussprache und Rechtschreibung Audio

Long and short vowels with an *Umlaut*

You have already learned that adding an **Umlaut** to the vowels **a**, **o**, and **u** changes their pronunciation. Vowels with an **Umlaut** have both long and short forms.

| **Räder** | **Männer** | **löhnen** | **löschen** | **Züge** | **fünf** |

The long **ä** is pronounced similarly to the *a* in the English word *bay*, without the final *y* sound. The short **ä** is pronounced like the *e* in *pet*.

| **Faxgerät** | **Unterwäsche** | **Fahrpläne** | **Spaziergänge** |

To produce the long **ö** sound, start by saying the German long **e**, but round your lips as if you were about to whistle. To produce the short **ö** sound, start by saying the short **e**, but keep your lips rounded.

| **Öl** | **öffentlich** | **schön** | **Töchter** |

To produce the long **ü** sound, start to say the German long **i**, but round your lips tightly. To produce the short **ü** sound, make the short **i** sound, but with tightly rounded lips. In some loanwords, the German **y** is pronounced like **ü**. In other loanwords, the German **y** is pronounced like the English consonant *y*.

| **Schüler** | **zurück** | **Typ** | **Physik** |

Suggestion To help students pronounce the long **ü** sound, have them position their tongues behind the back of the lower front teeth and round their lips, as if they were about to whistle.

1 **Aussprechen** Wiederholen Sie die Wörter, die Sie hören.

1. Rad / Räder
2. Kopf / Köpfe
3. Zug / Züge
4. Käse / Kästchen
5. mögen / möchten
6. fühlen / füllen
7. kämen / kämmen
8. lösen / löschen
9. Dünen / dünn
10. typisch
11. Audio-Player
12. Handy

2 **Nachsprechen** Wiederholen Sie die Sätze, die Sie hören.

1. In der Küche kocht die Köchin mit einem großen Kochlöffel.
2. Sie ändern morgen alle Fahrpläne für die Züge in Österreich.
3. Lösch alles auf der Festplatte, bevor du deinen PC verkaufst.
4. Jürgen fährt mit den öffentlichen Verkehrsmitteln zur Universität.
5. Grüne Fahrräder sind schöner als rote oder schwarze Fahrräder.
6. Der blonde Typ da hat sein Handy verloren.

3 **Sprichwörter** Wiederholen Sie die Sprichwörter, die Sie hören.

Ein goldener Schlüssel öffnet alle Türen.[1]

Der Apfel fällt nicht weit vom Stamm.[2]

[1] A golden key opens all doors.
[2] The apple doesn't fall far from the tree.

More activities

vhlcentral | LM p. 68 | Online activities

Ein Ende mit Schrecken

 Video

Sabite und Torsten gehen zusammen auf der Museumsinsel spazieren. Es ist Sabites Lieblingsort, aber es wird ein trauriger Tag.

Vorbereitung Have students read the episode title and try to predict what will happen in this episode. What do they think is going to end? Can they guess what **Schrecken** might mean? You may want to share with students the proverb **Besser ein Ende mit Schrecken als ein Schrecken ohne Ende.**

GEORGE Berlin hat die besten öffentlichen Verkehrsmittel! In Milwaukee haben wir nur Busse und kein S-Bahn-System.
HANS Hast du kein Auto?
GEORGE Doch, aber es ist alt und hat oft Pannen. Das Ölwarnlicht leuchtet ständig, und die Kupplung rutscht.
HANS Warum behältst du es?
GEORGE Es bringt mich zur Uni und zurück.

TORSTEN Sabite... es tut mir leid.
SABITE Wie bitte?
TORSTEN Es tut mir leid. An dem Abend im Restaurant, als ich von deinen Plänen erfahren habe...

SABITE Ich habe nicht darüber geredet, weil es nur eine Idee war. Ich hatte die Idee schon gehabt, bevor ich mit Lorenzo im Restaurant darüber gesprochen habe. Wir haben über Kunst geredet und da habe ich es zum ersten Mal laut ausgesprochen.
TORSTEN Ich habe das einfach nicht gewusst und bin wütend geworden.

SABITE Torsten, ich... ich glaube nicht...
TORSTEN Ich möchte nicht, dass du aus Berlin weggehst.
SABITE Warum?
TORSTEN Weil ich dich liebe.

SABITE Oh, Torsten, ich habe letzte Woche mit meiner Mutter zu Mittag gegessen. Wir haben etwas beschlossen. Meine ganze Familie verbringt den Sommer in der Türkei.

TORSTEN Ach so. Ich möchte nicht, dass du gehst, aber ich weiß, dass ich dich nicht davon abhalten kann. Du bist so stark, wie du schön bist. Was ich jetzt sagen muss, ist sehr schwer.
SABITE Torsten, machst du Schluss mit mir?
TORSTEN Liebst du mich?

ÜBUNGEN

1   **Richtig oder falsch?** Entscheiden Sie, ob die folgenden Sätze **richtig** oder **falsch** sind.

1. In Milwaukee gibt es Busse und ein S-Bahn-System. Falsch.
2. Georges Auto ist alt und hat oft Pannen. Richtig.
3. Sabite hat mit Lorenzo im Restaurant über Kunst gesprochen. Richtig.
4. Dort hat sie zum ersten Mal laut über die Türkei gesprochen Richtig.
5. Torsten war im Restaurant geduldig und ist ruhig geblieben. Falsch.

6. Sabite hat letzte Woche mit ihrer Mutter zu Abend gegessen. Falsch.
7. Torsten möchte, dass Sabite nach Istanbul geht. Falsch.
8. George und Hans fahren mit dem Bus in Berlin herum. Falsch.
9. Torsten hat mit Sabite auf der Museumsinsel Schluss gemacht. Richtig.
10. Sabite mag die Museumsinsel nicht. Falsch.

PERSONEN

 George   Hans   Meline   Sabite   Torsten

MELINE Hallo, Sabite. Wie geht's? Okay... Süße... es ist schon okay. Wo bist du? Bleib dort, ich bin gerade an einer U-Bahn-Station vorbeigekommen. Ich bin in einer Viertelstunde da. (*Zu sich selbst.*) Torsten. Er ist so dumm, wie er gemein ist.

GEORGE Sabite, hey. Hans und ich fahren mit der Bahn in der ganzen Stadt herum. Das ist die interessanteste Weise, Berlin zu sehen. Was? Jetzt mal ganz ruhig. Du bist wo? Er hat was? Wo sind wir?
HANS Spandau. Wir sind in der U-Bahn-Station Altstadt Spandau! Wo ist sie?
GEORGE Museumsinsel. Wir kommen so schnell wie möglich.

MELINE Er hat dich bis hierher zur Museumsinsel geschleppt, nur um mit dir Schluss zu machen?
SABITE Es war meine Idee, hierher zu kommen. Ich liebe diesen Ort. Ah, da kommen sie.
HANS Hey, Sabite, es tut mir so, so, so leid.
MELINE Hans. Hans!

HANS Also... du hast mit ihm Schluss gemacht?
SABITE Ich wollte mit ihm Schluss machen. Aber er... er war schneller als ich!

Nützliche Ausdrücke

- **die Panne**
  breakdown
- **Das Ölwarnlicht leuchtet ständig, und die Kupplung rutscht.**
  The oil warning light is always on, and the clutch slips.
- **erfahren (von)**
  to find out (about)
- **Wir haben über Kunst geredet und da habe ich es zum ersten Mal laut ausgesprochen.**
  We were talking about art, and that was the first time I said it out loud.
- **wütend**
  furious
- **Wir haben etwas beschlossen.**
  We decided something.
- **Ich möchte nicht, dass du gehst, aber ich weiß, dass ich dich nicht davon abhalten kann.**
  I don't want you to go, but I know I can't stop you.
- **vorbeikommen**   **herumfahren**
  to pass   *to ride around*
- **Wir kommen so schnell wie möglich.**
  We'll be there as soon as possible.
- **schleppen**
  to drag

8A.1
- **Berlin hat die besten öffentlichen Verkehrsmittel!**
  Berlin has the best public transportation!

8A.2
- **Ich hatte die Idee schon gehabt, bevor ich mit Lorenzo im Restaurant darüber gesprochen habe.**
  I'd already had the idea before Lorenzo and I discussed it at the restaurant.

Zum Besprechen Bilden Sie zu zweit einen Dialog zwischen Sabite und Torsten. Versuchen Sie, die Beziehung zu retten (*to save the relationship*). Answers will vary.

3 Vertiefung Finden Sie heraus, was für öffentliche Verkehrsmittel es in Berlin gibt. Sind die Fahrpreise billig oder teuer? Vergleichen Sie die öffentlichen Verkehrsmittel in Berlin mit den öffentlichen Verkehrsmitteln in Ihrer Stadt. Answers will vary.

3 Expansion Have students research the German **Autobahn** and compare it to the highway system in their country. How are the highways numbered? What are the speed limits?

More activities

vhlcentral   VM p. 15   Online activities

Suggestion Before they begin the reading, ask students: **Welche Autos kommen aus Deutschland? Was wissen Sie über die Autobahn in Deutschland?**

IM FOKUS

Die deutsche Autobahn Reading

DIE GESCHICHTE DER DEUTSCHEN Autobahn geht fast 100 Jahre zurück. Die AVUS (Automobil-Verkehrs- und Übungs-Straße), heute Teil der Autobahn A115, war die erste nur für Autos zugelassene° Straße Europas. Schon seit 1921 erstreckte sie sich° zwischen den Berliner Stadtteilen Charlottenburg und Nikolassee. Um einmal darüber zu fahren, musste man zehn Mark bezahlen. Damals war das ziemlich teuer!

Am 6. August 1932 eröffnete der Kölner Oberbürgermeister Konrad Adenauer die erste so genannte „Autobahn". Ihr Bau hatte drei Jahre gedauert. Sie war 20 Kilometer lang und erstreckte sich zwischen Köln und Bonn. In beide Fahrtrichtungen war sie zweispurig° und kreuzungsfrei° Damit entsprach° sie einer Autobahn, wie wir sie heute kennen, mit einem Unterschied: Es gab keinen Mittelstreifen°. Deshalb bekam der Abschnitt erst 1958, nach weiterem Ausbau°, den offiziellen Status der Autobahn.

Heute hat Deutschland eines der dichtesten Autobahnnetze° der Welt und der Bau geht immer weiter. Es gilt zwar in Deutschland eine Richtgeschwindigkeit° von 130 Kilometern pro Stunde, ein generelles Tempolimit° gibt es aber nicht. Trotzdem haben 45 Prozent aller deutschen Autobahnkilometer Tempolimits. An fast allen Autobahnen gibt es mittlerweile komfortable Raststätten°, wo es neben Tankstellen, Hotels, Restaurants und Läden sogar Kinderspielplätze gibt.

Längste Autobahnnetze der Welt	
Land	Strecke°
USA	260.000 km
China	130.000 km
Spanien	17.190 km
Deutschland	12.996 km

zugelassene *permitted* **erstreckte... sich** *extended* **zweispurig** *two-lane* **kreuzungsfrei** *intersection-free* **entsprach** *conformed to* **Mittelstreifen** *median strip* **Ausbau** *extension* **Autobahnnetze** *interstate highway networks* **Richtgeschwindigkeit** *target speed* **Tempolimit** *speed limit* **Raststätten** *service areas* **Strecke** *distance*

ÜBUNGEN

1 **Im Fokus** Richtig oder falsch? Korrigieren Sie die falschen Aussagen.

1. Die Geschichte der deutschen Autobahn geht fast 100 Jahre zurück. **Richtig.**
2. Deutschland hat das längste Autobahnnetz der Welt. **Falsch.** Die U.S.A haben weltweit das größte Autobahnnetz.
3. Man darf in Deutschland auf der Autobahn nur 130 Kilometer pro Stunde fahren. **Falsch.** 130 Kilometer pro Stunde sind nur eine generelle Richtgeschwindigkeit.

Diskussion Fahren Sie oft zu schnell oder respektieren Sie Tempolimits? Warum? Mit welchem Auto möchten Sie einmal auf einer deutschen Autobahn fahren?

2 **Die deutschsprachige Welt** Richtig oder falsch? Korrigieren Sie die falschen Aussagen.

1. In Deutschland haben mehr Haushalte Fahrräder als Autos. **Richtig.**
2. Fahrradfahrer dürfen nie in einer Einbahnstraße entgegen der Fahrtrichtung fahren. **Falsch.** Manchmal darf man in einer Einbahnstraße auch entgegen der Fahrtrichtung fahren.
3. In Fußgängerzonen müssen Fahrradfahren sehr langsam fahren. **Richtig.**

Diskussion Fahren Sie gern Fahrrad? Wo kann man in Ihrer Gegend (*area*) gut Fahrrad fahren?

DEUTSCH IM ALLTAG

Verkehrsschilder

die Kreuzung	*intersection*
das Stoppschild	*stop sign*
(die) Ausfahrt	*exit*
(die) Baustelle	*construction zone*
(die) Einbahnstraße	*one-way street*
(die) Umleitung	*detour*

DIE DEUTSCHSPRACHIGE WELT

Fahrrad fahren

In Deutschland besitzen mehr Haushalte° Fahrräder als ein Auto. Bei Familien haben sogar 96% der Haushalte Fahrräder. Deshalb gibt es in vielen Städten separate Fahrradwege°. Für das Fahrradfahren gibt es besondere Regeln°: Wenn es keinen Fahrradweg gibt, müssen Fahrradfahrer, die über 11 Jahre alt sind, auf der rechten Seite der Straße fahren. Besondere Schilder zeigen, wann Fahrradfahrer in Einbahnstraßen entgegen der Fahrtrichtung° fahren dürfen. In Fußgängerzonen° dürfen Radfahrer nur im Schritttempo° fahren. Außerdem muss jedes Fahrrad ein festes Fahrradlicht haben.

Haushalte *households* **Fahrradwege** *bike lanes* **Regeln** *rules* **entgegen der Fahrtrichtung** *against the flow of traffic* **Fußgängerzonen** *pedestrian zones* **Schritttempo** *walking speed*

PORTRÄT

Fräulein Stinnes' Weltreise°

Clärenore Stinnes kommt am 21. Januar 1901 als Tochter eines Großindustriellen zur Welt. Mit 24 Jahren nimmt sie zum ersten Mal an einem Autorennen° teil. Bis 1927 gewinnt sie 17 Rennen, darunter auch eine internationale Rallye in Russland. Sie ist die einzige Frau unter 53 Teilnehmern! Im Mai 1927 bricht Clärenore zu einer Weltreise auf. Sie finanziert die Reise mit Sponsoren wie Bosch und Aral. Auch das Außenministerium° und deutsche Auslandsvertretungen° unterstützen sie. Sie legt 47.000 Kilometer zurück und ist zwei Jahre und einen Monat unterwegs. Das Auto, ein Adler Standard 6, steht heute im Deutschen Museum in München.

Weltreise *world tour* **Autorennen** *car race* **Außenministerium** *Ministry of Foreign Affairs* **Auslandsvertretungen** *embassies*

🔗 IM INTERNET

Suchen Sie Informationen zu der Internationalen Automobil-Ausstellung (IAA). Wo und wann war die letzte Ausstellung?

Find out more at **vhlcentral.com**.

---

3 **Porträt** Richtig oder falsch? Korrigieren Sie die falschen Aussagen. Diskutieren Sie dann die letzte Frage mit einem Partner/ einer Partnerin.

1. Clärenore Stinnes war als Kind arm.
   Falsch. Ihre Eltern waren Großindustrielle und hatten viel Geld.
2. Stinnes´ Eltern finanzieren ihre Autoweltreise.
   Falsch. Stinnes hatte Sponsoren.
3. Als junge Frau gewinnt sie 17 Rennen. **Richtig.**

Diskussion Möchten Sie einmal eine Weltreise machen? Warum /Warum nicht?

4 **Lieblingstransportmittel** Sie möchten mit Freunden eine Reise von Sylt bis in die Alpen machen. Sie sind sportlich und möchten viel Kultur und Natur sehen. Wie kommen Sie von Sylt in die Alpen? Welche Transportmittel benutzen Sie? Planen Sie Ihre Reise und präsentieren Sie die Route im Kurs.

Suggestion Remind students that German trains are electric and an increasing number of cars are hybrids, and that one can transport a bike on a train.

8A.1

Das Plusquamperfekt Grammar Tutorial

Startblock Use the **Plusquamperfekt** tense to refer to a past event that occurred before another event in the past.

> Ich **hatte** die Idee schon **gehabt**, bevor ich mit Lorenzo im Restaurant darüber gesprochen habe.

> Wir **hatten** über Kunst **geredet** und da habe ich es zum ersten Mal laut ausgesprochen.

Das Plusquamperfekt

- To form the **Plusquamperfekt**, use the **Präteritum** form of **haben** or **sein** with the past participle of the verb that expresses the action.

  Ich **hatte vergessen**, die Tür zu schließen.
  *I **had forgotten** to close the door.*

  Jasmin **war** noch nie nach Zürich **gefahren**.
  *Jasmin **had** never **been** to Zurich.*

- Since the **Plusquamperfekt** refers to a past event that was completed prior to another past event, both events are often described in the same sentence.

Der Zug fährt ab.   Ich komme am Bahnsteig an.

14.45 Uhr   **Plusquamperfekt**   14.47 Uhr   **Perfekt/Präteritum**

PRÄTERITUM	PLUSQUAMPERFEKT
Als ich am Bahnsteig **ankam**, *When I **arrived** at the platform,*	**war** der Zug schon **abgefahren**. *the train **had** already **left**.*

Bevor Stefan in die Stadt gezogen ist, **hatte** er nie öffentliche Verkehrsmittel **benutzt**.
*Before Stefan moved to the city, he **had** never **used** public transportation.*

Nachdem der Mechaniker das Auto **repariert hatte**, **fuhr** er damit zur Tankstelle.
*After the mechanic **had fixed** the car, he **drove** it to the gas station.*

Bevor ich nach England **reiste, hatte** ich meinen Neffen noch nie **gesehen**.
*Before I **went** to England, I **had** never **met** my nephew.*

Als wir im Kino **ankamen, hatte** der Film schon **angefangen**.
*When we **got** to the movie theater, the film **had** already **started**.*

Conjunctions *als, bevor, nachdem*

Suggestion Tell students that subordinating conjunctions like **bevor**, **nachdem**, and **als** "send" or "kick" the verb to the end of the clause.

- Use the subordinating conjunctions **als** (*when*), **bevor** (*before*), and **nachdem** (*after*) to indicate the sequence in which two past events occurred.

  Als Jan ins Restaurant **kam**, **hatte** seine
  Freundin schon **bestellt**.
  *By the time Jan **got** to the restaurant, his girlfriend **had** already **ordered**.*

  Unsere Eltern sind erst nach Hause gekommen,
  nachdem wir schon ins Bett **gegangen waren**.
  *By the time our parents came home, we **had** already **gone** to bed.*

- When a clause begins with **als**, **bevor**, or **nachdem**, move the conjugated verb to the end of the clause.

  Bevor ich in Deutschland **wohnte**...
  *Before I **lived** in Germany...*

  Als Hanna **anrief**...
  *When Hanna **called**...*

- After **bevor** and **als**, use the **Perfekt** or **Präteritum** and put the main clause in the **Plusquamperfekt**.

  Als Tom zur Bushaltestelle **kam**, **war** der
  Bus schon **abgefahren**.
  *By the time Tom **got** to the bus stop, the bus **had** already **left**.*

  Bevor ich Kalifornien **besucht habe**, **hatte** ich
  noch nie Artischocken **gegessen**.
  *Before I **visited** California, I **had** never **eaten** artichokes.*

- After **nachdem**, use the **Plusquamperfekt** and put the main clause in the **Perfekt** or **Präteritum**.

  Der Bus **ist** endlich **gekommen**, **nachdem** wir
  schon 30 Minuten **gewartet hatten**.
  *The bus finally **came**, after we **had been waiting** for 30 minutes.*

  Nachdem Sara ins Bett **gegangen war**,
  hat ihre Mutter **angerufen**.
  *After Sara **had gone** to bed, her mother **called**.*

- If the clause with **bevor**, **nachdem**, or **als** is first in the sentence, the main clause after the comma begins with the verb. If that verb is in the **Plusquamperfekt** or **Perfekt**, put the helping verb first and the past participle at the end.

  Als wir am Flughafen **ankamen**, **war** das
  Flugzeug schon **abgeflogen**.
  *By the time we **got** to the airport, the plane **had** already **taken off**.*

  Das Flugzeug **war** schon **abgeflogen**, als wir am
  Flughafen **ankamen**.
  *The plane **had** already **taken off** by the time we **got** to the airport.*

Suggestion Point out to students that this word order is consistent with the "verb-in-second-position" rule. The dependent clause, set off by the comma, functions as the first sentence element, and the verb comes as the second element.

QUERVERWEIS

You will learn more about subordinating conjunctions in **10A.3**. To review coordinating conjunctions, see **6A.3**.

ACHTUNG

If the main clause comes first in the sentence, use the normal subject-verb word order.

Suggestion You may want to mention that in conversation, people often use the **Perfekt** tense instead of the **Plusquamperfekt** along with time expressions to help clarify the sequence of events: **Nachdem Ulrich einen Unfall gehabt hat, hat er sein Auto zum Mechaniker gebracht**.

More activities

vhlcentral

WB
pp. 107–108

LM
p. 69

Online activities

Jetzt sind Sie dran!   Schreiben Sie die Sätze ins Plusquamperfekt um.

1. Haben Sie Ihre Freundin angerufen?
   Hatten Sie Ihre Freundin angerufen?

2. Ich habe das Auto zum Mechaniker gebracht.
   Ich hatte das Auto zum Mechaniker gebracht.

3. Bist du zu spät aufgestanden?
   Warst du zu spät aufgestanden?

4. Benjamin ist noch nie in Berlin gewesen.
   Benjamin war noch nie in Berlin gewesen.

5. Ihr habt die Fahrkarte schon entwertet, nicht?
   Ihr hattet die Fahrkarte schon entwertet, nicht?

6. Die Mechanikerin hat den LKW schon repariert.
   Die Mechanikerin hatte den LKW schon repariert.

7. Oma und Opa sind gerade zurückgekommen.
   Oma und Opa waren gerade zurückgekommen.

8. Wir haben falsch geparkt.
   Wir hatten falsch geparkt.

9. Papa hat das Auto letzte Woche verkauft.
   Papa hatte das Auto letzte Woche verkauft.

10. Wir haben das Buch noch nicht gelesen.
    Wir hatten das Buch noch nicht gelesen.

11. Seid ihr in die Stadt gefahren?
    Wart ihr in die Stadt gefahren?

12. Hast du das gewusst?
    Hattest du das gewusst?

Anwendung

1 **Was passt zusammen?** Welche Sätze in der rechten Spalte ergänzen die Sätze in der linken Spalte?

_d_ 1. Nachdem Paul seine Sachen gepackt hatte,

_b_ 2. Als Amila nach Hause kam,

_a_ 3. Wir haben noch lange geredet,

_f_ 4. Bevor du zurückkamst,

_c_ 5. Hattest du meinen Geburtstag vergessen,

_e_ 6. Ich war sehr traurig,

a. nachdem wir gegessen hatten.

b. hatte ihre Familie schon mit dem Essen angefangen.

c. oder wolltest du mich überraschen?

d. hat er eine Karte an Greta geschrieben.

e. nachdem du weggegangen warst.

f. hatte ich dich überall gesucht.

2 **Was fehlt?** Ergänzen Sie die Sätze mit den richtigen Plusquamperfektformen.

1. Vor meiner Reise nach Paris _hatte_ ich viel darüber _gelesen_. (lesen)
2. Nachdem wir _gelandet_ _waren_, sind wir zuerst ins Hotel gefahren. (landen)
3. Wir _hatten_ kein Auto _gemietet_, sondern sind immer mit der U-Bahn gefahren. (mieten)
4. Jasmin _hatte_ ihr Geld in den Hotelsafe _gelegt_, bevor sie ausgegangen ist. (legen)
5. Sie sind ins Museum gegangen, nachdem sie _getankt_ _hatten_. (tanken)
6. Als sie dort ankamen, _hatten_ ihre Freunde schon lange auf sie _gewartet_. (warten)

3 **Dornröschen** Im Jahr 2020 wacht Dornröschen auf (*Sleeping Beauty wakes up*). Erzählen Sie, was für sie alles neu ist. Bilden Sie Sätze im Plusquamperfekt.

> **BEISPIEL** in einem Auto fahren
> *Sie war noch nie in einem Auto gefahren.*

1. in einem Flugzeug sein
Sie war (noch) nie in einem Flugzeug gewesen.
2. einen Film sehen
Sie hatte (noch) nie einen Film gesehen.
3. mit dem Zug reisen
Sie war (noch) nie mit dem Zug gereist.

4. ein Taxi nehmen
Sie hatte (noch) nie ein Taxi genommen.
5. eine Fahrkarte entwerten
Sie hatte (noch) nie eine Fahrkarte entwertet.
6. einen Sicherheitsgurt tragen
Sie hatte (noch) nie einen Sicherheitsgurt getragen.

4 **Was hatten sie gemacht?** Schreiben Sie zu jedem Bild einen Satz im Plusquamperfekt und erzählen Sie, was diese Personen gemacht hatten, bevor sie jemand fotografiert hat. Benutzen Sie Wörter aus der Liste oder Ihre eigenen. Seien Sie kreativ. Sample answers are provided.

▶ **BEISPIEL**

Manfred
war zur Tankstelle gefahren.

besuchen	kaufen
fahren	parken
gehen	warten (auf)

1. Herr Maier
hatte sein Auto geparkt.

2. Karl
hatte schon 15 Minuten auf Klara gewartet.

3. Birgit und Lara
hatten Fahrkarten gekauft.

4. Sebastian
war zur U-Bahn gegangen.

Kommunikation

5 **Faul oder fleißig** Besprechen Sie mit Ihrem Partner / Ihrer Partnerin, was Jan und Maria gestern gemacht haben. Wechseln Sie sich ab. Wer ist faul und wer ist fleißig? Warum? Schreiben Sie Ihre Antwort. Answers will vary.

BEISPIEL

S1: Maria hat um 8 Uhr gefrühstückt.
S2: Um 8 Uhr war Jan noch nicht aufgestanden.

	Jan	Maria
8.00	--	frühstücken
9.00	aufstehen	mit dem Bus zur Uni fahren
10.00	Kaffee trinken	Chemieprüfung schreiben
11.00	mit Freunden chatten	mit der Professorin sprechen
12.00	Musik hören	ins Fitnessstudio gehen
13.00	mit Martin Videospiele spielen	--

6 **Warum wohl?** Stellen Sie Ihrem Partner / Ihrer Partnerin zu jedem Bild eine Frage und erfinden Sie eine Antwort. Answers will vary.

die Küche nicht aufräumen	im Regen dreckig werden	keine Brille tragen
eine gute Note bekommen	kein Hotelzimmer buchen	zu spät nach Hause kommen

▶ **BEISPIEL**

S1: Warum hat Philip einen Unfall gehabt?
S2: Er war vielleicht zu schnell gefahren.

Philip / einen Unfall haben

1. Hasan und Greta / diskutieren

2. Sophia / Kopfschmerzen (*headache*) haben

3. Günther / laut singen

4. Paula und Rolf / Hund waschen

5. Ben und Hans / im Wald campen

6. Tom / einen Platten haben

7 **Wichtige Ereignisse** Sagen Sie Ihren Mitstudenten, in welchem Jahr Sie geboren sind. Ein anderer Student / eine andere Studentin nennt dann ein Ereignis (*event*), das schon vorher (*before that*) passiert war. Answers will vary.

BEISPIEL

S1: Ich bin 1994 geboren.
S2: 25 Jahre vorher waren Astronauten schon auf dem Mond gelandet.

1946: man baut das erste Mobiltelefon	1984: Steve Jobs stellt den ersten Mac vor
1959: die Barbiepuppe kommt auf den Markt	1989: die Berliner Mauer fällt
1973: in Deutschland gibt es eine Ölkrise	

5 **Partner Chat** You can also assign activity 5 on the Supersite. Students work in pairs to record the activity online. The pair's recorded conversation will appear in your gradebook.

7 **Suggestion** To prepare students for this activity, have them convert the information provided into complete **Plusquamperfekt** sentences. Ex.: **Man hatte das erste Mobiltelefon gebaut.**

8A.2

Comparatives and superlatives Grammar Tutorial

QUERVERWEIS

See **3A.2** to review the use of adjectives. See **4A.2** to review the use of adverbs.

Startblock Use the comparative and superlative forms of adjectives and adverbs to compare two or more people or things.

Mein Vater fährt gern **schneller als** 150.

Es ist einer der **schönsten** Orte in Berlin.

Der Komparativ

- There are three forms of adjectives and adverbs: **die Grundform** (**schnell**), **der Komparativ** (**schneller**), and **der Superlativ** (**am schnellsten**). When describing similarities between two people or things, use the expression **so... wie** (*as... as*) or **genauso... wie** (*just as... as*) with the **Grundform** of an adjective or adverb.

> Suggestion Model correct pronunciation of the **Grundformen** and comparative forms and have students repeat after you.

> Dieser LKW ist **so groß wie** ein Bus.
> *That truck is **as big as** a bus.*

> Der Zug fährt **genauso schnell wie** ein Auto.
> *The train goes **just as fast as** a car.*

- To describe differences between two people or things, you can use the expression **nicht so... wie** (*not as... as*), or you can use the **Komparativ**. Form the **Komparativ** by adding the ending **-er** to the **Grundform** of an adjective or adverb, followed by the word **als**.

> Lina fährt **nicht so langsam wie** Sara.
> *Lina **doesn't** drive **as slowly as** Sara.*

> Sara fährt **langsamer als** Lina.
> *Sara drives **more slowly than** Lina.*

ACHTUNG

The two-syllable word **gesund** (*healthy*) also has an umlaut on the **u** in the comparative form:

gesund ⟶ **gesünder**

For adjectives ending in **-el** or **-er**, German speakers usually drop the **-e-** before adding the comparative **-er** ending.

teuer ⟶ **teurer**
dunkel ⟶ **dunkler**

- Common one-syllable words with the stem vowel **a**, **o**, or **u** often have an umlaut on the vowel in the comparative.

a ⟶ ä		o ⟶ ö		u ⟶ ü	
alt	älter	groß	größer	dumm (*dumb*)	dümmer
lang	länger	oft	öfter	jung	jünger
stark	stärker	rot	röter	kurz	kürzer

> Meine Geschwister sind alle **älter** als ich.
> *My siblings are all **older** than I am.*

> Die Fahrt nach Frankfurt dauert mit dem Auto **länger** als mit dem Zug.
> *The trip to Frankfurt takes **longer** by car than by train.*

> Expansion Provide additional examples for each adjective or adverb. Ex.: **Sarahs Haare sind länger als Bens. Lady Gaga ist jünger als Madonna.**

- A small number of adjectives and adverbs have irregular comparative forms.

GRUNDFORM		KOMPARATIV
gern	⟶	lieber
gut	⟶	besser

Ich fahre **lieber** mit der U-Bahn als mit dem Bus.
*I'd **rather** take the subway than the bus.*

GRUNDFORM		KOMPARATIV
hoch	⟶	höher
viel	⟶	mehr

Benzin kostet in Deutschland **mehr** als in den USA.
*Gasoline is **more expensive** in Germany than in the USA.*

- When a comparative adjective precedes a noun, add the appropriate case ending after the **-er** ending.

Leider kostet der **schnellere** Zug mehr.
*Unfortunately the **faster** train costs more.*

Ich brauche einen **größeren** Koffer.
*I need a **bigger** suitcase.*

Der Superlativ

- Use the **Superlativ** form of an adjective or adverb to indicate that a person or thing has more of a particular quality than anyone or anything else.

Welches ist **das größte** Tier der Welt?
*What's **the biggest** animal in the world?*

Wie komme ich **am besten** zur Tankstelle?
*What's **the best** way to get to the gas station?*

- To form the superlative of an adjective, add **-st** to the **Grundform**. If the **Grundform** ends in **-d**, **-t**, or an **s** sound, add **-est**. When an adjective in the superlative precedes a noun, use a definite article before the superlative and add the appropriate case ending.

Warum habt ihr **die teuersten** Fahrkarten gekauft?
*Why did you buy **the most expensive** tickets?*

Wir wollten mit **dem schnellsten** Zug fahren.
*We wanted to take **the fastest** train.*

- To form the superlative of adverbs and of adjectives that come after **sein**, **werden**, or **bleiben**, use the word **am** before the adverb or adjective and add **-(e)sten** as the superlative ending.

Wer fährt **am langsamsten**?
*Who drives **the slowest**?*

Welches Auto ist **am schnellsten**?
*Which car is **the fastest**?*

- If an adjective or adverb has an added umlaut in the comparative, it will also have an umlaut in the superlative.

a → ä			o → ö			u → ü		
alt	älter	ältest-	rot	röter	rötest-	jung	jünger	jüngst-

- If an adjective or adverb is irregular in the comparative form, the superlative form is also irregular.

GRUNDFORM	KOMPARATIV	SUPERLATIV
gern	lieber	liebst-
groß	größer	größt-
gut	besser	best-
hoch	höher	höchst-
viel	mehr	meist-

QUERVERWEIS

See **3A.2** to review adjective agreement.

Expansion Bring in a few items or pictures that lend themselves to comparison, and ask questions that model comparative and superlative forms. Ex.: **Was ist größer, dieser Roman oder das Deutschbuch? Welcher Hut ist lustiger, der oder der? Welcher steht mir besser?**

ACHTUNG

The adjective **nah** (*near*) has a stem vowel change, as well as an additional spelling change in the superlative: **nah / näher / nächst-**

Most German speakers do not use the superlative form **öftest-**; instead, they use **(am) häufigst-** (*most often*).

More activities

vhlcentral

WB
pp. 109–110

LM
p. 70

Online activities

 Jetzt sind Sie dran! Ergänzen Sie die Lücken mit den richtigen Formen der Adjektive.

	Base form	*Komparativ*	*Superlativ*		Base form	*Komparativ*	*Superlativ*
1.	groß	*größer*	am größten	7.	*jung*	jünger	am jüngsten
2.	*gut*	besser	am besten	8.	kurz	kürzer	am *kürzesten*
3.	lang	länger	am *längsten*	9.	*gesund*	gesünder	am gesündesten
4.	klein	*kleiner*	am kleinsten	10.	einfach	einfacher	am *einfachsten*
5.	hoch	*höher*	am höchsten	11.	viel	*mehr*	am meisten
6.	spät	später	am *spätesten*	12.	*gern*	lieber	am liebsten

Anwendung

1 **Meinungen** Ergänzen Sie die Sätze mit dem Adjektiv oder dem Adverb im Superlativ.

BEISPIEL Von allen Verkehrsmitteln benutzen wir die U-Bahn
am häufigsten. (häufig)

1. Von allen Automodellen findet Ingrid einen Mercedes ___am schönsten___. (schön)
2. Von allen meinen Kursen finde ich Chemie ___am schwierigsten___. (schwierig)
3. Von allen Getränken trinkt Emil Tee ___am seltensten___. (selten)
4. Von allen Obstsorten schmecken dir Bananen ___am besten___? (gut)
5. Von allen meinen Kursen interessiert mich Mathematik ___am meisten___. (viel)
6. Von allen meinen Freunden habe ich Peter ___am liebsten___. (gern)

2 **Komparative** Bilden Sie Sätze im Komparativ. + bedeutet **-er als;** = bedeutet **(genau)so... wie;** und ≠ bedeutet **nicht so... wie.**

BEISPIEL ein Auto / ist / ≠ groß / ein LKW
Ein Auto ist nicht so groß wie ein LKW.

1. die Mozartstraße / ist / + lang / die Beethovenstraße Die Mozartstraße ist länger als die Beethovenstraße.
2. Kiara / fährt / + gut / Dana Kiara fährt besser als Dana.
3. der Verkehr am Freitagabend / ist / = schlecht / der Verkehr am Montagmorgen
Der Verkehr am Freitagabend ist (genau)so schlecht wie der Verkehr am Montagmorgen.
4. ich / reise / + gern / mit dem Zug / mit dem Flugzeug Ich reise lieber mit dem Zug als mit dem Flugzeug.
5. Die erste Klasse / ist / + teuer / die zweite Klasse Die erste Klasse ist teurer als die zweite Klasse.
6. heute / ist / es / ≠ warm / gestern Heute ist es nicht so warm wie gestern.

3 **Vergleichen Sie** Bilden Sie Sätze und benutzen Sie dabei die Komparativformen der angegebenen Adjektive. Sample answers are provided.

BEISPIEL ein Bus / ein Auto (klein)
Ein Auto ist kleiner als ein Bus.

1. eine U-Bahn / ein Flugzeug (schnell)
Ein Flugzeug ist schneller als eine U-Bahn.

2. Niklas / Lisa (alt)
Niklas ist nicht so alt wie Lisa.

3. Ben bezahlt 350 € Miete. / Jana bezahlt 320 € Miete. (viel)
Ben bezahlt mehr Miete als Jana.

4. Ihr esst Fisch einmal pro Monat. / Ihr esst Hähnchen einmal pro Woche. (gern)
Ihr esst lieber Hähnchen als Fisch.

Kommunikation

4 **Komparative** Ergänzen Sie die Fragen mit den Komparativformen der angegebenen Adjektive und beantworten Sie die Fragen Ihres Partners. Answers will vary.

BEISPIEL Wer ist _schüchterner_, du oder dein bester Freund? (schüchtern)

S1: *Wer ist schüchterner, du oder dein bester Freund?*
S2: *Ich bin viel schüchterner!*

1. Was isst du ___lieber___, Joghurt oder Schokolade? (gern)
2. Womit fährst du ___seltener___, mit dem Fahrrad oder mit dem Auto? (selten)
3. Welche Sängerin findest du ___besser___, Rihanna oder Beyoncé? (gut)
4. Welches Fach findest du ___interessanter___, Marketing oder Anthropologie? (interessant)
5. Wovon verstehst du ___mehr___, von Mode oder von Sport? (viel)
6. Was machst du am Wochenende ___häufiger___, Hausaufgaben oder schlafen? (häufig)

5 **Wie gut ist Ihr Allgemeinwissen?** Finden Sie mit Ihrem Partner / Ihrer Partnerin zu jedem Begriff (*concept*) zwei Sachen, die man vergleichen kann, und stellen Sie einem anderen Paar Ihre Fragen. Answers will vary.

BEISPIEL welcher Kontinent / groß

S1: *Welcher Kontinent ist größer, Europa oder Asien*
S2: *Natürlich ist Asien größer!*

1. welches Land / klein
2. welche Stadt / alt
3. welcher Fluss / lang
4. welcher Flughafen / groß
5. welches Auto / schnell
6. welches Hotel / teuer
7. welche Person / reich
8. welche Schule / gut

6 **Beschreiben Sie** Besprechen Sie mit einem Partner / einer Partnerin die Leute im Bild. Machen Sie so viele Vergleiche wie möglich.

BEISPIEL

S1: *Sarah ist so groß wie Sabrina.*
S2: *Ja, aber David ist am größten.*

Sabrina • David • Lukas • Sarah • Emma

7 **Ein kleines Interview** Interviewen Sie zwei Mitstudenten und schreiben Sie ihre Antworten auf. Stellen Sie dann Ihre Informationen vor. Benutzen Sie dabei Komparativ- und Superlativformen. Answers will vary.

BEISPIEL

S1: *Wie alt bist du, Emily?*
S2: *Ich bin 18. Und du, Michael?*
S3: *Ich bin 21.*
S1: *Ich bin älter als Emily und jünger als Michael. Michael ist am ältesten.*

Name:	
Wie alt bist du?	
Wie groß bist du?	
Wie viele Geschwister hast du?	
Wie oft machst du Sport?	

4 **Expansion** After students have done this activity with comparatives, have them ask each other similar questions using superlatives.

6 **Expansion** Have pairs of students choose two very different celebrities and write sentences comparing the two. You may want to have them bring in photographs and present their comparisons to the class.

6 **Partner Chat** You can also assign activity 6 on the Supersite. Students work in pairs to record the activity online. The pair's recorded conversation will appear in your gradebook.

Wiederholung

1 Vergleiche Schreiben Sie mit einem Partner / einer Partnerin auf, was Sie auf den Fotos sehen. Benutzen Sie so viele Vergleiche wie möglich. Arbeiten Sie dann mit einem anderen Paar zusammen: Diskutieren Sie, was sie über die Bilder geschrieben haben. Answers will vary.

BEISPIEL

S1: Taxis sind teurer als Busse.
S2: Aber Busse fahren nicht so schnell wie Taxis.

1.

2.

2 Diskutieren und kombinieren Sie und Ihr Partner / Ihre Partnerin bekommen von Ihrem Professor / Ihrer Professorin verschiedene Autostatistiken. Sehen Sie sich die Statistiken der vier Autos an und vergleichen Sie dann, wie schnell, wie stark und wie teuer die Autos sind. Entscheiden Sie auch, welches Auto den größten Kofferraum hat. Answers will vary.

BEISPIEL

2 Suggestion Pre-teach the vocabulary **Marke**, **Geschwindigkeit**, and **Kraft**, and explain that **PS** is short for **Pferdestärken** (*horsepower*). Make sure students know how to pronounce **VW**. Explain that all car brands are masculine.

S1: Wie schnell ist der Audi?
S2: Der Audi ist 247 Stundenkilometer schnell.
S1: Also ist der Audi am schnellsten.

3 Werbung Entwerfen Sie (*Design*) zu dritt ein Zukunftsfahrzeug (*vehicle of the future*). Wie heißt das Fahrzeug? Machen Sie auch eine Liste mit der Ausstattung (*features*). Schreiben Sie dann eine Werbung, in der Sie das Zukunftsfahrzeug mit einem Auto von heute vergleichen. Answers will vary.

BEISPIEL

S1: „Futura" – das Auto des 21. Jahrhunderts. Es kann CO_2 tanken.
S2: Unser Auto verbraucht viel weniger als die Autos von gestern.

3 Suggestion You may wish to provide markers and paper so that students can make their ads more colorful. Set a time limit and make sure everyone stays on task.

4 Suggestion Remind students to "kick" the verb to the end of the clause when using conjunctions like **bevor** or **nachdem**.

4 Arbeitsblatt Fragen Sie andere im Unterricht, was sie gestern gemacht haben. Berichten Sie dann, wer was wann gemacht hat. Benutzen Sie das Plusquamperfekt. Answers will vary.

BEISPIEL

S1: Bist du gestern zum Englischunterricht gegangen?
S2: Ja.
S1: Wann?
S2: Um 8.15 Uhr.
S1 (schreibt): Peter war schon zum Englischunterricht gegangen, bevor Julia Kaffee getrunken hat.

5 Die Party Sie geben eine Party mit Ihren Freunden. Besprechen Sie, was Sie alle gemacht haben, um die Party vorzubereiten. Answers will vary.

BEISPIEL

S1: Seid ihr einkaufen gegangen?
S2: Ja, aber bevor wir einkaufen gegangen sind, hatten wir die Küche geputzt.

6 Eine Reise nach Erfurt Sie planen eine Zugfahrt von Marburg nach Erfurt. Spielen Sie mit Ihrem Partner / Ihrer Partnerin ein Gespräch im Reisebüro der Deutschen Bahn. Der Reiseberater (*travel agent*) hilft dem Reisenden, sich für eine Zugverbindung zu entscheiden. Answers will vary.

6 Partner Chat You can also assign activity 6 on the Supersite.

BEISPIEL

S1: Wie kann ich Ihnen helfen?
S2: Ich möchte von Marburg nach Erfurt fahren und brauche eine Fahrkarte.
S1: Wann möchten Sie abfahren…?

TIPP

Here are some abbreviations used in train schedules.

Umst. = **Umsteigen** (*transfer*)
RE = **Regional-Express**
IC = **Intercity**
ICE = **Intercity-Express**

ZUG		Ihre Hinfahrtmöglichkeiten			
Bahnhof	**Zeit**	**Dauer**	**Umst**	**Produkte**	**Preis**
MARBURG ERFURT	ab **8.21** an **12.40**	4.19	2	RE, IC	51€
MARBURG ERFURT	ab **10.04** an **13.33**	3.29	1	IC, ICE	65€
MARBURG ERFURT	ab **10.56** an **14.40**	3.44	2	IC	51€
MARBURG ERFURT	ab **13.50** an **16.28**	2.38	1	IC	51€

S Video

Deutsche Automarken

1 **Vorbereitung** Besprechen Sie mit Ihrem Partner / Ihrer Partnerin die folgenden Fragen. Answers will vary.

1. Haben Sie einen Führerschein? Wie alt waren Sie, als Sie den Führerschein gemacht haben?

2. Welche Verkehrsmittel benutzen Sie?

Im Jahr 1886 bekam Carl Benz das Patent für das erste Automobil und legte den Grundstein° für eine schnelle Entwicklung der Autoindustrie in Deutschland. Neben Volkswagen, Audi und BMW gilt Mercedes Benz als die bekannteste Automarke.

legte den Grundstein *laid the foundation*

30 Jahre ADAC-Pannenstatistik

Nützliche Ausdrücke

der Führerschein, -e	*driver's license*
der Hersteller, -	*manufacturer*
die Panne, -en	*breakdown*
der Pannendienst, -e	*roadside assistance*
die Sicherheit	*safety*

2 **Verständnis** Beantworten Sie die Fragen mit den Informationen aus dem Video.

1. Wer ist der Mann im Video?

   a. Polizist   (b.) Pannendienst-Mitarbeiter   c. ein Tourist

2. Welche deutschen Automarken nennt der Mann?

   (a.) VW und Porsche   b. BMW und Volvo   c. Audi und Fiat

3. Warum denkt der Mann nicht sofort an Mercedes Benz?

   a. Weil es eine unbekannte Automarke ist.   b. Weil er nichts über Autos weiß.   (c.) Weil Mercedes Benz selten Pannen hat.

4. Das Video ist eine Werbung für ...

   a. den ADAC.   (b.) Mercedes Benz.   c. alle deutschen Automarken.

3 **Diskussion** Besprechen Sie zu zweit die folgende Frage. Answers will vary.

1. Gibt es Automarken mit einer langen Tradition in Ihrem Land? Vergleichen (*compare*) Sie diese Automarken mit Mercedes Benz.

4 **Präsentation** Wie kann man in Deutschland, Österreich oder in der Schweiz den Führerschein machen? Was ist das Mindestalter? Welche Prüfungen muss man machen? Recherchieren Sie im Internet und vergleichen Sie die deutschen, österreichischen oder Schweizer Regeln (*rules*) mit denen in Ihrem Land. Welches System finden Sie besser? Warum? Präsentieren Sie Ihre Ergebnisse im Kurs. Answers will vary.

More activities

S vhlcentral

Online activities

Technik und Medien

 Vocabulary Tools

Wortschatz

Technik bedienen	using technology
anmachen (macht... an)	to turn on
die App, -s	app
aufladen (lädt... auf)	to charge (a battery)
aufnehmen (nimmt... auf)	to record
ausmachen (macht... aus)	to turn off
das Blog, -s	blog
der Chat, -s	chat
drucken	to print
fernsehen (sieht... fern)	to watch television
funktionieren	to work, to function
herunterladen (lädt... herunter)	to download
hochladen (lädt... hoch)	to upload
löschen	to delete
online sein	to be online
schicken	to send
speichern	to save
starten	to start
im Internet surfen	to surf the Web
die Technik	**technology**
der Benutzername, -n	screen name
die Datei, -en	file
die Digitalkamera, -s	digital camera
das Dokument, -e	document
die E-Mail, -s	e-mail
der Kopfhörer, -	headphones
das Ladegerät, -e	battery charger
der Laptop, -s	laptop (computer)
das Mikrofon, -e	microphone
das Passwort, ̈er	password
das Programm, -e	program
der Sender, -	channel
das Smartphone, -s	smartphone
die SMS, -	text message
die Website, -s	Web site

Expansion Teach students the phrases that refer to sending a text: **simsen** or **eine SMS schicken**.

Suggestion Tell students that while **das Tablet** is treated as a neuter noun, it is short for **der Tablet-PC**, which is masculine, since **PC** refers to **der Computer**.

die Stereoanlage, -n
sound system

das Handy, -s

der Bildschirm, -e

die Festplatte, -n
hard drive

die Tastatur, -en
keyboard

die Maus, ̈e

das Tablet, -s

der Drucker, -

Anwendung

1 Bilder beschriften Wie heißen die Geräte auf den Fotos?

a. der Bluetooth-Drucker   c. der Fernseher   e. der Laptop
b. die Fernbedienung   d. die Digitalkamera   f. das Mikrofon

1. _c_   2. _d_   3. _f_

4. _a_   5. _b_   6. _e_

2 Ist das logisch? Sind die Aussagen die Sie hören logisch oder unlogisch?

	Logisch	Unlogisch		Logisch	Unlogisch
1.	☐	☑	4.	☑	☐
2.	☐	☑	5.	☐	☑
3.	☑	☐	6.	☑	☐

3 Was fehlt? Ergänzen Sie die Sätze mit einem passenden Wort aus der Vokabelliste.

1. Vergessen Sie nicht, Ihr Dokument zu ___speichern___, bevor Sie den Computer ausmachen.
2. Um das Handy aufzuladen, braucht man ein ___Ladegerät___.
3. Man soll nicht für jede Website dasselbe ___Passwort___ benutzen.
4. Recyceln Sie Ihren Computer nicht, ohne alle Dokumente zu ___löschen___.
5. Der Klingelton auf meinem ___Handy___ ist ein Lied von Lady Gaga.
6. X-Box und Playstation sind ___Spielkonsolen___.

4 Kategorien Finden Sie für jede Kategorie passende Wörter aus Ihrer Vokabelliste. Answers may vary slightly.

Computer	Telefon	Fernseher
die Maus	das Handy	fernsehen
die E-Mail	das Smartphone	die Fernbedienung
die Tastatur	klingeln	der Sender
speichern	die SMS	das Programm

5 Hören Sie zu Hören Sie sich die Dialoge 1-4 an. Welche Geräte brauchen die Personen? Schreiben Sie zu jedem Gerät die Nummer des passenden Dialogs. Answers will vary.

1. _4_ das Telefon   3. _2_ die Stereoanlage
2. _1_ die Kamera   4. _3_ die Fernbedienung

Das Telefon klingelt. (klingeln)
The phone rings.

die Fernbedienung, -en
remote control

der Fernseher, -
TV set

die Spielkonsole, -n
game console

Kommunikation

6 Im Elektronikladen

Was kann man hier im Elektronikladen (*electronics store*) alles kaufen? Fragen Sie Ihren Partner / Ihre Partnerin, wie er/sie die verschiedenen elektronischen Geräte findet. Answers will vary.

BEISPIEL

S1: Wie findest du den Laptop?
S2: Er ist in Ordnung. Die Festplatte ist ziemlich groß.

| der Bildschirm | die Festplatte | die Tastatur |
| der Fernseher | der Drucker | die Videokamera |

6 Suggestion Before beginning the activity, have the class look at the picture together. Ask students to tell you what they see, using as many vocabulary words as possible.

7 Diskutieren und kombinieren

Sie und Ihr Partner / Ihre Partnerin bekommen zwei verschiedene Versionen desselben Kreuzworträtsels (*crossword puzzle*). Lesen Sie sich gegenseitig die fehlenden Definitionen vor. Answers will vary.

BEISPIEL

S1: Eins senkrecht: Man macht das mit einem neuen Programm.
S2: Das ist HOCHLADEN.

7 Suggestion Before they begin this activity, have students prepare written definitions (in German) for the words in their **Kreuzworträtsel**, either in class or as homework.

8 Technische Geräte

Erzählen Sie zu zweit, welche technischen Geräte Sie und die Mitglieder Ihrer Familie haben und auch oft benutzen. Answers will vary.

BEISPIEL

S1: Meine Schwester kann ohne ihr Handy nicht leben. Sie schreibt bestimmt zweihundert SMS jeden Tag!
S2: Meine Eltern haben eine super Stereoanlage. Sie hören gern klassische Musik.

9 Wie macht man das?

Beschreiben Sie mit einem Partner / einer Partnerin zusammen möglichst genau, was Sie tun müssen, um die folgenden Tätigkeiten auszuführen (*carry out*). Answers will vary.

BEISPIEL

S1: Zuerst muss man die Fernbedienung finden.
S2: Dann macht man den Fernseher an und...

- einen Blog starten
- Fotos drucken
- ein Buch herunterladen
- Informationen für ein Referat finden
- eine SMS schicken

9 Suggestion Tell students to describe each process in at least five steps. Give them time to prepare, and provide vocabulary as needed.

Aussprache und Rechtschreibung 🔊 Audio

The German *l*

To pronounce the German **l**, place your tongue firmly against the ridge behind your top front teeth and open your mouth wider than you would for the English *l*.

lang	Laptop	Telefon	normal	stellen

Unlike the English *l*, the German **l** is always produced with the tongue in the same position, no matter what sound comes before or after it. Practice saying **l** after the following consonants and consonant clusters.

Platten	schlafen	Kleid	pflegen	fleißig

Practice saying **l** at the end of words and before the consonants **d**, **m**, and **n**. Be sure to use the German **l**, even in words that are spelled the same in English and German.

Ball	Spiel	Wald	Film	Zwiebeln

Practice saying the German **l** in front of the consonant clusters **sch** and **ch**.

solch	falsch	Milch	Kölsch	Elch

Suggestion Pronounce German and English cognates side by side, and ask students if they can hear the difference in the articulation of the **l** sound. Ex.: **Ball** and *ball*; **Spiel** and *spiel*.

1 **Aussprechen** Wiederholen Sie die Wörter, die Sie hören.

1. Lenkrad
2. Fahrplan
3. Öl
4. Klasse
5. schlank
6. Geld
7. Köln
8. welch

2 **Nachsprechen** Wiederholen Sie die Sätze, die Sie hören.

1. Viele warten an der Bushaltestelle auf den letzten Bus nach Ludwigsfelde.
2. Luise, kannst du das Nummernschild von dem LKW lesen?
3. Lothar hatte leider einen Platten auf einer verlassenen Landstraße.
4. Man soll den Ölstand im Auto regelmäßig kontrollieren.
5. Natürlich hat der Laptop eine Digitalkamera.
6. Klicken Sie auf das Bild, um den Film herunterzuladen.

3 **Sprichwörter** Wiederholen Sie die Sprichwörter, die Sie hören.

Wer im Glashaus sitzt, sollte nicht mit Steinen werfen.[1]

Ein Unglück kommt selten allein.[2]

[1] People in glass houses shouldn't throw stones.
[2] It never rains, but it pours. (lit. *Misfortune seldom comes alone.*)

More activities

vhlcentral | LM p. 72 | Online activities

Ein Spaziergang durch Spandau Video

George und Sabite haben Spaß zusammen, doch ein älteres Paar sieht mehr in ihnen. Hans und Meline haben leider nicht so viel Spaß.

NATIONAL
communication
cultures
STANDARDS

GEORGE Unter uns sind zwei Flüsse. Dieser Fluss ist die Havel, und das da ist die Spree. Die Spandauer Zitadelle wurde im 16. Jahrhundert anstelle einer alten Burg erbaut. Endlich besuche ich sie mal. Viel besser, als nur darüber im Internet zu lesen. Die Architektur Deutschlands ist sagenhaft!

SABITE Er hat nicht angerufen, keine E-Mail und keine SMS geschickt. Ich habe seine Nummer von meinem Handy gelöscht. Doch trotz meiner Gefühle habe ich seinen Schal behalten.
GEORGE Die Farbe steht dir gut.
SABITE Danke. Sie steht dir besser.

HANS Ich habe mich aus meiner Wohnung ausgeschlossen. Darf ich hier warten, bis George zurückkommt?
MELINE Wieso gehst du nicht in ein Café oder in die Bibliothek? Oder... oder... machst einen Spaziergang im Viertel.
HANS Mein Mantel, mein Handy und mein Geldbeutel sind in meiner Wohnung.

MELINE Hier ist etwas Geld und Lorenzos Pullover. Geh solange ins Café um die Ecke. Ich schicke George dann zu dir.
HANS Warum hast du den Pullover deines Ex-Freundes noch?
MELINE Tschüss, Hans.

GEORGE Wie nennst du es?
SABITE „Spandau... Spandau Ballet." Dein Handy klingelt.
GEORGE Es ist eine SMS von Meline. „Dein Mitbewohner, der Idiot, hat sich ausgeschlossen. Ich habe ihn ins Café geschickt. Bitte hol ihn dort ab. Lass dir Zeit."

MANN Berlin ist ein herrlicher Ort, um verliebt zu sein.
GEORGE Wie bitte?
FRAU Sie haben eine Verbindung. Wenn sie lacht, leuchten Ihre Augen.
MANN Katharinas Lächeln wärmt mein Herz noch immer.
FRAU Haben Sie noch viel Spaß.

ÜBUNGEN

1 **Wer ist das?** Welche Personen beschreiben die folgenden Sätze: George, Hans, Meline oder Sabite?

1. Er/Sie hat über die Spandauer Zitadelle im Internet gelesen. George
2. Er/Sie hat Torstens Nummer von seinem/ihrem Handy gelöscht. Sabite
3. Er/Sie hat sich aus seiner/ihrer Wohnung ausgeschlossen. Hans
4. Er/Sie hat Lorenzos Pullover behalten. Meline
5. Sein/Ihr Handy klingelt. George

6. Sein/Ihr Mitbewohner hat sich aus der Wohnung ausgeschlossen. George
7. Das ältere Paar glaubt, dass sie verliebt sind. George und Sabite
8. Er/Sie entschuldigt sich (apologizes) bei Hans. Meline
9. Er/Sie isst ein Stück Kuchen. Hans
10. Er/Sie hat ein Problem mit dem Computer. Meline

PERSONEN

 George
 Hans
 Meline
 Sabite
 Frau
 Mann

7

GEORGE Das ist verrückt. Wir sind Freunde. Gute Freunde.
SABITE Genau.

8

GEORGE Es tut mir leid, Sabite.
SABITE Es tut mir leid. Das war schrecklich.
GEORGE Ja, schrecklich. Die beiden waren trotz ihres Alters nicht wirklich weise.

9

MELINE Hans, es tut mir leid.
HANS Was willst du, Meline?
MELINE Ich? Nichts. Ich... ich bin unhöflich zu dir gewesen und bin hierher gekommen, um mich zu entschuldigen.
HANS Danke, ich nehme an. Setz dich doch. Kuchen?

10

MELINE Danke. Also, du kennst dich gut mit Computern aus?
HANS Ja...
MELINE Ich habe während eines Chats eine Datei runtergeladen, dann wurde mein Bildschirm plötzlich dunkel und die Festplatte hat angefangen, ein komisches Geräusch zu machen.
HANS Speichere deine Dateien ab und schalte den Computer aus.

Nützliche Ausdrücke

- **Die Spandauer Zitadelle wurde im 16. Jahrhundert anstelle einer alten Burg erbaut.**
  The Spandau Citadel was built during the 16th century, on the site of an old castle.

- **sagenhaft**
  legendary

- **das Gefühl**
  feeling

- **Die Farbe steht dir gut.**
  The color looks good on you.

- **Ich habe mich aus meiner Wohnung ausgeschlossen.**
  I'm locked out of my apartment.

- **das Viertel**
  neighborhood

- **der Geldbeutel**
  wallet

- **Berlin ist ein herrlicher Ort, um verliebt zu sein.**
  Berlin is a beautiful place to be in love.

- **Katharinas Lächeln wärmt mein Herz noch immer.**
  Katharina's smile still warms my heart.

- **schrecklich**
  terrible

- **unhöflich**
  rude

8B.1
- **Die beiden waren trotz ihres Alters nicht wirklich weise.**
  In spite of their age, those two weren't really wise.

8B.2
- **Dieser Fluss ist die Havel, und das da ist die Spree.**
  This river is the Havel and that one is the Spree.

---

2 **Zum Besprechen** Beschreiben Sie zu zweit, wie Sie Technologie täglich nutzen. Haben Sie einen Computer? Wofür benutzen Sie ihn? Schreiben Sie einen Blog? Chatten Sie? Was machen Sie, wenn Sie Probleme mit dem Computer haben? Answers will vary.

2 **Expansion** Have students write a blog entry about their reaction to George and Sabite's relationship.

2 **Video Virtual Chat** You can also assign activity 2 on the Supersite. Students record individual responses that appear in your gradebook.

3 **Vertiefung** Viele technische Erfindungen (*inventions*) kommen aus Deutschland, Österreich, Liechtenstein oder der Schweiz. Suchen Sie im Internet nach einer Erfindung und sprechen Sie im Kurs über den Erfinder, Ort und Zeit der Erfindung sowie den Zweck (*purpose*). Vergleichen Sie die deutsche technische Erfindung mit einer aus Ihrem Land.

Answers may include: automobile, combustion engine, movable type, aspirin, MP3s, Swiss Army knife.

More activities

vhlcentral | VM p. 16 | Online activities

IM FOKUS

Max-Planck-Gesellschaft°

 Reading

TIPP

Note that the German words **die Forschung** (*research*), **ein Forscher / eine Forscherin** (*researcher*), and **forschen** (*to research*) are all closely related.

MAX PLANCK (1858–1947) WAR EIN deutscher Physiker. Er entwickelte° die Quantentheorie und bekam dafür 1918 den Nobelpreis für Physik. Nach ihm ist die deutsche Max-Planck-Gesellschaft (MPG) benannt.

Diese Gesellschaft existiert seit 1948. Sie ist Nachfolgerin° der Kaiser-Wilhelm-Gesellschaft, die Kaiser Wilhelm II. 1911 in Berlin gegründet hatte. In beiden Gesellschaften bekamen und

bekommen Spitzenforscher° weltweit beste Arbeitsbedingungen°, um sich voll auf ihre Forschungsinteressen konzentrieren zu können. Niemand sagt ihnen, was sie machen müssen, und die Forscher dürfen sich ihre Mitarbeiter selber aussuchen.

Heute besteht die MPG aus 84 Instituten in den Bereichen° Natur-, Sozial- und Geisteswissenschaften°. Immer wieder entstehen° neue Institute in neuen Forschungsbereichen und alte Institute schließen wieder. Zwischen 1948 und 2014 waren 18 Nobelpreisträger Mitglieder° der MPG, ein weiteres Zeichen für die herausragende° Arbeit dieser Gesellschaft. Bisher war Christiane Nüsslein-Volhard die einzige Frau unter ihnen, aber das könnte sich ändern°. Im Jahre 2017 waren 14% der Wissenschaftler an den Instituten Frauen.

Nobelpreisträger der Max-Planck-Gesellschaft

Chemie	Medizin	Physik
Stefan W. Hell (2014)	Christiane Nüsslein-Volhard (1995)	Theodor Hänsch (2005)
Gerhard Ertl (2007)	Erwin Neher (1991)	Ernst Ruska (1986)
Paul Crutzen (1995)	Bert Sakmann (1991)	Klaus von Klitzing (1985)
Robert Huber (1988)	Georges Köhler (1984)	Walter Bothe (1954)
Hartmut Michel (1988)	Konrad Lorenz (1973)	
Johann Deisenhofer (1988)	Feodor Lynen (1964)	
Manfred Eigen (1967)		
Karl Zigler (1963)		

Gesellschaft *society* **entwickelte** *developed*
Nachfolgerin *successor* **Spitzenforscher** *top researchers*
Arbeitsbedingungen *work conditions* **Bereichen** *areas*
Geisteswissenschaften *humanities* **entstehen** *form*
Mitglieder *members* **herausragende** *outstanding*
sich ändern *to change*

1 **Im Fokus** Richtig oder falsch? Korrigieren Sie die falschen Aussagen. Diskutieren Sie dann die letzte Frage mit einem Partner/ einer Partnerin.

1. Für seine Quantentheorie bekam Max Planck 1918 den Nobelpreis für Physik. Richtig.

2. Die Max-Planck-Gesellschaft unterstützt nur Physiker.
Falsch. Die MPG unterstützt Spitzenforscher aus verschiedenen Natur-, Sozial- und Geisteswissenschaften.

3. Vor der Max-Planck-Gesellschaft gab es in Deutschland die Kaiser-Wilhelm-Gesellschaft. Richtig.

Diskussion Welche Bereiche der Wissenschaft interessieren Sie?

2 **Die deutschsprachige Welt** Richtig oder falsch? Korrigieren Sie die falschen Aussagen. Diskutieren Sie dann die letzte Frage mit einem Partner/ einer Partnerin.

1. Die Bertelsmann KGaA ist Europas zweitgrößtes Medienunternehmen.
Falsch. Die Bertelsmann KGaA ist Europas größtes Medienunternehmen.

2. Bertelsmann ist ein internationales Unternehmen mit Büchern, Fernsehen und Radio, Zeitschriften und Musik. Richtig.

3. Die Axel Springer AG verlegt mehr als 300 Zeitungen und Zeitschriften.
Falsch. Die Axel Springer AG verlegt mehr als 230 Zeitungen und Zeitschriften.

Diskussion Welche Technologien und digitale Medien benutzen Sie?

DEUTSCH IM ALLTAG

Wortfeld: machen

aufmachen	to open
durchmachen	to experience
mitmachen	to participate
nachmachen	to imitate
vormachen	to fool somebody
wettmachen	to make up for something
zumachen	to close

DIE DEUTSCHSPRACHIGE WELT

Deutsche Mediengiganten°

Die zwei deutschen Mediengiganten sind die Bertelsmann KGaA° und die Axel Springer AG. Die Bertelsmann KGaA, ein 1835 in Gütersloh gegründetes deutsches Familienunternehmen°, ist das größte Medienhaus Europas. Weltweit arbeiten 119.000 Mitarbeiter für dieses Unternehmen. Bertelsmann hat sechs Geschäftsbereiche: Bücher, Fernsehen und Radio, Zeitschriften, Dienstleistungen°, Druck° und Musik. Die 1946 gegründete Axel Springer AG ist der zweite deutsche Mediengigant. Sie verlegt° mehr als 230 Zeitungen und Zeitschriften°. Die bekannteste ist die *Bild*.

Mediengiganten *media giants*
KGaA=Kommanditgesellschaft auf Aktien *partnership limited by shares* **Familienunternehmen** *family-owned company* **Dienstleistungen** *services* **Druck** *print* **verlegt** *publishes* **Zeitschriften** *magazines*

PORTRÄT

Darmstadt

Darmstadt, eine Stadt in Hessen, gilt als Wissenschaftsstadt°. Hier wohnen zwar nur 157.000 Einwohner, aber es gibt drei Universitäten mit insgesamt mehr als 50.000 Studenten. Neben den Universitäten gibt es auch Forschungseinrichtungen° wie zum Beispiel das Europäische Raumflugkontrollzentrum° (ESOC), die Europäische Organisation für die Nutzung° meteorologischer Satelliten (EUMETSAT) und drei Institute der Fraunhofer-Gesellschaft. Im GSI Helmholtzzentrum für Schwerionenforschung° entdeckten Forscher 1994 das chemische Element Darmstadtium, das man unter der Ordnungsnummer 110 im Periodensystem finden kann. Zurzeit ist das internationale Beschleunigerzentrum° (FAIR) im Bau°.

Wissenschaftsstadt *city of science* **Forschungseinrichtungen** *research institutions* **Raumflugkontrollzentrum** *space flight control center* **Nutzung** *use* **Schwerionenforschung** *heavy ion research* **Beschleunigerzentrum** *particle accelerator facility* **im Bau** *under construction*

🔗 IM INTERNET

Suchen Sie Informationen über digitale Medien in der deutschsprachigen Welt. Was sind die neuesten Trends?

Find out more at **vhlcentral.com**.

---

3   **Porträt** Richtig oder falsch? Korrigieren Sie die falschen Aussagen. Diskutieren Sie dann die letzte Frage mit einem Partner/ einer Partnerin.

1. Darmstadt liegt in Bayern. **Falsch.** Darmstadt liegt in Hessen.

2. Darmstadt hat drei Universitäten mit insgesamt 50.000 Studenten. **Richtig.**

3. Die Galaxie Darmstadtium ist nach der Stadt benannt.
Falsch. Das chemische Element Darmstadtium ist nach der Stadt benannt.

Diskussion Wie kann die Technologie auf das öffentliche Leben angewendet werden? Zum Beispiel öffentliche Sicherheit (*safety*), öffentliche Verkehrsmittel, Verkehrsregelung, Internetzugang, usw.

4   **Wissenschaftsstädte** Welche Vorteile und Nachteile haben Wissenschaftsstädte oder -orte wie Silicon Valley für ihre Einwohner? Schreiben Sie einen kurzen Absatz und lesen Sie ihn im Kurs vor.

More activities

vhlcentral   Online activities

8B.1

Teaching Tip You may want to assign the grammar tutorial **8B.1 The genitive case** on the Supersite for students to watch before they come to class.

The genitive case Grammar Tutorial

Startblock German speakers often use constructions with **von** to indicate a relationship of ownership or close connection between two nouns. To talk about these relationships in more formal speech or writing, use the genitive case (**der Genitiv**).

- In conversation, the preposition **von** is used with a noun in the dative case to indicate ownership or a close relationship.

Hast du den neuen Klingelton **von meinem Handy** schon gehört?
*Have you heard **my cell phone's** new ringtone?*

Um die Website **von Doktor Giese** zu sehen, braucht man ein Passwort.
*You need a password to access **Doctor Giese's** website.*

- Another way to indicate ownership or a close relationship, especially in more formal speech and writing, is to use the genitive case.

Tim hat die Rede **des Bundespräsidenten** heruntergeladen.
*Tim downloaded **the president's** speech.*

Das Mikrofon **der Reporterin** hat nicht funktioniert.
***The reporter's** microphone didn't work.*

QUERVERWEIS

See **1A.3** to review the nominative case, **1B.1** and **3B.2** for the accusative case, and **4B.1** and **4B.2** for the dative case.

ACHTUNG

Possessive adjectives have the same genitive endings as the indefinite articles: **meines Druckers, meiner Festplatte, meines Handys, meiner E-Mails.**

- The forms of definite articles, indefinite articles, and possessive adjectives used with genitive nouns differ from the nominative, accusative, and dative forms. Masculine and neuter nouns also change in the genitive case: those with more than one syllable add **-s**, and those with only one syllable add **-es**.

definite articles				
	masculine	**feminine**	**neuter**	**plural**
nominative	der Drucker	die Festplatte	das Handy	die E-Mails
accusative	den Drucker	die Festplatte	das Handy	die E-Mails
dative	dem Drucker	der Festplatte	dem Handy	den E-Mails
genitive	des Druckers	der Festplatte	des Handys	der E-Mails

indefinite articles				
	masculine	**feminine**	**neuter**	**plural**
nominative	ein Drucker	eine Festplatte	ein Handy	keine E-Mails
accusative	einen Drucker	eine Festplatte	ein Handy	keine E-Mails
dative	einem Drucker	einer Festplatte	einem Handy	keinen E-Mails
genitive	eines Druckers	einer Festplatte	eines Handys	keiner E-Mails

Was ist der Preis **der Spielkonsole**?
*What is the price **of the game console**?*

Der Bildschirm **dieses Computers** ist sehr schmutzig.
***This computer's** screen is very dirty.*

Ich habe diese Fotos mit der Kamera **meines Vaters** gemacht.
*I took these photos with **my father's** camera.*

Ich kann die Telefonnummer **meiner Schwester** nicht finden.
*I can't find **my sister's** phone number.*

- You learned in **4B.1** that some masculine nouns add **-n** or **-en** in the accusative and dative cases: **der Herr, den Herrn, dem Herrn.** This is also true for the genitive case: **des Herrn.**

  Ich habe **dem Polizisten** meinen Personalausweis gezeigt.
  *I showed **the police officer** my ID card.*

  Die Kamera **des Touristen** funktioniert nicht.
  The tourist's camera isn't working.

- In the genitive case, an adjective *preceded* by an **ein**-word or a **der**-word always ends in **-en.** *Unpreceded* adjectives in the genitive case have the endings: **-en, -er, -en,** and **-er.**

  Ich mag das Aroma **schwarzen Kaffees.**
  *I like the smell **of black coffee.***

  Mögen Sie den Geschmack **grüner Paprikas**?
  *Do you like the taste **of green peppers**?*

- When using the name of a person or place in the genitive, add **-s** to the end of the name. If the name already ends with an **s** sound, add an apostrophe instead.

  Magst du **Laras** Website?
  *Do you like **Lara's** website?*

  Benjamin hat **Hans'** Ladegerät verloren.
  *Benjamin lost **Hans's** charger.*

- Most nouns in the genitive case follow the noun they modify. However, the name of a person or place comes before the noun it modifies.

  Die Eltern **meines Freundes** sind sehr nett.
  My boyfriend's *parents are really nice.*

  Jans Digitalkamera ist sehr klein.
  Jan's *digital camera is really small.*

- Use the genitive question word **wessen** to ask *whose?*

nominative	accusative	dative	genitive
wer?	wen?	wem?	wessen?

  Wessen Telefon klingelt?
  Whose phone is ringing?

  Ich glaube, es ist **Josefs** Handy.
  *I think it's **Josef's** cell phone.*

- The genitive case is also used after certain prepositions.

prepositions with the genitive			
(an)statt	*instead of*	trotz	*despite, in spite of*
außerhalb	*outside of*	während	*during*
innerhalb	*inside of, within*	wegen	*because of*

  Anstatt einer Stereoanlage bekam mein Bruder ein Handy zum Geburtstag.
  Instead of a stereo, *my brother got a cell phone for his birthday.*

  Trotz des Regens wollten unsere Freunde wandern gehen.
  Despite the rain, *our friends wanted to go hiking.*

QUERVERWEIS

See **2B.3, 3A.1, 3A.2,** and **4B.1** to review ein-words. See **3A.2** and **4B.1** to review der-words. You will learn more about **der**-words in **8B.2**

See **3B.2** to review accusative prepositions. See **4B.2** to review dative prepositions. See **5B.3** to review two-way prepositions.

ACHTUNG

Be careful not to confuse the genitive **-s** ending with the **'s** ending used in English. In German, the apostrophe is added instead of an **s,** never before it.

More activities

vhlcentral

WB
pp. 113–114

LM
p. 73

Online activities

Suggestion
Tell students that in colloquial German, people tend to use the dative instead of the genitive, especially with the prepositions **trotz** and **wegen.**

Jetzt sind Sie dran!   **Wählen Sie die richtigen Genitivformen.**

1. Das ist der Computer (meines Bruders / meinen Bruder).
2. Wo ist der Kopfhörer (der Schüler / der Schülerin)?
3. Der Fernseher (eures Vaters / euren Vater) steht im Wohnzimmer.
4. Die Website (der neuen Lehrerin / die neue Lehrers) ist sehr interessant.
5. Ich darf die Spielkonsole (meine ältere Schwester / meiner älteren Schwester) benutzen.
6. Der Bildschirm (unserem neuen Laptop / unseres neuen Laptops) ist kaputt.

Anwendung

1 Wessen? Beantworten Sie die Fragen mit einem ganzen Satz und benutzen Sie dabei den Genitiv der angegebenen Substantive.

▶ **BEISPIEL** Wessen Bücher sind das? (die Schülerin)
Das sind die Bücher der Schülerin.

1. Wessen Laptop ist das?
   (die Ingenieurin) Das ist der Laptop der Ingenieurin.
2. Wessen Fahrrad ist das? (das Kind)
   Das ist das Fahrrad des Kindes.
3. Wessen Auto war das? (Tobias)
   Das war Tobias' Auto.
4. Wessen Mikrofon ist das?
   (der Journalist) Das ist das Mikrofon des Journalisten.

5. Wessen Kamera ist das? (Johanna)
   Das ist Johannas Kamera.
6. Wessen Personalausweis ist das? (Julian)
   Das ist Julians Personalausweis.
7. Wessen Fahrplan ist das? (der Schaffner)
   Das ist der Fahrplan des Schaffners.
8. Wessen Abschlussparty war das?
   (die Deutschstudenten)
   Das war die Abschlussparty der Deutschstudenten.

2 Was fehlt? Ergänzen Sie die Sätze mit der Genitivform der Wörter in Klammern.

BEISPIEL

Das Auto *meiner kleinen Schwester* ist ein Mercedes. (meine kleine Schwester)

1. Gefällt dir die Farbe _meines tollen Kleides_? (mein tolles Kleid)
2. Der Blog _der neuen Dozentin_ ist sehr interessant. (die neue Dozentin)
3. Wir müssen immer über die Eskapaden _unserer jungen Hunde_ lachen.
   (unsere jungen Hunde)
4. Die Digitalkamera _des amerikanischen Touristen_ ist kaputt. (der amerikanische Tourist)
5. Der Klingelton _ihres billigen Handys_ ist sehr laut. (ihr billiges Handy)
6. Der Bildschirm _des teuren Fernsehers_ ist größer als ein Fenster. (der teure Fernseher)
7. Das Mikrofon _meines alten Computers_ funktioniert nicht mehr. (mein alter Computer)

3 Suggestion Remind students that **Neffe** (item 7) is an **n**-noun and does not take an -**s** in the genitive.

3 Dativ oder Genitiv? Schreiben Sie die Sätze so um, dass Sie statt des Dativs den Genitiv benutzen.

BEISPIEL Der Benutzername von meinem Partner ist wirklich sehr lustig.
Der Benutzername meines Partners ist wirklich sehr lustig.

1. Die Vorlesungen von unserem Professor sind interessant.
   Die Vorlesungen unseres Professors sind interessant.
2. Die Website von der Universität ist nicht sehr schön.
   Die Website der Universität ist nicht sehr schön.
3. Die Stereoanlage von Alexander ist alt.
   Alexanders Stereoanlage ist alt.
4. Die Festplatte von deinem Computer ist nicht groß.
   Die Festplatte deines Computers ist nicht groß.
5. Meine Eltern verkaufen das Auto von meinen Großeltern.
   Meine Eltern verkaufen das Auto meiner Großeltern.
6. Der Fußball von dem Jungen ist zwischen die geparkten Autos gefallen.
   Der Fußball des Jungen ist zwischen die geparkten Autos gefallen.
7. Die Katze von meinem Neffen ist sehr aggressiv.
   Die Katze meines Neffen ist sehr aggressiv.
8. Die neue App von Amazon ist gerade (*just now*) auf den Markt gekommen.
   Amazons neue App ist gerade auf den Markt gekommen.

Kommunikation

4 **Bilder beschreiben** Beschreiben Sie mit einem Partner / einer Partnerin zusammen, was man auf den Bilder sehen kann. Benutzen Sie den Genitiv und verwenden Sie dabei die Wörter aus der Liste. Answers will vary.

▶ **BEISPIEL**

S1: *Was sieht man auf diesem Bild?*
S2: *Man sieht den Bildschirm eines Fernsehers.*

| der Ausgang | der Motor | die Tastatur |
| der Bildschirm | der Seminarraum | |

1. Man sieht die Tastatur eines Computers.

2. Man sieht den Seminarraum einer Universität.

3. Man sieht den Motor eines Autos.

4. Man sieht den Ausgang eines Flughafens.

5 **Bedeutende Erfinder** Finden Sie zusammen mit einem Partner / einer Partnerin heraus, was diese Personen erfunden (*invented*) haben. Verwenden Sie in Ihren Antworten den Genitiv und wechseln Sie sich ab. Answers will vary.

BEISPIEL

S1: *Wer war Melitta Bentz?*
S2: *Sie war die Erfinderin des Kaffeefilters.*

der Bunsenbrenner	das Luftschiff
der Dieselmotor	die Röntgenstrahlen (*X-rays*)
die Jeans	der Rorschachtest
der Kaffeefilter	der Sportschuh

1. Rudolf Diesel
2. Levi Strauss
3. Wilhelm Röntgen
4. Ferdinand von Zeppelin

5. Hermann Rorschach
6. Robert Bunsen
7. Adi Dassler
8. Melitta Bentz

6 **Wann machst du das?** Fragen Sie Ihren Partner / Ihre Partnerin, wann er/sie diese Aktivitäten macht. Verwenden Sie bei Ihren Antworten einen Zeitausdruck aus jeder (*each*) Spalte. Lesen Sie Ihre Antworten im Kurs vor. Answers will vary.

BEISPIEL

S1: *Wann schreibst du die meisten Prüfungen?*
S2: *Ich schreibe die meisten Prüfungen am Ende des Semesters.*

Am Ende	das Semester
Am Anfang	die Woche
Während	der Tag
	das Jahr
	der Sommer
	die Ferien
	das Abendessen

1. Wann lernst du neue Mitstudenten kennen?
2. Wann surfst du im Internet?
3. Wann fährst du mal für ein paar Tage weg?
4. Wann rufst du deine Familie an?
5. Wann bekommst du deine Noten?
6. Wann suchst du einen Ferienjob?

5 **Suggestion** Tell students that Adi Dassler's name provides a clue about his invention. Dassler is the founder of the sportswear company **Adidas.**

5 **Suggested answers:**
1. Wer war Rudolf Diesel? Er war der Erfinder des Dieselmotors.

2. Wer war Levi Strauss? Er war der Erfinder der Jeans.

3. Wer war Wilhelm Röntgen? Er war der Erfinder der Röntgenstrahlen.

4. Wer war Ferdinand von Zeppelin? Er war der Erfinder des Luftschiffes.

5. Wer war Hermann Rorschach? Er war der Erfinder des Rorschachtests.

6. Wer war Robert Bunsen? Er war der Erfinder des Bunsenbrenners.

7. Wer war Adi Dassler? Er war der Erfinder des Sportschuhs.

8. Wer war Melitta Bentz? Sie war die Erfinderin des Kaffeefilters.

6 **Video Virtual Chat** You can also assign activity 6 on the Supersite. Students record individual responses that appearin your gradebook.

8B.2

Teaching Tip You may want to assign the grammar tutorial **8B.2 Demonstratives** on the Supersite for students to watch before they come to class.

Suggestion The humorous '90s song **Die Da!?!** by **Die Fantastischen Vier** can be found online and provides a good illustration of the use of demonstratives.

Demonstratives Grammar Tutorial

Startblock Use demonstrative pronouns and adjectives to refer to something that has already been mentioned, or to point out a specific person or thing.

Dieser Fluss ist die Havel, und **das** da ist die Spree.

Es war meine Idee, hierher zu kommen. Ich liebe **diesen** Ort.

Demonstrative pronouns

- Use demonstrative pronouns to refer to a person or thing that has already been mentioned or whose identity is clear, instead of repeating the noun.

Ist Greta online?
—Ja, **die** schreibt eine E-Mail.
Is Greta online?
—*Yes, **she**'s writing an e-mail.*

Gefällt dir dein neuer Drucker?
—Ja, **der** funktioniert sehr gut!
Do you like your new printer?
—*Yes, **it** works really well!*

- The forms of the demonstrative pronoun are identical to the definite article, except for the genitive and dative plural forms. Use the demonstrative pronoun that agrees in gender and number with the noun it is replacing.

demonstrative pronouns				
	masculine	**feminine**	**neuter**	**plural**
nominative	der	die	das	die
accusative	den	die	das	die
dative	dem	der	dem	denen
genitive	dessen	deren	dessen	deren

Dieser Laptop ist wirklich alt. **Den** habe ich schon seit Jahren.
*This laptop is really old. I've had **it** for years.*

Lara ist sehr zuverlässig. **Die** wird nicht zu spät kommen.
*Lara is very reliable. **She** won't come too late.*

Was sagen deine Eltern? Hast du **denen** schon dein Zeugnis gezeigt?
*What do your parents say? Have you shown **them** your report card yet?*

Ich habe nur eine Fernbedienung, aber mit **der** kann man alles an- und ausmachen.
*I only have one remote, but you can turn everything on and off with **it**.*

- Use the genitive demonstrative pronouns **dessen** or **deren** in cases where the possessive adjectives **sein** or **ihr** might cause confusion.

Erik hat Daniel auf **seinem** neuen Boot gesehen.
*Erik saw Daniel on **his** (Erik's? Daniel's?) new boat.*

Erik hat Daniel auf **dessen** neuen Boot gesehen.
*Erik saw Daniel on **his** (Daniel's) new boat.*

- Use **hier** or **da** with a demonstrative to distinguish between *this one* or *that one*.

Der da gefällt Klara besser.
*Klara likes **that one** better.*

Vergiss nicht, **das hier** zu drucken!
*Don't forget to print **this one**!*

Der-words

- **Der**-words include **dieser** (*this; that*), **jeder** (*each, every*) and its plural counterpart **alle** (*all*), **mancher** (*some*), and **solcher** (*such*), as well as the question word **welcher** (*which*).

Nina, **welcher** Laptop gefällt dir am besten?
*Nina, **which** laptop do you like best?*

Ich finde **diesen** Laptop am schönsten.
*I think **this** laptop is the nicest.*

- **Der**-words are so called because they have the same endings as the definite articles. The chart below shows only **dieser**, but all the other **der**-words have the same endings.

der-words			
	masculine	**feminine**	**neuter**	**plural**
nominative	dieser Mann	diese Frau	dieses Kind	diese Kinder
accusative	diesen Mann	diese Frau	dieses Kind	diese Kinder
dative	diesem Mann	dieser Frau	diesem Kind	diesen Kindern
genitive	dieses Mannes	dieser Frau	dieses Kindes	dieser Kinder

Mit **dieser** Tastatur können Sie viel
schneller tippen.
*With **this** keyboard, you can type much faster.*

Speichert dein neues Handy **jede** SMS?
*Does your new cellphone save **every** text message?*

Manche Sender haben keine guten Programme.
Some stations don't have any good programs.

Solche Websites gefallen mir nicht.
*I don't like **those kinds of** websites.*

- Adjectives after **der**-words have the same endings as adjectives after definite articles.

Diese kleine Digitalkamera macht sehr
schöne Fotos.
***That little** digital camera takes
great photos.*

Welchen neuen Film wollt ihr heute
Abend sehen?
***Which new** film do you want to
see tonight?*

Suggestion Provide students with a few memorable **so ein**
phrases to help them understand its idiomatic use. Ex.: **So ein Tag!**
So ein Zufall! So ein tolles Auto!

More
activities

vhlcentral

WB
pp. 115–116

LM
p. 74

Online
activities

Jetzt sind Sie dran! **Wählen Sie die passende Form.**

1. (Welches / Welcher) Mikrofon funktioniert am besten?
2. Simon speichert (jede / jedes) Dokument auf der Festplatte.
3. Frau Kaufmann hat einen neuen Laptop gekauft. (Die / Der) hat 700 € gekostet.
4. Von (welcher / welchem) Schwester hast du die Stereoanlage zum Geburtstag bekommen?
5. Danke für den guten Saft! (Den / Dem) trinken wir heute Abend.
6. Bringst du bitte das Ladegerät mit? (Das / Dem) brauche ich sofort (*right away*).
7. Mira speichert (manchen / manche) E-Mails und löscht den Rest.

8. Ich schreibe (jeder / jeden) Benutzernamen auf, um ihn nicht zu vergessen.
9. Mit (solche / solchen) Handys kann man E-Mails schreiben, SMS schicken und telefonieren.
10. Ihr wolltet den Fernseher mit der Fernbedienung anmachen, aber (die / das) war nirgendwo (*nowhere*) zu finden.
11. (Welches / Welcher) Freund hat dir mit deiner Website geholfen?
12. Antonia hat Nils und (dessen / deren) Frau das Dokument gezeigt.

Anwendung

1 Was fehlt? Ergänzen Sie die Sätze mit den richtigen Demonstrativpronomen.

1. Kennst du die Deutschdozentin? Nein, _die_ kenne ich nicht.
2. Welcher Computer ist der bessere? _Der_ da für 1.200 €.
3. Welches Kleid ziehst du auf die Party an? _Das_ da auf meinem Bett.
4. Welchem Kind gehört der Fußball? _Dem_ dort auf dem Spielfeld.
5. Haben Schmidts dich schon angerufen? _Deren_ Tochter hat letzte Woche ihren Abschluss gemacht.
6. Was machen deine Großeltern? Ach, _denen_ geht's leider nicht sehr gut.
7. Bringt ihr euren Hund ins Hundehotel während eurer Reise? Nein, _den_ nehmen wir natürlich mit.
8. Welcher Zug geht nach Kassel? _Der_ fährt dort drüben auf Bahnsteig 7A.

2 Was ist richtig? Wählen Sie die passenden der-Wörter.

1. (Solches / (Welches)) Auto hast du denn jetzt gekauft?
2. (Jede / (Manche)) Modelle haben nur einen kleinen Kofferraum.
3. Heute kann man mit ((jedem) / welchem) Handy im Internet surfen.
4. Hast du ((diese) / jede) Website schon gesehen? Die ist wirklich interessant!
5. (Manche / (Solche)) Probleme möchte ich haben!
6. Mit ((solchen) / welchen) Leuten kann man leider nicht reden.

3 Elektronische Geräte Beantworten Sie die Fragen mit ja oder nein. Verwenden Sie die der-Wörter in Klammern und ein passendes Adjektiv aus der Liste. Achten Sie auf die Adjektivendungen. Sample answers are provided.

> alt | amerikanisch | günstig | flach (flat) | kaputt | klein | nutzlos

> **BEISPIEL**
> Gefällt dir der Bildschirm meines Fernsehers? (dies-)
> *Ja, dieser flache Bildschirm gefällt mir.*

1. Kann man mit dem Smartphone auch SMS schreiben? (all-)

2. Kannst du mit deinem Laptop Videos herunterladen? (dies-)

3. Kann man diese Tastatur auch in Deutschland benutzen? (dies-)

4. Möchtest du die Videokamera meiner Mutter kaufen? (dies-)

5. Kannst du mit deinem Kopfhörer alles hören? (dies-)

Kommunikation

4 **Wie findest du das?** Fragen Sie Ihren Partner / Ihre Partnerin nach seiner/ihrer Meinung (*opinion*). Benutzen Sie Demonstrativpronomen und wechseln Sie sich ab. Answers will vary.

BEISPIEL

S1: Wie findest du die Band *Train*?
S2: Die ist einfach fantastisch!

Wie findest du...

1. die Musik von...?
2. die Kunst von...?
3. den Fernsehsender...?
4. den Film...?
5. die Kurse von Professor/Professorin...?
6. die Bücher von...?

egoistisch	langweilig
eingebildet	lustig
fade	romantisch
fantastisch	schlecht
hübsch	süß
intelligent	toll
interessant	

5 **Immer das Gleiche** Schreiben Sie, was Sie jeden Tag, jede Woche, jeden Monat und jedes Jahr machen, und dann interviewen Sie Ihre Mitstudenten. Answers will vary.

BEISPIEL

S1: Was machst du jeden Tag?
S2: Ich esse jeden Tag in der Mensa. Und du, was machst du jeden Tag?

jeden Tag:	
jede Woche:	
jeden Monat:	
jedes Jahr:	

6 **Rollenspiel: Im Modehaus** Sie sind Verkäufer / Verkäuferin in einem Modehaus. Leider hat der Kunde / die Kundin immer etwas auszusetzen (*criticize*). Erfinden Sie mit einem Partner / einer Partnerin einen Dialog. Answers will vary.

BEISPIEL

S1: Wie finden Sie diesen Pullover?
S2: Der ist viel zu klein!
S1: Und wie gefällt Ihnen dieses rote Kleid?
S2: So ein hässliches Kleid habe ich noch nie gesehen!

der Anzug	die Krawatte	billig	gestreift
die Baseballmütze	die Lederjacke	dunkel	hässlich
das Baumwollkleid	der Minirock	einfach	lang
die Halskette	die Sandalen	elegant	langweilig
die Handtasche	der Schal	eng	schmutzig
die Hose	das Trägerhemd	furchtbar	teuer

4 **Partner Chat** You can also assign activity 4 on the Supersite. Students work in pairs to record the activity online. The pair's recorded conversation will appear in your gradebook.

6 **Partner Chat** You can also assign activity 6 on the Supersite. Students work in pairs to record the activity online. The pair's recorded conversation will appear in your gradebook.

Wiederholung

NATIONAL communication STANDARDS

1 Logische Verbindungen
Sehen Sie sich mit einem Partner / einer Partnerin die Wortliste und die Bilder an. Welche Wörter passen zu welchen Bildern? Sample answers are provided.

▶ **BEISPIEL**

Das ist die Schwimmerin des Jahres.

1 Suggestion Make sure students understand that each of their answers must contain a genitive construction.

das Jahr	die Schülerin
der Monat	der Tag
das Restaurant	

1.
Das ist das Restaurant des Monats.

2.
Das sind die Bleistifte der Schülerin.

3.
Das ist das Auto des Jahres.

4.
Das ist der Koch des Restaurants.

2 Diskutieren und kombinieren
Sehen Sie sich die Tabelle mit statistischen Informationen über Deutschland, Liechtenstein und die Schweiz an. Fragen Sie Ihren Partner / Ihre Partnerin nach den fehlenden Informationen. **2 Suggestion** If you notice that students are having difficulty forming the questions, interrupt the activity to write the questions as a class.

BEISPIEL

S1: Wie lang ist der längste Fluss der Schweiz?
S2: Das ist der Rhein. Er ist 375 Kilometer lang.

3 Manche Leute
Viele Menschen machen komische Sachen (*strange things*). Was denken Sie und Ihr Partner / Ihre Partnerin darüber? Was sollen diese Menschen anders machen? **3 Suggestion** Encourage students to be creative, and provide vocabulary help as needed. If your class is fairly small, invite students to share their answers on the board.

BEISPIEL

S1: Manche Menschen tanzen im Regen.
S2: Solche Menschen sind dynamisch, aber sie sollen sich einen Regenschirm kaufen.

im Haus Rad fahren	draußen schlafen
unter dem Bett lesen	im Regen tanzen
auf dem Dach lesen	im Winter kurze Kleider tragen

4 Wem gehört's?
Sehen Sie sich die Bilder an. Fragen Sie einen Partner / eine Partnerin, wem die Dinge gehören. Wechseln Sie sich ab. Sample answers are provided.

▶ **BEISPIEL**

S1: Wessen Stereoanlage ist das?
S2: Das ist die Stereoanlage des Studenten.

meine Eltern	mein Opa
David	der Journalist
das Mädchen	der Student

1.
Das ist der Drucker meines Opas.

2.
Das ist die Videokamera des Journalisten.

3.
Das ist das Fotoalbum des Mädchens.

4.
Das ist der Fernseher meiner Eltern.

5 Arbeitsblatt
Fragen Sie andere im Unterricht, was ihnen gefällt. Schreiben Sie sich die Antworten auf.

BEISPIEL Autor: Stephen King / Jane Austen

S1: Wen liest du lieber, Stephen King oder Jane Austen?
S2: Mir ist Stephen King lieber.

6 Technologie
Unterhalten Sie sich mit Ihrem Partner / Ihrer Partnerin, über die Geräte, die sie besitzen. Was halten Sie von solchen Geräten? Benutzen sie viele Menschen? Sind sie für jeden geeignet (*suitable*)?

▶ **BEISPIEL**

S1: Ich habe eine Spielkonsole.
S2: Ich habe auch eine Spielkonsole. Viele Studenten mögen sie.
S1: Was spielst du am liebsten?
S2: Am liebsten spiele ich...

6 Partner Chat You can also assign activity 6 on the Supersite. Students work in pairs to record the activity online. The pair's recorded conversation will appear in your gradebook.

7 Die Deutsche Bahn AG Das Streckennetz° der Deutschen Bahn ist 34.000 Kilometer lang und macht es einfach und schnell, von einem Ort zum anderen zu kommen. Sehen Sie sich zu zweit diesen Fahrplan an und finden Sie heraus, wie lange die Zugfahrt dauert, wie oft man umsteigen muss und mit was für einem Zug man fährt.

Streckennetz *rail network*

BEISPIEL

S1: *Wohin fährst du?*
S2: *Ich fahre nach Saarbrücken.*
S1: *Wann fährst du hier in Erfurt ab?*
S2: *Der Zug fährt ...*

Expansion Ask students to guess what these acronyms stand for: **Hbf** (**Hauptbahnhof**), **ICE** (**Inter City Express**), and **RE** (**Regionalexpress**). Encourage them to find on a map the cities on this schedule.

Persönlicher Fahrplan
(gültig vom 08.04.2019 bis 14.04.2019)

Erfurt Hbf ⟶ Saarbrücken Hbf

Ab	Zug		An	Umsteigen	Ab	Zug		An	Dauer	Verkehrstage
8:17	ICE 1654	¶	10:36	Frankfurt(Main)Hbf	10:50	ICE 277	¶			Mo - Fr
			11:27	Mannheim Hbf	11:39	RE 4121		13:15	4:58	
8:17	ICE 1654	¶	11:15	Mainz Hbf	11:56	RE 29516		14:12	5:55	Mo - Sa
8:50	ICE 1636	¶	10:56	Frankfurt(Main)Hbf	11:08	RE 4256				Mo - Fr
			11:49	Mainz Hbf	11:56	RE 29516		14:12	5:22	
9:30	ICE 595	¶	12:27	Mannheim Hbf	12:39	RE 4123		14:15	4:45	Di - So
9:34	ICE 595	¶	12:27	Mannheim Hbf	12:39	RE 4123		14:15	4:41	Mo

Saarbrücken Hbf ⟶ Erfurt Hbf

Ab	Zug		An	Umsteigen	Ab	Zug		An	Dauer	Verkehrstage
10:58	TGV 9551	🍴	12:58	Frankfurt(Main)Hbf	13:19	ICE 1651	¶	15:38	4:40	täglich
11:47	RE 4106		13:21	Mannheim Hbf	13:32	ICE 598	¶	16:26	4:39	täglich
11:51	RE 29517		13:59	Mainz Hbf	14:10	RE 4261				Mo - Fr
			14:49	Frankfurt(Main)Hbf	15:02	ICE 1631	¶	17:07	5:16	

Legende

¶	=	Bordrestaurant
Ⓡ	=	Reservierungspflicht
🍴	=	Bordbistro

Alle Angaben ohne Gewähr
Softwareversion/Datenstand HAFAS-p2w-V1.4/DATAalls06 - 20.02.19

Genitivpräpositionen Schreiben Sie mit einem Partner / einer Partnerin ein Gedicht (*poem*) aus fünf Sätzen. Außer der letzten Zeile (*line*) muss jede Zeile mit einer Genitivpräposition beginnen.

BEISPIEL

Außerhalb der Stadt stürmt es.
Trotz des schlechten Wetters spielen wir Tennis.
Während des Spiels rollt der Ball in den Fluss.
Wegen des verlorenen Balls können wir nicht mehr spielen.
Das nächste Mal bleiben wir lieber mit der Spielkonsole zu Hause.

Wahrheiten und Lügen Schreiben Sie zwei Sätze darüber, was Sie schon vor Ihrem 14. Geburtstag gemacht haben. Eine der Aussagen ist wahr (*true*), eine Aussage ist eine Lüge (*lie*). Ihre Mitstudenten müssen erraten, welcher Satz die Lüge ist. Answers will vary.

9 Suggestion Provide a model with two truths and a lie about what you had already done before you turned 14. Have students guess which one is the lie.

BEISPIEL

Ich war schon zweimal nach Europa geflogen.
Ich hatte schon zwei Fremdsprachen gelernt.

 Mein Wörterbuch

Schreiben Sie noch fünf weitere Wörter in Ihr persönliches Wörterbuch zu den Themen **Verkehrsmittel** und **Technologie**.

Lektion 8B		
German	English	Definition

+ add word

| der Führerschein | driver's license | die Fahrerlaubnis |

↓ 🗑

ä ö ü ß ☐ ALL CAPS

Suggestion Write on the board the German words that students won't know for public transportation, and ask students to add them to Vocabulary Tools on the Sag mal Supersite.

Panorama Interactive Map

Hessen und Thüringen

Hessen in Zahlen

NATIONAL STANDARDS connections cultures

▶ **Fläche:** *21.114 km²*

▶ **Bevölkerung:** *6,3 Millionen Menschen*

▶ **Religion:** *evangelisch-lutherisch 38,9%, römisch-katholisch 24,3%*

▶ **Städte:** *Frankfurt (768.600 Einwohner), Wiesbaden (276.220), Kassel (198.000)*

▶ **Flüsse:** *der Main, der Neckar, die Fulda*

▶ **Wichtige Industriezweige:** *chemische Industrie, Pharmaindustrie, Fahrzeugbau, Banken Biotechnologie, Medizintechnik*

▶ **Touristenattraktionen:** *Römischer Grenzwall° Limes, Fossilienlagerstätte° Grube Messel, Benediktiner-Abtei° und Kloster° Lorsch
Touristen können in Marburg die Märchen der Gebrüder Grimm entdecken. Wirtschaftlich ist Hessen für die Banken in Frankfurt und die chemische und Pharmaindustrie bekannt.*

QUELLE: Landesportal Hessen

Thüringen in Zahlen

▶ **Fläche:** *16.172 km²*

▶ **Bevölkerung:** *2,15 Millionen Menschen*

▶ **Religion:** *evangelisch-lutherisch 23,3%, römisch-katholisch 7,7%*

▶ **Städte:** *Erfurt (210.000 Einwohner), Jena (110.320), Gera (94.750)*

▶ **Wichtige Industriezweige:** *Automobil, Metallverarbeitung, Lebensmittelindustrie, Optik, Tourismus*

▶ **Touristenattraktionen:** *Weimar, Wartburg (Eisenach), Schloss Friedenstein (Gotha)
Touristen können in Eisenach die Spuren berühmter Deutscher wie Luther und Bach entdecken. Wirtschaftlich ist Optik, Thüringen eines der erfolgreichsten° ostdeutschen Bundesländer.*

QUELLE: Thüringen Tourismus

Berühmte Hessen und Thüringer

▶ **Johann Sebastian Bach,** *Komponist (1685–1750)*

▶ **Johann Wolfgang von Goethe,** *Autor (1749–1832)*

▶ **Anne Frank,** *Autorin und Opfer° des Nationalsozialismus (1929–1945)*

römischer Grenzwall *Roman boundary wall* Fossilienlagerstätte *natural fossil deposit* Abtei *abbey* Kloster *monastery* erfolgreichsten *most successful* Opfer *victim* Karfreitag *Good Friday* Tanzverbot *ban on dancing* drohen *threaten* Geldstrafen *fines*

**Map labels:**
BREMEN · BRANDENBURG · NORDRHEIN-WESTFALEN · Fachwerkhäuser in Marburg · Wartburg in Eisenach · NATIONALPARK HAINICH · SACHSEN · Kassel · Eder · NATIONALPARK KELLERWALD-EDERSEE · HESSEN · Werra · Eisenach · Weimar · Erfurt · Saale · Marburg · Fulda · THÜRINGEN · Jena · Gera · WESTERWALD · Gießen · Schneekopf · THÜRINGER WALD · Großer Beerberg · Lahn · VOGELSBERG · Fulda · RHÖN · Wasserkuppe · Limburg · TAUNUS · Frankfurt am Main · Wiesbaden · Hanau · Offenbach · TSCHE · Darmstadt · ODENWALD · Main · RHEINLAND-PFALZ · Rhein · Neckar · BADEN-WÜRTTEMBERG · FRANKREICH · Bankenmetropole Frankfurt

Landesgrenzen
● Stadt
◉ Landeshauptstadt

0 — 25 Meilen
0 — 25 Kilometer

Unglaublich, aber wahr!

Am Karfreitag° und an anderen religiösen Feiertagen darf man in vielen Bundesländern nicht tanzen. Hessen und Thüringen sind zwei von dreizehn Bundesländern, in denen das Tanzverbot° am Karfreitag 24 Stunden dauert. Seit 1952 dürfen Diskotheken an diesem Tag keine Tanzveranstaltungen organisieren oder es drohen° hohe Geldstrafen°.

Suggestion Point out that the term **Bußgeld** typically refers to fines incurred for parking violations, speeding, or fare evasion, while **Geldstrafe** is a more general term for a fine or legal penalty.

Tanzverbot

Städte

Weimar

Suggestion Have students read a short poem by Goethe, such as *Wanderers Nachtlied II* or *Heidenröslein*.

Weimar ist die viertgrößte Stadt in Thüringen. Im Jahre 1919 beschloss die Nationalversammlung° hier die deutsche Verfassung°. Deshalb nennt man die erste deutsche Demokratie auch „Weimarer Republik". Für die Literatur ist Weimar wichtig, weil Autoren wie Goethe, Schiller und Nietzsche hier lebten. Berühmte Musiker, die in Weimar komponierten, waren Johann Sebastian Bach und Franz Liszt. Im Bereich der Architektur entwickelte° der Architekt Walter Gropius die Bauhaus-Schule in Weimar.

Kultur

Skat

Skat ist eines der beliebtesten Kartenspiele in Deutschland. Manche Menschen nennen es auch „das Spiel der Deutschen". Etwa 20 Millionen Deutsche spielen Skat. Das Spiel wurde circa 1810 in der thüringischen Stadt Altenburg erfunden°. Seit 1938 gibt es deutsche Meisterschaften°. Altenburg ist immer noch die Skathauptstadt der Welt, in welcher der Deutsche Skatverband seine Geschäftsstelle° hat. Hier gibt es auch die berühmte Kartenfabrik Altenburger Spielkarten. Die Kartenfabrik wurde 1832 gegründet.

Geographie

Wald und Jagd° in Deutschland

In Hessen und Thüringen bestehen große Landesflächen aus Wäldern. In Hessen gibt es 8.472 Quadratkilometer Wald, etwa 40% der Landesfläche. Damit liegt Hessen zusammen mit Rheinland-Pfalz an der Spitze der Bundesländer. Der Nationalpark Thüringer Wald bietet ein sehr beliebtes Urlaubsziel für Wanderer, Fahrradfahrer und Skifahrer an. Seit dem 19. Jahrhundert nennt man Thüringen „das grüne Herz Deutschlands". Auch Jäger° besuchen diese Region gerne zur Jagd von Rehen und Hirschen°.

Menschen

Heilige Elisabeth

Die heilige° Elisabeth, auch bekannt als Landgräfin Elisabeth von Thüringen, lebte zwischen 1207 und 1231. Sie war die Tochter des ungarischen° Königs Andreas II. und lebte die meiste Zeit ihres Lebens im hessischen Marburg. Sie starb im Alter von 24 Jahren, aber die Menschen liebten sie, weil sie sehr vielen Menschen während ihres Lebens geholfen hatte. Nur vier Jahre nach ihrem Tod sprach Papst Gregor IX. Elisabeth heilig°. In Marburg kann man heute ihr Grab° in der Elisabethkirche besuchen.

Musik Musik

Annenmaykantereit

Annenmaykantereit ist eine deutsche Rockgruppe. 2011 waren sie Straßenmusiker in Köln. Heute spielen sie in großen Hallen vor Tausenden.

Go to **vhlcentral.com** to find out more about **Annenmaykantereit**.

Nationalversammlung *national assembly* **Verfassung** *constitution* **entwickelte** *developed* **erfunden** *invented* **Meisterschaften** *championships* **Geschäftsstelle** *office* **Wald und Jagd** *forest and hunting* **Jäger** *hunters* **Rehen und Hirschen** *deer and stags* **heilige** *saint* **ungarischen** *Hungarian* **sprach… heilig** *canonized* **Grab** *grave*

---

1   **Was haben Sie gelernt?** Entscheiden Sie, ob die Sätze richtig oder falsch sind. Korrigieren Sie die falschen Sätze.

1. Die erste deutsche Demokratie nennt man auch die „Weimarer Republik." **Richtig.**
2. Die Musiker Johann Sebastian Bach und Franz Liszt haben in Weimar gelebt. **Richtig.**
3. Skat wurde circa 1610 in Altenburg in Thüringen erfunden. **Falsch.** Skat wurde circa 1810 in Altenburg erfunden.
4. Im Hessen sind fast 20% der Landesfläche Wald. **Falsch.** In Hessen sind etwa 40% der Landesfläche Wald.
5. In der Elisabethkirche in Marburg ist das Grab von Elisabeth. **Richtig.**

2   **Denken Sie nach** Diskutieren Sie die Frage mit einem Partner/einer Partnerin. Welchen Nationalpark haben Sie schon besucht? Was haben Sie dort gemacht? Was hat Ihnen besonders gut gefallen? Vergleichen Sie diesen Park mit dem Nationalpark Thüringer Wald.

Lesen Audio: Reading

Vor dem Lesen

Strategien

Identifying borrowed words: anglicisms

An anglicism (**der Anglizismus**) is a word or phrase from the English language that is adopted by another language. English words related to technology are often borrowed by German and other languages. The spelling of these words is often modified to fit the sounds of the languages that borrow them. Use the strategy of identifying anglicisms to help you understand new texts. This strategy can be especially useful when reading texts related to computer science or new technology.

 Untersuchen Sie den Text Sehen Sie sich mit einem Partner / einer Partnerin den Text und die Illustrationen an. Machen Sie eine Liste mit den Anglizismen. Worum geht es in dem Text?

Sample answers are provided.

Smartphone	Computer
relaxen	Apps
Präsenz	Handys
No-Screen-Policy	Mobbing

Umfrage machen Machen Sie eine Liste mit den Apps auf Ihrem Smartphone, die Sie am meisten benutzen. Fragen Sie dann im Kurs, welche Apps bei Ihren Mitstudenten / Mitstudentinnen am beliebtesten (*most popular*) sind. Welche fünf Apps verwenden alle am meisten? Warum und wofür benutzen Sie diese Apps? Answers will vary.

Suggestion Tell students to set the language on their smartphones to German to see what the common functions are named.

Das Smartphone

Für die Meisten von uns ist ein Leben ohne das Smartphone gar nicht mehr vorstellbar°. Wir benutzen unseren Mini-Computer 24 Stunden am Tag, 7 Tage die Woche. Das Smartphone sagt uns am Morgen, wann wir aufstehen müssen, und zeigt uns sofort den aktuellen Wetterbericht und die neuesten Nachrichten. Es informiert uns, wann wir wo sein müssen, was unsere Freunde gerade machen und ob unsere Lieblingsmusikerin ihr neues Video hochgeladen hat. Das Smartphone ist unser bester Freund geworden. Es ist immer dabei, egal wo wir sind. Wir gehen mit ihm einkaufen, es fährt mit uns im Bus oder zeigt uns, wie wir fahren müssen; es liegt neben uns auf dem Sofa und hilft uns zu relaxen, wenn wir mit ihm Filme anschauen, Spiele spielen oder Musik hören. Und jeden Tag gibt es neue Apps zum Runterladen, die unser Leben noch mehr vereinfachen. Das Smartphone kann alles, weiß alles, tut alles.

In Deutschland gibt es 65 Millionen Smartphone-Nutzer° und es werden Jahr für Jahr immer mehr. Drei Stunden pro Tag verbringt jeder Deutsche im Durchschnitt° am Handy. 66% kaufen sich jedes Jahr ein neues Modell, geben dafür circa 350 Euro aus und zahlen um die 22 Euro pro Monat für ihren Service.

Wofür nutzen die Deutschen ihr Smartphone am häufigsten°?

■ Social Media	49,7%
■ Musik hören	45,2%
■ Online Shoppen	34,6%
■ Spiele	33,8%
■ Filme und Videos	31,1%

Aber nicht alle Menschen freuen sich über die permanente Präsenz der Handys und Smartphones. Die Meisten stört° es, wenn im Zug, im Kino oder im Unterricht ein Handy klingelt oder wenn Smartphone-Nutzer Videos, Musik oder Spiele über Lautsprecher anhören.

Wo nutzen die Deutschen ihr Smartphone?

Zuhause	Unterwegs	Bei der Arbeit	Im Cafe/Restaurant	In der Schule/Uni
90%	87%	46%	28%	15%

In Deutschland ist das Thema „digitaler Unterricht" eine große Debatte. Sollen Schüler und Studenten ihre Smartphones in ihren Kursen benutzen dürfen? Es gibt keinen Konsens darüber und jede Schule und Universität, jeder Lehrer oder Professor vertritt° eine andere Meinung. Bayern hat als einziges Bundesland ein gesetzliches° Smartphone-Verbot°, aber seit Frankreich 2018 ein generelles Smartphone-Verbot an Schulen erlassen° hat, diskutiert man auch in Deutschland, ob ein solches Verbot sinnvoll ist.

Welche digitalen Geräte werden an Schulen und Universitäten am meisten benutzt?

80%	63%	53%	48%	21%
Tablets	Laptops	Smartphones	Smartboards	PCs

Für einige Lehrer und Professoren ist das Smartphone ein pädagogisches Plus. Es gibt aber auch viele Professoren, die eine „No-Screen-Policy" in ihren Kursen eingeführt° haben und sagen, dass ihre Studenten ohne den Computer wacher sind, besser lernen und so letztendlich° auch bessere Noten bekommen.

Smartphones im Unterricht

PRO ➕	KONTRA ➖
• Unterricht ist kreativer	• Schummeln° bei Tests und Hausaufgaben
• Hilfsmittel bei Projekten (Recherchen, Reportagen, digitales Wörterbuch)	• Klingeln stört die Konzentration
• Terminplaner (z.B. für Tests, Hausaufgaben)	• Permanente Erreichbarkeit° macht nervös
• Spiele mit Lernen kombinieren	• Mobbing in den Social Media
• Mehr Spaß im Unterricht durch interaktives Lernen	• Chatten und Spielen anstatt Lernen

Tatsache ist, dass wir in einer technologisierten Welt leben und arbeiten. Wir werden in der Zukunft nicht weniger Technologie benutzen, sondern immer mehr. Sollte es daher nicht die Aufgabe der Schulen und Universitäten sein, ihren Schülern und Studenten beizubringen°, wie man diese Technologie sinn- und nutzvoll im Leben einsetzt°?

vorstellbar *imaginable* **Nutzer** *user* **im Durchschnitt** *on average* **am häufigsten** *most frequently* **stört** *bothers* **vertritt** *advocates* **gesetzliches** *legal* **Verbot** *ban* **erlassen** *enact* **eingeführt** *introduced* **letztendlich** *all things considered* **Schummeln** *cheat* **Erreichbarkeit** *accessibility* **Mobbing** *bullying* **beizubringen** *teach* **einsetzt** *utilizes*

Nach dem Lesen

Richtig oder falsch Sind die Sätze **richtig** oder **falsch**? Korrigieren Sie die falschen Sätze. Sample answers are provided.

	richtig	falsch
1. Am häufigsten benutzen die Menschen das Smartphone zum Telefonieren. Man benutzt das Smartphone am häufigsten für Social Media.	☐	☑
2. In Deutschland leben 82 Millionen Menschen, und alle haben ein Smartphone. In Deutschland gibt es 65 Millionen Smartphone-Nutzer.	☐	☑
3. Mehr als die Hälfte aller Deutschen kauft sich jedes Jahr ein neues Smartphone.	☑	☐
4. Smartphones sind an deutschen Schulen verboten. Nur an Schulen in Bayern sind Smartphones verboten.	☐	☑
5. An deutschen Schulen benutzt man mehr Tablets als Laptops	☑	☐
6. Permanente Erreichbarkeit ist ein positiver Aspekt von Smartphones im Unterricht. Permanente Erreichbarkeit ist ein Argument gegen Smartphones im Unterricht, weil es Studenten nervös macht.	☐	☑

Zum Besprechen Deutsche benutzen ihr Smartphone circa 21 Stunden pro Woche, meistens zu Hause und am häufigsten für Social Media. Vergleichen Sie die Daten in den Grafiken zuerst mit Ihren eigenen Gewohnheiten (*habits*) und dann mit den Gewohnheiten Ihrer Mitstudenten. Welche Gemeinsamkeiten und Unterschiede gibt es? Answers will vary.

Zum Besprechen Encourage students to use comparatives and superlatives they learned in Lektion 8A.2.

BEISPIEL

S1: *An deutschen Unis gibt es mehr Laptops als PCs. An dieser Uni ist das ähnlich.*

S2: *Stimmt. Aber es gibt noch mehr Tablets als Laptops.*

Fragen Beantworten Sie die Fragen in ganzen Sätzen.

1. Digitale Technologie kann uns in vielen Lebensbereichen (*aspects of life*) helfen. Welche nennt der Text? Man kann mit dem Smartphone die neusten Nachrichten checken, Filme sehen oder Spiele spielen.

2. In welchen Lebenssituationen ist das Smartphone oft störend? Viele Leute stört es, wenn sie im Zug oder Kino das Smartphone klingeln hören, oder wenn Smartphone-Nutzer Videos, Musik oder Spiele über Lautsprecher anhören.

3. Worüber ist die Smartphone-Debatte in Deutschland? Die Debatte ist darüber, ob Schüler und Studenten ihre Smartphones in ihren Kursen benutzen dürfen.

4. Welche Argumente gibt es für und gegen den „digitalen Unterricht"? Argumente dafür sind, dass Technologie den Unterricht kreativer macht und als Hilfsmittel dient. Argumente dagegen sind, dass man mit digitalen Geräten bei Tests schummeln kann und dass diese Geräte die Konzentration stören.

Hören

Strategien

Recognizing the genre of spoken discourse

You will encounter many different types of speech in German. For example, you may hear a political speech, a radio interview, a commercial, a voicemail message, or a news broadcast. Try to identify the context of the speech you hear, so that you can activate your background knowledge about that type of discourse and identify the speakers' motives and intentions.

◁)) To practice this strategy, you will listen to two short selections. Identify the genre of each one.

Vorbereitung

Über was sollte man nachdenken, bevor man ein neues Handy kauft? Machen Sie eine Liste. Welche Funktionen sind Ihnen bei einem neuen Handy wichtig?

Zuhören

 Hören Sie Rolf und Karin zu, wie sie den Kauf eines neuen Handys diskutieren. Welche Funktionen von Ihrer Liste diskutieren Rolf und Karin? Kreisen Sie die richtigen Antworten ein. Hören Sie sich dann das Gespräch nochmal an. Schreiben Sie jetzt die anderen Antworten in die Tabelle. Answers may vary slightly.

Name + Kosten	Anbieter	Beschreibung	andere Merkmale
1. Samsung Galaxy (235 Euro)	T-Mobile	silbern	unbegrenztes Datenvolumen
2. Apple iPhone (450 Euro)	Vodafone	einfach zu benutzen	bis zu 8 Stunden Gesprächszeit
3. Doro PhoneEasy (129 Euro)	O2	rot	extra große Tasten
4. LG P700 (259 Euro)	E-Plus	dünn	Surf-Flatrate

Verständnis

Suggestion Point out to students that cell phone brand names are neuter: **das iPhone, das Samsung,** etc.

Welches Handy? Empfehlen Sie das passende Handy. Sample answers provided.

1. Ich will lange telefonieren.
   Kauf dir das iPhone.

2. Ich brauche nur ein einfaches Telefon.
   Kauf dir das Doro.

3. Ich will ein dünnes Telefon.
   Kauf dir das LG.

4. Ich habe nicht viel Geld für ein Handy.
   Kauf dir das Doro.

5. Ich will ein Telefon, damit ich viel im Internet surfen kann.
   Kauf dir das LG.

6. Ich will ein Telefon, das nicht sehr kompliziert ist.
   Kauf dir das iPhone.

7. Ich will viele Videos sehen und viel Musik hören.
   Kauf dir das Samsung.

Das beste Telefon Sie haben gehört, wie Rolf und Karin den Kauf eines neuen Handys diskutieren. Sprechen Sie mit einem Partner / einer Partnerin über die Vorteile der Handys. Entscheiden Sie, welches Handy das beste für Sie und Ihren Partner / Ihre Partnerin ist.

Suggestion Have students present their partner's preferences using **denn: Das LG ist am besten für meinen Partner, denn er surft viel im Internet mit seinem Handy.**

Expansion Use this listening activity as a lead-in to a discussion of the pros and cons of cell phones. Ask students how often they use their cell phones. Could they imagine giving up their phones? Do they ever see people use cell phones in a rude manner?

Schreiben

Thema

Schreiben Sie einen Bericht

Schreiben Sie einen Bericht (*review*) über ein Auto. Nennen Sie zuerst den Namen des Autos und sprechen Sie dann die folgenden Kategorien an. Bilden Sie sich zum Schluss eine eigene Meinung. Ist das ein gutes Auto?

- **Beschreibung**
  Wie groß ist das Auto? Wie viel wiegt (*weighs*) das Auto? Was für einen Motor hat es? Wie viele Liter verbraucht es je 100 Kilometer? Wie viele Gänge (*gears*) hat es? Was ist die Höchstgeschwindigkeit (*top speed*)? Wie viel Platz (*room*) haben die Passagiere? Wie groß ist der Kofferraum?

- **Ausstattung**
  Welche Farbe hat das Auto? Wie sieht es im Innenraum aus? Hat es hinten ein Kamerasystem zum Ein- und Ausparken? Kann es automatisch parken? Wie viele Türen hat das Auto? Hat es ein Sonnenfenster? Ist es ein Kombi (*station wagon*)?

- **Fahrzeugtyp**
  Ist es ein Familienauto? Ist es ein Sportauto? Ist es ein Geländewagen (*SUV*)?

- **Andere Funktionen**
  Welche Art von Elektronik hat das Auto? Wie bequem ist das Auto? Hat das Auto ein gutes Image? Wie viel kostet das Auto? Ist das Auto umweltfreundlich (*environmentally friendly*)? Wie ist der Wiederverkaufswert (*resale value*) des Autos?

Vocabulary Tools

Lektion 8A

Auto fahren
driving a car

die Autobahn, -en *highway*
der Fahrer, - / die Fahrerin, -nen *driver*
der Polizist, -en / die Polizistin, -nen
  police officer
die Straße, -n *street*
die Tankstelle, -n *gas station*
der Verkehr *traffic*

geradeaus fahren *to go straight ahead*
einen Platten haben *to have a flat tire*
einen Unfall haben *to have
  an accident*
parken *to park*

rechts/links abbiegen (biegt... ab)
  to turn right/left

Auto
car

das Benzin *gas*
die Bremse, -n *brakes*
der Kofferraum, ⁼e *trunk*
das Lenkrad, ⁼er *steering wheel*
der Mechaniker, - / die Mechanikerin,
  -nen *mechanic*
der Motor, -en *engine*
die Motorhaube, -n *hood*
das Nummernschild, -er *license plate*
das Öl, -e *oil*
der Scheibenwischer, -
  windshield wiper
der Scheinwerfer, - *headlight*
der Sicherheitsgurt, -e *seatbelt*
die Windschutzscheibe, -n *windshield*

reparieren *to repair*
tanken *to fill up*

die öffentlichen Verkehrsmittel
public transportation

der Bahnsteig, -e *track; platform*
die Bushaltestelle, -n *bus stop*
der Fahrkartenschalter, - *ticket office*
der Fahrplan, ⁼e *schedule*
das Bußgeld, -er *fine*
die erste/zweite Klasse, -n *first/
  second class*
der Schaffner, - *ticket collector*

(die Fahrkarte) entwerten *to validate
  (a ticket)*

das Verkehrsmittel
modes of transport

das Auto, -s *car*
das Boot, -e *boat*
der Bus, -se *bus*
das Fahrrad, ⁼er *bicycle*
der LKW, -s *truck*
das Schiff, -e *ship*
das Taxi, -s *taxi*
die U-Bahn, -en *subway*
der Zug, ⁼e *train*

*Das Plusquamperfekt
  See pp. 330–331.*
Comparatives and superlatives
  See pp. 334–335.

Lektion 8B

die Technik
technology

die App, -s *app*
der Benutzername, -n *username*
der Bildschirm, -e *screen*
das Blog,- s *blog*
der Chat, -s *chat*
die Datei, -en *file*
die Digitalkamera, -s *digital camera*
das Dokument, -e *document*
der Drucker, - *printer*
die E-Mail, -s *e-mail*
die Fernbedienung, -en *remote control*
der Fernseher, - *television*
die Festplatte, -n *hard drive*
das Handy, -s *cell phone*
der Kopfhörer, - *headphones*
das Ladegerät, -e *charger*
der Laptop, -s *laptop (computer)*
die Maus, ⁼e *mouse*
das Mikrofon, -e *microphone*
das Passwort, ⁼er *password*
das Programm, -e *program*
der Sender, - *TV channel*
das Smartphone, -s *smartphone*
die SMS, - *text message*
die Spielkonsole, -n *game console*
die Stereoanlage, -n *stereo system*
das Tablet, -s *tablet*
die Tastatur, -en *keyboard*
das Telefon, -e *telephone*
die Website, -s *Website*

Technik bedienen
operating technology

anmachen (macht... an) *to turn on*
aufladen (lädt... auf) *to charge
  (a battery)*
aufnehmen (nimmt... auf) *to record*
ausmachen (macht... aus) *to turn off*
drucken *to print*
fernsehen (sieht... fern) *to watch
  television*
funktionieren *to work, to function*
herunterladen (lädt... herunter)
  to download
hochladen (lädt... hoch) *upload*
klingeln *to ring*
löschen *to delete*
online sein *to be online*
schicken *to send*
speichern *to save*
starten *to start*
im Internet surfen *to surf the Web*

The genitive case *See pp. 348–349.*
Demonstratives *See pp. 352–353.*

More activities
vhlcentral | Online activities

KÖRPERAKUPUNKT...

COMMUNICATIVE GOALS
By the end of this chapter you will be able to:

🔊 **Los geht's!** Wo ist Meline? Warum ist sie da? Wer ist der Mann neben ihr? Was macht er?

LEKTION 9A

Discuss morning routines and personal hygiene.

To do so, you will use:

Kontext Seite 366–369
• Body parts. Personal hygiene

Strukturen Seite 374–387
9A.1 Reflexive verbs with accusative reflexive pronouns
9A.2 Reflexive verbs with dative reflexive pronouns
9A.3 Reciprocal verbs and reflexives used with prepositions

You will also learn about cultural products, practices, and perspectives related to:

Kultur Seite 372–373
• Die Kur
• Öffentliche Schwimmbäder
• Die Marke Nivea

Zapping Seite 387
• *Gesundheit bewegt uns*

LEKTION 9B

Talk about health.
Talk about remedies and well-being.

To do so, you will use:

Kontext Seite 388–391
• Words and phrases related to health
• Words and phrases related to symptoms and injuries
• Words related to the hospital

Strukturen Seite 396–405
9B.1 Der Konjunktiv II
9B.2 Würden with the infinitve

You will also learn about cultural products, practices, and perspectives related to:

Kultur Seite 394–395
• Die Apotheken
• Der Föhn
• Wilhelm Conrad Röntgen

WEITER GEHT'S

Seite 406–412
You will learn about Mecklenburg-Vorpommern und Brandenburg, their culture, industries, history, and famous inhabitants.

Panorama Seite 406–407
• **Mecklenburg-Vorpommern und Brandenburg**

And you will demonstrate that you can:
Lesen: Read for the main idea
Hören: Use background information
Schreiben: Create complex sentences using linking words

Die Alltagsroutine Vocabulary Tools

Wortschatz

im Badezimmer	*in the bathroom*
der Haartrockner, -	*hair dryer*
das Shampoo, -s	*shampoo*
der Körper, -	*body*
die Augenbraue, -n	*eyebrow*
der Bart, ⸚e	*beard*
das Gesicht, -er	*face*
das Haar, -e	*hair*
die Hand, ⸚e	*hand*
die Lippe, -n	*lip*
der Rücken, -	*back*
die Schulter, -n	*shoulder*
Verben	*verbs*
aufwachen (wacht...auf)	*to wake up*
(sich) duschen	*to take a shower*
ins Bett gehen	*to go to bed*
sich anziehen (zieht sich...an)	*to get dressed*
sich die Haare bürsten	*to brush one's hair*
sich die Zähne putzen	*to brush one's teeth*

ACHTUNG

The pronoun **sich** is used with reflexive verbs. You will learn more about reflexive verbs in the **Strukturen** for this lesson.

Suggestion Remind students that they learned to use the verb **anziehen** without a reflexive pronoun in 5B. Ex.: **Ich ziehe das Hemd an. Er zieht die Jacke an.**

Er rasiert sich. (sich rasieren) *He is shaving.*

Sie schminkt sich. (sich schminken) *She is putting on make-up.*

das Handtuch, ⸚er

der Lippenstift, -e *lipstick*

die Bürste, -n *brush*

der Rasierer, - *razor*

der Kamm, ⸚e *comb*

die Seife, -n

die Zahnbürste, -n

die Zahnpasta

der Hausschuh, -e

der Rasierschaum, ⸚e *shaving cream*

der Bademantel, ⸚

der Kopf, ⸚e
head

die Nase, -n

das Auge, -n

der Mund, ⸚er
mouth

das Ohr, -en

der Hals, ⸚e
neck

der Arm, -e

der Finger, -

der Ell(en)bogen, -
elbow

der Bauch, ⸚e

der Schlafanzug, ⸚e

das Bein, -e

der Fuß, ⸚e

das Knie, -
knee

der Zeh, -en
toe

Anwendung

1 Was passt nicht? Welches Wort passt nicht zu den anderen?

BEISPIEL Bart, Mund, Lippe, (Rücken)

1 Expansion Ask students to explain why each word doesn't belong.

1. Ohr, (Bauch), Auge, Nase
2. Zahnbürste, Mundwasser, (Mineralwasser), Zahnpasta
3. duschen, schminken, rasieren, (anziehen)
4. Shampoo, Seife, (Haar), Duschgel
5. (Gesicht), Lippenstift, Mascara, Make-up
6. Haartrockner, (Rasierer), Bürste, Kamm

2 Hören Sie zu Macht man das im Badezimmer?

2 Expansion Ask students additional personal questions: **Wie lange duschen Sie? Wie viel Zeit brauchen Sie am Morgen für ihre Morgenroutine? Wie oft waschen Sie sich die Haare?**

	Ja	Nein		Ja	Nein
1.	☑	☐	4.	☑	☐
2.	☐	☑	5.	☑	☐
3.	☐	☑	6.	☐	☑

3 Bild beschriften Wie heißen die verschiedenen Körperteile (*parts of the body*)?

1. ____der Kopf____
2. ____der Mund____
3. ____die Schulter____
4. ____die Hand____
5. ____der Rücken____
6. ____das Bein____
7. ____das Knie____
8. ____der Fuß____

Suggestion Tell students that the variants **Ellbogen** and **Ellenbogen** are used interchangeably to refer to the elbow.

4 Paulas Morgenroutine Hören Sie sich an, was Paula über ihre Morgenroutine erzählt. Bringen Sie danach ihre morgendlichen Aktivitäten in die richtige Reihenfolge.

1. __2__ Ich dusche mich.
2. __5__ Ich ziehe mich an.
3. __4__ Ich schminke mich.
4. __1__ Ich frühstücke.
5. __3__ Ich putze mir die Zähne.

4 Expansion Have students put the items in order according to their own morning routines.

Suggestion Call out the names of various body parts and have students point to each body part. Then move to "active recall" by pointing to a body part and asking: **Was ist das?**

Kommunikation

5 Was haben wir? Fragen Sie Ihren Partner / Ihre Partnerin, welche Badezimmer- und Kosmetikartikel er/sie besitzt und wie viele davon er/sie hat. Answers will vary.

▶ **BEISPIEL**

S1: Hast du einen Spiegel?
S2: Ja, ich habe einen. Wie viele Spiegel hast du?

5 Suggestion Quickly review the plural form of each noun by asking: **Was ist das? Und wenn ich zwei davon habe, wie heißt das denn?**

5 Partner Chat You can also assign activity 5 on the Supersite. Students work in pairs to record the activity online. The pair's recorded conversation will appear in your gradebook.

1.

2.

3.

4.

5.

6.

7.

8.

6 Diskutieren und kombinieren Sie und Ihr Partner / Ihre Partnerin bekommen zwei verschiedene Bilder Außerirdischer (*extraterrestrials*) von Ihrem Lehrer / Ihrer Lehrerin. Finden Sie die sieben Unterschiede auf den Bildern.

BEISPIEL

S1: Wie viele Augen hat dein Außerirdischer?
S2: Mein Außerirdischer hat drei Augen.
S1: Aha! Mein Außerirdischer hat nur ein Auge.

7 So ein Saustall! Sie und Ihr Partner / Ihre Partnerin wollen mal wieder das Badezimmer sauber machen. Aber leider sind diverse Kosmetikartikel in der ganzen Wohnung verstreut (*scattered*). Fragen Sie Ihren Partner / Ihre Partnerin, wo Ihre Sachen sind. Answers will vary.

7 Suggestion Remind students to use the dative with two-way prepositions when describing location.

BEISPIEL

S1: Wo ist mein Rasierer?
S2: Den habe ich in der Küche neben der Spüle gesehen. Aber wo ist mein...

6 Expansion Model the pronunciation of **Außerirdischer**. Have students come up with a fictional profile for their aliens. Have them ask one another: **Wie heißt dein Außerirdischer? Woher kommt er? Was sind seine Hobbys?** etc.

8 Berühmte Leute Wählen Sie eine berühmte Person und schreiben Sie sechs Dinge über das Aussehen dieser Person. Lesen Sie Ihre Aussagen zwei Mitstudenten vor, die erraten müssen, von welcher Person Sie sprechen. Answers will vary.

BEISPIEL

S1: Er ist Spanier, 1,85 Meter groß, hat dunkle Augen und dunkelbraune Haare. Er ist Linkshänder und hat die schnellsten Beine auf dem Tennisplatz.
S2: Ist es Rafael Nadal?
S1: Ja, genau!

8 Suggestion Circulate around the class to make sure students stay on task and to offer vocabulary support.

Aussprache und Rechtschreibung Audio

Vocalic *r*

After a vowel, the German **r** often sounds more like a vowel than a consonant. When the syllable **er** occurs at the end of a word, it is pronounced with the *vocalic* **r** sound, similar to the letter *a* in the English word *sofa*.

Schulter	**Pfleger**	**Schwester**	**guter**	**Badezimmer**

The vocalic **r** also appears in unstressed prefixes, such as **er-**, **ver-** or **zer-**. In these prefixes, the sound of the **e** and the vocalic **r** are pronounced as separate sounds, blended together in a single syllable.

Verletzung	**Erkältung**	**zerbrechen**	**verstauchen**	**erklären**

The vocalic **r** also appears at the end of words after a long vowel sound. After a long **a** sound, the vowel and the vocalic **r** blend together. Otherwise, the long vowel and the vocalic **r** are pronounced as two separate sounds in a single syllable.

Ohr	**vier**	**sehr**	**Haar**	**Bart**

1 **Aussprechen** Wiederholen Sie die Wörter, die Sie hören.

1. Mutter	4. schwanger	7. zerstechen	10. schwer
2. Vater	5. verstopft	8. verstehen	11. hier
3. Rasierer	6. erkälten	9. Paar	12. Fahrt

2 **Nachsprechen** Wiederholen Sie die Sätze, die Sie hören.

1. Mir tut das rechte Ohr weh.
2. Die Krankenschwester und der Krankenpfleger suchen den Rasierer.
3. Mein kleiner Bruder hatte eine verstopfte Nase und Fieber.
4. Ohne Haar und ohne Bart friert man im Winter sehr.
5. Wie konnte Oliver mit dem verstauchten Fuß den 400-Meter-Lauf gewinnen?
6. Der erkältete Busfahrer hat eine lange Fahrt vor sich.

3 **Sprichwörter** Wiederholen Sie die Sprichwörter, die Sie hören.

Es ist alles in Butter.[1]

Verbotene Früchte schmecken am besten.[2]

[1] Everything is just great. (lit. Everything is in butter.)
[2] Forbidden fruit tastes the sweetest.

More activities

vhlcentral   LM p. 76   Online activities

Guten Morgen, Herr Professor! Video

Meline schläft beim Lernen ein und hat einen interessanten Traum.
Er spielt in der Zukunft und wir begegnen einem guten Bekannten.

Vorbereitung Before showing students this episode, draw their attention to the reflexive verbs and other expressions used to talk about daily routines. Explain that reflexive pronouns always correspond to their subject pronouns. Ex.: **ich - mich/mir, du - dich/dir**, etc.

1

MELINE Schatz... es ist Zeit, dass du aufwachst und dich anziehst. Hase, ich habe um halb zehn eine Besprechung. Du musst dich für deinen ersten Unterrichtstag noch duschen und rasieren. Du darfst nicht zu spät kommen.

2

MELINE Da ist ja mein schöner Ehemann. Guten Morgen, Herr Professor.
HANS Wie haben wir uns nur so ineinander verliebt?
MELINE Tja, wahrscheinlich einfach Glück gehabt.

3

SABITE Meline? Meline, ist alles in Ordnung?
MELINE Hans?
SABITE Meline? Meline, beweg dich nicht. George? George!

4

MELINE Ich erinnere mich, du warst noch ein Junge. Dein Vater und ich – ist er schon aufgewacht? – dein Vater und ich haben uns diesen Tag immer vorgestellt. Wir haben nur nicht gedacht, dass er so schnell kommt. Heute machst du deinen Universitätsabschluss.

5

HANS Guten Morgen, mein Sohn.
WOLFGANG Paps.
HANS Mein Liebling.
WOLFGANG Mama, Paps, mir dreht sich der Magen um. Hört bitte auf, euch zu küssen.

MELINE Eines Tages, Wolfgang, wirst du erstaunt sein, wie es sich anfühlt, sich in jemanden zu verlieben. Ach Hans, putz dir die Zähne!
HANS Für dich tu ich doch alles, mein Liebling. Dann dusche ich mich, rasiere mich und wasche mir die Haare.

6

1 **Was fehlt?** Ergänzen Sie die Sätze mit den richtigen Informationen.

1. (Meline / Hans) hat um halb zehn eine Besprechung.
2. Hans muss sich noch duschen und (schminken / rasieren).
3. Er darf nicht zu (früh / spät) kommen.
4. Meline begrüßt ihren schönen (Schwiegervater / Ehemann).
5. In Melines Traum ist Hans (Professor / Ingenieur).
6. Wolfgang macht heute seinen (Universitätsabschluss / Urlaub).

7. Nach dem Frühstück geht Hans sich duschen, rasieren und die (Haare / Füße) waschen.
8. Als Meline aufwacht, liegt sie auf dem (Sofa / Boden).
9. Im Traum hat Meline gesagt, dass sie Hans (liebt / heiratet).
10. Sabite und George wollen Meline zum (Friseur / Arzt) bringen.

PERSONEN   **George**   **Hans**   **Meline**   **Sabite**   **Wolfgang**

7

HANS Heute ist ein besonderer Tag. Genießen wir ihn.

8

MELINE Besonderer Tag. Hans, ich liebe dich. Hans?
GEORGE Meline! Wach auf, Meline.
MELINE Hans?
GEORGE Ich bin's, George.

9

MELINE Oh, mein Kopf. Was ist passiert? Warum bin ich am Boden?
GEORGE Okay, Meline. Jetzt ganz langsam. Versuche, aufzustehen.

10

SABITE Sollen wir Hans holen?
MELINE Was? Nein. Warum wollt ihr ihn holen?
GEORGE Ähm, du hast gesagt, du liebst ihn.
MELINE Das ist nicht lustig. Jetzt wird mir erst recht schlecht.
SABITE Komm, wir bringen dich zum Arzt.

Nützliche Ausdrücke

- **Besprechung**
  meeting
- **Du darfst nicht zu spät kommen.**
  You don't want to be late.
- **Meline, beweg dich nicht.**
  Meline, don't move.
- **sich erinnern**
  to remember
- **sich vorstellen**
  to imagine
- **Mama, Paps, mir dreht sich der Magen um.**
  Mom, Dad, my stomach is churning.
- **Hört bitte auf, euch zu küssen.**
  Please stop kissing each other.
- **Eines Tages, Wolfgang, wirst du erstaunt sein, wie es sich anfühlt, sich in jemanden zu verlieben.**
  One day, Wolfgang, you will be amazed at what it feels like to fall in love with someone.
- **Heute ist ein besonderer Tag.**
  Today is a special day.
- **der Arzt**
  doctor

9A.1
- **Du musst dich für deinen ersten Unterrichtstag noch duschen und rasieren.**
  You need to shower and shave for your first day of classes.

9A.2
- **Ach Hans, putz dir die Zähne!**
  Oh, Hans, brush your teeth!

9A.3
- **Wie haben wir uns nur so ineinander verliebt?**
  How did we get to be so in love with each other?

---

2 **Zum Besprechen** Wählen Sie zu zweit eine Person aus dem Fotoroman und beschreiben Sie seinen/ihren Morgen im Badezimmer. Benutzen Sie Informationen dieser Episode und Ihre Fantasie. Answers will vary.

 2 Suggestion Before students begin this activity, ask them to brainstorm words and expressions used to talk about daily routines. Write these suggestions on the board for reference.

3 **Vertiefung** Im Deutschen gibt es viele Sprichwörter, die sich auf den Körper beziehen (*refer to*), zum Beispiel „Das geht mir nicht aus dem Kopf" (*It's always on my mind*). Finden Sie drei Sprichwörter mit Wörtern aus dieser Lektion. Machen Sie danach eine Liste von englischen Sprichwörtern, die sich auf den Körper beziehen, und vergleichen Sie sie mit den deutschen Sprichwörtern. Answers will vary.

3 Suggestion Encourage students to share their selected proverbs. As a class, discuss the meaning of each proverb.

More activities

 vhlcentral   VM p. 17   Online activities

Die Kur°

 Reading

Suggestion Read the first sentence out loud as a class and have students guess what a **Kurort** might be. Explain that in Germany, health spas are very common, and prescribing a long **Kur** is a fairly standard medical practice.

Suggestion Tell students that the designation **Bad** typically indicates that a location has natural hotsprings and was the site of ancient Roman baths.

IN DEUTSCHLAND GIBT ES UNGEFÄHR 300 Kurorte. An diesen Orten können Patienten sich erholen°. Nach einem schweren Unfall, bei psychischer Erschöpfung° oder wegen schwerer gesundheitlicher Probleme brauchen Patienten oft längere Pflege°: Kuraufenthalte° dauern normalerweise zwischen drei und sechs Wochen. Deutsche Krankenkassen° bezahlen einen großen Teil dieser Kurbesuche.

Kurorte in Deutschland bieten saubere Luft° und viel Ruhe°, damit Patienten sich auf ihre Gesundheit konzentrieren können. Patienten sollen in einer Kur physisch fit werden, indem sie wandern, schwimmen oder Rad fahren. Patienten sollen auch lernen, ihr Leben gesünder zu gestalten: Was kann man anders machen, damit man nicht wieder krank wird?

Einige der berühmtesten Kurorte in Deutschland sind Oberstdorf (Bayern), Bad Wörishofen (Bayern), Baden-Baden (Baden-Württemberg) und Westerland (Schleswig-Holstein). Oberstdorf liegt im Allgäu und ist die südlichste Gemeinde Deutschlands. Die Luft ist so klar, dass Patienten mit Allergien hier wenige Probleme haben. Hier hat man auch fantastische Wintersportmöglichkeiten. Das bayerische Bad Wörishofen im Allgäu ist berühmt wegen Sebastian Kneipp (1821–1897), einem katholischen Priester, der hier die Kneipp-Kur erfand. Teil der Kur ist Wassertreten° in einem kalten Wasserbad.

Baden-Baden liegt im Schwarzwald in der Nähe von Karlsruhe. Es ist bekannt für seine Thermalquellen°. Die Römer° haben die Stadt bereits im Jahr 80 nach Christus gegründet. Westerland liegt auf der Insel Sylt. Es ist ein sehr bekanntes Seeheilbad. Für Patienten ist die Nähe zur Nordsee und die Faszination des Wattenmeers° interessant.

Anzahl an Kurorten pro Bundesland	
Baden-Württemberg – 59	Nordrhein-Westfalen – 33
Bayern – 55	Rheinland-Pfalz – 18
Brandenburg – 8	Saarland – 4
Hessen – 31	Sachsen – 60
Mecklenburg-Vorpommern – 31	Sachsen-Anhalt – 4
	Schleswig-Holstein – 44
Niedersachsen – 45	Thüringen – 19

QUELLE: Portal Bäderland Deutschland

Kur health spa treatment **sich erholen** recover **Erschöpfung** exhaustion **Pflege** care **Kuraufenthalte** spa visits **Krankenkassen** health insurance **Luft** air **Ruhe** quiet **Wassertreten** treading water **Thermalquellen** hot springs **Römer** Romans **Wattenmeers** Wadden Sea (tidal flats)

ÜBUNGEN

1 **Im Fokus** Richtig oder falsch? Korrigieren Sie die falschen Aussagen. Diskutieren Sie dann die letzte Frage mit einem Partner/ einer Partnerin.

1. Patienten in Deutschland müssen ihren Kurbesuch selbst bezahlen.
   Falsch. Die Krankenkassen zahlen einen großen Teil des Kurbesuchs.
2. Die meisten Kurorte liegen in Bayern.
   Falsch. Baden-Württemberg hat die meisten Kurorte.
3. Ein Priester erfand das Wassertreten im 19. Jahrhundert. Richtig

Diskussion Wo kann man in Ihrer Region, zum Beispiel in Thermalquellen oder in einem Erholungsort (spa resort), eine Kur machen?

2 **Die deutschsprachige Welt** Richtig oder falsch? Korrigieren Sie die falschen Aussagen.

1. In Deutschland gibt es öffentliche Schwimmbäder erst seit kurzer Zeit.
   Falsch. Öffentliche Schwimmbäder gibt es seit 1860.
2. Die Deutschen gehen im Sommer gern ans Meer oder fahren Rad, aber sie gehen nicht so gern ins Freibad. Falsch. Fast jede deutsche Stadt hat ein Freibad, das normalerweise voll ist.
3. In einem Erlebnisbad kann man eine Sauna besuchen. Richtig.

Diskussion Wo gehen Sie gern schwimmen – auf dem Campus, im Fitness-Center oder in einem Fluss oder See? Warum?

Ausdrücke mit Körperteilen

Hand und Fuß haben	*to make sense*
jemandem ins Auge springen	*to catch somebody's eye*
sich die Augen aus dem Kopf weinen	*to cry one's eyes out*
Hals- und Beinbruch!	*Break a leg!*
Hand aufs Herz!	*Cross my heart!*

Öffentliche Schwimmbäder

Das erste öffentliche Schwimmbad° in Deutschland wurde 1860 in Marburg eröffnet. Heute gibt es viele verschiedene Arten von Schwimmbädern. Fast jede deutsche Stadt besitzt ein Freibad, das an warmen Sommertagen normalerweise voll ist. Dann gibt es auch noch Hallenbäder°, wo man das ganze Jahr über baden kann. Schwimmbäder mit moderneren Anlagen° wie Wellenbad°, Rutschen° und Saunen heißen entweder Spaßbad oder Erlebnisbad. Entlang der Meeresküsten gibt es Strandbäder, wo man in Meerwasser schwimmt, aber auch Flüsse und Seen, besonders Baggerseen°, sind sehr beliebt.

Schwimmbad *swimming pool* **Hallenbäder** *indoor swimming pools* **Anlagen** *facilities* **Wellenbad** *wave pool* **Rutschen** *slides* **Baggerseen** *quarry ponds*

Nivea

Suggestion Ask students if they use any Nivea products. Tell them that Germany's cosmetics industry is the third largest in the world, after the U.S. and Japan.

Die Marke Nivea gibt es schon seit 1911. Sie ist Teil der deutschen Firma Beiersdorf. Ihr bekanntestes Produkt ist die Nivea-Hautcreme°. Seit 1925 verkauft Nivea diese Hautcreme in der bekannten, blauen Dose°. Neben der traditionellen weißen Hautcreme gibt es heute auch viele andere Produkte, zum Beispiel Cremes für Babys, Rasiercremes, Aftershaves und verschiedene Sonnenschutzmittel°. Wichtig ist auch, dass bei der Entwicklung und Produktion von Nivea-Produkten keine Tierversuche° gemacht werden. Heute kann man Nivea auf allen Kontinenten und in fast allen Ländern kaufen.

Hautcreme *skin cream* **Dose** *jar* **Sonnenschutzmittel** *sunscreen* **Tierversuche** *animal testing*

◌ IM INTERNET

Suchen Sie im Internet den Katalog eines öffentlichen Schwimmbads. Was kann man hier alles machen? Wie viel kostet der Eintritt?

Find out more at **vhlcentral.com**.

---

3 **Porträt** Richtig oder falsch? Korrigieren Sie die falschen Aussagen. Diskutieren Sie dann die letzte Frage mit einem Partner/ einer Partnerin.

1. Nivea ist eine Firma. **Falsch.** Nivea ist eine Marke und gehört zur Firma Beiersdorf.

2. Tierversuche gibt es bei der Entwicklung von Nivea nicht. **Richtig.**

3. Nivea Hautcreme kann man nur in Deutschland und der Schweiz kaufen. **Falsch.** Man kann Nivea in fast allen Ländern der Welt kaufen.

Diskussion Sind Sie gegen Tierversuche, oder gibt es Situationen, in denen Tierversuche wichtig und sogar notwendig (*necessary*) sind?

4 **Ein Kurbesuch** Schreiben Sie eine kurze Broschüre für einen idealen deutschen Kurort und erklären Sie, was man dort für die Gesundheit machen kann. Informieren Sie potentielle Patienten auch über die Kosten der Kur. Stellen Sie Ihre Broschüre dann im Kurs vor.

More activities

vhlcentral | Online activities

9A.1

Reflexive verbs with accusative reflexive pronouns

Grammar Tutorial

Teaching Tip You may want to assign the grammar tutorial **9A.1 Reflexive verbs with accusative reflexive pronouns** on the Supersite for students to watch before they come to class.

Startblock A reflexive verb indicates an action you do to yourself or for yourself. The subject of a reflexive verb is also its object.

Du musst **dich** zum ersten Unterrichtstag **duschen** und **rasieren**.

Ich **erinnere mich**, du warst noch ein Junge.

ACHTUNG

The accusative reflexive pronouns are the same as the accusative personal pronouns, except that all of the third person pronouns and **Sie** are replaced by **sich**. Note that **sich** is never capitalized, even when it refers to **Sie**.

Suggestion Ask students: "If my subject is **ich**, what reflexive pronoun will I use?" etc.

- Reflexive verbs always use reflexive pronouns. When the subject of a reflexive verb is also its direct object, it takes an accusative reflexive pronoun.

personal pronouns						
nominative	ich	du	er/sie/es	wir	ihr	Sie/sie
accusative reflexive	mich	dich	sich	uns	euch	sich

- When a reflexive verb is conjugated, the verb and the reflexive pronoun must both agree with the subject. In the infinitive, reflexive verbs are always listed with the third person reflexive pronoun.

sich rasieren	
ich rasiere mich	wir rasieren uns
du rasierst dich	ihr rasiert euch
er/sie/es rasiert sich	Sie/sie rasieren sich

ACHTUNG

Verbs that are reflexive in German do not always have reflexive equivalents in English: **Ich frage mich, wo meine Schlüssel sind.** *I wonder where my keys are.*

Suggestion Note that students will learn to use **sich (etwas) vorstellen** to mean *to imagine (something)* in **9A.2**.

- Some verbs can be used both non-reflexively and reflexively. Note that certain verbs have a change in meaning when they are used reflexively.

non-reflexive verbs		reflexive verbs	
anziehen	*to put on*	sich anziehen	*to get dressed*
legen	*to put; to lay*	sich (hin)legen	*to lie down*
setzen	*to put; to set*	sich (hin)setzen	*to sit down*
fragen	*to ask*	sich fragen	*to wonder, ask oneself*
vorstellen	*to introduce*	sich vorstellen	*to introduce oneself*
umziehen	*to move*	sich umziehen	*to change clothes*
waschen	*to wash (something)*	sich waschen	*to wash (oneself)*

Ich **ziehe** den Mantel **an**.
I'm putting on my coat.

Ich **ziehe mich an**.
I'm getting dressed.

- A number of verbs related to daily routines, personal hygiene, and health take an accusative reflexive pronoun.

common reflexive verbs			
sich abtrocknen	*to dry oneself off*	sich entspannen	*to relax*
sich ausruhen	*to rest*	sich erkälten	*to catch a cold*
sich ausziehen	*to get undressed*	sich (wohl) fühlen	*to feel (well)*
(sich) baden	*to bathe, take a bath*	sich rasieren	*to shave*
sich beeilen	*to hurry*	sich schminken	*to put on makeup*
(sich) duschen	*to take a shower*	sich verspäten	*to be late*

Ich **fühle mich** nicht **wohl**.
I don't feel well.

Wir **haben uns** am Wochenende **entspannt**.
We relaxed this weekend.

- When the subject is the first word in a sentence, put the reflexive pronoun after the conjugated verb. When the verb and subject are inverted, put the reflexive pronoun after the subject.

Klara schminkt **sich** jeden Morgen.
Klara puts on makeup every morning.

Heute Morgen schminkt sie **sich** nicht.
She's not putting on makeup this morning.

Ziehst du **dich** an?
Are you getting dressed?

Setzen Sie **sich**, bitte!
Please be seated.

- In informal imperatives, since the pronoun **du** or **ihr** is dropped, the reflexive pronoun comes immediately after the verb.

Zieh **dich** bitte an!
Get dressed, please.

Setzt **euch**, bitte!
Please sit down.

- When the conjugated verb is a modal, the reflexive pronoun comes immediately after the modal, or immediately after the subject, if the word order is inverted.

Wir müssen **uns** beeilen.
We need to hurry up.

Möchtet ihr **euch** hier setzen?
Would you like to sit here?

- Use the auxiliary verb **haben** with reflexive verbs in the **Perfekt** and **Plusquamperfekt**.

Ich **habe mich** heute Morgen **rasiert**.
I shaved this morning.

Wir **hatten uns** schon **geduscht**.
We had already showered.

Suggestion Emphasize the point that *any* verb used reflexively takes **haben** in the perfect and the past perfect.

ACHTUNG

The verbs **baden** and **duschen** can also be used non-reflexively, with no difference in meaning: **Ich dusche jeden Morgen.**

Expansion Have students work in pairs to write a short text about getting ready for an evening out, using common reflexive verbs.

QUERVERWEIS

See **3B.3** to review the formation of imperatives.

See **3B.1** to review the use of modals.

See **5A.1** to review the **Perfekt** with **haben**.

See **8A.1** to review the **Plusquamperfekt**.

More activities

vhlcentral

WB
pp. 119–120

LM
p. 77

Online activities

Jetzt sind Sie dran! **Ergänzen Sie die Tabelle mit den fehlenden Formen.**

	sich fragen	sich beeilen	sich ausziehen
1. ich	ich frage mich	*ich beeile mich*	*ich ziehe mich aus*
2. du	du fragst dich	du beeilst dich	du ziehst dich aus
3. er/sie/es	er/sie/es fragt sich	er/sie/es beeilt sich	er/sie/es zieht sich aus
4. wir	wir fragen uns	wir beeilen uns	wir ziehen uns aus
5. ihr	ihr fragt euch	ihr beeilt euch	ihr zieht euch aus
6. sie	sie fragen sich	sie beeilen sich	sie ziehen sich aus
7. Sie	Sie fragen sich	Sie beeilen sich	Sie ziehen sich aus

Anwendung

1 **Reflexive Verben** Ergänzen Sie die Sätze mit den richtigen Reflexivformen der Verben in Klammern.

1. Birgit ist müde und ___legt sich___ (sich legen) aufs Sofa.
2. Wie ___fühlen___ Sie ___sich___ (sich fühlen) heute, Frau Neumann?
3. Bei dem schlechten Wetter ___erkälten sich___ (sich erkälten) manche Leute.
4. ___Beeil dich___ (sich beeilen)! Du musst vor 17 Uhr noch einkaufen.
5. Torsten ___duscht sich___ (sich duschen) schnell.
6. Ich ___schminke mich___ (sich schminken) nur, wenn ich ausgehe.
7. Jana! Erik! ___Setzt euch___ (sich setzen) hier zu uns an den Tisch!
8. Wir ___fragen uns___ (sich fragen), wie das passieren konnte.

2 **Sätze bilden** Bilden Sie Sätze und achten Sie dabei auf die Wortstellung. Answers may vary. Sample answers provided.

> **BEISPIEL**   Zuerst / Herr Bauer / sich duschen
> *Zuerst duscht sich Herr Bauer.*

1. Danach / er / sich rasieren / langsam
   Danach rasiert er sich langsam.

2. Seine Frau / sich schminken / vor dem Spiegel
   Seine Frau schminkt sich vor dem Spiegel.

3. Dann / sie / sich umziehen / schnell
   Dann zieht sie sich schnell um.

4. Die Kinder / sich anziehen / für die Schule
   Die Kinder ziehen sich für die Schule an.

5. Heute / alle in der Familie / sich verspäten
   Heute verspäten sich alle in der Familie.

6. Später / der Hund / sich legen / auf das Bett
   Später legt sich der Hund auf das Bett.

3 **Ein schlechter Tag** Gestern hat Claudia einen sehr schlechten Tag gehabt. Schreiben Sie ihre Geschichte ins Perfekt um.

> **BEISPIEL**   Claudia steht erst um halb zehn auf.
> Sie fühlt sich nicht wohl.
> *Claudia ist erst um halb*
> *zehn aufgestanden.*
> *Sie hat sich nicht wohl gefühlt.*

1. Sie duscht sich, und dann schminkt sie sich. Sie hat sich geduscht, und dann hat sie sich geschminkt.
2. Sie zieht sich schön an. Sie hat sich schön angezogen.
3. Sie beeilt sich, zur U-Bahn zu kommen. Sie hat sich beeilt, zur U-Bahn zu kommen.
4. Um 10.15 Uhr stellt sie sich bei der Firma *Werner Elektronik* vor.
   Um 10.15 Uhr hat sie sich bei der Firma *Werner Elektronik* vorgestellt.
5. Sie verspätet sich, und deshalb (*for that reason*) bekommt sie den Job nicht.
   Sie hat/hatte sich verspätet, und deshalb hat sie den Job nicht bekommen.
6. Sie geht traurig nach Hause, und dann legt sie sich aufs Sofa.
   Sie ist traurig nach Hause gegangen, und dann hat sie sich aufs Sofa gelegt.

Kommunikation

4 **Bilder beschreiben** Beschreiben Sie mit einem Partner / einer Partnerin, was die Personen auf den Bildern gerade machen. Benutzen Sie reflexive Verben. Sample answers are provided.

▶ **BEISPIEL**
Er zieht sich an.

1. Er duscht sich.
2. Das Kind wäscht sich.
3. Sie schminkt sich.
4. Er rasiert sich.
5. Sie legt sich hin.
6. Er beeilt sich.

4 **Suggestion** You may want to do this activity as a class. Ask: **Was macht der Mann? Was macht das Kind?** etc.

4 **Video Virtual Chat** You can also assign activity 4 on the Supersite. Students record individual responses that appear in your gradebook.

5 **Pantomimen** Sie spielen eine Tätigkeit (*activity*) aus der Liste vor und Ihre zwei Mitstudenten erraten, was Sie vorgespielt haben (*mimed*). Wechseln Sie sich ab. Answers will vary.

BEISPIEL
S1: (spielt „sich rasieren" vor)
S2: *Du hast dich rasiert!*

sich abtrocknen	sich umziehen
sich erkälten	sich vorstellen
sich hinsetzen	sich (nicht) wohl fühlen
sich rasieren	

5 **Suggestion** Act out a few reflexive verbs yourself, such as **sich kämmen** or **sich anziehen**. Ask: **Was habe ich gerade gemacht?**

6 **Machst du das?** Fragen Sie Ihre Mitschüler, ob (*whether*) sie diese Sachen machen. Finden Sie für jede Frage eine Person, die das macht. Präsentieren Sie Ihre Ergebnisse danach im Kurs. Answers will vary.

BEISPIEL
S1: *Verspätest du dich oft?*
S2: *Nein, ich verspäte mich nie!*
S3: *Ja, ich verspäte mich immer am Montagmorgen.*

Tätigkeiten	Name
sich oft verspäten	
sich vor einer Prüfung entspannen	
sich zweimal am Tag duschen	
sich nachmittags hinlegen	
sich am Abend duschen	
sich im Winter immer erkälten	

6 **Suggestion** Formulate the questions together before students begin circulating.

7 **Was soll ich machen?** Geben Sie Ihrem Partner / Ihrer Partnerin Ratschläge (*advice*) für seine/ihre Probleme. Wechseln Sie sich ab. Answers will vary.

BEISPIEL
S1: *Ich fühle mich so schmutzig!*
S2: *Du musst dich duschen.*

Die Probleme:

1. Ich bin sehr müde.
2. Ich kenne meinen Klassenkameraden nicht und möchte mit ihm sprechen.
3. Ich habe in fünf Minuten ein Seminar und muss mich noch anziehen.
4. Ich habe beim Essen mein neues T-Shirt schmutzig gemacht.

7 **Video Virtual Chat** You can also assign activity 7 on the Supersite. Students record individual responses that appear in your gradebook.

9A.2

Reflexive verbs with dative reflexive pronouns

 Grammar Tutorial

Startblock In **9A.1**, you learned that when the subject of a reflexive verb is also its direct object, it takes an accusative reflexive pronoun. When the subject of a reflexive verb is not its direct object, it takes a dative reflexive pronoun.

Dann dusche ich mich, rasiere ich mich und **wasche mir** die Haare.

Ach Hans, **putz dir** die Zähne!

- The dative reflexive pronouns are the same as the dative personal pronouns, except that all of the third person pronouns and the formal **Sie** are replaced by **sich**. Remember that the pronoun **sich** is never capitalized, even when it refers to the formal **Sie**.

personal pronouns						
nominative	ich	du	er/sie/es	wir	ihr	Sie/sie
accusative reflexive	mich	dich	sich	uns	euch	sich
dative reflexive	mir	dir	sich	uns	euch	sich

- Many verbs take an accusative reflexive pronoun when used on their own but a dative reflexive pronoun when used with a different direct object.

reflexive verbs used with direct objects	
sich (die Hände) abtrocknen	*to dry (one's hands)*
sich (eine Jacke) anziehen	*to put on (a jacket)*
sich (einen Mantel) ausziehen	*to take off (a coat)*
sich die Haare bürsten	*to brush one's hair*
sich die Haare färben	*to dye one's hair*
sich die Haare kämmen	*to comb one's hair*
sich die Zähne putzen	*to brush one's teeth*
sich (die Beine) rasieren	*to shave (one's legs)*
sich (die Augen) schminken	*to put on (eye) makeup*
sich (das Gesicht) waschen	*to wash (one's face)*
sich etwas vorstellen	*to imagine something (for oneself)*
sich etwas wünschen	*to wish for something (for oneself)*

Ich wasche **mich**.
I'm washing (myself).

Ich wasche **mir** das Gesicht.
I'm washing my face.

- Note that the meaning of the verb **sich vorstellen** changes when it is used with a direct object and a dative reflexive pronoun.

Hast du **dich** vorgestellt?
Did you introduce yourself?

Kannst du **dir** das vorstellen?
Can you imagine that?

- To refer to a part of the body or a particular piece of clothing after a reflexive verb in German, use a definite article where you would use a possessive adjective in English.

Ela putzt sich **die** Zähne.
*Ela is brushing **her** teeth.*

Habt ihr euch **die** Haare gebürstet?
*Did you brush **your** hair?*

Ich ziehe mir **den** Mantel aus.
*I'm taking off **my** coat.*

Zieh dir **die** Schuhe schnell an!
*Put **your** shoes on quickly!*

- Some verbs can be used reflexively to emphasize that the subject of the verb is also its indirect object.

Ich **bestelle (mir)** einen Kaffee.
*I'm ordering (**myself**) a coffee.*

Hast du **(dir)** eine Jacke **gekauft**?
*Did you **buy** (**yourself**) a jacket?*

- If the direct object is a *noun*, put the dative reflexive pronoun before it. If the direct object is a *pronoun*, put the dative reflexive pronoun after it.

Machst du **dir** eine Tasse Tee?
*Are you making (**yourself**) a cup of tea?*

Ja, ich habe sie **mir** schon gemacht.
*Yes, I've already made it (**for myself**).*

- In a sentence with more than one object, the dative object comes before the accusative object. However, when one object is a pronoun, the pronoun comes first. If there are two pronouns, the accusative pronoun comes before the dative.

Ich kaufe **meiner Schwester einen Hund**.
*I'm buying **my sister a dog**.*

Ich kaufe **ihn meiner Schwester**.
*I'm buying **it** for my sister.*

Ich kaufe **ihr** einen Hund.
*I'm buying **her** a dog.*

Ich kaufe **ihn ihr**.
*I'm buying **it for her**.*

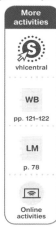

More activities

S
vhlcentral

WB
pp. 121–122

LM
p. 78

Online activities

Jetzt sind Sie dran!   **Ergänzen Sie die Sätze mit den richtigen Reflexivpronomen.**

1. Niklas kauft (sich)/ ihm) ein Sandwich.
2. Hast du (dich / (dir)) einen Salat gemacht?
3. Wir haben (euch / (uns)) ein kleines Auto gemietet.
4. Max und Lara haben (sich)/ ihnen) eine Pizza bestellt.
5. Nina wünscht (sich)/ ihm) eine Spielkonsole zum Geburtstag.
6. Ich backe (mich / (mir)) einen Schokoladenkuchen.

Anwendung

1 **Körperteile und Kleidung** Bilden Sie Sätze mit den reflexiven Verben in Klammern. Achten Sie (*Pay attention*) auf die Artikel!

> **BEISPIEL** ihre Beine (sich rasieren)
> Jasmin *rasiert sich die Beine*.

1. meine Nase (sich putzen)
Ich ___putze mir die Nase___.

2. deine Hände (sich abtrocknen)
Du ___trocknest dir die Hände ab___.

3. seine Uniform (sich anziehen)
Julius ___zieht sich die Uniform an___.

4. eure Füße (sich waschen)
Ihr ___wascht euch die Füße___.

5. deine Jacke (sich ausziehen)
Du ___ziehst dir die Jacke aus___.

6. meine Handschuhe (sich anziehen)
Ich ___ziehe mir die Handschuhe an___.

2 **Was machen sie?** Schreiben Sie die Sätze um.

> **BEISPIEL** Putzt du dir die Zähne? (ihr)
> *Putzt ihr euch die Zähne?*

1. Kauft David sich neue Hausschuhe? (du)
Kaufst du dir neue Hausschuhe?

2. Sie machen sich eine Tasse Tee. (ich)
Ich mache mir eine Tasse Tee.

3. Hat Anna sich die Haare gefärbt? (du)
Hast du dir die Haare gefärbt?

4. Ich bestelle mir etwas zu trinken. (Ben und Lisa)
Ben und Lisa bestellen sich etwas zu trinken.

5. Stell dir das vor! (Sie)
Stellen Sie sich das vor!

3 **Sätze mit Dativ** Schreiben Sie zu jedem Bild einen Satz. Benutzen sie ein reflexives Verb mit einem Reflexivpronomen im Dativ. Sample answers are provided.

 ▶ **BEISPIEL**
Lina
Lina schminkt sich die Lippen.

1. Fabian
Fabian rasiert sich das Gesicht.

2. du
Du wäschst dir die Haare.

3. wir
Wir waschen uns das Gesicht.

4. Nils
Nils bürstet sich die Haare.

5. ich
Ich putze mir die Zähne.

Kommunikation

4 **Was macht man damit?** Ihr kleiner Bruder möchte wissen, was man mit den Sachen unten macht. Schreiben Sie gemeinsam einen Dialog. Answers will vary.

BEISPIEL Haartrockner
S1: *Was ist das?*
S2: *Das ist ein Haartrockner.*
S1: *Und was machst du damit?*
S2: *Damit trockne ich mir die Haare.*

1. ein Lippenstift
2. ein Rasierer
3. ein Kamm
4. eine Zahnbürste
5. Shampoo
6. eine Kaffeemaschine

5 **Und nun?** Ihr Partner / Ihre Partnerin hat Probleme. Helfen Sie ihm/ihr mit guten Ratschlägen (*advice*). Benutzen Sie den Imperativ und wechseln Sie sich ab. Answers will vary.

BEISPIEL
S1: *Ich habe kalte Hände.*
S2: *Zieh dir doch Handschuhe an!*

> sich die Füße waschen
> sich die Haare kämmen
> sich einen Pullover anziehen
> sich etwas zu essen machen

1. Meine Füße sind sehr schmutzig.
2. Meine Haare hängen mir ins Gesicht.
3. Ich habe so einen Hunger!
4. Mir ist kalt.

6 **Wann machst du das?** Fragen Sie Ihren Partner / Ihre Partnerin, wann oder wie oft er/sie diese Dinge macht. Answers will vary.

BEISPIEL
S1: *Wann wäschst du dir die Haare?*
S2: *Ich wasche mir jeden zweiten Tag die Haare.*

> jeden Tag/Morgen/Abend | wenn ich Lust habe
> ein/zwei Mal am Tag | jeden zweiten Tag
> vor/nach dem Essen | wenn ich kalte Füße habe
> nie | bevor ich ins Bett gehe

1. sich die Haare waschen
2. sich die Zähne putzen
3. sich etwas zu essen machen
4. sich die Hände waschen
5. sich die Haare föhnen
6. sich Hausschuhe anziehen

7 **Gewonnen** Sie haben 500.000 Dollar gewonnen! Sagen Sie, was Sie sich zuerst kaufen, und dann fragen Sie Ihre Mitstudenten, was sie sich kaufen wollen. Answers will vary.

BEISPIEL
S1: *Ich kaufe mir ein großes Boot. Und was kaufst du dir, Tim?*
S2: *Ich kaufe mir ein Flugticket nach Sydney. Was kaufst du dir, Sophie?*
S3: *Ich gehe ins Restaurant und bestelle mir...*

4 **Video Virtual Chat** You can also assign activity 4 on the Supersite. Students record individual responses that appear in your gradebook.

5 **Video Virtual Chat** You can also assign activity 5 on the Supersite. Students record individual responses that appear in your gradebook.

6 **Partner Chat** You can also assign activity 6 on the Supersite. Students work in pairs to record the activity online. The pair's recorded conversation will appear in your gradebook.

7 **Suggestion** Circulate and provide vocabulary help, if needed. Set a time limit for this activity. As a follow-up, have students share answers, using the 3rd person. Ex.: **Sophie kauft sich einen Roboter.**

9A.3   Reciprocal verbs and reflexives used with prepositions

 Grammar Tutorial

Startblock Reciprocal verbs express an action done by two or more people or things to or for one another.

Hört bitte auf, **euch** zu **küssen**.

Torsten und ich **haben uns gestritten**.

Reciprocal verbs

- Because reciprocal verbs refer to more than one person, they are only used with the plural reflexive pronouns **uns**, **euch**, and **sich**.

Wir rufen **uns** jeden Tag an.
*We call **each other** every day.*

Woher kennt **ihr euch**?
*How do **you** know **each other**?*

Meine Großeltern lieben **sich** sehr.
*My grandparents love **each other** very much.*

Sie schrieben **sich** zweimal im Monat.
*They wrote to **one another** twice a month.*

- Here are some common verbs with reciprocal meanings.

common reciprocal verbs	
sich anrufen	*to call each other*
sich kennen	*to know each other*
sich kennen lernen	*to meet (each other) for the first time*
sich küssen	*to kiss (each other)*
sich lieben	*to love each other*
sich schreiben	*to write to one another*
sich streiten	*to argue (with one another)*
sich trennen	*to separate, split up*
sich treffen	*to meet up*
sich unterhalten	*to chat, have a conversation*
sich verlieben	*to fall in love (with one another)*

Wir **kennen uns** schon seit Jahren.
*We've **known each other** for years.*

Unsere Eltern **haben sich** vor fünfundzwanzig Jahren **verliebt**.
*Our parents **fell in love** twenty-five years ago.*

Habt ihr **euch** gestern **gestritten**?
*Did you **argue (with each other)** yesterday?*

Die Studenten **treffen sich** gern im Restaurant, um **sich zu unterhalten**.
*Students like to **meet (each other)** at the restaurant **to talk (with one another)**.*

- In some cases, it may be unclear whether a verb is being used reflexively or reciprocally. To clarify or emphasize a verb's reciprocal meaning, use the expression **einander** (*each other, one another*) instead of, or in addition to, a reflexive pronoun.

Sie haben **sich** vorgestellt.
They introduced themselves (to one another, or to someone else).

Sie haben sich **einander** vorgestellt.
They introduced themselves to one another.

Reflexive verbs with prepositions

- Some reflexive verbs are typically used in set phrases with a preposition. Use accusative reflexive pronouns with these verbs. The prepositions in the following fixed expressions also take the accusative case.

common reflexive verbs with prepositions	
sich ärgern über	*to get angry about*
sich erinnern an	*to remember*
sich freuen auf	*to look forward to*
sich freuen über	*to be happy about*
sich gewöhnen an	*to get used to*
sich informieren über	*to find out about*
sich interessieren für	*to be interested in*
sich verlieben in	*to fall in love with*
sich vorbereiten auf	*to prepare oneself for*

Suggestion Tell students that in some cases, reflexive pronouns can be used after prepositions to mean myself, herself, etc. Ex.: **Mein Freund denkt nur an** *sich*.

ACHTUNG

When using **einander** with a preposition, attach it to the end of the preposition to form a single word: **Die Kinder spielen immer so schön miteinander.**

Klara und Paul haben sich ineinander verliebt.

QUERVERWEIS

In **6B.2**, you learned to form the past participles of verbs with separable and inseparable prefixes. The verb **vorbereiten** has a separable prefix, but because its root verb, **bereiten**, has an inseparable prefix, there is no **-ge-** added to its past participle.

See **7A.2** to review other verbs that are used in set phrases with prepositions.

Mama **hat sich über** mein unordentliches Zimmer **geärgert.**
*Mom **got mad about** my messy room.*

Nach der Reise **freuten** wir **uns auf** ein warmes Bad.
*After our trip, we **were looking forward to** a warm bath.*

Meine kleine Schwester **interessiert sich für** Computer.
*My little sister **is interested in** computers.*

Ich **habe mich an** das kalte Wetter **gewöhnt.**
*I've **gotten used to** the cold weather.*

More activities

vhlcentral

WB pp. 123–124

LM p. 79

Online activities

Jetzt sind Sie dran! Geben Sie an, ob die Verben in den Sätzen eine reflexive oder reziproke Bedeutung (*meaning*) haben.

	reflexiv	reziprok		reflexiv	reziprok
1. Wir treffen uns um 16 Uhr im Café.	☐	☑	5. Seht ihr euch heute Abend?	☐	☑
2. Max und ich kennen uns seit drei Jahren.	☐	☑	6. Tom verliebte sich in Lena.	☑	☐
3. Die Schüler freuten sich auf die Ferien.	☑	☐	7. Lena freute sich sehr darüber.	☑	☐
4. Sara und Felix schreiben einander über 100 SMS am Tag.	☐	☑	8. Dana und ihr Freund streiten sich nur selten.	☐	☑

Anwendung

1 **Was fehlt?** Ergänzen Sie die Sätze mit den passenden Reflexivpronomen.

> **BEISPIEL** Mira und Hasan rufen ___sich___ dreimal pro Tag an.

1. Heute küssten sie ___sich___ zum ersten Mal.
2. Unsere Großeltern kennen ___sich___ seit 60 Jahren.
3. Es ist klar, dass ihr ___euch___ liebt.
4. Philip und Daniel unterhalten ___sich___ gern.
5. Wo sollen wir ___uns___ treffen?
6. Ich kann ___mich___ nicht an seinen Namen erinnern.
7. Hast du ___dich___ über den neuen Film informiert?
8. Ihr sollt ___euch___ vorstellen.

2 **Bilder beschreiben** Beschreiben Sie die Bilder mit reziproken reflexiven Verben. Benutzen Sie das Perfekt.

> **BEISPIEL** die Geschäftsleute
> *Die Geschäftsleute haben sich getroffen.*

sich jeden Tag anrufen	sich streiten
sich küssen	sich treffen
sich oft schreiben	sich unterhalten

Tobias und ich
1. haben uns geküsst.

Klara und Mia
2. haben sich jeden Tag angerufen.

Ihr
3. habt euch gestritten.

Wir
4. haben uns oft geschrieben.

Sie
5. haben sich unterhalten.

3 **Sätze schreiben** Schreiben Sie mindestens (*at least*) sechs logische Sätze mit Wörtern aus jeder Spalte.

> **BEISPIEL** *Die Studenten bereiten sich auf das Abschlussexamen vor.*

Julia	sich ärgern über	das Abschlussexamen
der Hotelgast	sich aufregen über	sein ehemaliger (*former*) Lehrer
die Enkelkinder	sich erinnern an	die Geburt ihres Enkelkindes
Simon	sich freuen auf	die Laptopangebote im Internet
Oma und Opa	sich freuen über	der schlechte Zimmerservice
die Passagierin	sich informieren über	ihr verlorenes (*lost*) Handgepäck
die Studenten	sich vorbereiten auf	die vielen Geschenke

Kommunikation

4 **Beste Freunde** Stellen Sie Ihrem Partner / Ihrer Partnerin Fragen über seinen besten Freund / ihre beste Freundin. Antworten Sie in ganzen Sätzen und wechseln Sie sich ab. Answers will vary.

BEISPIEL

S1: *Seit wann kennt ihr euch schon?*
S2: *Wir kennen uns schon seit 10 Jahren.*

1. Seit wann kennt ihr euch schon?
2. Wo und wie habt ihr euch kennen gelernt?
3. Wie oft seht ihr euch?
4. Wo trefft ihr euch meistens?

5. Schreibt ihr euch viele SMS?
6. Ruft ihr euch an? Wie oft?
7. Worüber unterhaltet ihr euch?
8. Streitet ihr euch manchmal? Worüber?

5 **Eine Liebesgeschichte** Schreiben Sie mit Ihrem Partner / Ihrer Partnerin eine Liebesgeschichte über Lisa und David. Verwenden Sie die reflexiven Verben aus der Liste und benutzen Sie das Perfekt. Answers will vary.

▶ **BEISPIEL** *Lisa und David haben sich auf einer Party kennen gelernt.*

sich anrufen	sich treffen
sich kennen lernen	sich trennen
sich küssen	sich unterhalten
sich schreiben	sich verlieben
sich streiten	sich vorstellen

6 **Interessen** Wofür interessieren sich Ihre Mitstudenten? Machen Sie eine kurze Umfrage in Ihrem Kurs. Answers will vary.

BEISPIEL

S1: *Ich interessiere mich für Technologie. Und du, Max, wofür interessierst du dich?*
S2: *Ich interessiere mich für Musik. Und du, Hanna, wofür interessierst du dich?*
S3: *Ich interessiere mich für...*

7 **Fragen über Fragen** Stellen Sie Fragen an Ihre Mitstudenten. Finden Sie für jede Frage mindestens eine Person, die sie mit ja beantwortet. Präsentieren Sie Ihre Ergebnisse danach im Kurs. Answers will vary.

BEISPIEL

S1: *Freust du dich auf das Semesterende?*
S2: *Ja, ich freue mich total auf das Semesterende. Und du, freust du dich auf das Semesterende?*
S1: *Nein, gar nicht! Ich muss in den Ferien arbeiten.*

	Name
sich auf das Semesterende freuen	
sich gern an den letzten Sommer erinnern	
sich für Politik interessieren	
sich über das Essen in der Cafeteria aufregen	
sich über schlechte Noten ärgern	

4 **Suggestion** As a class project, compile the stories into a "class book" of **Liebesgeschichten**.

4 **Video Virtual Chat** You can also assign activity 4 on the Supersite. Students record individual responses that appear in your gradebook.

7 **Suggestion** Formulate the questions as a class before students begin the group activity.

Wiederholung

1 Welches Bild?

Beschreiben Sie sich gegenseitig die Bilder und erraten Sie, welches Bild Ihr Partner / Ihre Partnerin beschreibt. Answers will vary.

BEISPIEL

S1: Es ist im Badezimmer...
S2: Auf Bild eins?
S1: Nein, es ist im Badezimmer vor dem Spiegel ...

1 **Partner Chat** You can also assign activity 1 on the Supersite. Students work in pairs to record the activity online. The pair's recorded conversation will appear in your gradebook.

1.

2.

3.

4.

5.

6.

2 Lebensregeln

Schreiben Sie eine Regelliste (*list of rules*) für Ihre Familie. Benutzen Sie reflexive Verben und Reflexivpronomen. Answers will vary.

2 **Expansion** Have the groups compare their lists and decide which rules are most important.

BEISPIEL

Alle in der Familie müssen einander jeden Tag helfen...

3 Arbeitsblatt

Schreiben Sie drei Aktivitäten auf, die Sie diese Woche gemacht haben. Dann fragen Sie vier Personen im Unterricht, was sie gemacht haben. Answers will vary.

BEISPIEL

S1: Hast du dich diese Woche über etwas geärgert?
S2: Ja.
S1: Worüber hast du dich geärgert?
S2: Über das schlechte Essen in der Cafeteria.

4 Körperteile

Arbeiten Sie mit einem Partner / einer Partnerin und beschreiben Sie Tätigkeiten, die mit den verschiedenen Körperteilen zu tun haben. Benutzen Sie die reflexiven Verben aus der Liste. Answers will vary.

4 **Expansion** Have students come up with additional statements involving parts of the body and reflexive verbs.

BEISPIEL

S1: Wir waschen uns das Gesicht.
S2: Wir kämmen uns die Haare.

A	B
Gesicht	sich abtrocknen
Haare	sich kämmen
Hände	sich waschen
Lippen	sich rasieren
Augen	sich schminken
Zähne	sich bürsten
Beine	sich putzen

5 Diskutieren und kombinieren

Sie und Ihr Partner / Ihre Partnerin bekommen zwei verschiedene Blätter mit Jasmins Alltagsroutine. Wechseln Sie sich ab und fragen Sie, was Jasmin jeden Abend und jeden Morgen macht. Answers will vary.

BEISPIEL

S1: Um 23 Uhr zieht sich Jasmin aus und zieht ihren Schlafanzug an. Was macht sie danach?
S2: Danach...

6 In der Stadt

Schreiben Sie mit einem Partner / einer Partnerin einen kurzen Text über eine Shoppingtour, die Sie zusammen am Wochenende machen wollen. Beantworten Sie die Fragen. Answers will vary.

BEISPIEL

S1: Wir treffen uns am Samstagmorgen um 9 Uhr auf dem Markt vor der Bank.
S2: Wir haben uns einen Monat lang nicht gesehen. Wir freuen uns auf den Tag zusammen.

- Wo und wann treffen Sie sich?
- Worauf freuen Sie sich?
- Was kaufen Sie sich?
- Worüber ärgern Sie sich?
- Gehen Sie in ein Restaurant oder in ein Café?
- Was bestellen Sie sich?
- Worüber unterhalten Sie sich?
- Was machen Sie noch?

Video

Gesundheit bewegt uns

1 **Vorbereitung** Besprechen Sie mit Ihrem Partner / Ihrer Partnerin die folgenden Fragen. Answers will vary.

1. Die meisten Menschen haben zumindest (*at least*) zwei Versicherungen. Welche Versicherungen kennen Sie?

2. Welche Dinge tun Sie in Ihrem Alltag, die sich positiv auf Ihre Gesundheit auswirken (*affect*)?

Central – Gesundheit bewegt uns.

Deutschland hat ein duales Krankenversicherungssystem°. Zum einen gibt es die gesetzliche° Krankenversicherung. Sie ist eine verpflichtende° Versicherung für alle Personen. Zum anderen gibt es private Unternehmen, die Krankenversicherungen anbieten. Die Central Krankenversicherung ist die älteste private Krankenversicherung Deutschlands. Sie zählt mit fast 900 Mitarbeitern zu den führenden° privaten Krankenversicherungen in Deutschland.

Nützliche Wörter:

die Behandlungsmethode, -n	*method of treatment*
das Herz-Kreislaufsystem, -e	*cardio-vascular system*
Was auch immer für... getan werden kann	*Whatever can be done for...*

Krankenversicherungssystem *health insurance system* **gesetzliche** *compulsory* **verpflichtende** *obligatory* **führenden** *leading*

2 **Verständnis** Sehen Sie sich das Video an. Sind die folgenden Aussagen richtig oder falsch? Korrigieren Sie die falschen Aussagen.

	Richtig	**Falsch**	
1. Das Video wirbt (*advertises*) für private Krankenhäuser.	☐	☑	Es wirbt für eine Krankenversicherung.
2. Der Mann sagt, dass es Spezialisten für das Herz-Kreislaufsystem gibt.	☑	☐	
3. Die Central ist Spezialist für alternative Behandlungsmethoden.	☐	☑	Die *Central* ist Spezialist für private Krankenversicherung.

3 **Diskussion** Diskutieren Sie die folgenden Fragen mit einem Partner / einer Partnerin. Answers will vary.

1. Welche Unterschiede gibt es zwischen dem Krankenversicherungssystem in Deutschland und dem System in Ihrem Land?

2. Kritiker des deutschen Krankenversicherungssystems sagen, dass Personen, die privat versichert sind, eine bessere medizinische Versorgung (*medical care*) bekommen als die gesetzlich Versicherten. Gibt es in Ihrem Land ähnliche Probleme? Vergleichen Sie.

4 **Präsentation** Wie sieht Ihrer Meinung nach ein gutes Krankenversicherungssystem aus? Erarbeiten (*develop*) Sie mit Ihrem Partner / Ihrer Partnerin ein Modell und präsentieren Sie es dann im Kurs. Answers will vary.

Beim Arzt Vocabulary Tools

Wortschatz

die Gesundheit	**health**
die Allergie, -n	allergy
die Apotheke, -n	pharmacy
allergisch sein (gegen)	to be allergic (to)
krank/gesund werden	to get sick/better
in guter/schlechter Form sein	to be in/out of shape
sich verletzen	to hurt oneself
zum Arzt gehen	to go to the doctor
Symptome	**symptoms**
der Schmerz, -en	pain
die verstopfte Nase	stuffy nose
Zahnschmerzen (*pl.*)	toothache
leicht	mild
schwer	serious
schwindlig	dizzy
übel	nauseous
im Krankenhaus	**at the hospital**
der Arzt, ¨e / die Ärztin, -nen	doctor
das Medikament, -e	medicine
die Grippe, -n	flu
der Krankenwagen, -	ambulance
die Notaufnahme, -n	emergency room
das Pflaster, -	adhesive bandage
das Rezept, -e	prescription
das Thermometer, -	thermometer
der Zahnarzt, ¨e / die Zahnärztin, -nen	dentist
sich (das Handgelenk / den Fuß) verstauchen	to sprain (one's wrist/ankle)
sich (den Arm / das Bein) brechen	to break (an arm / a leg)
weh tun (tut...weh)	to hurt
weinen	to cry
gesund	healthy
krank	sick

Expansion Ask students: **Wer hier studiert Medizin? Möchte jemand Arzt oder Krankenpfleger werden? Hat jemand hier sich schon mal was gebrochen, einen Arm oder ein Bein?** etc.

Suggestion Point out that when reporting symptoms, it's common to say: **Ich *habe* Husten und Schnupfen**, rather than using the conjugated verbs.

Suggestion Model pronunciation of **Patient** and **Patientin**.

Er hat Fieber.
He has a fever.

Sie hat Rückenschmerzen.
She has a backache.

Sie hustet. (husten)
She is coughing.

Sie gibt ihm eine Spritze.
She is giving him a shot.

der Patient, -en (die Patientin, -nen *f.*)

Sie ist schwanger.
She is pregnant.

die Tablette, -n

Er hat eine Erkältung.
He has a cold.

das Taschentuch, ¨er

Sie ist gesund.
She is healthy.

HATSCHI!

Er niest. (niesen)
He is sneezing.

die Verletzung, -en
injury

More activities

vhlcentral | WB pp. 125–126 | LM p. 80 | Online activities

ACHTUNG

To describe how you feel, use an adjective with a dative noun or pronoun:
Mir ist schwindlig. Ihr ist übel.

Also use a dative noun or pronoun with the phrase **weh tun**:
Tut dir das Bein weh? *Does your leg hurt?*

der Krankenpfleger, - *male nurse/orderly*

Sie treibt Sport. (Sport treiben) *She exercises.*

die Krankenschwester, -n *nurse*

Sie hat Kopfschmerzen. *She has a headache.*

Er hat Bauchschmerzen. *He has a stomachache.*

Anwendung

1 Assoziationen Wählen Sie ein Wort aus der Liste, das Sie mit einem der Ausdrücke assoziieren.

die Allergie	die Notaufnahme
die Apotheke	das Thermometer
das Ibuprofen	die Zahnschmerzen

1 Expansion Have students create four additional associations for a partner to complete.

1. sich den Arm brechen ____die Notaufnahme____
2. eine verstopfte Nase haben ____die Allergie____
3. zum Zahnarzt gehen ____die Zahnschmerzen____
4. 39 Grad Celsius Fieber haben ____das Thermometer____
5. Kopfschmerzen haben ____das Ibuprofen____
6. Medikamente kaufen ____die Apotheke____

2 Hören Sie zu Sind das typische Symptome für eine Erkältung?

	Ja	Nein		Ja	Nein
1.	☐	☑	4.	☐	☑
2.	☑	☐	5.	☑	☐
3.	☑	☐	6.	☐	☑

2 Expansion Ask students what they do when they catch a cold (**zur Apotheke gehen, Tee trinken, Hühnersuppe essen**, etc.)

3 Bilder beschriften Finden Sie ein passendes Wort oder einen passenden Ausdruck für jedes Bild. Sample answers are provided.

1. ____weinen____

2. ____Bauchschmerzen haben____

3. ____Fieber haben____

4. ____die Ärztin____

5. ____schwanger sein____

6. ____in schlechter Form sein____

4 Beim Arzt Hören Sie sich das Gespräch zwischen Elias und seinem Arzt an und markieren Sie dabei die Ausdrücke, die Sie hören.

1. Ich habe Halsschmerzen. ☑   6. Mir tut alles weh. ☑
2. Mir ist übel. ☐   7. Ich habe eine Erkältung. ☐
3. Ich habe Fieber. ☑   8. Meine Nase ist verstopft. ☑
4. Mein Bauch tut weh. ☐   9. Ich treibe Sport. ☐
5. Ich schlafe schlecht. ☑   10. Ich huste. ☑

4 Suggestion To prepare for the listening activity, ask students to be your "doctor." Provide a list of symptoms and have them diagnose the problem.

Kommunikation

5 Ratschläge geben

Sehen Sie sich mit einem Partner / einer Partnerin die Bilder an. Was ist passiert und welche Ratschläge (*advice*) geben Sie den Personen auf den Bildern, so dass es ihnen dann besser geht? Answers will vary.

▶ **BEISPIEL** Hanna

S1: Hanna hat Zahnschmerzen
S2: Sie soll den Zahnarzt anrufen.

5 Partner Chat You can also assign activity 4 on the Supersite. Students work in pairs to record the activity online. The pair's recorded conversation will appear in your gradebook.

1. Emma

2. Frau Schmidt

3. Jasmin

4. Moritz

5. Herr Meyer

6. Michaela

7. Klara

8. Jonas

6 Fragen und Antworten

Beantworten Sie mit einem Partner / einer Partnerin die Fragen. Answers will vary.

BEISPIEL

S1: Was machst du bei Kopfschmerzen?
S2: Ich lege mich ins Bett.

6 Virutal Chat You can also assign activity 5 on the Supersite.

1. Bist du gegen etwas allergisch?
2. Bekommst du jedes Jahr eine Spritze gegen die Grippe?
3. Hast du dir schon mal etwas gebrochen?
4. Wie oft gehst du zum Arzt?
5. Was machst du, um fit zu bleiben?

7 Diskutieren und kombinieren

Sie und Ihr Partner / Ihre Partnerin bekommen zwei verschiedene Blätter von Ihrem Professor / Ihrer Professorin. Fragen Sie Ihren Partner / Ihre Partnerin nach den Patienten, die in der Notaufnahme sind. Answers will vary.

BEISPIEL

S1: Wer hat sich den Arm gebrochen?
S2: Frau Zimmermann hat sich den Arm gebrochen. Welches Problem hat Herr Arslan?
S1: Er hat...

8 Wörter erraten

Erraten Sie mit zwei Mitstudenten Wörter aus Ihrer neuen Vokabelliste. Eine Person beschreibt ein Wort und die anderen zwei müssen es erraten. Wechseln Sie sich ab. Answers will vary.

BEISPIEL

S1: Man putzt sie sich, wenn sie verstopft ist.
S2: Die Nase!

8 Suggestion Give students a few minutes beforehand to prepare their definitions.

Aussprache und Rechtschreibung

 Audio

Syllabic Stress

When a syllable in a word is stressed, it is pronounced with more emphasis than the other syllables. In German, the main stress is usually on the first syllable of a word.

| **Sei**fe | **Na**se | **Au**ge | **Tech**niker | **fern**sehen |

You have already learned that separable prefixes are always stressed, while inseparable prefixes are never stressed.

| **auf**wachen | **an**kommen | be**sprech**en | Ver**kehr** | **wie**dersehen |

In compound words, the first part of the compound is usually stressed.

| **Schlaf**anzug | **Speise**karte | **Bade**mantel | **Zahn**pasta | **Haus**schuh |

In words borrowed from other languages, the placement of stress varies. In nouns ending with **–ei** or **-ie**, the final syllable is stressed. In verbs ending in **–ieren**, the stress is on the **ie** sound.

| Com**pu**ter | Stu**dent** | Bäcke**rei** | Aller**gie** | ra**sie**ren |

Expansion Give students examples of words that change meaning if stress is placed on the prefix: **wieder**holen *to repeat*, wieder**holen** *to fetch*; **über**fahren *to run over*, über**fahren** *to ferry*; **durch**schlagen *to smash*; durch**schlagen** *to split in two*.

---

1 **Aussprechen** Wiederholen Sie die Wörter, die Sie hören.

1. Rücken
2. duschen
3. anziehen
4. Einkauf
5. Gesicht
6. verlieren
7. überraschen
8. Handtuch
9. Bauchschmerzen
10. Hotel
11. Metzgerei
12. Psychologie

2 **Nachsprechen** Wiederholen Sie die Sätze, die Sie hören.

1. Ich nehme immer eine Zahnbürste, Zahnpasta und saubere Unterwäsche mit.
2. Mein Arzt verschreibt mir solche Medikamente nicht.
3. Robert rasiert sich nur mit Rasierschaum.
4. Die Studenten lernen am liebsten in der Bäckerei.
5. In den Ländern war die Demokratie nicht nur Theorie.
6. Wenn ich zu früh aufstehe, bekomme ich Kopfschmerzen.

3 **Sprichwörter** Wiederholen Sie die Sprichwörter, die Sie hören.

Was du heute kannst besorgen, das verschiebe nicht auf morgen.[1]

Aller Anfang ist schwer.[2]

[1] Never put off till tomorrow what you can do today.
[2] The first step is always the hardest. (lit. *Every beginning is hard.*)

More activities

vhlcentral   LM p. 81   Online activities

Im Krankenhaus Video

George und Sabite haben Meline ins Krankenhaus gebracht. Der Arzt möchte sie eine Nacht dabehalten und Meline beginnt wieder, von Hans zu träumen. Oder ist es gar kein Traum?

NATIONAL communication cultures STANDARDS

Vorbereitung Have students look at the video stills and guess what the episode will be about.

1

GEORGE Sie wird wieder gesund, Sabite. Sie ist auf den Kopf gefallen. Der Arzt untersucht sie gleich und dann gehen wir wieder nach Hause. Mein Bruder ist einmal aus einem Baum gefallen, ohne schwere Verletzungen zu haben.

5

ARZT Haben Sie ein Schwindelgefühl?
MELINE Ein bisschen.
ARZT Übelkeit?
MELINE Ahhh. Ja.
ARZT Ohrgeräusche?
MELINE Haben vor einer Stunde aufgehört.
ARZT Gut. Haben wir noch andere Symptome?
MELINE Außer Kopfschmerzen? Nein.

2

SABITE Was ist passiert?
GEORGE Er hat sich den Knöchel verstaucht. Und den Arm gebrochen. Und ihm war mehrere Stunden lang schlecht und schwindlig. Tage. Aber jetzt ist er gesund, in toller Form und schmerzfrei. Aber er meidet Bäume.

ARZT Okay. Hier ist ein Schmerzmittel. Lassen Sie mich die Schwester holen, damit wir eine Computertomographie machen können. Sie bleiben heute Nacht bei uns.
MELINE Och, Herr Doktor. Ich...
ARZT Frau... Meline. Es sieht so aus, als hätten Sie eine leichte Gehirnerschütterung.

3

ARZT Das ist eine schöne Beule auf Ihrem Kopf. Erinnern Sie sich, was passiert ist?
MELINE Ich habe gelernt und bin eingeschlafen. Und dann bin ich aufgewacht und vom Stuhl gefallen.
ARZT Und nachdem Sie das Bewusstsein wiedererlangt hatten?
MELINE Ich bin am Boden gelegen und meine Freunde haben mich gefunden.

4

MELINE Es geht mir gut, Dr. Klompenhouwer. Ist das holländisch?

ÜBUNGEN

1 **Richtig oder falsch?** Entscheiden Sie, ob die folgenden Sätze **richtig** oder **falsch** sind.

1. Meline ist auf ihren Arm gefallen. Falsch.
2. Georges Bruder ist einmal von der Garage gefallen. Falsch.

3. Georges Bruder hat sich einmal den Arm gebrochen. Richtig.
4. Meline hat eine Beule am Kopf. Richtig.
5. Sie ist aufgewacht und aus dem Bett gefallen. Falsch.

6. Jetzt hat sie ein Schwindelgefühl, Ohrgeräusche und Fieber. Falsch.
7. Dr. Klompenhouwer gibt Meline eine Spritze. Falsch.
8. Er will die Krankenschwester rufen, um eine CT zu machen. Richtig.
9. Meline hat wahrscheinlich eine leichte Gehirnerschütterung. Richtig.
10. Hans trägt einen Mundschutz (*face mask*), weil er Schnupfen und Husten hat. Richtig.

Expansion Point out that Meline says **bin am Boden gelegen** instead of **habe am Boden gelegen**. Explain that in Southern Germany and Austria, **sein** is used with **liegen** instead of **haben**. Explain also that the use of **am Boden** implies that she fell to the floor, whereas **auf dem Boden** would imply that she lay down intentionally.

PERSONEN

Dr. Klompenhouwer Hans George Meline Sabite

7

ARZT George Bachman, Sabite Yilmaz?
ARZT Wir würden Meline heute Nacht gern im Krankenhaus behalten. Es geht ihr gut. Wir möchten auf Nummer sicher gehen.
SABITE Können wir sie sehen?
ARZT Sie würde heute lieber keine Besucher mehr haben.

8

MELINE Dr. Klompenhouwer? Sind Sie Chirurg? Ich verstehe das nicht.
HANS Ich musste mit meinen eigenen Augen sehen, dass es dir gut geht.
MELINE Hans, ich liebe dich!

9

ARZT Ihre Freunde sind hier, um Sie abzuholen.
MELINE Oh, Dr. Klompenhouwer, ganz herzlichen Dank. Sie haben mein Leben gerettet. Sie sind ein ausgezeichneter Arzt.
ARZT Danke, Meline. Wenn Sie Symptome haben, dann rufen Sie uns bitte auf jeden Fall an.

10

MELINE Wo ist George?
SABITE Er wäre hier, wenn er keine Uni hätte. Hans ist mit mir gekommen.
HANS Na, wie geht es unserer Patientin heute morgen? Das hier hat mir die Schwester gegeben, weil ich Schnupfen und Husten habe. Ich soll ja niemanden anstecken.

Nützliche Ausdrücke

- **untersuchen**
  to examine
- **der Baum**
  tree
- **der Knöchel**
  ankle
- **meiden**
  to avoid
- **die Beule**
  bump
- **Und nachdem Sie das Bewusstsein wiedererlangt hatten?**
  And after you regained consciousness?
- **das Schmerzmittel**
  painkiller
- **die Gehirnerschütterung**
  concussion
- **der Chirurg**
  surgeon
- **abholen**
  to pick (someone) up
- **ausgezeichnet**
  excellent

9B.1
- **Er wäre hier, wenn er keine Uni hätte.**
  He would have come if he weren't in class.

9B.2
- **Wir würden Meline heute Nacht gern im Krankenhaus behalten.**
  We would like to keep Meline in the hospital tonight.

 Zum Besprechen Stellen Sie sich vor, Meline hat andere Symptome, als sie ins Krankenhaus kommt. Spielen Sie einen Dialog zwischen Meline und Dr. Klompenhouwer. Answers will vary.

2 **Expansion** Have students act out their dialogues for the class.

2 **Partner Chat** You can also assign activity 2 on the Supersite.

 Vertiefung Wilhelm Conrad Röntgen hat etwas erfunden, das heute in jedem Krankenhaus täglich benutzt wird. Finden Sie heraus, was es ist und wie er es erfunden hat. Haben Sie diese Erfindung schon einmal benutzt? Vergleichen Sie Ihre Erfahrung mit der Ihrer Mitstudenten. Answers may include X-rays or electromagnetic radiation.

More activities

vhlcentral VM p. 18 Online activities

IM FOKUS

Apotheken Reading

Suggestion Tell students that in Germany, supermarkets are not allowed to sell over-the-counter drugs. Before they read the article, have students skim for familiar words and cognates.

> **TIPP**
>
> **Die Medizin** refers to the practice of medicine, while **das Medikament** refers to medication.

In jeder Stadt ist immer mindestens eine Apotheke geöffnet. Das bedeutet, dass die Menschen 24 Stunden am Tag wichtige Medikamente bekommen können.

Apotheken sind Geschäfte, in denen man nicht nur Medikamente, sondern auch andere gesundheitsfördernde° Produkte kaufen kann. Neben Medikamenten findet man normalerweise auch Nahrungsergänzungsmittel° wie zum Beispiel Vitamine, Kosmetikprodukte, sowie Produkte für Diäten, Haut- und Fußpflege° und für die Kontaktlinsenpflege.

In Deutschland gibt es neben der traditionellen Medizin auch viele Menschen, die homöopathische Mittel° benutzen. Beide Medikamentensorten kann man in Apotheken kaufen, aber manche Ärzte und Apotheken spezialisieren sich auf die traditionelle Medizin oder auf die homöopathische Medizin.

DEUTSCHLAND IST DER GRÖSSTE Apothekenmarkt in Europa. Hier gibt es 19.750 Apotheken. Jede Apotheke muss von einem staatlich geprüften° Apotheker geleitet werden°. Apotheken sind keine Ketten°, daher darf ein Apotheker höchstens vier davon besitzen. Die Medikamentenpreise werden von der Regierung° reglementiert. Relativ neu sind Versandapotheken°, bei denen man im Internet Medikamente bestellen kann.

Typische homöopathische Mittel	
Belladonna	Fieber und Kopfschmerzen
Kamille	Ohren- und Zahnschmerzen
Echinacea	Erkältung und Fieber
Hopfen	Schlafstörung°

staatlich geprüften *state certified* **geleitet werden** *headed* **Ketten** *chains* **Regierung** *government* **Versandapotheken** *mail-order pharmacies* **gesundheitsfördernde** *health promoting* **Nahrungsergänzungsmittel** *dietary supplements* **Fußpflege** *foot care* **Mittel** *remedy* **Schlafstörung** *insomnia*

Expansion Have students compare and contrast German pharmacies with their local drugstores.

ÜBUNGEN

1 **Im Fokus** Richtig oder falsch? Korrigieren Sie die falschen Aussagen.

1. Deutsche Apotheken sind oft Teil einer sehr großen Kette.
   Falsch. Apotheken sind keine Ketten.
2. Jede Apotheke kann ihre Medikamentenreise selbst bestimmen (*determine*).
   Falsch. Die Regierung reglementiert alle Medikamentenpreise.
3. In einer Apotheke kann man normalerweise auch Nivea-Hautcreme oder Vitamine kaufen. Richtig.

Diskussion Deutsche Apotheken verkaufen homöopathische Medikamente. Benutzen Sie homöopathische Medikamente? Welche? Warum/Warum nicht?

2 **Die deutschsprachige Welt** Richtig oder falsch? Korrigieren Sie die falschen Aussagen.

1. Ein Fallwind ist ein Phänomen in Norddeutschland und kommt von der Nordsee. Falsch. Föhn kommt aus dem Süden über die Alpen nach Bayern.
2. Der Föhn ist ein trockener und warmer Wind. Richtig.
3. Viele Menschen mögen den Föhn, weil sie dann im Freien aktiver sein können. Falsch. Viele Menschen haben bei Föhn Kopfschmerzen.

Diskussion Welche wetterbedingten (*weather-related*) Symptome kennen Sie? Wie behandelt man diese Symptome?

DEUTSCH IM ALLTAG

Ausdrücke zur Gesundheit

der Blutdruck	blood pressure
der blaue Fleck	bruise
der Hitzschlag	heat stroke
der Muskelkater	sore muscles
der Sonnenbrand	sunburn
der steife Hals	stiff neck

DIE DEUTSCHSPRACHIGE WELT

10 °C   20 °C

Föhn

Suggestion Tell students that **der Föhn, -e** is also used as a synonym for **Haartrockner**.

Föhn heißt ein Windsystem in den Alpen. Dieser Wind, auch Fallwind genannt, ist sehr trocken°, weil er beim Aufsteigen° auf der Südseite der Alpen Wasser in der Form von Regen verliert. Wenn er von den Gipfeln° der Alpen nach Norden ins Voralpengebiet° weht°, ist die Luftmasse° trocken und warm. Das Wetter in Bayern ist bei Föhn sonnig und trocken. Aber viele Menschen haben bei Föhn Kopfschmerzen.

trocken dry **Aufsteigen** rising **Gipfeln** peaks **Voralpengebiet** foothills of the Alps **weht** blows **Luftmasse** air mass

PORTRÄT

Röntgen

Wilhelm Conrad Röntgen (1845–1923) war ein deutscher Physiker. Er arbeitete als Professor an der Universität Würzburg, als er 1895 zufällig° eine besondere Art von Strahlen° entdeckte: die X-Strahlen. Mit diesen Strahlen konnte man durch viele Materialien hindurchsehen. Für diese Entdeckung° bekam Röntgen 1901 als erster Wissenschaftler den Nobelpreis für Physik. Vor allem für die Medizin war diese Entdeckung sehr wichtig: Ärzte konnten mit den X-Strahlen zum Beispiel Knochenbrüche° diagnostizieren. In seinem Testament° schrieb Röntgen, dass die Strahlen nicht seinen Namen tragen dürfen. Trotzdem nennt man die X-Strahlen heute in Deutschland und in Polen Röntgenstrahlen.

zufällig accidentally **Strahlen** rays **Entdeckung** discovery **Knochenbrüche** bone fractures **Testament** will

🔗 IM INTERNET

Suchen Sie im Internet eine deutsche Versand-apotheke. Was kann man bei der Versandapotheke bestellen? Kann man hier homöopathische Mittel kaufen?

Find out more at **vhlcentral.com**.

---

3   **Porträt** Richtig oder falsch? Korrigieren Sie die falschen Aussagen. Diskutieren Sie dann die letzte Frage mit einem Partner/ einer Partnerin.

1. Vor Wilhelm Conrad Röntgens Erfindung konnte man das menschliche Skelett nicht direkt sehen. **Richtig.**

2. Röntgen war Arzt. **Falsch.** Röntgen hatte eine akademische Karriere.

3. In Deutschland und Polen nennt man die X-Strahlen Röntgenstrahlen. **Richtig.**

Diskussion Haben Sie schon einmal ein Röntgenbild von Ihrem Körper oder einem Körperteil gesehen? Hatten Sie einen Knochenbruch oder war es das Röntgenbild beim Zahnarzt?

4   **Meine Gesundheit** Schreiben Sie einen kurzen Text über Dinge, die Sie für Ihre Gesundheit machen. Vergleichen Sie Ihre Aktivitäten mit denen Ihrer Mitstudenten.

More activities

vhlcentral   Online activities

9B.1

Der Konjunktiv II Grammar Tutorial

Startblock Use the subjunctive, also called the **Konjunktiv II**, to talk about hypothetical or unreal conditions, to express wishes, and to make polite requests.

> Könnte es auch schlimmer sein?

> Er **wäre** hier, wenn er keinen Unterricht **hätte**.

Suggestion Run through the formation of the subjunctive with **sollen, wollen** and a few weak verbs, such as **machen**. Point out that **würden +** infinitive is often used in place of the subjunctive of weak verbs, to avoid confusion with the **Präteritum**. Students will learn about **würden +** infinitive in **9B.2**.

- To form the subjunctive of weak verbs and the modal verbs **sollen** and **wollen**, add the subjunctive endings -e, -est, -e; -en, -et, -en to the **Präteritum** stem. The subjunctive forms of these verbs are identical to their **Präteritum** forms.

wünschen (*to wish*)	
Präteritum	**Konjunktiv II**
ich wünschte	ich wünschte
du wünschtest	du wünschtest
er/sie/es wünschte	er/sie/es wünschte
wir wünschten	wir wünschten
ihr wünschtet	ihr wünschtet
Sie/sie wünschten	Sie/sie wünschten

Wir **sollten** vier Mal pro Woche Sport treiben.
*We **should** exercise four times a week.*

Ich **wünschte**, ich **spielte** besser Fußball.
*I **wish** I **played** soccer better.*

QUERVERWEIS

See **6A.1** to review the **Präteritum** of weak verbs, modals, mixed verbs, and strong verbs.
———
See **Appendix A** for a complete list of strong verbs and their **Präteritum** forms.

- To form the subjunctive of strong verbs, add the subjunctive endings to the **Präteritum** stem. If the stem vowel is **a, o,** or **u,** add an **Umlaut**. The verbs **sein** and **haben** and the modals **dürfen, können, mögen,** and **müssen** also follow this pattern.

Infinitiv	Präteritum	Konjunktiv II	Infinitiv	Präteritum	Konjunktiv II
bleiben	ich blieb	ich bliebe	dürfen	ich durfte	ich dürfte
geben	du gabst	du gäbest	können	du konntest	du könntest
gehen	er/sie/es ging	er/sie/es ginge	mögen	er/sie/es mochte	er/sie/es möchte
kommen	wir kamen	wir kämen	müssen	wir mussten	wir müssten
lassen	ihr ließt	ihr ließet	haben	ihr hattet	ihr hättet
tun	Sie/sie taten	Sie/sie täten	sein	Sie/sie waren	Sie/sie wären

ACHTUNG

In conversation, German speakers often shorten the **du** and **ihr** subjunctive endings to **-st** and **-t**: **du gingst, ihr gingt; du wärst, ihr wärt.**

- The only mixed verb commonly used in the subjunctive is **wissen**. Its subjunctive forms are the same as its **Präteritum** forms, but with an added **Umlaut** on the stem vowel.

Wüssten Sie, wo die Apotheke ist?
***Would** you **happen to know** where the pharmacy is?*

Wenn ich das nur **wüsste**!
*If only I **knew** that!*

Suggestion Point out that the red endings in the **Konjunktiv II** chart for **wünschen** are the same endings used with strong verbs. Have students practice deriving the full subjunctive conjugations of a few strong verbs, as well as **dürfen, können,** and **müssen**.

- Modals and the verbs **haben** and **sein** are often used in the subjunctive to make polite requests or ask questions.

  Hätten Sie Lust, diesen Film mit mir zu sehen?
  Do you feel like seeing this movie with me?

  Könntest du mir bitte ein Taschentuch reichen?
  Could you hand me a tissue, please?

- To express a wish that is contrary to reality, use the subjunctive form of **wünschen** with another clause in the subjunctive.

  Ich wünschte, wir hätten mehr Zeit!
  I wish we had more time!

  Ich wünschte, ich könnte heute schwimmen gehen.
  I wish I could go swimming today!

- The conjunction **wenn** (*if*) is often used with **nur** to mean *if only*. Move the conjugated verb to the end of a clause beginning with **wenn**.

  Wenn wir **nur** mehr Zeit **hätten**!
  If only we had more time!

  Wenn ich heute **nur** schwimmen gehen **könnte**!
  If only I could go swimming today!

- To express a condition that is hypothetical or contrary to fact, use a **wenn**-clause with a second clause that indicates what would happen if the **wenn**-clause were true.

  Wenn du Zeit **hättest, könnten** wir heute Abend ins Konzert gehen.
  If you had time, we could go to a concert this evening.

  Wenn mir die Füße nicht so **weh täten, käme** ich **gern** mit euch wandern.
  If my feet didn't hurt so much, I'd be happy to come hiking with you.

- You can use the conjunction **dann** to introduce the second clause in a hypothetical statement.

  Wenn du nicht so spät ins Bett **gingest**...
  If you didn't go to bed so late,...

  dann wärest du nicht so müde.
  then you wouldn't be so tired.

- Use **als ob** with the subjunctive, instead of **wenn**, to mean *as if*.

  Er tut, **als ob** er krank **wäre**.
  He's acting as if he were sick.

  Du siehst aus, **als ob** du eine Grippe **hättest**.
  You look as if you had the flu.

  Es hört sich an, **als ob** Paul Husten und Schnupfen **hätte**.
  It sounds like Paul has a cough and the sniffles.

  Sara tut so, **als ob** sie am besten Tennis **spielte**.
  Sara's acting like she's the best tennis player.

QUERVERWEIS

In **4A.1**, you learned to use the subjunctive forms of **mögen** to make polite requests.

Wenn and als ob are subordinating conjunctions. You learned about the subordinating conjunctions **bevor, nachdem**, and **als** in **8A.1**. You will learn more about subordinating conjunctions in **10A.3**.

ACHTUNG

Ich möchte is typically used instead of **ich wollte** as the polite equivalent of **ich will**. **Ich hätte gern** is also frequently used for ordering in a restaurant.

More activities

vhlcentral

WB
pp. 127–128

LM
p. 82

Online activities

Jetzt sind Sie dran!   **Wählen Sie die passenden Verbformen.**

1. Ich (habe / (hätte)) gern einen Kaffee, bitte.

2. (Soll / (Sollte)) man immer wegen Rückenschmerzen zum Arzt gehen?

3. Ihr tut immer, als ob ihr keine Zeit zum Rad fahren ((hättet) / habt).

4. Wenn ich dagegen nicht allergisch (bin / (wäre)), ((könnte) / kann) ich Erdbeeren essen.

5. Ich (will / (wollte)), mein Computer ((funktionierte) / funktioniert) besser!

6. Wenn ich nur ((wüsste) / weiß), wo das Rezept für die Tabletten ist!

7. Die Zahnärztin (wünscht / (wünschte)), dass nicht so viele Patienten vor ihr Angst (haben / (hätten)).

8. Wenn Sie mehr Sport (treiben / (trieben)), dann (sind / (wären)) Sie in besserer Form.

9. ((Könnten) / Können) Sie die Krankenschwester rufen, bitte?

10. Wenn Roland kein Fieber ((hätte) / hat), (kommen / (käme)) er mit uns ins Restaurant.

11. ((Dürfte) / Darf) ich bitte die Tabletten und ein Glas Wasser haben?

12. Wenn es Lina nur nicht so schlecht (geht / (ginge))!

Anwendung

1 **Expansion** Have students work in pairs to write about a hypothetical situation using the verbs from this activity.

1 **Konjunktivformen** Ergänzen Sie die Tabelle mit den fehlenden Verbformen im Präteritum und im Konjunktiv II.

Präsens	Präteritum	Konjunktiv II
wir kommen	wir kamen	wir kämen
ich gebe	ich gab	ich gäbe
sie will	sie wollte	sie wollte
ihr arbeitet	ihr arbeitetet	ihr arbeitetet
du hast	du hattest	du hättest
er geht	er ging	er ginge

2 **Hypothesen** Ergänzen Sie die Sätze mit den richtigen Konjunktivformen der Verben in Klammern.

> **BEISPIEL** Wenn ich das ___*wüsste*___ (wissen), könnte ich dir helfen.

1. Wenn Jan nicht krank wäre, ___könnte___ (können) er ins Konzert gehen.
2. Wenn das Baby nicht so laut ___weinte___ (weinen), könnte die Ärztin ihm eine Spritze geben.
3. Wenn Julian Zeit hätte, ___ginge___ (gehen) er mit uns zum Fußballspiel.
4. Es sieht aus, als ob Sophia sehr unglücklich ___wäre___ (sein).
5. Ali sieht aus, als ob er Fieber ___hätte___ (haben).

3 **Suggestion** Remind students of how the conjunction **wenn** impacts word order. Do the first few sentences together as a class.

3 **Wünsche** Was würden (*would*) die Personen sagen? Schreiben Sie zu jedem Bild einen Satz im Konjunktiv II und benutzen Sie die angegebenen Verben.

> ▶ **BEISPIEL**
>
> **Kopfschmerztabletten haben**
> *Wenn ich nur Kopfschmerztabletten hätte!*

1. nicht so früh aufwachen
   müssen ___Wenn ich nur nicht so früh aufwachen müsste!___

2. ihre Handynummer
   wissen ___Wenn ich nur ihre Handynummer wüsste!___

3. Tennis spielen können
   ___Wenn ich nur Tennis spielen könnte!___

4. nicht so viele Patienten
   haben ___Wenn ich nur nicht so viele Patienten hätte!___

Kommunikation

4 **Drei Wünsche** Fragen Sie einander, was Sie sich wünschen. Benutzen Sie dabei den Konjunktiv II. Answers will vary.

BEISPIEL

S1: *Was hättest du am liebsten?*
S2: *Ich hätte am liebsten ein Motorrad.*

1. Was hättest du am liebsten?
2. Wo wärest du am liebsten?
3. Was wüsstest du am liebsten?
4. Was möchtest du am liebsten?

5 **Stell dir mal vor...** Fragen Sie Ihren Partner / Ihre Partnerin, was er/ sie wäre, wenn er/sie eine andere Person, ein Tier oder ein Ding sein könnte. Answers will vary.

BEISPIEL

S1: *Wenn du ein Tier wärest, welches Tier wärest du und warum?*
S2: *Ich wäre ein Vogel, denn dann könnte ich fliegen. Und welches Tier wärest du?*

1. ein Tier
2. eine berühmte Person
3. ein Möbelstück
4. eine Person aus einem Film/Buch

6 **Wenn es nur anders wäre!** Erzählen Sie einander, was Sie stört (*bothers*) und was Sie sich wünschen. Benutzen Sie den Konjunktiv II. Answers will vary.

BEISPIEL

S1: *Ich habe nicht viel Zeit für meine Hobbys. Ich wünschte, ich hätte mehr Zeit!*
S2: *Mein Computer ist so langsam. Ich wünschte, mein Computer wäre schneller!*

7 **Rollenspiel: Im Restaurant** Sie sind im Restaurant. Fragen Sie den Kellner / die Kellnerin, was er/sie Ihnen empfehlen kann. Answers will vary.

BEISPIEL

S1: *Guten Tag, was möchten Sie trinken?*
S2: *Ich hätte gern ein Mineralwasser.*
S3: *Und könnte ich bitte Apfelsaft bekommen?*

Kellner(in)	Gäste
Möchten Sie etwas trinken/essen?	Dürfte/Könnte ich bitte...
Was hätten Sie gern?	Hätten Sie vielleicht...?
	Ich hätte gern...
	Könnten Sie etwas empfehlen?
	Könnten Sie mir/uns bitte sagen...?
	Wir möchten bitte...
	Was / Wie viel macht das?

Speisekarte

Vorspeisen
Tomatensuppe	€4,80
Großer Salatteller	€9,50
Kleiner Salatteller	€3,60
Brotteller (Wurst oder Käse)	€6,80

Nachspeisen
Schokoladentorte	€6,45
Apfelkuchen	€5,80
Gemischtes Eis	€5,30
Obstsalat mit Pfirsich, Melone, Erdbeeren und Birne	€4,10

Hauptspeisen
Currywurst mit Pommes frites	€8,20
Hähnchen mit Reis, Pilzen und Gemüse	€18,80
Wiener Schnitzel mit Kartoffeln und kleinem Salat	€15,60
Thunfisch mit Bratkartoffeln und grünen Bohnen	€21,30
Scampi: Garnelen mit Reis und Knoblauch	€20,50

Getränke
Mineralwasser 0,2 l	€1,50
Limonade (Cola, Orange, Zitrone) 0,2 l	€1,80
Saft (Apfel, Ananas, Orange) 0,2 l	€2,20
Tasse Kaffee, Tee	€1,50

4 Video Virtual Chat You can also assign activity 4 on the Supersite. Students record individual responses that appear in your gradebook.

5 Expansion Have students report what they learned about their partners to the class.

6 Partner Chat You can also assign activity 6 on the Supersite. Students work in pairs to record the activity online. The pair's recorded conversation will appear in your gradebook.

7 Suggestion Have students repeat the items in the word bank after you to practice pronunciation. Remind them to use the accusative with **Ich hätte gern...** and **Ich möchte...**

9B.2 *Würden* with the infinitive Grammar Tutorial

Startblock The subjunctive of **werden** is **würden**. It is the subjunctive form used most commonly in conversation.

Wir **würden** Meline heute Nacht gern im Krankenhaus behalten.

Sie **würde** heute lieber keine Besucher mehr haben.

- The subjunctive forms of **werden** are the same as its **Präteritum** forms, but with an added **Umlaut** on the stem vowel.

QUERVERWEIS

You will learn about other uses of **werden** in **12B.2**.

werden		
Indikativ	**Präteritum**	**Konjunktiv II**
ich werde	ich wurde	ich würde
du wirst	du wurdest	du würdest
er/sie/es wird	er/sie/es wurde	er/sie/es würde
wir werden	wir wurden	wir würden
ihr werdet	ihr wurdet	ihr würdet
Sie/sie werden	Sie/sie wurden	Sie/sie würden

- **Würden** functions like a modal verb. When you use it with an infinitive, place **würden** in the position of the conjugated verb and place the infinitive at the end of the clause.

Würden Sie mir bitte **helfen?**
*Would you **help** me, please?*

An deiner Stelle **würde** ich zum Arzt **gehen.**
*If I were you, I **would go** to the doctor.*

Ich glaube, ich **würde** mit ihr **gehen.**
*I think I **would go** with her.*

Wenn er nur **mitkommen würde!**
*If only he **would come** with us!*

- Since all weak verbs, and some strong and mixed verbs, have identical subjunctive and **Präteritum** forms, German speakers typically use **würden** with the infinitive to express a subjunctive meaning for those verbs.

Sie **rannte** nach Hause.
*She **ran** home. / She **would** run home.*

Sie **würde** nach Hause rennen.
*She **would** run home.*

Ich **fragte** die Krankenschwester nach einem Pflaster.
*I **asked** the nurse for a bandage. / I **would ask** the nurse for a bandage.*

Ich **würde** die Krankenschwester nach einem Pflaster **fragen.**
*I **would ask** the nurse for a bandage.*

- Use **würden** + *infinitive* with a **wenn**-clause in the subjunctive to describe a hypothetical situation.

Wenn du vorsichtiger **wärest**, **würdest** du dich nicht so oft **verletzen**.
*If you **were** more careful, you **wouldn't hurt** yourself so much.*

Wenn ich Zahnschmerzen **hätte**, **würde** ich zum Zahnarzt **gehen**.
*If I **had** a toothache, I **would go** to the dentist.*

Wenn du mehr **Sport treiben würdest**, **wärst** du in besserer Form.
*If you **exercised more**, you'd **be** in better shape.*

Wenn Jan und Susanna **sich** nicht so oft **streiten würden**, **dann würden** sie sich **nicht trennen**.
*If Jan and Susanna **didn't fight** with each other so much, they **wouldn't be splitting up**.*

ACHTUNG

The subjunctive forms of **haben**, **sein**, **wissen**, and the modal verbs are commonly used in conversation. These verbs are rarely used as infinitives with **würden**.

- Use **würden** + *infinitive* to express wishes, give advice, make polite requests, or ask questions.

Ich **würde** gern in die Türkei **reisen**.

An Ihrer Stelle **würde** ich die Wahrheit **sagen**.

Sie **würden gern** nach Bern **fahren**.
*They'd **love** to go to Bern.*

An deiner Stelle **würde** ich das nicht **tun**.
*I **wouldn't do** that if I were you.*

Würdest du bitte das Fenster **schließen?**
*Would you **close** the window, please?*

Wir **würden** das nie **tun**.
*We **would** never **do** that.*

Expansion Have students pick a famous person and give them a few words of advice: **An Ihrer Stelle würde ich...**

ACHTUNG

To give advice, use the expression **An deiner/Ihrer Stelle,** meaning *In your place...* or *If I were you...*

More activities

S vhlcentral

WB pp. 129–130

LM p. 83

Online activities

Jetzt sind Sie dran!   Geben Sie an, wie der Konjunktiv mit **würden** in jedem Satz verwendet wird (*is used*):
a. Frage b. Wunsch c. Ratschlag (*advice*) d. hypothetische Situation

1. _a_ Würden Sie die Tür bitte schließen?
2. _a_ Würdest du dich auf einen Besuch freuen?
3. _c_ An Ihrer Stelle würde ich mehr Gemüse essen.
4. _b_ Sie würden gern Musik hören.
5. _a_ Würden Sie bitte den Arzt rufen?
6. _c_ An seiner Stelle würde ich keinen Kaffee trinken.
7. _d_ Er würde sich nicht verletzen.
8. _d_ Wenn ich Rückenschmerzen hätte, würde ich mich hinlegen.
9. _b_ Ich würde gern nach Hause gehen.
10. _c_ An deiner Stelle würde ich zum Zahnarzt gehen.
11. _a_ Würdest du mir bitte das Thermometer geben?
12. _a_ Würden Sie lieber mit der Ärztin oder dem Arzt sprechen?

Anwendung

1 **Konjunktivformen** Schreiben Sie die Verben in die Konjunktivform mit **würden** + *Infinitiv* um.

BEISPIEL ich käme *ich würde kommen*

1. sie sagte ___sie würde sagen___
2. du nähmest ___du würdest nehmen___
3. ich gäbe ___ich würde geben___
4. wir zögen um ___wir würden umziehen___
5. er lernte ___er würde lernen___
6. ihr schriebet ___ihr würdet schreiben___
7. sie arbeitete ___sie würde arbeiten___
8. sie informierten sich ___sie würden sich informieren___

2 **Was tun?** Was würden Sie an Stelle dieser Personen machen? Schreiben Sie zu jedem Bild einen Satz mit **würden** + *Infinitiv*. Benutzen Sie die Wörter im Wortschatz. Lesen Sie Ihre Sätze im Kurs vor.

> den Automechaniker anrufen
> Brille tragen
> ein Boot bauen
>
> an Land schwimmen
> sehr still bleiben

▶ **BEISPIEL**
An seiner Stelle
würde ich ein Boot bauen.

1. An seiner Stelle
würde ich eine Brille tragen.

2. An ihrer Stelle
würde ich sehr still bleiben.

3. An seiner Stelle
würde ich den Automechaniker anrufen.

4. An ihrer Stelle
würde ich an Land schwimmen.

3 **Sätze umschreiben** Schreiben Sie die Sätze mit **würden** + *Infinitiv* um. Sample answers are provided.

BEISPIEL Öffnen Sie bitte die Tür!
Würden Sie bitte die Tür öffnen?

1. Räumt bitte eure Zimmer auf! Würdet ihr bitte eure Zimmer aufräumen?
2. Mach bitte den Fernseher aus! Würdest du bitte den Fernseher ausmachen?
3. Fahr bitte langsamer! Würdest du bitte langsamer fahren?
4. Zeigen Sie mir Ihre Bordkarte, bitte! Würden Sie mir Ihre Bordkarte zeigen, bitte?
5. Ladet dieses Dokument für mich herunter! Würdet ihr dieses Dokument für mich herunterladen?

Kommunikation

4 **An deiner Stelle würde ich...** Erzählen Sie Ihrem Partner / Ihrer Partnerin von Ihren Gesundheitsproblemen. Er/Sie sagt dann, was er/sie an Ihrer Stelle machen würde. Answers will vary.

▶ **BEISPIEL**

S1: Mir tun die Füße weh.
S2: An deiner Stelle würde ich mich öfter hinsetzen.

Probleme	Ratschläge (Advice)
Ich bin immer müde.	früher ins Bett gehen
Ich habe Rückenschmerzen.	mehr Sport treiben
Ich bin in schlechter Form.	sich öfter hinsetzen
Mir ist schwindlig.	sich hinlegen
Mir tun die Füße weh.	Tabletten nehmen
Ich bin allergisch gegen...	zum Arzt gehen

5 **Wenn es so wäre, ...** Erzählen Sie einander, was Sie machen würden, wenn diese Situationen echt wären. Answers will vary.

BEISPIEL

S1: Wenn ich mehr Zeit hätte, würde ich öfter ausgehen. Und du?
S2: Ich würde mehr Sport treiben.

1. Wenn es jetzt Sommer wäre, ...
2. Wenn ich wieder ein Kind wäre, ...
3. Wenn ich den ganzen Tag frei hätte, ...
4. Wenn ich eine Zeitmaschine hätte, ...
5. Wenn ich fliegen könnte, ...
6. Wenn ich viel Geld hätte, ...

6 **Austauschstudenten** Zwei Austauschstudenten (*exchange students*) aus Deutschland sind für ein paar Tage bei Ihnen. Diskutieren Sie, was Sie in der Zeit alles zusammen machen könnten. Benutzen Sie den Konjunktiv II. Answers will vary.

BEISPIEL

S1: Sollten wir vielleicht ins Kino gehen?
S2: Das wäre okay, aber ich würde lieber ein Museum besuchen.
S3: Wir könnten auch...

Wir könnten vielleicht...	Das wäre toll/langweilig/schön/okay...
Möchtet ihr...	Ich hätte nicht so viel Lust auf...
Sollten wir vielleicht...	Es würde bestimmt viel/keinen Spaß machen, zu...
Ich würde gern / lieber / am liebsten...	

7 **Ein neues Konzept** Was würden Sie an Ihrer Universität anders machen? Machen Sie einen Plan und überzeugen (*convince*) Sie dann Ihre Mitstudenten von den Vorteilen (*advantages*) Ihres Konzepts. Answers will vary.

BEISPIEL

S1: Wir würden zuerst allen Studenten einen Tag frei geben.
S2: Und Vorlesungen würden niemals vor 10 Uhr beginnen.

Wiederholung

1 **Suggestion** Point out that although some speakers still treat **backen** (item 2) as a strong verb, it is more frequently conjugated as a weak verb in current usage.

1 Als ob!

Diese Leute tun, als ob sie alles machen könnten. Beschreiben Sie mit einem Partner / einer Partnerin, was sie machen und wie sie sich benehmen (*act*). Sample answers are provided.

BEISPIEL Florian / vom Tennisspielen sprechen

S1: Florian spricht immer vom Tennisspielen.
S2: Als ob er am besten spielte!

1. Tim / vom
   Singen sprechen
   Als ob er am besten sänge!
2. Antonia und Jan / vom
   Backen sprechen
   Als ob sie am besten backten!
3. Simon / von seinen
   Reisen sprechen
   Als ob er am meisten reiste!

4. Mia / vom
   Laufen sprechen
   Als ob sie am schnellsten liefe!
5. Herr und Frau Schulz / vom
   Tanzen sprechen
   Als ob sie am schönsten tanzten!
6. Sara / vom
   Schreiben sprechen
   Als ob sie am schönsten schriebe!

2 Diskutieren und kombinieren

Sie und Ihr Partner / Ihre Partnerin bekommen zwei Blätter mit verschiedenen Informationen über Familie Weber. Was hat jedes Familienmitglied gemacht und was ist danach passiert? Finden Sie für jede Wirkung (*effect*) eine Ursache (*cause*). Answers will vary.

BEISPIEL

S1: Wie hat David sich den Arm gebrochen?
S2: Er ist beim Baseballspiel gefallen.

3 Wenn nur...

Schauen Sie sich mit einem Partner / einer Partnerin die Bilder an. Sagen Sie, was die Personen alles machen würden, wenn sie gesund wären. Answers will vary.

BEISPIEL

S1: Wenn Emma kein gebrochenes Bein hätte, könnte sie Fußball spielen.
S2: Auch könnte sie...

1. Emma
2. Herr Yildirim

3. Frau Krüger
4. Michael

4 Sätze bilden

Bilden Sie mit einem Partner / einer Partnerin logische Sätze. Verwenden Sie den Konjunktiv II für den Satzanfang und **würden** + *Infinitiv* für das Satzende. Sample answers are provided.

BEISPIEL ich / Zahnschmerzen haben / den Zahnarzt anrufen
Wenn ich Zahnschmerzen hätte, würde ich den Zahnarzt anrufen.

1. ich / mehr Geld haben / dir ein Geschenk mitbringen
   Wenn ich mehr Geld hätte, würde ich dir ein Geschenk mitbringen.

2. ihr / nicht so erkältet sein / campen gehen
   Wenn ihr nicht so erkältet wärt, würdet ihr campen gehen.

3. er / nicht arbeiten müssen / Zeit mit seiner Familie verbringen
   Wenn er nicht arbeiten müsste, würde er Zeit mit seiner Familie verbringen.

4. wir / spät ausgehen / morgen lange schlafen
   Wenn wir spät ausgingen, würden wir morgen lange schlafen.

5. du / nicht so viele Hausaufgaben haben / mehr Sport treiben
   Wenn du nicht so viele Hausaufgaben hättest, würdest du mehr Sport treiben.

5 Kritische Meinungen

Schauen Sie sich mit einem Partner / einer Partnerin die Bilder an. Fragen Sie ihn/sie, wie er/sie die Geräte findet. Answers will vary.

BEISPIEL

S1: Wie findest du das Handy?
S2: Ich fände es besser, wenn es nicht so alt wäre. Wie findest du es?

6 Arbeitsblatt

Wählen Sie eine schwierige Situation aus der Liste. Fragen Sie vier Personen, was sie in der Situation machen würden. Answers will vary.

BEISPIEL

S1: Was würdest du machen, wenn du einen Unfall sähest?
S2: Wenn ich einen Unfall sähe, würde ich den Krankenwagen rufen.

7 Heumann Tees

Die Firma Heumann Medikamente ist eines der bedeutendsten pharmazeutischen Unternehmen in Deutschland. Die Firma wurde 1913 von dem katholischen Pfarrer° Ludwig Heumann gegründet. Heumann produziert preiswerte Generika und qualitativ hochwertige Medikamente auf pflanzlicher Basis. Besonders beliebt ist das große Sortiment von Heumanns Tees, die aus Kräutern und Früchten hergestellt werden. Fragen Sie Ihren Partner / Ihre Partnerin, was er / sie bei Erkältungen und Kopf- oder Bauchschmerzen macht und was er / sie von Medikamenten aus Kräutern° oder anderen pflanzlichen Stoffen hält.

Pfarrer *priest*   **Kräutern** *herb*

BEISPIEL

S1: *Trinkst du einen Erkältungstee, wenn du dich erkältet hast?*

S2: *Nein, ich gehe zum Arzt und hole mir ein Rezept. Und du?*

S1: *Ich esse Hühnersuppe und …*

7 Suggestion List German words related to medicine on the board and ask students to add them to Vocabulary Tools on the Sag mal Supersite.

7 Expansion Bring a list of Heumann's „Vitaltees" and ask students what these teas might be good for. Which plant-based medicines are available in their own country?

Wird oft zusammen gekauft

HEU −37%[2] + HEUM/ Blasen- und I −37%[2] =

Heumann
Bronchialtee
Solubifix® T

Heumann Blasen-
und Nierentee
Solubitrat® Uro

AVP / UVP[1]: € ~~16,16~~

€ 10,17

inkl. MwSt. zzgl. Versand
Sie sparen[2] 37,00%

Beide Produkte in den Warenkorb

8 Ich wünschte, …

Sprechen Sie im Kurs über Ihre Wünsche. Verwenden Sie den Konjunktiv II mit **sein**, **haben**, **können**, **müssen** oder **dürfen**. Answers will vary.

BEISPIEL

S1: *Ich wünschte, ich müsste nicht so früh aufwachen. Was wünschst du dir?*

S2: *Ich wünschte, ich wäre in wirklich guter Form.*

9 Mir geht's nicht gut

Sagen Sie Ihrem Partner / Ihrer Partnerin, warum Sie sich nicht wohl fühlen. Beschreiben Sie alle Symptome. Der Partner / Die Partnerin sagt Ihnen, was Sie machen sollen, um sich besser zu fühlen. Answers will vary.

BEISPIEL

S1: *Ich fühle mich nicht gut. Ich habe eine verstopfte Nase, und ich huste. Ich glaube, ich habe auch Fieber.*

S2: *Es hört sich an, als ob du eine schwere Erkältung hättest. Du solltest…*

9 Partner Chat You can also assign activity 9 on the Supersite.

8 Expansion As a final project on the subjunctive, have students work in groups to prepare a poster with 10 statements about a hypothetical topic of their choice, such as their ideal world, what it would be like to be a cat, etc. Encourage them to use **würde** + infinitive constructions, except with the modals and **haben**, **sein**, **wissen**, **wünschen**.

Mein Wörterbuch

Schreiben Sie noch fünf weitere Wörter in Ihr persönliches Wörterbuch zu den Themen **Tagesroutine** und **Gesundheit**.

Lektion 9B		
German	English	Definition

+ add word

| sich ankleiden | to get dressed | sich anziehen |

↓ 🗑

ä ö ü ß ☐ ALL CAPS

Panorama Interactive Map

Mecklenburg-Vorpommern und Brandenburg

Mecklenburg-Vorpommern in Zahlen

NATIONAL connections cultures STANDARDS

▶ **Fläche:** *23.193 km²*

▶ **Bevölkerung:** *1,6 Millionen Menschen*

▶ **Städte:** *Rostock (208.000 Einwohner), Schwerin (96.000), Neubrandenburg (64.000)*

▶ **Wichtige Industriezweige:** *Schiffbau°, Reedereien°, Energiesektor, Tourismus*

▶ **Touristenattraktionen:** *Usedom, Rügen, Hiddensee, Greifswald, Stralsund*

Mecklenburg-Vorpommern zieht jedes Jahr viele Touristen an, die die Ostseeinseln° Usedom, Rügen und Hiddensee oder die historischen Hafenstädte° Rostock und Schwerin besuchen wollen.

QUELLE: Landesportal Mecklenburg-Vorpommern

Suggestion Tell students that **Buchenwald** was a concentration camp during the Nazi regime.

Brandenburg in Zahlen

▶ **Fläche:** *29.654 km²*

▶ **Bevölkerung:** *2,5 Millionen Menschen*

▶ **Städte:** *Potsdam (172.000 Einwohner), Cottbus (100.400), Brandenburg (71.700)*

▶ **Wichtige Industriezweige:** *Holzgewerbe°, Ernährungsindustrie°, Landwirtschaft°, Tourismus*

▶ **Touristenattraktionen:** *Potsdam, Schloss Sanssouci, Buchenwald im Grumsiner Forst*

Viele Touristen besuchen Potsdam mit seinen kaiserlichen Schlössern und Parkanlagen°.

QUELLE: Landesportal Brandenburg

Berühmte Menschen aus Mecklenburg-Vorpommern und Brandenburg

▶ **Heinrich von Kleist,** *Autor (1777–1811)*

▶ **Marie Christine Eleonora Prochaska,** *Soldatin (1785–1813)*

▶ **Heinrich Schliemann,** *Archäologe und Entdecker der Ruinen von Troja (1822–1890)*

▶ **Otto Lilienthal,** *Flugpionier (1848–1898)*

▶ **Gerhart Hauptmann,** *Autor und Literaturnobelpreisträger (1862–1946)*

Schiffbau *shipbuilding* **Reedereien** *shipping companies* **Ostseeinseln** *Baltic Sea islands* **Hafenstädte** *port cities* **Holzgewerbe** *wood industry* **Ernährungsindustrie** *food industry* **Landwirtschaft** *agriculture* **Parkanlagen** *parks* **Innere** *inside*

DÄNEMARK

OSTSEE

Schloss Güstrow

NATIONALPARK VORPOMMERSCHE BODDENLANDSCHAFT

RÜGEN

MECKLENBURGER BUCHT

Stralsund

SCHLESWIG-HOLSTEIN

Greifswald

POMMERSCHE BUCHT

Rostock

USEDOM

Wismar

MECKLENBURG-VORPOMMERN

Schwerin

Neubrandenburg

NATIONALPARK MÜRITZ

Müritz

Elbe

Havel

Oder

NIEDERSACHSEN

BRANDENBURG

POLEN

Oranienburg

BERLIN

Hafen von Rostock

Havel

Berlin

Frankfurt an der Oder

Brandenburg

Potsdam

Oder

Spree

Neiße

SACHSEN-ANHALT

Cottbus

Landesgrenzen
● Stadt
◎ Landeshauptstadt
✳ Hauptstadt

SACHSEN

0 _____ 25 Meilen

0 _____ 25 Kilometer

Segeln in Brandenburg

Suggestion You may want to mention the comedian Loriot as another example of a **berühmte Brandenburger**. Many of his classic sketches, such as **Die Nudel** or **Die Jodelschule**, can be found online.

TSCHECHIEN

Unglaublich, aber wahr!

Auf Rügen gibt es eine ungewöhnliche Touristenattraktion: Das „Haus-Kopf-über". Hier kann man ein Haus besuchen, das auf dem Dach steht. Besucher stehen auf der Unterseite des Hauses und können sich das Innere° des Hauses ansehen.

Architektur
Schloss Sanssouci

Suggestion Before they read about the Potsdam Conference, have students briefly share what they know about the situation in Germany in 1945.

Schloss Sanssouci war der Lieblingsort von Friedrich dem Großen, König von Preußen. Das Schloss war seine Sommerresidenz, in der er sein Privatleben genießen wollte. Der Name Sanssouci bedeutet „ohne Sorge°". Es wurde von 1745 bis 1747 von Georg Wenzeslaus von Knobelsdorff nach den Ideen des Königs auf einem terrassierten Weinberg° gebaut°. Es gilt als Hauptwerk deutscher Rokokoarchitektur. Die prächtigen° und eleganten Räume sind noch original ausgestattet°. Das Schloss und die Parks sind eine der größten Touristenattraktionen Brandenburgs.

Archäologie
Megalithgräber°

In Mecklenburg-Vorpommern bauten Menschen während der Jungsteinzeit° fast 5.000 große Grabmonumente. Diese Gräber heißen auch Megalithgräber. Die ersten Gräber stammen aus der Zeit um 3.500 vor Christus. Anfangs waren diese Gräber nur für Familienoberhäupter°, später wurden sie immer größer, und ganze Familien wurden in den Gräbern beerdigt°. Etwa 1.000 dieser Grabanlagen° gibt es noch, und wenn man durch die flache Landschaft Mecklenburg-Vorpommerns fährt, kann man sie heute noch gut erkennen.

Geographie
Rügen

Die Ostseeinsel Rügen ist mit 926 km² die größte deutsche Insel und gehört zum Bundesland Mecklenburg-Vorpommern. 70.000 Menschen leben hier ständig. Dazu kommen rund 800.000 Urlauber, die die Insel jedes Jahr besuchen.

Zu den meistbesuchten Touristen-attraktionen zählen die Kreidefelsen° im Nationalpark Jasmund und die rund 80 km langen Sand- und Naturstrände.

Geschichte
Die Potsdamer Konferenz

Zwischen dem 17. Juli und dem 2. August 1945 trafen sich in Potsdam die Alliierten Großbritannien, USA und UdSSR. Sie berieten°, was mit dem ehemaligen Kriegsgegner° Deutschland passieren sollte. Sie entschieden°, dass Deutschland eine Demokratie werden sollte, alle Naziparteien verboten werden. Konflikte zwischen Stalin und den anderen Alliierten führten aber später zur Teilung° Deutschlands.

Musik Musik

Mark Forster

Mark Forster hat Werbesongs geschrieben, bevor er zu einem der populärsten Sänger Deutschlands wurde. In seiner Freizeit engagiert er sich für Kinderhilfsorganisationen.

Go to **vhlcentral.com** to find out more about **Mark Forster**.

Sorge *worry* **Weinberg** *vineyard* **wurde... gebaut** *was built* **prächtigen** *grand* **ausgestattet** *furnished* **berieten** *deliberated* **Kriegsgegner** *wartime enemy* **entschieden** *decided* **Einheit** *unity* **Teilung** *division* **Kreidefelsen** *chalk rocks* **Megalithgräber** *megalith graves* **Jungsteinzeit** *New Stone Age* **Familienoberhäupter** *patriarchs* **wurden... beerdigt** *were buried* **Grabanlagen** *burial sites*

---

1 **Was haben Sie gelernt?** Entscheiden Sie, ob die Sätze richtig oder falsch sind. Korrigieren Sie die falschen Sätze.

1. Auf Rügen gibt es eine Kirche, die auf dem Kopf steht.
   Falsch. Auf Rügen gibt es ein Haus, das auf dem Kopf steht.
2. Schloss Sanssouci war das Schloss von Ludwig II.
   Falsch. Schloss Sanssouci war das Schloss von Friedrich dem Großen.
3. Die Potsdamer Konferenz fand im Jahre 1945 statt. **Richtig.**
4. Rügen liegt an der Ostsee und ist die größte deutsche Insel. **Richtig.**
5. Die großen Grabmonumente in Mecklenburg-Vorpommern heißen Megalithgräber. **Richtig.**

2 **Denken Sie nach** Diskutieren Sie die Frage mit einem Partner/einer Partnerin.

Suchen Sie Informationen über die Potsdamer Konferenz. Warum traf man sich in Potsdam? Was wollten die Alliierten mit Deutschland machen and warum?

Lesen Audio: Reading

Vor dem Lesen

Strategien

Reading for the main idea

You have already learned to make predictions about the content of a reading by looking at its format, titles, and subtitles, looking for cognates, skimming to get the gist, and scanning for specific information. Reading for the main idea involves locating the topic sentences of each paragraph to determine the author's purpose. Topic sentences can provide clues about the content of each paragraph, as well as the general organization of the reading. Your choice of which reading strategies to use will depend on the style and format of the reading selections you encounter.

Untersuchen Sie den Text

Sehen Sie sich beide Texte kurz an. Welche Ähnlichkeiten (*similarities*) und Unterschiede (*differences*) können Sie erkennen? Welche Strategien können Sie benutzen, um die Art (*type*) der Texte zu identifizieren? Vergleichen Sie Ihre Ideen mit denen eines Partners / einer Partnerin.

Vergleichen Sie die Texte

- Analysieren Sie das Format des ersten Texts. Gibt es eine Überschrift (*heading*)? Gibt es viele Abschnitte (*sections*)? Wie ist der Text gegliedert (*structured*)? Sehen Sie sich jetzt den Inhalt an. Was für Vokabeln benutzt man? Was ist die Hauptidee von jedem Abschnitt?

- Ist der zweite Text genauso gegliedert wie der erste? Gibt es Überschriften und verschiedene Abschnitte? Ist die Information ähnlich der im ersten Text? Welche Vokabeln werden benutzt? Was für eine Art Text ist es? Was ist die Hauptidee von jedem Abschnitt? Haben beide Texte das gleiche Thema?

Andis Blog

3. Juni 2012

Meine Gesundheitspläne

Kommentare

Vorheriger Eintrag

Nächster Eintrag

Archiv

Heute war ich beim Arzt für eine allgemeine Untersuchung°. Er hat mir gesagt, dass ich in keiner guten Form bin! Meine Blutdruckwerte sind zu hoch. Ich muss gesünder leben! Besser essen und mehr Sport treiben. Das soll ich machen:

Als Erstes muss ich mehr schlafen. Jeden Tag mindestens sieben Stunden. Vielleicht kann ich ja weniger Videospiele spielen!

Vor allem muss ich mich mehr bewegen°. Auf der Arbeit werde ich jeden Tag zum Büro Treppen steigen und nicht mit dem Aufzug° fahren! Ich bin früher immer gerne gelaufen. Also werde ich wieder anfangen zu joggen. Drei Mal die Woche möchte ich eine halbe Stunde joggen. Das wäre super! Ich habe einen tollen Artikel gefunden, der zeigt, wie man drei kurze Übungen machen kann, um fit zu werden. Ich möchte diese Übungen auch drei Mal die Woche machen.

Im Allgemeinen darf ich nicht so viel Stress in meinem Leben haben. Schlafen, Bewegung und besser essen sind ein guter Start. So hoffe ich, bald wieder gesünder zu sein.

Andi

Untersuchung *check-up* **mich... bewegen** *move around* **Aufzug** *elevator*

Fit in 10 Minuten!

Sie wollen fit werden? Hier sind 3 kurze Übungen für Bauch und Po°.
Machen Sie dreimal die Woche 5 bis 10 Wiederholungen jeder Übung.

Aufwärmen

Stehen sie aufrecht°, die Füße hüftweit° auseinander.
Gehen Sie 2 Minuten lang auf der Stelle. Die Arme schwingen mit.

Obere Bauchmuskeln

Legen Sie sich mit dem Rücken auf ein Handtuch.
Ziehen Sie jetzt die Knie an. Fassen Sie das
Handtuch mit den Händen an den Enden hinter
dem Kopf. Rollen Sie nun den Oberkörper°
langsam auf. Halten Sie kurz die Position und
rollen Sie langsam wieder in die erste Position.

Übung 1

Schräge° Bauchmuskeln

Legen Sie sich auf den Rücken und ziehen Sie die
Knie an. Heben Sie die Unterschenkel°, bis diese
parallel zum Boden sind. Verschränken° Sie nun die
Hände hinter dem Kopf. Jetzt heben Sie den linken
Ellenbogen zum rechten Knie und zurück, ohne dass
die rechte Schulter den Boden berührt°. Der Rücken
bleibt auf dem Boden. Wiederholen Sie die Übung
mit der anderen Seite.

Übung 2

Po

Hände und Knie berühren den Boden. Heben
Sie nun das linke Knie, bis Oberschenkel
und Boden etwa parallel sind. Halten Sie
kurz diese Position und senken Sie das Knie
langsam wieder zum Boden. Wiederholen
Sie die Übung auch mit der anderen Seite.

Übung 3

Suggestion If you have a lively class and a suitable
space, have students try out the exercises described.

Po *glutes* **aufrecht** *upright* **hüftweit** *hip-wide* **Oberkörper** *upper body* **Schräge** *Oblique*
Unterschenkel *lower leg* **Verschränken** *Cross* **berührt** *touches*

Nach dem Lesen

Was fehlt? Ergänzen Sie die Sätze.

1. Andi war heute beim _____Arzt_____.
2. Andi muss besser essen und mehr _____Sport_____ treiben.
3. Andi darf nicht so viel _____Stress_____ in seinem Leben haben.
4. Die Übungen, die Andi gefunden hat, sind für _____Bauch_____ und Po.
5. In der zweiten Übung verschränkt man die _____Hände_____ hinter dem Kopf.
6. In der dritten Übung berühren Hände und _____Knie_____ den Boden.

Richtig oder falsch? Sind die Sätze richtig oder falsch? Korrigieren Sie die falschen Sätze.

Sample answers are provided.

	richtig	falsch
1. Andis Arzt sagt, dass alles in Ordnung ist. Der Arzt sagt, dass Andi gesünder leben muss.	☐	☑
2. Andi muss sich mehr bewegen.	☑	☐
3. Andi will jeden Tag joggen gehen. Andi will 3 Mal die Woche joggen gehen.	☐	☑
4. Andi will jeden Tag mindestens 7 Stunden schlafen.	☑	☐
5. Vor der ersten Übung soll man die Muskeln aufwärmen.	☑	☐
6. In der ersten Übung liegt man mit dem Gesicht nach unten. In der ersten Übung liegt man auf dem Rücken.	☐	☑
7. In der zweiten Übung trainiert man die Rückenmuskeln. In der zweiten Übung trainiert man die Bauchmuskeln.	☐	☑
8. Alle Übungen kann man in 5 Minuten machen. Alle Übungen kann man in 10 Minuten machen.	☐	☑

Bessere Gesundheit Diskutieren Sie
mit einem Partner / einer Partnerin: Sie wollen
gesünder leben. Was müssen Sie machen? Welche
Ziele (*goals*) haben Sie? Wie können Sie diese Ziele
erreichen (*achieve*)?

BEISPIEL

S1: *Ich muss endlich gesünder leben.*
S2: *Was willst du machen?*
S1: *Ich will...*

Hören

Strategien

Using background information

Once you figure out the topic of a conversation, take a minute to consider what you already know about the subject. Using this background information will help you guess the meaning of unknown words or linguistic structures.

 To help you practice this strategy, you will listen to a short commercial. Once you figure out the topic, use your knowledge of the subject to listen for and jot down the main points mentioned.

Vorbereitung

Wie ist es, mit anderen Menschen zusammenzuwohnen? Schreiben Sie vier Dinge auf, die man mit Mitbewohnern planen oder diskutieren muss, damit das Zusammenwohnen ohne Probleme funktioniert. Answers will vary.

Zuhören

 Hören Sie sich den Dialog zwischen Marco, Annette und Simone an. Worüber diskutieren sie? Schreiben Sie mindestens sechs Sachen auf. Sample answers are provided.

Frühstück machen
Küche sauber machen
Badezimmer benutzen
Abfall raustragen
Zeitung lesen
Geschirr spülen

Verständnis

 Richtig oder falsch Sind die Sätze richtig oder falsch? Korrigieren Sie die falschen Sätze. Sample answers are provided.

1. Marco, Simone und Annette wohnen in einer Wohnung zusammen.
   Richtig.

2. Marco möchte um 7 Uhr ins Badezimmer.
   Falsch. Simone möchte um 7 Uhr ins Badezimmer.

3. Alle Personen bleiben 20 Minuten im Badezimmer.
   Falsch. Marco bleibt nur 15 Minuten im Badezimmer.

4. Simone wird sich nicht im Badezimmer schminken.
   Richtig.

5. Annette muss das Frühstück um 7 Uhr machen.
   Falsch. Annette muss das Frühstück vor 7 Uhr machen.

6. Um 7.20 Uhr darf Annette ins Badezimmer.
   Richtig.

7. Simone muss den Abfall runterbringen.
   Falsch. Annette muss den Abfall runterbringen.

8. Marco liest jeden Morgen Zeitung.
   Richtig.

 Morgenroutine Sie und Ihre Partner / Partnerinnen wohnen in einer Wohngemeinschaft (WG) zusammen. Wie funktioniert das Zusammenleben? Wer benutzt wann das Bad? Wie lange? Wie organisieren Sie das Frühstück? Wer räumt auf? Planen Sie die WG-Regeln.

BEISPIEL

S1: Zuerst müssen wir über das Badezimmer sprechen.
S2: Ich möchte als Erster ins Badezimmer.
S3: Und wann?
S1: Kann ich es um 7 Uhr benutzen?

Schreiben

Strategien

Using linking words

You can make your writing more sophisticated by using linking words (**Verbindungswörter**) to connect simple sentences or clauses, creating more complex sentences.

Consider these two passages.

Heute Morgen war ich beim Arzt. Ich hatte starke Kopfschmerzen. Ich hatte einen schlimmen Schnupfen. Es waren viele Leute im Wartezimmer. Ich musste über eine Stunde warten. Der Arzt hat mich behandelt. Er hat gesagt, dass ich eine Grippe habe.

Heute Morgen war ich beim Arzt, **denn** ich hatte starke Kopfschmerzen und einen schlimmen Schnupfen. Es waren viele Leute im Wartezimmer. **Deshalb** musste ich über eine Stunde warten. **Endlich** hat der Arzt mich behandelt. Er hat gesagt, dass ich eine Grippe habe.

Expansion Have students work in groups to create a plan and then pitch it to the rest of the class in a Q & A session.

Bio-Produkte haben's drauf.

Thema

 Unsere neue Firma

 Sie wollen eine Firma im Bereich Gesundheit gründen und brauchen einen Businessplan. Die neue Firma kann ein Fitness-Center, ein Wellness-Center, ein Bioladen (*health-food store*) oder etwas Ähnliches sein.

Schreiben Sie einen Businessplan für potentielle Investoren. Bevor Sie anfangen, überlegen Sie sich Antworten auf die folgenden Fragen:

- Warum gibt es Ihre Firma?
- Welche Art von Service oder welche Produkte bieten Sie an (*offer*)?
- Warum braucht man diesen Service oder diese Produkte?
- Wer sind die Kunden Ihrer Firma?
- Wie erfüllt Ihre Firma die Bedürfnisse (*needs*) Ihrer Kunden?
- Wie ist Ihre Firma anders als ähnliche Firmen?
- Wie heißt Ihre Firma?

Benutzen Sie Verbindungswörter, damit die Präsentation Ihrer Geschäftsidee überzeugend (*persuasive*) wird.

Verbindungswörter			
aber	*but*	**deswegen**	*that's why*
als erstes	*first*	**endlich**	*finally*
also	*so*	**manchmal**	*sometimes*
außerdem	*moreover*	**normalerweise**	*usually*
danach	*then, after that*	**oder**	*or*
dann	*then*	**oft**	*often*
denn	*because*	**sondern**	*however*
deshalb	*so*	**sowie**	*as well as*

Vocabulary Tools

Lektion 9A

der Körper
body

der Arm, -e *arm*
das Auge, -n *eye*
die Augenbraue, -n *eyebrow*
der Bart, ⸚e *beard*
der Bauch, ⸚e *belly*
das Bein, -e *leg*
der Ell(en)bogen, - *elbow*
der Finger, - *finger*
der Fuß, ⸚e *foot*
das Gesicht, -er *face*
das Haar, -e *hair*
der Hals, ⸚e *neck*
die Hand, ⸚e *hand*
das Knie, - *knee*
der Kopf, ⸚e *head*
die Lippe, -n *lip*
der Mund, ⸚er *mouth*
die Nase, -n *nose*
das Ohr, -en *ear*
der Rücken, - *back*
die Schulter, -n *shoulder*
der Zeh, -en *toe*

Verben

aufwachen (wacht...auf) *to wake up*
(sich) duschen *to take a shower*
ins Bett gehen *to go to bed*
sich anziehen (zieht sich...an)
    to get dressed
sich die Haare bürsten *to brush
    one's hair*
sich die Zähne putzen *to brush
    one's teeth*
sich rasieren *to shave*
sich schminken *to put on makeup*

im Badezimmer
bathroom

der Bademantel, ⸚ *bathrobe*
die Bürste, -n *brush*
der Haartrockner, - *hair dryer*
das Handtuch, ⸚er *towel*
der Hausschuh, -e *slipper*
der Kamm, ⸚e *comb*
der Lippenstift, -e *lipstick*
der Rasierer, - *razor*
der Rasierschaum *shaving cream*
der Schlafanzug, ⸚e *pajamas*
die Seife, -n *soap*
das Shampoo, -s *shampoo*
die Zahnbürste, -n *toothbrush*
die Zahnpasta
    (*pl.* Zahnpasten) *toothpaste*

Accusative reflexive pronouns
    See pp. 374–375.
Dative reflexive pronouns
    See pp. 378–379.
Reflexives used with prepositions
    See pp. 382–383.

Lektion 9B

im Krankenhaus
hospital

der Arzt, ⸚e / die Ärztin, -nen *doctor*
die Grippe, -n *flu*
der Krankenpfleger, - *nurse (m.)*
die Krankenschwester, -n *nurse (f.)*
der Krankenwagen, - *ambulance*
das Medikament, -e *medicine*
die Notaufnahme, -n *emergency room*
der Patient, -en / die Patientin,
    -nen *patient*
das Pflaster, -e *adhesive bandage*
das Rezept, -e *prescription*
die Tablette, -n *pill*
das Taschentuch, ⸚er *tissue*
das Thermometer, - *thermometer*
die Verletzung, -en *injury*
der Zahnarzt, ⸚e / die Zahnärztin,
    -nen *dentist*
sich (das Handgelenk / den Fuß)
    verstauchen *to sprain (one's
    wrist/ankle)*
sich (den Arm / das Bein) brechen *to
    break (an arm / a leg)*
eine Spritze geben *to give a shot*
weh tun (tut...weh) *to hurt*
weinen *to cry*
gesund *healthy*
krank *sick*
schwanger *pregnant*

Der Konjunktiv II

wünschen *to wish*

die Gesundheit
health

die Allergie, -n *allergy*
die Apotheke, -n *pharmacy*
die Erkältung, -en *cold*
allergisch sein (gegen) *to be
    allergic (to)*
krank/gesund werden *to get sick/better*
in guter/schlechter Form sein *to be in/
    out of shape*
sich verletzen *to hurt oneself*
Sport treiben *to exercise*
zum Arzt gehen *to go to the doctor*

Symptome
symptoms

die Bauchschmerzen (*pl.*) *stomachache*
die Kopfschmerzen (*pl.*) *headache*
die Rückenschmerzen (*pl.*) *backache*
der Schmerz, -en *pain*
die verstopfte Nase *stuffy nose*
die Zahnschmerzen (*pl.*) *toothache*
Fieber haben *to have a fever*
husten *to cough*
niesen *to sneeze*
leicht *mild*
schwer *serious*
schwindlig *dizzy*
übel *nauseous*

Der Konjunktiv II See pp. 396–397.
würden See pp. 400–401.

More activities

vhlcentral | Online activities

Stadtleben

COMMUNICATIVE GOALS
By the end of this chapter you will be able to:

🔊 **Los geht's!** Was machen Hans, George, Meline und Sabite?

LEKTION 10A

Talk about errands and banking.
Talk about businesses and places in town.

To do so, you will use:

Kontext Seite 414–417
- Places of business and government buildings
- Words and phrases related to running errands

Strukturen Seite 422–430
10A.1 Subordinating conjunctions
10A.2 Adjectives used as nouns
10A.3 Das Futur I

You will also learn about cultural products, practices, and perspectives related to:

Kultur Seite 420–421
- **Die Fußgängerzonen**
- **Die Heimat**
- **Die Deutsche Post**

Kurzfilm Seite 431–433
- *Bienenstich ist aus*

LEKTION 10B

Ask for and give directions.
Talk about parts of a city.

To do so, you will use:

Kontext Seite 434–437
- Words and phrases related to asking for and giving directions
- City traffic and buildings

Strukturen Seite 442–449
10B.1 Prepositions of direction
10B.2 Talking about nationality

You will also learn about cultural products, practices, and perspectives related to:

Kultur Seite 440–441
- **Das Kabarett**
- **Die Religion**
- **Matthias Schweighöfer**

WEITER GEHT'S

Seite 450–456
You will learn about Niedersachsen und Nordrhein-Westfalen, their industries, tourist attractions, and famous inhabitants.

Panorama Seite 450–451
- **Niedersachsen und Nordrhein-Westfalen**

And you will demonstrate that you can:
Lesen: Recognize and understand the use of repetition in poems
Hören: Guess the meaning of words from context
Schreiben: Use note cards to organize research information

Besorgungen Vocabulary Tools

Wortschatz

Orte	places
das Blumengeschäft, -e	flower shop
die Drogerie, -n	drugstore
das Kino, -s	movie theater
die Polizeiwache, -n	police station
das Rathaus, ¨er	town hall
der Waschsalon, -s	laundromat
geöffnet	open
geschlossen	closed

Suggestion Model the pronunciation of **Waschsalon**.

die Post	mail
die Adresse, -n	address
die Briefmarke, -n	stamp
der Briefumschlag, ¨e	envelope
die Postkarte, -n	postcard

in der Bank	at the bank
das Geld	money
das Kleingeld	change
das Konto (*pl.* die Konten)	bank account
die Münze, -n	coin
Geld abheben	to withdraw money
Geld einzahlen	to deposit money

Ausdrücke	expressions
das Bargeld	cash
bar bezahlen	to pay in cash
Besorgungen machen	to run errands
ein Formular ausfüllen	to fill out a form
mit der Karte bezahlen	to pay by (credit) card
unterschreiben	to sign

ACHTUNG

Post is short for **das Postamt, ¨er** or **die Postfiliale, -n**. It is also used to refer to the mail in general: **Wann kommt die Post?** *When does the mail arrive?*

Suggestion Ask students if they ever send or receive letters. Tell them that a pen pal is a **Brieffreund** or **Brieffreundin**.

Suggestion Point out the separable-prefix verbs on this page: **abschicken, abheben, einzahlen, ausfüllen**. Remind students that these are listed in the end-of-chapter **Wortschatz** with their 3rd-person forms in parentheses. Tell students that **unterschreiben** is an inseparable-prefix verb, and ask them to guess its past-tense forms.

das Schreibwarengeschäft, -e

das Juweliergeschäft, -e

das Internetcafé, -s

die Post

das Paket, -e

der Briefkasten, ¨

Sie schickt einen Brief ab.
(abschicken)
She is mailing a letter.

der Kiosk, -e

die Zeitschrift, -en
magazine

die Zeitung, -en
newspaper

More activities

| vhlcentral | WB pp. 131–132 | LM p. 84 | Online activities |

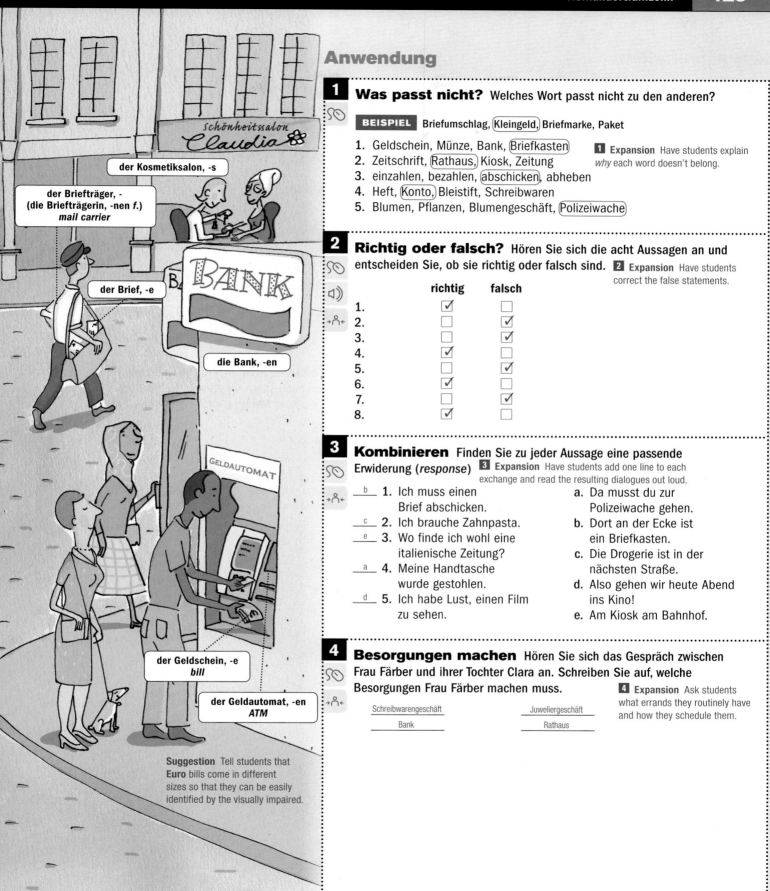

Anwendung

1 Was passt nicht? Welches Wort passt nicht zu den anderen?

BEISPIEL Briefumschlag, Kleingeld, Briefmarke, Paket

1. Geldschein, Münze, Bank, Briefkasten
2. Zeitschrift, Rathaus, Kiosk, Zeitung
3. einzahlen, bezahlen, abschicken, abheben
4. Heft, Konto, Bleistift, Schreibwaren
5. Blumen, Pflanzen, Blumengeschäft, Polizeiwache

1 Expansion Have students explain *why* each word doesn't belong.

2 Richtig oder falsch? Hören Sie sich die acht Aussagen an und entscheiden Sie, ob sie richtig oder falsch sind. **2** Expansion Have students correct the false statements.

	richtig	falsch
1.	☑	☐
2.	☐	☑
3.	☐	☑
4.	☑	☐
5.	☐	☑
6.	☑	☐
7.	☐	☑
8.	☑	☐

3 Kombinieren Finden Sie zu jeder Aussage eine passende Erwiderung (*response*) **3** Expansion Have students add one line to each exchange and read the resulting dialogues out loud.

_b_ 1. Ich muss einen Brief abschicken.

_c_ 2. Ich brauche Zahnpasta.

_e_ 3. Wo finde ich wohl eine italienische Zeitung?

_a_ 4. Meine Handtasche wurde gestohlen.

_d_ 5. Ich habe Lust, einen Film zu sehen.

a. Da musst du zur Polizeiwache gehen.

b. Dort an der Ecke ist ein Briefkasten.

c. Die Drogerie ist in der nächsten Straße.

d. Also gehen wir heute Abend ins Kino!

e. Am Kiosk am Bahnhof.

4 Besorgungen machen Hören Sie sich das Gespräch zwischen Frau Färber und ihrer Tochter Clara an. Schreiben Sie auf, welche Besorgungen Frau Färber machen muss. **4** Expansion Ask students what errands they routinely have and how they schedule them.

Schreibwarengeschäft _____ Juweliergeschäft _____

Bank _____ Rathaus _____

Kommunikation

Besorgungen Bringen Sie mit Ihrem Partner / Ihrer Partnerin die folgenden Sätze in eine logische Reihenfolge. Spielen Sie den Dialog dann im Kurs vor.

__7__ **MICHAELA** Ja, ich muss dir nämlich unbedingt erzählen, wen ich im Juweliergeschäft gesehen habe.

__3__ **MICHAELA** Weißt du was? Ich gehe mit dir auf die Post. Ich brauche sowieso Briefmarken. Und danach gehe ich dann auf die Bank, Geld abheben.

__6__ **JULIA** Klar, für einen Kaffee immer. Dann können wir uns dabei auch noch ein bisschen unterhalten.

__2__ **JULIA** Ich muss ein paar Besorgungen machen. Ich muss auf die Post, ein Paket an meine Freundin abschicken, und dann wollte ich noch nach einem Geburtstagsgeschenk für meinen Bruder suchen.

__1__ **MICHAELA** Hallo Julia! Was machst du heute Schönes in der Stadt?

__4__ **JULIA** Du, dort auf der anderen Straßenseite ist ein Geldautomat. Ich will auch noch Bargeld holen.

__8__ **JULIA** Ach ja?! Da bin ich jetzt aber neugierig. Also komm!

__5__ **MICHAELA** Okay, dann lass uns das schnell machen und dann können wir ja noch im Wiener Café einen Kaffee trinken. Hast du Zeit und Lust?

Definitionen Schreiben Sie zuerst zu jedem Begriff eine Definition und lesen Sie sie Ihrem Partner / Ihrer Partnerin vor. Er/sie muss dann den passenden Begriff aus der unten stehenden Liste identifizieren. Suggested answers provided.

BEISPIEL

6 Partner Chat You can also assign activity 6 on the Supersite.

S1: Es ist ein Automat, wo man Geld abheben kann.
S2: Ein Geldautomat!

1. Internetcafé Es ist kein Café, wo man nur Kaffee trinkt, sondern wo man im Internet surft.
2. Briefmarken Man macht sie auf einen Briefumschlag, um einen Brief abzuschicken.
3. Kiosk Hier kauft man Zeitungen und Zeitschriften.
4. Kreditkarte Mit ihr kann man ohne Bargeld bezahlen.
5. Briefträger Diese Person bringt die Post ans Haus.
6. Waschsalon Hier stehen viele Waschmaschinen und Wäschetrockner.

---

7 Diskutieren und kombinieren Sie und Ihr Partner / Ihre Partnerin bekommen zwei verschiedene Blätter von Ihrem Professor / Ihrer Professorin. Erzählen Sie abwechselnd, wohin Anna geht und was sie macht. Suggested answers provided.

BEISPIEL

S1: Um zehn Uhr geht Anna auf die Post, um Briefmarken zu kaufen.
S2: Danach...

7 Expansion Ask students to compare their day with Anna's. Ex.: **Haben Sie etwas gemacht, was Anna gemacht hat? Sind Sie auf die Post gegangen?**

---

8 Die perfekte Stadt Wählen Sie mit zwei Mitstudenten mindestens (*at least*) sechs Orte und Geschäfte, die Ihrer Meinung nach zu einer perfekten Stadt gehören. Answers will vary.

BEISPIEL

S1: Für mich muss es in einer perfekten Stadt ein Internetcafé geben.
S2: Gute Idee. Ich hätte auch gern eine leckere Konditorei.
S3: Ach, das ist doch nicht so wichtig! Was ich brauche, ist ...

Aussprache und Rechtschreibung

 Audio

The Glottal Stop

The glottal stop is the sound you hear in the middle of the English phrase *uh oh*. In German, there is a glottal stop before all words that begin with a vowel.

obwohl	Ampel	Innenstadt	abbiegen	einkaufen

Glottal stops occur within words, when one syllable ends with a vowel and the next syllable begins with a vowel. They also occur in compound words, when the second part of the compound begins with a vowel.

geradeaus	beeilen	Geldautomat	Zahnarzt	Wochenende

A glottal stop also occurs when one syllable of a word ends with a consonant and the next syllable begins with a vowel.

nachahmen	überall	nebenan	überaus	bergab

Suggestion Point out that the glottal stop is also used in English before words beginning with vowel sounds. Write the sentence *I eat an egg at eight*. Have students try saying it without using glottal stops between the words.

---

1 Aussprechen Wiederholen Sie die Wörter, die Sie hören.

1. abheben
2. Orte
3. einzahlen
4. Ecke
5. bearbeiten
6. Schlafanzug
7. Hausaufgaben
8. Freizeitaktivität
9. Mittagessen
10. hinab
11. fortan
12. bergauf

2 Nachsprechen Wiederholen Sie die Sätze, die Sie hören.

1. Auch am Abend kann man Geld vom Geldautomaten abheben.
2. Am Wochenende arbeitet Amanda in der Apotheke.
3. Im Internetcafé essen acht Engländer Erdbeereis.
4. Auf dem Briefumschlag steht die Adresse allerdings nicht.
5. Fortan bearbeitet ihr alles vor Ort.
6. Das Nadelöhr am Autobahndreieck wird ab morgen ausgebaut.

3 Sprichwörter Wiederholen Sie die Sprichwörter, die Sie hören.

Erst die Arbeit, dann das Vergnügen.[1]

Unkraut vergeht nicht.[2]

[1] Business before pleasure.
[2] Bad weeds grow tall. (*lit.,* Weeds don't die.)

More activities

vhlcentral | LM p. 85 | Online activities

Gute Neuigkeiten Video

Sabite bekommt einen Anruf vom Manager der Galerie. Die Freunde wollen die guten
Neuigkeiten feiern. Dann erzählt George von seinem Kuss mit Sabite...

Vorbereitung Have students read the title
of the episode and discuss in pairs what they
think will happen in the episode.

HANS Sind wir an einer Bank vorbeigekommen?
Ich muss Geld vom Bankautomaten abheben.
GEORGE Ich zahle nie bar. Ich zahle mit
meiner Bankkarte.
HANS Immer wenn ich eine Zeitung oder einen
Kaffee kaufe, zahle ich bar. Ich vergesse
immer, die kleinen Artikel aufzuschreiben, und
dann geht mir das Geld auf dem Bankkonto
aus. Ich gebe jede Woche gleich viel aus.
GEORGE Ich habe auf der anderen
Straßenseite eine Bank gesehen, dort.

MELINE Hallo? Oh, hallo Sabite. Was
gibt's Neues? Gutes oder Schlechtes?
Okay, okay. Ich komme gerade aus dem
Salon und treffe dich in einer Stunde im
Biergarten. Bis dann. „Ich sage es dir,
wenn ich dich sehe." Künstler sind
so dramatisch.

HANS Was musst du heute Nachmittag sonst
noch erledigen?
GEORGE Ich muss zur Post gehen und diese
Karten abschicken. Als ich die USA verlassen
habe, habe ich meiner kleinen Schwester Olivia
versprochen, ihr Postkarten zu schicken. Ich
habe sie schon geschrieben, habe sie aber noch
nicht in den Briefkasten geworfen.

GEORGE Hallo Sabite. Hat er angerufen?
Okay... okay. Wir sehen uns dann im
Biergarten. Das brauchst du nicht, er
steht direkt hier. Alles klar. Tschüss.
Sabite hat Neuigkeiten von der Galerie in
der Torstraße bekommen. Sie wollte sie
nicht am Telefon sagen. Wir werden beim
Blumengeschäft Halt machen müssen.

HANS Das müssen um die 20 Karten
sein. ... Potsdamer Platz, Alexanderplatz,
Brandenburger Tor, Jüdisches Museum,
Checkpoint Charlie...
GEORGE Ich werde sie in ein Päckchen legen
mit etwas Schokolade und diesem hier.

SABITE Es geht ihr jetzt wieder gut. Ja, was
komisch ist, ist, dass sie nach Hans gefragt
hat, als sie aufgewacht ist. Ich weiß. Ich
weiß. Oh, Mama, ich muss auflegen. Ich habe
auf diesen Anruf gewartet. Ok, ich gebe dir
Bescheid. Tschüss. Hallo, hier ist Sabite.
Guten Tag, Herr Kleinedler, wie geht es Ihnen?

1 Wer ist das? Welche Person(en) beschreiben die folgenden Sätze:
George, Hans, Meline oder Sabite?

1. __Hans__ muss Geld vom Bankautomaten abheben.

2. __George__ zahlt nie bar, sondern immer mit der Karte.

3. __Hans__ gibt jede Woche gleich viel Geld aus.

4. __George__ muss zur Post gehen und Karten abschicken.

5. __George__ will ein Päckchen mit Schokolade abschicken.

6. __Sabite__ bekommt einen Anruf von Herrn Kleinedler.

7. __Meline__ kommt gerade aus dem Salon.

8. __George__ möchte beim Blumengeschäft Halt machen.

9. __George__ erzählt Hans von dem Kuss.

10. __Sabite__ hat gute Neuigkeiten von der Galerie.

PERSONEN

 George Hans Meline Sabite

7

HANS Immer wenn etwas passiert, ruft sie dich an.
GEORGE Wir sind Freunde.
HANS Mehr nicht?
GEORGE Nein. Als wir uns geküsst haben, da wussten wir beide...
HANS Als ihr was?

8

GEORGE Wenn ich richtig liege, hast du gute Neuigkeiten. Komisch, ich habe es in deiner Stimme gehört, als du angerufen hast.
MELINE Herzlichen Glückwunsch, Sabite!

9

SABITE Danke. Wow. Wo ist Hans?
GEORGE Er, ähm...
MELINE Er hat ein Problem mit der Beziehung zwischen... dir und George.
SABITE Welche Beziehung? Wir sind Freunde.
GEORGE Ich habe ihm aus Versehen von unserem Kuss erzählt.

10

MELINE Von was?
SABITE Oh, George, wie konntest du nur?
GEORGE Frauen bringen mich ganz durcheinander.
MELINE So soll es ja auch sein. Hast du Hunger? Lass uns bestellen.

Nützliche Ausdrücke

- **vorbeikommen**
  to pass
- **aufschreiben**
  to write down
- **erledigen**
  to run an errand
- **verlassen**
  to leave
- **versprechen**
  to promise
- **einen Brief einwerfen**
  to mail a letter
- **das Päckchen**
  little package
- **auflegen**
  to hang up
- **Halt machen**
  to stop by
- **raten**
  to guess
- **die Beziehung**
  relationship
- **aus Versehen**
  by mistake
- **durcheinanderbringen**
  to confuse

10A.1
- **Ich werde sie in ein Päckchen legen mit etwas Schokolade und diesem hier.**
  I'm going to put them all in a little package with some chocolate and this.

10A.2
- **Was gibt's Neues? Gutes oder Schlechtes?**
  What's the news? Is it good or bad?

10A.3
- **Wenn ich richtig rate, hast du gute Neuigkeiten.**
  If I'm right, you have good news.

---

2 **Zum Besprechen** Machen Sie zu zweit Pläne für einen Tag in der Stadt. Entscheiden Sie, wohin Sie gehen und was Sie machen wollen. Erklären Sie Ihre Entscheidungen. Answers will vary.

2 **Expansion** Have students act out their dialogue in front of the class.

3 **Vertiefung** In den deutschsprachigen Ländern wird der Begriff ‚Kreditkarte' anders verwendet als in den USA. Benutzen Sie das Internet, um herauszufinden, wo genau die Unterschiede (*differences*) liegen.
Suggested answer: In German-speaking countries, the term refers to real credit cards as well as debit, prepaid, or charge cards.

More activities

vhlcentral | VM p. 19 | Online activities

IM FOKUS

Fußgängerzonen° Reading

IN VIELEN EUROPÄISCHEN STÄDTEN findet man im Stadtzentrum oder in der historischen Altstadt eine Fußgängerzone, in der man nur zu Fuß gehen darf. Radfahrer müssen langsam fahren oder das Fahrrad schieben°, und Autos dürfen hier nur fahren, wenn sie Geschäfte in der Fußgängerzone beliefern° oder zur Polizei, Feuerwehr oder anderen Notdiensten° gehören. Aber auch sie müssen hier Schritttempo° fahren und sehr vorsichtig sein.

Viele Leute kommen in die Fußgängerzone, weil man in den vielen Geschäften gut einkaufen und in schönen Cafés oder Restaurants im Freien sitzen kann.

Die erste Fußgängerzone Europas gibt es seit 1953 in der Lijnbaan im holländischen Rotterdam. Im selben Jahr eröffnete man in der Kasseler Treppenstraße, die erste Fußgängerzone Deutschlands. Nachdem große Teile Kassels während des Zweiten Weltkriegs zerstört wurden°, gab es einen Wiederaufbauwettbewerb°, um die Innenstadt Kassels neu zu gestalten°. 1961 folgte in Klagenfurt die erste Fußgängerzone in Österreich: die Kramergasse.

Historische Innenstädte° in Deutschland	
Dresden	Im 2. Weltkrieg wurde Dresden fast komplett zerstört. Heute kann man in der Altstadt wieder die Semperoper, den Zwinger und die Frauenkirche besuchen.
Heidelberg	Heidelberg, die Stadt mit der ältesten Universität im heutigen Deutschland, hat die längste Fußgängerzone Deutschlands.
Köln	Die Schildergasse in Köln ist die meistbesuchte Einkaufsmeile Europas.
Regensburg	Die Regensburger Altstadt geht auf die Römer° zurück. Das Schloss der Familie von Thurn und Taxis, die die erste Post in Deutschland gründete, ist Teil dieser Altstadt.

Fußgängerzonen *traffic-free zones* **schieben** *push* **beliefern** *supply* **Notdiensten** *emergency services* **Schritttempo** *walking pace* **zerstört wurden** *were destroyed* **Wiederaufbauwettbewerb** *reconstruction competition* **gestalten** *design* **Innenstädte** *city centers* **Römer** *Romans*

ÜBUNGEN

1 **Im Fokus** Richtig oder falsch? Korrigieren Sie die falschen Aussagen. Diskutieren Sie dann die letzte Frage mit einem Partner/ einer Partnerin.

1. Fußgängerzonen findet man meistens in der Innenstadt. **Richtig.**
2. Autos dürfen in den Fußgängerzonen fahren, wenn sie langsam fahren. **Falsch.** Nur sehr wenige Autos, zum Beispiel Polizeiautos, dürfen dort fahren.
3. Die Stadt Rotterdam hatte die erste Fußgängerzone in Europa. **Richtig.**

Diskussion Wo gehen Sie in Ihrer Stadt gern spazieren? Was möchten Sie dort sehen und machen?

 1 Diskussion Introduce the term **der Stadtbummel** *window shopping* and explain the German tradition to go for a walk through town on Sunday or when stores are closed to look at the window displays. Have students reflect on pros and cons of limited store hours.

2 **Die deutschsprachige Welt** Richtig oder falsch? Korrigieren Sie die falschen Aussagen.

1. Für Deutsche ist Heimat auch ein Ort, wo sie oft Urlaub machen. **Falsch.** Heimat ist der Ort, wo sie geboren und aufgewachsen sind.
2. An einem Heimatort haben oft schon viele Generationen der Familie gelebt. **Richtig.**
3. Deutsche, Schweizer und Österreicher assoziieren ihre Heimat oft mit ihrer Region und ihrem Dialekt. **Richtig.**

Diskussion Wie definieren Sie den Begriff (*term*) Heimat?

DEUTSCH IM ALLTAG

Geschäfte

der Antiquitätenladen	antiques shop
der Buchladen	bookshop
der Makler	real estate agent
der Schneider	tailor
der Schuster	shoemaker
das Spielwarengeschäft	toy store

DIE DEUTSCHSPRACHIGE WELT

Heimat

Für Deutsche, Österreicher und Schweizer ist Heimat ein sehr wichtiger Begriff°. Es ist der Ort, wo man geboren und aufgewachsen ist. Oft haben an diesem Ort schon mehrere Generationen einer Familie gelebt. Heimat bedeutet aber auch die Sprache, die man spricht, und zwar nicht nur Deutsch, sondern auch den Dialekt der Region. Heimat sind auch die Traditionen der Region. Im Allgemeinen ist Heimat ein sehr emotionales Konzept. Man kann dieses Wort nicht direkt ins Englische übersetzen. Oft sagt man *home* oder *homeland*.

Suggestion Ask students what place they consider home and why.
Begriff *term*

PORTRÄT

Die Deutsche Post

Die Post hat in Deutschland eine lange Tradition. Seit 1615 organisierte die Familie Thurn und Taxis in Deutschland den Postverkehr. Aus dieser Zeit stammt° auch das Symbol der Post: das Posthorn. Reiter benutzten es, wenn sie in Städte oder über Grenzen ritten. Ab 1660 führte die Familie Thurn und Taxis eine Fahrpost ein°, mit der sie Briefe und Personen beförderte°. Die erste Strecke führte von Halle über Magdeburg nach Hamburg. Ab 1710 gab es die ersten Briefträger in Deutschland und ab 1874 gab es dann in ganz Deutschland auch Briefkästen an Häusern. Heute ist die Deutsche Post kein staatliches Unternehmen° mehr, sondern eine private Aktiengesellschaft°.

Suggestion Point out that the **Deutsche Post** has become one of the world's largest courier companies.
stammt *stems* **führte ... ein** *instituted* **beförderten** *transported* **Unternehmen** *organization* **Aktiengesellschaft** *corporation*

IM INTERNET

Suchen Sie im Internet Informationen über eine bekannte Innenstadt in Deutschland. Was können Touristen und Besucher hier alles machen? Welche Geschäfte gibt es? Welche anderen Attraktionen?

Find out more at **vhlcentral.com**.

---

3 **Porträt** Richtig oder falsch? Korrigieren Sie die falschen Aussagen. Diskutieren Sie dann die letzte Frage mit einem Partner/ einer Partnerin.

1. Die Familie Thurn und Taxis hat 1615 in der Schweiz die erste Post organisiert. **Falsch.** Die Familie hat 1615 in Deutschland die erste Post organisiert.

2. Briefträger gibt es in Deutschland seit 1835. **Falsch.** Briefträger gibt es in Deutschland seit 1710.

3. Die erste deutsche Poststrecke ging von Halle über Magdeburg nach Hamburg. **Richtig.**

Diskussion Wo ist die Post in Ihrer Stadt? Waren Sie schon einmal da? Welche Paketdienste (*package delivery services*) benutzen Sie?

4 **Heimat** Was bedeutet Heimat für Sie? Können Sie Ihre Idee von Heimat – neben Ort, Region und Dialekt – auch mit anderen Traditionen assoziieren, zum Beispiel mit einer anderen Sprache, einer Küche (*cuisine*) oder auch mit Musik? Schreiben Sie einen kurzen Aufsatz über Ihre Heimat.

More activities

vhlcentral   Online activities

10A.1

Subordinating conjunctions Grammar Tutorial

You might want to assign the grammar tutorial **10A.1 Subordinating conjunctions** on the Supersite for students to watch before they come to class.

Suggestion Have students find the conjugated verbs in each example on this page. Ask if they notice a pattern.

Startblock Coordinating conjunctions combine two independent clauses in a single sentence. Use subordinating conjunctions to combine a subordinate clause with a main clause.

„Ich sage es dir, **wenn** ich dich sehe."

Wenn ich richtig rate, hast du gute Neuigkeiten.

QUERVERWEIS

See **6A.3** to review coordinating conjunctions. See **8A.1** to review the use of the subordinating conjunctions **bevor**, **nachdem**, and **als** with the **Plusquamperfekt**. See **9B.1** to review the use of the subordinating conjunction **wenn** in hypothetical statements.

- A subordinate clause explains how, when, why, or under what circumstances the action in the main clause occurs. Subordinate clauses always begin with a subordinating conjunction and normally end with the conjugated verb. Always use a comma to separate the subordinate clause from the main clause.

MAIN CLAUSE	SUBORDINATE CLAUSE
Ich lese die Zeitung,	**wenn** ich Zeit **habe**.
I read the newspaper	*when I **have** the time.*

Suggestion Tell students that **obwohl** is the "conjunction of contradictions." Give examples, ex: **Obwohl ich krank war, musste ich zu Arbeit gehen**.

- Here is a list of commonly used subordinating conjunctions:

subordinating conjunctions			
als	*as, when*	ob	*whether, if*
bevor	*before*	obwohl	*although*
bis	*until*	seit	*since*
damit	*so that*	während	*while; whereas*
dass	*that*	weil	*because*
nachdem	*after*	wenn	*when; whenever; if*

ACHTUNG

The conjunctions **denn** and **weil** both mean *because*. Since **denn** is a coordinating conjunction, it does not affect word order: **Ich komme nicht, denn ich bin krank.** Since **weil** is a subordinating conjunction, the verb moves to the end of the clause: **Ich komme nicht, weil ich krank bin.**

———

The conjunction **dass** is often used to report what somebody else said.

Jonas sagt, dass er seine Familie im Herbst besucht.

Vergiss nicht, **dass** wir nächste Woche ins Konzert **gehen**.
*Don't forget **that** we're going to a concert next week.*

Ich bezahle immer bar, **weil** ich keine Kreditkarte **habe**.
*I always pay cash, **because** I don't have a credit card.*

- When you begin a sentence with a subordinate clause, the entire clause is treated as the first element of the sentence. The verb in the main clause moves to second position, after the comma, and is followed by its subject.

Suggestion Remind students that the coordinating conjunctions *don't* cause subject-verb inversion and are simply inserted between two clauses.

SUBORDINATE CLAUSE	MAIN CLAUSE
Wenn ich nach Deutschland fahre,	**spreche** ich immer Deutsch.
Weil meine Familie deutsch ist,	**habe** ich als Kind Deutsch gelernt.
Obwohl ich Deutsch spreche,	**möchte** ich lieber in Italien wohnen.

- When using a separable prefix verb in a subordinate clause, attach the prefix to the beginning of the conjugated verb.

Ich **rufe dich** heute Abend **an**.
*I'll **call** you tonight.*

Ich warte, **bis** du mich **anrufst**.
*I'll wait **until** you **call** me.*

- When using a modal verb in a subordinate clause, put the conjugated form of the modal at the end of the clause, after the infinitive of the verb it modifies.

Wir **müssen** heute Nachmittag
Briefmarken **kaufen**.
*We **need to buy** stamps
this afternoon.*

Wir gehen zur Post, **weil** wir Briefmarken
kaufen müssen.
*We're going to the post office **because** we
need to buy stamps.*

- For a subordinate clause in the **Perfekt** or **Plusquamperfekt**, move the conjugated form of **sein** or **haben** to the end of the clause, after the past participle.

Ich **bin** heute früher nach
Hause **gegangen**.
*I **went** home early today.*

Ich habe Besorgungen gemacht, **bevor** ich
nach Hause **gegangen bin**.
*I ran some errands **before** I **went** home.*

- Use **als** to refer to a one-time event or continuing situation in the past. Use **wenn** to refer to a one-time event in the present or future. Use **(immer) wenn** to refer to a recurring event in the past, present, or future.

Als wir Kinder waren, gab uns Papa
Münzen aus anderen Ländern.
***When** we were kids, Dad used to give
us coins from other countries.*

Wenn du nächsten Sommer nach Hannover fährst,
musst du mir eine Postkarte schicken.
***When** you go to Hannover next summer, you'll
have to send me a postcard.*

Indirect questions

Expansion Write on the board: **ob** = *whether*. Then, have students complete the sentence, **Ich möchte wissen, ob…** and share their sentences.

- Indirect questions are a type of subordinate clause. They are introduced by a main clause beginning with a phrase such as **Weißt du**, **Ich möchte wissen**, **Kannst du mir sagen**, **Ich weiß nicht**, or **Ich frage mich**.

Ich möchte wissen, **ob** ich ein
Formular ausfüllen muss.
*I'd like to know **whether** I need
to fill out a form.*

Ich frage mich, **warum** es so viele
Internetcafés in Berlin gibt.
*I wonder **why** there are so many Internet
cafés in Berlin.*

Erzähl uns bitte, **was** passiert ist.
*Please tell us **what** happened.*

Sag mir, **wie viele** Briefmarken du brauchst.
*Tell me **how many** stamps you need.*

- Use the subordinating conjunction **ob** to ask indirect yes-or-no questions.

Wissen Sie, **ob** man hier mit der
Karte bezahlen kann?
*Do you know **if** I can pay by card here?*

Weißt du, **ob** die Post schon
da ist?
*Do you know **if** the mail has come yet?*

- For all other indirect questions, use the question words as subordinating conjunctions.

Sie wissen, **wohin** man gehen soll.
*They know **where** to go.*

Ich weiß, **wie** du dich fühlst.
*I know **how** you feel.*

QUERVERWEIS

See **1B.2** to review basic word order.

See **5B.2** to review the conjugations of the verb **wissen**.

See **2A.2** to review question words.

ACHTUNG

Both **ob** and **wenn** are sometimes translated as *if*, but only **ob** is used in indirect yes-or-no questions. Use **wann**, rather than **als** or **wenn**, to mean *when* in an indirect question.

Expansion Write two simple sentences, putting each word on a separate card. In class, distribute the cards and have students stand in the correct order to form the sentences. Then, add a card with a subordinating conjunction. Have students place the card between the sentences and rearrange themselves accordingly.

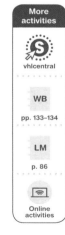

More
activities

vhlcentral

WB
pp. 133–134

LM
p. 86

Online
activities

Jetzt sind Sie dran! **Wählen Sie die richtigen Konjunktionen.**

1. Lara geht zur Post, (weil / ob) sie Briefmarken braucht.
2. Der Kunde erklärte der Verkäuferin, (dass / ob) er kein Kleingeld hat.
3. Ich habe ein Paket bekommen, (obwohl / ob) ich nichts bestellt habe.

4. (Damit / Nachdem) die Touristen im Internetcafé ihre E-Mails gelesen hatten, sind sie zum Hotel gegangen.
5. (Als / Bevor) man einen Brief abschickt, muss man die Adresse auf den Briefumschlag schreiben.
6. Weißt du, (ob / damit) es beim Kiosk noch Zeitungen gibt?

Anwendung

1 Ausflug nach München Ergänzen Sie die Sätze mit **als** oder **wenn**.

 BEISPIEL _Wenn_ wir nach München fahren, besuchen wir die Frauenkirche.

1. __Wenn__ es 12 Uhr mittags ist, sollte man am Münchner Rathaus das Glockenspiel anschauen.
2. __Als__ wir das letzte Mal in München waren, hat es nur geregnet.
3. __Wenn__ wir Ende September hier wären, könnten wir auch aufs Oktoberfest gehen.
4. Das erste Oktoberfest hat man 1810 gefeiert, __als__ Kronprinz Ludwig Prinzessin Therese heiratete.
5. Vielleicht fahren wir morgen zum Schloss Neuschwanstein, __wenn__ wir Zeit haben.
6. Ludwig II baute Schloss Neuschwanstein, __als__ er 1864 König (_king_) von Bayern wurde.

2 Suggestion Tell students that **Klatsch** means gossip.

2 Klatsch Schreiben Sie, was Anna sagt, und verbinden Sie die Sätze mit der Konjunktion **dass**.

BEISPIEL Mein kleiner Bruder will immer etwas kaputt machen.
Anna sagt, _dass ihr kleiner Bruder immer etwas kaputt machen will._

1. Max hat noch nie Sushi gegessen.
Anna sagt, dass Max noch nie Sushi gegessen hat.
2. Simon und Greta freuen sich nicht auf ihre Reise.
Anna sagt, dass Simon und Greta sich nicht auf ihre Reise freuen.
3. Die Katze hat eine Ratte im Garten gefangen.
Anna sagt, dass die Katze eine Ratte im Garten gefangen hat.
4. Die Eltern von Antonia haben sich getrennt.
Anna sagt, dass die Eltern von Antonia sich getrennt haben.
5. Mia kommt wegen Nina nicht auf die Feier mit.
Anna sagt, dass Mia wegen Nina nicht auf die Feier mitkommt.

3 Ein kurzes Interview Ändern Sie die direkten Fragen in indirekte Fragen um und verwenden Sie dabei die Ausdrücke aus der Liste. Sample answers provided.

BEISPIEL Warum lernst du Deutsch und nicht Spanisch?
Darf ich dich fragen, warum du Deutsch und nicht Spanisch lernst?

Darf ich dich fragen	Ich weiß nicht
Erzähl mir bitte	Kannst du mir sagen
Ich frage mich	Sag mir
Ich möchte gern wissen	Weißt du

1. Kommen deine Großeltern aus Deutschland?
Weißt du, ob deine Großeltern aus Deutschland kommen?
2. Hast du Geschwister?
Ich frage mich, ob du Geschwister hast.
3. Wie oft bist du schon nach Europa geflogen?
Sag mir, wie oft du schon nach Europa geflogen bist.
4. Welches Land möchtest du gern mal besuchen?
Erzähl mir bitte, welches Land du gern mal besuchen möchtest.

Kommunikation

4 **Besorgungen** Fragen Sie Ihren Partner / Ihre Partnerin, wohin er/sie geht, um die folgenden Besorgungen zu machen. Answers will vary.

> **BEISPIEL**
> **S1:** Wohin gehst du, wenn du einen
> schönen Ring kaufen willst?
> **S2:** Ich gehe zum Juweliergeschäft.

einen schönen
Ring kaufen

1. Geld abheben

2. schöne Rosen
kaufen

3. ein Paket
abschicken

4. eine Zeitung
kaufen

5. schmutzige
Wäsche waschen

5 **Was und wenn** Fragen Sie Ihren Partner / Ihre Partnerin, was er/sie normalerweise in den folgenden Situationen macht. Achten Sie auf die Wortstellung. Answers will vary.

BEISPIEL
S1: Was machst du normalerweise, wenn du richtig Hunger hast?
S2: Wenn ich richtig Hunger habe, esse ich einen Hamburger.

1. Hunger haben
2. sich schlecht fühlen
3. müde sein
4. sich verspäten
5. ein Paket abschicken wollen
6. traurig sein

6 **Was weißt du?**
A. Schreiben Sie vier Dinge auf, die Sie schon über die deutschsprachigen Länder gelernt haben. Beginnen Sie jede Aussage mit „**Ich weiß, dass...**". Answers will vary.

BEISPIEL
Ich weiß, dass Berlin die Hauptstadt Deutschlands ist.

B. Machen Sie jetzt ein kleines Quiz, um herauszufinden, ob Ihr Partner / Ihre Partnerin dasselbe Wissen hat. Beginnen Sie jede Frage mit **Weißt du, ...** und einem passenden Fragewort – **wer, was, wann, wo, wie**. Answers will vary.

BEISPIEL
S1: Weißt du, was die Hauptstadt Deutschlands ist?
S2: Natürlich! Berlin ist die Hauptstadt Deutschlands!

4 **Partner Chat** You can also assign activity 4 on the Supersite. Students work in pairs to record the activity online. The pair's recorded conversation will appear in your gradebook.

5 **Suggestion** Tell students that they can be creative with their answers.

6 **Expansion** After students complete part B, have everyone switch partners and repeat the quiz.

10A.2

Adjectives used as nouns Grammar Tutorial

Startblock Many adjectives in German can also be used as nouns.

Herr Miller ist ein sehr **alter** Mann.
*Mr. Miller is a very **old** man.*

Was sollen wir machen, um **den Alten** zu helfen?
*What should we do to help **the elderly**?*

QUERVERWEIS

See **3A.2** to review adjective endings in the nominative and accusative cases, **4B.1** to review dative endings, and **8B.1** to review genitive endings.

See **7B.3** to review indefinite words.

ACHTUNG

Common expressions with neuter adjectival nouns are **nichts Besonderes** (*nothing special*) and **etwas anderes** (*something else*). Notice that there is no capitalization in the expression **etwas anderes**.

Suggestion Emphasize that **etwas anderes** is an exception to the rule that adjectival nouns are always capitalized.

- The endings for adjectival nouns change depending on the gender, number, or case of the noun, and whether it is preceded by a **der**-word or an **ein**-word. When you use an adjective as a noun, add the same ending that you would add to the adjective form.

adjective	noun after a *der*-word	noun after an *ein*-word
arbeitslos *unemployed*	**der/die Arbeitslose** *unemployed person*	**ein Arbeitsloser / eine Arbeitslose**
bekannt *(well-)known*	**der/die Bekannte** *acquaintance*	**ein Bekannter / eine Bekannte**
erwachsen *grown(-up)*	**der/die Erwachsene** *adult*	**ein Erwachsener / eine Erwachsene**
jugendlich *young, youthful*	**der/die Jugendliche** *young person*	**ein Jugendlicher / eine Jugendliche**
verlobt *engaged*	**der/die Verlobte** *fiancé(e)*	**ein Verlobter / eine Verlobte**
verwandt *related*	**der/die Verwandte** *relative*	**ein Verwandter / eine Verwandte**

- When adjectival nouns refer to people, the gender of the noun matches the gender of the person. When they refer to previously mentioned objects, the gender of the noun matches the gender of the object.

Marias **Verlobter** ist sehr nett.
*Maria's **fiancé** is very nice.*

Welche **Krawatte** hast du gekauft?
***Which tie** did you buy?*

Seine **Verwandten** habe ich nicht so gern.
*I'm not so crazy about his **relatives**.*

Ich habe die **Blaue** gekauft.
*I bought the **blue one**.*

- Adjectival nouns that refer to concepts are always neuter and are only used in the singular. They often follow indefinite words such as **alles**, **etwas** and **nichts**, or the quantity words **viel** and **wenig** (*little, not much*). For adjectival nouns after **etwas**, **nichts**, **viel**, or **wenig**, use the endings for unpreceded neuter adjectives. After **alles**, use the endings you would use after a **der**-word. **Suggestion** Have students memorize the phrase **Alles Gute!** as a reminder that adjectival nouns after **alles** take the **-e** ending.

Wir wünschen dir **alles Gute**!
*We wish you **all the best**!*

Möchtest du **etwas Kaltes** trinken?
*Do you want **something cold** to drink?*

Suggestion Demonstrate the pattern by writing on the board **etwas Altes** and **etwas Neues**. Underline the capital letters and the **-es** endings. Have students guess how to say "*something blue,*" etc. Repeat with **wenig**, **viel**, and **nichts**.

Jetzt sind Sie dran! Wählen Sie das Wort, das in jedem Satz am besten passt.

1. Meine __c__ sind alle sportlich, vor allem mein Onkel.
2. Ich will dir etwas __a__ erzählen.
3. Du __e__! Hast du dich schwer verletzt?
4. Dein __b__ hat dir einen wunderschönen Ring geschenkt.
5. Amila bestellt alles __d__, das sie auf der Speisekarte sieht.

a. Lustiges
b. Verlobter
c. Verwandten
d. Leckere
e. Arme

Anwendung und Kommunikation

 1 **Was fehlt?** Ergänzen Sie die Sätze mit den richtigen Endungen der substantivierten Adjektive.

 1. Wer ist die hübsche Rothaarig_e_ dort drüben?

2. Ich finde, dass Tom nichts Interessant_es_ zu sagen hat.

3. Er ist ein Bekannt_er_, aber kein Freund.

4. In dem Gestreift_en_ siehst du wirklich gut aus.

5. Macht ihr heute noch etwas Besonder_es_?

 2 **Interview** Stellen Sie Fragen mit einem passenden Paar aus der Liste. Answers will vary.

BEISPIEL

S1: *Was isst du lieber, etwas Süßes oder etwas Scharfes?*
S2: *Ich esse lieber etwas Scharfes.*

einfach / kompliziert	kalt / warm
fantastisch / realistisch	lecker / gesund
hell / dunkel	modern / klassisch
italienisch / mexikanisch	süß / scharf

1. Was isst du lieber, ... ?

2. Was trinkst du am häufigsten, ... ?

3. Was schaust du dir im Fernsehen lieber an, ... ?

4. Welche Musik hörst du dir meistens an, ... ?

5. Welche Kleidung steht dir besser, ... ?

 3 **Bilder beschreiben** Beschreiben Sie mit einem Partner / einer Partnerin die Bilder und verwenden Sie dabei substantivierte Adjektive aus der Liste. Answers will vary.

dick	klein	verlobt
jugendlich	krank	verwandt

▶ **BEISPIEL**

Die Kleine hat einen Brief an den Weihnachtsmann geschrieben.

1.

2.

3.

4.

1 **Suggestion** Do the first few items as a class. After students have completed the activity, have them explain how they chose the correct endings.

2 **Partner Chat** You can also assign activity 2 on the Supersite. Students work in pairs to record the activity online. The pair's recorded conversation will appear in your gradebook.

3 **Suggestion** Have students work through this activity twice: first orally, with an emphasis on communication and content; then in writing, with an emphasis on accuracy.

comparisons STANDARDS

10A.3 Das Futur I Grammar Tutorial

QUERVERWEIS

See **2B.2** to review the use of the present tense with future meaning. See **1B.2** to review the present tense forms of **werden**.

In **11B.1**, you will learn about the future perfect tense, **das Futur II**.

ACHTUNG

Do not confuse the modal **wollen** with the future auxiliary **werden**: **Ich will gehen**. *I want to go.* BUT: **Ich werde** gehen. *I will go. / I'm going to go.*

In a subordinate clause, the infinitive of the modal comes at the end of the clause, preceded by the infinitive of the verb it modifies. The conjugated form of **werden** comes *before* both infinitives.: **Er weiß nicht, wie lange er wird arbeiten müssen**.

More activities

S
vhlcentral

WB
pp. 137–138

LM
p. 88

Online activities

Startblock You have already learned to make statements about the future using the present tense with future meaning. You can also use the future tense (**das Futur I**) to talk about the future, especially when the future meaning might not otherwise be clear from context.

Er **wird** bald hier **sein**.

Wir **werden** beim Blumengeschäft Halt machen **müssen**.

- To form the **Futur I**, use a present tense form of the verb **werden** with the infinitive of the verb that expresses the action.

  Wir **werden** uns in einer Woche wieder **treffen**.
  We'll meet again in one week.

  Werdet ihr am Wochenende Zeit **haben?**
  Will you have time on the weekend?

- In subordinate clauses, move the conjugated form of **werden** to the end of the clause, unless the clause contains a modal verb. When using a modal verb in the **Futur**, place the infinitive of the modal verb at the end of the clause, *after* the infinitive of the verb it modifies.

  Suggestion Tell students that a trick for remembering verb order with modals in future subordinate clauses is the acronym **AIM**: Auxiliary Infinitive Modal.

  Wir **werden** unsere Hausaufgaben **machen**, nachdem wir etwas essen.
  We'll do our homework after we eat something.

  Ich verspreche dir, dass ich dich immer **lieben werde**.
  I promise you that I will always love you.

  Bald **wird** man überall mit der Karte **bezahlen können**.
  Soon, you'll be able to pay by credit card everywhere.

  Sie **werden** ein Formular bei der Post **ausfüllen müssen**.
  You will have to fill out a form at the post office.

- The **Futur I** is commonly used to talk about assumptions or expectations concerning the present *or* future. Such sentences often include the words **wohl**, **wahrscheinlich**, **sicher**, or **schon**, all of which mean *probably* when used with the **Futur**.

  Daniel **wird wohl** noch bei der Ärztin **sein**.
  Daniel is probably still at the doctor's office.

  In 100 Jahren **wird** die Welt **sicher** sehr anders **aussehen**.
  In 100 years, the world will probably look very different.

Suggestion Since this is a common mistake among students, you may want to have your class highlight the first note in the **Achtung** box. Write on board: **Ich will** is NOT *I will*!

Jetzt sind Sie dran! **Bilden Sie Sätze im Futur.**

1. ich / bar bezahlen *Ich werde bar bezahlen.*
2. wir / machen keine Besorgungen
   Wir werden keine Besorgungen machen.
3. du / jetzt ins Bett gehen / ?
   Wirst du jetzt ins Bett gehen?
4. ihr / wahrscheinlich Hunger haben
   Ihr werdet wahrscheinlich Hunger haben.
5. ich / müssen / sich schnell anziehen
   Ich werde mich schnell anziehen müssen.

6. Nina / wohl / auf der Post / sein
   Nina wird wohl auf der Post sein.
7. das Kind / schon / schlafen
   Das Kind wird schon schlafen.
8. es / heute noch / regnen
   Es wird heute noch regnen.
9. wir / müssen / früh aufstehen
   Wir werden früh aufstehen müssen.
10. Onkel Gerhard / Diät machen
    Onkel Gerhard wird Diät machen.

Anwendung und Kommunikation

1 **Sätze schreiben** Schreiben Sie die Sätze um. Benutzen Sie das Futur.

BEISPIEL Wir kommen um 10 Uhr an.
Wir werden um 10 Uhr ankommen.

1. Ich koche morgen Abend. Ich werde morgen Abend kochen.
2. Müsst ihr am Abend noch lernen? Werdet ihr am Abend noch lernen müssen?
3. Andreas ärgert sich wohl darüber. Andreas wird sich wohl darüber ärgern.
4. Das Wetter wird bald besser. Das Wetter wird bald besser werden.
5. Das Flugzeug hat vier Stunden Verspätung. Das Flugzeug wird vier Stunden Verspätung haben.
6. Bist du nächstes Jahr schon 21? Wirst du nächstes Jahr schon 21 sein?
7. Will Michaela ein Zimmer buchen? Wird Michaela ein Zimmer buchen wollen?
8. Sie ziehen im Herbst in eine größere Wohnung um. Sie werden im Herbst in eine größere Wohnung umziehen.

2 **Meine Zukunftspläne** Fragen Sie einander nach Ihren Zukunftsplänen (*plans for the future*). Benutzen Sie die Futurformen. Answers will vary.

BEISPIEL

S1: *Was wirst du heute Abend machen?*
S2: *Heute Abend werde ich Deutsch lernen.*

1. heute Abend
2. am Wochenende
3. im Sommer
4. im Winter
5. nach dem Studium

2 **Expansion** Ask pairs to prepare a list of predictions about what they and their classmates will be doing in 10 years.

3 **Und dann** Schauen Sie sich mit Ihrem Partner / Ihrer Partnerin zusammen die Fotos an und entscheiden Sie, was wohl in den nächsten Minuten passieren wird. Benutzen Sie das Futur. Answers will vary.

3 **Partner Chat** You can also assign activity 3 on the Supersite. Students work in pairs to record the activity online. The pair's recorded conversation will appear in your gradebook.

BEISPIEL

S1: *Ich glaube, der Mann wird einen Käsekuchen kaufen.*
S2: *Ich glaube, er wird Brötchen fürs Frühstück kaufen.*

1.

2.

3.

4.

Wiederholung

1 Wer ist's?

Wählen Sie drei Adjektive aus der Liste und beschreiben Sie Ihrem Partner / Ihrer Partnerin zu jedem Adjektiv eine Person. Ihr Partner / Ihre Partnerin sagt, was für eine Person Sie beschreiben.

Answers will vary.

BEISPIEL

S1: *Dieser Mann hat seine Katze verloren. Er weint den ganzen Tag.*
S2: *Ist das der Traurige?*
S1: *Ja.*

1 Expansion Have students act out the characteristics described by the adjectival nouns.

dreckig	langweilig
intelligent	lustig
sportlich	nervös

1 Partner Chat You can also assign activity 1 on the Supersite.

2 Diskutieren und kombinieren

Sie und Ihr Partner / Ihre Partnerin bekommen verschiedene Arbeitsblätter. Fragen Sie Ihren Partner / Ihre Partnerin, welche Gegenstände die einzelnen Personen in dem Kaufhaus möchten.

BEISPIEL

S1: *Was für einen Pulli möchte Paul?*
S2: *Er möchte einen Roten.*

3 Unglaublich!

Wechseln Sie sich mit einem Partner / einer Partnerin ab: Was ist den Personen in den Bildern passiert? Beginnen Sie jede Beschreibung mit „Hast du gehört, dass ..." oder „Weißt du, dass ...". Ihr Partner / Ihre Partnerin wird auf die Neuigkeiten (*news*) reagieren.

Answers will vary.

3 Expansion Bring in additional pictures for students to work with.

BEISPIEL

S1: *Hast du gehört, dass Maria einen Autounfall hatte?*
S2: *Nein! Unglaublich! Sie fährt aber doch immer so langsam.*

1. Maria	2. Anna und Jonas	3. Emma und Felix

4. Max	5. Jan	6. Lisa und Erik

3 Partner Chat You can also assign activity 3 on the Supersite.

4 Versprechungen

Wählen Sie eine Person aus der linken Spalte und einen Zeitraum aus der rechten. Erzählen Sie Ihrem Partner / Ihrer Partnerin, was Sie jeder Person für diese Zeiträume versprochen haben.

Answers will vary.

4 Suggestion Remind students that **versprechen** takes a dative object.

BEISPIEL

S1: *Ich habe meinen Eltern versprochen, dass ich nach dem Abschluss einen Job finden werde.*
S2: *Gute Idee. Meinen Eltern habe ich versprochen, dass ...*

die Eltern	in drei Wochen
der Freund	im Sommer
der Professor	nach dem Studium
du	in fünf Jahren
die Schwester	vor dem 65. Lebensjahr
die Freundin	in 15 Jahren

4 Partner Chat You can also assign activity 4 on the Supersite.

5 Arbeitsblatt

Formulieren Sie zu dritt drei Fragen für eine Umfrage (*poll*): Wohin gehen andere Personen im Unterricht, wenn sie in die Stadt gehen? Was machen sie dort? Seien Sie höflich (*polite*), wenn Sie fragen! Answers will vary.

5 Suggestion Remind students to use the subjunctive for polite requests.

BEISPIEL

S1: *Entschuldigung, ich möchte gern wissen, wie oft du im Monat auf die Bank gehst.*
S2: *Vielleicht ein- oder zweimal im Monat.*
S1: *Aha, und könntest du mir sagen, ob ...*

6 Die Zukunft

Diskutieren Sie mit einem Partner / einer Partnerin, wie die Stadt der Zukunft aussehen wird.

Answers will vary.

BEISPIEL

S1: *In der Zukunft wird wohl kein Mensch mehr Auto fahren.*
S2: *Das stimmt. Wahrscheinlich werden Computer bald Auto fahren können.*

6 Partner Chat You can also assign activity 6 on the Supersite.

Video: Short Film

Bienenstich ist aus

Paul stottert und weigert sich (*refuses*) zu sprechen. Seine Eltern reisen viel und Paul ist oft alleine. Er hat keine Freunde. Aber er hat seine Oma, die er sehr lieb hat. In ihrem Garten essen sie oft zusammen Kuchen, am liebsten Bienenstich (*cream-filled cake*). Dort lernt er auch Emma und ihren Hund Anton kennen, die seine Freunde werden.

Vorbereitung

Suggestion Tell students that **Bienenstich** (literally "bee sting" cake) is filled with vanilla cream and topped with caramelized almonds. You may want to bring in a recipe to share with the class.

Nützliche Ausdrücke

- **das Apfelmus, -e**
  apple sauce
- **erschrecken**
  to frighten
- **Ich muss dann mal los.**
  I have to go now.
- **der Kirschkuchen, -**
  cherry cake
- **das Lied, -er**
  song
- **das Mittagsschläfchen, -**
  mid-day nap
- **der Seemann, ¨er**
  sailor
- **verrückt**
  crazy
- **wasserscheu**
  afraid of water

1 Was fehlt? Ergänzen Sie die Sätze mit einem passenden Wort oder Ausdruck aus den Listen.

1. Der ___Kirschkuchen___ kommt frisch aus dem Ofen.
2. Lina geht nicht gern schwimmen, weil sie ___wasserscheu___ ist.
3. Frau Müller ist im Krankenhaus, weil sie letzte Woche einen ___Schlaganfall___ hatte.
4. Diese laute Musik macht mich ganz ___verrückt___.
5. Mit Äpfeln, die vom Baum gefallen sind, können wir ___Apfelmus___ machen.
6. Mein Opa macht ein ___Mittagsschläfchen___, weil er müde ist.
7. Wir haben heute einen Baum im ___Schrebergarten___ gepflanzt.
8. Paul spricht nicht gern, weil er ___stottert___.
9. Die Schlangen ___erschrecken___ mich sehr.
10. Ich habe gestern ein schönes ___Lied___ im Radio gehört.

Über den Film sprechen

- **der Nachbar, - / die Nachbarin, -nen**
  neighbor
- **der Schlaganfall**
  stroke
- **der Schrebergarten**
  community garden
- **stottern**
  to stutter
- **vermissen**
  to miss

2 Partnerarbeit Besprechen Sie mit einem Partner / einer Partnerin die folgenden Themen.

1. In vielen deutschen Städten gibt es Schrebergärten. Gibt es solche Gärten auch in ihrer Stadt? Wie unterscheiden sie sich von anderen Gärten?
2. In Deutschland kauft man Brot und Kuchen oft bei einem Bäcker und nicht im Supermarkt. Ist dies in ihrem Land auch so? Diskutieren Sie die Vor- und Nachteile der beiden Läden.

Szenen: Bienenstich ist aus

Suggestion Tell students that the song featured in the film is **Seemann (deine Heimat ist das Meer)**, which was an international hit for the Viennese singer Lolita in 1960. You may want to find the lyrics online and have students sing the song in class. Alternatively, you could prepare a cloze activity where students listen to the song and fill in the missing lyrics.

TIM: Ey... Hast du seit Neuestem auch was auf den Augen, oder was?
STEFAN: Lass ihn doch!
TIM: Was, lass ihn doch? Der hätte doch wohl mal eben den Ball aufheben können.
STEFAN: Du weißt doch, wie er ist ...

VERKÄUFERIN: Der Bienenstich ist leider schon aus, tut mir leid. Darf ich dir denn irgendwas anderes geben? Wie wär's denn mit Kirschkuchen? Der ist ganz frisch aus dem Ofen. Ja? Zwei Stück, wie immer?

NACHBARIN: Ach, vielleicht hat sie sich ja auch was gebrochen.
NACHBAR: Gebrochen?
NACHBARIN: Ich weiß nicht, was das ist...
HERR SCHULTE: Das muss ganz plötzlich°, offensichtlich°... Eben hat sie noch gestanden. Ich verstehe das nicht.

HERR SCHULTE: Jetzt reicht's!° Stellen Sie die Musik leiser, Frau Hoffmann!
OMA: (singend) ... deine Freunde sind die Sterne, über Rio und Shanghai, über Bali und Hawaii...
HERR SCHULTE: Ja, ein Seemann müsste man sein. Dann hätte man wenigstens seine Ruhe!

EMMA: Meinst du nicht, dass es deiner Oma stinklangweilig° ist, so alleine im Krankenhaus? Sie vermisst dich bestimmt.
PAUL: Kommst du mit?

OMA: Och, der sieht doch noch ganz gut aus.
PAUL: Bienenstich gab's nicht mehr.
OMA: Mmm, boah°, ist der lecker!

Jetzt reicht's! *That does it!* **boah** *wow* **plötzlich** *suddenly* **offensichtlich** *obviously* **stinklangweilig** *really boring*

Analyse

3 **Richtig oder falsch?** Entscheiden Sie, ob die folgenden Sätze richtig oder falsch sind.

	richtig	falsch
1. Paul hat etwas auf den Augen und sieht nicht gut.	☐	☑
2. Seine Eltern sind nicht oft zu Hause.	☑	☐
3. Pauls Oma singt nicht gern.	☐	☑
4. Paul kann nicht sprechen und auch nicht singen.	☐	☑
5. Emmas Hund heißt Anton.	☑	☐
6. Anton hat alle vier Würstchen aufgegessen.	☑	☐
7. Im Schrebergarten wird Pauls Oma von einer Biene (*bee*) gestochen.	☐	☑
8. Die Nachbarn haben den Krankenwagen gerufen.	☑	☐

4 **Fortsetzung** Überlegen Sie sich mit einem Partner / einer Partnerin, wie der Kurzfilm weitergeht. Wird Pauls Oma wieder gesund? Wie können Paul und seine Eltern ihr dabei helfen? Kann Paul sein Stottern überwinden (*overcome*)? Schreiben Sie einen Dialog zwischen Paul und seinen Eltern sowie zwischen Paul und Emma.

5 **Diskutieren** Besprechen Sie die folgenden Themen im Kurs.

- Für Paul ist der Schrebergarten seiner Oma ein Ort, wo er sich gut und sicher fühlt. Wo fühlen Sie sich besonders wohl? Warum?

- Großeltern spielen eine wichtige Rolle im Leben von vielen Kindern. Besprechen Sie, warum Pauls Oma so wichtig für ihn ist.

- Werden Menschen diskriminiert, die stottern oder andere Sprachfehler haben? Was kann man tun, um einem Freund, der stottert, zu helfen?

6 **Nachgedacht** Lesen Sie die folgenden Zitate (*quotations*) des römischen Politikers Cicero und des schweizerischen Schriftstellers Curt Goetz. Welchen Bezug (*connection*) haben sie zum Film? Finden Sie, dass die beiden Zitate richtig sind? Begründen Sie Ihre Meinung. Besprechen Sie diese Fragen mit einem Partner / einer Partnerin.

„Reden lernt man nur durch Reden."
—Marcus Tullius Cicero

„Eine Gelegenheit (*opportunity*), den Mund zu halten, sollte man nie vorübergehen lassen."
— Curt Goetz

6 **Suggestion** Make sure students understand the meaning of the quotations before discussing them in pairs. Alternatively, you may wish to discuss them as a class.

In der Stadt

 Vocabulary Tools

Wortschatz

die Innenstadt	*downtown*
das Einkaufszentrum, (*pl.* Einkaufszentren)	*mall; shopping center*
das Gebäude, -	*building*
das Kaufhaus, ⁻er	*department store*
die Kirche, -n	*church*
die Stadt, ⁻e	*town*
das Viertel, -	*neighborhood*
Verkehr	*traffic*
die Allee, -n	*avenue; boulevard*
der Bürgersteig, -e	*sidewalk*
die Ecke, -n	*corner*
die Hauptstraße, -n	*main road*
der Zebrastreifen, -	*crosswalk*
Menschen	*people*
der Bürgermeister, - / die Bürgermeisterin, -nen	*mayor*
der Fußgänger, - / die Fußgängerin, -nen	*pedestrian*
Wo ist ...?	*Where is ...?*
abbiegen (biegt... ab)	*to turn*
folgen	*to follow*
bis zu	*until; up to*
gegenüber von	*across from*
geradeaus	*straight*
in der Nähe von	*close to*
in Richtung	*toward*
nah(e)	*near; nearby*
weit von	*far from*
Ausdrücke	*expressions*
(jemanden) mitnehmen	*to give (someone) a ride*
(die Straße) überqueren	*to cross (the street)*

Suggestion Remind students that they encountered the numerical meaning of **Viertel** when they learned to tell time in **2A.3**. Ex: **Es ist Viertel nach vier**. Point out that the English word quarter can also refer to a neighborhood or section of a city, as in the French Quarter of New Orleans.

die Brücke, -n

Sie geht die Treppe hoch.
(hochgehen)
She is going up the stairs.

die Statue, -n

Er geht die Treppe herunter.
(heruntergehen)
He is going down the stairs.

der Brunnen, -
fountain

Osten Süden
Norden Westen

Er hat sich verlaufen.
(sich verlaufen)
He is lost.

Sie findet sich zurecht.
(sich zurechtfinden)
She is finding her way.

ACHTUNG

Folgen is used with an object in the dative case: **Folge mir! Folgen Sie dem Bus!** To tell someone to follow a road, use **entlanggehen** if the person is on foot or **entlangfahren** for someone in a vehicle: **Gehen Sie die Hauptstraße entlang, bis Sie zur ersten Kreuzung kommen.**

die Ampel, -n
traffic light

die Kreuzung, -en
intersection

die Straße, -n

Suggestion Explain that telephone booths are used mainly with phone cards for international calls.

die Telefonzelle, -n

Suggestion Point out that when **die Bank** refers to a *bank* the plural form is **Banken**, and when it refers to a *bench*, the plural is **Bänke**.

die Bank, ⸚e

Anwendung

1 Paare finden Welche Tätigkeit verbinden Sie mit welcher Person oder mit welchem Ort?

_b_ 1. nach rechts abbiegen
_e_ 2. mit der Bürgermeisterin sprechen
_d_ 3. auf dem Bürgersteig gehen
_a_ 4. sich kurz hinsetzen
_c_ 5. telefonieren
_f_ 6. hochgehen

a. die Bank
b. die Kreuzung
c. die Telefonzelle
d. der Fußgänger
e. das Rathaus
f. die Treppe

2 Bilder beschriften Finden Sie ein passendes Wort für jedes Bild.

Sample answers provided.

1. ___die Ecke___
2. ___die Kirche___
3. ___der Brunnen___
4. ___die Ampel___
5. ___die Statue___
6. ___die Brücke___

3 Stimmt das? Hören Sie sich die Sätze an und entscheiden Sie, ob sie stimmen. **3 Expansion** Ask students to correct the false statements.

	Stimmt	Stimmt nicht		Stimmt	Stimmt nicht
1.	✓	☐	4.	✓	☐
2.	☐	✓	5.	✓	☐
3.	✓	☐	6.	☐	✓

4 Definitionen Lesen Sie die Definitionen und wählen Sie das dazu gehörige Wort aus Ihrer Vokabelliste.

1. Hier darf man die Straße überqueren. ___der Zebrastreifen___
2. Manchmal ist sie rot, gelb oder grün. ___die Ampel___
3. Man muss über sie gehen, um den Fluss zu überqueren. ___die Brücke___
4. Hier kreuzen sich zwei Straßen. ___die Kreuzung/die Ecke___
5. Man geht sie hoch oder herunter. ___die Treppe___
6. Eine Skulptur in Gestalt einer Person. ___die Statue___

5 Gespräche Wo finden sich diese Gespräche statt (*take place*)?

1. Brücke / (Einkaufszentrum)
2. (Bänke) / Kirchen
3. Kaufhaus / (Brunnen)
4. (Ampel) / Zebrastreifen
5. Kiosk / (Statue)

5 Expansion Have students close their books before you play the dialogues. Have them guess the locations without looking at the options.

Kommunikation

6 Wegbeschreibungen

 Sehen Sie sich den Stadtplan an und fragen Sie Ihren Partner / Ihre Partnerin, wie Sie zu den angegebenen Orten kommen. Ihre Ausgangsposition (*starting point*) ist mit einem "X" gekennzeichnet. **Wechseln Sie sich ab.** Answers will vary.

> **BEISPIEL**
>
> **S1:** *Entschuldigen Sie bitte, können Sie mir sagen, wie man zur Peterskirche kommt?*
> **S2:** *Gehen Sie auf der Karolinenstraße geradeaus bis zum Bismarckplatz! Dann…*

1. die Peterskirche
2. der Tiergarten
3. die Universitätsbibliothek
4. der Herkulesbrunnen
5. das Einkaufszentrum "Königsarkaden"
6. die Post

Suggestion Review the phrases listed on p. 88 under the headings **Wo ist…?** and **Ausdrücke**. To help students use these phrases correctly, begin with a listening task: Have students start at the "X" and move along the map as you give directions to different locations. Repeat a few times before having them work in pairs.

7 Nach der Ankunft

 Schreiben Sie zusammen mit Ihrem Partner / Ihrer Partnerin eine E-Mail an Toni, eine Freundin aus Österreich, die Sie nächste Woche besuchen kommt. Erklären Sie ihr, wie man am besten zu Ihnen nach Hause findet. Lesen Sie ihre E-Mail dann im Kurs vor. Ihre Mitstudenten zeichnen eine Karte nach der Wegbeschreibung. Answers will vary.

Von:	Vogel.Scheuche@online.de
An:	toni.meltzer@epost.au
Betreff:	Dein Besuch

Hallo Toni!

Wir freuen uns schon sehr auf deinen Besuch. Wenn du am Flughafen ankommst, solltest du erst mit dem Bus 51 in die Stadtmitte fahren. Dann…

8 Diskutieren und kombinieren

Sie und Ihr Partner / Ihre Partnerin bekommen zwei verschiedene Versionen dasselbe Kreuzworträtsels (*crossword puzzle*). Geben Sie einander die Definitionen der fehlenden Wörter, um die beiden Versionen des Kreuzworträtsels auszufüllen.

> **BEISPIEL**
>
> **S1:** *Eins waagerecht: Hier treffen sich vier Straßen.*
> **S2:** *Das ist eine Kreuzung.*

9 Mein Viertel

Zeichnen Sie zuerst eine Karte Ihres Viertels und beschreiben Sie es danach Ihrem Partner / Ihrer Partnerin. Er/Sie versucht eine eigene Karte zu zeichnen. Answers will vary.

> **BEISPIEL**
>
> **S1:** *Ich wohne um die Ecke, zwischen der Hauptstraße und dem Park. Wenn du bei mir aus der Haustür rausgehst und dann gleich nach rechts, dann…*

Aussprache und Rechtschreibung Audio

Loan Words (Part 1)

Some German words borrowed from other languages retain elements of their original pronunciation. For example, the German consonant **v** is normally pronounced like the *f* in the English word *fan*. But in certain loan words, the **v** is pronounced like the *v* in *van*.

Investor	Universität	Ventilator	Advokat	Vegetarier

The **ch** letter combination has a variety of pronunciations in loan words. Depending on the word, it may be pronounced like the *k* in *kitten*, like the *sh* in *shop*, or with a sound similar to the *j* in *jungle*. In some loan words, it is pronounced like the **ch** in the word **ich**.

Charakter	Chef	checken	Chemie	China

The **sk** in the German word **Ski** and related compound words is pronounced like the *sh* in *shirt*.

Skilift	Skier	Skiläufer	Skipiste	Skiurlaub

Suggestion Point out to students that many borrowed words are pronounced with standard German pronunciation, ex.: **informativ, aktiv**.

Suggestion Tell students about regional variations in pronunciation of **ch** at the beginning of loanwords. For example, an Austrian would typically pronounce **China**, "keen ah," while someone from Wuppertal might say "sheen ah."

1 **Aussprechen** Wiederholen Sie die Wörter, die Sie hören.

1. Interview
2. Vase
3. Video
4. investieren
5. Chaos
6. Champignon
7. Charter
8. Chance
9. chinesisch
10. Skifahrer
11. Skihütte
12. Skispringen

Suggestion Have students refer to the **Ausprache** and **Rechtschreibung** sections of **5B** and **6A** to review the pronunciation of **ch** in German words.

2 **Nachsprechen** Wiederholen Sie die Sätze, die Sie hören.

1. Der kreative und aktive Vegetarier war in Wirklichkeit ein Vampir.
2. Mit den chaotischen Zuständen in China kommt der Chef nicht zurecht.
3. Die Skiläufer fahren mit dem Skilift zu den Skipisten.
4. Das Interview mit dem Investor von der Bank war sehr informativ.
5. Auch im Winter essen wir oft Vanilleeis in unserer Villa in Venedig.
6. Der charmante Chemiker war ein Mann von Charakter.

3 **Sprichwörter** Wiederholen Sie die Sprichwörter, die Sie hören.

Auf dem Vulkan tanzen.[1]

„Wer nichts als Chemie versteht, versteht auch die nicht recht."[2]
–Georg Christoph Lichtenberg

[1] To laugh in the face of danger. (*lit.*, To dance on the volcano.)
[2] Whoever understands nothing other than chemistry, does not truly understand even that.

More activities

vhlcentral | LM p. 90 | Online activities

Fotoroman

Sabites Nacht Video

Die Freunde wollen ausgehen, um Sabites Erfolg zu feiern. Leider ist Berlin ziemlich groß. Wo war nochmal dieses spanische Restaurant?

Vorbereitung Have students look at scenes 5 and 6 and try to predict what the characters are reacting to. After they have watched the video, have them review their predictions.

communication cultures NATIONAL STANDARDS

1

GEORGE Hans? Hans! Du verlierst noch das Gehör, wenn du diese Dinger die ganze Zeit auf den Ohren trägst. Es sind jetzt schon drei Tage, Hans. Könntest du bitte mit mir darüber reden?
HANS Ich kann dich nicht hören.
GEORGE Geh heute Abend mit uns aus. Idiot.

5

MELINE Du bist Berlinerin, Sabite! Wie kann man sich denn hier verlaufen?
SABITE Ich bin noch nie in diesem Stadtteil gewesen.
GEORGE Ich habe zwei Häuserblocks weiter unten an der Kreuzung mit der Straßenampel ein koreanisches Restaurant gesehen. Wir sollten umkehren.
SABITE Ich will kein koreanisches Essen essen, ich wollte doch spanisches Essen. Es ist mein Abend.

2

GEORGE Sabite, ich bin's, George!
SABITE Ich komme! Kein Hans?
MELINE Hallo! Lass mal sehen. Sehr europäisch. Spricht Hans immer noch nicht mit dir? Idiot. Gib mir deine Schlüssel.

3

MELINE Hans, ich sage es nur einmal – hör also gut zu. Die Galerie in der Torstraße stellt Sabites Kunst in ein paar Wochen aus. Heute Abend feiern wir diese Neuigkeiten. Wir laufen nach Charlottenburg, um in einem spanischen Restaurant zu Abend zu essen. Und danach gehen wir in einen Club tanzen. George und Sabite sind nur Freunde. Das musst du einfach kapieren.

MELINE Mir ist es egal, wo wir essen gehen.
SABITE Hallo Hans. Wo bist du? Beweg dich nicht. Wir treffen dich dort in ein paar Minuten.

6

4

GEORGE Kommst du mit?
HANS Ich muss mich noch umziehen. Wir sehen uns dann in Kreuzberg.
SABITE Ich habe Melines Handtasche. Beeil dich. Wir treffen dich dann dort.

ÜBUNGEN

1

Was fehlt? Ergänzen Sie die Sätze mit den richtigen Informationen.

1. (George / Hans) spricht seit drei Tagen mit niemandem.
2. Die Galerie in der Torstraße will Sabites Kunst (kaufen / ausstellen).
3. Alle möchten diese Neuigkeiten in Charlottenburg (erzählen / feiern).
4. Sie wollen in einem (italienischen / spanischen) Restaurant essen gehen.
5. Anschließend wollen sie in einem Club (tanzen / singen).
6. George hat an der (Kreuzung / Brücke) ein koreanisches Restaurant gesehen.

7. Sabite möchte kein (koreanisches / spanisches) Essen.
8. Hans hat eine (Notiz / Karte) ausgedruckt, bevor er die Wohnung verlassen hat.
9. Sie müssen an der Kreuzung abbiegen und Richtung (Brücke / Tankstelle) gehen.
10. Das Restaurant ist gegenüber von einer (Telefonzelle / Statue).

PERSONEN

 George

 Hans

 Meline

 Sabite

SABITE Er ist an der U-Bahn-Station Görlitzer Bahnhof. Wir sind nicht weit weg davon. Ich kann mich erinnern, sie gesehen zu haben. Sie ist einen Häuserblock von der Falckensteinstraße entfernt. Wir sollten über diese Straße gehen und dann in diese Richtung weitergehen.

HANS Ich hatte es online nachgesehen, bevor ich die Wohnung verlassen habe. Ich habe uns eine Karte ausgedruckt. So, wir sind nicht weit vom Restaurant entfernt. Wir gehen einen Häuserblock weiter, biegen an der Kreuzung ab und gehen in Richtung Brücke. Es ist gegenüber von einer Statue.

GEORGE Es tut mir leid, Sabite.
SABITE Mir auch.
HANS Ich... Ich muss gehen.

SABITE Hans, warte! Hans! Geh ihm hinterher!
MELINE Ich laufe Jungen nicht hinterher, Sabite, Jungen laufen mir hinterher. Lass nicht zu, dass er uns den Spaß verdirbt. Essen und Tanzen warten auf dich. Es ist Sabites Nacht!

Nützliche Ausdrücke

- **das Gehör verlieren**
  to lose one's hearing
- **kapieren**
  to understand
- **umkehren**
  to turn around
- **sich bewegen**
  to move
- **Ich laufe Jungen nicht hinterher, Sabite, Jungen laufen mir hinterher.**
  I don't chase boys, Sabite; they chase me.
- **Lass nicht zu, dass er uns den Spaß verdirbt.**
  Don't let him ruin our fun.

10B.1
- **Wir sollten über diese Straße gehen und dann in diese Richtung weitergehen.**
  We should cross this street, and continue in this direction.

10B.2
- **Ich will kein koreanisches Essen essen, ich wollte doch spanisches Essen.**
  I don't want Korean food, I wanted Spanish food.

---

2 **Zum Besprechen** Stellen Sie sich vor, Hans kommt als Tourist in Ihre Stadt. Schreiben Sie einen Dialog, in dem Sie ihm drei Orte empfehlen, die er sehen sollte. Erklären Sie ihm den Weg von Ihrer Uni aus. Answers will vary.

2 **Expansion** Ask each pair of students what their three favorite places in town are and have them describe how you can get there.

3 **Vertiefung** Hans, George, Meline und Sabite wollen im Berliner Stadtteil (*district*) Charlottenburg spanisch essen gehen. Recherchieren Sie Charlottenburg im Internet und vergleichen Sie den Stadtteil mit einem Viertel in Ihrer Stadt. Welche Gemeinsamkeiten und Unterschiede gibt es?

3 **Expansion** Have students identify additional districts of Berlin and note which ones were formerly part of East Berlin.

More activities

vhlcentral   VM p. 20   Online activities

Kabarett Reading

Suggestion As a pre-reading activity, have students ask each other about their favorite comedians, late-night TV shows, and theater acts. Do any of these engage in social criticism or political satire?

TIPP

Many of the terms used to describe theatrical forms in German, like **Pantomime**, **Satire**, and **Komödie**, are similar to their English counterparts.

KABARETT IST EINE FORM DES THEATERS. Es wird auch Kleinkunst genannt. Beim Kabarett kombinieren und verbinden° Künstler Monologe, Dialoge, Pantomime und schauspielerische Szenen. Auch Aspekte der Lyrik (Gedichte° und Balladen) und Musik sind Teil° des Kabaretts. Im Kabarett kritisieren Künstler oft Aspekte der Gesellschaft°, indem sie Satire, Parodie, Sarkasmus und Ironie für diese Kritik benutzen. Dabei wollen sie auch das Publikum unterhalten° und zum Lachen bringen. Man kann Kabarett vor allem auf kleinen Bühnen° sehen. Die deutsche Kultshow „Mitternachtsspitzen", moderiert vom Kabarettisten Jürgen Becker, ist ein Beispiel dafür, dass es Kabarett auch im Fernsehen gibt.

Kabarett begann ursprünglich in Frankreich. 1901, etwa 20 Jahre später, gründete° Ernst von Wolzogen in Berlin das Kabarett „Überbrettl". Während des Kaiserreichs am Anfang des 20. Jahrhunderts und während des Dritten Reichs hatten Kabarettisten große politische Probleme. Erst nach dem 2. Weltkrieg durften Künstler im Kabarett wieder sagen, was sie wollten, und freie Kritik an Politik und Gesellschaft üben. In Mainz kann man heute das Deutsche Kabarettarchiv finden, wo es für die herausragenden° deutschen Kaberettisten ähnlich dem° *Hollywood Walk of Fame* einen Weg „Sterne der Satire" gibt.

Berühmte Kabarettisten	
Dieter Hallervorden (1935–)	Gründete 1960 das Kabarett *Die Wühlmäuse* und ist berühmt für die Figur *Didi*. In dem Film „Didi und die Rache der Enterbten" spielt Hallervorden sieben Rollen!
Dieter Hildebrandt (1927–2013)	Einer der wichtigsten Kaberettisten Deutschlands und Mitbegründer° der Münchner Lach- und Schießgesellschaft.
Urban Priol (1961–)	Berühmt für seine Arbeit im Kabarett und im Fernsehen. 2015 wurde ein Asteroid nach ihm benannt: (233880) Urbanpriol.

QUELLE: Das deutsche Kaberett Portal

Expansion One of the more accessible **Kabarett** artists for first-year students is the American Gayle Tufts, who performs in a language of her own invention: "Denglisch."

verbinden *combine* **Gedichte** *poems* **Teil** *part* **Gesellschaft** *society* **unterhalten** *entertain* **Bühnen** *stages* **gründete** *founded* **herausragenden** *outstanding* **ähnlich dem** *similar to the* **Mitbegründer** *co-founder*

1 **Im Fokus** Richtig oder falsch? Korrigieren Sie die falschen Aussagen.

1. Kabarett ist eine Kombination von vielen Kunstformen. **Richtig.**
2. Das Kabarett als Kunstform begann im kaiserlichen Österreich. **Falsch.** Das Kabarett als Kunstform begann in Frankreich.
3. Das Kabarett ist eine wichtige Form der Kritik an der Politik. **Richtig.**
4. 1901 gründete Ernst von Wolzogen in Berlin das Kabarett „Mitternachtsspitzen." **Falsch.** Das „Überbrettl" war ein Kabarett in Berlin im frühen 20. Jahrhundert.

Diskussion Welche Satiriker mögen Sie? Welche Aspekte der Gesellschaft kritisiert er / sie?

2 **Die deutschsprachige Welt** Richtig oder falsch? Korrigieren Sie die falschen Aussagen.

1. Die beiden größten Religionsgruppen in Deutschland sind der Katholizismus und der Protestantismus. **Richtig.**
2. Die religiöse Aufteilung Deutschlands geht auf den ersten Weltkrieg zurück. **Falsch.** Die religiöse Aufteilung Deutschlands geht auf den Dreißigjährigen Krieg zurück.
3. Etwa 25% der Deutschen sind evangelisch. **Richtig.**

Diskussion Wie wichtig ist Religion für Sie?

DEUTSCH IM ALLTAG

Orte der Kunst

die Freilichtbühne, -n	*open air theater*
die Galerie, -n	*gallery*
das Kabarett, -s	*cabaret*
das Museum, Museen	*museum*
die Oper, -n	*opera*
das Theater, -	*theater*

DIE DEUTSCHSPRACHIGE WELT

Religion

Die beiden größten Religionsgruppen in Deutschland sind der Katholizismus (die Römisch-Katholische Kirche) und der Protestantismus (Evangelische Landeskirchen). Etwa 30% der Deutschen sind römisch-katholisch und 26% evangelisch. Im Süden und Westen sind mehr Menschen katholisch. Im Norden sind mehr Menschen evangelisch. Diese Aufteilung° geht auf den Dreißigjährigen Krieg° zurück, als Länder im Norden die protestantische Seite unterstützten° und Länder im Süden die römisch-katholische Kirche. Neben den beiden Hauptreligionen ist der Islam mit 5% die drittgrößte Religionsgruppe, aber mehr als ein Drittel der Bevölkerung (36%), vor allem in Ostdeutschland, ist konfessionslos.

Aufteilung *division* **Krieg** *war* **unterstützten** *supported*

PORTRÄT

Matthias Schweighöfer

Matthias Schweighöfer wurde 1981 in der ehemaligen DDR geboren. Er kommt aus einer Schauspielerfamilie und ist einer der aktivsten Filmdarsteller° in Deutschland. Im Alter von 16 Jahren spielte er seine erste Rolle in dem Fernsehfilm *Raus aus der Haut*. Weitere Rollen in deutschen Fernsehserien folgten. Er hat mit seiner Schauspielerei viele Preise gewonnen, unter anderem den Deutschen Fernsehpreis als bester Nachwuchsdarsteller° (2001), den Bambi (2007 und 2013) und die Goldenen Kamera (2003 und 2010). Schweighöfer ist auch Filmproduzent, Teilhaber° eines Modelabels und gelegentlich° Synchronsprecher°. Seit 2016 tritt° er auch als Sänger auf. Mit der Thriller-Serie *You Are Wanted* beteiligte° er sich an dem ersten hauseigenen Angebot° des Streaming-Dienstleisters° Amazon in Deutschland.

Filmdarsteller *movie actors* **Nachwuchsdarsteller** *emerging actor* **Teilhaber** *partner* **gelegentlich** *occasionally* **Synchronsprecher** *dubbing actor* **tritt... auf** *performs* **beteiligt... an** *participated in* **hauseigenen Angebot** *in-house offering* **Dienstleisters** *service provider*

✆ IM INTERNET

Suchen Sie mehr Informationen zum Thema Religion in Deutschland: Welche Religionen gibt es in Deutschland? Welche religiösen Feste feiern die Deutschen? Welche offiziellen Feiertage gibt es?

Find out more at **vhlcentral.com**.

Suggestion Point out that the religious landscape of Germany is changing rapidly as immigrants bring their own beliefs with them.

---

3 **Porträt** Richtig oder falsch? Korrigieren Sie die falschen Aussagen. Diskutieren Sie dann die letzte Frage mit einem Partner/ einer Partnerin.

1. Matthias Schweighöfer spielte mit 16 in seinem ersten Kinofilm.
   Falsch. Er bekam mit 16 seine erste Fernsehrolle.
2. Schweighöfer konzentriert sich ausschließlich (*exclusively*) auf Filme.
   Falsch. Er ist auch Filmproduzent, Synchronsprecher und Sänger.
3. Schweighöfer arbeitet auch mit amazon.de an einer Thriller-Serie zusammen. **Richtig.**

4 **Kabarett!** Schreiben Sie mit einer Gruppe ein kurzes Kabarettstück, um es im Kurs vorzuspielen. Wählen Sie zuerst ein Thema. Überlegen Sie sich dann, was Sie darüber sagen oder zeigen wollen. Wollen Sie soziale oder politische Kommentare in Ihr Stück integrieren? Wollen Sie Satire integrieren? Wie können Sie Ihre Ideen und Ihre Kritik am besten ausdrücken (*express*): durch ein Gedicht (*poem*) oder Pantomime oder mit Musik?

More activities

vhlcentral   Online activities

QUERVERWEIS

See **3B.2**, **4B.2**, and **5B.3** to review the use of prepositions with the accusative and dative cases. See **7A.2** to review the use of prepositions to indicate locations.

You will learn more about country names in **10B.2**.

ACHTUNG

Remember that **nach Hause** means *(to) home*, while **zu Hause** means *(at) home*. Note that you cannot use **zu Hause** to express going to someone else's home.

Remember that certain prepositions are typically combined with the definite article to form a contraction. You have already learned the accusative contractions **ans**, **aufs**, **durchs**, **fürs**, **ins**, **ums** and the dative contractions **am**, **beim**, **im**, **vom**, **zum**, **zur**.

Suggestion Tell students that the patterns described here are helpful as guidelines, but that the use of prepositions is not always clear cut. Point out, for example, that the phrases **zum Kunstmuseum** and **ins Kunstmuseum** are both acceptable, but that **ins** emphasizes going *inside* to look at exhibits. Point out that **in**, **auf**, and **an** are also sometimes used interchangeably.

10B.1

Prepositions of direction Grammar Tutorial

Startblock Use prepositions to talk about where things are located. You can also use prepositions to talk about movement toward or away from a location.

Wir müssen **nach** Kreuzberg zurück.

Wir sollten **über** die Straße gehen und dann **in** diese Richtung weitergehen.

- Use **nach** with geographical place names to talk about traveling to a destination. Use **in** with the accusative if a place name includes a definite article.

  Fliegt ihr morgen **nach** Istanbul?
  *Are you flying **to** Istanbul tomorrow?*

  Wir wollten schon immer **in** die Türkei fahren.
  *We've always wanted to go **to** Turkey.*

- Use **zu** with the dative to talk about going to a destination within a town or city, such as a store or building. You can also use **zu** with a dative personal pronoun or a person's name or title to say that you are going to their home or business.

  Dieser Bus fährt **zum** Einkaufszentrum.
  *This bus goes **to** the shopping center.*

  Ich muss noch schnell **zu** Aldi, um Milch zu kaufen.
  *I still have to go **to** Aldi to buy milk.*

  Die Fahrt **zu** meinen Großeltern dauert zwei Stunden.
  *The drive **to** my grandparents' house takes two hours.*

  Vergiss nicht, dass du morgen **zur** Zahnärztin gehen musst!
  *Don't forget that you have to go **to** the dentist tomorrow!*

- Use **in** with the accusative to talk about going to a location inside a building, into a geographical area, or to a certain street.

  Heute Abend gehe ich **in** die Bibliothek.
  *I'm going **to** the library tonight.*

  Mia geht **in** den Waschsalon.
  *Mia's going **into** the laundromat.*

  Am Wochenende fahren wir gern **in** die Berge.
  *On weekends, we like to drive up **into** the mountains.*

  Biegen Sie links **in** die Waldstraße ab!
  *Take a left **onto** Wald Street!*

- Use **auf** with the accusative to talk about movement toward a horizontal surface, an open space, or a public building, and also in idiomatic expressions such as **auf eine Party gehen**.

  Legen Sie die Papiere bitte **auf** meinen Schreibtisch.
  *Please put the papers **on** my desk.*

  Am Sonntag gehen wir **auf** den Markt.
  *On Sunday, we're going **to** the market.*

  Könntest du bitte **auf** die Post gehen und Briefmarken kaufen?
  *Could you please go **to** the post office and buy some stamps?*

  Morgen fahren Herr und Frau Maier **aufs** Land.
  *Tomorrow, Mr. and Mrs. Maier are driving **out to** the country.*

- Use **an** with the accusative to talk about movement toward a vertical surface or a body of water.

Suggestion Encourage students to create flash-cards to help them memorize some of the more common directional expressions as "sound bites." Ex.: **ins Kino, ins Restaurant, ins Café, in die Stadt, in den Park, auf die Bank, auf die Post, auf eine Party, auf den Markt, aufs Land, zur Schule, zur Uni, zur Arbeit, an den Strand, ans Meer.**

Emma hängt ihre Poster **an** die Wand.
*Emma is putting her posters up **on** the wall.*

Im Sommer gehen wir immer **an** den Strand.
*We always go **to** the beach in the summer.*

Fahren wir zusammen **ans** Meer!
*Let's go **to** the seaside together!*

Sie fahren im Urlaub **an** die Nordsee.
*They're going **to** the North Sea on vacation.*

- Use **über** with the accusative to talk about movement over, across, or by way of something, such as a street, a bridge, or a mountain.

Radfahrer sollen ihre Fahrräder **über** die Straße schieben.
*Bicyclists are supposed to push their bikes **across** the street.*

Nur bei Grün darf man **über** die Kreuzung fahren.
*You can only drive **through** the intersection when the light is green.*

Sie fahren **über** München nach Salzburg.
*They're driving to Salzburg **by way of** Munich.*

Wir sind **über** die Berge nach Österreich gereist.
*We traveled **over** the mountains to Austria.*

- Use **aus** with place names to express where someone is from. If the place name includes a definite article, use the dative case.

Unsere Eltern kommen **aus** Österreich.
*Our parents are **from** Austria.*

Die beste Schokolade kommt **aus** der Schweiz.
*The best chocolate comes **from** Switzerland.*

- When using modals with prepositions of location, German speakers often omit the infinitive after the modal.

Wir müssen **nach Hause**.
*We have to **go home**.*

Ich will **ins Bett**.
*I want to **go to bed**.*

More activities

vhlcentral

WB
pp. 141–142

LM
p. 91

Online activities

🔊 **Jetzt sind Sie dran!** Wählen Sie die passenden Präpositionen.

1. Ich fliege morgen früh (nach/ in / auf) Spanien.
2. Tim und Greta fahren (in / auf / an) den Strand.
3. In zwei Wochen fliegen wir alle (über / nach/ zu) Hause.
4. Wie kommt man am schnellsten (an den / zum / in den) Deutschen Museum?
5. Ich fahre gern (in/ über / auf) die Schweiz.
6. Geht ihr am Wochenende (an / nach / auf) Annikas Party?
7. Schaut in beide Richtungen, bevor ihr (nach / über/ in) den Zebrastreifen lauft.
8. Der Professor hat seinen Namen (an/ in / nach) die Tafel geschrieben.
9. Warst du schon (in / zu / auf) der Post?
10. Fahren Sie (an / in/ auf) die Albstraße hinein und suchen Sie dort einen Parkplatz.
11. Mama, ich gehe (nach / über / zu) einer Freundin.
12. Der Mann ist bei Rot (zu / über/ aus) die Kreuzung gefahren.
13. Ich fliege morgen (zu / nach/ auf) München.
14. Wir gehen (zu / auf/ an) den Markt.

Anwendung

1 **Was fehlt?** Ergänzen Sie die Sätze mit **nach** oder **in**.

▶ **BEISPIEL** Italien
Nächsten Freitag fahre ich
nach Italien .

die Fußgängerzone
1. Zum Einkaufen
geht man
in die Fußgängerzone .

Paris
2. Macht ihr
eine Reise
nach Paris ?

die Schweiz
3. Jan und
Maria fahren
in die Schweiz .

Mexiko
4. Kiara würde gern
nach Mexiko
fliegen.

die Staatsbibliothek
5. Am Freitag
gehen wir
in die Staatsbibliothek .

2 **Kombinieren Sie** Ergänzen Sie die Sätze mit den passenden
Präpositionen: **an, auf, in, über, zu**.

BEISPIEL Kommst du nach dem Konzert noch mit uns _zu_ Paul?

1. Mein Opa legt sich nach dem Mittagessen immer _auf_ das Sofa.
2. Um zu Sarah zu kommen, musst du _über_ die Brücke fahren und dann links abbiegen.
3. Wisst ihr, ob Annika und Lena _in_ die Bibliothek gegangen sind?
4. Ich muss noch schnell _auf_ die Bank gehen und Geld abheben.
5. Warum fährst du im Winter nie in die Berge, sondern immer nur _an_ den Strand?

3 **Persönliche Fragen** Beantworten Sie die Fragen in ganzen Sätzen.
Achten Sie darauf, dass Sie die passenden Präpositionen bei Ihren
Antworten benutzen. Sample answers provided.

BEISPIEL Wohin werden Sie am Ende des Semesters fahren?
Ich werde zu meinen Eltern fahren.

1. Wohin gehen Sie, wenn Sie richtig Spaß haben wollen? Ich gehe zu meinem besten Freund.
2. Wohin gehen Sie, wenn Sie mal ganz allein sein wollen? Ich gehe in den Wald.
3. Wohin gehen Sie, wenn Sie ein schönes Geschenk für Ihre Mutter suchen?
Ich gehe in ein Juweliergeschäft.
4. Wohin gehen Sie, wenn Sie Briefmarken brauchen? Ich gehe auf die Post.
5. Wohin fahren Sie lieber: in die Berge oder an den Strand? Ich fahre lieber an den Strand.
6. Wohin möchten Sie in Urlaub fahren? Ich möchte gern in die Schweiz in Urlaub fahren.

Kommunikation

4 Wohin? Wohin sind die Leute in den Bildern gegangen, gefahren oder geflogen? Schreiben Sie Sätze mit einem Partner / einer Partnerin und benutzen Sie dabei das Perfekt und die passenden Präpositionen. Answers will vary.

Italien	der See	der Supermarkt
das Konzert	der Strand	

▶ **BEISPIEL** Simone und Emil

Simone und Emil sind an den See gefahren.

1. Herr und Frau Kaymaz

2. Julian

3. Mira

4. Familie Lehmann

5 Wie oft...? Fragen Sie Ihren Partner / Ihre Partnerin, wie oft er/sie zu den angegebenen Orten geht. Answers will vary.

BEISPIEL

S1: *Wie oft gehst du ins Theater?*
S2: *Vielleicht einmal im Jahr. Und wie oft gehst du auf eine Party?*
S1: *Jedes Wochenende.*

1. das Kino
2. das Einkaufszentrum
3. der Arzt
4. die Großeltern
5. die Bank

6 Spielen im Unterricht Zwei Studenten verlassen (*leave*) das Klassenzimmer. Der Rest der Klasse ändert die Position von ein paar Sachen im Klassenzimmer. Die zwei Studenten kommen wieder herein und müssen herausfinden, was die anderen Studenten gemacht haben. Answers will vary.

BEISPIEL

S1: *Ihr habt Bücher unter den Tisch gelegt.*
S2: *Und ihr habt einen Rucksack an die Wand gehängt.*

10B.2

Talking about nationality Grammar Tutorial

Startblock In German, both nouns and adjectives are used to talk about nationality.

ACHTUNG

The United States may be referred to as **Amerika**, **die USA** (*pl.*), or **die Vereinigten Staaten** (*pl.*). To talk about travelling to a country, use the preposition **in** with country names that begin with an article and **nach** with those that do not. **Ich fliege morgen** <u>**nach**</u> **Deutschland. Ich fahre dann** <u>**in**</u> **die Schweiz.**

Schweizer is used as an adjective in certain fixed expressions, such as **Schweizer Käse** and **Schweizer Schokolade**. It ends in **-er** regardless of the gender or number of the noun that follows it.

- Unlike in English, German adjectives of nationality are never capitalized and are rarely used to refer to people. To describe a person's nationality, use **sein** with a noun of nationality, dropping the article before the noun.

  Suggestion Point out that one can also form nouns and adjectives from city names. Ex: **Er ist Münchner. Ich esse gern Wiener Würstchen.**

  Magst du **deutsches** Essen?
  *Do you like **German** food?*

  Sarah ist **Deutsche**.
  *Sarah is **German**.*

countries and nationalities		
Amerika	der Amerikaner,- / die Amerikanerin,-nen	amerikanisch
China	der Chinese,-n / die Chinesin,-nen	chinesisch
Deutschland	der Deutsche,-n / die Deutsche,-n	deutsch
England	der Engländer,- / die Engländerin,-nen	englisch
Frankreich	der Franzose,-n / die Französin,-nen	französisch
Indien	der Inder,- / die Inderin,-nen	indisch
Italien	der Italiener,- / die Italienerin,-nen	italienisch
Japan	der Japaner, - / die Japanerin, -nen	japanisch
Kanada	der Kanadier,- / die Kanadierin,-nen	kanadisch
Korea	der Koreaner,- / die Koreanerin,-nen	koreanisch
Mexiko	der Mexikaner,- / die Mexikanerin,-nen	mexikanisch
Österreich	der Österreicher,- / die Österreicherin,-nen	österreichisch
Russland	der Russe,-n / die Russin,-nen	russisch
die Schweiz	der Schweizer,- / die Schweizerin,-nen	schweizerisch, Schweizer
Spanien	der Spanier,- / die Spanierin,-nen	spanisch
die Türkei	der Türke,-n / die Türkin,-nen	türkisch

QUERVERWEIS

Note that der/die Deutsche is an adjectival noun whose endings you learned about in **10A.2**.

Chinese, Franzose, and Russe are n-nouns. See **8B.1**. See **3A.2** to review adjective endings.

- You can use either **nicht** or **kein** before a noun of nationality.

  Marie **ist Französin**.
  *Marie **is French**.*

  Yasmin **ist keine Türkin**.
  *Yasmin **isn't Turkish**.*

  Max **ist nicht Kanadier**.
  *Max **isn't Canadian**.*

- Most nouns referring to languages are identical to the corresponding adjective of nationality, but are capitalized and have no added endings. Nouns referring to a language are always neuter. They do not take definite articles.

  Ben spricht fließend **Deutsch**.
  *Ben speaks **German** fluently.*

  Ihr **Französisch** ist sehr gut.
  *Your **French** is very good.*

  Wir sprechen **kein Italienisch**.
  *We don't speak **Italian**.*

  Ich spreche nicht so gut **Russisch**.
  *I don't speak **Russian** very well.*

More activities

vhlcentral

WB pp. 143–144

LM p. 92

Online activities

Jetzt sind Sie dran! **Wählen Sie das passende Wort.**

1. Niklas spricht (deutsch / Deutsch).
2. Ich finde (Chinesisches / chinesisches) Essen sehr lecker.
3. Arnold Schwarzenegger ist (Österreich / Österreicher).
4. Karl studiert seit zwei Jahren in Rom und spricht fließend (Italienisch / italienisch).
5. Die (Deutsche / deutsche) Flagge ist schwarz, rot und gold.
6. Lara kommt aus der Türkei und ist (eine Türkin / Türkin).
7. Daniela wohnt in Madrid und ist (spanisch / Spanierin).
8. In Kanada spricht man (englisch / Englisch) und Französisch.

Anwendung und Kommunikation

1 **Nationalitäten** Geben Sie die Nationalitäten und die Muttersprachen dieser Personen an.

> **BEISPIEL** Marie / Frankreich
> *Marie ist Französin. Sie spricht wohl Französisch.*

1. Manfred / Deutschland Manfred ist Deutscher. Er spricht (wohl) Deutsch.
2. Francesca / Italien Francesca ist Italienerin. Sie spricht (wohl) Italienisch.
3. Jasmin / Türkei Jasmin ist Türkin. Sie spricht (wohl) Türkisch.
4. Sergio / Spanien Sergio ist Spanier. Er spricht (wohl) Spanisch.
5. Emily / die USA Emily ist Amerikanerin. Sie spricht (wohl) Englisch.

2 **Was fehlt?** Ergänzen Sie die Sätze mit den Adjektiven, die zu den Orten in Klammern gehören. Benutzen Sie die richtigen Adjektivendungen.

> **BEISPIEL** (Türkei) Im Pergamonmuseum kann man etwas über die __türkische__ Geschichte lernen.

1. (Österreich) Das Wiener Schnitzel ist eine __österreichische__ Spezialität.
2. (Spanien) Das Guggenheim-Museum in der __spanischen__ Stadt Bilbao ist sehr modern.
3. (die Schweiz) Emmentaler und Münster sind __Schweizer__ Käse.
4. (Korea) Ich esse sehr gern __koreanisches__ Essen.
5. (Deutschland) Der __deutsche__ Journalist ist sehr neugierig.

3 **Aus aller Welt** Fragen Sie Ihren Partner / Ihre Partnerin, welche Sachen aus verschiedenen Ländern er/sie (nicht) gern mag. Benutzen Sie die Wörter aus der Liste oder Ihre eigenen. Schreiben Sie den Dialog auf und spielen Sie ihn dann im Kurs vor. Answers will vary.

> **BEISPIEL**
> **S1:** *Isst du gern Käse aus Holland?*
> **S2:** *Ja, ich esse gern holländischen Käse.*
>   *Am liebsten esse ich aber französischen Käse.*

Architektur (*f.*)	Musik (*f.*)
Essen (*n.*)	Olivenöl (*n.*)
Filme (*pl.*)	Schokolade (*f.*)
Käse (*m.*)	Tee (*m.*)
Kaffee (*m.*)	Würstchen (*n.*)
Literatur (*f.*)	Zeitungen (*pl.*)

3 **Partner Chat** You can also assign activity 3 on the Supersite. Students work in pairs to record the activity online. The pair's recorded conversation will appear in your gradebook.

Wiederholung

1 Diskutieren und kombinieren
Sie und Ihr Partner / Ihre Partnerin bekommen Blätter mit ähnlichen Bildern einer Straße. Suchen Sie die Unterschiede und notieren Sie sie. Answers will vary.

BEISPIEL

S1: Auf meinem Bild gibt es zwei Zeitungskioske. Wie viele hast du?
S2: Ich habe nur einen.

2 Geografie
Fragen Sie Ihren Partner / Ihre Partnerin, in welches Land man fahren muss, um die abgebildeten Sehenswürdigkeiten zu besichtigen. Sample answers are provided.

BEISPIEL

S1: Wohin reist man, wenn man den Eiffelturm sehen will?
S2: Wenn man den Eiffelturm sehen will, muss man nach Frankreich reisen.

der Eiffelturm in Paris
Nach Frankreich.

die Brooklyn-Brücke in New York   In die USA.

der Westminster-Palast in London   Nach England.

die Sultan-Ahmed-Moschee in Istanbul   In die Türkei.

das Matterhorn in den Alpen   In die Schweiz.

das Brandenburger Tor in Berlin   Nach Deutschland.

2 Expansion Have students name additional landmarks from other countries for their partners to guess.

2 Video Virtual Chat You can also assign activity 2 on the Supersite. Students record individual responses that appear in your gradebook.

3 In der Stadt
Wählen Sie eine Aktivität aus der Liste. Sagen Sie Ihrem Partner / Ihrer Partnerin, was Sie in der Stadt machen wollen. Er/Sie sagt Ihnen, wohin Sie gehen müssen, um das zu machen. Answers will vary.

BEISPIEL

S1: Ich möchte mit dem Bürgermeister sprechen.
S2: Hmmm, da musst du ins Rathaus.

> mit dem Bürgermeister sprechen
> schwimmen gehen
> eine Sportzeitschrift kaufen
> frisches Obst und Gemüse kaufen
> Blumen kaufen
> Wäsche waschen
> im Grünen spazieren gehen
> im Internet surfen

4 Wer isst das?
Erzählen Sie Ihrem Partner / Ihrer Partnerin, was Sie gerne essen würden. Ihr Partner / Ihre Partnerin sagt, in welches Restaurant Sie gehen sollen. Schreiben Sie den Dialog und spielen Sie ihn dann im Kurs vor. Answers will vary.

BEISPIEL

S1: Ich würde gern Pasta oder Pizza essen.
S2: Gehen wir doch in ein italienisches Restaurant!

5 Arbeitsblatt
Wählen Sie drei Orte in Ihrer Stadt aus. Fragen Sie zwei Personen, wie man von der Bibliothek zu jedem Ort kommt. Schreiben Sie die Antwort auf, und entscheiden Sie, welche Antwort besser ist. Answers will vary.

BEISPIEL

S1: Wie kommt man am besten von der Bibliothek zu Martins Waschsalon?
S2: Wenn du vor der Bibliothek stehst, geh erst nach links und dann geradeaus bis zum Broadway, dann...

6 Deutsche sind kulturbegeistert

Die Deutschen sind nicht nur sportbegeistert sondern auch kulturbegeistert°. Jeder deutsche Haushalt gibt im Durchschnitt° 260 Euro pro Monat für Unterhaltung° und Kultur aus. Sehen Sie sich das Kinoprogramm an. Fragen Sie Ihren Partner / Ihre Partnerin, welcher Film am interessantesten ist. Wie oft geht er / sie ins Kino, Konzert, und Theater?

kulturbegeistert *enthusiastic about culture* **im Durchschnitt** *on average* **Unterhaltung** *entertainment*

BEISPIEL

S1: *Welchen Film würdest du ansehen wollen?*
S2: *Ich würde „Wir" sehen. Ich mag Horrorfilme. Und du?*

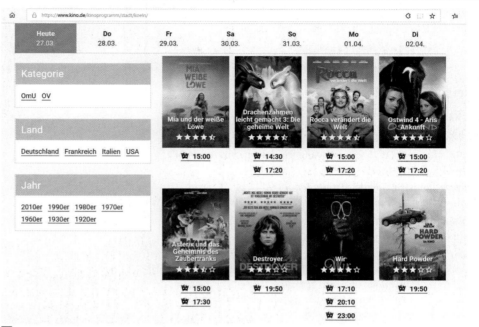

| Heute 27.03. | Do 28.03. | Fr 29.03. | Sa 30.03. | So 31.03. | Mo 01.04. | Di 02.04. |

Kategorie
OmU OV

Land
Deutschland Frankreich Italien USA

Jahr
2010er 1990er 1980er 1970er
1960er 1930er 1920er

Mia und der weiße Löwe ★★★★☆ 🛒 15:00

Drachenzähmen leicht gemacht 3: Die geheime Welt ★★★★☆ 🛒 14:30 🛒 17:20

Rocca verändert die Welt ★★★★☆ 🛒 15:00 🛒 17:20

Ostwind 4 - Aris Ankunft ★★★★☆ 🛒 15:00 🛒 17:20

Asterix und das Geheimnis des Zaubertranks ★★★☆☆ 🛒 15:00 🛒 17:30

Destroyer ★★★☆☆ 🛒 19:50

Wir ★★★★☆ 🛒 17:10 🛒 20:10 🛒 23:00

Hard Powder ★★★☆☆ 🛒 19:50

6 Suggestion Write on the board the German words that students won't know for entertainment and culture, and ask students to add them to Vocabulary Tools on the Sag mal Supersite.
6 Expansion Ask students how much they spend on entertainment a month.

7 Stadtführer
Wählen Sie mit einem Partner / einer Partnerin fünf Orte in Ihrer Stadt, die Besucher unbedingt sehen sollen. Beschreiben Sie jeden Ort. Besprechen Sie dann, wie man von einem Ort zum nächsten kommt. *Answers will vary.*

BEISPIEL

S1: *Ich finde, Besucher sollten das Kunstmuseum sehen.*
S2: *Du hast recht! Da kann man...*

8 Wer und woher?
Beschreiben Sie Ihrem Partner / Ihrer Partnerin eine berühmte Person. Er/Sie rät, wer das ist, und sagt, woher er/sie kommt. *Answers will vary.*

BEISPIEL

S1: *Man kennt diesen Mann durch seine Opern und Symphonien. Er war Österreicher und lebte im 18. Jahrhundert und ist jung gestorben.*
S2: *Das ist Mozart, der österreichische Musiker.*

🔹 Mein Wörterbuch

Schreiben Sie noch fünf weitere Wörter in Ihr persönliches Wörterbuch zu den Themen **Tagesroutine** und **Gesundheit**.

Lektion 10B

German	English	Definition
+ add word		
das Schmuckgeschäft	jewelry store	das Juweliergeschäft, der Juwelier

ä ö ü ß ☐ ALL CAPS

Panorama Interactive Map

Niedersachsen und Nordrhein-Westfalen

NATIONAL STANDARDS connections cultures

Niedersachsen in Zahlen

Suggestion Tell students that the people of Hannover are thought to speak the "purest" form of **Hochdeutsch**.

▸ **Fläche:** *47,634 km²*

▸ **Bevölkerung:** *8 Millionen Menschen*

▸ **Städte:** *Hannover (535.000 Einwohner), Braunschweig (251.000), Osnabrück (162.000)*

▸ **Wichtige Industriezweige:** *Automobil, Stahl°, Windenergie, Messen°*

▸ **Touristenattraktionen:** *Cuxhaven, Ostfriesische Inseln, Hannover, Otterndorf, Lüneburger Heide*

Touristen können in Niedersachsen Urlaub an der Nordseeküste machen oder die Natur in der Lüneburger Heide oder im Harz genießen. Die Industrie wird vor allem durch den Autohersteller VW mit seinem Sitz in Wolfsburg dominiert.

QUELLE: Landesportal Niedersachsen **Suggestion** Have students find some of the places mentioned on the map.

Nordrhein-Westfalen in Zahlen

▸ **Fläche:** *34,088 km²*

▸ **Bevölkerung:** *17,9 Millionen Menschen*

▸ **Städte:** *Köln (1.061.000 Einwohner), Düsseldorf (612.000), Dortmund (585.800)*

▸ **Wichtige Industriezweige:** *Maschinenbau, Elektroindustrie, Banken, Tourismus*

▸ **Touristenattraktionen:** *Teutoburger Wald, Siegerland, Wittgensteiner Land*

Viele Touristen besuchen Nordrhein-Westfalen wegen der schönen Natur und der vielen Bäder im Teutoburger Wald. Nordrhein-Westfalen ist nicht nur das Bundesland mit der größten Bevölkerung, sondern auch mit der stärksten Wirtschaft°.

Suggestion Tell students that the Teutoburger Wald was the site of a famous QUELLE: Landesportal Nordrhein-Westfalen battle in 9 A.D., in which the Germanic tribes ambushed the Roman army.

Berühmte Menschen aus Niedersachsen und Nordrhein-Westfalen

▸ **Wilhelm Busch,** *Autor (1832–1908)*

▸ **Lena Meyer-Landrut,** *Sängerin (1991–)*

▸ **Baron Münchhausen,** *Aristokrat (1720–1797)*

▸ **Michael Schumacher,** *Formel-1-Rennfahrer (1969–)*

▸ **Werner von Siemens,** *Erfinder° (1816–1892)*

Stahl *steel* **Messen** *trade shows* **Wirtschaft** *economy* **Erfinder** *inventor* **Würfen** *throws* **eine bestimmte Strecke schaffen** *complete a predetermined route* **freien Feldern** *open fields*

Karnevalskostüm in Köln

VW-Werk in Wolfsburg

Der Harz liegt in Niedersachsen, Sachsen-Anhalt und Thüringen

RUHRGEBIET

Map labels: NATIONALPARK NIEDERSÄCHSISCHES WATTENMEER · HAMBURG · Bremerhaven · BREMEN · Lüneburg · Elbe · LÜNEBURGER HEIDE · Oldenburg · NIEDERSACHSEN · Ems · Weser · Wolfsburg · Hannover · Braunschweig · NIEDERLANDE · Osnabrück · WESERBERGLAND · Münster · Bielefeld · NATIONALPARK HARZ · SACHSEN-ANHALT · Lippe · Paderborn · Wurmberg · HARZ · NORDRHEIN-WESTFALEN · Göttingen · Rhein · Ruhr · Langenberg · Düsseldorf · SAUERLAND · ROTHAARGEBIRGE · HESSEN · Köln · BERGISCHES LAND · Aachen · Bonn · BELGIEN · EIFEL · RHEINLAND-PFALZ · Gelsenkirchen · Dortmund · Duisburg · Essen · Bochum · Ruhr · Rhein

Legend: — Landesgrenzen · • Stadt · ◉ Landeshauptstadt · 0 50 Meilen · 0 50 Kilometer · 0 25 Meilen · 0 25 Kilometer

Unglaublich, aber wahr!

Boßeln ist ein Ballsport in Norddeutschland. Ein Spieler muss mit einem Ball in so wenig Würfen° wie möglich eine bestimmte Strecke schaffen°. Man kann auf freien Feldern° oder auf Straßen spielen. Normalerweise ist Boßeln ein Mannschaftssport.

Suggestion Tell students that Lena Meyer-Landrut is famous for winning the 2010 Eurovision Song Contest for her song "*Satellite.*"

Landschaftsarchitektur
Landschaftspark Duisburg-Nord

Suggestion Point out that the combination **ui** in **Duisburg** is pronounced **ü**.

Als die Stahlproduktion unrentabel° wurde, veränderte sich die gesamte Region. Aus dem Stahlwerk° in Duisburg-Meiderich ist so der Landschaftspark Duisburg-Nord geworden. Viele Industrieelemente sind im Park noch erhalten, aber sie wurden mit Bäumen, Blumen und Freizeitgeländen° kombiniert. Das Resultat ist eine bemerkenswerte Integration von Industriestrukturen und Landschaft. Der Landschaftspark gilt als eins der wichtigsten Projekte der Landschaftsarchitektur der Jahrtausendwende°.

Natur
Lüneburger Heide

Suggestion Have students scan for the following information: **Wo ist die Lüneberger Heide? Wie viele Touristen kommen jedes Jahr? Welche Tiere findet man dort?**

Die Lüneburger Heide° ist eine Naturlandschaft in Niedersachsen. Sie liegt zwischen Hamburg, Bremen und Hannover. Die Heide ist eine der wichtigsten Touristenattraktion in Niedersachsen: mehr als vier Millionen Touristen besuchen die Heide jedes Jahr. In dieser flachen Region kann man Wald- und Heidelandschaften finden. Im Naturschutzgebiet° darf man nicht mit dem Auto fahren. Selbst die Polizisten reiten auf Pferden°. Besonders interessant für Touristen sind die vielen Heidschnuckenherden°, die es auf der Heide gibt.

Berühmte Personen
Karl der Große°

Suggestion Tell students that **schweben** means *to float* or *to hover*, and that **die Wupper** is the river that runs through Wuppertal.

Karl der Große (circa 747–814) gilt als einer der bedeutendsten Herrscher° Europas. Er war ab dem Jahr 768 König des fränkischen Reiches° und ab dem Jahr 800 Römischer Kaiser. Er regierte das heutige Deutschland, Frankreich, die Niederlande, Belgien, Italien und Polen. Er gilt als der erste Europäer, weil er in dieser Region eine Art europäische Kultur geprägt° hat. Zum Beispiel war Latein die wichtigste Sprache in dem gesamten Reich. Nach seinem Tod wurde er in der Pfalzkapelle in seiner Residenzstadt Aachen begraben°, die heute in Nordrhein-Westfalen liegt.

Öffentlicher Verkehr
Schwebebahn° Wuppertal

In Wuppertal gibt es nicht nur Busse für den öffentlichen Verkehr, sondern auch eine Schwebebahn, die seit 1901 Menschen zwischen Vohwinkel und Oberbarmen transportiert. Sie ist das Wahrzeichen° der Stadt Wuppertal und steht seit 1997 unter Denkmalschutz. Im Jahr 1950 sollte der Elefant Tuffi zwischen zwei Stationen mit der Schwebebahn fahren. Der Elefant sprang aus der Schwebebahn und landete in der Wupper. Dem Tier passierte dabei nichts, aber die Stadt ist seither dafür berühmt.

Musik Musik

Anne-Sophie Mutter

Anne-Sophie Mutter ist eine weltberühmte deutsche Geigerin. Sie ist auch für ihre humanitäre Arbeit anerkannt.

Go to **vhlcentral.com** to find out more about **Anne-Sophie Mutter**.

---

unrentabel *unprofitable* **Stahlwerk** *steel mill* **Freizeitgeländen** *recreational facilities* **Jahrtausendwende** *turn of the millennium* **Heide** *heath* **Naturschutzgebiet** *protected landscape* **Pferden** *horses* **Heidschnuckenherden** *flocks of moorland sheep* **Schwebebahn** *suspended monorail* **Wahrzeichen** *landmark* **Karl der Große** *Charlemagne* **Herrscher** *rulers* **des fränkischen Reiches** *of the Frankish Empire* **geprägt** *shaped* **begraben** *buried*

---

1 **Was haben Sie gelernt?** Entscheiden Sie, ob die Sätze richtig oder falsch sind. Korrigieren Sie die falschen Sätze.

1. Boßeln ist ein Ballsport in Norddeutschland. **Richtig.**

2. Der Landschaftspark Duisburg-Nord ist ein Industriegebiet. **Falsch.** Der Landschaftspark Duisburg-Nord ist Freizeitgelände mit Industrieelementen und Landschaft.

3. Die Lüneburger Heide liegt zwischen Oldenburg und Münster. **Falsch.** Die Lüneburger Heide liegt zwischen Hamburg, Bremen und Hannover.

4. Die Wuppertaler Schwebebahn steht unter Denkmalschutz. **Richtig.**

5. Das Grab von Karl dem Großen ist in Rom. **Falsch.** Das Grab ist in Aachen.

2 **Denken Sie nach** Diskutieren Sie die Frage mit einem Partner/einer Partnerin. Welche Wahrzeichen gibt es in Ihrer Stadt oder Region? Beschreiben Sie sie.

Lesen Audio: Reading

Vor dem Lesen

Strategien

Repetition

Poets often use repetition of sounds, syllables, words, rhymes, or rhythms to emphasize certain images or themes, to establish a particular mood or tone, or to create a musical effect. A poet may also repeat a particular verse or phrase with slight variations, using these subtle differences to create a shift in tone or change of focus. Paying attention to the effects of recurring words, phrases, and sounds will help you gain insight into the meaning of a poem.

Untersuchen Sie den Text

Sehen Sie sich diese beiden Gedichte (*poems*) an. Beachten Sie die Wiederholung von Wörtern und Zeilen. Gibt es auch Wiederholungen mit kleinen Unterschieden (*differences*)?

Suggestion Ask students if they are familiar with any of Hesse's work, such as the novels *Steppenwolf* and *Demian*.

Autoren
Hermann Hesse

Der deutsche Schriftsteller (*writer*) Hermann Hesse (1877–1962) war weit gereist. In einigen Werken (z.B. seinem Roman *Siddhartha*) merkt man den Einfluss der indischen Kultur. Während beider Weltkriege wohnte Hesse in der Schweiz, wo er viel über Pazifismus schrieb.

Kurt Tucholsky

Kurt Tucholsky (1890-1935) ist in Berlin aufgewachsen und stammte aus einer jüdischen Familie. Als er 1918 aus dem ersten Weltkrieg nach Hause kam, konzentrierte er sich auf eine Karriere als Schriftsteller. Er schrieb kritisch über die Justiz, das Militär und den aufkommenden (*emerging*) Nationalsozialismus. In Deutschland verboten die Nazis seine Werke. Von 1924 bis zu seinem Tod lebte Tucholsky im Ausland.

Suggestion Explain to students that Tucholsky's poem is an example of the urban poetry, a genre that thematizes everyday life in an urban setting.

Allein

HERMANN HESSE

Es führen° über die Erde°
Strassen und Wege° viel,
Aber alle haben
Dasselbe Ziel°

Du kannst reiten und fahren
Zu zwein und zu drein°,
Den letzten Schritt°
Mußt du gehen allein.
Drum° ist kein Wissen
Noch Können so gut,
Als daß man alles Schwere
Alleine tut.

führen *lead* **Erde** *earth* **Wege** *paths*
Ziel *goal* **Zu zwein...zu drein** *in twos and threes* **Schritt** *step* **Drum** *Because of that*

Augen in der Großstadt

KURT TUCHOLSKY

Wenn du zur Arbeit gehst
am frühen Morgen,
wenn du am Bahnhof stehst
mit deinen Sorgen°:
da zeigt die Stadt
dir asphaltglatt°
im Menschentrichter°
Millionen Gesichter:
Zwei fremde Augen, ein kurzer Blick°,
die Braue°, Pupillen, die Lider -
Was war das? vielleicht dein Lebensglück...
vorbei, verweht°, nie wieder.

Du gehst dein Leben lang
auf tausend Straßen;
du siehst auf deinem Gang°, die
dich vergaßen.
Ein Auge winkt,
die Seele° klingt;
du hast's gefunden,
nur für Sekunden...
Zwei fremde Augen, ein kurzer Blick,
die Braue, Pupillen, die Lider -
Was war das? Kein Mensch dreht die Zeit zurück°...
Vorbei, verweht, nie wieder.

Du mußt auf deinem Gang
durch Städte wandern;
siehst einen Pulsschlag° lang
den fremden Andern.
Es kann ein Feind° sein,
es kann ein Freund sein,
es kann im Kampfe° dein
Genosse° sein.
Er sieht hinüber
und zieht vorüber ...
Zwei fremde Augen, ein kurzer Blick,
die Braue, Pupillen, die Lider -
Was war das?
Von der großen Menschheit° ein Stück!
Vorbei, verweht, nie wieder.

Sorgen worries
asphaltglatt asphalt-smooth
Menschentrichter funnel of people
Blick glance **Braue** eyebrow
verweht drifted away **Gang** walk
Seele soul
dreht die Zeit zurück turn back
time **Pulsschlag** pulse beat
Feind enemy **Kampf** fight
Genosse comrade **Menschheit** mankind

Nach dem Lesen

 Allein: Verständnis Beantworten Sie die Fragen. Sample answers are provided.

1. Wie ist die Stimmung (*mood*) in Hesses Gedicht?
   Die Stimmung ist traurig.
2. Wohin führen alle Straßen und Wege?
   Sie führen zum selben Ziel.
3. Was meint Hesse mit dem „letzten Schritt" im Leben?
   Der letzte Schritt ist der Tod.
4. Das Gedicht endet mit dem Satz „alles Schwere tut man allein". Wann ist etwas „schwer" im Leben? Dinge sind schwer, wenn man sie allein machen muss, ohne dass man Hilfe von anderen bekommen kann.
5. Welche Metaphern benutzt Hesse? Was bedeuten sie? Straßen und Wege, die über die Erde führen: das Ziel: der Tod; der letzte Schritt: das Sterben

 Augen in der Großstadt: Verständnis
Beantworten Sie die folgenden Fragen.
Sample answers are provided.
1. Welche Alltagssituationen beschreibt das Gedicht?
   Man fährt mit dem Zug, kommt am Bahnhof an und geht durch die Stadt zur Arbeit.
2. Welches Bild bekommt der Leser von den Menschen in einer Großstadt? Die Menschen haben Sorgen. Sie sehen Millionen von Menschen, aber haben keinen Kontakt. Man bleibt anonym in der Stadt.
3. Der Mensch in Tucholskys Gedicht ist einsam (*lonely*), aber hat Sehnsüchte (*desires*). Wonach sehnt sich das „du" in diesem Gedicht? Man sehnt sich nach dem Lebensglück, nach Kontakt, nach Freunden, die einen nicht vergessen.
4. Jede Strophe endet mit derselben Frage „was war das?" Welche Antworten gibt der Sprecher? Es könnte das Lebensglück sein, man kann jedoch die Zeit nicht zurückdrehen und man bleibt nur ein kleiner Teil der großen Menschheit.
5. Der Mensch hat mehrere Sinne: sehen, riechen, hören, schmecken, fühlen. Warum konzentriert sich der Sprecher auf „Augen"? Augen sind die Fenster zur Seele. Augen drücken Gefühle aus. Sie spiegeln das Innere.
6. Warum benutzt der Sprecher das Personalpronomen „du"? Der Sprecher will, dass man sich mit ihm und seiner Sichtweise identifiziert.

 Diskutieren Sie Welche Gemeinsamkeiten (*commonalities*) hat das „du" in Hesses Gedicht mit dem „du" in Tucholskys Gedicht? Wie ist das Leben in diesen beiden Gedichten dargestellt (*portrayed*)?
Answers will vary.

 Fragen Diskutieren Sie die Fragen mit einem
 Partner / einer Partnerin. Answers will vary.

- *Allein*
  Was sind laut Hermann Hesse sowohl dasselbe Ziel als auch der letzte Schritt? Hat Hesse recht? Ist man immer allein, wenn man stirbt?

- **Augen in der Großstadt**
  Tucholsky zeigt in seinem Großstadtgedicht die Einsamkeit (*loneliness*) und Anonymität des Individuums und die Distanz zu seinen Mitmenschen. Welche anderen Erfahrungen (*experiences*) bringt das Leben in der Großstadt mit sich?

 Schreiben Sie In beiden Gedichten wird die Thematik der Bewegung (*motion*) als Metapher für den Gang des Lebens benutzt. Auch in beiden Texten kommt das Modalverb „müssen" vor. Denken Sie, das Leben ist ein ständiges (*constant*) „müssen"?
Answers will vary.

Hören

Strategien

Guessing the meaning of words from context

When you hear an unfamiliar word, you can often guess its meaning based on the context in which it is used...

 To practice this strategy, you will listen to a tour guide talking about Bonn. Jot down some of the familiar words or place names that you hear. Then, listen again and try to guess the meaning of two unfamiliar words based on context. Suggested answers.

Hilfreiche Wörter	Unbekannte Wörter
Haupstadt, Berlin	Regierungssitz
Politiker, gearbeitet	Abgeordnetenhaus

Vorbereitung

Sehen Sie sich das Bild an. Was meinen Sie; welchen Beruf hat die Frau in der weißen Bluse?

Zuhören

 Hören Sie sich den Dialog an. Benutzen Sie den Kontext, um die Wörter in Spalte A zu verstehen. Welche Wörter in Spalte B passen zu den Wörtern in Spalte A?

Spalte A	Spalte B
1. _c_ Büro	a. Viertel
2. _d_ Umbau	b. Geschäfte
3. _b_ Läden	c. Arbeitszimmer für Geschäftsleute
4. _a_ Nachbarschaft	d. Renovierung eines Hauses
5. _e_ Tiefgarage	e. Parkplätze unter einem Haus

Suggestion Have students match the concepts in columns A and B *before* listening to the audio. Play the dialogue 2-3 times, and have students complete the true/false questions in **Verständnis**. Then, have them reevaluate their answers in **Zuhören**.

Verständnis

 Richtig oder falsch Sind die Sätze richtig oder falsch? Korrigieren Sie die falschen Sätze. Sample answers are provided.

1. Das renovierte Gebäude soll nur für Büros sein.
   Falsch. Das Gebäude soll für Läden, Büros und Wohnungen sein.

2. Das Gebäude soll 100 Büros haben.
   Falsch. Das Gebäude soll 200 Büros haben.

3. Der Umbau soll ein Jahr dauern.
   Richtig.

4. Es wird definitiv einen Supermarkt und ein Fitnessstudio in dem Gebäude geben.
   Falsch. Es könnten ein Supermarkt und ein Fitnessstudio in dem Gebäude sein.

5. Es wird Drei- und Vier-Zimmer-Wohnungen geben.
   Falsch. Es wird Zwei-, Drei- und Vier-Zimmer-Wohnungen geben.

6. Die Architektur ist eine Kombination aus alt und neu.
   Richtig.

7. Es werden neue Parkplätze neben dem Gebäude gebaut.
   Falsch. Man baut eine Tiefgarage.

8. Die Renovierung soll den Charakter der Nachbarschaft nicht verändern.
   Richtig.

 Neue Architektur Identifizieren Sie in einer Gruppe ein Gebäude in Ihrer Stadt, das man renovieren oder neu bauen sollte. Was sind die Vor- und Nachteile (*advantages and disadvantages*) einer Renovierung oder eines Neubaus? Was ist für die Bewohner und Nutzer des Gebäudes besser? Was ist effizienter? Was ist für die Nachbarschaft am besten?

Suggestion Play the **Strategien** recording once and ask comprehension questions: **Wie lange war Bonn die Hauptstadt Westdeutschlands? Wer hat früher in dem Alten Abgeordnetenhaus gearbeitet?** Then, play it again, and have students compile their word lists.

Schreiben

Strategien

Using note cards

When you write, note cards can help you organize and sequence the information you wish to present.

For example, if you were going to write an article about a new apartment complex being built in your town, you would jot down notes about each feature of the development on a different note card. Then you could easily organize the cards once you decide how you want to present the information. For example, you could include the best and worst features of the apartment complex, the different uses incorporated into the design, the size of the various facilities, etc.

Here are some helpful techniques:

- Label the top of each card with a general subject, such as **Geschäfte** or **Wohnungen**.

- Use only the front side of each note card so that you can easily flip through them to find information.

- On each card, jot down only those specifics that correspond to the topic of the card.

- As a last step, number the cards in each subject category in the upper right corner to help you organize them.

Wohnungskriterien   6

- *2–3 Schlafzimmer*
- *2 Badezimmer*
- *Einbauküche*
- *große Fenster*
- *Fitnesscenter im Haus*
- *Einkaufsmöglichkeiten im Haus*

Thema

 Eine virtuelle Stadttour

 Wählen Sie eine Stadt, die Sie kennen und mögen. Schreiben Sie einen Text für eine virtuelle Stadttour für deutschsprechende Besucher. Schreiben Sie für jede Besonderheit (*feature*) der Stadt eine Notizkarte mit einigen Details, die Sie beschreiben wollen.

- Jede Notizkarte soll ein allgemeines Thema und eine spezifische Sehenswürdigkeit (*point of interest*) haben. Ein allgemeines (*general*) Thema kann auf verschiedene Karten verteilt sein, jede mit einer anderen Sehenswürdigkeit. Wenn die Stadt zum Beispiel mehrere Viertel hätte, wäre „Viertel" das allgemeine Thema und jedes Viertel hätte seine eigene Karte mit einer Beschreibung.

- Benutzen Sie die Notizkarten, um die Tour zu organisieren. Sie können sie nach Nähe (*proximity*), Zweck (Wohnen, Geschäfte, Industrie, Unterhaltung), historischer Entwicklung (ältester Teil bis neuester Teil), saisonalen Interessen oder Art der Bewohner (Studenten, Geschäftsleute, Künstler (*artists*), Rentner (*retirees*)) organisieren.

- Wenn Sie die Tour beginnen, heißen Sie die Besucher willkommen und geben Sie eine allgemeine Übersicht (*orientation*) über die Stadt. Wenn Sie die Tour beenden, sagen Sie den Besuchern, dass Sie hoffen, dass ihnen die Tour gefallen hat und dass sie bald wiederkommen.

Vocabulary Tools

Lektion 10A

Orte

das Blumengeschäft, -e *flower shop*
die Drogerie, -n *drugstore*
das Internetcafé, -s *internet café*
das Juweliergeschäft, -e *jewelry store*
das Kino, -s *movie theater*
der Kiosk, -e *newspaper kiosk*
der Kosmetiksalon, -s *beauty salon*
die Polizeiwache, -n *police station*
das Rathaus, ⁻er *town hall*
das Schreibwarengeschäft, -e
  paper-goods store
der Waschsalon, -s *laundromat*

geöffnet *open*
geschlossen *closed*

die Post
the post office

die Adresse, -n *address*
der Brief, -e *letter*
der Briefkasten, ⁻ *mailbox*
die Briefmarke, -n *stamp*
der Briefträger, - / die Briefträgerin,
  -nen *mail carrier*
der Briefumschlag, ⁻e *envelope*
das Paket, -e *package*
die Post *post office*
die Postkarte, -n *postcard*

abschicken (schickt... ab) *to mail*

in der Bank
at the bank

die Bank, -en *bank*
das Geld *money*
der Geldautomat, -en *ATM*
der Geldschein, -e *bill*
das Kleingeld *change*
das Konto (*pl.* die Konten) *bank account*
die Münze, -n *coin*

abheben (hebt... ab) *to withdraw*
einzahlen (zahlt... ein) *to deposit*

Ausdrücke
expressions

das Bargeld *cash*
das Formular, -e *form*
die Zeitschrift, -en *magazine*
die Zeitung, -en *newspaper*

ausfüllen (füllt... aus) *to fill out*
bar bezahlen *to pay in cash*
Besorgungen machen *to run errands*
mit der Karte bezahlen *to pay by*
  (credit) card
unterschreiben *to sign*

Subordinating conjunctions
  See pp. 422–423.
Adjectives as nouns See p. 426.
Das Futur I See p. 428.

Lektion 10B

die Innenstadt
downtown

das Einkaufszentrum,
  (*pl.* Einkaufszentren) *mall;*
  shopping center
das Gebäude, - *building*
das Kaufhaus, ⁻er *department store*
die Kirche, -n *church*
die Stadt, ⁻e *town*
die Telefonzelle, -n *phone booth*
das Viertel, - *neighborhood*

Verkehr
traffic

die Allee, -n *avenue; boulevard*
die Ampel, -n *traffic light*
die Bank, ⁻e *bench*
die Brücke, -n *bridge*
der Brunnen, - *fountain*
der Bürgersteig, -e *sidewalk*
die Ecke, -n *corner*
die Hauptstraße, -n *main road*
die Kreuzung, -en *intersection*
die Statue, -n *statue*
die Straße, -n *street*
die Treppe, -n *stairs*
der Zebrastreifen, - *crosswalk*

Menschen
people

der Bürgermeister, - / die
  Bürgermeisterin, -nen *mayor*
der Fußgänger, - / die Fußgängerin,
  -nen *pedestrian*

Wo ist...?
where is. . . ?

abbiegen (biegt... ab) *to turn*
bis zu *until; up to*
folgen *to follow*
gegenüber von *across from*
geradeaus *straight*
in der Nähe von *close to*
in Richtung *toward*
nah(e) *near; nearby*
weit von *far from*

Ausdrücke

heruntergehen (geht... herunter)
  to go down
hochgehen (geht... hoch)
  to go up/climb
mitnehmen (nimmt... mit) *to give a ride*
sich verlaufen *to be/get lost*
sich zurechtfinden (findet sich...zurecht)
  to find one's way
überqueren *to cross*

Prepositions of direction
  See pp. 442–443.
Talking about nationality See p. 446.

Beruf und Karriere

COMMUNICATIVE GOALS
By the end of this chapter you will be able to:

🔊 **Los geht's!** Wo ist Meline? Was macht sie?

LEKTION 11A

Talk about jobs and qualifications.
Talk about job applications and interviews.

To do so, you will use:

Kontext Seite 458–461
- Looking for a job
- Office supplies
- On the phone

Strukturen Seite 466–472
11A.1 Relative pronouns
11A.2 The past tenses (review)

You will also learn about cultural products,
practices, and perspectives related to:

Kultur Seite 464–465
- **Familienunternehmen**
- **Die Kuckucksuhren**
- **Robert Bosch**

Kurzfilm Seite 473–475
- *Die Berliner Mauer*

LEKTION 11B

Discuss professions and work.

To do so, you will use:

Kontext Seite 476–479
- Words and phrases related to occupations
  and work

Strukturen Seite 484–489
11B.1 Das Futur II
11B.2 Adjective endings (review)

You will also learn about cultural products,
practices, and perspectives related to:

Kultur Seite 482–483
- **Die Sozialversicherungen**
- **Angestellte, Arbeiter, Beamte**
- **Der Marshallplan**

WEITER GEHT'S

Seite 490–496
You will learn about Baden-Württemberg,
Saarland, and Rheinland-Pfalz, their histories,
industries, and famous inhabitants.

Panorama Seite 490–491
- **Baden-Württemberg, das Saarland und
  Rheinland-Pfalz**

And you will demonstrate that you can:
Lesen: *Die Räuberbande*, von Leonhard Frank
Hören: Listen for linguistic cues
Schreiben: Write strong introductions
and conclusions

Im Büro

 Vocabulary Tools

Wortschatz

eine Stelle suchen	*looking for a job*
die Ausbildung, -en	education
der Beruf, -e	profession
die Berufsausbildung, -en	professional training
die Besprechung, -en	meeting
der Bewerber, - / die Bewerberin, -nen	applicant
das Empfehlungsschreiben, -	letter of recommendation
die Erfahrung, -en	experience
das (hohe/niedrige) Gehalt (*pl.* die (hohen/niedrigen) Gehälter)	(high/low) salary
das Geschäft, -e	business
das Praktikum (*pl.* die Praktika)	internship
die Referenz, -en	reference
die Stelle, -n	position; job
der Termin, -e	appointment
der Vertrag, -̈e	contract
Arbeit finden	to find a job
sich bewerben um (bewirbt sich)	to apply for
einen Termin vereinbaren	to make an appointment
Büromaterial	*office supplies*
die Büroklammer, -n	paperclip
das Büromaterial, -ien	office supplies
die Pinnwand, -̈e	bulletin board
der Hefter, -	stapler
am Telefon	*on the phone*
Bleiben Sie bitte am Apparat.	Please hold.
Wer spricht?	Who's calling?
eine Nachricht hinterlassen	to leave a message

Suggestion Tell students that **sich bewerben** is typically used with the preposition **um** (+ *acc.*). Ex.: **Julius bewirbt sich um eine Stelle bei einer Bank in Frankfurt**. However, some speakers also use it with **auf** or **für**. You may want to provide past tense forms: **bewarb sich, hat sich beworben**. Also remind students that complete conjugations for all verb types are listed in **Appendix A**.

More activities

vhlcentral WB pp. 145–146 LM p. 93 Online activities

ACHTUNG

In the singular, **Stellenangebot** typically refers to a specific job offer: **Die Firma macht dem Bewerber ein Stellenangebot.** In the plural, it usually refers to job listings: **Der Arbeitslose liest jeden Tag die Stellenangebote in der Zeitung.**

die Personalchefin, -nen
(der Personalchef, -s *m.*)
human resources manager

der Lebenslauf, ¨-e
résumé; CV

Personalbüro

das Vorstellungsgespräch, -e
job interview

die Assistentin, -nen
(der Assistent, -en *m.*)

der Hörer, -
receiver

das Stellenangebot, -e
job opening

Lotmeyer GmbH

die Firma (*pl.* die Firmen)

Suggestion Explain that **GmbH** stands for **Gesellschaft mit beschränkter Haftung**, a type of limited partnership, similar to "*Ltd.*" in English.

Anwendung

1 Hören Sie zu Sagt man das am Telefon?

	Ja	Nein		Ja	Nein
1.	☑	☐	4.	☑	☐
2.	☑	☐	5.	☑	☐
3.	☐	☑	6.	☐	☑

1 Expansion Ask students to write a short script for a phone call to make an appointment.

2 Bilder beschriften Wählen Sie das richtige Wort für jedes Foto.

1. (die Büroklammer)/ die Stellen

2. der Bewerber / (die Pinnwand)

3. (die Besprechung)/ der Vertrag

4. die Referenz / (der Hefter)

5. das Praktikum / (der Hörer)

6. (der Lebenslauf)/ das Gehalt

3 Definitionen Finden Sie die passende Definition.

1. _c_ die Personalchefin
2. _e_ der Beruf
3. _b_ das Praktikum
4. _f_ die Warteschleife
5. _a_ die Stellenangebote
6. _d_ das Empfehlungsschreiben

3 Expansion Have students write additional definitions and have classmates guess the words they refer to. Ex.: **In diesem Dokument steht meine Berufserfahrung. Was ist das? (der Lebenslauf)**

a. Die liest man, wenn man eine neue Stelle sucht.
b. Hier sammeln Studenten praktische Erfahrung für einen Beruf.
c. Mit dieser Person führt man ein Vorstellungsgespräch.
d. Das schickt man zusammen mit einer Bewerbung ab.
e. Das ist die Arbeit, die man jeden Tag macht.
f. Hier bleibt man oft lange, wenn zu viele Telefonanrufe zur selben Zeit ankommen.

4 Das Vorstellungsgespräch Hören Sie sich den Dialog an und zeigen Sie die Worte an, die die Bewerberin spricht.

1. Empfehlungsschreiben ☐	5. Bewerbung ☐
2. Gehaltshöhe ☑	6. Ausbildung ☑
3. Praktikum ☑	7. Berufserfahrungen ☐
4. Chefassistentin ☐	8. Vorstellungsgespräch ☑

4 Expansion After they complete the listening activity, ask students if they think Frau Mellert will get the job and why. Have them come up with additional interview questions to ask her.

Kommunikation

Bewerber Verwenden Sie die angegebenen Vorschläge (*suggestions*) und berichten Sie in ganzen Sätzen, welche Qualifikationen die Bewerber für die aufgelisteten Stellen brauchen. Sample answers are provided.

5 **Video Virtual Chat** You can also assign activity 5 on the Supersite. Students record individual responses that appear in your gradebook.

BEISPIEL

Für die Stelle als Fußballtrainer braucht der Bewerber mindestens fünf Jahre Erfahrung als Fußballspieler in der Bundesliga.

1. _f_ Fußballtrainer
2. _b_ Journalistin
3. _a_ Koch
4. _e_ Kosmetikerin
5. _d_ Mechaniker
6. _c_ Polizistin

a. fünf Jahre Berufserfahrung in einem Restaurant
b. ein abgeschlossenes (*completed*) Studium und ein Praktikum bei einer Zeitung, einer Zeitschrift oder einem Fernsehsender
c. eine zweijährige juristische (*legal*) Ausbildung in Praxis und Theorie
d. eine abgeschlossene technische Lehre (*apprenticeship*)
e. mindestens eine dreijährige Ausbildung in einer Drogerie oder einem Kosmetiksalon
f. mindestens fünf Jahre Erfahrung als Fußballspieler in der Bundesliga

---

Diskutieren und kombinieren Sie und Ihr Partner / Ihre Partnerin bekommen zwei verschiedene Blätter. Jedes Blatt hat fünf Schritte, die für jede Bewerbung notwendig sind. Bringen Sie alle zehn Schritte in die richtige Reihenfolge. Answers will vary.

6 **Suggestion** Make sure students understand all vocabulary before beginning the activity.

BEISPIEL

S1: *Als Erstes würde ich eine Liste mit Namen und Adressen einiger Firmen aufstellen. Was meinst du?*
S2: *Ich würde mich zuerst mal über mögliche Stellenangebote informieren, bevor ich eine Liste der Firmen aufstelle.*

6 **Expansion** Ask students questions about their personal experience with job searches. Ex.: **Haben *Sie* jemals eine Stelle gesucht? Haben Sie die Stelle bekommen? Was für eine Stelle war sie?**

---

7 **Stellenangebote** Wählen Sie zu dritt zwei der abgebildeten Fotos aus und schreiben Sie zu jedem Foto ein Stellenangebot. Es sollte Informationen über gewünschte Qualifikationen enthalten (*contain*), sowie über das Gehalt und die Anzahl der bezahlten Urlaubstage. Machen Sie Ihr Stellenangebot so attraktiv wie möglich. Answers will vary.

BEISPIEL

S1: *Wir suchen einen Piloten/eine Pilotin.*
S2: *Der/die ideale Bewerber (-in) sollte...*
S3: *Unsere Firma ist...*

Aussprache und Rechtschreibung Audio

Loan words (Part 2)

You have already learned that the main stress in German words usually falls on the first syllable. However, in words borrowed from other languages, the first syllable may not be stressed.

Kandidat **Immobilien** **Karriere** **Politiker** **Fabrik**

Some loan words in German are pronounced similarly to their English equivalents.

Computer **Sektor** **Komma** **Semester**

In other loan words, the stress falls on a different syllable in German than it does in English.

Referenz **Assistent** **Psychologe** **Material**

The stress in a loan word may shift to a different syllable in the plural form of a word, or in the feminine form of a noun.

Doktor **Doktorin** **Doktoren** **Sektor** **Sektoren**

1 **Aussprechen** Wiederholen Sie die Wörter, die Sie hören.

1. Jurist
2. Kosmetik
3. Identität
4. Hotel
5. Laptop
6. Thermometer
7. Sekretär
8. Temperatur
9. Akrobat
10. Student
11. Faktor
12. Faktoren

2 **Nachsprechen** Wiederholen Sie die Sätze, die Sie hören.

1. Am Computer sitzt der Student im ersten Semester.
2. Die Kandidaten werden vor der Wahl sehr nervös.
3. Der Atlas, den du suchst, liegt unter den anderen Atlanten.
4. In dem Sektor findet man weniger Arbeitslosigkeit als in den anderen Sektoren.
5. Die Assistentin kocht sich oft eine Tomatensuppe im Labor.
6. Aus diesem Katalog kann man sehr günstig Büromaterial bestellen.

3 **Sprichwörter** Wiederholen Sie die Sprichwörter, die Sie hören.

Je ärgrer Student, je frömmerer Pastor.[1]

Schlaf ist die beste Medizin.[2]

[1] The worse the student, the more devout the pastor.
[2] Sleep is the best medicine.

More activities

vhlcentral LM p. 94 Online activities

Sag niemals nie Video

Hans hat Meline seit Tagen nicht mehr gesehen. Er besucht sie, um sich für den Kuss zu entschuldigen. Aber dann kommt alles ganz anders.

communication cultures
NATIONAL STANDARDS

Vorbereitung Have students preview the images and write down 3 questions they want to have answered in the video.

SABITE Ich habe euch nicht mehr gesehen seit... Was macht ihr hier?
HANS Der Reichstag verkörpert deutsche Geschichte.

HANS Der Reichstag war bis 1918 Sitz des Parlamentes im Deutschen Kaiserreich. Hier verabschiedeten die Abgeordneten Gesetze, erließen Beschlüsse und wählten ihren Präsidenten. Nach dem Ersten Weltkrieg rief Philipp Scheidemann hier die Weimarer Republik aus. Ich habe vor, mich für ein Praktikum zu bewerben. Was genau machst du denn hier?

GEORGE Hans, mein Freund, vergiss es. Sie flirtet mit Männern, bekommt ihre Nummern und schmeißt sie danach in den Abfall.
SABITE Oh, George, du hast doch keine Ahnung von der Liebe. Hans, wenn Meline mit dir nicht geredet hat, ist es deshalb, weil sie Angst hat, dass ihr Herz gebrochen wird.

SABITE Der Reichstag bietet eine große Sammlung zeitgenössischer deutscher Kunst, die ich mir gern anschaue. Als ich ein Kind war, hat der Künstler Christo das gesamte Gebäude in Stoff verpackt. Ich schreibe darüber eine Hausarbeit.

MELINE Hallo?
HANS Hallo, Meline. Ich bin's, Hans. Leg bitte nicht auf. Ich bin draußen. Ich wollte mit dir reden über...

HANS Hast du Meline gesehen?
SABITE Ich weiß, dass sie viel zu tun hat und in Wien nach Arbeit sucht und Lebensläufe und Bewerbungsschreiben abgeschickt hat. Ich glaube, sie hat nächste Woche ein Vorstellungsgespräch. Ich habe sie nicht mehr gesehen seit...

1 **Richtig oder falsch?** Entscheiden Sie, ob die folgenden Sätze **richtig** oder **falsch** sind.

1. Der Reichstag war bis 1918 Sitz des Parlamentes im Deutschen Kaiserreich. Richtig.
2. Philipp Scheidemann rief im Reichstag die Weimarer Republik aus. Richtig.
3. Hans möchte sich als Geschäftsführer bewerben. Falsch.
4. Als Sabite ein Kind war, hat der Künstler Christo das Reichstagsgebäude in Stoff verpackt. Richtig.

5. Sie schreibt darüber ihr Examen. Falsch.
6. Meline sucht in Berlin nach Arbeit. Falsch.
7. Sie flirtet mit Männern, bekommt ihre Nummern und ruft sie an. Falsch.
8. Hans schreibt Meline eine SMS. Falsch.
9. Hans möchte sich für sein Verhalten entschuldigen. Richtig.
10. George glaubt, dass Meline und Hans zu unterschiedlich sind. Richtig.

PERSONEN

George

Hans

Meline

Sabite

7

HANS Also, ich bin hierhergekommen, um dir zu sagen, dass das, was neulich Abend passiert ist, nie wieder passieren wird. Ich möchte mich für mein Verhalten entschuldigen.
MELINE Ich bin froh, dass du das so siehst. Wir hätten das nicht tun sollen.

8

HANS Dann haben wir also eine Abmachung?
MELINE Ja.
HANS Du siehst hübsch aus, wenn du nicht total... fabelhaft aussiehst.
MELINE Danke, Hans. Das ist sehr nett von dir.

9

GEORGE Du liegst falsch, Sabite. Es würde zwischen den beiden niemals klappen. Sie sind zu unterschiedlich.
SABITE Glaubst du nicht, dass sich Gegensätze anziehen?
GEORGE Ich glaube nicht, dass Hans und Meline... Was ich gemeint habe, ist...

10

MELINE Genug. Alle raus. Ich muss arbeiten. Ja. Du auch, Sabite.

Nützliche Ausdrücke

- **verkörpern**
  to embody

- **ein Gesetz verabschieden**
  to pass a law

- **einen Beschluss erlassen**
  to adopt a resolution

- **ausrufen**
  to proclaim

- **das Gebäude**
  building

- **schmeißen**
  to throw

- **Oh, George, du hast doch keine Ahnung von der Liebe.**
  Oh, George, you don't know anything about love.

- **jemandem das Herz brechen**
  to break someone's heart

- **eine Abmachung haben**
  to have a deal

- **fabelhaft**
  fabulous

- **der Gegensatz**
  opposite

11A.1
- **Der Reichstag bietet eine große Sammlung zeitgenössischer deutscher Kunst, die ich mir gern anschaue.**
  The Reichstag holds a large collection of contemporary German art, which I like looking at.

11A.2
- **Der Reichstag war bis 1918 Sitz des Parlamentes im Deutschen Kaiserreich.**
  Until 1918, the Reichstag housed the parliament of the German Reich.

---

2 **Zum Besprechen** Was passiert zwischen Hans und Meline? Schreiben Sie in kleinen Gruppen einen kurzen Absatz darüber, wie es mit den beiden weitergehen wird. Bereiten Sie sich darauf vor, Ihre Prognose im Kurs zu präsentieren. Answers will vary.

 2 **Suggestion** Have all the groups read their predictions to the class. Ask them to keep their paragraphs until they watch the last episode, so that they can find out which predictions were correct.

3 **Vertiefung** Hans sagt, dass der Reichstag deutsche Geschichte verkörpert. Finden Sie mehr über das Reichstagsgebäude heraus. Wann wurde es gebaut? Welche historischen Ereignisse fanden hier statt? Vergleichen Sie dann die Geschichte und Symbolik des Reichstags mit Gebäuden und Plätzen in Ihrer Umgebung.

Possible answers: The Reichstag was built between 1884 and 1894. Philipp Scheidemann proclaimed the Weimarer Republik from the balcony in 1918. In 1990, the official German reunification ceremony took place in the Reichstag.

3 **Suggestion** Have students present their findings to the class.

More activities

vhlcentral | VM p. 21 | Online activities

IM FOKUS

Familienunternehmen

 ⑤ Reading

NATIONAL STANDARDS connections cultures

LAUT EINER STUDIE DES INSTITUTS für Mittelstandsforschung sind etwa 3 Millionen deutsche Firmen in Familienbesitz. Diese Familienunternehmen sind ungefähr 91% aller Firmen und Betriebe. Etwa 55% des Umsatzes° aller Firmen wird von Familienunternehmen erwirtschaftet°. Bei diesen Zahlen ist es kein Wunder, dass Experten Familienunternehmen den wichtigsten Aspekt der deutschen Wirtschaft nennen.

Die Liste bekannter deutscher Familienunternehmen ist lang. Die Familie Quandt (*oben im Bild*) besitzt zum Beispiel fast 50% des Automobilbauers BMW. Auch die Familie Bertelsmann ist mit dem größten deutschen Medienkonzern sehr erfolgreich. Die Familie Heraeus besitzt Heraeus Holding GmbH, die im Bereich Edelmetall° jährlich über 22 Milliarden Euro erwirtschaftet. Andere berühmte Familienunternehmen sind Henkel (Reinigungsmittel), Marquard und Bahls (Mineralöl) und Fresenius (Arzneimittel).

Neben diesen großen Unternehmen findet sich in ganz Deutschland eine große Anzahl kleinerer Familienunternehmen, die oft auf eine lange Tradition zurückschauen° können. Das Familienunternehmen Hipp produziert Babynahrung. Die Gebrüder Mehler produzieren Stoffe° im Bayerischen Wald. Und das Familienunternehmen Rombach & Haas stellt in der fünften Generation im Schwarzwald Kuckucksuhren° her.

Bekannte deutsche Familienunternehmen	
Meggle	(Butter) Gründer°: Josef Anton Meggle (1877)
Oetker	(Pudding) Gründer: August Oetker (1891)
Porsche	(Autos) Gründer: Ferdinand Porsche (1931)
Ritter Sport	(Schokolade) Gründer: Clara und Alfred E. Ritter (1912)
Steiff	(Plüschtiere°) Gründerin: Margarete Steiff (1880)

Umsatzes *sales* **erwirtschaftet** *generated*
Edelmetall *precious metal* **zurückschauen** *look back*
Stoffe *fabrics* **Kuckucksuhren** *cuckoo clocks*
Gründer *founder* **Plüschtiere** *stuffed animals*

ÜBUNGEN

1 **Im Fokus** Richtig oder falsch? Korrigieren Sie die falschen Aussagen. Diskutieren Sie dann die letzte Frage mit einem Partner/ einer Partnerin.

1. Die meisten deutschen Firmen sind Familienuntgernehmen. **Richtig.**

2. BMW gehört der Familie Quandt. **Falsch.** 50% von BMW gehören der Familie Quandt.

3. Die Familie Heraeus verdient viel Geld mit der Herstellung von Babynahrung. **Falsch.** Die Familie Heraeus verdient Geld durch den Handel mit Edelmetallen.

Diskussion Welche Familienunternehmen kennen Sie? Wie lange gibt es diese Unternehmen schon?

2 **Die deutschsprachige Welt** Richtig oder falsch? Korrigieren Sie die falschen Aussagen. Diskutieren Sie dann die letzte Frage mit einem Partner/ einer Partnerin.

1. Heute sind handgemachte Kuckucksuhren aus Plastik. **Falsch.** Handgemachte Kuckucksuhren sind auch heute noch aus Holz.

2. Manche Kuckucksuhren sind fast 300 Jahre alt. **Richtig.**

3. Um 12 Uhr mittags und um Mitternacht ruft ein mechanischer Kuckuck aus der Wanduhr. **Falsch.** Der mechanische Kuckuck ruft jede Stunde.

Diskussion Was zeigt Ihnen die Zeit an? Wer weckt Sie am Morgen? Woher wissen Sie, wann es Zeit ist, in den Unterricht zu gehen?

Expansion Have students repeat each phrase from the **Deutsch im Alltag** aloud after you. Have pairs write short dialogues using at least four of the words.

DEUTSCH IM ALLTAG

Im Büro

der Arbeitgeber	employer
der Arbeitnehmer	employee
die Abteilung	department
das Bewerbungsschreiben	cover letter
die Stellenanzeige	job advertisement
die Visitenkarte	business card

DIE DEUTSCHSPRACHIGE WELT

Kuckucksuhren

Kuckucksuhren haben in Deutschland und vor allem im Schwarzwald große Tradition. Die meisten Kuckucksuhren sind Wanduhren aus Holz. Jede volle Stunde° kommt ein Kuckuck mechanisch aus der Uhr und man kann einen Kuckucksruf° hören. Traditionelle Kuckucksuhren müssen alle 24 Stunden bis 8 Tage aufgezogen° werden, damit sie funktionieren. Im Schwarzwald werden heute noch viele dieser Uhren von Hand gemacht. Die ältesten Kuckucksuhren stammen aus dem 18. Jahrhundert.

volle Stunde top of the hour **Kuckucksruf** call of a cuckoo **aufgezogen** wound up

PORTRÄT

Robert Bosch

Robert Bosch, 1861 in Albeck geboren und 1942 in Stuttgart gestorben, war ein deutscher Erfinder°, Unternehmer°, Sozialreformer und Philanthrop. Seine bedeutendste Erfindung war die Zündkerze°, mit der man Autos leichter starten konnte. Diese Zündkerzen und andere Erfindungen machten sein Unternehmen bald zu einem multinationalen Unternehmen. Bosch war aber auch ein deutscher Philanthrop und Sozialreformer. In seinen Firmen mussten Arbeiter zum Beispiel nur acht Stunden am Tag arbeiten. Außerdem war ihm wichtig, dass es viel Licht und frische Luft in den Fabriken° gab. Bosch war auch ein spendabler Stifter°. Im Jahr 1910 schenkte er der Technischen Hochschule Stuttgart 1.000.000 Mark, um die Forschung zu unterstützen°. **Suggestion** Ask students whether they think Robert Bosch was a good boss, and why.

Erfinder inventor **Unternehmer** entrepreneur **Zündkerze** spark-plug **Fabriken** factories **spendabler Stifter** generous donor **Forschung zu unterstützen** to support research

🔗 IM INTERNET

Suchen Sie im Internet mehr Informationen über ein deutsches Familienunternehmen: Welche Informationen können Sie über die Familie finden?

Find out more at **vhlcentral.com**.

---

3 **Porträt** Richtig oder falsch? Korrigieren Sie die falschen Aussagen. Diskutieren Sie dann die letzte Frage mit einem Partner/ einer Partnerin.

1. Robert Boschs erste Erfindung war die Windschutzscheibe. **Falsch.** Seine erste Erfindung war die Zündkerze für Autos.
2. Boschs Arbeiter hatten am Tag mehr Freizeit als andere Arbeiter. **Richtig.**
3. Robert Bosch war in seinen Ideen zu Fairness und Gesundheit in der Industrie sehr progressiv. **Richtig.**

Diskussion Welche Philanthropen kennen Sie? Was machen sie?

4 **Geld und Geben** Wählen Sie mit einer Gruppe eine reiche Person und machen Sie eine Liste mit Fakten zu dieser Person. Woher kommt die Person? Was hat er/sie gegründet oder geschaffen (created)? Ist die Person philanthropisch tätig? Diskutieren Sie dann, wie er/sie Studenten helfen könnte.

comparisons **11A.1**

Teaching Tip You may want to assign the grammar tutorial **11A.1 Relative pronouns** on the Supersite for students to watch before they come to class.

QUERVERWEIS

See **10A.1** to review subordinate clauses.

ACHTUNG

Relative pronouns are not optional in German, even though they are sometimes omitted in English.

Suggestion Point out that the relative pronouns are identical to the definite articles except in the dative plural (**denen**) and the genitive forms (**dessen** and **deren**).

Relative pronouns Grammar Tutorial

Startblock In 8B.2, you learned to use demonstrative pronouns to refer to someone or something mentioned in a previous sentence. Demonstratives can also be used as relative pronouns, to introduce a subordinate clause that refers to someone or something mentioned in the main clause.

Er ist der Künstler, **der** im Central Park in New York das Kunstwerk „The Gates" errichtet hat.

Sie ist eine Frau, **die** mit Typen flirtet, ihre Telefonnummern bekommt und sie dann in den Abfall wirft.

- Use relative pronouns to combine two statements about the same subject into a single sentence. German relative pronouns correspond to the English relative pronouns *who, whom, whose, that,* and *which.*

relative pronouns				
	masculine	**feminine**	**neuter**	**plural**
nominative	der	die	das	die
accusative	den	die	das	die
dative	dem	der	dem	denen
genitive	dessen	deren	dessen	deren

Ich arbeite bei **einer** kleinen **Firma**.
*I work for **a** small **company**.*

Die Firma verkauft Möbel.
***The company** sells furniture.*

Ich arbeite bei einer kleinen Firma, **die** Möbel verkauft.
*I work for a small company **that** sells furniture.*

- Separate a relative clause from the main clause with a comma, and put the conjugated verb at the end. As in English, a relative clause may come in the middle of a main clause. In this case, put commas both before and after the relative clause.

Wer hat den Hefter genommen, **der** auf meinem Schreibtisch stand?
*Who took the stapler **that** was on my desk?*

Die Personalchefin, **die** meinen Anruf entgegengenommen hat, war sehr nett.
*The HR manager **who** took my call was very nice.*

- The gender and number of a relative pronoun matches the gender and number of the noun it refers to. The case depends on whether the relative pronoun is functioning as a subject, direct object, indirect object, or possessive in the relative clause.

Ich habe eine gute Freundin, **die** eine
Stelle sucht.
*I have a good friend **who** is looking
for a job.*

Die Bewerberin, **der** wir die Stelle anbieten,
hat sehr gute Referenzen.
*The applicant **to whom** we're offering the job
has very good references.*

Der Lebenslauf, **den** wir gestern bekommen
haben, hatte viele Schreibfehler.
*The résumé **(that)** we received yesterday had
a lot of spelling mistakes.*

Das ist der Geschäftsführer, **dessen** Tochter ein
Praktikum bei unserer Firma macht.
*That's the manager **whose** daughter is doing
an internship at our company.*

Suggestion You may want
to explain the concept of an
antecedent to students. Tell
them that the antecedent is
the word in the main clause
that the relative clause refers
to. Have students identify
the antecedent in each of the
example sentences.

- Use **was** as the relative pronoun if the noun in the main clause is an indefinite pronoun such as **alles, etwas, nichts, viel,** or **wenig.**

Ist das alles, **was** du mir
sagen wolltest?
*Is that all **(that)** you wanted to
say to me?*

Das ist etwas, **was** nur die Geschäftsführerin
entscheiden darf.
*That's something **(that)** only the manager
can decide.*

Expansion Teach students
the saying **Nicht alles, was
glänzt, ist Gold.** Have them
make up their own sayings
by completing the following
sentences: **Nichts, was…
Etwas, was… Viel, was…
Wenig, was…**

- If a relative pronoun is the object of a preposition, put the preposition at the beginning of the clause, *before* the relative pronoun. Remember to use a relative pronoun in the appropriate case for the preposition that precedes it.

Der Kalender, **auf den** ich meine Termine
schreibe, ist hinter den Schreibtisch gefallen.
*The calendar **on which** I write my
appointments fell behind the desk.*

Wie heißt die Firma, **für die** Sie gerne
arbeiten würden?
*What's the name of the company **(that)**
you'd like to work **for?***

- You may also use **wo** instead of a prepositional phrase to indicate location in a relative clause.

In dem Gebäude, **wo** ich arbeite, gibt es
ein gutes Restaurant.
*There's a good restaurant in the building
where I work.*

Ich kenne ein Geschäft, **wo** man Schweizer
Schokolade kaufen kann.
*I know a shop **where** you can buy
Swiss chocolate.*

More
activities

vhlcentral

WB
pp. 147–148

LM
p. 95

Online
activities

Jetzt sind Sie dran! **Wählen Sie die passenden Relativpronomen.**

1. Hast du das Paket bekommen, (<u>das</u>/ dem) ich dir letzte Woche geschickt habe?

2. Die Telefonnummer, (der/<u>die</u>) er mir gegeben hat, funktioniert nicht.

3. Die Firma, bei (die/<u>der</u>) Franz sich beworben hat, hat viele Angestellte.

4. Ich kenne den Geschäftsführer, mit (<u>dem</u>/ der) du sprichst, schon seit Jahren.

5. Ich muss den Lebenslauf, an (<u>dem</u>/ das) ich jetzt arbeite, bis morgen abschicken.

6. Ist das die Assistentin, (der/<u>die</u>) dir bei der Arbeit hilft?

7. Kennen Sie die Angestellten, (der/<u>die</u>) ihre Ausbildung in Wien gemacht haben?

8. Herr Vögele, (<u>dessen</u>/ der) Frau Geschäftsführerin ist, arbeitet als Personalchef.

9. Wie heißt die Bewerberin, mit (die/<u>der</u>) Sie gesprochen haben?

10. Das ist die nette Frau, (der/<u>die</u>) im Schreibwarengeschäft arbeitet.

11. Das Paket, auf (<u>das</u>/ dem) ich seit Wochen warte, ist heute angekommen.

12. Die Assistenten, (den/<u>denen</u>) der Personalchef gute Referenzen gegeben hat, freuten sich sehr.

Anwendung

1 **Falschbestellungen** Sie haben einige neue Artikel im Internet bestellt, aber bei der Bestellung gab es ein Durcheinander (*mix-up*). Sagen Sie, dass Sie diese Artikel nicht bestellt haben.

► **BEISPIEL** Computer

Das ist nicht der Computer, den ich bestellt habe.

Stuhl

1. Das ist nicht der Stuhl, den ich bestellt habe.

Uhr

2. Das ist nicht die Uhr, die ich bestellt habe.

Fahrrad

3. Das ist nicht das Fahrrad, das ich bestellt habe.

Schuhe

4. Das sind nicht die Schuhe, die ich bestellt habe.

Haartrockner

5. Das ist nicht der Haartrockner, den ich bestellt habe.

2 **Relativpronomen** Ergänzen Sie die Sätze mit den Relativpronomen aus der Liste.

| das | den | dessen | was |
| dem | der | die | wo |

BEISPIEL Dort ist der Student, *dessen* Eltern Immobilienmakler sind.

1. Meine Schwester hat einen neuen Freund, __den__ ich nicht mag.
2. Das Geschichteprojekt, an __dem__ die Studenten arbeiten, ist sehr interessant.
3. Die alte Frau, __der__ Martin immer beim Einkaufen hilft, ist heute krank.
4. An der Ecke ist eine Eisdiele, __wo__ es leckeres italienisches Eis gibt.
5. Die Brücke, über __die__ man gehen muss, um in die Altstadt zu kommen, ist für den Fahrverkehr geschlossen.
6. Es gibt nicht viel, __was__ mein Mann nicht isst.
7. Das ist das neue Handy, __dessen__ Display die Größe von einem Tablet-Computer hat.
8. Wo ist das Silberbesteck, __das__ wir zur Hochzeit bekommen haben?

3 **Die Tierarztpraxis** Ergänzen Sie den Dialog mit der richtigen Form der passenden Relativpronomen.

BEISPIEL **JASMIN:** Hanna, kennst du den Tierarzt, bei __dem__ Nina ihr Praktikum macht?

HANNA: Ja, ist das nicht der, (1) __dessen__ Büro gegenüber vom Juweliergeschäft Wagner ist?

JASMIN: Meinst du das Geschäft, (2)__wo / in dem__ es die tollen Halsketten gibt?

HANNA: Ja, genau. Und was sagt Nina so über die Arbeit, (3) __die__ sie da machen muss?

JASMIN: Sie sagt, sie lernt viele Dinge, von (4) __denen__ sie vorher nichts wusste.

Kommunikation

4 **Was passt zusammen?** Finden Sie mit einer Partnerin / einem Partner die richtige Definition für jeden Begriff und ergänzen Sie dann das passende Relativpronomen.

BEISPIEL

Ein Geschäftsführer ist eine Person,
die die Angestellten leitet.

1. Ein Geschäftsführer ist eine Person, _f_ .
2. Ein Praktikum ist eine Arbeit, _c_ .
3. Ein Gehalt ist Geld, _e_ .
4. Ein Personalchef ist ein Mann, _b_ .
5. Ein Bewerber ist eine Person, _a_ .
6. Ein Lebenslauf ist ein Dokument, _d_ .

a. _die_ sich um eine Stelle bewirbt.
b. _der_ Vorstellungsgespräche vereinbart.
c. _die_ oft unbezahlt ist.
d. _das_ zu einer Bewerbung gehört.
e. _das_ man für seine Arbeit bekommt.
f. _die_ die Angestellten leitet.

5 **Definitionen** Erfinden Sie mit einem Partner / einer Partnerin Ihre eigenen Definitionen und benutzen Sie Relativpronomen. Sample answers provided.

BEISPIEL Büromaterialien sind Sachen, *die man bei der Arbeit benutzt*

1. Ein Terminkalender ist ein Kalender, in den man wichtige Termine und Besprechungen schreibt.
2. Ein Vorstellungsgespräch ist ein Interview, das ein Bewerber mit einem Personalchef oder einem Geschäftsführer hat
3. Arzt ist ein Beruf, für den man lange studieren muss
4. Ein Kosmetiksalon ist ein Geschäft, in dem / wo man einen neuen Haarschnitt bekommen kann
5. Ein Briefträger ist ein Mann, der die Post bringt

6 **Stadt, Land, Fluss** Denken Sie sich mit Ihrem Partner / Ihrer Partnerin fünf Fragen zu den Themen Geografie, Sprachen, bekannte Leute und Architektur aus. Machen Sie dann ein Quiz mit zwei Mitstudenten. Benutzen Sie Relativsätze. Answers will vary.

BEISPIEL

S1: *Wie heißt der Fluss, der in Deutschland beginnt*
und ins Schwarze Meer fließt?
S2: *Das ist die Donau. Wie heißt der berühmteste*
Tennisspieler, der aus der Schweiz kommt?
S3: *Das ist Roger Federer.*

7 **Im Konferenzzimmer** Beschreiben Sie mit einem Partner / einer Partnerin, was in dieser Szene passiert. Verwenden Sie auch Ihre Fantasie dabei. Benutzen Sie Relativsätze. Answers will vary.

BEISPIEL

Die Angestellten sind in einer Besprechung,
in der sie über die Bewerberin für die Stelle
als Chefsekretärin reden. Frau Weber, die
eine der Bewerbungen liest, arbeitet schon
lange in der Firma und hat ein Gehalt, das...

7 **Partner Chat** You can also assign activity 7 on the Supersite. Students work in pairs to record the activity online. The pair's recorded conversation will appear in your gradebook.

11A.2 The past tenses (review) Grammar Tutorial

Startblock You have learned to use weak, strong, and mixed verbs, including verbs with separable and inseparable prefixes, in both the **Perfekt** and the **Präteritum**.

QUERVERWEIS

See **5A.1** and **6B.2** to review the formation of past participles. See **5B.1** to review verbs that use **sein** as the auxiliary in the **Perfekt**.

See **6A.1** and **7A.1** to review the formation of the **Präteritum**. See **Appendix A** for a complete list of strong verbs and their **Perfekt** and **Präteritum** forms.

Remember that the **Plusquamperfekt** is often used with subordinating conjunctions **als**, **bevor**, and **nachdem**. See **8A.1** to review the formation of the **Plusquamperfekt** and its use with these conjunctions.

- The **Perfekt** tense is used in conversation and informal writing to talk about the past. It is formed with a conjugated form of **haben** or **sein** and a past participle.

  Suggestion Make sure students remember the meanings of the verbs reviewed in this section.

    Hat Herr Schwartz eine Nachricht **hinterlassen**?
    *Did Mr. Schwartz **leave** a message?*

    Wir **sind** gestern erst sehr spät **angekommen.**
    *We **got here** very late yesterday.*

- To form the **Perfekt** of a reflexive verb, place the reflexive pronoun between the conjugated form of **haben** or **sein** and the past participle.

    Ich **habe mich** um fünfzehn Stellen **beworben.**
    *I **applied** for fifteen jobs.*

    Hast du **dir** die Zähne **geputzt**?
    *Did you **brush** your teeth?*

- The **Präteritum** is used to talk about the past in writing or in formal spoken contexts. **Präteritum** forms of **sein**, **haben**, **werden**, and the modal verbs are used more commonly than **Perfekt** forms, even in informal speech.

    Sie **suchten** Arbeit.
    *They **were looking for** work.*

    Lena **blieb** am Apparat.
    *Lena **stayed** on the line.*

- The **Plusquamperfekt** is used to talk about an action that happened before another event in the past. It is formed with the **Präteritum** of **haben** or **sein** and a past participle.

    Jasmin **hatte vergessen**, das Telefon aufzulegen.
    *Jasmin **had forgotten** to hang up the phone.*

    Sie **war** eine halbe Stunde in der Warteschleife **gewesen.**
    *She **had been** on hold for half an hour.*

ACHTUNG

Remember that the prefixes of separable prefix verbs are always stressed, while the prefixes of inseparable prefix verbs are never stressed: **Die Assistentin ist eingeschlafen. Der Chef hat viel verdient.**

verb type	*Infinitiv*	*Präteritum*	*Perfekt*	*Plusquamperfekt*
weak	suchen besuchen	suchte besuchte	hat gesucht hat besucht	hatte gesucht hatte besucht
modal	dürfen wollen	durfte wollte	hat gedurft hat gewollt	hatte gedurft hatte gewollt
mixed	bringen mitbringen	brachte brachte mit	hat gebracht hat mitgebracht	hatte gebracht hatte mitgebracht
strong	kommen ankommen	kam kam an	ist gekommen ist angekommen	war gekommen war angekommen

More activities

vhlcentral

WB
pp. 149–150

LM
p. 96

Online activities

Jetzt sind Sie dran! Ergänzen Sie die Tabelle mit den fehlenden Verbformen.

	Präteritum (er/sie/es)	Perfekt (er/sie/es)	Plusquamperfekt (er/sie/es)
abheben	*hob ab*	*hat abgehoben*	*hatte abgehoben*
sich anziehen	zog sich an	hat sich angezogen	hatte sich angezogen
haben	hatte	hat gehabt	hatte gehabt
nehmen	nahm	hat genommen	hatte genommen
sein	war	ist gewesen	war gewesen
mitbringen	brachte mit	hat mitgebracht	hatte mitgebracht
gehen	ging	ist gegangen	war gegangen

Anwendung und Kommunikation

1 **Was fehlt?** Ergänzen Sie die Sätze mit den Verben in Klammern. Benutzen Sie die richtigen Präteritumsformen.

1. Ben __bewarb sich__ (sich bewerben) um eine Stelle bei einer Bank.

2. Er __stand auf__ (aufstehen) und zog seinen besten Anzug an.

3. Nach dem Frühstück __wurde__ (werden) es Zeit, dass er sich auf den Weg machte.

4. Er __hatte__ (haben) nur noch fünfzehn Minuten, um zu seinem Termin zu kommen.

5. Er __wollte__ (wollen) einen guten Eindruck (*impression*) machen.

6. Aber als er die Kreuzung __überquerte__ (überqueren), hatte er einen Unfall!

7. Als er Stunden später bei seinem Vorstellungsgespräch __ankam__ (ankommen), sagte man ihm, dass er wieder gehen konnte.

8. Er __war__ (sein) sehr traurig.

2 **Sätze umschreiben** Schreiben Sie die Sätze um. Benutzen Sie das Perfekt anstelle des Präsens und das Plusquamperfekt anstelle des Perfekts.

1. Ich habe vier Karten für ein Konzert bekommen, also lade ich drei Freunde dazu ein.
Ich hatte vier Karten für ein Konzert bekommen, also habe ich drei Freunde dazu eingeladen.

2. Nachdem wir im Restaurant gegessen haben, fahren wir zusammen zum Konzert.
Nachdem wir im Restaurant gegessen hatten, sind wir zusammen zum Konzert gefahren.

3. Obwohl Jan die Wegbeschreibung (*directions*) im Internet heruntergeladen hat, biegen wir zweimal falsch ab.
Obwohl Jan die Wegbeschreibung im Internet heruntergeladen hatte, sind wir zweimal falsch abgebogen.

4. Als wir endlich in der Konzerthalle ankommen, hat das Konzert schon begonnen.
Als wir endlich in der Konzerthalle angekommen sind, hatte das Konzert schon begonnen.

3 **Im Märchenland** Wählen Sie mit Ihrem Partner / Ihrer Partnerin eine Märchenfigur (*fairy-tale character*). Auf was für eine Stelle würde diese Figur sich bewerben und wie würde ihr Lebenslauf aussehen? Schreiben Sie aus der Ich-Perspektive und benutzen Sie das Präteritum. Answers will vary.

> **BEISPIEL**
>
> **Aschenputtels Lebenslauf:**
>
> Meine Mutter starb, als ich sehr jung war. Ich musste also viele Jahre lang die ganze Hausarbeit für meine Stiefmutter und zwei Stiefschwestern machen. Ich putzte täglich das ganze Haus, kochte das Essen und hatte nie einen freien Tag …

3 **Expansion** Have students role-play a job interview with their fairy-tale character.

4 **Wer hat das gemacht?** Benutzen Sie die Verben aus der Liste und erfinden Sie mit einem Partner / einer Partnerin sechs Quizfragen zu dem Thema, was berühmte Leute gemacht haben. Stellen Sie Ihre Fragen dann zwei anderen Mitstudenten. Verwenden Sie das Perfekt und das Plusquamperfekt. Wechseln Sie sich ab. Answers will vary.

> **BEISPIEL**
>
> **S1:** Wer hat *Der Steppenwolf* geschrieben?
> **S2:** Hermann Hesse.

bauen	gewinnen	singen
bekommen	heiraten	(mit)spielen
entdecken	landen	sterben
erfinden	schreiben	verlieren

4 **Partner Chat** You can also assign activity 4 on the Supersite. Students work in pairs to record the activity online. The pair's recorded conversation will appear in your gradebook.

Wiederholung

1 Die Familie

Wählen Sie eine Person von der Liste aus. Beschreiben Sie die Person mit einem Relativsatz. Ihr Partner / Ihre Partnerin muss die Person erraten, die Sie beschreiben. Answers will vary.

1 Partner Chat You can also assign activity 1 on the Supersite.

BEISPIEL

S1: Das ist der junge Mann, dessen Vater mein Onkel ist.
S2: Ist es dein Cousin?

die Mutter	die Schwester
der Onkel	die Cousine
die Schwiegertochter	die Nichte
der Urgroßvater	die Tante

2 Diskutieren und kombinieren

Sie und Ihr Partner / Ihre Partnerin bekommen unterschiedliche Blätter. Fragen Sie Ihren Partner / Ihre Partnerin, was jede Person gemacht hat. Answers will vary.

BEISPIEL

S1: Was wollte die Geschäftsführerin?
S2: Sie wollte, dass die Assistentin Anrufe entgegennimmt.

3 Was trägst du?

Beschreiben Sie abwechselnd die Kleidung der Personen in Ihrer Gruppe. Die anderen erraten, wen Sie beschreiben. Verwenden Sie möglichst viele Relativsätze. Answers will vary.

BEISPIEL

S1: Ich denke an eine Frau, die eine schwarze Hose und eine weiße Bluse trägt.
S2: Denkst du an Sarah?

3 Expansion Have students describe the attributes of a famous person and have group members guess who is being described.

4 Arbeitsblatt

Fragen Sie drei Personen in der Gruppe, über welches Thema sie viel, alles, ein bisschen oder nichts wissen. Schreiben Sie die Antworten auf und lesen Sie sie im Kurs vor. Answers will vary.

BEISPIEL

S1: Worüber weißt du viel?
S2: Ich weiß viel über alles, was mit Mathematik zu tun hat.

5 Arbeitsuchender

Felix sucht eine neue Stelle. Sehen Sie mit einem Partner / einer Partnerin seinen Terminkalender an und besprechen Sie, was er gestern morgen gemacht hat, um eine Stelle zu finden. Benutzen Sie das Präteritum und das Plusquamperfekt. Answers will vary.

BEISPIEL

Felix hatte die Stellenangebote schon gelesen, bevor er gefrühstückt hat...

8.00	Stellenangebote lesen
9.00	Frühstück
10.00	dem Personalchef der Computerfirma meinen Lebenslauf schicken
11.00	mich aufs Vorstellungsgespräch vorbereiten
12.00	Vorstellungsgespräch bei „Maxifirma"
13.00	Mittagessen

6 Generationen

Diskutieren Sie mit einem Partner / einer Partnerin, wie das Leben der älteren Generationen war. Answers will vary.

BEISPIEL

S1: Meine Eltern sind beide 1978 geboren. Als sie Kinder waren, gab es kein Internet. Sie haben meistens Musik im Radio gehört.
S2: Das war bei meinen Eltern genauso. Aber meine Großeltern...

Arbeit	Kochen
Familie	Schule
Freizeit	Technologie
Gesundheit	Urlaub
Hausarbeit	

6 Suggestion Have students prepare notes individually, before they begin working with a partner.

S Video: Short Film

Die
Berliner
Mauer

Gewinner: Short
Film Jury Prize Hong
Kong International
Film Festival

Ein Film von Paul Cotter
mit Joost Siedhoff, Fritz Roth
und Dominik Bender

Die Berliner Mauer

Nach dem Tod seiner Ehefrau baut ein alter Mann eine Mauer (wall), wo die Berliner Mauer früher in seinem Dorf stand. Niemand weiß warum. Die Kinder in der Nachbarschaft (neighborhood) helfen ihm, während die Erwachsenen über die Bedeutung der neuen Mauer für Westdeutsche, Ostdeutsche und Ausländer diskutieren.

Vorbereitung

1 **Was fehlt?** Schreiben Sie die Wörter aus den zwei Listen, die die Sätze unten ergänzen.

1. Die Witwe war sehr ___einsam___ nach dem Tod ihres Ehemannes.
2. Wir wollen keinen ___Ärger___ mit der Polizei.
3. Viele Menschen glauben, dass sie zu hohe ___Steuern___ zahlen.
4. Sich nicht sicher zu sein ist kein ___Grund___, etwas nicht zu tun.
5. Ich weiß nicht, ob sie freundlich oder ___feindlich___ sind.
6. In diesem Land gibt es manchmal ___Diskriminierung___ von Ausländern.
7. Ist das Rauchen (smoking) ___erlaubt___ in diesem Gebäude?
8. Sie waren ___anscheinend___ glücklich, obwohl sie viele Probleme gehabt hatten.

2 **Diskutieren** Sprechen Sie über die folgenden Themen.

1. Was wissen Sie schon über die Berliner Mauer und die Wiedervereinigung (reunification) Deutschlands? Welche Probleme kann es geben, wenn Menschen, die sehr unterschiedliche Lebenserfahrungen gehabt haben, zusammenleben müssen?

2. Erzählen Sie einander über etwas, was Ihnen nicht erlaubt war, das Sie aber trotzdem getan haben. Glauben Sie, dass Sie das Richtige getan haben, obwohl es verboten war?

Nützliche Ausdrücke

- **anscheinend**
  apparently
- **der Ärger, -**
  trouble
- **Das reicht!**
  That's enough!
- **erlaubt**
  allowed
- **eingreifen**
  to intervene
- **ermutigen**
  to encourage
- **der Grund, ⸚e**
  reason
- **das Grundstück, -e**
  piece of land
- **die Steuer, -n**
  tax
- **zustimmen**
  to approve; to agree

Über den Film sprechen

- **der Ausländer, - / Ausländerin, -nen**
  foreigner
- **die Diskriminierung, -en**
  discrimination
- **einsam**
  lonely
- **feindlich (zu)**
  hostile (to)
- **hassen**
  to hate
- **der Nachbar, -n / Nachbarin, -nen**
  neighbor

Suggestion Point out that **Nachbar** is an **n**-noun.

Szenen: Die Berliner Mauer

MANN: Sie wird in Frieden ruhen°.

KATJA: Was macht er da?
KATJAS MANN: Ich hab' keine Ahnung°. Da macht er schon seit über einer Stunde 'rum.
KATJAS MANN: Werden wir auch so, wenn wir alt sind? Drehst du auch durch°, wenn ich sterbe?
KATJA: Der arme alte Mann. Sieht aus, als hätte er nicht mehr alle Tassen im Schrank.

MÄDCHEN: Aber wir sind schon fast fertig°!
POLIZIST: Das ist egal! Das ist ein öffentliches Grundstück. Hier können Sie nicht ohne Genehmigung° bauen. Da müssen Sie erst die Zustimmung° der Stadtplanung einholen. Und die haben Sie nicht, oder? Ja, dann muss es alles hier weg!

HELMUT: Herr Schlömerkemper, was machen Sie denn da? Sie können doch hier nicht einfach die Mauer wieder aufbauen. Die ist ja aus gutem Grund abgerissen worden°, nicht wahr? Sicher, es gibt schon Momente... da hätte ich sie auch schon gerne wieder, schon allein wegen des Gesindels° da, nicht wahr? Aber... Herr Schlömerkemper, das kann man nicht machen... Das ist nicht erlaubt!

HELMUT: Tut mir leid, Werner. Wir haben es versucht°.

POLIZIST: Okay! Stoppt, stoppt! Das reicht! Genug° jetzt! Die Mauer wird abgerissen! Räumen sie alle Ihre Gerätschaften° hier weg! Sie auch! Das muss hier alles weg!

in Frieden ruhen *rest in peace* **keine Ahnung** *no idea* **Drehst du...durch** *Will you go crazy*
ist... abgerissen worden *was torn down* **Gesindels** *scum* **Genug** *Enough* **Gerätschaften** *equipment*
fertig *finished* **Genehmigung** *permit* **Zustimmung** *approval* **haben...versucht** *tried*

Analyse

3 Verständnis
Lesen Sie die folgenden Sätze aus dem Film und bringen Sie sie in die richtige Reihenfolge (1-8).

__3__ „Werden wir auch so, wenn wir alt sind?"

__6__ „Aber wir sind fast fertig!"

__2__ „Ihr sollt nicht mal mit diesen Kindern spielen!"

__4__ „Herr Schlömerkemper, das kann man nicht machen."

__5__ „Die Mauer wird abgerissen!"

__8__ „Tut mir leid, Werner."

__7__ „Können wir das kleine Stückchen Mauer nicht einfach stehen lassen?"

__1__ „Sie wird in Frieden ruhen."

4 Dialoge
Erfinden Sie mit einem Partner / einer Partnerin einen Dialog zu einer der folgenden Situationen.

• Stellen Sie sich vor, dass Sie Katja und ihr Ehemann sind. Was besprechen Sie zusammen, nachdem die Polizei die Mauer zerstört (destroyed) hat? Wollen Sie Herrn Schlömerkemper und die anderen Nachbarn besser kennen lernen?

• Spielen Sie die Szene von dem Tag im Jahre 1962, als Werner Schlömerkemper und Theresa ihre Namen in den Stein eingeritzt (carved) haben. Welche Gedanken über die Zukunft hatten Sie? Was waren Ihre Träume für Ihr Leben zusammen?

5 Zum Besprechen
Diskutieren Sie die folgenden Sprichwörter. Glauben Sie an diese Sprichwörter? Welche Verbindung haben sie zu dem Film?

Stille Wasser sind tief.

Liebe deinen Nachbarn, reiß aber den Zaun (fence) nicht ein (tear down).

Suggestion Ask students if they can think of contemporary examples where the building of a wall or fence has been a source of controversy.

Berufe Vocabulary Tools

Wortschatz	
auf der Arbeit	*at work*
die Beförderung, -en	*promotion*
das Büro, -s	*office*
der Chef, -s / die Chefin, -nen	*boss*
der Erfolg, -e	*success*
die Gehaltserhöhung, -en	*raise*
die Gewerkschaft, -en	*labor union*
die Karriere, -n	*career*
anspruchsvoll	*demanding*
fertig	*ready; finished*
ganztags	*full-time*
halbtags	*part-time*
zuverlässig	*reliable*
Berufe	*occupations*
der Fabrikarbeiter, - / die Fabrikarbeiterin, -nen	*factory worker*
der Gärtner, - / die Gärtnerin, -nen	*gardener*
der Hausmann, ¨er / die Hausfrau, -en	*homemaker*
der Hausmeister, - / die Hausmeisterin, -nen	*caretaker; custodian*
der Klempner, - / die Klempnerin, -nen	*plumber*
der Politiker, - / die Politikerin, -nen	*politician*
der Rentner, - / die Rentnerin, -nen	*retiree*
der Richter, - / die Richterin, -nen	*judge*
Ausdrücke	*expressions*
arbeitslos sein	*to be unemployed*
entlassen	*to fire; to lay off*
kündigen	*to resign*
leiten	*to manage*
scheitern	*to fail*
Urlaub nehmen	*to take time off*
verdienen	*to earn*

Suggestion To help students personalize the new vocabulary, have them think of people they know who work in each of the professions listed.

Suggestion Tell students that **scheitern** takes **sein** as its auxiliary in the **Perfekt**. Point out that **entlassen** is a strong verb, and provide its past tense forms. You may want to note that **feuern** is often used in place of **entlassen** in informal speech.

die Wissenschaftlerin, -nen
(der Wissenschaftler, - *m.*)
scientist

$H_2O + C_2$

die Tierärztin, -nen
(der Tierarzt, ¨e *m.*)
veterinarian

die LKW-Fahrerin, -nen
(der LKW-Fahrer, - *m.*)
truck driver

die Buchhalterin, -nen
(der Buchhalter, - *m.*)
accountant

der Feuerwehrmann, *pl.*
die Feuerwehrleute
(die Feuerwehrfrau, -en *f.*)
firefighter

der Taxifahrer, -
(die Taxifahrerin, -nen *f.*)
taxi driver

der Koch, ¨e
(die Köchin, -nen *f.*)
cook

Suggestion Have students guess the meaning of the suffix -**los**.

Suggestion Remind students not to confuse the meaning of the words **Chef** and **Koch**. Point out that the compound **Chefkoch** means *head chef*.

More activities

 vhlcentral | WB pp. 151–152 | LM p. 97 | Online activities

der Bankangestellte, -n
(die Bankangestellte, -n f.)
bank employee

die Immobilienmaklerin, -nen
(der Immobilienmakler, - m.)
real estate agent

der Bauer, -n
(die Bäuerin, -nen f.)
farmer

die Elektrikerin, -nen
(der Elektriker, - m.)

der Psychologe, -n
(die Psychologin, -nen f.)

ACHTUNG

The adverbs **gut** and **schlecht** can be used with **verdienen** to indicate how well a person is paid: **Ich will gut verdienen.**

Anwendung

Suggestion Explain that **Bankangestellte(r)** is a compound adjectival noun, derived from the adjective **angestellt** (*employed*). Remind students that the ending of an adjectival noun changes depending on the article that precedes it.

1 Assoziationen Wählen Sie die Berufsbezeichnung, die Sie mit jedem Foto assoziieren.

_c_ 1. Feuerwehrmann   _e_ 3. LKW-Fahrer   _d_ 5. Bankangestellter
_f_ 2. Richterin   _a_ 4. Gärtnerin   _b_ 6. Tierärztin

a.   b.   c.

d.   e.   f.

2 Hören Sie zu Stimmt das?

2 Expansion Ask students to list the qualifications of different jobs: **Welche Qualifikationen braucht ein Tierarzt/ Buchhalter/Gärtner?**

	Ja	Nein		Ja	Nein
1.	☐	☑	4.	☑	☐
2.	☑	☐	5.	☐	☑
3.	☐	☑	6.	☑	☐

3 Vergleiche Ergänzen Sie die Vergleiche mit einem passenden Wort.

Suggested answers provided.

1. Garten : Gärtner :: Fabrik : ___Fabrikarbeiter___
2. Küche : Koch :: Labor (*lab*) : ___Wissenschaftler___
3. LKW : LKW-Fahrer :: Taxi : ___Taxifahrer___
4. Auto : Mechaniker :: Toilette : ___Klempner___
5. Musik : Musiker :: Politik : ___Politiker___

3 Expansion Have students explain which of these jobs they would or would not like to have, and why.

4 Die Beförderung Hören Sie sich das Gespräch zwischen Lukas und seinem Chef an, und entscheiden Sie dann, ob die folgenden Aussagen richtig oder falsch sind. **4 Expansion** Have groups of students write a conversation between a manager and an employee and then act it out.

	richtig	falsch
1. Der Chef hatte eine Besprechung mit dem Geschäftsführer.	☑	☐
2. Er bietet Lukas eine Halbtagsstelle an.	☐	☑
3. Lukas hat ein abgeschlossenes Studium.	☑	☐
4. Lukas nimmt das Angebot nicht an.	☐	☑
5. Der Buchhalter schickt Lukas einen neuen Vertrag.	☐	☑
6. Lukas bekommt eine Stelle als Assistent.	☑	☐
7. Die neue Stelle ist nicht sehr anspruchsvoll.	☐	☑
8. Der Chef denkt, dass Lukas eine große Karriere machen wird.	☑	☐

Kommunikation

5 Definitionen Schreiben Sie mit einem Partner / einer Partnerin zu
jedem Begriff eine Definition. Sample answers are provided.

BEISPIEL

Man gibt eine Stelle oder Position auf.

1. die Gehaltserhöhung Man bekommt ein höheres Gehalt.
2. halbtags arbeiten Man arbeitet nur zwanzig Stunden die Woche.
3. arbeitslos sein Man hat keine Arbeitsstelle und muss eine suchen.
4. die Gewerkschaft Das ist eine Organisation, die sich für die Interessen der Arbeiter oder Angestellten stark macht.
5. Urlaub nehmen Man nimmt sich ein paar Tage frei.
6. die Beförderung Man bekommt eine bessere Stelle.

5 **Expansion** Have partners play a guessing game. One student says the definition, and the other guesses the correct word.

6 Berufe raten Wählen Sie aus der Vokabelliste einen Beruf und beschreiben Sie,
was man in diesem Beruf macht. Ihr Partner / Ihre Partnerin muss erraten, um welchen
Beruf es geht. Answers will vary.

BEISPIEL

S1: Diese Frau arbeitet an biologischen, chemischen
oder physikalischen Experimenten.
S2: Ist sie Wissenschaftlerin?

7 Diskutieren und kombinieren Sie und Ihr
Partner / Ihre Partnerin bekommen zwei unterschiedliche
Bilder. Finden Sie die sieben Unterschiede auf den Bildern.
Wechseln Sie sich bei Ihren Fragen und Antworten ab.

BEISPIEL

S1: Sind auf deinem Bild Taxifahrer zu sehen?
S2: Ja, drei. Und auf deinem?
S1: Auf meinem sind zwei.

8 Heute im Büro Wählen Sie zwei der Zeichnungen
und erfinden Sie eine Geschichte, in der Sie erzählen, was
diesen Personen heute alles passiert ist. Sie können über
die zwei Zeichnungen getrennt erzählen oder sie zu einer
Geschichte verbinden. Lesen Sie Ihre Geschichte
im Kurs vor. Answers will vary.

BEISPIEL

S1: Heute Morgen hat Lisa zu lange geschlafen.
S2: Sie kam eine halbe Stunde zu spät zur Arbeit.
S3: Im Büro hat sie dann ...

Aussprache und Rechtschreibung Audio

Recognizing near-cognates

Because English and German belong to the same language family, the two languages share some related sounds. Knowing these relationships makes it easier to recognize English and German cognates. For example, for many English words that contain a *d* sound, the German equivalent has a **t** in the same position.

Tag	**unter**	**Brot**	**rot**	**Tür**

For many English words that contain a *p* sound, the German equivalent has an **f** or **pf** in the same position, while a *t* sound in an English word may correspond to a German **z** or **s** sound.

Pfanne	**Schiff**	**zwei**	**aus**	**essen**

In some German words, the **ch** corresponds to an English *k* or *gh*.

machen	**Buch**	**lachen**	**Nacht**	**hoch**

In many German words, the **d** corresponds to the English *th* sound, and in a few words, the **g** corresponds to an English *y*.

Bruder	**Donner**	**Leder**	**gestern**	**gelb**

Suggestion Tell students that these relationships are the result of the **Hochdeutsche Lautverschiebung** (High German consonant shift), which occurred between the 5th and 9th centuries A.D. Since English branched off from German prior to this shift, many of its consonant sounds correspond to the German spoken around 400 A.D. You may want to point out that the **Plattdeutsch** dialect likewise skipped the shift. For example, in **Plattdeutsch** *water* is **Water** and *ship* is **Schip**.

1 Aussprechen Wiederholen Sie die Wörter, die Sie hören.

1. trinken	4. zu	7. helfen	10. Bad
2. Wort	5. Pfeffer	8. brechen	11. recht
3. sitzen	6. Apfel	9. denken	12. Garn

2 Nachsprechen Wiederholen Sie die Sätze, die Sie hören.

1. Der alte Koch arbeitet nur noch halbtags.
2. Die Gärtnerin findest du unter einem großen Baum im Hinterhof.
3. Ich suche gerade seine Telefonnummer in meinem Adressbuch.
4. Wir wollen nicht den ganzen Tag vor einem Computer sitzen.
5. Es ist besser länger zu schlafen, als soviel Kaffee zu trinken.
6. Seit einer Woche leitet sie das Büro.

2 Expansion Have students underline the cognates and provide English equivalents.

3 Sprichwörter Wiederholen Sie die Sprichwörter, die Sie hören.

Wo sich Fuchs und Hase gute Nacht sagen.[1]

Die Nacht zum Tage machen.[2]

[1] In the middle of nowhere. (lit. Where the fox and hare say "good night" to each other.)
[2] To party all night. (lit. To turn the night into day.)

More activities

S vhlcentral	LM p. 98	Online activities

Schlechte Nachrichten Video

Sabite bekommt schlechte Nachrichten aus der Galerie. Zum Glück ist Hans gut in Wirtschaft und kann Sabite trösten.

NATIONAL
communication
cultures
STANDARDS

Vorbereitung Have students look at scene 1, and discuss with a partner why they think Sabite is sad. After they have watched the episode, have students get together with their partners again and check their predictions.

1

HERR KLEINEDLER Danke, dass Sie zu dieser Besprechung in die Galerie gekommen sind, Sabite. Ich hoffe, Sie mussten dafür nicht Ihre Uni ausfallen lassen.
SABITE Ich hatte heute nur einen Kurs. Dies ist die erste Ausstellung meiner Karriere, drum möchte ich... Herr Kleinedler, es gibt doch noch eine Ausstellung, oder?

2

HERR KLEINEDLER Sabite, sie sind eine junge und talentierte Künstlerin, aber es gibt noch so viele ausgezeichnete Künstler mit vielen neuen aufregenden Werken. Wir werden den Schwerpunkt unserer Ausstellung ändern auf Berlins Nachwuchskünstler. Wir werden nur zwei Ihrer Werke anstatt zehn brauchen.

3

SABITE Aber nur zwei Werke? Das ist nicht fair.
HERR KLEINEDLER Diese beiden Werke werden fünf Wochen in der Ausstellung sein, zusammen mit den Werken aller anderen Künstler. Dadurch werden viel mehr Leute Ihre Kunst sehen. Es ist die bessere Lösung.

4

MELINE Also, Hans, jetzt wohne ich schon seit fast einem Jahr neben dir, und ich weiß immer noch nicht einmal, was du studierst.
HANS Geschichte und Politik.
MELINE Willst du Politiker werden?
HANS Ich glaube nicht, dass ich ein guter Politiker wäre.

5

HANS Mein Vater ist Forscher und Wissenschaftler. Meine Mutter arbeitet in einer Versicherungsagentur. Sie ist Buchhalterin. Und Max plant eine Karriere als Psychologe.

MELINE Ich möchte, dass bereits etwas organisiert ist, wenn ich nach Wien komme.
HANS Ich war noch nie in Wien.
MELINE Wien ist eine wunderschöne Kulturstadt. Du solltest Wien besuchen kommen...

6

1 **Wer ist das?** Welche Person(en) beschreiben die folgenden Sätze: George, Hans, Meline, Sabite oder Herr Kleinedler?

1. Er/Sie hat die erste Ausstellung seiner/ihrer Karriere. Sabite
2. Er/Sie muss den Schwerpunkt der Ausstellung ändern. Herr Kleinedler
3. Er/Sie wird nur zwei seiner/ihrer Werke ausstellen können. Sabite
4. Er/Sie weiß nicht, was Hans studiert. Meline
5. Er/Sie glaubt nicht, dass er/sie ein guter Politiker/eine gute Politikerin wäre. Hans

6. Seine/Ihre Mutter arbeitet in einer Versicherungsagentur als Buchhalterin. Hans
7. Sein/Ihr Bruder möchte Psychologe werden. Hans
8. Er/Sie möchte eine Stelle in Wien finden. Meline
9. Er/Sie hatte in den letzten Monaten sehr viele Notfälle. Sabite
10. Es tut ihm/ihr leid, dass er/sie so anstrengend ist. Sabite

PERSONEN

Herr Kleinedler Hans Meline Sabite George

MELINE Hallo Sabite. Gut. Wir treffen dich dann in einer halben Stunde da. Mann. Sabite hatte in den letzten drei Monaten mehr Notfälle als ich in meinem ganzen Leben.

SABITE Und das alles, nachdem ich allen, die ich kenne, davon erzählt habe. Könnt ihr das glauben?
HANS Sabite, wir sind deine Freunde, die dich immer unterstützen. Aber Kleinedlers Idee ist wirklich nicht schlecht. Die Nachfrage nach deiner Kunst wird sich erhöhen, wenn weniger Werke über einen längeren Zeitraum ausgestellt werden.

MELINE VWL, Einführungskurs. Hans hat recht.
HANS Es werden auch Leute wegen der anderen Künstler kommen. Und die werden dann wieder deine Kunst gesehen haben, wenn sie wieder gehen.

SABITE Danke, Hans. Du überraschst mich immer wieder aufs Neue. Es tut mir leid, dass ich so anstrengend bin.
HANS Ist schon okay, Sabite.
MELINE Wenn ich es mir so recht überlege, Hans, könntest du doch auch ein guter Politiker sein.

Nützliche Ausdrücke

- **die Ausstellung**
  exhibition
- **der Künstler / die Künstlerin**
  artist
- **der Schwerpunkt**
  focus
- **der Nachwuchskünstler**
  emerging artist
- **die Lösung**
  solution
- **die Versicherungsagentur**
  insurance agency
- **Wien ist eine wunderschöne Kulturstadt.**
  Vienna is a beautiful cultural city.
- **der Notfall**
  emergency
- **die Nachfrage**
  demand
- **unterstützen**
  support
- **der Zeitraum**
  period of time
- **VWL, Einführungskurs.**
  Economics 101.

11B.1
- **Und die werden dann wieder deine Kunst gesehen haben, wenn sie wieder gehen.**
  Plus, they will have seen your art, too, by the time they leave.

11B.2
- **Sabite, sie sind eine junge und talentierte Künstlerin, aber es gibt noch so viele ausgezeichnete Künstler mit vielen neuen aufregenden Werken.**
  Sabite, you are a talented young artist, but there are so many new exciting works by other fine artists as well.

---

 2 Zum Besprechen Zuerst ist Sabite sehr enttäuscht (*disappointed*), dass Herr Kleinedler nur zwei ihrer Werke ausstellen kann. Schreiben Sie zu zweit einen Absatz, in dem Sie Sabite erklären, dass es besser ist, weniger Werke länger auszustellen. Answers will vary.

2 Suggestion Students can also write a conversation between Sabite and her friends.

 3 Vertiefung Meline sagt, dass Wien eine wunderschöne Kulturstadt ist. Finden Sie heraus, warum. Was gibt es in Wien zu sehen? Für welche Art von Kultur ist Wien besonders berühmt? Vergleichen Sie Wien mit historischen Orten in Ihrem Land. Welche Kulturstädte gibt es? Wofür sind sie bekannt? Answers will vary.

3 Suggestion On the board, make a list of the cultural highlights that students identified.

More activities

vhlcentral VM p. 22 Online activities

IM FOKUS

Sozialversicherungen Reading

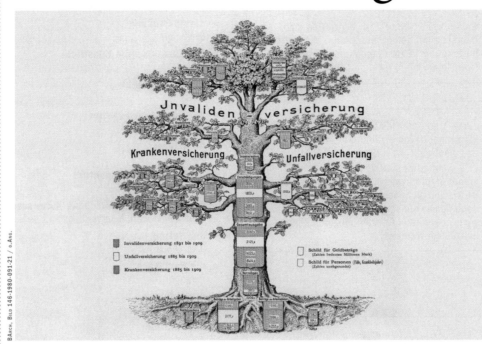

GESETZLICHE SOZIALVERSICHERUNGEN° gibt es in Deutschland schon seit Ende des 19. Jahrhunderts. Im Jahr 1883 führte° der deutsche Reichskanzler Otto von Bismarck die gesetzliche Krankenversicherung ein. Er wollte soziale Unruhen verhindern° und den Sozialismus bekämpfen°. Später kamen die Rentenversicherung und die Arbeitslosenversicherung hinzu.

Diese drei Versicherungen bilden heute die gesetzliche Sozialversicherung. Dieses System wird nicht durch Steuern°, sondern durch geteilte Beiträge° von Arbeitgebern und Arbeitnehmern° finanziert.

In Österreich und in der Schweiz gibt es ähnliche Systeme. In Österreich sind Unfall- Kranken-, Pensions- und Arbeitslosenversicherung Teil der gesetzlichen Sozialversicherungen. In der Schweiz gibt es eine Kranken- und eine Arbeitslosenversicherung sowie die Altersversicherung und die Invalidenversicherung. Anders als in Österreich und in Deutschland gibt es eine separate Versicherung für Erwerbsersatz° für den Fall, dass man Militär- oder Zivildienst leisten muss oder Erziehungsurlaub° machen muss.

Neben diesen Sozialversicherungen gibt es noch andere Ähnlichkeiten: festgelegte Wochenarbeitsstunden, ein gesetzliches Rentenalter° und eine bestimmte Anzahl an Urlaubstagen und Feiertage, an denen nicht gearbeitet wird.

Sozialversicherungen *social security* **führte... ein** *established* **soziale Unruhen verhindern** *avoid social unrest* **bekämpfen** *combat* **Steuern** *taxes* **geteilte Beiträge** *shared contributions* **Arbeitgebern und Arbeitnehmern** *employers and employees* **Erwerbsersatz** *compensation for loss of income* **Erziehungsurlaub** *maternity leave* **gesetzliches Rentenalter** *legal retirement age* **Zusatzleistungen** *job benefits*

Zusatzleistungen° in deutschsprachigen Ländern			
	Deutschland	**Österreich**	**Schweiz**
Wochenarbeitszeit (Stunden pro Woche)	35–42	40	42
gesetzliches Rentenalter	Männer: 67 Frauen: 67	Männer: 65 Frauen: 60	Männer: 65 Frauen: 64
Urlaubstage pro Jahr	30	28	20
gesetzliche Feiertage	9–13	17–18	8–14

ÜBUNGEN

1 **Im Fokus** Richtig oder falsch? Korrigieren Sie die falschen Aussagen. Diskutieren Sie dann die letzte Frage mit einem Partner/ einer Partnerin.

1. Otto von Bismarck führte in Deutschland den Sozialismus ein. **Falsch.** Bismarck führte soziale Reformen ein, denn er wollte den Sozialismus bekämpfen.
2. Die Sozialversicherung wurde von Arbeitern und der Industrie finanziert. **Richtig.**
3. Das größte Resultat der sozialen Reformen im späten 19. Jahrhundert waren mehr Versicherungen. **Richtig.**

Diskussion Welche Versicherungen haben Sie? Wer bezahlt sie? Welche Versicherungen finden Sie (nicht) wichtig? Warum?

2 **Die deutschsprachige Welt** Richtig oder falsch? Korrigieren Sie die falschen Aussagen.

1. Eine Arbeiterin bekommt in Deutschland normalerweise ein festes monatliches Gehalt. **Falsch.** Arbeiter und Arbeiterinnen bekommen Lohn.
2. An deutschen Schulen arbeiten Beamte. **Richtig.**
3. Angestellte findet man in Büros. **Richtig.**

Diskussion Haben Sie einen Job? Bekommen Sie einen Lohn oder ein Gehalt? Auf was für ein monatliches oder jährliches Gehalt hoffen Sie, wenn Sie mit Ihrem Studium fertig sind?

DEUTSCH IM ALLTAG

Berufe

der Fotograf, -en / die Fotografin, -nen	photographer
der Künstler, - / die Künstlerin, -nen	artist
der Optiker, - / die Optikerin, -nen	optician
der Schauspieler, - / die Schauspielerin, -nen	actor
der Schreiner, - / die Schreinerin, -nen	carpenter

DIE DEUTSCHSPRACHIGE WELT

Angestellte, Arbeiter, Beamte

Angestellte, Arbeiter und Beamte: Diese drei
Wörter bezeichnen° Personen, die arbeiten.
Was sind aber die Unterschiede zwischen
diesen Bezeichnungen? Angestellte sind
Personen, die vor allem in Büros arbeiten.
In Firmen haben sie oft auch eine leitende°
Funktion. Sie bekommen ein festes monatliches
Gehalt. Arbeiter sind Personen, die Lohn°
bekommen. Es kann zum Beispiel ein Stück-
oder Stundenlohn sein. Arbeiter verrichten
typischerweise manuelle Tätigkeiten°. Beamte
sind Personen, die für die Regierung arbeiten,
wie zum Beispiel Polizisten und Lehrer.

bezeichnen designate **leitende** managerial
Lohn wage **Tätigkeiten** tasks

PORTRÄT

Suggestion Tell students that in today's dollars,
the Marshall Plan would cost around $137.5 billion.

Der Marshallplan

Nach dem Zweiten Weltkrieg war Europa zu großen Teilen zerstört°. Am 3. April 1948
verabschiedete° der amerikanische Kongress einen Plan, den Marshallplan oder auch
European Recovery Program, um Westeuropa wieder aufzubauen°. Teil des Plans war es,
Kredite, Rohstoffe°, Lebensmittel und Waren nach Westeuropa zu schicken. Die drei Gründe
für den Marshallplan waren Hilfe für Westeuropa, Eindämmung° der Sowjetunion und des
Kommunismus, und Erschaffung° eines Marktes für amerikanische Waren. Das Volumen des
Plans betrug 1948 13,1 Milliarden Dollar. Der Plan war nach dem US-Außenminister George
C. Marshall benannt, der 1953 den Friedensnobelpreis bekam.

zerstört destroyed **verabschiedete** passed **aufzubauen** rebuild **Rohstoffe** raw materials
Eindämmung containment **Erschaffung** creation

🔗 IM INTERNET

Suchen Sie im Internet weitere Informationen zum
Marshallplan. Wie war die wirtschaftliche Situation
1948 in Deutschland? Was war die Reaktion auf
den Marshallplan in Europa?

Find out more at **vhlcentral.com**.

Suggestion Point out that the differences between **Angestellte**, **Arbeiter**, and **Beamter** are similar to the distinction in English between "blue-collar" and "white-collar" workers.

---

3 **Porträt** Richtig oder falsch? Korrigieren Sie die falschen Aussagen.
Diskutieren Sie dann die letzte Frage mit einem Partner/ einer Partnerin.

1. Der Marshall-Plan half, ganz Europa nach dem Zweiten Weltkrieg
wieder aufzubauen. **Falsch.** Dieser Plan half nur Westeuropa.

2. Der Marshall-Plan sollte auch für die USA finanziell profitabel sein. **Richtig.**

3. Der Marshall-Plan war eine französisch-britische Initiative.
Falsch. Diese Initiative kam von George C. Marshall, dem US-Außenminister.

Diskussion Sollte es heute auch noch Pläne wie den Marshall-
Plan geben? Warum (nicht)? Wo in der Welt könnte man so einen
Plan einsetzen (*put into action*)? Wer soll dafür bezahlen?

4 **Arbeitswelt** Schreiben Sie einen kurzen Aufsatz über Ihren idealen
Arbeitsplatz. Wo möchten Sie arbeiten? Mit wie vielen Mitangestellten
möchten Sie arbeiten? Oder wollen Sie der Chef oder die Chefin sein?
Möchten Sie für ein Start-up oder für eine große Firma arbeiten? Welche
Sozialleistungen (*benefits*) wären Ihnen wichtig?

11B.1

Suggestion Tell students that the **Futur II** is the "will-have-happened" tense.

Suggestion Summarize the pattern on the board: **werden** (conjugated) + **Partizip** + **haben/sein**.

ACHTUNG

The combination of the past participle and the infinitive of **haben** or **sein** is called a *past infinitive*.

QUERVERWEIS

See **10A.3** to review the **Futur I**. See **5A.1** and **5B.1** to review past participles and the use of **haben** and **sein** with verbs in the perfect tense.

More activities

vhlcentral

WB
pp. 153–154

LM
p. 99

Online activities

Das Futur II   Grammar Tutorial

Startblock In 10A.3 you learned about the future tense (**das Futur I**). Although it is rarely used, German also has a future perfect tense (**das Futur II**).

Bis zum Ende des Tages **werde** ich mit vier weiteren Künstlern **gesprochen haben**.

Die **werden** dann auch deine Kunst **gesehen haben**, wenn sie wieder gehen.

- Use the **Futur II** to indicate that an event is expected to have happened by or before a particular point in the future.

> Ich arbeite an einem Brief, den meine Chefin heute Nachmittag abschicken will.
> *I'm working on a letter that my boss wants to send this afternoon.*

> Bis heute Nachmittag **werde** ich den Brief **geschrieben haben**.
> *By this afternoon, I **will have written** the letter.*

- To form the **Futur II**, use the present tense of **werden** with the past participle of the verb that expresses the action plus the infinitive of **haben** or **sein**.

> Wir **werden** Urlaub **genommen haben**.
> *We **will have taken** time off.*

> Nils **wird** im Büro **geblieben sein**.
> *Nils **will have stayed** at the office.*

- Standard word order rules apply in the **Futur II**. Use **bis** to indicate the time by which a future action will have happened.

> Herr Mauer **wird bis** morgen die Arbeit **beendet haben**.
> *Herr Mauer **will have completed** the work **by** tomorrow.*

> Ich denke, dass er die ganze Nacht **gearbeitet haben wird**.
> *I think that he **will have worked** the whole night.*

- Use the **Futur II** with **wohl**, **wahrscheinlich**, **schon**, or **sicher**, to express the likelihood that something has happened or will have happened by or before a particular time.

> Peter wird **wahrscheinlich** heute gekündigt haben.
> *Peter **probably** (will have) quit today.*

> Bis nächste Woche wird er **wohl** eine neue Stelle gefunden haben.
> *By next week he will **likely** have found a new job.*

 Jetzt sind Sie dran!   Formulieren Sie die folgenden Sätze ins **Futur II** um.

1. Wir werden früh ins Bett gehen.
   Wir werden früh ins Bett gegangen sein.
2. Ich werde Arbeit finden.
   Ich werde Arbeit gefunden haben.
3. Die Assistentin wird kündigen.
   Die Assistentin wird gekündigt haben.

4. Ihr werdet einen wichtigen Termin haben.
   Ihr werdet einen wichtigen Termin gehabt haben.
5. Wie viele Fabrikarbeiter werden sie wohl entlassen?
   Wie viele Fabrikarbeiter werden sie wohl entlassen haben?
6. Dieses Projekt wird wohl scheitern.
   Dieses Projekt wird wohl gescheitert sein.

Anwendung und Kommunikation

1 **Was fehlt?** Ergänzen Sie die Sätze mit den Verben in Klammern. Benutzen Sie das **Futur II**.

> **BEISPIEL** Bis morgen Abend ___werden___ wir den Film schon _gesehen haben_. (sehen)

1. Bis heute Nachmittag ___werdet___ ihr schon die Besprechung mit eurem Chef ___gehabt haben___. (haben).

2. Bevor ich eine gute Stelle finde, ___werde___ ich schon bei vielen Vorstellungsgesprächen ___gewesen sein___. (sein)

3. Vor Ende der Woche ___wirst___ du bestimmt schon vom Personalchef ___gehört haben___. (hören)

4. Bis nächstes Frühjahr ___wird___ die Zahl (*number*) der Stellenangebote schon ___gestiegen sein___. (steigen)

5. Bis zum Ende des Jahres ___werden___ wohl viele Angestellte schon ___gekündigt haben___. (kündigen)

6. Vor Anfang September ___werden___ viele Geschäfte schon alle Sommerkleidung ___verkauft haben___. (verkaufen)

7. In zehn Jahren ___wird___ mein Vater schon in Rente ___gegangen sein___. (gehen)

8. Bis Dienstagnachmittag ___werden___ wir schon in unseren Urlaubsort ___abgeflogen sein___. (abfliegen)

2 **Bis zum 30. Geburtstag** Fragen Sie Ihren Partner / Ihre Partnerin, was er/sie wohl bis zum 30. Geburtstag alles gemacht haben wird. Benutzen Sie das **Futur II**. Answers will vary.

> **BEISPIEL**
>
> **S1:** Wirst du bis zu deinem 30. Geburtstag geheiratet haben?
> **S2:** Nein, ich werde nicht bis zu meinem 30. Geburtstag geheiratet haben. Und du, wirst du geheiratet haben?

> den Uni-Abschluss machen
> heiraten
> Kinder bekommen
> in ein anderes Land umziehen
> deinen Traumberuf (*dream job*) finden
> viel Geld verdienen
> nach Europa reisen

3 **Vor nächster Woche** Sagen Sie Ihrem Partner / Ihrer Partnerin vier Sachen, die Sie diese Woche machen müssen oder wollen. Benutzen Sie dabei das **Futur I**. Berichten Sie dann im Kurs, was Sie über Ihren Partner / Ihre Partnerin gelernt haben. Benutzen Sie dabei das **Futur II**. Answers will vary.

> **BEISPIEL**
>
> **S1:** Ich werde diese Woche zwei Referate schreiben. Ich werde auch ein neues Handy kaufen.
> **S2:** Paul wird bis nächste Woche zwei Referate geschrieben haben. Er wird auch ein neues Handy gekauft haben...

2 **Suggestion** Before students begin the activity, ask them which verbs in the word bank take **sein**, and verify that they know all of the past participles.

2 **Partner Chat** You can also assign activity 2 on the Supersite. Students work in pairs to record the activity online. The pair's recorded conversation will appear in your gradebook.

3 **Expansion** Ask students to make realistic predictions about what you will have done by the end of the week. Tell them whether or not their predictions are correct.

QUERVERWEIS

See **8B.2** to review **der**-words and **2B.3** to review **ein**-words.

Suggestion Point out that since **der**-words already carry information about case and gender, the adjective ending doesn't have to.

ACHTUNG

Remember that these endings are used with comparatives and superlatives, as well as with adjectival nouns.

Remember that adjectives that come directly after **sein**, **bleiben**, or **werden** do not have added endings.

Remember that adjectives ending in **-el** and **-er** drop the **-e-** when they take a case ending:

teuer → teure, teuren, teurer, teures

Suggestion Remind students that unpreceded adjectives and those after **ein**-words have "strong" endings because they must carry the case information that is not shown by the article.

More activities

vhlcentral

WB pp. 155–156

LM p. 100

Online activities

11B.2 Adjective endings (review) Grammar Tutorial

Startblock Adjectives that precede a noun take different endings depending on the case, gender, and number of the noun and whether they are preceded by a **der**-word, an **ein**-word, or neither.

- Adjectives that are preceded by **der**-words have the following endings.

	adjective endings after *der*-words			
	masculine	**feminine**	**neuter**	**plural**
nom.	der gute Chef	die gute Chefin	das gute Geschäft	die guten Stellen
acc.	den guten Chef	die gute Chefin	das gute Geschäft	die guten Stellen
dat.	dem guten Chef	der guten Chefin	dem guten Geschäft	den guten Stellen
gen.	des guten Chefs	der guten Chefin	des guten Geschäfts	der guten Stellen

- Adjectives that are preceded by **ein**-words have the following endings.

	adjective endings after *ein*-words			
	masculine	**feminine**	**neuter**	**plural**
nom.	ein guter Chef	eine gute Chefin	ein gutes Geschäft	keine guten Stellen
acc.	einen guten Chef	eine gute Chefin	ein gutes Geschäft	keine guten Stellen
dat.	einem guten Chef	einer guten Chefin	einem guten Geschäft	keinen guten Stellen
gen.	eines guten Chefs	einer guten Chefin	eines guten Geschäfts	keiner guten Stellen

Thomas hat eine sehr **gute** Stelle gefunden.
*Thomas found a really **good** job.*

Hast du mein **kleines** Adressbuch gesehen?
*Have you seen my **little** address book?*

- Unpreceded adjectives have the following endings.

	unpreceded adjective endings			
	masculine	**feminine**	**neuter**	**plural**
nom.	warmer Regen	helle Sonne	schönes Wetter	farbige Blumen
acc.	warmen Regen	helle Sonne	schönes Wetter	farbige Blumen
dat.	warmem Regen	heller Sonne	schönem Wetter	farbigen Blumen
gen.	warmen Regens	heller Sonne	schönen Wetters	farbiger Blumen

Jetzt sind Sie dran! **Wählen Sie die passenden Adjektivformen.** **Suggestion** Before students select the adjective endings, have them determine whether the article is a **der**-word or an **ein**-word, or if there is no article.

1. Ein Gärtner muss auch bei (schlechtes / schlechte / schlechtem) Wetter oft draußen arbeiten.

2. Wissenschaftler machen (wichtig / wichtige / wichtigen) Entdeckungen.

3. Ein (kaputter / kaputten / kaputte) Wäschetrockner ist für einen Elektriker kein Problem.

4. Die Immobilienmaklerin hat das Haus trotz des (hohes / hoch / hohen) Preises verkaufen können.

5. Unser Hausmeister geht nicht gern in den (dunkle / dunklen / dunkler) Keller.

6. Ingrid arbeitet seit (kurze / kurzen / kurzer) Zeit als Buchhalterin.

Anwendung und Kommunikation

1 **Beim Vorstellungsgespräch** Ergänzen Sie die Sätze mit den richtigen Formen der Adjektive in Klammern.

1. Wer träumt nicht von einer __erfolgreichen__ Karriere? (erfolgreich)

2. Auf ein __persönliches__ Vorstellungsgespräch sollte man sich gut vorbereiten. (persönlich).

3. Suchen Sie sich __nützliche__ Informationen über die Firma aus dem Internet. (nützlich)

4. Machen Sie dem Personalchef klar, dass Sie ein __zuverlässiger__ Mitarbeiter sind. (zuverlässig)

5. Sagen Sie, dass Sie an einer __längeren__ Zusammenarbeit interessiert sind. (länger)

6. Bleiben Sie immer freundlich und locker trotz __stressiger__ Fragen. (stressig)

7. Ziehen Sie sich lieber konservativ an und kommen Sie in __sauberer__ Kleidung zu Ihrem Termin. (sauber)

8. Zeigen Sie sich von Ihrer __besten__ Seite. (best-)

2 **Lebensläufe** Beschreiben Sie mit einem Partner / einer Partnerin die drei Personen auf dem Bild und erfinden Sie zu jeder Person einen kurzen Lebenslauf: Wer sind sie, woher kommen sie, was haben sie gemacht und so weiter. Verwenden Sie attributive Adjektive. Präsentieren Sie Ihre Beschreibungen im Kurs. Answers will vary.

> **BEISPIEL**
>
> **S1:** Die Frau in dem roten Kleid ist eine berühmte Musikerin.
> **S2:** Sie kommt aus einer kleinen Stadt in der Schweiz...

3 **Mein Traumjob** Fragen Sie einander, was Sie sich von Ihrem Traumberuf (nicht) erhoffen. Answers will vary.

> **BEISPIEL**
>
> **S1:** Was für eine Stelle möchtest du?
> **S2:** Ich möchte eine interessante, anspruchsvolle Stelle.

anspruchsvoll	großzügig	modern
dynamisch	intelligent	ordentlich
ernst	interessant	schön
freundlich	kreativ	zuverlässig

1. Was für eine Arbeitsstelle möchtest du (nicht)?

2. Was für ein Gehalt möchtest du (nicht)?

3. Was für einen Chef oder eine Chefin möchtest du (nicht)?

4. In was für einem Büro möchtest du (nicht) arbeiten?

5. Mit was für Mitarbeitern möchtest du (nicht) arbeiten?

1 **Expansion** For more practice, bring in assorted postcards and have students work in pairs to describe what they see on each card, using complete sentences and as many adjectives as possible. Collect the descriptions and correct any mistakes in adjective endings.

3 **Expansion** Allow students to focus on communication and content during the activity, but follow up by having them write down a few of their answers with a focus on accuracy. Have them trade with a partner and check each other's adjective endings.

3 **Video Virtual Chat** You can also assign activity 3 on the Supersite. Students record individual responses that appear in your gradebook.

Wiederholung

1 Diskutieren und kombinieren
Sie und Ihr Partner / Ihre Partnerin haben einige Personen, die Arbeit suchen, und einige Stellenangebote. Sprechen Sie über die Arbeitssuchenden und die Stellenangebote und entscheiden Sie, wer zu welcher Stelle passt. Answers will vary.

BEISPIEL

S1: Martin Richter hat sieben Jahre lang als Feuerwehrmann in Hamburg gearbeitet.
S2: Ich habe die perfekte Stelle für ihn. In Dresden gibt es einige Stellen für Feuerwehrleute.

1 Expansion Have students write a "want ad" together using the texts as models.

2 Semesterende
Was werden Sie vor Ende des Semesters gemacht haben? Vergleichen Sie Ihre Antworten mit denen Ihres Partners / Ihrer Partnerin. Answers will vary.

BEISPIEL

S1: Bis Ende des Semesters werde ich noch zwei Stücke auf dem Saxophon gelernt haben. Und du?
S2: Ich werde ... **2 Suggestion** Remind students to use the **Futur II**.

> Projekte fertig machen
> für die Abschlussprüfungen lernen
> ein Referat halten
> einen Ferienjob finden
> Aufsätze schreiben
> eine Sportveranstaltung besuchen
> Prüfungen schreiben
> aus meinem Zimmer ausziehen

3 Weltpolitik
Sagen Sie, was mit jedem der Länder auf der Liste in der Zukunft passieren wird. Sagen Sie auch, wann das passieren wird. Vergleichen Sie Ihre Antworten mit denen Ihres Partners / Ihrer Partnerin. Answers will vary.

BEISPIEL

S1: Bis 2035 wird China sicher eine Demokratie geworden sein.
S2: Ich glaube, dass es wohl ein kommunistisches Land geblieben sein wird.

3 Partner Chat You can also assign activity 3 on the Supersite. Students work in pairs to record the activity online. The pair's recorded conversation will appear in your gradebook.

Kanada	Russland
Österreich	Deutschland
die USA	die Schweiz

4 Der schönste Geburtstag
Beschreiben Sie Ihrem Partner / Ihrer Partnerin den schönsten Geburtstag Ihres Lebens. Benutzen Sie Adjektive, um den Tag zu beschreiben. Answers will vary.

BEISPIEL

Als ich neun wurde, habe ich den schönsten Geburtstag meines Lebens gehabt. Der Tag begann mit einem leckeren Frühstück. Wir aßen...

5 Kleine Geschichte
Schreiben Sie mit Ihrem Partner / Ihrer Partnerin die Geschichte von Frank, der in seinem Beruf nicht immer erfolgreich war. Gebrauchen Sie die angebenen Worte. Beachten Sie den Gebrauch des Präteritums. Lesen Sie Ihre Geschichte im Kurs vor. Answers will vary.

> eine Gehaltserhöhung bekommen
> eine große Überraschung sein
> die Firma verlassen
> ins Büro kommen
> eine Beförderung anbieten
> entlassen
> an der Qualität der Arbeit scheitern
> sich um eine neue Stelle bewerben

6 Arbeitsblatt
Fragen Sie drei Kommilitonen nach ihrer Lieblingsfarbe. Bitten Sie sie, zwei Dinge, die sie in dieser Farbe besitzen, detailliert zu beschreiben. Answers will vary.

BEISPIEL

S1: Was ist deine Lieblingsfarbe?
S2: Meine Lieblingsfarbe ist Grün.
S1: Was hast du alles in Grün?
S2: Ich habe eine warme, grüne Bettdecke, die mir meine Großmutter geschenkt hat...

6 Expansion Conduct a poll to find out students' favorite colors and the most common items they have in those colors.

7 Handwerksberufe

Wer in Deutschland nicht an die Uni will, macht nach dem Schulabschluss eine Lehre (*apprenticeship*) in einem Handwerksbetrieb oder einem anderen Industriesektor. In einer Lehre lernt und arbeitet man in einer Firma und geht gleichzeitig an ein oder zwei Tagen pro Woche in eine Berufsschule. Sehen Sie sich das Stellenangebot für einen Landschaftsgärtner. Diskutieren Sie sie mit Ihrem Partner / Ihrer Partnerin. Was bietet der Arbeitgeber?

BEISPIEL

S1: *Welche Qualifikationen braucht der Bewerber?*
S2: *Er oder sie muss eigenständig und verantwortungsvoll sein. Was noch?*

7 Suggestion Write on the board the German words that students won't know for apprenticeships and vocational schools, and ask students to add them to **Vocabulary Tools** on the **Sag mal** Supersite.

7 Expansion Ask additional questions about the ad: **Ab wann braucht das Unternehmen einen Landschaftsgärtner/Landschaftsgärtnerin? Wie soll man sich bewerben?**

8 Beim Immobilienmakler

Machen Sie zu zweit ein Rollenspiel. Sie sind ein(e) Immobilienmakler(in) und Ihr(e) Partner(in) ist Kunde / Kundin. Spielen Sie es dann im Kurs vor.

BEISPIEL

S1: *Ich suche ein kleines Haus auf dem Land nicht weit vom Meer. Ich brauche ein ziemlich großes Grundstück für meine drei Hunde.*
S2: *Hmmm... Ich habe hier drei Häuser, die Ihnen gefallen könnten.*

- Wie viele Zimmer brauchen Sie? Brauchen Sie besondere Zimmer oder Einrichtungen (*features*)?
- Würden Sie sich für ein Haus interessieren, das renoviert werden muss?
- Wie viel wollen Sie maximal bezahlen?

8 Video Virtual Chat You can also assign activity 8 on the Supersite.

Mein Wörterbuch

Schreiben Sie noch fünf weitere Wörter in Ihr persönliches Wörterbuch zu den Themen **Im Büro** und **Berufe**.

Panorama Interactive Map

Baden-Württemberg, das Saarland und Rheinland-Pfalz

Baden-Württemberg in Zahlen

▶ **Fläche:** *35.751 km²*

▶ **Bevölkerung:** *11 Millionen Menschen*

▶ **Städte:** *Stuttgart (628.000 Einwohner), Mannheim (306.000), Karlsruhe (307.800)*

▶ **Wichtige Industriezweige:** *Maschinenbau, Automobilindustrie, Metallerzeugnisse°*

▶ **Touristenattraktionen:** *Schwarzwald, Bodensee, Baden-Baden*

QUELLE: Tourismusportal Baden-Württemberg

Expansion Divide the class into small groups and assign each student one of these famous people to research and present to their group. You may want to provide additional names, ex.: **Hildegard von Bingen, Gottlieb Daimler, Oskar Lafontaine.**

Das Saarland in Zahlen

▶ **Fläche:** *2.569 km²*

▶ **Bevölkerung:** *1 Million Menschen*

▶ **Städte:** *Saarbrücken (178.000 Einwohner), Neunkirchen (48.000)*

▶ **Wichtige Industriezweige:** *Automobilbau, Keramikindustrie, Informatik*

▶ **Touristenattraktionen:** *Ludwigskirche in Saarbrücken, Völklinger Hütte, römische Villa in Borg*

QUELLE: Tourismus Zentrale Saarland GmbH

Suggestion Tell students that the **Limes** was a protective wall built by the ancient Romans to secure their territory and hold back Germanic invaders.

Rheinland-Pfalz in Zahlen

▶ **Fläche:** *19.853 km²*

▶ **Bevölkerung:** *4 Millionen Menschen*

▶ **Städte:** *Mainz (210.000 Einwohner), Ludwigshafen (167.000), Koblenz (113.000)*

▶ **Wichtige Industriezweige:** *Weinanbau°, chemische Industrie, pharmazeutische Industrie, Tourismus*

▶ **Touristenattraktionen:** *Speyerer Dom, Kulturlandschaft Oberes Mittelrheintal, Limes*

QUELLE: Rheinland-Pfalz Tourismus GmbH

Berühmte Baden-Württemberger, Saarländer und Rheinland-Pfälzer

▶ **Friedrich Schiller,** *Dichter° (1759–1805)*

▶ **Nicole (Seibert),** *Sängerin (1964–)*

▶ **Helmut Kohl,** *Politiker (1930–2017)*

Metallerzeugnisse *metal products* **Weinanbau** *vineyards* **Dichter** *poet* **Dom** *cathedral* **Kelten** *Celts* **Grab** *grave* **Fürstin** *princess* **starb** *died* **ausweichen** *yield*

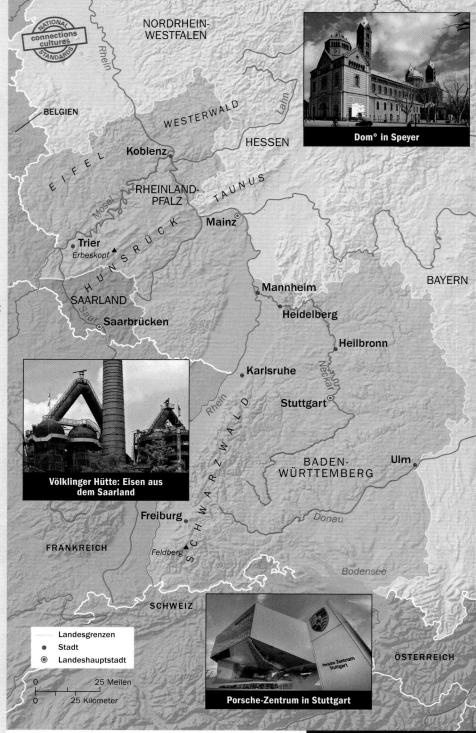

Dom° in Speyer

Völklinger Hütte: Eisen aus dem Saarland

—— Landesgrenzen
● Stadt
◎ Landeshauptstadt

0 ——— 25 Meilen
0 ——— 25 Kilometer

Porsche-Zentrum in Stuttgart

Unglaublich aber wahr!

Die Kelten° lebten früher in der Nähe der Donau im heutigen Baden-Württemberg, dem östlichen Frankreich und der Schweiz. Das älteste Grab° einer keltischen Fürstin° fand man 2010 in Ludwigsburg. Die Fürstin starb° etwa im Jahr 600 vor Christus. Erst später mussten die Kelten ins westliche Europa der britischen Inseln ausweichen°.

Geographie
Rhein

Der Rhein ist der längste Fluss Deutschlands. Er ist 1.233 Kilometer lang, 865 Kilometer davon fließen° durch Deutschland zwischen dem Bodensee im Süden und Holland im Norden. Er ist eine der verkehrsreichsten Wasserstraßen der Welt. Er ist auch eine wichtige Grenze° zwischen Deutschland und Frankreich. Die vielen Schlösser°, die man bei einer Bootsfahrt durch das Obere Mittelrheintal zwischen Bingen und Koblenz sehen kann, sind historische Beispiele der Grenzfunktion des Flusses.

Technologie
Gutenberg

Johannes Gutenberg (1400–1468) gilt als Erfinder des Buchdrucks mit beweglichen Metalllettern° in Europa. Diese Erfindung startete eine Medienrevolution. Mit Hilfe von Pamphleten konnte Martin Luther (1483–1546), der 1517 mit seinen 95 Thesen in direkte Konfrontation zur römisch-katholischen Kirche getreten war, seine neuen Ideen schnell und billig den Menschen mitteilen°. Ohne diese technische Neuerung wäre er isoliert und ohne Publikum gewesen.

Sport
Das Saarland bei Olympischen Spielen

An der Grenze zwischen Deutschland, Luxemburg und Frankreich liegt das Saarland, wegen seiner Bodenschätze ein oft umstrittenes° Land. 1952 war das Saarland politisch unabhängig°, gehörte wirtschaftlich aber zu Frankreich. Bei den ersten Olympischen Sommerspielen nach dem Zweiten Weltkrieg im finnischen Helsinki trat zum einzigen Mal eine saarländische Mannschaft bei der Olympiade an°. Sechsunddreißig saarländische Sportler fuhren nach Finnland, gewannen dort aber keine Medaille. Ab 1956 waren die Saarländer dann Teil der deutschen Mannschaft.

Kultur
Trier

Trier ist eine Stadt in Rheinland-Pfalz. Sie gilt als älteste Stadt Deutschlands. Vor mehr als 2000 Jahren gründeten die Römer die Stadt unter dem Namen Augusta Treverorum. Aus der Zeit der Römer kann man noch das Amphitheater, die Thermen°, die Konstantinbasilika und die Igeler Säule° besuchen. Die Römerbrücke ist die älteste Brücke Deutschlands. Das bekannteste Bauwerk° ist aber die Porta Nigra, ein römisches Stadttor° und Wahrzeichen° der Stadt. Alle diese Bauwerke sind Teil des UNESCO-Weltkulturerbes.

Musik Musik

Max Giesinger

Max Giesinger ist ein deutscher Sänger und Musikproduzent. Sein Lied „80 Millionen" wurde zur Hymne der deutschen Nationalmannschaft bei der Fußball-Europameisterschaft 2016.

Go to **vhlcentral.com** to learn more about **Max Giesinger.**

fließen *flow* **Grenze** *border* **Schlösser** *castles* **umstrittenes** *disputed* **unabhängig** *independent* **trat...an** *took part* **beweglichen Metalllettern** *movable metal type* **mitteilen** *communicate* **Thermen** *thermal baths* **Säule** *column* **Bauwerk** *building* **Stadttor** *city gate* **Wahrzeichen** *landmark*

---

1 **Was haben Sie gelernt?** Entscheiden Sie, ob die Sätze richtig oder falsch sind. Korrigieren Sie die falschen Sätze.

1. Die Kelten lebten zuerst im heutigen (*todays*) Deutschland und in Frankreich.
   Richtig.
2. Der Rhein ist eine wichtige Grenze zwischen Deutschland und Österreich.
   Falsch. Der Rhein ist eine wichtige Grenze zwischen Deutschland und Frankreich.
3. Das Saarland hat eine eigene Olympiamannschaft (*team*).
   Falsch. Nur bei den olympischen Spielen von 1952 hatte das Saarland eine eigene Mannschaft.
4. Johannes Gutenberg erfand den Buchdruck mit beweglichen Metalllettern.
   Richtig.
5. Das bekannteste Bauwerk Triers ist die Konstantinbasilika.
   Falsch. Das bekannteste Bauwerk Triers ist die Porta Nigra.

2 **Denken Sie nach** Diskutieren Sie die Frage mit einem Partner/einer Partnerin. Was sind die Ähnlichkeiten und Unterschiede zwischen der Erfindung des Buchdrucks mit beweglichen Metalllettern und dem Internet?

Lesen

Audio: Reading

Vor dem Lesen

Strategien

Analyzing characters

Two characters who are present in most
stories are the protagonist, or the hero,
and the antagonist, who opposes the hero.
Analyzing these characters and paying close
attention to the details the author provides in
the story can lead to a greater understanding
of the text and the dynamics of the plot.
Character analysis includes the relationships
between characters and how they treat one
another. What are their names? How do they
dress? What are their backgrounds? How do
the protagonist and antagonist act, and what
do their individual actions and attitudes tell
us about their character?

Untersuchen Sie den Text

Lesen Sie die ersten fünf Sätzen des Textes.
Was wissen Sie sofort? Wann und wo findet die
Geschichte statt? Wer ist der Protagonist und wer
der Antagonist in dem Text?

Autor
Leonhard Frank

Leonhard Frank (1882-1961)
war ein bekannter deutscher
Schriftsteller. Frank stammte
aus einer armen Familie
und ging nur wenige Jahre
auf die Schule. Mit seinem
autobiografischen Debütroman „Die Räuberbande"
hatte er 1914 großen Erfolg. Frank war Pazifist und
Sozialdemokrat. Während des Dritten Reichs waren
seine Bücher in Deutschland verboten und er verlor
seine deutsche Staatsbürgerschaft. Als der Zweite
Weltkrieg begann, wurde er in Frankreich interniert.
Er flüchtete und landete schließlich in den USA, wo er
als Drehbuchautor in Hollywood arbeitete. 1950 ging
Frank nach Deutschland zurück.

Suggestion Tell students that the spelling and puncutation in the
short story pre-date the German Spelling Reform of 1996.

(Ausschnitt°)

Die Räuberbande

LEONHARD FRANK

In der Werkstatt° des Mechanikers Tritt drückten die
Lehrjungen° sich ängstlich herum° und sahen auf die Uhr.
Der Geselle° war schon lange fortgegangen, die Werkstatt war
peinlich sauber aufgeräumt, die drei kleinen Drehbänke° blinkten,
auf dem Fußboden hätte man essen können.

Aber der Meister war noch immer nicht gekommen, um die
Erlaubnis° zum Fortgehen zu geben.

„Oldshatterhand", der jüngste der Lehrlinge, stand Wache°, um
die anderen benachrichtigen° zu können, wenn der Meister ankam.
Interessiert holte er aus der Tasche seines Mechanikerkittels° eine
kleine Feile und feilte eine Weile an seinen schwarzen Fingernägeln
herum. Dann suchte er weiter in seiner Tasche, zog einen Klumpen
öliger Putzwolle° heraus, aus der sich eine Pflaume und ein rundes
Handspiegelchen schälten°. Die Pflaume steckte er in den Mund;
das Spiegelchen rieb° er heftig° am Schenkel°
sauber und reflektierte damit die Sonne
einer Köchin ins Gesicht, die im vierten
Stock aus dem Fenster sah.

Erschrocken stürzte° er von
der Schmiede° in die Werkstatt.
Der Meister, ein Mann mit
gepflegtem rotem Spitzbart
und kalten, grünlichen Augen,
schritt° durch den Hof°, mit
seiner dreizehnjährigen
Tochter am Arm.

Der älteste Lehrling rieb
heftiger an einem Stück
Werkzeug, das er schon seit
einer Stunde rieb, immer
wieder mit Öl einstrich°
und rieb, und sah manchmal
von unten herauf nach dem
Meister, der jetzt an einer der
Drehbänke lehnte° und in der
Zeitung las. Es war sehr still,
man hörte nur das Reiben.

Der Meister sah langsam auf und starr° auf den Reibenden, der den Kopf senkte. Das Mädchen blickte° lächelnd zwischen ihm und dem Vater hin und her. Die anderen Lehrbuben standen atemlos° in den Ecken.

Oldshatterhand verrückte° die funkelnden° Zangen°, Hämmer und Pinzetten° auf der Werkbank um Millimeter.

Der Meister schritt auf ihn zu und sah, den Mund schiefgezogen°, auf ihn hinunter.

Gebannt° ließen Oldshatterhands Hände ab vom Werkzeug.

„Was soll denn das!"

„Ich le… leg das We… Werkzeug gr… gr… grad°."

„Ist das eine Arbeit? … Stotterndes Kamel!" Der Meister hatte seinen Blick in Oldshatterhands vergrößerte Augen eingehackt.

„Was bist du?"

Oldshatterhand wurde blutrot.

„Was bist du?"

„Ein st… st… stotterndes Ka… Ka… Kamel."

„Was reibst du denn! Schafskopf°!" schrie unvermittelt° der Meister den ältesten Lehrjungen an und biß auf seine Unterlippe. „Geht doch zum Teufel! … Eselsbande°!"

Das Mädchen schmiegte° sich an ihren Vater an und lächelte höhnisch°. Die Jungen entfernten° sich lautlos.

Oldshatterhand ging durch die Kaiserstraße. Vor einer Feinbäckerei blieb er stehen, sah die Kuchen an und schloß° manchmal die Augen, um besser riechen zu können, denn von unten aus dem Keller, wo der Backofen war, stieg durch das eiserne Gitter° der warme, süße Kuchenduft.

Oldshatterhand hatte es schlecht getroffen im Leben. Sein Vater war ein armer Mann. Und vom Schultyrannen Mager war Oldshatterhand zum Tyrannen Tritt geraten°.

Nach einem letzten lüsternen° Blick auf die Kuchen machte er sich auf den Heimweg.

Ausschnitt *excerpt* **Werkstatt** *workshop* **Lehrjungen** *apprentices* **drückten … herum** *hung around* **Geselle** *assistant to the master craftsman* **Drehbänke** *turning lathes* **Erlaubnis** *permission* **stand… Wache** *stood guard* **benachrichtigen** *notify* **Kittel** *smock* **Putzwolle** *polishing wool* **schälten** *emerged* **rieb** *rubbed* **heftig** *fiercely* **Schenkel** *thigh* **stürzte** *rushed* **Schmiede** *smithy* **schritt** *strutted* **Hof** *courtyard* **einstrich** *lubricated* **lehnte** *leaned* **starr** *stiffly* **blickte** *glanced* **atemlos** *breathless* **verrückte** *rearranged* **funkelnden** *sparkling* **Zangen** *pliers* **Pinzetten** *tweezers* **schiefgezogen** *drawn awry* **gebannt** *spellbound* **grad** *straight* **Schafskopf** *blockhead* **unvermittelt** *abruptly* **Eselsbande** *gang of donkeys* **schmiegte** *nuzzled* **höhnisch** *sardonically* **entfernten** *took off* **schloß** *closed* **Gitter** *bars* **geraten** *wound up with* **lüsternen** *yearning*

Nach dem Lesen

⟳ Richtig oder Falsch? Laut dieser Geschichte sind die Sätze richtig oder falsch?

	Richtig	Falsch
1. Die Lehrlinge haben Angst vor Herrn Tritt, dem Meister.	☑	☐
2. Oldshatterhand ist der älteste Lehrling.	☐	☑
3. Der Meister schreit Oldshatterhand an.	☑	☐
4. Herr Tritt nennt die Lehrlinge eine „Räuberbande".	☐	☑
5. Herrn Tritts Tochter hat Mitleid (*pity*) mit den Lehrlingen.	☐	☑
6. Oldshatterhand kommt aus einer armen Familie.	☑	☐

Expansion Ask students to correct the false statements.

⟳ Fragen Antworten Sie auf die folgenden Fragen.
Sample answers provided.

1. In was für einer Werkstatt arbeiten die Lehrjungen? Es ist eine Mechanikerwerkstatt.
2. Was hat Oldshatterhand in seiner Hosentasche? Er hat Putzwolle, eine Pflaume und einen Handspiegel in der Hosentasche.
3. Was macht Meister Tritt zuerst, wenn er in die Werkstatt kommt? Er lehnt an einer Drehbank und liest die Zeitung.
4. Was tut Tritts Tochter? Sie lächelt ihren Vater an.
5. Wie reagiert Oldshatterhand auf das Schreien des Meisters? Er wird blutrot.
6. Was macht Oldshatterhand auf dem Nachhauseweg? Er geht an einer Bäckerei vorbei und riecht die frisch gebackenen Kuchen.

⟳ Schreiben Schreiben Sie eine Interpretation der *Räuberbande*. Wie finden Sie die Geschichte? Ist sie traurig oder lustig? Beschreiben Sie auch Oldshatterhand. Wie ist er? Answers will vary.

⟳ Zum Besprechen Diskutieren Sie mit Ihrem Partner / Ihrer Partnerin, was man machen kann oder soll, wenn man in der Schule, an der Universität, bei der Arbeit oder zuhause gemobbt (*bullied*) wird. Answers will vary.

Hören

Strategien

Listening for linguistic clues

You can enhance your listening comprehension by listening for specific cues. For example, if you listen for the endings of conjugated verbs or for familiar constructions, such as the **Perfekt**, **Futur**, or **Konjunktiv**, you can find out whether a person did something in the past, is going to do something in the future, or would do something under certain conditions.

 To practice this strategy, you will listen to questions and statements from an interview. As you listen, note whether each question or statement refers to a past, present, or future action.

Vorbereitung

Sehen Sie sich das Bild an. Welche Art von Arbeit sucht wohl der Bewerber? Läuft das Bewerbungsgespräch gut oder schlecht? Glauben Sie, dass der Mann die Stelle bekommen wird?

Zuhören

 Hören Sie sich das Gespräch zweimal an. Machen Sie sich Notizen über den Bewerber, nachdem Sie das Gespräch ein zweites Mal gehört haben.

Name des Bewerbers: _Herr Huber_

Stelle: _Programmierer_

Studienabschluss: _Informatik_

Arbeitserfahrung: _keine_

Praktika: _zwei: Softwarefirmen in Karlsruhe und Mannheim_

Forschung (*research*): _Computerspiele_

Teilzeitarbeit: _Studentenjobs_

Verständnis

Richtig oder falsch Sind die Sätze richtig oder falsch?

1. Herr Huber ist gerade erst mit dem Studium fertig geworden.
   Richtig.

2. Herr Huber hat sein Studium mit der Note 1,5 beendet.
   Richtig.

3. Das erste Praktikum von Herrn Huber dauerte zwei Monate.
   Falsch.

4. Das erste Praktikum war bei einer Firma in Stuttgart.
   Falsch.

5. Das zweite Praktikum hat Herr Huber bei einer Softwarefirma gemacht.
   Richtig.

6. Das zweite Praktikum dauerte drei Monate lang.
   Richtig.

7. In seiner Forschung konzentrierte sich Herr Huber auf Softwareprogramme für die Buchhaltung.
   Falsch.

8. Herr Huber wird erst in zwei Wochen wieder von der Firma hören.
   Falsch.

Brief an den Interviewer Stellen Sie sich vor, dass Sie sich für ein Praktikum bei einer deutschen Firma beworben haben. Es war ein gutes Bewerbungsgespräch und Sie wollen sich bei der Firma bedanken. Schreiben Sie mit einem Partner / einer Partnerin einen Brief an den Interviewer: Bedanken Sie sich für das Interview und das Interesse der Firma. Wiederholen Sie nochmal Ihre Qualifikationen für die Stelle. Verwenden Sie die Sie-Form.

Schreiben

Strategien

Writing strong introductions and conclusions

Introductions and conclusions serve a similar purpose: both are intended to focus the reader's attention on the topic being discussed. The introduction presents a brief preview of the topic and informs the reader of the important points that will be covered in the body of the text. The conclusion reaffirms those points and concisely sums up the information that has been provided.

If you were writing a cover letter for a job application, you might start by identifying the job posting to which you are responding. The rest of your introductory paragraph could outline the areas you will cover in the body of your letter, such as your work experience and your reasons for wanting the job. In your conclusion, you might sum up the most important and convincing points of your letter and tie them together in a way that would leave your reader impressed and curious to learn more. You could, for example, use your conclusion to state why your qualifications make you the ideal candidate for the job and convince your reader of your enthusiasm for the position.

Suggestion You may want to share a few sample **Bewerbungsschreiben** with the class. Examples can be found online by searching with the keywords **Beispiele Bewerbungsschreiben** or **Muster Bewerbungsschreiben**.

Thema

 Bewerbungsschreiben

 Schreiben Sie eine Bewerbung, um sich auf Ihren Traumjob zu bewerben. Der Brief sollte drei Teile haben: Einleitung (*introduction*), Hauptteil (*body*) und Schluss (*conclusion*). Nennen Sie in der Einleitung kurz den Grund (*reason*) für den Brief. Beschreiben Sie dann im Detail Ihre Qualifikationen und Interessen. Fassen Sie am Ende die diversen Aspekte zusammen und erklären Sie, warum Sie ein guter Bewerber / eine gute Bewerberin für die Stelle sind.

Einleitung

- Nennen Sie den Titel der Stelle, um die Sie sich bewerben.
- Erklären Sie, warum Sie sich um die Stelle bewerben.

Hauptteil

- Fassen Sie Ihre (Schul-)Ausbildung und Erfahrungen zusammen.
- Beschreiben Sie, was Sie dadurch gelernt haben.
- Erklären Sie, warum Sie wegen dieser Erfahrungen für die Stelle qualifiziert sind.
- Beschreiben Sie, welche von Ihren Eigenschaften (*characteristics*) für die Firma wichtig sein könnten.

Schluss

- Bestätigen Sie (*Confirm*) Ihren Enthusiasmus für diese Stelle und Ihr Interesse daran.
- Erklären Sie, warum diese Stelle Ihrer Karriere helfen kann und auch, wie Sie dem Arbeitgeber nützen (*be of use*) können.

Vocabulary Tools

Lektion 11A

eine Stelle suchen
looking for a job

der/die Angestellte, -n *employee*
der Assistent, -en / die Assistentin,
 -nen *assistant*
die Ausbildung, -en *education*
der Beruf, -e *profession*
die Berufsausbildung, -en *professional
 training*
die Besprechung, -en *meeting*
der Bewerber, - / die Bewerberin,
 -nen *applicant*
das Empfehlungsschreiben, -
 letter of recommendation
die Erfahrung, -en *experience*
die Firma (*pl.* die Firmen) *firm;
 company*
das (hohe/niedrige) Gehalt (*pl.* die
 (hohen/niedrigen) Gehälter *(high/
 low) salary*
das Geschäft, -e *business*
der Geschäftsführer, - / die
 Geschäftsführerin, -nen *manager*
der Lebenslauf, ⁻e *résumé; CV*
der Personalchef, -s / die
 Personalchefin, -nen *human
 resources manager*
das Praktikum (*pl.* die
 Praktika) *internship*
die Referenz, -en *reference*
die Stelle, -n *position; job*
das Stellenangebot, -e *job opening*
der Termin, -e *appointment*
der Vertrag, ⁻e *contract*
das Vorstellungsgespräch, -e *job
 interview*

Arbeit finden *to find a job*
sich bewerben um (bewirbt sich) *to
 apply for*
einen Termin vereinbaren *to make
 an appointment*

Büromaterial
office supplies

die Büroklammer, -n *paperclip*
das Büromaterial, -ien *office supplies*
der Hefter, - *stapler*
die Pinnwand, ⁻e *bulletin board*

am Telefon
on the phone

der Hörer, - *receiver*
die Telefonnummer, -n *telephone
 number*

Bleiben Sie bitte am Apparat. *Please
 hold.*
Wer spricht? *Who's calling?*

auflegen *to hang up*
einen Anruf entgegennehmen *to
 answer the phone*
eine Nachricht hinterlassen *to leave
 a message*
in der Warteschleife sein *to be on hold*

Relative pronouns *See pp. 466–467.*
Perfekt versus *Präteritum* (review)
 See p. 470.

Lektion 11B

Berufe
occupations

der/die Bankangestellte, -n *bank
 employee*
der Bauer, -n / die Bäuerin,
 -nen *farmer*
der Buchhalter, - / die Buchhalterin,
 -nen *accountant*
der Elektriker, - / die Elektrikerin,
 -nen *electrician*
der Fabrikarbeiter, - / die
 Fabrikarbeiterin, -nen *factory worker*
der Feuerwehrmann (*pl.* die
 Feuerwehrleute) / die Feuerwehrfrau,
 -en *firefighter*
der Gärtner, - / die Gärtnerin,
 -nen *gardener*
der Hausmann, ⁻er / die Hausfrau,
 -en *homemaker*
der Hausmeister, - / die Hausmeisterin,
 -nen *caretaker; custodian*
der Immobilienmakler, - / die
 Immobilienmaklerin, -nen *real
 estate agent*
der Klempner, - / die Klempnerin,
 -nen *plumber*
der Koch, ⁻e / die Köchin, -nen
 cook, chef
der LKW-Fahrer, - / die LKW-Fahrerin,
 -nen *truck driver*
der Politiker, - / die Politikerin,
 -nen *politician*
der Psychologe, -n / die Psychologin,
 -nen *psychologist*
der Rentner, - / die Rentnerin,
 -nen *retiree*
der Richter, - / die Richterin,
 -nen *judge*
der Taxifahrer, - / die Taxifahrerin,
 -nen *taxi driver*
der Tierarzt, ⁻e / die Tierärztin,
 -nen *veterinarian*
der Wissenschaftler, - / die
 Wissenschaftlerin, -nen *scientist*

auf der Arbeit
at work

die Beförderung, -en *promotion*
das Büro, -s *office*
der Chef, -s / die Chefin, -nen *boss*
der Erfolg, -e *success*
die Gehaltserhöhung, -en *raise*
die Gewerkschaft, -en *labor union*
die Karriere, -n *career*

anspruchsvoll *demanding*
fertig *ready; finished*
ganztags *full-time*
halbtags *part-time*
zuverlässig *reliable*

Ausdrücke
expressions

arbeitslos sein *to be unemployed*
entlassen *to fire; to lay off*
kündigen *to resign*
leiten *to manage*
scheitern *to fail*
Urlaub nehmen *to take time off*
verdienen *to earn*

Das Futur II See p. 484.
Adjective endings (review) *See p. 486.*

More activities

vhlcentral | Online activities

COMMUNICATIVE GOALS
By the end of this chapter you will be able to:

🖱 **Los geht's!** Was machen Sabite und Karl?

LEKTION 12A

Talk about nature.
Talk about outdoor activities.

To do so, you will use:

Kontext Seite 498–501
• Nature
• Animals
• Words related being in nature

Strukturen Seite 506–515
12A.1 Der Konjunktiv der Vergangenheit
12A.2 Das Partizip Präsens

You will also learn about cultural products, practices, and perspectives related to:

Kultur Seite 504–505
• Landschaften Deutschlands
• Der Weißstorch
• Alexander von Humboldt

Kurzfilm Seite 513
• *Fünf Minuten Freundschaft*

LEKTION 12B

Talk about pollution.
Talk about the environment.

To do so, you will use:

Kontext Seite 516–519
• The environment
• Environmental problems and solutions

Strukturen Seite 524–531
12B.1 Der Konjunktiv
12B.2 The passive voice

You will also learn about cultural products, practices, and perspectives related to:

Kultur Seite 522–523
• Re-Use Berlin
• Umweltschutzorganisationen
• Michael Braungart

WEITER GEHT'S

Seite 532–538
You will learn about Sachsen-Anhalt und Sachsen, their people, culture, and politics.

Panorama Seite 532–533
• **Sachsen-Anhalt und Sachsen**

And you will demonstrate that you can:
Lesen: Understand the use of imagery in poetry
Hören: Improve listening comprehension by taking notes
Schreiben: Consider audience and purpose when writing

Suggestion Ask students to describe what they see in the photo. **Wo sind Sabite und Karl? In der Stadt? In einem Park? Im Wald? Wie ist das Wetter? Welche Jahreszeit ist es?**

In der Natur Vocabulary Tools

Wortschatz

die Natur	*nature*
der Bauernhof, ⸚e	*farm*
der Berg -e	*mountain*
das Blatt, ⸚er	*leaf*
das Feld, -er	*field*
der Fluss, ⸚e	*river*
die Küste, -n	*coast*
die Landschaft, -en	*countryside*
die Luft	*air*
das Meer, -e	*sea*
die Sonne, -n	*sun*
der Sonnenaufgang, ⸚e	*sunrise*
der Sonnenuntergang, ⸚e	*sunset*
der Wasserfall, ⸚e	*waterfall*
der Weg, -e	*path*
nass	*wet*
trocken	*dry*
Tiere	***animals***
der Fisch, -e	*fish*
das Huhn, ⸚er	*chicken*
die Maus, ⸚e	*mouse*
das Pferd, -e	*horse*
das Schaf, -e	*sheep*
Verben	***verbs***
aufgehen (geht...auf)	*to rise (sun)*
erforschen	*to explore*
untergehen (geht...unter)	*to set (sun)*
wandern	*to hike*

Suggestion Provide students with the past tense forms of the new verbs.

ACHTUNG

Kaninchen (*rabbits*) in the German-speaking world are almost exclusively domesticated. Their cousins **Hasen** (*hares*) are found in the wild.

Suggestion Point out that **aufgehen** and **untergehen** are used with other celestial bodies besides the sun.

Suggestion Have students brainstorm nature-related vocabulary they have already learned: **Blume**, **Pflanze**, **Park**, **Vogel**, **klettern**, **spazieren**, etc.

der Himmel *sky*

das Tal, ⸚er *valley*

der Baum, ⸚e *tree*

der Busch, ⸚e

der Wald, ⸚er *forest*

Sie machen ein Picknick (*n.*). *They are having a picnic.*

das Eichhörnchen, -

die Kuh, ⸚e

das Gras

More activities

vhlcentral | WB pp. 157–158 | LM p. 101 | Online activities

der Mond, -e

der Stern, -e

Expansion Bring in pictures of nature scenes. Divide the class into groups and have them describe what they see.

die Insel, -n
island

der See, -n
lake

die Klippe, -n
cliff

die Schlange, -n
snake

der Stein, -e
rock

der Hase, -n

Anwendung

1 Was passt zusammen? Wählen Sie das richtige Wort zu jedem Foto.

1. __a__ der Berg

2. __d__ der Wasserfall

3. __c__ das Feld

4. __b__ die Klippe

a.

b.

c.

d.

2 Hören Sie zu Hören Sie sich die Sätze an, und schreiben Sie die Substantive (*nouns*) in die passende Kategorie.

Pflanzen	Tiere	Erde	Himmel
(das) Blatt/Blätter	(die) Kuh/Kühe	(der) Berg	(der) Stern/Sterne
(der) Baum/Bäume	(das) Huhn/Hühner		(der) Mond
	(das) Eichhörnchen		
	(der) Fisch		

3 Kategorien Geben Sie zu jeder Kategorie drei passende Begriffe an.

Sample answers are provided.

> **BEISPIEL** Waldtiere *der Hase, die Maus, das Eichhörnchen*

1. Pflanzen *der Baum, das Gras, der Busch*

2. Landschaftliche Formationen *die Klippen, die Insel, das Tal*

3. Lebensräume (*habitats*) von wilden Tieren *der Wald, der Fluss, das Feld*

4. Gewässer (*bodies of water*) *das Meer, der See, der Wasserfall*

5. Tiere auf dem Bauernhof *die Kuh, das Schaf, das Pferd*

3 Expansion Have students come up with additional words for each category.

4 Momentaufnahmen Hören Sie sich die Dialoge an und entscheiden Sie, welches Bild am besten zu jeder Situation passt.

Schreiben Sie dann zu allen Bildern einen kurzen Satz. Sample answers are provided.
Suggestion Point out to students that **Hase** is an **n**-noun.

> **BEISPIEL** Sie hören:
>
> — Wie rosa der Himmel ist!
> — Ja, da hinten am Horizont geht die Sonne unter.

Gespräch __1__
Sie schauen sich einen Sonnenuntergang an.

1. Gespräch __4__
Sie machen ein Picknick.

2. Gespräch __3__
Sie schwimmen im See.

3. Gespräch __2__
Sie sehen sich die Sterne an.

Kommunikation

Ein schöner Urlaub Bringen Sie zusammen mit Ihrem Partner / Ihrer Partnerin die Sätze in eine logische Reihenfolge.

_5_ **FABIAN** Ja, nur gut, dass wir den Stall gefunden haben, wo wir uns unterstellen konnten. Wir wären sonst bis auf die Knochen (*to the bone*) nass geworden.

_1_ **FABIAN** Ich habe gerade nochmal die Fotos von unserem letzten Urlaub angeschaut. Ich glaube, das war der schönste Urlaub, den wir bis jetzt gemacht haben.

_4_ **LINA** Nicht nur an den. Auch an den Bergsee. Das Blau des Wassers—einfach unbeschreiblich! Und die vielen Tiere: die Kühe, die Schafe, die Hasen und die süßen Eichhörnchen! Leider zog dann am Nachmittag plötzlich ein Gewitter auf.

_3_ **FABIAN** Was waren wir kaputt am nächsten Tag! Denk mal an die vielen Kilometer, die wir gelaufen sind! Durch die Täler, über die Felder und dann auf den Berg hoch. Erinnerst du dich noch an den Wasserfall, der da senkrecht nach unten ging?

_2_ **LINA** Ich erinnere mich auch gern daran. Wir hatten so viel Spaß und haben so viel unternommen und gesehen. Die Wanderung, die wir gleich am zweiten Tag gemacht haben, war beeindruckend.

Richtig oder falsch? Entscheiden Sie mit einem Partner / einer Partnerin, ob die folgenden Aussagen richtig oder falsch sind. Korrigieren Sie die falschen Aussagen. Answers to false items may vary.

	richtig	falsch
1. Der Mond ist ein braves Haustier.		✓
2. Die Sonne geht im Osten unter.		✓
3. Aus Schafsmilch macht man Käse.	✓	
4. Der Rhein ist ein europäischer Fluss.	✓	
5. Hasen sind Pflanzenfresser.	✓	
6. Schafe sind kleiner als Mäuse.		✓
7. Eichhörnchen wohnen auf Bäumen.	✓	
8. Steine verlieren im Herbst ihre Blätter.		✓

6 Expansion Have pairs of students write four more true-false statements to exchange with another pair.

---

7 Diskutieren und kombinieren Sie und Ihr Partner / Ihre Partnerin bekommen zwei verschiedene Bilder. Finden Sie die sieben Unterschiede auf den Bildern. Wechseln Sie sich bei Ihren Fragen und Antworten ab. Sample answers are provided.

BEISPIEL

S1: Wie viele Flüsse sind auf deinem Bild zu sehen?
S2: Ein Fluss. Und auf deinem?
S1: Auf meinem Bild ist auch nur ein Fluss.

8 Der perfekte Tag Beschreiben Sie mit einem Partner / einer Partnerin, wie ein perfekter Tag in der freien Natur aussehen würde. Wie ist die Landschaft? Was würden Sie um sich herum sehen? Mit wem würden Sie den Tag verbringen? Was würden Sie machen? Und warum mögen Sie gerade diese Landschaft? Answers may vary.

BEISPIEL

S1: Mein perfekter Tag beginnt in den Bergen. Ich würde bei Sonnenaufgang aufstehen und ein großes Bauernfrühstück mit meiner Familie essen.
S2: Und was macht ihr nach dem Frühstück?
S1: Danach...

8 Expansion Have students take notes and describe their partner's perfect day to the class. Have the class identify similarities and differences.

Aussprache und Rechtschreibung Audio

Intonation

Intonation refers to the rise and fall of the voice in speaking. In German, different intonation is used for different types of questions and statements.

Es regnet.   **Es regnet?**   **Wenn es regnet...**

In general, statements and commands end with a drop in pitch. A speaker may use rising intonation at the end of a command or statement to communicate a friendly or encouraging tone.

Werfen Sie das nicht weg!   **Bring doch deine Schwester mit.**

Yes-or-no questions typically end with a rising intonation. Questions that begin with a question word end with falling intonation. In questions where multiple options are presented, the pitch rises before each pause and falls at the end of the last option.

Schwimmst du gern?   **Wo liegt diese Insel?**   **Ist das gut oder schlecht?**

The pitch neither rises nor falls at the end of incomplete sentences. It remains flat or neutral. This is also the case before a comma in a complex sentence. The final clause in a complex sentence usually ends with a drop in pitch.

Und wenn die Blätter bunt werden...   **Wenn die Sonne scheint, fahren wir.**

Suggestion Write an English sentence on the board to demonstrate how pitch functions in English. Have students say the sentence with different stress patterns to express questioning intonation, insistence, hesitation, friendliness, etc.

1 **Aussprechen** Wiederholen Sie die Sätze die Sie hören.

1. Der Müllwagen kommt zweimal in der Woche.
2. Wie retten wir uns vor der Erderwärmung?
3. Schlagen Sie eine bessere Lösung vor!
4. Warst du schon mal auf einem Bauernhof?
5. Willst du die Schafe, Kühe oder die Pferde sehen?
6. Wenn du nicht gleich ins Bett gehst, geht bald die Sonne auf.

2 **Nachsprechen** Wiederholen Sie die Sätze, die Sie hören.

1. Machen wir heute ein Picknick im Wald?
2. Ich weiß nicht, ob ich kommen kann.
3. Bleib stehen! Siehst du die Schlange nicht?
4. Wohnst du lieber in den Bergen oder an der Küste?

3 **Sprichwörter** Wiederholen Sie die Sprichwörter, die Sie hören.

Wo ein Wille ist, ist auch ein Weg.[1]

Es ist noch kein Meister vom Himmel gefallen.[2]

[1] Where there's a will, there's a way.
[2] No one is born an expert. (lit. No expert has dropped out of the sky yet.)

More activities

vhlcentral   LM p. 102   Online activities

Fotoroman

In der Kunstgalerie Video

Endlich ist der Tag für Sabites Ausstellung gekommen. Sabite und Karl, ein anderer Künstler, kommen sich näher, aber Meline und Hans haben Probleme.

 communication cultures NATIONAL STANDARDS

Vorbereitung Have students scan the script to find words and expressions related to nature.

KARL Ich finde deine Werke toll.
SABITE Danke, aber deine Kunst ist auch nicht schlecht. Und Herr Kleinedler hat mir gesagt, dass du noch nicht einmal eine formelle Ausbildung hast.

KARL Danke. Du bist sehr liebenswürdig. Erschaffen ist das, worin ich am besten bin. Durch die Arbeit mit meinen Händen erforsche ich meine Gefühle. Sag mir, liebst du die Natur? Ich gehe oft bei Sonnenaufgang in den Tiergarten, um unter den Eichen zu spazieren. Möchtest du mich morgen begleiten?

HANS Ciao, meine Damen! Na, wie geht's uns heute Abend?
SABITE Hans? Was trägst du da? Und deine Haare... sind sie... kürzer?
HANS Ich probiere einen eleganteren Look aus. Also, was meint ihr?
SABITE Ich glaube, du solltest du selbst sein. Wer immer das auch sein mag.

GEORGE Meline, was meinst du?
MELINE Fast so schön wie Lederhosen.
HANS Was ist an Lederhosen auszusetzen? Das Tragen von Lederhosen ist eine stolze urbayrische Tradition. Die Österreicher... ja, dein Großvater trug sicher auch Lederhosen! Diese Intoleranz macht mich rasend.

MELINE Hans, du verstehst nicht, worum es geht. Schon wieder nicht. Du bist manchmal so schwierig.
HANS Ich? Du bist die schwierigste Person, die ich jemals kennen gelernt habe!
MELINE Das stimmt nicht!

HANS Du hast recht. Es gibt schon etwas, das dir gefällt: du selbst!
MELINE Entschuldigt mich bitte.

---

1 **Was fehlt?** Ergänzen Sie die Sätze mit den richtigen Informationen.

1. Karl hat keine (Erfahrung / Ausbildung) als Künstler.
2. Durch die Arbeit mit seinen Händen erforscht er seine (Probleme / Gefühle).
3. Er geht oft in den Tiergarten, um unter den (Sternen zu schlafen / Eichen zu spazieren).
4. Hans probiert einen neuen (eleganteren / sportlicheren) Look aus.
5. Das Tragen von Lederhosen ist eine (bayrische / norddeutsche) Tradition.

6. Für Hans ist Meline die (schwierigste / schönste) Person, die er jemals kennen gelernt hat.
7. George findet, dass Hans sich (rasieren / entschuldigen) sollte.
8. Er denkt, Hans sollte Meline Zeit geben, sich zu (schminken / beruhigen).
9. Meline möchte nicht über (Hans / Kunst) reden.
10. Karl hat früher die Wälder erkundet und ist im (See / Fluss) geschwommen.

PERSONEN George Hans Meline Sabite Faik Karl Herr Kleinedler

7

HANS Ich hätte das nicht sagen sollen? Ich muss mich entschuldigen?
SABITE Noch nicht. Du würdest es nur schlimmer machen.
GEORGE Lass sie sich erst einmal beruhigen!
HANS Ich gehe nach Hause.

8

GEORGE Wer war das?
MELINE Mikhail Zagoruychenko.
GEORGE Russe?
MELINE Ja.
GEORGE Langweilig? Und Hans?
MELINE Ich möchte nicht darüber reden.

9

SABITE Hallo.
KARL Hallo. Schön, dass wir uns treffen.
SABITE Ich liebe diesen Ort.

10

SABITE Woher kommst du?
KARL Wir kommen aus einem Tal in der Nähe von Zürich. Wir haben die Wälder erkundet und sind im See geschwommen. Es war eine herrliche Landschaft mit singenden Vögeln und blühenden Blumen.

Nützliche Ausdrücke

- **liebenswürdig**
  amiable
- **erschaffen**
  to create
- **erforschen**
  to explore
- **die Eiche**
  oak tree
- **begleiten**
  to accompany
- **Wer immer das auch sein mag.**
  Whoever that may be.
- **Was ist an Lederhosen auszusetzen?**
  What's wrong with lederhosen?
- **rasend**
  furious
- **sich beruhigen**
  to calm down

12A.1
- **Ich hätte das nicht sagen sollen?**
  I shouldn't have said that?

12A.2
- **Es war eine herrliche Landschaft mit singenden Vögeln und blühenden Blumen.**
  It was a beautiful countryside with singing birds and blooming flowers.

---

2 **Zum Besprechen** Organisieren Sie ein Picknick für das nächste Wochenende. Wohin soll es gehen? Wann geht es los? Wie kommen Sie dorthin? Was gibt es zu essen? Wen laden Sie ein? Vergleichen Sie Ihre Pläne im Kurs. Answers will vary.

2 **Expansion** Ask students which group's picnic they would most like to attend and why.

3 **Vertiefung** Karl kommt aus einem Tal in der Nähe von Zürich. Finden Sie heraus, welche Freizeitaktivitäten unter freiem Himmel (*outdoors*) dieser Teil der Schweiz bietet. Was würden Sie dort am liebsten tun? Gibt es in Ihrer Nähe Orte, die ähnliche Aktivitäten anbieten? Beschreiben Sie sie. Answers will vary.

More activities		
S vhlcentral	VM p. 23	Online activities

IM FOKUS

Landschaften Deutschlands Reading

TIPP

The word **Art** generally means *type* or *kind*: **Welche Art Film hast du gern?** In biological contexts it refers to *species* and is often combined with other nouns: **Etwa 15.000 bis 30.000 Orchideenarten sind weltweit verbreitet.**

Vom Wattenmeer° im hohen Norden bis zu den bayerischen Alpen: Deutschland ist ein Land mit vielen verschiedenen Landschaften und einer Vielzahl an heimischen Tieren. Besonders in den Nationalparks findet man seltene Tiere, Vögel und Pflanzen.

Nationalpark Bayerischer Wald

Der Nationalpark Bayerischer Wald ist der älteste Nationalpark Deutschlands. Nirgendwo zwischen Atlantik und Ural gibt es einen so großen Wald, der sich ganz natürlich entwickeln° darf. Es ist ein wilder Wald, in dem es 17 Fledermausarten° gibt. Außerdem kann man Luchse° in freier Natur sehen und acht verschiedene Spechtarten° entdecken.

Biosphärenreservat Spreewald

Dieses Reservat in Brandenburg ist mit 500 Quadratkilometern eine der größten Fluss- und Auenlandschaften° Mitteleuropas. Die Flüsse und Kanäle sind hier etwa 1.500 Kilometer lang: ein Traum für Kanu- und Kajakfreunde. Wer Tiere mag, kann hier Otter, Biber°, Eisvogel° und Prachtlibelle° bewundern. Auch zu sehen sind etwa 1.600 Pflanzenarten wie zum Beispiel diverse Orchideen, Schwertlilien° und die Kuckuckslichtnelke°.

Nationalpark Sächsische Schweiz

Den Nationalpark Sächsische Schweiz, der in Sachsen liegt und an die Tschechische Republik angrenzt°, gibt es erst seit 1990. Er ist ein Paradies für Kletterfans und Wanderer. Seltene Pflanzen gibt es hier; das Gelbe Veilchen° ist noch ein Relikt aus der Eiszeit°. Vogelfans können hier Schwarzstörche, Uhus° und Wanderfalken° sehen. Außerdem gibt es Feuersalamander und Fischotter.

Suggestion Remind students that they read about another bio-diverse landscape, **National Park Niedersächsisches Wattenmeer**, in **Kapitel 7**.

Wattenmeer *intertidal zone* **entwickeln** *develop* **Fledermausarten** *bat species* **Luchse** *lynxes* **Spechtarten** *woodpecker species* **Auenlandschaften** *meadow landscapes* **Biber** *beaver* **Eisvogel** *kingfisher* **Prachtlibelle** *banded damselfly* **Schwertlilien** *irises* **Kuckuckslichtnelke** *ragged robin* **angrenzt** *borders* **Gelbe Veilchen** *twoflower violet* **Eiszeit** *Ice Age* **Uhus** *eagle owls* **Wanderfalken** *peregrine falcons* **Gefährdete** *Endangered* **Säugetiere** *mammals* **Weichtiere** *molluscs*

Gefährdete° Arten Deutschlands			
Säugetiere°:	6	Fische:	21
Vögel:	6	Weichtiere°:	9
Reptilien:	0	Pflanzen:	12

QUELLE: Rote Liste gefährdeter Arten (2018)

Expansion Ask students: **Welche Nationalparks haben Sie besucht? Was hat Ihnen da gefallen? Was haben Sie alles gesehen? Gibt es da irgendwelche besonderen Tiere, Pflanzen usw?**

ÜBUNGEN

1 **Im Fokus** Richtig oder falsch? Korrigieren Sie die falschen Aussagen. Diskutieren Sie dann die letzte Frage mit einem Partner/ einer Partnerin.

1. Naturparks in Deutschland sind wichtig, weil es dort nicht mehr viele Tiere gibt. Falsch. In Deutschland gibt es eine Vielzahl von Tieren.

2. Im Nationalpark Bayerischer Wald darf sich die Natur entwickeln. Richtig.

3. Das Biosphärenreservat Spreewald liegt in Brandenburg. Richtig.

Diskussion Wie wichtig ist Ihnen der Schutz (*protection*) von Tieren und Pflanzen? Warum (nicht)?

2 **Die deutschsprachige Welt** Richtig oder falsch? Korrigieren Sie die falschen Aussagen.

1. Im Winter findet man den Weißstorch im sonnigen Südwesten von Deutschland. Falsch. Der Weißstorch überwintert in Afrika.

2. Weißstörche benutzen jedes Jahr dasselbe Nest. Richtig.

3. In Deutschland gelten Störche als Glücksbringer. Richtig.

Diskussion Kennen Sie ähnliche Legenden von Tieren mit magischen Kräften?

DEUTSCH IM ALLTAG

Naturkatastrophen

das Erdbeben, -	*earthquake*
die Lawine, -en	*avalanche*
der Tornado, -s	*tornado*
der Treibsand	*quicksand*
der Vulkan, -e	*volcano*

DIE DEUTSCHSPRACHIGE WELT

Der Weißstorch

Der Weißstorch ist ein mitteleuropäischer Vogel, der vor allem in Deutschland, Österreich, Polen und der Schweiz zu finden ist. Er ist weiß mit schwarzen Flügeln°. Beine und Schnabel° sind rot. Er überwintert in Afrika. Der Storch kehrt jedes Jahr zum gleichen Nest zurück und so kann es nach vielen Jahren über eine Tonne wiegen. In Deutschland gelten Störche als Glücksbringer°. Der Sage° nach bringen sie auch die neugeborenen Kinder.

Flügeln *wings* **Schnabel** *beak* **Glücksbringer** *good luck charms* **Sage** *legend*

PORTRÄT

Alexander von Humboldt

Suggestion You may want to read students an excerpt from Daniel Kehlmann's popular book *Die Vermessung der Welt*, which offers a fictionalized account of Humboldt's travels through South America.

Friedrich Wilhelm Heinrich Alexander von Humboldt wurde am 14. September 1769 in Berlin geboren und starb dort am 6. Mai 1859. Er war Naturforscher und Begründer° der heutigen Geographie. Vor allem durch seine Reise nach Amerika, auf der er zwischen 1799 und 1804 das heutige Venezuela, Peru, Mexiko und die USA besuchte, wurde er weltweit berühmt. Seine Entdeckungen in den Bereichen der Botanik, Zoologie, Klimatologie und Ozeanographie dokumentierte er in seinem Werk *Kosmos*. Wegen seines großen Einflusses auf Botanik und Zoologie tragen heute eine Orchideen-, eine Lilien-, eine Kaktus°-, eine Pinguin-, eine Fledermaus- und mehrere Affenarten° seinen Namen. Allein in den USA heißen acht Städte Humboldt und der wichtige Humboldtstrom fließt entlang der Küste Südamerikas.

Begründer *founder* **Kakteen** *cactus* **Affenarten** *monkey species*

🔗 IM INTERNET

Suchen Sie im Internet eine europäische Pflanze oder ein europäisches Tier, über das Sie gerne mehr wissen möchten: Wie sieht es aus? Wo kann man es finden? Was frisst es?

Find out more at **vhlcentral.com**.

---

3 **Porträt** Richtig oder falsch? Korrigieren Sie die falschen Aussagen. Diskutieren Sie dann die letzte Frage mit einem Partner/ einer Partnerin.

1. Alexander von Humboldt hat wissenschaftliche Weltreisen gemacht. Richtig.

2. Humboldt hat sich auf *eine* Wissenschaft spezialisiert. Falsch. Humboldt interessierte sich für verschiedene Wissenschaften, wie zum Beispiel Botanik, Klimatologie und Ozeanographie.

3. In lateinamerikanischen Ländern ist Humboldt weniger bekannt. Falsch. Er hat viele Pflanzen- und Tierarten in Mexiko, Venezuela und Peru entdeckt und identifiziert.

Diskussion Gibt es eine Natur-Dokumentarserie, die Sie gern im Fernsehen sehen? Waren Sie schon einmal in einem berühmten Zoo, wie zum Beispiel in Washington D.C oder San Diego? Welche Tierarten sehen Sie besonders gern?

4 **An der Natur** Wählen Sie einen der Naturparks in Deutschland und beschreiben Sie Ihrer Gruppe verbal, was Sie dort gemacht und gesehen haben, als Sie neulich dort waren. Welche Tier- und Pflanzenarten haben Sie gesehen? Welche gefährdeten Arten haben Sie gesehen? Konnten Sie auch andere Aktivitäten machen?

12A.1

Der Konjunktiv der Vergangenheit Grammar Tutorial

Teaching Tip You may want to assign the grammar tutorial 12A.1 *Der Konjunktiv der Vergangenheit* on the Supersite for students to watch before they come to class.

Suggestion Point out that the **Konjunktiv der Vergangenheit** is often used to express regrets.

Expansion Have students convert other **Perfekt** or **Plusquamperfekt** sentences into the **Konjunktiv der Vergangenheit** by changing the auxiliary to the appropriate **Konjunktiv II** form. Make sure they understand the difference in meaning between the two sentences.

Startblock In 9B.1, you learned to use the **Konjunktiv II** to talk about hypothetical events or to express wishes about the present or the future. You can use a past form, **der Konjunktiv der Vergangenheit**, to speculate about events that could have happened, or to express wishes about the past.

Ich **hätte** nie **gedacht**, dass du solche Gefühle hast.

Das **hätte** ich nie **sagen sollen**.

- The formation of the **Konjunktiv der Vergangenheit** is similar to that of the **Plusquamperfekt**.

PLUSQUAMPERFEKT	KONJUNKTIV DER VERGANGENHEIT
Ich **hatte** ihm das **gesagt**.	Ich wünschte, ich **hätte** ihm das **gesagt**.
*I **had said** that to him.*	*I wish I **had said** that to him.*

QUERVERWEIS

See **9B.1** to review the formation and use of present forms of the **Konjunktiv II**.

ACHTUNG

Remember to use the subjunctive form of **wünschen** with a subjunctive clause to express a wish that is contrary to reality.

- To form the **Konjunktiv der Vergangenheit**, use the **Konjunktiv II** of **sein** or **haben** with a past participle.

Konjunktiv der Vergangenheit			
	wissen	**gehen**	**sich informieren**
ich	hätte gewusst	wäre gegangen	hätte mich informiert
du	hättest gewusst	wärest gegangen	hättest dich informiert
er/sie/es	hätte gewusst	wäre gegangen	hätte sich informiert
wir	hätten gewusst	wären gegangen	hätten uns informiert
ihr	hättet gewusst	wäret gegangen	hättet euch informiert
Sie/sie	hätten gewusst	wären gegangen	hätten sich informiert

Ich wünschte, ich **hätte** den Sonnenaufgang **gesehen**.
*I wish I **had seen** the sunrise.*

Wenn wir früher **angekommen wären**, **hätten** wir mehr Zeit **gehabt**.
*If we **had arrived** earlier, we **would have had** more time.*

Wenn du nur früher **aufgewacht wärest**!
*If only you **had woken up** earlier!*

Wenn ich mehr Zeit gehabt **hätte**, **hätte** ich **mich** besser darüber **informiert**.
*If I **had had** more time, I **would have found out** more about it.*

Suggestion Remind students that the auxiliary used with modals is always **haben**, and never **sein**.

- To use a modal in the **Konjunktiv der Vergangenheit**, replace the past participle with a double infinitive (verb infinitive + modal infinitive). This construction is most common with the modals **können**, **müssen**, and **sollen**.

Ich **hätte** es **wissen sollen**.
*I **should have known**.*

Sie **hätte** uns **helfen können**.
*She **could have helped** us.*

Sie **hätten** sich nicht **streiten sollen**.
*They **shouldn't have argued**.*

Du **hättest** den Wasserfall **fotografieren sollen**.
*You **should have taken a picture** of the waterfall.*

- In a subordinate clause with a modal, place the conjugated form of **haben** *before* the double infinitive at the end of the clause.

> Die Lehrerin hat Paul gesagt, dass er seine Hausaufgabe **hätte machen sollen**.
> *The teacher told Paul that he **should have done** his homework.*

> Wir wussten nicht, dass wir hier ein Picknick **hätten machen können**.
> *We didn't know that we **could have had** a picnic here.*

- When a modal is used without an accompanying infinitive, the **Konjunktiv der Vergangenheit** is formed as with other verbs.

> Er **hätte** das nicht **gekonnt**.
> *He **wouldn't have been able to do** that.*

> Wir **hätten** das nicht **gewollt**.
> *We **wouldn't have wanted** that.*

- Use the **Konjunktiv der Vergangenheit** to express wishes about events that are already past.

> Ich wünschte, ich **hätte** mehr Zeit **gehabt**, um den Wald zu erforschen.
> *I wish I **had had** more time to explore the forest.*

> Wenn wir nur länger auf der Insel **hätten bleiben können**!
> *If only we **could have stayed** on the island longer!*

- Use the **Konjunktiv der Vergangenheit** to make statements or ask questions about hypothetical situations in the past.

> Was **wäre passiert**, wenn ich dort nicht pünktlich **angekommen wäre**?
> *What **would have happened** if I **hadn't gotten** there in time?*

> Was **hättet** ihr an seiner Stelle **gemacht**?
> *What **would** you **have done** in his place?*

> Wenn das Wetter schön **gewesen wäre**, **hätten wir** ein Picknick **gemacht**.
> *If the weather **had been nice**, we **would have had** a picnic.*

> Wenn sie sehr krank **gewesen wäre**, **hätten** wir sie ins Krankenhaus **bringen müssen**.
> *If she **had been** really sick, we **would have had to take** her to the hospital.*

Suggestion Help students remember this word order with the acronym **AIM**: **A**uxiliary, then **I**nfinitive, then **M**odal.

More activities

vhlcentral

WB
pp. 159–160

LM
p. 103

Online activities

  Jetzt sind Sie dran!   **Wählen Sie die passenden Wörter.**

1. Wenn ich nur nichts gesagt (hätte/ wäre)!
2. Wir wünschten, wir (wären/ hätten) am Wochenende wandern gegangen.
3. Wenn er keinen Unfall (gehabt/ haben) hätte, hätte er sein Fahrrad nicht reparieren müssen.
4. Wenn die Klippe nicht so hoch (gewesen/ sein) wäre, wären wir hinaufgeklettert.
5. Ich wünschte, ich (haben/ hätte) als Kind ein Kaninchen gehabt.
6. Er wusste nicht, dass er den Hausmeister hätte (anrufen sollen/ sollen anrufen).
7. Wenn wir den Bauernhof (wären/ hätten) finden können, hätten wir frische Milch gekauft.
8. Welchen Weg (hättest/ wärest) du durch den Wald genommen?
9. Was für ein Wasserfall! Wenn ihr ihn nur hättet (sehen/ gesehen) können!
10. Ich (wäre/ hätte) gern mit euch aufs Land gefahren.

Anwendung

1 Sätze umschreiben Schreiben Sie die Sätze in den Konjunktiv der Vergangenheit um.

BEISPIEL

Wir kämen mit.
Wir wären mitgekommen.

Wir würden sie anrufen.
Wir hätten sie angerufen.

1. Ich schliefe länger. Ich hätte länger geschlafen.
2. Gingest du mit ihnen aus? Wärest du mit ihnen ausgegangen?
3. Er würde viel wandern. Er wäre viel gewandert.
4. Ihr solltet kündigen. Ihr hättet kündigen sollen.

5. Sie gäben eine Party. Sie hätten eine Party gegeben.
6. Ich könnte das nicht. Ich hätte das nicht gekonnt.
7. Wir müssten trainieren. Wir hätten trainieren müssen.
8. Sie würde nach Hause fahren. Sie wäre nach Hause gefahren.

2 Suggestion Quickly review the **Partizipien** of the verbs provided and have students identify which verbs take **hätte** and which take **wäre**.

2 Expansion Have students choose one sentence, build a scenario around it, and turn it into a short dialogue to share with the class.

2 Hypothesen Bilden Sie Sätze im Konjunktiv der Vergangenheit. Suggested answers provided.

BEISPIEL wenn der Manager / mich / nur / früher anrufen
Wenn der Manager mich nur früher angerufen hätte!

1. wenn die Assistentin / nur nicht / kündigen
Wenn die Assistentin nur nicht gekündigt hätte!
2. wenn seine Empfehlungsschreiben / nur / besser sein
Wenn seine Empfehlungsschreiben nur besser gewesen wären!
3. wenn ich / nur / mehr Geld haben Wenn ich nur mehr Geld gehabt hätte!
4. wenn die Katze / nur nicht / die Maus fangen Wenn die Katze nur nicht die Maus gefangen hätte!
5. wenn Jonas / nur nicht / seinen Schlüssel verlieren
Wenn Jonas nur nicht seinen Schlüssel verloren hätte!
6. wenn die Blätter / nur nicht / vom Baum fallen
Wenn die Blätter nur nicht vom Baum gefallen wären!
7. wenn das Gras / nur nicht / so nass werden Wenn das Gras nur nicht so nass geworden wäre!
8. wenn ich / nur / länger bleiben können Wenn ich nur länger hätte bleiben können!

3 Wenn es anders gewesen wäre Schreiben Sie die Sätze um.
Sagen Sie, was passiert wäre, wenn die Situation anders gewesen wäre.
Verwenden Sie dabei den Konjunktiv der Vergangenheit. Suggested answers provided.

BEISPIEL Ich bin spät nach Hause gekommen
und ich war am nächsten Tag müde.
*Wenn ich nicht spät nach Hause
gekommen wäre, wäre ich am
nächsten Tag nicht müde gewesen.*

1. Der Boden war so nass, dass die Frau hingefallen ist.
Wenn der Boden nicht so nass gewesen wäre, wäre die Frau nicht hingefallen.
2. Es hat einen Sturm gegeben und die Wanderer
konnten ihre Bergtour nicht machen.
Wenn es keinen Sturm gegeben hätte, hätten die Wanderer ihre Bergtour machen können.
3. Die Kinder haben Angst gehabt und sind ins Haus gelaufen.
Wenn die Kinder keine Angst gehabt hätten, wären sie nicht ins Haus gelaufen.
4. Wir hatten Vollmond (*full moon*) und ich habe nicht schlafen können.
Wenn wir keinen Vollmond gehabt hätten, hätte ich schlafen können.
5. Weil der Weg an einer Klippe endete, mussten sie zurückgehen.
Wenn der Weg nicht an einer Klippe geendet hätte, hätten sie nicht zurückgehen müssen.
6. Mein Hund hat nicht auf mich gehört und ist auf die Straße gerannt.
Wenn mein Hund auf mich gehört hätte, wäre er nicht auf die Straße gerannt.

Kommunikation

4 **Ich nicht** Schauen Sie sich die Bilder an und erzählen Sie sich, was Sie anders gemacht hätten. Benutzen Sie den Konjunktiv der Vergangenheit. Answers will vary.

> **BEISPIEL**
>
> **S1:** Ich wäre nicht so schnell gefahren!
> **S2:** Ich hätte länger an der Kreuzung gewartet!

5 **Wenn nur!** Was wäre wenn? Arbeiten Sie mit einem Partner / einer Partnerin und diskutieren Sie, was im letzten Jahr passiert wäre, wäre die Situation anders gewesen. Verwenden Sie dazu den Konjunktiv der Vergangenheit. Answers will vary.

BEISPIEL

S1: Was wäre (passiert), wenn ich fleißiger gelernt hätte?
S2: Du hättest vielleicht eine bessere Note bekommen!
S1: Was wäre passiert, wenn der Winter nicht so kalt gewesen wäre?
S2: Dann hätte ich nicht so viel gefroren.

6 **Was hättest du lieber gemacht?** Berichten Sie Ihrem Partner / Ihrer Partnerin von zwei Aktivitäten, die Sie letztes Wochenende gemacht haben. Erzählen Sie sich, was Sie lieber gemacht hätten, und verwenden Sie dabei den Konjunktiv der Vergangenheit. Answers will vary.

BEISPIEL

S1: Was hast du am Wochenende gemacht?
S2: Am Samstag habe ich ein Referat für Geschichte geschrieben und am Sonntag bin ich zum Waschsalon gefahren.
S1: Und was hättest du lieber gemacht?
S2: Ich hätte lieber länger geschlafen. Ich wäre auch lieber ins Kino gegangen.

7 **Vor 100 Jahren** Was hätten Sie (nicht) machen können, müssen oder dürfen, wenn Sie vor hundert Jahren gelebt hätten? Schreiben Sie vier Sätze und lesen Sie sie im Kurs vor. Answers will vary.

BEISPIEL

S1: Ich hätte nicht im Internet surfen können.
S2: Ich hätte keinen Minirock tragen dürfen.

4 **Suggestion** If students have difficulty spontaneously producing the past subjunctive in this activity, have them prepare their answers as written homework, and then share them with a partner during the next class.

4 **Partner Chat** You can also assign activity 4 on the Supersite. Students work in pairs to record the activity online. The pair's recorded conversation will appear in your gradebook.

6 **Video Virtual Chat** You can also assign activity 6 on the Supersite. Students record individual responses that appear in your gradebook.

12A.2 *Das Partizip Präsens* Grammar Tutorial

Startblock The present participle (**das Partizip Präsens**) can be used as an adjective or an adverb. It is used more often in writing than in spoken German.

ACHTUNG

Present participles used as adjectives can have comparative and superlative forms.: **der bedeutend<u>ere</u> Film; der bedeutend<u>ste</u> Film**

Remember that you do not need to add adjective endings to present participles used as predicate adjectives after **sein**, **bleiben**, or **werden**.

QUERVERWEIS

See **11B.2** to review adjective endings.
See **8A.2** to review the formation of comparatives and superlatives.

ACHTUNG

Past participles can also be used as adjectives and adverbs, following the same rules for adjective endings.

Auf der neu <u>entdeckten</u> Insel gab es sehr schöne Klippen und Wasserfälle.

Suggestion Explain that while an English present participle may be used as a noun (*smoking is prohibited*), German present participles cannot.

... es gibt auch von anderen ausgezeichneten Künstlern so viele neue **aufregende** Werke.

Es war eine herrliche Landschaft mit **singenden** Vögeln und **blühenden** Blumen.

- To form the present participle in German, add **-d** to the infinitive.

Suggestion Emphasize to students that *any* infinitive can be turned into an adjective or adverb by adding **-d**, followed by an adjective ending where necessary.

present participle	
klingelnd	*ringing*
lachend	*laughing*
wachsend	*growing*

Suggestion Point out that the second example sentence is a **Sprichwort**, similar to the English proverb, "Let sleeping dogs lie."

- When you use present participles as adjectives, follow the normal rules for adjective endings.

Der **aufgehende** Mond war sehr schön.
*The **rising** moon was beautiful.*

Schlafende Hunde soll man nicht wecken.
*You shouldn't wake a **sleeping** dog.*

Michael Hanekes Filme sind **bedeutend**.
*Michael Haneke's films are **important**.*

- Present participles can also be used as adverbs. When used as adverbs, they do not have added endings.

Nachdem der Junge vom Baum gefallen war, lief er **weinend** nach Hause.
*After the boy fell out of the tree, he ran home **crying**.*

Er sah ihr **suchend** in die Augen.
*He looked **searchingly** into her eyes.*

Suggestion Point out that a present participle and a past participle can be used together as attributive adjectives. Ex.: **die folgenden vergessenen historischen Orte.**

More activities

vhlcentral

WB
pp. 161–162

LM
p. 104

Online activities

Jetzt sind Sie dran! Wählen Sie die passenden Wörter.

1. Peter ist ein gut (aussehend / (aussehender) / aussehenden) Bauer.

2. Die (spielend / (spielenden) / spielende) Eichhörnchen sind niedlich (*cute*).

3. Wir fahren am (kommend / (kommenden) / kommendes) Wochenende an den See.

4. Hast du auch die (passend / passende / (passenden)) Schuhe zu diesem Kleid?

5. Das Mädchen lief ((singend) / singende / singender) durch den Wald.

6. Wo ist hier ein (funktionierend / (funktionierender) / funktionierenden) Drucker?

7. Die Kinder laufen ((lachend) / lachende / lachendes) durch das Feld.

8. Das war ein (überraschend / überraschenden / (überraschender)) Besuch!

9. ((Anschließend) / Anschließende / Anschließenden) gingen wir alle ins Kino.

10. Bitte beantworten Sie die (folgend / (folgenden) / folgende) Fragen.

Anwendung und Kommunikation

1 **Partizipien** Ergänzen Sie die richtigen Partizipendungen. Wenn Sie keine Endung brauchen, machen Sie einen Strich (*slash*).

> **BEISPIEL** Der Zirkus hatte einen tanzend*en* Bären (*bear*).
> Sein Tanzen war überraschend—— gut.

1. Die laufend*en* Kosten sind circa 120 Euro monatlich.
2. Sie hat das weinend*e* Baby nicht beruhigen (*calm down*) können.
3. Wir fahren in der kommend*en* Woche an den Strand.
4. Der Film war aufregend——.
5. Wegen stark steigend*er* Ölpreise wird alles teurer.
6. Ein schlafend*er* Hund liegt vor der Tür.
7. Die Prüfung war überraschend—— einfach.
8. Sein klingelnd*es* Handy ist allen auf die Nerven gegangen.

2 **Bilder beschreiben** Beschreiben Sie bei jedem Bild, was gerade passiert. Benutzen Sie dabei die Verben aus der Liste. Danach wiederholt Ihr Partner / Ihre Partnerin den Satz, aber er/sie muss das Verb in ein Partizip umändern (*change*). Answers will vary.

> klingeln | spielen
> scheinen | weinen
> schlafen |

▶ **BEISPIEL**
S1: Der Mond scheint hell diese Nacht.
S2: Ja, das ist ein hell scheinender Mond.

Der Mond...

Die Katze...

Das Kind...

Der Wecker...

Die Mädchen...

3 **Umweltprobleme** Schlagen Sie sich gegenseitig mögliche Lösungen (*solutions*) für die folgenden Probleme vor. Schreiben Sie eine Liste der besten Vorschläge und präsentieren Sie sie im Kurs. Answers will vary.

S1: Die Temperaturen steigen.
S2: Was können wir gegen die steigenden Temperaturen tun?
S1: Wir könnten weniger Auto fahren.

1. Die Temperaturen steigen.
2. Der Müll stinkt.
3. Die Regenwälder (*rainforests*) sterben.
4. Die Wasserqualität sinkt.

Wiederholung

1 Wie wäre es gewesen?
Wählen Sie eine Angabe (*condition*) aus der Liste und bilden Sie mit einem Partner / einer Partnerin eine logische Folgerung (*conclusion*) daraus. Benutzen Sie den Konjunktiv der Vergangenheit. Answers will vary.

BEISPIEL

Wenn wir früh aufgestanden wären, hätten wir den Sonnenaufgang gesehen.

früh aufstehen	mehr regnen
das Feld nicht so klein sein	auf den Berg steigen
wandern gehen	ein Boot haben

2 Diskutieren und kombinieren
Auf Ihrem Blatt finden Sie Informationen über vier Personen und vier Urlaubsorte. Berichten Sie Ihrem Partner / Ihrer Partnerin, was Ihre Personen gerne im Urlaub machen. Answers will vary.

2 Suggestion Give students time to read through each text and underline key words.

BEISPIEL

S1: Julian Koch liebt das Leben in der Stadt. Aber er segelt auch gerne und geht gerne klettern.
S2: Er sollte Salzburg besuchen. Da gibt es viele Theater und Konzerte. Die Berge sind sehr nah und es gibt auch Seen in der Nähe.

3 Was hätten Sie gemacht?
Sehen Sie sich mit einem Partner / einer Partnerin die Fotos an. Sagen Sie, was jede Person gemacht hat, und fragen Sie einander, was Sie in der gleichen Situation gemacht hätten. Benutzen Sie den Konjunktiv der Vergangenheit. Answers will vary.

3 Partner Chat You can also assign activity 3 on the Supersite.

BEISPIEL

S1: Sarah ist auf diesem Weg gelaufen. Wärest du darauf gelaufen?
S2: Nein. Obwohl dieser Weg sehr schön aussieht, wäre ich dort nicht gelaufen, weil es zu viele Insekten im hohen Gras gibt.

Sarah / laufen

 David / spielen
 Lara / schwimmen
 Nina / nahekommen

 Jonas / klettern gehen
 Max / angeln gehen
Hanna / springen

4 Arbeitsblatt
Zeichnen Sie (*draw*) ein Bild mit Tieren, die etwas Unerwartetes (*unexpected*) machen. Bitten Sie drei Personen im Unterricht, das Bild mit Partizipien der Gegenwart zu beschreiben. Schreiben Sie die Antworten auf. Answers will vary.

BEISPIEL

S1: Was siehst du auf meinem Bild?
S2: Die sprechende Kuh fragt das stehende Pferd, was das singende Huhn sagt.
S3: Das singende Huhn erzählt dem denkenden Pferd ...

5 Regeln
Schreiben Sie mit einem Partner / einer Partnerin Sicherheitsregeln für die folgenden Situationen. Answers will vary.

BEISPIEL in den Bergen wandern

S1: Wenn man in den Bergen wandert, soll man auf das Wetter achten.
S2: Wenn man in den Bergen wandert, muss man Trinkwasser mitbringen.

im Wald Fahrrad fahren	auf eine Klippe klettern
in einem See baden	unter einem Wasserfall baden
auf dem Meer segeln	ein Pferd reiten

6 Die Traumlandschaft
Beschreiben Sie einem Partner / einer Partnerin Ihre Traumlandschaft. Benutzen Sie so viele Details wie möglich für Ihre Beschreibung. Ihr Partner / Ihre Partnerin macht sich Notizen, um später allen diese Traumlandschaft beschreiben zu können. Answers will vary.

BEISPIEL

Neulich habe ich einen komischen Traum gehabt. Ich wanderte in den Bergen und kam auf ein Feld. Beim aufgehenden Mond sah ich einen laufenden Hasen aus dem Wald kommen. Der Hase...

S Video: Short Film

Fünf Minuten Freundschaft

Soldat Ralf Schaller patroulliert zum ersten Mal mit seinem Vorgesetzten (*superior*) die deutsch-deutsche Grenze in einem Wald in Ostdeutschland. Als der Vorgesetzte plötzlich den Weg verlässt (*departs*), muss Schaller entscheiden, ob er den Regeln folgt oder seinem Vorgesetzten vertraut.

Vorbereitung

Nützliche Ausdrücke

- **die Akte, -n**
  file
- **der Bau**
  (*colloq.*)
  slammer, prison
- **Das liegt ganz an Ihnen.**
  It is entirely up to you.
- **rasen**
  to hurry
- **rübermachen**
  to go from East- to West-Germany
- **schießen**
  to shoot
- **sich nähern**
  to approach
- **vorsichtig**
  carefully
- **warnen**
  to warn

Über den Film sprechen

- **der Genosse**
  comrade
- **die Grenze, -n**
  border
- **vertrauen**
  to trust
- **der Westempfang**
  the ability to receive West German broadcasts, literally: west reception

1 **Was fehlt?** Ergänzen Sie die Sätze mit einem passenden Wort oder Ausdruck aus den Listen.

1. Warum ____rast____ du denn so? Hast du's eilig?
2. Bitte haltet eure Pässe bereit, denn wir ____nähern____ uns der Grenze.
3. Mein bester Freund ist immer auf meiner Seite. Ich ____vertraue____ ihm.
4. Wie es nun weitergeht, ____liegt____ ganz an Ihnen.
5. Das ist gefährlich! Bitte sei ____vorsichtig____!
6. Hör dir den Westempfang nicht an, denn dafür kommt man jahrelang in den ____Bau____.
7. Stehen bleiben, oder ich ____schieße____!
8. Ich ____warne____ Sie! Legen Sie das ganz vorsichtig hin.

2 **Was wissen Sie schon?** Diskutieren Sie die Fragen mit einem Partner / einer Partnerin. Answers will vary.

1. Wie unterscheidet sich die ehemalige deutsch-deutsche Grenze von anderen Staats- und Landesgrenzen, die Sie kennen oder schon einmal überschritten haben?
2. Deutschland war zwischen 1949 und 1990 in Ost- und Westdeutschland geteilt. Diskutieren Sie, wie sich so eine Teilung auf das Leben der Menschen auswirkt.

3 **Die Hauptfiguren** Sehen Sie sich die Gesichter der beiden Hauptfiguren genau an und beschreiben Sie sie Ihrem Parter / Ihrer Partnerin. Answers will vary.

Genosse Gefreiter   Genosse Schaller

Suggestion Explain to students that **die deutsch-deutsche Grenze,** also called **die innerdeutsche Grenze,** was a heavily fortified and guarded border between **DDR** (**Deutsche Demokratische Republik,** formerly East Germany) and **BRD** (**Bundesrepublik Deutschland,** Federal Republic of Germany). It was built during the years following World War II and spanned almost 900 miles. The Berlin Wall was a smaller and separate structure that surrounded the city of West Berlin inside of East Germany. Both borders were opened in 1990, shortly before the reunification of Germany.

Szenen: Fünf Minuten Freundschaft

GENOSSE GEFREITER: Genosse, es ist die Aufgabe, die Grenze zu patroullieren.

GENOSSE SCHALLER: Jawohl, Genossse Gefreiter. Aber doch wohl nicht die ganze.

Suggestion Tell students that **Stasi** is the informal name for the **Staatssicherheitsdienst (SSD),** the secret state police agency of East Germany. Headquartered in Berlin, Stasi employees as well as a network of informants collected personal and political information on private citizens. In 1992 individuals were granted access to the Stasi files.

GENOSSE GEFREITER: Genosse, Schaller. Wovor haben sie euch in Berlin gewarnt?
GENOSSE SCHALLER: Sie haben gesagt, dass ihr hier auf alles schießt, was sich der Grenze nähert. Frauen und Kinder auch.

GENOSSE SCHALLER: Was machst du denn da? Hey, komm da raus, Mensch! Mensch, komm da raus, jetzt!

GENOSSE SCHALLER: Nimm die Hände hoch! Hände hoch! Und geh da rüber, jetzt.

Suggestion Tell students that in former East Germany all media were state-censored and it was forbidden to listen to West German radio or watch West German TV.

GENOSSE SCHALLER: Dafür kommt man in den Bau. Für ganz schön lange sogar. Das ist dir klar, oder?
GENOSSE GEFREITER: Liegt ganz an Ihnen. Ganz an Ihnen, Genosse Schaller.

Analyse

4 Richtig oder falsch?

Richtig oder falsch? Entscheiden Sie, ob die folgenden Aussagen richtig oder falsch sind. Korrigieren Sie danach die falschen Aussagen.

	richtig	falsch	
1. Genosse Schaller und Genosse Gefreiter patrouillieren die Grenze zwischen Deutschland und Frankreich.	☐	☑	**Falsch.** Sie patroullieren die deutsch-deutsche Grenze.
2. Genosse Gefreiter läuft sehr schnell.	☑	☐	
3. Genosse Gefreiter will nicht wissen, was man in Berlin über ihn sagt.	☐	☑	**Falsch.** Er will wissen, was man in Berlin über ihn sagt.
4. Genosse Schaller und Genosse Gefreiter kennen sich gut.	☐	☑	**Falsch.** Sie kennen sich nicht gut.
5. Genosse Gefreiter verlässt den vorgeschriebenen Weg.	☑	☐	
6. Genosse Gefreiter zieht seine Waffe, um auf einen Fuchs zu schießen.	☐	☑	**Falsch.** Genosse Schaller zieht seine Waffe nicht.
7. Genosse Gefreiter hat ein Radio im Wald versteckt.	☑	☐	
8. Wenn man Westradio hörte, konnte man in Ostdeutschland ins Gefängnis kommen.	☑	☐	
9. Genosse Schaller war ein Informant.	☑	☐	
10. Die beiden Männer treffen sich noch immer jedes Jahr.	☐	☑	**Falsch.** Sie treffen sich seit einem Jahr nicht mehr.

Fortsetzung Überlegen Sie sich mit einem Partner / einer Partnerin, wie der Kurzfilm weitergehen könnte. Werden sich die beiden Männer wieder treffen? Was kann Schaller tun, um die Freundschaft wieder aufzubauen? Schreiben Sie einen Dialog zwischen den beiden nun älteren Männern.

7 Nachgedacht

Nachgedacht Lesen sie die folgenden Sprichwörter. Was haben Sie mit dem Film zu tun? Finden Sie, dass die beiden Zitate richtig sind? Begründen Sie Ihre Meinung und besprechen Sie sie mit einem Partner / einer Partnerin.
Answers will vary.

„Misstrauen ist besser
als Zutrauen."
— deutsches Sprichwort

„Geflickte Freundschaft
wird selten
wieder ganz."
— deutsches Sprichwort

6 Diskutieren

Diskutieren Besprechen Sie die folgenden Themen im Kurs. Answers will vary.

1. Warum war es in Ostdeutschland nicht erlaubt, Westradio zu hören?

2. Die Stasi-Akten haben gezeigt, dass viele Menschen in der DDR Informanten waren und sogar über ihre Nachbarn, Freunde und Verwandten informiert haben. Wie denken Sie darüber? Können Sie sich eine Situtation vorstellen, in der Sie zum Informanten werden?

3. Was kann man tun, um das Vertrauen eines Freundes wiederzugewinnen?

Die Umwelt

 Vocabulary Tools

Suggestion Point out that Germany has announced plans to abandon nuclear energy by 2022, although some government officials have stated that this goal is unrealistic.

Wortschatz

die Umwelt	*environment*
die Art, -en	*species*
die Erde, -n	*earth*
die Gefahr, -en	*danger*
das Hochwasser, -	*flood*
das Licht, -er	*light*
die Ökologie	*ecology*
der Umweltschutz	*environmentalism*
die Welt, -en	*world*
biologisch	*organic*
gefährdet	*endangered*
ökologisch	*ecological*
umweltfreundlich	*environmentally friendly*
Energie	***energy***
die Windenergie	*wind energy*
Probleme	***problems***
das Aussterben	*extinction*
die Erderwärmung	*global warming*
der Giftmüll	*toxic waste*
die Überbevölkerung	*overpopulation*
Lösungen	***solutions***
das Gesetz, -e	*law*
die erneuerbare Energie (*pl.* die erneuerbaren Energien)	*renewable energy*
das Hybridauto, -s	*hybrid car*
die Regierung, -en	*government*
Verben	***verbs***
ausschalten (schaltet... aus)	*to turn off*
(den Planeten) retten	*to save (the planet)*
einschalten (schaltet... ein)	*to turn on*
entwickeln	*to develop*
erhalten	*to preserve*
schützen	*to protect*
verbessern	*to improve*
verschmutzen	*to pollute*
vorschlagen (schlägt... vor)	*to propose*
wegwerfen (wirft... weg)	*to throw away*

Suggestion Point out that environmental protection is an official national goal for Germany, and has been part of the German **Grundgesetz** since 1994. Ask students if they think environmental protection is a priority in their own country.

der saure Regen
acid rain

die Kernenergie
nuclear energy

die Sonnenenergie
solar energy

das Kernkraftwerk, -e
nuclear power plant

die Fabrik, -en
factory

Fabrik

die Verschmutzung
pollution

Sie bilden eine Fahrgemeinschaft.
They are carpooling.

Anwendung

ACHTUNG

The terms **Wiederverwertung** and **wiederverwerten** are sometimes used instead of the English loan words **Recycling** and **recyceln: Durch Wiederverwertung von Glas und Papier können wir alle unseren täglichen Haushaltsmüll stark reduzieren.**

der Müllwagen, -
garbage truck

Sie recycelt.
(recyceln)
She is recycling.

das Recycling

der Müll

1 Was passt nicht? Geben Sie an, welches Wort nicht zu den anderen passt.

1 Expansion Have students write one more group of words on a piece of paper. Have volunteers read their lists aloud and have their classmates find the word that doesn't belong.

1. Glas, Papier, (Gras), Plastik
2. erforschen, erfinden, entdecken, (einladen)
3. Smog, (Lösung), Wasserverschmutzung, Giftmüll
4. (Körperenergie), Windenergie, Sonnenenergie, Kernenergie
5. Regierung, Gesetz, Minister, (Gefahr)
6. biologisch, ökologisch, (gefährdet), umweltfreundlich

2 Hören Sie zu Entscheiden Sie, ob die Aussagen logisch oder unlogisch sind.

	Logisch	Unlogisch
1.	☑	☐
2.	☐	☑
3.	☐	☑
4.	☐	☑
5.	☑	☐
6.	☑	☐

3 Was ist richtig? Ergänzen Sie die Sätze mit einem passenden Ausdruck.

1. Um unsere Umwelt zu schützen, müssen wir alle mehr (recyceln) / wegwerfen).
2. Der saure Regen (verbessert / verschmutzt) die Wälder.
3. Viele Tierarten sind (gefährdet) / erneuerbar).
4. Wenn es plötzlich zu viel regnet, haben die Flüsse (Giftmüll / (Hochwasser)).
5. Es ist wichtig, dass die Regierung umweltfreundliche ((Gesetze) / Gefahren) vorschlägt.

4 Jeder muss seinen Teil tun Sie hören im Radio einen öffentlichen Aufruf (*public service announcement*) zum Thema Umweltschutz. Hören Sie zu und ergänzen Sie dann jeden Satz mit dem richtigen Wort.

1. Jeder muss seinen Teil (*part*) tun, um unsere ___Umwelt___ zu schützen.
2. Wir sollen Papier und ___Glas___ recyceln.
3. Wir können Strom (*electricity*) sparen, wenn wir nicht in allen Zimmern das ___Licht___ anlassen.
4. Man sollte weniger Produkte konsumieren, die ___Giftmüll___ produzieren.
5. Bio-Lebensmittel sind nicht nur gesünder, sondern auch ___umweltfreundlicher___.

4 Suggestion Prepare students for the listening activity by having them work in pairs to make a list of **Dinge in unserem täglichen Leben, die wir machen können, um die Erde zu retten.**

Kommunikation

5 Ein Umweltproblem
Lesen Sie den folgenden Artikel und ergänzen Sie mit einem Partner / einer Partnerin die Sätze. Sample answers are provided.

1. Wir haben eine Krise, weil zu viel __Energie__ verbraucht wird.
2. Alte Fabriken __verschmutzen__ den Planeten.
3. Es gibt viele __Lösungen__ für die Energiekrise.
4. Solar-, Wind- und Kernenergie sind __erneuerbare__ Energiequellen.
5. Öffentliche Verkehrsmittel und __Hybridautos__ verbrauchen weniger Energie pro Person.
6. Zusammen können wir den Planeten __retten__.

5 Expansion Ask students: **Was kann man sonst noch machen um den Planeten zu retten?**

Fokus Umwelt

ENERGIEVERBRAUCH

Die Energiekrise wird zu einem immer ernsteren Problem, das wir so schnell wie möglich angehen (*address*) müssen. Unsere Fabriken sind alt, verbrauchen (*use*) zu viel Energie und tragen (*contribute*) zur Verschmutzung des Planeten bei. Unsere Autos verbrauchen zu viel Benzin und verursachen (*cause*) Smog. Man kann die Energiekrise auf verschiedene Art und Weise lösen (*solve*). Erstens müssen wir weitere erneuerbare Energiequellen wie Solar-, Wind- oder Kernenergie verwenden. In der Stadt könnten wir alle öffentliche Verkehrsmittel oder Hybridautos benutzen. In den Häusern sollten wir versuchen, weniger Energie zu verbrauchen und unseren Stromverbrauch zu kontrollieren. Wir müssen zusammenarbeiten, um den Planeten zu retten!

6 Diskutieren und kombinieren
Sie und Ihr Partner / Ihre Partnerin bekommen zwei verschiedene Arbeitsblätter. Jeder von Ihnen hat nur die Hälfte der Informationen über die verschiedenen Umweltprobleme auf der Welt. Finden Sie heraus, welche Information Ihnen fehlt. Sample answers are provided.

BEISPIEL

S1: *Welches Land auf deiner Karte hat Probleme mit Smog?*
S2: *Mexiko hat Probleme mit Smog. Und auf deiner Karte?*
S1: *Großbritannien hat auch Probleme damit.*

7 Sätze bilden
Bringen Sie die Sätze zu einem logischen Schluss. Vergleichen Sie danach Ihre Antworten mit denen Ihres Partners / Ihrer Partnerin. Answers will vary.

BEISPIEL Das Gute an Hybridautos ist,...
dass sie die Luftverschmutzung in den Städten reduzieren.

1. Die größten Umweltprobleme sind...
2. Die Überbevölkerung ist ein weltweites Problem,...
3. Viele Tierarten sind vom Aussterben bedroht,...
4. Recyceln ist wichtig,...
5. Erneuerbare Energien sind solche,...
6. Um unseren Planeten zu retten,...

8 Karrieren mit Zukunftschancen
Erstellen Sie zu dritt eine Liste von Berufen, die Ihrer Meinung nach große Zukunftschancen haben. Beschreiben Sie für jeden Beruf die Tätigkeit (*type of work*), den Nutzen in der heutigen Zeit, und warum Ihrer Meinung nach dieser Beruf in der Zukunft noch wichtiger sein wird. Präsentieren Sie danach Ihre Liste im Kurs vor.
Answers will vary.

BEISPIEL

S1: *In der Zukunft wird die Erderwärmung weiter zunehmen.*
S2: *Ein nützlicher Beruf wäre deshalb einer, der...*

Aussprache und Rechtschreibung Audio

Tongue Twisters

Zungenbrecher (*Tongue twisters*) are a part of German culture. Mastering a tongue twister means being able to say it quickly several times in a row. One popular type of tongue twister reverses sounds, syllables or words.

Rauchlachs mit Lauchreis.   **Allergischer Algerier, algerischer Allergiker.**

. . . .

Other tongue twisters repeat syllables, words, or phrases that contain similar sounds.

In Ulm, um Ulm und um Ulm herum.   **Der dicke Dachdecker deckte das dicke Dach.**

. . . .

German allows for the construction of very long compound words. Many such compounds appear in tongue twisters, sometimes as nonsense words.

Postkutschkasten   **Fichtendickicht**   **Kirschenmirschen**

---

1 **Aussprechen** Wiederholen Sie die Zungenbrecher, die Sie hören.

1. zwischen zwei Zwetschgenzweigen
2. ein krummer Krebs kroch
3. der Cottbuser Postkutscher
4. allergischer Algerier

2 **Nachsprechen** Wiederholen Sie die Sätze, die Sie hören.

1. Hinter Hermann Hansens Haus hängen hundert Hemden raus.
2. Esel essen Nesseln nicht, Nesseln essen Esel nicht.
3. Der Cottbuser Postkutscher putzt den Cottbuser Postkutschkasten blank.
4. Fischers Fritz fischt frische Fische, frische Fische fischt Fischers Fritz.
5. Zehn Ziegen zogen zehn Zentner Zucker zum Zoo.
6. Es klapperten die Klapperschlangen, bis ihre Klappern schlapper klangen.

3 **Sprichwörter** Wiederholen Sie die Sprichwörter, die Sie hören.

Expansion Have students take turns trying to read these **Zungenbrecher** out loud. Have them search online for additional examples and variations.

Blaukraut bleibt Blaukraut und Brautkleid bleibt Brautkleid.[1]

Zwischen zwei Zwetschgenzweigen zwitschern zwei Schwalben.[2]

[1] You can't make a silk purse out of a sow's ear. (lit. *Red cabbage remains red cabbage and a wedding dress remains a wedding dress.*)
[2] Between two plum branches twitter two swallows.

More activities

vhlcentral — LM p. 106 — Online activities

Fotoroman

Auf Wiedersehen, Berlin! Video

Zum letzten Mal treffen sich unsere Freunde im Biergarten, um den Abschied von George zu feiern.

NATIONAL
STANDARDS
communication
cultures

Vorbereitung Have students read the title and discuss what they expect to happen in the episode.

HANS Hey, an was arbeitest du?
GEORGE Ich schreibe meine Hausarbeit über ökologische Architektur fertig. Damit der Planet gerettet werden kann, sollten erneuerbare Energien wie Solar- und Windenergie in neuen Gebäuden verwendet werden. Regierungen müssen Gesetze verabschieden, die die Umwelt erhalten. Die Bedrohung durch Abforstung und Verschmutzung darf nicht ignoriert werden. Außerdem...

HANS Ich habe meine Abschlussarbeit für das Semester gestern abgegeben.
GEORGE Ich schlage eine Lösung vor, die Fabriken helfen wird, weniger zu verschmutzen und mehr zu recyceln. Mein Professor sagt, es sei eine gute Sache.

HANS Meline, ich bin's. Bist du da? Es tut mir leid wegen neulich Abend in der Galerie. Können wir darüber reden? Meline?
SABITE Hans! Was machst du denn hier draußen? Oh, Mann.
HANS Meline?
SABITE Sie ist wohl nicht zu Hause.

HANS Sie ist mir immer noch böse, oder? Sie gibt mir gar keine Chance, mich zu entschuldigen. Manchmal verstehe ich sie überhaupt gar nicht. Ich glaube, George hatte recht, wir sind einfach zu unterschiedlich.
SABITE Vielleicht.

SABITE Bist du Hans immer noch böse? Es tut ihm wirklich leid.
MELINE Er hat sehr liebe Nachrichten hinterlassen. Ich bin ihm nicht böse. Ich glaube, dass er ein guter Mensch ist, aber ich... ja...
SABITE Du mochtest ihn mehr, als du ihn nicht mochtest.
MELINE Genau!

MELINE Hallo! George! Das ist für dich. Von uns.
HANS Öffne es, öffne es!
SABITE Vorsichtig!
GEORGE Das ist wunderbar. Habt vielen herzlichen Dank.
GEORGE Ich hätte keine besseren Freunde finden können. Wegen euch war das Jahr in Berlin so großartig.

1 **Richtig oder falsch?** Entscheiden Sie, ob die folgenden Sätze **richtig** oder **falsch** sind.

 1. George schreibt eine Hausarbeit über Ökotourismus. Falsch.

 2. Er schlägt vor, dass in neuen Gebäuden Solar- und Windenergie verwendet wird. Richtig.

3. Hans hat seine Abschlussarbeit für das Semester schon abgegeben. Richtig.

4. Georges Professor gefällt die Lösung nicht, die George vorschlägt. Falsch.

5. Meline versteckt sich in ihrem Zimmer, weil sie Hans nicht sehen möchte. Richtig.

6. Hans hat Meline einen Kuchen mitgebracht. Falsch.

7. Meline ist immer noch böse auf Hans. Falsch.

8. Seine Freunde schenken George einen Stadtplan von Milwaukee. Falsch.

9. Hans möchte mit George die nächsten paar Wochen verreisen. Falsch.

10. Meline und Hans möchten weiterhin Freunde sein. Richtig.

PERSONEN George Hans Meline Sabite

MELINE Ich hoffe, wir bleiben in Verbindung?
GEORGE Das werden wir. Ich möchte Wien besuchen.
HANS Ich habe gehört, es soll eine wunderschöne Kulturstadt sein.
SABITE Ähh, George, lass uns...
GEORGE Ja, definitiv.

HANS Das war nicht nett von mir, tut mir leid. Und wegen neulich Abend, ich... ich war wütend und ich hätte diese Dinge nicht zu dir sagen sollen.
MELINE Es ist schon okay, Hans. Du hast vielleicht gar nicht so falsch gelegen. Es tut mir leid, dass ich dich nicht angerufen habe.

HANS Max und ich, wir werden die nächsten paar Wochen verreisen, bevor ich wieder nach Hause zurückkehre, und ich... ich möchte dir nicht weh tun, aber ich kann mich im Moment nicht binden. Ich hoffe, du hast Verständnis dafür.
MELINE Ja, das habe ich. Können wir weiterhin Freunde sein?

HANS Auf ein tolles Jahr in Berlin, und neue Freunde.
GEORGE Richtig! Bravo!

Nützliche Ausdrücke

- **ein Gesetz verabschieden**
  to pass a law
- **neulich**
  the other day
- **unterschiedlich**
  different
- **eine Nachricht hinterlassen**
  to leave a message
- **in Verbindung bleiben**
  to stay in touch
- **falsch liegen**
  to be wrong

12B.1
- **Mein Professor sagt, es sei eine gute Sache.**
  My professor says it's a worthy cause.

12B.2
- **Die Bedrohung durch Abforstung und Verschmutzung darf nicht ignoriert werden.**
  The threat of deforestation and pollution shouldn't be ignored.

---

2 **Zum Besprechen** Am Ende dieser Episode trennen sich Hans und Meline. Denken Sie sich zu zweit ein alternatives Ende der Episode aus. Wie könnte es mit Hans und Meline weitergehen? Schreiben Sie ein Gespräch zwischen Hans und Meline und spielen Sie es im Kurs vor. Answers will vary.

2 **Expansion** Have students write a dialogue in which Hans and Meline meet again after Hans comes back from his vacation.

3 **Vertiefung** Suchen Sie im Internet nach dem „Grünen Punkt". Welches System steckt dahinter? Wann wurde es eingeführt (*introduced*)? In welchen Ländern gibt es den Grünen Punkt? Welche Hersteller in Ihrem Land haben Rücknahme und Recyclingprogramme für alte Elektronik? Haben Sie jemals alte Elektronik zum Recycling abgegeben? Welche?
Answers may include: recycling of packaging materials, Duales System Deutschland, introduced 1990 in Germany, most European countries participate.

More activities

vhlcentral   VM p. 24   Online activities

IM FOKUS

Re-Use Berlin – Wiederverwenden statt Wegwerfen

 Reading

NATIONAL connections cultures STANDARDS

DEUTSCHLAND HAT VIELE Recyclingprogramme. Trotzdem werden auch hier viele noch brauchbare Gegenstände weggeworfen und landen auf der Müllhalde°. Aber in vielen Städten gibt es *Zero-Waste*-Initiativen, um solche Gegenstände weiter zu verwerten°. **Re-Use Berlin** ist so eine Initiative. Sie wird von der Regierung der Hauptstadt organisiert. Die Bürger bringen ihre alten oder ungeliebten Gegenstände aus dem Haushalt zu diversen Sammelstellen in der Stadt. Elektrogeräte, Kleider, Geschirr, Spielsachen, CDs, Bücher und andere Artikel kann man zu diesen Sammelstellen bringen. Ihre Besitzer können sie dann auf dem Wochenmarkt° oder auf einem Tauschmarkt gegen andere Dinge tauschen°. Allerdings werden schwere Gegenstände wie Matrazen oder Möbel nicht akzeptiert. Es gibt auch Sammelstellen, die diese Gebrauchtwaren° an soziale Einrichtungen° weitergeben. Von dort aus finden sie dann ein neues Zuhause bei unterprivilegierten Menschen. Es gibt auch das **CRCLR-Haus** (*Circular Economy House*), wo man Gebrauchtwaren sehr preiswert kaufen kann. Der Berliner Senat lädt° die Einwohner auch dazu ein, neue Vorschläge für eine Zero-Waste Welt zu machen.

Grüne Berufe	Stellenbeschreibungen
Fischwirt/ Fischwirtin	Fischwirte arbeiten an den vielen Seen und Flüssen in Deutschland: sie fangen Fische und ziehen sie in Seen auf°.
Milchtechnologe/ Milchtechnologin	Milchtechnologen bedienen° die modernen Produktions- und Abfüllanlagen° und überwachen° die Produktionsprozesse von Milch und Milchprodukten wie Käse oder Jogurt.
Pferdewirt/ Pferdewirtin	Pferdewirte lernen, wie man Pferde richtig hält°, wie man sie reitet und wie man sie züchtet°.

Müllhalde *landfill* **weiter zu verwerten** *reuse*
Wochenmarkt *weekly market* **tauschen** *trade*
Gebrauchtwaren *second-hand goods*
Einrichtungen *institutions* **lädt... ein** *invites* **ziehen...**
auf *breed* **bedienen** *operate* **Abfüllanlagen** *bottling*
systems **überwachen** *monitor* **hält** *keeps* **züchtet** *breeds*

ÜBUNGEN

1 **Im Fokus** Richtig oder falsch? Korrigieren Sie die falschen Aussagen. Diskutieren Sie dann die letzte Frage mit einem Partner/ einer Partnerin.

1. Die Stadt Berlin verkauft noch brauchbare Dinge an andere Länder.
Falsch. In Berlin werden alte, noch brauchbare Gegenstände gesammelt und getauscht.

2. Wer arm ist und ein Haushaltsgerät braucht, kann es sehr wahrscheinlich bei einer sozialen Einrichtung bekommen. **Richtig.**

3. Die Re-Use Berlin Initiative ist ein perfektes Umweltprogramm. **Falsch.** Das Programm ist zwar praktisch, aber die Einwohner Berlins können es mit ihren Ideen noch verbessern.

Diskussion Finden Sie, dass Ihre Stadt eine praktische Initiative wie einen Wochenmarkt braucht, wo man alte Gegenstände hinbringen und sogar tauschen kann?

2 **Die deutschsprachige Welt** Richtig oder falsch? Korrigieren Sie die falschen Aussagen.

1. Umweltschutzorganisationen engagieren sich für den Klimaschutz.
Richtig.

2. Naturschutz in Österreich gibt es erst seit Kurzem.
Falsch. In Österreich gibt es schon seit 1913 organisierten Umweltschutz.

3. In der Schweiz gibt es 650 Naturschutzgebieten. **Richtig.**

Diskussion In welchen Regionen der USA sind Umweltorganisationen besonders aktiv? Warum sind solche Organisationen (nicht) wichtig?

DEUTSCH IM ALLTAG

Abfall und Recycling

der Abfall, ⁼e	waste
die Altkleider	second-hand clothing
das Altpapier	used paper
der Gartenabfall, ⁼e	yard waste
der Schrott	scrap metal
der Verpackungsmüll	packaging waste

DIE DEUTSCHSPRACHIGE WELT

Umweltschutzorganisationen°

Deutschland

Seit 1975 gibt es in Deutschland den Bund für Umwelt und Naturschutz. Diese Organisation engagiert° sich für ökologische Landwirtschaft, gesunde Lebensmittel, den Klimaschutz und den Ausbau° regenerativer Energien.

Österreich In Österreich gibt es seit 1913 den Naturschutzbund Österreich. Diese Organisation war bei der Gründung° der österreichischen Nationalparks sehr aktiv und hilft auch bei der Erhaltung des Wiener Waldes, der Krimmler Wasserfälle und der Hainburger Au.

Die Schweiz In der Schweiz setzt sich die Organisation Pro Natura seit 1909 für den Naturschutz ein°. Zu den Erfolgen dieser Organisation zählt ein Netz° von 650 Naturschutzgebieten°.

Umweltschutzorganisationen ecology groups **engagiert** gets involved in **Ausbau** development **Gründung** founding **setzt sich... ein** advocates **Netz** network **Naturschutzgebieten** nature reserves

PORTRÄT

Michael Braungart

Michael Braungart, ein Chemiker aus Schwäbisch-Gmünd, ist Professor an der Leuphana Universität Lüneburg. In den 80er Jahren war er aktives Mitglied° von Greenpeace Deutschland. Seither sucht er Antworten auf die folgenden Fragen: Wie kann der Mensch sich in das Leben auf der Erde integrieren? Wie kann er nicht nur wenig Schaden anrichten°, sondern wie kann er selbst einen Beitrag für die Umwelt leisten? Braungart ist bekannt für die Entwicklung von Umweltschutz-Konzepten und die Konzeption umweltverträglicher Produktionsverfahren°.

Mitglied member **Schaden anrichten** do damage **umweltverträglicher Produktionsverfahren** environmentally friendly production

🔗 IM INTERNET

Wählen Sie einen Umweltaspekt aus, der Sie besonders interessiert. Suchen Sie Informationen darüber. Machen Sie eine Liste mit Initiativen, die es auf diesem Gebiet gibt.

Find out more at **vhlcentral.com**.

---

3 **Porträt** Richtig oder falsch? Korrigieren Sie die falschen Aussagen. Diskutieren Sie dann die letzte Frage mit einem Partner/ einer Partnerin.

🔗 1. Michael Braungart ist schon seit über 30 Jahren ein engagierter Umweltschützer. Richtig.

 2. Braungart glaubt, dass die Menschen sich nicht in das Leben auf der Erde integrieren können. Falsch. Er sucht eine Antwort auf die Frage, wie der Mensch sich in das Leben auf der Erde integrieren kann.

Diskussion Was wird in Ihrer Stadt für Umweltschutz und Recycling getan? Wie finden Sie diese Initiativen?

4 **Die Umwelt** Schreiben Sie einen kurzen Aufsatz darüber, was Sie als Student oder Studentin im Alltag für die Umwelt machen. Welche Initiativen gibt es auf dem Campus? Woran beteiligen (participate) Sie sich?

12B.1

Suggestion Emphasize that the Konjunktiv I and Konjunktiv II have very different functions.

Der Konjunktiv I and indirect speech Grammar Tutorial

Startblock You learned in **9B.1** and **12A.1** about the **Konjunktiv II** and its present and past tense forms. There is another subjunctive, **der Konjunktiv I**, which is used to report what someone else has said.

Mein Professor sagt, es **sei** eine gute Sache.

Sie hat gesagt, sie **werde** sein Geschenk **mitnehmen**.

Suggestion You may may choose to emphasize recognition of the forms and uses of the **Konjunktiv I**, rather than expecting students to master production.

Suggestion Point out that the **-e** in the second person singular ending of **sein** is often omitted: **du seist**.

Der Konjunktiv I

- To form the present tense of the **Konjunktiv I**, add the endings **-e, -est, -e, -en, -et, -en** to the infinitive stem. Only the verb **sein** is irregular: its stem is **sei-** and the first and third person singular have no added endings.

Konjunktiv I Präsens				
	geben	**können**	**haben**	**sein**
ich	gebe	könne	habe	sei
du	gebest	könnest	habest	sei(e)st
er/sie/es	gebe	könne	habe	sei
wir	geben	können	haben	seien
ihr	gebet	könnet	habet	seiet
Sie/sie	geben	können	haben	seien

ACHTUNG

Verbs that are commonly used to introduce reported speech include **antworten, behaupten** (*to claim*), **berichten** (*to report*), **denken, erklären, erzählen, fragen, glauben, meinen**, and **sagen**.

———

When you use the subordinating conjunction **dass**, the verb comes at the end of the subordinate clause. In reported speech, **dass** may be omitted, in which case the verb remains the second element in the clause. **Max berichtete, er benutze seit Jahren eine Fahrgemeinschaft.**

Herr Braun sagt, die Erde **sei** wegen Erderwärmung gefährdet.
Herr Braun says the earth is in danger because of global warming.

Er meint, dass er die Lösung dafür **habe**.
He believes that he has the solution for it.

- To form the past tense of the **Konjunktiv I**, use the **Konjunktiv I** of **haben** or **sein** with the past participle.

Der *Spiegel* berichtete, dass es gestern sauren Regen **gegeben habe**.
Der Spiegel reported that acid rain fell yesterday.

Papa sagte, das Paket **sei** heute Morgen **gekommen**.
Dad said the package came this morning.

- Use the **Konjunktiv I** of **werden** with an infinitive to report a statement someone else has made about the future.

Frau Müller sagte, sie **werde** ein Hybridauto **kaufen**.
Ms. Müller said she would buy a hybrid car.

Wissenschaftler sagen, sie **werden** eine Lösung für die Erderwärmung **finden**.
Scientists say they will find a solution for global warming.

Indirect Speech

Expansion Bring in German-language newspapers, or printouts from online newspapers, and have students find statements containing the **Konjunktiv I**.

- In conversation, you can report what someone else said using the **Indikativ**, especially when you want to show that you agree with what was said or that you believe it to be true. If you wish to express skepticism or doubt, however, use the **Konjunktiv I**.

> Die Nachbarn sagten, sie **haben** eine Maus **gesehen**.
> *The neighbors said they **saw** a mouse.*

> Murat sagte, er **werde** später **wiederkommen**.
> *Murat said he **would come back** later.*

- In more formal contexts, such as news reports, political speeches, and scientific writing, the **Konjunktiv I** is used to report what people have said without implying that the information is necessarily true or accurate. It is typically introduced with a verb that denotes speech or belief, such as **sagen, berichten** (*to report*), **behaupten** (*to claim*), **meinen** (*to mean, to opine*), or **glauben**.

> Die *Zeit* berichtet, dass es einen Atomkraftwerkunfall **gegeben habe**.
> Die Zeit *reports that there **was** a nuclear power plant accident.*

> Wissenschaftler glauben, dass viele Menschen und Tiere in Gefahr **seien**.
> *Scientists believe that many people and animals **are** in danger.*

- The **Konjunktiv I** is used mainly with modals, **wissen, sein**, and third-person singular verbs. In cases where the **Konjunktiv I** conjugation is identical to the present-tense indicative, it is more common to use the **Konjunktiv II** or **würden** + infinitive.

> Thomas behaupte, er **habe** das nicht **gewusst**.
> *Thomas claimed he **didn't know** that.*

> Sarah sagte, dass sie uns vielleicht morgen **besuchen werde**.
> *Sarah said that she **might visit** us tomorrow.*

Suggestion Show students an ambiguous sentence in which the indicative and **Konjunktiv II** forms are identical. Ex.: **Natasha sagt, ich gebe Ihnen all mein Geld**. Then, restate it using the **Konjunktiv II** to avoid the ambiguity: **Natasha sagt, ich gäbe Ihnen all mein Geld**.

- To express imperatives in indirect speech, use the **Konjunktiv I** or **II** of the modals **sollen** or **müssen**. **Suggestion** Mention that the modal **mögen** can be used in indirect speech describing polite requests. Ex.: **Die Chefin sagte, der Bewerber möge jetzt eintreten**.

> Die Studenten meinen, die Uni **solle/sollte** nicht so viel Papier **verschwenden**.
> *The students feel that the school **shouldn't waste** so much paper.*

> Die Geschäftsführerin sagte, wir **müssten** mehr **recyceln**.
> *Our manager said we **should recycle** more.*

- The tense of the verb in indirect speech is the same as the tense in the original direct speech.

> Der Bundespräsident: „Unser Land **braucht** mehr Windenergie."
> *The President: "Our country **needs** more wind energy."*

> Der Bundespräsident meint, unser Land **brauche** mehr Windenergie.
> *The President believes that our country **needs** more wind energy.*

QUERVERWEIS

See **10A.1** to review indirect questions.

ACHTUNG

When you are reporting what someone else said, personal pronouns, possessive adjectives, and adverbs of time and place may need to be changed accordingly:

Paul: „Ich freue mich auf meinen Urlaub."

Paul sagte, dass er sich auf seinen Urlaub freue.

QUERVERWEIS

See **9B.1** and **9B.2** to review **Konjunktiv II** and the **würden** + infinitive construction.

More activities

vhlcentral

WB
pp. 165–166

LM
p. 107

Online activities

Jetzt sind Sie dran!   **Entscheiden Sie, ob die folgenden Sätze im Indikativ oder im Konjunktiv I stehen.**

Expansion Write two sentences on the board, one in the **Indikativ** and one in the **Konjunktiv I**. Ex.: **Er hat keine Schuhe. Er habe keine Schuhe.** Ask students to explain the difference in English.

	Indikativ	Konjunktiv I		Indikativ	Konjunktiv I
1. Maria sagte, sie sei krank.	☐	☑	7. Ihr sagt, ihr benutzt wenig Energie.	☑	☐
2. Du sagst, du fährst nur Hybridautos.	☑	☐	8. Er sagte, er werde Lösungen entwickeln.	☐	☑
3. Er meinte, die Umwelt bleibe in Gefahr.	☐	☑	9. Sie meinte, sie habe ihren Müll getrennt.	☐	☑
4. Sie sagte, sie habe eine Lösung vorgeschlagen.	☐	☑	10. Erika sagte, sie kaufe nur biologische Lebensmittel.	☐	☑
5. Max sagt, er wird Windenergie benutzen.	☑	☐	11. Alex sagt, er wird die Umwelt schützen.	☑	☐
6. Er glaubt, er werde den Planeten retten.	☐	☑	12. Ihr sagt, ihr habt keinen Giftmüll produziert.	☑	☐

Anwendung

1 **Was ist richtig?** Ihr Freund hat keine Lust mit Ihnen ins Konzert zu gehen. Berichten Sie Ihren anderen Freunden, was er gesagt hat. Wählen Sie die passenden Verbformen des Konjunktiv I.

> **BEISPIEL** Er sagte, er (war /sei) zu müde, um ins Konzert zu gehen.

Er sagte, ...

1. er (müsse / muss) noch für eine schwere Prüfung am nächsten Tag lernen.
2. er (hatte / habe) nicht genug Geld, eine Konzertkarte zu kaufen.
3. er (wollte / wolle) heute Abend früh ins Bett gehen.
4. das Konzert (werde / wird) schon ausverkauft (*sold out*) sein.
5. ich (solle / soll) jemand anders einladen.

2 **Welche Zeitform?** Markieren Sie die richtigen Zeitformen.

	Indikativ	Konjunktiv I Präsens	Konjunktiv I Vergangenheit	Konjunktiv I Zukunft
1. er habe nichts gemacht	☐	☐	☑	☐
2. sie werde ihn heiraten	☐	☐	☐	☑
3. ich dürfe das nicht	☐	☑	☐	☐
4. sie sind angekommen	☑	☐	☐	☐
5. du werdest kündigen	☐	☐	☐	☑
6. sie seien abgefahren	☐	☐	☑	☐
7. sie wollte umziehen	☑	☐	☐	☐
8. ihr habet eine Idee	☐	☑	☐	☐

3 Suggestion Do the first few items together as a class.

3 **Unsere Gegenwart** Formen Sie die Sätze in indirekte Rede um. Suggested answers provided.

> **BEISPIEL** „Der Wasserspiegel (*water level*) der Weltmeere steigt."Der Wissenschaftler erklärte, dass *der Wasserspiegel der Weltmeere steige*.

1. „Die Regenwald (*rainforest*) muss gerettet werden."
   Die Wissenschaftlerin sagte, dass _____ der Regenwald gerettet werden müsse _____.

2. „Die Solarzellen werden Ihre Energiekosten reduzieren."
   Der Elektriker sagte dem Mann, dass _____ die Solarzellen seine Energiekosten reduzieren würden _____.

3. „Wollen Sie in dieser Firma ein Praktikum machen?"
   Der Personalchef fragte mich, ob _____ ich in dieser Firma ein Praktikum machen wolle _____.

4. „Warum recycelst du nicht deinen alten Computer?"
   Jan fragte seine Freundin, warum _____ sie nicht ihren alten Computer recycle _____.

5. „Die Papierfabrik hat seit Jahren die Luft verschmutzt."
   Der Bürgermeister klagte (*complained*), dass _____ die Papierfabrik seit Jahren die Luft verschmutzt habe _____.

6. „Ich weiß nicht, ob man diesen Nationalpark erhalten kann."
   Die Innenministerin sagte, _____ sie wisse nicht, ob man diesen Nationalpark erhalten könne _____.

Kommunikation

4 Video Virtual Chat You can also assign activity 4 on the Supersite. Students record individual responses that appear in your gradebook.

4 Ein Streitgespräch Schreiben Sie mit einem Partner / einer Partnerin einen kurzen Dialog zu dem Bild. Dann berichten Sie zwei anderen Studenten, was die Leute auf dem Bild gesagt haben. Verwenden Sie den Konjunktiv I. Answers will vary.

> **BEISPIEL**
>
> *Dialog:*
> **Mann:** *Warum bist du so böse (angry) auf mich?*
> **Frau:** *Weil du niemals bei der Hausarbeit hilfst.*
> **Mann:** *Das ist nicht wahr! …*
>
> *Bericht:*
> *Der Mann hat die Frau gefragt, warum sie so böse auf ihn sei. Die Frau hat geantwortet, er helfe niemals bei der Hausarbeit. Der Mann hat dann gesagt, das sei nicht wahr. …*

5 Glaubst du das? Erzählen Sie zwei Partnern/Partnerinnen zwei Dinge über sich, die wahr oder eine Lüge (*lie*) sein könnten. Ein Partner / Eine Partnerin berichtet davon. Der andere Partner / Die andere Partnerin sagt, ob er/sie das glaubt oder nicht. Wechseln Sie sich ab. Answers will vary.

5 Suggestion Tell students to use statements with **Ich bin…, Ich habe…, Ich will…,** or **Ich kann…** Provide model subjunctive forms on the board: **Sie sagt, sie sei… Er sagt, er habe… Sie sagt, sie wolle… Er sagt, er könne…** Circulate and provide help as needed.

> **BEISPIEL**
>
> **S1:** *Ich bin 18 Jahre alt.*
> **S2:** *Melanie hat gesagt, sie sei 18 Jahre alt. Glaubst du das?*
> **S3:** *Nein, das glaube ich nicht. Ich glaube, sie ist 19.*

6 Klatschkolumnen Schreiben Sie mit Ihrem Partner / Ihrer Partnerin eine Klatschkolumne (*gossip column*) über einen Prominenten. Benutzen Sie Indikativformen. Tauschen Sie (*exchange*) Ihre Kolumne mit zwei Mitstudenten aus. Berichten Sie im Kurs, was in der Kolumne Ihrer Mitstudenten steht. Verwenden Sie dabei den Konjunktiv I. Answers will vary.

6 Suggestion After they swap columns, give students time to convert the verbs into indirect speech. It may be helpful to have them underline all of the verbs first. Point out that since they'll be using the 3rd person throughout their reports, the pattern will be: *verb stem* + -**e**.

> **BEISPIEL**
>
> **S1/S2:** *In der Klatschkolumne steht, dass die große Schauspielerin Tanja ihr ganzes Geld der Tierschutzorganisation „Ein Herz für Tiere" gegeben habe. Sie sei gestern in die Schweiz geflogen, habe das Geld abgehoben und dann ihre Konten gekündigt. Sie sei noch nie so glücklich gewesen, sagte Tanja.*

Die große Schauspielerin (*actress*) Tanja hat ihr ganzes Vermögen (*fortune*) der Tierschutzorganisation „Ein Herz für Tiere" gegeben. Sie ist gestern in die Schweiz geflogen, hat das Geld abgehoben und dann ihre Konten gekündigt. „Ich bin noch nie so glücklich gewesen", sagte Tanja.

12B.2

The passive voice Grammar Tutorial

Startblock Most sentences in German are in the *active* voice. Use the *passive* voice to put the focus on the action itself, or on the receiver of the action.

Suggestion Make sure students do not confuse passive voice constructions with the **Futur I**.

- To form a sentence using the passive voice, use a conjugated form of **werden** with the past participle of the verb that describes the action of the sentence. Sentences using the passive voice are usually in the present tense or the **Präteritum**.

  In diesem Land **wird** zu viel Müll **produziert**.
  *Too much trash **is being produced** in this country.*

  Im Jahr 2018 **wurden** 455 kg Müll pro Kopf **weggeworfen**.
  *In 2018, 455 kilos of trash per person **were thrown out**.*

- The subject of a passive sentence is the receiver of the action.

  Wir **schalten** immer die Lichter **aus**.
  *We always **turn out** the lights.*

  Die Lichter **werden ausgeschaltet**.
  *The lights **are being turned out**.*

- In a passive voice sentence, the doer of the action is often unidentified. To indicate who or what performed or is performing the action, use the preposition **von** after the conjugated form of **werden**, followed by a noun in the dative case.

  Neue Hybridautos werden (**von Wissenschaftlern**) entwickelt.
  *New hybrid cars are being developed (**by scientists**).*

  Das Wasser wurde (**von der Fabrik**) verschmutzt.
  *The water was polluted (**by the factory**).*

- In passive sentences with a modal verb, use the conjugated form of the modal and move the infinitive **werden** to the end of the sentence, after the past participle.

  Ein neues Gesetz **soll vorgeschlagen werden**.
  *A new law **needs to be proposed**.*

  Die Technologie **musste** erst **verbessert werden**.
  *The technology **had to be improved** first.*

- In an impersonal statement, where there is no specific subject, the sentence may begin with **es**, or with an adverb of time or place.

  Es wird hier nur Deutsch gesprochen.
  Only German is spoken here.

  Gestern wurde viel gearbeitet.
  *A lot of work was done **yesterday**.*

- You can often replace a statement in the passive voice with an active sentence using the indefinite pronoun **man** as the subject.

  In den USA **benutzt man** zu viel Benzin.
  ***People** in the U.S. **use** too much gasoline.*

  Man soll Energie sparen.
  ***We should save** energy.*

More activities

vhlcentral

WB pp. 167–168

LM p. 108

Online activities

Markieren Sie, ob die folgenden Sätze aktiv oder passiv sind.

	aktiv	passiv		aktiv	passiv
1. Es muss mehr getan werden.	☐	☑	4. Heute wird mehr wiederverwertet.	☐	☑
2. Viele Tierarten sind jetzt gefährdet.	☑	☐	5. Man muss mehr Wasser sparen.	☑	☐
3. Fahrgemeinschaften sollen oft benutzt werden.	☐	☑	6. Der Müll wurde von dem Müllfahrer abgeholt (*picked up*).	☐	☑

Anwendung und Kommunikation

1 Was fehlt? Ergänzen Sie die Sätze mit den Passivformen der Verben in Klammern.

BEISPIEL In meiner Familie ___werden___ keine Batterien
in den Müll _geworfen_. (werfen)

1. Innovative Ideen, unseren Planeten zu retten, ___werden___
dringend (*urgently*) ___gesucht___. (suchen)

2. Die Luft ___wird___ immer mehr ___verschmutzt___. (verschmutzen)

3. Stofftaschen (*Cloth bags*) statt Plastiktaschen sollen beim
Einkaufen ___benutzt___ ___werden___. (benutzen)

4. Wasserreservoirs, um Trinkwasser zu speichern, müssen
___gebaut___ ___werden___. (bauen)

5. In welchem Land ___wird___ das meiste Altpapier ___recycelt___? (recyceln)

6. Die Tier- und Pflanzenwelt darf nicht ___vergessen___ ___werden___. (vergessen)

2 Was wird hier gemacht? Beschreiben Sie mit einem Partner / einer Partnerin, was auf den Bildern gerade passiert. Benutzen Sie die Präsensformen des Passivs. Answers will vary.

BEISPIEL

S1: *Hier wird Mathematik gelernt.*

1.

2. 3. 4. 5.

Bücher / verkaufen	Müll / recyceln
ein Hund / baden	Pizza / essen
Mathematik / lernen	die Umwelt / verschmutzen

3 Lösungsvorschläge Diskutieren Sie mit einem Partner / einer Partnerin, was (nicht) gemacht werden kann/muss/soll/darf, um unsere Umweltprobleme zu lösen. Gebrauchen Sie Modalverben im Passiv. Präsentieren Sie Ihre Lösungsvorschläge danach im Kurs. Answers will vary.

BEISPIEL

S1: *Die Windenergie muss ausgebaut werden.*

ausbauen	das Kernkraftwerk / der Reaktor...
entwickeln	die Landschaft
erfinden	die Luft / das Wasser /...
finden	die Natur / die Flora / die Fauna...
recyceln	das Papier / das Glas / das Plastik / das Aluminium...
reduzieren	die Windenergie / die Solarenergie / die Kernenergie...
retten	die Wissenschaft
verbessern	

3 Expansion Ask students if they think people will start living in a more environmentally aware manner in the near future. Are they optimistic or pessimistic about the environment?

3 Partner Chat You can also assign activity 3 on the Supersite. Students work in pairs to record the activity online. The pair's recorded conversation will appear in your gradebook.

Wiederholung

1 Ein Zeitungsartikel

Identifizieren Sie mit einem Partner / einer Partnerin Beispiele indirekter Rede in dem Artikel über eine Umweltinitiative. Wechseln Sie sich dann ab und sagen Sie in indirekter Rede, was gesagt wurde.

Answers will vary.

BEISPIEL

S1: Die Polizei erklärte: „Am Wochenende haben mehr als 250.000 Menschen in ganz Deutschland für den Atomausstieg demonstriert."

Zehntausende demonstrieren für raschen Atomausstieg

Das Wochenende stand im Zeichen des Atomausstiegs (*nuclear phase-out*). Die Polizei erklärte, am Wochenende hätten mehr als 250.000 Menschen in ganz Deutschland für den Atomausstieg demonstriert. Sie berichtete außerdem, Demonstrationen hätten in 20 Städten stattgefunden. Atomgegener erzählten, es habe Demonstrationen in mehr als 20 Städten gegeben. Organisatoren meinten auch, diese Demonstrationen seien größer gewesen als die vorherigen Demonstrationen. Zu dem Protest aufgerufen hatten Umweltschutzinitiativen, Gewerkschaften und Parteien. Diese Organisationen sagten, sie wollten Druck (*pressure*) auf die Politiker in Berlin machen. Sie meinten auch, es sei Zeit für eine neue Umweltpolitik. Ohne Atomkraft hätten die Kinder eine Chance auf eine sicherere Welt.

2 Arbeitsblatt

Stellen Sie den anderen im Unterricht die Fragen auf dem Arbeitsblatt, das Sie bekommen. Schreiben Sie die Antworten auf. Diskutieren Sie dann mit der Gruppe, um zu sehen, was die typischsten Antworten waren. Answers will vary.

BEISPIEL

S1: Was wäre, wenn weniger Leute Kinder bekämen?
S2: Wenn weniger Leute Kinder bekämen, hätten wir kein Problem mit Überbevölkerung.

 2 Suggestion Make sure that students understand they will be practicing **Konjunktiv II** in this activity, not **Konjunktiv I**.

3 Wer hat's gesagt?

Entscheiden Sie, wer wahrscheinlich die folgenden Sätze gesagt hat. Berichten Sie, was die Personen gesagt haben. Wechseln Sie sich mit einem Partner / einer Partnerin ab. Sample answers are provided.

3 Video Virtual Chat You can also assign activity 3 on the Supersite.

BEISPIEL Man hat viele Tiere aus dem Tierheim adoptiert.

S1: Die Tierärztin war froh, dass man viele Tiere aus dem Tierheim adoptiert habe.
S2: Der Biologe berichtete, dass ...

die Bankangestellte	die Psychologin
der Biologe	der Rentner
der Elektriker	die Richterin
der Koch	die Tierärztin
der LKW-Fahrer	

1. Man muss jeden Tag arbeiten, bis das Restaurant schließt.
   Der Koch sagte, man müsse jeden Tag arbeiten, bis das Restaurant schließe.
2. Viele Menschen haben Depressionen.
   Die Psychologin berichtete, viele Menschen hätten Depressionen.
3. Niemand interessiert sich für alte Menschen.
   Der Rentner meinte, niemand interessiere sich für alte Menschen.
4. Es ist ein Problem, dass Benzin immer teurer wird.
   Der LKW-Fahrer sagte, es sei ein Problem, dass Benzin immer teurer werde.
5. Es gibt immer mehr Jugendliche, die Probleme mit dem Gesetz haben.
   Die Richterin sagte, es gebe immer mehr Jugendliche, die Probleme mit dem Gesetz hätten.
6. Online-Banking wird immer beliebter.
   Die Bankangestellte berichtete, Online-Banking werde immer beliebter.

4 Gut oder schlecht?

Bitten Sie Ihren Partner / Ihre Partnerin, auf die folgenden Fotos zu reagieren. Wie erklärt Ihr Partner / Ihre Partnerin diese Reaktion?

Answers will vary.

BEISPIEL

S1: Wie findest du die Insel im See?
S2: Ich finde sie schön, weil man da die frische Luft genießen kann.

1. 2. 3.

4. 5. 6.

4 Expansion Have students describe each picture in detail before giving their reactions.

4 Partner Chat You can also assign activity 4 on the Supersite. Students work in pairs to record the activity online. The pair's recorded conversation will appear in your gradebook.

5 Tier- und Wildparks

Im Berliner Zoo kann man über 20.000 Tiere aus aller Welt sehen. Im Unterschied dazu sieht man in dem kleinen Wildpark Christianental nur die Tiere, die in deutschen Wäldern oder Wiesen zuhause sind. Sehen Sie sich mit Ihrem Partner / Ihrer Partnerin die Anzeige° an und diskutieren Sie sie.

Anzeige *ad*

BEISPIEL

S1: *Welche Tiere gibt es in diesem Wildpark?*
S2: *Rotfüchse, Eichhörnchen und Wildschweine. Welche würdest du gern sehen?*
S1: *Die Wildkatzen. Gibt es die auch bei uns? ...*

5 Suggestion Write on the board the German words that students won't know for animals, and ask students to add them to **Vocabulary Tools** on the **Sag mal** Supersite.

6 In der Zukunft

Was muss man in der Zukunft machen, um der Umwelt zu helfen? Schreiben Sie zu dritt mindestens sechs Antworten auf diese Frage. Benutzen Sie das Futur I. Answers will vary.

6 Suggestion Remind students to use **werden** with an infinitive to form the **Futur I**.

BEISPIEL

S1: *In der Zukunft wird unsere Mensa das gesamte Papier und den gesamten Kunststoff recyceln.*
S2: *Ja, und es wird...*

7 Diskutieren und kombinieren

Auf Ihrem Arbeitsblatt finden Sie Informationen über Jasmin und ihre Mutter. Überlegen Sie sich, wie Jasmins Mutter reagieren würde, wenn Jasmin das machen würde, was Sie auf den Bildern sehen können. Answers will vary.

7 Suggestion Remind students that **werden** can be used in its subjunctive form for hypotheses and contrary-to-fact situations.

BEISPIEL

S1: *Was würde passieren, wenn Jasmin mit dem Flugzeug flöge?*
S2: *Wenn Jasmin mit dem Flugzeug flöge, würde ihre Mutter sie am Flughafen anrufen.*

8 Eine bessere Stadt

Schreiben Sie mit einem Partner / einer Partnerin eine Liste mit sechs Umwelt-problemen, die in Städten existieren. Schlagen Sie für jedes Problem eine Lösung vor. Benutzen Sie das Passiv. Answers will vary.

BEISPIEL

S1: *Zu viele Batterien werden in den Müll geworfen.*
S2: *Batterien sollen recycelt werden.*

Mein Wörterbuch

Schreiben Sie fünf weitere Wörter in Ihr persönliches Wörterbuch zu den Themen **In der Natur** und **Die Umwelt**.

Lektion 12B		
German	English	Definition
+ add word		
unbehandelt	untreated	biologisch, ungespritzt

ä ö ü ß ☐ ALL CAPS

Weiter geht's

Panorama Interactive Map

Sachsen-Anhalt und Sachsen

NATIONAL connections cultures STANDARDS

Sachsen-Anhalt in Zahlen

▸ **Fläche:** *20.446 km²*

▸ **Bevölkerung:** *2,2 Millionen Menschen*

▸ **Städte:** *Halle (238.000 Einwohner), Magdeburg (236.000)*

▸ **Wichtige Industriezweige:** *Chemieindustrie, die Logistik, erneuerbare Energien*

▸ **Touristenattraktionen:** *Lutherstadt Wittenberg, Bauhaus Dessau, Dessau-Wörtlitzer Gartenreich, Quedlinburg, Burg Falkenstein, das Grüne Band Deutschland, wo einmal die Mauer stand, Naumburger Dom*

Quelle: Investitions- und Marketinggesellschaft Sachsen-Anhalt mbH

Sachsen in Zahlen

Suggestion Tell students that the former no-man's land between East and West Germany remained relatively untouched for nearly 40 years and is now a protected area of rich biodiversity

▸ **Fläche:** *18.415 km²*

▸ **Bevölkerung:** *4 Millionen Menschen*

▸ **Städte:** *Leipzig (560.000 Einwohner), Dresden (544.000), Chemnitz (246.000)*

▸ **Wichtige Industriezweige:** *Automobilindustrie, Mikroelektronik, Maschinenbau*

▸ **Touristenattraktionen:** *Weihnachtsmärkte im Erzgebirge, Dresden, Meißener Porzellan
Dresden, das Elbflorenz, ist eine der größten Touristenattraktionen Sachsens. Touristen sollten den Zwinger, die Frauenkirche und die Semperoper besuchen.*

Quelle: Tourismus Marketing Gesellschaft Sachsen mbH

Berühmte Menschen aus Sachsen-Anhalt und Sachsen

▸ **Otto Fürst von Bismarck,** *Politiker (1815–1898)*

▸ **Erich Kästner,** *Autor (1839–1974)*

▸ **Gottfried Wilhelm Leibniz,** *Mathematiker und Wissenschaftler (1646–1716)*

▸ **Christiane Nüsslein-Volhard,** *Wissenschaftlerin (1942–)*

▸ **Katharina Witt,** *Sportlerin (1965–)*

Expansion For homework, have students research one of these famous individuals and find one piece of information about them to share with the class.

Kurfürst *prince-elector* **Manufaktur** *factory*
gekreuzten Schwerter *crossed swords*

Das Bauhaus in Dessau

Die Silhouette der Dresdener Innenstadt

Das Grüne Band Deutschland

Landesgrenzen
● Stadt
◉ Landeshauptstadt

0   25 Meilen
0   25 Kilometer

Unglaublich, aber wahr!

Im Jahr 1708 erfanden Johann Friedrich Böttger und Walther von Tschirnhaus das europäische Porzellan. 1710 gründete der sächsische Kurfürst° August der Starke dann die Porzellan-Manufaktur° Meißen. Dieses auch heute noch weltberühmte Porzellan trägt das Symbol der gekreuzten Schwerter°.

Technologie
Solar Valley

Suggestion Tell students that in 2014 Germany became the first country to generate more than half of its electricity supply from solar energy. Today China leads the world in solar power.

Das Solar Valley, auch Sonnenallee bezeichnet, liegt in Sachsen-Anhalt in der Nähe der Stadt Bitterfeld-Wolfen. Es gilt als eines der Zentren der Photovoltaikindustrie. Zu den Firmen, die hier vertreten° sind, gehören Q-Cells SE, Calyxo GmbH und Sontor GmbH.

Das Solar Valley gilt als einer der größten Solarstandorte Europas und ist Symbol für das deutsche Engagement im Bereich erneuerbarer Energiequellen. Bis zu 3.000 Menschen arbeiten in diesem Industriebereich in Sachsen-Anhalt.

Völker
Die Sorben

Die Sorben, ein westslawisches Volk, leben heute in der Ober- und Niederlausitz in den Bundesländern Brandenburg und Sachsen, wo Sorbisch eine offizielle Sprache ist. Es gibt heute noch etwa 60.000 Sorben in Deutschland, wo sie als offizielle Minderheit° anerkannt° sind. Die meisten Sorben sind deutsche Staatsangehörige°. Einer der bekanntesten sorbischen Bräuche° ist das alljährliche Osterreiten. Jährlich sehen mehr als 30.000 Besucher zu, wenn rund 1.700 Reiter in Frack und Zylinder° die Botschaft von der Auferstehung Jesu Christi verkünden°.

Musik
Barockmusiker aus Sachsen-Anhalt

Suggestion Play students clips of music by Händel, Telemann, and Bach. Ask students whether they have heard these pieces before, and whether they can identify each piece's composer.

Johann Sebastian Bach, Georg Philipp Telemann und Georg Friedrich Händel sind weltberühmte Barockmusiker aus Sachsen-Anhalt, deren Werke man heute noch hört. Telemann, der Musik im Selbststudium lernte, komponierte mehr als 3.600 Stücke. Bach ist vor allem für seine Chorwerke und Musik für Tasteninstrumente° berühmt. Händel hatte in England mit seinen dramatischen Opern und Oratorien großen Erfolg. Trotz der Entfernung waren Telemann und Händel gut befreundet, und alle drei studierten und führten die Musik der anderen auf°.

vertreten *represented* gewaltfreien *nonviolent* Wende *reunification* riefen *called* Minderheit *minority* anerkannt *recognized* Staatsangehörige *citizens* Bräuche *customs* Frack und Zylinder *tails and top hat* verkünden *announce* Musik für Tasteninstrumente *keyboard music* führten... auf *performed*

Politik
Leipziger Montagsdemonstrationen

Im Herbst 1989 kam es in der DDR zu der Friedlichen Revolution. Die gewaltfreien° Montagsdemonstrationen in Leipzig und einigen anderen ostdeutschen Städten galten als Katalysator für die Wende° und das Ende der DDR. Nachdem sich am 4. September 1.200 Demonstranten vor der Leipziger Nikolaikirche getroffen hatten, waren es am 6. November, drei Tage vor dem Fall der Berliner Mauer, 500.000 Menschen, die Slogans wie "Wir sind das Volk" oder "Für ein offenes Land mit freien Menschen" riefen°.

Musik Musik

Helene Fischer

Helene Fischer wurde 1984 in Sibirien geboren und kam mit drei Jahren nach Deutschland. Sie singt deutsche Schlager und ist eine der erfolgreichsten Sängerinnen Deutschlands.

Go to **vhlcentral.com** to find out more about **Helene Fischer**.

Was haben Sie gelernt? Entscheiden Sie, ob die Sätze richtig oder falsch sind. Korrigieren Sie die falschen Sätze.

1. 1710 gründete August der Starke die Porzellan-Manufaktur Meißen. Richtig.
2. Das Solar Valley ist in Kalifornien. Falsch. Das Solar Valley ist in Sachsen-Anhalt.
3. Die Berliner Mauer fiel im September 1989. Falsch. Die Mauer fiel im November 1989.
4. Die Sorben sind eine Minderheit in Westdeutschland. Falsch. Die Sorben sind eine Minderheit in Brandenburg und Sachsen.
5. Händels Opern und Oratorien hatten in England großen Erfolg. Richtig.

  2 **Denken Sie nach** Diskutieren Sie die Frage mit einem Partner/ einer Partnerin. Suchen Sie weitere Informationen über die Leipziger Montagsdemonstrationen und die Friedliche Revolution: Wann fingen diese Demonstrationen an? Wer organisierte sie? Welche Demonstrationen in Ihrem Land haben zu einem bedeutenden politischen Wandel (*change*) geführt?

Lesen   Audio: Reading

Vor dem Lesen

Strategien

Imagery

Poets often use vivid imagery to convey a particular sensory experience to the reader. A poet may also use specific images as symbols, to represent certain abstract themes or ideas, or as metaphors, to draw a comparison between apparently dissimilar objects or concepts. Paying close attention to the words of a poem and the images those words convey can help you to gain a deeper understanding of the poem.

Untersuchen Sie den Text

Lesen Sie einmal die beiden Gedichte. Welche Wörter und Bilder kommen in beiden Gedichten immer wieder vor?

Autoren
Rose Ausländer

Rose Ausländer (1901–1988) wurde in Czernowitz, Bukowina (damals Österreich-Ungarn) als Kind jüdischer Eltern geboren. 1921 wanderte sie nach Amerika aus, aber 1931 kam sie in ihre Heimatstadt zurück, um ihre Mutter zu pflegen (*care for*). Die Jahre von 1941 bis 1944 verbrachte sie mit ihrer Mutter und ihrem Bruder in einem Kellerversteck (*cellar hiding-place*). Nach dem Krieg wanderte sie wieder nach Amerika aus. Dort fing sie an, Gedichte auf Englisch zu schreiben. Erst im Jahre 1956 begann sie ihre Gedichte wieder auf Deutsch zu schreiben.

Rainer Maria Rilke

Rainer Maria Rilke (1875–1926) ist einer der bekanntesten Dichter (*poets*) der deutschen Sprache. Er stammte aus Prag, das damals zu Österreich-Ungarn gehörte. Neben Gedichten schrieb er Erzählungen, einen Roman und Aufsätze über Kunst und Kultur. Der Panther gilt als eines der berühmtesten Gedichte Rilkes.

Meine Nachtigall°

Rose Ausländer

❧

Meine Mutter war einmal ein Reh°
Die goldbraunen Augen
die Anmut°
blieben ihr aus der Rehzeit

Hier war sie
halb Engel° halb Mensch-
die Mitte° war Mutter
Als ich sie fragte was sie gern geworden wäre
sagte sie: eine Nachtigall

Jetzt ist sie eine Nachtigall
Nacht um Nacht höre ich sie
im Garten meines schlaflosen Traumes°
Sie singt das Zion der Ahnen°
sie singt das alte Österreich
sie singt die Berge und Buchenwälder°
der Bukowina
Wiegenlieder°
singt mir Nacht um Nacht
meine Nachtigall
im Garten meines schlaflosen Traumes

Nachtigall *nightingale* **Reh** *deer* **Anmut** *grace* **Engel** *angel*
Mitte *middle* **schlaflosen Traumes** *sleepless dream* **Ahnen** *ancestors*
Buchenwälder *beech tree forests* **Wiegenlieder** *lullabies*

∼ Der Panther ∼

Rainer Maria Rilke

Im Jardin des Plantes, Paris

Sein Blick° ist vom Vorübergehn° der Stäbe°
so müd geworden, daß er nichts mehr hält°.
Ihm ist, als ob es tausend Stäbe gäbe
und hinter tausend Stäben keine Welt.

Der weiche° Gang geschmeidig° starker Schritte,
der sich im allerkleinsten Kreise° dreht,
ist wie ein Tanz von Kraft um eine Mitte,
in der betäubt° ein großer Wille steht.

Nur manchmal schiebt der Vorhang der Pupille
sich lautlos° auf. – Dann geht ein Bild hinein,
geht durch der Glieder° angespannte Stille –
und hört im Herzen auf zu sein.

Blick *gaze* **Vorübergehn** *passing by* **Stäbe** *bars*
hält *holds* **weiche** *smooth* **geschmeidig** *sleek*
allerkleinsten Kreise *smallest circles*
betäubt *numbed* **lautlos** *silently* **Glieder** *limbs*

Nach dem Lesen

  Die Nachtigall Wählen Sie die richtige Antwort auf jede Frage.

1. Was wollte die Mutter laut Ausländers Gedicht werden?
   a. Sie wollte ein Reh werden.
   b. Sie wollte eine Nachtigall werden.

2. Was hatte die Mutter noch aus der Zeit, als sie ein Reh war?
   a. Sie hatte noch goldbraune Augen und Anmut.
   b. Sie hatte noch schlaflose Träume.

3. Was für Lieder singt die Nachtigall?
   a. Sie singt Wiegenlieder.
   b. Sie singt Volkslieder.

  Der Panther Wählen Sie die richtige Antwort auf jede Frage.

1. Wo lebt der Panther?
   a. Er lebt in der freien Natur.
   b. Er lebt in Gefangenschaft.

2. Warum sieht er die Welt nicht mehr?
   a. Weil er alt und blind geworden ist.
   b. Weil sein Blick müde geworden ist.

3. Wer hat laut Rilkes Gedicht einen großen Willen?
   a. Der Panther hat einen großen Willen.
   b. Die Welt hat einen großen Willen.

 Zum Besprechen Sprechen Sie mit einem Partner / einer Partnerin über die zwei Gedichte. Was finden beide Dichter so gut an den Tieren? Was unterscheidet die Situation der Nachtigall von der des Panthers? **Partner Chat** You can also assign this activity on the Supersite.

 Aufsatz Schreiben Sie einen Aufsatz über eins der folgenden Themen unde lesen Sie ihn im Kurs vor.

1. Wofür stehen die Tiere in den Gedichten? Was wollen die Autoren mit Hilfe der Tiere ausdrücken?

2. Gibt es Menschen, die wie der Panther in Rilkes Gedicht sind? Begründen Sie Ihre Meinung.

3. Welche Wörter und Verse kommen in beiden Gedichten immer wieder vor? Welche Wirkung (*effect*) hat die Wiederholung der Wörter und Verse?

4. Schreiben Sie ein Gedicht über ein Tier, das Sie besonders interessant finden.

Hören

Strategien

Taking notes

Jotting down notes while you listen can help you keep track of the important points of a speech or oral presentation. It will help you to focus actively on comprehension rather than on remembering what you heard.

 To practice this strategy, listen as Katrin Schneider describes her recent vacation. Jot down notes about the main points you hear. Suggested answers are provided.

Vorbereitung

Sehen Sie sich das Foto an: Wer sind diese Leute? Was machen sie? Warum protestieren sie? Was sagen sie vielleicht?

Zuhören

 Hören Sie dem Organisator zu, der mit den Demonstranten spricht, und nennen Sie die Themen, über die er spricht.

1. ____ Recycling
2. _X_ Abfall
3. _X_ Sonnenenergie
4. ____ Überbevölkerung
5. ____ Gesetz
6. _X_ Windenergie
7. _X_ Umwelt
8. ____ Waldsterben
9. _X_ Kernenergie
10. _X_ erneuerbare Energie
11. ____ Erderwärmung
12. _X_ Giftmüll

Suggestion For the first round of listening, have students keep their books closed and jot down as many words as they can catch. Ask them to share their lists and make a projection about the purpose of the speech.

Verständnis

 Alternativenergien Ergänzen Sie die Sätze mit der richtigen Antwort.

1. Die Demonstration ist gegen ___die Kernkraft___.
   a. die Sonnenenergie
   b. die Kernkraft
   c. die Windenergie

2. Die Demonstration findet in ___Berlin___ statt.
   a. Sachsen
   b. Berlin
   c. Schleswig-Holstein

3. Es sind ___30.000___ Menschen bei der Demonstration.
   a. 13.000
   b. 30.000
   c. 3.000

4. Windenergie wird vor allem in ___Schleswig-Holstein___ produziert.
   a. Sachsen
   b. Berlin
   c. Schleswig-Holstein

5. Die Technologie für Sonnenenergie wird in ___Sachsen___ entwickelt.
   a. Sachsen
   b. Berlin
   c. Schleswig-Holstein

Expansion Ask students to identify the rhetorical devices that they hear such as repetition of words, phrases, and structures, rhetorical questions, etc.

Suggestion Tell students that **Atomenergie** and **Solarenergie** are frequently used as synonyms for **Kernenergie** and **Sonnenenergie**, respectively.

 Neue Gesetze Ein Repräsentant einer internationalen Umweltorganisation besucht Ihre Universität, um Umweltprobleme und Umweltschutz zu diskutieren. Wählen Sie in kleinen Gruppen ein Umweltproblem aus, das heute sehr wichtig ist. Versuchen Sie den Repräsentanten zu überzeugen, dass Regierungen und Politiker mehr auf diesem Gebiet machen sollten. Sie müssen das Problem erklären können. Was muss sich ändern, damit es besser wird? Überlegen Sie sich auch neue Gesetze, die Sie dem Repräsentanten vorschlagen wollen.

Schreiben

Strategien

Considering audience and purpose

Before you begin a piece of writing, you must determine to whom you are addressing the piece and what you want to express to your reader. Once you have defined both your audience and your purpose, you will be able to decide which genre, vocabulary, and grammatical structures will best serve your composition.

Suppose you want to share your thoughts on local traffic problems. Your audience might be either the local government or the community. You could choose to write a newspaper article, a letter to the editor, or a letter to the city's governing board. You should first decide the focus of your piece:

1. Are there specific problems you want to highlight?

2. Is your goal to register a complaint or to increase public awareness?

3. Are you trying to persuade others to adopt your point of view?

4. Are you hoping to inspire others to take concrete actions?

The answers to these questions will help you establish the purpose of your writing and determine your audience. Of course, your writing may have more than one purpose. For example, you may intend both to inform others of a problem and to inspire them to take action.

Whatever the topic you choose, defining your purpose and your audience before you begin will help to make your writing more focused and effective.

Suggestion Remind students of the techniques introduced in earlier chapters for organizing their ideas, such as idea-maps and note cards, as well as linking words such as adverbs and conjunctions for creating logical connections and emphasis.

Thema

Schreiben Sie einen Brief oder einen Bericht

Schreiben Sie über ein Umweltproblem, das Ihrer Meinung nach (*in your opinion*) sehr wichtig ist. Beantworten Sie die folgenden Fragen.

1. Wählen Sie zuerst ein Problem, über das Sie schreiben wollen. Ist es ein Problem vor Ort (z. B., Recycling auf dem Schulgelände) oder ein Problem auf globaler Ebene (z. B. die Überbevölkerung)?

2. Wer sind die Leser Ihres Briefs/Berichts: Schreiben Sie einen Brief an einen Freund? Schreiben Sie einen Brief an einen Politiker? An den Umweltklub der Schule? Schreiben Sie einen Bericht oder einen Artikel für eine Zeitung oder eine Zeitschrift?

3. Nennen Sie den Grund für den Brief oder den Bericht: Informieren Sie die Leser oder wollen Sie auch Ihre Meinung sagen?

4. Schreiben Sie eine kurze Einleitung (*introduction*). Stellen Sie das Problem, das Sie ausgewählt haben, hier vor.

5. Wenn Sie Ihre Meinung sagen wollen, müssen Sie gute Gründe für ihre Position angeben, damit man Ihnen glaubt.

6. Schreiben Sie eine Schlussfolgerung (*conclusion*) für den Brief oder Bericht.

Expansion Before leaving the topic of the environment, ask students for their closing thoughts: **Wie sieht die Zukunft unseres Planeten aus? Möchten Sie versuchen, umweltfreundlicher zu leben? Warum, warum nicht? Wie? Kann der Einzelne was bewirken?**

Vocabulary Tools

Lektion 12A

die Natur
nature

der Bauernhof, ⸚e *farm*
der Baum, ⸚e *tree*
der Berg, -e *mountain*
das Blatt, ⸚er *leaf*
der Busch, ⸚e *bush*
das Feld, -er *field*
der Fluss, ⸚e *river*
das Gras, ⸚er *grass*
der Himmel *sky*
die Insel, -n *island*
die Klippe, -n *cliff*
die Küste, -n *coast*
die Landschaft, -en *countryside*
die Luft *air*
das Meer, -e *sea*
der Mond, -e *moon*
der See, -n *lake*
die Sonne, -n *sun*
der Sonnenaufgang, ⸚e *sunrise*
der Sonnenuntergang, ⸚e *sunset*
der Stein, -e *rock*
der Stern, -e *star*
das Tal, ⸚er *valley*
der Wald, ⸚er *forest*
der Wasserfall, ⸚e *waterfall*
der Weg, -e *path*

aufregend *exciting*
bedeutend *important*
nass *wet*
trocken *dry*

Tiere
animals

das Eichhörnchen, - *squirrel*
der Fisch, -e *fish*
der Hase, -n *hare*
das Huhn, ⸚er *chicken*
die Kuh, ⸚e *cow*
die Maus, ⸚e *mouse*
das Pferd, -e *horse*
das Schaf, -e *sheep*
die Schlange, -n *snake*

Verben

aufgehen (geht... auf) *to rise*
erforschen *to explore*
untergehen (geht... unter) *to set*
wandern *to hike*

ein Picknick (*n.*) machen *to have a picnic*

Der Konjunktiv der Vergangenheit
See pp. 506–507.
Das Partizip Präsens See p. 510.

Lektion 12B

die Umwelt
the environment

die Art, -en *species*
die Erde, -n *earth*
die Fabrik, -en *factory*
die Gefahr, -en *danger*
das Hochwasser, - *flood*
das Licht, -er *light*
der Müll *waste*
der Müllwagen, - *garbage truck*
die Ökologie *ecology*
der Umweltschutz *environmentalism*
die Welt, -en *world*

biologisch *organic*
gefährdet *endangered*
ökologisch *ecological*
umweltfreundlich *environmentally friendly*

Energie
energy

die Geothermie *geothermal energy*
die Kernenergie *nuclear energy*
das Kernkraftwerk, -e *nuclear power plant*
die Sonnenenergie *solar energy*
die Windenergie *wind energy*

Probleme
problems

das Aussterben *extinction*
die Erderwärmung *global warming*
der Giftmüll *toxic waste*
der saure Regen *acid rain*
die Überbevölkerung *overpopulation*
die Verschmutzung *pollution*

Lösungen
solutions

das Gesetz, -e *law*
die erneuerbare Energie (*pl.* die erneuerbaren Energien) *renewable energy*
die Fahrgemeinschaft, -en *carpool*
das Hybridauto, -s *hybrid car*
das Recycling *recycling*
die Regierung, -en *government*

Verben

ausschalten (schaltet... aus) *to turn off*
(den Planeten) retten *to save (the planet)*
einschalten (schaltet... ein) *to turn on*
entwickeln *to develop*
erhalten (erhält) *to preserve*
recyceln *to recycle*
schützen *to protect*
verbessern *to improve*
verschmutzen *to pollute*
vorschlagen (schlägt... vor) *to propose*
wegwerfen (wirft... weg) *to throw away*

Der Konjunktiv I See pp. 524–525.
The passive voice See p. 528.

Appendix A

Appendix B

Appendix C

Glossary of Grammatical Terms

ADJECTIVE Words that describe people, places, or things. An attributive adjective comes before the noun it modifies and takes an ending that matches the gender and case of the noun. A predicate adjective comes after the verb **sein**, **werden**, or **bleiben** and describes the noun that is the subject of the sentence. Predicate adjectives take no additional endings.

Thomas hat eine sehr **gute**
  Stelle gefunden.
Thomas found a really
  ***good** job.*

Hast du mein **kleines**
  Adressbuch gesehen?
*Have you seen my **little***
  address book?

Mein Bruder ist **klein**.
*My brother is **short**.*

Deine Schwester wird **groß**.
*Your sister is getting **tall**.*

Possessive adjectives Words that are placed before a noun to indicate ownership or belonging. Each personal pronoun has a corresponding possessive adjective. Possessive adjectives take the same endings as the indefinite article **ein**.

Meine Schwester ist hier.
My sister is here.

Wo ist **dein** Vater?
*Where is **your** father?*

ADVERB Words or phrases that modify a verb, an adjective, or another adverb. Adverbs and adverbial phrases describe *when*, *how*, or *where* an action takes place.

Der Kuchen ist **fast** fertig.
*The cake is **almost** ready.*

Du isst **viel zu** schnell.
*You eat **much too** quickly.*

ARTICLE A word that precedes a noun and indicates its gender, number, and case.

Definite article Equivalent to *the* in English. Its form indicates the gender and case of the noun, and whether it is singular or plural.

der Tisch (*m. s.*)
the table
die Tische (*m. pl.*)
the tables
die Tür (*f. s.*)
the door

die Türen (*f. pl.*)
the doors
das Fenster (*n. s.*)
the window
die Fenster (*n. pl.*)
the windows

Indefinite article Corresponds to *a* or *an* in English. It precedes the noun and matches its gender and case. There is no plural indefinite article in German.

ein Tisch (*m.*)
a table
eine Tür (*f.*)
a door

ein Fenster (*n.*)
a window

CASE There are four cases in German. The case indicates the function of each noun in a sentence. The case of a noun determines the form of the definite or indefinite article that precedes the noun, the form of any adjectives that modify the noun, and the form of the pronoun that can replace the noun.

Nominativ (*nominative*): **Der Professor** ist alt.
The professor is old.

Akkusativ (*accusative*): Ich verstehe **den Professor**.
*I understand **the professor**.*

Dativ (*dative*): Der Assistent zeigt **dem Professor** den
  neuen Computer.
*The assistant is showing **the professor** the new computer.*

Genitiv (*genitive*): Das ist der Assistent **des Professors**.
*This is **the professor's** assistant.*

The nominative case The grammatical subject of a sentence is always in the nominative case. The nominative case is also used for nouns that follow a form of **sein**, **werden**, or **bleiben**. In German dictionaries, nouns, pronouns, and numbers are always listed in their nominative form.

Das ist **eine gute Idee.**
*That's **a good idea.***

Die Kinder schlafen.
The kids are sleeping.

The accusative case A noun that functions as a direct object is in the accusative case.

Der Lehrer hat **den Stift**.
*The teacher has **the pen**.*

Sie öffnet **die Tür**.
*She's opening **the door**.*

Ich kaufe **einen Tisch**.
*I'm going to buy **a table**.*

Ich habe **ein Problem**.
*I have **a problem**.*

The dative case An object in the dative case indicates to whom or for whom an action is performed.

Ich bringe **dem Lehrer** einen Apfel.
*I'm bringing **the teacher** an apple.*

Zeig **der Professorin** deine Arbeit.
*Show your work **to the professor**.*

The genitive case A noun in the genitive case modifies another noun. The genitive case indicates ownership or a close relationship between the genitive noun and the noun it modifies, which may be a subject or an object.

Thorsten hat die Rede **des Bundespräsidenten**
  heruntergeladen.
*Thorsten downloaded **the president's** speech.*

Das Mikrofon **der Professorin** funktioniert nicht.
***The professor's** microphone doesn't work.*

CLAUSE A group of words that contains both a conjugated verb and a subject, either expressed or implied.

Main (or independent) clause A clause that can stand alone as a complete sentence.

Ich bezahle immer bar, weil ich keine Kreditkarte habe.
I always pay cash, because I don't have a credit card.

Subordinate clause A subordinate clause explains how, when, why, or under what circumstances the action in the main clause occurs. The conjugated verb of a subordinate clause is placed at the end of that clause.

Ich lese die Zeitung, **wenn** ich Zeit **habe.**
*I read the newspaper **when** I have the time.*

COMPARATIVE The form of an adjective or adverb that compares two or more people or things.

Meine Geschwister sind alle **älter** als ich.
*My siblings are all **older** than I am.*

Die Fahrt dauert mit dem Auto **länger** als mit dem Zug.
*The trip takes **longer** by car than by train.*

CONJUNCTION A word used to connect words, clauses, or phrases.

Coordinating conjunctions Words that combine two related sentences, words, or phrases into a single sentence. There are five coordinating conjunctions in German: **aber** (*but*), **denn** (*because; since*), **oder** (*or*), **sondern** (*but, rather*), **und** (*and*). All other conjunctions are subordinating.

Ich möchte eine große Küche, **denn** ich koche gern.
*I want a big kitchen, **because** I like to cook.*

Lola braucht einen Schrank **oder** eine Kommode.
*Lola needs a closet **or** a dresser.*

Subordinating conjunctions Words used to combine a subordinate clause with a main clause.

Ich lese die Zeitung, **wenn** ich Zeit **habe.**
*I read the newspaper **when** I have the time.*

DEMONSTRATIVE Pronouns or adjectives that refer to something or someone that has already been mentioned, or that point out a specific person or thing.

Ist Greta online? –Ja, **die** schreibt eine E-Mail.
*Is Greta online? –Yes, **she's** writing an e-mail.*

Gefällt dir dieser Sessel? –Ja, **der** ist sehr bequem!
*Do you like that chair? –Yes, **it's** very comfortable!*

DER-WORDS Words that take the same endings as the forms of the definite article **der**. These include the demonstrative pronouns **dieser** (*this; that*), **jeder** (*each, every*), **jener** (*that*), **mancher** (*some*), and **solcher** (*such*), and the question word **welcher** (*which*).

Welcher Laptop gefällt dir am besten?
Which laptop do you like best?

Ich finde **diesen** Laptop am schönsten.
*I think **this** laptop is the nicest.*

DIRECT OBJECT A noun or pronoun that directly receives the action of the verb. Direct objects are in the accusative.

Kennst du **diesen Mann?**   Ich mache **eine Torte.**
*Do you know **that man?**   I'm making **a cake.***

EIN-WORDS Words that take the same endings as the forms of the indefinite article **ein**. These include the negation **kein** and all of the possessive adjectives.

Hast du **einen** Hund?   Ich habe **keinen** Fußball.
*Do you have **a** dog?   I don't have **a** soccer ball.*

GENDER The grammatical categorization of nouns, pronouns, and adjectives as masculine, feminine, or neuter.

Masculine
articles: **der, ein**
pronouns: **er, der**
adjectives: **guter, schöner**

Feminine
articles: **die, eine**
pronouns: **sie, die**
adjectives: **gute, schöne**

Neuter
articles: **das, ein**
pronouns: **es, das**
adjectives: **gutes, schönes**

HELPING VERB *See VERB, Auxiliary verb.*

IMPERATIVE Imperatives are verb forms used to express commands, requests, suggestions, directions, or instructions.

Mach deine Hausaufgaben!   **Backen wir** einen Kuchen!
***Do** your homework!   **Let's bake** a cake!*

INDIRECT OBJECT A noun or pronoun that receives the action of the verb indirectly. The indirect object is often a person to whom or for whom the action of the sentence is performed. Indirect objects are in the dative case.

Manfred hat **seinem Bruder** ein Buch geschenkt.
*Manfred gave **his brother** a book.*

INFINITIVE The basic, unconjugated form of a verb. Most German infinitives end in **-en**. A few end in **-ern** or **-eln**.

sehen, essen, lesen, wandern, sammeln
to see, to eat, to read, to hike, to collect

NOUN A word that refers to one or more people, animals, places, things, or ideas. Nouns in German may be masculine, feminine, or neuter, and are either singular or plural.

der **Junge**, die **Katze**, das **Café**
*the **boy**, the **cat**, the **café***

Compound noun Two or more simple nouns can be combined to form a compound noun. The gender of a compound noun matches the gender of the last noun in the compound.

die Nacht + das Hemd = **das Nachthemd**
*night + shirt = **nightshirt***

NUMBER A grammatical term that refers to the quantity of a noun. Nouns in German are either singular or plural. The plural form of a noun may have an added umlaut and/or an added ending. Adjectives, articles, and verbs also have different endings, depending on whether they are singular or plural.

Singular:
der **Mann**, die **Frau**, das **Kind**
*the **man**, the **woman**, the **child***

Plural:
die **Männer**, die **Frauen**, die **Kinder**
*the **men**, the **women**, the **children***

NUMBERS Words that represent quantities.

Cardinal numbers Numbers that indicate specific quantities. Cardinal numbers typically modify nouns, but do not add gender or case endings.

zwei Männer, **fünfzehn** Frauen, **sechzig** Kinder
***two** men, **fifteen** women, **sixty** children*

Ordinal numbers Words that indicate the order of a noun in a series. Ordinal numbers add the same gender and case endings as adjectives.

der **erste** Mann, die **zweite** Frau, das **dritte** Kind
*the **first** man, the **second** woman, the **third** child*

PARTICIPLE A participle is formed from a verb but may be used as an adjective or adverb. Present participles are used primarily in written German. Past participles are used in compound tenses, including the **Perfekt** and the **Plusquamperfekt**.

Der **aufgehende** Mond war sehr schön.
*The **rising** moon was beautiful.*

Habt ihr schon **gegessen**?
*Have you already **eaten**?*

PREPOSITION A preposition links a noun or pronoun to other words in a sentence. Combined with a noun or pronoun, it forms a prepositional phrase, which can be used like an adverb to answer the question *when, how,* or *where.* In German, certain prepositions are always followed by a noun in the accusative case, while others are always followed by a noun in the dative case. A small number of prepositions are used with the genitive case.

ohne das Buch
without the book

mit dem Auto
by car

trotz des Regens
in spite of the rain

Two-way prepositions can be followed by either the dative or the accusative, depending on the situation. They are followed by the accusative when used with a verb that indicates movement toward a destination. With all other verbs, they are followed by the dative.

Stell deine Schuhe nicht **auf den Tisch**!
*Don't put your shoes **on the table**!*

Dein Schal liegt **auf dem Tisch**.
*Your scarf is lying **on the table**.*

PRONOUN A word that takes the place of a noun.

Subject pronouns Words used to replace a noun in the nominative case.

Maria ist nett.
***Maria** is nice.*

Der Junge ist groß.
***The boy** is tall.*

Sie ist nett.
***She** is nice.*

Er ist groß.
***He** is tall.*

Accusative pronouns Words used to replace a noun that functions as the direct object.

Wer hat **die Torte** gebacken?
*Who baked **the cake**?*

Ich habe **sie** gebacken.
*I baked **it**.*

Dative pronouns Words used to replace a noun that functions as the indirect object.

Musst du **deiner Oma** eine E-Mail schicken?
*Do you need to send an e-mail **to your grandma**?*

Nein, ich habe **ihr** schon geschrieben.
*No, I already wrote **to her**.*

Indefinite pronouns Words that refer to an unknown or nonspecific person or thing.

Jemand hat seinen Personalausweis vergessen.
Someone forgot his I.D. card.

Herr Klein will mit **niemandem** sprechen.
Mr. Klein doesn't want to speak with anyone.

Reflexive pronouns The pronouns used with reflexive verbs. When the subject of a reflexive verb is also its direct object, it takes an accusative reflexive pronoun. When the subject of a reflexive verb is not its direct object, it takes a dative reflexive pronoun.

Ich wasche **mich**.
I'm washing (myself).

Ich wasche **mir** das Gesicht.
I'm washing my face.

SUBJUNCTIVE A verb form (**der Konjunktiv II**) used to talk about hypothetical, unlikely or impossible conditions, to express wishes, and to make polite requests. German also has an additional subjunctive tense, der **Konjunktiv I**, used to report what someone else has said without indicating whether the information is true or false.

Ich **hätte** gern viel Geld.
I'd like to have a lot of money.

Wenn er sportlicher **wäre**, **würde** er häufiger trainieren.
If he were more athletic, he would exercise more.

SUPERLATIVE The form of an adjective or adverb used to indicate that a person or thing has more of a particular quality than anyone or anything else.

Welches ist **das größte** Tier der Welt?
What's the biggest animal in the world?

Wie komme ich **am besten** zur Tankstelle?
What's the best way to get to the gas station?

TENSE A set of verb forms that indicates if an action or state occurs in the past, present, or future.

Compound tense A tense made up of an auxiliary verb and a participle or infinitive.

Wir **haben** ihren Geburtstag **gefeiert**.
We celebrated her birthday.

VERB A word that expresses actions or states of being. German verbs are classified as *weak, mixed,* or *strong,* based on the way their past participles are formed.

weak: Ich **habe** eine Torte **gemacht**.
I made a cake.

strong: Wir **haben** Kekse **gegessen**.
We ate cookies.

mixed: Er **hat** eine CD **gebrannt**.
He burned a CD.

Auxiliary verb A conjugated verb used with the participle or infinitive of another verb. The auxiliary verbs **haben** and **sein** are used with past participles to form compound tenses including the **Perfekt** and **Plusquamperfekt**. **Werden** is used with an infinitive to form the future tense, and with a past participle to form a passive construction. Modals are also frequently used as auxiliary verbs.

Habt ihr den Tisch **gedeckt**?
Did you set the table?

Jasmin **war** noch nie nach Zürich **gefahren**.
Jasmin had never been to Zurich.

Wir **werden** uns in einer Woche wieder **treffen**.
We'll meet again in one week.

Es **wird** hier nur Deutsch **gesprochen**.
Only German is spoken here.

Modal verbs Verbs that modify the meaning of another verb. Modals express an attitude toward an action, such as permission, obligation, ability, desire, or necessity.

Ich **muss** Französisch **lernen**.
I have to study French.

Ich **will** Französisch **lernen**.
I want to learn French.

Principal parts German verbs are usually listed in dictionaries by their *principal parts* (**Stammformen**): the infinitive, the third-person singular present tense form (if the verb is irregular in the present), the third-person singular **Präteritum** form, and the past participle. Knowing the principal parts of a verb allows you to produce all of its conjugations in any tense.

geben (gibt)	**gab**	**gegeben**
to give (gives)	*gave*	*given*

Reflexive verbs Verbs that indicate an action you do to yourself or for yourself. The subject of a reflexive verb is also its object.

Ich **fühle mich** nicht **wohl**.
I don't feel well.

Wir **haben uns entspannt**.
We've been relaxing.

Reciprocal reflexive verbs Verbs that express an action done by two or more people or things to or for one another.

Wir rufen **uns** jeden Tag **an**.
We call each other every day.

Meine Großeltern lieben **sich** sehr.
My grandparents love each other very much.

Declension of articles

definite articles	masculine	feminine	neuter	plural
nominative	der	die	das	die
accusative	den	die	das	die
dative	dem	der	dem	den
genitive	des	der	des	der

der-words	masculine	feminine	neuter	plural
nominative	dieser	diese	dieses	diese
accusative	diesen	diese	dieses	diese
dative	diesem	dieser	diesem	diesen
genitive	dieses	dieser	dieses	dieser

indefinite articles	masculine	feminine	neuter	plural
nominative	ein	eine	ein	-
accusative	einen	eine	ein	-
dative	einem	einer	einem	-
genitive	eines	einer	eines	-

ein-words	masculine	feminine	neuter	plural
nominative	mein	meine	mein	meine
accusative	meinen	meine	mein	meine
dative	meinem	meiner	meinem	meinen
genitive	meines	meiner	meines	meiner

Declension of nouns and adjectives

nouns and adjectives with *der*-words			
	masculine	feminine	neuter	plural
nominative	der gute Rat	die gute Landschaft	das gute Brot	die guten Freunde
accusative	den guten Rat	die gute Landschaft	das gute Brot	die guten Freunde
dative	dem guten Rat	der guten Landschaft	dem guten Brot	den guten Freunden
genitive	des guten Rates	der guten Landschaft	des guten Brotes	der guten Freunde

nouns and adjectives with *ein*-words			
	masculine	feminine	neuter	plural
nominative	ein guter Rat	eine gute Landschaft	ein gutes Brot	meine guten Freunde
accusative	einen guten Rat	eine gute Landschaft	ein gutes Brot	meine guten Freunde
dative	einem guten Rat	einer guten Landschaft	einem guten Brot	meinen guten Freunden
genitive	eines guten Rates	einer guten Landschaft	eines guten Brotes	meiner guten Freunde

unpreceded adjectives			
	masculine	feminine	neuter	plural
nominative	guter Rat	gute Landschaft	gutes Brot	gute Freunde
accusative	guten Rat	gute Landschaft	gutes Brot	gute Freunde
dative	gutem Rat	guter Landschaft	gutem Brot	guten Freunden
genitive	guten Rates	guter Landschaft	guten Brotes	guter Freunde

Declension of pronouns

personal pronouns									
nominative	ich	du	Sie	er	sie	es	wir	ihr	Sie	sie
accusative	mich	dich	Sie	ihn	sie	es	uns	euch	Sie	sie
accusative reflexive	mich	dich	sich	sich	sich	sich	uns	euch	sich	sich
dative	mir	dir	Ihnen	ihm	ihr	ihm	uns	euch	Ihnen	ihnen
dative reflexive	mir	dir	sich	sich	sich	sich	uns	euch	sich	sich

Verb conjugation tables

Here are the infinitives of all verbs introduced as active vocabulary in **SAG MAL**. Each verb is followed by a model verb that follows the same conjugation pattern. The number in parentheses indicates where in the verb tables, pages **A10–19**, you can find the conjugated forms of the model verb. The word (*sein*) after a verb means that it is conjugated with **sein** in the **Perfekt** and **Plusquamperfekt**. For irregular reflexive verbs, the list may point to a non-reflexive model verb. A full conjugation of the simple forms of a reflexive verb is presented in Verb table 6 on page **A11**. Verbs followed by an asterisk (*) have a separable prefix.

abbiegen* (*sein*) like schieben (42)	**beschreiben** like bleiben (20)	**(sich) erkälten** like arbeiten (1)	**joggen** (*sein*) like machen (3)
abbrechen* like sprechen (47)	**besprechen** like sprechen (47)	**erkennen** like rennen (17)	**(sich) kämmen** like machen (3)
abfahren* (*sein*) like tragen (51)	**bestehen** like stehen (48)	**erklären** like machen (3)	**kaufen** like machen (3)
abfliegen* (*sein*) like schieben (42)	**bestellen** like machen (3)	**erzählen** like machen (3)	**kennen** like rennen (17)
abheben* like heben (29)	**besuchen** like machen (3)	**essen** (21)	**klettern** (*sein*) like fordern (26)
abschicken* like machen (3)	**(sich) bewegen** like heben (29)	**fahren** (*sein*) like tragen (51)	**klingeln** like sammeln (5)
abstauben* like machen (3)	**(sich) bewerben** like helfen (31)	**fallen** (*sein*) (22)	**kochen** like machen (3)
(sich) abtrocknen* like arbeiten (1)	**bezahlen** like machen (3)	**fangen** (23)	**kommen** (*sein*) (32)
adoptieren like probieren (4)	**bieten** like schieben (42)	**(sich) färben** like machen (3)	**können** (11)
anbieten* like schieben (42)	**bleiben** (*sein*) (20)	**faulenzen** like machen (3)	**korrigieren** like probieren (4)
anfangen* like fangen (23)	**braten** like schlafen (43)	**fegen** like machen (3)	**kosten** like arbeiten (1)
angeln like sammeln (5)	**brauchen** like machen (3)	**feiern** (2)	**küssen** like machen (3)
ankommen* (*sein*) like kommen (32)	**brechen** like sprechen (47)	**fernsehen*** like geben (27)	**lächeln** like sammeln (5)
anmachen* like machen (3)	**brennen** like rennen (17)	**finden** like trinken (52)	**lachen** like machen (3)
anrufen* like rufen (40)	**bringen** like denken (16)	**fliegen** (*sein*) like schieben (42)	**laden** like tragen (51)
anschauen* like machen (3)	**buchen** like machen (3)	**folgen** (*sein*) like machen (3)	**landen** (*sein*) like arbeiten (1)
anstoßen* like stoßen (50)	**büffeln** like sammeln (5)	**(sich) fragen** like machen (3)	**lassen** like fallen (22)
antworten like arbeiten (1)	**bügeln** like sammeln (5)	**(sich) freuen** (6)	**laufen** (*sein*) (33)
(sich) anziehen* like schieben (42)	**bürsten** like arbeiten (1)	**(sich) fühlen** like sich freuen (6)	**leben** like machen (3)
arbeiten (1)	**danken** like machen (3)	**füllen** like machen (3)	**legen** like machen (3)
(sich) ärgern like fordern (26)	**decken** like machen (3)	**funktionieren** like probieren (4)	**leiten** like arbeiten (1)
aufgehen* (*sein*) like gehen (28)	**denken** like denken (16)	**geben** (27)	**lernen** like machen (3)
auflegen* like machen (3)	**drücken** like machen (3)	**gefallen** like fallen (22)	**lesen** (34)
aufmachen* like machen (3)	**drucken** like machen (3)	**gehen** (*sein*) (28)	**lieben** like machen (3)
aufnehmen* like nehmen (38)	**durchfallen*** (*sein*) like fallen (22)	**gehören** like machen (3)	**liegen** (35)
aufräumen* like machen (3)	**durchmachen*** like machen (3)	**genießen** like fließen (25)	**löschen** like tragen (51)
aufstehen* (*sein*) like stehen (48)	**dürfen** (10)	**gewinnen** like schwimmen (44)	**lügen** (36)
aufwachen* (*sein*) like machen (3)	**(sich) duschen** like sich freuen (6)	**(sich) gewöhnen** like sich freuen (6)	**machen** (3)
ausfüllen like machen (3)	**einkaufen*** like machen (3)	**glauben** like machen (3)	**meinen** like machen (3)
ausgehen like gehen (28)	**einladen*** like tragen (51)	**gratulieren** like probieren (4)	**mieten** like arbeiten (1)
ausmachen like machen (3)	**einschlafen*** (*sein*) like schlafen (43)	**grüßen** like machen (3)	**mitbringen*** like denken (16)
(sich) ausruhen like sich freuen (6)	**einzahlen*** like machen (3)	**haben** like haben (7)	**mitkommen*** (*sein*) like kommen (32)
ausschalten* like arbeiten (1)	**empfehlen** like stehlen (49)	**handeln** like sammeln (5)	**mitmachen*** like machen (3)
(sich) ausziehen* like schieben (42)	**entdecken** like machen (3)	**hängen** like machen (3)	**mitnehmen*** like nehmen (38)
backen like mahlen (37)	**entfernen** like machen (3)	**heiraten** like arbeiten (1)	**mögen** (12)
(sich) baden like arbeiten (1)	**entgegennehmen*** like nehmen (38)	**heißen** (30)	**müssen** (13)
bauen like machen (3)	**entlassen** like fallen (22)	**helfen** (31)	**nachmachen*** like machen (3)
beantworten like arbeiten (1)	**(sich) entschließen** like fließen (25)	**heruntergehen*** (*sein*) like gehen (28)	**nehmen** (38)
bedeuten like arbeiten (1)	**(sich) entschuldigen** like machen (3)	**herunterladen*** like tragen (51)	**(sich) nennen** like rennen (17)
bedienen like machen (3)	**(sich) entspannen** like sich freuen (6)	**(sich) hinlegen*** like machen (3)	**niesen** like machen (3)
(sich) beeilen like sich freuen (6)	**entwerten** like arbeiten (1)	**(sich) hinsetzen*** like machen (3)	**öffnen** like arbeiten (1)
beginnen like schwimmen (44)	**entwickeln** like sammeln (5)	**hinterlassen** like fallen (22)	**packen** like machen (3)
behaupten like arbeiten (1)	**erfinden** like trinken (52)	**hochgehen*** (*sein*) like gehen (28)	**parken** like machen (3)
bekommen like kommen (32)	**erforschen** like machen (3)	**hören** like machen (3)	**passen** like machen (3)
belegen like machen (3)	**ergänzen** like machen (3)	**husten** like arbeiten (1)	**passieren** (*sein*) like probieren (4)
benutzen like machen (3)	**erhalten** like fallen (22)	**(sich) informieren** like probieren (4)	**probieren** (4)
berichten like arbeiten (1)	**(sich) erinnern** like fordern (26)	**(sich) interessieren** like probieren (4)	**putzen** like machen (3)

(sich) rasieren like probieren (4)
rauchen like machen (3)
recyceln like sammeln (5)
reden like arbeiten (1)
regnen like arbeiten (1)
reisen (*sein*) like machen (3)
reiten (*sein*) like pfeifen (39)
rennen (*sein*) (17)
reparieren like probieren (4)
retten like arbeiten (1)
sagen like machen (3)
schauen like machen (3)
scheitern (*sein*) like fordern (26)
schenken like machen (3)
schicken like machen (3)
schlafen (43)
schmecken like machen (3)
(sich) schminken like machen (3)
schneien like machen (3)
schreiben like bleiben (20)
schützen like machen (3)
schwänzen like machen (3)
schwimmen (*sein*) (44)
sehen like lesen (34)
sein (*sein*) (8)
(sich) setzen like machen (3)
singen like trinken (52)
sitzen (46)

sollen (14)
sortieren like probieren (4)
spazieren (*sein*) like probieren (4)
speichern like fordern (26)
spielen like machen (3)
sprechen (47)
springen (*sein*) like trinken (52)
spülen like machen (3)
starten (*sein*) like arbeiten (1)
staubsaugen like saugen (41)
stehen (48)
stehlen (49)
steigen (*sein*) like bleiben (20)
stellen like machen (3)
sterben (*sein*) like helfen (31)
(sich) streiten like pfeifen (39)
studieren like probieren (4)
suchen like machen (3)
surfen (*sein*) like machen (3)
tanken like machen (3)
tanzen like machen (3)
tragen (51)
träumen like machen (3)
(sich) treffen (*sein*) like sprechen (47)
treiben (*sein*) like bleiben (20)
(sich) trennen like sich freuen (6)
trinken (52)
tun (53)

üben like machen (3)
(sich) überlegen like machen (3)
übernachten like arbeiten (1)
überqueren like machen (3)
überraschen like machen (3)
umtauschen* like machen (3)
(sich) umziehen* (*sein*) like schieben (42)
untergehen* (*sein*) like gehen (28)
(sich) unterhalten* like fallen (22)
unterschreiben like bleiben (20)
(sich) verbessern like fordern (26)
verbringen like denken (16)
verdienen like machen (3)
vereinbaren like machen (3)
vergessen like essen (21)
verkaufen like machen (3)
verkünden like arbeiten (1)
(sich) verlaufen like laufen (33)
(sich) verletzen like machen (3)
(sich) verlieben like machen (3)
verlieren like schieben (42)
verschmutzen (*sein*) like machen (3)
(sich) verspäten like sich freuen (6)
(sich) verstauchen like machen (3)
verstehen like stehen (48)
versuchen like machen (3)
(sich) vorbereiten* like arbeiten (1)

vormachen* like machen (3)
vorschlagen* like tragen (51)
(sich) vorstellen* like machen (3)
wachsen (*sein*) like waschen (54)
wandern (*sein*) like fordern (26)
warten like arbeiten (1)
(sich) waschen (54)
wegräumen* like machen (3)
wegwerfen* like helfen (31)
weinen like machen (3)
werden (*sein*) (9)
wettmachen* like machen (3)
wiederholen like machen (3)
wiegen like schieben (42)
wischen like machen (3)
wissen (55)
wohnen like machen (3)
wollen (15)
(sich) wünschen like machen (3)
zeigen like machen (3)
ziehen (*sein*) like schieben (42)
zubereiten* like arbeiten (1)
zumachen* like machen (3)
(sich) zurechtfinden* like trinken (52)
zurückkommen* (*sein*) like kommen (32)
zuschauen* like machen (3)

Regular verbs: simple tenses

Infinitiv Partizip I Partizip II Perfekt	INDIKATIV			KONJUNKTIV I	KONJUNKTIV II		IMPERATIV
	Präsens	Präteritum	Plusquamperfekt	Präsens	Präsens	Perfekt	
1 arbeiten	arbeite	arbeitete	hatte gearbeitet	arbeite	arbeitete	hätte gearbeitet	
(to work)	arbeitest	arbeitetest	hattest gearbeitet	arbeitest	arbeitetest	hättest gearbeitet	arbeite
	arbeitet	arbeitete	hatte gearbeitet	arbeite	arbeitete	hätte gearbeitet	
arbeitend	arbeiten	arbeiteten	hatten gearbeitet	arbeiten	arbeiteten	hätten gearbeitet	arbeiten wir
gearbeitet	arbeitet	arbeitetet	hattet gearbeitet	arbeitet	arbeitetet	hättet gearbeitet	arbeitet
gearbeitet haben	arbeiten	arbeiteten	hatten gearbeitet	arbeiten	arbeiteten	hätten gearbeitet	arbeiten Sie
2 feiern	feiere	feierte	hatte gefeiert	feiere	feierte	hätte gefeiert	
(to celebrate)	feierst	feiertest	hattest gefeiert	feierest	feiertest	hättest gefeiert	feiere
	feiert	feierte	hatte gefeiert	feiere	feierte	hätte gefeiert	
feiernd	feiern	feierten	hatten gefeiert	feiern	feierten	hätten gefeiert	feiern wir
gefeiert	feiert	feiertet	hattet gefeiert	feiert	feiertet	hättet gefeiert	feiert
gefeiert haben	feiern	feierten	hatten gefeiert	feiern	feierten	hätten gefeiert	feiern Sie
3 machen	mache	machte	hatte gemacht	mache	machte	hätte gemacht	
(to make; to do)	machst	machtest	hattest gemacht	machest	machtest	hättest gemacht	mache/mach
	macht	machte	hatte gemacht	mache	machte	hätte gemacht	
machend	machen	machten	hatten gemacht	machen	machten	hätten gemacht	machen wir
gemacht	macht	machtet	hattet gemacht	machet	machtet	hättet gemacht	macht
gemacht haben	machen	machten	hatten gemacht	machen	machten	hätten gemacht	machen Sie
4 probieren	probiere	probierte	hatte probiert	probiere	probierte	hätte probiert	
(to try)	probierst	probiertest	hattest probiert	probierest	probiertest	hättest probiert	probiere/probier
	probiert	probierte	hatte probiert	probiere	probierte	hätte probiert	
probierend	probieren	probierten	hatten probiert	probieren	probierten	hätten probiert	probieren wir
probiert	probiert	probiertet	hattet probiert	probieret	probiertet	hättet probiert	probiert
probiert haben	probieren	probierten	hatten probiert	probieren	probierten	hätten probiert	probieren Sie
5 sammeln	sammle	sammelte	hatte gesammelt	sammle	sammelte	hätte gesammelt	
(to collect)	sammelst	sammeltest	hattest gesammelt	sammlest	sammeltest	hättest gesammelt	sammle
	sammelt	sammelte	hatte gesammelt	sammle	sammelte	hätte gesammelt	
sammelnd	sammeln	sammelten	hatten gesammelt	sammlen	sammelten	hätten gesammelt	sammeln wir
gesammelt	sammelt	sammeltet	hattet gesammelt	sammlet	sammeltet	hättet gesammelt	sammelt
gesammelt haben	sammeln	sammelten	hatten gesammelt	sammlen	sammelten	hätten gesammelt	sammeln Sie

Reflexive verbs

Infinitiv / Partizip I / Partizip II / Perfekt	INDIKATIV			KONJUNKTIV I	KONJUNKTIV II		IMPERATIV
	Präsens	Präteritum	Plusquamperfekt	Präsens	Präsens	Perfekt	
6 sich freuen	freue mich	freute mich	hatte mich gefreut	freue mich	freute mich	hätte mich gefreut	
(to be happy)	freust dich	freutest dich	hattest dich gefreut	freuest dich	freutest dich	hättest dich gefreut	freue/freu dich
	freut sich	freute sich	hatte sich gefreut	freue sich	freute sich	hätte sich gefreut	
sich freuend	freuen uns	freuten uns	hatten uns gefreut	freuen uns	freuten uns	hätten uns gefreut	freuen wir uns
sich gefreut	freut euch	freutet euch	hattet euch gefreut	freuet euch	freutet euch	hättet euch gefreut	freut euch
sich gefreut haben	freuen sich	freuten sich	hatten sich gefreut	freuen sich	freuten sich	hätten sich gefreut	freuen Sie sich

Auxiliary verbs

Infinitiv / Partizip I / Partizip II / Perfekt	INDIKATIV			KONJUNKTIV I	KONJUNKTIV II		IMPERATIV
	Präsens	Präteritum	Plusquamperfekt	Präsens	Präsens	Perfekt	
7 haben	habe	hatte	hatte gehabt	habe	hätte	hätte gehabt	
(to have)	hast	hattest	hattest gehabt	habest	hättest	hättest gehabt	habe/hab
	hat	hatte	hatte gehabt	habe	hätte	hätte gehabt	
habend	haben	hatten	hatten gehabt	haben	hätten	hätten gehabt	haben wir
gehabt	habt	hattet	hattet gehabt	habet	hättet	hättet gehabt	habt
gehabt haben	haben	hatten	hatten gehabt	haben	hätten	hätten gehabt	haben Sie
8 sein	bin	war	war gewesen	sei	wäre	wäre gewesen	
(to be)	bist	warst	warst gewesen	seiest/seist	wärst/wärest	wärst/wärest gewesen	sei
	ist	war	war gewesen	sei	wäre	wäre gewesen	
seiend	sind	waren	waren gewesen	seien	wären	wären gewesen	seien wir
gewesen	seid	wart	wart gewesen	seiet	wärt/wäret	wärt/wäret gewesen	seid
gewesen sein	sind	waren	waren gewesen	seien	wären	wären gewesen	seien Sie
9 werden	werde	wurde	war geworden	werde	würde	wäre geworden	
(to become)	wirst	wurdest	warst geworden	werdest	würdest	wärst geworden	werde
	wird	wurde	war geworden	werde	würde	wäre geworden	
werdend	werden	wurden	waren geworden	werden	würden	wären geworden	werden wir
geworden	werdet	wurdet	wart geworden	werdet	würdet	wärt geworden	werdet
geworden sein	werden	wurden	waren geworden	werden	würden	wären geworden	werden Sie

Compound tenses

Hilfsverb	INDIKATIV		KONJUNKTIV I		KONJUNKTIV II	
	Perfekt	Plusquamperfekt	Präsens	Perfekt	Präsens	Perfekt
haben	habe	hatte	habe		hätte	
	hast	hattest	habest	gemacht	hättest	gemacht
	hat gemacht	hatte gemacht	habe gearbeitet	gearbeitet	hätte gearbeitet	gearbeitet
	haben gearbeitet	hatten gearbeitet	haben studiert	studiert	hätten studiert	studiert
	habt studiert	hattet studiert	habet gefeiert	gefeiert	hättet gefeiert	gefeiert
	haben gefeiert	hatten gefeiert	haben gesammelt	gesammelt	hätten gesammelt	gesammelt
	haben gesammelt	hatten gesammelt				
sein	bin gegangen	war gegangen	sei gegangen		wäre gegangen	
	bist gegangen	warst gegangen	seiest/seist gegangen		wärst/wärest gegangen	
	ist gegangen	war gegangen	sei gegangen		wäre gegangen	
	sind gegangen	waren gegangen	seien gegangen		wären gegangen	
	seid gegangen	wart gegangen	seiet gegangen		wärt/wäret gegangen	
	sind gegangen	waren gegangen	seien gegangen		wären gegangen	

	Futur I/II		Futur I/II	Futur I/II
werden	werde machen / gemacht haben		werde machen / gemacht haben	würde machen / gemacht haben
	wirst machen / gemacht haben		werdest machen / gemacht haben	würdest machen / gemacht haben
	wird machen / gemacht haben		werde machen / gemacht haben	würde machen / gemacht haben
	werden machen / gemacht haben		werden machen / gemacht haben	würden machen / gemacht haben
	werdet machen / gemacht haben		werdet machen / gemacht haben	würdet machen / gemacht haben
	werden machen / gemacht haben		werden machen / gemacht haben	würden machen / gemacht haben

Modal verbs

Infinitiv Partizip I Partizip II Perfekt	INDIKATIV			KONJUNKTIV I	KONJUNKTIV II		IMPERATIV
	Präsens	Präteritum	Plusquamperfekt	Präsens	Präsens	Perfekt	
10 **dürfen**	darf	durfte	hatte gedurft	dürfe	dürfte	hätte gedurft	*Modal verbs are*
(to be permitted to)	darfst	durftest	hattest gedurft	dürfest	dürftest	hättest gedurft	*not used in the*
	darf	durfte	hatte gedurft	dürfe	dürfte	hätte gedurft	*imperative.*
dürfend	dürfen	durften	hatten gedurft	dürfen	dürften	hätten gedurft	
gedurft/dürfen	dürft	durftet	hattet gedurft	dürfet	dürftet	hättet gedurft	
gedurft haben	dürfen	durften	hatten gedurft	dürfen	dürften	hätten gedurft	
11 **können**	kann	konnte	hatte gekonnt	könne	könnte	hätte gekonnt	*Modal verbs are*
(to be able to)	kannst	konntest	hattest gekonnt	könnest	könntest	hättest gekonnt	*not used in the*
	kann	konnte	hatte gekonnt	könne	könnte	hätte gekonnt	*imperative.*
könnend	können	konnten	hatten gekonnt	können	könnten	hätten gekonnt	
gekonnt /können	könnt	konntet	hattet gekonnt	könnet	könntet	hättet gekonnt	
gekonnt haben	können	konnten	hatten gekonnt	können	könnten	hätten gekonnt	
12 **mögen**	mag	mochte	hatte gemocht	möge	möchte	hätte gemocht	*Modal verbs are*
(to like)	magst	mochtest	hattest gemocht	mögest	möchtest	hättest gemocht	*not used in the*
	mag	mochte	hatte gemocht	möge	möchte	hätte gemocht	*imperative.*
mögend	mögen	mochten	hatten gemocht	mögen	möchten	hätten gemocht	
gemocht /mögen	mögt	mochtet	hattet gemocht	möget	möchtet	hättet gemocht	
gemocht haben	mögen	mochten	hatten gemocht	mögen	möchten	hätten gemocht	
13 **müssen**	muss	musste	hatte gemusst	müsse	müsste	hätte gemusst	*Modal verbs are*
(to have to)	musst	musstest	hattest gemusst	müssest	müsstest	hättest gemusst	*not used in the*
	muss	musste	hatte gemusst	müsse	müsste	hätte gemusst	*imperative.*
müssend	müssen	mussten	hatten gemusst	müssen	müssten	hätten gemusst	
gemusst /müssen	müsst	musstet	hattet gemusst	müsset	müsstet	hättet gemusst	
gemusst haben	müssen	mussten	hatten gemusst	müssen	müssten	hätten gemusst	
14 **sollen**	soll	sollte	hatte gesollt	solle	sollte	hätte gesollt	*Modal verbs are*
(to be supposed to)	sollst	solltest	hattest gesollt	sollest	solltest	hättest gesollt	*not used in the*
	soll	sollte	hatte gesollt	solle	sollte	hätte gesollt	*imperative.*
sollend	sollen	sollten	hatten gesollt	sollen	sollten	hätten gesollt	
gesollt /sollen	sollt	solltet	hattet gesollt	sollet	solltet	hättet gesollt	
gesollt haben	sollen	sollten	hatten gesollt	sollen	sollten	hätten gesollt	
15 **wollen**	will	wollte	hatte gewollt	wolle	wollte	hätte gewollt	*Modal verbs are*
(to want to)	willst	wolltest	hattest gewollt	wollest	wolltest	hättest gewollt	*not used in the*
	will	wollte	hatte gewollt	wollev	wollte	hätte gewollt	*imperative.*
wollend	wollen	wollten	hatten gewollt	wollen	wollten	hätten gewollt	
gewollt/wollen	wollt	wolltet	hattet gewollt	wollet	wolltet	hättet gewollt	
gewollt haben	wollen	wollten	hatten gewollt	wollen	wollten	hätten gewollt	

Mixed verbs

Infinitiv / Partizip I / Partizip II / Perfekt	INDIKATIV			KONJUNKTIV I	KONJUNKTIV II		IMPERATIV
	Präsens	Präteritum	Plusquamperfekt	Präsens	Präsens	Perfekt	
16 denken	denke	dachte	hatte gedacht	denke	dächte	hätte gedacht	
(to think)	denkst	dachtest	hattest gedacht	denkest	dächtest	hättest gedacht	denke/denk
	denkt	dachte	hatte gedacht	denke	dächte	hätte gedacht	
denkend	denken	dachten	hatten gedacht	denken	dächten	hätten gedacht	denken wir
gedacht	denkt	dachtet	hattet gedacht	denket	dächtet	hättet gedacht	denkt
gedacht haben	denken	dachten	hatten gedacht	denken	dächten	hätten gedacht	denken Sie
17 rennen	renne	rannte	war gerannt	renne	rennte	wäre gerannt	
(to run)	rennst	ranntest	warst gerannt	rennest	renntest	wärest gerannt	renne/renn
	rennt	rannte	war gerannt	renne	rennte	wäre gerannt	
denkend	rennen	rannten	waren gerannt	rennen	rennten	wären gerannt	rennen wir
gerannt	rennt	ranntet	wart gerannt	rennet	renntet	wärt gerannt	rennt
gerannt sein	rennen	rannten	waren gerannt	rennen	rennten	wären gerannt	rennen Sie
18 senden	sende	sandte	hatte gesandt	sende	sendete	hätte gesandt	
(to send)	sendest	sandtest	hattest gesandt	sendest	sendetest	hättest gesandt	sende
	sendet	sandte	hatte gesandt	sende	sendete	hätte gesandt	
sendend	senden	sandten	hatten gesandt	senden	sendeten	hätten gesandt	senden wir
gesendet	sendet	sandtet	hattet gesandt	sendet	sendetet	hättet gesandt	sendet
gesendet haben	senden	sandten		senden	sendeten	hätten gesandt	senden Sie

Irregular verbs

Infinitiv / Partizip I / Partizip II / Perfekt	INDIKATIV			KONJUNKTIV I	KONJUNKTIV II		IMPERATIV
	Präsens	Präteritum	Plusquamperfekt	Präsens	Präsens	Perfekt	
19 bitten	bitte	bat	hatte gebeten	bitte	bäte	hätte gebeten	
(to ask)	bittest	batest	hattest gebeten	bittest	bätest	hättest gebeten	bitte
	bittet	bat	hatte gebeten	bitte	bäte	hätte gebeten	
bittend	bitten	baten	hatten gebeten	bitten	bäten	hätten gebeten	bitten wir
gebeten	bittet	batet	hattet gebeten	bittet	bätet	hättet gebeten	bittet
gebeten haben	bitten	baten	hatten gebeten	bitten	bäten	hätten gebeten	bitten Sie
20 bleiben	bleibe	bliebe	war geblieben	bleibe	bliebe	wäre geblieben	
(to stay)	bleibst	bliebst	warst geblieben	bleibest	bliebest	wärest geblieben	bleibe/bleib
	bleibt	blieb	war geblieben	bleibe	bliebe	wäre geblieben	
bleibend	bleiben	blieben	waren geblieben	bleiben	bleiben	wären geblieben	bleiben wir
geblieben	bleibt	bliebt	wart geblieben	bleibet	bliebet	wärt geblieben	bleibt
geblieben sein	bleiben	blieben	waren geblieben	bleiben	bleiben	wären geblieben	bleiben Sie

Infinitiv / Partizip I / Partizip II / Perfekt	INDIKATIV			KONJUNKTIV I	KONJUNKTIV II		IMPERATIV
	Präsens	**Präteritum**	**Plusquamperfekt**	**Präsens**	**Präsens**	**Perfekt**	
21 **essen**	esse	aß	hatte gegessen	esse	äße	hätte gegessen	
(to eat)	isst	aßest	hattest gegessen	essest	äßest	hättest gegessen	iss
	isst	aß	hatte gegessen	esse	äße	hätte gegessen	
essend	essen	aßen	hatten gegessen	essen	äßen	hätten gegessen	essen wir
gegessen	esst	aß	hattet gegessen	esset	äßet	hättet gegessen	esst
gegessen haben	essen	aßen	hatten gegessen	essen	äßen	hätten gegessen	essen Sie
22 **fallen**	falle	fiel	war gefallen	falle	fiele	wäre gefallen	
(to fall)	fällst	fielst	warst gefallen	fallest	fielest	wärest gefallen	falle/fall
	fällt	fiel	war gefallen	falle	fiele	wäre gefallen	
fallend	fallen	fielen	waren gefallen	fallen	fielen	wären gefallen	fallen wir
gefallen	fallt	fielt	wart gefallen	fallet	fielet	wäret gefallen	fallt
gefallen sein	fallen	fielen	waren gefallen	fallen	fielen	wären gefallen	fallen Sie
23 **fangen**	fange	fing	hatte gemacht	fange	finge	hätte gefangen	
(to catch)	fängst	fingst	hattest gemacht	fangest	fingest	hättest gefangen	fange/fang
	fängt	fing	hatte gemacht	fange	finge	hätte gefangen	
fangend	fangen	fingen	hatten gemacht	fangen	fingen	hätten gefangen	fangen wir
gefangen	fangt	fingt	hattet gemacht	fanget	finget	hättet gefangen	fangt
gefangen haben	fangen	fingen	hatten gemacht	fangen	fingen	hätten gefangen	fangen Sie
24 **flechten**	flechte	flocht	hatte geflochten	flechte	flöchte	hätte geflochten	
(to braid)	flichtst	flochtest	hattest geflochten	flechtest	flöchtest	hättest geflochten	flicht
	flicht	flocht	hatte geflochten	flechte	flöchte	hätte geflochten	
flechtend	flechten	flochten	hatten geflochten	flechten	flöchten	hätten geflochten	flechten wir
geflochten	flechtet	flochtet	hattet geflochten	flechtet	flöchtet	hättet geflochten	flechtet
geflochten haben	flechten	flochten	hatten geflochten	flechten	flöchten	hätten geflochten	flechten Sie
25 **fließen**	fließe	floss	war geflossen	fließe	flösse	wäre geflossen	
(to flow)	fließt	flossest/flosst	warst geflossen	fließest	flössest	wärest geflossen	fließe/fließ
	fließt	floss	war geflossen	fließe	flösse	wäre geflossen	
fließend	fließen	flossen	waren geflossen	fließen	flössen	wären geflossen	fließen wir
geflossen	fließt	flosst	wart geflossen	fließet	flösset	wärt geflossen	fließt
geflossen sein	fließen	flossen	waren geflossen	fließen	flössen	wären geflossen	fließen Sie
26 **fordern**	ford(e)re	forderte	hatte gefordert	fordere	forderte	hätte gefordert	
(to demand)	forderst	fordertest	hattest gefordert	forderest	fordertest	hättest gefordert	fordere/fordre
	fordert	forderte	hatte gefordert	fordere	forderte	hätte gefordert	
fordernd	fordern	forderten	hatten gefordert	forderen	forderten	hätten gefordert	fordern wir
gefordert	fordert	fordertet	hattet gefordert	forderet	fordertet	hättet gefordert	fordert
gefordert haben	fordern	forderten	hatten gefordert	forderen	forderten	hätten gefordert	fordern Sie
27 **geben**	gebe	gab	hatte gegeben	gebe	gäbe	hätte gegeben	
(to give)	gibst	gabst	hattest gegeben	gebest	gäbest	hättest gegeben	gib
	gibt	gab	hatte gegeben	gebe	gäbe	hätte gegeben	
gebend	geben	gaben	hatten gegeben	geben	gäben	hätten gegeben	geben wir
gegeben	gebt	gabt	hattet gegeben	gebet	gäbet	hättet gegeben	gebt
gegeben haben	geben	gaben	hatten gegeben	geben	gäben	hätten gegeben	geben Sie

Infinitiv / Partizip I / Partizip II / Perfekt	INDIKATIV			KONJUNKTIV I	KONJUNKTIV II		IMPERATIV
	Präsens	Präteritum	Plusquamperfekt	Präsens	Präsens	Perfekt	
28 gehen	gehe	ging	war gegangen	gehe	ginge	wäre gegangen	
(to go)	gehst	gingst	warst gegangen	gehest	gingest	wärest gegangen	gehe/geh
	geht	ging	war gegangen	gehe	ginge	wäre gegangen	
gehend	gehen	gingen	waren gegangen	gehen	gingen	wären gegangen	gehen wir
gegangen	geht	gingt	wart gegangen	gehet	ginget	wäret gegangen	geht
gegangen sein	gehen	gingen	waren gegangen	gehen	gingen	wären gegangen	gehen Sie
29 heben	hebe	hob	hatte gehoben	hebe	höbe	hätte gehoben	
(to lift)	hebst	hobst	hattest gehoben	hebest	höbest/höbst	hättest gehoben	hebe/heb
	hebt	hob	hatte gehoben	hebe	höbe	hätte gehoben	
hebend	heben	hoben	hatten gehoben	heben	höben	hätten gehoben	heben wir
gehoben	hebt	hobt	hattet gehoben	hebet	höbet/höbt	hättet gehoben	hebt
gehoben haben	heben	hoben	hatten gehoben	heben	höben	hätten gehoben	heben Sie
30 heißen	heiße	hieß	hatte geheißen	heiße	hieße	hätte geheißen	
(to be called)	heißt	hießest	hattest geheißen	heißest	hießest	hättest geheißen	heiß/heiße
	heißt	hieß	hatte geheißen	heiße	hieße	hätte geheißen	
heißend	heißen	hießen	hatten geheißen	heißen	hießen	hätten geheißen	heißen wir
geheißen	heißt	hießt	hattet geheißen	heißet	hießet	hättet geheißen	heißt
geheißen haben	heißen	hießen	hatten geheißen	heißen	hießen	hätten geheißen	heißen Sie
31 helfen	helfe	half	hatte geholfen	helfe	hälfe	hätte geholfen	
(to help)	hilfst	halfst	hattest geholfen	helfest	hälfest/hälfst	hättest geholfen	hilf
	hilft	half	hatte geholfen	helfe	hälfe	hätte geholfen	
helfend	helfen	halfen	hatten geholfen	helfen	hälfen	hätten geholfen	helfen wir
geholfen	helft	halft	hattet geholfen	helfet	hälfet/hälft	hättet geholfen	helft
geholfen haben	helfen	halfen	hatten geholfen	helfen	hälfen	hätten geholfen	helfen Sie
32 kommen	komme	kam	war gekommen	komme	käme	wäre gekommen	
(to come)	kommst	kamst	warst gekommen	kommest	kämest	wärest gekommen	komme/komm
	kommt	kam	war gekommen	komme	käme	wäre gekommen	
kommend	kommen	kamen	waren gekommen	kommen	kämen	wären gekommen	kommen wir
gekommen	kommt	kamt	wart gekommen	kommet	kämet	wäret gekommen	kommt
gekommen sein	kommen	kamen	waren gekommen	kommen	kämen	wären gekommen	kommen Sie
33 laufen	laufe	lief	war gelaufen	laufe	liefe	wäre gelaufen	
(to run)	läufst	liefst	warst gelaufen	laufest	liefest	wärest gelaufen	laufe/lauf
	läuft	lief	war gelaufen	laufe	liefe	wäre gelaufen	
laufend	laufen	liefen	waren gelaufen	laufen	liefen	wären gelaufen	laufen wir
gelaufen	lauft	lieft	wart gelaufen	laufet	liefet	wäret gelaufen	lauft
gelaufen sein	laufen	liefen	waren gelaufen	laufen	liefen	wären gelaufen	laufen Sie
34 lesen	lese	las	hatte gelesen	lese	läse	hätte gelesen	
(to read)	liest	la(se)st	hattest gelesen	lesest	läsest	hättest gelesen	lies
	liest	las	hatte gelesen	lese	läse	hätte gelesen	
lesend	lesen	lasen	hatten gelesen	lesen	läsen	hätten gelesen	les en wir
gelesen	lest	last	hattet gelesen	leset	läset	hättet gelesen	lest
gelesen haben	lesen	lasen	hatten gelesen	lesen	läsen	hätten gelesen	lesen Sie

Infinitiv Partizip I Partizip II Perfekt	INDIKATIV			KONJUNKTIV I	KONJUNKTIV II		IMPERATIV
	Präsens	**Präteritum**	**Plusquamperfekt**	**Präsens**	**Präsens**	**Perfekt**	
35 liegen	liege	lag	hatte gelegen	liege	läge	hätte gelegen	
(to lie; to be lying)	liegst	lagst	hattest gelegen	liegest	lägest	hättest gelegen	liege/lieg
	liegt	lag	hatte gelegen	liege	läge	hätte gelegen	
liegend	liegen	lagen	hatten gelegen	liegen	lägen	hätten gelegen	liegen wir
gelegen	liegt	lagt	hattet gelegen	lieget	läget	hättet gelegen	liegt
gelegen haben	liegen	lagen	hatten gelegen	liegen	lägen	hätten gelegen	liegen Sie
36 lügen	lüge	log	hatte gelogen	lüge	löge	hätte gelogen	
(to lie)	lügst	logst	hattest gelogen	lügest	lögest	hättest gelogen	lüge/lüg
	lügt	log	hatte gelogen	lüge	löge	hätte gelogen	
lügend	lügen	logen	hatten gelogen	lügen	lögen	hätten gelogen	lügen wir
gelogen	lügt	logt	hattet gelogen	lüget	löget	hättet gelogen	lügt
gelogen haben	lügen	logen	hatten gelogen	lügen	lögen	hätten gelogen	lügen Sie
37 mahlen	mahle	mahlte	hatte gemahlt/gemahlen	mahle	mahlte	hätte gemahlt/gemahlen	
(to grind)	mahlst	mahltest	hattest gemahlt/gemahlen	mahlest	mahltest	hättest gemahlt/gemahlen	mahle/mahl
mahlend	mahlt	mahlte	hatte gemahlt/gemahlen	mahle	mahlte	hätte gemahlt/gemahlen	
gemahlt/gemahlen	mahlen	mahlten	hatten gemahlt/gemahlen	mahlen	mahlten	hätten gemahlt/gemahlen	mahlen wir
gemahlt/gemahlen	mahlt	mahltet	hattet gemahlt/gemahlen	mahlet	mahltet	hättet gemahlt/gemahlen	mahlt
haben	mahlen	mahlten	hatten gemahlt/gemahlen	mahlen	mahlten	hätten gemahlt/gemahlen	mahlen Sie
38 nehmen	nehme	nahm	hatte genommen	nehme	nähme	hätte genommen	
(to take)	nimmst	nahmst	hattest genommen	nehmest	nähmest	hättest genommen	nimm
	nimmt	nahm	hatte genommen	nehme	nähme	hätte genommen	
nehmend	nehmen	nahmen	hatten genommen	nehmen	nähmen	hätten genommen	nehmen wir
genommen	nehmt	nahmt	hattet genommen	nehmet	nähmet	hättet genommen	nehmt
genommen haben	nehmen	nahmen	hatten genommen	nehmen	nähmen	hätten genommen	nehmen Sie
39 pfeifen	pfeife	pfiff	hatte gepfiffen	pfeife	pfiffe	hätte gepfiffen	
(to whistle)	pfeifst	pfiffst	hattest gepfiffen	pfeifest	pfiffest	hättest gepfiffen	pfeife/pfeif
	pfeift	pfiff	hatte gepfiffen	pfeife	pfiffe	hätte gepfiffen	
pfeifend	pfeifen	pfiffen	hatten gepfiffen	pfeifen	pfiffen	hätten gepfiffen	pfeifen wir
gepfiffen	pfeift	pfifft	hattet gepfiffen	pfeifet	pfiffet	hättet gepfiffen	pfeift
gepfiffen haben	pfeifen	pfiffen	hatten gepfiffen	pfeifen	pfiffen	hätten gepfiffen	pfeifen Sie
40 rufen	rufe	rief	hatte gerufen	rufe	riefe	hätte gerufen	
(to call)	rufst	riefst	hattest gerufen	rufest	riefest	hättest gerufen	rufe/ruf
	ruft	rief	hatte gerufen	rufe	riefe	hätte gerufen	
rufend	rufen	riefen	hatten gerufen	rufen	riefen	hätten gerufen	rufen wir
gerufen	ruft	rieft	hattet gerufen	rufet	riefet	hättet gerufen	ruft
gerufen haben	rufen	riefen	hatten gerufen	rufen	riefen	hätten gerufen	rufen Sie
41 saugen	sauge	saugte/sog	hatte gesaugt/gesogen	sauge	saugte/söge	hätte gesaugt/gesogen	
(to suck)	saugst	saugtest/sogst	hattest gesaugt/gesogen	saugest	saugtest/sögest	hättest gesaugt/gesogen	sauge/saug
saugend	saugt	saugte/sog	hatte gesaugt/gesogen	sauge	saugte/söge	hätte gesaugt/gesogen	
gesaugt/gesogen	saugen	saugten/sogen	hatten gesaugt/gesogen	saugen	saugten/sögen	hätten gesaugt/gesogen	saugen wir
gesaugt/gesogen	saugt	saugtet/sogt	hattet gesaugt/gesogen	sauget	saugtet/söget	hättet gesaugt/gesogen	saugt
haben	saugen	saugten/sogen	hatten gesaugt/gesogen	saugen	saugten/sögen	hätten gesaugt/gesogen	saugen Sie

Infinitiv Partizip I Partizip II Perfekt	INDIKATIV			KONJUNKTIV I	KONJUNKTIV II		IMPERATIV
	Präsens	**Präteritum**	**Plusquamperfekt**	**Präsens**	**Präsens**	**Perfekt**	
42 **schieben**	schiebe	schob	hatte geschoben	schiebe	schöbe	hätte geschoben	
(to push)	schiebst	schobst	hattest geschoben	schiebest	schöbest	hättest geschoben	schiebe/schieb
	schiebt	schob	hatte geschoben	schiebe	schöbe	hätte geschoben	
schiebend	schieben	schoben	hatten geschoben	schieben	schöben	hätten geschoben	schieben wir
geschoben	schiebt	schobt	hattet geschoben	schiebet	schöbet	hättet geschoben	schiebt
geschoben haben	schieben	schoben	hatten geschoben	schieben	schöben	hätten geschoben	schieben Sie
43 **schlafen**	schlafe	schlief	hatte geschlafen	schlafe	schliefe	hätte geschlafen	
(to sleep)	schläfst	schliefst	hattest geschlafen	schlafest	schliefest	hättest geschlafen	schlafe/schlaf
	schläft	schlief	hatte geschlafen	schlafe	schliefe	hätte geschlafen	
schlafend	schlafen	schliefen	hatten geschlafen	schlafen	schliefen	hätten geschlafen	schlafen wir
geschlafen	schlaft	schlieft	hattet geschlafen	schlafet	schliefet	hättet geschlafen	schlaft
geschlafen haben	schlafen	schliefen	hatten geschlafen	schlafen	schliefen	hätten geschlafen	schlafen Sie
44 **schwimmen**	schwimme	schwamm	war geschwommen	schwimme	schwömme	wäre geschwommen	
(to swim)	schwimmst	schwammst	warst geschwommen	schwimmest	schwömmest	wärest geschwommen	schwimme/schwimm
	schwimmt	schwamm	war geschwommen	schwimme	schwömme	wäre geschwommen	
schwimmend	schwimmen	schwammen	waren geschwommen	schwimmen	schwömmen	wären geschwommen	schwimmen wir
geschwommen	schwimmt	schwammt	wart geschwommen	schwimmet	schwömmet	wäret geschwommen	schwimmt
geschwommen sein	schwimmen	schwammen	waren geschwommen	schwimmen	schwömmen	wären geschwommen	schwimmen Sie
45 **schwören**	schwöre	schwor	hatte geschworen	schwöre	schwüre	hätte geschworen	
(to swear)	schwörst	schworst	hattest geschworen	schwörest	schwürest/schwürst	hättest geschworen	schwöre/schwör
	schwört	schwor	hatte geschworen	schwöre	schwüre	hätte geschworen	
schwörend	schwören	schworen	hatten geschworen	schwören	schwüren	hätten geschworen	schwören wir
geschworen	schwört	schwort	hattet geschworen	schwöret	schwüret	hättet geschworen	schwört
geschworen haben	schwören	schworen	hatten geschworen	schwören	schwüren	hätten geschworen	schwören Sie
46 **sitzen**	sitze	saß	hatte gesessen	sitze	säße	hätte gesessen	
(to sit)	sitzt	saßest	hattest gesessen	sitzest	säßest	hättest gesessen	sitze/sitz
	sitzt	saß	hatte gesessen	sitze	säße	hätte gesessen	
sitzend	sitzen	saßen	hatten gesessen	sitzen	säßen	hätten gesessen	sitzen wir
gesessen	sitzt	saßet	hattet gesessen	sitzet	säßet	hättet gesessen	sitzt
gesessen haben	sitzen	saßen	hatten gesessen	sitzen	säßen	hätten gesessen	sitzen Sie
47 **sprechen**	spreche	sprach	hatte gesprochen	spreche	spräche	hätte gesprochen	
(to speak)	sprichst	sprachst	hattest gesprochen	sprechest	sprächest	hättest gesprochen	sprich
	spricht	sprach	hatte gesprochen	spreche	spräche	hätte gesprochen	
sprechend	sprechen	sprachen	hatten gesprochen	sprechen	sprächen	hätten gesprochen	sprechen wir
gesprochen	sprecht	spracht	hattet gesprochen	sprechet	sprächet	hättet gesprochen	sprecht
gesprochen haben	sprechen	sprachen	hatten gesprochen	sprechen	sprächen	hätten gesprochen	sprechen Sie
48 **stehen**	stehe	stand	hatte gestanden	stehe	stünde/stände	hätte gestanden	
(to stand)	stehst	standest/standst	hattest gestanden	stehest	stündest/ständest	hättest gestanden	stehe/steh
	steht	stand	hatte gestanden	stehe	stünde/stände	hätte gestanden	
stehend	stehen	standen	hatten gestanden	stehen	stünden/ständen	hätten gestanden	stehen wir
gestanden	steht	standet	hattet gestanden	stehet	stündet/ständet	hättet gestanden	steht
gestanden haben	stehen	standen	hatten gestanden	stehen	stünden/ständen	hätten gestanden	stehen Sie

Infinitiv Partizip I Partizip II Perfekt	INDIKATIV			KONJUNKTIV I	KONJUNKTIV II		IMPERATIV
	Präsens	Präteritum	Plusquamperfekt	Präsens	Präsens	Perfekt	
49 stehlen	stehle	stahl	hatte gestohlen	stehle	stähle/stöhle	hätte gestohlen	
(to steal)	stiehlst	stahlst	hattest gestohlen	stehlest	stählest/stöhlest	hättest gestohlen	stiehl
	stiehlt	stahl	hatte gestohlen	stehle	stähle/stöhle	hätte gestohlen	
stehlend	stehlen	stahlen	hatten gestohlen	stehlen	stählen/stöhlen	hätten gestohlen	stehlen wir
gestohlen	stehlt	stahlt	hattet gestohlen	stehlet	stählet/stöhlet	hättet gestohlen	stehlt
gestohlen haben	stehlen	stahlen	hatten gestohlen	stehlen	stählen/stöhlen	hätten gestohlen	stehlen Sie
50 stoßen	stoße	stieß	hatte gestoßen	stoße	stieße	hätte gestoßen	
(to bump)	stößt	stießest/stießt	hattest gestoßen	stoßest	stießest	hättest gestoßen	stoße/stoß
	stößt	stieß	hatte gestoßen	stoße	stieße	hätte gestoßen	
stoßend	stoßen	stießen	hatten gestoßen	stoßen	stießen	hätten gestoßen	stoßen wir
gestoßen	stoßt	stießt	hattet gestoßen	stoßet	stießet	hättet gestoßen	stoßt
gestoßen haben	stoßen	stießen	hatten gestoßen	stoßen	stießen	hätten gestoßen	stoßen Sie
51 tragen	trage	trug	hatte getragen	trage	trüge	hätte getragen	
(to carry)	trägst	trugst	hattest getragen	tragest	trügest	hättest getragen	trage/trag
	trägt	trug	hatte getragen	trage	trüge	hätte getragen	
tragend	tragen	trugen	hatten getragen	tragen	trügen	hätten getragen	tragen wir
getragen	tragt	trugt	hattet getragen	traget	trüget	hättet getragen	tragt
getragen haben	tragen	trugen	hatten getragen	tragen	trügen	hätten getragen	tragen Sie
52 trinken	trinke	trank	hatte getrunken	trinke	tränke	hätte getrunken	
(to drink)	trinkst	trankst	hattest getrunken	trinkest	tränkest	hättest getrunken	trinke/trink
	trinkt	trank	hatte getrunken	trinke	tränke	hätte getrunken	
trinkend	trinken	tranken	hatten getrunken	trinken	tränken	hätten getrunken	trinken wir
getrunken	trinkt	trankt	hattet getrunken	trinket	tränket	hättet getrunken	trinkt
getrunken haben	trinken	tranken	hatten getrunken	trinken	tränken	hätten getrunken	trinken Sie
53 tun	tue	tat	hatte getan	tue	täte	hätte getan	
(to do)	tust	tatest	hattest getan	tuest	tätest	hättest getan	tue/tu
	tut	tat	hatte getan	tue	täte	hätte getan	
tuend	tun	taten	hatten getan	tuen	täten	hätten getan	tun wir
getan	tut	tatet	hattet getan	tuet	tätet	hättet getan	tut
getan haben	tun	taten	hatten getan	tuen	täten	hätten getan	tun Sie
54 waschen	wasche	wusch	hatte gewaschen	wasche	wüsche	hätte gewaschen	
(to wash)	wäschst	wuschest/wuschst	hattest gewaschen	waschest	wüschest/wüschst	hättest gewaschen	wasche/wasch
	wäscht	wusch	hatte gewaschen	wasche	wüsche	hätte gewaschen	
waschend	waschen	wuschen	hatten gewaschen	waschen	wüschen	hätten gewaschen	waschen wir
gewaschen	wascht	wuscht	hattet gewaschen	waschet	wüschet/wüscht	hättet gewaschen	wascht
gewaschen haben	waschen	wuschen	hatten gewaschen	waschen	wüschen	hätten gewaschen	waschen Sie
55 wissen	weiß	wusste	hatte gewusst	wisse	wüsste	hätte gewusst	
(to know)	weißt	wusstest	hattest gewusst	wissest	wüsstest	hättest gewusst	wisse
	weiß	wusste	hatte gewusst	wisse	wüsste	hätte gewusst	
wissend	wissen	wussten	hatten gewusst	wissen	wüssten	hätten gewusst	wissen wir
gewusst	wisst	wusstet	hattet gewusst	wisset	wüsstet	hättet gewusst	wisst
gewusst haben	wissen	wussten	hatten gewusst	wissen	wüssten	hätten gewusst	wissen Sie

Irregular verbs

The following is a list of the principal parts of all strong and mixed verbs that are introduced as active vocabulary in **SAG MAL**, as well as other sample verbs. For the complete conjugations of these verbs, consult the verb list on pages **A8–A9** and the verb charts on pages **A10–A19**. The verbs listed here are base forms. See **Strukturen 6B.2** and **7A.1** to review **Perfekt** and **Präteritum** forms of separable and inseparable prefix verbs.

Infinitiv		Präteritum	Partizip II
backen	*to bake*	backte	gebacken
beginnen	*to begin*	begann	begonnen
bieten	*to bid, to offer*	bot	geboten
binden	*to tie, to bind*	band	gebunden
bitten	*to request*	bat	gebeten
bleiben	*to stay*	blieb	(ist) geblieben
braten (brät)	*to fry, to roast*	briet	gebraten
brechen (bricht)	*to break*	brach	gebrochen
brennen	*to burn*	brannte	gebrannt
bringen	*to bring*	brachte	gebracht
denken	*to think*	dachte	gedacht
dürfen (darf)	*to be allowed to*	durfte	gedurft
empfehlen (empfiehlt)	*to recommend*	empfahl	empfohlen
essen (isst)	*to eat*	aß	gegessen
fahren (fährt)	*to go, to drive*	fuhr	(ist) gefahren
fallen (fällt)	*to fall*	fiel	(ist) gefallen
fangen (fängt)	*to catch*	fing	gefangen
finden	*to find*	fand	gefunden
fliegen	*to fly*	flog	(ist) geflogen
fließen	*to flow, to pour*	floss	(ist) geflossen
frieren	*to freeze*	fror	gefroren
geben (gibt)	*to give*	gab	gegeben
gehen	*to go, to walk*	ging	(ist) gegangen
gelten (gilt)	*to be valid*	galt	gegolten
genießen	*to enjoy*	genoss	genossen
geschehen (geschieht)	*to happen*	geschah	(ist) geschehen
gewinnen	*to win*	gewann	gewonnen
gleichen	*to resemble*	glich	geglichen
graben (gräbt)	*to dig*	grub	gegraben
haben (hat)	*to have*	hatte	gehabt
halten (hält)	*to hold, to keep*	hielt	gehalten
hängen	*to hang*	hing	gehangen
heben	*to raise, to lift*	hob	gehoben
heißen	*to be called, to mean*	hieß	geheißen
helfen (hilft)	*to help*	half	geholfen
kennen	*to know*	kannte	gekannt
klingen	*to sound, to ring*	klang	geklungen
kommen	*to come*	kam	(ist) gekommen
können (kann)	*to be able to, can*	konnte	gekonnt
lassen (lässt)	*to let, to allow*	ließ	gelassen
laufen (läuft)	*to run, to walk*	lief	(ist) gelaufen

Infinitiv		Präteritum	Partizip II
leiden	to suffer	litt	gelitten
leihen	to lend	lieh	geliehen
lesen (liest)	to read	las	gelesen
liegen	to lie, to rest	lag	gelegen
lügen	to lie, to tell lies	log	gelogen
meiden	to avoid	mied	gemieden
messen (misst)	to measure	maß	gemessen
mögen (mag)	to like	mochte	gemocht
müssen (muss)	to have, to must	musste	gemusst
nehmen (nimmt)	to take	nahm	genommen
nennen	to name, to call	nannte	genannt
preisen	to praise	pries	gepriesen
raten (rät)	to guess	riet	geraten
reiben	to rub, to grate	rieb	gerieben
riechen	to smell	roch	gerochen
rufen	to call, to shout	rief	gerufen
schaffen	to accomplish	schuf	geschaffen
scheiden	to divorce, to depart	schied	(ist) geschieden
scheinen	to shine, to appear	schien	geschienen
schieben	to push, to shove	schob	geschoben
schießen	to shoot	schoss	geschossen
schlafen (schläft)	to sleep	schlief	geschlafen
schlagen (schlägt)	to beat, to hit	schlug	geschlagen
schließen	to close	schloss	geschlossen
schlingen	to loop, to gulp	schlang	geschlungen
schneiden	to cut	schnitt	geschnitten
schreiben	to write	schrieb	geschrieben
schwimmen	to swim	schwamm	(ist) geschwommen
sehen (sieht)	to see	sah	gesehen
sein (ist)	to be	war	(ist) gewesen
senden	to send	sandte/sendete	gesandt/gesendet
singen	to sing	sang	gesungen
sinken	to sink	sank	(ist) gesunken
sitzen	to sit	saß	gesessen
sollen (soll)	to be supposed to	sollte	gesollt
sprechen (spricht)	to speak	sprach	gesprochen
stehen	to stand	stand	gestanden
stehlen (stiehlt)	to steal	stahl	gestohlen
steigen	to climb, to rise	stieg	(ist) gestiegen
sterben (stirbt)	to die	starb	(ist) gestorben
stoßen	to push, to thrust	stieß	gestoßen
streichen	to paint, to cancel	strich	gestrichen
streiten	to argue	stritt	gestritten
tragen (trägt)	to carry	trug	getragen
treffen (trifft)	to hit, to meet	traf	getroffen
treten (tritt)	to kick	trat	getreten
trinken	to drink	trank	getrunken
tun	to do	tat	getan
vergessen (vergisst)	to forget	vergaß	vergessen

Infinitiv		Präteritum	Partizip II
verlieren	*to lose*	verlor	verloren
wachsen (wächst)	*to grow*	wuchs	(ist) gewachsen
waschen (wäscht)	*to wash*	wusch	gewaschen
weisen	*to indicate, to show*	wies	gewiesen
wenden	*to turn, to flip*	wandte/wendete	gewandt/gewendet
werben (wirbt)	*to advertise*	warb	geworben
werden (wird)	*to become*	wurde	(ist) geworden
werfen (wirft)	*to throw*	warf	geworfen
winden	*to wind*	wand	gewunden
wissen (weiß)	*to know*	wusste	gewusst
wollen (will)	*to want*	wollte	gewollt
ziehen	*to pull, to draw*	zog	gezogen

Glossary

This glossary includes all active vocabulary introduced in **SAG MAL**, as well as some additional words and expressions. The singular and plural endings listed for adjectival nouns are those that occur after a definite article. See **10A.2** to review the complete set of endings.

Abbreviations used in this glossary

acc.	accusative	*gen.*	genitive	*poss.*	possessive
adj.	adjective	*inf.*	informal	*prep.*	preposition
adv.	adverb	*interr.*	interrogative	*pron.*	pronoun
conj.	conjunction	*m.*	masculine noun	*sing.*	singular
dat.	dative	*n.*	neuter noun	*v.*	verb
f.	feminine noun	*nom.*	nominative		
form.	formal	*pl.*	plural		

Deutsch-Englisch

A

abbiegen *v.* to turn **8A**
  rechts/links abbiegen *v.* to turn right/left **8A**
abbrechen *v.* to cancel **7B**
Abend, -e *m.* evening **2B**
  abends *adv.* in the evening **2A**
Abendessen, - *n.* dinner **4B**
aber *conj.* but **1B**
abfahren *v.* to leave **8A**
Abfall, ⁻e *m.* waste **12B**
abfliegen *v.* to take off **7B**
Abflug, ⁻e *m.* departure **7B**
abheben *v.* to withdraw (money) **10A**
Absatz, ⁻e *m.* paragraph **5B**
abschicken *v.* to send **11B**
Abschied, -e *m.* leave-taking; farewell **1A**
Abschluss, ⁻e *m.* degree **2A**
  einen Abschluss machen *v.* to graduate **5A**
Abschlusszeugnis, -se *n.* diploma (transcript) **2A**
abstauben *v.* to dust **6B**
sich abtrocknen *v.* to dry oneself off **9A**
acht eight **2A**
Achtung! Attention!
adoptieren *v.* to adopt **3A**
Adresse, -n *f.* address **10A**
Allee, -n *f.* avenue **10B**
allein *adv.* alone; by oneself **4A**
Allergie, -n *f.* allergy **9B**
allergisch (gegen) *adj.* allergic (to) **9B**
alles *pron.* everything **7B**
  Alles klar? Everything OK? **1A**
  alles Gute all the best **10A**
  Alles Gute zum Geburtstag! Happy birthday! **5A**
Alltagsroutine, -n *f.* daily routine **9A**
  im Alltag in everyday life
als *conj.* as; when **8A**
  als ob as if **10A**
also *conj.* therefore; so **9B**
alt *adj.* old **3A**
Altkleider *pl.* second-hand clothing **12B**
Altpapier *n.* used paper **12B**
Amerika *n.* America **10B**
amerikanisch *adj.* American **10B**
Amerikaner, - / Amerikanerin, -nen *m./f.* American **10B**
Ampel, -n *f.* traffic light **10B**
an *prep.* at; on; by; in; to **5B, 10B**
Ananas, - *f.* pineapple **4A**
anbieten *v.* to offer **12B**

anfangen *v.* to begin **4A**
Angebot, -e *n.* offer
  im Angebot on sale **5B**
angeln gehen *v.* to go fishing **2B**
angenehm *adj.* pleasant **3B**
  Angenehm. Nice to meet you. **1A**
angesagt *adj.* trendy **5B**
Angestellte, -n *m./f.* employee **11A**
Angst, ⁻e fear *f.* **7A**
  Angst haben (vor) *v.* to be afraid (of) **7A**
ankommen *v.* to arrive **4A**
Ankunft, ⁻e *f.* arrival **7B**
Anlass, ⁻e *m.* occasion **5A**
  besondere Anlässe *m. pl.* special occasions **5A**
anmachen *v.* to turn on **8B**
Anruf, -e *m.* phone call **11A**
  einen Anruf entgegennehmen *v.* to answer the phone **11A**
anrufen *v.* to call **4A**
  sich anrufen *v.* to call each other **9A**
anschauen *v.* to watch, look at **7A**
anspruchsvoll *adj.* demanding **11B**
anstatt *prep.* instead of **8B**
anstoßen *v.* to toast **5A**
Antwort, -en *f.*
antworten (auf) *v.* to answer **2A**
Anwendung *f.* application; usage
anziehen *v.* to put on **5B**
  sich anziehen *v.* to get dressed **9A**
Anzug, ⁻e *m.* suit **5B**
Apfel, ⁻ *m.* apple **1A**
Apotheke, -n *f.* pharmacy **9B**
App, -s, *f.* app **8B**
April *m.* April **2A, 7A**
Arbeit, -en *f.* work **11B**
  Arbeit finden *v.* to find a job **11A**
arbeiten (an) *v.* to work (on) **2A, 7A**
arbeitslos *adj.* unemployed **10A**
Arbeitszimmer, - *n.* home office **6A**
Architekt, -en / Architektin, -nen *m./f.* architect **3B**
Architektur, -en *f.* architecture **2A**
sich ärgern (über) *v.* to get angry (about) **9A**
arm *adj.* poor; unfortunate **3B**
Arm, -e *m.* arm **9A**
Art, -en *f.* species; type **12B**
Artischocke, -n *f.* artichoke **4A**
Arzt, ⁻e / Ärztin, -nen *m./f.* doctor **9B**
  zum Arzt gehen *v.* to go to the doctor **9B**
Assistent, -en / Assistentin, -nen *m./f.* assistant **11A**
Aubergine, -n *f.* eggplant **4A**

auch *adv.* also **1A**
auf *prep.* on, onto, to **5B**
  Auf Wiedersehen. Good-bye. **1A**
aufgehen *v.* to rise (sun) **12A**
aufladen *v.* to charge (a battery) **8B**
auflegen *v.* to hang up **11A**
aufmachen *v.* to open **8B**
aufnehmen *v.* to record **8B**
aufräumen *v.* to clean up **6B**
aufregend *adj.* exciting **12A**
aufrichtig *adj.* sincere **3B**
aufstehen *v.* to get up **4A**
aufwachen *v.* to wake up **9A**
Auge, -n *n.* eye **3A; 9A**
Augenbraue, -n *f.* eyebrow **9A**
August *m.* August **2A, 7A**
aus *prep.* from **4A**
Ausbildung, -en *f.* education **11A**
Ausdruck, ⁻e *m.* expression
Ausfahrt, -en *f.* exit **8A**
ausfüllen *v.* to fill out **10A**
  ein Formular ausfüllen *v.* to fill out a form **10A**
Ausgang ⁻e *m.* exit **7B**
ausgefallen *adj.* offbeat **5B**
ausgehen *v.* to go out **4A**
Ausland *n.* abroad **7B**
ausmachen *v.* to turn off **8B**
sich ausruhen *v.* to rest **9A**
ausschalten *v.* turn out, to turn off **12B**
Aussehen *n.* look (style) **5B**
außer *prep.* except (for) **4B**
außerhalb *prep.* outside of **8B**
Aussprache *f.* pronunciation
Aussterben *n.* extinction **12B**
sich ausziehen *v.* to get undressed **9A**
Auto, -s *n.* car **1A, 8A**
Autobahn, -en *f.* highway **8A**

B

Baby, -s *n.* baby **3A**
Bäckerei, -en *f.* bakery **4A**
Badeanzug, ⁻e *m.* bathing suit **5B**
Bademantel, ⁻ *m.* bathrobe **9A**
sich baden *v.* to bathe, take a bath **9A**
Badewanne, -n *f.* bathtub **6A**
Badezimmer, - bathroom *n.* **6A, 9A**
Bahnsteig, -e *m.* track; platform **8A**
bald *adv.* soon
  Bis bald. See you soon. **1A**
Balkon, -e/-s *m.* balcony **6A**
Ball, ⁻e *m.* ball **2B**

Ballon, -e/-s *m.* balloon **5A**
Banane, -n *f.* banana **4A**
Bank, ⁻e *f.* bench **10B**
Bank, -en *f.* bank **10A**
   auf der Bank *f.* at the bank **10B**
Bankangestellte, -n *m./f.* bank employee **11B**
bar *adj.* cash **10A**
   bar bezahlen *v.* to pay in cash **10A**
Bargeld *n.* cash **10A**
Bart, ⁻e *m.* beard **9A**
Baseball *m.* baseball **2B**
Basketball *m.* basketball **2B**
Bauch, ⁻e *m.* belly **9A**
Bauchschmerzen *m. pl.* stomachache **9B**
bauen *v.* to build **2A**
Bauer, -n / Bäuerin, -nen *m./f.* farmer **11B**
Bauernhof, ⁻e *m.* farm **12A**
Baum, ⁻e *m.* tree **12A**
Baumwolle *f.* cotton **5B**
Baustelle, -n *f.* construction zone **8A**
beantworten *v.* to answer **4B**
bedeuten *v.* to mean **2A**
bedeutend *adj.* important **12A**
bedienen *v.* to operate, use **8B**
sich beeilen *v.* to hurry **9A**
Beförderung, -en *f.* promotion **11B**
beginnen *v.* to begin **6A**
Begrüßung, -en *f.* greeting **1A**
behaupten *v.* to claim **12B**
bei *prep.* at; near; with **4B**
Beilage, -n *f.* side dish **4B**
Bein, -e *n.* leg **9A**
Beitrag ⁻e *m.* contribution **12B**
bekannt *adj.* well-known **10A**
bekommen *v.* to get, to receive **5A**
belegen *v.* to take (a class) **2A**
benutzen *v.* to use **8A**
Benutzername, -n *m.* screen name **8B**
Benzin, -e *n.* gasoline **8A**
Berg -e *m.* mountain **2B, 12A**
berichten *v.* to report **12B**
Beruf, -e *m.* profession; job **3B, 11A**
Berufsausbildung, -en *f.* professional
   training **11A**
bescheiden *adj.* modest **3B**
beschreiben *v.* to describe **2A**
Beschreibung, -en *f.* description **3B**
Besen, - *m.* broom **6B**
Besitzer, - / Besitzerin, -nen *m./f.* owner **3B**
besonderes special *adj.* **10A**
   nichts Besonderes *adj.* nothing special **10A**
besorgt worried *adj.* **3B**
Besorgung, -en *f.* errand **10A**
   Besorgungen machen *v.* to run errands **10A**
besprechen *v.* to discuss **7A**
Besprechung, -en *f.* meeting **11A**
besser *adj.* better **8A**
Besserwisser, - / Besserwisserin, -nen *m./f.* know-
   it-all **2A**
beste *adj.* best **8A**
Besteck *n.* silverware **4B**
bestehen *v.* to pass (a test) **1B**
bestellen *v.* to order **4A**
bestimmt *adv.* definitely. **4A**

besuchen *v.* to visit **4A**
Bett, -en *n.* bed **6A**
   das Bett machen *v.* to make the bed **6B**
   ins Bett gehen *v.* to go bed **9A**
Bettdecke, - n *f.* duvet **6B**
bevor *conj.* before **8A**
sich bewegen *v.* to move (around)
sich bewerben *v.* to apply **11A**
Bewerber, - / die Bewerberin, -nen *m./f.*
   applicant **11A**
Bewertung, -en *f.* rating **7B**
bezahlen *v.* to pay (for) **4A**
Bibliothek, -en *f.* library **1B**
Bier, -e *n.* beer **4B**
bieten *v.* to offer **9B**
Bild, -er *n.* picture **6A**
Bildschirm, -e *m.* screen **8B**
Bioladen, ⁻ *m.* health-food store **9B**
Biologie *f.* biology **2A**
biologisch *adj.* organic **12B**
Birne, -n *f.* pear **4A**
bis *prep.* until **3B**
   Bis bald. See you soon. **1A**
   Bis dann. See you later. **1A**
   Bis gleich. See you soon. **1A**
   Bis morgen. See you tomorrow. **1A**
   Bis später. See you later. **1A**
   bis zu *prep.* up to; until **10B**
Bitte. Please.; You're welcome. **1A**
Blatt, ⁻er *n.* leaf **12A**
blau *adj* blue. **3A**
   blaue Fleck, -e *m.* bruise **9B**
bleiben *v.* to stay **5B**
   Bleiben Sie bitte am Apparat. *v.* Please
   hold. **11A**
Bleistift, -e *m.* pencil **1B**
Blitz, -e *m.* lightning **7A**
Blog, -s, *n.* blog **8B**
blond *adj.* blond **3A**
   blonde Haare *n. pl.* blond hair **3A**
Blume, -n *f.* flower **1A**
Blumengeschäft, -e *n.* flower shop **10A**
Bluse, -n *f.* blouse **5B**
Blutdruck *m.* blood pressure **9B**
Boden, ⁻ *m.* floor; ground **6A**
Bohne, -n *f.* bean **4A**
   grüne Bohne *f.* green bean **4A**
Boot, -e *n.* boat **8A**
Bordkarte, -n *f.* boarding pass **7B**
braten *v.* to fry **2B**
brauchen *v.* to need **2A**
braun *adj.* brown **5B**
braunhaarig *adj.* brown-haired, brunette **3A**
brechen *v.* to break **2B**
   sich (den Arm / das Bein) brechen *v.* to break
   (an arm / a leg) **9B**
Bremse, -n *f.* brake **8A**
brennen *v.* to burn **5A**
Brief, -e *m.* letter **10A**
   einen Brief abschicken *v.* to mail a letter **10A**
Briefkasten, ⁻ *m.* mailbox **10A**
Briefmarke, -n *f.* stamp **10A**
Briefträger, - / Briefträgerin, -nen *m./f.* mail
   carrier **10A**

Briefumschlag, ⁻e *m.* envelope **10A**
Brille, -n *f.* glasses **5B**
bringen *v.* to bring **2A**
Brot, -e *n.* bread **4A**
Brötchen, - *n.* roll **4A**
Brücke, -n *f.* bridge **10B**
Bruder, ⁻ *m.* brother **1A**
Brunnen, - *m.* fountain **10B**
Buch, ⁻er *n.* book **1A**
buchen *v.* to make a (hotel) reservation **7B**
Bücherregal, -e *n.* bookshelf **6A**
Buchhalter, - / Buchhalterin, -nen *m./f.*
   accountant **11B**
büffeln *v.* to cram (for a test) **2A**
Bügelbrett, -er *n.* ironing board **6B**
Bügeleisen, - *n.* iron **6B**
bügeln *v.* to iron **6B**
Bundespräsident, -en / Bundespräsidentin,
   -nen *m./f.* (federal) president **8B**
bunt *adj.* colorful **10A**
Bürgermeister, - / Bürgermeisterin, -nen *m./f.*
   mayor **10B**
Bürgersteig, -e *m.* sidewalk **10B**
Büro, -s *n.* office **11B**
Büroklammer, -n *f.* paperclip **11A**
Büromaterial *n.* office supplies **11A**
Bürste, -n *f.* brush **9A**
bürsten *v.* to brush
   sich die Haare bürsten *v.* to brush one's hair **9A**
Bus, -se *m.* bus **8A**
Busch, ⁻e *m.* bush **12A**
Bushaltestelle, -n *f.* bus stop **8A**
Businessklasse *f.* business class **7B**
Bußgeld, -er *n.* fine (monetary) **8A**
Butter *f.* butter **4A**

C

Café, -s *n.* café **2A**
Camping *n.* camping **2B**
Chat, -s, *m.* chat **8B**
Chef, -s / Chefin, -nen *m./f.* boss **11B**
Chemie *f.* chemistry **2A**
China *n.* China **10B**
Chinese, -n / Chinesin, -nen *m./f.* Chinese
   (person) **10B**
Chinesisch *n.* Chinese (language) **10B**
Computer, - *m.* computer **1B**
Cousin, -s / Cousine, -n *m./f.* cousin **3A**

D

da there **1A**
   Da ist/sind... There is/are... **1A**
Dachboden, ⁻ *m.* attic **6A**
dafür *adv.* for it **6A**
daher *adv.* from there **6A**
dahin *adv.* there **6A**
damit *conj.* so that **10A**
danach *conj.* then, after that **9B**
danken *v.* to thank **2A**
   Danke. Thank you. **1A**
dann *adv.* then **7B**
daran *adv.* on it **6A**

darauf *adv.* on it **6A**
darin *adv.* in it **6A**
das *n.* the; this/that **1A**
dass *conj.* that **10A**
Datei, - en *f.* file **8B**
Datum (*pl.* Daten) *n.* date **7A**
davon *adv.* of it **6A**
davor *adv.* before it **6A**
Decke, -n *f.* blanket **6B**
decken *v.* to cover **6B**
  den Tisch decken *v.* to set the table **6B**
denken *v.* to think **5A**
  denken an *v.* to think about **7A**
denn *conj.* for; because **6A**
der *m.* the **1A**
deshalb *conj.* therefore; so **9B**
deswegen *conj.* that's why; therefore **9B**
deutsch German *adj.* **10B**
Deutsch German (language) *n.* **10B**
Deutsche *m./f.* German (man/woman) **10B**
Deutschland *n.* Germany **4A**
deutschsprachig *adj.* German-speaking
Dezember *m.* December **2A, 7A**
Diät, -en *f.* diet **4B**
  auf Diät sein *v.* to be on a diet **4B**
dick *adj.* fat **3A**
die *f./pl.* the **1A**
Dienstag, -e *m.* Tuesday **2A**
  dienstags *adv.* on Tuesdays **2A**
dieser/diese/dieses *m./f./n.* this; these **8B**
diesmal *adv.* this time **7B**
Digitalkamera, -s *f.* digital camera **8B**
Ding, -e *n.* thing
Diplom, -e *n.* diploma (degree) **2A**
diskret *adj.* discreet **3B**
doch *adv.* yes (contradicting a negative statement
  or question) **2B**
Dokument, -e *n.* document **8B**
Donner, - *m.* thunder **7A**
Donnerstag, -e *n.* Thursday **2A**
  donnerstags *adv.* on Thursdays **2A**
dort *adv.* there **1A**
Dozent, -en / Dozentin, -nen *m./f.* college
  instructor **2A**
draußen *prep.* outside; *adv.* out **7A**
  Es ist schön draußen. It's nice out. **7A**
dreckig *adj.* filthy **6B**
drei three **2A**
dritte third *adj.* **2A**
Drogerie, -n *f.* drugstore **10A**
drüben *adv.* over there **4A**
drücken *v.* to push **3B**; to print **8B**
Drucker, - *m.* printer **8B**
du *pron.* (*sing. inf.*) you **1A**
dumm *adj.* dumb **8A**
dunkel *adj.* dark **3A**
dunkelhaarig *adj.* dark-haired **3A**
dünn *adj.* thin **3A**
durch *prep.* through **3B**
durchfallen *v.* to flunk; to fail **1B**
durchmachen *v.* to experience **8B**
dürfen *v.* to be allowed to; may **3B**
(sich) duschen *v.* to take a shower **9A**
Dutzend, -e *n.* dozen **4A**

E

Ecke, -n *f.* corner **10B**
egoistisch *adj.* selfish **3B**
Ehe, -n *f.* marriage **5A**
Ehefrau, -en *f.* wife **3A**
Ehemann, ⁻er *m.* husband **3A**
Ei, -er *n.* egg **4A**
Eichhörnchen, - *n.* squirrel **12A**
eifersüchtig *adj.* jealous **3B**
ein/eine *m./f./n.* a **1A**
Einbahnstraße, -n *f.* one-way street **8A**
einfach *adj.* easy **2A**
einfarbig *adj.* solid colored **5B**
eingebildet *adj.* arrogant **3B**
einkaufen *v.* to shop **4A**
  einkaufen gehen *v.* to go shopping **4A**
Einkaufen *n.* shopping **5B**
Einkaufszentrum, (*pl.* Einkaufszentren) *n.* mall;
  shopping center **10B**
Einkommensgruppe, -n *f.* income bracket **6B**
einladen *v.* to invite **5A**
einmal *adv.* once **7B**
eins one **2A**
einschlafen *v.* to go to sleep **4A**
einzahlen *v.* to deposit (money) **10A**
Einzelkind, -er *n.* only child **3A**
Eis *n.* ice cream **5A**
Eisdiele, -n *f.* ice cream shop **4A**
Eishockey *n.* ice hockey **2B**
Eiswürfel, - *m.* ice cube **5A**
elegant *adj.* elegant **5B**
Elektriker, - / Elektrikerin, -nen *m./f.*
  electrician **11B**
elf eleven **2A**
Ell(en)bogen, - *m.* elbow **9A**
Eltern *pl.* parents **3A**
E-Mail, -s *f.* e-mail **8B**
empfehlen *v.* to recommend **2B**
Empfehlungsschreiben, - *n.* letter of
  recommendation **11A**
endlich *adv.* finally **9B**
Energie, -n *f.* energy **12B**
energiesparend *adj.* energy-efficient **6B**
eng *adj.* tight **5B**
England *n.* England **10B**
Engländer, - / Engländerin, -nen *m./f.* English
  (person) **10B**
Englisch *n.* English (language) **10B**
Enkelkind, -er *n.* grandchild. **3A**
Enkelsohn, ⁻e *m.* grandson **3A**
Enkeltochter, ⁻ *f.* granddaughter **3A**
entdecken *v.* to discover **6B**
entfernen *v.* to remove **6B**
entlang *prep.* along, down **3B**
entlassen *v.* to fire; to lay off **11B**
sich entschließen *v.* to decide **4B**
(sich) entschuldigen *v.* to apologize; to excuse
  Entschuldigen Sie. Excuse me. (*form.*) **1A**
  Entschuldigung. Excuse me. **1A**
sich entspannen *v.* to relax **9A**
entwerten *v.* to validate **8A**
  eine Fahrkarte entwerten *v.* to validate
  a ticket **8A**

entwickeln *v.* to develop **12B**
er *pron.* he **1A**
Erdbeben, - *n.* earthquake **12A**
Erdbeere, -n *f.* strawberry **4A**
Erde, -n *f.* earth **12B**
Erderwärmung *f.* global warming **12B**
Erdgeschoss, -e *n.* ground floor **6A**
Erfahrung, -en *f.* experience **11A**
erfinden *v.* to invent **7A**
Erfolg, -e *m.* success **11B**
erforschen *v.* to explore **12A**
ergänzen *v.* complete
Ergebnis, -se *n.* result; score **1B**
erhalten *v.* to preserve **12B**
sich erinnern (an) *v.* to remember **9A**
sich erkälten *v.* to catch a cold **9A**
Erkältung, -en *f.* cold **9B**
erkennen *v.* to recognize **7A**
erklären *v.* to explain **4A**
erneuerbare Energie, -n *f.* renewable energy **12B**
ernst *adj.* serious **3B**
erster/erste/erstes *adj.* first **2A**
erwachsen grown-up *adj.* **10A**
erzählen *v.* to tell **7A**
  erzählen von *v.* to talk about **7A**
es *pron.* it **1A**
  Es geht. (I'm) so-so. **1A**
  Es gibt... There is/are... **2B**
Essen, - *n.* food **4A**
essen *v.* to eat **2B**
  essen gehen *v.* to eat out **2B**
Esslöffel, - *m.* soup spoon **4B**
Esszimmer, - *n.* dining room **6A**
etwas *pron.* something **7B**
  etwas anderes something else **10A**
euer (*pl. inf.*) *poss. adj.* your **3A**

F

Fabrik, -en *f.* factory **12B**
Fabrikarbeiter, - / Fabrikarbeiterin, -nen *m./f.*
  factory worker **11B**
Fach, ⁻er *n.* subject **2A**
fade *adj.* bland **4B**
fahren to drive; to go *v.* **2B**
  Auto fahren *v.* to drive a car **8A**
  Fahrrad fahren *v.* to ride a bicycle **2B**
  geradeaus fahren *v.* to go straight ahead **8A**
Fahrer, - / Fahrerin, -nen *m./f.* driver **8A**
Fahrgemeinschaft, -en *f.* carpool **12B**
Fahrkarte, -n *f.* ticket **8A**
  eine Fahrkarte entwerten *v.* to validate a
  ticket **8A**
Fahrkartenschalter, - *m.* ticket office **8A**
Fahrplan, ⁻e *m.* schedule **8A**
Fahrrad, ⁻er *n.* bicycle **2B, 8A**
Fahrstuhl, ⁻e *m.* elevator **7B**
fallen *v.* to fall **2B**
Familie, -n *f.* family **3A**
Familienstand, ⁻e *m.* marital status **3A**
Fan, -s *m.* fan **2B**
fangen *v.* to catch **2B**
fantastisch *adj.* fantastic **10A**
Farbe, -n *f.* color **5B**

färben *v.* to dye
  sich die Haare färben *v.* to dye one's hair **9A**
fast *adv.* almost **4A**
faul *adj.* lazy **3B**
Februar *m.* February **2A, 7A**
fegen *v.* to sweep **6B**
feiern *v.* to celebrate **5A**
Feiertag, -e *m.* holiday **5A**
Feinkostgeschäft, -e *n.* delicatessen **4A**
Feld, -er *n.* field **12A**
Fenster, - *n.* window **1A**
Ferien *pl.* vacation **7A**
Fernbedienung, -en *f.* remote control **8B**
fernsehen *v.* to watch television **8B**
Fernsehen *n.* television (programming)
Fernseher, - *m.* television set **8B**
fertig *adj.* ready; finished **11B**
Fest, -e *n.* festival; celebration **5A**
Festplatte, -n *f.* hard drive **8B**
Feuerwehrmann, ⁻er / Feuerwehrfrau, -en
  (pl. Feuerwehrleute) *m./f.* firefighter **11B**
Fieber, - *n.* fever **9B**
  Fieber haben *v.* to have a fever **9B**
finden *v.* to find **2A**
Finger, - *m.* finger **9A**
Firma (pl. die Firmen) *f.* firm; company **11A**
Fisch, -e fish *m.* **4A, 12A**
Fischgeschäft, -e *n.* fish store **4A**
fit *adj.* in good shape **2B**
Flasche, -n *f.* bottle **4B**
Fleisch *n.* meat **4A**
fleißig *adj.* hard-working **3B**
fliegen *v.* to fly **7B**
Flug, ⁻e *m.* flight **7B**
Flughafen, ⁻ *m.* airport **7B**
Flugticket, -s *n.* (plane) ticket **7B**
Flugzeug, -e *n.* airplane **7B**
Flur, -e *m.* hall **6A**
Fluss, ⁻e *m.* river **3B, 12A**
folgen *v.* to follow **5A, 10B**
Form, -en *f.* shape, form
  in guter/schlechter Form sein *v.* to be in/out of
    shape **9B**
Formular, -e *n.* form **10A**
  ein Formular ausfüllen *v.* to fill out a form **10A**
Foto, -s *n.* photo, picture **1B**
Frage, -n *f.* question **1B**
fragen *v.* to ask **2A**
  fragen nach *v.* to ask about **7A**
  sich fragen *v.* to wonder, ask oneself **9A**
Frankreich *n.* France **10B**
Franzose, -n / Französin, -nen *m./f.* French
  (person) **10B**
Französisch *n.* French (language) **10B**
Frau, -en *f.* woman **1A**; wife **3A**
  Frau... Mrs./Ms.... **1A**
Freitag, -e *m.* Friday **2A**
  freitags *adv.* on Fridays **2A**
Freizeit, -en *f.* free time, leisure **2B**
Freizeitaktivität, - en *f.* leisure activity **2B**
Fremdsprache, -n *f.* foreign language **2A**
sich freuen (über) *v.* to be happy (about) **9A**
  Freut mich. Pleased to meet you. **1A**
  sich freuen auf *v.* to look forward to **9A**

Freund, -e / Freundin, -nen *m./f.* friend **1A**
freundlich *adj.* friendly **3B**
  Mit freundlichen Grüßen Yours sincerely **3B**
Freundschaft, -en *f.* friendship **5A**
Frischvermählte, -n *m./f.* newlywed **5A**
Friseur, -e / Friseurin, -nen *m./f.* hairdresser **3B**
froh *adj.* happy **3B**
  Frohe Ostern! Happy Easter! **5A**
  Frohe Weihnachten! Merry Christmas! **5A**
früh *adj.* early; in the morning **2B**
  morgen früh tomorrow morning **2B**
Frühling, -e *m.* spring **2B, 7A**
Frühstück, -e *n.* breakfast **4B**
frühstücken *v.* to have breakfast **4B**
fühlen *v.* to feel **2A**
  sich (wohl) fühlen *v.* to feel (well) **9A**
füllen *v.* to fill
fünf five **2A**
funktionieren *v.* to work, function **8B**
für *prep.* for **3B**
furchtbar *adj.* awful **7A**
Fuß, ⁻e *m.* foot **9A**
Fußball *m.* soccer **2B**
Fußgänger, - / Fußgängerin, -nen *m./f.* pedestrian **10B**

G

Gabel, -n *f.* fork **4B**
Gang, ⁻e *m.* course **4B**
  erster/zweiter Gang *m.* first/second course **4B**
ganz *adj.* all, total **7B**
ganztags *adj.* full-time **11B**
Garage, -n *f.* garage **5B**
Garnele, -n *f.* shrimp **4A**
Gartenabfall, ⁻e *m.* yard waste **12B**
Gärtner, - /Gärtnerin, -nen *m./f.* gardener **11B**
Gast, ⁻e *m.* guest **5A**
Gastfamilie, -n *f.* host family **4B**
Gastgeber, - / Gastgeberin, -nen *m./f.* host/
  hostess **5A**
Gebäck, -e *n.* pastries; baked goods **5A**
Gebäude, - *n.* building **10A**
geben *v.* to give **2B**
  Es gibt... There is/are... **2B**
Geburt, -en *f.* birth **5A**
Geburtstag, -e *m.* birthday **5A**
  Wann hast du Geburtstag? When is your
    birthday? **7A**
geduldig *adj.* patient **3B**
Gefahr, -en *f.* danger **12B**
gefährdet *adj.* endangered; threatened **12B**
gefallen *v.* to please **5A**
Gefrierschrank, ⁻e *m.* freezer **6B**
gegen *prep.* against **3B**
gegenüber (von) *prep.* across (from) **10B**
Gehalt, ⁻er *n.* salary **11A**
  hohes/niedriges Gehalt, -⁻er high/low salary *n.* **11A**
Gehaltserhöhung, -en *f.* raise **11B**
gehen to go *v.* **2A**
  Es geht. (I'm) so-so. **1A**
  Geht es dir/Ihnen gut? *v.* Are you all right?
    (*inf./form.*) **1A**
  Wie geht es Ihnen? (*form.*) How are you? **1A**
  Wie geht's (dir)? (*inf.*) How are you? **1A**

gehören *v.* to belong to **4B**
Geländewagen, - *m.* SUV **8B**
gelb *adj.* yellow **5B**
Geld, -er *n.* money **10A**
  Geld abheben/einzahlen *v.* to withdraw/deposit
    money **10A**
Geldautomat, -en *m.* ATM **10A**
Geldschein, -e *m.* bill (money) **10A**
gemein *adj.* mean **3B**
Gemüse, - *n.* vegetables **4A**
genau *adv.* exactly
  genauso wie just as **8A**
genießen *v.* to enjoy
geöffnet *adj.* open **10A**
Gepäck *n.* luggage **7B**
geradeaus straight ahead *adv.* **8A**
gern *adv.* with pleasure **2B**
  gern (+verb) to like to (+*verb*) **2B**
  ich hätte gern... I would like... **4A**
  Gern geschehen. My pleasure.; You're
    welcome. **1A**
Geschäft, -e *n.* business **11A**; store **4A**
Geschäftsführer, - / Geschäftsführerin, -nen
  m./f. manager **11A**
Geschäftsmann, ⁻er / Geschäftsfrau, -en
  (pl. Geschäftsleute) *m./f.* businessman/
  businesswoman **3B**
Geschenk, -e *n.* gift **5A**
Geschichte, -n *f.* history **2A**; story
geschieden *adj.* divorced **3A**
Geschirr *n.* dishes **6B**
  Geschirr spülen *v.* to do the dishes **6B**
geschlossen *adj.* closed **10A**
Geschmack, ⁻e *m.* flavor; taste **4B**
Geschwister *pl.* siblings **3A**
Gesetz, -e *n.* law **12B**
Gesicht, -er *n.* face **9A**
gestern *adv.* yesterday **5B**
gestreift *adj.* striped **5B**
gesund *adj.* healthy **8A; 9B**
  gesund werden *v.* to get better **9B**
Gesundheit *f.* health **9B**
geteilt durch divided by **1B**
Getränk, -e *n.* beverage **4B**
getrennt *adj.* separated **3A**
gewaltfrei *adj.* nonviolent **12B**
Gewerkschaft, -en *f.* labor union **11B**
gewinnen *v.* to win **2B**
Gewitter, - *n.* thunderstorm **7A**
sich gewöhnen an *v.* to get used to **9A**
gierig *adj.* greedy **3B**
Giftmüll *m.* toxic waste **12B**
Glas, ⁻er *n.* glass **4B**
glatt *adj.* straight **3A**
  glatte Haare *n. pl.* straight hair **3A**
glauben *v.* to believe **5A**
gleich *adj.* same
  ist gleich *v.* equals, is **1B**
Glück *n.* happiness **5A**
glücklich *adj.* happy **3B**
Golf *n.* golf **2B**
Grad *n.* degree **7A**
  Es sind 18 Grad draußen. It's 18 degrees out. **7A**
Gramm, -e *n.* gram **4A**

Granit, -e *m.* granite **6B**
Gras, ¨er *n.* grass **12A**
gratulieren *v.* to congratulate **5A**
grau *adj.* grey **5B**
grausam *adj.* cruel
Grippe, -n *f.* flu **9B**
groß *adj.* big; tall **3A**
großartig *adj.* terrific **3A**
Großeltern *pl.* grandparents **1A**
Großmutter, ¨ *f.* grandmother **3A**
Großvater, ¨ *m.* grandfather **3A**
großzügig *adj.* generous **3B**
grün *adj.* green **5B**
　grüne Bohne (*pl.* die grünen Bohnen) *f.* green
　　bean **4A**
Gruß, ¨e *m.* greeting
　Mit freundlichen Grüßen Yours sincerely **3B**
grüßen *v.* to greet **2A**
günstig *adj.* cheap **5B**
Gürtel, - *m.* belt **5B**
gut *adj.* good; *adv.* well **1A**
　gut aussehend *adj.* handsome **3A**
　gut gekleidet *adj.* well-dressed **5B**
　Gute Besserung! Get well! **5A**
　Guten Appetit! Enjoy your meal! **4B**
　Guten Abend! Good evening. **1A**
　Guten Morgen! Good morning. **1A**
　Gute Nacht! Good night. **1A**
　Guten Tag! Hello. **1A**

H

Haar, -e hair *n.* **3A, 9A**
Haartrockner, - *m.* hair dryer **9A**
haben to have *v.* **1B**
Hagel *m.* hail **7A**
Hähnchen, - *n.* chicken **4A**
halb half; half an hour before **2A**
Halbbruder, ¨ *m.* half brother **3A**
Halbschwester, -n *f.* half sister **3A**
halbtags *adj.* part-time **11B**
Hallo! Hello. **1A**
Hals, ¨e *m.* neck **9A**
　Hals- und Beinbruch! Break a leg! **5A**
Halskette, -n *f.* necklace **5B**
Hand, ¨e *f.* hand **9A**
handeln *v.* to act
　handeln von *v.* to be about; have to do with **7A**
Handgelenk, -e *n.* wrist **9B**
Handgepäck *n.* carry-on luggage **7B**
Handschuh, -e *m.* glove **5B**
Handtasche, -n *f.* purse **5B**
Handtuch, ¨er *n.* towel **9A**
Handy, -s *n.* cell phone **8B**
hängen *v.* to hang **5B**
Hase, -n *m.* hare **12A**
hässlich *adj.* ugly **3A**
Hauptspeise, -n *f.* main course **4B**
Hauptstraße, -n *f.* main road **10B**
Haus, ¨er *n.* house **6A**
　nach Hause *adv.* home **5B**
　zu Hause *adv.* at home **4A**
Hausarbeit *f.* housework **6B**
　Hausarbeit machen *v.* to do housework **6B**

Hausaufgabe, -n *f.* homework **1B**
Hausfrau, -en / Hausmann, -¨er *f./m.*
　homemaker **11B**
hausgemacht *adj.* homemade **4B**
Hausmeister, - / Hausmeisterin, -nen *m./f.*
　caretaker; custodian **11B**
Hausschuh, -e *m.* slipper **9A**
Haustier, -e *n.* pet **3A**
Heft, -e *n.* notebook **1B**
Hefter, - *m.* stapler **11A**
heiraten *v.* to marry **3A**
heiß *adj.* hot **7A**
heißen *v.* to be named **2A**
　Ich heiße... My name is... **1A**
helfen *v.* to help **2B**
　helfen bei *v.* to help with **7A**
hell *adj.* light **3A**; bright **5B**
Hemd, -en *n.* shirt **5B**
herauf *adv.* up; upwards **6A**
heraus *adv.* out **6A**
Herbst, -e *m.* fall, autumn **2B, 7A**
Herd, -e *m.* stove **6B**
Herr Mr. **1A**
herunter *adv.* down; downwards **6A**
heruntergehen *v.* to go down **10B**
　die Treppe heruntergehen *v.* to go
　　downstairs **10B**
herunterladen *v.* to download **8B**
Herz, -en *n.* heart
　Herzlichen Glückwunsch! Congratulations! **5A**
heute *adv.* today **2B**
　Heute ist der... Today is the... **2A**
　Welcher Tag ist heute? What day is it today? **7A**
　Der Wievielte ist heute? What is the date
　　today? **2A**
hier *adv.* here **1A**
　Hier ist/sind... Here is/are... **1B**
Himmel *m.* sky **12A**
hin und zurück there and back **7B**
sich hinlegen *v.* to lie down **9A**
sich hinsetzen *v.* to sit down **9A**
hinter *prep.* behind **5B**
hinterlassen *v.* to leave (behind)
　eine Nachricht hinterlassen *v.* to leave
　　a message **11A**
Hobby, -s *n.* hobby **2B**
hoch *adj.* high **8A**
hochgehen *v.* to go up, climb up **10B**
　die Treppe hochgehen *v.* to go upstairs **10B**
hochladen *v.* upload **8B**
Hochwasser, - *n.* flood **12B**
Hochzeit, -en *f.* wedding **5A**
Hochzeitstag, -e, *m.* wedding anniversary **5B**
Hockey *n.* hockey **2B**
Höflichkeit, -en *f.* courtesy; polite expression **1A**
Holz, ¨er *n.* wood **6B**
hören *v.* to hear; listen to **2A**
Hörer, - *m.* receiver **11A**
Hörsaal (*pl.* Hörsäle) *m.* lecture hall **2A**
Hose, -n *f.* pants **5B**
　kurze Hose *f.* shorts **5B**
Hotel, -s *n.* hotel **7B**
　Fünf-Sterne-Hotel *n* five-star hotel. **7B**
Hotelgast, ¨e *m.* hotel guest **7B**

hübsch *adj.* pretty **3A**
Hund, -e *m.* dog **3A**
Hundewetter *n.* terrible weather **7A**
husten *v.* to cough **9B**
Hut, ¨e *m.* hat **5B**
Hybridauto, -s *n.* hybrid car **12B**

I

ich *pron.* I **1A**
Idee, -n *f.* idea **1A**
Ihr (*form., sing/pl.*) *poss. adj.* your **3A**
ihr (*inf., pl.*) *pron.* you **1A**; *poss. adj.* her, their **3A**
immer *adv.* always **4A**
Immobilienmakler, - / Immobilienmaklerin,
　-nen *m./f.* real estate agent **11B**
in *prep.* in **5B**
Inder, - / Inderin, -nen *m./f.* Indian (person) **10B**
Indien *n.* India **10B**
indisch *adj.* Indian **10B**
Informatik *f.* computer science **2A**
sich informieren (über) *v.* to find out (about) **9A**
Ingenieur, -e / Ingenieurin, -nen *m./f.*
　engineer **3B**
Innenstadt, ¨e *f.* city center; downtown **10B**
innerhalb *prep.* inside of, within **8B**
Insel, -n *f.* island **12A**
intellektuell *adj.* intellectual **3B**
intelligent *adj.* intelligent **3B**
interessant *adj.* interesting **2A**
sich interessieren (für) *v.* to be interested (in) **9A**
Internet *n.* Web **8B**
　im Internet surfen *v.* to surf the Web **8B**
Internetcafé, -s *n.* internet café **10A**
Italien *n.* Italy **10B**
Italiener, - / Italienerin, -nen *m./f.* Italian
　(person) **10B**
Italienisch *n.* Italian (language) **10B**

J

ja yes **1A**
Jacke, -n *f.* jacket **5B**
Jahr, -e *n.* year **7A**
　Ein gutes neues Jahr! Happy New Year! **5A**
　Ich bin... Jahre alt. I am... years old **1B**
Jahrestag, -e *m.* anniversary **5A**
Jahreszeit, -en *f.* season **7A**
Januar *m.* January **2A, 7A**
Japan *n.* Japan **10B**
Japaner, - / Japanerin, -nen *m./f.* Japanese
　(person) **10B**
Japanisch *n.* Japanese (language) **10B**
Jeans *f.* jeans **5B**
jeder/jede/jedes *adj.* any, every, each **8B**
jemand *pron.* someone **7B**
jetzt *adv.* now **4A**
joggen *v.* to jog **2B**
Joghurt, -s *m.* yogurt **4A**
Journalist, -en / Journalistin, -nen *m./f.*
　journalist **3B**
Jugendherberge, -n *f.* youth hostel **7B**
jugendlich *adj.* young; youthful **10A**
Juli *m.* July **2A, 7A**

jung *adj.* young **3A**
Junge, -n *m.* boy **1A**
Juni *m.* June **2A, 7A**
Juweliergeschäft, -e *n.* jewelry store **10A**

K

Kaffee, -s *m.* coffee **4B**
Kaffeemaschine, -n *f.* coffeemaker **6B**
Kalender, - *m.* calendar **1B**
kalt *adj.* cold **7A**
sich (die Haare) kämmen *v.* to comb (one's hair) **9A**
Kanada *n.* Canada **10B**
Kanadier, - / Kanadierin, -nen *m./f.*
  Canadian **10B**
Kandidat, -en *m.* candidate **11A**
Kaninchen, - *n.* rabbit **12A**
Karotte, -n *f.* carrot **4A**
Karriere, -n *f.* career **11B**
Karte, -n *f.* map **1B**, *f.* card **2B; 5A**
  eine Karte lesen *v.* to read a map **7B**
  mit der Karte bezahlen *v.* to pay by (credit)
    card **10A**
Kartoffel, -n *f.* potato **4A**
Käse, - *m.* cheese **4A**
Katze, -n *f.* cat **3A**
kaufen *v.* to buy **2A**
Kaufhaus, ̈er *n.* department store **10B**
Kaution, -en *f.* security deposit **6A**
kein *adj.* no **2B**
  Keine Zufahrt. Do not enter. **3B**
Keks, -e *m.* cookie **5A**
Keller, - *m.* cellar **6A**
Kellner, - / Kellnerin, -nen *m./f.* waiter/
  waitress **3B, 4B**
kennen *v.* to know, be familiar with **5B**
  sich kennen *v.* to know each other **9A**
  (sich) kennen lernen *v.* to meet (one another) **1A**
Keramik, -en *f.* ceramic **6B**
Kernenergie *f.* nuclear energy **12B**
Kernkraftwerk, -e *n.* nuclear power plant **12B**
Kind, -er *n.* child **1A**
Kino, -s *n.* movie theater **10A**
Kiosk, -e *m.* newspaper kiosk **10A**
Kirche, -n *f.* church **10B**
Kissen, - *n.* pillow **6B**
Klasse, -n *f.* class **1B**
  erste/zweite Klasse, -n first/second class **8A**
**Klassenkamerad, -en / Klassenkameradin,
  -nen** *m./f.* (K-12) classmate **1B**
Klassenzimmer, - *n.* classroom **1B**
klassisch *adj.* classical **10A**
Kleid, -er *n.* dress **5B**
Kleidergröße, -n *f.* clothing size **5B**
Kleidung *f. pl.* clothes **5B**
klein *adj.* small; short (stature) **3A**
Kleingeld *n.* change (money) **10A**
Klempner, - / Klempnerin, -nen *m./f.* plumber **11B**
klettern *v.* to climb (mountain) **2B**
klingeln *v.* to ring **8B**
Klippe, -n *f.* cliff **12A**
Knie, - *n.* knee **9A**
Knoblauch, -e *m.* garlic **4A**
Koch, ̈e / Köchin, -nen *m./f.* cook, chef **4B**

kochen *v.* to cook **2B**
Koffer, - *m.* suitcase **7B**
Kofferraum, ̈e *m.* trunk **8A**
Kombi, -s *m.* station wagon **8B**
Komma, -s *n.* comma **1B**
kommen *v.* to come **2A**
Kommilitone, -n / Kommilitonin, -nen *m./f.*
  (university) classmate **1B**
Kommode, -n *f.* dresser **6A**
kompliziert *adj.* complicated **10A**
Konditorei, -en *f.* pastry shop **4A**
können *v.* to be able, can **3B**
Konto (pl. Konten) *n.* bank account **10A**
Konzert, -e *n.* concert **5B**
Kopf, ̈e *m.* head **9A**
Kopfhörer, - *m.* headphones **8B**
Kopfschmerzen *m. pl.* headache **9B**
Korea *n.* Korea **10B**
der Koreaner, - / die Koreanerin, -nen *m./f.*
  Korean (person) **10B**
Koreanisch *n.* Korean (language) **10B**
Körper, - *m.* body **9A**
korrigieren *v.* to correct **2A**
Kosmetiksalon, -s *m.* beauty salon **10A**
kosten *v.* to cost **2A**
  Wie viel kostet das? *v.* How much is that? **4A**
krank *adj.* sick **9B**
  krank werden *v.* to get sick **9B**
Krankenhaus, ̈er *n.* hospital **9B**
Krankenpfleger, - / Krankenschwester, -n *m./f.*
  nurse **9B**
Krankenwagen, - *m.* ambulance **9B**
Krawatte, -n *f.* tie **5B**
Kreuzfahrt, -en *f.* cruise **7B**
Kreuzung, -en *f.* intersection **10B**
Küche, -n *f.* kitchen **6A**
Kuchen, - *m.* cake; pie **4A**
Kuh, ̈e *f.* cow **12A**
kühl *adj.* cool **7A**
Kühlschrank, ̈e *m.* refrigerator **6B**
Kuli, -s *m.* (ball-point) pen **1B**
Kunde, -n / Kundin, -nen *m./f.* customer **5B**
kündigen *v.* to resign **11B**
Kunst, ̈e *f.* art **2A**
Kunststoff, -e *m.* plastic **6B**
kurz *adj.* short **3A**
  kurze Haare *n. pl.* short hair **3A**
  kurze Hose *f.* shorts **5B**
kurzärmlig *adj.* short-sleeved **5B**
Kurzfilm, -e *m.* short film
Kuss, ̈e *m.* kiss **5A**
küssen *v.* to kiss **5A**
  sich küssen *v.* to kiss (each other) **9A**
Küste, -n *f.* coast **12A**

L

lächeln *v.* to smile **3B**
lachen *v.* to laugh **3B**
Ladegerät, -e *n.* battery charger **8B**
Lage, -n *f.* location **7B**
Laken, - *n.* sheet **6B**
Lampe, -n *f.* lamp **6A**

Land, ̈er *n.* country **7B**
landen *v.* to land **7B**
Landkarte, -n *f.* map **7B**
Landschaft, -en *f.* landscape; countryside **12A**
lang *adj.* long **3A**
  lange Haare *n. pl.* long hair **3A**
langärmlig *adj.* long-sleeved **5B**
langsam *adj* slow. **3B**
  Langsam fahren. Slow down. **3B**
langweilig *adj.* boring **2A**
Laptop, -s *m./n.* laptop (computer) **8B**
lassen *v.* to let, allow **2B**
laufen *v.* to run **2B**
leben *v.* to live **2A**
Lebenslauf, ̈e *m.* résumé; CV **11A**
Lebensmittelgeschäft, -e *n.* grocery store **4A**
Lebenspartner, - / Lebenspartnerin, -nen *m./f.*
  life partner **3A**
lecker *adj.* delicious **4B**
Leder, - *n.* leather **5B**
ledig *adj.* single **3A**
legen *v.* to lay **5B**; *v.* to put; lay **9A**
Lehrbuch, ̈er *n.* textbook (university) **1B**
Lehrer, - / Lehrerin, -nen *m./f.* teacher **1B**
leicht *adj.* light **4B**; mild **9B**
Leichtathletik *f.* track and field **2B**
leider *adv.* unfortunately **4A**
leiten *v.* to manage **11B**
Lenkrad, ̈er *n.* steering wheel **8A**
lernen *v.* to study; to learn **2A**
lesen *v.* to read **2B**
letzter/letzte/letztes *adj.* last **2B**
Leute *pl.* people **3B**
Licht, -er *n.* light **12B**
Liebe, -n *f.* love **5A**
  Lieber/Liebe *m./f.* Dear **3B**
lieben *v.* to love **2A**
  sich lieben *v.* to love each other **9A**
lieber *adj.* rather **8A**
liebevoll *adj.* loving **3B**
Liebling, -e *m.* darling
  Lieblings- favorite **4B**
liegen *v.* to lie; to be located **5B**
lila *adj.* purple **5B**
Linie, -n *f.* line
Lippe, -n *f.* lip **9A**
Lippenstift, -e *m.* lipstick **9A**
Literatur, -en *f.* literature **2A**
LKW, -s *m.* truck **8A**
LKW-Fahrer, - / LKW-Fahrerin, -nen *m./f.* truck
  driver **11B**
lockig *adj.* curly **3A**
  lockige Haare *n. pl.* curly hair **3A**
Los! Start!; Go! **2B**
löschen *v.* to delete **8B**
Lösung, -en *f.* solution **12B**
  eine Lösung vorschlagen *v.* to propose a
    solution **12B**
Luft, ̈e *f.* air **12A**
lügen *v.* to lie, tell a lie
Lust, ̈e *f.* desire
  Lust haben *v.* to feel like **7B**
lustig *adj.* funny **3B**

M

machen *v.* to do; make **2A**
  Mach's gut! *v.* All the best! **3B**
Mädchen, - *n.* girl **1A**
Mahlzeit, -en *f.* meal **4B**
Mai *m.* May **2A, 7A**
Mal, -e *n.* time
  das erste/letzte Mal the first/last time **7B**
  zum ersten/letzten Mal for the first/last
    time **7B**
mal times **1B**
Mama, -s *f.* mom **3A**
man *pron.* one **7B**
mancher/manche/manches *adj.* some. **8B**
manchmal *adv.* sometimes **7B**
Mann, ¨er *m.* man **1A**; *m.* husband **3A**
Mannschaft, -en *f.* team **2B**
Mantel, ¨ *m.* coat **5B**
Markt, ¨e *m.* market **4A**
Marmelade, -n *f.* jam **4A**
Marmor *m.* marble **6B**
März *m.* March **2A, 7A**
Material, -ien *n.* material **5B**
Mathematik *f.* mathematics **2A**
Maus, ¨e *f.* mouse **8B**
Mechaniker, - / Mechanikerin, -nen *m./f.*
  mechanic **8A**
Medikament, -e *n.* medicine **9B**
Medizin *f.* medicine **2A**
Meer, -e *n.* sea; ocean **12A**
Meeresfrüchte *f. pl.* seafood **4A**
mehr *adj.* more **8A**
mein *poss. adj.* my **3A**
meinen *v.* to mean; to believe; to
  maintain **12B**
Meisterschaft, -en *f.* championship **2B**
Melone, -n *f.* melon **4A**
Mensa (*pl.* Mensen) *f.* cafeteria (college/
  university) **1B**
Mensch, -en *m.* person
Messer, - *n.* knife **4B**
Metzgerei, -en *f.* butcher shop **4A**
Mexikaner, - / Mexikanerin, -nen *m./f.* Mexican
  (person) **10B**
mexikanisch *adj.* Mexican **10B**
Mexiko *n.* Mexico **10B**
Miete, -n *f.* rent **6A**
mieten *v.* to rent **6A**
Mikrofon, -e *n.* microphone **8B**
Mikrowelle, -n *f.* microwave **6B**
Milch *f.* milk **4B**
Minderheit, -en *f.* minority **12B**
Mineralwasser *n.* sparkling water **4B**
minus minus **1B**
mir *pron.* myself, me **7A**
  Mir geht's (sehr) gut. *v.* I am (very) well. **1A**
  Mir geht's nicht (so) gut. *v.* I am not (so)
    well. **1A**
mit with **4B**
Mitbewohner, - / Mitbewohnerin, -nen *m./f.*
  roommate **2A**
mitbringen *v.* to bring along **4A**

mitkommen *v.* to come along **4A**
mitmachen *v.* to participate **8B**
mitnehmen *v.* to bring with **10B**
  jemanden mitnehmen *v.* to give someone a
    ride **10B**
Mittag, -e *m.* noon **2A**
Mittagessen *n.* lunch **4B**
Mitternacht *f.* midnight **2A**
Mittwoch, -e *m.* Wednesday **2A**
  mittwochs *adv.* on Wednesdays **2A**
Möbel, - *n.* furniture **6A**
Möbelstück, -e *n.* piece of furniture **6A**
möbliert *adj.* furnished **6A**
modern *adj.* modern **10A**
modisch *adj.* fashionable **5B**
mögen *v.* to like **4B**
  Ich möchte... I would like… **4B**
Monat, -e *m.* month **2A, 7A**
Mond, -e *m.* moon **12A**
Montag, -e *m.* Monday **2A**
  montags *adv.* on Mondays **2A**
Morgen, - *m.* morning **2B**
  morgens *adv.* in the morning **2A**
morgen *adv.* tomorrow **2B**
  morgen früh tomorrow morning **2B**
Motor, -en *m.* engine **8A**
Motorhaube, -n *f.* hood (of car) **8A**
müde *adj.* tired **3B**
Müll *m.* trash **6B**; *m.* waste **12B**
  den Müll rausbringen *v.* to take out the trash **6B**
Müllwagen, - *m.* garbage truck **12B**
Mund, ¨er *m.* mouth **9A**
Münze, -n *f.* coin **10A**
Musiker, - / Musikerin, -nen *m./f.* musician **3B**
müssen *v.* to have to; must **3B**
mutig *adj.* brave **3B**
Mutter, ¨ *f.* mother **1A**
Mütze, -n *f.* cap **5B**

N

nach *prep.* after; to; according to **4B**; *prep.* past
  (time) **2A**
  nach rechts/links to the right/left **6A**
nachdem *conj.* after **10A**
nachmachen *v.* to imitate **8B**
Nachmittag, -e *m.* afternoon **2B**
  nachmittags *adv.* in the afternoon **2A**
Nachname, -n *m.* last name **3A**
Nachricht, -en *f.* message **11A**
  eine Nachricht hinterlassen *v.* to leave a
    message **11A**
nächster/nächste/nächstes *adj.* next **2B**
Nacht, ¨e *f.* night **2B**
Nachtisch, -e *m.* dessert **4B**
Nachttisch, -e *m.* night table **6A**
nah(e) *adj.* near; nearby **10B**
Nähe *f.* vicinity **10B**
  in der Nähe von *f.* close to **10B**
naiv *adj.* naïve **3B**
Nase, -n *f.* nose **9A**
  verstopfte Nase *f.* stuffy nose **9A**
nass *adj.* wet **12A**

Natur, *f.* nature **12A**
Naturkatastrophe, -n *f.* natural disaster **12A**
Naturwissenschaft, -en *f.* science **2A**
Nebel, - *m.* fog; mist **7A**
neben *prep.* next to **5B**
Nebenkosten *pl.* additional charges **6A**
Neffe, -n *m.* nephew **8B**
nehmen *v.* to take **2B**
nein no **1A**
nennen *v.* to call **5A**
nervös *adj.* nervous **3B**
nett *adj.* nice **3B**
neugierig *adj.* curious **3B**
neun nine **2A**
nicht *adv.* not **2B**
  nicht schlecht not bad **1A**
nichts *pron.* nothing **7B**
nie *adv.* never **4A**
niedrig *adj.* low **11A**
niemals *adv.* never **7B**
niemand *pron.* no one **7B**
niesen *v.* to sneeze **9B**
noch *adv.* yet; still; in addition **4A**
normalerweise *adv.* usually **9B**
Notaufnahme, -n *f.* emergency room **9B**
Note, -n *f.* grade (on an assignment) **1B**
Notfall, ¨e *m.* emergency **11B**
Notiz, -en *f.* note **1B**
November *m.* November **2A, 7A**
Nummernschild, -er *n.* license plate **8A**
nur *adv.* only **4A**
nützlich *adj.* useful **2A**
nutzlos *adj.* useless **2A**

O

ob *conj.* whether; if **10A**
Obst *n.* fruit **4A**
obwohl *conj.* even though **6A**; *conj.* although **10A**
oder *conj.* or **1B**
Ofen, ¨ *m.* oven **6B**
öffentlich *adj.* public **8A**
  öffentliche Verkehrsmittel *n.* public
    transportation **8A**
öffnen *v.* to open **2A**
oft *adv.* often **4A**
ohne *prep.* without **3B**
Ohr, -en *n.* ear **9A**
Ökologie *f.* ecology **12B**
ökologisch *adj.* ecological **12B**
Oktober *m.* October **2A, 7A**
Öl, -e *n.* oil **4A**
Olivenöl, -e *n.* olive oil **4A**
Oma, -s *f.* grandma **3A**
online sein *v.* to be online **8B**
Opa, -s *m.* grandpa **3A**
orange *adj.* orange **5B**
Orange, -n *f.* orange **4A**
ordentlich *adj.* neat, tidy **6B**
Ort, -e *m.* place **1B**
Österreich *n.* Austria **10B**
Österreicher, - / Österreicherin, -nen *m./f.*
  Austrian (person) **10B**

P

Paar, -e *n.* couple **3A**
packen *v.* to pack **7B**
Paket, -e *n.* package **10A**
Papa, -s *m.* dad **3A**
Papier, -e *n.* paper
    Blatt Papier (*pl.* Blätter Papier) *n.* sheet of paper **1B**
Papierkorb, ⁝e *m.* wastebasket **1B**
Paprika, - *f.* pepper **4A**
    grüne/rote Paprika *f.* green/red pepper **4A**
Park, -s *m.* park **1A**
parken *v.* to park **8A**
    Parkverbot. No parking. **3B**
Party, -s *f.* party **5A**
    eine Party geben *v.* to throw a party **5A**
Passagier, -e / Passagierin, -nen *m./f.* passenger **7B**
passen *v.* to fit; to match **5A**
passieren *v.* to happen **5B**
Passkontrolle, -n *f.* passport control **7B**
Passwort, ⁝er *n.* password **8B**
Pasta *f.* pasta **4A**
Patient, -en / Patientin, -nen *m./f.* patient **9B**
Pause, -n *f.* break, recess **1B**
Pension, -en *f.* guesthouse **7B**
Person, -en *f.* person **1A**
Personalausweis, -e *m.* ID card **7B**
Personalchef, -s / die Personalchefin, -nen *m./f.* human resources manager **11A**
persönlich *adj.* personal **3B**
Pfanne, -n *f.* pan **6B**
Pfeffer, - *m.* pepper **4B**
Pferd, -e *n.* horse **2B**
Pfirsich, -e *m.* peach **4A**
Pflanze, -n *f.* plant **6A**
Pfund, -e *n.* pound **4A**
Physik *f.* physics **2A**
Picknick, -s, *n.* picnic **12A**
    ein Picknick machen *v.* to have a picnic **12A**
Pilz, -e *m.* mushroom **4A**
Pinnwand, ⁝e *f.* bulletin board **11A**
Planet, -en *m.* planet **12B**
    den Planeten retten *v.* to save the planet **12B**
Platten, - *m.* flat tire **8A**
    einen Platten haben *v.* to have a flat tire **8A**
Platz, ⁝e *m.* court **1A**
plus plus **1B**
Politiker, - / Politikerin, -nen *m./f.* politician **11B**
Polizeiwache, -n *f.* police station **10A**
Polizist, -en / Polizistin, -nen *m./f.* police officer **8A**
Post *f.* post office; mail **10A**
    zur Post gehen *v.* to go to the post office **10A**
Poster, - *n.* poster **6A**
Postkarte, -n *f.* postcard **10A**
Praktikum (*pl.* die Praktika) *n.* internship **11A**
prima *adj.* great **1A**
probieren *v.* to try **3B**
    Probieren Sie mal! Give it a try!
Problem, -e *n.* problem **1A**
Professor, -en / Professorin, -nen *m./f.* professor **1B**
Programm, -e *n.* program **8B**

Prost! Cheers! **4B**
Prozent, -e *n.* percent **1B**
Prüfung, -en *f.* exam, test **1B**
Psychologe, -n / Psychologin, -nen *m./f.* psychologist **11B**
Psychologie *f.* psychology **2A**
Pullover, - *m.* sweater **5B**
Punkt, -e *m.* period **1B**
pünktlich *adj.* on time **7B**
putzen *v.* to clean **6B**
    sich die Zähne putzen *v.* to brush one's teeth **9A**

Q

Querverweis, -e *m.* cross-reference

R

Radiergummi, -s *m.* eraser **1B**
Rasen, - *m.* lawn, grass **3B**
    Betreten des Rasens verboten. Keep off the grass. **3B**
sich rasieren *v.* to shave **9A**
Rasierer, - *m.* razor **9A**
Rasierschaum, ⁝e *m.* shaving cream **9A**
Rathaus, ⁝er *n.* town hall **10A**
rauchen *v.* to smoke
    Rauchen verboten. No smoking. **3B**
rausbringen *v.* to bring out **6B**
    den Müll rausbringen *v.* to take out the trash **6B**
realistisch *adj.* realistic **10A**
Rechnung, -en *f.* check **4B**
Rechtsanwalt, ⁝e / Rechtsanwältin, -nen *m./f.* lawyer **3B**
Rechtschreibung *f.* spelling
recyceln *v.* to recycle **12B**
reden *v.* to talk **5A**
    reden über *v.* to talk about **7A**
Referat, -e *n.* presentation **2A**
Referenz, -en *f.* reference **11A**
Regen *m.* rain **7A**
Regenmantel, ⁝ *m.* raincoat **7A**
Regenschirm, -e *m.* umbrella **7A**
Regierung, -en *f.* government **12B**
regnen *v.* to rain **2A, 7A**
reich *adj.* rich **3B**
Reis *m.* rice **4A**
Reise, -n *f.* trip **7B**
Reisebüro, -s *n.* travel agency **7B**
reisen *v.* to travel **2A**
Reisende, -n *m./f.* traveler **7B**
Reiseziel, -e *n.* destination **7B**
reiten *v.* to ride **2B**
rennen *v.* to run **5A**
Rente, -n *f.* pension
    in Rente gehen *v.* to retire **5A**
Rentner, - / Rentnerin, -nen *m./f.* retiree **11B**
reparieren *v.* to repair **8A**
Restaurant, -s *n.* restaurant **4B**
retten *v.* to save **12B**
Rezept, -e *n.* recipe **4A**; prescription **9B**
Richter, - / Richterin, -nen *m./f.* judge **11B**
Richtung, -en *f.* direction **10B**
    in Richtung *f.* toward **10B**

Rindfleisch *n.* beef **4A**
Rock, ⁝e *m.* skirt **5B**
rosa *adj.* pink **5B**
rot *adj.* red **3A**
rothaarig *adj.* red-haired **3A**
Rücken, - *m.* back **9A**
Rückenschmerzen *m. pl.* backache **9B**
Rucksack, ⁝e *m.* backpack **1B**
ruhig *adj.* calm **3B**
Russe, -n / Russin, -nen *m./f.* Russian (person) **10B**
Russisch *n.* Russian (language) **10B**
Russland *n.* Russia **10B**

S

Sache, -n *f.* thing **1B**
Saft, ⁝e *m.* juice **4B**
sagen *v.* to say **2A**
Salat, -e *m.* lettuce; salad **4A**
Salz, -e *n.* salt **4B**
salzig *adj.* salty **4B**
Samstag, -e *m.* Saturday **2A**
    samstags *adv.* on Saturdays **2A**
sauber *adj.* clean **6B**
saurer Regen *m.* acid rain **12B**
Saustall *n.* pigsty **6B**
    Es ist ein Saustall! It's a pigsty! **6B**
Schach *n.* chess **2B**
Schaf, -e *n.* sheep **12A**
Schaffner, - / Schaffnerin, -nen *m./f.* ticket collector **8A**
Schal, -s *m.* scarf **5B**
scharf *adj.* spicy **4B**
schauen *v.* to look **7A**
Scheibenwischer, - *m.* windshield wiper **8A**
Scheinwerfer, - *m.* headlight **8A**
scheitern *v.* to fail **11B**
schenken *v.* to give (a gift) **5A**
schicken *v.* to send **8B**
Schiff, -e *n.* ship **8A**
Schinken, - *m.* ham **4A**
Schlafanzug, ⁝e *m.* pajamas **9A**
schlafen *v.* to sleep **2B**
Schlafzimmer, - *n.* bedroom **6A**
Schlange, -n *f.* line **7B**; *f.* snake **12A**
    Schlange stehen *v.* to stand in line **7B**
schlank *adj.* slim **3A**
schlecht *adj.* bad **3B**
    schlecht gekleidet *adj.* badly dressed **5B**
schließlich *adv.* finally **7B**
Schlüssel, - *m.* key **7B**
schmecken *v.* to taste **4B**
Schmerz, -en *m.* pain **9B**
sich schminken *v.* to put on makeup **9A**
schmutzig *adj.* dirty **6B**
Schnee *m.* snow **7A**
schneien *v.* to snow **7A**
schnell *adj.* fast **3B**
schon *adv.* already, yet **4A**
schön *adj.* pretty; beautiful **3A**
    Schön dich/Sie kennen zu lernen. Nice to meet you. **1A**
    Schönen Tag noch! Have a nice day! **1A**
    Es ist schön draußen. It's nice out. **7A**

Schrank, ⸚e *m.* cabinet; closet **6A**
schreiben *v.* to write **2A**
  schreiben an *v.* to write to **7A**
  sich schreiben *v.* to write one another **9A**
Schreibtisch, -e *m.* desk **1B**
Schreibwarengeschäft, -e *n.* paper-goods store **10A**
Schublade, -n *f.* drawer **6A**
schüchtern *adj.* shy **3B**
Schuh, -e *m.* shoe **5B**
Schulbuch, ⸚er *n.* textbook (K–12) **1B**
Schule, -n *f.* school **1B**
Schüler, - / Schülerin, -nen (K–12) *m./f.* student **1B**
Schulleiter, - / Schulleiterin, -nen *m./f.* principal **1B**
Schulter, -n *f.* shoulder **9A**
Schüssel, -n *f.* bowl **4B**
schützen *v.* to protect **12B**
schwach *adj.* weak **3B**
Schwager, ⸚ *m.* brother-in-law **3A**
Schwägerin, -nen *f.* sister-in-law **3A**
schwanger *adj.* pregnant **9B**
schwänzen *v.* to cut class **1B**
schwarz *adj.* black **5B**
schwarzhaarig *adj.* black-haired **3A**
Schweinefleisch *n.* pork **4A**
Schweiz (die) *f.* Switzerland **7A**
Schweizer, - / Schweizerin, -nen *m./f.* Swiss (person) **10B**
schwer *adj.* rich, heavy **4B**; *adj.* serious, difficult **9B**
Schwester, -n *f.* sister **1A**
Schwiegermutter, ⸚ *f.* mother-in-law **3A**
Schwiegervater, ⸚ *m.* father-in-law **3A**
schwierig *adj.* difficult **2A**
Schwimmbad, ⸚er *n.* swimming pool **2B**
schwimmen *v.* to swim **2B**
schwindlig *adj.* dizzy **9B**
sechs six **2A**
See, -n *m.* lake **12A**
sehen *v.* to see **2B**
sehr *adv.* very **3A**
Seide, -n *f.* silk **5B**
Seife, -n *f.* soap **9A**
sein *v.* to be **1A**
  (gleich) sein *v.* to equal **1B**
sein *poss. adj.* his, its **3A**
seit since; for **4B**
Sekt, -e *m.* champagne **5A**
selten *adv.* rarely **4A**
Seminar, -e *n.* seminar **2A**
Seminarraum, -räume *m.* seminar room **2A**
Sender, - *m.* TV channel **8B**
September *m.* September **2A, 7A**
Serviette, -n *f.* napkin **4B**
Sessel, - *m.* armchair **6A**
setzen *v.* to put, place **5B**; *v.* to put, set **9A**
Shampoo, -s *n.* shampoo **9A**
sicher *adv.* probably **10A**
Sicherheitsgurt, -e *m.* seatbelt **8A**
sie *pron.* she/they **1A**
Sie *pron.* (*form., sing./pl.*) you **1A**
sieben seven **2A**

Silvester *n.* New Year's Eve **5A**
singen *v.* to sing **2B**
sitzen *v.* to sit **5B**
Ski fahren *v.* to ski **2B**
Smartphone, -s *n.* smartphone **8B**
SMS, - *f.* text message **8B**
Snack, -s *m.* snack **4B**
so *adv.* so **4A**
Socke, -n *f.* sock **5B**
Sofa, -s *n.* sofa; couch **6A**
  Sofa surfen *v.* to couch surf **7B**
Sohn, ⸚e *m.* son **3A**
solcher/solche/solches *pron.* such **8B**
sollen *v.* to be supposed to **3B**
Sommer, - *m.* summer **2B, 7A**
sondern *conj.* but rather; instead **6A**
Sonne, -n *f.* sun **12A**
Sonnenaufgang, ⸚e *m.* sunrise **12A**
Sonnenbrand, ⸚e *m.* sunburn **9B**
Sonnenbrille, -n *f.* sunglasses **5B**
Sonnenenergie *f.* solar energy **12B**
Sonnenuntergang, ⸚e *m.* sunset **12A**
sonnig *adj.* sunny **7A**
Sonntag, -e *m.* Sunday **2A**
  sonntags *adv.* on Sundays **2A**
Sozialwissenschaft, -en, *f.* social sciences **2A**
Spanien *n.* Spain **10B**
Spanier, - / Spanierin, -nen *m./f.* Spanish (person) **10B**
Spanisch *n.* Spanish (language) **10B**
spannend *adj.* exciting **10A**
Spaß fun *m.* **2B**
  Spaß haben/machen *v.* to have fun/to be fun **2B**
  (keinen) Spaß haben *v.* to (not) have fun **5A**
spät *adj.* late
  Wie spät ist es? What time is it? **2A**
spazieren gehen *v.* to go for a walk **2B**
Spaziergang, ⸚e *m.* walk
speichern *v.* to save **8B**
Speisekarte, -n *f.* menu **4B**
Spiegel, - *m.* mirror **6A**
Spiel, -e *n.* match, game **2B**
spielen *v.* to play **2A**
Spieler, - / Spielerin, -nen *m./f.* player **2B**
Spielfeld, -er *n.* field **2B**
Spielkonsole, -n *f.* game console **8B**
Spitze! *adj.* great! **1A**
Sport *m.* sports **2B**
  Sport treiben *v.* to exercise **9B**
Sportart, -en *f.* sport; type of sport **2B**
Sporthalle, - n *f.* gym **2A**
sportlich *adj.* athletic **3A**
sprechen *v.* to speak **2B**
  sprechen über *v.* to speak about **7A**
Spritze, -n *f.* shot **9B**
  eine Spritze geben *v.* to give a shot **9B**
Spüle, -n *f.* (kitchen) sink **6B**
spülen *v.* to rinse **6B**
  Geschirr spülen *v.* to do the dishes **6B**
  Spülmaschine, -n *f.* dishwasher **6B**
Stadion (pl. Stadien) *n.* stadium **2B**
Stadt, ⸚e *f.* city **5B**; *f.* town **10B**
Stadtplan, ⸚e *m.* city map **7B**
Stahl *m.* steel **6B**

stark *adj.* strong **3B**
starten *v.* to start **8B**
statt *conj.* instead of
Statue, -n *f.* statue **10B**
staubsaugen *v.* to vacuum **6B**
Staubsauger, - *m.* vacuum cleaner **6B**
stehen *v.* to stand **5B**
  Schlange stehen *v.* to stand in line **7B**
stehlen *v.* to steal **2B**
steif *adj.* stiff **9B**
steigen *v.* to climb **5B**
Stein, -e *m.* rock **12A**
Stelle, -n *f.* place, position **10A**; job **11A**
  an deiner/Ihrer Stelle *f.* if I were you **10A**
  eine Stelle suchen *v.* to look for a job **11A**
stellen *v.* to put, place **5B**
Stellenangebot, -e *n.* job opening **11A**
sterben *v.* to die **5B**
Stereoanlage, -n *f.* stereo system **8B**
Stern -e *m.* star **12A**
Stiefel, - *m.* boot **5B**
Stiefmutter, ⸚ *f.* stepmother **3A**
Stiefsohn, ⸚e *m.* stepson **3A**
Stieftochter, ⸚ *f.* stepdaughter **3A**
Stiefvater, ⸚ *m.* stepfather **3A**
Stift, -e *m.* pen **1B**
Stil, -e *m.* style **5B**
still *adj.* still **4B**
  stilles Wasser *n.* still water **4B**
Stipendium, (pl. Stipendien) *n.* scholarship, grant **2A**
Stock, ⸚e *m.* floor **6A**
  erster/zweiter Stock first/second floor **6A**
stolz *adj.* proud **3B**
Stoppschild, -er *n.* stop sign **8A**
Strand, ⸚e *m.* beach **2B**
Straße, -n *f.* street **8A**
sich streiten *v.* to argue **9A**
Strom, ⸚e *m.* stream **12A**
Student, -en / Studentin, -nen *m./f.* (college/university) student **1A**
Studentenwohnheim, -e *n.* dormitory **2A**
studieren *v.* to study; major in **2A**
Studium (pl. Studien) *n.* studies **2A**
Stuhl, ⸚e *m.* chair **1A**
Stunde, -n *f.* lesson **1B**; hour **2A**
Stundenplan, ⸚e *m.* schedule **2A**
Sturm, ⸚e *m.* storm **7A**
suchen *v.* to look for **2A**
  eine Stelle suchen *v.* to look for a job **11A**
Supermarkt, ⸚e *m.* supermarket **4A**
Suppe, -n *f.* soup **4B**
surfen *v.* to surf **8B**
  im Internet surfen *v.* to surf the Web **8B**
süß *adj.* sweet, cute **3B, 4B**
Süßigkeit, -en *f.* candy **5A**
Sweatshirt, -s *n.* sweatshirt **5B**
Symptom, -e *n.* symptom **9B**

T

Tablet, -s *n.* tablet **8B**
Tablette, -n *f.* pill **9B**
Tafel, -n *f.* board, black board **1B**

Tag, -e *m.* day **1A, 7A**
  Welcher Tag ist heute? What day is it today? **7A**
täglich *adv.* every day; daily **4A**
Tal, ⁼er *n.* valley **12A**
tanken *v.* to fill up **8A**
Tankstelle, -n *f.* gas station **8A**
Tante, -n *f.* aunt **3A**
tanzen *v.* to dance **2B**
Taschenrechner, - *m.* calculator **1B**
Taschentuch, ⁼er *n.* tissue **9B**
Tasse, -n *f.* cup **4B**
Tastatur, -en *f.* keyboard **8B**
Taxi, -s *n.* taxi **8A**
Taxifahrer, - / Taxifahrerin, -nen *m./f.* taxi
  driver **11B**
Technik *f.* technology **8B**
  Technik bedienen *v.* to use technology **8B**
Tee, -s *m.* tea **4B**
Teelöffel, - *m.* teaspoon **4B**
Telefon, -e *n.* telephone **8B**
  am Telefon on the telephone **11A**
Telefonnummer, -n *f.* telephone number **11A**
Telefonzelle, -n *f.* phone booth **10B**
Teller, - *m.* plate **4B**
Tennis *n.* tennis **2B**
Teppich, -e *m.* rug **6A**
Termin, -e *m.* appointment **11A**
  einen Termin vereinbaren *v.* to make an
    appointment **11A**
teuer *adj.* expensive **5B**
Thermometer, - *n.* thermometer **9B**
Thunfisch, -e *m.* tuna **4A**
Tier, -e *n.* animal **12A**
Tierarzt, ⁼e / Tierärztin, -nen *m./f.*
  veterinarian **11B**
Tisch, -e *m.* table, desk **1B**
  den Tisch decken *v.* to set the table **6B**
Tischdecke, -n *f.* tablecloth **4B**
Toaster, - *m.* toaster **6B**
Tochter, ⁼ *f.* daughter **3A**
Toilette, -n *f.* toilet **6A**
Tomate, -n *f.* tomato **4A**
Topf, ⁼e *m.* pot **6B**
Tor, -e *n.* goal (in soccer, etc.) **2B**
Tornado, -s *m.* tornado **12A**
Torte, -n *f.* cake **5A**
Touristenklasse *f.* economy class **7B**
tragen *v.* to carry; wear **2B**
Trägerhemd, -en *n.* tank top **5B**
trainieren *v.* to practice (sports) **2B**
Traube, -n *f.* grape **4A**
träumen *v.* to dream **7A**
traurig *adj.* sad **3B**
treffen *v.* to meet; to hit **2B**
  sich treffen *v.* to meet (each other) **9A**
treiben *v.* to float; to push
  Sport treiben *v.* to exercise **9B**
Treibsand *m.* quicksand **12A**
sich trennen *v.* to separate, split up **9A**
Treppe, -n *f.* stairway **6A**
trinken *v.* to drink **3B**
Trinkgeld, -er *n.* tip **4B**
trocken *adj.* dry **12A**

trotz *prep.* despite, in spite of **8B**
Tschüss. Bye. **1A**
T-Shirt, -s *n.* T-shirt **5B**
tun *v.* to do **9B**
  Es tut mir leid. I'm sorry. **1A**
  weh tun *v.* to hurt **9B**
Tür, -en *f.* door **1B**
  Türen schließen. Keep doors closed. **3B**
Türkei (die) *f.* Turkey **10B**
Türke, -n / die Türkin, -nen *m./f.* Turkish
  (person) **10B**
Türkisch *n.* Turkish (language) **10B**
Turnschuhe *m. pl.* sneakers **5B**

U-Bahn, -en *f.* subway **8A**
übel *adj.* nauseous **9B**
über *prep.* over, above **5B**
übernachten *v.* to spend the night **7B**
überall *adv.* everywhere **4A**
Überbevölkerung *f.* overpopulation **12B**
überlegen *v.* to think over **4A**
übermorgen *adv.* the day after tomorrow **2B**
überqueren *v.* to cross **10B**
überraschen *v.* to surprise **5A**
Überraschung, -en *f.* surprise **5A**
überzeugend *adj.* persuasive **9B**
Übung, -en *f.* practice, exercise
Uhr, -en *f.* clock **1B**
  um... Uhr at... o'clock **2A**
  Wie viel Uhr ist es? *v.* What time is it? **2A**
um *prep.* around; at (time) **3B**
  um... zu in order to **7B**
Umleitung, -en *f.* detour **8A**
umtauschen *v.* to exchange **6B**
Umwelt, -en *f.* environment **12B**
umweltfreundlich *adj.* environmentally
  friendly **12B**
Umweltschutz *m.* environmentalism **12B**
umziehen *v.* to move **6A, 9A**
  sich umziehen *v.* to change clothes **9A**
unangenehm *adj.* unpleasant **3B**
und *conj.* and **1B**
Unfall, ⁼e *m.* accident **8A**
  einen Unfall haben *v.* to have an accident **8A**
Universität, -en *f.* university; college **1B**
unmöbliert *adj.* unfurnished **6A**
unser *poss. adj.* our **3A**
unter *prep.* under, below **5B**
untergehen *v.* to set (sun) **12A**
sich unterhalten *v.* to chat, have a
  conversation **9A**
Unterkunft, ⁼e *f.* accommodations **7B**
Unterricht, -e *m.* class **1B**
unterschreiben *v.* to sign **10A**
Unterwäsche *f.* underwear **5B**
Urgroßmutter, ⁼ *f.* great grandmother **3A**
Urgroßvater, ⁼ *m.* great grandfather **3A**
Urlaub, -e *m.* vacation **7B**
  Urlaub machen *v.* to go on vacation **7B**
  Urlaub nehmen *v.* to take time off **11B**
USA (die) *pl.* USA **10B**

Vase, -n *f.* vase **6A**
Vater, ⁼ *m.* father **3A**
Veranstaltung, -en *f.* class; course **2A**
Verb, -en *n.* verb **9A**
verbessern *v.* to improve **12B**
verbringen *v.* to spend **4A**
verdienen *v.* to earn **11B**
Vereinigten Staaten (die) *pl.* United States **10B**
Vergangenheit, -en *f.* past **12A**
vergessen *v.* to forget **2B**
verheiratet *adj.* married **3A**
verkaufen *v.* to sell **4A**
Verkäufer, - / Verkäuferin, -nen *m./f.*
  salesperson **5B**
Verkehr *m.* traffic **8A**
Verkehrsmittel *n.* transportation **8A**
  öffentliche Verkehrsmittel *n. pl.* public
    transportation **8A**
verkünden *v.* to announce **12B**
sich verlaufen *v.* to get lost **10B**
sich verletzen *v.* to hurt oneself **9B**
Verletzung, -en *f.* injury **9B**
sich verlieben (in) *v.* to fall in love (with) **9A**
verlieren *v.* to lose **2B**
verlobt *adj.* engaged **3A**
Verlobte, -n *m./f.* fiancé(e) **3A**
verschmutzen *v.* to pollute **12B**
Verschmutzung *f.* pollution **12B**
sich verspäten *v.* to be late **9A**
Verspätung, -en *f.* delay **7B**
Verständnis, -se *n.* comprehension
sich (das Handgelenk / den Fuß) verstauchen *v.* to
  sprain (one's wrist/ankle) **9B**
verstehen *v.* to understand **2A**
verstopfte Nase *f.* stuffy nose **9B**
versuchen *v.* to try **7B**
Vertrag, ⁼e *m.* contract **11A**
verwandt *adj.* related **10A**
Verwandte, -n *m.* relative **3A**
viel *adv.* much, a lot (of) **4A**
  Viel Glück! Good luck! **5A**
  Vielen Dank. Thank you very much. **1A**
vielleicht *adv.* maybe **4A**
vier four **2A**
Viertel, - *n.* quarter **2A**; neighborhood **10B**
  Viertel nach/vor quarter past/to **2A**
Visum(*pl.* Visa) *n.* visa **7B**
Vogel, ⁼ *m.* bird **3A**
voll *adj.* full **7B**
  voll besetzt *adj.* fully occupied **7B**
Volleyball *m.* volleyball **2B**
von *prep.* from **4B**
vor *prep.* in front of, before **5B**; *prep.* to **2A**
vorbei *adv.* over, past **7A**
vorbereiten *v.* to prepare **4A**
  sich vorbereiten (auf) *v.* to prepare oneself
    (for) **9A**
  Vorbereitung, -en *f.* preparation
Vorhang, ⁼e *m.* curtain **6A**
Vorlesung, -en *f.* lecture **2A**
vormachen *v.* to fool **8B**

Vormittag, -e *m.* midmorning **2B**
vormittags *adv.* before noon **2A**
Vorspeise, -n *f.* appetizer **4B**
vorstellen *v.* to introduce **9A**
  sich vorstellen *v.* to introduce oneself **9A**
  sich (etwas) vorstellen *v.* to imagine
    (something) **9A**
Vorstellungsgespräch, -e *n.* job interview **11A**
Vortrag, ⁻e *m.* lecture **6B**
Vulkan, -e *m.* volcano **12A**

W

wachsen *v.* to grow **5B**
während *prep.* during **8B**
wahrscheinlich *adv.* probably **10A**
Wald, ⁻er *m.* forest **2B**, **12A**
Wand, ⁻e *f.* wall **5B**
wandern *v.* to hike **2A**
wann *interr.* when **2A**
  Wann hast du Geburtstag? When is your
    birthday? **2B**
warm *adj.* warm **10A**
warten *v.* to wait (for) **2A**
  warten auf *v.* to wait for **7A**
  in der Warteschleife sein *v.* to be on hold **11B**
warum *interr.* why **2A**
was *interr.* what **2A**
  Was geht ab? What's up? **1A**
  Was ist das? What is that? **1B**
Wäsche *f.* laundry **6B**
waschen *v.* to wash **2B**
  sich waschen *v.* to wash (oneself) **9A**
  Wäsche waschen *v.* to do laundry **6B**
Wäschetrockner, - *m.* dryer **6B**
Waschmaschine, -n *f.* washing machine **6B**
Waschsalon, -s *m.* laundromat **10A**
Wasser *n.* water **4B**
Wasserfall, ⁻e *m.* waterfall **12A**
Wasserkrug, ⁻e *m.* water pitcher **4B**
Website, -s *f.* web site **8B**
Weg, -e *m.* path **12A**
wegen *prep.* because of **8B**
wegräumen *v.* to put away **6B**
wegwerfen *v.* to throw away **12B**
weh tun *v.* to hurt **9B**
Weihnachten, - *n.* Christmas **5A**
weil *conj.* because **10A**
Wein, -e *m.* wine **4B**
weinen *v.* to cry **3B**
weise *adj.* wise **3B**
weiß *adj.* white **5B**
weit *adj.* loose; big **5B**; *adj.* far **10B**
  weit von *adj.* far from **10B**
  weiter geht's moving forward
welcher/welche/welches *interr.* which **2A**
  Welcher Tag ist heute? What day is it today? **7A**
Welt, -en *f.* world **12B**
wem *interr.* whom (*dat.*) **4B**
wen *interr.* whom (*acc.*) **2A**

Wende, -n *f.* turning point **12B**
wenig *adj.* little; not much **10A**
wenn *conj.* when; whenever; if **10A**
  wenn... dann if… then **10A**
  wenn... nur if… only **10A**
wer *interr.* who **2A**
  Wer ist das? Who is it? **1B**
  Wer spricht? Who's calling? **11A**
werden *v.* to become **2B**
werfen *v.* to throw **2B**
Werkzeug, -e *n.* tool kit
wessen *interr.* whose **8B**
Wetter *n.* weather **7A**
  Wie ist das Wetter? What's the weather like? **7A**
Wetterbericht, -e *m.* weather report **7A**
wichtig *adj.* important **7B**
wie *interr.* how **2A**
  wie viel? *interr.* how much? **1B**
  wie viele? *interr.* how many? **1B**
  Wie alt bist du? How old are you? **1B**
  Wie heißt du? (*inf.*) What's your name? **1A**
wiederholen *v.* to repeat **2A**
Wiederholung, -en *f.* repetition; revision
wiegen *v.* to weigh **8B**
willkommen welcome **1A**
  Herzlich willkommen! Welcome! **1A**
Windenergie *f.* wind energy **12B**
windig *adj.* windy **7A**
Windschutzscheibe, -n *f.* windshield **8A**
Winter, - *m.* winter **2B**, **7A**
wir *pron.* we **1A**
wirklich *adv.* really **4A**
Wirtschaft, -en *f.* business; economy **2A**
wischen *v.* to wipe, mop **6B**
wissen *v.* to know (information) **5B**
Wissenschaftler, - / Wissenschaftlerin, -nen *m./f.*
  scientist **11B**
Witwe, -n *f.* widow **3A**
Witwer, - *m.* widower **3A**
wo *interr.* where **2A**
woanders *adv.* somewhere else **4A**
Woche, -n *f.* week **2A**
Wochenende, -n *n.* weekend **2A**
woher *interr.* from where **2A**; **6A**
wohin *interr.* where to **2A**
wohl *adv.* probably **10A**
wohnen *v.* to live (somewhere) **2A**
Wohnheim, -e *n.* dorm **6A**
Wohnung, -en *f.* apartment **6A**
Wohnzimmer, - *n.* living room **6A**
Wolke, -n *f.* cloud **7A**
wolkig *adj.* cloudy **7A**
Wolle *f.* wool **5B**
wollen *v.* to want **3B**
Wörterbuch, ⁻er *n.* dictionary **1B**
Wortschatz, ⁻e *m.* vocabulary
wünschen *v.* to wish **9A**
  sich (etwas) wünschen *v.* to wish (for
    something) **9A**
Würstchen, - *n.* sausage **4A**

Z

Zahn, ⁻e *m.* tooth **9A**
  sich die Zähne putzen *m.* to brush one's teeth **9A**
Zahnarzt, ⁻e / Zahnärztin, -nen *m./f.* dentist **9B**
Zahnbürste, -n *f.* toothbrush **9A**
Zahnpasta (*pl.* **Zahnpasten)** *f.* toothpaste **9A**
Zahnschmerzen *m. pl.* toothache **9B**
Zapping *n.* channel surfing
Zebrastreifen, - *m.* crosswalk **10B**
Zeh, -en *m.* toe **9A**
zehn ten **2A**
zeigen *v.* to show **4B**
Zeit, -en *f.* time **2A**
Zeitschrift, -en *f.* magazine **10A**
Zeitung, -en *f.* newspaper **7B, 10A**
Zelt, -e *n.* tent **7B**
Zeltplatz, ⁻e *m.* camping area **7B**
Zeugnis, -se *n.* report card, grade report **1B**
ziehen *v.* to pull **3B**
ziemlich *adv.* quite **4A**
  ziemlich gut pretty well **1A**
Zimmer, - *n.* room **5A**
  Zimmer frei vacancy **6A**
Zimmerservice *m.* room service **7B**
Zoll, ⁻e *m.* customs **7B**
zu *adv.* too **4A**; *prep.* to; for; at **4B**
  bis zu *prep.* until **10B**
  um... zu (in order) to **7B**
  Zum Wohl! Cheers! **4B**
zubereiten *v.* to prepare **7A**
zuerst *adv.* first **7B**
Zug, ⁻e *m.* train **8A**
zumachen *v.* to close **8B**
sich zurechtfinden *v.* to find one's way **10B**
zurückkommen *v.* to come back **4A**
zusammen *adv.* together **3A**
zuschauen *v.* to watch **4A**
Zutat, -en *m.* ingredient **4A**
zuverlässig *adj.* reliable **11B**
zwanzig twenty **2A**
zwei two **2A**
zweite *adj.* second **2A**
Zwiebel, -n *f.* onion **4A**
Zwilling, -e *m.* twin **3A**
zwischen *prep.* between **5B**
zwölf twelve **2A**

Englisch-Deutsch

A

a ein/eine **1A**
able: to be able to können *v.* **3B**
about über *prep.* **5B**
 to be about handeln von *v.* **7A**
above über *prep.* **5B**
abroad Ausland *n.* **7B**
accident Unfall, ⁻e *m.* **8A**
 to have an accident einen Unfall haben *v.* **8A**
accommodation Unterkunft, ⁻e *f.* **7B**
according to nach *prep.* **4B**
accountant Buchhalter, - / Buchhalterin, -nen *m./f.* **11B**
acid rain saurer Regen *m.* **12B**
across (from) gegenüber (von) *prep.* **10B**
address Adresse, -n *f.* **10A**
adopt adoptieren *v.* **3A**
afraid: to be afraid of Angst haben vor *v.* **7A**
after nach *prep.* **4B**; nachdem *conj.* **10A**
afternoon Nachmittag, -e *m.* **2B**
 in the afternoon nachmittags *adv.* **2A**
against gegen *prep.* **3B**
air Luft, ⁻e *f.* **12A**
airplane Flugzeug, -e *n.* **7B**
airport Flughafen, ⁻ *m.* **7B**
all ganz *adj.* **7B**; alle *pron.* **7B**
allergic (to) allergisch (gegen) *adj.* **9B**
allergy Allergie, -n *f.* **9B**
allow lassen *v.* **2B**
 to be allowed to dürfen *v.* **3B**
almost fast *adv.* **4A**
alone allein *adv.* **4A**
along entlang *prep.* **3B**
already schon **4A**
alright: Are you alright? Alles klar? **1A**
also auch *adv.* **4A**
although obwohl *conj.* **10A**
always immer *adv.* **4A**
ambulance Krankenwagen, - *m.* **9B**
America Amerika *n.* **10B**
American amerikanisch *adj.* **10B**; **(person)** Amerikaner, - / Amerikanerin, -nen *m./f.* **10B**
 American football American Football *m.* **2B**
and und *conj.* **1B**
animal Tier, -e *n.* **12A**
angry böse *adj.*
 to get angry (about) sich ärgern (über) *v.* **9A**
anniversary Jahrestag, -e *m.* **5A**
announce verkünden *v.* **12B**
answer antworten *v.* **2A**; beantworten *v.* **4A**; Antwort, -en *f.*
 to answer the phone einen Anruf entgegennehmen *v.* **11A**
anything: Anything else? Noch einen Wunsch? **4B**; Sonst noch etwas? **4A**
apartment Wohnung, -en *f.* **6A**
app App, -s *f.* **8B**
appetizer Vorspeise, -n *f.* **4B**
apple Apfel, ⁻ *m.* **1A**
applicant Bewerber, - / Bewerberin, -nen *m./f.* **11A**

apply sich bewerben *v.* **11A**
appointment Termin, -e *m.* **11A**
April April *m.* **2A**
architect Architekt, -en / Architektin, -nen *m./f.* **3B**
architecture Architektur, -en *f.* **2A**
argue sich streiten *v.* **9A**
arm Arm, -e *m.* **9A**
armchair Sessel, - *m.* **6A**
around um *prep.* **3B**
arrival Ankunft, ⁻e *f.* **7B**
arrive ankommen *v.* **4A**
arrogant eingebildet *adj.* **3B**
art Kunst, ⁻e *f.* **2A**
artichoke Artischocke, -n *f.* **4A**
as als *conj.* **8A**
 as if als ob **10A**
ask fragen *v.* **2A**
 to ask about fragen nach *v.* **7A**
assistant Assistent, -en / Assistentin, -nen *m./f.* **11A**
at um *prep.* **3B**; bei *prep.* **4B**; an *prep.* **5B**
 at...o'clock um...Uhr **2A**
athletic sportlich *adj.* **2B**
ATM Geldautomat, -en *m.* **10A**
Attention! Achtung!
attic Dachboden, ⁻ *m.* **6A**
August August *m.* **2A**
aunt Tante, -n *f.* **3A**
Austria Österreich *n.* **10B**
Austrian österreichisch *adj.* **10B**; **(person)** Österreicher, - / Österreicherin, -nen *m./f.* **10B**
autumn Herbst, -e *m.* **2B**
avenue Allee, -n *f.* **10B**
awful furchtbar *adj.* **7A**

B

baby Baby, -s *n.* **3A**
back Rücken, - *m.* **9A**
backache Rückenschmerzen *m. pl.* **9B**
backpack Rucksack, ⁻e *m.* **1B**
bad schlecht *adj.* **3B**
 badly dressed schlecht gekleidet *adj.* **5B**
baked goods Gebäck *n.* **5A**
bakery Bäckerei, -en *f.* **4A**
balcony Balkon, - e *m.* **6A**
ball Ball, ⁻e *m.* **2B**
balloon Ballon, -e *m.* **5A**
ball-point pen Kuli, -s *m.* **1B**
banana Banane, -n *f.* **4A**
bank Bank, -en *f.* **10A**
 at the bank auf der Bank *f.* **10B**
bank account Konto (*pl.* Konten) *n.* **10A**
bank employee Bankangestellte, -n *m./f.* **11B**
baseball Baseball *m.* **2B**
basketball Basketball *m.* **2B**
bath: to take a bath sich baden *v.* **9A**
bathing suit Badeanzug, ⁻e *m.* **5B**
bathrobe Bademantel, ⁻ *m.* **9A**
bathroom Badezimmer, - *n.* **9A**
bathtub Badewanne, -n *f.* **6A**
battery charger Ladegerät, -e *n.* **8B**

be sein *v.* **1A**
 Is/Are there... Ist/Sind hier...? *v.* **1B**; Gibt es...? **2B**
 There is/are... Da ist/sind... *v.* **1A**; Es gibt... **2B**
beach Strand, ⁻e *m.* **2B**
bean Bohne, -n *f.* **4A**
beard Bart, ⁻e *m.* **9A**
beautiful schön *adj.* **3A**
beauty salon Kosmetiksalon, -s *m.* **10A**
because denn *conj.* **6A**; weil *conj.* **10A**
 because of wegen *prep.* **8B**
become werden *v.* **2B**
bed Bett, -en *n.* **6A**
 to go to bed ins Bett gehen *v.* **9A**
 to make the bed das Bett machen *v.* **6B**
bedroom Schlafzimmer, - *n.* **6A**
beef Rindfleisch *n.* **4A**
beer Bier, -e *n.* **4B**
before vor *prep.* **5B**; bevor *conj.* **8A**
 before noon vormittags *adv.* **2A**
begin anfangen *v.* **4A**; beginnen *v.* **6A**
behind hinter *prep.* **5B**
believe glauben *v.* **5A**; meinen *v.* **12B**
belly Bauch, ⁻e *m.* **9A**
belong gehören *v.* **4B**
below unter *prep.* **5B**
belt Gürtel, - *m.* **5B**
bench Bank, ⁻e *f.* **10B**
best beste/bester/bestes *adj.* **8A**
 All the best! Mach's gut! *v.* **3B**; alles Gute **10A**
better besser *adj.* **8A**
 to get better gesund werden *v.* **9B**
between zwischen *prep.* **5B**
beverage Getränk, -e *n.* **4B**
bicycle Fahrrad, ⁻er *n.* **2B**
big groß, weit *adj.* **3A**
bill (money) Geldschein, -e *m.* **10A**
biology Biologie *f.* **2A**
bird Vogel, ⁻ *m.* **3A**
birth Geburt, -en *f.* **5A**
birthday Geburtstag, -e *m.* **5A**
 When is your birthday? Wann hast du Geburtstag? **2B**
black schwarz *adj.* **5B**
 black board Tafel, -n *f.* **1B**
 black-haired schwarzhaarig *adj.* **3A**
bland fade *adj.* **4B**
blanket Decke, -n *f.* **6B**
blog Blog, -s *n.* **8B**
blond blond *adj.*
 blond hair blonde Haare *n. pl.* **3A**
blood pressure Blutdruck *m.* **9B**
blouse Bluse, -n *f.* **5B**
blue blau *adj.* **3A**
board Tafel, -n *f.* **1B**
boarding pass Bordkarte, -n *f.* **7B**
boat Boot, -e *n.* **8A**
body Körper, - *m.* **9A**
book Buch, ⁻er *n.* **1A**
bookshelf Bücherregal, -e *n.* **6A**
boot Stiefel, - *m.* **5B**
boring langweilig *adj.* **2A**
boss Chef, -s / Chefin, -nen *m./f.* **11B**

bottle Flasche, -n *f.* **4B**
bowl Schüssel, -n *f.* **4B**
boy Junge, -n *m.* **1A**
brakes Bremse, -n *f.* **8A**
brave mutig *adj.* **3B**
bread Brot, -e *n.* **4A**
break brechen *v.* **2B**
  to break (an arm / a leg) sich (den Arm/Bein) brechen *v.* **9B**
  Break a leg! Hals- und Beinbruch! **5A**
breakfast Frühstück, -e *n.* **4B**
bridge Brücke, -n *f.* **10B**
bright hell *adj.* **5B**
bring bringen *v.* **2A**
  to bring along mitbringen *v.* **4A**
  to bring out rausbringen **6B**
  to bring with mitnehmen *v.* **10B**
broom Besen, - *m.* **6B**
brother Bruder, ⸚ *m.* **1A**
brother-in-law Schwager, ⸚ *m.* **3A**
brown braun *adj.* **5B**
  brown-haired braunhaarig *adj.* **3A**
bruise blauer Fleck, -e *m.* **9B**
brush Bürste, -n *f.* **9A**
  to brush one's hair sich die Haare bürsten *v.* **9A**
  to brush one's teeth sich die Zähne putzen *v.* **9A**
build bauen *v.* **2A**
building Gebäude, - *n.* **10A**
bulletin board Pinnwand, ⸚e *f.* **11A**
burn brennen *v.* **5A**
bus Bus, -se *m.* **8A**
bus stop Bushaltestelle, -n *f.* **8A**
bush Busch, ⸚e *m.* **12A**
business Wirtschaft, -en *f.* **2A**; Geschäft, -e *n.* **11A**
  business class Businessklasse *f.* **7B**
businessman / businesswoman Geschäftsmann, -⸚er / Geschäftsfrau, -en *m./f.* (*pl.* Geschäftsleute) **3B**
but aber *conj.* **1B**
  but rather sondern *conj.* **6A**
butcher shop Metzgerei, -en *f.* **4A**
butter Butter *f.* **4A**
buy kaufen *v.* **2A**
by an *prep.* **5B**; bei; von **4B**
Bye! Tschüss! **1A**

<h2 style="text-align:center">C</h2>

cabinet Schrank, ⸚e *m.* **6A**
café Café, -s *n.* **2A**
cafeteria Cafeteria, (*pl.* Cafeterien) *f.*; (**college/ university**) Mensa, Mensen *f.* **1B**
cake Kuchen, - *m.* **4A**; Torte, -n *f.* **5A**
calculator Taschenrechner, - *m.* **1B**
calendar Kalender, - *m.* **1B**
call anrufen *v.* **4A**; sich anrufen **9A**; nennen *v.* **5A**
  Who's calling? Wer spricht? **11A**
calm ruhig *adj.* **3B**
(to go) camping campen gehen *n.* **2B**
camping area Zeltplatz, ⸚e *m.* **7B**
can können *v.* **3B**
Canada Kanada *n.* **10B**

Canadian kanadisch *adj.* **10B**; (**person**) Kanadier, - / Kanadierin, -nen *m./f.* **10B**
cancel abbrechen *v.* **7B**
candidate Kandidat, -en *m.* **11A**
candy Süßigkeit, -en *f.* **5A**
cap Mütze, -n *f.* **5B**
car Auto, -s *n.* **1A**
  to drive a car Auto fahren *v.* **8A**
card Karte, -n *f.* **2B**
career Karriere, -n *f.* **11B**
caretaker Hausmeister, - / Hausmeisterin, -nen *m./f.* **11B**
carpool Fahrgemeinschaft, -en *f.* **12B**
carrot Karotte, -n *f.* **4A**
carry tragen *v.* **2B**
carry-on luggage Handgepäck *n.* **7B**
cash bar *adj.* **10A**; Bargeld *n.* **10A**
  to pay in cash bar bezahlen *v.* **10A**
cat Katze, -n *f.* **3A**
catch fangen *v.* **2B**
  to catch a cold sich erkälten *v.* **9A**
celebrate feiern *v.* **5A**
celebration Fest, -e *n.* **5A**
cell phone Handy, -s *n.* **8B**
cellar Keller, - *m.* **6A**
ceramic Keramik, -en *f.* **6B**
chair Stuhl, ⸚e *m.* **1A**
champagne Sekt, -e *m.* **5A**
championship Meisterschaft, -en *f.* **2B**
change Kleingeld *n.* **10A**
  to change clothes sich umziehen *v.* **9A**
channel (**TV**) Sender, - *m.* **8B**
  channel surfing Zapping *n.*
charge (a battery) aufladen *v.* **8B**
chat sich unterhalten *v.* **9A**
  chat Chat, -s *m.* **8B**
cheap günstig *adj.* **5B**
check Rechnung, -en *f.* **4B**
Cheers! Prost! **4B**; Zum Wohl! **4B**
cheese Käse, - *m.* **4A**
chemistry Chemie *f.* **2A**
chess Schach *n.* **2B**
chicken Huhn, -⸚er *n.* **12A**; (**food**) Hähnchen, - *n.* **4A**
child Kind, -er *n.* **1A**
China China *n.* **10B**
Chinese (**person**) Chinese, -n / Chinesin, -nen *m./f.* **10B**; (**language**) Chinesisch *n.* **10B**
Christmas Weihnachten, - *n.* **5A**
church Kirche, -n *f.* **10B**
city Stadt, ⸚e *f.* **5B**
  city center Innenstadt, ⸚e *f.* **10B**
claim behaupten *v.* **12B**
class Klasse, -n *f.* **1B**; Unterricht *m.* **1B**; Veranstaltung, -en *f.* **2A**
  first/second class erste/zweite Klasse **8A**
classical klassisch *adj.* **10A**
classmate Kommilitone, -n / Kommilitonin, -nen; Klassenkamerad, -en / Klassenkameradin, -nen *m./f.* **1B**
classroom Klassenzimmer, - *n.* **1B**
clean sauber *adj.* **6B**; putzen *v.* **6B**
  to clean up aufräumen *v.* **6B**
cliff Klippe, -n *f.* **12A**

climb steigen *v.* **5B**
  to climb (mountain) klettern *v.* **2B**
  to climb (stairs) (die Treppe) hochgehen *v.* **10B**
clock Uhr, -en *f.* **1B**
  at... o'clock um... Uhr **2A**
close zumachen *v.* **8B**; nah *adj.* **10B**
  close to in der Nähe von *prep.* **10B**
closed geschlossen *adj.* **10A**
closet Schrank, ⸚e *m.* **6A**
clothes Kleidung *f.* **5B**
cloud Wolke, -n *f.* **7A**
cloudy wolkig *adj.* **7A**
coast Küste, -n *f.* **12A**
coat Mantel, ⸚ *m.* **5B**
coffee Kaffee, -s *m.* **4B**
coffeemaker Kaffeemaschine, -n *f.* **6B**
coin Münze, -n *f.* **10A**
cold kalt *adj.* **7A**; Erkältung, -en *f.* **9B**
  to catch a cold sich erkälten *v.* **9A**
college Universität, -en *f.* **1B**
college instructor Dozent, -en / Dozentin, -nen *m./f.* **2A**
color Farbe, -n *f.* **5B**
  solid colored einfarbig *adj.* **5B**
colorful bunt *adj.* **10A**
comb Kamm, ⸚e *m.* **9A**
  to comb (one's hair) sich (die Haare) kämmen *v.* **9A**
come kommen *v.* **2A**
  to come along mitkommen *v.* **4A**
  to come back zurückkommen *v.* **4A**
comma Komma, -s *f.* **1B**
compact disc CD, -s *f.* **8B**
company Firma (*pl.* die Firmen) *f.* **11A**
complicated kompliziert *adj.* **10A**
computer Computer, - *m.* **1B**
computer science Informatik *f.* **2A**
concert Konzert, -e *n.* **5B**
congratulate gratulieren *v.* **5A**
  Congratulations! Herzlichen Glückwunsch! **5A**
construction zone Baustelle, -n *f.* **8A**
contract Vertrag, ⸚e *m.* **11A**
conversation: to have a conversation sich unterhalten *v.* **9A**
cook kochen *v.* **2B**; Koch, ⸚e / Köchin, -nen *m./f.* **4B**
cookie Keks, -e *m.* **5A**
cool kühl *adj.* **7A**
corner Ecke, -n *f.* **10B**
correct korrigieren *v.* **2A**
cost kosten *v.* **2A**
cotton Baumwolle *f.* **5B**
couch Sofa, -s *n.* **7B**
  to couch surf Sofa surfen *v.* **7B**
cough husten *v.* **9B**
country Land, ⸚er *n.* **7B**
countryside Landschaft, -en *f.* **12A**
couple Paar, -e *n.* **3A**
courageous mutig *adj.*
course Veranstaltung, -en *f.* **2B**; Gang, -⸚e *m.* **4B**
  first/second course erster/zweiter Gang *m.* **4B**
  main course Hauptspeise, -en *f.* **4B**

court Platz, ⁓e *m.* **1A**
cousin Cousin, -s / Cousine, -n *m./f.* **3A**
cover decken *v.* **6B**
cow Kuh, ⁓e *f.* **12A**
cram (for a test) büffeln *v.* **2A**
cross überqueren *v.* **10B**
   to cross the street die Straße überqueren *v.* **10B**
cross-reference Querverweis, -e *m.*
crosswalk Zebrastreifen, - *pl.* **10B**
cruel grausam *adj.*; gemein *adj.* **3B**
cruise Kreuzfahrt, -en *f.* **7B**
cry weinen *v.* **3B**
cup Tasse, -n *f.* **4B**
curious neugierig *adj.* **3B**
curly lockig *adj.* **3A**
curtain Vorhang, ⁓e *m.* **6A**
custodian Hausmeister, - / Hausmeisterin,
   -nen *m./f.* **11B**
customer Kunde, -n /Kundin, -nen *m./f.* **5B**
customs Zoll *m.* **7B**
cut Schnitt, -e *m.* **5B**
   to cut class schwänzen *v.* **1B**
cute süß *adj.* **3B**
CV Lebenslauf, ⁓e *m.* **11A**

D

dad Papa, -s *m.* **3A**
daily täglich *adv.* **4A**
   daily routine Alltagsroutine *f.* **9A**
dance tanzen *v.* **2B**
danger Gefahr, -en *f.* **12B**
dark dunkel *adj.* **3A**
   dark-haired dunkelhaarig *adj.* **3A**
darling Liebling, -e *m.*
date Datum (*pl.* Daten) *n.* **7A**
   What is the date today? Der wievielte ist
   heute? **2A**
daughter Tochter, ⁓ *f.* **3A**
day Tag, -e *m.* **1A**
   every day täglich *adv.* **4A**
Dear Lieber/Liebe *m./f.* **3B**
December Dezember *m.* **2A**
decide sich entschließen *v.* **4B**
definitely bestimmt *adv.* **4A**
degree Abschluss, ⁓e *m.* **2A**; Grad *n.* **7A**
   It's 18 degrees out. Es sind 18 Grad draußen. **7A**
delay Verspätung, -en *f.* **7B**
delete löschen *v.* **8B**
delicatessen Feinkostgeschäft, -e *n.* **4A**
delicious lecker *adj.* **4B**
demanding anspruchsvoll *adj.* **11B**
dentist Zahnarzt, ⁓e / Zahnärztin, -nen *m./f.* **9B**
department store Kaufhaus, ⁓er *n.* **10B**
departure Abflug, ⁓e *m.* **7B**
deposit (money) (Geld) einzahlen *v.* **10A**
describe beschreiben *v.* **2A**
description Beschreibung, -en *f.* **3B**
desk Schreibtisch, -e *m.* **1B**
despite trotz *prep.* **8B**
dessert Nachtisch, -e, *m.* **4B**
destination Reiseziel, -e *n.* **7B**
detour Umleitung, -en *f.* **8A**
develop entwickeln *v.* **12B**

dictionary Wörterbuch, ⁓er *n.* **1B**
die sterben *v.* **5B**
diet Diät, -en *f.* **4B**
   to be on a diet auf Diät sein *v.* **4B**
difficult schwierig *adj.* **2A**
digital camera Digitalkamera, -s *f.* **8B**
dining room Esszimmer, - *n.* **6A**
dinner Abendessen, - *n.* **4B**
diploma Abschlusszeugnis, -se *n.* **2A**; Diplom,
   -e *n.* **2A**
direction Richtung, -en *f.* **10B**
dirty schmutzig *adj.* **6B**
discover entdecken *v.* **6B**
discreet diskret *adj.* **3B**
discuss besprechen *v.* **4A**
dish Gericht, -e *n.* **4B**
dishes Geschirr *n.* **6B**
   to do the dishes Geschirr spülen **6B**
dishwasher Spülmaschine, -n *f.* **6B**
dislike nicht gern (+*verb*) **3A**
divided by geteilt durch **1B**
divorced geschieden *adj.* **3A**
dizzy schwindlig *adj.* **9B**
do machen *v.* **2A**; tun *v.* **9B**
   to do laundry Wäsche waschen *v.* **6B**
   to do the dishes Geschirr spülen *v.* **6B**
   to have to do with handeln von **7A**
doctor Arzt, ⁓e / Ärztin, -nen *m./f.* **9B**
   to go to the doctor zum Arzt gehen *v.* **9B**
document Dokument, -e *n.* **8B**
dog Hund, -e *m.* **3A**
door Tür, -en *f.* **1B**
dormitory (Studenten)wohnheim, -e *n.* **6A**
down entlang *prep.* **3B**; herunter *adv.* **6A**
   to go down heruntergehen *v.* **10B**
download herunterladen *v.* **8B**
downtown Innenstadt, ⁓e *f.* **10B**
dozen Dutzend, -e *n.* **4A**
   a dozen eggs ein Dutzend Eier **4A**
drawer Schublade, -n *f.* **6A**
dream träumen *v.* **7A**
dress Kleid, -er *n.* **5B**
   to get dressed sich anziehen *v.* **9A**
   to get undressed sich ausziehen *v.* **9A**
dresser Kommode, -n *f.* **6A**
drink trinken *v.* **3B**
drive fahren *v.* **8A**
   to drive a car Auto fahren *v.* **8A**
driver Fahrer, - / Fahrerin, -nen *m./f.* **8A**
drugstore Drogerie, -n *f.* **10A**
dry trocken *adj.* **12A**
   to dry oneself off sich abtrocknen *v.* **9A**
dryer Wäschetrockner, - *m.* **6B**
dumb dumm **8A**
during während *prep.* **8B**
dust abstauben *v.* **6B**
duvet Bettdecke, - n *f.* **6B**
dye (one's hair) sich (die Haare) färben *v.* **9A**

E

ear Ohr, -en *n.* **9A**
early früh *adj.* **2B**
earn verdienen *v.* **11B**

earth Erde, -n *f.* **12B**
earthquake Erdbeben, - *n.* **12A**
easy einfach *adj.* **2A**
eat essen *v.* **2B**
   to eat out essen gehen *v.* **2B**
ecological ökologisch *adj.* **12B**
ecology Ökologie *f.* **12B**
economy Wirtschaft, -en *f.* **2A**
   economy class Touristenklasse *f.* **7B**
education Ausbildung, -en *f.* **11A**
egg Ei, -er *n.* **4A**
eggplant Aubergine, -n *f.* **4A**
eight acht **2A**
elbow Ell(en)bogen, - *m.* **9A**
electrician Elektriker, - / Elektrikerin,
   -nen *m./f.* **11B**
elegant elegant *adj.* **5B**
elevator Fahrstuhl, ⁓e *m.* **7B**
eleven elf **2A**
e-mail E-Mail, -s *f.* **8B**
emergency Notfall, ⁓e *m.* **11B**
emergency room Notaufnahme, -n *f.* **9B**
employee Angestellte, -n *m./f.* **11A**
endangered gefährdet *adj.* **12B**
energy Energie, -n *f.* **12B**
energy-efficient energiesparend *adj.* **6B**
engaged verlobt *adj.* **3A**
engine Motor, -en *m.* **8A**
engineer Ingenieur, -e / Ingenieurin, -nen
   m./f. **3B**
England England *n.* **10B**
English (person) Engländer, - / Engländerin,
   -nen *m./f.* **10B**; **(language)** Englisch *n.* **10B**
enjoy genießen *v.*
   Enjoy your meal! Guten Appetit! **4B**
envelope Briefumschlag, ⁓e *m.* **10A**
environment Umwelt, -en *f.* **12B**
   environmentally friendly umweltfreundlich
   adj. **8B**
environmentalism Umweltschutz *m.* **12B**
equal (gleich) sein *v.* **1B**
eraser Radiergummi, -s *m.* **1B**
errand Besorgung, -en *f.* **10A**
   to run errands Besorgungen machen *v.* **10A**
even though obwohl *conj.* **6A**
evening Abend, -e *m.* **2B**
   in the evening abends *adv.* **2A**
every jeder/jede/jedes *adv.* **8B**
everything alles *pron.* **7B**
   Everything OK? Alles klar? **1A**
everywhere überall *adv.* **4A**
exam Prüfung, -en *f.* **1B**
except (for) außer *prep.* **4B**
exchange umtauschen *v.* **6B**
exciting spannend *adj.* **10A**; aufregend *adj.* **12A**
Excuse me. Entschuldigung. **1A**
exercise Sport treiben *v.* **9B**
exit Ausgang, ⁓e *m.* **7B**; Ausfahrt, -en *f.* **8A**
expensive teuer *adj.* **5B**
experience durchmachen *v.* **8B**; Erfahrung,
   -en *f.* **11A**
explain erklären *v.* **4A**
explore erforschen *v.* **12A**
expression Ausdruck, ⁓e *m.*

extinction Aussterben *n.* **12B**
eye Auge, -n *n.* **3A**
eyebrow Augenbraue, -n *f.* **9A**

F

face Gesicht, -er *n.* **9A**
factory Fabrik, -en *f.* **12B**
factory worker Fabrikarbeiter, - / Fabrikarbeiterin,
 -nen *m./f.* **11B**
fail durchfallen *v.* **1B**; scheitern *v.* **11B**
fall fallen *v.* **2B**; (season) Herbst, -e *m.* **2B**
 to fall in love (with) sich verlieben (in) *v.* **9A**
familiar bekannt *adj.*
 to be familiar with kennen *v.* **5B**
family Familie, -n *f.* **3A**
fan Fan, -s *m.* **2B**
fantastic fantastisch *adj.* **10A**
far weit *adj.* **10B**
 far from weit von *adj.* **10B**
farm Bauernhof, ¨e *m.* **12A**
farmer Bauer, -n / Bäuerin, -nen *m./f.* **11B**
fashionable modisch *adj.* **5B**
fast schnell *adj.* **3B**
fat dick *adj.* **3A**
father Vater, ¨ *m.* **3A**
father-in-law Schwiegervater, ¨ *m.* **3A**
favorite Lieblings- **4B**
fear Angst, ¨e *f.* **7A**
February Februar *m.* **2A**
feel fühlen *v.* **2A**; sich fühlen *v.* **9A**
 to feel like Lust haben *v.* **7B**
 to feel well sich wohl fühlen *v.* **9A**
fever Fieber, - *n.* **9B**
 to have a fever Fieber haben *v.* **9B**
fiancé(e) Verlobte, -n *m./f.* **3A**
field Spielfeld, -er *n.* **2B**; Feld, -er *n.* **12A**
file Datei, -en *f.* **8B**
fill füllen *v.*
 to fill out ausfüllen *v.* **10A**
 to fill up tanken *v.* **8A**
filthy dreckig *adj.* **6B**
finally schließlich *adv.* **7B**
find finden *v.* **2A**
 to find one's way sich zurechtfinden *v.* **10B**
 to find out (about) sich informieren
 (über) *v.* **9A**
fine (monetary) Bußgeld, -er *n.* **8A**
 I'm fine. Mir geht's gut. **1A**
finger Finger, - *m.* **9A**
fire entlassen *v.* **11B**; Feuer, - *n.*
firefighter Feuerwehrmann, ¨er / Feuerwehrfrau,
 -en (*pl.* Feuerwehrleute) *m./f.* **11B**
firm Firma (*pl.* die Firmen) *f.* **11A**
first erster/erste/erstes *adj.* **2A**; zuerst *adv.* **7B**
 first course erster Gang *m.* **4B**
 first class erste Klasse *f.* **8A**
fish Fisch, -e *m.* **4A**
 to go fishing angeln gehen *v.* **2B**
fish store Fischgeschäft, -e *n.* **4A**
fit passen *v.* **5A**; fit *adj.* **2B**
five fünf **2A**
flat tire Platten, - *m.* **8A**
 to have a flat tire einen Platten haben *v.* **8A**

flavor Geschmack, ¨e *m.* **4B**
flight Flug, ¨e *m.* **7B**
flood Hochwasser, - *n.* **12B**
floor Stock, ¨e *m.*; Boden, ¨ *m.* **6A**
 first/second floor erster/zweiter Stock **6A**
flower Blume, -n *f.* **1A**
 flower shop Blumengeschäft, -e *n.* **10A**
flu Grippe, -n *f.* **9B**
flunk durchfallen *v.* **1B**
fly fliegen *v.* **7B**
fog Nebel, - *m.* **7A**
follow folgen *v.* **5A**
food Essen, - *n.* **4A**
foot Fuß, ¨e *m.* **9A**
football American Football *m.* **2B**
for für *prep.* **3B**; seit; zu *prep.* **4B**
foreign language Fremdsprache, -n *f.* **2A**
forest Wald, ¨er *m.* **2B**
forget vergessen *v.* **2B**
fork Gabel, -n *f.* **4B**
form Formular, -e *n.* **10A**
 to fill out a form ein Formular ausfüllen *v.* **10A**
fountain Brunnen, - *m.* **10B**
four vier **2A**
France Frankreich *n.* **10B**
French (person) Franzose, -n / Französin,
 -nen *m./f.* **10B**; (language) Französisch *n.* **10B**
free time Freizeit, -en *f.* **2B**
freezer Gefrierschrank, ¨e *m.* **6B**
Friday Freitag, -e *m.* **2A**
 on Fridays freitags *adv.* **2A**
friend Freund, -e / Freundin, -nen *m./f.* **1A**
friendly freundlich *adj.* **3B**
friendship Freundschaft, -en *f.* **5A**
from aus *prep.* **4A**; von *prep.* **4B**
 where from woher *interr.* **2A**
front: in front of vor *prep.* **5B**
fruit Obst *n.* **4A**
fry braten *v.* **2B**
full voll *adj.* **7B**
full-time ganztags *adj.* **11B**
fully occupied voll besetzt *adj.* **7B**
fun Spaß *m.* **2B**
 to be fun Spaß machen *v.* **2B**
 to (not) have fun (keinen) Spaß haben *v.* **5A**
function funktionieren *v.* **8B**
funny lustig *adj.* **3B**
furnished möbliert *adj.* **6A**
furniture Möbel, - *n.* **6A**
 piece of furniture Möbelstück, ¨e *n.* **6A**

G

game Spiel, -e *n.* **2B**
game console Spielkonsole, -n *f.* **8B**
garage Garage, -n *f.* **5B**
garbage truck Müllwagen, - *m.* **12B**
gardener Gärtner, - / Gärtnerin, -nen *m./f.* **11B**
garlic Knoblauch *m.* **4A**
gas Benzin, -e *n.* **8A**
gas station Tankstelle, -n *f.* **8A**
generous großzügig *adj.* **3B**
German (person) Deutsche *m./f.* **10B**;
 (language) Deutsch *n.* **10B**

Germany Deutschland *n.* **4A**
get bekommen *v.* **5A**
 to get up aufstehen *v.* **4A**
 to get sick/better krank/gesund werden *v.* **9B**
gift Geschenk, -e *n.* **5A**
girl Mädchen, - *n.* **1A**
give geben *v.* **2B**
 to give (a gift) schenken *v.* **5A**
glass Glas, ¨er *n.* **4B**
glasses Brille, -n *f.* **5B**
global warming Erderwärmung *f.* **12B**
glove Handschuh, -e *m.* **5B**
go gehen *v.* **2A**; fahren *v.* **2B**
 to go out ausgehen *v.* **4A**
 Go! Los! **2B**
goal (in soccer) Tor, -e *n.* **2B**
golf Golf *n.* **2B**
good gut *adj.*; nett *adj.* **1A**
 Good evening. Guten Abend! **1A**
 Good morning. Guten Morgen! **1A**
 Good night. Gute Nacht! **1A**
 Good-bye. Auf Wiedersehen! **1A**
 Good luck! Viel Glück! **5A**
government Regierung, -en *f.* **12B**
grade Note, -n *f.* **1B**
grade report Zeugnis, -se *n.* **1B**
graduate Abschluss machen, ¨e *v.* **5A**
graduation Abschluss, ¨e *m.* **1B**
gram Gramm, -e *n.* **4A**
 100 grams of cheese 100 Gramm Käse **4A**
granddaughter Enkeltochter, ¨ *f.* **3A**
grandson Enkelsohn, ¨e *m.* **3A**
grandchild Enkel, - *m.* **3A**; Enkelkind, -er *n.* **3A**
grandfather Großvater, ¨ *m.* **3A**
grandma Oma, -s *f.* **3A**
grandmother Großmutter, ¨ *f.* **3A**
grandpa Opa, -s *m.* **3A**
grandparents Großeltern *pl.* **1A**
grape Traube, -n *f.* **4A**
grass Gras, ¨er *n.* **12A**
gray grau *adj.* **5B**
great toll *adj.* **3B**; prima *adj.*; spitze *adj.* **1A**
great grandfather Urgroßvater, ¨ *m.* **3A**
great grandmother Urgroßmutter, ¨ *f.* **3A**
greedy gierig *adj.* **3B**
green grün *adj.* **5B**
green bean grüne Bohne (*pl.* die grünen
 Bohnen) *f.* **4A**
greet grüßen *v.* **2B**
greeting Begrüßung, -en *f.* **1A**; Gruß, ¨e *m.* **1A**
grocery store Lebensmittelgeschäft, -e *n.* **4A**
ground floor Erdgeschoss, -e *n.* **6A**
grow wachsen *v.* **5B**
grown-up erwachsen *adj.* **10A**
guest Gast, ¨e *m.* **5A**
 hotel guest Hotelgast, ¨e *m.* **7B**
guesthouse Pension, -en *f.* **7B**
gym Sporthalle, -n *f.* **2A**

H

hail Hagel *m.* **7A**
hair Haar, -e *n.* **3A**
hair dryer Haartrockner, - *m.* **9A**

hairdresser Friseur, -e / Friseurin, -nen *m./f.* **3B**
half halb *adj.* **2A**
half brother Halbbruder, -̈ *m.* **3A**
half sister Halbschwester, -n *f.* **3A**
hall Flur, -e *m.* **6A**
ham Schinken, - *m.* **4A**
hand Hand, -̈e *f.* **9A**
handsome gut aussehend *adj.* **3A**
hang hängen *v.* **5B**
  to hang up auflegen *v.* **11A**
happen passieren *v.* **5B**
happiness Glück *n.* **5A**
happy glücklich *adj.* **3B** froh *adj.* **3B**
  Happy birthday! Alles Gute zum Geburtstag! **5A**
  Happy Easter! Frohe Ostern! **5A**
  Happy New Year! Ein gutes neues Jahr! **5A**
  to be happy (about) sich freuen (über) *v.* **9A**
hard schwer *adj.* **9B**
hard drive Festplatte, -en *f.* **8B**
hard-working fleißig *adj.* **3B**
hare Hase, -n *m.* **12A**
hat Hut, -̈e *m.* **5B**
have haben *v.* **1B**
  Have a nice day! Schönen Tag noch! **1A**
  to have breakfast frühstücken *v.* **4B**
  to have to müssen *v.* **3B**
he er *pron.* **1A**
head Kopf, -̈e *m.* **9A**
headache Kopfschmerzen *m. pl.* **9B**
headlight Scheinwerfer, -e *m.* **8A**
headphones Kopfhörer, - *m.* **8B**
health Gesundheit *f.* **9B**
health-food store Bioladen, -̈ *m.* **9B**
healthy gesund *adj.* **8A**
hear hören *v.* **2A**
heat stroke Hitzschlag, -̈e *m.* **9B**
heavy schwer *adj.* **4B**
hello Guten Tag!; Hallo! **1A**
help helfen *v.* **2B**
  to help with helfen bei *v.* **7A**
her ihr *poss. adj.* **3A**
here hier *adv.* **1A**
  Here is/are... Hier ist/sind... **1B**
high hoch *adj.* **8A**
highway Autobahn, -en *f.* **8A**
hike wandern *v.* **2A**
his sein *poss. adj.* **3A**
history Geschichte, -en *f.* **2A**
hit treffen *v.* **2B**
hobby Hobby, -s *n.* **2B**
hockey Hockey *n.* **2B**
hold: to be on hold in der Warteschleife
  sein *v.* **11B**
  Please hold. Bleiben Sie bitte am Apparat! **11A**
holiday Feiertag, -e *m.* **5A**
home Haus, -̈er *adv.* **5B**
  at home zu Hause *adv.* **4A**
home office Arbeitszimmer, - *n.* **6A**
homemade hausgemacht *adj.* **4B**
homemaker Hausfrau, -en / Hausmann,
  -̈er *f./m.* **11B**
homework Hausaufgabe, -n *f.* **1B**
hood Motorhaube, -en *f.* **8A**
horse Pferd, -e *n.* **2B**

hospital Krankenhaus, -̈er *n.* **9B**
host / hostess Gastgeber, - / Gastgeberin,
  -nen *m./f.* **5A**
host family Gastfamilie, -n *f.* **4B**
hot heiß *adj.* **7A**
hotel Hotel, -s *n.* **7B**
  five-star hotel Fünf-Sterne-Hotel *n.* **7B**
hour Stunde,-n *f.* **2A**
house Haus, -̈er *n.* **6A**
housework Hausarbeit *f.* **6B**
  to do housework Hausarbeit machen *v.* **6B**
how wie *interr.* **2A**
  How are you? (form.) Wie geht es Ihnen? **1A**
  How are you? (inf.) Wie geht's (dir)? **1A**
  how many wie viele *interr.* **1B**
  how much wie viel *interr.* **1B**
human resources manager Personalchef, -s / die
  Personalchefin, -nen *m./f.* **11A**
humble bescheiden *adj.*
hurry sich beeilen *v.* **9A**
hurt weh tun *v.* **9B**
  to hurt oneself sich verletzen *v.* **9B**
husband Ehemann, -̈er *m.* **3A**
hybrid car Hybridauto, -s *n.* **12B**

I ich *pron.* **1A**
ice cream Eis *n.* **5A**
ice cream shop Eisdiele, -n *f.* **4A**
ice cube Eiswürfel, - *m.* **5A**
ice hockey Eishockey *n.* **2B**
ID card Personalausweis, -e *m.* **7B**
idea Idee, -n *f.* **1A**
if wenn *conj.;* ob *conj.* **10A**
  as if als ob **10A**
  if I were you an deiner/Ihrer Stelle *f.* **10A**
  if... only wenn... nur **10A**
  if... then wenn... dann **10A**
imagine sich (etwas) vorstellen *v.* **9A**
imitate nachmachen *v.* **8B**
important wichtig *adj.* **7B;** bedeutend *adj.* **12A**
improve verbessern *v.* **12B**
in in *prep.* **5B**
  in the afternoon nachmittags *adv.* **2A**
  in the evening abends *adv.* **2A**
  in the morning morgens *adv.* **2A**
  in spite of trotz *prep.* **8B**
India Indien *n.* **10B**
Indian indisch *adj.* **10B;** **(person)** Inder, - /
  Inderin, -nen *m./f.* **10B**
ingredient Zutat, -en *f.* **4A**
injury Verletzung, -en *f.* **9B**
inside (of) innerhalb *prep.* **8B**
instead sondern *conj.* **6A**
  instead of statt *prep.;* anstatt *prep.* **8B**
intellectual intellektuell *adj.* **3B**
intelligent intelligent *adj.* **3B**
interested: to be interested (in) sich interessieren
  (für) *v.* **9A**
interesting interessant *adj.* **2A**
internet café Internetcafé, -s *n.* **10A**
internship Praktikum (*pl.* die Praktika) *n.* **11A**
intersection Kreuzung, -en *f.* **10B**

introduce: to introduce (oneself) (sich)
  vorstellen *v.* **9A**
invent erfinden *v.* **7A**
invite einladen *v.* **5A**
iron Bügeleisen, - *n.* **6B;** bügeln *v.* **6B**
ironing board Bügelbrett, -er *n.* **6B**
island Insel, -n *f.* **12A**
it es *pron.* **1A**
Italian (person) Italiener, - / Italienerin,
  -nen *m./f.* **10B; (language)** Italienisch *n.* **10B**
Italy Italien *n.* **10B**
its sein *poss. adj.* **3A**

jacket Jacke, -n *f.* **5B**
jam Marmelade, -n *f.* **4A**
January Januar *m.* **2A**
Japan Japan *n.* **10B**
Japanese (person) Japaner, - / Japanerin,
  -nen *m./f.* **10B; (language)** Japanisch *n.* **10B**
jealous eifersüchtig *adj.* **3B**
jeans Jeans, - *f.* **5B**
jewelry store Juweliergeschäft, -e *n.* **10A**
job Beruf, -e *m.* **11B;** Stelle, -n *f.* **11A**
  to find a job Arbeit finden *v.* **11A**
job interview Vorstellungsgespräch, -e *n.* **11A**
job opening Stellenangebot, -e *n.* **11A**
jog joggen *v.* **2B**
journalist Journalist, -en / Journalistin,
  -nen *m./f.* **3B**
judge Richter, - / Richterin, -nen *m./f.* **11B**
juice Saft, -̈e *m.* **4B**
July Juli *m.* **2A**
June Juni *m.* **2A**
just as genauso wie **8A**

key Schlüssel, - *m.* **7B**
keyboard Tastatur, -en *f.* **8B**
kind nett *adj.*
kiosk Kiosk, -e *m.* **10A**
kiss Kuss, -̈e *m.* **5A;** küssen *v.* **5A**
  to kiss (each other) sich küssen *v.* **9A**
kitchen Küche, -n *f.* **6A**
knee Knie, - *n.* **9A**
knife Messer, - *n.* **4B**
know kennen *v.* **5B;** wissen *v.* **5B**
  to know each other sich kennen *v.* **9A**
know-it-all Besserwisser, - / Besserwisserin
  -nen *m./f.* **2A**
Korea Korea *n.* **10B**
Korean (person) Koreaner, - / Koreanerin,
  -nen *m./f.* **10B; (language)** Koreanisch *n.* **10B**

labor union Gewerkschaft, -en *f.* **11B**
lake See, -n *m.* **12A**
lamp Lampe, -n *f.* **6A**
land landen *v.* **7B;** Land, -̈er *n.* **7B**
landscape Landschaft, -en *f.* **12A**
laptop (computer) Laptop, -s *m./n.* **8B**

last letzter/letzte/letztes *adj.* **2B**
last name Nachname, -n *m.* **3A**
late spät *adj.* **2A**
  to be late sich verspäten *v.* **9A**
laugh lachen *v.* **2A**
laundromat Waschsalon, -s *m.* **10A**
laundry Wäsche *f.* **6B**
  to do laundry Wäsche waschen *v.* **6B**
law Gesetz, -e *n.* **12B**
lawyer Rechtsanwalt, ⸚e / Rechtsanwältin,
  -nen *m./f.* **3B**
lay legen *v.* **5B**
lazy faul *adj.* **3B**
leaf Blatt, ⸚er *n.* **12A**
learn lernen *v.* **2A**
leather Leder, - *n.* **5B**
leave abfahren *v.* **8A**
lecture Vorlesung, -en *f.* **2A**; Vortrag, ⸚e *m.* **6B**
lecture hall Hörsaal (*pl.* Hörsäle) *m.* **2A**
leg Bein, -e *n.* **9A**
leisure Freizeit *f.* **2B**
lesson Stunde, -n *f.* **1B**
let lassen *v.* **2B**
letter Brief, -e *m.* **10A**
  to mail a letter einen Brief abschicken *v.* **10A**
  letter of recommendation
    Empfehlungsschreiben, - *n.* **11A**
lettuce Salat, -e *m.* **4A**
library Bibliothek, -en *f.* **1B**
license plate Nummernschild, -er *n.* **8A**
lie liegen *v.* **5B**
  to lie down sich (hin)legen *v.* **9A**
  to tell a lie lügen *v.*
life partner Lebenspartner, - / Lebenspartnerin,
  -nen *m./f.* **3A**
light hell *adj.* **3A**; leicht *adj.* **4B**; Licht,
  -er *n.* **12B**
lightning Blitz, -e *m.* **7A**
like mögen *v.* **4B**; gern (+*verb*) *v.* **2B**; gefallen *v.* **5A**
  I would like... ich hätte gern… **4A**;
    Ich möchte… **4B**
line Schlange, -n *f.* **7B**; Linie, -n *f.*
  to stand in line Schlange stehen *v.* **7B**
lip Lippe, -n *f.* **9A**
lipstick Lippenstift, -e *m.* **9A**
listen (to) hören *v.* **2A**
literature Literatur, -en *f.* **2A**
little klein *adj.* **3A**; wenig *adj.* **10A**
live wohnen *v.* **2A**; leben *v.* **2A**
living room Wohnzimmer, - *n.* **6A**
load laden *v.* **8B**
location Lage, -n *f.* **7B**
long lang *adj.* **3A**
  long-sleeved langärmlig *adj.* **5B**
look schauen *v.* **7A**
  to look at anschauen *v.* **7A**
  to look for suchen *v.* **2A**
  to look forward to sich freuen auf *v.* **9A**
loose weit *adj.* **5B**
lose verlieren *v.* **2B**
  to get lost sich verlaufen *v.* **10B**
love lieben *v.* **2A**; Liebe *f.* **5A**
  to fall in love (with) sich verlieben (in) *v.* **9A**
  to love each other sich lieben *v.* **9A**

loving liebevoll *adj.* **3B**
low niedrig *adj.* **11A**
luggage Gepäck *n.* **7B**
lunch Mittagessen, - *n.* **4B**

M

magazine Zeitschrift, -en *f.* **10A**
mail Post *f.* **10A**
  to mail a letter einen Brief abschicken *v.* **10A**
mail carrier Briefträger, - / Briefträgerin,
  -nen *m.* **10A**
mailbox Briefkasten, ⸚ *m.* **10A**
main course Hauptspeise, -n *f.* **4B**
main road Hauptstraße, -n *f.* **10B**
major: to major in studieren *v.* **2A**
make machen *v.* **2A**
makeup: to put on makeup sich schminken *v.* **9A**
mall Einkaufszentrum (*pl.* Einkaufszentren) *n.* **10B**
man Mann, ⸚er *m.* **1A**
manage leiten *v.* **11B**
manager Geschäftsführer, - / die
  Geschäftsführerin, -nen *m./f.* **11A**
map Karte, -n *f.* **1B**; Landkarte, -n *f.* **7B**
  city map Stadtplan, ⸚e *m.* **7B**
  to read a map eine Karte lesen *v.* **7B**
marble Marmor *m.* **6B**
March März *m.* **2A**
marital status Familienstand, ⸚e *m.* **3A**
market Markt, ⸚e *m.* **4A**
marriage Ehe, -n *f.* **5A**
married verheiratet *adj.* **3A**
marry heiraten *v.* **3A**
match Spiel, -e *n.* **2B**; passen *v.* **5A**
material Material, -ien *n.* **5B**
mathematics Mathematik *f.* **2A**
May Mai *m.* **2A**
may dürfen *v.* **3B**
maybe vielleicht *adv.* **4A**
mayor Bürgermeister, - / Bürgermeisterin,
  -nen *m./f.* **10B**
meal Mahlzeit, -en *f.* **4B**
mean bedeuten *v.* **2A**; meinen *v.* **12B**;
  gemein *adj.* **3B**
meat Fleisch *n.* **4A**
mechanic Mechaniker, - / Mechanikerin,
  -nen *m./f.* **8A**
medicine Medizin *f.* **2A**; Medikament, -e *n.* **9B**
meet (sich) treffen *v.* **2B**; **(for the first time)** (sich)
  kennen lernen *v.* **9A**
  Pleased to meet you. Schön dich/Sie kennen zu
    lernen! **1A**
meeting Besprechung, -en *f.* **11A**
melon Melone, -n *f.* **4A**
menu Speisekarte, -n *f.* **4B**
Merry Christmas! Frohe Weihnachten! **5A**
message Nachricht, -en *f.* **11A**
Mexico Mexiko *n.* **10B**
Mexican mexikanisch *adj.* **10B**; **(person)**
  Mexikaner, - / Mexikanerin, -nen *m./f.* **10B**
microphone Mikrofon, -e *n.* **8B**
microwave Mikrowelle, -n *f.* **6B**
midmorning Vormittag, -e *m.* **2B**
midnight Mitternacht *f.* **2A**

mild leicht *adj.* **9B**
milk Milch *f.* **4B**
minority Minderheit, -en *f.* **12B**
minus minus **1B**
mirror Spiegel, - *m.* **6A**
mist Nebel, - *m.* **7A**
modern modern *adj.* **10A**
modest bescheiden *adj.* **3B**
mom Mama, -s *f.* **3A**
Monday Montag, -e *m.* **2A**
  on Mondays montags *adv.* **2A**
money Geld, -er *n.* **10A**
month Monat, -e *m.* **2A**
moon Mond, -e *m.* **12A**
mop wischen *v.* **6B**
more mehr *adj.* **8A**
morning Morgen, - *m.* **2B**
  in the morning vormittags **2A**
  tomorrow morning morgen früh **2B**
mother Mutter, ⸚ *f.* **1A**
mother-in-law Schwiegermutter, ⸚ *f.* **3A**
mountain Berg, -e *m.* **2B**; **12A**
mouse Maus, ⸚e *f.* **8B**
mouth Mund, ⸚er *m.* **9A**
move umziehen *v.* **6A**; sich bewegen *v.*
movie Film, -e *m.*
movie theater Kino, -s *n.* **10A**
Mr. Herr **1A**
Mrs. Frau **1A**
Ms. Frau **1A**
much viel *adv.* **4A**
mushroom Pilz, -e *m.* **4A**
musician Musiker, - / Musikerin, -nen *m./f.* **3B**
must müssen *v.* **3B**
my mein *poss. adj.* **3A**
myself mich *pron.*; mir *pron.* **9A**

N

naïve naiv *adj.* **3B**
name Name, -n *m.* **1A**
  to be named heißen *v.* **2A**
  What's your name? Wie heißen Sie? (form.) /
    Wie heißt du? (inf.) *v.* **1A**
napkin Serviette, -n *f.* **4B**
natural disaster Naturkatastrophe, -n *f.* **12A**
nature Natur, -en *f.* **12A**
nauseous übel *adj.* **9B**
near bei *prep.* **4B**; nah *adj.* **10B**
neat ordentlich *adj.* **6B**
neck Hals, ⸚e *m.* **9A**
necklace Halskette, -n *f.* **5B**
need brauchen *v.* **2A**
  to need to müssen *v.* **3B**
neighborhood Viertel, - *n.* **10B**
nephew Neffe, -n *m.* **8B**
nervous nervös *adj.* **3B**
never nie *adv.* **4A**; niemals *adv.* **7B**
New Year's Eve Silvester *n.* **5A**
newlywed Frischvermählte, -n *m./f.* **5A**
newspaper Zeitung, -en *f.* **7B**
next nächster/nächste/nächstes *adj.* **2B**
  next to neben *prep.* **5B**

nice nett *adj.* 3B
  It's nice out. Es ist schön draußen. 7A
  Nice to meet you. Schön dich/Sie kennen zu lernen! 1A
  The weather is nice. Das Wetter ist gut. 7A
night Nacht, ¨e *f.* 2B
  to spend the night übernachten *f.* 7B
night table Nachttisch, -e *m.* 6A
nine neun 2A
no nein 1A; kein *adj.* 2B
no one niemand *pron.* 7B
nonviolent gewaltfrei *adj.* 12B
noon Mittag, -e *m.* 2A
nose Nase, -n *f.* 9A
not nicht *adv.* 2B
  Do not enter. Keine Zufahrt. 3B
  not bad nicht schlecht 1A
  not much wenig *adj.* 10A
note Notiz, -en *f.* 1B
notebook Heft, -e *n.* 1B
nothing nichts *pron.* 7B
November November *m.* 2A
now jetzt *adv.* 4A
nuclear energy Kernenergie *f.* 12B
nuclear power plant Kernkraftwerk, -e *n.* 12B
nurse Krankenpfleger, - / Krankenschwester, -n *m./f.* 9B

O

ocean Meer, -e *n.* 12A
occasion Anlass, ¨e *m.* 5A
  special occasions besondere Anlässe *m. pl.* 5A
October Oktober *m.* 2A
offer Angebot, -e *n.* 5B; bieten *v.* 9B; anbieten *v.* 12B
office Büro, -s *n.* 11B
office supplies Büromaterial, -ien *n.* 11A
often oft *adv.* 4A
oil Öl, -e *n.* 4A
old alt *adj.* 3A
  How old are you? Wie alt bist du? 1B
  I am... years old. Ich bin... Jahre alt. 1B
olive oil Olivenöl, -e *n.* 4A
on an *prep.*; auf *prep.* 5B
once einmal *adv.* 7B
one eins 2A; man *pron.* 7B
  by oneself allein *adv.* 4A
one-way street Einbahnstraße, -n *f.* 8A
onion Zwiebel, -n *f.* 4A
online: to be online online sein *v.* 8B
only nur *adv.* 4A
  only child Einzelkind, -er *n.* 3A
on-time pünktlich *adj.* 7B
onto auf *prep.* 5B
open öffnen *v.* 2A; aufmachen *v.* 8B; geöffnet *adj.* 10A
or oder *conj.* 1B
orange Orange, -n *f.* 4A; orange *adj.* 5B
order bestellen *v.* 4A
organic biologisch *adj.* 12B
our unser *poss. adj.* 3A
out draußen *adv.* 7A; heraus *adv.* 6A
  It's nice out. Es ist schön draußen. 7A

to go out ausgehen *v.* 4A
  to bring out rausbringen 6B
outside draußen *prep.* 7A
  outside of außerhalb *prep.* 8B
oven Ofen, ¨ *m.* 6B
over über *prep.* 5B; vorbei *adv.* 7A
  over there drüben *adv.* 4A
overpopulation Überbevölkerung *f.* 12B
owner Besitzer, - / Besitzerin, -nen *m./f.* 3B

P

pack packen *v.* 7B
package Paket, -e *n.* 10A
pain Schmerz, -en *m.* 9B
pajamas Schlafanzug, ¨e *m.* 9A
pan Pfanne, -n *f.* 6B
pants Hose, -n *f.* 5B
paper Papier, -e *n.* 1B
  sheet of paper Blatt Papier (*pl.* Blätter) Papier *n.* 1B
paperclip Büroklammer, -n *f.* 11A
paper-goods store Schreibwarengeschäft, -e *n.* 10A
paragraph Absatz, ¨e *m.* 5B
parents Eltern *pl.* 3A
park Park, -s *m.* 1A; parken *v.* 8A
  No parking. Parkverbot. 3B
participate mitmachen *v.* 8B
part-time halbtags *adj.* 11B
party Party, -s *f.* 5A
  to go to a party auf eine Party gehen *prep.* 10B
  to throw a party eine Party geben *v.* 5A
pass (a test) bestehen *v.* 1B
passenger Passagier, -e *m.* 7B
passport control Passkontrolle, -n *f.* 7B
password Passwort, ¨er *n.* 8B
past Vergangenheit, -en *f.* 12A; nach *prep.* 2A
pasta Pasta *f.* 4A
pastries Gebäck *n.* 5A
pastry shop Konditorei, -en *f.* 4A
path Weg, -e *m.* 12A
patient geduldig *adj.* 3B; Patient, -en / Patientin, -nen *m./f.* 9B
pay (for) bezahlen *v.* 4A
  to pay by (credit) card mit der Karte bezahlen *v.* 10A
  to pay in cash bar bezahlen *v.* 10A
peach Pfirsich, -e *m.* 4A
pear Birne, -n *f.* 4A
pedestrian Fußgänger, - / Fußgängerin, -nen *m./f.* 10B
pen Kuli, -s *m.* 1B
pencil Bleistift, -e *m.* 1B
people Leute *pl.* 3B; Menschen *pl.*
pepper Paprika, - *f.* 4A; Pfeffer, - *m.* 4B
percent Prozent, -e *n.* 1B
period Punkt, -e *m.* 1B
person Person, -en *f.* 1A; Mensch, -en *m.*
personal persönlich *adj.* 3B
pet Haustier, -e *n.* 3A
pharmacy Apotheke, -n *f.* 9B
phone booth Telefonzelle, -n *f.* 10B
photo Foto, -s *n.* 1B

physics Physik *f.* 2A
picnic Picknick, -s *n.* 12A
  to have a picnic ein Picknick machen *v.* 12A
picture Foto, -s *n.* 1B; Bild, -er *n.* 6A
pie Kuchen, - *m.* 4A
pigsty Saustall, ¨e *n.* 6B
  It's a pigsty! Es ist ein Saustall! 6B
pill Tablette, -n *f.* 9B
pillow Kissen, - *n.* 6B
pineapple Ananas, - *f.* 4A
pink rosa *adj.* 5B
place Ort, -e *m.* 1B; Lage, -n *f.* 7B; setzen *v.* 5B
  in your place an deiner/Ihrer Stelle *f.* 10A
plant Pflanze, -n *f.* 6A
plastic Kunststoff, -e *m.* 6B
plate Teller, - *m.* 4B
platform Bahnsteig, -e 8A
play spielen *v.* 2A
player Spieler, - / Spielerin, -nen *m./f.* 2B
pleasant angenehm *adj.* 3B
please bitte 1A; gefallen *v.* 5A
  Pleased to meet you. Freut mich! 1A
plumber Klempner, - / Klempnerin, -nen *m./f.* 11B
plus plus 1B
police officer Polizist, -en / Polizistin, -nen *m./f.* 8A
police station Polizeiwache, -n *f.* 10A
politician Politiker, - / Politikerin, -nen *m./f.* 11B
pollute verschmutzen *v.* 12B
pollution Verschmutzung *f.* 12B
poor arm *adj.* 3B
pork Schweinefleisch *n.* 4A
position Stelle, -n *f.* 11A
post office Post, - *f.* 10A
  to go to the post office zur Post gehen *v.* 10A
postcard Postkarte, -n *f.* 10A
poster Poster, - *n.* 6A
pot Topf, ¨e *m.* 6B
potato Kartoffel, -n *f.* 4A
pound Pfund, -e *n.* 4A
  a pound of potatoes ein Pfund Kartoffeln 4A
practice (sports) trainieren *v.* 2B; Übung, -en *f.*
pregnant schwanger *adj.* 9B
preparation Vorbereitung, -en *f.*
prepare vorbereiten *v.* 4A; zubereiten *v.* 7A
  to prepare oneself (for) sich vorbereiten (auf) *v.* 9A
prescription Rezept, -e *n.* 9B
presentation Referat, -e *n.* 2A
preserve erhalten *v.* 12B
president Präsident, - / Präsidentin, -nen *m./f.* 8B
  federal president Bundespräsident, - / Bundespräsidentin, -nen *m./f.* 8B
pretty hübsch *adj.* 3A
  pretty well ziemlich gut *adv.* 1A
principal Schulleiter, - *m.* / Schulleiterin, -nen *f.* 1B
print drucken *v.* 8B
printer Drucker, - *m.* 8B
probably wohl ; wahrscheinlich *adv.* 10A; sicher *adv.* 10A
problem Problem, -e *n.* 1A
profession Beruf, -e *m.* 3B
professional training Berufsausbildung, -en *f.* 11A

professor Professor, -en / Professorin, -nen *m./f.* **1B**
program Programm, -e *n.* **8B**
promotion Beförderung, -en *f.* **11B**
pronunciation Aussprache *f.*
propose vorschlagen *v.* **12B**
protect schützen *v.* **12B**
proud stolz *adj.* **3B**
psychologist Psychologe, -n / Psychologin, -nen *m./f.* **11B**
psychology Psychologie *f.* **2A**
public öffentlich *adj.* **8A**
  public transportation öffentliche Verkehrsmittel *n. pl.* **8A**
pull ziehen *v.* **3B**
purple lila *adj.* **5B**
purse Handtasche, -n *f.* **5B**
push drücken *v.* **3B**
put stellen *v.* **5B**; legen *v.* **9A**; setzen *v.* **9A**
  to put away wegräumen *v.* **6B**
  to put on anziehen *v.* **5B**

Q

quarter Viertel, - *n.* **2A**
  quarter past/to Viertel nach/vor **2A**
question Frage, -n *f.* **1B**
quicksand Treibsand *m.* **12A**
quite ziemlich *adv.* **4A**

R

rabbit Kaninchen, - *n.* **12A**
rain Regen *m.* **7A**; regnen *v.* **2A**
raincoat Regenmantel, ⸚ *m.* **7A**
raise Gehaltserhöhung, -en *f.* **11B**
rarely selten *adv.* **4A**
rather lieber *adj.* **8A**
rating Bewertung, -en *f.* **7B**
razor Rasierer, - *m.* **9A**
read lesen *v.* **2B**
ready fertig *adj.* **11B**
real estate agent Immobilienmakler, - / Immobilienmaklerin, -nen *m./f.* **11B**
realistic realistisch *adj.* **10A**
really wirklich *adv.* **4A**
receive bekommen *v.* **5A**
receiver Hörer, - *m.* **11A**
recess Pause, -n *f.* **1B**
recipe Rezept, -e *n.* **4A**
recognize erkennen *v.* **7A**
recommend empfehlen *v.* **2B**
record aufnehmen *v.* **8B**
recycle recyceln *v.* **12B**
red rot *adj.* **3A**
  red-haired rothaarig *adj.* **3A**
reference Referenz, -en *f.* **11A**
refrigerator Kühlschrank, ⸚e *m.* **6B**
related verwandt *adj.* **10A**
relative Verwandte, -n *m.* **3A**
relax sich entspannen *v.* **9A**
reliable zuverlässig *adj.* **3B**
remember sich erinnern (an) *v.* **9A**
remote control Fernbedienung, -en *f.* **8B**

remove entfernen *v.* **6B**
renewable energy erneuerbare Energie, -en *f.* **12B**
rent Miete, -n *f.* **6A**; mieten *v.* **6A**
repair reparieren *v.* **8A**
repeat wiederholen *v.* **2A**
repetition Wiederholung, -en *f.*
report berichten *v.* **12B**
report card Zeugnis, -se *n.* **1B**
reservation: to make a (hotel) reservation buchen *v.* **7B**
resign kündigen *v.* **11B**
rest sich ausruhen *v.* **9A**
restaurant Restaurant, -s *n.* **4B**
result Ergebnis, -se *n.* **1B**
résumé Lebenslauf, ⸚e *m.* **11A**
retire in Rente gehen *v.* **5A**
retiree Rentner, - / Rentnerin, -nen *m./f.* **11B**
review Besprechung, -en *f.* **8B**
rice Reis *m.* **4A**
rich reich *adj.* **3B**
ride fahren *v.* **2B**; reiten *v.* **2B**
  to give (someone) a ride (jemanden) mitnehmen *v.* **10B**
  to ride a bicycle Fahrrad fahren *v.* **2B**
ring klingeln *v.* **8B**
rinse spülen *v.* **6B**
rise (sun) aufgehen *v.* **12A**
river Fluss, ⸚e *m.* **3B**
rock Stein, -e *m.* **12A**
roll Brötchen, - *n.* **4A**
room Zimmer, - *n.* **5A**
room service Zimmerservice *m.* **7B**
roommate Mitbewohner, - / Mitbewohnerin, -nen *m./f.* **2A**
rug Teppich, -e *m.* **6A**
run laufen *v.* **2B**; rennen *v.* **5A**
Russia Russland *n.* **10B**
Russian (person) Russe, -n / Russin, -nen *m./f.* **10B**; **(language)** Russisch *n.* **10B**

S

sad traurig *adj.* **3B**
salad Salat, -e *m.* **4A**
salary Gehalt, ⸚er *n.* **11A**
  high/low salary hohes/niedriges Gehalt, ⸚er *n.* **11A**
sale Verkauf, ⸚e *m.*
  on sale im Angebot **5B**
salesperson Verkäufer, - / Verkäuferin, -nen *m./f.* **5B**
salt Salz, -e *n.* **4B**
salty salzig *adj.* **4B**
same gleich *adj.*
Saturday Samstag, -e *m.* **2A**
  on Saturdays samstags *adv.* **2A**
sausage Würstchen, - *n.* **4A**
save speichern *v.* **8B**; retten *v.* **12B**
  to save the planet den Planeten retten *v.* **12B**
say sagen *v.* **2A**
scarf Schal, -s *m.* **5B**
schedule Stundenplan, ⸚e *m.* **2A**; Fahrplan, ⸚e *m.* **8A**
scholarship Stipendium (*pl.* Stipendien) *n.* **2A**

school Schule, -n *f.* **1B**
science Naturwissenschaft, -en *f.* **2A**
scientist Wissenschaftler, - / Wissenschaftlerin, -nen *m./f.* **11B**
score Ergebnis, -se *n.* **1B**
screen Bildschirm, -e *m.* **8B**
screen name Benutzername, -n *m.* **8B**
sea Meer, -e *n.* **12A**
seafood Meeresfrüchte *f. pl.* **4A**
season Jahreszeit, -en *f.* **7A**
seatbelt Sicherheitsgurt, -e *m.* **8A**
second zweite *adj.* **2A**
  second-hand clothing Altkleider *pl.* **12B**
see sehen *v.* **2B**
  See you later. Bis später! **1A**
  See you soon. Bis gleich! / Bis bald! **1A**
  See you tomorrow. Bis morgen! **1A**
selfish egoistisch *adj.* **3B**
sell verkaufen *v.* **4A**
seminar Seminar, -e *n.* **2A**
seminar room Seminarraum (*pl.* Seminarräume) *m.* **2A**
send schicken *v.* **8B**; abschicken *v.* **11B**
separate (sich) trennen *v.* **9A**
separated getrennt *adj.* **3A**
September September *m.* **2A**
serious ernst *adj.* **3B**; schwer *adj.* **9B**
set setzen *v.* **9A**; **(sun)** untergehen *v.* **12A**
  to set the table den Tisch decken *v.* **6B**
seven sieben **2A**
shampoo Shampoo, -s *n.* **9A**
shape Form, -en *f.* **9B**
  in good shape fit *adj.* **2B**
  to be in/out of shape in guter/schlechter Form sein *v.* **9B**
shave sich rasieren *v.* **9A**
shaving cream Rasierschaum, ⸚e *m.* **9A**
she sie *pron.* **1A**
sheep Schaf, -e *n.* **12A**
sheet Laken, - *n.* **6B**
  sheet of paper Blatt Papier (*pl.* Blätter) Papier *n.* **1B**
ship Schiff, -e *n.* **8A**
shirt Hemd, -en *n.* **5B**
shoe Schuh, -e *m.* **5B**
shop einkaufen *v.* **4A**; Geschäft, -e *n.* **4A**
  to go shopping einkaufen gehen *v.* **4A**
shopping Einkaufen *n.* **5B**
shopping center Einkaufszentrum, -(*pl.* Einkaufszentren) *n.* **10B**
short kurz *adj.* **3A**; **(stature)** klein *adj.* **3A**
  short film Kurzfilm, -e *m.* **10A**
  short-sleeved kurzärmlig *adj.* **5B**
shorts kurze Hose, -n *f.* **5B**
shot Spritze, -n *f.* **9B**
  to give a shot eine Spritze geben *v.* **9B**
shoulder Schulter, -n *f.* **9A**
show zeigen *v.* **4B**
shower: to take a shower (sich) duschen *v.* **9A**
shrimp Garnele, -n *f.* **4A**
shy schüchtern *adj.* **3B**
siblings *pl.* Geschwister **3A**
sick krank *adj.* **9B**
  to get sick krank werden *v.* **9B**

side dish Beilage, -n *f.* **4B**
sidewalk Bürgersteig, -e *m.* **10B**
sign unterschreiben *v.* **10A**; Schild, -er *n.*
silk Seide, -n *f.* **5B**
silverware Besteck *n.* **4B**
since seit **4B**
sincere aufrichtig *adj.* **3B**
 Yours sincerely Gruß, ⁻e **3B**
sing singen *v.* **2B**
single ledig *adj.* **3A**
sink Spüle, -n *f.* **6B**
sister Schwester, -n *f.* **1A**
sister-in-law Schwägerin, -nen *f.* **3A**
sit sitzen *v.* **5B**
 to sit down sich (hin)setzen *v.* **9A**
six sechs **2A**
size Kleidergröße, -n *f.* **5B**
ski Ski fahren *v.* **2B**
skirt Rock, ⁻e *m.* **5B**
sky Himmel *m.* **12A**
sleep schlafen *v.* **2B**
 to go to sleep einschlafen *v.* **4A**
slim schlank *adj.* **3A**
slipper Hausschuh, -e *m.* **9A**
slow langsam *adj.* **3B**
 Please speak more slowly. Sprechen Sie bitte langsamer! **3B**
 Slow down. Langsam fahren. **3B**
small klein *adj.* **3A**
smartphone Smartphone, -s *n.* **8B**
smile lächeln *v.* **5A**
smoke rauchen *v.*
 No smoking. Rauchen verboten. **3B**
snack Snack, -s *m.* **4B**
snake Schlange, -n *f.* **12A**
sneakers Turnschuhe *m. pl.* **5B**
sneeze niesen *v.* **9B**
snow Schnee *m.* **7A**; schneien *v.* **7A**
so so *adv.* **4A**
 so far, so good so weit, so gut **1A**
 so that damit *conj.* **10A**
soap Seife, -n *f.* **9A**
soccer Fußball *m.* **2B**
social science Sozialwissenschaft, -en *f.* **2A**
sock Socke, -n *f.* **5B**
sofa Sofa, -s *n.* **6A**
soil verschmutzen *v.* **6B**
solar energy Sonnenenergie *f.* **12B**
solid colored einfarbig *adj.* **5B**
solution Lösung, -en *f.* **12B**
some mancher/manche/manches *pron.* **8B**
someone jemand *pron.* **7B**
something etwas *pron.* **7B**
 something else etwas anderes *n.* **10A**
sometimes manchmal *adv.* **7B**
somewhere else woanders *adv.* **4A**
son Sohn, ⁻e *m.* **3A**
soon bald **1A**
 See you soon. Bis bald.; Bis gleich. **1A**
sorry: I'm sorry. Es tut mir leid. **1A**
so-so (I'm so-so) Es geht. **1A**
soup Suppe, -n *f.* **4B**
soup spoon Esslöffel, - *m.* **4B**
Spain Spanien *n.* **10B**

Spanish (person) Spanier, - / Spanierin, -nen *m./f.* **10B**; **(language)** Spanisch *n.* **10B**
sparkling water Mineralwasser *n.* **4B**
speak sprechen *v.* **2B**
 to speak about sprechen über; reden über *v.* **7A**
special besonderes *adj.* **10A**
 nothing special nichts Besonderes *adj.* **10A**
species Art, -en *f.* **12B**
spelling Rechtschreibung *f.*
spend verbringen *v.* **4A**
spicy scharf *adj.* **4B**
split up sich trennen *v.* **9A**
spoon Löffel, - *m.* **4B**
sport Sport *m.* **2B**; Sportart, -en *f.* **2B**
sprain (one's wrist/ankle) sich (das Handgelenk / den Fuß) verstauchen *v.* **9B**
spring Frühling, -e *m.* **2B**
squirrel Eichhörnchen, - *n.* **12A**
stadium Stadion (*pl.* Stadien) *n.* **2B**
stairs Treppe, -n *f.* **6A**
 to go up/down stairs die Treppe hochgehen/ heruntergehen *v.* **10B**
stamp Briefmarke, -n *f.* **10A**
stand stehen *v.* **5B**
 to stand in line Schlange stehen *v.* **7B**
stapler Hefter, - *m.* **11A**
star Stern, -e *m.* **12A**
start starten *v.* **8B**; anfangen *v.* **4A**; beginnen *v.* **6A**
station wagon Kombi, -s *m.* **8B**
statue Statue, -n *f.* **10B**
stay bleiben *v.* **5B**
steal stehlen *v.* **2B**
steering wheel Lenkrad, ⁻er *n.* **8A**
stepbrother Halbbruder, ⁻ *m.* **3A**
stepdaughter Stieftochter, ⁻ *f.* **3A**
stepfather Stiefvater, -s⁻ *m.* **3A**
stepmother Stiefmutter, ⁻ *f.* **3A**
stepsister Halbschwester, -n *f.* **3A**
stepson Stiefsohn, ⁻ *m.* **3A**
stereo system Stereoanlage, -n *f.* **8B**
still noch *adv.* **4A**; still *adj.* **4B**
 still water stilles Wasser *n.* **4B**
stomachache Bauchschmerzen *m. pl.* **9B**
stop sign Stoppschild, -er *n.* **8A**
store Geschäft, -e *n.* **4A**
storm Sturm, ⁻e *m.* **7A**
stove Herd, -e *m.* **6B**
straight glatt *adj.* **3A**
 straight hair glatte Haare *n. pl.* **3A**
 straight ahead geradeaus *adv.* **8A**
strawberry Erdbeere, -n *f.* **4A**
stream Strom, ⁻e *m.* **12A**
street Straße, -n *f.* **8A**
 to cross the street die Straße überqueren *v.* **10B**
striped gestreift *adj.* **5B**
strong stark *adj.* **3B**
student Schüler, - / Schülerin, -nen *m./f.* **1B**; **(college/university)** Student, -en / Studentin, -nen *m./f.* **1A**
studies Studium (*pl.* Studien) *n.* **2A**
study lernen *v.* **2A**
stuffy nose verstopfte Nase *f.* **9B**
style Stil, -e *m.* **5B**
subject Fach, ⁻er *n.* **2A**

subway U-Bahn, -en *f.* **8A**
success Erfolg, -e *m.* **11B**
such solcher/solche/solches *pron.* **8B**
suit Anzug, ⁻e *m.* **5B**
suitcase Koffer, - *m.* **7B**
summer Sommer, - *m.* **2B**
sun Sonne, -n *f.* **12A**
sunburn Sonnenbrand, ⁻e *m.* **9B**
Sunday Sonntag, -e *m.* **2A**
 on Sundays sonntags *adv.* **2A**
sunglasses Sonnenbrille, -n *f.* **5B**
sunny sonnig *adj.* **7A**
sunrise Sonnenaufgang, ⁻e *m.* **12A**
sunset Sonnenuntergang, ⁻e *m.* **12A**
supermarket Supermarkt, ⁻e *m.* **4A**
supposed: to be supposed to sollen *v.* **3B**
surf surfen *v.* **8B**
 to surf the Web im Internet surfen *v.* **8B**
surprise überraschen *v.* **5A**; Überraschung, -en *f.* **5A**
sweater Pullover, - *m.* **5B**
sweatshirt Sweatshirt, -s *n.* **5B**
sweep fegen *v.* **6B**
sweet süß *adj.* **3B**
swim schwimmen *v.* **2B**
swimming pool Schwimmbad, ⁻er *n.* **2B**
Switzerland die Schweiz *f.* **7A**
Swiss schweizerisch, Schweizer *adj.* **10B**; **(person)** Schweizer, - / Schweizerin, -nen *m./f.* **10B**
symptom Symptom, -e *n.* **9B**

T

table Tisch, -e *m.* **1B**
 to set the table den Tisch decken **6B**
tablecloth Tischdecke, -n *f.* **4B**
tablet Tablet, -s *n.* **8B**
take nehmen *v.* **2B**
 to take (a class) belegen *v.* **2A**
 to take out the trash den Müll rausbringen **6B**
 to take a shower (sich) duschen *v.* **9A**
 to take off abfliegen *v.* **7B**
talk reden *v.* **5A**
 to talk about erzählen von; sprechen/reden über *v.* **7A**
tall groß *adj.* **3A**
tank top Trägerhemd, -en *n.* **5B**
taste schmecken *v.* **4B**; Geschmack, ⁻e *m.* **4B**
taxi Taxi, -s *n.* **8A**
taxi driver Taxifahrer, - / Taxifahrerin, -nen *m./f.* **11B**
tea Tee, -s *m.* **4B**
teacher Lehrer, - / Lehrerin, -nen *m./f.* **1B**
team Mannschaft, -en *f.* **2B**
teaspoon Teelöffel, - *m.* **4B**
technology Technik *f.* **8B**
 to use technology Technik bedienen *v.* **8B**
telephone Telefon, -e *n.* **8B**
 on the telephone am Telefon **11A**
telephone number Telefonnummer, -n *f.* **11A**
television Fernsehen *n.*
 television (set) Fernseher -*m.* **8B**
tell erzählen *v.* **7A**
 to tell a story about erzählen von *v.* **7A**

temperature Temperatur, -en *f.*
What's the temperature? Wie warm/kalt ist es? **7A**
tennis Tennis *n.* **2B**
tent Zelt, -e *n.* **7B**
ten zehn **2A**
terrific großartig *adj.* **3A**
test Prüfung, -en *f.* **1B**
text message SMS, - *f.* **8B**
textbook Lehrbuch, ⁻er *n.*; Schulbuch, ⁻er *n.* **1B**
thank danken *v.* **2A**
Thank you. Danke! **1A**
Thank you very much. Vielen Dank! **1A**
that das **1A**; dass *conj.* **10A**
the das/der/die **1A**
their ihr poss. *adj.* **3A**
then dann *adv.* **7B**
there da **1A**
Is/Are there...? Ist/Sind hier...? **1B**; Gibt es...? **2B**
There is/are... Da ist/sind... **1A**; Es gibt... **2B**
there and back hin und zurück **7B**
over there drüben *adv.* **4A**
therefore also; deshalb *conj.* **9B**
thermometer Thermometer, - *n.* **9B**
these diese *pron.* **8B**
These are... Das sind... **1A**
they sie *pron.* **1A**
thick dick *adj.* **3A**
thin dünn *adj.* **3A**
thing Sache, -n *f.* **1B**; Ding, -e *n.*
think denken *v.* **5A**
to think about denken an *v.* **7A**
to think over überlegen *v.* **4A**
third dritter/dritte/drittes *adj.* **2A**
this das **1A**; dieser/diese/dieses *pron.* **8B**
This is... Das ist... **1A**
three drei **2A**
through durch *prep.* **3B**
throw werfen *v.* **2B**
to throw away wegwerfen *v.* **12B**
thunder Donner, - *m.* **7A**
thunderstorm Gewitter, - *n.* **7A**
Thursday Donnerstag, -e *m.* **2A**
on Thursdays donnerstags *adv.* **2A**
ticket Flugticket, -s *n.* **7B**; Fahrkarte, -n *f.* **8A**
ticket collector Schaffner, - / Schaffnerin,
-nen *m./f.* **8A**
ticket office Fahrkartenschalter, - *m.* **8A**
tidy ordentlich *adj.* **6B**
tie Krawatte, -n *f.* **5B**
tight eng *adj.* **5B**
time Zeit, -en *f.* **2A**; Mal, -e *n.* **7B**
for the first/last time zum ersten/letzten
Mal **7B**
the first/last time das erste/letzte Mal **7B**
this time diesmal *adv.* **7B**
What time is it? Wie spät ist es?; Wie viel Uhr
ist es? **2A**
times mal **1B**
tip Trinkgeld, -er *n.* **4B**
tired müde *adj.* **3B**
tissue Taschentuch, ⁻er *n.* **9B**
to vor *prep.* **2A**; nach; zu *prep.* **4B**; auf, an *prep.* **5B**
(in order) to um...zu **7B**
to the right/left nach rechts/links **6A**

toast anstoßen *v.* **5A**
toaster Toaster, - *m.* **6B**
today heute *adv.* **2B**
Today is... Heute ist der... **2A**
What day is it today? Welcher Tag ist heute? **7A**
toe Zeh, -en *m.* **9A**
together zusammen *adv.* **3A**
toilet Toilette, -n *f.* **6A**
tomato Tomate, -n *f.* **4A**
tomorrow morgen *adv.* **2B**
the day after tomorrow übermorgen *adv.* **2B**
tomorrow morning morgen früh **2B**
too zu *adv.* **4A**; auch *adv.* **1A**
tool kit Werkzeug, -e *n.*
tooth Zahn, ⁻e *m.* **9A**
toothache Zahnschmerzen *m. pl.* **9B**
toothbrush Zahnbürste, -n *f.* **9A**
toothpaste Zahnpasta (*pl.* Zahnpasten) *f.* **9A**
tornado Tornado, -s *m.* **12A**
toward in Richtung *f.* **10B**
towel Handtuch, ⁻er *n.* **9A**
town Stadt, ⁻e *f.* **10B**
town hall Rathaus, ⁻er *n.* **10A**
toxic waste Giftmüll *m.* **12B**
track Bahnsteig, -e *m.* **8A**
track and field Leichtathletik *f.* **2B**
traffic Verkehr *m.* **8A**
traffic light Ampel, -n *f.* **10B**
train Zug, ⁻e *m.* **8A**
transportation Verkehrsmittel, - *n.* **8A**
public transportation öffentliche
Verkehrsmittel *n. pl.* **8A**
trash Müll *m.* **6B**
to take out the trash den Müll rausbringen **6B**
travel reisen *v.* **2A**
travel agency Reisebüro, -s *n.* **7B**
traveler Reisende, -n *m./f.* **7B**
tree Baum, ⁻e *m.* **12A**
trendy angesagt *adj.* **5B**
trip Reise, -n *f.* **7B**
truck LKW, -s *m.* **8A**
truck driver LKW-Fahrer, - / LKW-Fahrerin,
-nen *m./f.* **11B**
trunk Kofferraum, ⁻e *m.* **8A**
try probieren *v.* **3B**; versuchen *v.* **7B**
Give it a try! Probieren Sie mal!
T-shirt T-Shirt, -s *n.* **5B**
Tuesday Dienstag, -e *m.* **2A**
on Tuesdays dienstags *adv.* **2A**
tuition fee Studiengebühr, -en *f.* **2A**
tuna Thunfisch, -e *m.* **4A**
Turkey die Türkei *f.* **10B**
Turkish (person) Türke, -n / Türkin,
-nen *m./f.* **10B**; **Turkish**
(language) Türkisch *n.* **10B**
turn abbiegen *v.* **10B**
to turn right/left rechts/links abbiegen *v.* **8A**
to turn off ausmachen *v.* **8B**; einschalten *v.* **12B**
to turn on anmachen *v.* **8B**; auschalten *v.* **12B**
turning point Wende, -n *f.* **12B**
twelve zwölf **2A**
twenty zwanzig **2A**
twin Zwilling, -e *m.* **3A**
two zwei **2A**

U

ugly hässlich *adj.* **3A**
umbrella Regenschirm, -e *m.* **7A**
under unter *prep.* **5B**
understand verstehen *v.* **2A**
underwear Unterwäsche *f.* **5B**
undressed: to get undressed sich ausziehen *v.* **9A**
unemployed arbeitslos *adj.* **10A**
unfortunate arm *adj.* **3B**
unfortunately leider *adv.* **4A**
unfurnished unmöbliert *adj.* **6A**
university Universität, -en *f.* **1B**
unpleasant unangenehm *adj.* **3B**
until bis *prep.* **3B**; bis zu *prep.* **10B**
up herauf *adv.* **6A**
to get up aufstehen *v.* **4A**
to go up hochgehen *v.* **10B**
upload hochladen *v.* **8B**
USA die USA *pl.*; die Vereinigten Staaten *pl.* **10B**
use benutzen *v.* **8A**; bedienen *v.* **8B**
to get used to sich gewöhnen an *v.* **9A**
useful nützlich *adj.* **2A**
useless nutzlos *adj.* **2A**

V

vacancy Zimmer frei *f.* **6A**
vacation Ferien *pl.*; Urlaub, -e *m.* **7B**
to go on vacation Urlaub machen *v.* **7B**
vacuum staubsaugen *v.* **6B**
vacuum cleaner Staubsauger, - *m.* **6B**
validate entwerten *v.* **8A**
to validate a ticket eine Fahrkarte
entwerten *v.* **8A**
valley Tal, ⁻er *n.* **12A**
vase Vase, -n *f.* **6A**
vegetables Gemüse *n.* **4A**
verb Verb, -en *n.* **9A**
very sehr *adv.* **3A**
very well sehr gut **1A**
veterinarian Tierarzt, ⁻e / Tierärztin,
-nen *m./f.* **11B**
visa Visum (*pl.* Visa) *n.* **7B**
visit besuchen *v.* **4A**
vocabulary Wortschatz, ⁻e *m.*
volcano Vulkan, -e *m.* **12A**
volleyball Volleyball *m.* **2B**

W

wait warten *v.* **2A**
to wait for warten auf *v.* **7A**
waiter / waitress Kellner, - / Kellnerin,
-nen *m./f.* **3B**
Waiter! Herr Ober! **4B**
wake up aufwachen *v.* **9A**
walk Spaziergang, ⁻e *m.*
to go for a walk spazieren gehen *v.* **2B**
wall Wand, ⁻e *f.* **5B**
want wollen *v.* **3B**
warm warm *adj.* **10A**
wash waschen *v.* **2B**
to wash (oneself) sich waschen *v.* **9A**

washing machine Waschmaschine, -n *f.* **6B**
waste Müll *m.* **12B**; Abfall, ⸚e *m.* **12B**
wastebasket Papierkorb, ⸚e *m.* **1B**
watch zuschauen *v.* **4A**; anschauen *v.* **7A**
  to watch television fernsehen *v.* **8B**
water Wasser *n.*
  sparkling water Mineralwasser *n.* **4B**
  still water stilles Wasser *n.* **4B**
water pitcher Wasserkrug, ⸚e *m.* **4B**
waterfall Wasserfall, ⸚e *m.* **12A**
we wir *pron.* **1A**
weak schwach *adj.* **3B**
wear tragen *v.* **2B**
weather Wetter *n.* **7A**
  What's the weather like? Wie ist das Wetter? **7A**
weather report Wetterbericht, -e *m.* **7A**
Web Internet *n.* **8B**
  to surf the Web im Internet surfen *v.* **8B**
Web site Website, -s *f.* **8B**
wedding Hochzeit, -en *f.* **5A**
wedding anniversary Hochzeitstag, -e *m.* **5B**
Wednesday Mittwoch, -e *m.* **2A**
  on Wednesdays mittwochs *adv.* **2A**
week Woche, -n *f.* **2A**
weekend Wochenende, -n *n.* **2A**
weigh wiegen *v.* **8B**
welcome (herzlich) willkommen **1A**
  You're welcome. Gern geschehen! **1A**
well gut *adv.*
  I am (very) well. Mir geht's (sehr) gut. **1A**
  I am not (so) well. Mir geht's nicht (so) gut. **1A**
  Get well! Gute Besserung! **5A**
well-dressed gut gekleidet *adj.* **5B**
well-known bekannt *adj.* **10A**
wet nass *adj.* **12A**
what was *interr.* **2A**
  What is that? Was ist das? **1B**
  What's up? Was geht ab? **1A**
when wann *interr.* **2A**
whenever wenn *conj.* **10A**
where wo *interr.* **2A**
  where from woher *interr.* **2A**
  where to wohin *interr.* **2A**
whether ob *conj.* **10A**
which welcher/welche/welches *interr.* **2A**
white weiß *adj.* **5B**
who wer *interr.* **2A**
  Who is it? Wer ist das? **1B**
whom wen *acc. interr.* **2A**; wem *dat. interr.* **4B**
whose wessen *interr.* **8B**
why warum *interr.* **2A**
widow Witwe, -n *f.* **3A**
widower Witwer, - *m.* **3A**
wife Ehefrau, -en *f.* **3A**
win gewinnen *v.* **2B**
wind energy Windenergie *f.* **12B**
window Fenster, - *n.* **1A**
windshield Windschutzscheibe, -n *f.* **8A**
windshield wiper Scheibenwischer, - *m.* **8A**
windy windig *adj.* **7A**
wine Wein, -e *m.* **4B**
winter Winter, - *m.* **2B**
wipe wischen *v.* **6B**

wise weise *adj.* **3B**
wish wünschen *v.* **9A**
  to wish (for something) sich (etwas) wünschen *v.* **9A**
with mit **4B**
withdraw (money) (Geld) abheben *v.* **10A**
within innerhalb *prep.* **8B**
without ohne *prep.* **3B**
woman Frau, -en *f.* **1A**
wonder sich fragen *v.* **9A**
wood Holz *n.* **6B**
wool Wolle *f.* **5B**
work Arbeit, -en *f.* **11B**; arbeiten *v.* **2A**; funktionieren *v.* **8B**
  at work auf der Arbeit **11B**
  to work on arbeiten an *v.* **7A**
world Welt, -en *f.* **12B**
worried besorgt *adj.* **3B**
write schreiben *v.* **2A**
  to write to schreiben an *v.* **7A**
  to write to one another sich schreiben *v.* **9A**

Y

year Jahr, -e *n.* **7A**
yellow gelb *adj.* **5B**
yes ja **1A**; (contradicting) doch *adv.* **2B**
yesterday gestern *adv.* **5B**
yet noch *adv.* **4A**
yogurt Joghurt, -s *m.* **4A**
you du/ihr/Sie *pron.* **1A**
young jung *adj.* **3A**; jugendlich *adj.* **10A**
your euer/Ihr *poss. adj.* **3A**
youth hostel Jugendherberge, -n *f.* **7B**

Index

Europa

die Welt

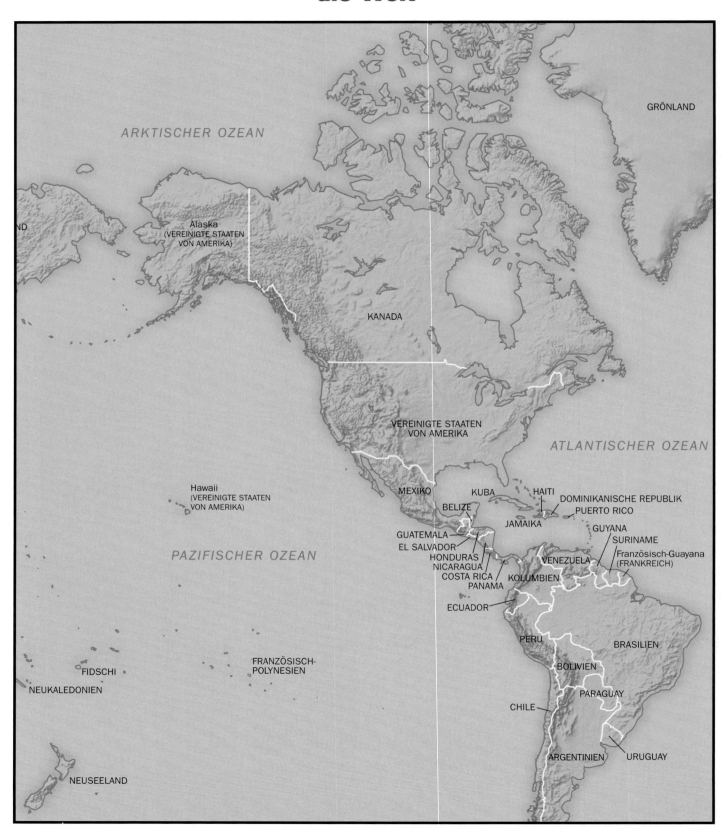

ARKTISCHER OZEAN

GRÖNLAND

Alaska
(VEREINIGTE STAATEN
VON AMERIKA)

KANADA

VEREINIGTE STAATEN
VON AMERIKA

ATLANTISCHER OZEAN

Hawaii
(VEREINIGTE STAATEN
VON AMERIKA)

MEXIKO

KUBA HAITI DOMINIKANISCHE REPUBLIK
PUERTO RICO

BELIZE

JAMAIKA

GUATEMALA
EL SALVADOR
HONDURAS
NICARAGUA
COSTA RICA
PANAMA

GUYANA
SURINAME
Französisch-Guayana
(FRANKREICH)

VENEZUELA

KOLUMBIEN

ECUADOR

PAZIFISCHER OZEAN

PERU

BRASILIEN

BOLIVIEN

FIDSCHI

FRANZÖSISCH-
POLYNESIEN

NEUKALEDONIEN

PARAGUAY

CHILE

ARGENTINIEN URUGUAY

NEUSEELAND

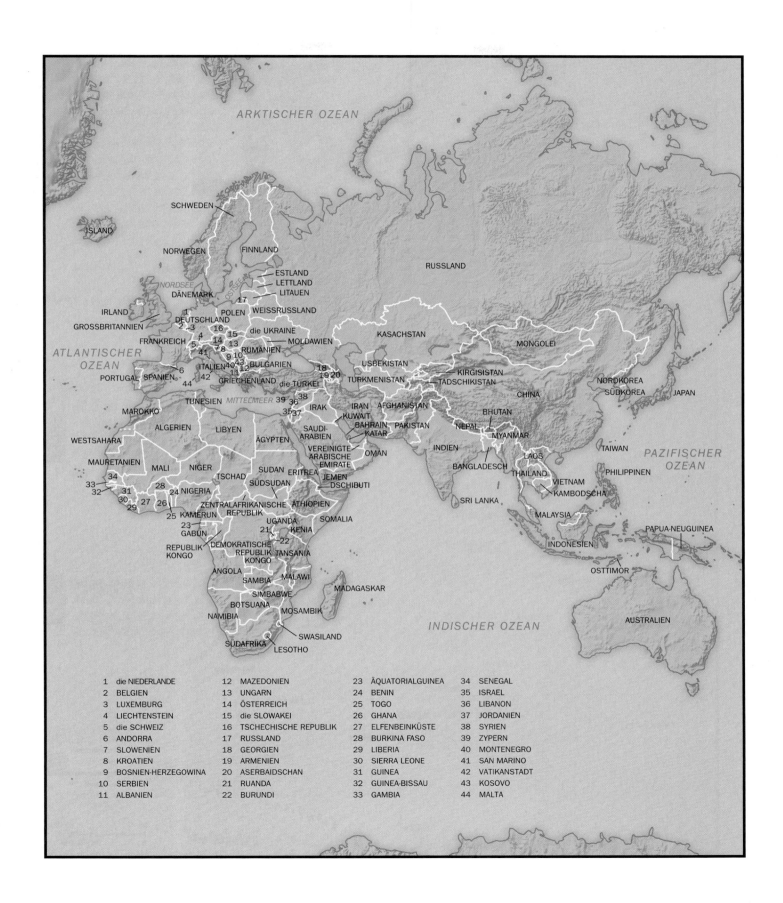

1	die NIEDERLANDE	12	MAZEDONIEN	23	ÄQUATORIALGUINEA	34	SENEGAL
2	BELGIEN	13	UNGARN	24	BENIN	35	ISRAEL
3	LUXEMBURG	14	ÖSTERREICH	25	TOGO	36	LIBANON
4	LIECHTENSTEIN	15	die SLOWAKEI	26	GHANA	37	JORDANIEN
5	die SCHWEIZ	16	TSCHECHISCHE REPUBLIK	27	ELFENBEINKÜSTE	38	SYRIEN
6	ANDORRA	17	RUSSLAND	28	BURKINA FASO	39	ZYPERN
7	SLOWENIEN	18	GEORGIEN	29	LIBERIA	40	MONTENEGRO
8	KROATIEN	19	ARMENIEN	30	SIERRA LEONE	41	SAN MARINO
9	BOSNIEN-HERZEGOWINA	20	ASERBAIDSCHAN	31	GUINEA	42	VATIKANSTADT
10	SERBIEN	21	RUANDA	32	GUINEA-BISSAU	43	KOSOVO
11	ALBANIEN	22	BURUNDI	33	GAMBIA	44	MALTA

Deutschland

OSTSEE

NORDSEE

DÄNEMARK

SCHLESWIG-HOLSTEIN

Kiel

Rostock

Lübeck

BREMEN

Schwerin

MECKLENBURG-VORPOMMERN

Bremerhaven

Hamburg

HAMBURG

Bremen

Weser

NIEDERSACHSEN

Elbe

BRANDENBURG

BERLIN

Oder

POLEN

Aller

Potsdam

Berlin

Ems

Hannover

Leine

Braunschweig

Magdeburg

die NIEDERLANDE

Münster

Bielefeld

SACHSEN-ANHALT

NORDRHEIN-WESTFALEN

Essen

Dortmund

Elbe

Düsseldorf

Halle

Leipzig

SACHSEN

Köln

Dresden

Aachen

Fulda

Erfurt

Chemnitz

Bonn

Rhein

THÜRINGEN

BELGIEN

HESSEN

Frankfurt am Main

LUXEMBURG

Mosel

Wiesbaden

Main

RHEINLAND-PFALZ

Mainz

TSCHECHISCHE REPUBLIK

SAARLAND

Mannheim

Nürnberg

BÖHMERWALD

Saarbrücken

Karlsruhe

Regensburg

Stuttgart

Donau

BAYERN

SCHWARZWALD

BADEN-WÜRTTEMBERG

Augsburg

FRANKREICH

München

Lech

BAYERISCHE ALPEN

Bregenz

die SCHWEIZ

LIECHTENSTEIN

ÖSTERREICH

Landesgrenzen
Stadt
Landeshauptstadt
Hauptstadt

0   50 Meilen
0   50 Kilometer

Österreich

die SLOWAKEI

TSCHECHISCHE REPUBLIK

NIEDERÖSTERREICH

UNGARN

KROATIEN

Neusiedler See

Eisenstadt

Donau

Wien

WIEN

Krems an der Donau

Leitha

BURGENLAND

St. Pölten

Wiener Neustadt

Melk

SLOWENIEN

Graz

Mur

Leoben

STEIERMARK

Wolfsberg

KÄRNTEN

Klagenfurt

Linz

Steyr

OBERÖSTERREICH

Traun

Enns

Traunsee

Schärding

Inn

Braunau

Salzburg

Attersee

St. Wolfgang

Bad Ischl

Spittal

Villach

Zell am See

SALZBURG

Bad Gastein

Salzach

Drau

Kitzbühel

Lenz

TIROL

DEUTSCHLAND

Innsbruck

TIROL

ITALIEN

50 Meilen

50 Kilometer

Bregenz

Dornbirn

VORARLBERG

Vaduz

LIECHTENSTEIN

die SCHWEIZ

Landesgrenzen

Stadt

Landeshauptstadt

Hauptstadt

Liechtenstein

die Schweiz

About the Authors

Christine Anton, a native of Germany, is Associate Professor of German and Director of the Language Resource Center at Berry College. She received her B.A. in English and German from the Universität Erlangen and her graduate degrees in Germanic Languages and Literatures from the University of North Carolina at Chapel Hill. She has published two books on German realism and German cultural memory of National Socialism, and a number of articles on 19th and 20th century German and Austrian literature, as well as on second language acquisition. Dr. Anton has received several awards for excellence in teaching and was honored by the American Association of Teachers of German with the Duden Award for her "outstanding efforts and achievement in the teaching of German." Dr. Anton previously taught at the State University of New York and the University of North Carolina, Chapel Hill.

Tobias Barske, a native of Bavaria, is an Associate Professor of German and Applied Linguistics at the University of Wisconsin-Stevens Point. He has a Ph.D. in German Applied Linguistics from the University of Illinois at Urbana-Champaign with emphases on language and social interaction as well as language pedagogy. He has also studied at the Universität Regensburg in Germany. Tobias has over 10 years of experience teaching undergraduate and graduate courses at the university level and has earned numerous awards for excellence in teaching.

Credits

Every effort has been made to trace the copyright holders of the works published herein. If proper copyright acknowledgment has not been made, please contact the publisher and we will correct the information in future printings.

Photography and Art Credits

All images © by Vista Higher Learning unless otherwise noted.

Cover: Geber86/E+/Getty Images.

Front Matter (SE): xiii: Guteksk7/Fotolia.

Front Matter (IAE): IAE-15: Mike Flippo/Shutterstock.

Chapter 1: 1: Xavier Roy; **4:** Paula Díez; **8:** Laurence Mouton/Media Bakery; **9:** (tl) Michaeljung/iStockphoto; (tr) Sashagala/Shutterstock; (b) Imac/Alamy; **13:** (tl) Anne Loubet; (tm) Igor Tarasov/Fotolia; (tr) Jack Hollingsworth/Corbis; (bl) Gualtiero Boffi/Shutterstock; (bml) Tupungato/Shutterstock; (bmr) Nicole Winchell; (br) Tabitha Patrick/iStockphoto; **15:** (tl) Lazar Mihai-Bogdan/Shutterstock; (tr) Vanessa Bertozzi; (ml, mr, bm) Nicole Winchell; (mm) Anne Loubet; (bl) Gudrun Hommel; (br) Paula Díez; **16:** Auremar/Fotolia; **28:** Woodapple/Fotolia; **29:** (tl) ChristArt/Fotolia; (tr) Arnd Wiegmann/RTR/Newscom; (b) Kyle Monk/Blend Images/Getty Images; **36:** (all) Nicole Winchell; **38:** Sarah2/Shutterstock; **39:** © 2018 Pelikan Vertriebsgesellschaft mbH & Co. KG; **40:** (t) Shishic/iStockphoto; (m) PeterSVETphoto/Shutterstock; (b) Hollandse Hoogte/Redux; **41:** (tl) Vaclav Volrab/Shutterstock; (tr) Steve Raymer/Corbis Documentary/VCG/Getty Images; (bl) CrazyD/iStockphoto; (bm) Horst Galuschka/DPA/Corbis; (br) Peter Röther/Panther Media GmbH/Alamy; **44:** Chris Schmidt/iStockphoto; **45:** StockLite/Shutterstock.

Chapter 2: 47: Xavier Roy; **50:** Chris Schmidt/Track5/E+/Getty Images; **54:** Sabine Lubenow/AGE Fotostock; **55:** (tl) Heinz-Peter Bader/Reuters/Newscom; (tr) Ingolf Pompe/AGE Fotostock; (b) Laviana/Shutterstock; **56:** (l) Nicole Winchell; (r) Martín Bernetti; **58:** Nicole Winchell; **66:** (left col: t) IDP Manchester Airport Collection/Alamy; (left col: ml) Javier Larrea/AGE Fotostock; (left col: mm) Noam/Fotolia; (left col: mr) Martín Bernetti; (left col: bl) Ana Cabezas Martín; (left col: bm) Tetra Images/Alamy; (left col: br) Jacob Wackerhausen/iStockphoto; (right col) Martinap/Shutterstock; **74:** Roland Syba/Shutterstock; **75:** (tl) Imagebroker.net/SuperStock; (tr) Jan Woitas/DPA Picture-Alliance/Newscom; (m) DPA Picture-Alliance/Alamy; (b) Allan Grosskrueger/Shutterstock; **78:** (t, br) Nicole Winchell; (ml) Polka Dot Images/JupiterImages; (mm) Martín Bernetti; (mr) Robert Michael/Media Bakery; (bl) Losevsky Photo and Video/Shutterstock; (bm) Gudrun Hommel; **83:** Janne Hämäläinen/Shutterstock; **84:** Auremar/Shutterstock; **85:** (tl) Ilyashenko Oleksiy/Shutterstock; (tm) Martín Bernetti; (tr) Cheryl Ann Quigley/123RF; (bl) Karen Struthers/123RF; (bml) Val Thoermer/Deposit Photos; (bmr) Ben Blankenburg/Corbis; (br) Danny Warren/iStockphoto; **86:** (l) Neustockimages/iStockphoto; (r) Photos.com/Getty Images; **88:** (tl) Gudrun Hommel; (tr) Noppasinw/Fotolia; (ml) Nicole Winchell; (mr) VVO/Shutterstock; (b) Bettmann/Getty Images; **89:** (tl) Riccardo Sala/Alamy; (tr) Lexan/123RF; (m) AKG-Images; (bl) Philip Lange/Shutterstock; (br) Derek Storm/Splash News/Newscom; **90–91:** Patrick Seeger/DPA Picture-Alliance/Alamy; **92:** Jack Hollingsworth/Cardinal/Corbis; **93:** (t) Paylessimages/123RF; (b) Nadezda Verbenko/Shutterstock.

Chapter 3: 95: Xavier Roy; **102:** Westend61/Getty Images; **103:** (tl) John Dowland/Getty Images; (tr) Bildquelle/ullstein bild/Getty Images; (b) Wrangler/Shutterstock; **105:** George Olsson/iStockphoto **106:** (tl, tr, bl, bmr) Martín Bernetti; (tm) Ray Levesque; (bml) David N. Madden/Shutterstock; (br) Prism68/Shutterstock; **112:** (t) Aspen Stock/AGE Fotostock; (ml) Xalanx/123RF; (mm) Zoran Orcik/123RF; (mr) Alexander Rochau/Fotolia; (bl) Imag'In Pyrénées/Fotolia; (bm) Pixtal/AGE Fotostock; (br) Robert Berry/Shutterstock; **116:** (top row: tl) José Blanco; (top row: tm) Michael Jung/iStockphoto; (top row: tr) Anne Loubet; (top row: bl) Rasmus Rasmussen/iStockphoto; (top row: bml) Ana Cabezas Martín; (top row: bmr) Javier Larrea/AGE Fotostock; (top row: br) Martín Bernetti; (bottom row: l) Vanessa Nel/Shutterstock; (bottom row: r) Photoinjection/Shutterstock; **120:** OneInchPunch/Shutterstock; **121:** (tl) Tatiana Lebedeva/Shutterstock; (tr) Axel Heimken/dpa/AGE Fotostock; (b) Sonya Etchison/Shutterstock; **123:** Anne Loubet; **125:** Minerva Studio /Shutterstock; **131:** Nicole Winchell; **132:** (left col: tl) Lichtmeister/Shutterstock; (left col: tr, br) Gudrun Hommel; (left col: bl) Martín Bernetti; (right col) Anne Loubet; **133:** © 2019 by zooplus AG; **134:** (tl) Andre Jenny/Alamy; (tr) ShyMan/iStockphoto; (m) RosaIreneBetancourt 3/Alamy; (b) Frymire Archive/Alamy; **135:** (tl) Aspen Rock/Shutterstock; (tr) Ruggles Susan/AGE Fotostock; (bl) MWaits/Shutterstock; (bm) Sergey Peterman/Shutterstock; (br) PictureLux/The Hollywood Archive/Alamy; **136:** Aleksandar Mijatovic/Shutterstock; **137:** Serg64/Shutterstock; **138:** Gudrun Hommel; **139:** Gudrun Hommel.

Chapter 4: 141: Xavier Roy; **143:** (tl) VHL; (tr) Smit/Shutterstock; (bl) Susan Schmitz/Shutterstock; (bml) Smileus/Shutterstock; (bmr, br) Vanessa Bertozzi; **144:** (tl) Nancy Camley; (tr, bl) Vanessa Bertozzi; (bml) Nicole Winchell; (bmr) Monkey Business Images/Shutterstock; (br) Martín Bernetti; **148:** Ernst Wrba/Image Broker/Newscom; **149:** (l) Karandaev/Fotolia; (r) Ted Soqui/Corbis Entertainment/Getty Images; (b) StockPixstore/Fotolia; **151:** Tyler Olson/Shutterstock; **153:** (tl) Rafael Rios; (tr) Steve Debenport/iStockphoto; (bl) Nicole Winchell; (bml) Oscar Artavia Solano; (bmr) Anne Loubet; (br) MAEWJPHO/Shutterstock; **155:** (tl) Muzsy/Shutterstock; (tr) Alexey

Text Credits

87: Courtesy of By Graziela; **177:** Courtesy of Der Standard, (published 23.7.2017) https://derstandard.at/2000061646859/Der-Oesterreicher-liebstes-Obst-und-Gemuese; **269:** Courtesy of CHECK24 GmbH; **357:** Courtesy of Deutsche Bahn AG; **405:** Courtesy of Sanofi-Aventis Deutschland GmbH; **452:** "Allein" from Hermann Hesse, Sämtliche Werke in 20 Bänden. Herausgegeben von Volker Michels. Band 10: Die Gedichte. © Suhrkamp Verlag Frankfurt am Main 2002. All rights with and controlled by Suhrkamp Verlag Berlin; **489:** Courtesy of Garten- und Landschaftsbau Kowalski; **492:** "Die Räuberbande" by Leonhard Frank. © Aufbau Verlag GmbH & Co. KG, Berlin 1957, 2008; © Aufbau Verlag GmbH & Co. KG, Berlin 1957, 2008; **534:** "Meine Nachtigall" by Rose Ausländer. Gesammelte Weke in sieben Bänden. Band II, Die Sichel mäht die Zeit zu Heu. Gedichte 1957-1965. ©1985 S.Fischer Verlag GmbH, Frankfurt am Main.

Video Credits

21: Courtesy of Deutsche Bahn AG; **67:** Courtesy of NDR/Studio Hamburg; **113:** "Minkas Naturkost - aus Liebe gemacht" by ZooRoyal GmbH, Creative Commons Attribution 4.0 International (CC BY 4.0); **161:** Mit Filmproduktion und ggfs. sonstigen Dritten abzustimmen, die Rechte haben, z.B.: Agency: Jung von Matt, Film production: Film Deluxe GmbH; **203:** Courtesy of It's Us Media GmbH; **251:** Courtesy of NDR/Studio Hamburg; **295:** ZDF Enterprises GmbH; **339:** Courtesy of Daimler AG; **387:** Courtesy of Central Krankenversicherung AG and Philipp und Keuntje GmbH; **431:** Courtesy of Sarah Winkenstette, Director, Writer and Producer; **473:** Courtesy of Kurzfilm Agentur Hamburg; **513:** A short film by Dino Weisz. Courtesy of Wunderwelt Pictures.